(Continued on inside back cover)

For Reference

Not to be taken from this room.

Encyclopedia of

Animal Science

Encyclopedia of

Animal Science

edited by

Wilson G. Pond • Alan W. Bell

MARCEL DEKKER

NEW YORK

ISBN: Print: 0-8247-5496-4
ISBN: Online: 0-8247-5495-6
ISBN: Combo: 0-8247-4796-8

Library of Congress Cataloging-in-Publication Data.
A catalog record of this book is available from the Library of Congress.

This book is printed on acid-free paper.

Headquarters
Marcel Dekker
270 Madison Avenue, New York, NY 10016, U.S.A.
tel: 212-696-9000; fax: 212-685-4540

World Wide Web
http://www.dekker.com

Current printing (last digit):
10 9 8 7 6 5 4 3 2 1

PRINTED IN THE UNITED STATES OF AMERICA

List of Contributors

Charles W. Abdalla / *The Pennsylvania State University, University Park, Pennsylvania, U.S.A.*

N. R. Adams / *CSIRO Livestock Industries, Wembley, Western Australia*

R. Michael Akers / *Virginia Polytechnic Institute and State University, Blacksburg, Virginia, U.S.A.*

C. Z. Alvarado / *Texas Tech University, Lubbock, Texas, U.S.A.*

David B. Anderson (Retired) / *Elanco Animal Health, Greenfield, Indiana, U.S.A.*

Kenneth E. Anderson / *North Carolina State University, Raleigh, North Carolina, U.S.A.*

R. C. Anderson / *United States Department of Agriculture, Agricultural Research Service, College Station, Texas, U.S.A.*

R. P. Ansotegui / *Montana State University, Bozeman, Montana, U.S.A.*

Michael C. Appleby / *The Humane Society of the United States, Washington, D.C., U.S.A.*

Todd J. Applegate / *Purdue University, West Lafayette, Indiana, U.S.A.*

Jimmy Avery / *Mississippi State University, Stoneville, Mississippi, U.S.A.*

Janice Bahr / *University of Illinois, Urbana, Illinois, U.S.A.*

Clifton A. Baile / *University of Georgia, Athens, Georgia, U.S.A.*

David H. Baker / *University of Illinois, Urbana, Illinois, U.S.A.*

R. L. Baldwin / *University of California, Davis, California, U.S.A.*

Douglas D. Bannerman / *United States Department of Agriculture, Agricultural Research Service, Beltsville, Maryland, U.S.A.*

Dale E. Bauman / *Cornell University, Ithaca, New York, U.S.A.*

Fuller W. Bazer / *Texas A&M University, College Station, Texas, U.S.A.*

Jason M. Behrends / *Texas A&M University, College Station, Texas, U.S.A.*

Donald C. Beitz / *Iowa State University, Ames, Iowa, U.S.A.*

Alan W. Bell / *Cornell University, Ithaca, New York, U.S.A.*

Donald D. Bell / *University of California, Riverside, California, U.S.A.*

R. A. Bellows / *United States Department of Agriculture, Agricultural Research Service, Bozeman, Montana, U.S.A.*

Eric P. Berg / *University of Missouri, Columbia, Missouri, U.S.A.*

S. F. Bilgili / *Auburn University, Auburn, Alabama, U.S.A.*

Kenneth M. Bischoff / *United States Department of Agriculture, Agricultural Research Service, College Station, Texas, U.S.A.*

Stephen C. Bishop / *Roslin Institute (Edinburgh), Roslin, Midlothian, U.K.*

Dominique Blache / *The University of Western Australia, Crawley, Australia*

Harvey Blackburn / *United States Department of Agriculture, Agricultural Research Service, Fort Collins, Colorado, U.S.A.*

Olga U. Bolden-Tiller / *The University of Texas–M.D. Anderson Cancer Center, Houston, Texas, U.S.A.*

Eric Bradford / *University of California, Davis, California, U.S.A.*

Suzanne Broussard / *University of Illinois, Urbana, Illinois, U.S.A*

Dan L. Brown / *Cornell University, Ithaca, New York, U.S.A.*

Michael S. Brown / *West Texas A&M University, Canyon, Texas, U.S.A.*

Veerle Bruggeman / *K.U. Leuven, Leuven, Belgium*

David S. Buchanan / *Oklahoma State University, Stillwater, Oklahoma, U.S.A.*

Leonard S. Bull / *North Carolina State University, Raleigh, North Carolina, U.S.A.*

Thomas D. Bunch / *Utah State University, Logan, Utah, U.S.A.*

Larry G. Burditt / *Oklahoma State University, Stillwater, Oklahoma, U.S.A.*

Robert C. Burghardt / *Texas A&M University, College Station, Texas, U.S.A.*

Jeanne L. Burton / *Michigan State University, East Lansing, Michigan, U.S.A.*

Jason H. Byrd / *Texas Tech University, Lubbock, Texas, U.S.A.*

Todd R. Callaway / *United States Department of Agriculture, Agricultural Research Service, College Station, Texas, U.S.A.*

C. C. Calvert / *University of California, Davis, California, U.S.A.*

Anthony V. Capuco / *United States Department of Agriculture, Agricultural Research Service, Beltsville, Maryland, U.S.A.*

Kristen M. Carnagey / *Iowa State University, Ames, Iowa, U.S.A.*

John Carr / *Iowa State University, Ames, Iowa, U.S.A.*

L. E. Chase / *Cornell University, Ithaca, New York, U.S.A.*

Muhammad M. Chaudry / *Islamic Food and Nutrition Council, Chicago, Illinois, U.S.A.*

D. J. R. Cherney / *Cornell University, Ithaca, New York, U.S.A.*

J. H. Cherney / *Cornell University, Ithaca, New York, U.S.A.*

Lee I. Chiba / *Auburn University, Auburn, Alabama, U.S.A.*

Vern L. Christensen / *North Carolina State University, Raleigh, North Carolina, U.S.A.*

N. Andy Cole / *United States Department of Agriculture, Agricultural Research Service, Bushland, Texas, U.S.A.*

Steven R. Cooper / *Oklahoma State University, Stillwater, Oklahoma, U.S.A.*

Tawni L. Crippen / *United States Department of Agriculture, Agricultural Research Service, College Station, Texas, U.S.A.*

Gary L. Cromwell / *University of Kentucky, Lexington, Kentucky, U.S.A.*

Matthew A. Cronin / *ENTRIX, Inc., Anchorage, Alaska, U.S.A.*

Larry V. Cundiff / *United States Department of Agriculture, Agricultural Research Service, Clay Center, Nebraska, U.S.A.*

Patricia A. Curtis / *Auburn University, Auburn, Alabama, U.S.A.*

Stanley E. Curtis / *University of Illinois, Urbana, Illinois, U.S.A.*

Michael Czarick / *University of Georgia, Athens, Georgia, U.S.A.*

Greg Dana / *Pioneer Hi-Bred International, Inc., Johnston, Iowa, U.S.A.*

Duane L. Davis / *Kansas State University, Manhattan, Kansas, U.S.A.*

Lionel J. Dawson / *Oklahoma State University, Stillwater, Oklahoma, U.S.A.*

Eddy Decuypere / *K.U. Leuven, Leuven, Belgium*

Cornelis F. M. de Lange / *University of Guelph, Guelph, Ontario, Canada*

Christopher L. Delgado / *International Food Policy Research Institute (IFPRI), Washington, D.C., U.S.A.; International Livestock Research Institute (ILRI), Nairobi, Kenya*

Mary Anne Della-Fera / *University of Georgia, Athens, Georgia, U.S.A.*

Alyssa R. Dodd / *The Pennsylvania State University, University Park, Pennsylvania, U.S.A.*

Matthew E. Doumit / *Michigan State University, East Lansing, Michigan, U.S.A.*

C. Robert Dove / *University of Georgia, Athens, Georgia, U.S.A.*

Hugh Dove / *CSIRO Plant Industry, Canberra, Australia*

David A. Dunn / *University of Rochester Medical Center, Rochester, New York, U.S.A.*

Frank R. Dunshea / *Department of Primary Industries, Werribee, Victoria, Australia*

Catherine M. Dwyer / *Scottish Agricultural College, Edinburgh, Scotland, U.K.*

Jackson M. Dzakuma / *Prairie View A&M University, Prairie View, Texas, U.S.A.*

Maurice Lenuel Eastridge / *The Ohio State University, Columbus, Ohio, U.S.A.*

S. E. Echternkamp / *United States Department of Agriculture, Agriculture Research Service, Clay Center, Nebraska, U.S.A.*

Tom S. Edrington / *United States Department of Agriculture, Agricultural Research Service, College Station, Texas, U.S.A.*

Susan D. Eicher / *United States Department of Agriculture, Agricultural Research Service, West Lafayette, Indiana, U.S.A.*

Joan H. Eisemann / *North Carolina State University, Raleigh, North Carolina, U.S.A.*

Steven Ellis / *Clemson University, Clemson, South Carolina, U.S.A.*

William C. Ellis / *Texas A&M University, College Station, Texas, U.S.A.*

Carole R. Engle / *University of Arkansas, Pine Bluff, Arkansas, U.S.A.*

Galen Erickson / *University of Nebraska, Lincoln, Nebraska, U.S.A.*

Jeffery Escobar / *Baylor College of Medicine, Houston, Texas, U.S.A.*

K. D. Evans / *University of California, Davis, California, U.S.A.*

Brian D. Fairchild / *University of Georgia, Athens, Georgia, U.S.A.*

Scott William Fausti / *South Dakota State University, Brookings, South Dakota, U.S.A.*

James D. Ferguson / *University of Pennsylvania, Kennett Square, Pennsylvania, U.S.A.*

C. L. Ferrell / *United States Department of Agriculture, Agricultural Research Service, Clay Center, Nebraska, U.S.A.*

Daniel L. Fletcher / *University of Georgia, Athens, Georgia, U.S.A.*

Harry J. Flint / *Rowett Research Institute, Aberdeen, U.K.*

William L. Flowers / *North Carolina State University, Raleigh, North Carolina, U.S.A.*

Hugh Galbraith / *University of Aberdeen, Aberdeen, U.K.*

Duane L. Garner / *University of Nevada, Reno, Nevada, U.S.A.*

Rodney D. Geisert / *Oklahoma State University, Stillwater, Oklahoma, U.S.A.*

Kenneth J. Genovese / *United States Department of Agriculture, Agricultural Research Service, College Station, Texas, U.S.A.*

Ifigenia Geornaras / *Colorado State University, Fort Collins, Colorado, U.S.A.*

Stanley E. Gilliland / *Oklahoma State University, Stillwater, Oklahoma, U.S.A.*

Eric Gingerich / *University of Pennsylvania School of Veterinary Medicine, Kennett Square, Pennsylvania, U.S.A.*

Robert A. Godke / *Louisiana State University, Baton Rouge, Louisiana, U.S.A.*

Arthur Goetsch / *Langston University, Langston, Oklahoma, U.S.A.*

Ian Gordon / *University College, Dublin, Republic of Ireland*

Temple Grandin / *Colorado State University, Fort Collins, Colorado, U.S.A.*

Marion Greaser / *University of Wisconsin, Madison, Wisconsin, U.S.A.*

M. P. Green / *University of Missouri, Columbia, Missouri, U.S.A.*

L. Wayne Greene / *Texas A&M University, Amarillo, Texas, U.S.A.*

Barbara Grisdale-Helland / *AKVAFORSK, Sunndalsøra, Norway*

Deana L. Hancock / *Elanco Animal Health, Greenfield, Indiana, U.S.A.*

Robert H. Harms / *University of Florida, Gainesville, Florida, U.S.A.*

John F. Hasler / *AB Technology, Pullman, Washington, U.S.A.*

J. L. Hatfield / *United States Department of Agriculture, Agricultural Research Service, Ames, Iowa, U.S.A.*

D. B. Hausman / *University of Georgia, Athens, Georgia, U.S.A.*

Gary J. Hausman / *United States Department of Agriculture, Agricultural Research Service, Athens, Georgia, U.S.A.*

Virgil W. Hays / *University of Kentucky, Lexington, Kentucky, U.S.A.*

Rodney K. Heitschmidt / *United States Department of Agriculture, Agricultural Research Service, Miles City, Montana, U.S.A.*

Ståle J. Helland / *Aquaculture Protein Centre—CoE, Sunndalsøra, Norway*

Becca Hendricks / *National Pork Board, Des Moines, Iowa, U.S.A.*

Kevin Hillman / *Scottish Agricultural College, Aberdeen, U.K.*

Harold F. Hintz / *Cornell University, Ithaca, New York, U.S.A.*

William V. Holt / *Zoological Society of London, London, United Kingdom*

Katherine Albro Houpt / *Cornell University, Ithaca, New York, U.S.A.*

T. Richard Houpt / *Cornell University, Ithaca, New York, U.S.A.*

Alexander N. Hristov / *University of Idaho, Moscow, Idaho, U.S.A.*

Suzanne M. Hubbard / *United States Department of Agriculture, Agricultural Research Service, Beltsville, Maryland, U.S.A.*

Gerald B. Huntington / *North Carolina State University, Raleigh, North Carolina, U.S.A.*

Keith Inskeep / *West Virginia University, Morgantown, West Virginia, U.S.A.*

Han Jianlin / *International Livestock Research Institute (ILRI), Nairobi, Kenya*

Anna Kerr Johnson / *National Pork Board, Des Moines, Iowa, U.S.A.*

Barbara McBride Johnson / *Prairie View A&M University, Prairie View, Texas, U.S.A.*

Greg A. Johnson / *Texas A&M University, College Station, Texas, U.S.A.*

Rodney W. Johnson / *University of Illinois, Urbana, Illinois, U.S.A.*

G. Kannan / *Fort Valley State University, Fort Valley, Georgia, U.S.A.*

Larry S. Katz / *Rutgers University, New Brunswick, New Jersey, U.S.A.*

Robert G. Kauffman / *University of Wisconsin, Madison, Wisconsin, U.S.A.*

Cleon V. Kimberling / *Colorado State University, Fort Collins, Colorado, U.S.A.*

David A. King / *Texas A&M University, College Station, Texas, U.S.A.*

Brian Kinghorn / *University of New England, Armidale, Australia*

John Klindt / *United States Department of Agriculture, Agricultural Research Service, Clay Center, Nebraska, U.S.A.*

Terry J. Klopfenstein / *University of Nebraska, Lincoln, Nebraska, U.S.A.*

James E. Knight / *Montana State University, Bozeman, Montana, U.S.A.*

Travis J. Knight / *Iowa State University, Ames, Iowa, U.S.A.*

Kari Kolstad / *AKVAFORSK, Ås, Norway*

Nadège Krebs / *Texas Tech University, Lubbock, Texas, U.S.A.*

Liangxue Lai / *University of Missouri, Columbia, Missouri, U.S.A.*

J. David Latshaw / *The Ohio State University, Columbus, Ohio, U.S.A.*

Donald C. Lay, Jr. / *United States Department of Agriculture, Agricultural Research Service, Livestock Behavior Research Unit, West Lafayette, Indiana, U.S.A.*

Xin Gen Lei / *Cornell University, Ithaca, New York, U.S.A.*

Ronald Martin Lewis / *Virginia Polytechnic Institute and State University, Blacksburg, Virginia, U.S.A.*

Ehud Lipkin / *The Hebrew University of Jerusalem, Jerusalem, Israel*

H. Lippke / *Texas Agricultural Experiment Station, Uvade, Texas, U.S.A.*

Adam L. Lock / *Cornell University, Ithaca, New York, U.S.A.*

Joan K. Lunney / *United States Department of Agricultural Research Service, Beltsville, Maryland, U.S.A.*

Christopher John Lupton / *Texas A&M University, San Angelo, Texas, U.S.A.*

Michael D. MacNeil / *United States Department of Agriculture, Agricultural Research Service, Miles City, Montana, U.S.A.*

Donald C. Mahan / *The Ohio State University, Columbus, Ohio, U.S.A.*

Phelix Majiwa / *International Livestock Research Institute, Nairobi, Kenya*

Irek Malecki / *The University of Western Australia, Crawley, Australia*

Samantha A. Malusky / *University of Illinois, Urbana, Illinois, U.S.A.*

Elaine V. Marchello / *University of Arizona, Tucson, Arizona, U.S.A.*

John A. Marchello / *University of Arizona, Tucson, Arizona, U.S.A.*

Graeme B. Martin / *The University of Western Australia, Crawley, Australia*

Michael J. Martin / *University of Rochester Medical Center, Rochester, New York, U.S.A.*

Scott A. Martin / *University of Georgia, Athens, Georgia, U.S.A.*

J. H. Matis / *Texas A&M University, College Station, Texas, U.S.A.*

Robert W. Mayes / *Macaulay Institute, Aberdeen, U.K.*

Robert H. McCusker / *University of Illinois, Urbana, Illinois, U.S.A*

Lee R. McDowell / *University of Florida, Gainesville, Florida, U.S.A.*

John J. McGlone / *Texas Tech University, Lubbock, Texas, U.S.A.*

Lyle G. McNeal / *Utah State University, Logan, Utah, U.S.A.*

David Meisinger / *National Pork Board, Des Moines, Iowa, U.S.A.*

Joy A. Mench / *University of California, Davis, California, U.S.A.*

Margaret Merchant / *Macaulay Institute, Aberdeen, U.K.*

Robert A. Merkel / *Michigan State University, East Lansing, Michigan, U.S.A.*

Harry J. Mersmann / *Children's Nutrition Research Center, Baylor College of Medicine, Houston, Texas, U.S.A.*

Mark F. Miller / *Texas Tech University, Lubbock, Texas, U.S.A.*

John A. Milne / *The Macaulay Institute, Aberdeen, U.K.*

Alva D. Mitchell / *United States Department of Agriculture, Agricultural Research Service, Beltsville, Maryland, U.S.A.*

Diane E. Moody / *Purdue University, West Lafayette, Indiana, U.S.A.*

Edwin T. Moran, Jr. / *Auburn University, Auburn, Alabama, U.S.A.*

Saqib Mukhtar / *Texas A&M University, College Station, Texas, U.S.A.*

Michael R. Murphy / *University of Illinois at Urbana–Champaign, Urbana, Illinois, U.S.A.*

Tony Musoke / *International Livestock Research Institute, Nairobi, Kenya*

Laura A. Muzinic / *Kentucky State University, Frankfort, Kentucky, U.S.A.*

R. O. Myer / *University of Florida, NFREC Marianna, Florida, U.S.A.*

C. Jamie Newbold / *University of Wales, Aberystwyth, U.K.*

John A. Nienaber / *United States Department of Agriculture, Agricultural Research Service, Clay Center, Nebraska, U.S.A.*

David J. Nisbet / *United States Department of Agriculture, Agricultural Research Service, College Station, Texas, U.S.A.*

Dan Nonneman / *United States Department of Agriculture, Agricultural Research Service, Clay Center, Nebraska, U.S.A.*

Amy C. Norman / *University of Illinois at Urbana–Champaign, Urbana, Illinois, U.S.A.*

H. Duane Norman / *United States Department of Agriculture, Agricultural Research Service, Beltsville, Maryland, U.S.A.*

Jan E. Novakofski / *University of Illinois, Urbana, Illinois, U.S.A*

Charles M. Nyachoti / *University of Manitoba, Winnipeg, Manitoba, Canada*

A. M. Oberbauer / *University of California, Davis, California, U.S.A.*

Olav T. Oftedal / *Smithsonian Institution, Washington, D.C., U.S.A.*

James Oldfield / *Oregon State University, Corvallis, Oregon, U.S.A.*

L. Ollivier / *National Institute for Agricultural Research, Jouy-en-Josas, France*

Elizabeth A. Branford Oltenacu / *Cornell University, Ithaca, New York, U.S.A.*

Okanlawon Onagbesan / *K.U. Leuven, Leuven, Belgium*

Fred Owens / *Pioneer Hi-Bred International, Inc., Johnston, Iowa, U.S.A.*

Max J. Paape / *United States Department of Agricultural Research Service, Beltsville, Maryland, U.S.A.*

Wendy C. Palmore / *Texas Tech University, Lubbock, Texas, U.S.A.*

Young W. Park / *Fort Valley State University, Fort Valley, Georgia, U.S.A.*

John E. Parks / *Cornell University, Ithaca, New York, U.S.A.*

Geri Parsons / *Colorado State University, Fort Collins, Colorado, U.S.A.*

Gary G. Pearl / *Fats and Proteins Research Foundation, Inc., Bloomington, Illinois, U.S.A.*

R. Anne Pearson / *University of Edinburgh, Centre for Tropical Veterinary Medicine, Scotland, U.K.*

Carl A. Pinkert / *University of Rochester Medical Center, Rochester, New York, U.S.A.*

Jeffrey L. Platt / *Mayo Clinic, Rochester, Minnesota, U.S.A.*

Matthew H. Poore / *North Carolina State University, Raleigh, North Carolina, U.S.A.*

Jesus M. Porres / *Universidad de Granada, Grenada, Spain*

Sylvia P. Poulos / *United States Department of Agriculture, Agricultural Research Service, Athens, Georgia, U.S.A.*

J. Mark Powell / *United States Dairy Forage Research Center, Madison, Wisconsin, U.S.A.*

Randall S. Prather / *University of Missouri, Columbia, Missouri, U.S.A.*

Wayne D. Purcell / *Virginia Tech, Blacksburg, Virginia, U.S.A.*

Vernon G. Pursel / *United States Department of Agriculture, Agricultural Research Service, Beltsville, Maryland, U.S.A.*

M. Rassette / *Kansas State University, Manhattan, Kansas, U.S.A.*

Carrie E. Regenstein / *University of Wisconsin, Madison, Wisconsin, U.S.A.*

Joe M. Regenstein / *Cornell University, Ithaca, New York, U.S.A.*

R. M. Roberts / *University of Missouri, Columbia, Missouri, U.S.A.*

Gary A. Rohrer / *United States Department of Agriculture, Agricultural Research Service, Clay Center, Nebraska, U.S.A.*

Bernard E. Rollin / *Colorado State University, Fort Collins, Colorado, U.S.A.*

Michael N. Romanov / *Michigan State University, East Lansing, Michigan, U.S.A.*

Tilahun Sahlu / *Langston University, Langston, Oklahoma, U.S.A.*

Janeen L. Salak-Johnson / *University of Illinois, Urbana, Illinois, U.S.A.*

James Sales / *University of Maryland, College Park, Maryland, U.S.A.*

Tirath S. Sandhu / *Cornell University Duck Research Laboratory, Eastport, New York, U.S.A.*

P. T. Sangild / *Royal Veterinary and Agricultural University, Frederiksberg, Denmark*

Thomas E. Sauber / *Pioneer Hi-Bred International, Inc., Johnston, Iowa, U.S.A.*

Jeffrey W. Savell / *Texas A&M University, College Station, Texas, U.S.A.*

Lawrence R. Schaeffer / *University of Guelph, Guelph, Ontario, Canada*

A. C. Schlink / *CSIRO Livestock Industries, Wembley, Western Australia*

Armin Scholz / *United States Department of Agriculture, Agricultural Research Service, Beltsville, Maryland, U.S.A.*

Jon Tate Self / *Texas A&M University, College Station, Texas, U.S.A.*

Jeff S. Sharp / *The Ohio State University, Columbus, Ohio, U.S.A.*

C. M. Sherwin / *University of Bristol, Langford, U.K.*

Julie Stepanek Shiflett / *Juniper Economic Consulting, Byers, Colorado, U.S.A.*

Randall S. Singer / *University of Illinois at Urbana–Champaign, Urbana, Illinois, U.S.A.*

Lawrence C. Smith / *Université de Montréal, Quebec, Canada*

Michael F. Smith / *University of Missouri, Columbia, Missouri, U.S.A.*

Timothy P. L. Smith / *United States Department of Agriculture, Agricultural Research Service, Clay Center, Nebraska, U.S.A.*

John N. Sofos / *Colorado State University, Fort Collins, Colorado, U.S.A.*

Morris Soller / *The Hebrew University of Jerusalem, Jerusalem, Israel*

Brian K. Speake / *Scottish Agricultural College, Ayr, U.K.*

Thomas E. Spencer / *Texas A&M University, College Station, Texas, U.S.A.*

Rebecca K. Splan / *Virginia Tech, Blacksburg, Virginia, U.S.A.*

Chad A. Stahl / *University of Missouri, Columbia, Missouri, U.S.A.*

Hans H. Stein / *South Dakota State University, Brookings, South Dakota, U.S.A.*

Jeffrey S. Stevenson / *Kansas State University, Manhattan, Kansas, U.S.A.*

Nathan M. Stone / *University of Arkansas, Pine Bluff, Arkansas, U.S.A.*

James R. Stouffer / *Cornell University, Ithaca, New York, U.S.A.*

Peter F. Surai / *Scottish Agricultural College, Ayr, U.K.*

J. C. Swanson / *Kansas State University, Manhattan, Kansas, U.S.A.*

R. Mark Thallman / *United States Meat Animal Research Center, Clay Center, Nebraska, U.S.A.*

W. W. Thatcher / *University of Florida, Gainesville, Florida, U.S.A.*

Kenneth R. Thompson / *Kentucky State University, Frankfort, Kentucky, U.S.A.*

L. D. Thompson / *Texas Tech University, Lubbock, Texas, U.S.A.*

Paul B. Thompson / *Michigan State University, East Lansing, Michigan, U.S.A.*

Michael L. Thonney / *Cornell University, Ithaca, New York, U.S.A.*

Thomas L. Thurow / *University of Wyoming, Laramie, Wyoming, U.S.A.*

Michael J. Toscano / *United States Department of Agriculture, Agricultural Research Service, West Lafayette, Indiana, U.S.A.*

Ian A. Trounce / *University of Melbourne, Victoria, Australia*

Duane E. Ullrey / *Okemos, Michigan, U.S.A.; Michigan State University, East Lansing, Michigan, U.S.A.*

Peter J. Van Soest / *Cornell University, Ithaca, New York, U.S.A.*

Nguyen van Thu / *Cantho University, Can Tho City, Vietnam*

Vincent H. Varel / *United States Department of Agriculture, Agricultural Research Service, Clay Center, Nebraska, U.S.A.*

Martin Vavra / *United States Department of Agriculture, Forest Service, La Grande, Oregon, U.S.A.*

Trygve L. Veum / *University of Missouri, Columbia, Missouri, U.S.A.*

Martha M. Vogelsang / *Texas A&M University, College Station, Texas, U.S.A.*

Park W. Waldroup / *University of Arkansas, Fayetteville, Arkansas, U.S.A.*

Robert J. Wall / *United States Department of Agriculture, Agricultural Research Service, Beltsville, Maryland, U.S.A.*

Kangling Wang / *Sichuan Agricultural University, Yaan, Sichuan, China*

Simon Ward / *Fur Commission USA, Paranaque, Philippines*

Paul F. Watson / *Royal Veterinary College, London, United Kingdom*

Carl D. Webster / *Kentucky State University, Frankfort, Kentucky, U.S.A.*

James E. Wells / *United States Department of Agriculture, Agricultural Research Service, Clay Center, Nebraska, U.S.A.*

William L. Wendorff / *University of Wisconsin, Madison, Wisconsin, U.S.A.*

Robert P. Wettemann / *Oklahoma State University, Stillwater, Oklahoma, U.S.A.*

Matthew B. Wheeler / *University of Illinois, Urbana, Illinois, U.S.A.*

Bryan A. White / *University of Illinois at Urbana–Champaign, Urbana, Illinois, U.S.A.*

Gerald Wiener / *Roslin Institute, Edinburgh, U.K.*

Dale R. Woerner / *Texas Tech University, Lubbock, Texas, U.S.A.*

William R. Wolters / *United States Department of Agriculture, Agricultural Research Service, and University of Maine, Orono, Maine, U.S.A.*

J. D. Wood / *University of Bristol, Bristol, United Kingdom*

Guoyao Wu / *Texas A&M University, College Station, Texas, U.S.A.*

R. J. Xu / *University of Hong Kong, Hong Kong, China*

Hong Yang / *ADM Alliance Nutrition, Inc., Quincy, Illinois, U.S.A.*

Jong-Tseng Yen / *United States Department of Agriculture, Agricultural Research Service, Clay Center, Nebraska, U.S.A.*

Curtis R. Youngs / *Iowa State University, Ames, Iowa, U.S.A.*

Gideon Zeidler / *University of California, Riverside, California, U.S.A.*

Guolong Zhang / *Oklahoma State University, Stillwater, Oklahoma, U.S.A.*

Contents

xix

Preface

Domestic animals are an integral part of human existence. The human population approaches 7 billion in 2004 and is predicted to reach 10 billion by 2050. Food of animal origin provides about one-sixth of human food energy and one-third of human food protein, and demand is accelerating with the growth in population and affluence, especially in developing countries. Animal products make a crucial contribution to the continuing struggle to alleviate alarmingly prevalent malnutrition in the world. Social and environmental stability depend on efforts to balance natural resources with human needs and animals play a key role in this delicate effort.

The nearly 300 entries in this volume, covering the broad field of Animal Science, complement the vast information contained in the companion volumes in Marcel Dekker's Agropedia and underscore the interdependence of production agriculture, and economic and environmental sustainability in contributing to a stable and flourishing world society.

The Encyclopedia of Animal Science is a key reference work for policy makers, governmental bodies, private and public research professionals, agricultural producers, students, and the public. It is intended to be a ready source of current information covering a broad spectrum of topics related to the biology, production, and uses of animals and their products in a complex, diverse, and rapidly changing world.

Entry topics, arranged alphabetically in the volume, include a comprehensive array of categories, including: production characteristics, husbandry, and taxonomic classification of domestic farm animals; contributions of domestic animals to society, and their geographic distribution; comparative biological systems, e.g., genetics, nutrition, reproduction, growth and development, body composition; biological diversity; biotechnology; animal well-being; animal health management; feed resources for animals and from animals; fiber and integument resources from animals; plant-animal ecosystems; ecological balance and environmental quality; food safety; and factors influencing the future of animal science. Entries are succinct overviews, each of about 2000 words, designed to help the reader acquire basic familiarity with the key terms and current knowledge of the subject, augmented by selected literature citations. Specific features of the volume include both printed and on-line versions, the latter to be updated quarterly to ensure that the content remains current and relevant. We invite suggestions from users for additional important topics and/or changes to be addressed in on-line updates.

This volume resulted from the vision of Russell Dekker and a dedicated and creative Advisory Board consisting of 19 members, representing countries on all continents. The diligent efforts of this Board and of entry authors are deeply appreciated. In addition, we are indebted to the many reviewers whose constructive suggestions and insights materially enhanced the quality of individual entries and of the volume in total. We are especially grateful to the staff at Marcel Dekker, particularly Alison Cohen, for superb leadership in the handling of massive correspondence with authors, reviewers, and the editors.

Wilson G. Pond
Alan W. Bell
Cornell University
Ithaca, NY

Adaptation and Stress: Animal State of Being

Stanley E. Curtis
University of Illinois, Urbana, Illinois, U.S.A.

INTRODUCTION

Sound animal husbandry depends on application of scientific knowledge of many aspects of the biology of the animals we keep. Environmental aspects of animal care are based on application of principles of animal ecology in design, operation, troubleshooting, and correcting deficiencies. They are crucial to both economical animal production and responsible animal stewardship.

ADAPTATION

Any environment has factors that threaten to overwhelm its inhabitants. Animals are driven to adapt to their environments, and thereby remain fit. Adaptation is an animal's adjustment to its environment, especially a nonideal one, so its life and species can continue.

Realistic Expectations

Animals sometimes fail to adapt; they experience stresses of various kinds. So they may feel well, fair, or ill (described later). We should expect an animal to experience well-being mostly, fair-being sometimes, ill-being once in a while. When an animal shows signs of failing to adapt, correcting the problem may not be easy.

Animal Responses

An animal's environment consists of a complex of elements, each of which varies over time, across space, in intensity. Most combine in additive fashion as they affect an animal.

Internal steady state

An animal normally maintains steady states over time in the various aspects of its internal environment. This mechanism—homeokinesis—is the general basis of environmental adaptation. When an animal perceives a threat or actual shift in some internal or external feature, it reacts to preempt or counteract that change. It attempts to keep an internal steady state, and thereby to survive and thrive. The essence of an animal's homeokinetic mechanisms is similar to that of a home's simple thermostat: a negative-feedback control loop.

Coping

An environmental adaptation refers to any behavioral, functional, immune, or structural trait that favors an animal's fitness—its ability to survive and reproduce under given (especially adverse) conditions. When an animal successfully keeps or regains control of its bodily integrity and psychic stability, it is said to have coped.

A given stimulus complex provokes different responses by different animals, and even by the same animal from time to time. Tactics vary. Its response depends on the individual's inherent adaptability, accumulated life experiences, current adaptation status, and current ability to muster extraordinary responses.

STRESS

Failure to Adapt

Stress occurs when the stimulation an animal is experiencing goes beyond that individual's ability to adapt. Environmental stress may ensue when the environment changes, adaptation status changes, or an animal is moved to another environment. When an animal has coped, its response is an adaptive response. But there always are limits to adaptability. When attempts to adapt fail, the response is a stress response, the stimulus a stressor.

Failure to adapt—stress—has negative consequences for animal state of being. Understanding untoward consequences of such breakdowns for bodily integrity is relatively clear-cut. But psychic disturbance or collapse is often not even recognized. It is now believed that humans can survive stress only to the extent we can cope

Encyclopedia of Animal Science
DOI: 10.1081/E-EAS 120019427

psychologically. Likewise, Ian J. H. Duncan[1] thinks that animal state of being has to do with animal feelings.

COPING

The numerous possible strategies and tactics for counteracting stimuli an animal usually has at its disposal imbue flexibility and power to the animal's adaptive responses when it faces an adverse environment. But when an animal responds to environmental stimuli, it is not necessarily under stress or distress. Responding to stimuli is a normal biological feat routinely carried out by every normal, unstressed creature that lives. Typical scenarios of environmental stimuli and animal responses run a wide gamut. Modified versions of nine schemes created by Donald M. Broom and Kenneth G. Johnson[2] follow:

1. In the face of stimuli, internal steady state is maintained with ordinary basal responses. State of being is very well.
2. Complete adaptation achieved with minor extraordinary response. Stimuli provoke adaptation. Fitness and performance may be briefly compromised, but wellness promptly returns.
3. Sometimes, animal response to stimuli over time is neither extraordinary nor adequate. For so long as the impingement continues, fitness and performance may be reduced—minor stress and fairness ensue—but after that, wellness returns.
4. Stimuli elicit some minor extraordinary response, but over time this is inadequate for complete adaptation. Both fitness and performance decrease awhile (fairness), after which wellness returns. Stress is present at scheme 4 and above.
5. An animal's extraordinary response over a long period achieves only incomplete adaptation. Although fitness remains relatively high, performance is reduced. The animal experiences overall fair-being.
6. To completely adapt, an animal sometimes must mount an extreme response. During adaptation and recovery periods, fitness and performance decline. The animal is only fair.
7. Despite some extraordinary response to stimuli, complete adaptation is not achieved long term. Fitness and performance decline; the animal becomes ill.
8. In some cases, an extreme response does not result in complete adaptation—even long term—reducing the ill animal's fitness and performance.
9. An environmental stimulus may be so enormous and swift that the animal succumbs before it can respond.

Measuring Impacts

Impacts of environmental impingements are estimated by measuring their effects on the animal. The same environment that would quickly chill to death a newborn piglet might be well-tolerated by the sow. Differences in thermal adaptabilities of the two put the same environment in the piglet's cold zone, the sow's neutral zone.

Tolerance Limits, Collapse, and Death

An animal ordinarily is confronted by more than one stimulus at a time. Stimuli also impinge sequentially. Animals in practical settings generally need to cope with multiple stimuli.

A range of tolerance sets limits for an environmental factors within which an animal can readily cope, thrive, reproduce, survive—i.e., experience wellness. Outside this range are the upper and lower ranges of resistance. If an animal resides long enough outside its tolerance range, it eventually will die due to environmental stress.

Kinds of Stress Response

There are four kinds of stress response. Some reduce an animal's state of being; others enhance it. *Understress* occurs in simple environments that lack certain features (social companions, play items) (stimulus underload). Sometimes animals give behavioral signs of understress (lethargy; exaggerated, repetitive activity apparently devoid of purpose (stereotypy); some other disturbed behavior). *Eustress* (good stress): situations of extraordinary responses, but which the animal finds tolerable or even enjoyable. *Overstress*: environmental situations that provoke minor stress responses. *Distress* (bad stress): circumstances that provoke major stress responses. Judging from signs of negative emotions (anxiety, fear, frustration, pain), distress causes an animal to suffer, but to what extent is not yet known.

STATE OF BEING

An animal's state of being is determined by any response the environment requires and the extent to which the animal is coping. When readily adapting, the animal is well. When having some difficulty, it is fair. When frankly unable to cope, it is ill. In reality, environments that make animals ill are not uncommon. But it is our moral responsibility to minimize such occasions and correct them to the extent possible.

Scientific Assessment

Our understanding of an animal's state of being depends on generally accepted observations, scientific laws and theories, and unique individual experiences. In 1983, Marian Stamp Dawkins and Ian J. H. Duncan believed that the terms ''well-being'' and ''suffering'' would be very difficult to define.[3] That remains the case two decades later. Until more is known, it is unlikely that kept animals will enjoy more of the objectively defined well-being for which we all should hope. Following are some questions to be asked in assessing animal state of being.[4] Is the animal

- Having its actual needs met, achieving internal integrity and psychic stability, coping, adapting?
- Showing frank signs of sickness, injury, trauma, emotional disturbance?
- As free of suffering as possible, experiencing mostly neutral and positive emotional states?
- To some extent able to control its environment, predict it, live harmoniously in it?
- Performing—growing, reproducing, lactating, competing, working—at a high level?
- Showing signs of imminent illness or being in a vulnerable state?

Animal Needs

When an animal *actually* needs something it does not have, it is experiencing a deficiency. At any moment, an animal has specific needs based on its heredity; life experiences; bodily, psychic, and environmental conditions. Given its needs at a given point, then, the biological, chemical, and physical elements of its environment determine whether those needs are being fulfilled.

Functional Priorities Under Stress

A performing animal is one that is producing some product, progeny, or work or performing some activity useful to humans. The rate of performance of a constitutionally fit animal usually is the best single indicator of that animal's state of being.[5] When its performance wanes, the animal probably is not as well is it could be.

When bodily resources become limiting—as often happens during stress—some processes must be downplayed so others more vital at the moment can ascend. The goals of individual survival (maintenance) and species perpetuation (reproduction)—in that order—are an ani-

mal's top priorities. Other performance processes may not be critical to an individual's survival or reproduction, so they are least protected and least spared.

When an animal responds to any stimulus, its maintenance needs invariably increase. Resource expenditures in support of maintenance processes increase progressively along with stress intensity, so the animal's potential performance capabilities progressively decrease.

How Animal Responses Affect Performance

Environmental stimuli provoke an animal to respond, which in turn can influence performance processes in five ways.[5] Responses:

1. Alter internal functions. As an unintentional consequence, certain stress hormones secreted as part of long-term adaptive or stress responses can reduce a foal's growth rate.
2. Divert nutrients from other maintenance processes and performance. A nursling piglet that increases metabolic rate simply to keep its body warm in a chilly environment will have fewer nutrients left for disease resistance and growth.
3. Directly reduce animal productivity. Thermoregulatory responses to hot environments sometimes include reducing internal heat production. Eggs laid by heat-stressed hens weigh less than normal, due partly to decreased feed intake, partly to a homeokinetic reduction in egg synthesis (which gives off heat).
4. Impair disease resistance. As a consequence, e.g., individual feedlot cattle under social stress due to aggressive group mates are more likely to become infected and diseased.
5. Increase variation in animal performance. Individual animals differ in responses to stimuli—and therefore in performance—even when residing in the same adverse environment. Stress increases individual variation in performance.

Other Considerations

Other environmental aspects of animal care include the concepts of optimal stimulation, enrichment, predictability, controllability, frustration, and helplessness.[6]

CONCLUSION

Foundations of success in environmental aspects of animal care are the fundamental principles of animal ecology and their application. Every situation is complex and unique. There are no general recipes in these matters. The fundamental principles have been set forth here.

REFERENCES

1. Duncan, I.J.H. Feelings of Animals. In *Encyclopedia of Animal Rights and Animal Welfare*; Bekoff, M., Meaney, C.A., Eds.; Greenwood Press: Westport, CT, 1998.
2. Broom, D.M.; Johnson, K.G. *Stress and Animal Welfare*; Kluwer Academic Publishing: Amsterdam, 1993.
3. Duncan, I.J.H.; Dawkins, M.S. The Problem of Assessing "Well-Being" and "Suffering" in Farm Animals. In *Indicators Relevant to Farm Animal Welfare*; Smidt, D., Ed.; Martinus Nijhoff Publishers: Boston, 1983.
4. CAST. *The Well-being of Agricultural Animals*; Curtis, S.E., Ed.; Council on Agricultural Science and Technology: Ames, IA, 1997.
5. Curtis, S.E.; Widowski, T.M.; Johnson, R.W.; Dahl, G.E.; McFarlane, J.M. *Environmental Aspects of Animal Care*; Blackwell Publishing Professional: Ames, IA, 2005.
6. *The Biology of Animal Stress: Basic Principles and Implications for Animal Welfare*; Moberg, G.P., Mench, J.A., Eds.; CABI Publishers: New York, 2000.

Adaptation and Stress: Neuroendocrine, Physiological, and Behavioral Responses

Janeen L. Salak-Johnson
University of Illinois, Urbana, Illinois, U.S.A.

INTRODUCTION

During the daily routines of animals, the animal responds to numerous challenges with a variety of responses, including structural and behavioral changes in the brain and body, which enable both behavioral and physiological stability to be maintained. In some incidences, adaptive physiological changes are not sufficient to achieve the animal's requirements and in these situations, defense mechanisms are initiated, which are collectively referred to as stress responses. Stress is a term that is generally associated with negative consequences, but stress is not always bad. Often, organisms seek stress and relish the euphoric feeling and reward associated with stressful experiences (e.g., skiing, copulation). The term stress is full of ambiguities; thus, no clear universal definition has emerged. For this discussion, "stress" is defined as a perceived threat to homeostasis, which elicits behavioral and physiological responses. The stress response consists of a complex array of behavioral and physiological adaptive changes that are initiated as a means of restoring homeostasis. Exposure to adverse stimuli results in a well-orchestrated series of responses that can typically cause alterations in autonomic, neuroendocrine, or immune function along with complex changes in behavior. These homeostatic mechanisms enable the organism to maintain behavioral and physiological stability despite fluctuating environmental conditions.

HISTORICAL—CONCEPT OF STRESS

Life exists by maintaining a complex of dynamic equilibrium or homeostasis that is constantly challenged by internal and external adverse stimuli;[1] often these stressful conditions are too demanding for the animal to adapt. However, animals have evolved mechanisms that enable them to adapt to the numerous stressors in their lives. An animal can initiate several types of biological responses to alleviate stress. These responses often result in shifts or alterations in biological resources that are normally used for other basal functions. Thus, under most circumstances the biological cost (in terms of biological function) is minimal for acute stressors, but during prolonged stress the cost is significant, thus leading to a prepathological or pathological state.[2] The stress response elicited by a stressor protects the animal and restores homeostasis, thus enhancing the probability of survival.

The stress response initiated by a stressor results in the release of neurotransmitters and hormones that serve as the central nervous system's (CNS) messengers to other parts of the body. The CNS obtains information from the external environment and signals to the organism that a particular danger or threat to homeostasis has been perceived. The perception of the threat is mostly related to prior experience and the physiological state of the animal (Fig. 1). Once the threat has been perceived, adaptive responses are initiated by evoking well-orchestrated defenses that include behavioral and physiological adjustments. Neuroendocrine changes are initiated to meet energy requirements for behavioral responses and to maintain homeostasis. It is the final stage of the stress response that determines whether the animal is simply experiencing a brief disruption in homeostasis with no significant consequences or experiencing extreme difficulty, which may lead to the development of disease. Oftentimes, the consequences of the stress response are adaptive in nature. However, if the animal reaches a state in which the intensity and duration of the stressor is severe and uncontrollable, compromising health and reproduction, this condition may lead to development of a prepathological state or pathology.

NEUROENDOCRINE RESPONSES

The neuroendocrine responses to stressors are important adaptation and coping mechanisms that occur in response to a threatening stimulus. The adaptive changes initiated by stressors involve activation of the hypothalamic-pituitary-adrenal (HPA) axis. The hypothalamus and the

Encyclopedia of Animal Science
DOI: 10.1081/E-EAS 120034100

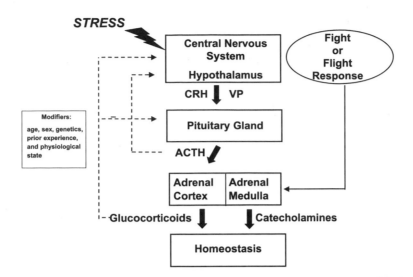

Fig. 1 This diagram depicts the activation of the HPA axis in response to stress. The response is perceived and organized in the CNS, which in turn activates either the endocrine pathway or fight-or-flight response so that the animal can return to homeostasis. The type of response(s) the animal initiates is dependent upon various modifiers.

brainstem are pivotal regions of the brain that control the animal's response to stress. Once the threat to homeostasis is perceived, the HPA axis is activated and the hormones corticotropin releasing hormone (CRH) and vasopressin (VP) are released from the neurons of the paraventricular nuclei (Fig. 1). CRH stimulates the pituitary gland to secrete adrenocorticotropin hormone (ACTH) and other peptides (i.e., β-endorphin). VP plays a role in sustaining HPA responsiveness and, along with CRH, has a synergistic impact on ACTH secretion. Elevated ACTH stimulates the adrenal cortex to increase synthesis and production of glucocorticoid hormones and regulates the secretion of glucocorticoids.

The glucocorticoids influence homeostasis and the biological response to stress. The glucocorticoids are essential for regulating basal activity of the HPA axis and terminating the stress response. Glucocorticoids terminate the stress response through an inhibitory feedback loop at the pituitary and hypothalamus (Fig. 1). Further responsiveness within the HPA is dependent upon this negative feedback, which is influenced by HPA facilitation. In addition, stress activates the secretion of the catecholamines, which influence the HPA axis, and mediates many changes associated with the stress response.

Cortisol and CRH Expression

Cortisol is secreted under diverse conditions that impact both physiology and behavior.[3] Short-term cortisol release is protective and facilitates normal physiological and behavioral adaptive processes, whereas high levels of cortisol have detrimental effects on various regulatory processes such as immune and neuroendocrine systems. The behavioral and physiological effects of CRH and cortisol are often independent of one another; however, cortisol can influence CRH neurons by inhibiting and affecting the responsiveness of CRH neurons. Cortisol can lead to increases in CRH production and expression in various regions of the brain. In fact, behavioral responses are influenced by cortisol, facilitating CRH expression.

PHYSIOLOGICAL RESPONSES

Numerous physiological changes are associated with the stress response that enables the animal to adapt to aversive stimuli. Short-term activation of the HPA axis results in changes in metabolic responses such as rapid mobilization of energy stores for initiation of the fight-or-flight response. In the long run, suppression and changes in other physiological responses such as anabolic processes, energy stores, and the immune system have negative consequences. Stress results in mobilization of energy stores to maintain normal brain and muscle function while increasing glucose utilization, which are essential to maintaining physiological stability. Cardiovascular output and respiration are enhanced during stress to mobilize glucose and oxygen for the tissues. The gastrointestinal tract during acute stress is inhibited. Many of these changes are associated with stressful events that prepare the animal for fight or flight. These precise physiological changes are geared to alter the internal milieu in order to increase survivability, but if activated frequently and for too long, the results can be detrimental.

The immune response and processes involving cellular growth and reproduction are temporarily inhibited during stress to allow the animal to utilize biological resources for other purposes (such as flight). Long-term stress can cause disruptions in reproductive physiology and sexual behavior. Stress modulates the immune system. Acute or short-term stress may suppress, enhance, or have no effect on the immune system. Chronic or long-term stress can suppress the immune system, thus making it more difficult for the animal to fight disease effectively. Glucocorticoids and other components may contribute to stress-induced immunosuppression, but can also serve as a protective mechanism against stress. In addition, feed intake, appetite, and other catabolic and anabolic processes are altered in response to stress. Physiological responses to stressful situations are critical to the adaptability of the animal, but repeated exposure to stressors or a massive single stressful experience may lead to pathological consequences.

BEHAVIORAL RESPONSES

Stress elicits a broad range of behavioral responses in which the profile is dependent upon characteristics of the organism (i.e., coping ability, dominance order) and the stressor (i.e., severity, duration). Most often these behaviors are indicative of fear and anxiety. Animals frequently exhibit decreases in exploratory activity and social interaction while exhibiting increases in locomotor activity, vocalization, and inappropriate behaviors (e.g., stereotypies) in response to stressors. Typically, stress causes changes in normal behaviors instead of causing new behaviors. In general, behavioral adjustments to stress are adaptive in nature. It has been suggested that at the onset or during mild bouts of stress, behavioral adjustments can modulate the animal back to ''normal'' without eliciting a physiological response.[4] During mild thermal stress one can only detect behavioral adjustments in response to thermal stress (end of the comfort zone), which may be enough to help the animal cope. In fact, it's not until the thermal environment changes further that the animal requires measurable behavioral and physiological adjustments. Despite these adjustments, the homeokinetic responses are within normal range.[4] Essentially, it's not until the animal experiences

stress for a prolonged period of time or is in a state in which behavioral adjustments are no longer adequate that other physiological processes are affected, leading to a prepathological state or development of pathology. It is this point in which behavioral adjustments are no longer adequate to return to homeostasis.

The central state of the brain orchestrates the behavioral responses in anticipation of and in adaptation to environmental events.[5] Behavioral responses to stress involve neuronal systems in which peptides function as neurotransmitters. It has been suggested that CRH coordinates behavioral responses to stress such as feed intake, anxiety-like behaviors, arousal, learning, and memory–just to name a few. CRH is a critical mediator of stress-related behaviors and its influence on behavior is dependent on the baseline arousal state of the animal. In nonstressed animals under low levels of arousal, CRH is behaviorally activating while under stressful conditions, exogenous CRH causes enhanced behavioral responses. Neuropeptides prepare the animal to perceive stimuli and cause an animal to behave a certain way, which enables it to respond appropriately to environmental changes. Other neuropeptides are probably involved in the behavioral responses to stress, but few have been described at this time.

CONCEPT OF ALLOSTASIS

A new concept called allostasis has evolved in order to encompass the various degrees and outcomes of stress responses across species. Allostasis is a process that supports homeostasis in which stability is achieved through change.[3] Thus, the physiological parameters change as environments and other life history stages change. Allostasis involves the whole brain and body and is regulated by the brain's attempt to alter and sustain behavioral and physiological adjustments in response to changing environments and challenges. Thus, the concept of allostasis incorporates the adaptive function of regulating homeokinetic responses to the pathological effects of the inability to adapt.[5]

An allostatic state leads to an imbalance of the primary mediators of allostasis (i.e., glucocorticoids, catecholamines), overproduction of some and underproduction of others.[6] Allostatic load is the cumulative effect of an allostatic state. Allostatic load can increase dramatically if additional loads of unpredictable events in the environment occur in addition to adaptive responses to seasonal or other demands. In essence, the mediators of allostasis are protective and adaptive, thus increasing survival and health.[3] However, they can be damaging.

CONCLUSION

In terms of short-term goals, the stress response initiated by a particular stressor provides a series of homeostatic mechanisms as well as behavioral and physiological adaptations. On the other hand, allostasis enables an organism to maintain physiological and behavioral stability despite adverse and fluctuating environmental conditions. The responses to stress involve numerous endocrine and neural systems that contribute to orchestrating defenses that enable the animal to adapt and maintain behavioral and physiological stability. Behavioral and physiological processes work in conjunction to regulate the viability of the internal milieu. During acute stress, the biological cost to an animal is minimal, but maximal during chronic stress. The inability to initiate an appropriate and adequate stress response can be highly deleterious, thus affecting health and reproduction, which in turn impacts survivability and well-being.

REFERENCES

1. Chrousos, G.P.; Gold, P.W. The concepts of stress system disorders: Overview of behavioral and physical homeostasis. J. Am. Med. Assoc. **1992**, *267* (9), 1244–1252.
2. Moberg, G.P. Biological Response to Stress: Implications for Animal Welfare. In *The Biology of Animal Stress*; Moberg, G.P, Mench, J.A., Eds.; CABI Publishing: New York, 2000; 1–21.
3. McEwen, B.S.; Wingfield, J.C. The concept of allostasis in biology and biomedicine. Horm. Behav. **2003**, *43* (1), 2–15.
4. McGlone, J.J. What is animal welfare? J. Agric. Environ. Ethics **1993**, *6*, 26–36.
5. Schulkin, J. Allostasis: A neural behavioral perspective. Horm. Behav. **2003**, *43* (1), 21–27.
6. Koob, G.F.; LeMoal, M. Drug addiction, dysregulation of reward, and allostasis. Neuropsychopharmacology **2001**, *24* (2), 97–129.

Amino Acids: Metabolism and Functions

Guoyao Wu
Jon Tate Self
Texas A&M University, College Station, Texas, U.S.A.

INTRODUCTION

An amino acid contains both amino and acid groups. The names for amino acids are largely derived from Greek (e.g., glycine from the Greek word ''glykos,'' meaning sweet). Over 300 amino acids occur in nature, but only 20 serve as building blocks of proteins. Amino acids are substrates for the synthesis of many biologically active substances (including NO, polyamines, glutathione, nucleic acids, hormones, creatine, and neurotransmitters) that regulate metabolic pathways essential to the life and productivity of animals. Their abnormal metabolism disturbs whole-body homeostasis, impairs animal growth and development, and may even cause death. Thus, knowledge of amino acid biochemistry and nutrition is of enormous importance for both animal agriculture and medicine.

AMINO ACID CHEMISTRY

Except for glycine, all amino acids have an asymmetric carbon and exhibit optical activity.[1] The absolute configuration of amino acids (L- or D-isomers) is defined with reference to glyceraldehyde. Except for proline, all protein amino acids have both a primary amino group and a carboxyl group linked to the α-carbon atom (hence α-amino acids). In β-amino acids (e.g., taurine and β-alanine), an amino group links to the β-carbon atom. Posttranslationally modified amino acids (e.g., 4-hydroxyproline, 5-hydroxylysine, 3-methylhistidine, and dimethylarginines) occur in some proteins. The biochemical properties of amino acids vary because of their different side chains. The amino and acid groups of all amino acids are completely ionized (zwitterionic form) at physiological pH.

Amino acids are stable in aqueous solution at physiological temperature, except for glutamine, which is slowly cyclized to pyroglutamate (<2%/day at 1 mM), and cysteine, which undergoes rapid oxidation to cystine. Acid hydrolysis of protein results in almost complete destruction of tryptophan, the oxidation of cysteine to cystine, and some degradation of methionine, serine, threonine, and tyrosine. Alkaline hydrolysis is used for tryptophan determination because of its relative stability. Both acid and alkaline hydrolysis are accompanied by deamination of glutamine and asparagine.

AMINO ACID METABOLISM

Amino Acid Synthesis

Microorganisms in the digestive tract can synthesize all amino acids in the presence of ammonia, sulfur, and carbohydrates.[2] All animals can synthesize tyrosine as well as the following amino acids and their carbon skeletons: alanine, asparagine, aspartate, cysteine, glutamate, glutamine, glycine, proline, and serine. The ability to synthesize citrulline and its carbon skeleton varies among species, but arginine can be made from citrulline in all animal cells.

Because of its large mass (representing 45% of adult body weight), skeletal muscle accounts for the majority of glutamine and alanine synthesis from branched-chain amino acids (BCAA) in animals. These synthetic pathways also occur in extrahepatic tissues, including the brain, adipose tissue, intestine, kidney, lung, placenta, and lactating mammary gland. The liver and kidney are the major sites for the synthesis of tyrosine from phenylalanine by phenylalanine hydroxylase, whereas hepatic transsulfuration is primarily responsible for cysteine synthesis from methionine. There is no conversion of tyrosine into phenylalanine or cysteine into methionine. In contrast, there is reversible interconversion of serine into glycine by hydroxymethyltransferase in tissues, including the liver, kidney, lactating mammary tissue, placenta, and intestine. Proline can be synthesized from arginine in animal cells containing mitochondria, and from glutamine and glutamate in most mammals (e.g., pigs and ruminants).[3]

Utilization of precursors for the synthesis of L-amino acids is of practical importance in animal production. Most D-amino acids, except for D-lysine, D-threonine, D-cystine, D-arginine and D-histidine, can be converted into L-amino acids in animals via widespread D-amino acid oxidase and transamination.[4] The efficiency of D-amino acid utilization, on a molar basis of the L-isomer,

Encyclopedia of Animal Science
DOI: 10.1081/E-EAS 120019428

may be 20 to 100%, depending on species and substrates. Most of the α-ketoacids can be transaminated to form L-amino acids in animals.

Amino Acid Degradation

Microorganisms in the digestive tract degrade all amino acids, with ammonia, fatty acids (including branched-chain fatty acids, acetate, propionate and butyrate), H_2S, and CO_2 being major products. In animals, amino acids are catabolized by cell- and tissue-specific pathways. The liver is the principal organ for the catabolism of all amino acids except for BCAA and glutamine. There is growing recognition that the mammalian small intestine extensively degrades essential and nonessential amino acids, such that circulating glutamate, aspartate, and glutamine arise almost entirely from endogenous synthesis.[3]

Although each amino acid has its own unique catabolic pathway(s), the catabolism of all amino acids exhibits a number of common characteristics (Table 1). Their important products include glucose, ketone bodies, fatty acids, urea, uric acid, and other nitrogenous substances (Table 2). Complete oxidation of amino acids occurs only if their carbon skeletons are ultimately converted to acetyl-CoA, which is oxidized via the Krebs cycle. On a molar basis, oxidation of amino acids is less efficient for ATP production compared with fat and glucose. Glutamine, however, is a major fuel for rapidly dividing cells, including enterocytes, immunologically activated lymphocytes, and tumors.[1]

Ammonia is an essential substrate in intermediary metabolism, but at high concentrations it is toxic to animal cells (particularly in the brain). Thus, plasma levels of ammonia (primarily NH_4^+) must be precisely regulated. Syntheses of urea (via hepatic and intestinal urea cycles) and uric acid (via hepatic purine metabolism) represent the major pathways for ammonia detoxification in mammals and birds, respectively. Hepatic ureagenesis is subject to both short- and long-term regulation: 1) availabilities of substrates and N-acetylglutamate, and 2) adaptive changes in the amounts of urea cycle enzymes.[5] Glutamine synthetase is a major regulatory enzyme for uric acid synthesis in uricotelic species.

Species Differences in Amino Acid Metabolism

Metabolic pathways for most amino acids are generally similar between microorganisms and animals, but important differences do occur. For example, N-acetylglutamate is an intermediate of and an allosteric activator for arginine synthesis in microorganisms and animal cells, respectively.[2,5] Second, deiminase plays a significant role in microbial arginine degradation to form citrulline and ammonia; animal cells, however, lack this pathway. Third, the conversion of proline into pyrroline-5-carboxylate is catalyzed by $NAD(P)^+$-dependent proline dehydrogenase in microorganisms, but by oxygen-dependent proline oxidase in animal cells. Regarding differences among animals, most mammals (except for cats and ferrets) can convert glutamine, glutamate, and proline into citrulline in enterocytes, whereas birds do not. Similarly, ammonia detoxification pathways differ remarkably between ureotelic and uricotelic organisms.

Table 1 Reactions initiating amino acid catabolism in animals

Reactions	Examples	
Transamination	Leucine + α-Ketoglutarate ⇌ α-Ketoisocaproate + Glutamate	(1)
Deamidation	Glutamine + H_2O → Glutamate + NH_4^+	(2)
Oxidative deamination	Glutamate + NAD^+ ⇌ α-Ketoglutarate + NH_3 + NADH + H^+	(3)
Decarboxylation	Ornithine → Putrescine + CO_2	(4)
Hydroxylation	Arginine + O_2 + NADPH + H^+ → NO + Citrulline + $NADP^+$	(5)
Reduction	Lysine + α-Ketoglutarate + NADPH + H^+ → Saccharopine + $NADP^+$	(6)
Dehydrogenation	Threonine + NAD^+ → 2-Amino-3-ketobutyrate + NADH + H^+	(7)
Hydrolysis	Arginine + H_2O → Ornithine + Urea	(8)
Dioxygenation	Cysteine + O_2 → Cysteinesulfinate	(9)
One-carbon unit transfer	Glycine + N^5-N^{10}-methylene-THF ⇌ Serine + THF	(10)
Condensation	Methionine + Mg-ATP → S-Adenosylmethionine + Mg-PPi + Pi	(11)
Oxidation	Proline + $\frac{1}{2}O_2$ → Pyrroline-5-carboxylate + H_2O	(12)

Enzymes that catalyze the indicated reactions are: 1) BCAA transaminase; 2) glutaminase; 3) glutamate dehydrogenase; 4) ornithine decarboxylase; 5) NO synthase; 6) lysine:α-ketoglutarate reductase; 7) threonine dehydrogenase; 8) arginase; 9) cysteine dioxygenase; 10) hydroxymethyltransferase; 11) S-adenosylmethionine synthase; and 12) proline oxidase. THF, tetrahydrofolate. Tetrahydrobiopterin is required for hydroxylation of arginine, phenylalanine, tyrosine, and tryptophan.

Table 2 Important nitrogenous products of amino acid metabolism in animals

Precursors	Products	Functions
Arginine	NO	Vasodilator; neurotransmitter, signaling molecule; angiogenesis; cell metabolism; apoptosis (programmed cell death); immune response
	Agmatine	Signaling molecule; inhibitor of NO synthase and ornithine decarboxylase; brain and renal function
Cysteine	Taurine	Antioxidant; muscle contraction; bile acid conjugates; retinal function
Glutamate	γ-Aminobutyrate	Neurotransmitter; inhibitor of glutamatergic, serotonin, and NEPN activities
Glutamine	Glu and Asp	Neurotransmitters; fuels for enterocytes; components of the malate shuttle
	Glucosamine	Glycoprotein and ganglioside formation; inhibitor of NO synthesis
	Ammonia	Renal regulation of acid–base balance; synthesis of carbamoylphosphate, glutamate and glutamine
Glycine	Serine	One-carbon unit metabolism; ceramide and phosphatidylserine formation
	Heme	Hemoproteins (e.g., hemoglobin, myoglobin, catalase, cytochrome C)
Histidine	Histamine	Allergic reaction; vasodilator; gastric acid and central acetylcholine secretion
Methionine	Homocysteine	Oxidant; inhibitor of NO synthesis; risk factor for cardiovascular disease
	Betaine	Methylation of homocysteine to methionine; one-carbon unit metabolism
	Choline	Synthesis of betaine, acetylcholine (neurotransmitter and vasodilator) and phosphatidylcholine
	Cysteine	An important sulfur-containing amino acid; formation of disulfide bonds
Phenylalanine	Tyrosine	A versatile aromatic amino acid containing a hydroxyl group
Serine	Glycine	Antioxidant; bile acid conjugates; neurotransmitter; immunomodulator
Tryptophan	Serotonin	Neurotransmitter; smooth muscle contraction; hemostasis
	N-acetylserotonin	Inhibitor of sepiapterin reductase and thus tetrahydrobiopterin synthesis
	Melatonin	Circadian and circannual rhythms; free radical scavenger; antioxidant
Tyrosine	Dopamine	Neurotransmitter; apoptosis; lymphatic constriction
	EPN and NEPN	Neurotransmitters; smooth muscle contraction; cAMP production; glycogen and energy metabolism
	Melanin	Dark-color pigment; free radical scavenger; chelator of metals
	T3 and T4	Gene expression; tissue differentiation and development; cell metabolism
Arg and Met	Polyamines	Gene expression; DNA and protein synthesis; ion channel function; apoptosis; signal transduction; antioxidants; cell function, proliferation, and differentiation
Gln and Asp	Nucleic acids	Gene expression; cell cycle and function; protein and uric acid synthesis
Gln and Trp	NAD(P)	Coenzymes for oxidoreductases; substrate of poly(ADP-ribose) polymerase
Arg, Pro or Gln	Ornithine	Glutamate, glutamine, and polyamine synthesis; mitochondrial integrity
Arg, Met, Gly	Creatine	Energy metabolism in muscle and nerve; antioxidant; antiviral; antitumor
Cys, Glu, and Gly	Glutathione	Free radical scavenger; antioxidant; formation of leukotrienes, mercapturate, glutathionylspermidine, glutathione-NO adduct and glutathionylproteins; signal transduction; gene expression; apoptosis; spermatogenesis; sperm maturation; cellular redox state
Gln, Glu, and Pro	Citrulline	Free radical scavenger; arginine synthesis
Lys, Met, and Ser	Carnitine	Transport of long-chain fatty acids into mitochondria; storage of energy as acetylcarnitine

EPN, epinephrine; NEPN, norepinephrine; T3, triiodothyronine; T4, thyroxine.

REGULATORY FUNCTIONS OF AMINO ACIDS

Through the production of diversified metabolites, amino acids regulate cell metabolism and play vital roles in animal homeostasis (Table 2). For example, arginine stimulates the secretion of insulin, growth hormone, pro-lactin, glucagon, and placental lactogen, thereby modulating protein, lipid, and glucose metabolism. Second, arginine activates N-carbamoylglutamate synthase, which uses glutamate as a substrate. Thus, arginine and glutamate maintain the urea cycle in an active state. Third, through signaling pathways involving the mammalian target of rapamycin protein kinase, leucine increases protein synthesis and inhibits proteolysis in skeletal muscle. Fourth, alanine inhibits pyruvate kinase, thereby regulating gluconeogenesis and glycolysis to ensure net glucose production by hepatocytes during periods of food deprivation. Fifth, glutamate and aspartate mediate the transfer of reducing equivalents across the mitochondrial membrane and thus regulate glycolysis and cellular redox state. Finally, coordination of amino acid metabolism among the liver, skeletal muscle, intestine, and immune cells maximizes glutamine availability for renal ammoniagenesis and therefore the regulation of acid–base balance in acidotic animals.[1]

CONCLUSION

Amino acids display remarkable metabolic and regulatory versatility. They serve as essential precursors for the synthesis of proteins and other biologically important molecules and also regulate metabolic pathways vital to the health, growth, development, and functional integrity of animals. Future studies are necessary to elucidate the mechanisms that regulate amino acid metabolism at cellular, tissue, and whole-body levels. Better understand-

ing of these processes will lead to improved efficiency of protein production by animals.

ACKNOWLEDGMENT

Work in our laboratory is supported, in part, by USDA grants.

REFERENCES

1. Brosnan, J.T. Amino acids, then and now—A reflection on Sir Hans Krebs' contribution to nitrogen metabolism. IUBMB Life **2001**, *52*, 265–270.
2. Voet, D.; Viet, J.G. *Biochemistry*; John Wiley & Sons Inc.: New York, NY, 1995.
3. Wu, G. Intestinal mucosal amino acid catabolism. J. Nutr. **1998**, *128*, 1249–1252.
4. Baker, D.H. Utilization of precursors for L-amino acids. In *Amino Acids in Farm Animals*; D'Mello, J.P.F., Ed.; CAB International: Wallingford, 1994; 37–61.
5. Morris, S.M., Jr. Regulation of enzymes of the urea cycle and arginine metabolism. Annu. Rev. Nutr. **2002**, *22*, 87–105.

Angora Goats: Production and Management

Christopher John Lupton
Texas A&M University, San Angelo, Texas, U.S.A.

A

INTRODUCTION

Dogs, goats, and sheep were the first animals to be domesticated by man. Domestication of the goat is considered to have occurred at least 10,000 years ago in the Near East and Africa. The animals were used for production of meat, milk, skins, and fiber. Fiber-producing goats have occupied the area between the Black Sea and the Mediterranean Ocean for at least 2000 years. The white, lustrous-fleeced goat called the Angora (*Capra hircus aegagrus*) was developed on the Turkish plains close to Ankara, from which the name of the goat was derived. The original Turkish Angora goats were described as small, refined, and delicate and annually produced 1–2 kg of mohair in ringlets 20–25 cm in length. The primary and secondary follicles of Angora goats produce fibers of similar diameter and length, giving rise to a nonshedding single-coated fleece that is quite distinct from cashmere and the fleece of other goats that produce double coats. The first recorded shipment of Angora goats out of Turkey occurred in 1554. Shipments to South Africa (1838), the United States (1849), Australia (1850s), and the United Kingdom (1881) followed. Mohair production flourished in South Africa and the United States. By 1909, 1.34 million Angora goats were shorn in Texas. The population increased to 4.61 million by 1965 but subsequently declined to the present-day 220,000. In recent years, the South African Angora goat population peaked in 1989 with 3.0 million animals. By 2003, this number had declined to 1.1 million. Meanwhile, the population in Turkey had declined to about 100,000 Angora goats.

NUTRITION

Most Angora goats (Figs. 1 and 2) are maintained on native rangelands that are diverse in grasses, forbs, and shrubs.[1,2] To support their high rate of fiber production, Angora goats are highly selective browsers, choosing the most nutritious plants or plant parts when available. Maintaining an Angora goat on monocultures such as Bermuda grass can cause nutrition-related problems. Similarly, holding the animals on depleted rangeland

without adequate supplementation can also result in many problems. An Angora doe will continue to produce fiber at close to an optimal level even when nutrition is inadequate. At such times, fiber production takes priority over maintenance of body weight or continuation of pregnancy. However, poor nutrition eventually results in production of short (but finer), matted mohair, lower fleece weights, lower reproduction rates, and abortion. An authoritative bulletin[3] contains energy, protein, mineral, and vitamin requirements of Angora goats for a wide range of body weights, different levels of activity, fiber production, growth, and milk production, and different stages of pregnancy. For year-round grazing on Texas rangeland, light, medium, and heavy stocking rates are considered to be one goat per 6.6, 3.3, and 2.2 acres, respectively.[4] Supplementation of Angora goats (e.g., for development of kids, flushing of does, or inadequate forage on the range) and related economics are the subjects of many texts[3,5] and computer programs.[6]

Adequate nutrition is important after shearing, which decreases insulation and results in increased energy demand, especially in cold, wet, or windy weather. Providing freshly shorn goats with ample feed before returning them to the range can help avoid catastrophic postshear death losses.

REPRODUCTION

Angora goats have a reputation for low reproduction rates. This causes problems for the producer in terms of lost income from sale of excess animals, making progress in herd improvement, and maintaining herd numbers. There are various reasons for low reproductive efficiency. The most important is inadequate nutrition at one or more stages of growth or during the reproductive cycle. Many reproductive problems can be cured with adequate nutrition and/or increased management inputs that must be considered in light of anticipated economic returns.

The reproductive processes of Angora goats are similar to those of other goats. Major exceptions are the pronounced seasonality of mating in Angoras and problems associated with the high and competing

Encyclopedia of Animal Science
DOI: 10.1081/E-EAS 120030226

Fig. 1 Angora goats grazing in western Texas. (Photograph courtesy of J.W. Walker.) (*View this art in color at www. dekker.com.*)

demands of fiber production. Most Angora goats will attain puberty and breed at 18 months of age. Well-fed, well-developed kids occasionally breed at 6–8 months of age. Both males and females are seasonal breeders, the female having recurring estrual periods during fall/winter if not bred. Estrous cycles last from 19 to 21 days, with estrus itself lasting about one day. Gestation length is 149 days (range 143–153 days). The body weight and development of the doe are major sources of variation in ovulation and kidding rates, the ovulation rate decreasing with lower body weights.

Normal birth weight of kids ranges from 2 to 3 kg. Larger kids cause birthing difficulties for their dams, whereas smaller kids have low survival rates. A normal kid crop for commercial herds is in the range of 40 to 80%. Kid crops of 150% (i.e., 50% of does raised twins) have been reported in well-managed, small flocks. Low-kid crops can be a result of failure to ovulate or conceive, loss of embryo (resorption or abortion), or death of kid after birth. Most of these problems can be affected in a positive manner by improving nutrition and increasing the level of management. An example of the former would include a period of supplemental feeding before and during breeding. Examples of the latter would include kidding in small pastures or through a barn instead of on the range. Again, cost-effectiveness of all extra inputs is a major consideration for producers.

GENETICS AND SELECTION

Because the majority of income from Angora goats traditionally has come from fiber, much of the selection pressure has been for increased fiber production. Recently, more interest has been focused on selecting for a

dual-purpose Angora goat. Hence, more emphasis has been placed on body traits such as gain and mature weight. In its current form, the Angora goat produces fiber more efficiently than any other animal to which it has been compared. Selection for fine fiber (i.e., more valuable fiber) and against medullated (hollow) fibers has been practiced also. Most of the commonly measured and economically important production traits are inherited in a quantitative manner (i.e., under control of many genes). Derivation of comprehensive indices to assist with selection programs (though beyond the scope of this article) requires knowledge of the economic value, variability, and heritability of each trait, and the relationships among traits.

Because economic values change over time, average values calculated over a long period of time are most useful (unless there is a clear indication or guarantee of future value). Shelton[5] reported "consensus values" for heritability of the various traits. Highly heritable (>0.25) values include lock length; clean yield; mature weight; face, neck, and belly covering; secondary/primary follicle ratio; and scrotal division. Moderately heritable (0.15–0.25) values include fleece weight, fleece density, average fiber diameter, kemp (medullation) content, and weaning weight, and lowly heritable values include reproductive rate, longevity, and adaptability. Because Angora goat breeders are interested in many animal and fleece traits, developing a comprehensive selection index for Angora goats is a difficult task. To further complicate the issue, few of the traits are completely independent, and all are affected to some degree by such factors as age, nutrition, year, sex, and type of birth. The index for ranking yearling males on the Texas Agricultural Experiment Station annual central performance test[7] has received wide acceptance in the Texas industry.

Fig. 2 Angora goat fleece, illustrating the whiteness and luster for which mohair is famous. (*View this art in color at www. dekker.com.*)

HEALTH CONSIDERATIONS

Angora goats are susceptible to a broad range of diseases, consideration of which is beyond the scope of this article. When maintained under semiarid, extensive conditions (similar to those under which they were developed originally in Turkey), they generally thrive so long as adequate nutrition and fresh water are available. Problems tend to arise when animals are concentrated into small areas, particularly when conditions are damp. Diseases (e.g., pinkeye, soremouth, caseous lymphadenitis, pneumonia, bluetongue, dysentery, mastitis, caprine arthritis encephalitis, urinary calculi) and parasites (e.g., roundworms, coccidiosis, lice, scabies, etc.) that tend to be more prevalent in Angora goats, and how the industry deals with these problems, are the subjects of authoritative coverage elsewhere.[5,8]

CALENDAR OF OPERATIONS

In Texas, Angora does are bred in October to kid in March. Two to three weeks before and after males are introduced (one male to 20–25 does), does may be supplemented nutritionally to enhance ovulation rates. Throughout winter, range and forage conditions are evaluated in conjunction with the body condition of does so that a timely decision on required supplementation can be made. Also, internal parasites are monitored so the goats can be treated with anthelmintics after first frost, when fecal egg counts indicate treatment is warranted. Does are sheared just before kidding, a practice that seems to encourage them to seek out a sheltered place in which to give birth. In range flocks, kids typically remain with their dams until weaning in August, when the kids are sheared for the first time. Replacement selections are made from the 18-month-old does and males at this time, and older animals are inspected for possible culling. A few weeks after shearing, all animals may be treated for external parasites with prescribed pesticides.

CONCLUSION

The present-day Angora goat is an animal breeding success, with its ability to produce more than twice as much fiber compared to 100 years ago. However, the ability to produce more fiber almost certainly has been achieved with a concurrent loss in adaptability. Except in very favorable years, today's animals must be supplemented at critical times in order to maintain satisfactory levels of kid, meat, and mohair production. Further, the high priority the goat now has to produce fiber appears to have made it more susceptible to nutrition-related health problems, compared to other breeds. The long decline in the world's Angora goat population is a direct result of the inability of this animal enterprise to provide producers with adequate, consistent income. This in turn is a consequence of changing fashion trends and a general decline in demand for and use of animal fibers in modern textiles, in favor of cheaper synthetics. Although mohair is still one of the most important of the specialty animal fibers, its consumption is not expected to increase dramatically, despite the best efforts of producers' promotional groups and federal support programs.

ACKNOWLEDGMENTS

The author is indebted to his colleagues at the Texas Agricultural Experiment Station, San Angelo—M. Shelton, J. E. Huston, and M. C. Calhoun—for their willingness to share their substantial knowledge of Angora goats with this fiber scientist and many others in the goat industry.

ARTICLES OF FURTHER INTEREST

Mohair: Biology and Characteristics, p. 645
Mohair: Production and Marketing, p. 649

REFERENCES

1. Van der Westhuysen, J.M.; Wentzel, D.; Grobler, M.C. *Angora Goats in South Africa*, 3rd Ed.; 1988; 258 pp.
2. *Mohair South Africa*; The Green Room Design Company; http://www.mohair.co.za. Accessed February, 2004.
3. National Research Council. *Nutrient Requirements of Domestic Animals, No. 15. Nutrient Requirements of Goats: Angora, Dairy, and Meat Goats in Temperate and Tropical Climates.* National Academy Press: Washington, DC, 1981; 91 pp.
4. Taylor, C.A.; Fuhlendorf, S.D. *Contribution of Goats to the Sustainability of Edwards Plateau Rangelands*; Texas Agricultural Experiment Station Technical Report 03-1; Texas Agricultural Experiment Station: Sonora, 2003.
5. Shelton, M. *Angora Goat and Mohair Production*; Mohair Council of America: San Angelo, TX, 1993; 233 pp.
6. Huston, J.E.; Lupton, C.J. *Livestock Management Solutions (Available in Lotus and Excel Versions)*; Texas Agricultural Experiment Station: San Angelo, 2003.
7. Waldron, D.F.; Lupton, C.J. *Angora Goat Performance Test Report*; Texas Agricultural Experiment Station Research Center Technical Report 2003-3; Texas Agricultural Experiment Station: San Angelo, 2003.
8. Linklater, K.A.; Smith, M.C. *Color Atlas of Diseases and Disorders of the Sheep and Goat*; Wolfe Publishing, An Imprint of Mosby-Year Book Europe Limited: London, UK, 1993; 256 pp.

Animal Agriculture and Social Ethics for Animals

Bernard E. Rollin
Colorado State University, Fort Collins, Colorado, U.S.A.

INTRODUCTION

The social demand for a comprehensive ethic governing all areas of human use of animals did not appear until the 1960s. Historically, although society did have some ethical prescriptions for animal use, they were extremely minimalistic, focusing on forbidding deviant, willful, extraordinary, purposeless, sadistic infliction of pain and suffering on animals or outrageous neglect, such as not feeding or watering. Although this ethic of forbidding overt cruelty was incorporated into the legal system (i.e., into the visible articulation of social ethics) in most countries beginning in about 1800, it is in fact readily evidenced in the Old Testament, for example, in the injunction not to muzzle the ox when the animal is being used to mill grain or in the commandment to avoid yoking together an ox and an ass to a plow because of those animals' inherent inequality in size and strength. The Rabbinical tradition explained this ethic in terms of respecting animals' capability of suffering. In Catholic theology, as articulated by Thomas Aquinas, on the other hand, cruelty is forbidden not for the sake of the animals, but because people who perpetrate cruelty on animals are likely to graduate to perpetrating cruelty on people, an insight confirmed by modern psychological research.

HUSBANDRY AND THE ANTICRUELTY ETHIC

For most of human history, the anticruelty ethic and laws expressing it sufficed to encapsulate social concern for animal treatment for one fundamental reason: During that period, and today as well, the majority of animals used in society were agricultural, utilized for food, fiber, locomotion, and power. Until the mid-20th century, the key to success in animal agriculture was good husbandry, a word derived from the old Norse term for "bonded to the household."[1] Humans were in a contractual, symbiotic relationship with farm animals, with both parties living better than they would outside of the relationship. We put animals into optimal conditions dictated by their biological natures, and augmented their natural ability to survive and thrive by protecting them from predation, providing food and water during famine and drought, and giving them medical attention and help in birthing. The animals in turn provided us with their products (e.g., wool and milk), their labor, and sometimes their lives, but while they lived, their quality of life was good. Proper husbandry was sanctioned by the most powerful incentive there is—self-interest! The producer did well if and only if the animals did well. Husbandry was thus about putting square pegs in square holes, round pegs in round holes, and creating as little friction as possible doing so. Had a traditional agriculturalist attempted to raise 100,000 chickens in one building, they would all have succumbed to disease within a month.

Thus, husbandry was both a prudential and an ethical imperative, as evidenced by the fact that when the psalmist wishes to create a metaphor for God's ideal relationship to humans in the 23rd Psalm, he uses the Good Shepherd, who exemplifies husbandry.

> The Lord is my shepherd, I shall not want. He maketh me to lie down in green pastures; he leadeth me beside still waters; he restoreth my soul.

We want no more from God than what the Good Shepherd provides to his sheep. Thus, the nature of agriculture ensured good treatment of animals, and the anticruelty ethic was only needed to capture sadists and psychopaths unmoved by self-interest.

THE END OF HUSBANDRY

Symbolically, this contract was broken in the mid-20th century when academic departments of animal husbandry changed their names to departments of animal science. As the textbooks put it, animal science became "the application of industrial methods to the production of animals." This change occurred in America for a variety of reasons.[1] With projections of burgeoning population and shrinking amounts of agricultural land, agricultural scientists feared shortages in the food supply. The Depression and Dust Bowl had driven many people out of agriculture, as had World War II, which exposed young men to faster, more exciting lives than rural America afforded. As the lyrics of a song popular during World

Encyclopedia of Animal Science
DOI: 10.1081/E-EAS 120025129

War I went, ''How you gonna keep 'em down on the farm, now that they've seen Paree?''

WELFARE PROBLEMS OF INDUSTRIALIZED AGRICTULTURE

For these reasons, the values of industry—business efficiency and productivity—supplanted the values and way of life of husbandry. One casualty was animal welfare, as technological sanders such as antibiotics, vaccines, air-handling systems, and hormones allowed us to force, as it were, round pegs into square holes. Productivity was severed from well-being, with animals now suffering in ways that were irrelevant to productivity and profit. Industrialized confinement agriculture in fact brought with it at least four major new sources of suffering and welfare problems:

1. So-called production diseases that would not be a problem but for the means of production (e.g., liver abscesses in feedlot cattle arising from feeding too much grain and not enough roughage).
2. Truncated environments that prevent the animals from actualizing their physical, psychological, and social natures (e.g., gestation crates for sows, cages for egg-laying hens).
3. The huge scale of confinement operations militates against attention to and concern for individual animals (e.g., dairy herds of 6000; 100,000 chickens in one building), because part of the point in developing such systems was using capital to replace labor. However, nothing in principle prohibits reintroducing more individual attention, particularly if such attention is vectored into the design of these systems.
4. In confinement systems, workers are not animal-smart; the intelligence, such as it is, is in the mechanized system. (Instead of husbandry people, for example, workers in swine factories are low-wage, often illegal-immigrant labor who have no empathy with, knowledge of, or concern for the animals.) Once again, this could be changed with greater attention to selection and training of workers. Indeed, agriculture could take advantage of better educated urban people's desire to leave the cities.

NEED FOR A NEW ETHIC

This change from a fair-contract-with-animals agriculture to far more exploitative agriculture took place between World War II and the 1970s. And, as society became cognizant of the change, beginning in Britain in the 1960s with the publication of Ruth Harrison's *Animal Ma-*

chines,[2] and spreading throughout Western Europe, it needed a way to express its moral concern about the precipitous change. The traditional anticruelty ethic did not fit, for confinement agriculturalists were not sadistic or cruel, but rather were simply attempting to produce cheap and plentiful food. Similarly, social reservations about toxicological use of animals and research on animals—wherein, unlike the situation in husbandry, animals were harmed but received no compensatory benefit—also drove the demand for a new ethic for animals.

ORIGIN AND NATURE OF THE NEW ETHIC

Plato points out that new ethical systems are not created ex nihilo; rather, they build on previously established ethics, as when the Civil Rights Movement reminded society, in Plato's phrase, that segregation was incompatible with basic American ideals of equality. In the case of animals, society looked to its ethics for the treatment of humans and adapted it, with appropriate modifications, to animals.

The part of the ethic that was adapted is the part designed to deal with a fundamental problem confronting all societies—the conflict between the good of the group and the good of the individual.[3] Thus, when we tax the wealthy to help feed the poor, the rich person does not benefit but rather society as a whole. Similarly, if a person is drafted to serve in a war, the society benefits but not the individual who may be wounded or killed. Many totalitarian societies simply favor the corporate entity. Western democratic societies, however, strike a wise balance. These societies do make most of their decisions by reference to the general welfare but also protect certain fundamental aspects of the individual, based on a reasonable theory of human nature, even *from* the general welfare. These legal/moral protections of key aspects of human nature—speech, belief, property, assembly, etc.—are called rights.

APPLICATION OF THE NEW ETHIC TO ANIMALS

Animals too have natures: the cowness of the cow, the pigness of the pig. Although these natures were protected in husbandry, they are now compromised in industrialized agriculture. So, society, in essence, has come to say that if these animals' rights are no longer presuppositional to animal agricultural, they must be socially imposed on producers, i.e., they must be legislated. Not surprisingly, studies show that the vast majority of the public affirms that animals have rights, as do many husbandry agriculturalists. A Gallup poll published in May of 2003 indicated that fully 75% of Americans wish to see laws protecting animals in agriculture (available at http://www.gallup.com).

The clearest example of this new ethic can be found in the Swedish law of 1988, which essentially ended Sweden confinement agriculture as the United States knows it, and required an agriculture that fits the animals' biological and psychological natures. Tellingly, the *New York Times* called this law a ''Bill of Rights for farm animals.''[5] More recently, this approach has been adopted by the European Union, and inexorably will spread to the United States when the public realizes that agriculture is no longer Old McDonalds' farm.

SOCIAL REASONS FOR CONCERN ABOUT ANIMALS

Several other factors besides social concern for restoration of husbandry have vectored into the significant proliferation of animal welfare ethics as a major social concern. First, demographic changes and agricultural productivity have created a society in which only 1.5% of the public produces food for the rest. In this regard, therefore, the paradigm in the social mind for an animal is no longer a horse or cow as it was in 1900 when half the population was engaged in agriculture—it is now the pet or companion animal, which most people see as a member of the family.

Second, over the past 50 years, society has undergone a great deal of ethical soul-searching with regard to the disenfranchised—blacks, women, persons with disabilities, and others. Inevitably, the same ethical imperative has focused on animals and the environment, with many leaders of the animal movement coming from other social movements.

Third, the media have discovered that animals sell papers and that the public has an insatiable hunger for animal stories. According to a *New York Times* reporter who did a count, animal stories and shows occupy the single largest block of time on New York cable television.

Fourth, animal issues have been championed by highly intelligent philosophers and scientists, and by many celebrities with great influence on social thought. Books on animal ethics sell very well—Peter Singer's seminal *Animal Liberation* has been in print steadily since 1975, and has gone through three editions.[5]

CONCLUSION

Far too many people in animal industries and in academic animal science have failed to attend to the many signs that society is seriously concerned with animal treatment in agriculture, preferring to believe that these concerns are the sole purview of extremists and will go away if ignored. All evidence indicates that this is not the case and that if agriculture is to maintain its autonomy and avoid onerous legislation penned by concerned but agriculturally naive citizens, it must temper its quest for efficiency and productivity by a return to the principles of animal husbandry. Any profession or subgroup of society allowed the freedom by society to pursue its goals in its own way must always be able to assure society in general that its activities are in harmony with consensual social ethical concerns.

REFERENCES

1. Rollin, B.E. *Farm Animal Welfare*; Iowa State University Press: Ames, IA, 1995.
2. Harrison, R. *Animal Machines*; Vincent Stuart: London, 1964.
3. Rollin, B.E. *Animal Rights and Human Morality*; Prometheus Books: Buffalo, NY, 1982. (Second edition, 1993).
4. Singer, P. *Animal Liberation*; New York Review of Books Press: New York, 1975.
5. *Swedish Farm Animals Get a Bill of Rights*; P.I. New York Times, October 25, 1998.

Animal By-Products: Biological and Industrial Products

Gary G. Pearl

Fats and Proteins Research Foundation, Inc., Bloomington, Illinois, U.S.A.

A

INTRODUCTION

The terms by-products and coproducts as they relate to animal production are often used interchangeably. The need to debate, which is most appropriate or descriptive, is not extremely important, except to draw attention to one fact. By-product is defined as a secondary product obtained during the manufacture of a principal commodity. Coproduct possesses the meaning of being together or joined. Thus, the important facts for the animal production and processing industries are the utilization and opportunities that exist for the by-products that are produced ancillary to the production of meat, milk, and eggs for human food consumption. The actual value of animal by-products in comparison to the food components has not been determined in composite, nor have published economic projections for the alternative uses for animal-derived tissues, when used as biological and industrial products, been made available. But as one reviews the array of significant products that are derived from animal production and the technical opportunities that exist, one acquires a greater appreciation for their contributions to society.

BIOLOGICALS

Serum, vaccines, antigens, and antitoxins are derived from many food-animal tissues acquired both during the slaughter and processing of and by primary extraction from hyperimmunized animals. The true biologicals serve as preventive and treatment regimes in both humans and animals and are primarily derived from blood. Other animal tissues have been primary for the replication of cell-culture vaccines. Biotechnology continues to alter vaccine production processes, but animal by-products and their extractions are still important components. Purified animal blood is fractionated into many vital end products for numerous medical applications. Examples include thrombin, which is used for blood coagulation agents and skin graft procedures, fibrin used in surgical repair of internal organs, and fibrinolysin, an enzyme used to assist digestive and vaginal infections, as well as for wound cleaning agents.

Biological applications extend into uses for numerous pharmaceuticals, neutraceuticals, nutritional supplements, glandular extracts, and enzymes. Tissue implants, hormones, organs, glands, and tissue meats are considered to possess specific custom or health benefits. Other than heart, tongue, liver, kidney, pancreas/thymus (sweetbread), brain, stomach (tripe), and intestines that are used as food, all other noncarcass material, though edible biologically, is generally referenced as by-product tissue.

GLANDULAR EXTRACTS, HORMONES, AND ENZYMES

Glandular extracts, hormones, and enzyme collections are specific to the species, age, and sex of respective animals. Major products such as pepsin, rennin and other digestive enzymes, lipase and trypsin enzymes extracted from the pancreas, bile from the liver, adrenocortical steroids from the adrenal glands, and female reproductive hormones from the ovary are all medically significant products. Though insulin has been referenced as one of the prime pharmaceutical products derived from animal by-products, it is now synthesized by other procedures. This is true for a number of other pharmaceuticals, but reliance on the natural production and extraction is still an important source of medical treatment and prevention compounds.

IMPLANTS AND GRAFTING

Tissue transplants and grafting with animal tissues are routine human treatment regimes. Of particular note are the use of skins for initial treatment of burn patients and arteries, heart values, bone cartilage, and bone fragments, which are used as substitutes for diseased or damaged human tissue parts. In many of these treatment areas, there are no synthetic products that function or perform equally well. Historically, animal by-products have been used for these pharmaceutical and biological medical treatments for centuries. Rather crude applications based primarily on folklore preceded the extensive medical research and technology that guided their use in more modern times. The biological properties of the component tissues and

Encyclopedia of Animal Science
DOI: 10.1081/E-EAS 120019430

their extracts of animal by-products have provided the scientific basis for the development of synthetic substitutes. Many of the animal by-products are still indispensable as treatment regimes and research assets for the development of new and improved applications. A significant market has accompanied the biotechnical age in research work related to cell media, bioactive peptides, immunochemicals, molecular biology, tissue culture media, and reagents.

NEUTRACEUTICALS

Much has been referenced recently regarding various neutraceutical effects from a variety of foodstuffs that include those derived from animal by-products. A neutraceutical is vaguely defined. Though not defined as a specific required nutrient, the effects of identified compounds in specific tissues and their alleged benefit to certain health conditions is an expanding market. The majority of the neutraceuticals do not possess FDA approval for specific indications, but are marketed over-the-counter as nutritional supplements. Though the health food shelves are laden with products for nearly all ailments, an exemplary example of the product types are glucosamine hydrochloride and chondroitin sulfate. The supplements are labeled as an aid to the promotion of healthy cartilage and joint support. These supplements are extracts from animal by-product cartilage such as bovine trachea. There are numerous such supplements extracted or processed from animal by-products and made available for domestic and international markets. The Asian market has traditionally used and continues to expand its usage of nutritional supplements.

GELATIN

Gelatins obtained from both inedible and edible tissues are water-soluble protein derived from collagen extracted from animal connective tissues such as bone, cartilage, skin, and tendons. A variety of uses have been made of the various grades and types of gelatin. These include the primary use as food from edible processes and glue from inedible processes. Other significant uses are photographic film, adhesives, and gelatin coatings for pharmaceutical products. To dispel past beliefs, the only protein tissue that can yield gelatin or animal glue is collagen. Therefore, animal parts such as horns, hair, and hooves, which are composed of distinctly different proteins, cannot be used to make gelatin.

HIDES, SKIN, AND WOOL/HAIR

The largest component, based on value and volume, of animal by-products derived from the slaughter of food animals is the hide, in particular the hides derived from cattle. The skin of virtually every animal can be used to produce leather. Animal skins have been the source of clothing attire for man since historical times. Leather is used in a remarkable number of applications, including automobile and furniture upholstery, shoes, sporting goods, luggage, garments, gloves, and purses. A representative of the leather industry categorized leather utilization as 40% for upholstery, 50% for shoes and shoe leather, and 10% for other uses.[2] Leather garments are again increasing in vogue around the world. A very high percentage of hides, especially from cattle, produced in the United States are currently exported to China and Korea and, in lesser volume, to Mexico.

Pork skins are likewise a popular tissue used for garments and footwear, as are other skins from a number of minor species. Similarly, wool and hair have multiple uses based on their fiber properties. These qualities guide their usage into fabric, building insulation, and absorptive products. Synthetically derived products have challenged hide, skins, wool, and hair in nearly all of their traditional uses and will undoubtedly continue to do so in the future.

INDUSTRIAL USE

Certain animal by-products have found complementary outlets in many industrial niche markets, but with the exception of tallow and other species fat, animal by-product protein factions have been processed for their utilization as livestock, poultry, companion animal, and aquaculture feed ingredients. Tallow gained its prominence as an industrial ingredient for the soap, candle, cosmetic, and oleochemical industries. Animal fat utilization typically involves the production of lubricants, fatty acids, and glycerol. These fatty acids have primary industrial manufacturing uses for surfactants, soaps, plastics, resins, rubber, lubricants, and defoaming agents. Actual volume utilization for industrial uses of animal fats is not available. Worldwide, all the animal fats represent approximately 15% of the total production of all fats and oils. Tallow and grease are important commodities, and when lard is added to the total volume, rendered meat fats constitute the third largest commodity after soybean oil and palm oil.[3] The United States produces in excess of 50% of the world's tallow and grease. Tallow has been the primary animal fat for soap making, as lard and grease yield lower-quality soap. The USDA estimate of the current usage of tallow in producing soap is now less than

6% of domestic production, compared to 72% in 1950 and 27% in 1965. Thus, the usage in soap is still an important volume, but its use as feed ingredients—both domestically and as a product for export—now commands its largest utilization.

BIOENERGY USES

Renewable and recyclable sourced fuels are now recognized as being an important part of U.S. as well as global energy plans. As such, fats, oils, and recycled greases are feedstocks now used as biofuels. Biodiesel is defined as a monoalkyl ester of long-chain fatty acids that are derived from animal fats, vegetable oils, and recycled cooking oils/restaurant grease. Production by the reaction of a fat or oil with an alcohol in the presence of a catalyst results in an alternative or additive fuel to petroleum diesel. The methyl esters produced by this same process are used in a broad area of industrial chemicals for use as solvents and cleaners.

The use of rendered animal fats as burner fuel resources that are alternatives to natural gas, #2 fuel oil, and #6 fuel oil has now evolved as a viable and often economical use of feedstocks for energy alternatives. Both the protein and fat fractions from rendered animal by-products have potential for generation of captured energy. The lipid factions, however, have many more opportunities for use of this resource.

CONCLUSIONS

Animal by-products are the direct result of the production and processing of animals for food. Providing meat, milk, and eggs for the global table results in the ancillary production of inedible by-products. The total volume of such by-products approximates the total volume of edible meat when these animals are processed. This volume is increasing annually as the trend for more table-ready meat preparations increases. The utilization and the exploration for new utilizations as biological, industrial, and other value-added products must remain a priority in concert with the most economical, environmentally friendly, biosecure, and ecologically appropriate production of animal-derived foods.

ACKNOWLEDGMENTS

The author is grateful to many members of the Fats and Proteins Research Foundation, Inc., for providing valuable information needed to write this article.

REFERENCES

1. Ockerman, H.W. *Pharmaceutical and Biological Products. Inedible Meat By-Products*; Pearson, A.M., Dutson, T.R., Eds.; Advances on Meat Research; Elsevier Science Publishers, Ltd. Barking, U.K., 1992; Vol. 8, 304–305. Chapter 12.
2. Qualtification of the Utilization of Edible and Inedible Beef By-Products. In *Final Report of the National Cattlemen's Beef Association*; Field, T.G., Garcia, J., Ohola, J., Eds.; Colorado State University: Fort Collins, CO, February 1996.
3. McCoy, R.J. *Fats and Oils—A Global Market Complex, Chapter 5, The Original Recyclers*; The Animal Proteins Producers Industry, The Fats and Proteins Research Foundation and The National Renderers Association, 1996.

Animal Handling-Behavior

Temple Grandin
Colorado State University, Fort Collins, Colorado, U.S.A.

INTRODUCTION

People who understand the natural behavior patterns of farm animals will be able to handle them more easily. This will help reduce stress, improve animal welfare, and reduce accidents. Common domestic animals such as cattle, sheep, pigs, goats, poultry, and horses are prey species of grazing or foraging animals. Their wild ancestors survived in the wild by flight from predators. This is why domestic animals today are easily frightened by potentially threatening stimuli such as sudden movement. It is important to handle animals calmly; calm animals are safer and easier to handle than excited ones. If an animal becomes agitated, it is advisable to let it calm down for 20 to 30 minutes.

WIDE-ANGLE VISION

Prey species animals have a wide-angle visual field that enables them to scan their surroundings for signs of danger. Both grazing mammals and birds are especially sensitive to rapid movement and high contrasts of light and dark. Most grazing mammals are dichromats and are partially color-blind. Their eyes are most sensitive to yellowish-green and blue-purple light.[1] However, some birds have full-color vision. If an animal refuses to walk through a handling facility it may be due to seeing small distractions that people often do not notice. It may balk and refuse to walk past a small swinging chain or shadows that make harsh contrasts of light and dark.[2] A leaf blowing in the wind may make a horse "spook" and jump. To locate the distractions that impede animal movement, people should walk through the chutes to see what the animal sees. Ruminants, pigs, and equines may refuse to move through a chute for veterinary procedures if they see people moving up ahead, sparkling reflections on a wet floor, or vehicles. One simple way to improve animal movement through a handling facility is to put up a solid fence, so that the animals do not see things that frighten them through the fence.[3] This is especially important for animals that are not accustomed to close contact with people.

For wild ruminants such as bison, solid fences to block vision will keep them calmer during vaccinations and other procedures. Covering the eyes with a completely opaque blindfold also keeps them calmer. Deer and poultry producers handle these animals in darkened rooms to prevent excitement. Illumination with faint blue lights is often used in poultry processing plants. The blue lights provide sufficient illumination for people to see, and they keep the birds calm.

Lighting in a handling facility will affect animal movement. Animals are attracted to light unless it is blinding sun. They may refuse to move through a chute that is directly facing the sun. Chutes should face away from the rising or setting sun. In indoor facilities, lamps can be used to attract animals into chutes. On a bright, sunny day, cattle and pigs may refuse to enter a dark building. One of the best ways to solve this problem is to install white translucent panels in the building to admit abundant shadow-free light.

HEARING

Cattle, horses, and other grazing animals are much more sensitive to high-pitched noise than people are. Cattle are most sensitive at 8000 hz,[4] and people are most sensitive at meq 1000 to 3000 hz. Research has shown that people yelling will raise the heart rate of cattle more than the sound of a gate slamming.[5] People working with animals should be quiet and refrain from yelling and whistling. In one study, cattle with an excitable temperament that became agitated in an auction ring were more sensitive to sudden movement and yelling, compared to calmer cattle.[6]

FLIGHT ZONE AND POINT OF BALANCE

A tame riding horse or a show dairy cow has no flight zone, and leading it with a halter is the best way to move it. Most mammals and birds that are used in production agriculture are not completely tame, and they will keep a certain distance from a person. This is the flight zone, or the animal's safety zone.[3,7] There are three basic factors that determine the flight zone: 1) genetics; 2) the amount of contact with people; and 3) the quality of the contact, either calm and quiet or rough and aversive. Animal

Encyclopedia of Animal Science
DOI: 10.1081/E-EAS 120019431

Fig. 1 Cattle will turn and face the handler when the person is outside their flight zone. (Photo by Temple Grandin.)

head and poking it on the rear to make it go forward. Doing this signals the animal to move forward and back at the same time.

Ruminants, pigs, or equines standing in a chute can be induced to move forward by quickly walking past the point of balance in the direction opposite of desired movement. The animal will move forward when the balance line is crossed. This principle can also be used for moving cattle in pens or on pasture. The handler walks inside the group flight zone in the direction opposite of desired movement and walks outside the flight zone in the same direction as desired movement.

movement patterns during herding are similar in herding both mammals and poultry.

When a person is outside the flight zone, the animals will turn and face the person (Fig. 1). When the person enters the flight zone, both livestock and poultry will move away (Fig. 2). If an animal rears up when it is confined in a chute, this is usually due to a person deeply penetrating the flight zone with the animal unable to move away. The person should back up and get out of the flight zone. The animal will usually settle back down when the person backs away.

The point of balance is an imaginary line at the animal's shoulder. To induce an animal to move forward, the person must be behind the point of balance at the shoulder.[8,9] To back an animal up, the person should stand in front of the shoulder. People handling animals should not make the mistake of standing at the animal's

HANDLING FACILITIES AND RESTRAINT

Curved, single-file races (chutes) work efficiently because they take advantage of the grazing animal's natural tendency to move back to where they came from. Large ranches, feedlots, meat plants, and sheep operations have used curved chute systems for years. To help keep animals calmer and to facilitate movement through the facility, the following areas should have solid fences to block vision: the single-file chute (race); the restraining device for holding the animal (squeeze chute); and the crowd pen, crowd gate, and truck loading ramp. Solid sides are especially important for extensively reared animals with a large flight zone. If an animal is completely tame and can be led with a halter, the use of solid sides is less important. Figure 3 illustrates a well-designed curved, single-file chute with solid sides.

Both mammals and poultry will be less stressed if they are restrained in a comfortable, upright position. Inverting either mammals or birds into an upside down position

Fig. 2 When the handler enters the flight zone, the cattle will move away. The best place to work is on the edge of the flight zone. (Photo by Temple Grandin.)

Fig. 3 A curved, single-file chute with solid sides is more efficient than a straight chute for moving cattle. (Photo by Temple Grandin.)

is very stressful. In all species, an inverted animal will attempt to right itself by raising its head.

HANDLING BULLS AND BOARS

Research has shown that bull calves reared in physical isolation from their own species are more likely to be aggressive and dangerous after they mature than bull calves reared on a cow in a herd.[10] Dairies have learned from experience that bucket-fed Holstein bull calves can be made safer by rearing them in group pens after they reach six weeks of age. Young male calves must learn at a young age that they are cattle. If they grow up without social interactions with their own species, they may attempt to exert dominance over people instead of fighting with their own kind. Young bulls that are reared with other cattle are less likely to direct dangerous behaviors toward people.

People handling bulls should be trained to recognize a broadside threat. A bull will stand sideways so that either the person or the bull he intends to attack can see him from the side. He does this to show his adversary how big he is. This broadside threat will occur prior to an actual attack. Bulls that threaten or attack people should be culled, because bull attacks are a major cause of fatal accidents with cattle. Accidents with boars can be reduced by always handling the most dominant boar first. A boar is more likely to attack if he smells a subordinate's smell on a person.

CONCLUSIONS

Understanding the natural behavior patterns of animals will make handling more efficient and safer for both persons and animals. Some of the most important points are wide-angle vision, acute hearing, flight zone, and point of balance. The use of curved chutes with solid sides will help facilitate handling and keep mammals calmer.

Poultry will remain calmer in a darkened room. These principles are especially important for extensively raised animals. Finally, raising young bull calves in a social group where they interact with their own species will help prevent bulls from attacking people. The dominant male should be handled first.

REFERENCES

1. Jacobs, G.H.; Deegan, J.F.; Neitz, J. Photo pigment basis for dichromatic colour vision in cows, goats and sheep. Vis. Neurosci. **1998**, *15*, 581–584.
2. Grandin, T. Factors that impede animal movement at slaughter plants. J. Am. Vet. Med. Assoc. **1996**, *209*, 757–759.
3. Grandin, T. Animal handling. Vet. Clin. North Am., Food Anim. Pract. **1987**, *79*, 827–831.
4. Heffner, R.S.; Heffner, H.E. Hearing in large mammals: Horse (*Equus Cabellas*) and cattle (*Bos Taurus*). Behav. Neurosci. **1983**, *97*, 299–309.
5. Waynert, D.E.; Stookey, J.M.; Schwartzkopf-Gerwein, J.M.; Watts, C.S. Response of beef cattle to noise during handling. Appl. Anim. Behav. Sci. **1999**, *62*, 27–42.
6. Lanier, J.L.; Grandin, T.; Green, R.D.; McGee, K. The relationship between reaction to sudden intermittent movements and sounds to temperament. J. Anim. Sci. **2000**, *78*, 1467–1474.
7. Grandin, T. Behavioral Principles of Handling Cattle and Other Grazing Animals Under Extensive Conditions. In *Livestock Handling and Transport*; Grandin, T., Ed.; CAB International: Wallingford, 2000; 63–85.
8. Grandin, T. Handling methods and facilities to reduce stress on cattle. Vet. Clin. North Am., Food Anim. Pract. **1998**, *14*, 325–341.
9. Kilgour, R.; Dalton, L. *Livestock Behaviour a Practical Guide*; Granada Publishing: Progmore, St. Albans, United Kingdom, 1984.
10. Price, E.O.; Wallach, S.J.R. Physical isolation of hand reared Hereford bulls increases their aggressiveness towards humans. Appl. Anim. Behav. Sci. **1990**, *27*, 263–267.

Animal Health: Diagnostics

Phelix Majiwa
Tony Musoke
International Livestock Research Institute, Nairobi, Kenya

INTRODUCTION

A healthy, productive animal is the most useful to its owner. Disease constrains animal productivity in many parts of the world. Accurate diagnosis of disease is therefore an essential component of control of the disease, and for this reliable diagnostic kits are required. Diagnostic reagents are usually based upon defined molecules from either the infectious agent or the infected host. Sometimes, a crude component of an infectious agent or the infected host is used in diagnostic assays. In genetic diseases, tissue from the affected host is normally used as the analyte.

Diagnostics are required for assessment of disease surveillance and control programmes, determining more accurately the incidence of disease, and better defining the factors that affect disease transmission. Diagnostics 1) make it possible to determine the health status of an animal; 2) allow for collection of accurate data used in impact assessment and modeling of health constraints to animal production; 3) support deployment of vaccines and therapeutics; and 4) enable access to domestic and international markets through evaluation of the safety and quality of animal products. Thus, affordable, rapid, sensitive, and specific penside diagnostic tests for animal diseases are desirable. However, such tests are currently lacking for many of the animal diseases common in developing countries, thus forming a major constraint to effective disease control. This article focuses on diagnostic tests for animal health care.

THE ROLE OF DIAGNOSTICS

Animals need to be protected from ravages of infection and disease in order to remain healthy and productive. This protection can be conferred most effectively through vaccination. However, the development of vaccines and the evaluation of their performance require relevant diagnostics. Thus, companies that develop veterinary products find diagnostics useful during product development, validation, and deployment.[1] Diagnostic technologies are recognized as one of the top ten most important biotechnology products likely to improve general human and animal welfare.[2,3] Diagnostics facilitate understanding of the basis of pathology in relation to pathogens and disease dynamics.

Diagnostic testing of animals and their products is conducted for economic, public health, and environmental reasons. Risk assessment is a central element in animal disease management to ascertain their disease or pathogen status. Therefore, keepers of animals benefit from the availability of user-friendly and reliable diagnostics.

HEALTHY, PRODUCTIVE ANIMALS

Animals are kept for various purposes. In order to be useful, the animals must be healthy, but constraints to animal health vary with the production systems in which they are kept. A majority of the constraints are in the category of feeds and health. Feed quality and utilization can be improved in ways that do not involve the use of diagnostics. The threat of disease must be minimized or removed in order for animals and their keepers to remain healthy. Effective detection of pathogens and diagnosis of diseases require appropriate and reliable diagnostics. An important function of diagnostics in connection with animal disease is to contribute to improved welfare and productivity of the animals through the control of diseases.[3]

A majority of animal diseases that occur in the developed world have been controlled through a combination of effective diagnosis, treatment, and vaccination. However, in the developing world, many diseases pose a serious threat to the welfare of animals and their keepers. A partial list of economically important animal diseases is given in Table 1.[4] Diagnostic tests that have been developed for some of the listed diseases are not efficiently linked with other indicator systems to provide meaningful decision support tools for therapy, strategy development, and trade in animal products.

To be appropriate for the tasks in animal health care, diagnostic test components should be of known identity; pure in quality, produced in vitro synthetically or through recombinant DNA; precise and specific in identifying disease; linked to important traits or phenotypes; and able

Encyclopedia of Animal Science
DOI: 10.1081/E-EAS 120019432

Table 1 Selected pathogens that cause diseases in animals and humans, their distribution, and the assays commonly used to detect exposure

Pathogen	Disease name	Species affected	Distribution	Test system	Diagnostic performance
Bacteria					
Bacillus anthracis	Anthrax	All livestock species, humans	Worldwide	Serological (Ab-ELISA) PCR	Requires improvement
Clostridium chauvaei	Black-leg	Cattle, sheep	Worldwide	Serological (IFA)	Requires improvement
Clostridium botulinum	Botulism	All livestock species, humans	Worldwide	Neutralization of toxins	Requires improvement
Brucella abortus	Brucellosis	All livestock species	Worldwide	Rose bengal plate agglutination PCR, DNA probes, CFT ELISA	Good
B. melitensis	Brucellosis	All livestock species	Worldwide	Rose bengal plate agglutination PCR, DNA probes, CFT ELISA	Good
Chlamydia trachomatis	Chlamydial infections	All livestock species, humans	Worldwide	Cell culture, PCR, Ab-ELISA	Good
Chlamydia suis	Chlamydial infections	Porcine, humans	Worldwide	Cell culture, PCR, Ag-EILSA	Good
Mycoplasma mycoides mycoides	Contagious bovine pleuropneumonia (CBPP)	Cattle	Africa, Asia	CFT, C-ELISA	Good in combination
Mycoplasma mycoides capri	Contagious caprine pleuropneumonia (CCPP)	Sheep, goats	Africa, Middle East	CFT, latex agglutination	Good in combination
Dermatophilus congolensis	Dermatophilosis	Cattle, sheep, goats	Africa	Giemsa, IFA	Insensitive
Pasteurella multocida	Fowl cholera	Poultry	Worldwide	Culture, PCR	Good
Salmonella pullorum, S. gallinarum	Fowl typhoid	Poultry	Worldwide	Culture, serum agglutination test, PCR	Good
Leptospira spp	Leptospirosis	All livestock species (not poultry), humans	Worldwide	Microscopic agglutination test, Ab-ELISA	Need improved assay for chronic cases
Listeria monocytogenes	Listerosis	All livestock species, humans	Worldwide	Culture, PCR	Good
Brucella metitensis	Malta fever	Sheep, goats, humans	Worldwide	C-ELISA, CFT, PCR, FPA	Good
Mycobacterium paratuberculosis	Paratuberculosis, (Johne's disease) (Para-TB)	Cattle	Worldwide	Culture, AGID Ab-ELISA, PCR	Good
Mycobacterium bovis	Tuberculosis (TB)	Cattle, humans	Africa	Culture, Tuberculin test PCR	Good
Parasites					
Babesia bigemina	Babesiosis	Cattle	Worldwide	Ab-ELISA, PCR	Good
B. bovis	Babesiosis	Cattle	Worldwide	C-ELISA, PCR	Good
Coccidia spp.	Coccidiosis	All livestock species	Worldwide	Parasitological	Inadequate
Taenia saginata (Cysticercus bovis)	Cysticercosis (beef tapeworm)	Humans, cattle	Worldwide	Ag-ELISA for both humans and animals	Lacks required specificity

Agent	Disease	Species	Distribution	Diagnostic method	Status
Theileria parva	East Coast Fever (ECF)	Cattle	East, Central, Southern Africa	Ab-ELISA, PCR	Good
Gastro-intestinal (GI) parasitism (helminthosis) (e.g., *Haemonchus, Ostertagia, Onchocerca, Ascaris, Trichostrongylus, Bunostomum, Cooperia, Strongyloides, Nematodirus, Toxocara, Trichuris*, etc.)	Various helminth species	All livestock species	Worldwide	Parasitological	Molecular/immunological assays needed
Haemonchus contortus	Haemonchosis	Cattle, sheep, goats	Worldwide	Parasitological	Molecular/immunological assays needed
Echinococcus granulosus, E. multilocularis, and other *Echinococcus* spp.	Hydatidosis (hydatid disease)	All livestock species, humans	Worldwide	Necropsy/organ examination	Molecular/immunological assays needed
Fasciola hepatica, F. gigantica	Fascioliasis (liver fluke)	Buffalo, cattle, sheep, goats	Worldwide	Parasitological, Ab-ELISA	Good
Dirofilaria immitis	Filariasis	All livestock species	Worldwide	PCR, Ab-ELISA	Good
Various species of ticks	Tick infestation	All livestock species	Worldwide	Toxonomy	Good
Trypanosoma evansi	Surra	Buffalo, cattle, camels, horses, donkeys, mules	Africa, Asia, South America	CATT, PCR	Good
Trypanosoma congolense, T. brucei sl. *T. vivax, T. brucei*	Trypanosomosis	Cattle, sheep, humans	Africa, South America	Parasitological IFA	Needs improvement
Theileria annulata	Tropical theileriosis	Cattle	North Africa, Middle East, Asia, China, continental Europe	Ab-ELISA, IFA	Good
Rickettsia					
Anaplasma marginale	Anaplasmosis	Cattle, sheep, goats	Worldwide	Ab-ELISA, C-ELISA, PCR	Good
Cowdria ruminantium	Heartwater	Cattle, sheep, goats	Africa, Caribbean	Ab-ELISA, PCR	Fair, needs improvement
Viruses					
Iridovirus	African swine fever (ASF)	Pigs	Africa	Ab-ELISA, PCR IFA	Good
Rhinovirus (various serotypes)	Foot-and-mouth disease (FMD)	Cattle, sheep, goats, pigs	Worldwide	VN, Ab-ELISA, CR	Good
Pox virus	Fowl pox	Poultry	Worldwide	VN, IFA Ab-ELISA	Good
IBD virus	Gumboro disease (infectious bursal disease, IBD)	Poultry	Worldwide	AGID, VN, Ab-ELISA	Good
Pox virus	Lumpy skin disease	Cattle	Africa	Virus neutralization	Insensitive

A

(Continued)

Table 1 Selected pathogens that cause diseases in animals and humans, their distribution, and the assays commonly used to detect exposure (*Continued*)

Pathogen	Disease name	Species affected	Distribution	Test system	Diagnostic performance
Pox virus	Sheep and goat pox	Sheep, goats	Africa, Middle East, China	VN, AGID, IFA	Insensitive
Ganjam group virus	Nairobi sheep disease	Sheep, goats	East Africa	IFA, CFT	Insensitive but satisfactory
Paramyxovirus	Newcastle disease (ND)	Poultry	Worldwide	Hemoagglutination-inhibition	Good
Morbillivirus	Peste des petits ruminants (PPR)	Sheep, goats	Africa, Middle East	VN, C-ELISA	Good
Morbillivirus	Rinderpest (RP)	Cattle, buffalo, pigs sheep, goats	Africa, southern Asia	C-ELISA, VN	Good
Lyssavirus	Rabies	All livestock species (not poultry), humans	Worldwide	VN, IFA, RREID	Good
Bunyavirus	Rift Valley fever (RVF)	Sheep, cattle, goats, humans	Africa	VN, ELISA	Good
Rhabdoviridae	Vesicular stomatitis	Horses, cattle, pigs Sheep, goats, humans	Americas	Liquid-phase blocking ELISA, VN	Good
Orbivirus	Blue tongue	Sheep	Africa	C-ELISA	Good
Orbivirus	African horse sickness	Horses	Africa, Middle East	VN, ELISA, CFT	Good

Abbreviations: CFT: complement fixation test; C-ELISA: competitive-enzyme linked immunosorbent assay; Ag-ELISA: antigen-ELISA; Ab-ELISA: antibody-ELISA; VN: virus neutralization; PCR: polymerase chain reaction; IFA: immuno-fluorescent assay; RREID: rapid enzyme immunodiagnosis; AGID: agar gel immunodiffusion; FPA: fluorescence polarization assay.

to provide an index of host morbidity. Diseases for which diagnostics are required include infectious diseases, diseases with impact on general socioeconomic development, zoonotic diseases, genetic diseases, and diseases of intensification. A diagnostic test needs to have been validated. The validation process quantifies the performance of the test, the possible errors, and the likelihood of their occurrence. Additionally, it gives criteria of reliability, reproducibility, and relevance.

DISCOVERY, DEVELOPMENT, AND DEPLOYMENT OF DIAGNOSTICS

Methods for discovering diagnostics exploit the information generated through research in physical genomics for many animals and their pathogens. The strategy is to search genome-wide for the appropriate molecules that form the basis for development of the diagnostics.[5]

The conceptual framework for development of the diagnostics incorporates epidemiological considerations. Selection of candidate molecules for further development is based upon genomic information, followed by the evaluation of fitness to function as a diagnostic. The availability of diagnostics and the accompanying services is determined largely by considerations of cost of the test and returns to the investment made in their development. This, in turn, depends on the purpose for which the diagnosis is performed.

The availability of accurate and user-friendly diagnostics usable at the point of care encourages the keeping of only the most productive animals, provided that commensurate disease intervention options are also available. This discourages overstocking, spares the fragile environment, and improves the welfare of animals and their owners. For general animal health care, the diagnostics available should be suitable for use by veterinarians, extension workers, and technicians operating in individual country laboratories, regional laboratories, and commercial laboratories.

DIAGNOSTIC TEST FORMAT

Diagnostics exist in various formats, depending on the disease and the market. An ideal diagnostic should differentiate animals that have been vaccinated or simply exposed to antigenic molecules of an infectious agent from those with an active infection. An ideal test is one that can be conducted in a single-step procedure, with the result observable in minutes as either clearly positive or negative based on visual inspection, with minimal requirement for sophisticated equipment, processing, or technical expertise.

CONCLUSION

Robust diagnostics have use in animal disease epidemiology, control, surveillance, prevention, and treatment. With the anticipated increase in the demand for animal products,[6] the intensification of animal production, and the increase in human population and climate change,[7] the role of animal disease diagnostics will gain greater prominence.

ACKNOWLEDGMENT

We thank all our colleagues who contributed to this article in various ways.

REFERENCES

1. OIE. *Manual of Standards for Diagnostic Tests and Vaccines*, 4th Ed.; Office International des Epizooties, 2000; 957 pp.
2. Daar, A.S.; Thorsteindotir, H.; Martin, D.K.; Smith, A.C.; Nast Shauna; Singer, P.A. Top ten biotechnologies for improving health in developing countries. Nat. Genet. **2002**, *32*, 229–232.
3. FAO. *New Technologies in the Fight Against Trans-Boundary Animal Diseases*; FAO Animal Production and Health Paper 44, Food and Agricultural Organization of the United Nations: Rome, 1999; 118 pp.
4. Perry, B.D.; Randolph, T.F.; McDermott, J.J.; Sones, K.R.; Thornton, P.K. *Investing in Animal Health Research to Alleviate Poverty*; ILRI (International Livestock Research Institute): Nairobi, Kenya, 2002; 148 pp.
5. Jordan, J.A. New technologies for life sciences: Real-time detection of PCR products and microbiology. Trends Microbiol. Elsevier Sci. **December 2000**, 61–66.
6. Delgado, C.; Rosegrant, M.; Steinfeld, H.; Ehui, S.; Courbois, C. *Livestock to 2020: The Next Food Revolution*; Food, Agriculture, and the Environment. Discussion Paper 228, IFPRI (International Food Policy Research Institute), FAO (Food and Agriculture Organization of the United Nations), and ILRI (International Livestock Research Institute). IFPRI (International Food Policy Research Institute): Washington, DC, 1999; 72 pp.
7. Thornton, P.K.; Kruska, R.L.; Henninger, N.; Kristjanson, P.M.; Reid, R.S.; Atieno, F.; Odero, A.N.; Ndegwa, T. *Mapping Poverty and Livestock in the Developing World*; ILRI (International Livestock Research Institute): Nairobi, Kenya, 2002; 124 pp.

A

Animal Source Food: Nutritional Value

Kristen M. Carnagey
Donald C. Beitz
Iowa State University, Ames, Iowa, U.S.A.

INTRODUCTION

During the 20th century, animal foods played an increasingly important role in the diets of Americans. As household incomes increase and families find themselves with more expendable income, consumption of animal products tends to increase in the United States as well as in other countries throughout the world. Generally speaking, proteins from animal products more closely match the amino acid requirements of humans than do plant-derived foods. Currently, foods of animal origin contribute a significant portion of daily calories to the typical American diet. Animal products supply about 60% of dietary protein and 40% of dietary fat. Also, many vitamins, especially water-soluble vitamins, are provided primarily by foods of animal origin. Animal products are the sole source of dietary cholesterol and provide about 70% of dietary saturated fatty acids.

MEAT

One of the most obvious foods of animal origin—meat—includes all muscle foods. Beef, pork, and lamb are considered red meat. Chicken, turkey, and duck are poultry. Finfish and shellfish are fish, but the two are often differentiated.

The protein composition of most meats is very similar. The amino acid composition of muscle protein remains relatively constant among animal species, so the value of the protein as a food remains virtually unchanged between species. The amount and type of fat in meat can vary greatly depending on the source and cut of meat. Red meat usually contains more total fat and saturated fatty acids than does poultry or fish. This fact is probably the primary reason for the decrease in per capita beef consumption and the increase in poultry consumption in the past 25 years (Fig. 1). During that time, per capita pork consumption has remained stable. One possible reason for the stability of pork consumption is the widely publicized theme that pork is "the other white meat," is more healthful than beef or lamb, and is as healthful as poultry. Ocean fish have higher concentrations of the heart-healthy omega-3 fatty acids than do land animals or farmed fish, a finding

that has slightly increased consumption of fish such as tuna, halibut, and salmon in recent years.

Meats contain a variety of water-soluble vitamins and minerals. The B family vitamins (except thiamine, which is higher in pork) are present in about the same concentrations in most meats, whereas minerals, especially phosphorus, zinc, and iron, are more variable and found in higher concentrations in red meats. Vitamin B_{12} is found virtually only in foods of animal origin, and zinc and iron in meats are more bioavailable than the same minerals found in plant sources. Iron in meat is in the heme form, which is much more easily digested than the form found in plants.[1] Zinc absorption is facilitated by amino acids such as histidine, methionine, and cysteine.[2] These amino acids are found in the protein of meat, so zinc can be readily absorbed.

DAIRY

Dairy products include a vast array of products ranging from fluid milk to ice cream and several foods in between. Low-fat dairy products are often touted as being very healthful food choices.

One nutrient that prevents some people from enjoying dairy products is lactose. Many adults are lactose intolerant and experience gastrointestinal disturbances if they consume too much. There are products in stores, such as acidophilus milk and products that contain lactase, that can help alleviate this problem by converting each molecule of lactose into glucose and galactose which are easily absorbed.

Foods from ruminant animals, including milk, contain conjugated linoleic acid (CLA), which has been reported to have positive health benefits. Diets rich in CLA decrease cardiac disease and the risk of cancer and improve immune function.[3]

One cup of reduced-fat (2%) milk provides balanced amounts of carbohydrate (lactose), protein, and fat. Choosing low-fat (1%) or fat-free (skim) milk can decrease dietary fat intake. All fluid milks, regardless of fat content, have the same concentration of calcium. One cup provides about 30% of the recommended daily intake of calcium for healthy adults. Fluid milk is fortified with

Encyclopedia of Animal Science
DOI: 10.1081/E-EAS 120019436

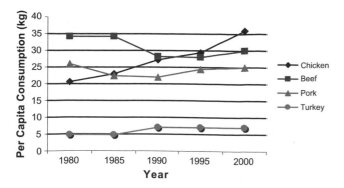

Fig. 1 Average annual meat comsumption. (Adapted from Ref. 4.) (*View this art in color at www.dekker.com.*)

vitamin D (400 IU per quart) to prevent deficiencies of this vitamin in the population.

One serving of yogurt provides as much calcium as a cup of milk, but yogurts often contain large amounts of added sucrose. Recently, yogurts that contain aspartame or sucralose as low-calorie sweeteners have appeared on store shelves. Some yogurts are made with low-calorie sweeteners and skim milk to form a product with half the calories of regular yogurt. All yogurts contain bacterial cultures. Most cultures are alive and promote gastrointestinal health by inoculating the intestines with bacteria that aid in digestion of food.

The nutrients found in cheese vary greatly depending on the kind of cheese. Some types, such as cottage and ricotta, contain relatively low amounts of fat. Harder cheeses, such as cheddar, contain higher concentrations

of fat, making them more calorie-dense. All cheeses provide protein and calcium, but the amounts are variable between cheeses.

Other dairy products—cream, half-and-half, sour cream, ice cream, and butter, for example—contain varying amounts of fat, protein, and lactose. These products generally are not consumed in large quantities, so even though they may be more calorie-dense, they do not contribute significantly to the diets of most people.

EGGS

Chicken eggs contain ovalbumin, which often is used as the gold standard for comparison of proteins from other sources. The ovalbumin of egg white is highly digestible and has a good balance of amino acids to promote health. The yolk contains primarily lipids as both triacylglycerols and phospholipids. The lipids contain mostly heart-friendly mono- and polyunsaturated fatty acids.[5] Egg yolk contains fat-soluble vitamins that are essential for proper health. Two of these vitamins are vitamin A (also in the form of β-carotene) and vitamin E. Cholesterol also is found in the egg yolk in relatively high concentrations. One yolk from a large egg contains about 213 mg of cholesterol.[6] When you consider that the upper limit for daily cholesterol consumption is 300 mg cholesterol per day, consuming one egg a day does not allow for consumption of many other animal-derived products.[6] However, the cholesterol in egg yolk is not efficiently absorbed, making it reasonable to consume eggs in moderation. During the past 20 to 25 years, egg substitutes

Table 1 Nutritive value of animal foods and animal food alternatives

Product	Measure of edible portion	Component per 1 oz (28 g)				
		Calories (kcal)	Total fat (g)	Saturated fatty acids (g)	Cholesterol (mg)	Protein (g)
Lean beef	3 oz (85 g)	54.7	2	0.8	25	8.6
Lean pork	3 oz (85 g)	56.6	2.3	0.8	23	8.6
Poultry						
White	3 oz (85 g)	46.2	1	0.3	23.8	8.8
Dark	3 oz (85 g)	48.4	1.3	0.4	26.1	7.6
Salmon	3 oz (85 g)	60.6	3	0.5	24.4	7.6
Milk						
Whole	1 cup (244 g)	17	1	0.6	3.8	0.9
Skim	1 cup (245 g)	9.8	Tr[a]	Tr	Tr	0.9
Whole egg	1 large (50 g)	42	2.8	0.9	119	3.4
Kidney beans	1 cup (177 g)	37.9	0.2	Tr	0	2.4
Lentils	1 cup (198 g)	32.5	0.1	Tr	0	2.5
Tofu (firm)	0.25 block (81 g)	21.4	1.4	0.2	0	2.4
Peanut butter	1 tbs (16 g)	166	14	3	0	7

[a]Trace.
(Adapted from Ref. 7.)

have emerged. These egg products are most often made of egg whites and do not contain the lipids, including cholesterol, present in yolk.

COMPARISON OF ANIMAL PRODUCTS AND ALTERNATIVES

When people choose not to consume animal products, they often cite nutrition as one of the major factors affecting their decision. Table 1 shows the nutritive value of some animal products as compared with some animal food alternatives. Ounce for ounce, animal products have approximately the same calorie density as plant products. Fat content is less variable in low-fat animal products than in vegetable products. Animal products do contain more saturated fat, and cholesterol is found only in animal products. The protein content in solid animal products is higher than that in most plant products. Consuming low-fat animal products can provide good-quality protein without adding large amounts of fat or calories.

CONCERNS ABOUT CONSUMING ANIMAL PRODUCTS

In the past decade, safety of animal products has become a major factor in the consumption of these foods. Consumers have become aware of the connection between animal products, especially meat, and some diseases. Some diseases worth noting are bovine spongiform encephalopathy (BSE), gastrointestinal disturbances caused by *Escherichia coli (E. coli)*, the parasite trichina, and colon cancer. BSE is a neural disease that is caused by an altered prion present in the brain and spinal cord of infected cattle. BSE is only transferred by consumption of infected tissue. *E. coli* is a bacteria found in all animals that can cause illness when its pathogenic form is present in the stomach and small intestine in addition to the colon. Trichinosis is a disease caused by the parasite trichina. Trichina used to be prevalent in the pork population but has been eradicated. A small but significant increase in the occurrence of colon cancer in people who consume red and processed meat is evident.[8]

IMPROVING NUTRITIONAL VALUE OF ANIMAL PRODUCTS

With recent advances in the biological sciences, improving nutrition provided by animal products is becoming a reality. In the near future, red meat might contain less total fat, and the fat that is present might be of a more healthful composition. Meats, beef especially, might be consistently tender and therefore more palatable. Products from ruminant animals might contain greater concentrations of CLA and omega-3 fatty acids. The ideal egg would have decreased cholesterol content and more unsaturated and omega-3 fatty acids. Though these ideas may sound as if they are many years away, researchers currently are working to make them reality.

CONCLUSION

Foods of animal origin supply Americans with a large proportion of their daily nutrient intakes. Animal products supply protein of nearly unequalled quality, as well as fat and carbohydrates (in milk). Along with these macronutrients, foods of animal origin supply numerous vitamins and minerals. Although the U.S. food supply is among the safest in the world, some concerns about the safety of consuming animal products remain. Consumption of animal products helps people meet recommended daily intakes of many required nutrients.

REFERENCES

1. Fairbanks, V. Iron in Medicine and Nutrition. In *Modern Nutrition in Health and Disease*, 8th Ed.; Shils, M.E., Olson, J.A., Shike, M., Ross, A.C., Eds.; Lippincott Williams and Wilkins: Philadelphia, 1994.
2. King, J.C.; Keen, C.L. Zinc. In *Modern Nutrition in Health and Disease*, 8th Ed.; Shils, M.E., Olson, J.A., Shike, M., Ross, A.C., Eds.; Lippincott Williams and Wilkins: Philadelphia, 1994.
3. D'Orazio, N.; Ficoneri, C.; Riccioni, G.; Conti, P.; Theoharides, T.C.; Bollea, M.R. Conjugated linoleic acid a functional food? Int. J. Immunopathol. Pharmacol. **2003**, *16*, 215–220.
4. Anonymous. American Meat Institute. In *Overview of U.S. Meat and Poultry Production and Consumption*; 2003. http://www.meatami.com/Content/NavigationMenu/PressCenter/FactSheets_InfoKits/FactSheetMeatProductionand-Consumption.pdf. (accessed 11/13/03).
5. Gunstone, F.D.; Harwood, J.L.; Padley, F.B. *The Lipid Handbook*, 2nd Ed.; Chapman & Hall: London, 1994; 193–194.
6. Anonymous. *A Prospective Study of Egg Consumption and Risk of Cardiovascular Disease in Men and Women*; 2003. http://www.americanheart.org/presenter.jhtml?identifier=3057. (accessed 12/03/03).
7. Gebhardt, S.E.; Thomas, R.G. *Nutritive Value of Foods*; USDA Agricultural Research Service: Beltsville, MD, 2002.
8. Norat, T.; Lukanova, A.; Ferrari, P.; Riboli, E. Meat consumption and colorectal cancer risk: Dose-response meta-analysis of epidemiological studies. Int. J. Cancer **2002**, *98*, 241–256.

Animal Source Food: Quality and Safety—Meat and Poultry

Ifigenia Geornaras
John N. Sofos
Colorado State University, Fort Collins, Colorado, U.S.A.

INTRODUCTION

The quality of foods is influenced by chemical and physical changes associated with their intrinsic properties or environmental variables. Loss of quality may also occur due to enzymatic changes brought about by intrinsic or microbial enzymes. Food products of animal origin are easily contaminated with microorganisms, the extent of which depends on hygienic practices; sanitation and processing procedures; and conditions under which the products are harvested, processed, handled, distributed, and stored. The levels and types of microorganisms contaminating meat and poultry products at the end of processing may have important consequences on the spoilage and quality of the food. Furthermore, microbial contamination of food products with foodborne pathogens, as well as chemical (e.g., chemical residues) and physical (e.g., bone, glass, wood) hazards, may compromise the safety of foods. Loss of food quality and compromise of its safety lead to economic losses; foodborne illness may also lead to human suffering and death.

QUALITY

Meat quality is described by a range of physical and chemical attributes including color, flavor, tenderness, juiciness, and texture. These characteristics are influenced by intrinsic and extrinsic factors such as animal species and age, muscle structure and its chemical composition, antemortem stress, product handling, processing, and storage conditions. Color is an important attribute of meat, as the consumer uses it to judge the product's freshness and wholesomeness. The concentration and chemical state of the pigment—myoglobin—determines the color of meat, and is dependent upon a number of antemortem factors, including the animal species and age, the physiological function of the muscle, the nutritional status of the animal, and the dietary regime.[1] It is thus due to these reasons that beef muscle has a bright, cherry-red color compared to the lighter color of pork or poultry meat; that meat from an older animal appears darker than that from a younger animal; and that breast meat from poultry is lighter than its leg counterpart.[2] The color of meat is also affected by storage conditions, such as the gaseous environment, storage time, and temperature. For example, the lack of oxygen in vacuum-packaged beef results in conversion of oxymyoglobin to deoxymyglobin of purple-red or brown color, which is perceived as undesirable by consumers.[2]

The flavor of meat is composed of: 1) meat flavors derived from water-soluble compounds; 2) species flavors derived from fat-soluble compounds that are stored in the lipid depots of the animal; and 3) off-flavor development due to lipid oxidation or other chemical reactions.[2] Lipid peroxidation or oxidative rancidity occurs when molecular oxygen reacts with unsaturated lipids to form lipid peroxides, which are colorless, tasteless, and odorless. Decomposition of these primary products, however, gives rise to a complex mixture of low-molecular weight compounds that have distinctive flavor and odor characteristics (e.g., rancid, fatty, pungent). Cooking of meat results in an increase in lipid oxidation in muscle and to the development of warmed-over flavor (WOF) in refrigerated cooked meat. This flavor defect can also be encountered in uncooked emulsion-type, ground, flaked, or restructured meat products in which the muscle structure is disrupted, exposing muscle lipids to a pro-oxidative environment. Lipid peroxidation is positively linked to pigment oxidation, and also affects the odor of meat, its nutritive value, and potentially the safety of the meat.[2,3] Factors affecting the flavor of meat include species, sex, age, and diet of the animal.[1,2]

Meat tenderness is a quality attribute determined by the connective tissue and type and state of muscle fibers, whereas texture is determined by the definition and fineness of muscle fiber, as well as by the amount and distribution of fat in the muscle. Juiciness is a sensory term indicating the moisture content of meat, which is critically affected by its water-holding capacity.[1] More details on these aspects of quality can be found in other sections of this encyclopedia.

Encyclopedia of Animal Science
DOI: 10.1081/E-EAS 120019437

The quality of meat is also affected by the metabolic activity of microorganisms.[4] Substrates utilized for growth by spoilage bacteria include glucose, glucose-6-phosphate, amino acids, proteins, and lactic acid, whereas major end products of metabolism of these bacteria include sulfides, amines, acids (lactic, acetic, isovaleric, isobutyric), esters, and nitriles.[4,5] Spoilage characteristics of meat and poultry are similar, despite the differences in properties among muscle tissues of different animal and bird species.[6] Spoilage of meat and poultry is characterized by an offensive appearance (e.g., green, brown, or gray discolorations) and/or an off-odor (e.g., sour, fruity, cheesy, putrid) or off-flavor. The growth of bacteria on the surface of meat reportedly accelerates the oxidation of meat pigments, resulting in discoloration of the product.[3] Off-odors are sensorially detectable first, when bacterial numbers exceed 10^7 per cm^2, whereas bacterial slime becomes evident when numbers reach 10^8 per cm^2.[7]

The spoilage flora of refrigerated meat and poultry is composed of psychrotrophic bacteria, including *Pseudomonas* spp., Enterobacteriaceae (*Serratia liquefaciens*, *Hafnia alvei*, *Enterobacter agglomerans*), *Brochothrix thermosphacta*, lactic acid bacteria (*Lactobacillus*, *Carnobacterium*, *Pediococcus*, *Streptococcus*, *Lactococcus*, and *Leuconostoc* spp.), *Shewanella putrefaciens*, and species of *Moraxella*, *Psychrobacter*, *Acinetobacter*, and *Aeromonas*.[8] Under aerobic storage conditions, *Pseudomonas* spp., specifically *Pseudomonas fragi*, *Pseudomonas fluorescens*, and *Pseudomonas lundensis*, usually predominate (normally >50%), while under modified atmosphere or vacuum conditions, lactic acid bacteria (e.g., species of *Carnobacterium*, *Lactobacillus*, and *Leuconostoc*) and *Brochothrix thermosphacta* are dominant.[7,8] Thus, under aerobic and chill conditions, Gram-negative bacteria predominate, whereas under modified atmospheres, Gram-positive bacteria form the major portion of the spoilage flora. Processed meats (e.g., cooked ham, corned beef, emulsion-type sausages, luncheon meats) stored at cold temperatures and packed under vacuum or modified atmosphere are also predominantly spoiled by lactic acid bacteria. Spoilage in these products is characterized by a sour odor and flavor, greening, gas production, and slime formation. Yeast and mold spoilage of meat and poultry can also occur, but only under conditions where bacterial competition is reduced (e.g., reduced water activity, presence of preservatives or antimicrobial treatments, and long-term storage).[4,9]

SAFETY

Three types of hazards can compromise the safety of meat and poultry (i.e., physical, chemical, and biological). Bone chips and foreign materials such as metal, glass, wood, plastic, stones, etc. are considered physical hazards. Chemical hazards include natural and synthetic environmental contaminants. Included in this category are chemical residues, which result from the use of animal drugs and pesticides, or from chemicals present in the animal's environment.[9] Antimicrobials are administered to animals for their therapeutic value, and also to enhance their growth and feed efficiency. Regulatory agencies and consumers are concerned about the presence of residues in animal tissues and their products, as they may lead to allergic reactions, hypersensitivity, and toxicity. Furthermore, there is increasing concern that subtherapeutic and therapeutic use of antimicrobials in food animals gives rise to antimicrobial-resistant bacteria and that these antimicrobial-resistant bacteria may be transmitted from animals to humans.[10] The United States has a complex residue control program in an effort to prevent violative residues from entering the food supply chain. The Food and Drug Administration and Environmental Protection Agency are responsible for establishing tolerances (maximum permissible levels) for chemical residues in foods, while the U.S. Department of Agriculture Food and Safety Inspection Service enforces these tolerances through its various residue control programs. If a product containing violative levels of residues is found, it is considered adulterated and subject to condemnation (http://www.fsis.usda.gov/OPHS/blue2000/).

Biological hazards associated with meat and poultry are bacteria, viruses, parasites, and bovine spongiform encephalopathy. It is estimated that bacterial agents are responsible for 30% of human foodborne illnesses, while viruses and parasites cause 67% and 3% of the illnesses, respectively.[11] Biological hazards associated with foods of animal origin are discussed in more detail in other sections of this encyclopedia.

CONCLUSION

Animal source foods, including meat and poultry, are highly perishable foods. Loss of quality occurs from physical and chemical changes caused by their inherent properties, as well as by extrinsic factors, including processing, storage, and handling conditions. They are also able to support the growth of spoilage microorganisms that are mainly acquired from the production and processing environment; thus, loss of quality also occurs as a result of their metabolic activities. Furthermore, due to their nature and origin, meat and poultry products may also be associated with microorganisms that cause foodborne illness. In addition, the presence of chemical residues in these foods raises safety concerns. Procedures to control the quality and safety of meat and poultry foods require an integrated approach encompassing all sectors of the food supply chain, including the producers, processors, distributors, retailers, and consumers. This includes, among others, good production practices on the farm, slaughtering of animals that are disease-free, processing of carcasses under sanitary and hygienic conditions, use of decontamination intervention strategies to reduce microbial levels, maintenance of the cold chain during distribution, and proper storage and preparation procedures by the consumer.

ARTICLES OF FURTHER INTEREST

REFERENCES

1. Xiong, Y.L.; Ho, C.-T.; Shahidi, F. *Quality Attributes of Muscle Foods*; Kluwer Academic/Plemum Publishers: New York, 1999.

2. Kinsman, D.M.; Kotula, A.W.; Breidenstein, B.C. *Muscle Foods: Meat, Poultry and Seafood Technology*; Chapman & Hall, Inc.: New York, 1994.

3. Decker, E.A.; Faustman, C.; Lopez-Bote, C.J. *Antioxidants in Muscle Foods: Nutritional Strategies to Improve Quality*; John Wiley & Sons, Inc.: New York, 2000.

4. Davies, A.; Board, R. *The Microbiology of Meat and Poultry*; Blackie Academic & Professional: London, 1998.

5. Lund, B.M.; Baird-Parker, T.C.; Gould, G.W. *The Microbiological Safety and Quality of Food*; Aspen Publishers, Inc.: Gaithersburg, 2000; Vol. 1.

6. Doyle, M.P.; Beuchat, L.R.; Montville, T.J. *Food Microbiology: Fundamentals and Frontiers*, 2nd Ed.; ASM Press: Washington, DC, 2001.

7. International Commission on Microbiological Specifications for Foods (ICMSF). *Microorganisms in Foods 6, Microbial Ecology of Food Commodities*; Blackie Academic and Professional: London, UK, 1998.

8. Jay, J.M. *Modern Food Microbiology*, 6th Ed.; Aspen Publishers Inc.: Gaithersburg, 2000.

9. Pearson, A.M.; Dutson, T.R. *Quality Attributes and Their Measurements in Meat, Poultry and Fish Products*; Blackie Academic and Professional: Glasgow, UK, 1994.

10. Mitchell, J.M.; Griffiths, M.W.; McEwen, S.A.; McNab, W.B.; Yee, A.J. Antimicrobial drug residues in milk and meat: Causes, concerns, prevalence, regulations, tests, and test performance. J. Food Prot. **1998**, *61*, 742–756.

11. Mead, P.S.; Slutsker, L.; Dietz, V.; McCaig, L.F.; Bresee, J.S.; Shapiro, C.; Griffin, P.M.; Tauxe, R.V. Food-related illness and death in the United States. Emerg. Infect. Dis. **1999**, *5*, 607–625.

Animal Source Food: Quality and Safety—Milk and Eggs

Ifigenia Geornaras
John N. Sofos
Colorado State University, Fort Collins, Colorado, U.S.A.

INTRODUCTION

The quality of animal food products such as milk and eggs, as well as foods, is largely based on their sensorial characteristics. Loss of food quality is brought about by chemical and physical changes to the food's intrinsic properties, which bring about deterioration in food appearance, flavor and texture, and/or the development of off-odors. These changes are the result of physical phenomena or the action of intrinsic or microbial enzymes, the latter resulting from the growth of spoilage microorganisms that become associated with foods during rearing, harvesting, processing, distribution, and/or storage procedures.

The safety of foods may be compromised by three types of hazards: physical, chemical, and biological. Physical hazards (e.g., glass, plastic) tend to be of lower safety risk than chemical or biological contaminants, as they usually cause only injury and affect a small number of consumers. Chemical hazards include chemical residues, which may be of environmental or synthetic nature, whereas biological hazards include bacteria, viruses, and parasites, which may lead to foodborne illness and death.

MILK

Quality

Quality, in reference to milk, includes its composition and aesthetic factors such as flavor, odor, and appearance. Approximately 60% of variation in milk composition is caused by genetic factors, with environmental factors such as feeding, nutrition, climate, disease, processing, etc. making up the remainder of the variation. Off-flavors and/or odors may be: 1) feed induced; 2) environmentally or chemically induced; 3) indigenous milk enzyme induced; or 4) bacteria induced. Off-flavors or odors described as cowy or barny may be a result of unsanitary housing or milking conditions. Chemical or chemical-induced off-flavors may result from improper use of sanitizers, old or poorly maintained equipment, or

prolonged exposure to sunlight, resulting in light-induced oxidized off-flavors. Hydrolytic rancidity or rancid flavors arise through the action of lipases, which originate from indigenous milk lipoprotein lipase or from bacterial contamination.[1]

Sources of bacterial contamination of raw milk include the cow's udder, the exterior of the animal (e.g., bedding, soil, manure, feed residues), and the environment (e.g., milk-handling equipment and personnel, water, air).[2–4] Raw milk is pasteurized to extend its shelf life, or quality, during refrigerated storage (by minimizing numbers of spoilage microorganisms), and to ensure its microbiological safety (by eliminating pathogenic microorganisms, which caused major health problems before pasteurization was implemented). The extent to which pasteurization reduces microbial levels depends on the initial number of contaminants and the types of microorganisms. The primary spoilage organisms of raw and pasteurized milk are psychrotrophic bacteria, including species of *Pseudomonas*, *Alcaligenes*, and *Flavobacterium*.[3] Most of these microorganisms are heat-labile, although some may survive at low levels. Additional microorganisms may be introduced as postpasteurization contaminants. During refrigerated storage, these bacteria proliferate and produce proteinases and lipases, which affect the quality of milk. Proteolysis results in bitter, putrid, fermented, unclean, and fruity off-flavors and coagulation, while lipolysis and lipid oxidation result in hydrolytic or oxidative rancidity.[1] Organoleptic defects become evident when microbial levels reach 10^6 to 10^7 per ml. Pasteurized milk may also be spoiled by surviving spore-formers (e.g., *Bacillus* and *Clostridium* spp.) or thermoduric species (microorganisms that survive pasteurization, but do not grow at high temperatures).[2,3] Lactic acid bacteria (e.g., *Lactococcus*, *Leuconostoc*, *Enterococcus*, *Pediococcus*, and *Streptococcus* spp.) become the dominant spoilage organisms when milk is stored at high enough temperatures that allow these organisms to outgrow the psychrotrophs.[4] Lactic acid bacterial spoilage results in sour odors, malty flavors, and ropiness.[4] Spoiled raw milk may also exhibit ropiness due to exopolysaccharide production by *Alcaligenes viscolatis*.[2,3]

Encyclopedia of Animal Science
DOI: 10.1081/E-EAS 120034144

Safety

Potential safety concerns associated with milk include bacterial pathogens and chemical residues. Foodborne pathogens associated with milk include those that may be associated with cows, milk-handlers, equipment, and the environment.[2] Raw milk thus serves as an important vehicle of transmission of several pathogens including *Campylobacter* spp., *Brucella* spp., Shiga toxin-producing *Escherichia coli*, *Corynebacterium diphtheriae*, *Salmonella* (including multidrug-resistant strains), *Mycobacterium bovis*, *Listeria monocytogenes*, *Yersinia enterocolitica*, *Staphylococcus aureus*, and *Clostridium perfringens* (http://www.cdc.gov/).[2,5] Pathogens that have been involved in the majority of outbreaks linked to the consumption of raw milk or pasteurized milk that has been inadequately heat treated or contaminated postpasteurization include *Salmonella*, *Campylobacter* spp., and *Listeria monocytogenes*, among others.[5] During the period of 1972–2000, *Salmonella* was the cause of 17 out of 58 (29%) raw milk-associated outbreaks (http://www.cdc.gov/).

Chemical residues in milk are caused by antibiotics used on dairy cows to help control diseases such as mastitis, hormones, disinfectants used to sterilize milking and processing sites, pesticides, mycotoxins, toxic metals, and dioxins.[6] In order to regulate the level of these residues in milk, authorities set maximum residue limits that should not be exceeded if good agricultural practice is followed by the dairy industry.

EGGS

Quality

The quality of shell eggs is described by external and internal factors. External factors refer to the strength, texture, porosity, shape, cleanliness, soundness, and color of the shell, whereas internal factors refer to the presence of inclusions (blood and meat spots, and chalazae), the quality of the albumen, the color and uniformity of the yolk, and the odor and taste of the egg. Extrinsic factors affecting shell quality include temperature, hen age, and nutrition. Loss of shell egg quality begins immediately after the egg is laid, due to water loss, which leads to thinning of the albumen and an increase in the size of the air cell. Furthermore, due to migration of carbon dioxide from the egg, an increase in albumen pH occurs as well as a decrease in the strength of the vitelline (yolk) membrane. Off-flavors and odors associated with eggs may be caused by the ration fed to the hens.[7]

Loss of shell egg quality may also occur as a result of microbial growth (i.e., spoilage). Freshly laid eggs may be contaminated through two primary routes: transovarian or trans-shell infection.[2] Transovarial transmission occurs when bacteria infect the hen's ovaries or oviducts, resulting in contamination of the egg during its formation. The more common route of microbial contamination of eggs, however, is via trans-shell infection. This occurs when the physical (e.g., the cuticle, shell, and shell membranes) and chemical (e.g., lysozyme) antimicrobial barriers of the egg are compromised, resulting in contamination of the internal contents of the egg.[2,5] Microorganisms contaminating the egg after laying originate from the intestines when the egg passes through the cloaca, as well as from nest materials, litter, or incubator surfaces.[2] The rate at which microorganisms penetrate the egg depends on factors such as storage temperature, age of the eggs, and level of contamination.[3]

The most common form of bacterial spoilage of eggs is rotting, caused primarily by Gram-negative bacteria; the type of rot depends on the bacterial species/strain(s) present. For example, fluorescent green rots are caused by *Pseudomonas putida*; fluorescent blue rots by *Pseudomonas aeruginosa*; pink rots by *Pseudomonas fluorescens*; colorless rots by *Acinetobacter/Moraxella* spp.; black rots by *Proteus vulgaris*, *Aeromonas liquefaciens*, and species of *Pseudomonas*, *Alcaligenes*, and *Enterobacter*; and red rots by *Serratia marcescens*.[2,3,5] Mold spoilage of eggs may also occur during refrigerated storage when the humidity is high. Growth of molds on the egg surface is referred to as whiskers and is often associated with *Cladosporium herbarum*, whereas pinspots are caused when fungal (mycelia) growth occurs inside the egg.[2,3]

Safety

An important safety aspect associated with eggs is their contamination with *Salmonella*, and in particular, transovarial contamination with *Salmonella* Enteritidis. The estimated rate of transovarian contamination of eggs with this pathogen in the United States is one in 20,000 eggs. During 1985–1998, raw or undercooked shell eggs were reportedly responsible for 279 out of 360 (82%) *Salmonella* Enteritidis outbreaks with a confirmed source (http://www.cfsan.fda.gov/~dms/fs-eggs3.html-authors). Other pathogens that have been recovered from egg shells include species of *Campylobacter*, *Listeria*, and *Aeromonas* (http://apresslp.gvpi.net/apfmicro/lpext.dll?f=templates&fn=main-hit-h.htm&2.0).

The presence of chemical residues is also a safety concern in eggs as veterinary drugs and growth promoters are administered to birds to prevent disease and enhance their growth. A residue control program (http://www.fsis.usda.gov/OPHS/blue2000/) is used by regulatory agencies in the United States to prevent eggs with illegal levels of chemical residues from entering the food chain.

Although not regarded as a safety aspect per se, it is worth mentioning the cholesterol content of egg yolks (200–250 mg per egg), as it is a major health concern due to its link to the development of coronary heart disease. There have been countless efforts to reduce the cholesterol content of whole eggs through genetic selection and nutritional and pharmacological manipulation, with minimal success.[8] Feeding of hens with high levels of a variety of grains reportedly can reduce the cholesterol concentration by 15 to 20%. Higher reductions can be achieved through the use of cholesterol synthesis blocking agents. These blocking agents, however, may have negative side effects, such as a reduction or complete termination of egg production.[7]

CONCLUSION

Economic losses are incurred by the deterioration of quality and compromise of safety of milk and eggs, whether the loss results from product recalls or destruction of product. Furthermore, consumption of products contaminated with pathogenic bacteria can also lead to human suffering. In order to improve the quality and safety of milk and eggs, a multifaceted approach is needed, including good agricultural, hygienic, sanitation, processing, distribution, and storage practices. More specifically, with regard to milk, it is important that dairy cows are disease-free, that milk-handling and pasteurization equipment is clean and sanitized, and that environmental contamination is controlled. Similarly, using *Salmonella* Enteritidis–free chicks or pullets, cleaning and disinfecting hen houses between flocks, washing eggs properly, and refrigerating eggs promptly after collection can improve the quality and safety of eggs.

ARTICLES OF FURTHER INTEREST

Antibiotics: Microbial Resistance, p. 39
Antibiotics: Subtherapeutic Levels, p. 42
Eggs: Processing, Inspection, and Grading, p. 318
Feed Supplements: Antibiotics, p. 370

REFERENCES

1. DeLorenzo, M.A.; Harris, B., Jr.; Shearer, J.K.; Staples, C.R.; Thatcher, W.W.; Umphrey, J.E.; Webb, D.W. *Large Dairy Herd Management*; American Dairy Science Association: Illinois, 1992.
2. International Commission on Microbiological Specifications for Foods (ICMSF). *Microorganisms in Foods 6, Microbial Ecology of Food Commodities*; Blackie Academic and Professional: London, UK, 1998.
3. Jay, J.M. *Modern Food Microbiology*, 6th Ed.; Aspen Publishers Inc.: Gaithersburg, 2000.
4. Doyle, M.P.; Beuchat, L.R.; Montville, T.J. *Food Microbiology: Fundamentals and Frontiers*, 2nd Ed.; ASM Press: Washington, D.C., 2001.
5. Lund, B.M.; Baird-Parker, T.C.; Gould, G.W. *The Microbiological Safety and Quality of Food*; Aspen Publishers, Inc.: Gaithersburg, 2000; Vol. 1.
6. Harding, F. *Milk Quality*; Blackie Academic and Professional: Glasgow, UK, 1995.
7. Bell, D.D.; Weaver, W.D., Jr. *Commercial Chicken Meat and Egg Production*; Kluwer Academic Publisher: Massachusetts, 2002.
8. Griffin, H.D. Manipulation of egg yolk cholesterol: A physiologist's view. World's Poult. Sci. J. **1992**, *48*, 101–112.

Antibiotics: Microbial Resistance

Bryan A. White
Randall S. Singer
University of Illinois at Urbana-Champaign, Urbana, Illinois, U.S.A.

INTRODUCTION

Antibiotics are compounds that either inhibit or cease the growth of microbes by targeting cellular functions that are required for maintenance or replication. Resistance to antibiotics can arise by point mutations that alter the target such that the antibiotic no longer exerts an inhibitory effect. Microbes can also acquire a gene or genes that confer resistance to the antibiotic's inhibitory effect. This acquisition is commonly mediated by horizontal transfer of the resistance gene(s) by a plethora of mechanisms. Microbial resistance to antibiotics can emerge as a result of exposure to antibiotics in the environment or when they are used therapeutically to prevent or cure diseases. This exposure exerts a selective pressure on the susceptible microbes and can result in the selective advantage of the resistant microbe, an up-regulation of the resistance protein, or an enhanced horizontal transfer of the resistance gene(s).

GENERAL MODES OF RESISTANCE

Antibiotic resistance mechanisms fall into various categories for both resistance to specific antibiotics and for multidrug resistance.[1,2] In general, the mechanisms for resistance to specific antibiotics include: 1) mutations that prevent the antibiotic from affecting the target, 2) porins or other cytoplasmic membrane proteins that actively pump the antibiotic out of the cell, 3) enzymatic inactivation of the antibiotic, 4) modification or protection of the antibiotic target, 5) circumvention of the effects of the antibiotic, and 6) failure to activate the antibiotic. The mechanisms used for multidrug resistance include: 1) efflux pumps in the cytoplasmic membrane that actively pump multiple antibiotics out of the cell, 2) alterations to the cytoplasmic membrane or cell wall such that the antibiotics do not enter the cell, and 3) formation of protective biofilms that restrict exposure of the microbes to antibiotics.

MAJOR CLASSES OF ANTIBIOTICS: MODES OF MICROBIAL RESISTANCE

β-Lactam Antibiotics

This class of antibiotic includes the penicillins, cephalosporins, carbapenems, and monobactams, which inhibit the formation of the bacterial cell wall by inhibiting the transpeptidation step in peptidoglycan synthesis. These antibiotics can also bind penicillin-binding proteins and stimulate autolysins, which then lyse the bacterial cell. Resistance to β-lactam antibiotics is commonly mediated by enzymatic inactivation of the antibiotic by a class of enzymes called β-lactamases.[3] The presence of a β-lactamase can be overcome by combining a β-lactam antibiotic with a β-lactamase inhibitor such as clavulanic acid or sulbactam. However, bacteria can also become resistant to these β-lactamase inhibitors. Resistance to β-lactams can also be conferred by mutations to the penicillin-binding proteins, which results in reduced affinity of these proteins for the β-lactam antibiotic. Finally, bacteria can alter the cell wall to reduce the uptake of β-lactams, or use an active efflux pump system to remove the antibiotic from the cytoplasm, although these mechanisms are rare.

Glycopeptide Antibiotics

Glycopeptide antibiotics such as vancomycin and teichoplanin bind the D-alanine dipeptide and inhibit the transglycosylation and transpeptidation steps in peptidoglycan synthesis of the cell wall. Gram-negative bacteria are generally not affected by glycopeptide antibiotics as these antibiotics cannot transverse the outer membrane and gain access to the peptidoglycan in the cell wall. Glycopeptide antibiotic resistance in Gram-positive bacteria is most often mediated by changes in the peptidoglycan side-chain thus circumventing the effects of the antibiotic.[2,4]

Encyclopedia of Animal Science
DOI: 10.1081/E-EAS 120019441

Aminoglycosides

The commonly used aminoglycoside antibiotics, kanamycin, gentamicin, streptomycin, tobramycin, and amikacin, interfere with protein synthesis by binding to the 30S ribosomal subunit. Resistance to aminoglycosides is usually mediated by inactivation of the antibiotic by glycoside-modifying enzymes. The covalent modification of aminoglycosides can be carried out by aminoglycoside acetyltransferases, aminoglycoside nucleotidyltransferases, or aminoglycoside phosphotransferases. There are also reports of aminoglycoside resistance mediated by mutations to ribosomal RNA, or by active efflux systems.[2,5]

Tetracyclines

Tetracycline and the derivatives oxytetracycline, doxycycline, and minocycline inhibit protein synthesis by binding to the 30S ribosomal subunit. Resistance to tetracyclines is mediated by one of two mechanisms. Both energy-dependent efflux pumps and protection of the ribosome by production of a protein that interacts with the ribosome and renders it unaffected by tetracycline are widely used by bacteria to confer resistance to these antibiotics.[2,6] There is also a rare resistance to tetracycline that is mediated by inactivation of the antibiotic. The significance of this mode of tetracycline resistance is not known.

Macrolides, Lincosamides, and Streptogramin (MLS) Antibiotics

MLS antibiotics that bind to the 50S ribosomal subunit and inhibit protein synthesis include tylosin, tilmicosin, erythromycin, clindamycin, and lincomycin. Streptogramins are also part of the multiantibiotic formulation Synercid. The most common resistance to macrolides and lincosamides is by posttranscriptional covalent modification of the 23S ribosomal RNA by adenine-N^6-methyltransferase. Efflux pump systems for exporting MLS antibiotics out of the cell have become increasingly encountered, and these vary in their specificity, exporting either specific MLS antibiotics only or groups of MLS antibiotics. Moreover, resistance can be conferred by inactivation of specific MLS antibiotics by hydrolysis or removal of functional groups. Covalent modification of lincosamides has also been detected.[2]

Fluoroquinolones

Antibiotics such as ciprofloxacin and norfloxacin inhibit bacterial topoisomerases and DNA gyrase, thus affecting DNA replication and partitioning. Mutations in the genes for these enzymes, affecting drug binding efficiencies, are the most dominant mode of resistance to fluoroquinolones. There is also a report of fluoroquinolone resistance mediated by an active efflux system.[2]

Sulfonamides

Trimethoprim, Septra, and Bactrim inhibit folate metabolism. Trimethoprim inhibits the enzyme dihydrofolate reductase, which is essential for tetrahydrofolate synthesis, whereas sulfonamides inhibit dihydropteroate synthase. Resistance to these antibiotics involves circumventing the effects of the antibiotic by either overprotection of dihydrofolate reductase or acquisition of a gene encoding a resistant form of the enzyme. Mutations to dihydrofolate reductase structural gene can also confer resistance.[2]

Chloramphenicols

Chloramphenicol and florfenicol affect protein synthesis by binding to the 50S ribosomal subunit and inhibiting the peptidyltransferase step. Resistance to chloramphenicol can be mediated by inactivation of the antibiotic by an acetyltransferase, but these enzymes are typically inactive against florfenicol. Bacteria can also alter the cell membrane to reduce the uptake of chloramphenicol and florfenicol, or use an active efflux pump system to remove the antibiotic from the cytoplasm.[2]

Others

Rifampin inhibits RNA synthesis by binding to the β-subunit of RNA polymerase. As with fluoroquinolone resistance, mutations in the target enzyme are the most common mechanism of resistance.[2]

Metronidazole interferes with DNA replication and is particularly useful against anaerobic bacteria and protozoa. Resistance to metronidazole is via failure to activate the antibiotic and apparently involves the decreased production of flavadoxin, a protein that activates metronidazole.[4]

Oxazolidinones such as Zyvox inhibit protein synthesis by binding to the 50S ribosomal subunit. Resistance to oxazolidinones is mediated by mutations to the 23S ribosomal RNA.

DEVELOPMENT AND TRANSFER OF ANTIBIOTIC RESISTANCE

It is clear that the development of resistance to antibiotics can be accomplished in many ways.[1,2] Mutations that alter antibiotic targets are a common mechanism, and these mutations occur at a background mutation rate in the absence of selection pressure. Organisms can also become resistant by acquiring a resistance gene or genes from other organisms by horizontal transfer. DNA carrying the gene(s) can be acquired from other microbes by: 1) conjugation, direct cell-to-cell transfer of DNA through a membrane protein complex; 2) transduction with a bacteriophage; and 3) transformation, the uptake of naked DNA from the environment. Conjugative DNA elements that carry antibiotic resistance genes include plasmids and conjugative transposons. These genetic elements can carry more than one antibiotic resistance gene, contributing to multidrug resistance. In animal agriculture, these plasmids containing multiple antibiotic resistance genes are often seen in *E. coli*, and the plasmids can often be very large (>50 kb). Tetracycline, florfenicol, and β-lactamase resistance genes are often found on these plasmids. Integrons are another genetic element responsible for the evolution of multidrug resistance.[7] These elements carry cassettes of genes that can integrate into plasmids or other genetic elements, thus contributing to multidrug resistance. Integrons commonly possess a sulfonamide resistance gene, sulI, in the 3′ conserved region, and thus sulfonamide resistance is often used as a potential indicator of the presence of integrons. Within the gene cassettes, genes conferring resistance to extended-spectrum β-lactamases, aminoglycosides, trimethoprim, and macrolides have been reported. Finally, the multidrug resistance of *Salmonella enterica* typhimurium DT104 deserves special mention.[8] The standard resistance phenotype in *Salmonella* DT104 includes resistance to ampicillin, chloramphenicol, streptomycin, sulfonamides, and tetracylines (ACSSuT). Some of the genes conferring this resistance in *Salmonella* DT104 are located within gene cassettes within integrons. All of the resistance genes are located together in the chromosome and form what is known as a genomic island. Typically, this chromosomal antibiotic resistance gene cluster is thought to be stable and nonmobile, and thus a clonal spread of *Salmonella* DT104 is required for the dissemination of this gene cluster. However, recent evidence of very similar multidrug resistance gene clusters in other *Salmonella* suggests the possibility that this gene cluster can be horizontally transferred.

CONCLUSION

Whenever an antibiotic is used, a selective pressure is applied that affects the interactions and competitions of the microbial populations in contact with the antibiotic. Due to selectively advantageous mutations or to the acquisition of resistance determinants by horizontal transfer, antibiotic resistance in the affected microbial populations can be expected to increase following this selective pressure. Moreover, the emergence of multidrug resistance can be expected because of this selective pressure. However, the long-term impacts of these changes in the resistant and susceptible microbial populations are unclear. Many of the resistance mechanisms can persist in the absence of an obvious selection pressure.[9,10,11]

REFERENCES

1. Schwarz, S.; Chaslus-Dancla, E. Use of antimicrobials in veterinary medicine and mechanisms of resistance. Vet. Res. **2001**, *32*, 201–225.
2. Salyers, A.A.; Whitt, D.D. How Bacteria Become Resistant to Antibiotics. In *Bacterial Pathogenesis: A Molecular Approach*; Salyers, A.A., Whitt, D.D., Eds.; ASM Press: Washington, DC, 2002; 168–184.
3. Kotra, L.P.; Samama, J.; Mobashery, S. β-Lactamases and Resistance to β-Lactam Antibiotics. In *Bacterial Resistance to Antimicrobials*; Lewis, K., Salyers, A.A., Taber, H.W., Wax, R.G., Eds.; Marcel Dekker: New York, 2002; 123–161.
4. Pootoolal, J.; Neu, J.; Wright, G.D. Glycopeptide antibiotic resistance. Annu. Rev. Pharmacol. Toxicol. **2002**, *42*, 381–408.
5. Wright, G.D. Mechanisms of Aminoglycoside Antibiotic Resistance. In *Bacterial Resistance to Antimicrobials*; Lewis, K., Salyers, A.A., Taber, H.W., Wax, R.G., Eds.; Marcel Dekker: New York, 2002; 91–122.
6. Roberts, M.C. Tetracycline resistance determinants: mechanisms of action, regulation of expression, genetic mobility, and distribution. FEMS Microbiol. Rev. **1996**, *19*, 1–24.
7. Carattoli, A. Importance of integrons in the diffusion of resistance. Vet. Res. **2001**, *32*, 243–259.
8. Cloeckaert, A.; Schwarz, S. Molecular characterization, spread and evolution of multidrug resistance in *Salmonella enterica* typhimurium DT104. Vet. Res. **2001**, *32*, 301–310.
9. Salyers, A.A.; Amabile-Cuevas, C.F. Why are antibiotic resistance genes so resistant to elimination? Antimicrob. Agents Chemother. **1997**, *41*, 2321–2325.
10. Lipsitch, M. The rise and fall of antimicrobial resistance. Trends Microbiol. **2001**, *9*, 438–444.
11. Levy, S.B. Multidrug resistance—A sign of the times. N. Engl. J. Med. **1998**, *338*, 1376–1378.

Antibiotics: Subtherapeutic Levels

Virgil W. Hays
University of Kentucky, Lexington, Kentucky, U.S.A.

INTRODUCTION

The word "antibiotic," though meaning antilife, has been commonly accepted as a term for antibacterial or antimicrobial agents, particularly those synthesized by bacteria or other microorganisms. Those antibacterial agents produced by chemical synthesis are often referred to as chemotherapeutics. Certain compounds containing arsenic, sulfur, and copper are members of this grouping and may be included in discussions of antibiotic usages. Subtherapeutic use has been accepted as a term for using these substances at relatively low levels in situations in which there is no apparent or detectable disease involved.

EFFECTIVE SUBTHERAPEUTIC USE OF ANTIBACTERIAL AGENTS IN SWINE PRODUCTION

For 50 plus years, the subtherapeutic uses of antibacterial agents have played a significant role in the efficiency of animal production, particularly for swine and poultry. The major discovery of antibiotic use for this purpose came as a by-product of the evaluation of fermentation products as sources of APF (animal protein factor or antipernicious anemia factor). Following Fleming's[1] report of the bacterial inhibitory effects of a certain mold, it was a decade later before Chain and coworkers[2] identified the active substance, penicillin. The miraculous effects of penicillin stimulated extensive searches for other antimicrobial agents that might have similar uses. At the same time, extensive research was in progress to find alternative sources and to identify the active substance in APF, a factor associated with animal protein. Researchers at Lederle Laboratories (The American Cyanimid Co.) had two independent teams, one involved in searching for antibacterial agents and the other searching for APF sources. The antibiotic team discovered the highly effective antibiotic Aureomycin (chlortetracycline) produced by *Streptomyces aureofaciens*.[3] Some time passed before the APF team tested the same organism. When Stockstad and coresearchers[4] tested the *S. aureofaciens*, they found a growth-stimulating effect greater than could be accredited to APF. Subsequent tests using crys-talline chlortetracycline and APF (by this time determined to be vitamin B_{12}) demonstrated that the additional growth stimulation was an effect of the antibacterial agent. This naturally led others to confirm these results and to determine if other antibiotics available at that time resulted in similar improvements in performance.

These studies on antibiotics were taking place at a time when other major changes were taking place in swine production. Pigs were being weaned at a younger age, major changes were being made in type and capacity of housing, more pigs were being reared in close confinement, herd sizes were increasing, and soybean meal was becoming even more economically competitive with milk, meat by-products, and fish meal as a supplemental protein. Antibiotics and vitamin B_{12} allowed greater application of these changes.

These observations were the forerunners of the widespread testing and subsequent use of numerous antimicrobial agents in swine and poultry production. Rapers[5] reported that more than 300 antibacterial substances had been identified. No doubt some of these were duplications as the reports were often published before complete identification of the active principle had been established and verified. To date, the number of antibiotics would far exceed this; however, a relatively small number has been adequately tested and approved for use as feed additives for the purposes of improving growth and feed conversion in pigs.

The effective antibiotics vary in chemical structure and in the relative amount absorbed. Some are readily absorbed and others are hardly absorbed at all. The absorptive capacity certainly influences their effectiveness against systemic infections; however, the absorption pattern is less readily associated with their effectiveness in improving growth rate and efficiency of feed conversion in apparently healthy animals. At least three modes of action have been postulated and have varying degrees of support: 1) *a metabolic effect*, in which the chemical constituency of the antibiotic, in some way, alters the rate or the pattern of the metabolic processes; 2) *a nutrient-sparing effect*, which reduces the dietary requirement for certain nutrients, either by allowing the growth of desirable organisms that synthesize essential nutrients, by depressing organisms that compete with the host

Encyclopedia of Animal Science
DOI: 10.1081/E-EAS 120019443

animal for nutrients, or by improving the absorption of nutrients by the host animal; and 3) *a disease-control effect* through suppression of organism causing clinical or subclinical manifestations of disease.

Due consideration should be given to the first two or even other ways antibacterial agents may be affecting improved performance in pigs and chicks. However, the evidence for the first two modes of action would indicate they are of relatively minor importance, highly variable, and of questionable significance. Most diets can be adequately fortified with appropriate levels of all nutrients, though there may be some localities or extenuating circumstances that would limit availability of an optimum diet. There is evidence that the intestinal wall is thinner and interpreted to be more healthy with antibiotics and some experiments suggest this results in improved absorption. The greatest benefits are from limiting the effects of harmful organisms or preventing adverse effects of organisms that may or may not result in identifiable disease situations. At subtherapeutic or feed additive levels, antibiotics improve performance in the absence of clinical signs of harmful organisms.

There are numerous feeding, housing, and management programs that will affect the observed response to antibiotics. Also, the response is greater (percentage wise) in younger animals than in animals that are more mature or older. If it were economically and physically practical to house animals in a germ-free environment or in an environment free of any harmful organisms, there would be no need for antibiotics as feed additives or for therapeutic purposes. There are numerous reports that demonstrate that cleanliness in the environment improves performance and reduces the relative response to antibacterial agents. Wacholz and Heidenriech[6] reported the results of an experiment in which pigs were housed in previously used dirt lots or in a clean barn. The observed responses to antibiotics were much greater in the dirt lots; however, the performance was much higher with the combination of a clean barn plus antibiotics. Hays and Speer[7] reported the results of trials in facilities that differed in cleanliness at the start of the experiments. In one, the building was completely emptied, thoroughly cleaned, and all pigs moved in the same day. In the other experiment, pens were emptied and cleaned for one replication at a time, but the building was not completely emptied and thoroughly cleaned. The response to antibiotics was less (33%) in the cleaner environment than in the unclean barn (75%), but the overall performance was greater for the clean environment plus the antibiotic.

Mixing pigs of different ages, mixing pigs from different farms, or even mixing pigs from other buildings on the same farm can expose them to harmful organisms and higher incidents of clinical and subclinical disease. When such exposure is necessary, the adverse effects can be lessened with the appropriate use of antibiotics as feed additives.

CONTINUED EFFECTIVENESS OF ANTIBIOTICS WHEN USED AS FEED ADDITIVES

In the early years of antibiotic usage, there was concern that the popularly used antibiotics, such as chlortetracycline, oxytetracycline, penicillin, tylosin, and others would eventually lose their effectiveness because of resistance development in harmful organisms or by selecting for harmful organisms that were naturally resistant. Certain bacteria do develop resistance and this should be considered in antibiotics use programs. However, the problem is not as great as some suggest. Appropriate management of therapeutic and subtherapeutic use in combination with sound housing, management, and nutrition programs has resulted in profitable benefits from these antibacterial agents for more than half a century. Comprehensive statistical evaluations of experiments conducted over a period of more than 25 years show that those antibiotics first introduced are still effective.[8] This report[8] also included the results of an experiment that demonstrated positive responses to tetracycline in a facility in which tetracycline had been used continuously in the feed for three years prior to the experiment. The pigs used in the experiment had been fed diets containing tetracycline prior to being allocated to diets with or without the tetracycline. A positive response to the antibiotic continued. Over the years, numerous antibacterial agents have been tested singly or in combination with others. Some combinations provide greater antibacterial activity and greater improvements in rates of gain or efficiency of feed conversion. Some have been effective, but never approved for use, either because they showed no unique advantage or because they were uncompetitive cost-wise.

CONCLUSION

After more than half a century of extensive usage worldwide, the use of low levels of antibacterial agents in the feed or water for livestock and poultry continues to be effective in increasing growth rate, improving feed conversion, and reducing morbidity and mortality. Those first introduced, such as tetracyclines, penicillin, streptomycin, and certain compounds containing arsenic continue to be effective. As would be expected, those agents with a wide antibacterial spectrum are, on average, more effective as routine additives.

ARTICLE OF FURTHER INTEREST

Feed Supplements: Antibiotics, p. 369

REFERENCES

1. Fleming, A. On the antibacterial action of cultures of a Penicillium, with special reference to their use in the isolation of B influenzae. Brit. J. Exp. Pathol. **1929**, *10*, 226.
2. Chain, E.; Florey, H.W.; Gardner, A.D.; Heatley, N.G.; Jennings, M.A.; Orr-ewing, J. Penicillin as a therapeutic agent. Lancet **1940**, *2*, 226.
3. Dugger, B.M. Aureomycin: A product of the continuing search for new antibiotics. Ann. N.Y. **1940**, *51*, 177.
4. Stockstad, E.L.R.; Jukes, T.H.; Pierce, J.V.; Page, A.C.; Franklin, A.L. The multiple nature of the animal protein factor. J. Biol. Chem. **1949**, *180*, 647.
5. Raper, K.B. A decade of antibiotics in America. Mycologia **1952**, *44*, 1.
6. Wachholz, D.E.; Heidenreich, C.J. Effect of tylosin on swine growth in two environments. J. Anim. Sci. **1970**, *31*, 104.
7. Hays, V.W.; Speer, V.C. Effect of spiromycin on growth and feed utilization of young pigs. J. Anim. Sci. **1960**, *19*, 938.
8. Hays, V.W. *Effectiveness of Feed Additive Usage of Antibacterial Agents in Swine and Poultry Production*; Office of Technology Assessment, U. S. Congress, Washington, D.C., 1977.

Antimicrobial Use in Food Animals: Potential Alternatives

Kenneth M. Bischoff
Todd R. Callaway
Tom S. Edrington
Kenneth J. Genovese
Tawni L. Crippen
David J. Nisbet
United States Department of Agriculture, Agricultural Research Service, College Station, Texas, U.S.A.

INTRODUCTION

For over fifty years, antimicrobials have been used in food-animal production to maintain animal health and to increase productivity. The resulting increase in antimicrobial resistance among enteric bacteria has created two principal concerns: 1) The prevalence of drug-resistant pathogens leaves the producer with fewer tools to manage disease; and 2) a reservoir of antimicrobial-resistant bacteria has the potential for transmission to humans via the food chain. The most logical intervention strategy to combat the increase in antimicrobial resistance is to reduce selection pressure by limiting the availability and promoting prudent use of antimicrobial drugs, but such measures may not be effective, because linkage of resistance genes allows a single selection pressure to coselect for resistance to multiple agents. Thus, simultaneous reductions of all coselecting agents may be required to reverse the persistence of antimicrobial resistance. This necessitates the development of alternative, nonantimicrobial methods to maintain animal health and productivity. This article reviews some of the intervention strategies that are being developed as alternatives to antimicrobials for the control of enteric pathogens in food animals. The application of alternative pathogen control measures will decrease the total usage of antimicrobial drugs and should reduce antimicrobial resistance among enteric bacteria in food animals.

NONANTIMICROBIAL ALTERNATIVES FOR NONSPECIFIC CONTROL OF ENTERIC PATHOGENS

Competitive Exclusion

Competitive exclusion (CE) is the prophylactic treatment of young animals with suspensions of enteric bacteria obtained from healthy adults. It is a highly effective method of controlling gut colonization by *Salmonella* and other enteric pathogens, particularly when cultures are administered to animals shortly after birth while the ecology of the gastrointestinal (GI) tract is relatively naive.[1] The mechanism by which CE cultures confer protection is not clearly understood but may involve one or more of the following factors: 1) blockage of potential attachment sites; 2) production of bacteriocins by endogenous bacterial species; 3) maintenance of gut pH by volatile fatty acids; and 4) competition for nutrients.

In many countries, the use of undefined mixed bacterial cultures for competitive exclusion is acceptable, but in the United States, the Food and Drug Administration (FDA) restricts the use of such cultures as undefined drugs. Use of continuous-culture technology (i.e., continuous-flow chemostats) has allowed for the selection, testing, and maintenance of defined CE cultures, and has led to the development of an efficacious CE culture, called CF3, for use in controlling *Salmonella* in poultry.[2] Similar products are being developed for use in controlling *Salmonella* and enterotoxigenic *E. coli* in swine.[3]

Prebiotics

Prebiotics are nondigestible food ingredients that benefit the host by promoting the growth of beneficial bacteria in the gastrointestinal tract. Beneficial species of bacteria such as bifidobacteria and lactobacilli readily ferment the prebiotic oligosaccharides (oligofructose and inulin), whereas pathogenic bacteria such as *Salmonella* and *E. coli* do not.[4] The potential of prebiotics to replace antimicrobials for pathogen control or performance enhancement has not been proven conclusively, because feed supplements can have mixed effects depending on the bacterial species, the animal, and its age.[4] Existing data from studies with chickens suggest that oligofructose can reduce cecal concentrations of *Salmonella* but not *Campylobacter*. In swine, oligofructose can reduce mortality and morbidity due to infectious *E. coli* but showed no effect on weight gain or feed efficiency in neonatal and weaned pigs and only mixed effects in growing pigs.

Encyclopedia of Animal Science
DOI: 10.1081/E-EAS 120025130

45

Potentiators of Innate Immunity

The use of cytokines for the preventive activation of the nonspecific innate immune system may be an effective alternative to antibiotics, particularly in neonates whose acquired immune system has yet to mature.[5] Chickens, for example, are extremely susceptible to opportunistic pathogens in the first week post-hatch and rely primarily on their innate immune system.[6] Splenic T cells from adult chickens immunized against *Salmonella enteritidis* secrete factors, collectively called immune lymphokines (ILK), that can activate the bactericidal activities of heterophils, one of the main effector cells of the avian innate response.[7] The activation of heterophils in ILK-treated birds is strongly associated with protection against *Salmonella* organ invasion and reduction of *Salmonella*-induced mortality.[8] A similar preparation for swine has been shown to significantly reduce *Salmonella* colonization and organ invasion in neonatal and weaned pigs.[9] Although the functional activities of ILK have been well documented, the molecular composition of ILK remains largely undefined. Identification of its active components is still required for the development of a defined cocktail of immunopotentiators that will fully activate innate resistance.

NONANTIMICROBIAL ALTERNATIVES FOR SPECIFIC CONTROL OF PATHOGENS

Exploitation of Facultative Metabolism in *Escherichia coli* and *Salmonella* spp.

Some facultative gastrointestinal bacteria, including *E. coli* and *Salmonella*, possess a respiratory nitrate reductase enzyme that allows the coupling of anaerobic nitrate reduction to oxidative phosphorylation.[10] This enzyme is also capable of reducing chlorate, an analogue of nitrate, to the cytotoxic product chlorite. Administration of chlorate in feed or water should therefore selectively eliminate facultative anaerobes from the gastrointestinal tract but retain many of the beneficial obligate anaerobes.

Experimental chlorate products have been shown to be effective for the control of *E. coli* O157:H7 and *Salmonella* in cattle, swine, and poultry.[11–13] They are being developed primarily as preharvest interventions at terminal feedings to reduce intestinal *E. coli* O157:H7 and *Salmonella* levels in livestock before slaughter, which will subsequently decrease the risk of transmission of these pathogens to consumers via meat products.

Bacteriophage Therapy

Lytic bacteriophages are viruses that can infect and kill bacteria. Their use for the prevention and treatment of infectious disease offers another attractive alternative to antimicrobials, because they are highly specific to a bacterial species, are nontoxic to the animal host, and can increase in titre as they infect and kill their target bacteria.[14] In experimentally infected animals, bacteriophages have been shown to prevent and treat *E. coli*–induced diarrhea in calves, piglets, and lambs, and to prevent *E. coli* respiratory infections in broiler chickens.[15,16]

Vaccines

Vaccines confer protection against specific pathogens by exploiting the specificity and memory of the acquired immune response. The host is first exposed to the pathogen through a preparation of the pathogen's antigens that elicits a primary acquired immune response without developing clinical symptoms of disease in the host. Subsequent exposures to the same antigens elicit faster and more effective secondary immune responses to the offending microbe. Although many vaccines consist of killed bacteria or of live attenuated strains,[17] the antigens in the vaccine need not be associated with whole cells. Recombinant forms of virulence factors, such as fimbriae or heat-labile toxin from enterotoxigenic *E. coli*, may be sufficient to induce an effective immunologic response.[18]

CONCLUSION

Despite the best efforts to control and treat infectious disease with antimicrobials, bacteria will continue to adapt and survive. As resistance to these drugs increases, producers are left with fewer options for maintaining herd health and productivity. This article has presented some of the strategies that are being developed as alternatives to antimicrobials for controlling enteric pathogens in food animals. Chlorate supplementation, immune lymphokines, and competitive exclusion cultures show promising commercial potential, as do other areas of product development including, prebiotics, vaccine development, and bacteriophage. It is unlikely that any single product will meet all the needs of the producer, but each alternative has its effective place along the production continuum, and combinations of alternatives may have synergistic effects. Ultimately the application of these products will decrease the need for antimicrobials and will likely have a large impact on the reduction of antimicrobial resistance among enteric bacteria in food animals.

REFERENCES

1. Nisbet, D.J. Use of competitive exclusion in food animals. J. Am. Vet. Med. Assoc. **1998**, *213* (12), 1744–1746.

2. Nisbet, D.J. Defined competitive exclusion cultures in the prevention of enteropathogen colonization in poultry and swine. Antonie van Leeuwenhoek **2002**, *81*, 481–486.

3. Genovese, K.J.; Anderson, R.C.; Harvey, R.B.; Nisbet, D.J. Competitive exclusion treatment reduces the mortality and fecal shedding associated with enterotoxigenic *Escherichia coli* infection in nursery-raised neonatal pigs. Can. J. Vet. Res. **2000**, *64* (4), 204–207.

4. Flickinger, E.A.; Loo, J.V.; Fahey, G.C. Nutritional responses to the presence of inulin and oligofructose in the diets of domesticated animals: A review. Crit. Rev. Food Sci. Nutr. **2003**, *43* (1), 19–60.

5. Toth, T.E.; Veit, H.; Gross, W.B.; Siegel, P.B. Cellular defense of the avian respiratory system: Protection against *Escherichia coli* airsacculitis by *Pasteurella multocida*-activated respiratory phagocytes. Avian Dis. **1988**, *32* (4), 681–687.

6. Lowenthal, J.W.; Connick, T.E.; McWaters, P.G.; York, J.J. Development of T cell immune responsiveness in the chicken. Immunol. Cell Biol. **1994**, *72* (2), 115–122.

7. Kogut, M.H.; McGruder, E.D.; Hargis, B.M.; Corrier, D.E.; DeLoach, J.R. Dynamics of avian inflammatory response to *Salmonella*-immune lymphokines. Inflammation **1994**, *18* (4), 373–388.

8. Kogut, M.H.; Tellez, G.I.; McGruder, E.D.; Hargis, B.M.; Williams, J.D.; Corrier, D.E.; DeLoach, J.R. Heterophils are decisive components in the early responses of chickens to *Salmonella* enteritidis infections. Microb. Pathog. **1994**, *16* (2), 141–151.

9. Genovese, K.J.; Anderson, R.C.; Nisbet, D.E.; Harvey, R.B.; Lowry, V.K.; Buckley, S.; Stanker, L.H.; Kogut, M.H. Prophylactic administration of immune lymphokine derived from T cells of *Salmonella enteritidis*-immune pigs. Protection against *Salmonella choleraesuis* organ invasion and cecal colonization in weaned pigs. Adv. Exp. Med. Biol. **1999**, *473* (1), 299–307.

10. Stewart, V. Nitrate respiration in relation to facultative metabolism in enterobacteria. Microbiol. Rev. **1988**, *52* (2), 190–232.

11. Anderson, R.C.; Callaway, T.R.; Buckley, S.A.; Anderson, T.J.; Genovese, K.J.; Sheffield, C.L.; Nisbet, D.J. Effect of oral sodium chlorate administration on *Escherichia coli* O157:H7 in the gut of experimentally infected pigs. Int. J. Food Microbiol. **2001**, *71* (2–3), 125–130.

12. Callaway, T.R.; Anderson, R.C.; Genovese, K.J.; Poole, T.L.; Anderson, T.J.; Byrd, J.A.; Kubena, L.F.; Nisbet, D.J. Sodium chlorate supplementation reduces *E. coli* O157:H7 populations in cattle. J. Anim. Sci. **2002**, *80* (6), 1683–1689.

13. Jung, Y.S.; Anderson, R.C.; Byrd, J.A.; Edrington, T.S.; Moore, R.W.; Callaway, T.R.; McReynolds, J.; Nisbet, D.J. Reduction of *Salmonella Typhimurium* in experimentally challenged broilers by nitrate adaptation and chlorate supplementation in drinking water. J. Food Prot. **2003**, *66* (4), 660–663.

14. Summers, W.C. Bacteriophage therapy. Annu. Rev. Microbiol. **2001**, *55*, 437–451.

15. Huff, W.E.; Huff, G.R.; Rath, N.C.; Balog, J.M.; Xie, H.; Moore, P.A., Jr.; Donoghue, A.M. Prevention of *Escherichia coli* respiratory infection in broiler chickens with bacteriophage (SPR02). Poult. Sci. **2002**, *81* (4), 437–441.

16. Smith, H.W.; Huggins, M.B. Effectiveness of phages in treating experimental *Escherichia coli* diarrhoea in calves, piglets and lambs. J. Gen. Microbiol. **1983**, *129* (Pt. 8), 2659–2675.

17. Lillehoj, E.P.; Yun, C.H.; Lillehoj, H.S. Vaccines against the avian enteropathogens *Eimeria*, *Cryptosporidium* and *Salmonella*. Anim. Health Res. Rev. **2000**, *1* (1), 47–65.

18. Yu, J.; Cassels, F.; Scharton-Kersten, T.; Hammond, S.A.; Hartman, A.; Angov, E.; Corthesy, B.; Alving, C.; Glenn, G. Transcutaneous immunization using colonization factor and heat-labile enterotoxin induces correlates of protective immunity for enterotoxigenic *Escherichia coli*. Infect. Immun. **2002**, *70* (3), 1056–1068.

Aquaculture: Production, Processing, Marketing

Carole R. Engle
Nathan M. Stone
University of Arkansas, Pine Bluff, Arkansas, U.S.A.

INTRODUCTION

Aquaculture is broadly defined as the culture of aquatic organisms under controlled conditions. More than 210 species of finfish, crustaceans, mollusks, and aquatic plants are raised, with the vast majority (99%) grown for human consumption. Fish and other aquatic organisms account for 16% of the animal protein consumed worldwide, with an average per capita fish consumption of 15.8 kg. In clear contrast to terrestrial animal production, most fish consumed are caught from the wild. However, the harvest from capture fisheries has peaked. Declining populations of wild fish and restrictions on fishing vessels, effort, and gear have increased costs, whereas new technologies have reduced the costs of aquaculture production. Aquaculture has been the source of continued increase in the world supply of aquatic products, providing 34% (48.4 million mt; $61.7 billion) of the worldwide fisheries supply in 2001.

PAST AND CURRENT STATUS OF AQUACULTURE

The earliest recorded evidence of aquaculture was 900 B.C.[1] However, for most species of fish, scarcities due to overfishing in the late 1900s provided adequate incentive to domesticate aquatic plants and animals. Technologies developed rapidly, and aquaculture industries have grown rapidly through the 1990s (Fig. 1).

China leads the world in aquaculture production. With the exception of Chile, the top 10 countries in world aquaculture production are all Asian countries.[2] Most of these (with the exception of Japan) are lesser-developed nations. The majority of aquaculture production consists of a mixture of carp species raised for family and local consumption. However, aquaculture has increasingly become a source of foreign exchange through export. The United States alone imported $18.5 billion worth of edible and nonedible fisheries products in 2001.

Once envisioned as a blue revolution that would save the world from starvation, aquaculture has come under increasing criticism from environmentalists who allege biological, organic, and chemical pollution; habitat modification; and use of fish protein as a feed ingredient.[3] Like other forms of agriculture supporting human life, aquaculture modifies the natural environment and has the potential to degrade it.[4]

UNIQUE ASPECTS

Aquaculture includes a wide diversity of species raised in diverse aquatic environments that include freshwater, brackish, and marine systems (Table 1).[2] Aquaculture products are farmed for food consumption, for sportfishing, for bait, for clothing (alligator skins), for pets (ornamental fish and feeders), and for industrial processes (seaweeds for agar and carrageenan).[5] Polyculture is an appealing concept that maximizes production by stocking different species in the same pond, thus exploiting various trophic levels in a pond environment.

Aquaculture is limited by the nature of aquatic organisms and the medium of their water environment. Unlike all other domesticated livestock, fish and invertebrates are cold-blooded and require a narrow temperature range for good growth. In water, gravity is nearly overcome by the buoyancy of the medium, reducing energy expended in daily movements. Oxygen is a limiting factor because it is relatively insoluble in water. Depending on temperature and salinity, water is saturated with oxygen at 5.2 to 14.6 mg/L; in contrast, air contains approximately 21% oxygen. Water is an excellent solvent for nitrogenous wastes, which makes them difficult to concentrate and remove. In ponds, fish wastes stimulate growth of phytoplankton and bacteria that are difficult to control or concentrate for removal. Water quality in warmwater fishponds is to a large extent controlled by the plankton community.[6]

PRODUCTION

Aquaculture production occurs in ponds, raceways, cages, rafts, baskets, lines, recirculating systems, and by ocean and reservoir ranching.[5] The majority of finfish and crustacean production worldwide occurs in earthen ponds,

Encyclopedia of Animal Science
DOI: 10.1081/E-EAS 120019444

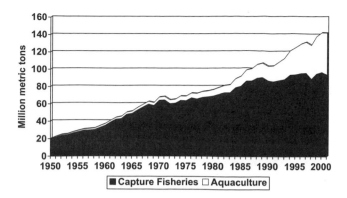

Fig. 1 Volume of capture fisheries and aquaculture production. (Figure courtesy of Ref. [2].)

but fish can be raised in open waters by confining them to cages or net pens. Salmon and freshwater paddlefish are ranched by releasing young into the wild for recapture and sale as adults. Very intensive indoor recirculating systems rely on biofilters or hydroponics to remove the dilute nitrogenous waste products of fish. Shellfish are cultured on rafts, in baskets, and on lines.

Species that are good aquaculture candidates: 1) are easy to reproduce in a controlled fashion; 2) accept prepared feeds; 3) are hardy; 4) tolerate a wide range of water quality conditions; and 5) have high market value. Seed for aquaculture production often closely resembles its wild counterpart. Although some carp strains have undergone selective breeding for decades, there has been little genetic improvement of most aquaculture stocks. Recent bioengineering advances have come under intense scrutiny by those opposed to genetic manipulation. Seed production in aquaculture is further complicated by complex life cycles (as many as 20+ larval stages of some crustaceans) and the small-sized larvae of many marine species.

Most forms of aquaculture production rely on artificial feeds. Diet formulations are complex due to the range of dietary habits. Fish such as tilapia and some carp are primarily herbivores, fish such as catfish have omnivorous dietary habits, and salmon are essentially carnivores. There is no parallel in terrestrial agriculture for large-scale production of carnivorous species as food. In spite of the range of natural dietary habits, typical crude protein levels in commercial, pelletized fish diets range from 28–45% protein.

Mechanical aeration is used frequently to maintain acceptable levels of dissolved oxygen. Ammonia removal technologies are required in very intensive systems. Harvesting, holding, and transportation of aquatic animals are complicated by requirements to maintain adequate water quality (Fig. 2).

Management intensity and risk vary with the species produced and the culture system employed. Some crops require only a few months of production, whereas others require several years. Increasing intensification can be accompanied by increasing problems of fish health. Aquaculture industries lag behind other forms of animal agriculture in understanding disease transmission and in development of effective control mechanisms.

Most aquaculture businesses are classified as small businesses. In the United States, 84% of catfish, 93% of baitfish, and 95% of trout farms are small businesses.[7] Some integration has occurred, but the extent of consolidation of aquaculture supply and marketing chains has lagged behind that of other animal production industries. The broiler industry has been widely cited as a model path for aquaculture industry evolution, but the nature of aquatic species, systems, and market channels is more complex. The greater degree of perishability of seafood products and the consequent consumer demand for freshness have slowed consolidation of distribution networks. Salmon, shrimp, and catfish are the commercial large-scale aquaculture businesses most likely to follow the poultry industry integration model.

In the United States, the U.S. Department of Agriculture (USDA) is the lead agency in aquaculture and is supported by the National Oceanic and Atmospheric Association (NOAA). Private associations of producers, such as the Catfish Farmers of America, the U.S. Trout Farmers Association, and the American Tilapia Association, are all affiliated with the umbrella trade group, the National Aquaculture Association. The U.S. Aquaculture Society, a chapter of the World Aquaculture Society, provides professional support for aquaculture. The gateway to aquaculture resources on the web is AquaNic: the Aquaculture Network Information Center (http://aquanic.org).

PROCESSING

Aquaculture products are sold live, fresh, frozen, canned, smoked, salted, pickled, and dried. Fish are processed as whole-dressed or fillets, fresh (packed on ice), or frozen [in blocks for wholesale markets or individually quick-frozen (IQF)]. Crustaceans are sold head on or off, peeled, or shell on. There is increasing interest in expanding value-added offerings beyond the traditional breaded and glazed products. Rapid processing and preservation are necessary because fish and shellfish spoil easily. As poikilotherms (cold-blooded organisms), fish contain enzymes that function at relatively low temperatures, which leads to the rapid decomposition of harvested fish.

Table 1 Worldwide aquaculture production of selected species and groups for 2001, in metric tons

Species/group	Quantity produced (mt)
Finfish	
Freshwater	
Cyprinids (carps, barbels, etc.)	16,427,626
Tilapia and other cichlids	1,385,223
Channel catfish	271,075
Other freshwater finfish	2,718,287
Freshwater finfish total	**20,802,211**
Diadromous	
Atlantic salmon	1,025,287
Rainbow trout	510,055
Milkfish	495,250
Eels	230,992
Seabass (*Lates calcarifer*)	15,546
Other diadromous finfish	16,330
Diadromous finfish total	**2,293,460**
Marine finfish	
Japanese seabream	873
Mandarin fish	116,423
European seabass and gilthead seabream	44,637
Mullets	10,648
Other marine finfish	890,045
Marine finfish total	**1,062,626**
Total finfish	**24,158,297**
Crustaceans	
Marine shrimp	1,270,875
Crabs	164,232
Freshwater prawns and other crustaceans	514,451
Red swamp crawfish	13,847
Other crustaceans	36,278
Crustaceans total	**1,999,683**
Molluscs	
Oysters	4,207,818
Clams, cockles	3,109,024
Scallops, pectens	1,219,127
Mussels	1,370,631
Freshwater molluscs	10,399
Abalones, winkles, conchs	5,425
Squids, cuttlefish, octopus	16
Other marine mollusks	1,344,763
Molluscs total	**11,267,203**
Miscellaneous animals (frogs, turtles, tunicates)	**164,883**
Seaweeds	
Brown seaweeds	4,691,210
Red seaweeds	2,215,193
Green seaweeds	31,913
Miscellaneous aquatic plants	3,623,963
Seaweeds total	**10,562,279**
Aquaculture total, excluding seaweeds	**37,590,066**
Aquaculture total, including seaweeds	**48,152,345**

(From Ref. [2].)

Fig. 2 Recording channel catfish biomass weights loaded per tank on an 18-wheeled transport truck, after harvesting from a commercial pond. (*View this art in color at www.dekker.com.*)

The rate of decomposition is species-dependent and relatively faster in fattier, cold-water fish.[8]

MARKETING

Unlike animal and row crop agriculture, aquaculture growers find themselves competing in the marketplace with wild-caught seafood products. Salmon and catfish are two examples of aquaculture products whose supply has grown to surpass that of the wild catch. Market channels reflect the local nature of seafood product availability and historically have tended to involve small-scale jobbers that fulfilled wholesaling and transportation functions. In more recent years, major seafood distributors have consolidated and supply chains have become more globalized as major buyers source seafood products from around the world. In retail markets, seafood marketing margins typically are high (25–35%), reflecting a premium for risk of spoilage and the luxury nature of most seafood in the United States.

Trade in aquaculture products has acquired an important international focus. Shrimp is a global commodity, with over $8.4 billion traded internationally each year. More than 27% of the shrimp traded internationally is from aquaculture. Moreover, trade disputes related to

salmon, crawfish, catfish, and shrimp have had major international political ramifications in recent years.

CONCLUSION

Aquaculture is stunning in its diversity and complexity. It is the equivalent of combining all forms of animal agriculture together as what might be called terrestrial culture. The growth of aquaculture has provided the supply to fuel the increase in total growth of the world supply of fisheries products. This growth is occurring during times of increased environmental concerns and continued population increases that challenge our ability to feed populations. Aquaculture represents a mechanism to contribute both to feeding the poor and to supplying a diversity of high-valued products that generate economic growth through business development. Continued growth, however, will depend upon developing solutions to the challenges posed by declining resource availability and continued population pressure.

REFERENCES

1. Avault, J.W., Jr. *Fundamentals of Aquaculture: A Step-by-Step Guide to Commercial Aquaculture*; AVA Publishing Company, Inc.: Baton Rouge, LA, 1996.
2. FAO. *The State of World Fisheries and Aquaculture 2002*; Food and Agriculture Organization, United Nations: Rome, Italy, 2002.
3. Tidwell, J.H.; Allan, G.L. Fish as food: Aquaculture's contribution. World Aquac. **2002**, *33* (3), 44–48.
4. Tomasso, J. *Aquaculture and the Environment in the United States*; U.S. Aquaculture Society, World Aquaculture Society: Baton Rouge, LA, 2002.
5. Stickney, R.R. *Encyclopedia of Aquaculture*; John Wiley & Sons, Inc.: New York, 2000.
6. Boyd, C.E.; Tucker, C.S. *Pond Aquaculture Water Quality Management*; Kluwer Academic Publishers: Norwell, MA, 1998.
7. USDA/NASS. *Census of Aquaculture*; United States Department of Agriculture/National Agricultural Statistics Service: Washington, DC, 1998.
8. Martin, R.E.; Flick, G.J. *The Seafood Industry*; Van Nostrand Reinhold: New York, 1990.

Aquatic Animals: Fishes—Major

Carl D. Webster
Kenneth R. Thompson
Laura A. Muzinic
Kentucky State University, Frankfort, Kentucky, U.S.A.

INTRODUCTION

Aquaculture, the culture of aquatic organisms, has been practiced by people for several thousand years. It is said that the Romans cultured oysters, and China has been growing fish in ponds for 3000 years. Globally, in 2001, approximately 97 million tonnes (tonne = metric ton: 2205 pounds) of aquatic animals and mollusks (excluding aquatic plants) were harvested, of which 60 million tonnes were derived from capture fisheries and 37 million tonnes were derived from aquaculture. Global aquaculture production consisted of 15.2 million tonnes from marine areas and 22.6 million tonnes from inland areas. In 2002, production of finfish represented more than 50% of all aquaculture production, mollusks were 23.4%, aquatic plants were 22.2%, crustaceans were 3.6%, and other species represented 0.3% (Fig. 1A). As a percentage of value, there are shifts in the percent compared by each category. Finfish represent 55.9% of the value of all aquaculture products, mollusks represent 16.8%, crustaceans represent 16.6%, aquatic plants represent 9.9%, and other aquaculture items represent 0.8% of the total value (Fig. 1B).

Two hundred and ten different species of animals and plants are currently cultured around the world. China produces 71% of the total volume (Fig. 2A) and almost 50% of the total value (Fig. 2B) of global aquaculture production. Carp production constitutes 68% of the total global finfish aquaculture production; they are grown and consumed mainly in China and India (Fig. 3). Although there are many species of fish, shellfish, and crustaceans cultured in the world, this article will focus on the most commonly cultured fish species, their scientific names, the amount produced, the country or region that is the lead producer, and the types of culture systems most commonly used in production. This listing is by no means complete. There are fish species that may not be listed, although they may have a large local or regional production, but it is hoped that this list will serve as a brief introduction to the fish that constitute the majority of global finfish production.

MOST COMMONLY CULTURED SPECIES

Atlantic salmon (*Salmo salar*) is one of the most-produced fish in the global aquaculture industry, with Norway and Chile being two of the largest producers. In 1980, only 10,000 tonnes were produced globally, but by 2010 it is expected that over 2 million tonnes will be produced.[1] Marine net pens are the most commonly used culture system, and production reached 1.4 million tonnes in 2002.

Bighead carp (*Aristichthys nobilis*) are native to the lowland rivers of China and feed principally on zooplankton (although they do eat larger phytoplankton and detritus) in the upper layer of water in a pond. Bighead carp are typically cultured in ponds and can grow rapidly, although growth is dependent upon the fertility of the water, or the quality and amount of prepared food. Generally, bighead carp are not directly fed a diet, and they are cultured extensively with other carp species. Production for 2002 was approximately 1.75 million tonnes.

Catla (*Catla catla*) is one of the three Indian major carps that are commercially cultured in India and the Indian subcontinent. India is the second largest carp producer in the world, next only to China, and produces approximately 1.7 million tonnes of India major carps each year. Catla are mostly grown in freshwater ponds; however, some brackish water ponds have been used to successfully grow catla in India. Production in 2002 was approximately 546,000 tonnes (personal communication; Dr. B.B. Jana, India).

Channel catfish (*Ictalurus punctatus*) are the most widely cultured fish in the United States, representing approximately 50% of that country's aquaculture industry (roughly $600,000 a year). Channel catfish are a popular finfish and are most often grown in ponds, although small farmers can grow the fish successfully in cages. It may not be unreasonable to state that more is known of the nutrient requirements of the channel catfish than any other fish species in the world. Production is estimated to be 305,000 tonnes in 2003.[2]

Encyclopedia of Animal Science
DOI: 10.1081/E-EAS 120019447

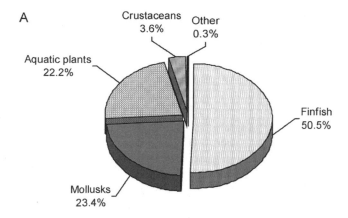

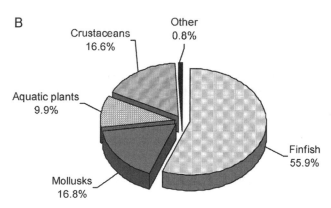

Fig. 1 (A) The percentage of major groups of cultured organisms and plants in 2000–2002 (by weight). The total amount of cultured products was 45.7 million tonnes. (B) The percentage of value represented by the major groups of cultured organisms and plants in 2002. Total value was $56.5 billion. (Data adapted from FAO, accessed August 2003.)

Common carp (*Cyprinus carpio*) is a member of the family Cyprinidae and is the third most commonly produced fish in global aquaculture. In 2002, approximately 2.9 million tonnes were produced, with a value of $2.8 billion. China is the largest single producer of common carp. Common carp are traditionally cultured in ponds or rice paddies. However, more intensive culture systems have been used recently including irrigation ponds, flow-through raceways, and net pens. In the past, low-cost supplemental diets have been fed to carp, but as production has intensified, especially in China, more complete diets are being fed so as to maximize growth and production yields.

Crucian carp (*Carassius carassius*) is another Chinese carp, and most food-fish production of this fish occurs in China, where 1.5 million tonnes were produced in 2002. As in most carp production, ponds are used for grow-out of the fish, generally in polyculture with other carp species. Crucian carp feed on plants, zooplankton, and benthic invertebrates.

Grass carp (*Ctenopharyngodon idella*), also called white amur, is the most commonly produced fish in the world. It is one of the Chinese carps and is native to large rivers in China and Siberia, such as the Yangtze and Amur, respectively. It has been extensively cultured in ponds in China, but Thailand, Taiwan, Indonesia, the Philippines, and Hong Kong also grow grass carp commercially. It is a hearty fish that consumes many species of aquatic vegetation. In some countries where grass carp is not native, concern over the adverse environmental impact that grass carp could cause if established in the wild has led to the fish being banned from pond stocking, unless they are certified triploid (triploid grass carp cannot reproduce). Production in 2002 was approximately 3.75 million tonnes.

Milkfish (*Chanos chanos*) is an important food fish in several countries in the Indo-Pacific region (principally the Philippines, Indonesia, and Taiwan). Herbivorous by nature, milkfish can consume prepared diets and can tolerate a wide range of salinities (0–150 ppt). Milkfish are most commonly grown in ponds or cages. Production in 1999 was approximately 460,000 tonnes.[3]

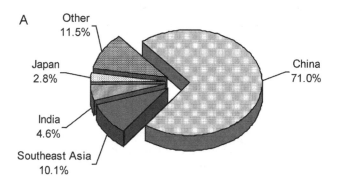

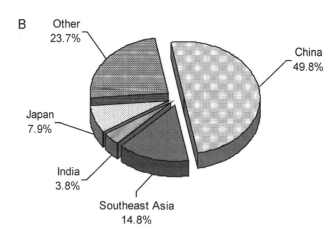

Fig. 2 (A) The percentage of total aquaculture production in 2000–2002, by country. (B) The percentage of value of cultured products in 2000, by country. (Data adapted from FAO, accessed August 2003.)

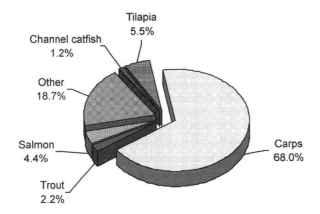

Fig. 3 The percentage of total finfish production in 2000–2002 (23 million tonnes) that were comprising various species groups. There are five major groups represented: carps, tilapias, salmonids, trout, and channel catfish. All other fish species cultured in the world are represented by Other. (Data adapted from FAO, accessed August 2003.)

Mrigal (*Cirrhinus mrigala*) is another of the Indian major carps (see Catla), and production in 2002 was approximately 517,000 tonnes (personal communication; Dr. B.B. Jana, India). Mrigal are mostly grown in ponds and consumed locally within India.

Rainbow trout (*Oncorhynchus mykiss*) is an euryhaline fish species that primarily inhabits fresh water. They can adapt to seawater once they reach the juvenile stage (approx. 100 g) by gradually increasing the salinity of the culture water. Rainbow trout is the most widely cultured trout in the world, being grown in the United States, Canada, Britain, Denmark, France, Italy, and Chile. In Chile, rainbow trout are grown in marine cages, whereas in most other countries, including Chile, they are grown in fresh water using raceways (a flow-through water supply). France, Chile, Denmark, and Italy accounted for approximately 50% of global production in 1995, while the United States accounted for 7–8% of global production. Production worldwide in 2000 was approximately 326,000 tonnes.

Rohu (*Labeo rohita*) is another of the Indian major carps (see Catla), and production in 2002 was 567,000 tonnes (personal communication; Dr. B.B. Jana, India). Rohu are produced in earthen ponds and mostly consumed locally (within India).

Silver carp (*Hypophthalmichthys molitrix*) is the food fish with the second-highest production of any cultured finfish species in the world. The majority of production occurs in China, although Japan and Poland grow a very small percentage (<2%) of the global supply. For the most part, silver carp are produced, sold, and consumed in China. Ponds are the principal culture method for silver carp, generally in polyculture with other carp species. Silver carp filter phytoplankton from the water, but they can eat zooplankton and prepared diets. Production in 2002 was approximately 3.5 million tonnes.

Tilapia are a group of fish species that are the second-largest group of farmed finfish in the world (behind carp and ahead of salmon), with an annual growth rate of about 10% per year. There are two genera that compose the cultured tilapias: *Tilapia*, which spawn on substrate and are generally macrophagous feeders, and *Oreochromis*, which are mouth-brooders and microphagous feeders. The species most commonly cultured are Nile tilapia (*Oreoochromis niloticus*), of which 1.3 million tonnes were produced in 2002; Blue tilapia (*O. aureus*); Mossambique tilapia (*O. mossambicus*); and hybrid (Red) tilapia (*O. niloticus* × *O. aureus*). Tilapia are generally cultured in ponds, but large floating cages are also a successful culture method. Tilapia are grown in many countries throughout the world, with some of the largest production occurring in South and Central America. China is the largest single producer.

CONCLUSION

The 13 fish species (or groups) described in this chapter represent approximately 82% of the total global fish production. These species will continue to be the massive foundation of global aquaculture production into the foreseeable future.

ACKNOWLEDGMENTS

We thank Michelle Coyle for typing this manuscript; and B. R. Lee, Sam Wise, and D. R. Wynn for technical assistance.

REFERENCES

1. Storebakken, T. Atlantic Salmon, *Salmo salar*. In *Nutrient Requirements and Feeding of Finfish for Aquaculture*; Webster, C.D., Lim, C., Eds.; CAB International Publishing: Wallingford, United Kingdom, 2002; 79–102.
2. Harvey, D. Aquaculture outlook. Aquac. Mag. **2003**, *29* (4), 28–34.
3. Bagarinao, T. *Ecology and Farming of Milkfish*; SEAFDEC, Aquaculture Department: Tigbaun, Iloilo, Philippines, 1999; 1–171.

Aquatic Animals: Fishes—Minor

Carl D. Webster
Kenneth R. Thompson
Laura A. Muzinic
Kentucky State University, Frankfort, Kentucky, U.S.A.

INTRODUCTION

In the article "Aquatic Animals: Fishes—Major," fish species that represented the largest share of global aquaculture were listed. In this article, fish species that are produced in lesser quantities globally but are still vital aquaculture industries are briefly discussed. Unlike the species that dominate production data (which have had large, stable production during the past decade), many of these minor species have undergone dramatic increases in production (e.g., gilthead sea bream and hybrid striped bass). Further, the culture of some of those species has taken commercial fishing pressure off wild stocks (e.g., European sea bass). Finally, production data are lacking for a number of the listed species because the species has only recently been considered a candidate for culture (e.g., pacu) or because production is more regional (*Pangasius* catfish) with little recorded production data available. However, many of these minor aquaculture species are extremely important to local/regional economies and/or diets, and production of some species may increase in the future to high levels. Although this list is by no means complete, it is hoped that it will serve as a brief introduction to the fish that constitute the majority of global finfish production.

MINOR FISH SPECIES

Arctic char (*Salvelinus alpinus*) has the most northern distribution of any freshwater fish species and is common in the Arctic and subarctic regions of North America, Europe, and Asia. It is a relatively new aquaculture species that, as yet, does not have much production. However, it is easy to culture, has wide consumer acceptance, and should return a fairly high price to producers.

Asian sea bass (*Lates calcarifer*), also known as baramundi, is a carnivorous fish that spends its first 2–3 years in freshwater and then migrates into the ocean to mature and spawn. Asian sea bass can be cultured in freshwater and brackish-water ponds, as well as in marine cages. Most production currently uses marine cages.

Countries that produce Asian sea bass are Malaysia, Indonesia, Taiwan, Thailand, Hong Kong, Singapore, and Australia. Production for 2002 was 16,000 tonnes.[1]

Atlantic halibut (*Hippoglossus hippoglossus*) is primarily produced in Norway, either in tanks or in marine net pens. Fish reach market size (5 kg) in about 3–4 years. Production for 1999 was approximately 400 tonnes.[2]

Blue catfish (*Ictalurus furcatus*) has many of the same desirable culture traits as channel catfish, yet most catfish production is of the latter species (see Channel catfish). This is probably due to the ease of spawning of channel catfish at a younger age and smaller size. However, a blue catfish/channel catfish hybrid is currently being evaluated for commercial production.

Bluefin tuna (Southern, *Thunnus maccoyii*; Northern, *T. thynnus*). The southern bluefin tuna is being developed as an aquaculture species in Australia, and the northern bluefin tuna is being grown in the Mediterranean, North America, and Japan. Tuna is grown primarily in large marine net pens. In Australia, tuna is caught from the wild, transferred to marine net pens, and cultured until attaining market size. In 2002, approximately 9000 tonnes of Southern bluefin tuna was grown to market size in Australia (personal communication; Dr. Geoff Allen, Australia).

Clariid catfish (*Clarias* sp.) are a family of walking catfish that have the ability to survive for extended periods of time out of water because they can breathe air directly. The pectoral fins are modified so that they can be used to walk across land, often traveling from pond to pond. *Clarius batrachus* and *C. macrocephalus* are important species in Asia, where they are cultured in Thailand, India, and the Philippines. In Africa, *C. gariepinus* (the sharptooth catfish) is most commonly cultured. Several hybrids are produced, but little production information on these exists. Most production occurs in ponds, although raceways with flow-through water are also used. Ponds tend to have very steep banks and fencing around the pond to keep the walking catfish from escaping. Production in 2002 was approximately 100,000 tonnes.

Cod (*Gadus morhua*) is a fish species that has attracted great interest for culture in Europe and Canada due to the overfishing of wild stocks. Cod can be grown in sea cages

Encyclopedia of Animal Science
DOI: 10.1081/E-EAS 120026647

and can grow to market size (2.5 kg) in 18–28 months. Little production data can be found, although the literature is replete with potential production values. If financially feasible, cod production could supply a highly desirable product to consumers in the future.

Coho salmon (*Oncorhynchus kisutch*) is cultured mainly in Chile and is the other major salmonid (second to the Atlantic salmon) species grown for food. Atlantic salmon and coho salmon represent approximately 98% of the cultured salmonids. Marine cages are used as the most popular method of producing Coho salmon, and production in 2002 was approximately 110,000 tonnes.

European catfish (*Silurus glanis*) is the largest freshwater fish in Europe, reaching a length of 2 meters or more. Production occurs in ponds; however, data are difficult to obtain. Poland produced approximately 70 tonnes in 2002; however, other countries' production data on this fish are lacking.

European eel (*Anguilla anguilla*) is produced in several countries in Europe, with Italy as the major producer, growing them in tanks or ponds. Recently, however, eels have been cultured in The Netherlands and Denmark, which use recirculating indoor/outdoor systems. Production in 2002 was 10,000 tonnes.

European sea bass (*Dicentrarchus labrax*) is highly prized throughout its native range where they have been heavily fished. Aquaculture production exceeds the wild catch by almost a 3:1 margin. Sea bass is grown mostly in sea cages with Greece, Turkey, and Italy being the largest producers. Production in 2002 was approximately 41,000 tonnes.

Gilthead sea bream (*Sparus aurata*) is generally grown in sea cages, as this is more profitable than raising the fish in ponds and raceways. The major producers are Greece, Turkey, and Spain, which account for over 70% of the production of approximately 64,000 tonnes in 2002. The desirability of gilthead sea bream is shown by the dramatic increase in production since the mid-1980s, when 100 tonnes was cultured.

Hybrid striped bass is the fourth most valuable food-fish species in the United States, with an estimated 5250 tonnes produced in 2002 (Fig. 1), for which consumers paid $US 26 million (personal communication; Dr. Jim Carlberg, United States). Hybrid striped bass can be either Palmetto bass (female striped bass, *Morone saxatilis* × male white bass, *M. chrysops*) or Sunshine bass (female white bass × male striped bass). The Sunshine bass is the most widely used cross due to the ease of obtaining white bass females. Hybrid striped bass can be cultured in ponds (57% of production) or tanks (43% of production).

Japanese flounder (*Paralichthys olivaceus*) is primarily produced in Japan, where it is the fourth highest produced marine finfish. Japanese flounder are generally fed locally available trash fish; however, prepared dry

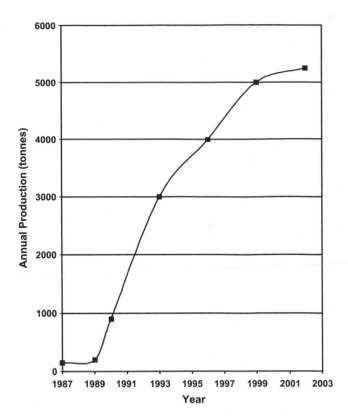

Fig. 1 Annual production data (tonnes) for hybrid striped bass in the United States.

diets are becoming more commonly used. Production in 1997 was approximately 8600 tonnes.[3]

Pacu (*Piaractus mesopotamicus*). Great interest has been shown in South America, especially Brazil, to grow this desirable fish species for the food and for the fee-fishing industries. A related fish, tambaqui (*Colossoma macropomum*), is also cultured in Brazil. Pacu and tambaqui are produced in ponds, but little information on production data can be found.

***Pangasius* catfish** is widely cultured in southeast Asian countries. Two species are predominantly produced: striped catfish (*Pangasius sutchi*) and black-ear catfish (*P. lamaudii*). Both species are fast-growing fish that have a high dress-out percentage, similar to channel catfish (*Ictalurus punctatus*). *Pangasius* catfish can be grown in earthen ponds or cages moored in rivers or lakes.

Red drum (*Sciaenops ocellatus*), also known as redfish or channel bass, is native to the Gulf of Mexico and the Atlantic Ocean. Juvenile fish are primarily grown in ponds before their release into the wild for stock enhancement, but food-fish have been cultured in a wide variety of systems including ponds, cages, net pens, raceways, and tanks using recirculating systems. The primary producer of red drum is the United States.

Red sea bream (*Pagrus major*) is one of the most popular food-fishes in Japan and its production ranks second in Japan, behind only the yellowtail. Since the late 1980s, production of red sea bream has almost doubled in Japan to 82,500 tonnes.[4]

Silver perch (*Bidyanus bidyanus*) is a freshwater fish endemic to southeast Australia. It has attracted the interest of Australian aquaculturists due to its ease of culture, mild-flavored fillet, and 40% dress-out percentage. Most production occurs in earthen ponds, although cage-culture may be a feasible culture method. Approximately 454 tonnes was produced in 2002.

Snakehead (*Channa striatus*), also known as murrel or serpent-headed fish, is found in South Africa, India, Burma, Thailand, and several other southeast Asian countries. Culture methods include growing fish in ponds or in cages. In Thailand, snakehead represents 5–10% of total freshwater-fish production and represents an industry worth an estimated $US 5–10 million.

Sturgeon (*Acipenser* spp.) is a primitive fish with several unique digestive features, including a spiral valve (like a shark) and ciliated epithelium in the intestines. Sturgeon is mostly prized for its caviar but is becoming increasingly threatened as a species due to pollution, overfishing, and poaching. Three main species are cultured: the White sturgeon (*Acipenser transmontanus*), the Siberian sturgeon (*A. baeri*), and the Adriatic sturgeon (*A. naccarii*). About 1000 tonnes are grown in circular or rectangular tanks and raceway systems, although cages and ponds are used to a lesser extent.

Yellow perch (*Perca flavescens*) is an important freshwater food-fish in the north-central region of the United States. Ponds are the most commonly used method of culture. Production in 2002 was approximately 2300 tonnes.

Yellowtail (*Seriola quinqueradiata*) is the most cultured marine fish in Japan in terms of volume and dollars, representing 70% of Japanese aquaculture production in 1997. Market size is 2–5 kg and fish are generally grown in marine net pens. Production in 2002 was approximately 145,000 tonnes.

Walleye (*Stizostedion vitreum*) is an important food-fish in the north-central region of the United States. Ponds are the most commonly used method to grow walleye to market size. Production in 2002 was approximately 2300 tonnes.

CONCLUSION

The fish species described in this article represent between 3% and 10% of the global cultured fish production and are among the species that have exhibited the greatest increases in production during the past decade. Although these species may account for a minor portion of global production, their industries are nonetheless of vital importance to local/regional economies.

ACKNOWLEDGMENTS

We thank Michelle Coyle for typing this manuscript and B. R. Lee, Sam Wise, and D. R. Wynn for technical assistance.

REFERENCES

1. Boonyaratpatin, M.; William, K. Asian Sea Bass, Lates Calcarifer. In *Nutrient Requirements and Feeding of Finfish for Aquaculture*; Webster, C.D., Lim, C., Eds.; CAB International Publishing: Wallingford, UK, 2002; 40–50.
2. Grisdale-Helland, B.; Helland, S.J. Atlantic Halibut, Hippoglossus Hippoglossus. In *Nutrient Requirements and Feeding of Finfish for Aquaculture*; Webster, C.D., Lim, C., Eds.; CAB International Publishing: Wallingford, UK, 2002; 103–112.
3. Kikuchi, K.; Takeuchi, T. *Nutrient Requirements and Feeding of Finfish for Aquaculture*; Webster, C.D., Lim, C., Eds.; CAB International Publishing: Wallingford, UK, 2002; 113–120.
4. Statistical Information Department. *Annual Statistics of Fishery as Aquaculture in 1998*; Ministry of Agriculture, Forestry, and Fisheries: Tokyo, Japan, 2000; 1–300.

Beef: Carcass Composition and Quality

Mark F. Miller
Dale R. Woerner
Texas Tech University, Lubbock, Texas, U.S.A.

INTRODUCTION

Beef carcasses are sorted in a grading system regulated by the U.S. Department of Agriculture (USDA), Agricultural Marketing Service (AMS), Livestock and Seed Division (LSD). When officially graded, the grade of steer, heifer, cow, or bullock carcass consists of the yield grade and (or) quality grade. USDA Yield Grade is an estimator of carcass composition, and USDA Quality Grade is an indicator of carcass quality. USDA beef grades were created with the intention of developing a uniform marketing system for beef based on composition (red meat yield) and quality (overall palatability).

CARCASS COMPOSITION

Beef Yield Grading

The indicated yield of closely trimmed (1/2 inch of fat or less), boneless retail cuts expected to be derived from the major wholesale cuts (round, sirloin, short loin, rib, and square-cut chuck) of a carcass is indicated by the USDA Yield Grade.[1] Yield grades are the most convenient and practical indicators of carcass composition that are utilized in the beef industry today. The beef yield-grading equation utilizes four measurable traits of each individual carcass. These include the amount of external fat (subcutaneous); the amount of kidney, pelvic, and heart fat (perinephric); the area of the ribeye (longissimus dorsi); and the hot weight of the carcass. The measured values of each of the four traits are placed into the yield-grading equation and result in values ranging from 1.0 to 5.9. Generally, the calculated value is considered solely by its whole-number value. For example, if the computation results in a designation of 3.9, the final yield grade is 3; it is not rounded to 4.[1] The USDA Yield Grade equation is as follows:

USDA Yield Grade

$$
\begin{aligned}
= \; & 2.50 + (2.50 \times \text{adjusted fat thickness in inches}) \\
& + (0.20 \times \text{percent kidney, pelvic, and heart fat}) \\
& + (0.0038 \times \text{hot carcass weight in pounds}) \\
& - (0.32 \times \text{ribeye area in square inches}) \qquad (1)
\end{aligned}
$$

The amount of external fat is measured by the thickness of the fat over the ribeye muscle, measured perpendicular to the outside surface at a point three fourths of the length of the ribeye from its chine bone end. This measurement may be adjusted, as necessary, to reflect unusual amounts of fat on other parts of the carcass. The amount of kidney, pelvic, and heart fat is a subjective measurement considered in the equation. It includes the kidney knob, lumbar, and pelvic fat in the loin and round region, and heart fat in the chuck and brisket area. The area of the ribeye muscle is measured where this muscle is exposed by ribbing the carcass between the 12th and 13th ribs. The actual hot carcass weight (or chilled carcass weight × 102%) is utilized in Eq. 1.

Beef Yield Grading and Its Relevance to Composition

The yield grading equation has been shown to effectively categorize and rank beef carcass in terms of composition based on lean meat (muscle), fat (subcutaneous, intermuscular, and perinephric), and bone.[2] Beef carcasses are expected to yield greater than 52.3%, 52.3–50.0%, 50.0–47.7%, 47.7–45.4%, and 45.4% or less of lean meat after bone and excess fat have been removed for yield grades 1, 2, 3, 4, and 5, respectively.[3]

Quality Grade and Its Relevance to Composition

Even though the quality grade of a beef carcass does not largely affect the composition, there are evident trends in the overall composition of carcasses with higher and lower marbling scores. Obviously, with an increase in marbling score (intramuscular fat) there will be an increase in the total amount of fat in the animal, also contributing to lower percentages of moisture in the lean tissues.[4] Beef animals tend to have increased numerical yield grades and hot carcass weights with an increase in marbling score.[5] This trend is due the animals' ability to produce greater amounts of marbling at a more mature age while being on a higher plane of nutrition that results in heavier slaughter weights and greater amounts of external

Encyclopedia of Animal Science
DOI: 10.1081/E-EAS 120019459

fat. Moreover, animals that marble more readily also have tendencies to deposit greater amounts of seam (intermuscular) fat.

BEEF QUALITY

Beef Quality Grading

The USDA Quality Grade is determined by considering the degree of marbling, as observed in the cut surface of the ribeye between the 12th and 13th ribs, in relation to the overall maturity of the carcass. Marbling scores are assigned to the carcass depending on the degree of intramuscular fat that is present in the cut surface of the ribeye. Marbling scores have been established by the LSD and are referenced in the form of photographs[1] (Fig. 1). The marbling scores are Abundant, Moderately Abundant, Slightly Abundant, Moderate, Modest, Small, Slight, Traces, and Practically Devoid. Mean percent chemical fat has been determined in the ribeye muscle as 10.42%, 8.56%, 7.34%, 5.97%, 4.99%, 3.43%, 2.48%, and 1.77% for marbling scores of Moderately Abundant, Slightly Abundant, Moderate, Modest, Small, Slight, Traces, and Practically Devoid, respectively.[4] Before the marbling score is evaluated, the USDA has mandated a ten-minute (minimum) bloom period between the time that the carcass has been ribbed until grading, to allow for consistency.[1]

Prior to assigning an official USDA Quality Grade, the maturity of the carcass must be evaluated and determined. Maturity scores of A, B, C, D, and E are assigned to each carcass. These scores correlate to the balance of skeletal maturity (the ratio of cartilage to bone in the cartilaginous buttons of the vertebral column) and the

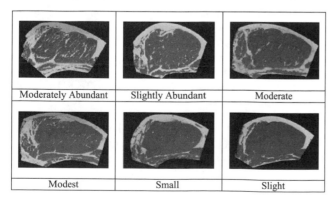

Fig. 1 USDA standard marbling scorecards. Reproductions of the official USDA marbling photographs prepared by the National Livestock and Meat Board for the U.S. Department of Agriculture. (From Ref. 1.) (*View this art in color at www.dekker.com.*)

Table 1 Beef muscle color and texture of each maturity group

Maturity	Muscle color	Muscle texture
A	Light cherry red	Fine
B	Slightly dark red	Fine
C	Slightly dark red	Moderately fine
D	Moderately dark red	Slightly coarse
E	Dark red	Coarse

(From Ref. 6.)

lean maturity (based on the color and texture of the exposed ribeye). As an animal matures, the cartilaginous (soft, white, pliable) connective tissue of the skeletal system is changed into bone (hard, dense, spongy) via the ossification process. Such changes occur in a definite sequence so that the relative degree of ossification (cartilage to bone) is a reliable indicator of maturity.[6] A, B, C, D, and E scores for skeletal maturity have 0–10%, 11–35%, 36–70%, 71–90%, and greater than 90% ossification in the first three thoracic buttons, respectively.[6] A carcass in the A-lean maturity group has a bright, cherry-red color of lean with a very fine texture, while a carcass in the E-lean maturity group has a dark, moderately brown-colored lean with extremely coarse texture (Table 1). Carcasses with balanced maturity scores of A, B, C, D, and E are 9–30, 30–42, 42–72, 72–96, and greater than 96 months of age at slaughter, respectively.[6] Beef carcasses classified as B maturity and younger are considered to be young, and maturity scores of C and older are considered old.[6]

Marbling and maturity scores are combined to determine the overall USDA Quality Grade. These are combined as illustrated in Fig. 2[1] and may be referenced to result in different levels of the final USDA Quality Grades: Prime, Choice, Select, Standard, Commercial, Utility, Cutter, and Canner. An exception to this system includes carcasses classified as bulls, whose grade consists of yield grade only. Additionally, bull and bullock carcasses must be further identified.[1]

Even though wholesomeness, cleanliness, and nutritional value are often confused as aspects of quality, the eating quality or overall palatability of the beef is of primary concern when dealing with "quality." USDA Quality Grades are assigned to beef carcasses with the intention of predicting overall palatability. The factors used to determine the USDA Quality Grade, including marbling and maturity scores, have been proven to have effects on palatability. Research shows that with increased marbling score, sensory panel ratings increase, including factors such as juiciness, tenderness, flavor desirability, and overall palatability.[7] In support of this, increasing marbling score also has shown lower shear force values (less resistance).[7] Youthfulness (maturity) is also an

Relationship Between Marbling, Maturity, and Carcass Quality Grade*

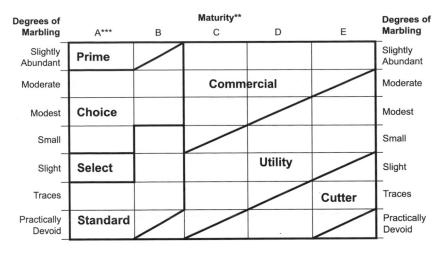

* Assumes that firmness of lean is comparably developed with the degree of marbling and that the carcass is not a "dark cutter."
** Maturity increases from left to right (A through E).
*** The A maturity portion of the figure is the only portion applicable to bullock carcasses.

Fig. 2 USDA quality grading chart. (From Ref. 1.)

indicator of tenderness in beef carcasses due to the minimal cross-linking of connective tissues (collagen) in muscles of young animals.

CONCLUSION

The carcass beef grades identify two separate general considerations: The estimated composition of carcasses in terms of red meat yield predicted by USDA Yield Grades, as well as the overall quality, or palatability, predicted by USDA Quality Grades. Trends associated with each—yield and quality grade—exist in terms of carcass composition, primarily including variation in percentages of fat, protein, and moisture.

REFERENCES

1. United States Department of Agriculture, Agricultural Marketing Service, Livestock and Seed Division. *United States Standards for Grades of Carcass Beef*; USDA, 1997; 1–20.

2. Griffin, D.B.; Savell, J.W.; Morgan, J.B.; Garrett, R.P.; Cross, H.R. Estimates of subprimal yields from beef carcasses as affected by USDA grades, subcutaneous fat trim level, and carcass sex class and type. J. Anim. Sci. **1992**, *70*, 2411–2430.

3. Savell, J.W.; Smith, G.C. Beef Carcass Evaluation. *Meat Science Laboratory Manual*, 7th Ed.; American Press: Boston, MA, 2000; 175–194.

4. Savell, J.W.; Cross, H.R.; Smith, G.C. Percentage ether extractable fat and moisture content of beef longissimus muscle as related to USDA marbling score. J. Anim. Sci. **1986**, *51* (3), 838, 840.

5. Brackebusch, S.A.; McKeith, F.K.; Carr, T.R.; McLaren, D.G. Relationship between longissimus composition and the composition of other major muscles of the beef carcass. J. Anim. Sci. **1991**, *69*, 631–640.

6. Miller, M.F.; Davis, G.W.; Ramsey, C.B.; Patterson, L.L.; Alexander, C.D.; Miller, J.D. *The Texas Tech University Meat Judging Manual*, 7th Ed.; Texas Tech University Meat Laboratory: Lubbock, TX, 2003; 21–28.

7. Dolezal, H.G.; Smith, G.C.; Savell, J.W.; Carpenter, Z.L. Comparison of subcutaneous fat thickness, marbling and quality grade for predicting palatability of beef. J. Anim. Sci. **1982**, *47*, 397–401.

Beef Cattle Management: Crossbreeding

Michael D. MacNeil
*United States Department of Agriculture, Agricultural Research Service,
Miles City, Montana, U.S.A.*

B

INTRODUCTION

Crossbreeding is one of the most beneficial management strategies for commercial beef production. Heterosis may significantly increase weaning weight per cow exposed with only a minor increase in energy consumed by cow-calf pairs. Exploiting heritable differences among breeds involves using breeds in specialized roles as sire and dam lines. Use of a terminal sire breed may further increase the amount of retail product produced per cow in the breeding herd. Beef producers may consequently derive economic benefits from capturing heterosis and use of specialized sire and dam lines in a planned crossbreeding system. The primary concern of this article is to discuss logistical factors affecting implementation of a crossbreeding system on an individual farm or ranch operation.

GENERAL CHARACTERISTICS OF CROSSBREEDING SYSTEMS

Rotational crossbreeding systems facilitate capture of a sizeable fraction of the approximately 26% increase in weaning weight per cow exposed resulting from heterosis.[1] This increase in productivity may be realized with only about a 1% increase in energy consumed by cow-calf pairs.[2] A two-breed rotation system is shown in Fig. 2. All females sired by bulls of breed A are bred to bulls of breed B, and vice versa. This system can be effectively approximated by using bulls of breed A for two or three years, switching to bulls of breed B for two or three years, then back to bulls of breed A, and so on. The rotation systems can also be expanded to include a third or fourth breed, if desired. Breeds used in rotation systems should combine both desirable maternal qualities and desirable growth and carcass characteristics.

Use of a terminal sire breed may increase the amount of retail product produced per cow in the breeding herd by 8%.[1] However, using a terminal sire breed adds an additional level of complexity to rotational crossbreeding systems. A terminal sire system is shown in Fig. 3. The base cow herd is produced as a two-breed rotation. All females less than four years of age (about 50% of the cow herd) are bred in the two-breed rotation, as described above. Breeding young cows to bulls of compatible size should keep calving difficulty at a manageable level. Replacement females all come from this phase of the system. Older cows, with their greater potential for milk production and reduced likelihood of calving difficulty, are bred to a terminal sire breed of bull. All calves sired by the terminal sire breed are sold for ultimate harvest. Terminal sire systems also give commercial producers an opportunity to change sires rapidly, so calves can be quickly changed in response to market demands.

Breeds are used in more specialized roles in a terminal sire system. Therefore, greater attention should be given to maternal qualities in choosing breeds for the rotation part of the system. In choosing the terminal sire breed, more attention should be given to growth rate and carcass composition.

Using composite breeds whose ancestry traces back to several straightbreds is another viable crossbreeding system. Using composites in place of a straightbred provides an opportunity to take some advantage of heterosis, even in very small herds. For very large herds, composites can simplify management relative to rotational crossbreeding systems. Use of composites also facilitates fixing the breed composition, thus holding the influence of each breed constant. Net effects on income can be illustrated comparing generic straightbred, rotation, multi-breed composite, and terminal sire systems (Fig. 1). Heterosis effects are particularly important for cow-calf producers who market their produce at weaning. Use of specialized sire and dam lines appears to be more advantageous when ownership is retained through harvest.

FACTORS INVOLVED IN CHOOSING A CROSSBREEDING SYSTEM

There are nine factors to consider in helping identify a feasible crossbreeding system. Those factors are: 1) relative merit of breeds available; 2) market endpoint for the calves produced; 3) pasture resources available; 4) size of the herd; 5) availability of labor at calving time; 6) availability of labor just before the breeding season; 7) method of obtaining replacements; 8) system of

Encyclopedia of Animal Science
DOI: 10.1081/E-EAS 120027674

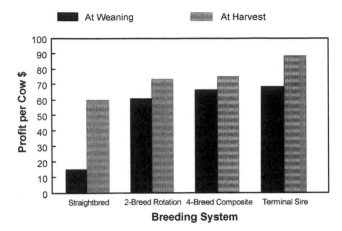

Fig. 1 Profit from breeding systems at weaning and harvest endpoints.

identifying cows; and 9) managerial ability and desire to make the system work.

Relative Merit of Breeds

What are the relative merits of breeds of cattle available? This question is addressed by Cundiff in this volume.[3] Growth rate is important in having cattle reach market weights in a desirable length of time. However, more rapid growth is generally associated with increased mature size and the increased energy needed to sustain each animal. Consumers are continually demanding leaner and leaner meat products, but fat is important to the biological function of the beef cow. External fat serves as insulation and internal fat serves as reserve energy for continuing productive function in times of restricted energy availability. The age at which a female attains sexual maturity indicates her potential for reproduction. Overuse of late-maturing types will result in inadequate conception rates in yearling heifers. Adequate milking ability of the cow is necessary for her calf to express its genetic potential for

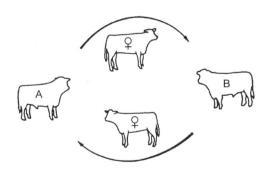

Fig. 2 A two-breed rotation crossbreeding system implemented with bulls of breeds A and B.

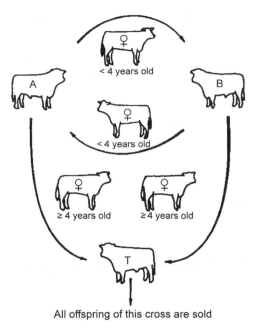

All offspring of this cross are sold

Fig. 3 A crossbreeding system with a terminal sire breed (T) used with females produced from a two-breed rotation of breeds A and B.

growth early in life. However, the cow must convert feed energy to milk and maintain the machinery required to produce the milk. Cows with high potential levels of milk production and large mature size need better nutritive environments than cows with lesser genetic potentials.

Some breeds are useful only at restricted levels. In northern environments, some restriction on the percentage of *Bos indicus* germplasm is prudent. Likewise, under warmer and more humid conditions some restriction on the percentage of *Bos taurus* germplasm is probably warranted. When heterosis effects are large relative to differences among breeds, there is less concern with using breeds in specialized roles and more with using a number of breeds in general-purpose roles. As breed differences become more important, using a particular breed characterized by high genetic potential for lean tissue growth rate in the role of a terminal sire becomes increasingly advantageous. When a terminal sire system is adopted, heterosis and maternal characteristics should be further emphasized in the cow herd.

Market Endpoint for Calves

If calves are sold at weaning, then heterosis is relatively more important and breed differences are of lesser importance. As ownership is retained to endpoints closer to the ultimate consumer, heterosis becomes relatively less important and breed differences are of increased importance. Calves also may be marketed to a middleman, and a premium may be received based on their anticipated future performance. Similarly, some producers will choose to participate in branded beef programs that specify breed composition. These marketing strategies effectively reduce the importance of heterosis and increase the importance of breed differences. However, heterosis still results in a 7% increase in the production of retail cuts per cow.

Pasture Resource Availability

The number of pastures and their relative sizes can have a major influence on which crossbreeding systems are feasible. Some very effective crossbreeding systems, such as multibreed composites, can be conducted in a single breeding pasture. These systems allow relatively efficient use of heterosis, but do not allow as much opportunity to exploit breed differences as when multiple breeding pastures are available. In most cases, using a terminal sire breed will require one breeding pasture that is larger than the rest (or a group of breeding pastures that can be used similarly). If artificial insemination is an option, then the number of pastures available for use during the breeding season is less important.

Size of the Herd

Herd size, as defined by the number of bulls required to breed the cows, is of primary concern. The inventory of cows is a secondary consideration. To efficiently implement rotation or terminal sire systems minimally requires the use of two to six bulls. Composite breeds are appropriate for herds that require only one bull. If

artificial insemination is feasible, then efficient use of bulls is not a concern and more complex crossbreeding systems can be implemented with fewer cows.

Availability of Labor at Calving Time

If labor is in short supply at calving time, then an option would be to mate all yearling heifers to a smaller breed of bull to reduce the frequency of assisted calving. This complicates a crossbreeding system by effectively reducing the herd size, requiring additional pasture resources, and producing calves with another breed composition. Selecting bulls based on their expected progency difference or breeding value for direct calving ease may accomplish the same goal without using a different breed of bull on yearling heifers.

Availability of Labor Prior to Breeding

To implement rotation and terminal sire crossbreeding systems, labor may be required to sort cows into different breeding herds before the start of the breeding season. Composite systems do not have this requirement.

Method of Obtaining Replacements

Producing replacement females may require the commitment of 40 to 60% of the cow herd. However, that proportion of the herd need not be dedicated to producing replacement females if replacements are purchased. This enables a greater proportion of cows to be bred to a terminal sire. Scarcity of consistent, reliable, and affordable sources for replacement females may make

Table 1 Resource and managerial requirements of crossbreeding systems

| System | Pastures | | Sorting of cows | Herd size[a] |
	No.	Sizes		
Straightbred	1		None	vs
Composite breed	1		None	vs
Two-breed rotation	2	1:1	Sire	sm
Terminal sire on:				
Straightbred	2	1:1	Age	sm
Composite breed	2	1:1	Age	sm
Three-breed rotation	3	1:1:1	Sire	md
Terminal sire on two-breed rotation	3	2:1:1	Sire, age	lg
Four breed rotation	4	1:1:1:1	Sire	lg
Terminal sire on three-breed rotation	4	3:1:1:1	Sire, age	vl

[a]A very small (vs) herd implies one bull, a small (sm) herd implies two bulls, a moderate (md) herd implies three bulls, a large (lg) herd implies four bulls, and a very large (vl) herd implies six bulls.

purchasing them an unattractive option in many cases. However, producing first-cross females to market as commercial replacement heifers represents a significant niche market.

System of Identifying Cows

There is no requirement for cow identification when using a composite system, but implementing a rotation system requires knowing each cow's breed of sire. Terminal sires can be used on composite females if the age of the cow is known. More complex identification schemes that record both age and breed of sire are required for using a terminal sire breed on older cows from a rotation system.

Managerial Ability

Jointly considered, the factors just discussed are indicative of feasible crossbreeding systems. Determining which systems are practical requires a willingness to make the selected system work. No benefit comes without an expenditure of managerial capital. The previously discussed managerial and resource requirements of various crossbreeding systems are summarized in Table 1. How much, if any, managerial capital your customer will invest in a crossbreeding system depends on the perceived returns.

CONCLUSION

Crossbreeding can increase the efficiency of beef production. Opportunities exist to use breed differences in producing cattle that better fit market requirements than existing breeds, and to exploit heterosis to do so more efficiently. To select a workable crossbreeding system for an individual operation requires matching physical and natural resources of the ranch with genetic potentials of the livestock. Almost all operations will find some crossbreeding systems within their resource capabilities.

REFERENCES

1. MacNeil, M.D.; Cundiff, L.V.; Gregory, K.E.; Koch, R.M. Crossbreeding systems for beef production. Appl. Agric. Res. **1988**, *3*, 44–54.
2. Brown, M.A.; Dinkel, C.A. Efficiency to slaughter of calves from Angus, Charolais, and reciprocal cross cows. J. Anim. Sci. **1982**, *55*, 254–262.
3. Cundiff, L.V.; et al. *Beef Cattle: Breeds and Genetics.* Encyclopedia of Animal Science, Dekker: New York, 2005.

Beef Cattle Management: Extensive

Michael D. MacNeil
Rodney K. Heitschmidt
United States Department of Agriculture, Agricultural Research Service, Miles City, Montana, U.S.A.

INTRODUCTION

Extensive systems of beef production capitalize on land resources that cannot be effectively used in crop production. Precipitation is often sparse on such lands, which limits forage production and, ultimately, beef production per unit area of land. This in turn limits the number of management interventions that are cost-effective in the production system. In addition to the limited production capacity of the natural resource base typically used for extensive beef production systems, both the quantity and the quality of forage produced tend to be highly and sometimes unpredictably variable over time and space. This variation encourages inclusion of various risk management strategies in designing successful management systems to be employed in extensive beef production. Exploiting heterosis and additive breed differences through crossbreeding facilitates achieving an optimal level of beef production. Matching biological type of the cow to the environment is important in managing risk and ensuring optimal levels of animal performance, given constraints imposed by the natural resource.

RESOURCE UTILIZATION

Grazing indigenous grasslands is considered one of the most sustainable of all agricultural production systems.[1] Dependence of extensive beef production on the underlying natural resource base necessitates that the first level of management addresses that foundation. Establishing a constant or increasing long-term trend in carrying capacity is seen as essential to economic sustainability of the production system. This is accomplished by blending ecological, economic, and animal management principles.[2] Attention to stocking rate, grazing systems, class of cattle, and season of use provide management with critical control points to individually and collectively affect this trend.

Stocking rate is the primary determinant affecting the relative success of any grazing management strategy.[3] This is because stocking rate determines the amount of forage available per animal. On a short-term basis, increasing stocking rate above a site-specific threshold results in forage intake per animal that is less than optimal, and thus individual animal performance declines (Fig. 1). Moreover, because grazing animals such as beef cattle are selective grazers (i.e., they prefer certain plants and plant parts over others), the frequency and severity of defoliation vary among individual plants. Thus, as stocking rate is increased, competitive relationships among plant species are altered, potentially causing changes in plant species composition that favor undesirable plant species over desirable species. The resulting long-term effect is a further decline in animal performance.

The effect of stocking rate on production per unit area of land is a direct function of individual animal performance and stocking density. Thus, production per unit area increases as stocking rate increases, up to some maximum beyond which it rapidly declines (Fig. 1).

The fundamental relationships are further complicated by variation over time and space in the amount of forage available for animal consumption. Therefore, the optimal stocking rate for maximizing production per unit area varies broadly over time and space and only becomes apparent in retrospect. In extensive beef production systems, the management challenge to optimize production in a highly variable (i.e., high risk) environment is truly formidable.

Grazing systems serve to alter the distribution of grazing intensities over time and space. Reducing grazing pressure on plants when they are vegetative allows them greater opportunity to accumulate energy reserves and thus increase their vitality. Conversely, increasing grazing pressure on plants when they are vegetative affords them less opportunity to accumulate energy reserves and thus decreases their vitality. However, the nutritional value of perennial plants is greatest while they are vegetative. Hence, a grazing system must manage the tradeoff to achieve its maximum long-term benefit. A practical and effective grazing system is characterized by six principles:[2] 1) It satisfies physiological requirements and is suited to life histories of primary forage species; 2) it improves the vigor of desirable species that are low in vigor or maintains desirable species in more vigorous condition; 3) it is adapted to existing soil conditions; 4) it will promote high forage productivity; 5) it is not overly detrimental to animal performance; and 6) it is consistent with operational constraints and managerial capabilities.

Encyclopedia of Animal Science
DOI: 10.1081/E-EAS 120019449

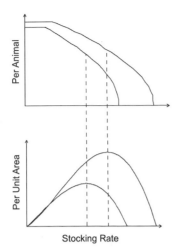

Fig. 1 A conceptual model showing relationships between stocking rate and livestock production. The upper panel illustrates production per animal and the lower panel illustrates production per unit land area. In each panel, the upper curve indicates the functional relationship during periods of high forage productivity relative to periods of more limited productivity illustrated by the lower curve. Vertical dashed lines indicate the relationship between maximum production per unit area (lower panel) and production per animal (upper panel).

Fencing the resource into pastures facilitates grazing management in many production systems. However, the capital investment in fencing should be evaluated relative to financial returns from the use of an appropriate grazing system. Alternative management interventions may achieve some goals usually attributed to grazing systems. For example, developing additional watering points, strategic placement of salt, and herding can also be used to alter the distribution of grazing pressure and may be more economically viable tactics in extensive beef production systems. Shifts in the time of calving and weaning can also affect grazing pressure, in response to changes in the energy requirements of lactating versus nonlactating cows.[4]

Grazing multiple classes of cattle may offer significant advantages to beef producers. For example, a cow calf enterprise of a magnitude that can be maintained by the natural resource base in all but the least productive years and a stocker enterprise that uses surplus forage when it is available may be a more efficient production system than either enterprise separately.

BREEDING SYSTEMS

Heterosis, which is of greater magnitude in harsh environments than in environments that are more favorable,

can return economic benefits to cow calf producers upwards of $70 per cow per year.[5,6] In low feed resource situations, such as characterize extensive beef production, heterosis and the risk associated with improperly matching the biological type of cow with the environment tend to be greater than with more abundant feed resources. Thus, crossbreeding is an important technology for extensive beef production. Like all technologies, successful implementation of a crossbreeding system depends on management. Crossbreeding systems that use sires of two or more breeds may increase variability in the calves to be marketed. Some crossbreeding systems also require multiple breeding pastures and the identification of cows by their year of birth and/or the breed of their sire.

It is important to match the biological type of cow to the environment in which she is to produce.[7] In an environment characterized by high annual precipitation, abundant high-quality forage during the grazing season, and plentiful winter feed, the proper biological type would be a high-milking and fast-growing cow with an early age at puberty. However, if the environment is more limiting, as would be typical of most extensive beef production systems, then the proper biological type of cow would have reduced potential for both milk production and growth, but would retain the ability to reach puberty at an early age. Figure 2 can be used as a way of visualizing this matching process. Being conservative in the matching process wastes feed resources and forgoes income. Over matching the environment by using cows that require too much energy for maintenance and production increases

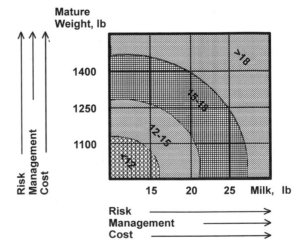

Fig. 2 Matching maternal biological type (as characterized by weight and milk production) to the forage environment (as determined by precipitation). Values within the shaded areas of the figure reflect increments of annual precipitation and/or represent availability of feed resources.

sensitivity of output to the naturally occurring variation in feed resources.

Using terminal sire breeds allows producers in extensive production situations the opportunity to match maternal genetic resources with the environment, and simultaneously to match composition of the beef produced with consumer expectations. Crossbreeding systems that employ a terminal sire breed also provide greater flexibility for rapid adaptation to changing markets.

MARKETING

Extensive beef production systems lack the energy dense feeds currently used in finishing beef cattle for harvest. However, participation in an alliance, forward contracting, or retained ownership provide options to capture benefits that result from improved feed conversion and carcass merit due to the selection of breeding stock. Alternatively, managers of extensive beef production systems may choose to market their livestock through competitive pricing at the time the cattle leave their possession. The latter approach requires less managerial input, and it may reduce risk relative to alternatives in which the change in ownership occurs nearer harvest.

RISK MANAGEMENT

Variability in the profit (or loss) stream results from variation in weather, forage production, livestock performance, and prices; that is, these factors all contribute to economic risk. In managing risk, variation in profit derived from the production system is reduced, albeit with a simultaneous reduction in average profit over time. Thus, minimizing risk is inconsistent with maximizing profit. However, managing risk may ensure the long run economic sustainability of extensive beef production systems. Commonly used risk management strategies include: scaling production systems conservatively; stockpiling feed for later use; choosing animal genetic resources that have energy demands consistent with the nutritional and climatic environment; and employing

marketing strategies that capture the value of products produced.

CONCLUSION

Challenges to extensive beef production systems stem from the use of highly variable natural resources with limited agronomic production potential. Livestock production from these resources justifies only limited capital investment in technologically sophisticated production systems. Naturally occurring variation in weather, forage production, livestock performance, and prices all indicate the importance of management tactics that minimize economic risk while capturing the value of livestock produced.

REFERENCES

1. Heitschmidt, R.K.; Short, R.E.; Grings, E.E. Ecosystems, sustainability, and animal agriculture. J. Anim. Sci. **1996**, *74* (6), 1395–1405.
2. Vallentine, J.F. Introduction to Grazing. In *Grazing Management*; Academic Press, Inc.: San Diego, CA, 1990.
3. Heitschmidt, R.K.; Taylor, C.A. Livestock Production. In *Grazing Management: An Ecological Perspective*; Heitschmidt, R.K., Stuth, J.W., Eds.; Timber Press, Inc.: Portland, OR, 1991; 161–178.
4. Grings, E.E.; Short, R.E.; Heitschmidt, R.K. Effects of Calving Date and Weaning Age on Cow and Calf Production in the Northern Great Plain. Proceedings of the Western Section American Society of Animal Science, Phoenix, AZ, June 22–26, 2003; Vol. 54, 335–338.
5. MacNeil, M.D.; Newman, S. Using Heterosis to Increase Profit. Proceedings of the International Beef Symposium, Great Falls, MT, January 15–17, 1991; 129–133.
6. Davis, K.C.; Tess, M.W.; Kress, D.D.; Doornbos, D.E.; Anderson, D.C. Life cycle evaluation of five biological types of beef cattle in a cow-calf range production system: II. Biological and economic performance. J. Anim. Sci. **1994**, *72* (10), 2591–2598.
7. Kress, D.D.; MacNeil, M.D. *Crossbreeding Beef Cattle for Western Range Environments*, 2nd Ed.; The Samuel Robert Noble Foundation: Ardmore, OK, 1999.

Beef Cattle Management: Intensive

Galen Erickson
University of Nebraska, Lincoln, Nebraska, U.S.A.

INTRODUCTION

Intensive beef cattle management in the United States consists of feedlots where cattle are managed more efficiently and fed to gain more weight than in extensive production systems. This article discusses technologies and management issues common to U.S. feedlots.

INTENSIVE CATTLE PRODUCTION

Each year, approximately 28 million head of feedlot cattle are marketed from feedlots for beef production. This production phase is unique to the United States by virtue of its large commercial cattle-feeding enterprises. In the United States in 2001, 26.9 million head of cattle were fed and 87% of those were from feedlots larger than 1000 head capacity. The total number of feedlots in the United States has steadily decreased by approximately 3500 each year. The amount of beef produced per animal has increased, owing to increased carcass weights over this same period. Figure 1 depicts cattle on feed by month for 2001, 2002, and 2003. Each year, the number of cattle in feedlots varies some across months and is generally lowest during summer months.

Cattle are fed diets that are energy-dense, consisting primarily of grain. Current feedlot production and management efficiently produce highly marbled beef that is subsequently low in price for consumers. Cattle are generally fed to an end point that is desirable by consumers, i.e., safe, flavorful, and tender. This end point is generally 28% to 30% carcass fat, U.S. Department of Agriculture Choice grade (indication of marbling or intramuscular fat), with 0.4 to 0.5 in. of backfat.

Numerous types of cattle are fed and generally classified either as calves for finishing (also commonly referred to as calf-feds) or as yearlings. However, many variations exist—from calves being weaned and directly entering feedlots, to calves that are weaned and then backgrounded on forage, pasture, or growing diets for 30 to 300 days prior to entering the feedlot. The different classes of cattle have large impacts on health, initial and market weights, amount of time in the feedlot, and overall performance. Feedlot performance is measured as dry matter intake (DMI), average daily gain (ADG), and efficiency of feed utilization, which can be measured as ADG/DMI (feed efficiency) or DMI/ADG (feed conversion). These three parameters are each important; however, feed conversion is the most common measure used by feedlots.

Performance data have been collected by Professional Cattle Consultants as part of eMerge Interactive. Data were summarized from 1996 to 2002 for cattle fed in U.S. northern, central, and southern plains regions from member feedlots. The dataset included 13.94 million head of steers, with the average animal weighing 338 kg initially, gaining 1.42 kg per day, consuming 8.84 kg of DM per day, weighing 554 kg at market, and requiring 153 days on feed.[1]

Cattle performance is dependent upon numerous factors including cattle type, nutrition program, health, overall management, and climate. A few of these important management considerations will be outlined, along with issues facing the feedlot industry now and in the future.

Nutrition

Feeding grain is common in U.S. feedlots. Corn or maize is the most prevalent, followed by grain sorghum (milo), barley, and wheat. Grain use is based on price, availability, and geographic region. Corn is a relatively abundant and inexpensive energy source containing approximately 70% starch. Feedlot diets generally contain 85% grain such as corn; 5 to 12% forage or roughage such as alfalfa hay, corn silage, or grasses; and 3 to 8% supplement. Diets may contain numerous types of by-product feeds such as corn gluten feed, distiller's grains, potato wastes, molasses, beet pulp, etc. that may replace 5–40% of the grain, depending on supply, cost, protein, and energy of the by-product feed. Supplements provide protein, minerals, vitamins, and feed additives at appropriate levels based on nutrient requirements of cattle. In feedlot diets, calcium supplementation is required in all cases, owing to the low concentrations of calcium in basal ingredients such as grain. In most cases, unless high-protein by-products are fed, protein supplementation is required to ensure optimal growth of both microbes and the animal. For more information on nutrient requirements and protein nutrition, the reader is referred to the

Encyclopedia of Animal Science
DOI: 10.1081/E-EAS 120019450

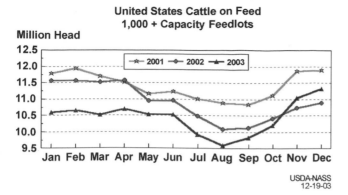

**United States Cattle on Feed
1,000 + Capacity Feedlots**

USDA-NASS
12-19-03

Fig. 1 Graph of cattle on feed or present in feedlots on the first day of each month for 2001, 2002, and 2003. As a general rule, cattle numbers tend to decrease in the summer months, and are greatest in the fall when calves enter feedlots following weaning and as yearlings are brought into feedlots from summer pastures. (*View this art in color at www.dekker.com.*)

National Research Council's 1996 publication, "Nutrient Requirements of Beef Cattle." The average feedlot diet, based on a survey of nutritionists, is provided in Table 1,[2] which illustrates how diets are formulated to meet nutrient requirements.

To understand feedlot nutrition, a rudimentary knowledge of ruminants is required. The distinguishing feature for ruminants is the fermentation, digestion, and microbial growth that occurs in the reticulo-rumen. During normal fermentation, microbes digest feed, grow, and produce acid compounds as by-products of their digestion. These acids are referred to as volatile fatty acids (VFAs) and are used by the animal for energy and growth. Common short-chain VFAs produced during fermentation include acetic, proprionic, and butyric acids.

The importance of understanding rumen fermentation is critical for two reasons: 1) when starch (i.e., corn or other grains) is digested too rapidly, cattle may experience negative consequences referred to as subacute and acute acidosis, or too much VFA; and 2) cattle must be slowly adapted from forage diets to feedlot diets (grain-based) over an 18- to 28-day period, commonly referred to as grain adaptation or step-up programs. Acidosis is defined as a series of biochemical events resulting in low rumen pH and reduced DMI (pH<5.6; subacute acidosis) or more severe symptoms including death at very low pH (pH<5.0; acute acidosis). Acidosis is a critical condition that feedlots manage daily to ensure good performance and health.[3]

Grain is normally processed, but can be fed whole. In most large operations, grain may be dry-rolled, fed as high-moisture (24–30% moisture) ensiled grain, or steam-flaked. There is a cost to processing; however, animal performance is improved through improved starch digestion. The effects of corn processing on digestion[4] and on performance[5] has been reviewed, and direct comparisons have been made.[6,7] However, as processing intensity increases, ruminal starch digestion will increase and may cause acidosis-related challenges.

By-product feeding is important in intensive beef production systems, particularly corn gluten feed,[8,9] distiller's grains,[10] and potato by-products.[11]

Other Technologies

Implants are steroids usually consisting of estrogenic and androgenic hormones given to cattle for improved growth. Implanting cattle is safe, cost-efficient, effective technology for feedlot operators to utilize. Implants have little impact on tenderness or quality grade of cattle if compared at equal end points[12] and markedly increase finished weight of cattle, by 20 to 40 kg.[13]

Feed additives are commonly used to control disease challenges, improve feed efficiency, or increase weight. Ionophores are a class of compounds that manipulate rumen fermentation, resulting in more proprionic acid

Table 1 Dietary assumptions on nutrients

Nutrient	Average concentration	Minimum concentration	Maximum concentration
CP, % of DM	13.31	12.50	14.0
P, % of DM[a]	0.31	0.25	0.50
Ca, % of DM	0.70	0.60	0.90
K, % of DM	0.74	0.60	1.00
Mg, % of DM	0.21	0.15	0.30
S, % of DM	0.19	0.10	0.34
Na, % of DM	0.138	0.098	0.197
Cu, mg/kg	14.8	6.0	20.0
Zn, mg/kg	74	50	150
Se, mg/kg	0.21	0.10	0.30

[a]Maximum concentration of P increased to 0.50%, due to by-product feeding in certain regions (From Ref. 2.)

compared to acetic acid. The shift in VFA profiles improves feed efficiency 4%[14] to 7.5%[15] in feedlot diets for monensin. Antibiotics are occasionally fed to beef cattle for health challenges, and for control of liver abscesses. Another class of feed additives called beta-agonists was recently approved for use in beef feedlot cattle. Ractopamine was approved in 2003 for use during the last 28 to 42 days before marketing for increased weight gain and improved feed efficiency.

CONCLUSION

All indications are that beef production will continue to consolidate, with fewer producers producing the same or greater amounts of beef. Consumer demand and economics are currently favorable for beef. Three important challenges facing the beef industry are food safety, environmental challenges, and data management or traceability. Food safety concerns are *E. coli* O157:H7 in beef products and the recent bovine spongiform encephalopathy cases in North America. The predominant environmental issues facing beef feedlots that are currently being addressed are nitrogen volatilization and P distribution. Some perceive runoff control from open-lot production systems as an environmental challenge, but most operations with greater than 1000-head capacity already control runoff. Finally, numerous changes will be initiated in beef production in the next few years related to tracing beef products from conception to consumption. Although tracing beef animals will create some challenges, it will be required to minimize repercussions from foreign and domestic animal disease and food pathogen outbreaks. Many positive steps have been taken by the beef industry in the past 10 years, focusing on consumers and beef products. Continued focus will only improve beef demand in the future, because beef is a wholesome, nutritious, and safe food product.

REFERENCES

1. Professional Cattle Consultants. *Newsletter 1996 to 2002*; an eMerge Interactive Service: Weatherford, OK.

2. Galyean, M.L.; Gleghorn. *Summary of the 2000 Texas Tech University Consulting Nutritionist Survey*; Texas Tech University, 2001. Available at: http://www.asft. ttu.edu/burnett_center/progress_reports/bc12.pdf. Accessed on 15 Jun 2002.

3. Stock, R.A.; Britton, R.A. Acidosis in Feedlot Cattle. In *Scientific update on Rumensin/Tylan for the Professional Feedlot Consultant*; Elanco Animal Health: Indianapolis, IN, 1993; p A-1.

4. Huntington, G.B. Starch utilization by ruminants: From basics to the bunk. J. Anim. Sci. **1997**, *75*, 852–867.

5. Owens, F.N.; Secrist, D.S.; Hill, W.J.; Gill, D.R. The effect of grain source and grain processing on performance of feedlot cattle: A review. J. Anim. Sci. **1997**, *75*, 868–879.

6. Cooper, R.J.; Milton, C.T.; Klopfenstein, T.J.; Jordon, D.J. Effect of corn processing on degradable intake protein requirement of finishing cattle. J. Anim. Sci. **2002a**, *80*, 242–247.

7. Cooper, R.J.; Milton, C.T.; Klopfenstein, T.J.; Scott, T.L.; Wilson, C.B.; Mass, R.A. Effect of corn processing on starch digestion and bacterial crude protein flow in finishing cattle. J. Anim. Sci. **2002b**, *80*, 797–804.

8. Stock, R.A.; Lewis, J.M.; Klopfenstein, T.J.; Milton, C.T. Review of new information on the use of wet and dry milling feed byproducts in feedlot diets. Proc. Am. Soc. Anim. Sci. **1999**. Available at: http://www.asas.org/jas/ symposia/proceedings/0924.pdf.

9. Erickson, G.E. Recent Research on Byproduct Feeds for Beef Feedlot and Cow-Calf Operations. Proc. 3rd Nat. Symp. Alternative Feeds for Livestock and Poultry, Kansas City, MO; Eastridge, M.L., Ed.; Ohio State University Extension, 2003; 103–114.

10. Klopfenstein, T.J. Feeding Distillers Grains to Ruminants. Proc. 3rd Nat. Symp. Alternative Feeds for Livestock and Poultry, Kansas City, MO; Eastridge, M.L., Ed.; Ohio State University Extension, 2003; 53–64.

11. Nelson, M. Nutritive Value of Wet Potato (Solanum Tuberosum) Processing Byproducts for Ruminants. Proc. 3rd Nat. Symp. Alternative Feeds for Livestock and Poultry, Kansas City, MO; Eastridge, M.L., Ed.; Ohio State University Extension, 2003; 77–84.

12. Nichols, W.T.; Galyean, M.L.; Thomson, D.U.; Hutcheson, J.P. Review: Effects of steroid implants on the tenderness of beef. Prof. Anim. Sci. **2002**, *18*, 202–210.

13. Guiroy, P.J.; Tedeschi, L.O.; Fox, D.G.; Hutcheson, J.P. The effects of implant strategy on finished body weight of beef cattle. J. Anim. Sci. **2002**, *80*, 1791–1800.

14. Stock, R.A.; Laudert, S.B.; Stroup, W.W.; Larson, E.M.; Parrott, J.C.; Britton, R.A. Effects of monensin and monensin and tylosin combinations on feed intake variation of feedlot steers. J. Anim. Sci. **1995**, *73*, 39–44.

15. Goodrich, R.D.; Garrett, J.E.; Gast, D.R.; Kirick, M.A.; Larson, D.A.; Meiske, J.C. Influence of monensin on the performance of cattle. J. Anim. Sci. **1984**, *58*, 1484–1498.

16. CAST. *Animal Diet Modification to Decrease the Potential for Nitrogen and Phosphorus Pollution. Issue Paper No. 21*; Council for Agricultural Science and Technology: Ames, IA, 2002.

Beef Cattle: Behavior Management and Well-Being

Michael J. Toscano
Donald C. Lay, Jr.
Agricultural Research Service–USDA, West Lafayette, Indiana, U.S.A.

B

INTRODUCTION

Managing beef cattle effectively requires substantial knowledge of nutrition, health, reproduction, and behavior. Beef cattle have specific requirements in each of the mentioned categories, and deviations from these requirements can induce a state of impaired well-being. The following information is designed to inform the reader of normal behavior and to highlight areas that are prone to cause poor well-being in cattle.

COW–CALF BEHAVIOR

Cows strive to isolate themselves at birth to allow for calf bonding during the initial 24 to 48 hours after birth. When cows are kept in close confinement, preventing isolation from the herd, it is not uncommon for a calf to become orphaned or to incompletely bond with its dam. This has obvious well-being consequences because nonbonded calves are unable to obtain milk from their dams and are subject to starvation. Ensuring an isolated area for each cow will prevent this problem. Another area of concern for calves is unthriftiness, weak calf syndrome, and calves that do not suck, a condition known as dummy calf syndrome. Close observation of newborn calves will identify these problems. If calves can be helped to suckle during the first several days, they often learn to suck on their own and regain a healthful status.

During the first week or more of life the calf will be left on its own away from the herd, which is termed hiding behavior. Good management dictates that producers find each calf to ensure that it is in good health and receiving adequate nutrition. The cow should respond to the stockperson's approach by coming to the side of her calf. It is also common for calves to form nurseries, in which calves congregate while their dams graze elsewhere. At least one cow will stay close to the nursery. If they are disturbed, the cow will vocalize, at which point her calf comes to her and the cows in the herd return to their own calves. Nursery formation is normal and should not be taken as a sign that the cow has abandoned her calf.

In terms of maternal care, there is a necessary balance between a protective dam and an aggressive dam. Cow–calf production on the range requires that dams are protective of their calves. However, overly aggressive dams are dangerous to stockpersons and should be culled to prevent injuries. Care should be taken by producers to not select overly passive cows that may in turn neglect their calves.

WEANING

Weaning is the next critical event in the calf's life. Weaning deprives the calf of nutrients derived from suckling, but breaking the social attachment between calf and dam is much more stressful. Research on wild and feral cattle shows that calves may stay with their dams for an entire year. Thus, weaning at six months is premature to the nature of cattle and has the potential for distress. The amount of stress the calf is experiencing can be observed from the amount of fence pacing and bawling the calf performs after weaning. These behaviors, along with the stressful state, dissipate over a period of several weeks. Researchers have used several methods to reduce the stress of weaning. Price et al.[1] found that separating the dam and the calf, but allowing fence line contact, reduced distress and minimized weight loss.[1] Haley et al.[2] used nose rings that prevented the calf from nursing for 14 days prior to weaning. Upon weaning, the calves exhibited fewer signs of distress.

TRANSPORT

Transport of cattle to slaughter is a common practice in modern agriculture. Cattle are predominantly shipped via road transport, although rail transport is used when distances exceed 800 km.[3] Transportation is generally considered stressful to animals, as indicated by studies employing physiological and behavioral techniques. Reducing transport stress is of great interest to producers, government, and consumers, because transport can result in reduced meat quality, bruised carcasses which must be trimmed, and potential suffering that compromises well-being. Stressors from transport include irregular social

Encyclopedia of Animal Science
DOI: 10.1081/E-EAS 120019451

interactions and physical fatigue from loading and maintaining balance. The interaction between animals and the individuals' response to transport can greatly affect how cattle cope with transport stress, thus necessitating attention to behavior.

Cattle have definitive social hierarchies placing individual cows above or below their herd mates. When cows within this social order are confined in a trailer and unable to distance themselves from each other, aggression often results in the form of increased head-butting, pushes, and fights. Similarly, unfamiliar animals that have not established a social order will often interact aggressively. Kenny and Tarrant[4] demonstrated that transporting a higher density of cattle resulted in a reduced appearance of such interactions. Such a strategy offers obvious financial benefits (i.e., fewer trips for more animals). Higher stocking densities result in reduced aggressive behaviors, most likely because the animals are less able to move. Despite this benefit, particularly in high-density groups where cows are unlikely to lie, the inability to move is likely to induce physical fatigue, often causing the animal to fall. Once the animal is down, it is nearly impossible to regain a standing posture as other animals "close over" it.[5] Fallen animals can be severely bruised or trampled, and can cause other animals to fall, which makes loss of balance the major hazard during transport.[5] Despite these problems, critics of low stocking density argue that more space per animal impairs animals from providing physical support to each other during transport.

Cattle's response to transport suggests that transportation is stressful. Such responses include increases in cortisol, heart rate, and urination. Interestingly, once cattle appear to adapt to the rigors of transport, associated stress responses are reduced as well, suggesting that the initial novelty of the experience is the major stressor for this typically flighty animal. Trunkfield and Broom[6] concluded that appropriate social contact and positive previous experiences with transportation and related events could exploit this adaptive quality and reduce transport-associated stress.

FEEDLOT CATTLE

Feedlot cattle are exposed to a variety of stressors, including abnormal behaviors such as buller-steer syndrome, difficulties in adjusting to and finding the provided diet, and effectively dealing with extreme temperatures.

Buller-steer syndrome, or the abnormal occurrence of individual steers (bullers) to stand for mounting by others, has long been known to occur. However, the phenomenon appears to have increased with the development of feedlot systems. It can become a major problem

as the buller, unable to escape, becomes exhausted and collapses. Although causes have not been identified (as reviewed by Blackshaw et al., 1997),[7] high densities, use of hormonal implants, and specific social interactions, among other factors, have been correlated with the syndrome.

When stocker cattle arrive at the feedlot, the transition is typically stressful and coincides with decreased feed intake, weight gain, and reduced benefit from the antibiotics being administered. The source of this stress may be a number of factors, but it most likely involves difficulty in adapting to the new environment, regrouping of animals, and feeding routines. Because many of these cattle were previously on pasture, the use of a feed bunk is foreign. Exploiting cattle's gregarious behavior and propensity for socially induced foraging behavior can assist in getting cattle on feed. Loerch and Fluharty (2000)[10] found that housing newly arrived animals with those already adapted to the feeding process facilitated the feeding of these newly arrived animals.

Another problem for cattle in feedlot systems is effective temperature management. Given the choice, cattle will seek an environment to maintain thermal homeostasis, such as shade when provided. Shade and misters are often used in hot environments, and have been studied extensively.[8] However, the myriad environmental conditions call for careful application of each. Misting during summer months must be applied appropriately or it can result in excessive cooling of the cattle's surface, causing constriction of exterior vessels and preventing dissipation of central heat.[9] Windbreaks, used to reduce wind exposure in winter months, must be strategically placed so as not to reduce evaporative cooling during the summer. Lastly, feeding in the late afternoon will cause cattle to have their metabolic peak during cooler parts of the day, and thus reduce heat stress.[9]

WELL-BEING

The well-being of beef cattle can be ensured by attention to health and the minimization of stress. Exposure to some environments and management techniques may cause both physical and psychological stress. In turn, stressful states cause the animal to develop an impaired immune system, thereby causing it to succumb to disease. Thus, keeping basic behavioral principles in mind and allowing cattle to exhibit normal behaviors, while at the same time decreasing deleterious behaviors, will optimize well-being. Some management procedures are inherently stressful, such as weaning and transportation. Thus, care should be taken during these times to minimize stress. Keen behavioral observations of individual animals will allow the stockperson to detect stressed animals and act accordingly to reduce this negative state.

CONCLUSIONS

Management of beef cattle includes multiple instances when appropriate behavior management is required to minimize exposure to stress and maintain healthy animals. These instances can range from reducing transport stress to providing for the expression of appropriate maternal behavior. If successful, animals will be maintained in conditions that optimize well-being.

REFERENCES

1. Price, E.O.; Harris, J.E.; Borgwardt, R.E.; Sween, M.L.; Connor, J.M. Fence line contact of beef calves with their dams at weaning reduces the negative effects of separation on behavior and growth rate. J. Anim. Sci. **2003**, *81*, 116–121.

2. Haley, D.B.; Stookey, J.M.; Bailey, D.W. A Procedure to Reduce the Stress of Weaning on Beef Cattle: On-Farm Trials of Two Step Weaning. In *Proceedings International Society for Applied Ethology*, Fifth North American Regional Meeting of the ISAE, July 20–21, 2002; Haley, D., Harris, M., Pajor, E., Bergeron, R., Eds.; Universite Laval: Canada, 2002; 8.

3. Tarrant, P.V. Transportation of cattle by road. Appl. Anim. Behav. Sci. **1990**, *28*, 153–170.

4. Kenny, F.J.; Tarrant, P.V. The physiological and behavioural response of crossbred Friesan steers to short-haul transport by road. Livestock Production Science **1987**, *17*, 63–75.

5. Tarrant, P.V.; Kenny, F.J.; Harrington, D. The effect of stocking density during 4 hour transport to slaughter on behavior, blood constituents and carcass bruising in Friesian steers. Meat Sci. **1988**, *24*, 209–222.

6. Trunkfield, H.R.; Broom, D.M. The welfare of calves during handling and transport. Appl. Anim. Behav. Sci. **1990**, *28*, 135–152.

7. Blackshaw, J.K.; Blackshaw, A.K.; McGlone, J.J. Buller steer syndrome review. Appl. Anim. Behav. Sci. **1997**, *54*, 97–108.

8. West, J.W. Effects of heat-stress on production in dairy cattle. J. Dairy Sci. **2003**, *86* (6), 2131–2144.

9. Mader, T. *Keep Feedlot Cattle Cool Even in Drought*, 2000. Available http://ianrnews.unl.edu/static/0006200.shtml (accessed December 15, 2003).

10. Loerch, S.C.; Fluharty, F.L. Use of trainer animals to improve performance and health of newly arrived feedlot calves. J. Anim. Sci. **2000**, *78*, 1117–1124.

Beef Cattle: Breeds and Genetics

Larry V. Cundiff
*United States Department of Agriculture, Agricultural Research Service,
Clay Center, Nebraska, U.S.A.*

INTRODUCTION

Genetic variation has accrued between populations of cattle throughout their evolution. Natural selection for fitness in diverse environments or selection directed by man toward different goals (e.g., draft, milk, meat, fatness, size, color, horn characteristics) has led to significant diversity among breeds of cattle.

HETEROSIS

Breeds can be considered as mildly inbred lines. Inbreeding and genetic uniformity (homozygosity of genes) have gradually and inevitably increased within pure breeds since their formation. Even in breeds with a large population size, it is not uncommon for inbreeding levels to increase about 0.5% per generation. Heterosis, the difference between the mean of reciprocal F1 crosses (A × B and B × A) and the mean of two parental breeds (breeds A and B), is the reverse of inbreeding depression. Diallel crossing experiments with *Bos taurus* (nonhumped cattle) breeds in temperate climates have demonstrated that weaning weight per cow exposed to breeding was increased by about 23%. This increase was due to beneficial effects of heterosis on survival and growth of crossbred calves and on reproduction rate and weaning weight of calves from crossbred cows.[1] More than half of this advantage is due to the use of crossbred cows. Effects of heterosis are greatest for lifetime production of cows (30%), longevity (15%), and calf crop percentages weaned (5 to 7% for reproduction rate and 3 to 5% for calf survival). Effects of heterosis are important, but they are of more intermediate magnitude for growth rate (3 to 5%) and maternal performance of F1 dams. Effects of heterosis on carcass and meat traits have been relatively small (3% or less). Crossing of *Bos indicus* (thoracic-humped cattle) and *Bos taurus* breeds (e.g., Brahman × Hereford) yields even higher levels of heterosis,[2] averaging about twice as high as those reported for corresponding traits in crosses of two *Bos taurus* breeds.

BREED DIFFERENCES

Topcross performance of 36 different sire breeds has been evaluated in the ongoing Germplasm Evaluation Program at the U.S. Meat Animal Research Center.[3] Results have provided the basis for classifying the breeds into biological types (Table 1). In the table, increasing Xs indicate relatively greater growth rate and mature size, lean-to-fat ratios, marbling, beef tenderness, age at puberty of females, milk production, and tropical adaptation.

In the 1970s Continental breeds (breeds that originated in Continental Europe; e.g., Charolais, Simmental, Braunvieh, Gelbvieh, Maine Anjou, Chianina) had significantly greater growth rates and heavier body weights at weaning, yearling, and mature ages than British breeds (originating in the British Isles, e.g., Angus, Hereford, Shorthorn, Red Poll). However, recent results indicate that British breeds are comparable to Continental breeds in growth rate.[4] The advantage of Continental breeds over British breeds in retail product yield is about the same today as in the early 1970s. British breeds, especially Angus, Red Angus, and Shorthorn, still excel in marbling, relative to Continental breeds. *Bos taurus* breeds have advantages over *Bos indicus* breeds or *Bos indicus*-influenced breeds (Brangus, Beefmaster) in tenderness of longissimus steaks.

Females sired by breeds with large mature size and relatively high lean-to-fat ratios (e.g., Chianina, Charolais) have tended to be older at puberty than those sired by breeds of smaller mature size and greater propensity to fatten. However, the relationships between mature size and age at puberty can be offset by increased genetic potential for milk production. Breeds that have been selected for milk production reach puberty earlier than breeds that have not been selected for milk production. *Bos indicus* breeds (Brahman, Nellore, Sahiwal, Boran) reach puberty at older ages than *Bos taurus* breeds.

UTILIZATION OF BREEDS

Significant levels of heterosis are maintained by use of rotational cross breeding systems[5] or by use of

Encyclopedia of Animal Science
DOI: 10.1081/E-EAS 120019452

Table 1 Breeds grouped into biological types for seven criteria[a]

Breed group	Growth rate and mature size	Lean-to-fat ratio	Marbling (Intramuscular fat)	Tenderness	Age at puberty	Milk production	Tropical adaptation
Jersey	X	X	XXXX	XXX	X	XXXXX	XX
Longhorn	X	XXX	XX	XX	XXX	XX	XX
Wagyu	X	XXX	XXXX	XXX	XX	XX	XX
Angus	XXXX	XX	XXXX	XXX	XX	XXX	X
Red angus	XXXX	XX	XXXX	XXX	XX	XXX	X
Hereford	XXXX	XX	XXX	XXX	XXX	XX	X
Red poll	XX	XX	XXX	XXX	XX	XXXX	X
Devon	XX	XX	XXX	XXX	XXX	XX	X
Shorthorn	XXXX	XX	XXXX	XXX	XX	XXX	X
Galloway	XX	XXX	XXX	XXX	XXX	XX	X
South devon	XXX	XXX	XXXX	XXX	XX	XXX	X
Tarentaise	XXX	XXX	XX	XX	XX	XXX	X
Pinzgauer	XXXX	XXX	XXX	XXX	XX	XXX	X
Braunvieh	XXX	XXXX	XXX	XX	XX	XXXX	XX
Gelbvieh	XXXX	XXXX	X	XX	XX	XXXX	X
Holstein	XXXXX	XXXX	XXX	XX	XX	XXXXXX	X
Simmental	XXXXX	XXXX	XX	XX	XXX	XXXX	X
Maine anjou	XXXXX	XXXX	XX	XX	XXX	XXX	X
Salers	XXXX	XXXX	XX	XX	XXX	XXX	X
Norwegian red	XXXX	XXXX	XXX	XX	XX	XXXX	X
Swed. red and white	XXXX	XXXX	XXX	XX	XX	XXXX	X
Friesian	XXXX	XXXX	XXX	XX	XX	XXXX	X
Piedmontese	XX	XXXXXX	X	XXX	XX	XX	XX
Belgian blue	XXX	XXXXXX	X	XXX	XX	XX	X
Limousin	XXX	XXXXX	X	XX	XXXX	X	X
Charolais	XXXXX	XXXXX	XX	XX	XXXX	XX	X
Chianina	XXXXX	XXXXX	XX	XX	XXXX	X	XX
Tuli	XX	XXX	XXX	XX	XXX	XXX	XXX
Romosinuano	X	XXX	XX	XX	XXX	XXX	XXX
Brangus	XXXX	XXX	XXX	XX	XXX	XXX	XXX
Beefmaster	XXXX	XXX	XX	XX	XXX	XXX	XXX
Bonsmara	XXX	XXX	XX	XX	XXX	XXX	XXX
Brahman	XXXX	XXXX	XX	X	XXXXX	XXXX	XXXX
Nellore	XXXX	XXXX	XX	X	XXXXX	XXX	XXXX
Sahiwal	XX	XXXX	XX	X	XXXX	XXXX	XXXX
Boran	XXX	XXX	XX	X	XXXX	XXX	XXXX

[a]Increasing numbers of Xs indicate relatively higher value.

composite populations.[6] Two breed rotations involving the use of two breeds of sire in alternate generations maintain about 68% of F1 heterosis. Adding a third breed to the rotation maintains 86%. Composite populations are established by the inter se mating of animals founded by crossing two or more breeds. Fifty percent of F1 heterosis is retained in composite populations founded by crossing two breeds, and 75% in composite populations founded with equal contributions from four breeds. Uniformity of cattle and consistency of end product can be provided with greater precision using F1 seedstock or composite populations than by rotational crossing of diverse breeds, in which breed composition fluctuates from one generation to the next (e.g., 1/3 to 2/3 in two-breed rotations). For example, with current pricing systems, cattle with 50:50 ratios of Continental to British inheritance have more optimal carcass characteristics—experiencing fewer severe discounts for excessive fatness (yield grade 4 or more) or for low levels of marbling (USDA standard quality grades or less)—than cattle with lower or higher ratios of Continental to British inheritance.

Use of *Bos indicus* × *Bos taurus* crosses is favored in the subtropical regions of the United States. In one experiment, weaning weight per cow exposed was significantly greater for *Bos indicus* × *Bos taurus* F1 crosses (Brahman × Hereford, Brahman × Angus, Sahiwal × Hereford, Sahiwal × Angus) than for *Bos taurus* × *Bos taurus* F1 crosses (Hereford × Angus, Angus × Hereford, Pinzgauer × Hereford, Pinzgauer × Angus) in both Florida and Nebraska, but the advantage was 22% greater in Florida than in Nebraska.[7] In the hotter and more humid climates of the Gulf Coast, about 50:50 ratios of *Bos indicus* to *Bos taurus* inheritance may be optimal.

SELECTION

Rate of change from selection has been greatly accelerated by use of artificial insemination and expected progeny differences (EPDs), computed from records performance on individuals and their relatives.[8] Significant progress has been made to make calving easier in response to selection for lighter-birthweight EPDs. Likewise, significant change has been made for direct and maternal components of weaning weight, as well as for yearling weight. Some breeds have used EPDs for measurements of scrotal circumference in yearling bulls, primarily to reduce age at puberty and improve the conception rate in yearling females. EPDs have only recently been introduced by a few breed associations for mature weight, and as indicators of reproduction rate and longevity of cows. EPDs have been introduced in some breeds based on use of ultrasound technology to estimate fat thickness, rib-eye area, and marbling in live animals.

Current research is focused on development of molecular genetics approaches. Comprehensive genomic maps including more than two thousand DNA markers spanning all 30 chromosomes of the bovine have been developed.[9] Chromosomal regions (quantitative trait loci, QTL) in cattle have been identified that possess genes with a significant effect on expression of measures of ovulation rate, growth, carcass composition, marbling, and estimates of beef tenderness.[10] DNA tests are being used commercially to identify cattle with favorable genotypes for leanness, marbling, polledness, and coat color. Molecular approaches will play an increasingly important role in the genetic evaluation and selection of beef cattle.

CONCLUSIONS

The beef industry is challenged to: 1) reduce costs of production to remain competitive in global markets; 2) match genetic potential with the climate and feed resources available in diverse environments; 3) reduce fat and increase leanness of products to gain greater acceptance by consumers; and 4) improve palatability, tenderness, and consistency of beef products. Use of heterosis and breed differences through the use of crossbreeding or composite populations, and selection of breeding stock to exploit genetic variation within breeds can all be used to help meet these challenges. Selection based on the use of EPDs has accelerated the rate of genetic change for calving ease and growth rate in most breeds of beef cattle. Effectiveness of selection is likely to be enhanced by molecular genetic tools that are being developed to provide for more accurate genetic prediction.

REFERENCES

1. Cundiff, L.V.; Gregory, K.E.; Koch, R.M. Effects of heterosis on reproduction in Hereford, Angus and Shorthorn cattle. J. Anim. Sci. **1974**, *38*, 711–727.
2. Long, C.M. Crossbreeding for beef production: Experimental results (A review). J. Anim. Sci. **1980**, *51*, 1197–1223.
3. Cundiff, L.V.; Szabo, F.; Gregory, K.E.; Koch, R.M.; Crouse, J.D. Breed Comparisons in the Germplasm Evaluation Program at MARC. Proc. Beef Improvement Federation Meeting, Ashville, NC, May 26–29, 1993; 124–136.
4. Cundiff, L.V.; Gregory, K.E.; Wheeler, T.L.; Shackelford, S.D.; Koohmaraie, M.; Freetly, H.C.; Lunstra, D.D. *Preliminary Results from Cycle VII of the Germplasm Evaluation Program at the Roman L. Hruska U.S. Meat Animal Research Center*, Germplasm Evaluation Program Progress Report No. 21; USDA, ARS, June 2001; 1–13. www.marc.usda.god.
5. Gregory, K.E.; Cundiff, L.V. Crossbreeding in beef cattle. Evaluation of systems. J. Anim. Sci. **1980**, *51*, 1224–1241.
6. Gregory, K.E.; Cundiff, L.V.; Koch, R.M. *Composite Breeds to use Heterosis and Breed Differences to Improve Efficiency of Beef Production.* Technical Bulletin 1875; U.S. Department of Agriculture, Agricultural Research Service, 1999; 1–75.
7. Olson, T.A.; Euclides, F. K.; Cundiff, L.V.; Koger, M.; Butts, W.T., Jr.; Gregory, K.E. Effects of breed group by location interaction on crossbred cattle in Nebraska and Florida. J. Anim. Sci. **1991**, *69*, 104–114.
8. *Guidelines for Uniform Beef Improvement Programs. Beef Improvement Federation,* 8th Ed.; Hohenboken, W.D., Ed.; 2002; 1–161. www.beefimprovement.org.
9. Kappes, S.M.; Keele, J.W.; Stone, R.T.; McGraw, R.A.; Sonstegard, T.S.; Smith, T.P.L.; Lopez-Coralles, N.L.; Beattie, C.W. A second generation linkage map of the bovine genome. Genome Res. **1997**, *7*, 235–249.
10. Stone, R.T.; Keele, J.W.; Shackelford, S.D.; Kappes, S.M.; Koohmaraie, M. A primary screen of the bovine genome for quantitative trait loci affecting carcass and growth traits. J. Anim. Sci. **1999**, *77*, 1379–1384.

Beef Cattle: Housing

John A. Nienaber

United States Department of Agriculture, Agricultural Research Service, Clay Center, Nebraska, U.S.A.

INTRODUCTION

Cattle are among the most hardy domestic species with respect to climatic conditions. It has been shown that the lower critical temperature of a beef animal on feed is below $-20°C$ and upper threshold as high as 25 to 30°C, depending on associated humidity, thermal radiation, and wind speed. So why consider housing for beef cattle? If selected, what features should be considered? These issues are addressed in this article.

ENVIRONMENTAL TEMPERATURE TOLERANCE

Full-fed beef animals have a very high tolerance for cold temperatures.[1–3] This is illustrated by the story of feeder cattle brought into a loafing barn for routine observations before noon one day, and later found to be strangely affected by some unknown condition. A virulent disease was feared and the animals were moved outside and isolated for observation, where they quickly recovered. The unknown condition was heat stress, and the stressful temperature was 0°C. The animals had become acclimated to $-30°C$ over the previous month, which demonstrates adaptability and acclimation. A second story involves more than 5000 cattle that died in northeastern Nebraska during a 1999 two-day heat wave.[4] When studying some of the affected feedyards seven days later, we found very few animals in distress, even though climatic conditions were more severe than the area had experienced during the heat wave. Again, adaptation and acclimation were factors. Both stories demonstrate a climatic stressor that may be more important than temperature alone: extreme variability of thermal conditions.

COLD WEATHER HOUSING

The heat and moisture production and manure generation of cattle combine to make ventilation primary in design of beef housing, regardless of climatic conditions. Adequate ventilation in cold climates means removal of moisture generated by respiration and evaporated from urine and feces. Given the limited moisture-holding capacity of cold air, insulation of the structure is important to limit condensation.

The performance advantage for housing beef in cold climates results from blocking wind, precipitation, and accumulation of snow.[2,5–8] For very cold climates, warm housing may be economically feasible, but results have been mixed.

Regardless of climatic conditions or type of structure, effective separation of accumulated waste from the animal is the key to comfort and sanitation. Concerns over odor issues have heightened interest in housing beef animals as a tool for reducing and/or controlling odor and nitrogen volatilization.[9] The value of this management practice is not fully known and requires additional research. Floor design, space, and diet formulation are critical elements of proper manure management.

FLOOR DESIGN

Floor design requires draining liquids from the surface as quickly as possible to limit evaporation and odor generation. Firm surfaces and the absence of deep mud are important factors in beef confinement.[10] Flooring types range from dirt to concrete to slats over pits. Although least complex in construction and least expensive, dirt and/or concrete require the most maintenance to provide sanitary conditions, and require some type of bedding or very low stocking density. When pen space is limited (<2.5 m^2/head), and animals are confined to the barn, a deep storage manure pit covered with slats provides a suitable surface without frequent maintenance.[7] If the deep pit option is selected, extreme caution must be taken because hazardous gases may be emitted from the pit and affect environment within the pit and structure during pump-out. To prevent asphyxiation and possible death, no human should ever enter pit without an approved self-contained breathing apparatus and harness, with at least two people outside the pit with a rescue line. Animals should be removed from the structure during pump-out.[11]

DIET FORMULATION

Diet formulation is critical because characteristics of manure reflect diet roughage level.[12] As digestibility

Encyclopedia of Animal Science
DOI: 10.1081/E-EAS 120019454
Published 2005 by Marcel Dekker, Inc. All rights reserved.

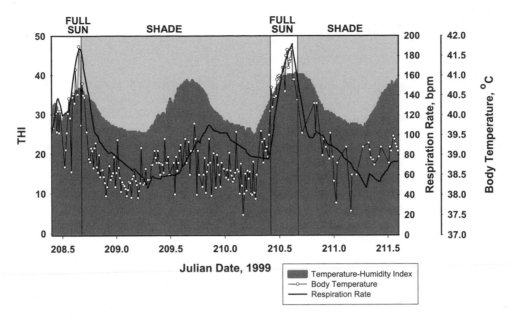

Fig. 1 Respiration rate and body temperature responses of a steer provided with no shade (days 208 and 210) during a heat wave near Columbia, Missouri. (From Ref. 14.)

decreases, the volume of generated manure increases as much as 100%. Furthermore, moisture content and handling characteristics are affected. Manure from cattle fed high-roughage diets is more dry and bulky than

from high-concentrate diets.[13] Minimizing manure volume and higher moisture content is optimal for slatted floors, while drier manure is better suited to bedded systems. This author helped move a drag the full

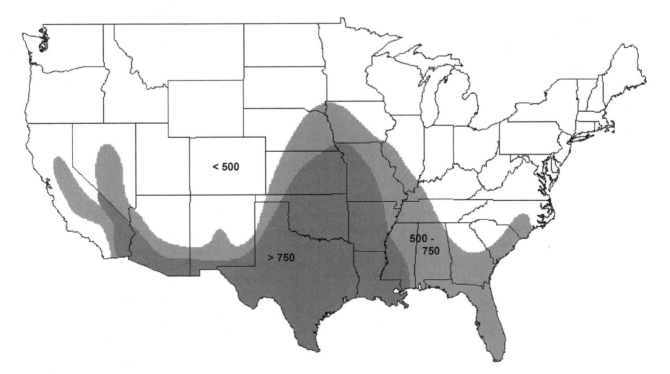

Fig. 2 Areas of the mainland United States having selected categories of yearly hours above 29.4°C (Ref. 4; taken from Ref. 17). Nonshaded sections of the map indicate no significant yearly benefit of providing shade within the feedyard if less than 500 hours per year of temperatures above 29.4°C. The dark areas represent locations expected to experience annual benefits from shaded feedlots with an expected 750 hours of temperatures above 29.4°C. (*View this art in color at www.dekker.com.*)

distance of the barn when a five-day accumulation of manure directly behind/beneath the feedbunk was too dry (high-roughage diet) for the drag to handle. That same drag was prone to freezing during Nebraska winters. Drags designed for heated dairy barns may not be appropriate pit cleaners.

FLOOR SPACE

Although proportional to construction costs, floor space impacts animal performance and health, as well as environmental quality. During the surge in beef housing in the mid-1970s, a minimum floor space of 1.8 m²/500 kg was recommended. However, this animal spacing did not support optimal performance, and many of those barns were abandoned. Current recommendations are 2.5 to 3 m²/head,[11] but even with this amount of space, producers report reduced performance compared to outdoor penned animals (under ideal conditions). Floor space can be effectively and efficiently increased by extending pens beyond the structure, giving cattle shelter during inclement periods, while protecting the feed line.[6] The primary drawback is the need to provide two types of manure management to handle material within the shelter, and to control precipitation runoff generated from outdoor areas.

HOT WEATHER HOUSING

The primary benefit of shelter in high-temperature conditions is shade. Figure 1 shows results from an animal instrumented with continuous body temperature and respiration rate sensors under shade and no shade.[14] The figure shows the nearly instantaneous drop in core body temperature and respiration rate as the animal is moved into shade from direct sunlight. Responses can be compared for the same animal on successive days under shade one day and direct sunlight the next day (before the animal was moved). Environmental temperatures were comparable for four days, as shown in Fig. 1. Additional information has supported these results in subsequent studies,[15] and most recently in an unshaded feedlot in which cattle with dark-pigmented skin had higher respiration rates and surface temperatures than those with light skin pigment, when environmental temperatures exceeded 35°C.[16] W. N. Garrett[17] proposed that northern latitudes experiencing fewer than 500 h per year above 29.4°C would not have an economically viable response to shade, whereas those experiencing more than 750 h per year above 29.4°C would benefit from shade (Fig. 2 from Ref. 4). Regardless of feedlot design, an adequate supply of clean, fresh water is vital to survival and performance.[11]

CONCLUSIONS

There are advantages and disadvantages to beef housing. Whereas housing provides shelter from winter winds and precipitation, reduces solar heat loads during hot summer conditions, reduces mud and dust problems of open feedyards, and improves the operator's control over manure and possibly odors, there are substantial cost increases. These include both capital and maintenance costs, as well as possible performance reductions. Reducing space allotment reduces the capital cost, but at the expense of performance. Under current economic conditions, the advantages of manure control will most likely dictate the feasibility of beef housing under moderate climates. However, shade structures have been shown to be beneficial. Warm housing in severe cold climates may be beneficial, but protection from wind and precipitation provides the primary benefit to performance.

REFERENCES

1. Hahn, G.L. Environmental Requirements of Farm Animals. In *Handbook of Agricultural Meteorology*; Griffiths, J., Ed.; Oxford Univ Press: New York, 1994; 220–235.
2. Milligan, J.D.; Christison, G.I. Effects of severe winter conditions on performance of feedlot steers. Can. J. Anim. Sci. **1974**, *54*, 605–610.
3. Young, B.A. Cold stress as it affects animal production. J. Anim. Sci. **1981**, *52*, 154–163.
4. Hahn, G.L.; Mader, T.; Spiers, D.; Gaughan, J.; Nienaber, J.; Eigenberg, R.; Brown-Brandl, T.; Hu, Q.; Griffin, D.; Hungerford, L.; Parkhurst, A.; Leonard, M.; Adams, W.; Adams, L. Heat Wave Impacts on Feedlot Cattle: Considerations for Improved Environmental Management, Proc., Sixth Int'l Livestock Environment Symp, Louisville, KY, May 21–23, 2001. ASAE Publication No. 701P0201. Amer. Soc. of Agr. Engr.: St. Joseph, MI.
5. Hoffman, M.P.; Self, H.L. Shelter and feedlot surface effects on performance of yearling steers. J. Anim. Sci. **1970**, *31*, 967–972.
6. Leu, B.M.; Hoffman, M.P.; Self, H.L. Comparison of confinement, shelter and no shelter for finishing yearling steers. J. Anim Sci. **1977**, *44*, 717–721.
7. Meador, N.F.; Jesse, G.W. *Facility Effects on Finishing Beef Animals—UMC Tests*; ASAE Paper No. 81-4058, Amer. Soc. of Agr. Engr.: St. Joseph, MI, 1981.
8. Smith, R.E.; Hanke, H.E.; Lindor, L.K. *A Comparison of Five Housing Systems for Feedlot Cattle*, Minnesota Cattle Feeder's Report; Agr. Ext. Serv. and Agr. Exp. Sta., Univ. of Minnesota, 1972; 3–32.
9. Borton, L.R.; Rotz, C.A.; Person, H.L.; Harrigan, T.M.; Bickert, W.G. *Simulation to Evaluate Dairy Manure Systems*; ASAE Paper No. 934572, Amer. Soc. of Agr. Engr.: St. Joseph, MI, 1993.
10. Bond, T.E.; Garrett, W.N.; Givens, R.L.; Morrison, S.R.

Comparative effects of mud, wind and rain on beef cattle performance. Int'l. J. Farm Bldg. Res. **1970**, *5*, 3–9.

11. MWPS. *Beef Housing and Equipment Handbook*, 4th Ed.; Midwest Plan Service: Ames, IA, 1987. MWPS-6.

12. Erickson, G.E.; Auvermann, B.; Eigenberg, R.; Greene, L.W.; Klopfenstein, T.; Koelsch, R. Proposed Beef Cattle Manure Excretion and Characteristics Standard for ASAE. Proc. 9th Anim. Ag. and Food Process Wastes, Research Triangle Park, NC, October 12–15, 2003; ASAE: St. Joseph, MI, 269–276. ASAE Pub. 701P1203.

13. Gilbertson, C.B.; Nienaber, J.A. The Effect of Ration on Materials Handling and Processing Methods of Beef Cattle Manure. In *Proc., 1974 Cornell Agricultural Waste Management Conference*; Cornell: Rochester, NY, 1974; 342–355.

14. Hahn, G.L.; Spiers, D.E.; Eigenberg, R.A.; Brown-Brandl, T.M.; Leonard, M. *Dynamic Thermoregulatory Responses of Feedlot Cattle to Shade vs. No Shade During Heat Stress*; ASAE Paper 004073, Amer. Soc. of Agr. Engr.: St. Joseph, MI, 2000.

15. Brown-Brandl, T.M.; Nienaber, J.A.; Eigenberg, R.A.; Hahn, G.L.; Freetly, H.C. *Thermoregulatory Responses of Feeder Cattle*; ASAE Paper No. 024180, Amer. Soc. of Agr. Engr.: St. Joseph, MI, 2002.

16. Brown-Brandl, T.M.; Nienaber, J.A.; Eigenberg, R.A.; Mader, T.L.; Morrow, J.L.; Dailey, J.W. *Relative Heat Tolerance Among Cattle of Different Genetics*; ASAE Paper No. 034035, Amer. Soc. of Agr. Engr: St. Joseph, MI, 2003.

17. Garrett, W.N. *Importance of Environment and Facilities in Beef Production*; ASAS 55th Annual Meeting, Corvallis, OR, 1963.

Beef Cattle: Marketing

Scott William Fausti
South Dakota State University, Brookings, South Dakota, U.S.A.

INTRODUCTION

In 2001, U.S. farm commodity cash receipts totaled $207.7 billion.[1] Crop sales accounted for 46.4% and livestock and livestock products for 53.6% of total receipts. Cattle and calf cash receipts accounted for $40.44 billion or 19.5% of total receipts. The production of beef is the largest individual contributor to total U.S. farm commodity cash receipts.

The marketing channel is complex. However, the majority of slaughter cattle are sold on a direct cash basis. A majority of cash sales are by pen and the transaction price is an average price per head.

Large meat packing firms dominate the slaughter and processing segment of the beef industry. Increasing market concentration in the meat packing industry since the late 1980s has been alluded to as a potential anti-competitive trend in the beef industry.[2]

Consumer demand for beef products is dependent upon how consumers make their purchases. Higher quality beef products are desired in the hotel-restaurant and retail markets. Fast-food industry firms, on the other hand, purchase lower quality beef products. While total beef consumption has increased over the last 40 years, beef's market share of total red meat consumption has been declining since the late 1970s.

THE EFFECT OF INDUSTRIAL STRUCTURE ON BEEF MARKETING

The structure of the beef industry's supply chain, relative to the pork and poultry industries, exhibits great diversity. The beef industry's supply chain contains a number of different management and marketing alternatives coordinated by market forces to move beef products from the producer to the consumer. The majority of production and processing of cattle is located in the central U.S. from Texas north to the Canadian border. The structure of the supply chain is outlined in Fig. 1.

Figure 1 provides a general overview of the present feeding, marketing, and distribution alternatives in the beef industry today. Small independent producers dominate the cow-calf segment of the beef industry. Ownership and management responsibilities of beef cattle are often transferred several times between the postweaning and the preslaughter phases of an animal's life cycle. For example, 1) meat packers can act as integrators, acquiring and maintaining ownership of an animal from the cow-calf operation until the consumer purchases the beef product from a retail outlet, or 2) cow-calf producers can retain ownership until slaughter. However, ownership across different production stages in the beef industry is minimal relative to the pork and poultry industries.

The production and processing of slaughter cattle have changed dramatically over the last 50 years. Increased concentration in the packing and feedlot segments of the beef industry has resulted in a dramatic decline of the number of firms involved in both the feeding and processing segments of the beef industry. In the feedlot industry the number of firms declined from 104,000 in 1972 to 41,000 in 1995. In the meat packing industry, the number of plants required (processing more than 2000 head annually) to report to GIPSA[3] declined from 856 in 1974 to 204 in 1999.

In the feedlot industry, prior to 1962, almost 64% of marketed fed cattle were fed in farmer-owned feedlots with an annual capacity of less than 1,000 head. Today, less than 25% are marketed from these small feedlots. The largest 400 feedlots in the United States market 50% of the fed cattle.[3]

The USDA estimated that the four largest meat packing firms slaughtered 81.5% of all marketed finished steers and heifers in 2000. Increased concentration in the processing segment of the beef industry has been driven by firms seeking to reduce production costs. Meat packing firms have moved from urban areas with terminal markets to feed-grain production regions of the Midwest. As a result, packer purchases from public markets (all cattle types) declined from 46% in 1960 to 14% in 1999.[3] This structural shift has been driven by economics as it is more cost-effective to process slaughter cattle in grain producing regions and ship boxed beef to urban areas than ship live cattle to urban areas for processing. It is the general consensus of agricultural economists and regulatory authorities that increased concentration in the feeding and processing segments of the beef industry has affected price discovery in the slaughter cattle market. Recent passage of federal livestock mandatory price reporting

Encyclopedia of Animal Science
DOI: 10.1081/E-EAS 120019455

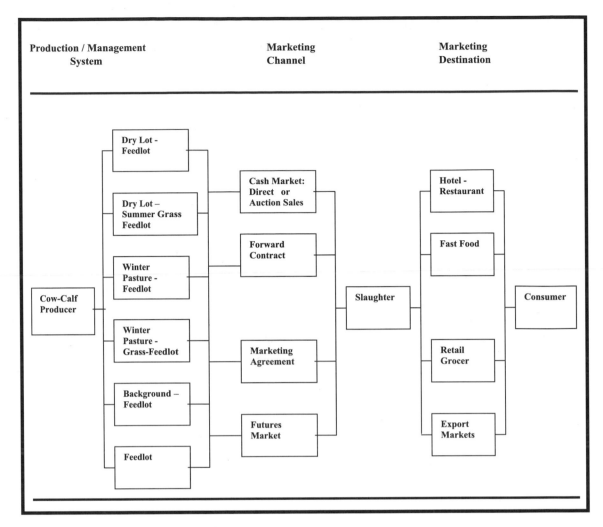

Fig. 1 U.S. beef industry supply chain.

legislation and ongoing Congressional hearings on the competitive impact of packer ownership of slaughter cattle provide anecdotal support for this statement.

THE PRICING OF BEEF CATTLE

Slaughter cattle, as indicted in Fig. 1, can be marketed numerous ways. However, slaughter cattle are priced in predominantly three ways: 1) live weight, 2) dressed weight, or 3) by a value-based pricing system. The premium and discount structure of a value-based pricing system is firm-dependent and varies across the industry. These value-based pricing systems are often referred to as a grid pricing system.[4]

The interaction of supply and demand for beef and beef by-products determines the market price for slaughter

cattle or what economists refer to as price determination. Price discovery is the process by which buyers and sellers arrive at a transaction price for a given quality and quantity of a product. Price discovery begins with the market price level. The actual transaction price will be dependent on: 1) pricing method, 2) number of buyers and sellers in the market, and 3) the amount of information on the quality of the product being sold. Price determination and price discovery are interrelated economic concepts. Market concentration, captive supply, and incomplete information can all affect the price discovery process. Feedlot and packer market concentration cannot affect market price if competitive market forces are maintained in the beef industry.

Meat packers represent the demand side of the slaughter cattle market and the supply side of the box beef and beef by-product markets. Therefore, a packer's profit is derived from the transformation of live cattle into beef products destined for consumer markets. When a meat packing firm is making a slaughter cattle–purchasing decision, the firm begins by establishing a bid price for slaughter cattle. First, the packer estimates sales revenue from the sale of beef and beef by-products. Next, the packer subtracts processing cost and a profit target to determine the price the packer would be willing to pay for slaughter cattle. Beginning with a basic profit equation,

$$\text{Profit} = \text{Total Revenue} - \text{Total Cost} \qquad (1)$$

Eq. 1 can be expanded to incorporate relevant variables into the packer's profit equation:

$$
\begin{aligned}
\text{Profit} = &(P_{\text{boxed-beef}}\, Q_{\text{boxed-beef}} \\
&+ P_{\text{byproduct}}\, Q_{\text{byproduct}}) - (P_{\text{cattle}}\, Q_{\text{cattle}} \\
&+ \text{Costs of slaughter and fabricating})
\end{aligned} \qquad (2)
$$

where P is price and Q is quantity.

Eq. 2 can be rearranged into a general bid price equation:

Bid price per head

$$
\begin{aligned}
= &((P_{\text{boxed-beef}}\, Q_{\text{boxed-beef}} \\
&+ P_{\text{byproduct}}\, Q_{\text{byproduct}}) \\
&- (\text{Costs of slaughter and fabricating} \\
&+ \text{profit target}))/\text{No. of head}
\end{aligned} \qquad (3)
$$

Key points associated with the general bid equation:

1. When boxed beef and/or beef by-product prices change, then the fed cattle bid price will change.
2. Bid price will vary across individual packers because cost structure and profit targets vary across firms.
3. Profit targets shrink when fed cattle are in short supply and increase when fed cattle supply is high.

The bid price presented in Eq. 3 is a starting point for the packer. The actual offering price for a particular pen of cattle will be dependent on the marketing method selected by the seller.[5]

THE MARKETING OF BEEF CATTLE

GIPSA reported that in 1999 the packing industry purchased only 3% of the steers and heifers slaughtered through public markets. The sale of slaughter cattle in a public market is conducted on a live weight basis, and cattle are usually sold by lot or pen. This implies that individual animals are sold at an average per-head price.

Direct purchases of slaughter cattle either in the cash market or through one of the contractual methods listed in Fig. 1 can be conducted on a live, dressed-weight, or value-based pricing system. GIPSA reported that in 1991 48% of slaughter cattle were purchased on a live-weight basis. This implies that 52% were purchased on a carcass basis. However, Ward[6] reported that only 20% of direct purchases are made on individual carcass quality merit basis. Therefore, approximately 32% of slaughter cattle are purchased on a dressed-weight basis. Ward's findings indicate that approximately 80% of slaughter cattle are purchased at an average price per head.

The issue of average pricing of slaughter cattle has been named as a major contributor to the beef industry's continuing problem of inconsistent product quality and excess fat production.[7] Recent research on the economic consequences of average pricing of slaughter cattle suggests that average pricing introduces carcass quality estimation error into the pricing mechanism for slaughter cattle.[4] Average pricing favors producers who sell below-average quality cattle and penalizes producers who sell above-average quality cattle. Average pricing therefore interferes with the transmission of consumer preferences for specific type of beef product to producers because producers are receiving the same price for above and below average animals when sold by the pen at an average price.

The beef industry's solution to the average pricing problem has been a movement toward marketing slaughter cattle on a value-based marketing pricing system. Value-based pricing systems today are commonly referred to as grid pricing systems. A typical grid will apply premiums and discounts based on the following carcass quality characteristics: 1) quality grade, 2) yield grade, and 3) hot carcass weight. A grid pricing system begins with the packer establishing the market value for yield grade 3, quality grade choice carcass weighing between 550 and 950 pounds. This industry standard for carcass quality is then used to establish the grid system's base price. Carcasses failing to meet any of the minimum yield, quality, or weight specifications of the grid are discounted. Carcasses that exceed the minimum yield and quality specifications are given a premium.

CONCLUSION

The marketing of beef will continue to be affected by concentration in the feeding and packing segments of the beef industry. Agricultural economists expect that average pricing will continue to dominate the market for slaughter cattle in the future. Unfortunately, grid pricing has captured only approximately 20% of total slaughter after a decade of promotion by beef industry groups and agricultural economists. This implies that excess fat production and product quality problems will be issues the beef industry will continue to grapple with in the future.

REFERENCES

1. USDA-NASS. *Agricultural Statistics 2003*; United States Government Printing Office: Washington, DC, 2003.
2. Ward, C.E. Market Structure Dynamics in the Livestock-Meat Subsector: Implications for Pricing and Price Reporting. In *Key Issues in Livestock Pricing: A Perspective for the 1990's*; Purcell, W., Rowsell, W., Eds.; Research Institute in Livestock Pricing: Blacksburg, VA, 1987; 8–53.
3. USDA-GIPSA. *Packers and Stockyards Statistical Report: 1999 Reporting Year, GIPSA SR-02-1*; United States Government Printing Office: Washington, DC, 2002.
4. Fausti, S.W.; Feuz, D.M.; Wagner, J.J. Value based marketing for fed cattle: A discussion of the issues. Int. Food Agribus. Manag. Rev. **1998**, *1* (1), 73–90.
5. Feuz, D.M.; Schroeder, T.C.; Ward, C.E. *Fed Cattle Pricing. Institute of Agriculture and Natural Resources, G98-1353-A*; University of Nebraska, 1998.
6. Ward, C.E.; Feuz, D.M.; Schroeder, T.C. *Formula Pricing and Grid Pricing for Fed Cattle: Implications for Pricing Discovery and Variability*; Research Bulletin 1–99, Research Institute in Livestock Pricing: Blacksburg, VA, Jan. 1999; 3–16.
7. Cross, H.R.; Savell, J.W. What do we need for a value-based beef marketing system? Meat Sci. **1994**, *36*, 19–27.

Beef Cattle: Nutritional Management

Gerald B. Huntington
Matthew H. Poore
North Carolina State University, Raleigh, North Carolina, U.S.A.

INTRODUCTION

Humans have managed cattle for thousands of years. *Bos indicus* was domesticated somewhere between 4,000–6,000 years ago, and *Bos taurus* was domesticated in Europe about 2000 years ago. This long tradition gives cattle management an important role in human culture that continues today; the lives and language of human herders in North and South America, Europe, Africa, and Asia revolve around the activities and business of managing cattle. Therefore, economic and social success depend on successful management techniques.

There are four main segments of cattle production of food (beef) for human consumption in the United States: 1) production of weaned calves from herds of brood cows, 2) growing weaned calves until they weigh about 350 kg, 3) finishing the growth process when the animals weigh about 550 kg, and 4) production of purebred males and females of specific breeds or other genetic criteria for use as replacements in the herds that produce calves.

Because the cost of feeding animals usually accounts for 40–80% of all operating costs, nutritional management is a topic of major interest to cattle producers. Nutritional management revolves around three major themes: 1) the nutritional needs of the animal in a given situation; 2) the availability of feeds to meet those nutritional needs; and 3) the economics, or profitability, of a given feeding system or production strategy. Successful beef cattle managers are highly skilled and motivated people who balance these nutritional themes with other variables such as weather, market conditions, and ecological concerns.

MANAGEMENT BY CLASSES OF NUTRIENTS

Water

Good management requires access to clean water at all times. For a given size (body weight) and production status, water intake will change as ambient temperature changes and as amount and type of feed consumed changes (Table 1). Water sources should allow adequate access for the size of the herd, and should be constructed or managed to prevent damage to pastures or riparian areas, and to avoid conditions that promote propagation of disease.

Energy and Protein

Energy is not a nutrient, but managers evaluate diets and animals' requirements on an energy basis. Usually, optimal economic return from this conversion is predicated upon maximizing consumption of forage; the more forage they eat, the better. Managing forages as energy and protein sources centers on managing the agronomic aspects of the forage to take full advantage of its nutrient potential, and on predicting the nutrient content of a given forage at the time it is grazed or harvested as hay. Knowing nutrient content (Table 2) and accurately predicting forage consumption allow a good manager to formulate a supplement that complements the forage nutrient supply to meet nutritional requirements and minimizes feed costs. Nutrition-related diseases, such as grass tetany, acute bovine pulmonary emphysema, or nitrate toxicity, can have lethal effects on grazing ruminants.[1,2] Legumes, such as alfalfa and clover, are good sources of energy and protein for beef cattle; however, beef cattle may die from bloat caused by rapid consumption of legumes.[1]

An important aspect of beef production is the use of by-products as feedstuffs. By-products such as recycled poultry bedding, whole cottonseeds, and soybean hulls are cost-efficient sources of energy and protein. In fact, many of these unusual feed sources are rated for their value relative to corn grain, soybean meal, or alfalfa hay, which allows managers to make intelligent feed purchase decisions.[3]

Beef cattle gain weight rapidly on high-grain diets, but excessive consumption of grain can upset the fermentation balance in the rumen, which can lead to potentially lethal acidosis.[1] Acidosis is controlled by feeding approved compounds (ionophores, buffers) as well as by astute management of feed composition and supply to the animals.

The relatively high cost of supplemental protein obliges a manager to consult technical information and formulate diets that meet but do not exceed the animal's requirements. Degradability of dietary protein in the

Table 1 Nominal daily dry matter intake and nutrient requirements for beef cattle[a]

	Weaned calf 200–350 kg BW	Growing–finishing, 350–500 kg BW	Mature cow	Mature bull
Dry matter, kg	4–10	10–12	6–12	6–9
Nutrient				
Water, L	15–56	28–78	23–61	30–78
Protein, g	400–1000	600–1000	500–1300	800–1000
Metabolizable energy, Mcal	12–17	15–27	12–27	21–28
Calcium, g	12–35	15–29	12–42	27–33
Phosphorus, g	9–18	13–21	12–31	22–33
Sodium chloride, g	10–20	10	15–36	15–36

[a]Specific requirements[4] for a given type of animal and productive purpose should be used for formulating and evaluating diets.

rumen varies among feedstuffs.[4] Managers can mix protein sources of differing ruminal degradabilities to optimize efficiency of nutrient use for weight gain. Concern about the contribution of animal waste to nutrient loads in ecosystems encourages managers to tightly manage nitrogen supply and use.

Energy and protein requirements vary with age, environment, and productive state (Table 1). In general, if forage intake equals 2–3% of the animal's live weight, the forage will be close to providing the animal's maintenance energy needs, and if that forage contains at least 8% crude protein, it will be close to providing the animal's maintenance protein needs.

Minerals

Several essential minerals may be limited in beef cattle diets. Supplemental feeds usually contain minerals to meet nutritional requirements (Table 1). Supplements usually provide salt (NaCl), Ca, P, and trace minerals such as Mn, Cu, Co, Zn, I, and Se. Concentrations of each mineral are based on estimates of voluntary intake and daily requirements.[2] Supplements can contain supplemental protein or energy as well as minerals, or can contain other compounds (e.g., ionophores) that modulate

fermentation to improve nutrient use or reduce the chance of a nutrition-related disease, depending on the management scheme.

Mineral deficiencies or imbalances are the most likely problems, but isolated areas may have toxic levels of minerals, such as Se.[5] In most instances, problems linked to improper mineral nutrition are subtle, such as slightly reduced weight gain and reduced probability of pregnancy in breeding females. Effective managers need to know local conditions and need to routinely analyze feedstuffs to distinguish problems caused by improper mineral nutrition from problems with other causes unrelated to nutrition. Blood, liver, and hair samples are taken from cattle to pinpoint potential problems with mineral status.

Vitamins

Essentially all the water-soluble vitamins (B-vitamins) and fat-soluble vitamin K required by beef cattle are synthesized by the ruminal microbes.[3] These vitamins are provided in mother's milk to young calves before their rumens begin functioning. At normal intakes, fat-soluble vitamins A, D, and E are adequate in common feedstuffs. In most situations, animals are exposed to sufficient sunlight to adequately synthesize vitamin D to supplement

Table 2 Dry matter (DM) and nutrient composition of examples of feedstuffs for beef cattle

	Bromegrass	Bermudagrass	Alfalfa	Corn grain	Soybean meal	Whole cottonseed	Recycled poultry bedding
DM, g/kg	270–920	290–900	200–910	770–890	890–900	870–900	770–820
Protein, g/kg DM	60–171	70–140	149–225	890–112	477–540	200–244	225–320
Metabolizable energy, Mcal/kg DM	1.8–2.8	1.5–2.3	2.1–2.4	3.2–3.7	2.9–3.4	3.2–3.5	1.5–2.1
Calcium, g/kg DM	2.6–3.8	4.2–5.5	11.9–16.9	0.2–0.3	2.9–4.0	1.5–2.0	15–40
Phosphorus, g/kg DM	1.6–2.6	1.8–2.7	2.1–3.3	3.3	6.8–7.1	5–7.5	7–25

Source: Ref. [3], personal experience of authors.

dietary sources. Managers need to respond to unusual conditions, when the diet or ambient conditions are not compatible with adequate supplies of vitamins. For example, animals fed poor-quality, old hay, or animals that have access to sparse, mature grass in pastures may need supplemental vitamin A. Animals housed indoors may need supplemental vitamin D. Animals eating forages in geographic areas with soils low in Se may need supplemental vitamin E. The relatively low cost and minimal risk of toxicity of vitamins A, D, and E prompt many managers to routinely include them in completely mixed diets or supplements to meet requirements.[2]

Lipids and Fats

Fats and fatty acids can be added to diets of beef cattle to increase the energy density, but the amount is limited to about 5% of the dietary dry matter. Fats are toxic to some ruminal bacteria, specifically those involved in fermentation of fiber, so levels higher than 5% have unacceptable negative effects on fiber fermentation and hence voluntary intake of high-fiber feeds.[6]

MANAGEMENT BY NUTRIENT NEEDS

Information on nutrient requirements is available for almost all possible animal classifications and production levels.[4] The annual cycle of reproduction is a useful calendar to formulate nutritional schemes to meet the animals' requirements. A nationally accepted and implemented system of visual body condition scores is a simple yet powerful evaluation tool.[3,4] Successful implementation of the tool keeps animals from becoming too thin or too fat to meet production goals. For example, during the 100 days around calving (30 days before calving, 70 days after), nutrient requirements of females increase to about 1.5 times their maintenance needs. The manager monitors body condition scores of the females and provides access to feed accordingly.

Both bulls and breeding females may be fed extra feed to improve probability of conception. However, it is important that virgin (first calf) heifers gain weight at a prescribed rate to avoid over- or under-condition at their first calving. Available tables[4] allow managers to fit breed, age, weather, and other conditions to recommended ration formulations and feeding levels.

Specific information on postweaning growth of calves likewise is available to match a variety of genetic, physiological, and ambient conditions to desired rates of weight gain.[4] These factors, plus nutrient composition of feedstuffs, are factored into equations that help managers provide amounts of feed that are compatible with the animals' nutrient requirements and economic considerations.

Managers of purebred herds have special nutrient considerations that center on the physical appearance of the animals. Much of this management is subjective and has more to do with the reputation of the breeder than the nutrient requirements of the animals.

CONCLUSION

Effective nutritional management of beef cattle depends on skillful integration of the animal's nutrient needs, the environment, feed composition and supply, and the economics of growth and production. Information and recommendations are readily available from governmental, university, and private sources.

REFERENCES

1. Essig, H.W.; Huntington, G.B.; Emerick, R.J.; Carlson, J.R. Nutritional Problems Related to the Gastro-Intestinal Tract. In *The Ruminant Animal, Digestive Physiology and Nutrition*; Church, D.C., Ed.; Prentice Hall: Englewood Cliffs, NJ, 1988; 468–492.
2. Schultz, L.H.; Mayland, H.F.; Emerick, R.J. Metabolic Problems Related to Nutrition. In *The Ruminant Animal, Digestive Physiology and Nutrition*; Church, D.C., Ed.; Prentice Hall: Englewood Cliffs, NJ, 1988; 493–542.
3. Ensminger, M.A.; Perry, R.C. *Beef Cattle Science*, 7th Ed.; Interstate Publishers, Inc.: Danville, IL, 1997.
4. *Nutrient Requirements of Beef Cattle*, 7th Rev. Ed.; National Academy Press: Washington, DC, 1996.
5. Mortimer, R.G.; Dargatz, D.A.; Corah, L.R. *Forage Analyses from Cow/Calf Herds in 23 States*; USDA: Aphis:VS, Centers for Epidemiology and Animal Health: Fort Collins, CO, 1999. #N303.499. http://www.aphis.usda.gov/vs/ceah/cahm/Beef_Cow-Calf/BF97FORG.pdf (Accessed September, 2003).
6. Moore, J.A.; Swingle, R.S.; Hale, W.H. Effects of whole cottonseed, cottonseed oil or animal fat on digestibility of wheat straw diets by steers. J. Anim. Sci. **1986**, *63*, 1267–1273.

Beef Cattle: Reproduction Management

R. A. Bellows
United States Department of Agriculture, Agricultural Research Service,
Bozeman, Montana, U.S.A.

R. P. Ansotegui
Montana State University, Bozeman, Montana, U.S.A.

INTRODUCTION

Successful reproduction management of beef cattle results from decisions and actions made by a manager. Without goals, production systems drift and decisions involve reacting to situations rather than making positive, goal-driven actions. The goal is profitable beef cattle production and it is achieved by correctly manipulating genetic and environmental variables to obtain predicted outcomes.

GENETICS

The beef herd can be straightbred or crossbred, or combinations thereof.[1–3] Heterosis (hybrid vigor) derived from breed crossing increases reproductive performance in cows and bulls. Production involving crossbred cows bred to a bull of a third breed can increase total production by up to 20%. Genetic goals can be attained through planned matings, culling, and selection. Selection progress depends on trait heritability, accuracy of trait measurement, and intensity of selection.[4] Heritabilities of reproductive performance are low, but must not be ignored. Heritabilities of reproduction components, e.g., age at puberty, are higher, and selection response is more rapid. A selection/culling strategy for improving reproduction should include: 1) selecting cows and replacement females that calve early in the calving season, that calve with minimal obstetrical difficulty, that have superior maternal ability and sound udders with moderate milk production, and are physically sound; and 2) culling nonpregnant and late-calving females. Sires (natural service) must exceed minimum criteria for testicle size (scrotal circumference), semen quality, mating capacity, and physical soundness, in addition to desired growth and carcass traits. Sires used for artificial insemination (AI) are selected on individual and offspring performance records appropriate for achieving management goals.

ENVIRONMENT

Puberty

Replacement beef heifers are bred to produce their first calf at approximately 2 years of age, requiring attainment of puberty and conception by 14 to 16 months of age.[1] Heifers conceiving and calving early their first breeding and calving season, respectively, will produce more and heavier calves during their lifetime. Puberty is critically dependent on adequate nutrition.[5] Heifers should reach a target weight equal to approximately 65% of their mature body weight a minimum of three weeks prior to breeding. Example: A replacement heifer weighs 225 kg on November 1, three weeks before breeding occurs on May 1, 180 days later. Assuming the target weight is 340 kg, the heifer must gain 115 kg in 180 days, for a daily gain of 0.64 kg. Heifers must reach this weight and puberty goal prior to the breeding season to prevent breeding at their first (pubertal) estrus (heat), because conception rates improve approximately 15% from breeding at a later estrus, compared to breeding at the pubertal estrus. Excessive feeding is costly and has detrimental effects on fertility, subsequent calving ease, and milk production. Ionophore feed additives will improve weight gains and hasten puberty. Separation of heifers into heavy- and lightweight groups for feeding can improve the puberty percentage by reducing social competition. Commercial heifer development and breeding companies are available.

Gestation

Pregnancy diagnosis is performed by manual palpation or ultrasound examination of the reproductive tract, or by analyzing blood or milk samples for hormone content. Manual tract manipulation should not be attempted before 50 days after breeding to prevent damage to the developing fetus. Once pregnancy is established in a disease-free animal the probability is high that it will be maintained to calving, but if excessive losses occur a

Encyclopedia of Animal Science
DOI: 10.1081/E-EAS 120019458

disease or toxic nutritional problem (e.g., pine needle-induced abortion) should be suspected. Gestation is the physiological period during which the fetus develops and the dam prepares for a short postpartum interval (calving to first estrus) and successful rebreeding. All nutrient requirements must be met.[5] Body condition scores are used to determine adequacy of gestation management and rebreeding potential. Scores are visual or palpated estimates of body fleshing and fat cover of the dam. Numerical values are assigned, from 1=very thin and emaciated to 9=very fat.[3] Separating pregnant females into heifers, females with low condition scores, and females with high condition scores is excellent, because feeding levels can be adjusted critically and social competition minimized. The key condition score goal is a minimum 5 at calving, indicating gestation nutrient requirements for dam and fetus have been met. Calves from 5-score dams are more vigorous and less susceptible to disease than calves from lower-score dams. The 5 score indicates that body reserves are present to maintain the dam during the critical postpartum nutritional period, from calving until forage is adequate to maintain bodyweight in the lactating dam. Maintaining dams in condition scores higher than 7 is costly and results in increased dystocia. Nutrient requirements, feed intake, and digestibility are negatively affected by cold temperatures. In dams with a heavy winter hair coat, a 6°C decrease (includes chill factor) in temperature increases the metabolizable energy requirement for maintenance by approximately 8%. Physical activity (e.g., walking) increases nutrient requirements. High environmental temperatures reduce birth weights and the subsequent milk production and fertility of the dam.

Parturition (Calving)

Perinatal calf deaths rank second in importance of factors depressing the net calf crop. Dystocia (calving difficulty) is the major cause of calf deaths up to 72 hours postpartum, occurring most frequently in primaparous (first-calf) heifers. Severe dystocia also depresses postpartum dam fertility and calf gains. Up to 45% of heifers may require obstetrical assistance to complete the birth process, emphasizing the need for close observation, adequate obstetrical facilities and equipment, and trained personnel available throughout the calving season. Knowledge of parturition physiology (stages 1, 2, and 3 of labor) is mandatory to determine when and how correct obstetrical assistance must be given.[3] The major cause of dystocia is a disproportion between the size of the calf and the size of the birth canal. Careful sire selection can control birth weight and dystocia. Adequate nutrition for developing replacement heifers will maximize skeletal growth, resulting in larger birth canal openings. Selection of heifers with large pelvic openings to reduce dystocia is only partially successful, but will result in increased body frame size. Feeding the pregnant dam late in the evening can prevent calving from 1 A.M. to 6 A.M., but this practice is not 100% successful.

Postpartum/Lactation

Adequate nutrition[5] is essential both before and after calving if timely estrus and rebreeding are to be obtained. Lactation increases nutrient requirements of the dam, which can be met with pastures containing sufficient nutrients. If pastures are inadequate, lactation will continue at the expense of the dam's body tissue stores, and supplemental hay and/or grain feeding is required. Calf deaths from pneumonia or scours (diarrhea) can be high during the first six weeks postcalving and may result from poor nutrition of the dam during the last trimester of gestation. Suckling delays return to estrus, and primaparous dams have longer postpartum intervals than cows. Breeding replacement heifers to calve 20 to 30 days before the cow herd allows more time for recovery.

Breeding

Whether breeding will be by natural service or AI, the season, and duration of the breeding period are important decisions. Artificial insemination requires planning for facilities, animal management, labor, and sire selection. Sire records can be used to predict offspring performance to attain production goals for either AI or natural service breeding. Sire selection based entirely on visual appraisal decreases the probability of goal attainment. Minimum scrotal circumference in yearling breeding bulls should exceed 33 cm.

A 60-day breeding season is considered maximum. Estrous synchronization can shorten the breeding season to 45 days using one AI and two subsequent natural service breedings. Synchronization of estrus with progestogen–prostaglandin combinations or intravaginal devices can be used for either AI or natural service breeding. If natural service is used in synchronized herds, a bull ratio of 1:15 is adequate, whereas a ratio of 1:30 is adequate for nonsynchronized herds. Bull ratios of 2:80 cows in natural service have given high pregnancy rates. Some synchronization protocols involve 48-hour calf removal, requiring management of calves during this period. Early weaning terminates suckling effects and lactation nutrient demands, and stimulates occurrence of estrus in females. This practice can be used in adverse feeding conditions (e.g., drought), but requires management of the early-weaned calf.

Season of breeding (spring or fall) must be evaluated for forage availability and supplemental feeding requirements. Combining spring and fall breeding seasons can perpetuate poor reproductive performance if cows that do not conceive in one breeding season are moved to the later breeding period and given another chance for conception. Season consideration must include when and where marketing will occur as well as evaluation of retained ownership.

Bull Management

Natural service requires bull management to ensure optimum semen production and libido. Nutrient requirements for a 770-kg bull are approximately equivalent to that of a 545-kg lactating cow producing 4.5 kg of milk daily. Unless severe, effects of nutrition on sperm production are inconclusive, but underfeeding and overfeeding are detrimental to libido. The testicular sperm-production cycle in the bull requires eight weeks to complete, so concern for body condition and nutrient requirements[5] must begin well before the breeding season. A breeding soundness examination (BSE) is a wise investment, particularly in young bulls or if the bull is used in a single-sire herd. If a socially dominant bull in a multiple-sire herd is of low fertility, herd pregnancy rates will be depressed. The exam will detect abnormal sperm morphology, testicular and tract abnormalities, and damage from conditions including fever or frozen scrotum. The BSE results in classification of the bull as a satisfactory or an unsatisfactory breeder.[4] Bulls classifying unsatisfactory can be retested in approximately two weeks, as classification can change, especially in young bulls.

Diseases

A disease prevention and control program for bulls, cows, and calves must be developed in consultation with a qualified veterinarian. The plan must include all common reproductive diseases, calf diseases, and control of both internal and external parasites.

Records

Effective reproductive management depends on records, including individual animal identification and records that identify poor and high producers. A livestock scale allows for determining the adequacy of feeding regimens. Computer software programs are available for formulating and balancing diets, evaluating changes in production protocols, determining applicable cost–benefit ratios, etc. University beef extension specialists can supply valuable record-keeping information.

CONCLUSIONS

Reproduction management includes using existing technology, being aware of horizon technology, and predicting how new developments can be used to attain desired goals. Responsibilities of the manager are increasing exponentially and include choices not directly related to production. These include environmental and ethical issues, political decisions, international market and production changes, population growth and consumer attitudes, and pressures from various advocacy groups. But goal setting and attainment will be the key to successful reproduction management in beef cattle.

REFERENCES

1. Dziuk, P.J.; Bellows, R.A. Management of reproduction of beef cattle, sheep and pigs. J. Anim. Sci. **1983**, *57* (Suppl. 2), 355–379.
2. Thomas, V.M. *Beef Cattle Production, An Integrated Approach*; Waveland Press, Inc.: Prospect Heights, IL, 1992; 270.
3. Field, T.G.; Taylor, R.E. *Beef Production and Management Decisions,* 4th Ed.; Prentice-Hall: Upper Saddle River, NJ, 2002; 714.
4. Guidelines for Uniform Beef Improvement Programs. *Beef Improvement Federation,* 8th Ed.; University of Georgia: Athens, GA, 2002; 65.
5. National Research Council. *Nutrient Requirements of Beef Cattle,* 7th Ed.; National Academy Press: Washington, DC, 1996; 46.

Behavior: Aberrant

John J. McGlone
Nadège Krebs
Texas Tech University, Lubbock, Texas, U.S.A.

B

INTRODUCTION

Aberrant refers to something that deviates from the usual or natural type. Interchanged in the literature with the term aberrant is the term abnormal in reference to deviations from normal behaviors. Abnormal behavior has been defined as behavior "that deviates in form, frequency, or sequence from a defined, comparable standard. Such a standard may be a behavioral inventory typical for a given genotype, age group, sex, nutritional level, housing condition, or management system, etc."[2]

Behaviors are not classified as aberrant or abnormal simply because of their level of behavioral frequency or duration. Some behaviors are expressed at a low frequency, yet they are critical (example: defecation is an infrequent, yet critical behavior). In contrast, tongue rolling in calves may be expressed at a low frequency, but it lacks purpose and thus can be classified as an aberrant behavior. To be classified as aberrant, a behavior must be lacking purpose; harmful to the animal, other animals, or property; or maladaptive. To suggest a behavior lacks purpose requires a complete understanding of the context of the behavior and the evolutionary development of the species. For example, some ritualized sexual displays may at first seem to lack purpose, but they have been incorporated into sequences of behaviors that on the whole are adaptive.

TYPES OF ABERRANT BEHAVIORS

Self-Directed Aberrant Behaviors

These are directed at the animal or at inanimate objects. These may or may not injure the animal.[1,2]

Stereotyped behaviors are behaviors that vary little in form, sequence, and time. Chewing food is a stereotyped behavior. Rumination is a variation of chewing that is found in a highly stereotyped form in cattle. Some behaviors occur regularly, but are a special form of stereotyped behavior referred to as stereotypies. Stereotypies are stereotyped behaviors composed of relatively invariant sequences of movements that serve no obvious purpose.

Many examples of self-directed aberrant behaviors are given in Table 1. Some behaviors are directed toward

the animal itself (including to the air)[4,5] and some are directed toward components of the environment. Some self-directed aberrant behaviors can be harmful to the animal. Others seem obsessive-compulsive in nature.

Some stereotypies are thought to be related to feeding motivation[6] in that restricted feeding may increase the rate of expression of stereotypies. In sows, stereotypies can be present 10–15% of the time; in horses, the average can be 8%, but can reach 30% in racing stables.[7] Ruminants express less stereotyped behaviors,[8] but they may show tongue rolling or other forms of oral behaviors. Brain mechanisms that cause stereotypies are not known, but they may be related to the brain dopamine system involved in the control of movements and to opiate peptides.[9]

Social Aberrant Behaviors

These are directed toward other animals of the same species or toward other species.

Aberrant behaviors directed toward others can be damaging to the body of animals receiving the behavior.[10] Tail biting,[11] feather pecking, and wool-pulling are relatively common aberrant behaviors. Other aberrant social behaviors that do not involve oral behaviors include excessive mounting as in the Buller Steer Syndrome.[12] The Buller Steer Syndrome is not considered a reproductive behavior because it is usually observed among castrated males. Injury from oral and nonoral aberrant behaviors can be severe because modern confinement systems have limited space that does not allow flight from the offending animal(s).

Parental-Neonatal Aberrant Behaviors

These include those shown by the mother or father toward the young, or of the young toward their mother.[13,14]

The mother may not accept her newborn. This problem can have life-threatening consequences to the neonatal animal. Lack of acceptance of the neonate is found in all farm mammal species. Besides ambivalence of the mother toward her newborn, some mothers (and fathers) actually attack and, if allowed, will kill their offspring.

Encyclopedia of Animal Science
DOI: 10.1081/E-EAS 120019462

Table 1 Examples of aberrant behaviors and possible causes among farm animals

Type of behavior	Description of the behavior	Possible causes
Overeating, anorexia, polydipsia	Excess or reduced eating or drinking	Abnormal brain chemistry, (ex. of hypothalamus?)
Abnormal standing and lying or abnormal postures; changes in activity (hyper or hypo active); hysteria; pacing; weaving	Aberrant frequency, duration, or sequence of standing, lying, posture or locomotion; ataxia; head shaking or nodding	Slippery floors Lack of space (therefore, weakness) and movement, weak legs because lack of calcium (osteomyelitis, osteoporosis), infectious disease
Self-mutilation; mutilation of others	Vigorous body mutilation; excessive rubbing, licking, biting, chewing; kicking directed at self or other animals; feather or body pecking; wool pulling; tail biting; egg eating; Buller Steer Syndrome (excessive mounting to the point of injury)	Parasitism, gastrointestinal problems, pain, confinement and isolation; early weaning
Oral–nasal–facial (ONF) behaviors such as sham chewing, tongue rolling, bar biting, licking, cribbing, drinker pressing, anal massage, belly nosing, intersucking, wind sucking, eye rolling	Movements of the mouth without food present. Generally associated with standing, sitting, or lying, mouth and face movements; may have frothing and foaming	Individual housing, lack of oral stimulation or enrichment
Aggressive/agonistic behaviors	Excessive threat or attack of another animal (or of human); movements of head (bite), butting and kicking (cattle, horses), biting (horses), chasing (poultry), charging (goats and sheep)	Confinement, housing system effects; inappropriate olfactory environment; restricted space
Neonatal rejection; maternal failure; stealing young; killing young/cannibalism	First-day postpartum desertion or aggression (butting, striking, driving away, biting); more common in first parity; unresponsiveness of the mother	Separation from newborn, breed, disturbance at parturition, genetic, stress, crowding, Rearing system (isolation), possibly low estrogens or progesterone
Reproductive behaviors; mounting; silent heat, impotence; coital disorientation; intromission impotence, inappropriate mounting	Mounting, Excessive dysfunctional sexual technique	Isolation in monosexual groups High densities, hormone administration, vaccine, stress, genetics, inexperience, confinement

The precise physiological mechanisms of aberrant behaviors are not known.
(Adapted from Ref. [3].)

Reproductive Aberrant Behaviors

Several aberrant reproductive behaviors can be observed among farm animals. One class involves a lack of appropriate sexual behavior.[15] This may be due to inexperience or lack of ability. While these aberrant reproductive behaviors do not directly threaten the animal's health, they cause problems for completing reproductive cycles.

Feeding Aberrant Behaviors

Feeding behaviors may become aberrant. Aberrant feeding behaviors include those associated with the mouth, face, or snout with or without ingestion of substrate. Also, feed or water intake may be excessive (hyper) or inadequate (hypo) for body maintenance.

POSSIBLE CAUSES OF ABNORMAL BEHAVIORS

Aberrant behavior can be provoked by a range of environmental factors such as limited space, high animal density, competition for feeding space, reduced flight or escape opportunities, slippery floors, and by neuronal diseases (e.g., transmissible spongiform encephalopathy), metabolic diseases (e.g., milk fever), specific nutrient deficiencies, transportation, and traumatic experiences. Because stress-induced behaviors generally serve a purpose such as to reduce negative effects of stress, they are not generally considered aberrant behaviors. Some aberrant behaviors appear more often among confined farm animals (they may not exist at all in natural conditions), and some are an excessive expression of a natural behavior, but the frequency, intensity, context, and consequences make the behavior aberrant.

CONCLUSION

Many aberrant behaviors are common in several farm animal species. Among some of the common causes are heredity, housing systems, nutrient deficiencies, and lack of enrichment. Providing enriched environments or more space may alleviate some aberrant behaviors.

REFERENCES

1. *Merriam-Webster Online*; 2004. Aberrant. http://www.m-w.com/cgi-bin/dictionary. Accessed 25 April, 2004.
2. Hurnik, J.F.; Webster, A.B.; Siegel, P.B. Abnormal Behavior. In *Dictionary of Farm Animal Behavior*; Iowa State University: Ames, IA, 1995.
3. Fraser, A.F.; Broom, D.M. *Farm Animal Behaviour and Welfare*, 3rd Ed.; Bailliere Tindall, 1990.
4. Lane, J.G.; Mair, T.S. Observations on headshaking in the horse. Equ. Vet. J. **1987**, *19*, 331–336.
5. Cook, W.R. Headshaking in horses: An afterword. The compendium on continuing education for the practicing veterinarian. Appl. Anim. Behav. Sci. **1992**, *14*, pp. 1369–1371, 1376.
6. Lawrence, A.B.; Terlouw, E.M.C. A review of behavioral factors involved in the development and continued performance of stereotypic behaviors in pigs. J. Anim. Sci. **1993**, *71*, 2815–2825.
7. Waters, A.J.; Nicol, C.J.; French, N.P. Factors influencing the development of stereotypic and redirected behaviours in young horses: Findings of a four year prospective epidemiological study. Equ. Vet. J. **2002**, *6*, 572–579.
8. Houpt, K.A. Abnormal Behavior. In *The Veterinary Clinics of North America 3,2*; Price, E.O., Ed.; Farm Animal Behavior, Saunders: Philadelphia, 1987; 357–367.
9. Cronin, G.M.; Wiepkema, P.R.; van Ree, J.M. Endogeneous opioids are involved in abnormal stereotyped behaviors of tethered sows. Neuropeptides **1985**, *6*, 527–530.
10. Lidfors, L.; Isberg, L. Intersucking in dairy cattle—Review and questionnaire. Appl. Anim. Behav. Sci. **2003**, *80*, 207–231.
11. Breuer, K.; Sutcliffe, M.E.M.; Mercer, J.T.; Rance, K.A.; Beattie, V.E.; Sneddon, I.A.; Edwards, S.A. The effect of breed on the development of adverse social behavior in pigs. Appl. Anim. Behav. Sci. **2003**, *84*, 59–74.
12. Blackshaw, J.K.; Blackshaw, A.W.; McGlone, J.J. Buller Steer Syndrome. Appl. Anim. Behav. Sci. **1997**, *54*, 97–108.
13. Houpt, K.A. Equine Maternal Behavior and Its Aberrations. In *Recent Advances in Companion Animal Behavioral Problems*; International Veterinary Information Service: Ithaca, NY, 2000. http://www.ivis.org/advances/Behavior_Houpt/houpt-foal/chapter_frm.asp?LA=1. Accessed 27 April, 2004.
14. Duncan, P. Foal killing by stallions. Appl. Anim. Ethol. **1982**, *8*, 567–570.
15. Pickett, B.W.; Squires, E.L.; Voss, J.L. *Normal and Abnormal Sexual Behavior of the Equine Male*; General Series, Colorado State University Experimental Station, 1981; Vol. 1004. 33p.ill.http://www.neosoft.com/~iaep/pages/protected/jissues/j1804/j1804p212.html. Accessed 27 April, 2004.

B

Behavior: Feeding

T. Richard Houpt
Katherine Albro Houpt
Cornell University, Ithaca, New York, U.S.A.

INTRODUCTION

All animals supply their nutritional needs by eating feed in such a way that the internal body expenditure of nutrients for energy purposes, growth, and other body uses (such as milk production) is balanced by the quantity and quality of feed eaten. This balance is determined by several physiological control systems that determine when and how much feed will be eaten. This results in a stable body weight—or in the young, a steady uniform growth. However, the feeding behavior and digestive mechanisms of the common domestic animals vary widely, from the relatively simple food of a typical carnivore (such as the cat) to the bulky, tough, and difficult-to-digest feed of the herbivorous cow or horse. This wide variety of eating habits and diet—and the accompanying modifications of the digestive system—calls for a corresponding variety of physiological mechanisms to bring about the desirable matching of body needs and eating behavior.

THE PIG AS A MODEL OF OMNIVOROUS MAMMALS

The eating habits of the domestic pig closely resemble those of the human, with respect to both what it eats and the pattern of meals. In young pigs, the pattern of eating consists of periodic meals separated by intermeal intervals of a few hours' duration. Much of the water consumed is drunk in close association with meals.

It is presumed that during the intermeal intervals deficits of nutrients slowly develop as they are consumed in body metabolism. These deficits are then corrected at subsequent meals. The physiological mechanisms using hormonal and neural pathways will be emphasized here as determining how much food will be consumed in the meals. It should be recognized, however, that the body learns through previous experience how much food should be consumed to satisfy the deficit. In other words, eating is calibrated by experience to match the amount eaten with the metabolic need. This learned control of food intake is difficult to evaluate as part of the combination that includes the mechanistic, physiological control of eating.

It is instructive to consider what kinds of signals could be used by the body to initiate satiation, so that the amount eaten as the meal proceeds matches the need (deficit). These physiological feedback signals that are activated by the presence of food in the digestive tract and that determine the size of each meal are summarized for a typical mammal in Fig. 1. The first and most obvious change caused by the foodstuff as it passes into the mouth, pharynx, and esophagus is distention of these structures and tactile stimulation of their inner surfaces. This oropharyngeal metering of food ingestion plays a small role in controlling the amount eaten in the meal. If this metering acted alone to limit the size of the meal, the meal size would be excessive—as much as two or three times the normal size. But such metering does not act alone; there are other signals from the mouth and the rest of the gastrointesinal tract. The taste of the food as it is chewed may oppose further eating, or an attractive taste may act as positive feedback and increase the amount eaten in the meal. An extremely bitter or unpleasant taste (perhaps resembling a toxin) may block eating entirely.

The arrival of the ingested meal in the stomach causes further distension, which is detected by the numerous stretch or distension receptors in the mucosa and wall of the stomach. This distension is a powerful inhibitory influence on eating behavior. By the time the foodstuffs arrive at the small intestine much liquification has occurred, with solubilization of many products of digestion. The duodenum is the site of many sensory receptors, as well as endocrine cells. Most important are the release of the hormone cholecystokinin (CCK), the response of osmoreceptive mechanisms to the concentrated intestinal content, and the absorption of glucose from the chyme. All have a satiation effect that generally strengthens as the meal proceeds, until strong enough to bring the meal to an end.[1]

In addition to these rapid, short-term control systems that operate in the time span of a meal, there are long-term controls that operate over days and weeks. An example is the leptin system. Leptin is released from body fat stores and acts centrally to inhibit eating. Over time, as the fat stores slowly increase, the levels of leptin increase. Leptin depresses food intake and limits body weight increase. Note that the controls of food intake are predominantly

Encyclopedia of Animal Science
DOI: 10.1081/E-EAS 120019463

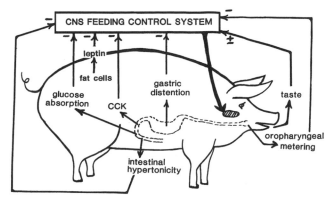

Fig. 1 Controls of food intake in the pig.

inhibitory. Eating is a tonic activity interupted periodically by these inhibitory signals that are initiated by the presence of food in the digestive tract.[2] An intermeal interval follows, and not until those satiety signals weaken does the next meal begin.

THE COW AS AN EXAMPLE OF THE LARGE HERBIVORES

In contrast to the eating habits of the omnivorous pig, most herbivores eat food of quite a different character and follow a different pattern of eating. The plant material eaten by herbivores is in large part not digestible by the ordinary mammalian digestive enzymes—that is, not by the digestive juices of the salivary glands (amylase), stomach (pepsin), pancreas (amylase, lipase, etc.), intestine (peptidases), and so on. For the usual omnivore or carnivore such as the pig or dog, this means that the enormous store of nutritionally usable chemical energy stored up in plant structure, and originally derived from the energy of the sun, is not available. For access to these stores of energy the cow is dependent upon the enzymes synthesized by the symbiotic microorganisms that inhabit the gastrointestinal tract, particularly the rumen. These microbial digestive enzymes can make much of the plant energy available.

The prime example of these plant materials is cellulose, the most abundant carbohydrate on earth. Cellulose is abundant, but nutritionally inaccessible to the nonherbivore. The key problem for the mammal who ingests cellulose is that the usual digestive enzymes do not have the ability to break up the long polymers of glucose that compose the cellulose molecules. Although the starch can be split by the salivary and pancreatic amylases into the component glucose molecules, the mammalian digestive enzymes cannot break the bonds between glucose molecules in cellulose. The result is that although cellulose

contains about the same amount of glucose as an equivalent amount of cornstarch, its glucose is unavailable to the mammals that ingest it.

The herbivores, such as the cow, have solved this problem of the nutritional inaccessibility of cellulose by anatomical and physiological adaptations that permit the development of large populations of microorganisms within the body. Many of these associated microorganisms—bacteria and protozoa mainly—can synthesize the enzyme cellulase, which can attack the cellulose molecules. Breakdown of these molecules results in making glucose available for absorption and utilization in the metabolic machinery of the animal.

The calorically dilute nature of the plant material consumed by the cow requires that large amounts must be ingested. A cow can spend eight or more hours grazing on pasture or consuming hay in the barn, and then another eight hours in the process of rumination, where the ingesta is retrieved from the rumen and remasticated. This extensive grinding of plant material is necessary to make cellulose and other complex carbohydrates located within the plant structure accessible to microbial action. The unique process of digestion and absorption of nutrients in ruminants requires unique satiety signals, summarized for the cow in Fig. 2 as the following three steps:

1. As the bulky plant material is ingested, the immediate consequence is distension of the GI tract. There are ample stretch receptors located in the wall of the reticulorumen. When distended, they give rise to inhibitory impulses to the CNS, limiting further eating. As indicated in the figure, the degree of distention depends on the amount of bulky food ingested and the rate of removal of the ingesta, either by fermentative breakdown or by passage from the reticulorumen into the omasum.

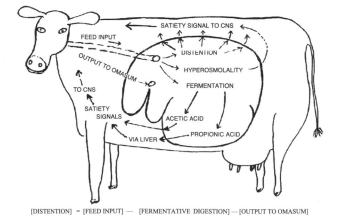

[DISTENTION] = [FEED INPUT] — [FERMENTATIVE DIGESTION] — [OUTPUT TO OMASUM]

Fig. 2 Controls of food intake in the ruminant.

2. If the food being ingested is of a more concentrated, water-soluble nature, then the osmolality of the ruminal fluid rises significantly, due to both the solutes in the feed going into solution and the release of ions and molecules in the microbial fermentation of the foodstuffs. This change in the ruminal fluid acts as a satiety signal to the CNS that, as it grows stronger, brings the meal to an appropriate end. The exact site of reception of this hyperosmolality is unclear.

3. The fermentative action of the ruminal microbes results in the endproducts acetic acid, propionic acid, and butyric acid. These short-chain fatty acids are known as volatile fatty acids (VFAs). There is some evidence that these VFAs act at receptor sites either in the ruminal wall (acetic acid) or in the vascular bed of the liver (propionic acid), giving rise to satiety signals to the CNS that inhibit further eating.[3]

CONCLUSIONS

Body weight depends on equality between food intake and expenditures of nutrients and energy. This balance is largely achieved by controlling the intake of nutrients based on the size and frequency of meals. Intake is assessed by a pattern of signals eminating from the digestive tract as a meal is in progress. The characteristics of the food and the products of its digestion are used to inform the CNS continuously as to the amounts of nutrient ingested. This information is in the form of satiety signals that may be chemical signals or nerve impulses. As the meal proceeds, these satiety signals become progressively stronger, until they cause the meal to end at an appropriate size. In the subsequent intermeal interval, these satiety signals weaken as nutrients are consumed within the body again until the tonic influences driving eating behavior initiate eating.

REFERENCES

1. Houpt, T.R.; Houpt, K.A.; Swan, A.A. Duodenal osmoconcentration and food intake in pigs after ingestion of hypertonic nutrients. Am. J. Physiol. **1983**, *245*, R181–R189.

2. Houpt, K.A. *Domestic Animal Behavior*, 3rd Ed.; Iowa State University Press: Ames, Iowa, 1997.

3. Forbes, J.M. *Voluntary Food Intake and Diet Selection in Farm Animals*; CAB International: Wallingford, UK, 1995.

Behavior: Maternal

Catherine M. Dwyer
Scottish Agricultural College, Edinburgh, Scotland, U.K.

INTRODUCTION

Maternal behaviors include all those behaviors carried out by a parturient mother that influence the lives of her offspring, both those that indirectly affect the offspring (e.g., nest site selection, increased food intake in pregnancy) and behaviors that are directly displayed to the offspring. Maternal behaviors have evolved as they promote the survival of the offspring, and they are expressed by nearly all mammals and birds, and by some fish, reptile, and invertebrate species. Maternal behaviors are species-specific, but they serve a similar purpose in all species: that is, to protect, feed, and nurture the young until they are able to perform these behaviors themselves. Behavioral expression is affected by species factors: maternal social behavior, reproductive strategy, offspring development at birth, environmental niche, and paternal care. Typically, man has domesticated animals that are social, polygynous (one male mates with several females), and show exclusively maternal care.

MATERNAL CARE IN MAMMALS

Mammalian mothers express a high degree of maternal behavior. Offspring are dependent on their mothers and are fed from her bodily resources via lactation. This maternal strategy has reduced the need for male assistance to raise the young, and only 3% of mammalian species show paternal care. The degree and type of maternal care provided are related to offspring need, whether the young are immature (altricial) or well-developed at birth (precocial).

Behavior of Mothers of Altricial Offspring

These species are often predators and frequently solitary, or they live in family groups (e.g., rodents, dogs, cats). Altricial offspring are generally born in large litters, and individuals are small relative to maternal bodyweight. Maternal investment in each individual is, therefore, relatively low, and the survival of some of the litter takes precedence over the survival of all offspring. Mothers of altricial offspring construct a den or nest in which to give birth and maintain the litter for the initial period of

development. The nest is important to provide warmth and protection for the vulnerable young, and mothers show a high degree of defensive aggression to intruders. Altricial offspring are largely helpless at birth, so other maternal behaviors consist of licking or grooming (sometimes to stimulate voiding in the young), retrieval of offspring to the nest if they become scattered, gathering the young together to suck, and the adoption of a nursing posture to aid their sucking. The young do, however, have some influence over the expression of maternal behavior by their responses (e.g., vocalizations), which may indicate their degree of need to the mother.

Behavior of Mothers of Precocial Offspring

These species are generally grazing prey animals and live in large social groups of several females with a male (e.g., horse) or matrilineal groups (e.g., sheep). Litters comprise one or two large (relative to the maternal body weight), well-developed, and mobile young. A specific birth site may be selected, sometimes remote from the social group, but nest building does not occur. Behaviors immediately following birth are usually directed toward recognition of their individual offspring and formation of a social bond between mother and young. Delivery of the young is quick and frequently followed by a period of intense maternal licking (Fig. 1), when the mother forms an olfactory memory of her offspring. Social prey species often breed seasonally, thus all the young are born within a short period. This behavior allows the dam to reliably recognize her own young among other similar young within the group.

Within this class of maternal behavior there are two main maternal strategies, termed hiders and followers.[1] Follower species (e.g., horse, sheep) are accompanied by their offspring from birth, are seldom more than a few meters from their young, and show frequent sucking bouts. Both partners show intense distress on separation. Hider species (e.g., cattle, deer), following birth and initial licking of the young, leave the young concealed and the mother rejoins the social group. Mothers return to their young to suckle on a few occasions during the day and maintain large spatial distances from their offspring. The young animals eventually join the social group with their mothers but still maintain large mother–young distances,

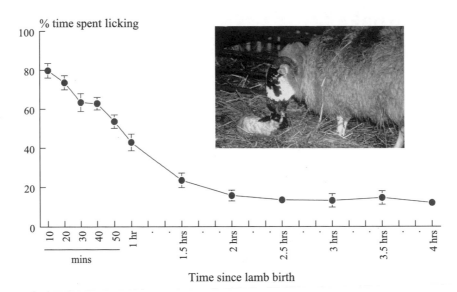

Fig. 1 Average amount of time spent licking lambs by maternal ewes in a four-hour period after the birth of the lamb (lamb born at time zero). Intense licking occurs in the first hour after delivery (ewes spent 38 minutes of the first hour licking the lamb), but ewes are still spending some time licking the lamb four hours after birth. (From C. M. Dwyer, drawn from unpublished data.) (*View this art in color at www.dekker.com.*)

forming peer groups with similarly aged calves—sometimes as a crèche under the supervision of a single mother.

Intermediate Mothers

A few species do not fall easily into either of these groups. These include the pig, where the piglets are well developed and mobile, but have poor thermoregulatory abilities and are born into a large litter. The sow, therefore, builds a large nest to group the piglets together and keep them warm. Sows are extremely passive and non-responsive mothers (Fig. 2), which may reduce piglet deaths from maternal crushing. They also have an unusual lactation pattern, where milk ejection occurs only for a few seconds each suckle, and the piglets are called to the udder before milk ejection by a specific vocalization—a suckling grunt. Other intermediate groups include primates, with relatively developed semiprecocial offspring that have limited locomotor abilities. An important maternal behavior in these species is carrying of the young, which may facilitate observational learning.

CONTROL AND REGULATION OF MATERNAL BEHAVIOR

Species-specific maternal behavior appears spontaneously after delivery, even in naïve animals. Prior to birth many females are indifferent, or even aggressive, to

neonates, but maternal behavior is expressed immediately at the birth of their own young. The rapid onset of maternal care requires hormonal priming by an increase in ovarian hormones (estrogen and progesterone) and

Fig. 2 Passive maternal behavior shown by the pig (a) in comparison to the active behaviors shown by sheep (b). [Photos by S. Jarvis (a) and C. M. Dwyer (b).] (*View this art in color at www.dekker.com.*)

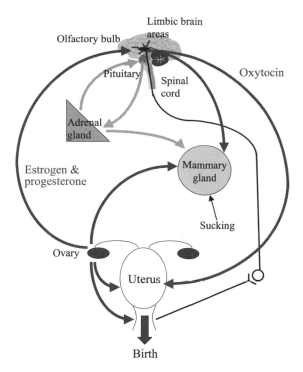

Fig. 3 Schematic diagram of the neuroendocrine events occurring during pregnancy and at birth that lead to the onset of maternal behavior in mammals. (Derived from data given in Ref. [2].) (*View this art in color at www.dekker.com.*)

particularly by the substantial changes in the relative concentrations of these hormones that precedes birth. This priming functions to prepare the maternal brain by increasing oxytocin receptors in key brain regions. At birth, neural impulses travel up through the spinal cord when the birth canal stretches by the passage of the foetus (the Ferguson Reflex) and these impulses stimulate the release of oxytocin in the brain and into the periphery (Fig. 3). This acts as a trigger for the expression of the suite of maternal behaviors.[2] For example, in the sheep it causes maternal licking of the newborn lamb and many low-pitched bleats or "rumbles" (a specific vocalization made by ewes to their lambs). Other chemicals (e.g., opioids, glucocorticoids) act as modulators of maternal behavior expression.

In many species, females that are maternal for the first time (primiparas) often show poorer expression of maternal behavior, and mortality of offspring of these mothers is higher than with experienced dams. For most species, the act of giving birth and showing maternal care causes a maturation of the hormonal processes described above.[3] In some species, such as primates, young females can gain experience of maternal behavior through allomothering, where they share in the care of their younger siblings or the offspring of their older siblings.

MATERNAL BEHAVIOR IN BIRDS

Birds express a diversity of parental styles: nest parasitism, maternal care, paternal care, and biparental care. Paternal care in birds is more common than in mammals, and 90% of bird species show paternal behavior. Birds need to provision their chicks after hatching because, with the exception of some birds (e.g., pigeon) that produce crop milk, they are unable to feed their young from their own bodily resources. Maternal behavior in birds is affected by the risks of the environment, the social group, and the stage of development of the chicks at hatch. Species that hatch altricial chicks (blind, featherless) require biparental care to ensure the survival of the young by providing food simultaneously with keeping the chicks warm and protected. Bird species that hatch precocious chicks (e.g., galliforms) can show just maternal behavior, because the hen is able to rear her chicks without paternal assistance.

Maternal behavior commences before lay with the selection of a nest site and the construction of a nest. After egg-laying, the eggs are incubated and the hen shows broodiness, crouching over the eggs and emitting specific clucks or vocalizations. In some species a brood patch develops: An area of the chest becomes highly vascularized and devoid of feathers to enhance heat transfer to the eggs and chicks. After hatch, precocial chicks imprint onto their mothers and accompany her immediately. Maternal behaviors are concerned with defense against predators, ensuring that the chicks remain with her, and teaching the chicks about appropriate food sources: what to eat, where to find it, and how to obtain it. Parents of altricial chicks also show defense of the nest and chicks against predators, and are strongly motivated to feed the chicks by their gaping mouths.

ROLE OF MATERNAL BEHAVIOR IN OFFSPRING DEVELOPMENT

Recent interest in maternal behavior has focused on the role played by maternal behavior in the development of offspring responses. Mothers teach offspring about food acquisition and associated skills (e.g., hunting). However, offspring also learn about social interactions from their mothers, acquiring sexual preferences and social status, and learning species-specific social cues and signals. Cultural transmission of environmental information from mother to young also occurs (from shelter and water locations in hefted hill sheep to tool use in chimpanzees). Variation in the expression of maternal behavior, or its absence, can have a profound effect on the development of stress-coping behaviors in the offspring as adults, and can influence their reactivity to the environment.[4] Under domestication, this process is often disrupted—or entirely prevented—by early weaning of offspring (e.g., dairy calves, pigs) or by artificial incubation and rearing in same-age groups (e.g., chickens).

CONCLUSIONS

The function of maternal behavior is to facilitate the survival of her offspring. What is required to ensure offspring survival is influenced by the riskiness of the environment and the degree of development or vulnerability of the young. As a result, maternal behaviors are very diverse across species. Common features of maternal behavior are the provision of food and warmth to the young, and their protection from harm. Maternal behavior is also important to teach the young animal about its environment, and to equip the adult with the skills it requires to survive. Recent research suggests this also includes modification of offspring responses to stress, and even the subsequent expression of maternal behaviour by the offspring.

ARTICLES OF FURTHER INTEREST

Domestication of Animals, p. 294
Pregnancy: Maternal Response, p. 747

REFERENCES

1. Lent, P.C. Mother–Infant Relationships in Ungulates. In *The Behavior of Ungulates and Its Relationship to Management*; Geist, V., Walther, F., Eds.; IUCN Publication: Switzerland, 1974; Vol. 24, 14–55.
2. Kendrick, K.M. Oxytocin, motherhood and bonding. Exp. Physiol. **2000**, *85*, 111S–124S.
3. Keverne, E.B.; Lévy, F.; Guevara-Guzman, R.; Kendrick, K.M. Influence of birth and maternal experience on olfactory bulb neurotransmitter release. Neuroscience **1993**, *56* (3), 557–565.
4. Meaney, M.J. Maternal care, gene expression, and the transmission of individual differences in stress reactivity across generations. Annu. Rev. Neurosci. **2001**, *24*, 1161–1192.

Behavior: Reproductive

Larry S. Katz
Rutgers University, New Brunswick, New Jersey, U.S.A.

INTRODUCTION

Animal scientists study reproductive behavior for a variety of reasons, including seeking tools for obtaining direct economic benefit through improved reproductive performance. Learning how reproductive behavior develops and is regulated affords the ability to facilitate the expression of sexual behavior, a goal in many breeding systems. Also, understanding how to inhibit reproductive behavior is advantageous in some production systems, such as feedlots. Domesticated livestock are also useful models for understanding the behavior of non-domesticated species or even humans.

Reproductive behavior, like other behaviors, is shaped by the ongoing interplay of the genotype, environment, and experience. An animal takes part in a continuous dialogue with the environment, which includes external stimuli such as social interactions or interspecific exchanges, contact with humans or predatory interactions, and relations with the inanimate world. In addition to developmental events, livestock reproductive behaviors—like other traits—are subject to both artificial selection and natural selection in the domesticated environment. Intensively managed livestock that are used in hand-breeding, artificial insemination, or single-sire mating schemes have experienced reduced selective pressure for traits such as sexual motivation or other physiological or structural attributes that enhance mating efficiency.

Many studies have been published that reveal the multiple physiological mechanisms controlling the expression of sexual behavior. These studies include descriptions of how the endocrine system facilitates the development of neural substrates involved in sexual behavior, referred to as the organizational actions of hormones. Also, studies have addressed the activational actions of hormones, i.e., how hormones stimulate sexual behaviors in adulthood. A smaller body of literature describes the physiological adjustments an animal makes in response to the expression of reproductive behavior. New findings in this area will help us more fully understand the range of behavioral and physiological adaptations animals can make. The topics presented in this article are primarily ethological (behavioral) in focus, and relate to production problems that may have behavioral solutions. The topics include courtship and mating systems; the sexual performance, motivation, and stimulation of males; and female attractivity, proceptivity, and receptivity.

COURTSHIP AND MATING SYSTEMS

Courtship

The specific motor patterns and physical displays associated with courtship behavior vary among livestock species and can also vary among individuals within a species. Some individuals may display frequent precopulatory behaviors, whereas others may attempt to copulate with little or no courtship. Detailed descriptions of courtship displays of domesticated animals are available.[1] In many nondomesticated species these displays serve to: regulate species recognition and ensure reproductive isolation; bring males and females into close proximity; synchronize the pair to bring about sexual readiness; and lead to actual fertilization or copulation. Breeding practices extending over many generations in domesticated species have modified the selective pressures that influence the frequency, but not necessarily the form, of courtship displays. In intensively managed livestock systems, animals that mate quickly with few precopulatory courtship displays may have been selected as the preferred behavioral phenotype. Thus, over time, courtship displays have become less pronounced in many domesticated species.

Mating Systems

Ecological and evolutionary considerations, such as the availability of food resources and unequal investment by the sexes in offspring, underlie differences in the mating systems employed by most species. Mating systems include promiscuity, polygamy (either polygyny or polyandry), and monogamy. These systems can manifest themselves in a simultaneous or serial manner, and can be expressed annually or seasonally. Farm animals are typically promiscuous or polygynous. Promiscuous animals have no exclusive breeding rights over any other individual. Typically, much copulation occurs during periods of female receptivity, yet no pair bonds or

Encyclopedia of Animal Science
DOI: 10.1081/E-EAS 120019466

extended associations are formed. This is the mating system most commonly observed among cattle, sheep, goats, swine, and chickens. Some promiscuous species can also show simultaneous polygyny, in which the mating system may involve a male forming a bond with many females for variable periods. Simultaneous polygyny is typical of species in which the male forms harems, such as in horses. Mating systems in intensive confinement may differ from those in a more natural environment due to housing and management. Domestic fowl, for example, are really a polygynous species, but in intensive production systems the male is unable to maintain a harem, and the mating system becomes promiscuous instead. The promiscuous and polygynous mating systems of most livestock species served as a preadaptation that contributed to the success of domestication, because monogamy or other pair bond formation would likely have hindered animal breeding programs.

SEXUAL PERFORMANCE, MOTIVATION, AND STIMULATION OF MALES

Within a species, motor patterns associated with courtship and copulation are species-specific and relatively invariant, although the sequence of behaviors exhibited varies within and among individuals. Large variation in the frequency or intensity of displays of sexual behavior does occur in farm animals and is likely due to relaxation of natural selection.[2,3] For example, single-sire mating systems enable animals with poor sexual performance to produce large numbers of offspring. This would not occur normally in wild animals, because competition among males would continue to exert intense selective pressure for high sexual performance. The number of males displaying inadequate sexual performance is significant, and this lack of performance has direct economic consequences.

This variation in sexual performance has contributed to the need for animal scientists and producers to develop tests of sexual behavior in males. With animal agriculture the need still exists for males that express high levels of sexual activity. This is true for those used for semen collection and for those used for natural service. In natural breeding systems, males with high sexual performance and a combination of high sexual motivation and superior endurance, strength, and coordination will likely breed more females early in the breeding season. Males with lower sexual motivation and/or low sexual performance will inseminate fewer females, thus either reducing herd production or extending the breeding season, as more estrous cycles will be required to impregnate the group. Sexual performance tests, also referred to as serving capacity tests, have been developed to identify and select high performers and to cull low performers.[3–5] These tests measure copulation frequency within a short period, but they are inconsistent in predicting either field reproductive performance or how well young males will perform when they are mature. High sexual performance depends on a male having high motivation to mate and also possessing the physical ability to do so. Low sexual performance may be caused by low sexual motivation, or by physical attributes such as poor structural conformation or genital abnormalities.[3] Current tests identify physical limitations but not necessarily motivational ones. New behavior tests to measure sexual motivation in farm animals are necessary to develop better behavioral tools for assessing reproductive performance and thus enhance animal productivity.

Research on the sexual performance of males has yielded interesting findings that remind us that the domesticated animal is a social animal with species-typical perceptual abilities and responses. Providing sexual arousal for males improves the efficiency of sexual performance tests. Male pigs, horses, goats, and cattle—but not sheep—are sexually stimulated by the opportunity to view estrous females or other sexual activity. Male sheep are aroused, however, when exposed to other male sheep that have either recently mated or recently contacted estrous females.[6] Promiscuous farm species, if given the opportunity, will form social systems consisting of groups of mature females with their offspring, bands of juvenile males, and individual adult males. Cows and female goats, respectively, will engage in female-to-female sexual activity. This activity provides a visual signal that attracts and arouses the males. In contrast, estrual sheep do not form groups of mounting females. Instead, female sheep seek the male. Thus the selective forces shaping the development of arousal mechanisms differ among farm species.

FEMALE ATTRACTIVITY, PROCEPTIVITY, AND RECEPTIVITY

Artificial insemination requires that humans, in lieu of conspecific males, detect estrus in females.[7] However, developing techniques to regulate timing of ovulation and artificial insemination might eliminate the need for managers to detect estrus in females in the near future.[8] Nevertheless, understanding the ethology and physiology of female sexual and social behavior can improve female fertility, health, and welfare. Attractivity, proceptivity, and receptivity are three components of female sexual behavior that have been defined.[9] Attractivity refers to the stimulus value of the female. It is measured by observing the behaviors performed by the male that are directed toward the female. Proceptivity includes behaviors performed by the female that bring the male into closer proximity and maintain his proximity and sexual motivation in order for mating to occur. Finally, receptivity describes the behaviors and postures exhibited by a female that allow successful intromission and intravaginal ejaculation to occur. Production demands and housing systems can interfere with the expression of female reproductive behavior. Studies aimed at learning how physiological and environmental signals are integrated could improve reproductive performance.[10]

CONCLUSION

Ethology is the field of study that describes animal behavior and attempts to understand an animal's continuous interaction with its environment. Natural selection affected the ancestors of domesticated livestock and continues to operate on farmed species. In addition, artificial selection and its correlated unintended selective pressures influence genotypic and phenotypic variations in behavior. Studies of reproductive behavior that can aid in the identification of high-performing males and females will contribute to improved animal fertility and productivity.

ARTICLES OF FURTHER INTEREST

Environment: Accommodations for Animals, p. 332

REFERENCES

1. Hafez, E.S.E. *The Behaviour of Domestic Animals*; Bailliere, Tindall & Cassell: London, 1969.
2. Price, E.O. Behavioral aspects of animal domestication. Q. Rev. Biol. **1984**, *59* (1), 1–33.
3. Price, E.O. Sexual behavior of large domestic farm animals: An overview. J. Anim. Sci. **1985**, *61* (Suppl. 3), 62–74.
4. Blockey, M.A. deB. Serving capacity—A measure of the serving efficiency of bulls during pasture mating. Theriogenology **1976**, *6* (4), 393–398.
5. Chenowith, P.J. Libido and mating behavior in bulls, boars and rams: A review. Theriogenology **1981**, *16* (2), 155–177.
6. Maina, D.; Katz, L.S. Scent of a ewe: Transmission of a social cue by conspecifics affects sexual performance in male sheep. Biol. Reprod. **1999**, *60* (6), 1373–1377.
7. Foote, R.H. Estrus detection and estrus detection aids. J. Dairy Sci. **1975**, *58* (2), 248–256.
8. Schmitt, E.J.P.; Diaz, T.; Drost, M.; Thatcher, W.W. Use of a gonadotropin-releasing hormone agonist or human chorionic gonadotropin for timed insemination in cattle. J. Anim. Sci. **1996**, *74* (5), 1084–1091.
9. Beach, F.A. Sexual attractivity, proceptivity, and receptivity in female mammals. Horm. Behav. **1976**, *7* (1), 105–138.
10. Katz, L.S.; McDonald, T.J. Sexual behavior of farm animals. Theriogenology **1992**, *38* (2), 239–253.

Beta Adrenergic Agonists

David B. Anderson (Retired)
Elanco Animal Health, Greenfield, Indiana, U.S.A.

Diane E. Moody
Purdue University, West Lafayette, Indiana, U.S.A.

Deana L. Hancock
Elanco Animal Health, Greenfield, Indiana, U.S.A.

INTRODUCTION

Beta adrenergic agonists (β-agonists, repartitioning agents) have been studied in livestock species for more than two decades for their effects as lean efficiency enhancing agents. Work began at several pharmaceutical laboratories in the late 1970s. Patents were issued and initial reports were made in the mid-1980s.[1–3] More recently, data have been generated to meet registration requirements, define the physiological effects, and define parameters needed to optimize responses. Two compounds have regulatory approval to be used in livestock. Zilpaterol is approved for cattle in South Africa and Mexico (Intervet), and ractopamine is approved for use in swine in 21 countries including the United States and for use in cattle in the United States (Elanco Animal Health). Several reviews of β-agonist use in livestock have been published. Anderson et al.[4] provide an extensive review with over 360 citations, Moloney et al.[5] provide an especially complete summarization of efficacy for various compounds, and an updated review of mechanism of action is provided by Mersmann[6] and Moody et al.[7]

β-AGONIST LEAN EFFICIENCY ENHANCING AGENTS

The compounds most commonly studied include: cimaterol, clenbuterol, L-644,969, ractopamine, salbutamol, and zilpaterol (Fig. 1). They are orally active and administered as feed ingredients. They belong to a class of compounds called phenethanolamines. This class of compounds has been used safely and effectively in human medicine for more than 30 years as bronchodilators for asthma treatment, uterine relaxants to treat pregnant women to arrest premature labor, and cardiostimulants to treat cardiac irregularities.[8] The compounds that have been studied for their effects on lean efficiency (Fig. 1) have demonstrated effects on the metabolism of fat and muscle in livestock species. They have no antibiotic activity and, therefore, are not acting as antibiotic growth promoters, nor are they anabolic steroids.

SUMMARY OF EFFICACY

β-agonist lean efficiency enhancing agents are often referred to as repartitioning agents because of their ability to redirect nutrients away from adipose tissue and toward muscle.[9] In general, the effects of β-agonists are improved feed utilization efficiency, increased leanness, increased dressing percentage (carcass weight/live weight), and increased rate of weight gain. These effects have been demonstrated in lambs, broilers, turkeys, beef cattle, and swine.[4] Several factors including diet, dosage and duration of treatment, age, weight, and genetics have been shown to influence the response to β-agonists (Table 1) and are important to the successful implementation of β-agonists to livestock.

HOW β-AGONISTS WORK

β-agonists specifically enhance the growth of muscle and give a small reduction in the growth of fat. β-agonists' effects are mediated by modifying specific metabolic signals in muscle and fat cells with a resulting increase in nutrients directed toward lean growth. Directing nutrients to tissues of highest priority is a normal metabolic process. This nutritive flow takes place as an ongoing hourly, daily, and weekly adjustment directed by internal body signals. In young growing pigs, more energy is directed toward lean than fat; however, in more mature, heavier pigs, a larger proportion of energy is directed toward fat. β-agonists modify the metabolic signals within muscle and fat cells to direct more nutrients to lean growth (Fig. 2).

The binding of β-agonists with specific receptors on the surface of muscle and fat cells (β-adrenergic receptors) generates these signals. When β-agonists bind

Encyclopedia of Animal Science
DOI: 10.1081/E-EAS 120019468

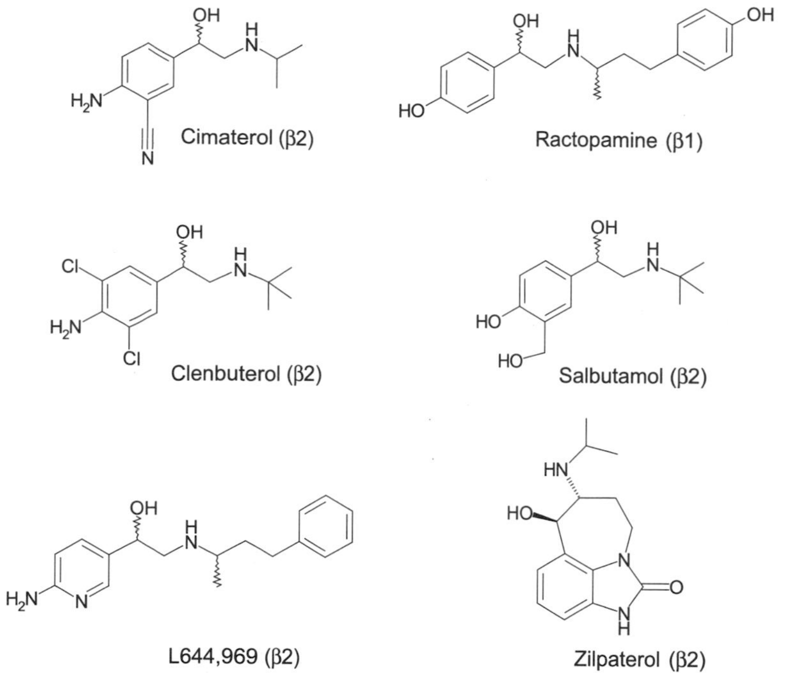

Fig. 1 Structure of several phenethanolamines evaluated as leanness enhancers in livestock. Current classifications of receptor subtype selectivity (β1 or β2 adrenergic receptor) are indicated.

to these receptors on the surface of the fat cell, biochemical signals are produced inside the cell that decrease fat synthesis and increase fat degradation, resulting in a slower rate of fat deposition. In muscle cells, the outcome of the internal signaling is a substantial increase in the rate of muscle protein synthesis and deposition. As a result, muscle synthesis is faster and fat synthesis is slower. Because it takes only half the energy to deposit lean compared to fat, the outcome is a leaner animal that utilizes feed more efficiently. Because this effect is primarily on muscle in the carcass, dressing percentage is increased.

A more detailed description of the proposed mechanism by which β-agonists affect muscle and fat cell synthesis through interaction with β-adrenergic receptors on the surface of muscle and fat cells is shown in Fig. 3. Activation of β-adrenergic receptors is coupled to Gs proteins and activation of adenyl cyclase (AC), which converts adenosine triphosphate (ATP) to cyclic adenosine monophosphate (cAMP), an intracellular signaling

Table 1 Factors that influence response to treatment with β-agonists

Factor	Requirement	Compounds studied	Species studied
Dietary protein	Greater response with higher dietary protein	Clenbuterol BRL47672 Ractopamine	Pigs, broilers, rats
Duration of treatment	Greater response during final finishing phase	Cimaterol Clenbuterol L-644969 Ractopamine	Pigs, cattle, sheep
Dosage	Differential effect on growth and leanness	Ractopamine	Pigs
Age or weight	Greater response with older, heavier animals	Cimaterol Ractopamine	Pigs, cattle
Genetics	Effective in both fat and lean genetics	Cimaterol Ractopamine	Pigs, mice

(From Ref. [7].)

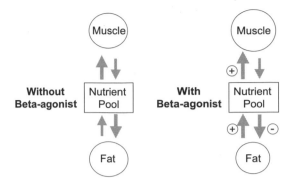

Fig. 2 β-agonists modify the metabolic signals in muscle and fat cell to enhance the rate of lean (muscle) growth.

Table 2 Effect of β-agonists on myofiber diameter in swine

	Paylean treatment (ppm)	
	0	20
Number of animals	23	22
Red, μ^2	2,480	2,564
Intermediate, μ^2	1,783	2,216[a]
White, μ^2	3,467	4,048[a]

[a]Significantly different from control (P<0.05).
(From Ref. [10].)

molecule. The cAMP binds to the regulatory subunit of protein kinase A (PKA) to release its catalytic subunit. Regulation of intracellular enzymes is then accomplished through phosphorylation by protein kinase A. Activation of β-adrenergic receptors and the cAMP signaling pathway by β-agonists results in the activation of rate-limiting enzymes in lipolysis and inactivation of lipogenic enzymes involved in de novo synthesis of fatty acids and triglycerides.[7]

The effects of β-agonists on muscle result in muscle cell hypertrophy (Table 2) and increased lean mass. This effect is generally attributed to activation of the β-adrenergic receptor pathway. The outcome of the intracellular signaling in muscle is an increase in the abundance of total RNA and mRNA for myofibrillar proteins, which is reflected in an increase in the fractional rate of protein synthesis in vivo. Results from these studies support the hypotheses that protein synthesis is substantially enhanced and that β-agonists do not affect protein degradation in muscle.[7]

SAFETY ISSUES

The β-agonist clenbuterol was the subject of considerable negative publicity in the early 1990s when its illegal use was linked to cases of acute food poisoning in Europe.[11] Clenbuterol was initially designed with a long half-life as a pharmaceutical medicine used in treatment of respiratory and other diseases, and the desired properties of such medicines are totally opposite to what is required for a feed ingredient. Later generation β-agonists were developed with structural differences that resulted in shorter

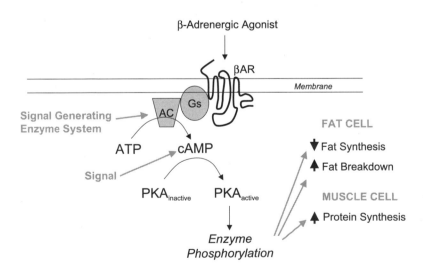

Fig. 3 Mechanism of signal transduction from β adrenergic receptors (βAR). The β adrenergic receptor is activated by an agonist and interacts with Gs proteins. The Gs proteins stimulate adenylyl cyclase (AC) to convert adenosine triphosphate (ATP) to cyclic adenosine monophosphate (cAMP), which acts as an intracellular signaling molecule. Increased levels of cAMP activate protein kinase A (PKA) to phosphorylate many enzymes and regulatory factors important in metabolic regulation. (From Ref. [7].)

half-lives and lower oral potencies allowing safe development for use in livestock.[12] Therefore, the problems that arose from the illegal treatment of animals with clenbuterol are no longer problems with current β-agonists. Any approved β-agonists' lean efficiency enhancer must meet or exceed stringent human food safety standards.

CONCLUSIONS

β-agonists that have been approved as feed ingredients for livestock feeds have been shown to benefit the producer, the packer, the processor, the consumer, and the environment.[4–7] The development and use of β-agonists have the potential to impact all aspects of the meat and livestock industries. Producers will be able to raise livestock more efficiently, meat packers will have higher-yielding carcasses, and meat processors will have the opportunity to more efficiently develop new low-fat meat products.[7] In addition, consumers will benefit from products with reduced cholesterol[13] and reduced calories. Finally, the use of β-agonist lean enhancing agents will provide environmental benefits. Less land will be required to produce the feedstuffs needed for the meat that is consumed, and the greater nitrogen retention in the animal for lean tissue growth will result in less nitrogen excreted as waste.[14] β-agonist lean enhancing agents that are demonstrated to be safe and efficacious will provide the meat industry with a powerful tool to aid in the production of health-conscious meat products.

REFERENCES

1. Asato, G.; Baker, P.K.; Bass, R.T.; Bentley, T.J.; Chari, S.; Dalrymple, R.H.; France, D.J.; Gingher, P.E.; Lences, B.L.; Pascavage, J.J.; Pensack, J.M.; Ricks, C.A. Repartitioning agents, 5-[1-hydroxy-2(isopropylamino)ethyl]-anthranilonitrile and related phenethanolamines, agents for promoting growth, increasing muscle accretion and reducing fat deposition in meat-producing animals. Agric. Biol. Chem. **1984**, *48*, 2883–2888.
2. Convey, E.M.; Rickes, E.; Yang, Y.T.; McElligot, M.A.; Olson, G. Effects of the beta-adrenergic agonist L-644,969 on growth performance, carcass merit and meat quality. Proc. Recip. Meat Conf. **1987**, *40*, 47–55.
3. Veenhuizen, E.L.; Schmiegel, K.K.; Waitt, W.P.; Anderson, D.B. Lipolytic, growth, feed efficiency and carcass responses to phenethanolamines in swine. J. Anim. Sci. **1987**, *65* (Suppl. 1), 130.
4. Anderson, D.B.; Veenhuizen, E.L.; Schroeder, A.L.; Jones, D.J.; Hancock, D.L. The Use of Phenethanolamines to Reduce Fat and Increase Leanness in Meat Animals. Proceedings of Symposium on Fat and Cholesterol Reduced Foods—Advances in Applied Biotechnology Series; Portfolio Publishing Company: New Orleans, 1991; 43–73.
5. Moloney, A.; Allen, P.; Joseph, R.; Tarrant, V. Influence of Beta-Adrenergic Agonists and Similar Compounds on Growth. In *Growth Regulation in Farm Animals*; Pearson, A.M., Dutson, T.R., Eds.; Elsevier: New York, 1991; 455–513.
6. Mersmann, H.J. Overview of the effects of beta-adrenergic receptor agonists on animal growth including mechanisms of action. J. Anim. Sci. **1998**, *76*, 160–172.
7. Moody, D.E.; Hancock, D.L.; Anderson, D.B. Chapter 4. Phenethanolamine Repartitioning Agents. In *Farm Animal Metabolism and Nutrition: Critical Reviews*; D'Mello, J.P.F., Ed.; CAB International: WallingfordOxon, UK, 2000; 65–96.
8. Hoffman, B.B.; Lefkowitz, R.J. Catecholamines, Sympathomimetic Drugs, and Adrenergic Receptor Antagonists. In *Goodman and Gilman's: The Pharmacological Basis of Therapeutics*; Hardman, J.G., Limbird, L.E., Eds.; McGraw-Hill: New York, 1996; 100–248.
9. Ricks, C.A.; Baker, P.K.; Dalrymple, R.H. Use of repartitioning agents to improve performance and body composition of meat animals. Proc. Recip. Meat Conf. **1984**, *37*, 5–11.
10. Aalhus, J.L.; Schaefer, A.L.; Murray, A.C.; Jones, S.D.M. The effect of ractopamine on myofibre distribution and morphology and their relation to meat quality in swine. Meat Sci. **1992**, *31*, 397–409.
11. Kuiper, H.A.; Noordam, M.Y.; van Dooren-Flipsen, M.M.; Schilt, R.; Roos, A.H. Illegal use of beta-adrenergic agonists: European community. J. Anim. Sci. **1998**, *76*, 195–207.
12. Smith, D.J. The pharmacokinetics, metabolism and tissue residues of beta-adrenergic agonists in livestock. J. Anim. Sci. **1998**, *76*, 173–194.
13. Perkins, E.G.; McKeith, F.K.; Jones, D.J.; Mowrey, D.H.; Hill, S.E.; Novakofski, J.; O'Connor, P.L. Fatty acid and cholesterol changes in pork longissimus muscle and fat due to ractopamine. J. Food Sci. **1992**, *57*, 1266–1268.
14. Carroll, A.L.; Anderson, D.B.; Elam, T.E.; Sutton, A.L. *Environmental Benefits of Paylean in Finisher Swine: An Example Based on Adoption in the United States*; Purdue Extension Publication AS-551-W, 2001; 1–6. http://www.ces.purdue.edu/extmedia/AS/AS-551-W.pdf.

Bioavailability: Amino Acids

Charles M. Nyachoti
University of Manitoba, Winnipeg, Manitoba, Canada

Hans H. Stein
South Dakota State University, Brookings, South Dakota, U.S.A.

INTRODUCTION

The main goal in formulating animal feeds is to supply nutrients in amounts and relative proportions that optimize performance. This is particularly important with respect to amino acids (AAs), as the feed ingredients used to supply AA are often expensive. Furthermore, any AA supplied in excess is deaminated and the resulting nitrogen excreted, thus posing a potential environmental problem. Because animals do not store excess AAs in the body, the exact needs for protein synthesis need to be supplied each day. Therefore, the AA requirements of the animal and the dietary concentration of AAs need to be known. However, availability of AAs in many feedstuffs is not known, and thus, digestibility measurements are used as reasonable estimates of availability. This article covers aspects of bioavailability of AAs in feed ingredients with particular emphasis on pig nutrition. The determination of AA digestibility coefficients and the application to estimate bioavailability are discussed.

DIETARY SUPPLY OF AMINO ACIDS

Bound protein in feedstuffs and pure forms of crystalline AA supply AAs in pig diets. Crystalline AAs are assumed to be completely absorbed from the gut and utilized by the animal. In contrast, animals are only able to utilize a portion of the AAs contained in bound protein for metabolic functions. Therefore, the total amount of AAs in a diet is not equal to the amount of AAs that are available to the animal for metabolic functions. As a consequence, estimates of bioavailability of dietary AAs are used in formulating swine diets to match the supply with requirements.

The Concept of Bioavailability

The bioavailability of an AA refers to the proportion of that AA that is in a form that can be digested, absorbed, and used for metabolic functions.[1] Bioavailability coefficients of AAs in feedstuffs are determined in slope ratio growth assays. These assays are laborious and time consuming and only allow determination of the bioavailability of a single AA at a time, which is costly. Consequently, there are only a limited number of ingredients and AAs for which bioavailability coefficients have been determined and such coefficients of AA are not routinely used in feed formulation.

The use of bioavailability coefficients is important for heat-processed or long-stored ingredients because of the negative impact of these treatments on the bioavailability of the AA lysine. Lysine is rendered biologically unavailable by complexing with reducing compounds in the feed.

There are considerable efforts to develop simpler methods for estimating AA bioavailability in feedstuffs. A method known as the reactive lysine technique for assessing the bioavailability of lysine in feedstuffs that have undergone heat processing or that have been stored for a long time under conditions that might compromise lysine availability has been proposed.[2] A method for determining the so-called metabolic availability of AAs in feed ingredients has also been developed.[3] Thus far, this method has been used to estimate the metabolic availability (i.e., the proportion that is used for body protein synthesis) of lysine in a small number of ingredients and there are still several questions that must be addressed before it can find use in routine assessment of AA bioavailability in feedstuffs.

The Concept of Digestibility

Digestibility is a measure of the disappearance of a nutrient from the digestive tract and is assumed to equate the degree of absorption of the nutrient from the gut lumen. Digestibility measurements do not provide any indication of the fate of the absorbed nutrient, but they are used as a reasonable estimate of AA availability.[4]

Amino acid digestibility

Ileal AA digestibility coefficients provide better estimates of AA availability in swine feed ingredients than faecal

Encyclopedia of Animal Science
DOI: 10.1081/E-EAS 120019469

Table 1 Techniques used in collecting ileal digesta from pigs

Cannulation techniques
   Simple T-cannula
   Post-valve T-cannula (PVTC)
   Steered ileal-caecal valve cannula
   Re-entrant cannula
Isolation of the large bowel
   Ileo-rectal anastomosis
   Ileostomy
Slaughter and ileal dissection

digestibility coefficients[4] because AAs that disappear from the hindgut are not available to the animal. The measurement of ileal AA digestibility coefficients requires sampling of digesta at the distal ileum. Techniques used for this purpose have been reviewed in detail.[5] The techniques can be grouped into three main categories, namely those that involve cannulation, isolation of the large bowel, and slaughter of the animal (Table 1). Each of these techniques has limitations that create specific challenges in their use as discussed elsewhere.[5]

Estimating Bioavailable Amino Acid Content in Feedstuffs

Apparent ileal digestibility coefficients

In conventional digestibility studies, it is not possible to distinguish between nondigested dietary AAs and non-reabsorbed endogenous AAs that are present in the digesta captured at the distal ileum. Calculated digestibility coefficients are, therefore, referred to as apparent digestibility coefficients. However, apparent ileal digestibility coefficients of AAs in a mixed diet may underestimate the amount of AAs that are actually available to the pig. This is particularly true if low-protein feed ingredients such as cereal grains are included in the diet.[6] The reason for this underestimation is that apparent ileal digestibility coefficients may not be additive in a mixture of feed ingredients (Fig. 1), thus creating challenges in accurately formulating diets to supply the desired amount of AAs in the diet. The use of digestibility coefficients to estimate bioavailability is improved considerably when apparent ileal digestibility coefficients are corrected for endogenous gut AA losses. For a complete review of endogenous gut AA losses in pigs and the methods used for their estimation, please refer to Nyachoti et al.[5] and Boisen and Moughan.[7] Endogenous gut AA losses can be divided into two categories, namely, basal (diet-independent) losses and

diet-specific (additional) losses. Basal endogenous AA losses are obligatory losses closely associated with the metabolic functions of the animal and are independent of the type of diet fed. Specific endogenous AA losses are dependent on the composition of the diet.

Standardized ileal amino acid digestibility coefficients

Standardized ileal AA digestibility coefficients, which are sometimes incorrectly referred to as true ileal digestibility coefficients, are derived by correcting apparent ileal digestibility coefficients for basal endogenous AA losses.[8] Compared with apparent digestibility coefficients, standardized ileal digestibility coefficients are believed to provide a better estimate of AA bioavailability in pig feeds. It is important, however, to recognize that estimates of basal endogenous AA losses vary widely among studies and that there is no general agreement on the best estimate of basal endogenous AA losses.[7]

True ileal amino acid digestibility coefficients

True ileal AA digestibility coefficients are estimated when the recovery of specific endogenous AAs in the ileal digesta is determined and used to correct apparent digestibility coefficients. This requires that the specific endogenous gut AA losses in ileal digesta be quantified. The required techniques are relatively tedious, thus making it more difficult to generate true ileal digestibility coefficients for routine feed formulation. However, when the goal is to understand how different feed ingredients or dietary components influence AA utilization in pigs, true ileal digestibility coefficients should be determined.

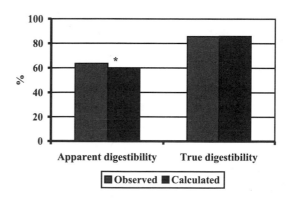

Fig. 1 Observed and calculated apparent and true ileal lysine digestibilities in a barley-canola meal-based diet fed to growing pigs. (Adapted from Ref. [9].) (*View this art in color at www. dekker.com.*)

Effects of gut microbes on estimation of amino acid digestibility

Although the majority of the gut microflora in monogastric animals reside in the hindgut, a large microbial population also inhabits the upper gut (i.e., small intestine). Gut microbes may deaminate dietary AAs or synthesize new AAs. This will influence the digestibility measurements. The significance of such an effect on determining ileal AA digestibility coefficients is not known yet and deserves further attention.

CONCLUSION

Formulating pig diets to closely match the supply of AAs with the AA requirements of the animals presents a significant economic benefit and helps minimize nitrogen excretion in pig manure, thus reducing the environmental impact of livestock production on the environment. To achieve this goal, knowledge of the bioavailability of AAs in pig feed ingredients is required. Due to the difficulties involved in determining the content of bioavailable AAs in feedstuffs on a routine basis, ileal digestible AAs are used. To this end, it is recommended to use standardized ileal digestible AA coefficients as estimates of bioavailable AA. Such values should be determined for the specific feeding situation. Continued efforts to develop and/or refine current methods for determining bioavailability of AAs for routine application are warranted.

REFERENCES

1. Batterham, E.S. Availability and utilization of amino acids for growing pigs. Nutr. Res. Rev. **1992**, *5* (1), 1–18.
2. Moughan, P.J.; Rutherfurd, S.M. A new method for determining digestible reactive lysine in foods. J. Agric. Food Chem. **1997**, *45* (4), 1189–1194.
3. Ball, R.O. *Definition of Amino Acid Requirements in Pigs: Partitioning between Gut and Muscle*; Canadian Society of Animal Science—SCSA: Quebec City, Canada, July 21 2002; 17–25.
4. Sauer, W.C.; Ozimek, L. Digestibility of amino acids in swine: Results and their practical applications. A review. Livest. Prod. Sci. **1986**, *15* (4), 367–388.
5. Nyachoti, C.M.; de Lange, C.F.M.; McBride, B.W.; Schulze, H. Significance of endogenous gut protein losses in the nutrition of growing pigs: A review. Can. J. Anim. Sci. **1997a**, *77* (1), 149–163.
6. Fan, M.Z.; Sauer, W.C.; Hardin, R.T.; Lien, K.A. Determination of apparent ileal amino acid digestibility in pigs: Effect of dietary amino acid level. J. Anim. Sci. **1994**, *72* (11), 2851–2859.
7. Boisen, S.; Moughan, P.J. Dietary influences on endogenous ileal protein and amino acid loss in the pig—A review. Acta Agric. Scand., A Anim. Sci. **1996**, *46* (2), 154–164.
8. Stein, H.H.; Kim, S.W.; Nielsen, T.T.; Easter, R.A. Standardized amino acid digestibilities in growing pigs and sows. J. Anim. Sci. **2001**, *79* (8), 2113–2122.
9. Nyachoti, C.M.; de Lange, C.F.M.; Schulze, H. Estimating endogenous amino acid flows at the terminal ileum and true ileal amino acid digestibilities in feedstuffs for growing pigs using the homoarginine method. J. Anim. Sci. **1997b**, *75* (12), 3206–3213.

Bioavailability: Energy

C. L. Ferrell
United States Department of Agriculture, Agricultural Research Service,
Clay Center, Nebraska, U.S.A.

INTRODUCTION

Energy is defined as the potential to perform work and is required by the animal to perform the "work of living." Some of the more obvious examples of the expenses of living include thermoregulation, voluntary and involuntary muscular activity, ingestion of food, digestion, absorption, excretion, metabolite transport, cell turnover, tissue or product formation (e.g., wool, milk, eggs), etc. There are inefficiencies or waste associated with all of these processes. Energy requirements depend on the additive needs of individual cells, which vary according to physiological needs imposed upon them. Gross dietary requirement is the sum of all cellular needs plus losses. Bioavailability of energy is an expression of the value of an energy source toward meeting the cumulative energy needs of all cells to perform the "work of living" of the animal.

Energy is an abstraction that can only be measured in its transformation from one form to another. Bioenergetics, the study of energy transformations in biological systems, is based on the fundamental principles stated by the laws of thermodynamics and the law of Hess. Simply stated, these laws assert that: 1) energy can be neither created nor destroyed, but may be converted from one form to another, 2) all forms of energy can be quantitatively converted to heat, and 3) heat generated in a net transformation is independent of the path of conversion. Energy is available to the animal from three sources: diet, body reserves, and to some extent, from its external environment (via radiation, convection, and conduction). This article will concentrate primarily on energy availability from dietary sources and, to a lesser extent, from body tissues.

PARTITION OF DIETARY ENERGY

A generalized flow of energy in the animal is shown in Fig. 1. Briefly, heat of combustion of food consumed is termed intake energy (IE). A substantial 20–80% of the food energy consumed is voided from the animal as fecal energy (FE) and the difference (IE−FE) is termed apparently digested energy (DE). Portions of IE are also lost as combustible gaseous energy (GE) and as urinary energy (UE). The remainder (IE−FE−GE−UE) is termed metabolizable energy (ME). ME may be recovered (RE) as product such as tissue (TE), milk (LE), conceptus (YE), egg or ovum (OE), wool or hair (VE), etc., or may be transferred to the environment as heat (HE). Heat energy may be the result of a variety of functions including digestion and absorption (H_dE), fermentation (H_fE), waste formation and excretion (H_wE), basal metabolism (H_eE), activity (H_jE), thermal regulation (H_cE), and product formation (H_rE). An increase in heat production following feeding is termed heat increment (H_iE) and includes increases in H_dE, H_fE, H_wE, and H_rE. This scheme may be summarized by the equation: IE = FE + UE + GE + HE + RE. This identity partitions the food energy into the major components associated with animal energetics. It may be expanded to include a few or many of the intermediate steps involved, and each component can be divided into component parts. The inclusion or exclusion of intermediate transformations does not prejudice the balance of the equation. All energy balance techniques and all systems of expressing relationships between the animal's requirements and the usefulness of a food to supply those needs are related to this classical energy balance identity (see Ref. [1]).

GROSS ENERGY

The gross energy content or total energy contained in dry feed (IE) varies depending on the carbohydrate, protein, lipid, and mineral content, but is of little value in assessing the value of a diet or dietary component as a source of energy for the animal. For example, starch and cellulose, both polymers of glucose, have similar heats of combustion. Starch is readily digested by most mammalian species, eventually to glucose. In contrast, cellulose is not attacked by mammalian digestive enzymes, and thus does not provide energy substrates to animals such as humans. In contrast, starch or cellulose may be digested in animals having pregastric microbial fermentation (e.g., ruminants) by amylolytic and cellulolytic microbes, resulting in the production of volatile fatty acids (VFA), CH_4, water, and CO_2, but the patterns of VFA and

Encyclopedia of Animal Science
DOI: 10.1081/E-EAS 120019470

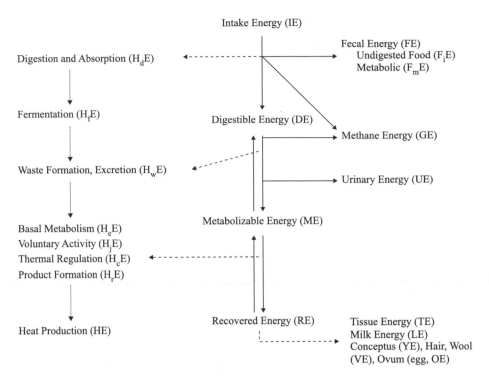

Fig. 1 Schematic partition of energy in the animal.

quantities produced differ.[2] Starch and cellulose may also be digested in animals having a postgastric fermentation (e.g., horse, rabbit), such that much of the starch is digested and absorbed in the stomach and small intestine. Some starch, as well as the cellulose, is digested by microbial fermentation in the cecum and large intestine, but availability of the VFAs produced is reduced compared to the ruminant.

DIGESTIBLE ENERGY

Digestible energy is defined as intake energy minus fecal energy (DE = IE − FE). The word ''apparent'' is often associated with this definition, which acknowledges that FE includes materials of metabolic (F_mE) as well as of food (F_iE) origin. There are additional losses of energy associated with the digestion of food that are not included in the conventional determination of DE. These losses include methane (GE), heat of fermentation (H_fE), and heat of digestion and absorption (H_dE). ''True'' digestibility, which attempts to account for those additional losses, is greater than estimated by apparent digestibility for most feeds.

Fecal energy represents a major loss of dietary energy. In herbivores that consume a wide variety of diets, FE varies from 15–20% of dietary intake on a high grain diet

to about 80% of intake on a low-quality forage diet. The primary determinants of FE, hence DE, are the physical and chemical characteristics of the food consumed, both of which may be influenced extensively by processing. These characteristics influence the site of digestion, rate and extent of digestion, and the amounts and proportions of products available for absorption. Total tract digestibility, as measured in most digestion studies, considers only total disappearance, and may not reflect the nature of the products absorbed from the gut. Site and rate of digestion, as well as total tract digestibility of dietary energy may differ among animals due to species, age, breed, intake level, and temperature. For species of animals or feeding situations in which a relatively few dietary ingredients are used and the animals' dietary requirements have been determined using similar feeds, levels of intake and animal production, DE may be a satisfactory method of assessing energy available to the animal. Digestible energy has been used extensively as the basis to formulate diets and estimate the energy requirements of swine, as well as other species. However, for ruminants, a major weakness is that DE overvalues high-fiber (hays, straws) in relation to low-fiber (grains) feedstuffs. A substantial portion of this discrepancy may be attributable to energy losses unaccounted for by apparent digestibility and to differences in digestive end-products.

METABOLIZABLE ENERGY

Metabolizable energy (ME) is an estimate of the dietary energy available for metabolism by the tissues of the animal and is defined by the relationship: ME=IE − (FE+UE+GE). Metabolizable energy is an improvement over DE for use as a measure of energy available to the animal and animal requirements because it incorporates urinary and gaseous losses, but has some of the same limitations as DE. The total digestible nutrient (TDN) system of feed evaluation accounts for the higher energy concentration of lipids by multiplying digested lipid by 2.25, but does not incorporate a similar correction for protein. As a result, TDN is a hybrid measure (not precisely DE or ME) that maintains many of the limitations of DE. Physiological fuel values (PFV) are essentially ME values derived by the use of average heats of combustion and average digestion coefficients for protein, fat, and carbohydrates, with values for protein corrected for urinary nitrogen loss. The physiological fuel values commonly quoted (4, 4, and 9 kcal/g of protein, carbohydrate, and fat) may give reasonable estimates of ME and have long served as the basis to formulate diets and express requirements of humans. Metabolizable energy has major significance as a reference unit and as a starting point for nearly all systems that are based on the net energy concept.

NET ENERGY

The equations and energy balance identity indicate that ME can appear in only two forms: heat (HE) or in formed products (RE). Thus, ME = HE + RE. Total heat production (HE) includes all energy that is transferred from the animal to the environment in a form other than combustible energy. Recovered energy (RE) is the heat of combustion of all animal products (TE, LE, YE, OE, VE, etc.) that may be produced or lost with a given energy intake not accounted for in any other category. It is evident that if two of the three terms in the previous equation are measured, the third may be obtained by difference. Thus, by measurement of ME and HE (as done in indirect or direct calorimetry) RE may be determined, or by measurement of ME and RE (as done by comparative slaughter approaches) HE can be determined.[3–5]

The general relationships between RE and HE to ME intake are shown in Fig. 2. At zero food intake, body tissues are metabolized to provide energy for necessary body functions. Fasting heat production (FHP) is the heat produced at zero food or ME intake and is about 70 kcal/kg$^{0.75}$/d. Estimates of FHP vary with animal age or maturity, physiological state, prior nutritional status, environmental adaptation, breed, gender, etc. As ME intake increases, dietary energy provides increasingly higher proportion of the required energy supply, and body tissues provide a lower proportion. The ME intake at which net recovered energy is zero, or HE is equal to ME intake, is termed maintenance. Maintenance is often considered to be a constant, but in actuality may vary substantially for numerous reasons. It is also important to note that maintenance refers to the whole system, whereas components of the system may not equal zero. For example, a lactating animal may have a net loss of body tissue in combination with milk production, with the sum of those processes resulting in zero RE.

Although the relationship between RE and ME intake is nonlinear over the full range of intake (as shown in Fig. 2), the relationship is usually approximated by two linear relationships, which intersect at maintenance. Efficiency of dietary energy use below maintenance is high, in part because its efficiency of use is relative to efficiency of use of body tissue energy. Estimates of the efficiency of use of body tissues for maintenance or milk production are typically 0.80 to 0.90, whereas typical estimates of efficiency of ME use below maintenance (k_m) are about 0.70, but vary depending on dietary source, environmental temperature, etc. Efficiency of ME use above maintenance for milk production (k_l) is similar to k_m, whereas efficiencies of use for accretion of body tissue (k_g; 0.40), conceptus development (k_p; 0.13), etc., are generally lower. Dietary differences, contributing to differences in metabolites available, and variation in functions for which those metabolites are used contribute

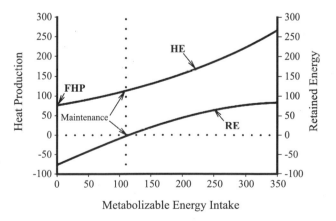

Fig. 2 Relation of heat production and retained energy to metabolizable energy intake.

to variation in efficiencies of ME use by the animal. Some of those issues have been reviewed.[5,6]

CONCLUSIONS

A brief synopsis of classical approaches for assessing the availability of energy for meeting the cumulative energy needs of all cells to perform the "work of living" of the animal has been presented. These concepts and approaches remain the standards on which animal requirements and the value of energy sources to meet those requirements are based. As knowledge of energy transactions in the animal increases, and systems to describe those transactions become more refined and complex, the classical notions of requirements and feed value become less clear. The classical separation of energy from other nutrients, such as amino acids, becomes more difficult to justify. Mathematical modeling approaches, such as those described by Baldwin,[1] are valuable to incorporate

knowledge of the entire system for describing animal needs and the value of energy sources to meet those needs.

REFERENCES

1. Baldwin, R.L. *Modeling Ruminant Digestion and Metabolism*; Chapman & Hall: New York, 1995.
2. Baldwin, R.L; Allison, M.J. Rumen metabolism. J. Anim. Sci. **1983**, *57* (Suppl. 2), 461–477.
3. ARC. *The Nutrient Requirements of Farm Livestock. No. 2 Ruminants*; Agricultural Research Council: London, 1965.
4. Lofgreen, G.P.; Garrett, W.N. A system for expressing the net energy requirements and feed values for growing and finishing cattle. J. Anim. Sci. **1968**, *27*, 793–806.
5. van Milgen, J.; Noblet, J. Partitioning of energy intake to heat, protein, and fat in growing pigs. J. Anim. Sci. **2003**, *81* (E. Suppl. 2), E86–E93.
6. Reynolds, C.K. Economics of visceral energy metabolism in ruminants: Toll keeping or internal revenue service? J. Anim. Sci. **2002**, *80* (E. Suppl. 2), E74–E84.

Bioavailability: Fat-Soluble Vitamins

David H. Baker
University of Illinois, Urbana, Illinois, U.S.A.

INTRODUCTION

Bioavailability of fat-soluble vitamins in their crystalline state or as they exist in foods and feeds is influenced by heat, moisture, oxidation, and trace minerals. These factors are reviewed in this article, and readers are referred to previous reviews for more detailed information on bioavailability of fat-soluble vitamins.

VITAMIN A

Vitamin nomenclature policy[1-3] dictates that the term "vitamin A" be used for all B-ionone derivatives, other than provitamin A carotenoids, exhibiting the biological activity of all-*trans* retinol (i.e., vitamin A alcohol or vitamin A_1). Esters of all-*trans* retinol should be referred to as retinyl esters.

Vitamin A is present in animal tissues, whereas most plant materials contain only provitamin A carotenoids, which must be split in the intestinal tract to form vitamin A. In blood, vitamin A is transported as retinol, but it is stored, primarily in the liver, as retinyl palmitate. Absorption efficiency of vitamin A is relatively constant over a wide range of doses, but higher doses of carotenoids are absorbed much less efficiently than lower doses.[4]

Vitamin A esters are more stable in feeds and premixes than retinol. The hydroxyl group as well as the four double bonds on the retinol side chain are subject to oxidative losses. Thus, esterification of vitamin A alcohol does not totally protect this vitamin from oxidative losses. Current commercial sources of vitamin A are generally "coated" esters (e.g., acetate or palmitate) that contain an added antioxidant such as ethoxyquin or butylated hyroxytoluene (BHT).

The water content of premixes and feedstuffs has a negative effect on vitamin A stability. Moisture causes vitamin A beadlets to soften and become more permeable to oxygen. Thus, both high humidity and the presence of free choline chloride (hygroscopic) enhance vitamin A destruction. Trace minerals also exacerbate vitamin A losses in premixes exposed to moisture. For maximum retention of vitamin A activity, premixes should be as moisture-free as possible and should be made to have a pH above 5. Low pH causes isomerization of all-*trans* vitamin A to less potent *cis* forms and also results in de-esterification of vitamin A esters to retinol. Likewise, heat processing, especially extrusion, can reduce vitamin A bioavailability.

Crystalline β-carotene is absorbed from the gut more efficiently than β-carotene existing in foods and feeds. Some of the β-carotene in foods is complexed with protein. Fiber components of feeds, especially pectins, have been shown to reduce β-carotene absorption from the gut in chicks.

Ullrey[5] reviewed the bioavailability aspects of vitamin A precursor materials for swine and reported that pigs were far less efficient than rats or chicks in converting carotenoid precursors to active vitamin A. Thus, bioefficacies (wt/wt) ranging from 7 to 14% were observed for corn carotenes in pigs relative to all-*trans* retinyl palmitate. Hence, carotenoid precursors in corn (also corn gluten meal) have no more than 261 IU/mg vitamin A activity when consumed by swine. This is decidedly less than the theoretical potency of 1667 IU/mg (assuming all the carotenoids are all-*trans*-β carotene), which is assumed for the rat.[3] Corn carotenoids consist of about 50% cryptoxanthin, 25% β-zeacarotene, and 25% β-carotene.

Quantification of vitamin A bioavailability is difficult. Accumulation of vitamin A in the liver may be the most acceptable method.[4]

VITAMIN D

The term "vitamin D" is appropriate for all steroids having cholecalciferol biological activity. Cholecalciferol itself is synonymous with vitamin D_3, as distinguished from ergocalciferol, which is also called vitamin D_2. Commercially, vitamin D_3 is available as a spray-dried product or (frequently in combination with vitamin A) as gelatin-coated beadlets; one international unit is equal to 0.025 µg of cholecalciferol.[3] These products are quite stable if stored as the vitamin itself at room temperature. In complete feeds and mineral-vitamin premixes, 4 to 6 mo. of storage may cause activity losses of up to 30%.[2]

Vitamin D precursors are present in plant (ergosterol) and animal (7-dehydrocholesterol) feedstuffs, but they

Encyclopedia of Animal Science
DOI: 10.1081/E-EAS 120019472

require ultraviolet irradiation for conversion into active D_2 and D_3, respectively. Vitamin D_3 has more biological activity than D_2. Hydroxylated forms of cholecalciferol [25-OH D_3, 1α-OH D_3, 1,25(OH)$_2$ D_3] contain more D_3 bioactivity than D_3 itself.

VITAMIN E

Vitamin E is the generic term for all tocol and tocotrienol derivatives having α-tocopherol biological activity. There are eight naturally occurring forms of vitamin E: α-, β-, γ-, and δ- tocopherols and α-, β-, γ-, and δ-tocotrienols. Among these, D-α-tocopherol possesses the greatest biological activity.[6] One international unit of vitamin E is the activity of 1 mg of DL-α-tocopheryl acetate. All racemic (i.e., DL-α-tocopherol) has about 70% of the activity of pure D-α-tocopherol. Bieri and McKenna[6] consider β-tocopherol and γ-tocopherol to have only 40 and 10% of the activity, respectively, of α-tocopherol (set at 100%). The only other natural form to possess activity is α-tocotrienol, which on the rating scale used above was estimated to contain a biopotency of 25%.

Vitamin E is subject to destruction by oxidation, and this process is accelerated by heat, moisture, unsaturated fat, and trace minerals. Losses of 50–70% have been observed to occur in alfalfa hay stored at 32°C for 12 wk; losses up to 30% have been known to occur during dehydration of alfalfa. Treatment of high-moisture grains with organic acids also greatly enhances vitamin E destruction. However, even mildly alkaline conditions of vitamin E storage are detrimental to vitamin E stability. Thus, finely ground limestone or MgO coming in direct contact with vitamin E can markedly reduce its bioavailability.

VITAMIN K

This fat-soluble vitamin exists in three series: phylloquinones (K_1) in plants, menaquinones (K_2) formed by microbial fermentation, and menadiones (K_3), which are synthetic. All three forms of vitamin K are biologically active. Only water-soluble forms of menadione are used to supplement animal diets. The commercially available forms of K_3 supplements are menadione sodium bisulfite (MSB), menadione sodium bisulfate complex (MSBC), menadione dimethyl pyrimidinol bisulfite (MPB), and menadione nicotinamide bisulfite (MNB). These contain 52, 33, 46, and 46% menadione, respectively. Stability of these K_3 supplements in premixes and diets is impaired by moisture, choline chloride, trace elements, and alkaline conditions. It has been suggested that MSBC or MPB may lose almost 80% of bioactivity if stored for 3 mo. in a vitamin-trace-mineral premix containing choline, but losses are lower if stored in a similar premix containing no choline.[2] Coated K_3 supplements are generally more stable than uncoated supplements. Bioactivity of MPB and MNB is greater than either MSB or MSBC for chicks and pigs.[2] Although certain feed ingredients are known to be rich in vitamin K activity (e.g., alfalfa meal), little quantitative information exists on the bioavailability of vitamin K in feedstuffs.

CONCLUSIONS

Bioavailability of fat-soluble vitamins and their precursors needs greater attention. Potential metabolic functions for carotenoids such as lutein and lycopene as well as cis- and trans- forms of provitamin A carotenoids are important issues in nutrition. Also, the bioavailability and antioxidant capacity of the various forms and isomers of vitamin E are in need of attention.

REFERENCES

1. Zhuge, Q.; Klopfenstein, C.F. Factors affecting storage stability of vitamin A, riboflavin and niacin in a broiler diet premix. Poult. Sci. **1976**, *65*, 987.
2. Baker, D.H. Vitamin Bioavailability. In *Bioavailability of Nutrients for Animals: Amino Acids, Minerals, and Vitamins*; Ammerman, C.B., Baker, D.H., Lewis, A.J., Eds.; Academic Press, Inc.: San Diego, CA, 1995.
3. Anonymous. Nomenclature policy: Generic descriptors and trivial names for vitamins and related compounds. J. Nutr. **1979**, *109*, 8.
4. Erdman, J.W., Jr.; Poor, C.L.; Dietz, J.M. Processing and dietary effects on the bioavailability of vitamin A, carotenoids and vitamin E. Food Technol. **1988**, *42*, 214.
5. Ullrey, D.E. Biological availability of fat-soluble vitamins: Vitamin A and carotene. J. Anim. Sci. **1972**, *35*, 648.
6. Bieri, J.G.; McKenna, M.C. Expressing dietary values for fat-soluble vitamins: Changes in concepts and terminology. Am. J. Clin. Nutr. **1981**, *34*, 289.

Bioavailability: Mineral Elements

Xin Gen Lei
Cornell University, Ithaca, New York, U.S.A.

Hong Yang
ADM Alliance Nutrition, Inc., Quincy, Illinois, U.S.A.

Kangling Wang
Sichuan Agricultural University, Yaan, Sichuan, China

INTRODUCTION

Bioavailability of minerals or any group of nutrients has been defined in a variety of ways. It usually refers to the portion of a given source of mineral that can be absorbed and/or utilized for a specific biochemical or an integrated metabolic function by a given species. Recently, body immunity and health values of animal products have also been considered criteria of mineral bioavailability. In practice, bioavailability of minerals is listed in percentage, either as absolute values that represent the actual proportion of the mineral that can be absorbed or utilized, or relative values that are in relation to a response obtained with a highly available standard reference mineral source.

METHODOLOGY FOR MINERAL BIOAVAILABILITY ESTIMATION

Many different methods have been used to determine mineral bioavailability because of its broad definition or interpretation.[1,2] Traditionally, a large portion of data has been derived from whole-body responses including absorption, retention, growth, reproduction, and prevention of deficiency disease. There are some data based on tissue responses such as bone strength and blood hormone levels. Recently, more data have been generated from impacts of minerals on gene expression, protein synthesis, enzyme activity, and immune function.[3,4] Radioactive or stable isotopes and in vitro cell culture models have become increasingly used in mineral bioavailability assays.

Digestion and Balance Study

Digestion trials are used to estimate the absorption rate of an element by animals. There are apparent and true absorptions. Apparent absorption is defined as total intake minus total fecal excretion of the element, and that difference is often expressed as a percentage of the total intake. Fecal excretion of the element consists of the unabsorbed portion of the element and the absorbed portion that is subsequently excreted into the gastrointestinal tract. The latter portion of the total fecal excretion is designated as "total endogenous fecal excretion." It can be estimated by extrapolating responses of fecal losses of the element to zero dietary intake or by monitoring fecal loss of an injected element isotope. True absorption corrects for the portion of total endogenous excretion and is calculated as follows:

$$\text{True absorption} = [\text{total intake} - (\text{total fecal excretion}$$
$$- \text{ total endogenous fecal excretion})]$$
$$/\text{total intake} \times 100$$

The value for true absorption is greater than that for apparent absorption. True absorption is more accurate than apparent absorption for elements such as calcium, phosphorus, zinc, and copper, as the gastrointestinal tract is a major pathway of excretion for these elements.[5] For both apparent and true absorption measures, the limitation lies in the fact that not all the absorbed elements are available for storage or physiological use by the animals.

Balance trials are used to estimate the retention of an element. It is defined as total intake minus total excretion (total fecal plus total urinary) of the element. As urine is a major pathway of excretion for minerals such as potassium, magnesium, and iodine,[5] retention is a useful indicator of their bioavailability. However, in many situations, the mineral element excreted in the urine represents a portion that has been utilized in metabolism. In such cases, net retention is not a good indicator of bioavailability.

Both radioactive and stable isotopes can be used to determine absorption and retention of mineral elements.[1] The procedure usually involves a single oral dose, followed by measurements of the administered radioactive or

Encyclopedia of Animal Science
DOI: 10.1081/E-EAS 120019471

stable isotope in blood, target organs, or whole body. This approach is specific so it can sort out the unavailable portion from the endogenous loss of the testing elements. The disadvantage of this method is the need for special equipment to detect both types of isotopes and the very limited manipulating time.

Animal Feeding Trial

Comparing responses of animals fed a particular mineral in purified or practical diets with those fed a reference mineral is a routine method for determining mineral bioavailability. As an important economic trait, growth performance is often used to measure mineral bioavailability. Young chicks have been frequently chosen, as larger animals are somewhat less desirable for this purpose. Milk production and reproduction can also be bioavailability indicators. Bone ash and bone breaking strength are considered two of the most reliable response criteria for estimating bioavailability of calcium and phosphorus. Tibia in chicken and metacarpals and metatarsals in swine are the commonly sampled bones for these assays.[6] Accumulation of the mineral elements such as copper and iron in target organs has also been found to be well-related to their bioavailability. Tissue uptake of the element can be measured following dietary supplementation of physiological doses for a long period or supplementation of high (pharmacological) levels for a short period. Both methods may provide similar tissue concentrations of the test elements.[2] The pharmacological type of assay can be performed with high dietary mineral levels formulated with natural ingredients and relatively short period of time. The physiological type of assay may require semipurified diets.

Many minerals are essential components of catalytic enzymes or hormones. Examples include iron in hemoglobin and selenium in glutathione peroxidases. Thus, effects of minerals on the gene, protein, and activity expressions of those factors are good bioavailability measures for these minerals.[4]

In Vitro or Cultured-Cell Models

Because of the cost and other issues of using animals for mineral bioavailability determination, in vitro systems and cultured cells have been explored as alternative testing models. An in vitro system has been developed to assay for feed phosphorus bioavailability.[7] Ferritin analysis of Caco-2 cells cultured with filtered samples treated with simulated stomach and intestine digestions has been used to determine iron bioavailability.[8] Although it is convenient to use these systems to screen for large numbers of samples at relatively low costs, caution should be given in relating the data to physiological conditions.

DETERMINANTS OF MINERAL BIOAVAILABILITY

Bioavailability of a given mineral depends on many factors. All these factors can be simply classified into three categories: the mineral itself, the target animals, and the dietary conditions. In many cases, bioavailability of any particular mineral is a function of these three-way interactions.

Nature and Level of Testing Mineral

Animals receive their mineral supply mainly from feedstuffs and mineral supplements. In most cases, minerals from the former are less bioavailable than those from the latter. Bioavailability of the naturally occurring minerals in feedstuffs varies with their sources. For example, phosphorus bioavailability in soybean meal to simple-stomached species is approximately tenfold greater than that in sunflower seed meal or cottonseed meal.[9] Mineral supplements are primarily inorganic salts of sulfate, oxide, and carbonates. Chemical forms of mineral affect its bioavailability. Recently, a number of ''organic'' trace mineral complexes have been developed as mineral supplements. These complexes include metal–polysaccharide, metal–proteinate, and metal–amino acid, along with metal–amino acid chelates. A limited amount of research has shown that ''organic'' minerals are more available than corresponding inorganic reference sources. However, bioavailability estimates of organic mineral complexes are not well defined and are rather inconsistent among different experiments. It seems true to all mineral elements that bioavailability is higher when the elements are deficient than when the elements meet or exceed the requirements of the animal.

Species, Age, and Physiological State of Target Animals

Bioavailability of some minerals such as phytate-phosphorus differs between ruminant and nonruminants because of differences in their digestive systems. True digestibility of phytate-phosphorus can be as high as 63% in sheep, but usually less than 30% in nonruminants.[5] Bioavailability of minerals appears to be lower for adult than for young animals. Copper absorption is low (<1.0–10.0%) in weaned lambs, but high (70–85%) in young, milk-fed lambs that do not have a functional rumen.[10] The low absorption of copper in adult ruminants is largely due to complex interactions that occur in rumen. Early growth, gestation, and lactation use minerals more efficiently than occurs at later stages. Duodenal coccidiosis caused by *Eimeria acervulina* inoculation in the young broiler decreased zinc bioavailability, but increased bioavailability of manganese, copper, cobalt, and iron.

Dietary Factors

Normal utilization of dietary calcium and phosphorus by animals requires adequate active vitamin D and an appropriate ratio of these two elements. Mineral interactions often result in a reduced absorption and retention of one mineral under the influence of another. High dietary calcium levels, in particular in the presence of high levels of phytate, reduce zinc bioavailability. Occasionally, interactions may be beneficial, as in the case of improvement of iron utilization by a small amount of copper supplementation. But, a large amount of copper supplementation can decrease iron bioavailability.[5] Dietary fiber may affect mineral bioavailability due to its association with minerals in the feedstuff and/or binding of minerals to undigested fiber constituents in the gastrointestinal tract. Furthermore, dietary fiber may accelerate the rate of digesta passage through the gastrointestinal tract and thus reduce absorption of minerals. Ascorbic acid decreases copper absorption and utilization, but enhances absorption of iron in several species.[2] Adding citric acid and phytase to a corn–soy diet for growing pigs improves their phytate-phosphorus utilization.[11] Feeding monensin has been shown to improve absorption of magnesium, phosphorus, zinc, and selenium, but has inconsistent effect on absorption of calcium, potassium, and sodium.[2] Processing may affect both the total quantity of the mineral and its bioavailability. Grinding adds metals such as iron, copper, and zinc to the feed, and pelleting improves the availability of phosphorus in plant ingredients to chicks.

CONCLUSION

Bioavailability of minerals has been defined and determined in many different ways. In general, it refers to the portion of a given source of mineral that can be absorbed, retained, or utilized for a specific function. Thus, the values of mineral bioavailability are often derived from digestion, balance, and feeding trials, using a highly available mineral as a reference. Cultured-cell and in vitro models have also been developed for assay of mineral bioavailability. Modifying factors of mineral bioavailability include the chemical form, source, and level of the testing compound; the species, age, and physiological states of the target animals; and the conditions of diets to which the testing mineral is added.

REFERENCES

1. McDowell, L.R. *Minerals in Animal and Human Nutrition*, 2nd Ed.; Elsevier: Amsterdam, The Netherlands, 2003.
2. Ammerman, C.B.; Baker, D.H.; Lewis, A.J. *Bioavailability of Nutrients for Animals: Amino Acids, Minerals, and Vitamins*; Academic Press: New York, NY, 1995.
3. Gengelbach, G.P.; Spears, J.W. Effects of dietary copper and molybdenum on copper status, cytokine production, and humoral immune response of calves. J. Dairy Sci. **1998**, *81*, 3286–3292.
4. Lei, X.G.; Dann, H.M.; Ross, D.A.; Cheng, W.H.; Combs, G.F., Jr.; Roneker, K.R. Dietary selenium supplementation is required to support full expression of three selenium-dependent glutathione peroxidases in various tissues of weanling pigs. J. Nutr. **1998**, *128*, 130–135.
5. Underwood, E.J.; Suttle, N.F. *The Mineral Nutrition of Livestock*, 3rd Ed.; CABI Publishing: New York, NY, 1999.
6. Augspurger, N.R.; Webel, D.M.; Lei, X.G.; Baker, D.H. Efficacy of *E. coli* phytases expressed in yeast for releasing phytate-bound phosphorus in young chicks and pigs. J. Anim. Sci. **2003**, *81*, 47–483.
7. Liu, J.Z.; Ledoux, D.R.; Veum, T.L. In vitro prediction of phosphorus availability in feed ingredients for swine. J. Agric. Food Chem. **1998**, *46*, 2678–2681.
8. Glahn, R.P.; Wien, E.M.; Van-Campen, D.R.; Miller, D.D. Caco-2 cell iron uptake from meat and casein digests parallels in vivo studies: Use of a novel in vitro method for rapid estimation of iron bioavailability. J. Nutr. **1996**, *126*, 332–339.
9. Kornegay, E.T. Nutritional, Environmental, and Economic Considerations for Using Phytase in Pig and Poultry Diets. In *Nutrient Management of Food Animals to Enhance and Protect the Environment*; Kornegay, E.T., Ed.; CRC Press: New York, NY, 1996; 277–302.
10. Spears, J.W. Trace mineral bioavailability in ruminants. J. Nutr. **2003**, *133*, 1506S–1509S.
11. Han, Y.M.; Roneker, K.R.; Pond, W.G.; Lei, X.G. Addition of wheat middlings, microbial phytase, and citric acid to corn–soybean meal diets for growing pigs may replace inorganic phosphorus supplementation. J. Anim. Sci. **1998**, *76*, 2649–2656.

Bioavailability: Water-Soluble Vitamins

David H. Baker
University of Illinois, Urbana, Illinois, U.S.A.

INTRODUCTION

There are two primary concerns regarding bioavailability of water-soluble vitamins in animal diets and premixes: 1) stability of crystalline vitamins in vitamin and vitamin-mineral premixes as well as in diets and supplements; and 2) utilization efficiency of B-vitamin precursors contained in plant- and animal-source feed ingredients. Readers are referred to other reviews for details concerning factors affecting the stability of crystalline vitamins in diets and premixes. Regarding bioavailability of water-soluble vitamins in feed ingredients, a paucity of research data exists, and few feed ingredients have been evaluated. Feedstuffs contain B-vitamins in precursor, coenzyme, or bound forms, and enzymes are required to release the free form of these vitamins prior to absorption from the gut.

BIOTIN

Commercial D-biotin has no specific unit of activity. Thus, 1 g of D-biotin equals 1 g of activity. Pelleting or heat has little effect on biotin activity in feeds, but oxidative rancidity severely reduces biotin bioavailability. Much of the biotin in feed ingredients exists in a bound form, ε-N-biotinyl-L-lysine (biocytin), which is a component of protein. Crystalline biotin is absorbed well from the small intestine, but the bioavailability of biotin in biocytin varies widely and is dependent on the digestibility of the proteins in which it is found.[1,2] Avidin, a glycoprotein found in egg albumen, binds biotin and makes it totally unavailable. Proper heat treatment of egg white will denature avidin and prevent it from binding biotin. Based on bioassay results using biotin-depleted chicks, it is apparent that among the cereal grains, bioavailability of biotin in corn is high (100%), whereas that in wheat, barley, and sorghum is about 50%.[2] Buenostro and Kratzer[3] estimated that biotin is 100% available in soybean meal and 86% available in meat-and-bone meal for laying hens.

CHOLINE

In mammalian but not avian species, the dietary need for choline can be replaced by excess methionine. In crystalline form, choline chloride (74.6% choline) is hygroscopic, and therefore it is considered a stress agent to other vitamins in a vitamin-mineral premix. Crystalline choline is considered quite stable in animal feeds and premixes. Crude plant oils (e.g., corn and soybean oil) contain choline as phospholipid-bound phosphatidyl choline. The bioavailability of choline in this form is at least 100%.[4] Refined plant oils generally have been subjected to alkaline treatment and bleaching, and these processes almost totally remove phospholipids, including phospholipid-bound choline.

Choline bioavailability (relative to crystalline choline chloride) in oilseed meals for chicks has been estimated at 83% in soybean meal, 76% in peanut meal, and only 24% in canola meal.[2] Also in chicks, excess dietary protein has been observed to markedly increase the dietary requirement for choline.

FOLACIN

The folacin present in feeds and foods exists largely as polyglutamates. In plants, folacin exists as a polyglutamate conjugate containing a γ-linked polypeptide chain of (primarily) seven glutamic acid residues. The normal gut proteases do not cleave the glutamate residues from this compound. Instead, a group of intestinal enzymes known as conjugases (folyl polyglutamate hydrolases) removes all but the last glutamate residue. Only the monoglutamyl form is thought to be absorbed into the enterocyte. Most of the folic acid taken up by the brush border is reduced to tetrahydrofolate (FH_4) and then methylated to N^5-methyl-FH_4, the predominant form of folate in blood plasma. The majority of the N^5-methyl-FH_4 in plasma is bound to protein.

Like thiamin, folic acid has a free amino group (on the pteridine ring), and this makes it very sensitive to losses in activity due to heat treatment, particularly if heat is applied to foods or feeds containing reducing sugars such as lactose or glucose. Whether the free amino group of folacin (or thiamin) can bind to the free aldehyde moiety of pyridoxal or pyridoxalphosphate is not known. Intestinal conjugase inhibitors may be present in certain beans and pulses, and these may impede folacin absorption.[5] Only 38% retention of folacin activity

Encyclopedia of Animal Science
DOI: 10.1081/E-EAS 120023791

occurs when folic acid is stored for 3 wk at 45°C in a mineral-free premix; even greater losses occur when minerals are included in the premix.[2]

NIACIN

Niacin is a very stable vitamin when added to feed or premixes, being little affected by heat, oxygen, moisture, or light. In plant-source feed ingredients, much of the niacin activity, mostly nicotinamide nucleotides, is bound and therefore unavailable. Roughly 85–90% of the niacin activity in cereal grains and 40% in oilseeds is in a bound unavailable form.[2] Alkaline hydrolysis is the only means by which niacin can be efficiently released from its bound state in these ingredients. Meat and milk products, on the other hand, contain no bound niacin, but instead contain free nicotinic acid, nicotinamide, and nicotinamide nucleotides.

Because excess tryptophan is converted to nicotinic acid and because all common feed ingredients contain tryptophan as well as nicotinic acid, there is no good way to assess the bioavailability of niacin per se. Thus, 50 mg of tryptophan yields 1 mg of nicotinic acid.[6,7] Iron is required in two metabolic reactions in the pathway of tryptophan to nicotinate mononucleotide. Oduho et al.[8] established that Fe deficiency in chicks will reduce the conversion efficiency of tryptophan to niacin [i.e., from 42:1 to 56:1 (wt:wt)].

Niacin activity can be purchased as either free nicotinic acid or free nicotinamide. Relative to nicotinic acid, nicotinamide has been observed to be roughly 120% bioavailable in delivering niacin bioactivity.[9,10]

PANTOTHENIC ACID

This B vitamin is generally sold as either D- or DL-Ca pantothenate, and only the D-isomer has bioactivity.[2] Thus, 1 g of D-Ca pantothenate equals 0.92 g pantothenic acid (PA) activity, and 1 g DL-Ca pantothenate equals 0.46 g of PA activity. Crystalline PA is relatively stable to heat, oxygen, and light, but it can lose activity rapidly when exposed to moisture.

Feed ingredients contain PA in the form of coenzyme A, and in this form it may not be fully available for gut absorption. Chick bioassay work has suggested that the PA in corn and soybean meal is 100% bioavailable, whereas that in barley, wheat, and sorghum is about 60% bioavailable.[11] Processed feed ingredients may exhibit losses in PA bioavailability, although definitive animal data are lacking on this subject. Sauberlich[12] estimated that PA in the typical adult American diet was only 50% bioavailable. He further suggested that processing

(freezing, canning, refining, etc.) may decrease bioavailability further.

RIBOFLAVIN

This vitamin is relatively labile, being reduced in bioactivity by light, alkali, and oxygen. In feedstuffs, it exists primarily as nucleotide coenzymes, in which form the bioavailability is probably less than 100%. Chung and Baker[13] estimated that riboflavin bioavailability in a corn-soybean meal diet is 60% for chicks relative to crystalline riboflavin. Gadient[14] suggested that 95–100% of riboflavin bioactivity in pelleted feeds remains following storage for 3 mo at room temperature.

Sauberlich[12] suggested that several factors may reduce the bioavailability of riboflavin in foods. Among the suggested factors antagonizing riboflavin were excess dietary levels of tetracycline, Fe, Zn, Cu, ascorbate, and caffeine. Patel and Baker[15] used chick growth bioassays to evaluate dietary excesses of Fe (420 mg/kg), Zn (448 mg/kg), Cu (245 mg/kg), ascorbic acid (1000 mg/kg), caffeine (200 mg/kg), and chortetracycline (500 mg/kg), which were added to riboflavin-deficient soy-isolate semipurified diets. None of these supplements was found to decrease the utilization of crystalline riboflavin.

THIAMIN

Thiamin is available to the food and feed industries as thiamin-Cl-HCl (79% thiamin) or thiamin-NO_3 (81% thiamin). These compounds are stable up to 100°C and are readily soluble in water.[16] One international unit of thiamin activity is equivalent to 3 μg of crystalline thiamin-HCl. Because it contains a free amino group, heat processing can rapidly destroy thiamin bioactivity via the Maillard reaction. Likewise, any processing procedure that involves alkaline treatment leads to loss of thiamin activity. The thiamin contained in feed ingredients is present largely in phosphorylated forms, either as protein-phosphate complexes or as thiamin mono-, di-, or triphosphates. Some raw ingredients (e.g., fish) contain thiaminases, which can destroy thiamin in diets to which it is added. Whereas thiaminases are of particular concern in the nutrition of cats and fur-bearing animals, they are of little consequence in food-animal production. Fish and meat meals have essentially no bioavailable thiamin activity, primarily due to high-temperature processing of these products.

Pelleting results in some loss of thiamin activity, as does premix storage in the presence of minerals.[14] About 48 and 95% retention of thiamin activity occurs when thiamin is stored in the form of the HCl and NO_3, respectively, in a premix for 21 days at 40°C and 85% relative humidity.[2] In a complete feed stored under similar conditions, thiamin-HCl retains only 21% of its activity, whereas thiamin-NO$_3$ retains 97% of its activity. Thus, the mononitrate form of thiamin would seem to be the more stable form when storage in hot environments is anticipated.

VITAMIN B$_6$

Vitamin B$_6$ is not routinely added in supplemental crystalline form to practical-type diets for swine and poultry, because both corn and soybean meal are plentiful in this B vitamin. Vitamin B$_6$ is about 40% bioavailable in corn and about 60% bioavailable in soybean meal.[17] Moderate heat treatment (80–120°C) of corn seems to enhance B$_6$ bioavailability, whereas greater heat treatment (160°C) decreases availability. Most of the vitamin B$_6$ activity in corn exists as pyridoxal and pyridoxamine, forms that are more heat-labile than pyridoxine. Plant-source feedstuffs may contain B$_6$ as either pyridoxine glucoside or pyridoxallysine, and both of these compounds have minimal B$_6$ bioactivity.[18]

In premixes, vitamin B$_6$ can lose bioactivity, particularly when minerals in the form of carbonates or oxides are present. High temperatures enhance loss of activity. Loss of B$_6$ activity in stored, pelleted complete feeds averages about 20% during 3 mo of storage at room temperature.[14]

When vitamin B$_6$ is added at supplemental levels to animal diets, it is generally added in the form of pyridoxine-HCl. To become active metabolically, pyridoxine must be converted to pyridoxal phosphate, and riboflavin is required for this conversion. Thus, riboflavin deficiency can markedly reduce the effectiveness of supplemental pyridoxine.[19]

VITAMIN B$_{12}$

Cyanocobalamin, or B$_{12}$, is available in crystalline form, but this vitamin is essentially devoid in plant-source feed ingredients, existing instead in animal-source proteins and fermentation products, where it is considered (but not proved) to be 100% available.

Both animal- and fermentation-based feedstuffs contain B$_{12}$ as methylcobalamin or adenosylcobalamin, which are bound to protein. As in humans, but unlike in sheep and horses, an intrinsic factor is required for gut absorption of B$_{12}$ in swine and poultry. Crystalline vitamin B$_{12}$ is considered quite stable in feeds and premixes.[2]

VITAMIN C

There is little concern about the bioavailability of vitamin C (ascorbic acid), because food animals (unlike humans, apes, and guinea pigs) are capable of synthesizing this vitamin. Nonetheless, vitamin C is often included in vitamin premixes for use in purified animal diets because of its antioxidant and putative antistress properties. Stored diets or premixes can lose vitamin C activity. Coating ascorbate with ethylcellulose minimizes the loss. Gadient[14] noted that both pelleting and extruding can markedly reduce the bioactivity of supplemental ascorbate added to feeds or premixes. Losses due to oxidation are well known, as ascorbic acid (reduced form) can be reversibly oxidized to dehydroascorbic acid, which in turn can be further irreversibly oxidized to diketogulonic acid. Both reduced and oxidized forms of ascorbate retain scurvy-preventing ascorbate activity, but diketogulonic acid has no activity. Both ascorbate and dehydroascorbate are heat labile, particularly when heat is applied in the presence of trace minerals such as Cu, Fe, or Zn.

CONCLUSIONS

Most of the B vitamins in foods and feeds exist as precursor compounds or coenzymes that are often bound or complexed in some manner. Hence, gut processes are required to either release or convert vitamin precursors or complexes to usable and absorbable chemical entities. Generally speaking, these processes are not 100% efficient. Moreover, storage, as well as feed and food processing, can also reduce the utilization of food-containing vitamins. Bioavailability of water-soluble vitamins in foodstuffs relative to that of crystalline forms of the same vitamins is an issue that deserves greater attention.

REFERENCES

1. Zhuge, Q.; Klopfenstein, C.F. Factors affecting storage stability of vitamin A, riboflavin and niacin in a broiler diet premix. Poult. Sci. **1976**, *65*, 987.
2. Baker, D.H. Vitamin Bioavailability. In *Bioavailability of Nutrients for Animals: Amino Acids, Minerals, and Vitamins*; Ammerman, C.B., Baker, D.H., Lewis, A.J., Eds.; Academic Press, Inc.: San Diego, CA, 1995.
3. Buenostro, J.L.; Kratzer, F.H. Use of plasma and egg yolk biotin of white leghorn hens to assess biotin availability from feedstuffs. Poult. Sci. **1984**, *63*, 1563.
4. Emmert, J.L.; Garrow, T.A.; Baker, D.H. Development of an experimental diet for determining bioavailable choline concentration, and its application in studies with soybean lecithin. J. Anim. Sci. **1996**, *74*, 2738.

5. Bailey, L.B. Factors affecting folate bioavailability. Food Technol. **1988**, *42*, 206.

6. Anonymous. Nomenclature policy: Generic descriptors and trivial names for vitamins and related compounds. J. Nutr. **1979**, *109*, 8.

7. Czarnecki, G.L.; Halpin, K.M.; Baker, D.H. Precursor (amino acid):product (vitamin) interrelationship for growing chicks as illustrated by tryptophan-niacin and methionine-choline. Poult. Sci. **1983**, *62*, 371.

8. Oduho, G.; Han, Y.; Baker, D.H. Iron deficiency reduces the efficacy of tryptophan as a niacin precursor for chicks. J. Nutr. **1994**, *124*, 444.

9. Baker, D.H.; Yen, J.T.; Jensen, A.H.; Teeter, R.G.; Michel, E.N.; Burns, J.H. Niacin activity in niacinamide and coffee. Nutr. Rep. Int. **1976**, *14*, 115.

10. Oduho, G.; Baker, D.H. Quantitative efficacy of niacin sources for the chick: nicotinic acid, nicotinamide, NAD and tryptophan. J. Nutr. **1993**, *123*, 2201.

11. Southern, L.L.; Baker, D.H. Bioavailable pantothenic acid in cereal grains and soybean meal. J. Anim. Sci. **1981**, *53*, 403.

12. Sauberlich, H. Bioavailability of vitamins. Prog. Food Nutr. Sci. **1985**, *9*, 1.

13. Chung, T.K.; Baker, D.H. Riboflavin requirement of chicks fed purified amino acid and conventional corn-soybean meal diets. Poult. Sci. **1990**, *69*, 1357.

14. Gadient, M. Effect of Pelleting on Nutritional Quality of Feed. In *Proc. of the Maryland Nutr. Conf.*; 1986; p. 73.

15. Patel, K.; Baker, D.H. Supplemental iron, copper, zinc, ascorbate caffeine and chlortetracycline do not affect riboflavin utilization in the chick. Nutr. Res. **1996**, *16*, 1943.

16. National Research Council. *Vitamin Tolerance of Animals*; National Academy Press: Washington, DC, 1987.

17. Yen, J.T.; Jensen, A.H.; Baker, D.H. Assessment of the concentration of biologically available vitamin B_6 in corn and soybean meal. J. Anim. Sci. **1976**, *42*, 866.

18. Gregory, J.F., III; Kirk, J.R. The bioavailability of vitamin B6 in foods. Nutr. Rev. **1981**, *39*, 1.

19. Baker, D.H.; Edwards, H.M., III; Strunk, C.S.; Emmert, J.L.; Peter, C.M.; Mavromichalis, I.; Parr, T.M. Single versus multiple deficiencies of methionine, zinc, riboflavin, vitamin B-6 and choline elicit surprising growth responses in young chicks. J. Nutr. **1999**, *129*, 2239.

Biodiversity: Germplasm Banks

Paul F. Watson
Royal Veterinary College, London, U.K.

William V. Holt
Zoological Society of London, London, U.K.

INTRODUCTION

Germplasm banking (genetic resource banking, GRB) refers to the storage of gametes or embryos for future use in the breeding of a species or breed, as a means of combating the extinction of groups of animals because of human activity. This generally means cryopreservation by storage at $-196°C$, although other methods such as vitrification or freeze-drying are possible.

AIMS

Germplasm banking has two important applications, which differ in their overall aims and therefore in the choice of material to store: GRB for species conservation and maintaining biodiversity, and GRB for rare and traditional breeds to enable the recovery of the breed after a total wipe-out. The aim of the former is to contribute to the conservation of the genetic diversity of a particular species and involves harvesting a wide representation of the genes of the species without consideration of the phenotype. In contrast, GRB for breed conservation aims to store the particular gene combinations that represent the breed most aptly, and therefore selects the best examples for preservation. The key contrast lies in the terms ''diversity'' and ''gene combination''; in the one instance, the desire is to store genetic variations of the representative population in the frequencies in which they occur, and in the second instance, the plan is to preserve a desirable combination of genes representing a particular subpopulation of the species (i.e., breed). Although the techniques are similar, the genetic management is determined by the aims.

METHODS

Freezing

The methods available are those developed for sperm, oocyte, and embryo freezing or vitrification.[1–3] In principle, the material is suspended in a supportive solution of ions and other additives, of the correct osmotic strength and the appropriate pH. One or more cryoprotective agents are added and the suspension is packaged into plastic straws or tubes designed to withstand cooling to $-200°C$ and rewarming. The samples are frozen carefully by cooling in a controlled-rate freezer designed for the purpose, or in the vapour phase over the surface of liquid nitrogen. The material is stored under the surface of liquid nitrogen ($-196°C$) or more recently, responding to concerns about cross contamination, in the vapour phase. For recovery of the material, thawing is generally rapid (to avoid damaging recrystallization of ice) often in a water bath to increase the rate of heat transfer. Stored material has an indefinite time-span estimated at hundreds of years because metabolic processes are arrested, leaving only cosmic radiation to cause DNA damage.

However, the frozen sample is subjected to severe stresses during cooling and rewarming that result in considerable cell damage. Only about 50% of spermatozoa will survive an optimized cryopreservation protocol, and success with embryos depends on species. Oocytes have been cryopreserved with only modest success. The stresses arise from one or more of the following: 1) osmotically driven water movements across the cell membranes caused by the addition and removal of cryoprotectant; 2) the removal of water as ice during freezing and its dissolution during rewarming; and 3) cytotoxicity from high concentrations of cryoprotectants used.

Vitrification

Vitrification[2] eliminates the removal of water as ice. However, it requires combinations of cryoprotectants allowing greater concentration whilst avoiding toxicity, and a sufficient cooling rate to prevent removal of water as ice; instead, the entire solution reaches its glass transition temperature and forms a solid, trapping the cells. It has been found to offer promise for oocytes and embryos but the toxicity of cryoprotectants remains a problem for spermatozoa.

Encyclopedia of Animal Science
DOI: 10.1081/E-EAS 120019478

ORGANIZATIONAL CONSIDERATIONS

Germplasm banking has its greatest value as part of an integrated strategy for maintaining the availability of the genetics of today for the benefit of tomorrow. Thus, there is a need to develop a planned genetic management of the total resources including the in situ resources, the ex situ resources (zoos, wildlife parks, botanic gardens), and the frozen resources.[4] Because they are expected to be available and utilized over a period of many years, the frozen resources need to be updated and replaced as use dictates. For long-term success, there are a number of considerations to be taken into account: disease control, genetic management, curatorship and record keeping, ownership, and security. Too often, enthusiasm to develop such resources has not addressed these issues, and the collection has soon become unusable.

Disease Control

Disease transgresses national borders. Living tissues can harbor viruses, bacteria, and prions responsible for transmissible encephalopathies. Cryostorage does not destroy such infectious agents. Indeed, evidence is accumulating to suggest that infectious agents released into the liquid nitrogen may pass to uncontaminated specimens and result in cross-infection.

Consequently, the international exchange of frozen germplasm is governed by restrictions regarding the health status of the donor animal. For some countries, e.g., Australia, stringent import restrictions apply to protect local animal health. In other countries, the requirements vary depending on the history of the material and the animals from which it was derived. As a precaution before material is stored, as much information as possible about the health status of the donor animal should be obtained. Inevitably, regulations continue to be updated as new disease organisms are identified and situations arise that could not have been foreseen. A blood sample should also be stored for future investigations of health status. It is not possible to predict whether material stored today could be transferred in the future, and therefore it is best to store germplasm in the country (or at least continent) of origin or of likely intended use.

Genetic Management

The management of a biodiversity germplasm bank should be based upon knowledge of the genetics of the population being resourced. Planned utilization can then be arranged to ensure the least inbreeding and preserve the genetic diversity of the population.[5] For this approach, a skin or blood sample should be stored for future analysis of novel genetic markers. For conservation of breeds, the

Food and Agriculture Organization of the United Nations (FAO) has been formulating a global strategy for domestic animal genetic management including the use of germplasm banking.[6]

Curatorship and Record Keeping

A GRB needs to have clear management responsibility. If there are competing needs, what priorities are set and who judges their relative importance? On these decisions the success of the venture hangs. For these judgements, detailed records need to be maintained reliably in the long term. Failure of record keeping has limited the value of several GRBs in the past.

Ownership

When gametes are collected and stored from exotic locations, the question of ownership (and, therefore, involvement in the subsequent utilization of the resource) becomes an issue. Are the stored gametes the property of the agency of the country in which they are harvested, the technical team whose expertise made this possible, or the funding body that provided financial support? These issues should be considered and resolved before

Fig. 1 Rough Fell (above) and Herdwick (below) sheep, heritage breeds being conserved by the Heritage Genebank Project. (Photo kindly provided by The Sheep Trust.) (*View this art in color at www.dekker.com.*)

the collection is established to avoid legal disputes in the future.

Security

Breakdown of nitrogen storage vessels is the most common catastrophe facing frozen storage. Another crisis can arise from outbreak of notifiable animal disease (e.g., foot-and-mouth disease in the U.K.) resulting in a movement restriction of material in or out of the store; while this persists, the bank becomes unusable. Apart from proper alarms fitted to storage dewars, it is a good policy for the collection to be divided between two storage sites geographically separated from each other.

UTILIZATION OF THE FROZEN GERMPLASM

Stored genetic resources should be used on a regular and systematic basis, and not considered a frozen museum archive. The strategies for maintaining genetic diversity should be managed by a governing body, as exemplified by the Conservation Breeding Specialist Group of the International Union for Conservation of Nature and Natural Resources, now known as IUCN-The World Conservation Union.[7] In Great Britain, the Heritage Genebank Project, managed by The Sheep Trust,[8] was established during the recent foot-and-mouth disease outbreak to ensure the survival of rare and regional breeds of sheep, e.g., the Rough Fell and the Herdwick breeds (Fig. 1).

Examples where a germplasm bank has been valuable are the black-footed ferret in North America and the cheetah. Artificial insemination has been used successfully in the giant panda[9] and the elephant[10] although in the latter, cryopreserved semen was not used. These examples of flagship species help to publicize the importance of

Fig. 2 Koalas born after artificial insemination with fresh semen—a promise for the future for germplasm banking. (Photograph supplied by Dr. Steve Johnston, courtesy of the Lone Pine Koala Sanctuary, Queensland, Australia.) (*View this art in color at www.dekker.com.*)

GRB and give promise of future developments. However, there is currently need for further research to develop suitable methods for each species since existing methods are rarely applicable without modification.[4] In some instances (e.g., the koala), basic sperm cell physiology is largely unknown and requires more extensive research, but some work is in progress (Fig. 2).

CONCLUSION

Germplasm banks have produced only a few successes so far, but these have stimulated much thought about the proper establishment of the banks for the long-term future. There is a need for clear planning in the establishment of a useful resource, and the limited knowledge currently available calls for continued research. If the concept of GRBs is utilized, they have much to contribute to the maintenance of biodiversity.

REFERENCES

1. *Cryobanking: Banking the Genetic Resource: Wildlife Management for the Future?*; Watson, P.F., Holt, W.V., Eds.; Taylor and Francis: London, 2001.
2. Liebermann, J.; Nawroth, F.; Isachenko, V.; Isachenko, E.; Rahimi, G.; Tucker, M.J. Potential importance of vitrification in reproductive medicine. Biol. Reprod. **2002**, *67* (6), 1671–1680.
3. Kusakabe, H.; Szczygiel, M.A.; Whittingham, D.G.; Yanagimachi, R. Maintenance of genetic integrity in frozen and freeze-dried mouse spermatozoa. Proc. Natl. Acad. Sci. U. S. A. **2001**, *98* (24), 13501–13506.
4. Wildt, D.E.; Ellis, S.; Howard, J.G. Linkage of reproductive sciences: From 'quick fix' to 'integrated' conservation. J. Reprod. Fertil. **2001**, *57* (Suppl), 295–307.
5. Bennett, P.M. Establishing Germplasm Resource Banks for Wildlife Conservation: Genetic, Population and Evolutionary Aspects. In *Cryobanking: Banking the Genetic Resource: Wildlife Management for the Future?*; Watson, P.F., Holt, W.V., Eds.; Taylor and Francis: London, 2001; 47–67.
6. http://dad.fao.org/en/Home.htm/. Management of Small Populations at Risk (accessed May 2003).
7. http://www.cbsg.org/. The conservation breeding specialist group of the IUCN (accessed May 2003).
8. http://www.thesheeptrust.org/. The Sheep Trust (accessed May 2003).
9. Moore, H.D.M.; Bush, M.; Celma, M.; Garcia, A.L.; Hartman, T.D.; Hearn, J.P.; Hodges, J.K.; Jones, D.M.; Knight, J.A.; Monsalve, L.; Wildt, D.E. Artificial insemination in the giant panda (Ailuropoda melanoleuca). J. Zool. **1984**, *203*, 269–278.
10. Brown, J.L.; Goeritz, F.; Hermes, R.; Pratt-Hawkes, N.; Galloway, M.; Hildebrandt, T.B. Artificial insemination in the Asian elephant. Biol. Reprod. **2002**, *66* (Suppl. 1), No. 399.

Biodiversity: Grazing Management

Martin Vavra
United States Department of Agriculture, Forest Service, La Grande, Oregon, U.S.A.

INTRODUCTION

Grazing by livestock, or any other herbivore, has the potential to impact biodiversity. Biodiversity is simply defined as the great variety of life-forms present. The term can be scale-dependent, referring to a backyard, a landscape, a continent, or the planet. Scientists generally recognize two scales, community (alpha diversity) and landscape (beta diversity). There are three types of biodiversity: habitat diversity, genetic diversity, and species diversity. Livestock grazing has the potential to affect all three (either positively or negatively), but can have the most direct effect on habitat diversity. All herbivores consume selected plants and plant parts from their environment. This selective defoliation through the removal of photosynthetic or reproductive tissues impedes the grazed plant's ability to compete with other ungrazed plants in the community. Grazing animals are important agents of environmental change, acting to create spatial heterogeneity, accelerate successional processes, and control switching between alternative states. Chronic herbivory can change composition, structure, and production of plant communities (habitat). With a decline in habitat diversity a concomitant decline in species diversity can be expected; some species simply have no place to live. If populations of individual species fail to persist because of declining habitat diversity, then genetic diversity is reduced. However, one must consider that some changes in plant structure, composition, and production may in fact improve or have no effect on species diversity because new habitats are created. Some species may decline, but others will increase. Such variables as season of use, intensity of defoliation, frequency of defoliation, and forage selectivity separately and together impact the grazed plant community. Knowledge of these variables can be of use to managers designing grazing systems to minimize the impacts on biodiversity.

ECOLOGICAL DISTURBANCE

Most ecosystems across the planet are disturbance based. That means that periodically some form of disturbance, usually fire, decimates all or selected portions of plant communities, and the process of plant colonization must occur in the aftermath of the disturbance. Typically, if the disturbance is severe enough to destroy most plants in the community, the first recolonizing plant communities are simplistic and over time increase in complexity. This progression of plant communities is termed succession. Disturbance does not usually destroy or uniformly modify a given landscape. Therefore, at any one time there are varying communities that exist at different time intervals from the last disturbance event. These different stages of succession provide habitat diversity across the landscape and provide the potential for species diversity. As species occupy various habitats that may be somewhat dissimilar, over time their genes are altered through selection to adapt to the different habitats, providing genetic diversity.

Humans have drastically altered landscapes through their management. Livestock grazing certainly has been a major force of change, both in the past and today, particularly in parts of the world where education in land management has not occurred. Livestock grazing in the western United States in the late nineteenth and early twentieth centuries devastated ecosystems. Damages still persist. Unmanaged livestock grazing can lead to a dominance of unpalatable, chemically defended plants, some of which may be invasive. Other management practices have also greatly influenced landscapes; fire suppression in forests and rangelands, alteration of stream channels for irrigation, and logging forests are a few examples. To assess the influence of livestock grazing on biodiversity, one must also take into consideration human actions on the landscape. Wild herbivores provide yet another confounding influence. In the western United States deer and elk are significant forces of influence on plant community structure and composition; in the East, it is primarily white-tailed deer. These other confounding influences may, in some cases, have greater impacts than livestock grazing.

PLANT COMMUNITY STRUCTURE AND COMPOSITION

Species composition of plant communities can be altered by selective foraging of ungulates, and this phenomenon is a trademark of plant-ungulate relations.[1,2] By altering the competitive relations among plants, differential tolerances of co-occurring plant species appear to be important determinants of how woody and herbaceous plants respond to herbivory. On a landscape inhabited by herbivores that prefer one class of forage, that preferred forage will, through the defoliation process, be less competitive than those species not grazed. In areas grazed by cattle without a mitigating grazing system, grasses can be expected to decline while unpalatable shrubs and trees should increase. Poorly managed cattle grazing often reduces the cover of grasses, forbs, and shrubs, as well as vegetation biomass.[3] Additionally, this reduction in plant cover coupled with soil disturbance from animal trafficking provides the potential for invasion of undesirable exotic plant species.

Because livestock grazing has the potential to alter structure and composition of plant communities, habitat diversity can be directly affected by reducing the structure of vegetation short-term through the eating process, and long-term by changing and simplifying the composition. Therefore, some species will decline due to a reduction in habitat required by them, new species may colonize because new habitats are created, and still others may be unaffected.

NUTRIENT CYCLING

When grazing animals reduce biomass and litter and/or change plant species composition, nutrient cycling and energy flow can also be altered. This alteration has an indirect effect on biodiversity in that changes in nutrient cycling can initiate changes in habitat diversity. If grazing animals suppress nitrogen-fixing plants, less nitrogen may be available to the system. Because herbivores feed selectively, their food items usually have higher nutrient content than vegetation not selected. These same highly digestible plants are also those that, if allowed to become litter, would decompose relatively rapidly. If grazing is not managed to prevent the decline of preferred forage plants and the concomitant increase of unpalatable, less-degradable plants, rates of nutrient cycling may decline. Aboveground herbivory can decrease aboveground biomass, belowground production, soil elevation, and expansion of the root zone. Grazing can have a negative effect on the soil-building process.

Conversely, grazing can increase nutrient cycling through the deposition of urine and dung to contribute to the pool of nitrogen in the soil that is readily available for plant growth. This process decreases the carbon-to-nitrogen ratio of the soil, which increases litter decomposition rates. Also in some cases, higher availability of soil nitrogen enhances the productivity of deciduous species, while low availability enhances conifer production.

Deciduous species have more potential as forage plants and themselves provide more readily decomposed litter than conifers.

MANAGEMENT IMPLICATIONS

Unrestricted livestock grazing can have potentially negative impacts on biodiversity. However, grazing systems can be established that mitigate the potential negative effects and may enhance some aspects of diversity. Grazing systems can provide rest or deferment from defoliation, thereby providing improved physiological and ecological fitness for grazed plants. This improved fitness levels the competition playing field between grazed and ungrazed plants and can prevent species composition changes. Declines in habitat diversity can then be prevented.

Livestock do not graze rangelands or pastures uniformly. Preferred foraging areas are selected because of a variety of characteristics. Likewise, other areas are avoided for another set of characteristics, at least until preferred areas are fully exploited and animals are forced to go elsewhere. This is a typical occurrence on rangelands simply because of the physical characteristics of the landscape: steepness of slopes, limited water availability, or areas of unpalatable forages. Variation in vertical structure and canopy cover of the herb layer, as well as areas of species composition change, all occur as a result of an uneven pattern of grazing across a landscape. The disturbance of grazing has the potential to improve the habitat diversity of a community and a landscape, and this knowledge can be incorporated into specifically designed grazing systems. In fact strategic livestock grazing systems can be designed as manipulative tools to create specific habitats.[4,5]

CONCLUSIONS

Livestock grazing can be viewed as a chronic disturbance factor on landscapes with the potential to have positive, neutral, or negative impacts on biodiversity. Habitat diversity is the most directly affected attribute of biodiversity. A decline in habitat diversity leads to a decline in species diversity, which, in turn, leads to a decline in genetic diversity. Grazing can have an effect on habitat diversity through the process of selective grazing. Changes in plant community structure and function can occur from the lack of proper grazing management. Grazing may also have indirect effects on plant community composition by impacting nutrient cycling and energy flow. However, other land management practices, both past and present, or other natural events, often interact with grazing to affect biodiversity. Grazing managers can mitigate the potential negative effects of grazing with the implementation of grazing systems designed to provide for the physiological and ecological needs of forage species. Additionally, with knowledge of animal behavior traits, vegetation, and landscape variables, managers can design grazing systems that are neutral or even complementary to biodiversity.

REFERENCES

1. Hobbs, N.T. Modification of ecosystems by ungulates. J. Wildl. Manage. **1996**, *60*, 695–713.

2. Augustine, D.J.; McNaughton, S.J. Ungulate effects on the functional species composition of plant communities: Herbivore selectivity and plant tolerance. J. Wildl. Manage. **1998**, *62*, 1165–1183.

3. Jones, A. Effects of cattle grazing on North American arid ecosystems: A quantitative review. West. N. Am. Nat. **2000**, *60*, 155–164.

4. Severson, K.E.; Urness, P.J. Livestock Grazing: A Tool to Improve Wildlife Habitat. In *Ecological Implications of Livestock Herbivory in the West*; Vavra, M., Laycock, W.A., Pieper, R.E., Eds.; Soc. Range Manage. 1994; 232–249.

5. Bryant, F.C.; Payne, N.F. Rangeland Management Techniques: Controlled Grazing and Prescribed Burning. In *Techniques for Wildlife Habitat Management of Uplands*; Bryant, F.C., Payne, N.F., Eds.; McGraw-Hill, Inc., 1994; 347–412.

Biotechnology: Artificial Insemination

William L. Flowers
North Carolina State University, Raleigh, North Carolina, U.S.A.

INTRODUCTION

Genetic improvement is the main reason artificial insemination is used in breeding programs. Ejaculates from most male livestock contain more spermatozoa than are needed to achieve adequate fertility. As a result, if semen is collected and diluted, a greater number of females can be bred with artificial insemination than with natural service. In order to accomplish successful artificial insemination, semen must be collected, extended, stored, and inseminated.

SEMEN COLLECTION

Digital pressure or massage and use of an artificial vagina are the two most common methods of semen collection in livestock species.[1] The decision as to which one is best for à given animal is based on several factors, including male reproductive physiology and behavior, quality of semen obtained, and the technical expertise required for a successful collection. The best collection procedure for a given animal is the one that most closely simulates the social and physiological stimuli that occur during natural mating (Table 1).

Digital Pressure or Massage

Pressure applied to the end of the penis is the most common collection technique for swine and poultry. The primary stimulus for mounting behavior in boars is an object that resembles an immobile sow, and the primary stimulus for ejaculation is pressure on the end of the penis. Therefore, most boars can be trained to mount a bench called a collection dummy, or dummy sow. After mounting, boars will begin to thrust forward until the penis protrudes from the sheath. Manual pressure is applied by grasping the tip of the penis with a gloved hand. The pressure on the tip of the penis mimics cervical contractions during natural mating and results in full extension of the penis and ejaculation. In male birds, the cloaca is the exit for the reproductive system and contains small nipple-like projections called papillae. Collection of semen is achieved by massaging the papillae. The area surrounding the vent is massaged while simultaneously stroking the back. These actions stimulate a spinal reflex arc that causes the male to become aroused sexually and causes the papillae to become erect. Once erect, the papillae are gently massaged until ejaculation occurs.

Artificial Vagina

An artificial vagina is a device that imitates the female vagina and provides the appropriate thermal and mechanical stimulation required for ejaculation in horses, sheep, goats, and cattle. Most artificial vaginas have the same basic design, which includes an outer casing, an inner lining, and an insulated pouch that is attached to one end of the outer casing. Water added to the space between the outer casing and inner lining prior to collection is used to regulate the temperature and pressure to which the penis is exposed during collection. During collection from bulls, rams, or bucks, the male is allowed to mount a female or a neutered male. Stallions can be trained to mount a mare or a collection dummy called a phantom. When the male mounts, his sheath is gently deflected to the side and, as he thrusts forward to breed, the artificial vagina is placed over the end of his penis. The male ejaculates into the artificial vagina.

SEMEN EXTENSION AND PRESERVATION

After collection, semen is diluted with semen extender and stored prior to insemination (Table 1). For horses, swine, poultry, sheep, and goats, semen is stored at temperatures above 0°C and is referred to as fresh semen. For cattle, semen is stored at temperatures below 0°C and is referred to as frozen semen. The decision to use fresh or frozen semen is based primarily on fertility. In most species, fertility is considerably lower with frozen than with fresh semen. Therefore, fresh semen is the preferred choice. In cattle, frozen semen is equivalent to fresh semen in terms of fertility. As a result, frozen semen is used with cattle because it allows for much longer periods of storage prior to insemination, compared to fresh semen.

Extenders used in the preservation of semen perform several basic functions, including providing nutrients for sperm metabolism, neutralizing metabolic wastes, stabilizing sperm membranes, preventing drastic changes in

Encyclopedia of Animal Science
DOI: 10.1081/E-EAS 120019481

Table 1 Preferred collection and storage conditions for semen from cattle, chickens, horses, sheep and goats, swine, and turkeys

Animal	Collection technique	Type of semen	Storage temperature	Maximum storage length
Cattle	Artificial vagina	Frozen	−196°C	>1 year
Chickens	Manual massage	Fresh	5°C	24–48 hours
Horses	Artificial vagina	Fresh	5 to 20°C	24–36 hours
Swine	Digital pressure	Fresh	15 to 18°C	2–5 days
Sheep/goats	Artificial vagina	Fresh	5°C	4–6 days
Turkeys	Manual massage	Fresh	5°C with aeration	12–24 hours

the osmolarity of semen, and retarding bacterial growth. The chemical compositions of semen extenders are similar across species. Common ingredients in extenders include glucose, sodium bicarbonate, phosphate buffers, organic zwitterionic compounds, sodium citrate, potassium chloride, albumin and other proteins, and antibiotics.[2] Extenders used for preparing frozen semen include these ingredients as well as cryoprotectants, which protect spermatozoa during freezing and thawing.

INSEMINATION

Decisions associated with the insemination process are considered to be the most important components of artificial insemination. These include the insemination dose, the insemination regimen (frequency and timing), and the insemination technique.

Insemination Dose and Insemination Regimen

The insemination dose consists of the number of spermatozoa and the total volume of extended semen. Semen processing procedures, viability of spermatozoa,

and the insemination technique are the main factors that influence the individual characteristics of insemination doses. Likewise, the insemination regimen is determined by the length of estrus, the timing of ovulation during estrus, and the viability of spermatozoa in the female reproductive tract. Characteristics of insemination doses and regimens most commonly used in cattle, sheep, goats, horses, chickens, turkeys, and swine are summarized in Table 2.

Insemination Technique

Female reproductive anatomy determines the type of insemination technique that is used.[2] From an anatomical perspective, the goal of insemination is to deposit semen as close as possible to the uterus or in the posterior portion of it.

Cattle

In cattle, a rectovaginal procedure is used. One hand is positioned so that it grasps the cervix through the ventral floor of the rectum. An insemination gun or rod, which resembles a long, thin needle with a blunt end, is inserted into the vulva and guided by the other hand through the

Table 2 Characteristics of insemination of cattle, chickens, horses, sheep and goats, swine, and turkeys

Animal	Insemination dose	Insemination location	Insemination strategies	Normal pregnancy rates
Cattle	15–25 million sperm in 0.5–1.0 ml	Uterus	Once, 12–18 hours after detected estrus	60–70%
Chickens	150–200 million sperm in 0.2–0.5 ml	Caudal portion of oviduct	Once per week during breeding season	80–90%
Horses	250–500 million sperm in 10–25 ml	Uterus or cervix	Every other day of estrus, beginning on day 2 or 3	65–75%
Swine	2–4 billion sperm in 60–80 ml	Cervix	Once each day of estrus	80–90%
Sheep/goats	100–300 million sperm in 0.1–0.5 ml	Cervix	Once each day of estrus	70–80%
Turkeys	150–250 million sperm in 0.2–0.5 ml	Caudal portion of oviduct	Once per week during breeding season	80–90%

vagina and cervix and into the uterus. Gentle manipulation of the cervix through the rectum facilitates movement of the insemination rod through the cervical rings. Semen is deposited by pushing the plunger forward, which physically pushes the semen out of the tip of the insemination rod. Gentle massaging of the clitoris for at least 10 seconds prior to insemination is a technique that has been shown to improve conception rates in beef cows, and it is a practice often used on repeat breeders.

Sheep and Goats

In sheep and goats, an instrument called a speculum and a long, narrow insemination rod are used to deposit semen in the cervix. The speculum is inserted into the vagina and positioned just caudal to the external opening of the cervix. Visualization of the cervical os is enhanced by the use of a standard medical head lamp. When the cervix is located, the insemination rod is inserted through the speculum and threaded into the cervix at least 3 cm. Once the insemination rod is correctly positioned, a syringe or bottle with semen is attached to the other end of the insemination rod and semen is deposited.

Horses

The insemination catheter, or pipette, used in mares is a flexible plastic tube with a rounded tip. The insemination dose is loaded into a syringe with a plastic plunger and connected to the catheter with a short piece of pliable tubing. The tip of the catheter is placed in the palm of the hand with the index finger covering the tip. The gloved hand and insemination pipette are then passed into the cranial portion of the vagina, where the index finger is used to locate the cervix. The insemination catheter is advanced through the cervix into the uterine body and semen is slowly deposited.

Swine

In swine, the vagina becomes progressively smaller as it approaches the cervix and forms a smooth junction. The central canal of the cervix in the pig is a left-handed, or counterclockwise spiral. Specialized catheters with left-handed spirals or compressible foam tips are used for insemination. Insemination doses are packaged in small bottles, tubes, or flexible bags. With the tip pointed up, the catheter is passed through the vulva and into the vagina until resistance is encountered. The catheter is then rotated counterclockwise. When rotation becomes difficult, insertion is stopped the insemination dose is connected, and the semen is slowly deposited. Physical stimulation of the sow by massaging her back and rear enhances sperm deposition and transport of semen inside the sow.

Turkeys and Chickens

For birds, the insemination rod resembles a medicine dropper or small plastic rod connected to a 1 ml syringe by flexible tubing. The female is held so that her vent is exposed, and the area around the vent is massaged at the same time her back is stroked. As the hen become sexually aroused, the vent turns inside out and an opening resembling a rosette appears on the left side. The tip of the insemination rod is inserted about 1 cm into the opening and semen is deposited.

CONCLUSION

Artificial insemination currently is used successfully in most livestock species for genetic improvement, because semen from superior males can be used to breed increased numbers of females. For most species, fertility with artificial insemination is equivalent to or exceeds that normally achieved with natural service, if it is performed correctly.

REFERENCES

1. Hafez, E.S.E. Artificial Insemination. In *Reproduction in Farm Animals,* 6th Ed.; Hafez, E.S.E., Ed.; Lea and Febiger: Philadelphia, 1993; 424–439.
2. Flowers, W.L. Artificial Insemination, in Animals. In *Encyclopedia of Reproduction*; Knobil, E., Neill, J.D., Eds.; Academic Press: San Diego, 1999; Vol. 1, 291–302.

Biotechnology: Cloning Animals

Liangxue Lai
Randall S. Prather
University of Missouri, Columbia, Missouri, U.S.A.

INTRODUCTION

Animal cloning has been the subject of scientific experiments for many years, but garnered little attention until the birth of the first mammal cloned from an adult cell, a sheep named Dolly.[1] Since Dolly, scientists have cloned other animals, including cows,[2] mice,[3] pigs,[4] goats,[5] cats,[6] and rabbits.[7] The ability to clone animals has many important applications, but has also sparked fierce debates among scientists, politicians, and the general public about the use and morality of cloning plants, animals, and possibly humans.

DEFINITION

Cloning is making a biological copy of another organism with the identical genetic makeup of the founding individual. It is an asexual method of reproduction. Natural examples of cloning include organisms such as bacteria and yeast. Bacteria that result from asexual reproduction are genetically identical. Specifically, animal cloning refers to the creation of a new genetic replica of an original living or dead animal. The only clones produced naturally in mammals are identical twins. These are formed when cells produced by the early divisions of the fertilized egg separate and independently develop into two new individuals. They are therefore genetically identical to each other but not identical to their parents.

Animals can be cloned by three processes: embryo splitting, blastomere dispersal, and nuclear transfer. Our focus will be cloning by nuclear transfer (NT). Nuclear transfer involves the complete removal of genetic material (chromosomes) from an egg to produce an enucleated cell (cytoplast). It is replaced by a nucleus containing a full complement of chromosomes from a suitable donor cell (the karyoplast), which is introduced into the recipient cytoplast by direct microinjection or by fusion of the donor and recipient cells. The egg is then implanted in another adult female for normal gestation and delivery (Fig. 1). Depending upon the source of donor nuclei, cloning by nuclear transfer can be classified into embryonic cell (unspecialized) NT and somatic cell (differentiated) NT. Somatic cell NT is the most important process used for animal cloning and has most potential applications.

HISTORY OF ANIMAL CLONING

The first successful cloning experiments in vertebrates arose from the desire of embryologists to know whether the process of cell differentiation from an egg involved permanent or stable changes in the genome. One idea was that, as cells differentiate, the genes no longer needed (such as skin genes in intestinal cells) could be lost or permanently repressed. The other idea was that all genes are present in all cell types, and that cell differentiation involved the selective activation and repression of genes appropriate to the cell type. The transfer of nuclei from differentiated cells to an egg could answer these important questions. In 1952, the first successful transplantation of nuclei from early embryo cells was achieved with the American frog *Rana pipiens*.[8]

In the late 1980s, scientists took cloning to the next stage by cloning other mammals (cattle, sheep, pigs, mice, and rhesus monkeys).[9] This is seen as the first step toward the cloning of mammals closest to humans. But they were limited in their success to using the early unspecialized embryo cells, i.e., not adult cells. All this background work led to Dolly, the first mammal to develop from the nucleus of an adult somatic cell.[1]

SUCCESSFULLY CLONED SPECIES

We have seen that the published data suggest that nuclear transfer in some animals is much less successful than in other species. Part of this difference may reflect the intensity of research, and part may be real and reflect another component critical for the successful reprogramming of the donor nucleus—nuclear remodeling. In order for a differentiated nucleus to redirect development in the environment of the egg, its particular constellation of regulatory proteins must be replaced by those of the egg in time for the embryo to be able to use the genome of the donor nucleus to transcribe the genes it needs for normal development. It should be noted that scientists have not

Encyclopedia of Animal Science
DOI: 10.1081/E-EAS 120019482

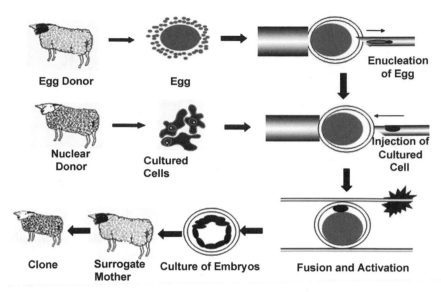

Fig. 1 Schematic of procedures for cloning by nuclear transfer. Nuclear transfer requires a source of recipient eggs. The genetic material is removed from the recipient egg (enucleation) using a glass micropipette. Donor cells are collected, cultured, and transferred next to the cytoplast. The cytoplast and donor cell are then fused together and activated so that development begins. The resulting NT embryo is cultured prior to transfer to a surrogate mother.

yet succeeded in making cloned dogs or monkeys by somatic cell NT cloning.

FACTORS AFFECTING EFFICIENCY OF SOMATIC NUCLEAR TRANSFER

The efficiency of somatic cell nuclear transfer, when measured as development to term as a proportion of oocytes used, has been very low (1–2%). A number of variables influence the ability to reproduce a specific genotype by cloning. These include species, source of recipient ova, cell type of nuclei donor, treatment of donor cells prior to NT, method of artificial oocyte activation, embryo culture, possible loss of somatic imprinting in the nuclei of reconstructed embryos, failure of reprogramming the transplanted nucleus adequately, and techniques employed for NT.[10]

APPLICATIONS OF SOMATIC NUCLEAR TRANSFER

Making Clones for Research Purposes

Inbred strains of animals have been a major mainstay of biological research for years. These animals have been bred by brother-sister mating for many generations until they are essentially all genetically identical within each sex. Experimental analysis is then simplified, because variations in response to experimental treatment due to variations in genetic background can be eliminated.

Clearly, generating homozygous inbred lines in larger animals with long generation times and small numbers of offspring is not readily achievable. By somatic cell nuclear transfer, we can produce larger numbers of genetically identical animals, which reduces variability in experiments. This consequently reduces the number of animals needed for an experiment.

Propagating Desirable Stocks

In animal breeding strategies, rapid spread of desirable traits within stocks of domestic animals is of obvious commercial importance. Nuclear transfer cloning, especially from adult nuclei, could provide an additional means of increasing the genetic merit of a given generation of animals. The ability to make identical copies of adult prize cows, sheep, and pigs is a feature unique to nuclear transfer technologies.

Improving Generation and Propagation of Transgenic Livestock

Transgenic technology developed to add genes has been widely applied to livestock species because it is technically simple, although it is inefficient. Not all injected eggs will develop into transgenic animals, and then not all transgenic animals will express the transgene in the desired manner. Characterizing a transgenic line of livestock is a slow and expensive business. Nuclear transfer would speed the expansion of a successful transgenic line, but—perhaps more important—it would allow more efficient generation of transgenic animals in the first place. Foreign DNA could be introduced into cell lines in culture, and cells containing the transgene in the correct configuration could be grown and used as a source of nuclei for transfer, ensuring that all offspring are transgenic.[11–13]

Generating Targeted Gene Alterations

The most powerful technology for genetic manipulation in mammals—gene targeting—was developed in mice, and depends on the ability of mammalian DNA, when added to cells in culture, to recombine homologously with identical DNA sequences in the genome and to replace them. In mice, this can be achieved by the use of embryonic stem (ES) cells. However to date, there are no fully validated ES cell lines in domestic animals. Nuclear transfer from nonpluripotent cell lines provides an alternative to the ES cell route for the introduction of targeted gene alterations into the germ line. Successful production of cloned pigs for xenotransplantation resulting from the combination of somatic nuclear transfer with specific modification (knock out) of fetal fibroblasts has been reported.[14]

Rederiving Endangered and Extinct Animals

Endangered species such as the giant panda that have difficulty reproducing in zoos may be preserved using this nuclear transfer technology. This underscores the importance of such conservation efforts as preserving cells of animals that are in danger of extinction to create a genetic trust for future cloning. In addition, cross-species NT technology confers certain advantages over traditional conservation efforts, such as the possibility of cloning extinct animals such as the wooly mammoth.

CONCLUSION

Although somatic nuclear transfer cloning has helped answer many fundamental questions in developmental biology and has many potential applications, the efficiency of somatic cell nuclear transfer is very low. Scientists are currently working on improving the efficiency of the procedures and applying the technology to the creation of animals with targeted genetic modifications.

ACKNOWLEDGMENTS

The authors would like to acknowledge support from Food for the 21st Century, and the National Institutes of Health (RR13438).

REFERENCES

1. Wilmut, I.; Schnieke, A.E.; McWhir, J.; Kind, A.J.; Campbell, K.H.S. Viable offspring derived from fetal and adult mammalian cells. Nature **1997**, *385*, 810–813.
2. Kato, Y.; Tani, T.; Sotomaru, Y.; Kurokawa, K.; Kato, J.; Doguchi, H.; Yasue, H.; Tsunoda, Y. Eight calves cloned from somatic cells of a single adult. Science **1998**, *282*, 2095–2098.
3. Wakayama, T.; Perry, A.C.; Zuccotti, M.; Johnson, K.R.; Yanagimachi, R. Full-term development of mice from enucleated oocytes injected with cumulus cell nuclei. Nature **1998**, *394*, 369–374.
4. Onishi, A.; Iwamoto, M.; Akita, T.; Mikawa, S.; Takeda, K.; Awata, T.; Hanada, H.; Perry, A.C.F. Pig cloning by microinjection of fetal fibroblast nuclei. Science **2000**, *289*, 1188–1190.
5. Baguisi, A.; Behboodi, E.; Melican, D.T.; Pollock, J.S.; Destrempes, M.M.; Cammuso, C.; Williams, J.L.; Nims, S.D.; Porter, C.A.; Midura, P.; Palacios, M.J.; Ayres, S.L.; Denniston, R.S.; Hayes, M.L.; Ziomek, C.A.; Meade, H.M.; Godke, R.A.; Gavin, W.G.; Overstrom, E.W.; Echelard, Y. Production of goats by somatic cell nuclear transfer. Nat. Biotechnol. **1999**, *17*, 456–461.
6. Shin, T.; Kraemer, D.; Pryor, J.; Liu, L.; Rugila, J.; Howe, L.; Buck, S.; Murphy, K.; Lyons, L.; Westhusin, M. A cat cloned by nuclear transplantation. Nature **2002**, *415*, 859.
7. Chesne, P.; Adenot, P.; Viglietta, C.; Baratte, M.; Boulanger, L.; Renard, J.P. Cloned rabbits produced by nuclear transfer from adult somatic cells. Nat. Biotechnol. **2002**, *20* (4), 366–369.
8. Briggs, R.; King, T.J. Transplantation of living cell nuclei from blastula cells into enucleated frogs' eggs. Proc. Natl. Acad. Sci. U. S. A. **1952**, *38*, 455–463.
9. Lai, L.; Prather, R.S. Progress in producing knockout models for xenotransplantation by nuclear transfer. Annal. Med. **2002**, *34*, 501–506.
10. Prather, R.S.; Kuhholzer, B.; Lai, L.; Park, K.-W. Changes in the structure of nuclei after transfer to oocytes. Cloning **2000**, *2* (3), 117–122.
11. Cibelli, J.B.; Stice, S.L.; Golueke, P.J.; Kane, J.J.; Jerry, J.; Blackwell, C.; Ponce de Leon, F.A.; Robl, J.M. Cloned transgenic calves produced from nonquiescent fetal fibroblasts. Science **1998**, *280*, 1256–1258.
12. Zou, X.; Wang, Y.; Cheng, Y.; Yang, Y.; Ju, H.; Tang, H.; Shen, Y.; Mu, Z.; Xu, S.; Du, M. Generation of cloned goats (*Capra hircus*) from transfected foetal fibroblast cells, the effect of donor cell cycle. Mol. Reprod. Dev. **2002**, *61* (2), 164–172.
13. Park, K.W.; Cheong, H.T.; Lai, L.; Im, G.S.; Kühholzer, B.; Bonk, A.; Samuel, M.; Rieke, A.; Day, B.N.; Murphy, C.N.; Carter, D.B.; Prather, R.S. Production of nuclear transfer-derived swine that express the enhanced green fluorescent protein. Anim. Biotechnol. **2001**, *12*, 173–181.
14. Lai, L.; Kolber-Simonds, D.; Park, K.W.; Cheong, HT.; Greenstein, J.L.; Im, G.S.; Samuel, M.; Bonk, A.; Rieke, A.; Day, B.N.; Murphy, C.N.; Carter, D.B.; Hawley, R.J.; Prather, R.S. Production of alpha-1,3-galactosyltransferase knockout pigs by nuclear transfer cloning. Science **2002**, *295*, 1089–1092.

B

Biotechnology: Embryo Technology for Cattle

Robert A. Godke
Louisiana State University, Baton Rouge, Louisiana, U.S.A.

Curtis R. Youngs
Iowa State University, Ames, Iowa, U.S.A.

INTRODUCTION

Embryo transfer in food animals began in the 1930s using sheep and goats; however, it was not until the early 1950s, following successful embryo transfers producing live offspring in cattle and swine, that agricultural interest began to develop for this assisted reproductive technology. The first use of embryo transfer by commercial units in North America did not occur until the early 1970s. Initially, embryos were recovered from valuable donor cattle and transferred to recipient females by time-consuming and labor-intensive surgical collection and surgical transfer methods. The popularity of embryo transfer increased markedly when the nonsurgical embryo collection and transfer procedures became available to the commercial industry in 1976. Currently, embryo transfer is more often used today by the dairy producers than by beef cattle producers.

EMBRYO TRANSFER UPDATE

Historically, the process of embryo transfer involved the selection of genetically superior cows followed by a five-day treatment with follicle-stimulating hormone to cause the release of multiple ova (instead of one) at the time of ovulation. This donor female was artificially inseminated with semen from a genetically elite bull, and after 7 or 8 days the embryos were recovered and transferred to recipient females whose estrous cycles were synchronized with that of the donor female.

Embryo transplantation has evolved from a few centralized transplant stations to many smaller clinics offering on-farm services. Although actual methodology has changed little since the 1970s, two major improvements are the use of less follicle-stimulating agent over fewer days in donor cows and the need for fewer sperm for donor insemination. With experienced professionals, the embryo recovery rates are expected to be >75%, with four to eight good-quality embryos per donor collection.

In recent years, a single-embryo on-the-farm collection approach has become popular with progressive dairymen. This approach uses no follicle stimulatory hormones to treat donor cows. Single embryos are collected from the highest producing cows in the herd and are then transferred individually to cows in the lowest producing group of the herd. Also, frozen embryos can be purchased commercially by producers for transplantation on a year-round basis. Pregnancy rates following transfer of excellent-quality frozen-thawed embryos are similar to those obtained after transfer of fresh embryos. The use of cryopreserved embryos is predicted to be the market growth area, with the potential for the use of frozen embryos in cattle herds being virtually unlimited.

IN VITRO FERTILIZATION

For over two decades researchers have been fine tuning in vitro (test-tube) fertilization (IVF) procedures for cattle. The IVF technology has only been commercially available at embryo transplant stations for cattle producers since the early 1990s because IVF is a complex multi-step process that requires a well-equipped laboratory and a skilled technician. From good-quality oocytes harvested from cattle ovaries, one would expect a 90% in vitro maturation rate and >80% cleavage rates.

The resulting IVF-derived embryos are held at cow body temperature in an incubator for 7 or 8 days, with the expectation of 35–50% reaching the morula and blastocyst stages of development. Embryos are then nonsurgically transferred to females at the appropriate stage of their estrous cycle. The pregnancy rate obtained with good-quality IVF-derived embryos is expected to range from 50–65%. Although viable healthy calves have been produced from frozen-thawed IVF-derived embryos, the pregnancy rate is generally lower than with unfrozen embryos.

Encyclopedia of Animal Science
DOI: 10.1081/E-EAS 120019483

OOCYTE COLLECTION FROM DONOR FEMALES

The IVF procedure offers an alternative to producers who have genetically valuable cows that for some reason are unable to produce viable embryos through standard embryo collection procedures. This technology can be used with oocytes harvested from older nonovulating cows, females with physical injuries (e.g., lameness), and problem breeding cows (e.g., abnormal cervix). Good success has been reported using IVF procedures on supplemental oocytes harvested from cows with cystic ovarian disease.

Today, oocytes are harvested from females by transvaginal ultrasound-guided collection procedures. To retrieve the oocytes for IVF, a trained professional inserts an ultrasound-guided stainless steel needle through the wall of the vagina near the cervix to extract oocytes from both ovaries of the donor female. This approach can also be used to harvest oocytes from prepubertal heifers and during the first trimester of gestation in pregnant cows.

With IVF the potential exists for more embryos to be produced in a shorter period of time because the collection procedure can be repeated on the same cow multiple times per month. Oocytes can be harvested from an early postpartum cow before the female begins cyclic activity. Good-quality embryos have been produced with IVF from oocytes harvested from cows as early as 10 days after calving. The approach allows the opportunity to produce one or more extra calves from the cow before she is mated to establish a pregnancy.

EMBRYO SEXING

Microsurgical methods have been developed to extract individual cells (blastomeres) from early stage embryos. The cells remaining in the biopsied embryo generally survive and develop into a viable offspring. The individual cells removed from both early- and later-stage embryos can be used to determine the sex of each embryo prior to its transfer to a recipient female. Embryo sexing using the DNA amplification procedure known as the polymerase chain reaction (PCR), with specific Y-chromosome DNA probes, is remarkably accurate for sexing cattle embryos.[1] This procedure is now user-friendly, and can be completed within 5 hours after the embryos are harvested from donor animals. Sexing later-stage embryos (6 to 8 days of age) before transplantation is now possible at embryo transplant stations. The capability of sexing embryos gives producers the option of selecting bull or heifer calves for market and for reproductive management purposes.

EMBRYO CLONING

In the 1980s, procedures were developed to produce genetically identical twin offspring (clones) by bisecting or splitting individual sheep, goat, swine, cattle, and horse embryos (5–8 days of age). A glass needle or a razor blade is used to bisect the embryo, and the pregnancy rates (45–70%) obtained in cattle after the transfer of one-half of a bisected embryo (''half'' embryo or demi-embryo) are similar to those obtained with intact embryos from the same donor female. Today, methods are available to bisect animal embryos with a glass microscope slide and a hand-held razor blade.[2] This low-cost microsurgery procedure is simple and relatively easy to learn.

Embryo bisection offers the potential of doubling the number of viable embryo transplant offspring produced from valuable donor females. For example, 100 good-quality cattle embryos may result in 65 transplant offspring born, whereas 100 similar-quality embryos divided into halves would yield 200 demi-embryos, which then may result in 130 demi-embryo transplant calves born (130% pregnancy rate from 100 embryos). Twin calves produced by microsurgery will result in genetically identical offspring of the same sex. This removes the concern for freemartinism, if both demi-embryos are transferred to the same recipient female.

A new cloning method called nuclear transfer (transferring individual undifferentiated embryonic cells to enucleated oocytes) emerged in the mid 1980s.[3] Multiple nuclear transfer-derived offspring from individual blastomeres from a single early-stage embryo have been produced in several farm animal species (e.g., sheep, cattle). Nuclear transfer-derived offspring have been produced four generations from a single cattle embryo. Unexpectedly, some of the nuclear transplant calves have extended gestation lengths, and there are reports of abnormally large term offspring (e.g., calves, lambs) that need assistance at birth. The reason for these problems is not clear, although laboratory culture conditions have been implicated as a potential cause. Even though improvements in the nuclear transfer methodology are still needed, this approach has a lot of potential for seedstock producers.

SOMATIC CELL CLONING

More recently, there has been a major breakthrough in the animal nuclear transfer procedure. With Dolly, the famous sheep, cells were harvested from the mammary gland (adult cells) of a mature ewe for cloning. These cells were multiplied to produce a larger cell population for the cloning procedure. The production of cloned sheep was important because Dolly was the first mammal ever produced from an adult differentiated body cell (somatic cell).

The cloning of an adult sheep, reported in 1997, stimulated strong interest in nuclear transfer technology by the livestock industry. To construct cloned embryos with this new approach, a somatic cell is taken from a developing fetus or an adult animal (male or female) and microsurgically transferred into an unfertilized oocyte from which the nuclear DNA has been removed (enucleation). The enucleated oocyte with a newly introduced donor cell becomes activated, and then the reprogrammed nucleus directs embryonic development into a cloned embryo for recipient transplantation. Once the donor cell population has been prepared, hundreds of cloned embryos can be produced weekly in the laboratory, using oocytes extracted from abattoir ovaries.

The potential for the use of this new technology has left the world in amazement. Somatic cell clones have been produced in mice, rabbits, cats, sheep, goats, swine, domestic beef and dairy cattle, as well as exotic cattle and sheep. Most recently, cloned mules and a cloned horse have been produced. Cloning would provide the cattle producer an opportunity to reproduce valuable seedstock, clone animals that have suffered an injury and can no longer reproduce, or clone males that had been castrated. Cloning technology would also provide livestock producers with ready access to production-tested breeding stock, thus increasing the accuracy of selection in their breeding herds.

CONCLUSION

Advances in the development and application of assisted reproductive technologies have accelerated over the past decade. Although the availability and cost-effectiveness of some of these new technologies still remain in question, there is little doubt about their potential impact on livestock production in the future.[4] Utilization of these emerging technologies will require more intensive management by the cattle producer. These new technologies, if economically practical, will provide producers with the opportunity to change the genetic potential of cattle at a faster rate than is possible by the conventional methods presently in use.

REFERENCES

1. Herr, C.M.; Reed, K.C. Micromanipulation of bovine embryos for sex determination. Theriogenology **1991**, *35* (1), 45–54.
2. Rorie, R.W.; McFarland, C.W.; Overskei, T.L.; Voelkel, S.A.; Godke, R.A. A new method of splitting embryos without the use of a commercial micromanipulator unit. Theriogenology **1985**, *23* (1), 224. (abstract).
3. Willadsen, S.M. Nuclear transplantation in sheep embryos. Nature **1986**, *320* (6), 63–65.
4. Hansel, W.; Godke, R.A. Future prospectives on animal biotechnology. Anim. Biotechnology **1992**, *3* (1), 111–137.

Biotechnology: Genetically Modified Feeds

Fred Owens
Thomas E. Sauber
Greg Dana
Pioneer Hi-Bred International, Inc., Johnston, Iowa, U.S.A.

INTRODUCTION

Genetic modification (GM) is the transfer of genes across barriers that are normally impervious. Transfer within or across species, genera, and kingdoms results in transgenic or genetically modified organisms (GMOs). These genes can change crop characteristics or nutritive value. Transgenic crops can alter the supply and quality of feed, diet formulation, and animal productivity.

BACKGROUND

Production of transgenic crops increased more than thirtyfold from 1996 to 2002,[1] primarily from four crops (soybeans, 63%; corn, 19%; cotton, 13%; canola, 3% of total transgenic crops) grown primarily in four countries (United States, 63%; Argentina, 23%; Canada, 6%; China, 4% of transgenic cropland). Land area devoted to transgenic crops in the United States is shown in Fig. 1.[2]

IMPACTS OF GM ON LIVESTOCK FEED QUALITY AND COST

Production Traits

Most transgenic plants possess traits that alter crop production (often called input traits; Table 1). Through altering crop production procedures, they reduce feed contaminants (e.g., pesticides and herbicides). By reducing crop damage from insect pests, viruses, and fungi, they stabilize feed supplies and help modulate volatility in feed prices. By reducing the need for soil tillage, they help to conserve water and soil and expand crop production into new regions.[3,4]

Product Traits

Transgenic crops with improved product (also called output) traits have altered value for animal feeding or for industrial use. These include increased content or availability of energy and nutrients or compounds that improve animal health or value of animal products (improved flavor and tenderness, extended shelf life).[5] For example, both increased phosphorus availability and improved amino acid balance reduce dietary needs and excretion of nutrients by nonruminants.[6] Unfortunately, ruminants benefit from neither of these traits, illustrating how value of a trait can differ among end users. A product trait has value when the crop is identity-preserved during production, handling, and marketing—a challenge to traditional grain handlers who blend commercial grains. Furthermore, rapid assay procedures are needed to verify presence of the desired trait.

Limitations of Feeds from GM Crops

In most countries, products from transgenic plants are considered acceptable when they are substantially equivalent to products not derived by GM. However, consumer concerns have precipitated governmental restrictions in certain countries; these hamper the international trade of GM crops. Because GM food crops have been grown on more than 230 million cumulative hectares worldwide over the past seven years[1] without any verified instances of adverse nutritional effects on livestock or humans, most researchers have become convinced that products from transgenic plants are safe.[7]

Safety of transgenic crops entails two scientific questions. First, can an introduced gene be transferred to

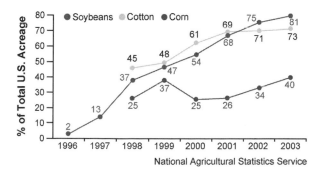

Fig. 1 Percentage of land area in the United States devoted to transgenic crops. (From Ref. 2.) (*View this art in color at www.dekker.com.*)

Encyclopedia of Animal Science
DOI: 10.1081/E-EAS 120019484

Table 1 Current and pending transgenic agricultural products

Characteristic	Target crop	Company	Trade name or biological function
Herbicide tolerance			
Glufosinate tolerance	Canola, cotton[a] Rice,[a] soybeans[a]	Bayer	Libertylink products
	Corn	Aventis	Libertylink corn
	Alfalfa,[a] canola, corn, cotton, lettuce[a] soybeans, sugar beets[a]		
Glyphosate tolerance	Turf grass,[a] wheat	Monsanto	Roundup ready products
	Corn[a]	Syngenta	Glyphosate-tolerant
	Strawberries[a]	DNA Plant Tech	
Insect resistance			
Corn borer resistance	Corn	Bayer	Libertylink corn
	Corn	Dow/Pioneer	Herculex I
	Corn	Monsanto	Yieldgard
	Corn	Mycogen	Natureguard
	Corn	Syngenta	Knockout, yieldgard
	Sweet corn	Syngenta	Attribute
Rootworm protection	Corn	Monsanto	Maxgard
	Corn[a]	Dow/Pioneer	Rootworm-resistant
Borer and rootworm-resistant	Corn[a]	Syngenta	Insect-resistant corn
Bollworm protection	Cotton	Monsanto	Bollgard
Broad-spectrum pest resistance	Cotton[a]	Dow	Insect-protected cotton
Broad-spectrum pest resistance	Cotton[a]	Syngenta	Vegetative insecticidal protein
Codling moth protection	Apples[a]	Monsanto	Bt insect-protected
Insect protection	Soybeans[a]	Monsanto	Insect-protected soybeans
Fungi-resistant			
Black sigatoka fungus resistance	Bananas[a]	DNA Plant Tech	Disease-resistant bananas
Fusarium blight (scab)-resistant	Wheat[a]	Syngenta	Fusarium-resistant wheat
Fungi-resistant	Strawberries[a]	DNA Plant Tech	
Ringspot virus-resistant	Papaya	Cornell	Rainbow, sunup
Sclerotina-resistant	Canola[a]	DuPont	Disease-resistant canola
Altered composition			
Amylase expression	Corn[a]	Syngenta	Amylase for enhanced ethanol
Greater digestibility	Corn[a]	DuPont	Increased energy availability
Higher energy density	Corn[a]	Dow	Nutritionally enhanced
Improved protein functionality	Soybeans[a]	DuPont	Improved protein function
Increased phosphorus digestion	Feeds[a]	Syngenta	Phytase for animal feed
Lauric acid-rich seed	Rapeseed	Calgene	Laurical
Lengthened shelf life	Bananas[a]	Syngenta	Long shelf life bananas
No trans fatty acids	Canola	Dow	Natreon naturally stable
No trans fatty acids	Sunflowers	Mycogen	Naturally stable
Oleic acid-rich nuts	Peanuts	Mycogen	Flavor runner naturally stable
Altered growth or appearance			
Delayed ripening, longer lasting	Raspberries[a] Tomatoes[a]	Agritrope	Long shelf life fruits and vegetables
Drought resistance	Corn[a]	DuPont	Improved drought response
Mauve (violet) color	Carnations	Florigene	Moondust

[a]Transgenic crops expected to be produced commercially by 2008.
(From Ref. 4.)

animals and alter genetics or productivity? Second, will protein synthesized by the transferred gene cause adverse reactions (e.g., allergies, toxicoses)?

Gene Transfer

Nature has endowed animals with barriers that prevent foreign DNA from entering the genome or synthesizing foreign proteins. Compositionally, the DNA of a transgenic plant is the same as DNA consumed as part of normal diets; it shares a similar fate. Food processing and ingredient extraction remove or inactivate some DNA. Next, DNA is degraded within the digestive tract.[8] Transfer of genes from normal or altered plants to the intestinal microflora and enterocytes has been speculated.[9] Using methods to detect ultratrace gene fragments, no transfer of transgenes to humans could be detected.[8] Considering that animals and humans have been exposed to DNA from plants and bacteria for centuries, dietary genes appear innocuous.[10]

ALTERED PROTEINS

Allergic reactions among commercial livestock are rare even though many traditional feed ingredients contain allergenic proteins, e.g., milk, eggs, legumes (peanut and soy), tree nuts, and cereals. To avoid allergens in transgenic crops, safety tests are conducted, e.g., susceptibility of transgenic protein to acidified pepsin. The development of GM crops has advanced scientific understanding about allergens and led to crops devoid of their normal allergens. Reducing digestion inhibitors (e.g., trypsin inhibitors, lectins, and viscous compounds) and eliminating indigestible components (e.g., oligosaccharides) can enhance digestibility and reduce the need for extensive feed processing. This can improve amino acid availability and energy availability. Transgenic crops are monitored for presence of compounds that adversely affect nontarget species and gastrointestinal microbes, but organisms closely related to a target can be impacted. For example, because the genus *Coleoptera* includes both the corn borer—a target species—and the Monarch butterfly, crops toxic for the corn borer are toxic to both species. Fortunately, differences in habitat and food selection patterns between target and nontarget species generally avoid adverse effects.

SAFEGUARDS

In the United States, the safety of transgenic crops is monitored by biotech firms, academia, and governmental regulators from the Food and Drug Administration, the Environmental Protection Agency, and the Department of Agriculture.[11–13] Test strategies are scientifically robust and proportionate to other areas of safety evaluation.[14,15] To become commercial, a GM crop must be considered as safe as crops currently produced and nonobjections from governmental agencies must be on file. In addition, isolation zones can be imposed to avoid pollen transfer, refuge areas specified to postpone insect resistance, and prohibition regions established to avoid habitats of endangered species. The benefits of a transgenic crop— e.g., increased yield or nutritional value, reduced insecticide and herbicide use, reduced fungal damage, decreased nutrient waste by animals—must outweigh adverse effects on other plants or nontarget species. Safety evaluation is more stringent and more extensive for GM crops than for conventional crops. Biotech companies and academic groups conduct voluntary stewardship trials to test the nutritive value of transgenic crops and products. In numerous trials and field tests with poultry, swine, dairy and beef cattle, and fish,[2,16–19] no adverse effects of transgenic plants or plant products on productivity have been detected.[10]

CONCLUSION

Close scrutiny by the biotech industry, academicians, governmental regulators, and consumer advocacy groups has helped assure that GM plant and animal products are as safe as crops developed by other selection procedures. Through transgenic modification, the use of pesticides and herbicides on crops is being reduced, the stability of yields and crop supplies is being improved, and the nutritive value and potential health benefits of plant products are being enhanced. Combined, these effects help reduce the environmental footprints of animal and plant production. The potential to further improve the nutritive value, safety, and quality of food and feed resources through GM alteration of plants is limited only by the imagination of researchers.

REFERENCES

1. International Service for the Acquisition of Agri-Biotech Applications. *Preview: Global Status of Commercialized Transgenic Crops*; International Service for the Acquisition of Agri-Biotech Applications, 2002. Brief no. 27. http://www.isaaa.org (accessed September 2003).
2. Council for Biotechnology Information, 2003. http://www.whybiotech.com (accessed September 2003).
3. Barnes, R.L. *Why the American Soybean Association Supports Transgenic Soybeans*; 2002. http://www.asa-europe.org/pdf/barnes.pdf (accessed September 2003).

4. National Corn Growers Association and U.S. Grains Council. *2003 Ag Biotechnology Reference Guide*; 2003. http://www.ncga.com/biotechnology/pdfs/biotech guide817.pdf (accessed September 2003).

5. DuPont Biotechnology. *Crops Derived from Biotechnology in the Animal Production Industry*; 2003. http://www.dupont.com/biotech/science_knowledge/feed_livestock/scientific_narrative.htm (accessed September 2003).

6. Coon, C. *The Present and Future Utilization of Biotechnology in the Feed Industry: A Poultry Nutritionist's Perspective*; 2002. http://www.asa-europe.org/pdf/present.pdf (accessed September 2003).

7. American Medical Association Council on Scientific Affairs. *Genetically Modified Crops and Food*; 2000. Report No. 10. http://www.ama-assn.org/ama1/pub/mm/-1/csa10cropsandfoods.pdf (accessed September 2003).

8. Netherwood, T.; Martin-Orue, S.M.; O'Donnell, A.G.; Gockling, S.; Graham, J.; Mathers, J.C.; Gilbert, H.J. Assessing the survival of transgenic plant DNA in the human gastrointestinal tract. Nat. Biotechnol. **2004**, *22*, 204–209.

9. Beever, D.E.; Phipps, R.H. The fate of plant DNA and novel proteins in feeds for farm livestock: A United Kingdom perspective. J. Anim. Sci. **2001**, *79* (E. Suppl.), E290–E295.

10. Federation of Animal Science Societies. *The Composition and Quality of Meat, Milk and Eggs from Animals Fed Biotech Crops and Attempts to Detect Transgenic DNA and Protein in Meat, Milk and Eggs from Animals Fed Biotech Crops*; 2001. http://www.animalbiotechnology.org/abstc.pdf. (accessed September 2003).

11. U.S. Food and Drug Administration, Center for Food Safety and Applied Nutrition. *Biotechnology*; 2003. http://www.cfsan.fda.gov/~lrd/biotechm.html (accessed September 2003).

12. Environmental Protection Agency. *Regulation of Biotechnology for Use in Pest Management*; 2002. http://www.epa.gov/pesticides/biopesticides/reg_of_biotech/eparegofbiotech.htm (accessed September 2003).

13. United States Department of Agriculture. *Agricultural Biotechnology. Permitting, Notification, and Deregulation*; 2002. http://www.aphis.usda.gov/brs (accessed September 2003).

14. FAO/WHO2002. http://www.who.int/fsf (accessed September 2003).

15. *Codex Alimentarius*; 2002. http://www.foodlaw.rdg.ac.uk/news/in-02012.htm.

16. Food Safety Network. *GM Food Animal Feeding Study References and Reviews*; 2000. http://www.foodsafetynetwork.ca/animal/Ontarion-feedingstudies.htm (accessed September 2003).

17. Thomas, B.R. *Biotech Food Safety Assessment. Seed Biotechnology Center*; 2001. http://sbc.ucdavis.edu/outreach/resource/gm_food_safety.htm#Feed%20References (accessed September 2003).

18. Clark, J.H.; Ipharraguerre, I.R. Livestock performance: Feeding biotech crops. J. Dairy Sci. **2002**, *84* (Suppl. E), E9–E18.

19. International Life Sciences Institute. *Genetic Modification Technology and Food: Consumer Health and Safety*; 2003. http://www.ilsi.org/publications/pubslist.cfm?pubentityid=%2D1&publicationid=418 (accessed September 2003).

Biotechnology: Sexing Sperm

Duane L. Garner
University of Nevada, Reno, Nevada, U.S.A.

INTRODUCTION

Sex can be predetermined in the offspring of mammals by separating the sex-determining sperm prior to insemination with a flow cytometer/cell sorter. This sexing technology has advanced to commercialization in cattle with marketable applications in other domestic species impending.

BIOLOGICAL BASIS OF SPERM SEXING

Separation of sperm according to the sex chromosome is based on the DNA content of the sperm. Mammalian semen can be sexed because the X-chromosome-bearing sperm that produce females contain about 4% more DNA than do the Y-chromosome-bearing sperm that produce males. The procedure is 85-95% accurate for the selected sex.[1–3] Sorting of live mammalian sperm according to their DNA content first was developed the USDA Beltsville Agricultural Research Center.[4] This flow cytometric sorting procedure for sperm[5–8] is patented and exclusively licensed worldwide for non-human mammals to XY, Inc., a private company. For the sorting procedure, freshly collected sperm are stained with a DNA-specific bisbenzimidazole dye, Hoechst 33342, for approximately 1 hr prior to sorting.[9] Hoechst 33342-stained sperm fluoresce bright blue when exposed to a laser beam of short wavelength light and the X-bearing sperm are differentiated from the Y-bearing sperm because they fluoresce brighter due to their greater DNA content. The fluorescence of each stained sperm is measured in a stream of fluid as it passes in front of a photomultiplier tube (PMT).[10] The resultant data are integrated using a powerful computer. Only the DNA content of properly oriented sperm can be measured because the flat surface of each sperm head must be properly oriented relative to the PMT.[1,2]

FLOW SORTING SYSTEM

As the liquid stream containing sperm exits the sorter nozzle, it is vibrated at about 75,000 to 85,000 oscillations/

sec to break the stream into individual droplets.[9] Although not all of these formed droplets contain sperm, those that do are electrically charged, either positive or negative, according to the DNA content information previously provided by detector. Droplets containing improperly oriented sperm, more than one sperm, or dead sperm, as determined by uptake of a vital dye, are disposed of as waste because no charge is applied to these droplets. As the droplets pass by an oppositely charged plate they are deflected into a collection vessel according to the DNA content of the sperm. Those droplets containing Y-sperm are simultaneously directed to a separate collection vessel by applying an opposite charge to those drops to deflect them toward the opposing-charged plate. Opposing charges are applied to droplets containing X-sperm so that they are directed toward a separate vessel. Three streams of droplets containing X-sperm, Y-sperm, or no sperm as well as too many sperm are collected into separate vessels. Approximately 40% of the living sperm going through the sorter at a speed of approximately 75 km/hr can be accurately sexed and collected. Thus, at an event rate of 28,000 total sperm/sec, nearly 5000 live sperm/sec of each sex can be sorted simultaneously with 85–95% accuracy.[8] The current system can produce approximately 10 to 15×10^6 live bovine sperm/hr of each sex-determining gamete. Considerable numbers of sperm are, however, lost in the centrifugation and other postsorting steps making actual yields somewhat lower.[1,2] Sperm of other species tend to sort at somewhat slower rates. Sorted sperm are dilute so they must be reconcentrated prior to being used for artificial insemination (AI) or in vitro fertilization (IVF).

UTILIZATION OF SEX-SORTED SPERM

The first sex-selected mammalian offspring were rabbits born following surgical insemination of sexed sperm.[5] Later, in a milestone achievement, a similar system was used to produce sex-selected piglets, demonstrating the utility of the system for pre-selecting the sex of offspring in domestic livestock.[6] The first calves born were from embryos derived from IVF with sex-sorted sperm, but most of the recent work in cattle has been done using AI.[1,2,8,9]

Encyclopedia of Animal Science
DOI: 10.1081/E-EAS 120019487

Cattle

Sex-sorted bovine sperm must be reconcentrated by centrifugation[11] before they can be properly packaged in 0.25-ml French straws at doses of 1 to 6×10^6 sperm/straw. This is contrasted to conventional AI procedures that use at least 20×10^6 sperm/straw making the insemination dose for sex-sorted bovine sperm about 1/20 to 1/3 that of a normal AI dose. This is necessary because it takes some time to sort each dose, even at the high sort rates now being achieved. Fortunately, sexed bovine sperm can be cryopreserved, thereby allowing efficient use in AI. Current sexing technology has been applied mainly in heifers due to their inherently higher fertility. Several regimens have been used successfully to synchronize estrus to optimize insemination with low doses of sexed sperm.[3] Pregnancy rates from the use of sexed, cryopreserved sperm have been about 60–80% of controls inseminated with 7–20 times more sperm or higher insemination dose.[3,4] With sex-sorted sperm, some differences in pregnancy rates have been noted among bulls, suggesting that only sperm from highly fertile bulls should be sorted for predetermining sex of their offspring. Until recently, field trials with sexed sperm were conducted by sorting the gametes in fluid pressurized to 50 psi. This pressure level, however, was found to be detrimental to sperm.[4] With the latest procedures, where the pressure has been lowered to 40 psi, pregnancy rates in heifers inseminated with sexed sperm have been 60–80% of controls, depending on the particular bull, inseminator skills, and management level of the herd.[4]

Swine

The first sexed piglets were from sows surgically inseminated with sex-sorted sperm.[6] Even with recent technological improvements in sorting efficiency, production of adequate numbers of boar sperm for uterine insemination of swine is limiting because normally 3 to 5×10^9 sperm/dose are used with the insemination being repeated two to three times during each estrus.[12] A system must be developed to deliver fewer sperm deeper into the porcine reproductive tract before sex-sorted sperm can be used effectively with AI of swine. Recently, this endoscopic approach has been replaced with a newly designed, flexible catheter for deep nonsurgical insemination.[13] A 1.3-m-deep uterine insemination catheter was used to deposit 7.5 ml containing 150×10^6 unsexed sperm in the upper end of the uterine horn of sows in natural postweaning estrus. Sows inseminated one time 32 hr post onset of estrus achieved pregnancy rates of 83.3% (50/60 sows) for sexed sperm and 87.3% (48/55) unsexed sperm.[14] Adequate fertility rates were achieved with only 2–5% of the sperm used conventionally for AI in pigs. These preliminary data suggest that this approach may be suitable for efficiently producing single sex litters.

Sheep

Early efforts to predetermine the sex of lambs used low doses of freshly sorted ram sperm that were surgically deposited directly into the uteri of estrous-synchronized ewes.[8] Pregnancy rates were low, but demonstrated that live lambs could be produced with sex-sorted ram sperm. Recent trials in Australia with sex-sorted ram sperm resulted in pregnancy rates of 25% for ewes inseminated with 4×10^6 X-sorted sperm and 15% for Y-sorted sperm. Control inseminations with 140×10^6 cryopreserved, thawed sperm yielded 54% pregnant ewes.[15] In this trial, thawed sperm were deposited either by standard laproscopic methods or placed into the uterotubal junction with a catheter after minilaparotomy. It is likely that pregnancy rates with sexed sperm could be improved by increasing sperm/dose and precisely controlling the time of insemination relative to ovulation.

Horses

The first sex-selected filly was produced by surgical insemination with a limited number of flow-sorted X-sperm. This effort was followed by nonsurgical artificial insemination of mares with flow-sorted sperm. Reasonable conception rates with sorted stallion sperm have been achieved only if the timing of insemination was optimized relative to ovulation induced with hCG or GnRH. Although stallion sperm do not sort as efficiently as those from bulls, semen from some stallions can be sorted at rates greater than 2000 sperm/sec producing nearly 5×10^6 live sperm/hr of each sex. Thus, with low-dose insemination, several doses of sexed sperm can be produced with a sorter each day.[8]

A hysteroscopic insemination technique, which arose from clinical examination of the mare's reproductive tract using the videoendoscope, has been used to inseminate mares with many fewer sperm than used with conventional equine artificial insemination.[16] Very low numbers of sperm are placed directly onto the oviductal papillus at the uterotubal junction with the videoendoscope. Application of this technique to deposit small numbers of sex-sorted sperm deep into the reproductive tract appears to make predetermination of sex a practical possibility in horses. Recently, 38% of mares hysteroscopically inseminated with 5×10^6 fresh, sex-sorted motile sperm became pregnant compared to 40% when mares were inseminated with 5 million nonsorted motile sperm.[17]

Other Mammals

Living sperm from several other mammalian species have been successfully sorted according to their DNA content including sperm from humans, rabbits, bison, elk, cats, and even sperm from white-sided dolphins.[2]

CONCLUSION

Additional refinements in the system are needed, but sexing sperm using flow sorting has been commercialized for cattle in Great Britain and is being developed for commercial application in horses, swine, sheep, and some exotic mammalian species.

REFERENCES

1. Seidel, G.E., Jr.; Garner, D.L. Current status of sexing mammalian spermatozoa. Reproduction **2002**, *124*, 733–743.

2. Garner, D.L.; Seidel, G.E., Jr. Past, present and future perspectives on sexing sperm. Can. J. Anim. Sci. **2003**, *83*, 375-384.

3. Seidel, G.E., Jr.; Schenk, J.L.; Herickhoff, L.A.; Doyle, S.P.; Brink, Z.; Green, R.D.; Cran, D.G. Insemination of heifers with sexed sperm. Theriogenology **1999**, *52*, 1407–1420.

4. Seidel, G.E., Jr.; Brink, Z.; Schenk, J.L. Use of heterospermic insemination with fetal sex as the genetic marker to study fertility of sexed sperm. Theriogenology **2003**, *59*, 515.

5. Johnson, L.A.; Flook, J.P.; Hawk, H.W. Sex preselection in rabbits: Live births from X and Y sperm separated by DNA and cell sorting. Biol. Reprod. **1989**, *41*, 199–203.

6. Johnson, L.A. Gender preselection in domestic animals using flow cytometrically sorted sperm. J. Animal Sci. **1992**, *70* (Suppl. 2), 8–18.

7. Amann, R.P. Issues affecting commercialization of sexed sperm. Theriogenology **1999**, *52*, 1441–1457.

8. Johnson, L.A.; Welch, G.R. Sex preselection: High-speed flow cytometric sorting of X and Y sperm for maximum efficiency. Theriogenology **1999**, *52*, 1323–1341.

9. Garner, D.L. Sex-sorting mammalian sperm: Concept to application in animals. J. Androl. **2001**, *22*, 519–526.

10. Gledhill, B.L.; Lake, S.; Steinmetz, L.L.; Gray, J.W.; Crawford, J.R.; Dean, P.N.; VanDilla, M.A. Flow microfluorometric analysis of sperm DNA content: Effect of cell shape on the fluorescence distribution. J. Cell. Physiol. **1976**, *87*, 367–376.

11. Schenk, J.L.; Suh, T.K.; Cran, D.G.; Seidel, G.E., Jr. Cryopreservation of flow-sorted bovine sperm. Theriogenology **1999**, *52*, 1375–1391.

12. Rath, D.; Long, C.R.; Dobrinsky, J.R.; Welch, G.R.; Schreier, L.L.; Johnson, L.A. In vitro production of sexed embryos for gender preselection: High speed sorting of X-chromosome-bearing sperm to produce piglets after embryo transfer. J. Anim. Sci. **1999**, *77*, 3346–3352.

13. Vazquez, J.M.; Martinez, E.A.; Parrilla, I.; Cuello, C.; Gil, M.A.; Lucas, X.; Roca, J.; Vazquez, J.L.; Didion, B.A.; Day, B.N. Deep Intrauterine Insemination in Natural Postweaning Estrus Sows. In *Proc. Sixth International Conference on Pig Reproduction*; University of Missouri: Columbia, MO, 2001; 134 pp.

14. Martinez, E.A.; Vazquez, J.M.; Roca, J.; Lucas, X.; Gil, M.A.; Vazquez, J.L. Deep Intrauterine Insemination and Embryo Transfer. In *Proc. Sixth International Conference on Pig Reproduction*; University of Missouri: Columbia, MO, 2001; 129 pp.

15. Hollinshead, F.K.; O'Brien, J.K.; He, L.; Maxwell, W.M.C.; Evans, G. Pregnancies after insemination of ewes with sorted, cryopreserved ram spermatozoa. Proc. Soc. Reprod. Biol. **2001**, *32*, 20.

16. Morris, L.H.A.; Hunter, R.H.F.; Allen, W.R. Hysteroscopic insemination of small numbers of spermatozoa at the uterotubal junction of preovulatory mares. J. Reprod. Fert. **2000**, *118*, 95–100.

17. Lindsey, A.C.; Morris, L.H.A.; Allen, W.R.; Schenk, J.L.; Squires, E.L.; Bruemmer, J.E. Hysteroscopic insemination of mares with low numbers of nonsorted or flow sorted spermatozoa. Equine Vet. J. **2002**, *34*, 128–132.

Biotechnology: Stem Cell and Germ Cell Technology

Matthew B. Wheeler
Samantha A. Malusky
University of Illinois, Urbana, Illinois, U.S.A.

INTRODUCTION

In mammals, stem cells are defined as a unique cell population characterized by nearly unlimited self-renewal and capacity to differentiate via progenitor cells into terminally differentiated somatic cells. Stem cells may be of embryonic or adult origin. Adult stem cells are located in many specialized tissues, including the liver, skin, brain, fat, bone marrow, and muscle. As a result of stem cell activity, adult tissues are continuously renewed, even in the absence of injury, to ensure maintenance of cell type throughout the life of the animal. Pluripotency in mammals is restricted to the zygote, early embryonic cells, primordial germ cells, and the stem cells derived from embryonic carcinomas. Embryonic stem (ES) cells are derived from the inner cell mass of the blastocyst. In contrast to adult stem cells, ES cells are pluripotent, contribute to all three primary germ layers (endoderm, mesoderm, and ectoderm), indefinitely proliferate, and maintain an undifferentiated phenotype. Embryonic germ (EG) cells are derived from primordial germ cells, which are progenitor cells of the sperm and egg in the adult animal. EG cells reintroduced to the early embryo are capable, like ES cells, of colonizing fetal cell lineages and also possess the ability to differentiate in vitro to a variety of cell types. ES and EG cell lines from mammalian species other than the mouse have not been reported in published literature to successfully colonize the germ line of chimeric animals. The potential of stem-cell technology makes it a valuable and exciting science. Adult and embryonic stem cells may possess the ability to restore or replace tissue that has been damaged by disease or injury. Pluripotent, in vitro cell lines offer an opportunity to study the early stages of embryonic development not accessible in utero and are a powerful tool to facilitate genetic modification of animal genomes.

ADULT STEM CELLS

Adult stem cells are anchored permanent residents of a particular tissue that are involved in repair and mainte-nance. Adult bone marrow, brain, skeletal muscle, liver, pancreas, fat, skin, and gastrointestinal tract have all been shown to possess stem or progenitor cells.[1] It was originally believed that adult stem-cell function was restricted to cell lineages present in the organ from which they were derived. Recent studies suggest that these adult stem cells are multipotent and can transdifferentiate into different cell lineages.[2] Adult stem cells have a reduced differentiation potential compared to embryo-derived stem cells. Among all presently known adult stem or progenitor cells, cell populations from bone marrow have shown the highest potential with respect to multi-lineage differentiation. Potential adult stem cells are progenitors arising from a hierarchal pathway of cells dependent upon the tissue type and, in a healthy state, are part of the transit population. Injury can induce these potential stem cells to regenerate the entire lineage through clonal expansion, including the anchored stem cell, to maintain tissue integrity. Effective markers for anchored stem cells or potential stem cells do not exist outside of the hematopoietic lineage. The absence of a reliable identification system has made the study of these crucial cells limited.

EMBRYONIC STEM CELLS

Teratocarcinoma and Embryonic Carcinoma

The first pluripotent embryonic cells were isolated from teratocarcinomas, a spontaneous tumor of the testes in mice and humans. The tumors resembled a disorganized fetus consisting of a wide variety of tissues including hair, muscle, bone, and teeth. Developmental biologists dis-covered teratocarcinomas could be artificially induced by transferring mouse embryos to extrauterine sites and that they contained undifferentiated stem cells.[3] These embryonic carcinoma (EC) stem cells, once isolated, could grow in culture without losing the capacity to differentiate. When these cells were introduced into a blastocyst, they formed chimeras and could contribute to all somatic tissues. EC cells exhibit an unstable karyotype,

Encyclopedia of Animal Science
DOI: 10.1081/E-EAS 120019488

which reduces their experimental value despite their capacity to differentiate into all three germ layers.

Embryonic Stem Cells

The early mammalian embryo is composed of cells that have the potential to contribute to all tissue types in the body, a property termed pluripotency. As the embryo develops to blastocyst stage, it forms an outer cell layer and an inner cluster of cells referred to as the inner cell mass (ICM). The outer cells become the trophectoderm and ultimately the placenta. The ICM cells create all tissues in the body, as well as nontrophoblast structures that support the embryo. Embryonic stem cells are derived in vitro from the ICM. ES cells were successfully developed from mouse blastocysts in 1981.[4,5] ES cells contribute to all three germ layers in the developing fetus, proving that they are pluripotent, but ES cells fail to contribute to the trophectoderm, revealing that they are not totipotent. ES cells, when removed from feeder layers, begin to differentiate into multilayered differentiated

structures called embryoid bodies. In addition to blastocyst injection, the in vivo developmental potential of ES cells can be tested by injecting ES cells into severe combined immunodeficient (SCID) mice.[6] Benign teratomas form where the cells are injected and contain tumors representing all three germ layers.

Embryonic stem cell criteria

Pluripotent cells do not all possess the same characteristics. Listed below are defining properties of mouse ES cells:

- Stable diploid karyotype
- Clonogenic property
- Ability to recover after freezing and thawing
- Ability to survive and proliferate in vivo indefinitely
- High telomerase activity
- Teratoma and embryoid body formation
- Chimera formation and germ line colonization
- Undifferentiated state

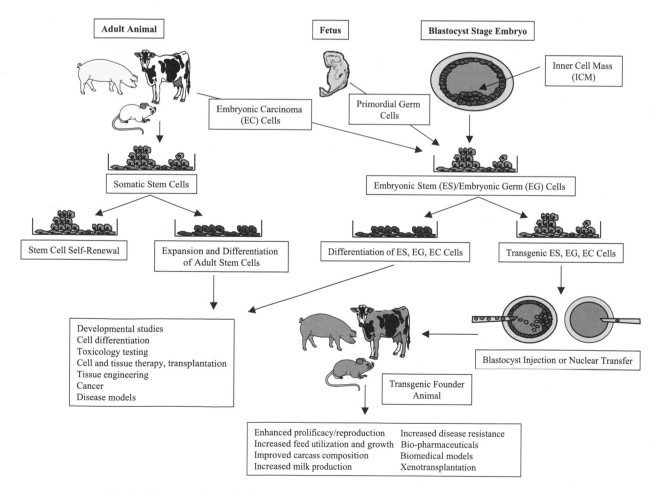

Fig. 1 Sources and applications of stem cells. (*View this art in color at www.dekker.com.*)

Embryonic Germ Cells

Pluripotent embryonic germ cells can be isolated from the genital ridge of the developing mammalian fetus. EG cells closely resemble ES cell lines in the morphology of colonies, response to induced differentiation, and ability to create chimeric offspring. ES and EG cells are not the same in all respects. Differences exist in the conditions required for their isolation, culture, lifespan in vitro, and differentiation capacity. An important difference is genetic modifications that occur in the deoxyribonucleic acid (DNA) of primordial germ (PG) cells that result in erasure of genomic imprints. The DNA modifications that occur can compromise the developmental potential of the EG cells.

Agricultural Applications for ES and EG Cells

The establishment of ES and/or EG cells from a wide variety of species will allow more flexibility in direct genetic manipulation of livestock as well as agricultural, gene-regulation, and developmental biology research. The use of ES cells in mouse developmental biology research is well documented. However, the production of a chimeric livestock species (swine and cattle) produced from ES cells has only recently been reported.[7,8] The use of ES or EG cells for the production of transgenic animals from DNA-transformed, individually derived and screened embryonic cell lines could allow large numbers of genetically identical animals to be established. There are many potential applications of stem cell–mediated transgenesis to develop new and improved strains of livestock. Practical applications of stem cell transgenic technology in livestock production include enhanced prolificacy and reproductive performance, increased feed utilization and growth rate, improved carcass composition, improved milk production and/or composition, and increased disease resistance (Fig. 1).

CONCLUSION

Stem cells have revolutionized many areas of biology, and with continued research more information will be learned regarding these unique cells. Comparisons of prospective applications between mammalian adult, ES, EG, and EC cells indicate varying levels of potential. Adult stem cell potential has not been as extensively investigated compared to ES cells due to the difficulty of identifying adult stem cells in a population of cells. EG cells have limited ability to recapitulate normal development due to genetic modifications affecting imprinting status of the cells. EC cells contain karyotypic abnormalities and have limited potential to transmit through the germ line of chimeric animals. ES cells do not possess any major limiting characteristics in comparison to the other cell types, which demonstrates their preferential use in scientific studies. ES cells offer a multitude of applications including access to a population of precursor cells difficult to identify in vivo, ability to identify novel genes during early embryonic development and differentiation processes, use as a standardized in vitro model to test embryotoxic effects of chemicals,[9] the study of targeted mutations of genes that may be lethal in vivo but can be studied in vitro, and less expensive teratogen testing that does not involve isolating embryos or sacrificing animals. The potential applications of stem-cell technology in livestock production are tremendous. The utility of this technology is limited only by our ability to identify appropriate genes and gene functions to manipulate in our production of livestock species.

REFERENCES

1. Passier, R.; Mummery, C. Origin and use of embryonic and adult stem cells in differentiation and tissue repair. Cardiovasc. Res. **2003**, *58*, 324–335.
2. Medvinsky, A.; Smith, A. Fusion brings down barriers. Nature **2003**, *422*, 823–825.
3. Van der Heyden, M.A.; Defize, L.H. Twenty one years of P19 cells: What an embryonal carcinoma cell line taught us about cardiomyocyte differentiation. Cariovasc. Res. **2003**, *58*, 292–302.
4. Martin, G.R. Isolation of a pluripotent cell line from early mouse embryos cultured in medium conditioned by teratocarcinoma stem cells. Proc. Natl. Acad. Sci. U. S. A. **1981**, *787*, 634–638.
5. Evans, M.J.; Kaufman, M.H. Establishment in culture of pluripotent cells from mouse embryos. Nature **1981**, *292*, 154–156.
6. Foley, G.L.; Rund, L.A.; Wheeler, M.B. Factors affecting murine embryonic stem cell teratoma development. Biol. Reprod. **1994**, *50* (Suppl 1), 291.
7. Wheeler, M.B.; Walters, E.M. Transgenic technology and applications in swine. Theriogenology **2001**, *56*, 1345–1370.
8. Cibelli, J.B.; Stice, S.L.; Golueke, P.J.; Kane, J.J.; Jerry, J.; Blackwell, C.; Ponce deLeon, F.A.; Robl, J.M. Transgenic bovine chimeric offspring produced from somatic cell-derived stem-like cells. Nat. Biotechnol. **1998**, *16*, 642–646.
9. Spielmann, H.; Pohl, I.; Doring, B.; Liebsch, M.; Moldenhauer, F. The embryonic stem cell test, an in vitro embryotoxicity test using two permanent mouse cell lines: 3T3 fibroblasts and embryonic stem cells. Toxicol in Vitro **1997**, *10*, 119–127.

Biotechnology: Transgenic Animals

Vernon G. Pursel
Robert J. Wall
*United States Department of Agriculture, Agricultural Research Service,
Beltsville, Maryland, U.S.A.*

INTRODUCTION

The genetic composition of all living creatures is continually undergoing alteration by mutation, natural selection, and genetic drift. Beginning at the onset of plant and animal domestication, humans have further manipulated the genetic composition of plant and animals to enhance their health and usefulness to humans by selecting for specific phenotypic traits. Development of recombinant DNA technology has enabled scientists to isolate single genes, analyze and modify their nucleotide structures, make copies of these isolated genes, and insert copies of these genes into the genome of plants or animals. The procedure used to insert these isolated genes is called gene transfer; an animal that contains the inserted gene or genes is called a transgenic animal; and the transferred gene is called a transgene.

The first intentional transfer of a transgene into the genome of an animal was achieved in 1980 in mice.[1] Gene transfer methodology was subsequently successfully applied to pigs, sheep, and rabbits.[2] Gene transfer has thus far been used most extensively for basic research on all aspects of biology and genetics, but it has numerous potential applications for genetic improvement of farm animals. Practical applications of gene transfer in livestock production include improved milk production and composition, increased growth rate, improved feed use and carcass composition, increased disease resistance, enhanced reproductive performance, and increased prolificacy. Gene transfer in farm animals has also been investigated extensively for potential to produce human pharmaceutical products, and the alteration of cell or tissue characteristics has been investigated for potential use in organ transplantation in humans.

GENE TRANSFER METHODS

Pronuclear Microinjection

The primary method used to produce transgenic farm mammals has been the direct microinjection of the transgene into the pronucleus of a zygote (recently fertilized ovum or egg). As in the mouse, pronuclei of rabbit, sheep, and goat zygotes can be readily seen using phase-contrast microscopy or differential interference contrast (DIC) microscopy. Lipid granules in the cytoplasm interfere with visualization of pronuclei in pig and cow zygotes. Centrifugation of pig and cow zygotes can be used to stratify the cytoplasm so that pronuclei are visible with the use of DIC microscopy.[3]

To permit microinjection, ova are placed on a depression slide in a microdrop of media that is overlaid with silicone or paraffin oil to prevent evaporation. The microscope must be equipped with two micromanipulators, one for an egg-holding pipette and the other for an injection pipette. The holding pipette and injection pipette are each fitted with a tube leading to a syringe that permits either gentle suction or carefully controlled fluid injection. As an ovum is held with light suction by the holding pipette, the tip of the injection pipette is inserted through the zona pellucida and cytoplasm into the most visible pronucleus. Several hundred copies of the gene are expelled into the pronucleus. The person performing the injection carefully observes the pronucleus and withdraws the pipette when the pronuclear structure has visibly enlarged. After microinjection, cow embryos are usually cultured in vitro until they are morulae or blastocysts before nonsurgical transfer into the uterus of a synchronous host cow. The injected zygotes of other species are usually cultured only a few hours before they are surgically transferred directly into the oviduct of synchronous host females.

The mechanism by which a transgene integrates into a chromosome is unknown. A transgene usually integrates in a single site on a chromosome, but multiple integrations can occur. Frequently, multiple copies of the transgene integrate in head-to-tail array. Breeding studies with transgenic pigs and sheep indicate mosaicism is a definite problem, with about 20% of founder transgenics failing to transmit the transgene to progeny and another 20–30% transmitting the transgene to less than 50% of their progeny, presumably due to mosaicism in the germ cells as a consequence of integration occurring a few cleavage cycles after microinjection.

The efficiency is usually lower for integration of transgenes into farm animals than into mice. The percentage of gene-injected zygotes that develop into transgenic animals

Encyclopedia of Animal Science
DOI: 10.1081/E-EAS 120019489

varies from 0.3–4.0% for pigs, 0.1–4.4% for sheep, 1.0–1.7% for goats, and 0.3–2.6% for cattle. A few transgenic chickens have been produced by microinjection of genes into the germinal disk of the recently fertilized egg.[4] After microinjection, the chick embryos were cultured in a host eggshell until hatching time.

Retroviral Insertion

Retroviruses can be modified by recombinant DNA techniques to make them replication-defective and to replace part of the viral DNA with a desired transgene so it can then be used as a gene vector. Retroviral-mediated gene transfer was originally used to insert transgenes into mice embryos[5] and blostodermal cells of chicken eggs.[6] In comparison to microinjection, retroviral infection offers the following advantages: 1) integration of single copies of the gene; and 2) retroviral DNA integrates into a high percentage of embryos when exposed to high concentrations of viral stock by coculture with infected cells in vitro, or in the case of chickens, by microinjection into the blastodisk. The disadvantages are: 1) it requires added work to produce a retrovirus carrying the transgene; 2) the gene being transferred must be smaller than 10 kb in size; 3) resulting transgenic animals are frequently highly mosaic, which necessitates extensive outbreeding to establish pure transgenic lines; and 4) unresolved problems with hypermethylation can interfere with expression of the transgene.

More recently, retrovirus-mediated gene transfer has been used to produce transgenic cattle by insertion of retroviruses into metaphase II oocytes to avoid mosaicism and ensure that a high percentage of the offspring are transgenic.[7]

Many laboratories involved in the production of transgenic livestock have not embraced the use of retroviral insertion technology because of concerns about public perception and the potential consequences of recombination events between the viral vectors and endogenous retroviruses to generate new pathogenic agents.

Cellular Insertion

The third method of introducing genes into the germ line is a two-step process involving first the transfection of a transgene into embryonic stem (ES) cells, embryonic germ (EG) cells (also known as primordial germ cells), or fetal somatic cells during in vitro culture, and then the incorporation of the transgenic ES or EG cells into an inner-cell mass of an embryo or the insertion of the transgenic cell's nucleus into an enucleated oocyte by nuclear transfer (NT). The advantage of this procedure is that a particular genotype can be selected during in vitro culture before introduction of the cells

into the embryo or NT. In addition, this technique provides the ability for site-specific insertion of a transgene by homologous recombination.

This approach with ES cells has been used extensively in the mouse but has not been effective in other mammalian animals because of extreme difficulty in isolating and maintaining ES or EG cells in the undifferentiated state during in vitro culture. Nuclear transfer (also known as animal cloning) is currently being extensively investigated in cattle, goats, and pigs. Consequently, cellular insertion by NT may become the method of choice for gene transfer in these species, because relatively few recipient hosts are required to produce transgenic founder animals.

Sperm-Mediated Gene Transfer

The simplest, but most controversial, method of gene transfer involves merely mixing a transgene with spermatozoa and using them to fertilize oocytes, either in vitro or by artificial insemination. The use of sperm-mediated transfer in mice by Dr. Lavitrano[8] was initially discounted as unrepeatable by many investigators. During the past decade, research on this procedure has persisted and many investigators report successful gene transfers by this technique. Unfortunately, only a few studies have provided convincing evidence that the transgene was unaltered before or during the integration process and capable of expressing appropriately in the resulting transgenic animals.[9]

EVALUATION OF TRANSGENIC ANIMALS

Integration

The primary way that presence of the transgene is confirmed is by removing a piece of tail tissue at birth, extracting the DNA from the tissue, and analyzing the DNA for the presence of the transgene by Southern blot hybridization, slot-blot hybridization, or polymerase chain reaction using a unique segment of the transgene as a probe. If performed correctly, the Southern blot analysis provides information on presence, intactness, copy number, and orientation of the transgene.

Expression

Mere presence of the transgene in the transgenic animal does not guarantee that the transgene will be expressed or expressed appropriately. Expression is usually evaluated by assay of appropriate tissues or fluids recovered from the transgenic animal for presence of the transgene transcription by Northern blot analysis of the mRNA, by presence of the protein using Western immunoblot analysis, or by some other assay that is appropriate for specific transgene.

Transmission

The primary aim of transgenesis is to establish a new genetic line of animals in which the trait is stably transmitted to succeeding generations. This can be determined only by mating the transgenic animal to a nontransgenic animal and evaluating subsequent progeny for the presence and expression of the transgene.

CONCLUSION

Transgenic animals were initially produced by pronuclear microinjection. During the past two decades a number of other gene transfer methods have been developed and include the use of retroviral vectors, cellular insertion, and sperm-mediated transfer. Additional details regarding each of these procedures can be found in *Transgenic Animal Technology: A Laboratory Handbook*.[10]

REFERENCES

1. Gordon, J.W.; Scangos, G.A.; Plotkin, D.J.; Barbosa, J.A.; Ruddle, F.H. Genetic transformation of mouse embryos by microinjection of purified DNA. Proc. Natl. Acad. Sci. U. S. A. **1980**, *77* (12), 7380–7384.
2. Hammer, R.E.; Pursel, V.G.; Rexroad, C.E., Jr.; Wall, R.J.; Bolt, D.J.; Ebert, K.M.; Palmiter, R.D.; Brinster, R.L. Production of transgenic rabbits, sheep and pigs by microinjection. Nature **1985**, *315* (6021), 680–683.
3. Wall, R.J.; Pursel, V.G.; Hammer, R.E.; Brinster, R.L. Development of porcine ova that were centrifuged to permit visualization of pronuclei and nuclei. Biol. Reprod. **1985**, *32* (3), 645–651.
4. Love, J.; Gribbin, C.; Mather, C.; Sang, H. Transgenic birds by DNA microinjection. Biotechnology **1994**, *12* (1), 60–63.
5. Soriano, P.; Cone, R.D.; Mulligan, R.C.; Jaenisch, R. Tissue-specific and ectopic expression of genes introduced into transgenic mice by retroviruses. Science **1986**, *234* (4782), 1409–1413.
6. Salter, D.W.; Smith, E.J.; Hughes, S.H.; Wright, S.E.; Crittenden, L.B. Transgenic chickens: Insertion of retroviral genes into the chicken germ line. Virology **1987**, *157* (1), 236–240.
7. Chan, A.W.; Homan, E.J.; Ballou, L.U.; Burns, J.C.; Bremel, R.D. Transgenic cattle produced by reverse-transcribed gene transfer in oocytes. Proc. Natl. Acad. Sci. U. S. A. **1998**, *95* (24), 14028–14033.
8. Lavitrano, M.; Camaioni, A.; Fazio, V.M.; Dolci, S.; Farace, M.G.; Spadafora, C. Sperm cells as vectors for introducing foreign DNA into eggs: Genetic transformation of mice. Cell **1989**, *57* (5), 717–723.
9. Wall, R.J. New gene transfer methods. Theriogenology **2002**, *57* (1), 189–201.
10. Pinkert, C.A. *Transgenic Animal Technology: A Laboratory Handbook*, 2nd Ed.; Academic Press: San Diego, 2002.

Biotechnology: Xenotransplantation

Jeffrey L. Platt
Mayo Clinic, Rochester, Minnesota, U.S.A.

INTRODUCTION

Xenotransplantation refers to transplantation of cells, tissues, or organs from individuals of one species into individuals of another species. Xenotransplantation has long been envisioned as a way of addressing the severe shortage of human organs and tissues for transplantation, as the number of available organs is as low as 5% of the number needed.

The first serious efforts at xenotransplantation were made in the early 20th century; however, these attempts at xenotransplantation failed, as did early attempts at human-to-human transplantation (allotransplantation), because the immune system of the recipients inevitably rejected the graft. This barrier was addressed in part by the advent of immunosuppressive drugs in the late 1950s, and the era of clinical allotransplantation began. However, as human donors were limited, animals, such as chimpanzees and baboons, were used once again as a source. Those primate-to-human xenografts functioned for weeks to months, but ultimately failed, whereas human-to-human transplants sometimes functioned indefinitely. This experience suggested that the immunological barrier to xenotransplantation was more severe than the barrier to allotransplantation. Recent years have brought a better understanding of the barriers to xenotransplantation and have raised the possibility of applying genetic engineering to that barrier.

RATIONALE FOR XENOTRANSPLANTATION

Xenotransplantation has been viewed as a plentiful source of organs and tissues for transplantation (Table 1).[1,2] However, xenotransplantation may even be preferred over allotransplantation in certain circumstances. Where organ failure is caused by a viral infection, e.g., hepatitis, xenotransplantation might be preferred because the transplant would resist reinfection by the virus that caused organ failure.[3] Xenotransplantation might also be preferred as a way of delivering genes of therapeutic importance. For example, an animal source might be genetically engineered to express a gene at a high level or under regulated conditions.

An important consideration today is how to weigh xenotransplantation against other potential approaches to treating organ failure (Table 2).[4] Though some new technologies, such as stem cells, tissue engineering, and cardiac assist devices, have received much attention, they have also received less scrutiny than xenotransplantation because their development is so recent. Most likely, these technologies will be applied in ways that fill therapeutic niches, such as repairing local defects or injury of tissues. Devices may eventually be used to replace the heart, but application for other organs is more remote. On the other hand, cell transplantation, stem-cell transplantation, and tissue engineering seem less promising for replacement of the function of structurally complex organs such as the kidney, lungs, and heart. For replacement of these organs, organogenesis (the de novo formation of organs) or xenotransplantation may be necessary. Xenotransplantation may also find application in conjunction with organogenesis. For example, one might envision growing human organs, perhaps derived from stem cells, as a xenograft in an animal host and then transplanting the organs to human patients.[2]

SOURCE OF XENOGRAFTS

Many species have been used as sources of tissues and organs for xenotransplantation. Xenografts from sources phylogenetically closer to the recipient would be expected to provoke less immunity and be more physiologically compatible with the recipient. Consistent with that idea, experimental cardiac xenografts from monkeys to baboons have survived greater than a year, and renal xenografts from chimpanzees in humans have survived and functioned up to 9 months (Table 1). However, some biological barriers to xenotransplantation derive from expression of one or very few genes in the donor or recipient. These barriers do not relate directly to overall genetic difference.

The genetic barrier of greatest current interest and importance is the expression of $\alpha 1,3$-galactosyltransferase, a glycosyltransferase that catalyzes synthesis of Galα1-3Gal (Table 3). Galα1-3Gal is a saccharide expressed by lower mammals and New World monkeys but not by humans or Old World monkeys. Humans and Old World monkeys have natural antibodies specific for this saccharide that trigger severe reactions when organs containing Galα1-3Gal are transplanted. Indeed, many of the efforts in

Encyclopedia of Animal Science
DOI: 10.1081/E-EAS 120019490

Table 1 Some clinical attempts at xenotransplantation

Year	Donor	Organ	Maximum survival
1906	Pig, goat	Kidney	2 Days
1964	Chimpanzee	Kidney	9 Months
1964	Baboon	Kidney	60 Days
1984	Baboon	Kidney	20 Days
1992	Baboon	Liver	70 Days

(Adapted from Ref. 8.)

genetic engineering and immunosuppression for xenotransplantation are directed respectively at eradicating expression of the sugar or suppressing immunity directed against it.

Today most efforts in xenotransplantation focus on the pig as a potential source of tissues and organs. The most important reason for favoring the pig is that pigs are available in large numbers. (It is estimated that more than 1 million would be needed for transplants worldwide each year.) Another reason for favoring pigs as a source of xenografts is that pigs can be bred and genetically manipulated, as described later in this article. Still another reason for favoring the pig is that the organs are large enough to fulfill the needs of full-sized humans, and some strains of pigs, such as the mini-pig, may at maturity approximate human size. Finally, the microorganisms harbored by pigs that are potentially infectious for humans are well known, and measures for screening for these organisms are well established.[5] In contrast, some viruses of non-human primates are poorly known and potentially lethal for humans.

Although the experience is limited, the best current evidence suggests that the heart, lung, and kidneys of the pig would function sufficiently to sustain the life of a human. Whether the liver would function sufficiently is a matter of controversy because of the metabolic complexity of that organ and because of the possibility that complex cascades, such as complementing coagulation, could be incompatible between pig and human.

HURDLES TO XENOTRANSPLANTATION

The main hurdle to xenotransplantation is the immune reaction of the recipient against the graft (see Ref. 2 for a review). Much of the immune response is directed against Galα1-3Gal. Another problem with the pig is that the proteins of that species are so different from the proteins of humans that they too provoke strong immune reactions, thus increasing the challenge of developing an effective approach to immunosuppression. Still another hurdle to

using pigs as a source of xenografts in humans is the possibility that infectious agents might transfer from the graft to the recipient. As indicated above, most infectious agents potentially transmitted from pigs to humans are known, and the means exist to eliminate those agents from potential sources of xenografts. One exception, however, may be the porcine endogenous retrovirus (PERV), which exists in the porcine genome. PERV has been transmitted from porcine cells to the cells of humans and nonhuman primates under a variety of experimental circumstances. Although the subject of much investigation, to date no evidence has emerged that PERV can be transmitted to human cells in vivo as a result of xenotransplantation.[6] This subject will be an active area of investigation until a decisive answer is achieved.

GENETIC ENGINEERING AND XENOTRANSPLANTATION

The ability to genetically engineer and breed animals has stimulated recent excitement about xenotransplantation. This excitement stems in part from the idea that if genetic engineering might be used to optimally modify the source of a transplant to make it compatible with the recipient, then the need for immunosuppression might be decreased or eliminated. This has been achieved only in part.

Transgenic techniques have been used to express human genes for complement regulatory proteins and carbohydrate-modifying enzymes in lines of pigs. For example, the human decay-accelerating factor and CD59 genes, which inhibit complement reactions, have been introduced into lines of pigs in an effort to prevent complement-mediated tissue injury. These efforts have prevented the severest form of complement-mediated rejection, hyperacute rejection.[7] Genes that would modify synthesis of Galα1-3Gal, such as H transferase, have also been expressed, but expression of that sugar has not been fully eradicated by this approach.

Table 2 Technologies for organ replacement

Technology	Potential applications
Allotransplantation	Heart, lung, liver, kidney, pancreas
Implantable devices	Heart, pancreas
Cell transplantation	Heart, liver, pancreas
Stem cells	Heart, liver, pancreas
Tissue engineering	Liver
Organogenesis	Kidney, lung
Transplantation	Heart, lung, liver, kidney, pancreas

(Adapted from Ref. 9.)

Table 3 Phylogeny of expression of Galα1-3Gal

Species	Functional α1,3GT	Galα1-3Gal	AntiGalα1-3Gal antibodies
Mouse	+	+	−
Pig	+	+	−
New World monkey	+	+	−
Baboon	−	−	+
Human	−	−	+

(Adapted from Ref. 10.)

Recent efforts have focused on eliminating α1,-3-galactosyltransferase by gene targeting. Gene targeting in pigs was recently made feasible by advances in reproductive cloning. At the time of this writing, several groups have targeted one allele and one group has generated pigs fully deficient in α1,3-galactosyltransferase. Though these advances have stimulated excitement, preliminary work in several laboratories suggests that targeting this gene will not fully eradicate immune reactions against pig cells.

Genetic engineering may be applied in other ways in xenotransplantation. One potential application is to eliminate endogenous viruses, such as PERV, should these viruses be found to cause human pathology. Another potential application of genetic engineering is to eliminate or replace porcine genes that pose a physiologic hurdle to the success of transplantation or toxicity to the recipient. For example, porcine coagulation factors may be incompatible with human control proteins, and hence genes for human coagulation factors might replace the genes for these factors in pigs. Still another application might be to introduce genes whose expression could provide therapeutic benefit for the recipient of a transplant. For example, human genes might be expressed in a pig, potentially under specific regulation. The genes would then be expressed in the human individual who receives a transplant from the pig. In this way, a genetically engineered pig cell might be used as a vehicle for expressing genes of therapeutic interest, such as enzymes, growth factors, antitumor agents, etc.

CONCLUSION

At the time of this writing, xenotransplantation is not applied routinely for any medical purpose. However, clinical trials using porcine cells for the treatment of Parkinson's disease and various metabolic diseases have been conducted, and new trials of various types are planned. Because the immune reactions suffered by transplanted cells are far less severe than the immune reactions suffered by transplanted organs, it can be anticipated that xenogeneic cellular transplants may provide a first step toward full clinical application. It is hoped that new insights gained from the immune response to cellular xenografts and application of gene targeting in swine will eventually allow the transplantation of intact porcine organs into humans. Such an advance would certainly revolutionize the treatment of organ failure.

ARTICLE OF FURTHER INTEREST

Xenotransplantation: Biological Barriers, p. 894

REFERENCES

1. Evans, R.W. Coming to Terms with Reality: Why Xeno-Transplantation is a Necessity. In *Xenotransplantation*; ASM Press: Washington, DC, 2001; 29–51.
2. Cascalho, M.; Platt, J.L. Xenotransplantation and other means of organ replacement. Nat. Rev., Immunol. **2001**, *1*, 154–160.
3. Mueller, Y.M.; Davenport, C.; Ildstad, S.T. Xenotransplantation: Application of disease resistance. Clin. Exp. Pharmacol. Physiol. **1999**, *26*, 1009–1012.
4. *Future Strategies for Tissue and Organ Replacement*; Polak, J.M., Hench, L.L., Kemp, P., Eds.; Imperial College Press: London, 2002.
5. National Research Council of the National Academies. *Animal Biotechnology: Science-Based Concerns*; The National Academies Press: Washington, DC, 2002.
6. Paradis, K.; Langford, G.; Long, Z.; Heneine, W.; Sandstrom, P.; Switzer, W.M.; Chapman, L.E.; Lockey, C.; Onions, D. Search for cross-species transmission of porcine endogenous retrovirus in patients treated with living pig tissue. Science **1999**, *285*, 1236–1241.
7. McCurry, K.R.; Kooyman, D.L.; Alvarado, C.G.; Cotterell, A.H.; Martin, M.J.; Logan, J.S.; Platt, J.L. Human complement regulatory proteins protect swine-to-primate cardiac xenografts from humoral injury. Nat. Med. **1995**, *1*, 423–427.
8. Taniguchi, S.; Cooper, D.K.C. Clinical Xenotransplantation — A Brief Review of the World Experience. In *Xenotransplantation 2*; Springer-Verlag: Berlin, 1997; 776–784.
9. Ogle, B.M.; Platt, J.L. Approaches to the replacement of the function of failing organs. Curr. Opin. Organ Transpl. **2002**, *7*, 28–34.
10. Galili, U. Interaction of the natural anti-Gal antibody with α-galactosyl epitopes: A major obstacle for xenotransplantation in humans. Immunol. Today **1993**, *14*, 480–482.

Body Composition: Breed and Species Effects

Michael L. Thonney
Cornell University, Ithaca, New York, U.S.A.

INTRODUCTION

Body composition of agricultural animals is described by proportions of muscle, fat, and bone in the carcass or by proportions of chemically measured amounts of water, protein, lipid, and ash in the whole body. Animals with better conformation have been assumed to produce carcasses with more meat in the high-priced cuts, but dissection studies in cattle and sheep have shown little variation in muscle distribution among breeds of widely different shapes. The principal determinant of composition at a given weight is stage of growth, which is defined as weight in relation to mature weight. Thus, mature size is the genetic trait that determines the composition, use, and economic value of domestic farm animals.

MATURE SIZE

Body composition is a primary determinant of the value of agricultural animals, because composition determines nutrient requirements as well as the value of meat. There is wide variation among breeds within species in body composition at specific weights. Most of this variation is due to differences in mature size. The amounts of carcass muscle, fat and bone for a hypothetically large-mature-size and a hypothetically small-mature-size animal are plotted against carcass weight in Fig. 1. The underlying allometry square[1] shows the different patterns of tissue growth. The mature carcasses of both large-mature-size and small-mature-size animals contain 50% muscle, 35% fat, and 15% bone,[2] but the mature carcass of the small-mature-size animal is 75% of the weight of the mature carcass of the large-mature-size animal.

As an animal grows, bone and muscle are gained rapidly at first. The rate of bone and muscle growth slows as the animal approaches its genetically predetermined maximum skeletal size and muscle weight. Well-fed animals can continue gaining weight after reaching maximum bone and muscle size, but the gain consists mostly of fat. The percentage of fat in mature animals varies with stage of reproduction and lactation. Although there is variation of mature fat concentration among breeds and among animals within breeds, it is not clear what proportion of this variation is independent of mature size.

Dietary and environmental effects on composition in time-limited growth studies are primarily a function of differences in stage of growth at slaughter because animals that grow faster reach heavier weights than animals that grow slower.

The effect of mature size on growth has been modeled into genetic size–scaling rules[3] and has important implications for speed and efficiency of growth and for carcass composition. Although about 75 kJ of metabolizable energy is required to gain a gram of either protein or lipid,[4] the water content of muscle is about 70%, whereas that of fat is only about 20%. Thus, muscle is accumulated much more efficiently than fat. At comparable immature weights, large-mature-size animals will have gained more muscle and less fat than small-mature-size animals (Fig. 1), so they have leaner carcasses, their maintenance requirements will have been similar, and they will have required less feed per unit of gain than small-mature-size animals. Because the large-mature-size animals will have consumed at least as much feed per day as small-mature-size animals, they will have grown faster.

An example of the effects of stage of growth and mature size on composition, efficiency, and growth of lambs[5] is given in Table 1. As expected based upon the relationships shown in Fig. 1, lighter lambs were leaner and accumulated more weight per unit of feed than lambs slaughtered at heavier weights. Also as expected, lambs from large-mature-size rams and ewes were leaner and accumulated more weight per unit of feed than lambs from small-mature-size rams and ewes slaughtered at the same weight.

Identifying genetic variation of body composition independently of mature weight could be important for improving the value of agricultural animals. As an example, chemical composition of small-mature-size Dorset rams was compared with that of large-mature-size Suffolk rams slaughtered across a range of ages from 1 to 600 days.[6] Because the rams were continuously fed a high-energy diet, the oldest and heaviest rams contained almost 50% lipid. This provides an example of how choosing mature weight is difficult, because mature animals gain and lose lipid in response to nutrient demands and availability. In place of the mature-body-weight estimates for the rams, four lipid-free estimates of breed mature-size were used: 1) mature amount of water;

Encyclopedia of Animal Science
DOI: 10.1081/E-EAS 120019505

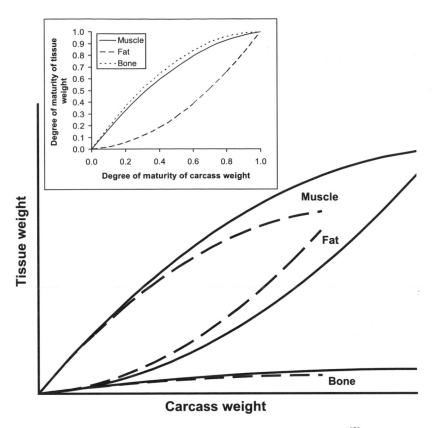

Fig. 1 Growth of the carcass to mature proportions of 50% muscle, 35% fat, and 15% bone.[2] Solid lines represent data for a large-mature-size animal. Dashed lines represent data for a small-mature-size animal. Note that muscle, fat, and bone weights must add to carcass weight. Inset: The underlying genetically standardized allometry square[1] with *q*-values of 1.8, 0.1, and 2.0 for muscle, fat, and bone, respectively.

2) mature amount of the combination of water, protein, and ash; 3) metacarpal bone length; and 4) metacarpal bone weight. When the chemical composition of the Dorset and Suffolk rams was described in genetically standardized allometry squares, the same conclusion was reached using any of the lipid-free estimates of breed mature-size: Water, protein, and ash had about the same standardized growth, whereas lipid accumulated faster than expected in Suffolk rams at advanced stages of growth.

MUSCLE DISTRIBUTION

Given that mature size is the primary trait affecting the amount of muscle at a particular weight, the other possible effect on carcass value could be differences in muscle distribution. In their classic book on cattle growth, Berg and Butterfield[7] summarized several studies of dissectible muscle distribution of breeds with widely different conformations. Data from one of those studies are summarized in Table 2. Similar data were summarized for sheep by Butterfield.[2]

The breeds in Table 2 represent widely different shapes and purposes. For example, Hereford cattle have been selected over centuries for beef, whereas Holstein and Jersey cattle have been selected for milk production and against the supposedly more meaty shape associated with Herefords and Shorthorns. And yet, the proportion of muscle weight in the high-priced cuts has not been changed through selection. The small differences among breeds of cattle and sheep—and the necessity for anatomical dissection of progeny to detect genetic differences of muscle-weight distribution of breeding stock—make the payoff unlikely to be profitable. Selection for animals with bulgier and shorter muscles (better conformation) may be important in situations where shape can be used as a marketing tool, as in the case of lambs produced for rib chops. Some beef cattle slaughtered at heavy weights, however, contain such bulgy muscles that they produce steaks unacceptably large for most consumers.

In addition to increased breast muscle size in selected turkeys and chickens, there are two examples of increased proportions of carcass muscle in cattle and sheep. Generalized muscle hypertrophy in double-muscled cattle

Table 1 Effect of mature size on growth and body composition of sheep

Item	Ewe size:	Small				Large			
	Lambs:	Single		Twins		Single		Twins	
	Slaughter weight kg:	36	54	36	54	36	54	36	54
54-kg ram									
	Number of ewes		9		2		5		5
	Ewe weight, kg		47		44		65		67
	Total feed per ewe, kg		448		510		538		609
	Lamb slaughter weight, kg	36.2	54.2	38.2	55.6	36.2	53.8	36.9	53.9
	Total feed per lamb, kg	143	391	118	537	130	365	83	513
	Lamb weight/feed	0.25	0.14	0.32	0.10	0.28	0.15	0.45	0.11
	Fat trim per lamb, kg	1.5	5.5	2.2	6.9	1.5	4.3	1.3	5.0
118-kg ram									
	Number of ewes		10		1		4		9
	Ewe weight, kg		49		49		68		72
	Total feed per ewe, kg		450		513		574		622
	Lamb slaughter weight, kg	44.0	53.9	37.0	55.6	36.3	54.2	35.7	55.2
	Total feed per lamb, kg	118	350	91	459	78	279	73	421
	Lamb weight/feed	0.37	0.15	0.41	0.12	0.47	0.19	0.49	0.13
	Fat trim per lamb, kg	1.0	4.6	1.3	5.3	0.7	3.9	0.7	3.9

(Adapted from Table 8 of Ref. 5.)

results from mutations in the myostatin gene.[8] The increased muscle of purebred animals is associated with so much calving difficulty that delivery by cesarean section is common in countries, such as France, with a high proportion of breeds carrying one of the mutations. An ideal increase in muscle hypertrophy occurs in heterozygous lambs inheriting the Callipyge mutation from their sires.[9] Differentially faster muscle growth in the high-priced cuts of the loin and leg in Callipyge lambs begins when the lambs are about three weeks old. Unfortunately, this ideal mutation comes at the expense of tougher meat,[10] and such lambs are discriminated against commercially.

Table 2 Distribution of muscle weight in breed groups of bulls and steers

Item	Hereford	Shorthorn cross	Hybrid and other crosses	Holstein	Jersey
Bulls:					
Number of animals	13	12	22	8	8
Days of age	461	361	430	386	407
Live weight, kg	465	386	489	415	294
Expensive muscles, %	53.2	53.3	53.2	53.7	53.2
Hind quarter, %	46.7	47.8	47.6	48.7	47.6
Fore quarter, %	53.3	52.2	52.4	51.3	52.4

Item	Hereford	Shorthorn cross	Hybrid and other crosses	Holstein	Brown Swiss cross
Steers:					
Number of animals	11	22	32	6	14
Days of age	402	383	434	480	404
Live weight, kg	373	376	461	466	456
Expensive muscles, %	54.3	54.2	54.4	54.4	54.7
Hind quarter, %	50.2	49.9	49.5	49.5	49.7
Fore quarter, %	49.8	50.1	50.5	50.5	50.3

(Adapted from Table 5.7 of Ref. 7.)

CONCLUSIONS

Body composition of agricultural animals is mainly determined by the stage of growth at which the animals are slaughtered. Large-mature-size animals are leaner and grow faster and more efficiently to acceptable slaughter weights than small-mature-size animals. Large-mature-size breeding stock require more nutrients for maintenance, so efficient production systems breed small-to moderate-mature-size females to large-mature-size terminal sires to produce animals for slaughter. In cattle and sheep, obvious differences in muscle shape do not translate into differences in muscle-weight distribution, although there are some genetic exceptions that may be useful in the future if associated problems in management and meat toughness can be solved. Animal scientists need to look for additional opportunities to improve body composition of agricultural animals independently of mature size.

REFERENCES

1. Taylor, S.C.S. *Genetic Aspects of Mammalian Growth and Survival in Relation to Body Size*; University of Queensland: Brisbane, 1987.
2. Butterfield, R.M. *New Concepts of Sheep Growth*; Department of Vet Anatomy, University of Sydney: Epping, NSW Australia, 1988.
3. Taylor, S.C.S. Genetic size-scaling rules in animal growth. Anim. Prod. **1980**, *30*, 161–165.
4. Thonney, M.L.; Arnold, A.M.; Ross, D.A.; Schaaf, S.L.; Rounsaville, T.R. Energetic efficiency of rats fed low or high protein diets and grown at controlled rates from 80 to 205 grams. J. Nutr. **1991**, *121*, 1397–1406.
5. Hogue, D.E. A sheep production model for maximum nutritional efficiency. In *Proceedings of the Sheep Industry Development Symposium*; Ohio Agricultural Research and Development Center: Wooster, OH, 1968; 1–20.
6. Oberbauer, A.M.; Arnold, A.M.; Thonney, M.L. Genetically size-scaled growth and composition of Dorset and Suffolk rams. Anim. Prod. **1994**, *59*, 223–234.
7. Berg, R.T.; Butterfield, R.M. *New Concepts of Cattle Growth*; John Wiley & Sons: New York, 1976.
8. Grobet, L.; Martin, L.J.; Poncelet, D.; Pirottin, D.; Brouwers, B.; Riquet, J.; Schoeberlein, A.; Dunner, S.; Ménissier, F.; Massabanda, J.; Fries, R.; Hanset, R.; Georges, M. A deletion in the bovine myostatin gene causes the double-muscled phenotype in cattle. Nat. Genet. **1997**, *17*, 171–174.
9. Cockett, N.E.; Jackson, S.P.; Snowder, G.D.; Shay, T.L.; Berghmans, S.; Beever, J.E.; Carpenter, C.; Georges, M. The callipyge phenomenon: Evidence for unusual genetic inheritance. J. Anim. Sci. **1999**, *77*, 221–227.
10. Duckett, S.K.; Snowder, G.D.; Cockett, N.E. Effect of the callipyge gene on muscle growth, calpastatin activity, and tenderness of three muscles across the growth curve. J. Anim. Sci. **2000**, *78*, 112836–112841.

Body Composition: Chemical Analysis

Harry J. Mersmann
USDA/ARS Children's Nutrition Research Center, Houston, Texas, U.S.A.

INTRODUCTION

The primary purpose of animal production is to generate skeletal muscle, a palatable and economically acceptable protein source for human consumption, milk, or hair. Regardless of the desired endpoint, products of lesser economic value, such as fat and bone, are a burden to the producer's profitability.

To measure the value of a particular genetic, husbandry, nutritional, or pharmacological practice, body composition analysis is necessary. Thus, an intervention that increases body mass might not be very profitable if it increases fat to a greater extent than muscle. Usually, the carcass is used for body composition analysis, because it contains most of the products for human consumption. However, from a biological standpoint, the empty body (entire animal but with gastrointestinal contents removed), water content or water compartments (extracellular and intracellular), specific elements in the mineral fraction, individual amino acids in proteins, and fatty acids in lipids may be important. Also, the composition of secondary products such as the head, feet, viscera, blood, skin, hair, etc. might be necessary endpoints for a complete understanding of the utilization of feed resources for animal growth.

BODY COMPARTMENTS

Body composition analysis must divide the whole into component parts (Fig. 1). Depending on the scientific question, those parts are different. They might be the chemical elements, e.g., carbon, hydrogen, oxygen, sodium, etc.; they might be anatomical entities, e.g., intestinal tract, liver, muscles, skeleton, etc.; or they might be defined by cellular location, e.g., cell mass, extracellular space, extracellular water, etc. Of pragmatic interest to animal scientists is the division of the eviscerated body or carcass into skeletal muscle, fat, bone, and sometimes skin. Dissection of the carcass into these components is a viable but laborious approach for large animals. The water, protein, fat, and mineral content of the body or carcass is an approximation of the muscle, fat, and bone

mass. Carbohydrate is a very small percentage of the total and usually is not analyzed. The simplest compartmentalization of the body or carcass is into fat mass plus fat-free mass. This two-compartment model can be obtained by underwater weighing using estimates of the density of the two compartments.

Extensive reviews of body composition are available although they usually are slanted toward a single species, e.g., humans[1] or pigs.[2] Techniques have been developed to approximate body composition without the laborious procedures necessary for chemical composition. The fat-free mass (muscle plus bone) may be approximated using ^{40}K determination of intact animals, assuming that ions, including potassium, are primarily present in tissues with a high water concentration, e.g., muscle, bone, internal organs, but are present at very low concentrations in fat. Some methods determine the water or ionic compartment to approximate muscle mass using techniques based on the water space or electrical conductance (bioelectric impedance). Other techniques employ imaging by ultrasound, X-ray–based computer-assisted tomography, or magnetic resonance imaging. The latter two techniques can evaluate internal organs in an intact animal, as well as the muscle, fat, and bone mass. Most of these techniques can be used with a live animal, although the imaging techniques require anesthesia to eliminate movement.

COMMINUTION OF SAMPLES

To analyze animal body composition or composition of a specific portion of an animal, a homogeneous sample representing the total must be produced. Large animals can be ground in screw-type grinders with powerful motors. Grinding is facilitated by freezing the specimen. To obtain homogeneity, the sample must be ground several times with progressively smaller face-plate openings and then thoroughly mixed to ensure that the small analytical sample represents the whole. Because large grinders are unavailable for very large animals, or to diminish the labor involved or to reduce the economic loss, a representative portion of the animal might be used;

Encyclopedia of Animal Science
DOI: 10.1081/E-EAS 120019497

159

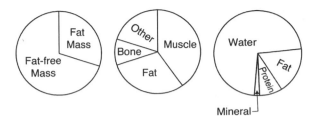

Fig. 1 Body composition compartmentalization.

it is rather common to analyze a rib section to estimate the composition of cattle.[3,4] Small animals, such as rodents, or small animal parts can be homogenized in a blender with a measured amount of water and an aliquant of the homogenate used as a sample. Hair is difficult to uniformly distribute in ground or homogenized samples and should be removed, collected, and weighed and/or further analyzed separately.

TECHNIQUES FOR CHEMICAL ANALYSIS

Many techniques are available to analyze the chemical components of the body. It is strongly recommended that only tested and reproducible methods be used.[5] A general scheme for analysis is presented in Fig. 2.

Water

Total water is usually measured by oven-drying to constant weight; the sample can also be lyophilized or dried by microwave heating. Water spaces can be measured by dilution techniques using the appropriate markers. For example, total body water may be measured by dilution of a known dose of urea or water labelled with ^2H, ^3H, or ^{18}O. The extracellular water space can be measured using bromine, which does not enter cells.

Fat

Fat is determined by extraction with solvents. Most methods use a dried sample that has been ground or homogenized, because fine particles increase the efficiency of extraction. The classical approach is the Soxhlet method, wherein a weighed sample is continuously extracted in a specialized apparatus to heat, condense, and cycle the solvent over the sample in a continuous process for 18–24 hours. The sample is then dried; the difference between pre- and postextraction weights is the

lipid weight. Diethyl ether is the standard solvent for these extractions, but petroleum ether may be substituted to reduce the danger of fire and explosion. Wet samples are usually extracted with chloroform-methanol or sometimes petroleum ether-diethyl ether. The solvent dictates the efficiency and composition of the extracted lipids. Chloroform-methanol completely extracts all neutral lipids (triglycerides, cholesterol, etc.), plus most phospholipids. Extraction with petroleum ether, chloroform, or methylene chloride alone will not remove the more hydrophilic phospholipids.

Protein

The diverse physical properties of proteins preclude a simple extraction method. Protein usually is not determined directly, but nitrogen is determined on the totally hydrolyzed sample. The nitrogen concentration of the average protein is 16%; consequently, the nitrogen concentration is multiplied by 6.25 to give the protein concentration. This average factor (6.25) may not be applicable to unique samples that contain a large amount of a specialized protein, e.g., collagen. There are other compounds in the body that contain nitrogen, e.g., nucleic acids, some phospholipids, etc., but these represent a small portion of the total nitrogen and are ignored in body composition determinations.

Usually nitrogen is determined after fat extraction. Heated sulfuric acid digestion of the sample is the most common approach, with clarification of the charred material by addition of hydrogen peroxide or other

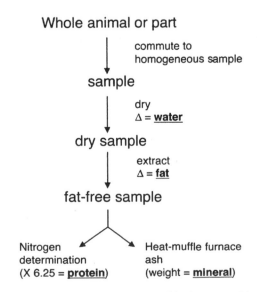

Fig. 2 Chemical determination of body composition.

Table 1 Body composition during growth

	Cattle[a]			Pigs[b]			Sheep[c]		
Weight, kg	45	364	682	5	27	92	5	32	82
Water, %	72	58	44	68	58	39	76	59	53
Protein, %	20	19	16	12	15	12	15	18	18
Fat, %	4	19	38	13	24	47	4	18	24
Ash, %	4	4	3	3	3	2	5	6	6

[a]Adapted from Ref. 8 and based on empty body weight.
[b]Adapted from Ref. 9 and based on empty body weight.
[c]Adapted from Ref. 10 and based on carcass weight.

oxidizing agents. Perchloric acid digestion is sometimes used. The hydrolysis product is ammonia. In the standard Kjeldahl nitrogen method, the ammonia is distilled into weak sulfuric acid that is then titrated. In some cases, the nitrogen is determined using a colorimetric method that can readily be automated.

There are alternative methods to determine protein concentration. These colorimetric methods, e.g., biuret, Lowry, Bradford, etc., are faster than the nitrogen methods, but many interfering substances are a major problem when using complex samples from an entire animal. Consequently, these methods are not used for body composition, but are generally reserved for determination of protein concentration in more specialized samples in the laboratory.

The total amino acid content could be used to determine the protein content, but this approach is cumbersome, complex, and difficult with a heterogeneous sample from an entire animal. Determination of the amino acid composition of particular organs is very important to understand metabolic interrelationships among the diet, the animal, and the individual organs.

Minerals

The mineral concentration of the body is determined by weighing a sample before and after heating to a very high temperature to convert complex molecules to individual elements. The carbon, nitrogen, oxygen, etc. are volatilized, leaving the heavier mineral elements, i.e., the ash. A fat-free sample is generally used. Although there are minerals in every cell in the body, the bulk of the mineral content is derived from the skeleton. Thus, the ash concentration is used to represent the skeletal mass.

Individual minerals may be determined on the ash sample. Generally, atomic absorption methods are used, but specialized chemical methods are available for some elements. Whole-body techniques using detection of natural radiation from particular elements, e.g., ^{40}K,

or elements made radioactive by neutron activation are available.

DISTRIBUTION OF PROTEIN, FAT, AND BONE

Protein, fat, and minerals are concentrated in skeletal muscle, adipose tissue, and bone, respectively. However, all tissues, including the adipose tissue and bone, contain protein and all tissues contain minerals and fat. The proportion of the whole represented by muscle, fat, and bone changes as animals grow.[6,7] The bone and muscle masses increase until the animal reaches the adult body size, whereas the fat mass continues to grow as long as the animal is fed a balanced diet containing more energy than necessary to achieve maintenance (Table 1).

CONCLUSION

Body composition is an important endpoint in animal growth research and in estimation of the economics of animal production. The labor involved in the determination of chemical composition has elicited many less intense methods using instrumental determinations or prediction equations based on measurement of fat depths, areas, or weights coupled with measurement of specific muscle depth or area (usually the longissimus muscle). For economic estimates of meat production, the carcass (minus head, hide, feet, and viscera) is used. However, from a biological or an energetic perspective, all components are important. Prediction equations used to extrapolate to the whole animal should be tailored to the specific species and perhaps need to account for age, breed, diet, sex, treatment, etc. Ultimately, using established methods and good sample preparation, chemical analysis is the gold standard for all body composition measurements.

REFERENCES

1. Ellis, K.J. Human body composition: In vivo methods. Physiol. Rev. **2000**, *80* (2), 649–680.
2. Mitchell, A.D.; Scholz, A.M. Techniques for Measuring Body Composition of Swine. In *Swine Nutrition*, 2nd Ed.; Lewis, A.J., Southern, L.L., Eds.; CRC Press: Boca Raton, FL, 2001; 917–960.
3. Hankins, O.G.; Howe, P.E. *Estimation of the Composition of Beef Carcasses and Cuts*; Technical Bulletin No. 926, U.S. Department of Agriculture: Washington, DC, 1946; 1–20.
4. Crouse, J.D.; Dikeman, M.E. Methods of estimating beef carcass chemical composition. J. Anim. Sci. **1974**, *38*, 1190–1196.
5. *The Official Methods of Analysis of AOAC International (OMA), E17*; Horwitz, W., Ed.; AOAC International: Gaithersburg, MD, 2003.
6. Berg, R.T.; Walters, L.E. The meat metal: Changes and challenges. J. Anim. Sci **1983**, *57* (Suppl. 2), 133–146.
7. Mitchell, A.D.; Scholz, A.M.; Mersmann, H.J. Growth and Body Composition. In *Biology of the Domestic Pig*; Pond, W.G., Mersmann, H., Eds.; Comstock Publishing Associates, a division of Cornell University Press: Ithaca, NY, 2001; 225–308.
8. Berg, R.T.; Butterfield, R.M. *New Concepts of Cattle Growth*; John Wiley & Sons: New York, NY, 1976.
9. Ferrell, C.L.; Cornelius, S.G. Estimation of body composition of pigs. J. Anim. Sci. **1984**, *58*, 903–912.
10. Jenkins, T.G.; Leymaster, K.A. Estimates of maturing rates and masses at maturity for body components of sheep. J. Anim. Sci. **1993**, *71*, 2952–2957.

Body Composition: Genetic Influence

Harry J. Mersmann
USDA/ARS Children's Nutrition Research Center, Houston, Texas, U.S.A.

INTRODUCTION

The variety of domesticated animal breeds within any given species existing worldwide indicates great diversity of body size and composition. In domesticated animals, intense genetic selection for body composition was not applied until the 20th century. In developed countries, genetic selection produced remarkable changes in the body composition of the common species raised for meat production, particularly in the latter decades of the century. Currently, cattle, pigs, and sheep are considerably more muscular and less fat than in earlier times. The impetus for these changes was to increase the economic return for the producer by increasing the marketable product, muscle, and concomitantly reducing the fat mass, a product whose value declined with the replacement of by-products made from fat by oil-derived moieties. During the last quarter of the 20th century, consumers began to demand that retail meat products have less fat, so fat was trimmed as a waste product and animals were bred for less fat mass.

GENETIC DIVERSITY

There is obvious divergence in body composition between breeds in cattle, pigs, and sheep.[1] Perhaps the most extreme example is the difference in the market pig in the early 1900s compared to the early 2000s. The earlier pig was extremely fat, because fat was a valued product, not only as a source of fat-based by-products, but also because it provided an energy-dense dietary component required by the human consumer who performed very energy-intensive work in the home and in the workplace. Fatty meats provided much of the caloric density required for survival. During the 1900s, with the development of oil-based products and especially as humans automated many of the energy-intensive types of work, demand for fat became limited. Carcass fat is highly heritable, so much progress was made to produce leaner, more muscular animals.

In addition to the genetic selection for muscle mass and against fat mass within breeds, there are breeds of cattle, e.g., Belgian Blue, and sheep, e.g., Callipyge, that are

extremely muscular.[2] In pigs, the majority of marketed animals are cross-breeds, and the sires are usually more muscular breeds, e.g., Hampshire or Duroc, or some cross-breed with a considerable contribution from muscular breeds. There have been several experimental selection projects in pigs to study the heritability of fat deposition; these have produced extremely fat pigs (also lightly muscled) in relatively few generations.[3]

BREED DIFFERENCES

The proportion of fat to muscle in animals continually changes during growth so that comparison of breeds must consider whether animals are being compared at constant weight or constant chronological age.[2,4,5] Comparison at constant weight is often used, because the weight chosen approximates the market weight for that species. This comparison has practical outcomes regarding production of lean meat. The difficulty with constant-weight comparisons is that different breeds have different mature size and growth rates and reach maturity of body composition at different ages. Thus, comparison at a given weight can represent comparison of animals at divergent stages of maturity. Because fat deposition is a predominant aspect of later-stage growth, earlier maturing animals will be fatter than later maturing animals at a given weight. For example, comparison of two breeds with mature body weights of 100 and 125 kg at 95-kg body weight would show one breed at 95% of mature composition (i.e., more fat) and the other breed at 76% of mature composition (i.e., less fat). This is the result of comparing early maturing cattle, e.g., Angus, with later maturing cattle, e.g., Simmental, at constant weight. Comparison at constant age contrasts breeds that may have different weights or maturity, i.e., stages of achieving mature body composition; these comparisons have important biological implications regarding growth.

Comparison of different breeds of cattle at constant age (Table 1) indicates considerable diversity in weight, fatness, and yield of retail product. If these animals are examined at later ages, they have more fat and less retail product.[6] The earlier maturing breeds, e.g., Angus, have

Encyclopedia of Animal Science
DOI: 10.1081/E-EAS 120019500

Table 1 Growth of cattle[a]

Breed	Carcass weight, kg	Fat thickness, mm	Fat trim, %	Retail product, %	Marbling score
Angus	277	14.6	21.5	66.97	13.3
Hereford	273	14.2	19.0	68.4	9.1
Gelbvieh cross	303	9.3	16.6	70.7	9.2
Chianina cross	304	8.0	12.3	73.8	8.0

[a]Carcass composition at constant age (473 days).
(Adapted from Ref. 6.)

a higher percentage of fat and a lower percentage of retail product than the later maturing breeds, e.g., Chianina, regardless of the time of comparison. An approximation of maturity can be made at constant fat-trim percentage;[6] the assumption is that all breeds will eventually achieve the same percentage carcass fat. This assumption may not apply when extremes in mature body composition are compared, e.g., Angus vs. Chianina.

Comparison of breeds of pigs at constant weight (Table 2) indicates that the rate of gain is quite divergent, as is the rate of gain for lean, fat, and nonfat viscera. The larger and faster growing Landrace breed also has greater gain of lean mass than the Duroc breed; both Landrace and Duroc are considerably greater than the fat breed shown in Table 2. The lean gain/total gain is 43 and 42% for Landrace and Duroc, respectively, during growth from 85 to 105 kg. However, the fat gain is 26 and 32% of the total gain, respectively, for the two breeds during the same period of growth. Also, the gain in viscera during this period is 6.4% of the total gain in the Landrace breed, but 8.9% in the Duroc breed; this has implications on the efficiency of growth because the viscera require considerable energetic input.

The Callipyge lamb represents an animal with a single gene mutation that produces exceptional muscle growth. When compared at constant weight, the Callipyge carcass is slightly heavier than the normal carcass and has more muscle and less fat. The accretion rates (g/day) for protein are higher in Callipyge lambs than in normal lambs, whereas fat accretion rates are lower in Callipyge lambs than normal lambs (Table 3). The differences between Callipyge lambs and normal lambs were observed at

constant weight, constant age, and constant 12th-rib fat depth. [7]

DISTRIBUTION OF FAT

Species differ greatly in the distribution of fat in the body. Rats have small omental and perivisceral depots, modest subcutaneous depots, and large perigonadal and perirenal depots. In contrast, pigs deposit approximately 70% of fat in the subcutaneous depots with a modest perirenal depot and smaller omental, perivisceral, and perigonadal depots. Cattle and sheep deposit much less fat in the subcutaneous depot than pigs, and deposit more fat in the perirenal and especially the omental and perivisceral depots. The deposition of fat in intermuscular depots (between the individual muscles) is common in cattle, pigs, and sheep and tends to be accentuated in the forequarters. In developed countries, intermuscular fat can be a negative factor in the marketing of meat cuts because of the aversion to dietary intake of fat. By contrast, there are market segments that favor considerable fat deposition in the intramuscular depot (i.e., marbling), at least in specific retail meat cuts. Interestingly, there are no great differences between breeds within a species in the distribution of fat, although Japanese Kobe beef have a very high level of intramuscular fat. Also, cattle breeds bred for muscle production have more subcutaneous and less internal fat, whereas the breeds bred for milk production have less subcutaneous and more internal fat. No other species have been selected for such extreme product production as cattle; perhaps if such selection were practiced

Table 2 Growth of pigs (g/d)[a]

Breed	Weight	Carcass lean	Fat	Nonfat viscera
Landrace	1049	454	277	67
Duroc	906	381	291	81
Fat, slow grow line	817	301	348	73

[a]Growth rate between 85 and 105 kg.
(Adapted from Ref. 10.)

Table 3 Growth of Callipyge lambs

Breed	Accretion rate, g/day	
	Protein	Fat
Callipyge	12.5	35.2
Normal	10.2	42.1

(Adapted from Ref. 7.)

in other species, the same extremes of fat distribution would ensue.

RELATION BETWEEN BODY COMPOSITION AND NUTRIENT REQUIREMENTS

To achieve maximal growth, the nutritional input must be optimal. The protein content and amino-acid composition must be appropriate to foster muscle and bone growth. Thus, animals selected for increased rates of muscle growth have an increased requirement for dietary protein and amino acids to maintain maximal growth. The energy content must be sufficient to support the desired anabolic processes for muscle and bone growth, and the vitamin and mineral content must be adequate. However, excess energy and even amino-acid intake relative to needs of the animal produce excess fat accretion. For most domesticated species, access to high-quality rations ad libitum results in excess fat accretion. Limiting intake to less than ad libitum can produce essentially the same deposition of muscle, but less deposition of fat.[8,9] For example, pigs fed 100, 92.5 or 85% of ad libitum had daily gains of 833, 802, and 771 g/d, respectively.[9] The protein deposition was 47, 48, and 48% of the total gain, respectively, whereas the fat gain was 25, 22, and 20% of the total gain, respectively. Thus, feeding less than ad libitum can emphasize the maximal production of the desired muscle product and reduce the undesired fat product. Amino-acid, vitamin, and mineral intake must be maintained at optimal concentrations, and the energy-to-protein ratio must also be optimal.

CONCLUSION

Modern breeds of cattle, pigs, and sheep have been selected for production of muscle mass and against production of fat mass. Within a species, there is considerable diversity among breeds in body composition. Much of the diversity results from different rates of growth and the age at which mature body composition is achieved. Thus, a comparison of breeds at a given weight may compare breeds at different stages of maturity. Genetic selection has been and continues to be very effective in changing the composition within a breed. The high degree of heritability of fat growth is a major contributing factor. There are extremes of muscling in several breeds of cattle and in sheep. Several experimental strains of pigs have been genetically selected for extreme fatness.

REFERENCES

1. Briggs, H.M. *Modern Breeds of Livestock*; The Macmillan Company, Collier-Macmillan, Ltd: London, 1969.
2. Marple, D. Fundamental Concepts of Growth. In *Biology of Growth of Domestic Animals*; Scanes, C.G., Ed.; Iowa State Press: Ames, IA, 2003; 9–19.
3. Mersmann, H.J. Characteristics of Obese and Lean Swine. In *Swine Nutrition*; Miller, E.R., Ullrey, D.E., Lewis, A.J., Eds.; Butterworth-Heinemann: Stoneham, MA, 1991; 75–89.
4. Berg, R.T.; Walters, L.E. The meat animal: Changes and challenges. J. Anim. Sci. **1983**, *57* (Suppl. 2), 133–146.
5. Mitchell, A.D.; Scholz, A.M.; Mersmann, H.J. Growth and Body Composition. In *Biology of the Domestic Pig*; Pond, W.G., Mersmann, H.J., Eds.; Comstock Publishing Associates, a division of Cornell University Press: Ithaca, NY, 2001; 225–308.
6. Koch, R.M.; Dikeman, M.E.; Lipsey, R.J.; Allen, D.M.; Crouse, J.D. Characterization of biological types of cattle—cycle II: III. Carcass composition, quality and palatability. J. Anim. Sci. **1979**, *49*, 448–460.
7. Freking, B.A.; Keele, J.W.; Nielsen, M.K.; Leymaster, K.A. Evaluation of the ovine callipyge locus: II. Genotypic effects on growth, slaughter, and carcass traits. J. Anim. Sci. **1998**, *76*, 2549–2559.
8. Hays, V.W.; Preston, R.L. Nutrition and Feeding Management to Alter Carcass Composition of Pigs and Cattle. In *Low-Fat Meats Design Strategies and Human Implications*; Hafs, H.D., Zimbelman, R.G., Eds.; Academic Press: San Diego, CA, 1994; 13–33.
9. Leymaster, K.A.; Mersmann, H.J. Effect of limited feed intake on growth of subcutaneous adipose tissue layers and on carcass composition in swine. J. Anim. Sci. **1991**, *69*, 2837–2843.
10. Kolstad, K.; Brenoe, U.T.; Vangen, O. Genetic differences in energy partitioning in growing pigs. Acta Agric. Scand., Sect. A Anim. Sci. **2002**, *52*, 213–220.

Body Composition: Indirect Measurement

Alva D. Mitchell
Armin Scholz
United States Department of Agriculture, Agricultural Research Service,
Beltsville, Maryland, U.S.A.

INTRODUCTION

Historically meat animals have been evaluated and selected using subjective methods based primarily on visual appraisal. However, a variety of indirect methods for the measurement of body composition are now available to assist in the evaluation process. Most of the newer techniques are based on tissue interaction at the atomic or molecular level that result in signals that can be analyzed quantitatively.

DILUTION METHODS

Dilution techniques for body composition analysis are based on the principle that water occupies a relatively fixed fraction of the fat-free mass. This technique involves the introduction (e.g., orally, intravenous injection) of a known amount of a tracer that will then equilibrate throughout a given compartment (e.g., total body water) in the body. The concentration of the (nontoxic) tracer is measured in a sample of the compartment, assuming that the tracer has the same distribution volume as the compartment, and in the case of water, is exchanged by the body in a similar manner. This approach can be applied to animals of wide-ranging body size.[1] To extrapolate from total body water to other compartments of body composition such as fat or lean mass, a validation of the relationship to reference values for the particular species and physiological state is required. The primary reference method for the indirect techniques in (farm) animals is chemical analysis or, in some cases, total body dissection.

Deuterium Oxide

The most widely used dilution approach for measuring total body water is that of deuterium oxide (D_2O, or heavy water). After allowing for equilibration (time depends on species, body weight, age), a blood sample is obtained. Sample analysis by infrared spectroscopy is simple and inexpensive.[2]

TISSUE INTERACTION

Bioelectrical Impedance (BIA)

When a low-level alternating electrical current is applied to a biological system, a voltage drop or impedance to the electrical flow is detected. Conductance, which is the opposite of impedance, is greatest in the electrolyte-rich body water and is lower in lipids and bone mineral. Two sets of electrodes at defined locations on the animal serve for the measurement of the impedance. In addition, body weight and the distance between detector electrodes are measured. Because this system is portable, inexpensive, and simple to operate, it is frequently used to estimate the fat-free mass in humans[2] and in animals as well.[1]

Total Body Electrical Conductivity

By applying similar principles, instead of the electrodes used in BIA, an electromagnetic coil provides the basis for the measurement of energy absorption with total body electrical conductivity (TOBEC). The energy absorption signal is primarily a function of the volume of the fat-free mass measured as the difference between the coil impedance when the subject is inside or outside the coil.[1] The amount of energy absorbed is a function of the area, the magnetic field strength, and the conductivity per unit volume at a specific frequency.

Dual-Energy X-Ray Absorptiometry

A different attenuation of low- and high-energy X-rays by fat and nonfat or bone tissues is the basic principle for the measurement of body composition by dual energy X-ray absorptiometry (DXA). The fat and lean (nonfat) content is determined for each pixel of a scan that does not overlie bone and is reported to be virtually independent of tissue thickness. In addition to whole-body or regional composition values of fat and lean content (Fig. 1), DXA provides estimates for bone mineral content, bone mineral density, and total mass of soft tissues. DXA has been used with poultry,[3] swine,[4] and recently with calves.[5]

Encyclopedia of Animal Science
DOI: 10.1081/E-EAS 120019501

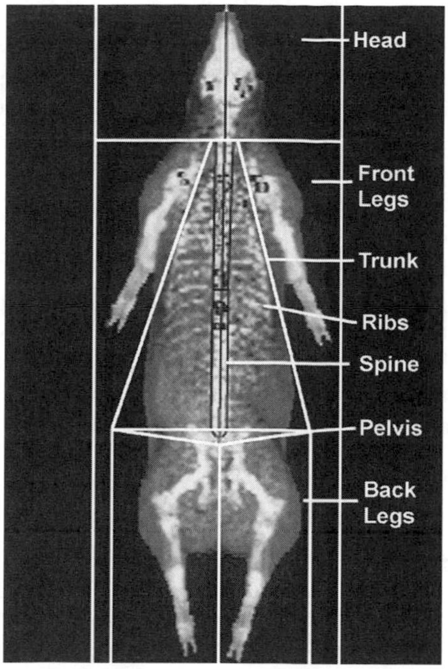

Fig. 1 Image produced by a DXA scan of a live pig with defined regions of interest.

ATOMIC ANALYSIS

Total Body Potassium

The determination of total body potassium based on a total body count of naturally occurring ^{40}K can be used to estimate total-body cell mass or lean mass. With proper calibration, shielding of background radiation, and correction for body geometry, an accurate measurement of total body potassium can be obtained. However, the equipment is expensive and is available at only a few locations. In animal studies, this technique has been tested with live pigs,[6] lambs,[7] and cattle.[8]

Neutron Activation

Neutron activation (NA) is the only method available for multielemental analysis of the body. NA analysis consists of irradiating the subject with fast neutrons during a total-body scan. Elements within the body such as hydrogen, carbon, nitrogen, oxygen, calcium, phosphorus, sodium, and chlorine capture the neutrons, resulting in unstable isotopes. After returning to a stable condition, they emit one or more gamma rays at specific energy levels. Only a few NA instruments are currently available, because NA is quite expensive, requires considerable expertise, and is

slow (15–60 min). Contrary to a number of human NA body composition studies,[2] animal studies such as in swine or sheep[9] are restricted.

IMAGE ANALYSIS

Magnetic Resonance Imaging

A magnetic resonance image (MRI) is produced by placing a subject in a static magnetic field and exciting certain atoms in the body with pulses of radiofrequency waves. The excited atoms produce signals transformed to (a series of) images that can be analyzed to measure the volume of muscle or adipose within a region of the body (Fig. 2). Although MRI is widely available for human clinical studies, the equipment is expensive to purchase and operate. MRI has been used for body composition analysis in several species, including poultry, sheep, and swine.[10,11]

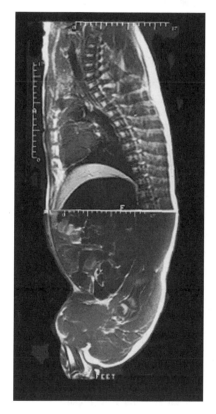

Fig. 2 A composite of sagittal MRI images of a pig. The top portion is through the middle line of the thoracic region, and the bottom portion, through the abdominal region, is off-set to bisect one of the back legs.

X-Ray Computed Tomography

Generally, computed topography (CT) or X-ray computed axial tomography (CAT) images of the body's interior look quite similar to MRI images. However, CT images originate from transmission data created by a rotating X-ray tube. The CT image produces good contrast between fat and lean tissue, but lacks the ability of MRI to provide detailed contrast among or within various tissues and organs in the lean-tissue category. CT is also widely available for human clinical studies, but the equipment is expensive to purchase. CT has been used for body composition analysis in several species, including poultry,[12] rabbits,[13] swine,[14,15] and, most extensively, sheep.[16]

Ultrasound

Because of the technological development of real-time linear-array ultrasonic transducers and scanners in the medical field during the last decade, this technique has become the most common in vivo (and postmortem) technology in (farm) animal body composition assessment,[1] ranging from simple distance to area measurements using A-mode, B-mode, or M-mode devices. Two-dimensional ultrasound images provide information about adipose tissue depots and cross-sectional areas of muscles. In principle, the ultrasound device uses a probe to convert electronic energy to high-frequency ultrasonic energy that is capable of penetrating the body in short pulses. When these ultrasonic waves encounter an interface between two tissues that differ in acoustical properties, part of the ultrasonic energy is reflected back to the receiver probe. Variations in tissue depths result in time differences in reflected signals. Real-time images result from rapid electronic switching or linear array transducers. The practical application of ultrasound measurements of the live animal and carcass are being extended to genetic selection programs[17] and on-line carcass evaluation.[18]

CONCLUSION

Advances in techniques for body/carcass composition analysis are based on the development of electronic/computer-based methods, thus avoiding destructive, labor-intensive, or subjective approaches. In general, the choice of a particular technique (Table 1) will depend on the purpose or application, technical aspects (accuracy, reliability, and the type of information needed), and

Table 1 Comparison of methods for indirect measurement of body composition

Method[a]	Measurement	Advantages	Disadvantages
D₂O	Total body water	Wide range of body size, simple, inexpensive	Slow, accuracy depends on reference studies
BIA	Lean mass	Simple, rapid, inexpensive, portable	Accuracy depends on reference studies
TOBEC	Lean mass	Simple, rapid, can be automated	Accuracy depends on reference studies, sedation required for most animals, moderately expensive
DXA	Fat, lean, bone mineral, and total tissue mass	Accurate, simple, rapid analysis, region of interest analysis	Moderately expensive, sedation necessary, radiation exposure
⁴⁰K	Total body potassium (cell mass)	Wide range of body size, rapid	Expensive, accuracy depends on reference studies
NA	Various elements (e.g., nitrogen, carbon, oxygen)	Accurate	Expensive, radiation exposure, technical expertise, sedation necessary
MRI	Visualization of fat, muscle, and other soft tissues	Accurate, multiple levels of analysis	Expensive, technical expertise, sedation necessary, slow
CAT or CT	Visualization of fat, lean, and bone	Accurate, multiple levels of analysis	Expensive, technical expertise, sedation necessary, slow, radiation exposure
US	Visualization of subcutaneous fat and underlying lean	Portable, extensive database for some species, can be automated	Moderately expensive, accuracy depends on reference studies

[a]D2O = deuterium oxide, BIA = bioelectrical impedance, TOBEC = total body electrical conductivity, DXA = dual energy X-ray absorptiometry, ⁴⁰K = total body potassium counting, NA = neutron activation analysis, MRI = magnetic resonance imaging, CAT = X-ray computer axial tomography, CT = X-ray computer tomography, US = ultrasound.

practical aspects (cost, portability, need for restraint or anesthesia, speed, ease of use or training required, safety, and size of the animal to be measured).

ARTICLE OF FURTHER INTEREST

Body Composition: Chemical Analysis, p. 159

REFERENCES

1. Speakman, J.R. *Body Composition Analysis of Animals*; Cambridge University Press: New York, 2001.
2. Lukaski, H.C.; Johnson, P.E. A simple, inexpensive method of determining total body water using a tracerdose of D_2O and infrared absorption of biological fluids. Am. J. Clin. Nutr. **1985**, *41* (2), 363–370.
3. Mitchell, A.D.; Rosebrough, R.W.; Conway, J.M. Body composition analysis of chickens by dual energy x-ray absorptiometry. Poult. Sci. **1997**, *76* (12), 1746–1752.
4. Mitchell, A.D.; Conway, J.M.; Scholz, A.M. Incremental changes in total and regional body composition of growing pigs measured by dual-energy x-ray absorptiometry. Growth Dev. Aging **1996**, *60* (2), 95–105.
5. Scholz, A.M.; Nüske, S.; Förster, M. Body composition and bone mineralization measurement in calves of different genetic origin by using dual-energy X-ray absorptiometry. Acta Diabetol. **2003**, *40*, S91–S94.
6. Siemens, A.L.; Lipsey, R.J.; Martin, W.M.; Siemens, M.G.; Hedrick, H.B. Composition of pork carcasses by potassium-40 liquid scintillation detection: Estimation and validation. J. Anim. Sci. **1991**, *69* (1), 47–53.
7. Judge, M.D.; Stob, M.; Kessler, W.V.; Christian, J.E. Lamb carcass and live lamb evaluation by potassium-40 and carcass measurements. J. Anim. Sci. **1963**, *22* (2), 418–421.
8. Johnson, J.E.; Ward, G.M. Body composition of live animals as determined by K40. I. A crystal-type, whole-body counter for determining body composition of live animals. J. Dairy Sci. **1966**, *49* (9), 1163–1165.
9. Mitra, S.; Wolff, J.E.; Garrett, R. Calibration of a prototype in vivo total body composition analyzer using 14 MeV neutron activation and the associated particle technique. Appl. Radiat. Isotopes **1998**, *49* (5/6), 537–539.
10. Baulain, U. Magnetic resonance imaging for the in vivo determination of body composition in animal science. Comput. Electron. Agric. **1997**, *17*, 189–203.
11. Mitchell, A.D.; Scholz, A.M.; Wang, P.C.; Song, H. Body composition analysis of the pig by magnetic resonance imaging. J. Anim. Sci. **2001**, *79* (7), 1800–1813.
12. Brenøe, U.T.; Kolstad, K. Body composition and development measured repeatedly by computer tomography during growth in two types of turkeys. Poult. Sci. **2000**, *79* (4), 546–552.
13. Szendrõ, Zs.; Horn, P.; Kövér, Gy.; Berényi, E.; Radnai, I.; Bíróné Németh, E. In vivo measurment of the carcass traits of meat type rabbits by X-ray computerised tomography. J. Appl. Rabbit Res. **1992**, *15*, 799–809.
14. Skjervold, H.; Grønseth, K.; Vangen, O.; Evensen, A. In vivo estimation of body composition by computerized tomography. Z. Tierz. Züchtgsbiol. **1981**, *98*, 77–79.
15. Leymaster, K.A. Tomography to estimate changes in body tissues. J. Anim. Sci. **1986**, *63* (Suppl. 2), 89–95.
16. Lambe, N.R.; Young, M.J.; McLean, K.A.; Conington, J.; Simm, G. Prediction of total body tissue weights in Scottish Blackface ewes using computed tomography scanning. Anim. Sci. **2003**, *76*, 191–197.
17. Wilson, D.E. Application of ultrasound for genetic improvement. J. Anim. Sci. **1992**, *70*, 973–983.
18. Brøndum, J.; Agerskov, E.M. Busk, J. On-line pork carcass grading with the Autofom ultrasound system. J. Anim. Sci. **1998**, *76*, 1859–1868.

Body Composition: Linear Dimensions

Robert G. Kauffman
University of Wisconsin, Madison, Wisconsin, U.S.A.

Eric P. Berg
University of Missouri, Columbia, Missouri, U.S.A.

INTRODUCTION

Animal species vary in composition due to their stage of growth, nutritional history, and genetic base. This is significant for livestock producers, the meat industry, and consumers, because the economic value of meat-producing animals depends greatly on composition. Economic forces have reduced the fat composition of livestock in general in response to consumer demands for more lean meat. To successfully assess body composition of both the live animal and its carcass, many procedures have been studied, and of these, linear measurements including width, depth, length, and area, as well as weight, density, and visual shape, have been used separately and collectively with varying degrees of accuracy. More accurate techniques such as nuclear magnetic resonance (NMR) imaging, electromagnetic scanning, bioelectrical impedance, anyl-ray, computerized tomography, chemical analyses of body fluids, video imaging, and whole-body potassium isotope counting exist. These techniques are usually ignored because they are too slow, too complicated, or too expensive to be practical or to serve as substitutes for dissection and chemical analysis when accurate composition is required for research. The following is a discussion of meat-animal composition and of linear dimensions used as means of assessing composition of livestock and their carcasses.

COMPOSITION

Composition is the aggregate of ingredients, their arrangement, and the integrated interrelationships that form a unified, harmonious whole. Steel spikes and steel tacks contain 100% steel. Even though differing in shape, size, weight, depth, length, and width, all have identical compositions. Unlike steel nails, meat animals consist of many components, as shown in Fig. 1.[1] They contain muscles, tendons, ligaments, bones, fat, organs, skin, blood, ingesta, and excreta. Each of these is subdivided into more specific categories and is expressed as a proportion of the live animal or any of its parts. For instance, the largest muscle in most animals is the longissimus thoracis et lumborum (commonly referred to as the rib and loin muscle), which spans the length of the back. By weight it represents about 4% of the live animal, 7% of the carcass, 12% of the total musculature, and 51% of the back muscles. The greatest economic emphasis is placed on increasing the mass of muscles in the animal in relation to everything else. The proportion of an animal's compositional endpoints is related to several criteria, but the three most important are visceral proportions, fatness, and muscling as expressed by the muscle/bone ratio. Livestock possessing high proportions of viscera are undesirable, as these organs have little value. A high proportion of fat is undesirable, as it requires trimming from the musculature. A low muscle/bone ratio is undesirable because it indicates the animal contains proportionately more low-value bone than high-value muscle.

Livestock at various stages of prenatal and postnatal growth vary in composition. Therefore, when variations in composition are assessed accurately, there is need to identify quantifiable measurements and factors affecting them.[2] Such factors include stage of growth, physiological maturity, nutrition, and genetics. The proportion of muscle in livestock can vary from below 35% to over 50%. This variation is more complicated when average compositions of species are considered as depicted in Table 1. Species alone accounts for at least 15% of the variation in muscle mass, because species differences in dressing percentages and muscle/bone ratios may vary by 30% and 3.2 respectively. As illustrated in Fig. 2,[1] there are several factors influencing dressing percentage including contents of the alimentary canal, pregnancy, presence of abnormalities (trimmed bruises, broken bones, etc.), methods of slaughter, sex, stage of growth, muscling, and condition of the hide or fleece, fatness, species and condition of the hide or fleece.

Figure 3[1] shows the interrelationships of muscle, bone, fat, and noncarcass components as influenced by stage of growth, fatness, muscling, and fill. For instance, when the effects of growth, fatness, and fill are constant, heavier-muscled livestock have proportionately more muscle, less bone, less fat, and higher dressing percentages than angular-shaped ones. Livestock that have more fill have proportionately less muscle.

Encyclopedia of Animal Science
DOI: 10.1081/E-EAS 120019503

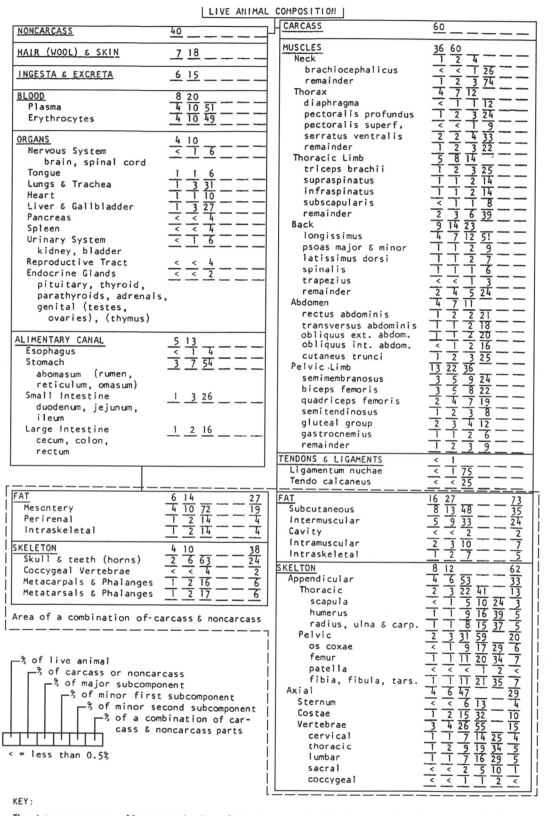

Fig. 1 Summary of the composition of meat animals.

Table 1 Average compositional variations among species of meat animals

	Beef	Veal	Pork	Venison	Lamb	Turkey	Chicken	Catfish
Live weight, kg	550	160	110	70	50	15	2	0.7
Proportion of live weight								
Noncarcass, %	38	46	27	42	48	18	23	37
Carcass skin, %	—	—	5	—	—	9	9	—
Carcass fat, %	17	7	23	10	17	6	7	—
Carcass bone, %	10	15	9	8	10	17	22	12
Carcass muscle, %	35	32	36	40	25	50	39	51
Total	100	100	100	100	100	100	100	100
Dressing percent	62	54	73	58	52	82	77	63
Carcass muscle/bone	3.5	2.1	4.0	5.0	2.5	2.9	1.8	4.3

METHODS TO MEASURE COMPOSTION OF LIVESTOCK AND THEIR CARCASSES

Some of the following methods are not strictly linear by definition but are included because they are associated with linear dimensions.

Visual Appraisal

Subjective visual assessment of live animals or their carcasses is an inexpensive and rapid technique that is often used to supplement linear measurements. Distinguishing between muscling and fatness is difficult. Therefore, visual assessment of muscling is more effective within a narrow range of fatness, particularly when fat levels are low. However, visual prediction is difficult to standardize. Comparative photographs that subjectively depict degrees of muscling and fatness are effective standards that can be used to classify extremes in composition, especially for carcasses. Nevertheless, for the sake of accuracy visual appraisal is not recommended.[1]

Weight

Live or carcass weight is useful when combined with other variables such as external fat depth. Obviously, weight is used as the denominator in calculating proportions of leanness and is related to stage of biological maturity, frame size, and fatness. The only time weight alone becomes a reliable predictor of composition is when all other factors remain constant.[2]

Depths

An inexpensive ruler is used to measure external fat thickness as well as length and width of muscles and has been used extensively to make linear measurements of livestock and their carcasses. For livestock, the back-fat probe was one of the first methods used.[3] Recently, more sophisticated techniques have been developed such as

noninvasive real-time ultrasound to determine external fat and muscle depth on livestock and invasive optical light reflectance probes on carcasses.[1]

Other Linear Measurements

Lengths, widths, and circumferences are taken on livestock and carcasses using anatomically identified reference locations. Measurements include hip or shoulder height, heart girth circumference, length or circumference of cannon bone, hind saddle length, and carcass length. Most of these are related to weight and will provide some insight into variations of skeletal size, but usually they are

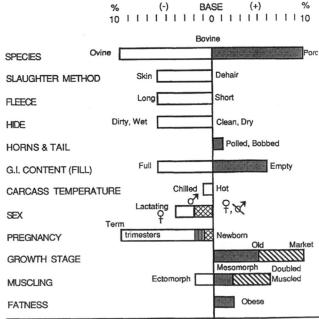

1 Some traits are interrelated such as species, slaughter method and fleece.

2 Condemnations (due to bruising, disease, contamination, etc.) and weighing errors are not included but could change yields slightly to excessively.

Fig. 2 Effects of various traits on dressing percentage.

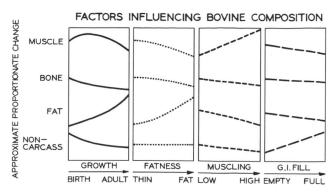

Fig. 3 Factors influencing bovine composition.

not related directly to composition. Of all linear measurements, fat depth in combination with weight contributes most significantly to the prediction of lean body mass.[4]

Areas

Measurements of muscle area expressed in square inches (or centimeters) contribute to the improvement of prediction equations used to estimate cutability grades in livestock and their carcasses. Muscle area is measured on the surface of the transverse section of a specific muscle at a specific anatomical location. For example, rib muscle area on beef carcasses is obtained on the surface of the rib muscle sectioned at the interface between the 12th and 13th ribs. For any constant weight or size of animal or carcass, the size of individual or groups of muscles is related to lean content. For a given frame size, muscles having larger areas are associated with higher muscle mass and a higher muscle/bone ratio. However, fatness is the single most important factor affecting composition. When muscling is represented by muscle area and included in a prediction equation, the estimate of composition improves.[4,5] It is obligatory to use ultrasonic measurements for livestock whereas a plastic grid is used to determine muscle areas for carcasses. The loin muscle is used as a point of reference for muscle areas of beef, pork, and lamb. This area is used in combination with fat depth and weight to predict leanness. Occasionally, areas of intermuscular (seam) fat have been assessed. However, the difficulty in standardizing anatomical locations has made such areas less practical.

Density

Fat, bone, and muscle possess different densities and this procedure is used for estimating carcass composition. Such differences are discernable when carcasses are weighed in water and then in air to indirectly measure water displacement. Based on the arbitrary value of 1.0 as the density of water, fat (0.9) is less dense than the fat-free

carcass, and bone (1.8) has greater density than either fat or muscle (1.1). In addition to the method being slow, it assumes that the carcass muscle/bone ratio is constant.

CONCLUSIONS

The conversion of plants by livestock to provide meat for humans is important to agriculture. Because of consumer demands for lean, high-quality meat and the economical efficiencies of converting plants into lean meat rather than fat, there is need to understand how livestock vary in composition and how to accurately determine these variations. Stage of maturity, level of nutrition, and genetic makeup are important for understanding body composition. Nevertheless, other factors such as species, pregnancy, and dressing percentages contribute significantly to this understanding.

To successfully understand the variables responsible for composition of market livestock, the parents from which they originate, and the ultimate carcasses they yield for lean, high-quality meat production, it is essential to have practical, accurate, inexpensive, and rapid methods to ascertain composition, and there are numerous ways to estimate it in both livestock and their carcasses. However, most methods fail in one or more of the four required criteria: 1) practicality; 2) accuracy; 3) inexpensiveness; and 4) rapidity. Using the combination of weight, fat depth, and muscle area through ultrasonic evaluation for livestock and optical-light reflectance probes for carcasses proves reliable for both scientific research and commercial marketing.

REFERENCES

1. Kauffman, R.G.; Breidenstein, B.C. Meat-Animal Composition and Its Measurement. In *Muscle Foods*; Kinsman, D.M., Kotula, A.W., Breidenstein, B.C., Eds.; Chapman and Hall: New York, NY, 1994; 224–247.
2. Topel, D.G.; Kauffman, R. Live Animal and Carcass Composition Measurement. In *Designing Foods*; Committee on Technological Options to Improve the Nutritional Attributes of Animal Products, Board on Agriculture, National Research Council, Eds.; National Academy Press: Washington, DC, 1988; 258–272.
3. Hazel, L.N.; Kline, E.A. Mechanical measurement of fatness and carcass value of live hogs. J. Anim. Sci. **1952**, *11*, 313–318.
4. Fahey, T.J.; Schaefer, D.M.; Kauffman, R.G.; Epley, R.J.; Gould, P.F.; Romans, J.R.; Smith, G.C.; Topel, D.G. A comparison of practical methods to estimate pork carcass composition. J. Anim. Sci. **1977**, *44*, 8–17.
5. National Pork Board. *Pork Composition and Quality Assessment Procedures*; Berg, E.P., Ed.; National Pork Board #04412-4/2000: Des Moines, IA, 2000; 1–40.

Body Composition: Nutritional Influence

Cornelis F. M. de Lange
University of Guelph, Guelph, Ontario, Canada

INTRODUCTION

The essence of animal production is to convert nutrients supplied by a range of feedstuffs into high-quality animal products. In meat-producing animals, this conversion encompasses relationships between nutrient intake and chemical body composition, as well as those between chemical and physical body composition. In terms of physical body composition, the amount of muscle tissue and its distribution are of prime concern, as they are the main determinants of the amount and quality of consumable products that can be derived from the animal's carcass. Relationships between nutrient intake and body composition also influence the efficiency of animal production and are affected by a range of factors associated with animal type, nutrition, environment, and stage of growth. An understanding of these relationships, and of factors affecting them, is required to identify means to manipulate animal product quality and production efficiencies.

PHYSICAL AND CHEMICAL BODY COMPOSITION

The main body tissues in growing animals are muscle or lean tissue, fat, visceral organs, bones, and skin. The other tissues, including nervous, lymphatic, and vascular tissue, and blood contribute less than 10% to empty body weight in growing animals and are discussed in detail elsewhere in this encyclopedia. The three main chemical constituents in the animal's empty body are water, protein, and lipid. Most of the body water and body protein is contained in muscle tissue, whereas body lipid is largely present in fat tissue. The animal's body contains only minor amounts of carbohydrates, which largely represent glycogen stores in the liver and muscle. The mineral and vitamin content in animal products is low relative to the three main chemical constituents, but animal products represent an important source of these essential nutrients for humans. Moreover, the bio-availability of nutrients in animal products is generally higher than that in plant products.

In terms of chemical body composition, body water is closely associated with body protein, reflecting the association between water and protein in muscle.[1] The latter implies that variation in chemical and physical body composition of animals reflects largely variation in the ratios between body protein and body lipid mass and between muscle and fat tissue, respectively. It should be noted that across animal types, variation in hide and visceral organ mass contributes to variation in chemical and physical body composition as well.

The physical and chemical body composition that growing animals attempt to achieve is ultimately controlled by the animal's genotype.[1] However, the rate and composition of body weight gain—and thus the actual body composition of growing animals—are influenced by the animal's environment and by the intake of available nutrients in particular.

EFFECTS OF AMINO ACID AND ENERGY INTAKE ON BODY COMPOSITION

Insufficient dietary supply of any of the essential nutrients will reduce animal growth performance and is likely to influence the animal's body composition. For this reason, practical animal diets are generally overfortified with vitamins and minerals, which are relatively inexpensive nutrients. Special consideration should be given to amino acids and energy-yielding nutrients.

At the tissue level, animals require amino acids for the synthesis of body proteins.[2] Of the approximately 20 amino acids present in body protein, 12 amino acids can be considered essential or semiessential and must be supplied in the diet or derived from microbial protein that is generated in the rumen of ruminant animals. Animals must be supplied with sufficient quantities of nitrogen for synthesis of indispensable amino acids as well. Insufficient supply of amino acids at the tissue level will limit the growing animal from expression of its protein deposition potential.

Based on carefully controlled animal experiments, the relationship between intake of a specific indispensable amino acid and body protein deposition may be represented using a broken line–linear plateau model (Fig. 1). The linear increase in body protein deposition with amino acid intake—represented by the sloped line in Fig. 1—indicates that the marginal efficiency of using available amino acid intake for body protein deposition is constant

Encyclopedia of Animal Science
DOI: 10.1081/E-EAS 120019504

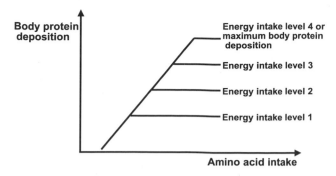

Fig. 1 Schematic representation of the relationship between dietary intake of an essential amino acid and body protein deposition in growing animals at different levels of energy intake. (From Refs. 3 and 4.)

over a rather wide range of amino acid intake levels. The marginal postabsorptive efficiency of using the first limiting amino acid for retention in body protein is less than 1, due to inevitable amino acid catabolism.[5] The plateaus in body protein deposition represented in Fig. 1 may be determined by the intake of another essential nutrient, energy intake, or the animal's operational body protein deposition potential. The latter reflects the body protein deposition potential that an animal can achieve under practical conditions and when fed ad libitum a palatable diet that is not limiting in essential nutrients. The animal's operational body protein deposition potential is influenced by body weight and approaches 0 when the animal reaches maturity.

Energy-yielding nutrients are required as fuels to support a variety of processes associated with the maintenance of body function and integrity and growth.[1] Energetically, growth may be represented as body lipid and body protein deposition (Fig. 2). When energy intake

exceeds requirements for maintenance and maximum body protein deposition, additional energy intake is used only to support lipid deposition and fat tissue growth. However, even when energy intake is insufficient to maximize body protein deposition, some of the absorbed energy-yielding nutrients are partitioned toward the deposition of (essential) body lipid (Fig. 2). Only at extreme low levels of energy intake can animals mobilize some of the body fat reserves to support body protein deposition. This implies that the fatness of the animal's body increases with energy intake level, and this increase in fatness is greatest once energy intake exceeds requirements for maximum body protein deposition. The relationship between energy intake and body protein deposition appears to be influenced by body weight as well. At the same level of energy intake above maintenance energy requirements, more energy is partitioned toward body lipid deposition with increasing body weight, even when energy intake is insufficient to maximize body protein deposition. The efficiency of using dietary energy for various body functions is addressed elsewhere in this encyclopedia.

DIETARY MANIPULATION OF FATTY ACID PROFILE AND NUTRIENT CONTENT OF ANIMAL PRODUCTS

Manipulation of the fatty acid profile of body lipid and of vitamin and mineral content in slaughter animals should be considered, as it influences storage and sensory properties of animal products. It also provides a means to supply fatty acids and nutrients in animal products that are beneficial to human health.

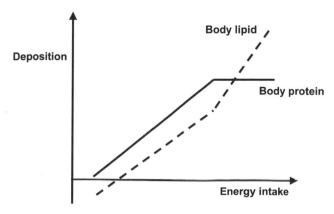

Fig. 2 Schematic representation of the relationship between energy intake and accretion of body protein and body lipid in growing animals. (From Refs. 3,6,7.)

Table 1 Fatty acid composition (% of deposited body lipid) in female broiler chickens fed diets containing 10% from different sources between 8 and 42 days of age[a]

	Dietary fat source				
	None (control)	**Tallow**	**Olive oil**	**Sunflower oil**	**Linseed oil**
C16:0	25.9	23.1	17.0	10.7	10.9
C16:1 n-7	7.41	5.42	1.99	0.67	1.06
C18:0	6.86	8.28	4.77	4.12	4.52
C18:1 n-9	31.8	39.4	55.2	18.6	18.2
C18:1 n-7	2.27	2.34	2.10	0.49	0.77
C18:2 n-6	20.0	13.6	14.9	61.9	17.8
C18:3 n-6	0.52	0.16	0.17	0.35	0.05
C18:3 n-3	1.47	1.39	1.22	0.99	43.0

[a]Values represent means from 10 individual chickens.
(From Ref. 8.)

Table 2 Effect of dietary dosage and duration of supplemental vitamin E on tissue content of α-tocopherol in cattle[a]

		Tissue content, μg/g fresh tissue			
Dosage, IU/d	Duration, d	Liver	Subcutaneous fat	Gluteus medius muscle	Longissimus muscle
0	38–266	2.9	2.7	1.8	1.4
360	211–252	12.0	9.5	5.3	4.1
1280	211–252	25.2	19.6	8.6	6.8
3560	196–266	31.2	22.5	–	7.6

[a]Values represent observations obtained in several studies.
(From Ref. 9.)

Fatty acids incorporated into body lipid can either be synthesized de novo by the animal (largely palmitic, C16:0; stearic, C18:0; and oleic acid, C18:1 n-9) or derived directly from dietary fat. Because animals preferentially use dietary fatty acids for the synthesis of body lipids, manipulation of the content and fatty acid composition of dietary fat represents a means to influence the fatty acid composition of body fat.[8] This applies in particular to monogastric animals. Microbes in the gastrointestinal tract of ruminant animals can alter the dietary fatty acid profile before it is absorbed. The high content of oleic (C18:1 n-9), linoleic (C18:2 n-6), and linolenic acid (C18:3 n-3) content in olive oil, sunflower oil, and linseed oil, respectively, is reflected in the high content of these fatty acids in body lipid when these fat sources are fed to broiler chickens (Table 1).

A nutrient whose level in the various tissues is manipulated easily by changing dietary intake is vitamin E (Table 2).[5] An increased level of tocopherol provides protection of lipid and myoglobin oxidation during harvesting and storage of fresh meat products, and thus extends the stability of lipid and color in these animal products.

CONCLUSION

The chemical and physical body composition of growing animals is ultimately determined by the animal's genotype. However, body composition can be manipulated substantially by altering feeding level and diet composition. This applies in particular to the body lipid–to–body protein ratio, which is closely related to the fat tissue–to–muscle tissue ratio. Diet manipulation also represents a means to influence the fatty acid profile of body lipid and the content of some vitamins and minerals in the animal's body.

REFERENCES

1. Lawrence, T.J.L.; Fowler, V.R. Growth of Farm Animals; CABI Publishing: CAB International: Wallingford, 2002.
2. Martin, D.W.; Mayes, P.A.I.; Rodwell, V.W. Harper's Review of Biochemistry, 18th Ed.; Lange Medical Publications: Los Altos, CA, USA, 1981.
3. Campbell, R.G.; Taverner, M.R. Genotype and sex effects on the relationship between energy intake and protein deposition in growing pigs. J. Anim. Sci. **1988**, *66*, 676–686.
4. Möhn, S.; Gillis, A.M.; Moughan, P.J.; de Lange, C.F.M. Influence of dietary lysine and energy intakes on body protein deposition and lysine utilization in growing pigs. J. Anim. Sci. **2000**, *78*, 1510–1519.
5. Moughan, P.J. Protein Metabolism in the Growing Pig. In *Quantitative Biology of the Pig*; Kyriazakis, I., Ed.; CABI Publishing: CAB International: Wallingford, 1999; 299–332.
6. de Greef, K.H.; Verstegen, M.W.A.; Kemp, B.; van der Togt, P.L. The effect of body weight and energy intake on the composition of deposited tissue in pigs. Anim. Prod. **1994**, *58*, 263–270.
7. Kyriazakis, I.; Emmans, G.C. The effects of varying protein and energy intakes on the growth and body composition of pigs: 2. The effects of varying both energy and protein intake. Br. J. Nutr. **1992**, *68*, 615–625.
8. Crespo, N.; Esteve-Garcia, E. Nutrient and fatty acid deposition in broilers fed different dietary fatty acids profiles. Poultry Sci. **2002**, *81*, 1533–1542.
9. Arnold, R.N.; Arp, S.C.; Scheller, K.K.; Williams, S.N.; Schaefer, D.M. Tissue equilibration and subcellular distribution of vitamin E relative to myoglobin and lipid oxidation in displayed beef. J. Anim. Sci. **1993**, *71*, 105–118.

Body Composition: Technical Options for Change

Harry J. Mersmann
USDA/ARS Children's Nutrition Research Center, Houston, Texas, U.S.A.

INTRODUCTION

Animals raised for meat production are usually marketed before they reach adult body composition. During growth, various body compartments (skeleton, muscle, fat, and viscera) are in a dynamic state, with each having its own trajectory toward maturity. Within a species, individual breeds have distinct mature sizes and rates of maturation for body composition, so harvesting different breeds at a fixed weight yields differences in body composition. In addition, some breeds are genetically more muscular and some are fatter. Furthermore, the environment (climate and husbandry practices) and nutrition are important contributors to the ultimate body composition exhibited by a particular breed.

Many experimental and production-oriented approaches have been used to change body composition. Effective experimental technologies sometimes are not practical or they are cost-prohibitive. Some technologies may later become practical because of changes in husbandry, scientific or technological advances, or favorable economics. For example, a half-century ago it was shown that somatotropin modified growth of mammals, but the available somatotropin extracted from pituitary glands made its use cost-prohibitive. Many years later, recombinant somatotropin became available; it is cost-effective and is used to modify mammalian growth in countries where it is approved by the regulatory bodies.

TECHNIQUES TO CHANGE BODY COMPOSITION

Genetics

Genetic selection has been and continues to be the major tool to change body composition in species raised for the production of meat.[1,2] Previously, fat was a feedstock for many by-products, but most uses were supplanted by oil-derived products. Fat is also an energy-dense product and was important as food in earlier times when humans expended large amounts of energy to accomplish tasks that in developed countries are now performed by or assisted by machines. In developing and developed countries, as modernization progresses, there is less need for energy-dense diets. The tendency of modern societies toward being overweight or obese has changed the demand toward lean meat. Genetic selection for less body fat and more muscle is successful because of the high and moderate degree of heritability of fat and muscle deposition, respectively.[3] For example, in pigs selected for and against backfat thickness, it changed approximately 3.5% per generation.[4]

As more is known about the role of specific genes or combinations of genes in the regulation of body composition, genetic selection can be directed toward those genes.[5] The double-muscled condition in cattle results from mutations in a protein, myostatin, involved in differentiation and growth of muscle. Selection for these types of mutations may lead to more muscular animals. Selection for less function of genes associated with adipose tissue accretion may lead to leaner animals. Animal growth is complex and regulated by a multitude of genes, so selection for a single gene may not produce the desired effects. Determination of anonymous markers in the genome associated with variation in quantitative traits (quantitative trait loci) allows discovery and mapping of genetic loci that should be valuable in future selection projects. Fine mapping of these regions can then be used to discover a particular gene or genes involved with the desired traits.

Environment and Nutrition

In some species, it may be economically feasible to modify the temperature, humidity, air flow, photoperiod, etc. to provide a more favorable environment for optimal animal growth. At less-than-optimal temperatures, energy is expended to maintain body temperature, whereas at elevated temperatures, animals decrease feed intake to diminish heat production. Both extremes produce less-than-optimal growth. Shelters of various design and even enclosed buildings may be economically advantageous in raising some species, e.g., poultry and pigs in temperate climates.

Nutrition is an important determinant of body composition. The diet must be optimal for vitamin, mineral, and energy content. Insufficient protein or an inappropriate

Encyclopedia of Animal Science
DOI: 10.1081/E-EAS 120019508

amino acid composition leads to lesser growth of skeletal muscle and more deposition of fat. However, provision of a high-quality ration ad libitum leads to excess fat deposition. In pigs fed ad libitum, 92.5% ad libitum, and 85% ad libitum, the carcass protein was 100%, 97%, and 94%, respectively, whereas the fat was 100%, 86%, and 75%, respectively.[6] The groups fed 92.5% and 85% ad libitum required 5% and 10% less feed per unit protein produced. Many experiments indicate the advantage of less than ad libitum feeding. Experimental limit feeding uses individually penned animals or computer-controlled feed delivery systems. Practical implementation of limited feeding is difficult. In group-penned animals fed limited quantities, socially dominant animals eat at greater than ad libitum and submissive animals eat less than required. Biomedical research to understand neural control of feeding behavior may lead to strategies to control feed intake in animals raised for meat production. Leptin, a protein produced and secreted by adipocytes, binds to receptors in the brain to diminish feed intake. Also, some dietary fatty acids, e.g., n-3 polyunsaturated fatty acids or conjugated linoleic acids, favor less fat deposition in rodents and other species, including pigs. The practicality and economics of using such technologies are yet to be demonstrated.

Endocrinology and Pharmacology

Experimental demonstration of endocrine effects on body composition is extensive.[7,8] For example, excess glucocorticoid hormones produce decreased muscle and increased fat deposition. Insufficient thyroid hormone leads to excess fat production. Sex hormones have marked effects on body composition with mammalian males being more muscular and less fat than females or castrated males. However, because of aggressiveness and sexual activity, males are usually castrated. In some countries, male pigs are raised but are marketed at a younger age to avoid behavioral problems and boar-taint (an off-flavor developing with sexual maturity). In the United States,

cattle are regularly implanted with sex steroids to augment growth and favor muscle production.[7,8]

Exogenous somatotropin (growth hormone) leads to increased muscle and visceral organ growth (Table 1), along with decreased fat deposition and feed intake.[7,8] Somatotropin is used to promote efficient muscle production in some countries. Experimental strategies stimulate endogenous somatotropin production or release through growth hormone–releasing hormone or by decreasing activity of somatostatin (that is, diminishing somatotropin release). Insulin-like growth factor 1 (IGF-1) may be the mediator of many somatotropin effects, so its regulation can also control body composition. Selected compounds that stimulate β-adrenergic receptors (βAR agonists) increase muscle and decrease fat deposition (Table 1) with little effect on visceral growth and usually a decrease in feed consumption.[7,8] The βAR agonists are used in cattle and pigs in some countries.

In addition to the administration of exogenous hormones or synthetic analogs, endocrine function can be controlled by immunological approaches. Animals can be immunized against a peripheral endocrine substance to decrease its circulating levels or against a pituitary factor that modifies peripheral production and release of hormones. An example is the immunocastration of male mammals, wherein intact males can be raised to take advantage of the favorable growth characteristics and then they can be neutered by immunocastration to eliminate the later ensuing negative aspects of male behavior.

Using molecular biology techniques, transgenic animals that produce an excess of the transgene product have been created; animals with nonfunctional genes produce less of the gene product. Pigs were made transgenic for somatotropin.[9] The approach has not become practical because the expression of the gene is irregular and variable in different tissues. As the function of gene promoters (that part of the gene that controls expression or production of messenger RNA and subsequent protein synthesis) and tissue-specific expression of genes is better understood, it is expected that these techniques will have practical value in animal production. An intriguing approach is a gene therapy that implants a DNA construct for growth hormone–releasing hormone (GHRH) in skeletal muscle.[10] This construct then functions to produce and secrete GHRH. In the central nervous system GHRH causes release of somatotropin with consequent increase in IGF-1, an increase in muscle, and a decrease in fat mass. Thus, administration of exogenous somatotropin is avoided with its negative consumer biases. Other molecular biology approaches will present themselves in the future as the control of gene function is understood and methods are devised to selectively stimulate or disengage gene function in a specific tissue at particular

Table 1 Effect of somatotropin and β-adrenergic agonists in lambs

Variable	Somatotropin[a]	β-Adrenergic agonists[b]
Gain	+14	+22
Feed/gain	−22	−14
Protein g/d	+36	+12.2
Fat g/d	−30	−20

[a]Adapted from Table 2 of Ref. 7.
[b]Adapted from Table 4 of Ref. 7.

times. Increased or decreased production of a hormone or growth factor at select times during growth will be possible. It should be possible to decrease fat synthesis or increase fat mobilization or oxidation at stages when these functions are less critical to the animal and over-function or under-function leads to excess fat deposition.

Immunology

In rats, chickens, pigs, and sheep, fat deposition is decreased by injecting antibodies against adipocyte membranes from the same species.[11] This technique, like many immunological approaches, has not been practically implemented because it is not yet possible to control the immunological response. When the immunological response can be controlled, immunological technologies probably will become a part of the armamentarium of the producer.

CONCLUSION

Genetic selection has been the primary approach to change body composition for many years. As knowledge of bioregulation of animal growth continues to unfold, selection will be directed toward specific genes and proteins that impact growth of muscle and fat. Additionally, selection may be directed toward factors that control regulation of cell differentiation or specific metabolic pathways. Molecular biology technology continues to reveal additional potential targets for genetic selection, pharmacological intervention or specific immunization to enhance or diminish a function. In the future, there will be an abundance of new targets to explore, as well as some not yet conceived.

REFERENCES

1. Berg, R.T.; Walters, L.E. The meat animal: Changes and challenges. J. Anim. Sci. **1983**, *57* (Suppl. 2), 133–146.
2. Marple, D. Fundamental Concepts of Growth. In *Biology of Growth of Domestic Animals*; Scanes, C.G., Ed.; Iowa State Press: Ames, IA, 2003; 9–19.
3. Miller, R.H. A Compilation of Heritability Estimates for Farm Animals. In *A Handbook of Animal Science*; Putnam, P.A., Ed.; Academic Press: San Diego, CA, 1991; 151–169.
4. Hetzer, H.O.; Harvey, W.R. Selection for high and low fatness in swine. J. Anim. Sci. **1967**, *26*, 1244–1251.
5. Clutter, A.C. Genetics and Growth. In *Biology of Growth of Domestic Animals*; Scanes, C.G., Ed.; Iowa State Press: Ames, IA, 2003; 263–279.
6. Leymaster, K.A.; Mersmann, H.J. Effect of limited feed intake on growth of subcutaneous adipose tissue layers and on carcass composition in swine. J. Anim. Sci. **1991**, *69*, 2837–2843.
7. Beermann, D.H. Carcass Composition of Animals Given Partitioning Agents. In *Low-Fat Meats: Design Strategies and Human Implications*; Hafs, H.D., Zimbelman, R.G., Eds.; Academic Press: San Diego, CA, 1994; 203–232.
8. Scanes, C.G. *Biology of Growth of Domestic Animals*; Iowa State Press: Ames, IA, 2003.
9. Pursel, V.G.; Solomon, M.B.; Wall, R.J. Genetic Engineering of Swine. In *Advances in Swine in Biomedical Research*; Tumbleson, M.E., Schook, L.B., Eds.; Plenum Press: New York, 1996; 189–206.
10. Draghia-Akli, R.; Ellis, K.M.; Hill, L.-A.; Malone, P.B.; Fiorotto, M.L. High-efficiency growth hormone-releasing hormone plasmid vector administration into skeletal muscle mediated by electroporation in pigs. FASEB J. **2003**, *17*, 526–528.
11. Hill, R.A.; Pell, J.M.; Flint, D.J. Immunological Manipulation of Growth. In *Biology of Growth of Domestic Animals*; Scanes, C.G., Ed.; Iowa State Press: Ames, IA, 2003; 316–341.

By-Product Feeds: Animal Origin

Lee I. Chiba
Auburn University, Auburn, Alabama, U.S.A.

INTRODUCTION

The competition between humans and animals for quality sources of nutrients is likely to increase continuously because of the ever-increasing world population. It is therefore imperative not only to improve feed efficiency but also to explore all the sources as a potential feed ingredient. Animal by-products have been used as a source of nutrients for many years, but they will play even more important roles in the future. The objective of this article is to review briefly selected by-product feeds of animal and marine origins used for food animal production.

ANIMAL BY-PRODUCTS IN GENERAL

Although there are some standards,[1,2] considerable variations exist in the classification and quality of animal fats and fish oils. Similarly, other animal and marine by-products are generally more variable than plant feeds in terms of their nutrient content and quality because of the source of raw materials and heat processing used for dehydration and sterilization.[3] The composition of selected animal by-product feeds is presented in Tables 1 and 2. For complete information, readers are referred to the National Research Council (NRC)[4–7] and other[1–3,8–11] publications. Since the first diagnosis in the mid-1980s, there has been some impact of bovine spongiform encephalopathy (BSE) on the food animal industries in many countries. In light of BSE, regulations on the use of some animal by-products may differ depending on the country, species, and/or product, and they are subject to change. For complete information on this issue, readers are referred to, among others, the United Nations Food and Agriculture Organization (FAO) Web site.[11]

ANIMAL FATS AND FISH OILS

General

Both animal fats and fish oils are highly digestible energy sources for animals, and fish oils are also an excellent source of omega-3 fatty acids and vitamins A and D. The quality of feed-grade fats can be assessed by the composition, hardness, color, impurities, and stability.

Composition refers to the fatty acid profile, and hardness is affected by chain length and degree of unsaturation of fatty acids. Color may not be associated with nutritional value, but it can indicate the product composition or source. Moisture or unsaponifiable matters have no nutritional value, whereas ether insolubles can reduce the fat quality. Moisture can also deteriorate fat. Fats and oils are prone to oxidation, which can reduce palatability and quality, and thus must be stabilized with antioxidants.

Animal and Poultry Fats

Feed-grade animal fats consist of rendered fats from beef or pork by-products, which are mainly slaughterhouse offal or supermarket trimmings from the packaging of meats, and poultry fat includes fats from 100% poultry offal. Some fats are also produced from inedible tissues by rendering plants. Choice white grease is primarily rendered pork fat, but it can be a blend of animal fats. In addition to fats of animal origin, restaurant greases—which can be mixtures of various animal fats and vegetable oils—are being recycled and used for food animal production.

Fish Oils

Fish caught specifically for the production of fish meals are high in body oil content, much of which is extracted before making meal. There has been some interest in feeding fish oils to food animals to increase the omega-3 fatty acid content of meat, milk, and eggs and the reproductive performance of swine. Although feeding fish oils may have beneficial effects, problems such as softening of body fat, development of a fish-like odor in edible tissues, and reduced protein and fat contents in milk have been reported. It is therefore necessary to consider an optimum inclusion rate and/or a chemical treatment of oils to ensure acceptable final products.

MEAT ANIMAL BY-PRODUCTS

General

Protein sources from the meat-processing industry generally contain highly digestible protein, and their amino acid (AA) pattern is often very similar to dietary needs. Beef

Encyclopedia of Animal Science
DOI: 10.1081/E-EAS 120019512

Table 1 Composition of selected animal by-products (% or Mcal/kg for ME and NE, data on DM basis)[a]

Protein source	DM	ME (Sw)	ME$_n$ (Po)	NE$_m$ (Ru)	NE$_g$ (Ru)	Eth Ex	Lino acid
Animal fats:[b]							
Beef tallow	–	7.68	7.16	4.53	3.12	100.0	3.10
Choice white grease	–	7.96	–	–	–	–	11.60
Lard	–	7.95	8.56	–	–	100.0	10.20
Poultry fat	–	8.18	9.48	–	–	99.8	19.50
Restaurant grease	–	8.21	–	–	–	–	17.50
Beef scrap, dried	87.8	–	–	–	–	15.0	–
Blood meal, conventional	91.7	2.55	3.01	2.00	1.34	1.6	0.10
Blood meal, spray/ring-dried	93.0	3.17	3.68	–	–	1.2	0.15
Bone meal, steamed	97.0	–	–	–	–	–	–
Casein	91.3	3.88	4.45	–	–	0.7	0.03
Crab meal	95.0	–	1.56	–	–	2.3	–
Feather meal, hydrolyzed	93.2	2.67	2.54	1.93	1.29	6.1	0.89
Fish meal, anchovy, mech ext	92.0	2.93	2.80	2.13	1.46	5.8	0.26
Fish meal, herring, mech ext	93.0	3.51	3.43	–	–	10.3	0.16
Fish meal, menhad, mech ext	91.7	3.65	3.07	2.09	1.41	10.4	0.13
Fish meal, white, mech ext	91.0	3.09	2.85	–	–	5.2	0.09
Fish oils:[b]							
Anchovy	–	8.11	–	–	–	–	1.20
Herring	–	8.33	–	–	–	100.0	1.15
Menhaden	–	8.14	8.45	–	–	100.0	2.15
Fish solubles, condensed	51.0	3.19	2.86	–	–	13.1	–
Fish solubles, dried	92.0	3.31	3.08	–	–	9.1	0.13
Meat and bone meal, rend	93.3	2.39	2.31	1.71	1.09	11.0	0.58
Meat meal, rend	93.4	2.76	2.39	1.98	1.32	11.0	0.58
Milk, skim, dried	96.0	3.87	2.74	–	–	0.9	0.01
Oyster, shells, ground[b]	–	–	–	–	–	–	–
Plasma protein, spray-dried	91.0	–	–	–	–	2.2	–
Poult by-product meal, rend	93.0	3.08	3.17	–	–	13.8	2.73
Poult litter, cage, dried	89.0	–	–	–	–	1.9	–
Poult litter, floor, dried	85.0	–	–	–	–	2.7	–
Shrimp meal	90.0	2.34	–	–	–	4.3	–
Whey, dried	94.5	3.32	2.04	–	–	0.9	0.01
Whey, liquid	13.9	–	–	1.96	1.41	0.7	–
Whey, low lactose, dried	93.5	3.03	2.30	–	–	1.1	0.03

[a]ME=metabolizable energy; NE=net energy; DM = dry matter; ME (Sw)=ME for swine; ME$_n$ (Po)=N-corrected ME for poultry; NE$_m$ (Ru)=NE for maintenance for ruminants; NE$_g$ (Ru)=NE for growth for ruminants; Eth Ex=ether extract; Lino Acid=linoleic acid; mech ext=mechanically extracted; menhad=menhaden; rend=rendered; Poult=poultry. Dash=no available data.
[b]No available moisture, ether insoluble, or unsaponifiable matter content or DM content; thus, the values are on as-fed basis.
(Data from Refs. 1 and 4–9.)

scrap or meal, meat meal, and meat and bone meal are, however, low in tryptophan, and blood meal is low in isoleucine. Meat meal and meat and bone meal are excellent sources of many minerals and vitamins, especially Ca, P, and vitamin B$_{12}$. Blood meals are generally a poor source of vitamins and minerals, except Fe. Bone meal is a good source of Ca and P.

Meat By-Product Meals and Blood Products

Beef scrap is made from the waste materials of the beef-slaughtering operations. Steamed bone meal is produced by heating bones in a pressurized cooker to remove fat

and other materials. Meat meal and meat and bone meal are made from carcass trimming, condemned carcasses and livers, offal, and bones. They are also prepared from the rendering of dead animals. Meat meal consists of mostly meat trimmings and organs, and is distinguished from meat and bone meal based on its P content. If the product contains more than 4.4% P, it is considered meat and bone meal. Blood meal produced by conventional vat cooking and drying processes has poor palatability and low lysine availability. Spray-drying and flash-drying procedures have improved the quality of blood meal. The plasma fraction of blood yields a fine, light-tan powder. Spray-dried product, plasma protein, is highly palatable and may have a positive effect on the immune system of the young pig.

MILK BY-PRODUCTS

Casein is the solid residue obtained from the coagulation of defatted milk. In skim milk, most of the fat and fat-soluble vitamins are removed. Liquid whey is the part of milk that separates from the curd during cheese production, and can be fed to animals as-is or dried and can also be used for animal and human diets. A large portion of lactose can be removed to produce low-lactose dried whey. Dried skim milk and dried whey have been used for young animals and in some pet foods. Milk products are

very palatable and an excellent source of AA. Dried skim milk and dried whey are a good source of vitamins and minerals, but they are low in vitamins A and D, and perhaps Fe and Cu.

MARINE BY-PRODUCTS

Crab and Shrimp Meals, and Oyster Shell

By-products from the processing of crabs or shrimp can be dried and ground to produce crab or shrimp meal. Both meals are high in chitin, which contains unavailable N. Chitin is structurally similar to cellulose but not digested by cellulase. Other N fractions contributed by the viscera

Table 2 Contents of selected animal by-products (%, data on DM basis)[a]

Animal by-product	CP	RUP	Lys	Trp	Thr	Met	Ash	Ca	P
Animal fats:[b]									
Beef tallow	0.0	–	0.00	0.00	0.00	0.00	0.00	0.00	0.00
Choice white grease	–	–	–	–	–	–	–	–	–
Lard	0.0	–	0.00	0.00	0.00	0.00	0.00	0.00	0.00
Poultry fat	0.0	–	0.00	0.00	0.00	0.00	0.00	0.00	0.00
Restaurant grease	–	–	–	–	–	–	–	–	–
Beef scrap, dried	68.3	–	–	–	–	–	12.7	9.67	4.76
Blood meal, conventional	89.8	74.2	7.69	1.30	3.93	0.84	2.6	0.42	0.34
Blood meal, spray/ring-dried	95.5	–	8.25	1.53	4.14	1.12	–	0.44	0.32
Bone meal, steamed	13.2	60.0	–	–	–	–	71.0	30.71	12.86
Casein	90.4	–	7.89	1.13	4.26	2.84	3.5	0.64	0.99
Crab meal	31.6	–	1.47	0.32	1.26	0.53	32.6	18.95	1.58
Feather meal, hydrolyzed	88.9	63.8	2.34	0.59	4.10	0.63	3.5	0.56	0.58
Fish meal, anchovy, mech ext	70.6	53.7	5.53	0.84	3.07	2.12	16.0	4.11	2.70
Fish meal, herring, mech ext	75.5	–	5.88	0.85	3.28	2.26	11.2	2.52	1.86
Fish meal, menhad, mech ext	67.3	62.5	5.08	0.63	2.78	1.85	20.2	5.50	3.16
Fish meal, white, mech ext	69.2	–	4.97	0.73	2.84	1.89	26.4	7.67	4.07
Fish oils:[b]									
Anchovy	–	–	–	–	–	–	–	–	–
Herring	0.0	–	–	–	–	–	–	–	–
Menhaden	0.0	–	–	–	–	–	–	–	–
Fish solubles, condensed	62.9	–	3.39	0.61	1.69	0.98	19.6	0.51	1.32
Fish solubles, dried	69.5	–	3.33	0.47	1.50	1.08	13.4	0.97	1.57
Meat and bone meal, rend	54.6	54.8	2.74	0.30	1.79	0.73	30.4	10.81	5.19
Meat meal, rend	58.1	44.4	3.25	0.39	1.99	0.83	22.1	8.79	4.28
Milk, skim, dried	36.0	–	2.98	0.53	1.69	0.96	8.7	1.36	1.04
Oyster, shells, ground[b]	–	–	–	–	–	–	–	38.0	0.10
Plasma protein, spray-dried	85.7	–	7.52	1.49	5.19	0.82	–	0.16	1.88
Poult by-product meal, rend	66.7	–	3.45	0.46	2.34	1.13	20.2	4.01	2.21
Poult litter, cage, dried	32.2	–	0.44	0.60	0.39	0.13	29.8	8.76	2.47
Poult litter, floor, dried	29.8	–	0.58	–	0.61	0.15	16.6	2.94	1.88
Shrimp meal	44.3	–	2.41	1.40	1.57	0.91	–	10.81	2.04
Whey, dried	13.3	–	0.99	0.20	0.86	0.19	10.3	0.91	0.78
Whey, liquid	14.4	5.3	1.08	0.22	0.87	0.21	9.8	1.05	0.85
Whey, low lactose, dried	18.0	–	1.59	0.29	1.08	0.51	20.2	2.11	1.25

[a]See Table 1 for the dry matter (DM) content. CP=crude protein; RUP=ruminal undegradable protein, % CP; mech ext=mechanically extracted; menhad=menhaden; rend=rendered; Poult=poultry. Dash=no available data.
[b]No available moisture, ether insoluble, or unsaponifiable matter content or DM content; thus, values are on as-fed basis.
(Data from Refs. 1 and 4–9.)

and residual meat can be of good quality, and thus their nutritional value may depend on the proportion of nonchitinous residues in those meals. They are relatively high in Ca and low in P content. Shrimp meal is a good protein source for nonruminant species. Crab meal does not show much promise even for ruminants, but it can be a low-cost alternative to replace some protein supplements. Dried and ground oyster shell is an excellent source of Ca.

Fish Meals and Fish Solubles

Fish meals are produced from fish caught specifically for making meals—such as anchovy, herring, and menhaden—or from the residues remaining after processing fish mostly for human consumption. Whitefish meal is produced from whitefish or whitefish waste. Fish meals are high in protein and indispensable AA and a good source of most vitamins and minerals. However, fish meal produced from degraded raw material is of low quality and can be toxic to animals because of high histamine concentrations.[11] Feeding fish meal may result in the development of a fish-like odor in final products. Fish solubles are by-products of the fish canning and fish oil industries. After centrifuging to remove the oil, the remaining fraction can be condensed or dried to make solubles. Fish solubles contain high-quality protein and are an excellent source of the B vitamins.

POULTRY BY-PRODUCTS

Poultry feathers are virtually indigestible in their natural state, and disulfide bonds in feather keratin must be destroyed before the protein can be used by animals. The most widely used commercial product is hydrolyzed feather meal, which is deficient in methionine, lysine, histidine, and tryptophan, but rich in many other AA. Poultry by-product meal consists of the ground, rendered, clean parts of slaughtered poultry, exclusive of feathers. It has a good AA balance and is a good source of minerals and vitamins. Dried poultry litter from caged layers or broiler operations is not suitable for nonruminant species because of the nonprotein N content, and neither of them is permitted to be fed to lactating dairy cows, but they can be used as a source of N for ruminants under some situations.

OTHER ANIMAL BY-PRODUCT FEEDS

Dried liver meal consists mostly of dried, condemned livers. Hydrolyzed hair or leather meal is produced by cooking the hair or leather under pressure for a long period to hydrolyze the protein. These meals can be used by ruminant species. Condensed or dried buttermilk, dried whole milk, and other milk products may be available, but they are usually too expensive for use as animal feed. Fish

protein concentrate, which has higher protein and lower ash content than fish meals, can be produced by extracting the oil and screening or settling out the bones. Fish silage can be made from minced whole fish and/or fish offal by the combined action of the body enzymes and added acids. Shells of hatched eggs, infertile and unhatched eggs, culled chicks, and others can be used to make poultry hatchery by-product meal. Other animal by-product feeds can be used for food animal production, and readers are referred to Refs. 2, 8, and 11 and other publications for this information.

CONCLUSION

Because of the competition between humans and animals for quality sources of nutrients, it is necessary not only to improve feed efficiency but also to fully explore all the sources of potential feed ingredients. Animal and marine by-product feeds are generally more variable than plant feeds in terms of nutrient content and quality. Having accurate information is therefore important for the efficient utilization of those by-products and for developing environmentally friendly, optimum feeding strategies for successful and sustainable food animal production.

REFERENCES

1. Seerley, R.W. Major Feedstuffs Used in Swine Diets. In *Swine Nutrition*; Miller, E.R., Ullrey, D.E., Lewis, A.J., Eds.; Butterworth-Heinemann: Boston, 1991; 451–481.
2. *Livestock Feeds and Feeding*; Kellems, R.O., Church, D.C., Eds.; Prentice Hall: Upper Saddle River, 1998.
3. Chiba, L.I. Protein Supplements. In *Swine Nutrition*, 2nd Ed.; Lewis, A.J., Southern, L.L., Eds.; CRC Press: Boca Raton, 2001; 803–837.
4. NRC. *Nutrient Requirements of Poultry*, 9th Ed.; National Academy Press: Washington, DC, 1994.
5. NRC. *Nutrient Requirements of Beef Cattle*, 7th Ed.; National Academy Press: Washington, DC, 1996.
6. NRC. *Nutrient Requirements of Swine*, 10th Ed.; National Academy Press: Washington, DC, 1998.
7. NRC. *Nutrient Requirements of Dairy Cattle*, 7th Ed.; National Academy Press: Washington, DC, 2001.
8. Dale, N. Ingredient analysis table: 2001 Edition. Feedstuffs **2001**, *73* (29), 28–37.
9. USDA. *USDA National Nutrient Database for Standard Reference, Release 15*; Agricultural Research Service, USDA: Washington, DC, 2002. http://www.nal.usda.gov/fnic/foodcomp/data/index.html (accessed April 2003).
10. *Nontraditional Feed Sources for Use in Swine Production*; Thacker, P.A., Kirkwood, R.N., Eds.; Butterworth: Boston, 1990.
11. FAO. *Animal Feed Resources Information System*; Agriculture Department, Food and Agriculture Organization of the United Nations: Rome, 2003. http://www.fao.org/ag/aga/agap/frg/afris/default.htm (accessed April 2003).

By-Product Feeds: Plant Origin

Terry J. Klopfenstein
University of Nebraska, Lincoln, Nebraska, U.S.A.

INTRODUCTION

Plants are important sources of feed (food) for animals and humans. Most plant products, such as cereal grains, are processed prior to consumption by humans. Corn, wheat, rice, and soybeans are the primary crops used to produce human foods. By-products from the processing of these grains are good feed resources for animals, and because they are relatively high in fiber, they are better utilized by ruminants (cattle, sheep) than by nonruminants (pigs, poultry).

SOYBEAN-PROCESSING BY-PRODUCTS

Soybeans are processed to produce soybean oil and isolated protein for human consumption. The resulting soybean meal, originally considered a by-product, is now considered a primary product. The soybean hull, removed during oil extraction, is now the major by-product. Soybean hulls contain 10–12% protein and high amounts of fiber. However, there is essentially no lignin in the soyhull, so the fiber is very highly digestible in beef and dairy cattle[1,2] diets. In contrast, cereal grains (which contain starch) are digested rapidly by cattle, producing volatile fatty acids that lower ruminal pH and inhibit fiber digestion (negative associative effect). Although soyhulls are highly digested, the rate of digestion is less rapid than that for starch, thereby producing more moderate pH values and less negative associative effects. Further, the same microorganisms digest the fiber in soyhulls and in the forage being supplemented. Soyhulls are an excellent energy supplement for beef cows or calves and dairy cows. Soyhulls are of benefit in a dairy-cow diet by reducing starch without decreasing diet energy density.[2]

WHEAT-MILLING BY-PRODUCTS

The primary product from the milling of wheat is flour for human consumption. Wheat is ground and sieved to produce flour. The resulting by-products are primarily wheat bran and wheat middlings. The bran is the hull of the wheat kernel and the middlings are a mixture of hull (bran) starch and protein (gluten). Wheat midds contain

about 18% starch and 18% protein. The remainder is primarily fiber, which is not digested by ruminants as well as soyhull fiber. Midds have good feeding value but are different from soyhulls, primarily because of the starch. Midds are used by the feed-manufacturing industry as a carrier and pelleting aid, as well as a source of protein, minerals, energy, and fiber for commercial livestock feeds. Midds are widely used in dairy-cattle diets,[3] in beef-feedlot diets, and in beef forage-based diets.[4]

CORN-PROCESSING BY-PRODUCTS

Corn is the most widely grown crop in the United States. The corn grain is used as a feedstock for three important milling industries—one wet-milling and two dry-milling.

Corn Dry-Milling By-Products—Hominy

The corn dry-milling industry that produces grits, meals, and flours for human consumption is very different from the dry-milling industry that produces ethanol. In dry-milling to produce grits, meals, and flours, the corn grain is ground and separated into component parts by aspiration, screening, etc. The by-product of this process is mostly hominy feed that contains over 50% starch, 11–12% protein, and 25–26% fiber. For beef-cattle finishing diets, 40% of diet dry matter seems to be a practical upper limit.[5] Up to that level, the hominy has an energy value of 87% that of corn grain. Hominy is widely used as an ingredient in dairy-cattle diets.

Dry-Milling By-Products—Distillers

The dry-milling industry ferments the starch in grain (corn, sorghum, barley) to ethanol. The dry grain is ground, mixed with water, and cooked, and then an enzyme is added to convert the starch to glucose. The glucose is fermented to ethanol using added yeast. When the alcohol is removed, the resulting stillage is high in moisture and usually separated into wet grains and thin stillage by screening or centrifuging. In the past, these by-products were dried in drum dryers to produce dried distiller's grains (DDG) or dried distillers grains with solubles (DDGS). The solubles are commonly used in

Encyclopedia of Animal Science
DOI: 10.1081/E-EAS 120019514

beef-cattle feedlots as either a dietary ingredient or a carrier for liquid supplements.

In the early 1980s, researchers started evaluating the feeding of distillers grains and/or solubles wet.[6] Klopfenstein and Grant[7] summarized 11 experiments in which wet distillers by-products were fed in beef cattle finishing diets. At 17.4% of the diet dry matter, this by-product had 150% the feeding value of corn, and when fed at 40% of the diet, 136% the value of corn. The protein in distillers grains is about 30% and the fat is about 12%. Typically, DDG (or DDGS) are used as a protein supplement in ruminant diets. Feed manufacturers use DDG in beef and dairy supplements and feeds. Many larger dairies use DDG as a commodity feed ingredient for use in total mixed rations.[7] Initially, beef-cattle feedlots were reluctant to use wet distillers products as an energy source in beef-cattle finishing diets. However, the practice of feeding wet distillers by-products within 100 to 150 miles of an ethanol plant is becoming common.

DDG and DDGS are excellent sources of rumen-undegraded protein. This is an advantage for ruminants such as lactating beef or dairy cows that have high protein requirements. The relatively high fat content ensures a high energy content diet. The corn fiber (hull) in forage-based diets is highly digested by cattle. The high protein and bypass, high fat, and fiber contents of DDG are especially useful in lactating dairy diets.[7]

Corn Wet-Milling By-Products

The corn wet-milling process is more complex than either of the dry-milling processes. Large plants are necessary for efficiency of production. Dry-milling ethanol plants may use 30,000 to 50,000 bushels of corn per day, whereas wet-milling plants grind 150,000 to over 500,000 bushels per day. The wet-milling process produces alcohol and several human food products including sweeteners and corn oil. In the first step, corn is steeped in weak acid and then milled (ground). After grinding, the kernel is separated into four parts—the germ, the starch, the bran (hull), and the gluten meal (protein). The oil is extracted from the germ. The starch is used for human consumption or ethanol production. The primary by-product is corn gluten feed, which contains the bran, steep liquor, and germ meal. This product is 16–24% protein and 40–50% fiber. The corn fiber is highly digestible by ruminants, probably even more rapidly digested than soyhull fiber.[8]

The majority (70–75%) of dry corn-gluten feed is shipped to Europe.[6] In the future, the amount produced will probably increase and the amount exported will probably decrease, making more gluten feed available for feeding in the United States. The practice of feeding wet corn-gluten feed to beef-feedlot cattle or dairy cows has been widely accepted.[7] The wet gluten feed has 100–

110% the feeding value of dry rolled corn in beef-cattle feedlot diets when fed as 20–40% of the diet dry matter.[6]

BREWER BY-PRODUCTS

Another by-product in alcohol production is brewer's grains. These grains are widely used in dairy- and beef-cattle diets fed both wet and dry by-products. Brewers grains differ from DDG because the brewer's grains are not fermented and because barley is the grain commonly used, rather than corn. The resulting by-product is higher in fiber and the fiber is less digestible than that in corn by-products. Because of the fiber content, brewer's grains are fed primarily in forage-based cattle diets including lactating-dairy-cattle diets.[9]

POTATO-PROCESSING BY-PRODUCTS

Potatoes are an important human food and many potatoes are processed before marketing. It is estimated that 33 kg of waste is produced for each 100 kg of potatoes processed.[10] Considerable processing occurs in the northwest United States, and much of the waste (by-product) is fed wet to beef cattle in feedlots. Because of the high starch content, potato waste has high feed value—similar in energy to corn or barley. The practical limit of its use in cattle diets is 30–40% of the dry matter. This is a high-value by-product and is essentially the basis for the cattle-feeding industry in Idaho and Washington.[11]

CITRUS-PROCESSING BY-PRODUCTS

Approximately 39% of processed citrus fruit is by-product.[10] The by-product includes the peel, pulp, and seeds, which are processed and dried. Citrus pulp is relatively low in protein (6.5%), but is an excellent source of fiber. This by-product is widely used in dairy diets in the southeast and southwest United States.[12,13]

FRUITS AND VEGETABLE BY-PRODUCTS

Although some fruits and vegetables are marketed without processing, most are processed to some degree. The wastes generally are high in water content, perishable, and seasonally produced.[10] The by-products tend to be low-protein, high-carbohydrate materials. Energy values for feeding to ruminants vary but may be quite high.

RICE-MILLING BY-PRODUCTS

Rice bran and rice hulls are produced in the processing of rice for humans.[14] Both are high in fiber. The bran is similar in feeding value to wheat bran, but the hulls have little feeding value.

CONCLUSION

By-products in general are high in fiber, but the fiber is highly digested. These by-products are excellent feed sources for ruminants. They vary in content of energy, protein, and phosphorus and can be included in ruminant diets to supply the needed nutrients. Because the by-products are primarily produced in the production of further-processed human foods, it is anticipated that quantities of products available will increase in the future. Production of fuel ethanol will also increase by-product availability. Ruminants provide a means of maximizing utilization of most of these by-products.

REFERENCES

1. Anderson, S.J.; Merill, J.K.; Klopfenstein, T.J. Soybean hulls as an energy supplement for the grazing ruminant. J. Anim. Sci. **1988**, *66*, 2959–2964.
2. Weidner, S.J.; Grant, R.J. Soyhulls as a replacement for forage fiber in diets for lactating dairy cows. J. Dairy Sci. **1994**, *77*, 513–521.
3. Depies, K.K.; Armentano, L.E. Partial replacement of alfalfa fiber with fiber from ground corn cobs or wheat middlings. J. Dairy Sci. **1995**, *78*, 1328–1335.
4. Sunvold, G.D.; Cochran, R.C.; Vanzant, E.S. Evaluation of wheat middlings as a supplement for beef cattle consuming dormant bluestem-range forage. J. Anim. Sci. **1991**, *69*, 3044–3054.
5. Larson, E.M.; Stock, R.A.; Klopfenstein, T.J.; Sindt, M.H.; Shain, D.H. Energy value of hominy feed for finishing ruminants. J. Anim. Sci. **1993**, *71*, 1092–1099.
6. Stock, R.A.; Lewis, J.M.; Klopfenstein, T.J.; Milton, C.T. Review of new information on the use of wet and dry milling by-products in feedlot diets. Proc. Am. Soc. Anim. Sci **2000**, E20. (www.asas.org).
7. Klopfenstein, T.J.; Grant, R. Uses of Corn Products in Beef and Dairy Rations, Proc 62nd Minnesota Nutrition Conference, Bloomington, MN, Sept. 11–12, 2001.
8. Firkins, J.L. *Fiber Value of Alternative Feeds*; Eastridge, M.L., Ed.; Proc. Alternative Feeds for Dairy and Beef Cattle. 2nd Natl. Alternative Feeds Symp.; Univ. Missouri: Columbia, 1995; 221–232.
9. Younker, R.S.; Winland, S.D.; Firkins, J.L.; Hull, B.L. Effects of replacing forage fiber or nonfiber carbohydrates with dried brewers grains. J. Dairy Sci. **1998**, *81*, 2645–2656.
10. NRC. *Underutilized Resources as Animal Feedstuffs*; Natl. Acad. Sci. National, Academy Press: Washington, DC, 1983.
11. Nelson, M.L.; Busboom, J.R.; Cronrath, J.D.; Falen, L.; Blankenbaker, A. Effects of graded levels of potato by-products in barley- and corn-based beef feedlot diets: I. Feedlot performance, carcass traits, meat composition, and appearance. J. Anim. Sci. **2000**, *78*, 1829–1836.
12. Harris, B. *Value of High-Fiber Alternative Feedstuffs as Extenders of Roughage Sources*; Jordon, E.R., Ed.; Proc. Alternative Feeds for Dairy and Beef Cattle; University Missouri: Columbia, 1991; 138.
13. Ammerman, C.B.; Henry, P.R. *Citrus and Vegetable Products for Ruminant Animals*; Jordon, E.R., Ed.; Proc. Alternative Feeds for Dairy and Beef Cattle; University Missouri: Columbia, 1991; 103.
14. Fadel, J.G.; Asmus, J.N. *Production, Geographical Distribution and Environmental Impact of By-Products*; Eastridge, M.L., Ed.; Proc. Alternative Feeds for Livestock and Poultry; The Ohio State University: Columbus, 2003; 1.

Camelids

Han Jianlin
International Livestock Research Institute (ILRI), Nairobi, Kenya

INTRODUCTION

Camelids comprise three genera of *Camelus* found exclusively in the Old World; *Lama* and *Vicugna* in the New World or South America of the Camelidae family, including four domesticated species: (1) domestic Bactrian or two-humped camels (*C. bactrianus*; Linnaeus, 1758), (2) dromedaries, or Arabian or one-humped camels (*C. dromedarius*; Linnaeus, 1758), (3) llamas (*L. glama*; Linnaeus, 1758), and (4) alpacas (*V. pacos;* formerly *L. pacos*; Linnaeus, 1758); and three wild species: wild Bactrian camels (*C. ferus* or *C. bactrianus ferus*; Przewalski, 1883), guanacos (*L. guanicoe*; Muller, 1776), and vicunas (*V. vicugna*; Molina, 1782). The overlap in distribution of domestic Bactrian camels and dromedaries is limited to small areas in central Asia. However, the distribution of all four of the South American camelids overlap in large areas in the Andes. The Old World camels may produce fertile hybrids. Hybridizations among all four South American species have also been confirmed through DNA analyses. Today, domestic camelid rearing is central to the economies of the poorest nomads in dry and cold Central Asia, dry and hot Middle East and North Africa, and the high and chilly Andes.

ORIGIN AND DOMESTICATION

Fossil records trace early evolution of Camelidae in North America. The predecessors of *Camelus* migrated to the Old World by the Bering Straits into Eurasia in the Pliocene to early Pleistocene. Others migrated from North America to South America about this time and became the founders of the South American camelids. Camelidae became extinct in North America, possibly due to overhunting, 12,000–14,000 years ago.

Recent studies on phylogenetic divergences between dromedary and domestic Bactrian camels postulate speciation of their ancestors in the early Pliocene prior to migration from North America to Eurasia, accommodating the hypothesis of separate domestications of dromedary in ancient Arabic territory and Bactrian camel in central Asia 4000–5000 years ago.[1,2] Genetic distinctions between the wild and domestic Bactrian camels portray them as reciprocally monophyletic,

recognizing the wild Bactrian camels as an independent taxonomic unit.[2,3] Wild Bactrian camels, with fewer than 900 survivors in northwestern China and southwestern Mongolia, have been included on the United Nations' (UN) list of the most threatened species since September 2002.[4]

Archaeozoological and genetic evidence favors independent domestications of llama from guanaco and alpaca from vicuna supposedly 6000–7000 years ago in the Peruvian puna. Today guanacos remain in the wild in Chile and Argentina, whereas vicunas survive in Chile, Argentina, and Ecuador under protection.[5,6]

DISTRIBUTION AND NUMBERS

Dromedaries, uniquely adapted to hot and dry climates, are found in about 35 countries from the east of India to the west of Senegal and from the south of Kenya to the north of Turkey, with an estimated global population of 17.7 million in 2002. There are around 6.2 million dromedaries in Somalia, where they are the main livestock sources of milk and meat.[7] A feral dromedary population was established in Australia after 1928 following importations from Africa and Asia.

Domestic Bactrian camels are found in the desert steppes of Central Asian countries, in Turkmenistan, Kazakhstan, Kyrgyzstan, and northern Pakistan and India, overlapping to varying degrees with dromedaries, and further eastward to southern Russia, and down to northwestern China and western Mongolia. The total population is about 0.82 million, of which 0.35 million were in Mongolia and 0.28 million in China by 2002.[7]

Llamas and alpacas are found in Andean semidesert rangelands at altitudes of 3800–5000 m for llamas and 3500–5000 m for alpacas in Peru, Chile, Bolivia, Ecuador, and Argentina. Additionally, Columbia has a few llamas. The total population of llamas and alpacas is about 3.8 million, respectively.[6,7]

PHYSIOLOGICAL AND ANATOMICAL CHARACTERISTICS

Camelids have 37 pairs of chromosomes. Because camelids evolved in desert and semidesert environments,

Encyclopedia of Animal Science
DOI: 10.1081/E-EAS 120019515
Copyright © 2005 by Marcel Dekker, Inc. All rights reserved.

Table 1 Reproductive parameters of camelids

Species	Puberty (years)	First breeding age (years)	Reproductive life span (years)	Gestation length (days±SD)	Birth weight (kg)
Dromedary, male	2.5–3	5–7	15		35–54
Dromedary, female	3–4	4–6	20	375±27	26–48
Bactrian camel, male	3	5–6	15		35–54
Bactrian camel, female	3–4	3–4	20	400±35	32–48
Llama, male	1	2–3	15		9.5–14.5
Llama, female	1	1.5–2	15	348±7	7.0–11.5
Alpaca, male	1	2–3	15		7.0–8.5
Alpaca, female	1	1.5–2	15	343±2	6.0–7.5

(Data from Refs. 6–9.)

they developed sophisticated physiological adaptations for dehydration and extreme cold or heat in their habitats. Old World camelids are much larger, have a single broad footpad and a lighter hairy coat, and are adapted to extreme temperatures and scarce food supplies. South American camelids are small and cloven-hoofed, and have a dense and fine wool coat, enabling them to survive under extremely low temperatures in the snowy semidesert of the Andes.

Hump

The dromedary has one hump and the Bactrian camel has two, about 25–35 cm high, for storing fat. South American camelids have no hump.

Water Balance

The unusual water balance in camelids is characterized by a low level of evaporation and greatly delayed dehydration, enabling them to consume dry food for long periods. Camelids usually take water only once or twice a week but in large amounts, up to 70 kg. They can safely survive a water loss equivalent to 40% of their body weight. Their erythrocytes, being highly elastic, can continue circulating under increased blood viscosity. Their kidneys are capable of markedly concentrating their urine to reduce water loss. They can also extract water from their fecal pellets.

Digestive Tract

Camelids have a complex, three-compartmented stomach. Although not considered ruminants, they regurgitate and rechew ingested forage. They are more efficient at feed conversion than true ruminants in extracting protein and energy from poor-quality forages.

Body Temperature Fluctuation

Camelids are adapted to have a large fluctuation in body temperature, from 34.5 to 41°C, depending on the time of day and water availability.

Reproduction

Males are seasonal breeders, corresponding with that of the females. Spermatogenesis continues throughout the year but at a higher rate during the breeding season. Females do not have regular estrous cycles but are induced ovulators. Ovulation can occur within 48 hours for Old World camelids and within 24–36 hours for South American camelids following mating.[8] They demonstrate polyestrus seasonally, which occurs with the decrease of day length from October to May for Old World camelids and during the rainy months from December to April for South American camelids. Further, Old World camelids calve a single baby every 2 years and wean newborns at 12–18 months, whereas South American camelids calve every year and wean newborns at 6–12 months (Table 1).

USES

Camelids are multipurpose animals that supply meat, milk, fiber, transport, and draught power.

Meat

Meat, mostly eaten fresh, is the main source of animal protein for nomads of western Asia, northern and eastern Africa, and the Andes. Bactrian camel meat has coarser fibers than beef with low market demand.

Table 2 Body measurement and productive performance of adult camelids

Species	Height at wither (cm)	Liveweight (kg)	Dressing percentage (%)	Milk yield (kg/day)	Fleece weight (kg/animal/year)
Dromedary, male	170–220	360–720	50–57		1.5–4.0
Dromedary, female	165–205	320–630	47–55	3.5–20.0	1.3–3.5
Bactrian camel, male	172–195	525–775	43–52		12.0–15.0
Bactrian camel, female	166–182	450–595	35–47	1.0–3.5	6.0–8.0
Llama, male	105–120	80–115	45–55		1.0–2.0
Llama, female	95–105	75–105	40–52		1.0–2.0
Alpaca, male	80–95	62–90	51–59		1.5–3.2
Alpaca, female	75–88	61–75	45–55		1.2–2.8

(Data from Refs. 6,7,9.)

Milk

Dromedaries produce about 3.5–20 kg of milk per day during lactation, which ranges from 8–24 months. Their milk is rich in protein, fat, and mainly vitamin C. It is mostly consumed fresh or is made into fermented products, butter, and cheese.[9] Bactrian camels produce smaller amounts of milk. Llamas and alpacas are milked (Table 2).

Fiber

Alpacas are primarily kept for wool, which is highly prized by the textile industry. However, the quality of their fleece has degenerated, supposedly due to extensive crossbreeding with llamas and uncontrolled breeding between the fine and extrafine breeds since the Spanish.[5,6] Llamas have long and coarse fleece fiber, which is made into string bags, sacks, blankets, and clothing. Bactrian camel fleece consists of long and coarse hair used for making rope, and short and fine fiber used for making padded clothes and quilts. Dromedaries in the north produce less coarse fiber (Table 2).

Transport

Bactrian camels, dromedaries, and llamas are kept primarily for pack and transport, but this has declined in the last two decades due to mechanization, which has led to rapid population reduction, particularly in Bactrian camels.

Sport

Dromedary racing is a popular sport in Arabic countries.

Other

Skins are raw materials for traditional currier and tannery. Dung is used as fertilizer and fuel. In north-ern Kenya, camel blood supplies vitamin D, salt, and other nutrients. Camelids are also considered sacrificial animals.

CONCLUSIONS

Camelids are managed under transhumant systems that support the poorest populations in marginalized desert and semidesert regions and highland steppes. The utilization and development of camelids could potentially enhance their livelihood and prevent human migration into already overcrowded villages and towns.

Currently, breed names of camelids take after the ethnic group keeping them or the geographic regions where they are found. Therefore, little is known about genetic differences between these different groups or within any type of camelids.[2,5,10] Modern technologies to improve reproductive efficiency and economic traits in camelids have been tried but not extensively used in the field.[8]

There are huge variations in body conformation and milk production in the Old World camelids (Table 2). Some dromedary breeds likely have high potential for milk production.[9] Llamas and alpacas have been introduced into North America, Europe, Australia, and New Zealand for the primary purpose of fiber production under well-controlled breeding schemes and management systems. It is expected that experience and knowledge gained from these small herds may be applied to the genetic improvement of South American camelids in their home countries.

REFERENCES

1. Peters, J.; von den Driesch, A. The two-humped camel (*Camelus bactrianus*): New light on its distribution,

management and medical treatment in the past. J. Zool., Lond. **1997**, *242*, 651–679.

2. Jianlin, H. Origin, Evolution and Genetic Diversity of Old World Genus of Camelus. Doctoral Dissertation; Lanzhou University: P.R. China, 2002.

3. Jianlin, H.; Jiexia, Q.; Zhenming, M.; Yaping, Z.; Wen, W. Three unique restriction fragment length polymorphisms of EcoRI, PvuII, and ScaI digested mitochondrial DNA of bactrian camels (*Camelus bactrianus ferus*) in China. J. Anim. Sci. **1999**, *77*, 2315– 2316.

4. Marzuola, C. Camelid comeback. Sci. News **2003**, *163* (2), 26–28.

5. Kadwell, M.; Fernandez, M.; Stanley, H.F.; Baldi, R.; Wheeler, J.C.; Rosadio, R.; Bruford, M.W. Genetic analysis reveals the wild ancestors of the llama and the alpaca. Proc. R. Soc. Lond., B **2001**, *268*, 2575–2584.

6. Wheeler, J.C. Evolution and present situation of the South American camelidae. Biol. J. Linn. Soc. **1995**, *54*, 271– 295.

7. FAO-STAT. http://apps.fao.org/; FAO-DAD-IS. http:// dad.fao.org/en/Home.htm (accessed June 2003).

8. Bravo, P.W.; Skidmore, J.A.; Zhao, X.X. Reproductive aspects and storage of semen in Camelidae. Anim. Reprod. Sci. **2000**, *62*, 173–193.

9. Yagil, R. *Camels and Camel Milk*; FAO Animal Production and Health Paper, FAO of the United Nations: Rome, Italy, 1982; Vol. 26.

10. Mburu, D.N.; Ochieng, J.W.; Kuria, S.G.; Jianlin, H.; Kaufmann, B.; Rege, J.E.O.; Hanotte, O. Genetic diversity and relationships of indigenous Kenyan dromedary (*Camelus dromedarius*) populations: Implications for their classification. Anim. Genet. **2003**, *34*, 26–32.

Carcass Composition and Quality: Genetic Influence

Marion Greaser
University of Wisconsin, Madison, Wisconsin, U.S.A.

INTRODUCTION

Genetic background has been known for many years to affect the quantity and quality of meat from food animals. Improvements in the ratios of muscle to fat in carcasses from meat animals have been dramatic. In addition to the benefits for animal selection from analyzing meat quality, a number of genetic conditions have also provided new insights on biological mechanisms involved in muscle contraction, muscle growth, and postmortem metabolism. The current entry describes some of these genetic factors.

BOS TAURUS VERSUS BOS INDICUS

Most cattle used for food are members of two different species. Those of European origin (i.e., Angus, Hereford, Charolois breeds) are *Bos taurus*, while those with humped backs (Brahman, zebu) are *Bos indicus*. Animals with *B. indicus* breeding give meat that is much less tender than that from the *B. taurus* breeds.[1] The reason for this difference has been ascribed to the level of calpastatin in the muscle.[2] Calpastatin is an inhibitor of calpains, a class of calcium-activated proteases that are believed to be involved in the tenderness improvement that occurs during postmortem aging. Thus *B. indicus* muscle has more calpastatin and less postmortem protein breakdown.

DOUBLE-MUSCLE CONDITION IN CATTLE

Double-muscle animals have hypertrophied muscles in both the front- and hindquarters due to a mutation in the myostatin gene.[3] The increased muscling is visible at birth, and the larger size also contributes to difficulty with calving. The increased muscle size is due to an approximate doubling in the number of muscle fibers in these animals without significant change in average muscle diameter.[4] Carcasses show bulging muscles and a minimum of exterior fat covering (Fig. 1). The double-muscle condition results in a somewhat paler muscle color

and a reduction in intramuscular fat. The tenderness of the muscle, however, is largely unaffected.

PALE, SOFT, EXUDATIVE (PSE) AND PORCINE STRESS SYNDROME (PSS) IN PIGS

An unusual condition occurs in pig muscle postmortem that is referred to as PSE.[5] The muscle is pale in color, soft in texture, and may exude as much as 10% of the muscle weight in liquid (also called drip) (Fig. 2). The condition is genetic in nature and has been linked to a recessive mutation in the ryanodine receptor.[6] The latter is a protein that serves as a calcium channel in the sarcoplasmic reticulum. In normal muscle, this channel releases calcium to activate muscle contraction. However, the mutant protein leaks calcium and thus partially activates the contractile system. Such activation dramatically increases the postmortem ATP splitting and the rate of glycolysis. Muscle pH drops rapidly while the temperature is still high, and this pH–temperature combination denatures the myosin, resulting in decreased muscle water binding. The extent of this glycolysis acceleration is highly variable, being affected by numerous antemortem conditions including ambient temperature, climatic change, and stress.[7] The incidence of the PSE condition has remained at about 10–15% of the pig population for many years. Animals with the mutant gene are often leaner and more heavily muscled, so visual breed stock selection has worked against eliminating the mutation. A similar condition occurs in humans and is called "malignant hyperthermia." The name is actually a misnomer; it is unrelated to cancer. Humans containing a ryanodine receptor mutation respond to anesthesia by developing muscle rigidity and extreme increases in body temperature, often leading to death unless the condition can be stopped by drug intervention. More than 20 different ryanodine receptor mutations have been found in humans; it seems fairly likely that additional pig mutations will also be identified in the future.

Porcine stress syndrome is caused by the same ryanodine receptor mutation found in PSE, but occurs in

Encyclopedia of Animal Science
DOI: 10.1081/E-EAS 120019518

Fig. 1 Carcass from a double-muscled steer. Note the bulging muscles and the minimal external fat covering. (Photograph courtesy of Morse Solomon, United States Department of Agriculture, Beltsville, Maryland.) (*View this art in color at www.dekker.com.*)

postmortem glycolysis is normal, but the final or ultimate pH in the longissimus muscle is often around 5.3–5.4 instead of the more typical 5.5 to 5.6. This phenotype results from a dominant mutation termed *RN-*. The letters are an abbreviation for Rendement (French for yield) Napole (name of a test for ham processing yield). The condition is also referred to as "acid meat" and the "Hampshire effect" since the mutation is prevalent in the Hampshire breed. The lower ultimate pH, along with a lower protein content, causes the water-holding capacity of the meat to be diminished and the processed ham yield to be reduced. Carriers were formerly identified by measuring the "glycolytic potential" (the sum of the lactic acid concentration plus $2 \times$ [glycogen glucose+glucose+glucose-6 phosphate content]).[9] Since muscle is a closed system postmortem, the time of sampling after death will not affect the glycolytic potential. Glycolytic potential values are typically around 125 μM/gram in normal muscle, but often range from 180–300 μM/gram in animals with the mutation. The *RN-* locus is on chromosome 15 in the region coding for the gamma

the live animal. PSS pigs under stress may show muscle tremors and rigidity, skin splotchiness, and increased body temperature. In many cases, these conditions will lead to death. Even the stress of loading the animals on a truck to transport them to market may be fatal.

Testing for carriers of the ryanodine receptor mutation was formerly conducted using a challenge with the anesthetic halothane; carriers would show muscle tremors and rigidity. A genetic test now is available for the single pig ryanodine receptor mutation identified to date; however, some pigs develop PSE meat in spite of having a normal genetic result.

Some turkeys and chickens also have accelerated postmortem glycolysis that has been termed a PSE-like condition. It is not currently known whether a ryanodine receptor mutation is the causative agent.

RN-CONDITION IN PIGS

Certain pigs have unusually high glycogen levels in their muscle at the time of death.[8] The time course of

Normal

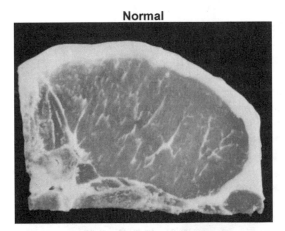

Pale, Soft Exudative

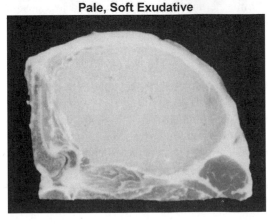

Fig. 2 Loin chops from a normal and a pale, soft, exudative (PSE) pig. Note that the PSE condition does not affect all muscles equally. (*View this art in color at www.dekker.com.*)

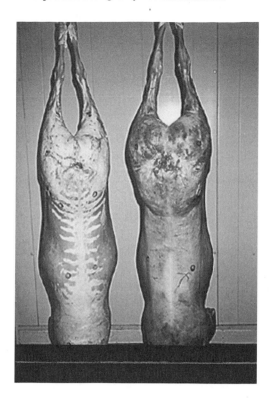

Fig. 3 Carcasses from normal (L) and callipyge (R) lambs. The extreme muscularity of the hind legs is evident. (Photograph courtesy of Sam Taylor, Texas Tech University.) (*View this art in color at www.dekker.com.*)

subunit of a muscle-specific adenosine-monophosphate-activated protein kinase PRKAG3.[10] This kinase normally inactivates glycogen synthase, but this inactivation does not occur in the mutant animals.

Meat from *RN* carriers has greater cooking loss and is inferior for use in processed meat products. However, this type of meat is more tender than normal pork.

CALLIPYGE SHEEP

An unusual genetic condition in sheep results in animals with hypertrophied muscles primarily in their hindquarters. The word callipyge was derived from the Greek *calli* = beautiful and *pyge* = buttocks. The phenotypic trait only appears after the lambs are 4 to 6 weeks of age. The callipyge condition is transmitted by a remarkable inheritance mode called polar overdominance, where only heterozygous offspring from carrier males express the phenotype. The mutation locus appears to be a single A- to -G replacement on chromosome 18.[11] Callipyge carcasses have increased muscle content and reduced fat

levels.[12] A picture showing a comparison of a normal and callipyge lamb carcass is shown in Fig. 3. Unfortunately, muscles from these animals also have reduced tenderness. Increased calpastatin content has been linked to the tenderness problem.[13]

CONCLUSION

The influence of genetics on meat quality will continue to be an important area of research. The rapid progress toward sequencing the genomic DNA from the agricultural animal species will speed the identification of new factors affecting muscle foods.

REFERENCES

1. Johnson, D.D.; Huffman, R.D.; Williams, S.E.; Hargrove, D.D. Effects of percentage Brahman and Angus breeding, age-season of feeding and slaughter end point on meat palatability and muscle characteristics. J. Anim. Sci. **1990**, *68*, 1980–1986.
2. Ferguson, D.M.; Jiang, S.T.; Hearnshaw, H.; Rymill, S.R.; Thompson, J.M. Effect of electrical stimulation on protease activity and tenderness of M. longissimus from cattle with different proportions of *Bos indicus* content. Meat Sci. **2000**, *55*, 265–272.
3. Grobet, L.; Martin, L.J.; Poncelet, D.; Pirottin, D.; Brouwers, B.; Riquet, J.; Schoeberlein, A.; Dunner, S.; Menissier, F.; Massabanda, J.; Fries, R.; Hanset, R.; Georges, M. A deletion in the bovine myostatin gene causes the double-muscled phenotype in cattle. Nat. Genet. **1997**, *17*, 71–74.
4. Wegner, J.; Albrecht, E.; Fiedler, I.; Teuscher, F.; Papstein, H.J.; Ender, K. Growth- and breed-related changes of muscle fiber characteristics in cattle. J. Anim. Sci. **2000**, *78*, 1485–1496.
5. Cassens, R.G. Historical perspectives and current aspects of pork meat quality in the USA. Food Chem. **2000**, *69*, 357–363.
6. Fujii, J.; Otsu, K.; Zorzato, F.; de Leon, S.; Khanna, V.K.; Weiler, J.E.; O'Brien, P.J.; MacLennan, D.H. Identification of a mutation in porcine ryanodine receptor associated with malignant hyperthermia. Science **1991**, *253*, 448–451.
7. Greaser, M.L. Conversion of Muscle to Meat. In *Muscle as Food*; Bechtel, P.J., Ed.; Academic Press: New York, 1986; 37–102.
8. Estrade, M.; Vignon, X.; Rock, E.; Monin, G. Glycogen hyperaccumulation in white muscle fibres of *RN*-carrier pigs. A biochemical and ultrastructural study. Comp. Biochem. Physiol. B **1993**, *104*, 321–326.
9. Monin, G.; Sellier, P. Pork of low technological meat

quality with a normal rate of muscle pH fall in the immediate post mortem period. Meat Sci. **1985**, *13*, 49–63.

10. Milan, D.; Jeon, J.T.; Looft, C.; Amarger, V.; Robic, A.; Thelander, M.; Rogel-Gaillard, C.; Paul, S.; Iannuccelli, N.; Rask, L.; Ronne, H.; Lundstrom, K.; Reinsch, N.; Gellin, J.; Kalm, E.; Roy, P.L.; Chardon, P.; Andersson, L. A mutation in PRKAG3 associated with excess glycogen content in pig skeletal muscle. Science **2000**, *288*, 1248–1251.

11. Smit, M.; Segers, K.; Carrascosa, L.G.; Shay, T.; Baraldi, F.; Gyapay, G.; Snowder, G.; Georges, M.; Cockett, N.; Charlier, C. Mosaicism of Solid Gold supports the causality of a noncoding A-to-G transition in the determinism of the callipyge phenotype. Genetics **2003**, *163*, 356–453.

12. Jackson, S.P.; Miller, M.F.; Green, R.D. Phenotypic characterization of rambouillet sheep expressing the callipyge gene: III. Muscle weights and muscle weight distribution. J. Anim. Sci. **1997**, *75*, 133–138.

13. Koohmaraie, M.; Shackelford, S.D.; Wheeler, T.L.; Lonergan, S.M.; Doumit, M.E. A muscle hypertrophy condition in lamb (callipyge): Characterization of effects on muscle growth and meat quality traits. J. Anim. Sci. **1995**, *73*, 3596–3607.

Carcass Composition and Quality: Postmortem

Marion Greaser
University of Wisconsin, Madison, Wisconsin, U.S.A.

INTRODUCTION

Numerous factors affect the quality of muscle in its use for food. The genetic background of the animals, the age at harvest, the feeding program used, and the way the animals are handled before harvest all have important effects on meat quality. Muscle foods are also influenced by the metabolism and changes that occur during the postmortem time period. This article summarizes the biochemical and physical alterations that occur in muscle after death, and discusses some conditions that modify these alterations.

MUSCLE METABOLISM

Muscle tissue is specialized for movement in humans and animals. The compound adenosine triphosphate (ATP) contains high-energy phosphate bonds, and these bonds can be broken to convert chemical energy into work by the myofibrils. Muscle contraction occurs when a nerve signal causes the depolarization of the muscle cell membrane and the release of calcium from the sarcoplasmic reticulum to activate the myofibril contractile proteins. Adenosine triphosphate is required to power the contraction as well as to pump the calcium back into the sarcoplasmic reticulum and restore the sodium and potassium at the cell membrane.[1] A diagram showing the pathways for ATP production and utilization is shown in Fig. 1. In the living animal, the most efficient pathways of ATP production involve conversion of pyruvate into carbon dioxide in the mitochondria. However, after the animal dies, substrates such as glucose, fatty acids, and oxygen from the bloodstream are no longer available. Creatine phosphate (CP) can regenerate a small amount of ATP, but only the glycolysis pathway remains active. In postmortem muscle, the glycogen is converted to lactic acid and the latter accumulates. The pH also declines to below 6.0 in most cases, and the final or ultimate pH depends on species and muscle type. A typical pattern for the postmortem changes in several chemical and physical factors is shown in Fig. 2. Although this pattern is for normal pig muscle, other species would display similar patterns except for differences in the time axis.

RIGOR MORTIS

Adenosine triphosphate is required to power muscle contraction, but it also functions to dissociate the myosin and actin bonds after a contraction. Therefore, resting muscle is easily stretchable and extensible. However, if the ATP supply is depleted, the myosin and actin form tight bonds so that the muscle filaments no longer slide over one another.[3] This inextensibility is referred to as rigor mortis (Latin for the stiffness of death). The time course of rigor mortis is directly related to the muscle ATP content (see Fig. 2). It also varies with species (beef—12 to 24 hours; lamb—8 to 12 hours; pig—4 to 6 hours; chicken and turkey—2 to 3 hours). The time course is also related to the muscle temperature, with glycolysis generally more rapid at higher temperatures.

PROTEIN CHANGES

Although the metabolic changes in muscle postmortem are essentially completed within the first day after death, additional alterations occur in some of the structural proteins of muscle. The calpain proteases are believed to be responsible for the proteolytic cleavage of several proteins including desmin, troponin T, titin, and nebulin.[4] The postmortem time course of these protein changes parallels the improvement in tenderness of cooked meat. This process, termed aging, is mostly completed within the first few days in chickens, but extends over a one- to two-week period in beef.

UNUSUAL TYPES OF POSTMORTEM METABOLISM

Thaw Rigor

Muscle tissue that is frozen before rigor mortis occurs and is then rapidly thawed undergoes a process termed thaw rigor. Freezing causes the formation of ice crystals inside the sarcoplasmic reticulum, resulting in a large release of calcium upon thawing[5] and a marked shortening (down to 20–25% of the initial length). The thawed muscle also

Encyclopedia of Animal Science
DOI: 10.1081/E-EAS 120019517

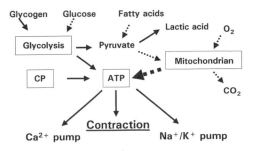

Fig. 1 Diagram showing an overview of muscle metabolism. The dotted arrows are pathways that become nonfunctional in postmortem muscle. (From Ref. 2. Reprinted courtesy of Marcel Dekker, Inc.) (*View this art in color at www. dekker.com.*)

releases a large amount (as much as 25% by weight) of its fluid (called drip).

Cold Shortening

The typical dependence of postmortem metabolism on temperature is invalid under certain conditions. Muscles from beef and lamb have a higher rate of ATP breakdown and pH decline at 4°C than at 10°C. Muscles from these species, when excised from the carcass, undergo a slow contraction called cold shortening.[6] The muscles shorten by as much as 50% of their length. This shortening also reduces meat tenderness. Cold shortening can occur on the carcass as well, particularly under conditions with high efficiency and rapid cooling.

Pale, Soft, Exudative (PSE) Condition

Pigs that have the ryanodine receptor mutation[7] have an unusually rapid rate of postmortem glycolysis. The muscle pH may drop below 5.5 within the first 15–30 minutes postmortem instead of the normal 4 to 6 hours. The rapid pH decline while the muscle temperature is still high results in myosin denaturation and loss of water-binding activity. Stress and high ambient temperatures at the time of harvest increase the severity of the PSE condition.

Dark Cutter (Beef) and Dark, Firm, Dry (Pigs)

Both of these conditions occur when the muscle glycogen has been largely depleted before the animal dies. In bovine animals, this occurs quite often with bulls that have been socially regrouped.[8] The incidence is 2–5% among steers and heifers, but may approach 15% in bulls. Stress and fights lead to the glycogen depletion. With pigs, the dark, firm, dry meat results from the same ryanodine receptor mutation that causes PSE, but in the former case, the glycogen has also been depleted before harvest. In

both cases, the ultimate pH is between 6.2 and 6.8. The high pH results in higher water-binding activity and a darker surface color.

INTERVENTIONS THAT ALTER POSTMORTEM METABOLISM

Extremely rapid postmortem chilling has been adopted to reduce bacterial growth and improve food safety. A modest improvement in pig meat quality can be achieved by rapid chilling, but no economically feasible cooling system has been devised to prevent the most severe PSE meat. Injection of muscle early postmortem with sodium bicarbonate can prevent the PSE condition, apparently by decreasing the rate and extent of pH decline.[9]

Rapid chilling may result in an undesirable decline in meat tenderness, especially in beef and lamb. An alternative method to speed postmortem glycolysis is early postmortem electrical stimulation.[10] Electrical stimulation of the carcass (within the first 30 minutes after death) results in vigorous muscle contraction and rapid glycolysis. In beef carcasses, the pH may drop to around 6.3 after a couple minutes of stimulation. Unfortunately, a wide variety of stimulation voltages and stimulation equipment types has been adopted, so comparing results from different studies has been difficult. Electrical stimulation in most cases provides a modest increase in meat tenderness.[11]

CONCLUSION

The metabolic and proteolytic activities of muscle tissue do not cease at the time of death. Postmortem metabolism should be slowed in pig muscle, but accelerated in bovine

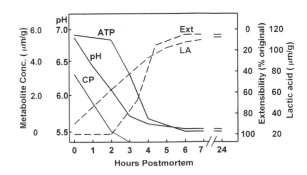

Fig. 2 Chemical and physical changes that occur in muscle postmortem. The time course corresponds to that occurring in normal pig muscle. Abbreviations: ATP—adenosine triphosphate; CP—creatine phosphate; LA—lactic acid; Ext—extensibility. (From Ref. 2. Reprinted courtesy of Marcel Dekker, Inc.) (*View this art in color at www.dekker.com.*)

and ovine muscle for optimum meat quality. It remains a challenge to control and/or manipulate the various enzymatic activities postmortem to ensure uniform meat products with desirable eating quality.

ACKNOWLEDGMENTS

This work was supported by the College of Agricultural and Life Sciences, University of Wisconsin—Madison.

REFERENCES

1. Greaser, M.L. Conversion of Muscle to Meat. In *Muscle as Food*; Bechtel, P.J., Ed.; Academic Press: New York, 1986; 37–102.
2. Greaser, M.L. Post-Mortem Muscle Chemistry. In *Meat Science and Applications*; Hui, Y.H., Nip, W.-K., Rodgers, R.W., Young, O.A., Eds.; Marcel Dekker, Inc.: New York, 2001; 21–37.
3. Bendall, J.R. Postmortem Changes in Muscle. In *The Structure and Function of Muscle*, 2nd Ed.; Bourne, G.H., Ed.; Academic Press: New York, 1973; Vol. 2, 243–309.
4. Ho, C.Y.; Stromer, M.H.; Robson, R.M. Effect of electrical stimulation on postmortem titin, nebulin, desmin, and troponin-T degradation and ultrastructural changes in bovine longissimus muscle. J. Anim. Sci. **1996**, *74*, 1563–1575.
5. Kushmerick, M.J.; Davies, R.E. The role of phosphate compounds in thaw contraction and the mechanism of thaw rigor. Biochim. Biophys. Acta **1968**, *153*, 279–287.
6. Locker, R.H.; Hagyard, C.J. A cold shortening effect in beef muscles. J. Sci. Food. Agric. **1963**, *14*, 787–793.
7. Fujii, J.; Otsu, K.; Zorzato, F.; de Leon, S.; Khanna, V.K.; Weiler, J.E.; O'Brien, P.J.; MacLennan, D.H. Identification of a mutation in porcine ryanodine receptor associated with malignant hyperthermia. Science **1991**, *253*, 448–451.
8. Tarrant, P.V. The Occurrence, Causes, and Economic Consequences of Dark-Cutting Beef—A Survey of Current Information. In *The Problem of Dark Cutting Beef*; Hood, D.E., Tarrant, P.V., Eds.; Martinus Nijhoff: Hague, The Netherlands, 1998; 3–34.
9. Kauffman, R.G.; van Laack, R.L.J.M.; Russell, R.L.; Pospiech, E.; Cornelius, C.A.; Suckow, C.E.; Greaser, M.L. Can pale, soft, exudative pork be prevented by postmortem sodium bicarbonate injection? J. Anim. Sci. **1998**, *76*, 3010–3015.
10. Bendall, J.R. The Electrical Stimulation of Carcasses of Meat Animals. In *Developments in Meat Science*; Lawrie, R., Ed.; Applied Science Publishers LTD: London, 1980; Vol 1, 37–59.
11. Roeber, D.L.; Cannell, R.C.; Belk, K.E.; Tatum, J.D.; Smith, G.C. Effects of a unique application of electrical stimulation on tenderness, color, and quality attributes of the beef longissimus muscle. J. Anim. Sci. **2000**, *78*, 1504–1509.

Channel Catfish

William R. Wolters
United States Department of Agriculture, Agricultural Research Service, Orono, Maine, U.S.A.

Jimmy Avery
Mississippi State University, Stoneville, Mississippi, U.S.A.

INTRODUCTION

Channel catfish, *Ictalurus punctatus*, is a member of the catfish family Ictaluridae. The larger members of the catfish family—blue catfish (*Ictalurus furcatus*) and flathead catfish (*Pylodictus olivarus*)—are important commercial and sport fish. The Ictaluridae family also includes the white catfish (*Ameiurus catus*), bullheads (*Ameuirus* sp.), and madtoms (*Noturus* sp.). Catfish as a group are morphologically distinguished from other fish by their scaleless bodies, broad flat heads, a single spine in the front of each dorsal and pectoral fin, a small adipose fin between the tail and dorsal fin, and long barbells above and below the mouth. Catfish are omnivores, usually nocturnal, and generally locate feed by taste and touch through the numerous taste and sensory cells located along the barbells and other external skin areas. Catfish spawn or deposit their eggs in nests, which are generally shoreline or bottom cavities and depressions. All catfish species are considered benthic fish and inhabit a wide range of stream, river, lake, and pond habitats.

CHARACTERISTICS AND GEOGRAPHIC DISTRIBUTION

Channel catfish is the most widely utilized catfish species for commercial production.[1–3] The native range originally was from the Great Lakes and Sakatchewan River southward to the Gulf of Mexico, but introductions have greatly increased the distribution for both sport fishing and aquaculture. Coloration is white on the belly (ventrum), silver to gray on the sides, and gradually darkening to almost black on the top (dorsum) (Fig. 1). Albinism, caused by a single recessive gene, can be common in commercial culture and the aquarium industry, but is rare in nature.

Commercial production of channel catfish began more than 40 years ago and has become one of the most successful aquaculture enterprises in the United States.[4] Major processors processed more than 630 million pounds of catfish in 2002.[5] A recent survey reported 174,900 acres of ponds in production in the four major producing states of Alabama, Arkansas, Louisiana, and Mississippi.[6] Mississippi leads all states with 106,000 acres, followed by Arkansas (33,500 acres), Alabama (26,000 acres), and Louisiana (9400 acres). The sustained growth of the catfish industry is due to increased per capita consumption of seafood products, development of an effective industry infrastructure, successful marketing, and research support.

CHANNEL CATFISH PRODUCTION

Optimum growth and production of channel catfish necessitate maintaining optimum environmental conditions. Although catfish farmers utilize a variety of management practices that are specific to individual farms, general management practices or production schemes have been developed to optimize production efficiency. The catfish production system or production practices described in this summary provide brief recommendations for culture systems, biology and management of different life stages (adults, juveniles, and foodfish), and harvesting and processing. The information provided is not inclusive, and detailed information can be obtained from the references provided.

Culture Systems

Channel catfish are typically cultured in large earthen ponds, although a variety of other systems including raceways, cages, and tanks have been utilized. Ponds are usually constructed on flat land to form levee ponds covering 10 to 15 surface acres, with an average depth of 4 feet (Fig. 2). Smaller ponds are often constructed in rolling terrain by constructing a levee across a watershed or drainage area, but most water for filling and maintaining pond water levels is from a groundwater (well) source. In the southeastern United States, catfish are generally cultured for two growing seasons and reach market size in

Encyclopedia of Animal Science
DOI: 10.1081/E-EAS 120019520

Fig. 1 Photograph of a channel catfish. (*View this art in color at www.dekker.com.*)

18 to 30 months, depending on stocking and feeding rates.[3]

Biology and Management

Broodfish and hatchery management

Proper management and care of broodfish are critical for high reproductive or spawning success. Many factors such as water quality, stocking density, and management outside the spawning season can affect catfish reproduction. Spawning success can be as high as 20 to 30% in two-year-old fish, but best reproduction is obtained from three- and four-year-old fish. The industry average for spawning success is estimated to be around 30 to 40%, and for egg hatching around 60%. A sex ratio of 1:1 or 2:1 females to males is desirable and should be closely monitored each year, because males have higher mortality rates than females. Male and female catfish are sexually dimorphic. Males typically are darker in color and have larger heads, whereas females are lighter in color and typically have swollen abdomens during the spawning season, because of ovary development. Broodfish should

be stocked at no more than 1200 pounds per acre into ponds that have been drained, allowed to dry, and recently reflooded. After the spawning season, broodfish can be moved and restocked into ponds at 3000 to 4000 pounds per acre. Broodfish should be fed a nutritionally complete floating commercial diet, with at least 28% protein, at 2% of body weight per day when water temperatures are above 70°F, and at 1% per day with a slow-sinking pellet at temperatures between 55° and 70°F. Generally, no feed is offered below 50°F.

Spawning activity will begin in the spring when water temperatures are consistently around 75°F. Maintaining optimum water quality in spawning ponds is important, because low levels of dissolved oxygen and excessive algae and aquatic weed growth will inhibit spawning success. Commercial farmers place 50 to 75 spawning cans into ponds for each 500 females. Spawning cans can be checked every two days during the spawning season. Eggs should not be crowded into transport containers and transport water should not become warmer than 85°F before transport to the hatchery.

Well water with temperatures between 75°F and 82°F is preferred for hatching catfish eggs. Eggs are usually incubated in long, shallow troughs or tanks with aeration paddles or diffused aeration (Fig. 3). Dissolved oxygen levels should be maintained above 6.0 ppm, total water hardness and alkalinity at >20 ppm, pH between 7.5 and 8.5, and total gas pressure at 100% of saturation, or less. Maintaining optimum water temperatures, cleaning hatchery equipment, and using formalin and iodophores will minimize bacterial and fungal infections on eggs. Eggs hatch in five to seven days after spawning, and fry will actively start swimming and begin feeding three to four

Fig. 2 Aerial view of levee ponds used for channel catfish culture. (*View this art in color at www.dekker.com.*)

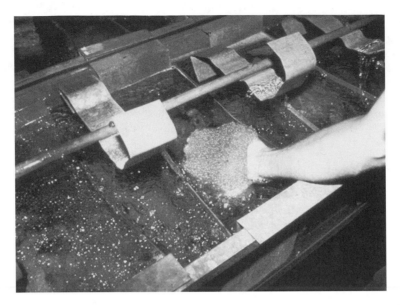

Fig. 3 Catfish eggs being incubated in a hatching trough. (*View this art in color at www.dekker.com.*)

days after hatching. Fry must be fed a high-protein diet (usually 45% protein) at least 12 to 24 times per day.

Fingerling culture

Growth and survival of catfish fry to fingerling size depend on maintaining water quality, controlling disease, and providing enough feed to achieve the desired harvest size. Although the industry average for survival of fry to fingerling has been estimated at 65%, with a yield of about 3000 pounds per acre, acute problems with disease and water quality can drastically affect survival and yield in fingerling ponds. Fry/fingerling ponds should be drained and dried to kill all trash fish and vegetation before filling with well water. Ponds must be fertilized, checked for zooplankton populations, and have predaceous insects controlled, following recommended management guidelines. Fry can be counted volumetrically or by weight prior to stocking into ponds, and should be stocked at 7 to 10 days old, after they are actively feeding. Fry are normally stocked at a rate of 75,000 to 125,000 fry per

Fig. 4 Catfish are harvested from ponds using tractors to pull large seines. (*View this art in color at www.dekker.com.*)

acre. Morning dissolved oxygen readings should be above 5 ppm, and stocking should be completed before water temperatures exceed 85°F. Vaccination of fry against bacterial diseases may improve survival.

After stocking, catfish fry should be fed finely ground feed (usually 40 to 50% protein) two to three times daily (20 to 30 lbs/acre/day) until fish are observed feeding and swimming on the pond surface. Fry should be observed feeding on the surface within three to five weeks after stocking. At this time, a small-pellet floating feed can be fed to satiation daily, once the fish are actively feeding. Supplemental aeration is necessary for fingerling ponds, and addition of salt to maintain chloride levels of 100 ppm is often recommended. At the onset of cool weather in the fall, when morning pondwater temperatures begin to drop below 80°F, fish can be placed on a restricted feeding regime on alternate days, or every second day. Feed containing antibiotics (Romet[®] or Terramycin[®]) is often used if juvenile or fingerling fish are diagnosed with bacterial infections and a diagnostic laboratory has recommended treatment.

Foodfish culture

No single, well-defined production schedule is used on commercial farms because food-size fish are harvested and fingerlings are stocked year-round. Management practices for stocking density, sizes, feeding practices, and water-quality management are often specific to individual farms. Fingerlings are typically stocked into growout ponds at 5000 to 8000 fish per acre, and rates of up to 10,000 fish per acre are not uncommon. Maintaining optimum water quality is critical for high production levels and profitability. Most production ponds are monitored daily for water quality parameters and have electrical aeration to maintain dissolved oxygen levels. Chloride levels should be maintained around 100 ppm to prevent nitrite toxicosis and enhance osmoregulation. Industry average mortality is estimated to be 2% per month. Fingerlings typically reach marketable size in 150 to 300 days. Catfish are harvested from ponds using large seines pulled by tractors (Fig. 4), and then are transported alive to processing plants.

CONCLUSION

As suggested in the introduction, the following references contain detailed information on channel catfish culture.[7–10] The information is provided in clear, nontechnical language covering overviews of catfish biology, reproduction, genetics, environmental requirements, nutrition, culture systems, and disease control. Although channel catfish production was stable or lower in 2003 because of reduced farm-gate prices and lower economic returns, the future potential of the industry is favorable, because channel catfish production is a sustainable and environmentally compatible aquaculture production system.

REFERENCES

1. Pflieger, W.L. *The Fishes of Missouri*; Missouri Department of Conservation, 1975; 343 pp.
2. Eddy, S. *The Freshwater Fishes*; William C. Brown Company: Dubuque, IA, 1975; 286 pp.
3. Tucker, C.S. Channel Catfish Culture. In *Encyclopedia of Aquaculture*; Stickney, R.R., Ed.; John Wiley and Sons, Inc.: New York, 2000; pp 153–170, 1063.
4. *Culture of Non-Salmonid Fishes*; Stickney, R.R., Ed.; CRC Press: Boca Raton, FL, 1993; 331 pp.
5. USDAa. *Catfish Processing. January 2003*; National Agricultural Statistics Service, Agricultural Statistics Board, USDA: Washington, DC, 2003; 6 pp.
6. USDAb. *Catfish Production. July 2003*; National Agricultural Statistics Service, Agricultural Statistics Board, USDA: Washington, DC, 2003; 8 pp.
7. Brunson, M.W. *Channel Catfish Fingerling Production*; MSU Cooperative Extension Service Publication 1460: Mississippi State, MS, 1992; 15 pp.
8. Steeby, J.A.; Brunson, M.W. *Fry-Pond Preparation for Rearing Channel Catfish*; MSU Cooperative Extension Service, Publication 1553: Mississippi State, MS, 1996; 2 pp.
9. Steeby, J.A.; Brunson, M.W. *Pond Preparation for Spawning Channel Catfish*; MSU Cooperative Extension Service, Publication 1565: Mississippi State, MS, 1997; 2 pp.
10. Tucker, C.S.; Robinson, H. *Channel Catfish Farming Handbook*; Kluwer Academic Publishers: Boston, 1990; 454 pp.

Chickens: Behavior Management and Well-Being

Joy A. Mench
University of California, Davis, California, U.S.A.

INTRODUCTION

Commercial poultry production has grown rapidly in the last 50 years, and billions of chickens are now raised annually for meat (broilers) or egg-laying (layers) under highly intensified conditions. These conditions impose many constraints on the birds, and a number of serious welfare concerns have arisen for both egg-laying (layers) and meat-type (broiler) chickens, particularly regarding behavioral restriction, health, and distress.

NATURAL BEHAVIOR OF CHICKENS

Chickens were domesticated in Asia about 8000 years ago. Despite many years of selection for production traits, the behavior of chickens is surprisingly similar to that of their wild ancestors, the red junglefowl.[1,2] Like junglefowl, chickens are highly social animals. They form dominance hierarchies (peck orders) and communicate using visual signals (appearance, posture) and vocalizations. In a naturalistic environment, they are exploratory and active, and they spend a large proportion of their day foraging for food. Significant time is also spent caring for the plumage, primarily by preening, during which oil from a gland at the base of the tail is worked through the feathers, and by dustbathing, during which loose material like dirt is worked through the feathers to absorb excess oils. The usual social group consists of a dominant rooster and a harem of 4–12 hens and their chicks. This group affiliates closely and feeds and roosts together. When the hens are ready to lay eggs, they separate themselves from the group and make a rudimentary nest in a secluded area, in which they lay and incubate. In the commercial environment, many of these behaviors are severely restricted, particularly for laying hens.

LAYING HENS

In the United States, about 99% of laying hens are housed in so-called battery (or conventional) cages (Fig. 1). This type of housing provides the hen with protection against predators and soil-borne diseases, and although hens are kept in natural-sized social groups of 3–10 birds, their behavior is also restricted. A space allowance of about 72 in^2 is required for a hen to be able to stand, turn around, and lie comfortably, although hens may be given less than this amount. Even more space is required, however, for the hen to groom herself and perform other behaviors such as wing-flapping. Even given sufficient space, typical conventional cages are barren and lack the features that the hen needs to perform dustbathing, perching, and nestbuilding behaviors, all considered important for welfare.[3,4]

Because of concerns about behavioral restriction, conventional cages will be outlawed in Europe as of 2012. Potential alternatives are free-range systems and barn-type systems similar to those in which broilers are raised (as described in the next section), with or without access to range.[2] These systems are not perfect alternatives, however, and they can present other welfare problems, including poorer air quality, much larger group sizes, more cannibalism, and generally higher mortality than for chickens in cages. A middle ground is the furnished (or modified) cage, which contains a perch, dustbath, and nesting area. The feasibility of using these cages on a commercial scale is currently being evaluated.[2]

Most laying hens are beak-trimmed to reduce injuries and mortality associated with feather pecking and cannibalism. These are abnormal behaviors whose causes are still incompletely understood, but large group size (as in free-range and barn systems) and lack of foraging opportunity (as in cages) are both contributing factors.[1] Beak trimming involves removal of one-third to one-half of the upper beak. Birds explore their environment using their beaks, and consequently the beak is highly enervated. Although cannibalism is a serious welfare issue, beak trimming causes acute pain and can also cause chronic pain if the bird is trimmed when older.[5] Genetic selection for hens that do not show these behaviors has been successful experimentally, and it may be possible for the industry to discontinue beak trimming by using selected stocks.[2,5]

Another controversial practice is induced molting. Birds in the wild normally molt their feathers periodically. The function of a natural molt is to improve feather condition, but the molt is also associated with changes in the hen's reproductive system. The industry uses this link between molting and reproduction to control egg production rates. By inducing the molt artificially when egg

Encyclopedia of Animal Science
DOI: 10.1081/E-EAS 120019522

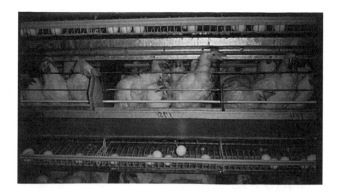

Fig. 1 Battery (or conventional) cages house about 99% of laying hens in the United States.

production starts to decline, all hens molt simultaneously and subsequently return to a higher rate of egg production. Although in the wild the trigger for a molt is declining daylength, the most common method to induce the molt is to withdraw feed from the hens for periods ranging from 4–21 days. This causes hunger, and since fowl normally spend a considerable portion of their day in activities associated with foraging, it can also lead to boredom, frustration, and the development of abnormal behaviors like stereotyped pecking and pacing.[4] Molt programs that do not involve feed withdrawal are being developed and evaluated.

A final concern relates to the disposal of hens at the end of their productive life (spent hens).[6] These hens used to be sent to a nearby processing plant to be used in products such as pet foods, but since broiler meat is so inexpensive, spent hen meat now has little economic value. Spent hens may have to be transported long distances to places where there are specialty markets for their meat, or be killed on-farm. Hens have osteoporosis because of their high rates of calcium utilization for formation of eggshell, and many hens suffer broken bones during catching and transport, so the transport process is particularly stressful for them. Current on-farm killing methods are not optimal, and there is an urgent need for the development of practical and humane methods for on-farm depopulation.

BROILER CHICKENS

Broilers are typically housed on litter-covered floors in buildings holding groups of tens of thousands of birds (Fig. 2). They generally have sufficient room to move (at least when they are younger) and can perform many of their normal behaviors, so behavioral restriction is not as much of a concern as it is for laying hens. However, like turkeys, broilers have been selected and are managed for

rapid growth, growing to full body weight in a mere 6 weeks. As a consequence, they share many of the same health problems as turkeys. These are described elsewhere in this encyclopedia and will not be discussed in detail here, but they include skeletal disorders that can lead to lameness, footpad and hock lesions, and eye and cardiovascular problems. The incidence and the severity of these disorders vary from one flock to another and are influenced by many factors, including genetics, lighting and feeding programs, ventilation, quality of litter management, and housing density (crowding). Other potential housing and management problems are poor air quality (especially high ammonia levels, which can cause eye, foot, and respiratory problems), infectious disease, and death losses due to heat stress. There is increasing emphasis on the adoption of on-farm monitoring and management practices to decrease these problems.[7]

A related issue concerns the management of the parent flocks of broiler chickens. Unlike turkeys, chickens are still produced by natural mating. However, since broiler strains have been selected for such fast growth, the parent birds become obese unless their daily allowance of feed is strictly controlled. Like molting, this causes hunger and can lead to the development of abnormal behaviors.[8]

Another area of concern relates to catching, transportation, and slaughter. Broilers are typically hand-caught and carried, in groups, upside-down by their legs. They are loaded into crates and transported by road over varying distances to the processing plant. Rough handling and poor transport conditions can cause stress, bruising, bone breakage, and mortality. It is estimated that 0.3% of birds die in transit to the processing plant. This is a small number in percentage terms, but given the scale of broiler production it translates to more than 120 million birds

Fig. 2 Broiler chickens typically are housed in large buildings holding thousands of birds, but with more freedom of movement and fewer behavioral problems than laying hens.

annually worldwide.[9] The primary cause of transport mortality is heat stress, although factors such as trauma due to rough handling are also important. There are catching machines that cause less stress and injury to the birds than human handling, and while these are routinely used in a few countries, technical problems have slowed industry-wide adoption. Improved transport vehicles that allow closer control of temperature and humidity are also available, and these can significantly decrease bird mortality due to thermal stress.

When the birds arrive at the processing plant, they are typically dumped from the crates, hung upside-down on shackles, and then stunned electrically prior to having their throats cut. Because electrical stunning is not always effective in producing unconsciousness, gas or modified-atmosphere stunning (e.g., using carbon dioxide mixtures, argon, or nitrogen), which more reliably renders the birds unconscious, is now being recommended as an alternative.[2,4] A particular welfare advantage of gas stunning is that the birds can be stunned in the crates, which eliminates the need for conscious birds to be handled and shackled.

CONCLUSION

Commercial rearing conditions impose many constraints on chickens that can affect their well-being. Welfare issues of concern include restriction of normal behavior, poor health, and distress due to management practices such as feed withdrawal, beak-trimming, transport, and slaughter methods.

REFERENCES

1. Mench, J.A.; Keeling, L.J. The Social Behaviour of Domestic Birds. In *Social Behaviour in Farm Animals*; Keeling, L.J., Gonyou, H., Eds.; CAB International: Wallingford, UK, 2001; 177–210.
2. Appleby, M.C.; Mench, J.A.; Hughes, B.O. *Poultry Behaviour and Welfare*; CAB International: Wallingford, UK, *in press.*
3. Mench, J.A. The welfare of poultry in modern production systems. Poult. Sci. Rev. **1992**, *4*, 107–128.
4. Duncan, I.J.H. Animal welfare issues in the poultry industry: Is there a lesson to be learned? J. Appl. Anim. Welf. Sci. **2001**, *4*, 207–222.
5. Hester, P.Y.; Shea-Moore, M. Beak trimming egg-laying strains of chickens. World's Poult. Sci. J. **2003**, *59*, 458–474.
6. Newberry, R.C.; Webster, A.B.; Lewis, N.J.; Van Arnam, C. Management of spent hens. J. Appl. Anim. Welf. Sci. **1999**, *2*, 13–29.
7. *Measuring and Auditing Broiler Welfare*; Weeks, C.A., Butterworth, A., Eds.; CAB International: Wallingford, UK, *in press.*
8. Mench, J.A. Broiler breeders: Feed restriction and welfare. World's Poult. Sci. J. **2002**, *58*, 23–29.
9. Weeks, C.A.; Nicol, C.J. Poultry Handling and Transport. In *Livestock Handling and Transport*, 2nd Ed.; Grandin, T., Ed.; CAB International: Wallingford, UK, 2000; 363–384.

Chickens: Broiler Housing

Brian D. Fairchild
Michael Czarick
University of Georgia, Athens, Georgia, U.S.A.

INTRODUCTION

Broilers are chickens raised for meat production and have long been selected for increased meat yields. In the 1950s, it took approximately 11 weeks to raise a 3.5-pound broiler.[1,2] Nowadays, a 5-pound broiler can be raised in 6 to 7 weeks. While genetic and nutritional contributions are extremely important, the full potential of broilers cannot be reached unless the proper environment is maintained in the broiler house. The basic needs of a broiler include: a source of heat during brooding and cold weather, cooling during hot weather, good air quality, food, water, and protection from disease. Broiler houses are designed to meet these needs in a cost-efficient manner.

HOUSE CONSTRUCTION

Broiler houses are typically 40 to 50 ft in width, and 400 to 600 ft in length (Fig. 1). Wood or metal scissor trusses are used, resulting in sloped ceilings. Side walls are typically 6 to 8 ft in height with ceiling peaks running 10 to 16 ft. To minimize heat loss during cold weather and heat gain during hot weather, insulation is either directly under the metal roof (open ceiling house) or at the bottom cord of the truss (dropped ceiling house). Open ceiling houses are typically insulated with 1- to $1\frac{1}{2}$-inch insulation made of polystyrene boards with an R-value of 5 to 9. In a dropped ceiling house, a plastic vapor barrier is attached to the bottom cord of a truss with either batt or blown insulation (R-value 12–21) installed above the vapor barrier.

Most broiler houses have 2- to 5-ft curtains on each side of the house to facilitate natural ventilation or to use in case of a power failure. With some farms using fan ventilation throughout the year, many houses are now equipped with solid side walls. Houses with solid side walls as well as many curtain-sided houses are equipped with a generator that automatically starts in the case of a power failure.

The floor in most broiler houses is typically compacted soil or concrete. The surface of the floor is covered with bedding material known as litter. Materials used as litter mostly consist of wood shavings, wood chips, sawdust, peanut hulls, or rice hulls. Whatever material is used, its primary functions are to absorb moisture and promote drying of the house, reduce contact between birds and manure by diluting the fecal material, and provide an insulation and protective cushion between the birds and the floor.

HEATING SYSTEMS

Heating of a broiler house is important, as chicks are not able to maintain a constant body temperature until approximately 14 days of age. Until then, it is crucial that floor temperature be maintained between 90–95°F with little variation. The easiest way to heat a broiler house is using a forced-air furnace. This type of heat source uses an open flame to heat air being pulled through the unit. Although they are very successful in providing heat for older birds, these heaters are problematic during brooding. Furnaces are basically top-down heating systems. The hot air coming from a furnace does not move along the floor and keep the chicks warm, but rises quickly to the ceiling of the house. Therefore, in order to get the hot air down to chick level, you have to fill up the ceiling of the house with hot air until you have added enough heat to make it down to floor level.

Because of the need for warm floor temperatures, radiant heat is an efficient way of accomplishing this. The most common types of radiant heat sources are pancake and radiant brooders. One of the advantages of radiant heat is that roughly 50% of the heat energy is directed to the floor, making it possible to maintain a floor temperature well above air temperature. When brooders are used, the floor temperature is warmest directly under the brooder, with temperatures decreasing as the distance from the brooder increases. Research studies have demonstrated that floor temperatures between 80–110°F are beneficial in getting optimum broiler performance. The advantage to this is that birds have some ability to control the amount of heat they receive. The closer they move to a brooder, the more radiant heat they receive. As they move away from the brooder, they receive less heat.

Encyclopedia of Animal Science
DOI: 10.1081/E-EAS 120019525

Fig. 1 Tunnel-inlet end of a commercial broiler house. Evaporative cooling system, air inlets, and 36-inch exhaust fans can been seen. (*View this art in color at www.dekker.com.*)

COLD WEATHER VENTILATION

During colder weather, the amount of air entering the broiler house has to be tightly controlled. The grower has to bring in enough fresh air to minimize excess moisture buildup, minimize dust, limit the buildup of harmful gases, and provide oxygen for respiration. Overventilation must be avoided because this can cause drafts that can chill the birds and results in excessive fuel usage.

Negative Pressure/Inlet Ventilation

Exhaust fans actively remove the air present in a broiler house and create a negative pressure. The negative pressure within the house causes air to enter through adjustable inlets in the ceiling that are designed to direct the air along the ceiling (Fig. 2). As air moves along the ceiling, it heats up. As the air is heated, the moisture-holding ability increases, which helps remove moisture from the house as air is pulled out by the exhaust fans. Fans are controlled with a combination of interval timers and thermostats. Interval timers allow growers to adjust air quality by fan run time. This allows the grower to run one or two fans at various intervals during brooding, while increasing both the number of fans and run times as the birds get older. The width of the inlet opening is automatically adjusted by a machine to maintain a desired static pressure level. The typical static pressure is between .05 and .10 inches of water column to promote proper air mixing.

HOT WEATHER VENTILATION

The purpose of hot weather ventilation is to ensure air exchange every minute, prevent excessive heat buildup, and provide a wind speed of at least 400 ft/min. Air movement is one of the most effective methods of cooling birds during hot weather. As air moves over a bird's body, heat is removed from the bird, making it feel cooler (i.e., windchill). Birds will not only think the house is cooler when exposed to air movement during hot weather, but will continue to eat and grow as if the air temperature is 10 degrees lower than it actually is. To get the desired cooling effect, wind speed needs to be between 400–600 ft/min, depending on factors such as bird age, house temperature, and bird density.

In curtain-sided houses, curtains are 4–5 ft in height which are fully opened during hot weather to facilitate

Fig. 2 Commercial broiler house prior to chick placement. Water lines, feed lines, radiant brooders, circulation fans, exhaust fans, and air inlets can be observed. (*View this art in color at www.dekker.com.*)

Fig. 3 Tunnel-fan end of commercial house, where 48-inch cone fans are used to move air down and out of the house. This particular house is curtain-sided and has a pocket at the top of the curtain opening to allow for a tight seal during brooding and tunnel ventilation. (*View this art in color at www.dekker.com.*)

maximum air exchange. One 36-inch fan for every 750 to 1500 ft² is typically used to blow air over the birds to increase convective cooling. To get total floor coverage, it takes a large number of fans and it creates safety hazards and increases operating costs and maintenance.

In tunnel-ventilated houses, exhaust fans are located in one end of the building and two large openings are installed in the opposite end (Fig. 3). Air is drawn through these openings and then down the house in a wall-like fashion. This provides uniform air movement across the birds, creating the windchill effect discussed earlier. The air entering the house can be cooled by drawing it through evaporative cooling pads, or by the use of misting nozzles located throughout the house.

EVAPORATIVE COOLING

Evaporative cooling is when the energy in the form of heat is used to evaporate water, resulting in air temperature cooling. Evaporative cooling systems are divided into two groups: fogging systems and pad systems. Fogging systems are found in naturally ventilated houses while pad systems are exclusively in tunnel-ventilated houses.

A typical fogging system found in a curtain/naturally ventilated house will have polyvinyl chloride (PCV) pipe with 10 fogging nozzles for every 1000 ft². A booster pump is used to pump water through the system at 100–200 pounds per square inch, resulting in a fine water vapor that evaporates quickly, which removes heat from the air without wetting the floors. Fogging systems are effective in reducing air temperature, but when not used correctly, the water will not evaporate and wet litter problems sometimes result.

A typical pad evaporative cooling system includes a PVC pipe with small holes placed above the pads in a shroud that directs the water pumped through the holes onto the top of the pad. The water flows down the pad into a gutter. The gutter collects the water and funnels it into a storage tank. A pump in the tank pumps the water back into the PVC pipe over the pad where the process is repeated. The advantages of any type of pad system are that they get the water out of the house and produce more cooling with less mess and maintenance than traditional fogging systems. Houses with pad systems tend to stay cleaner and because the equipment in houses with pad systems stays drier, it may last longer.

HOUSE CONTROLLERS

The brain of the modern broiler house is the computer controller, which monitors house environmental conditions and adjusts the equipment as necessary to keep temperatures constant. Controllers can monitor temperature in six or more locations within the house. Humidity can also be monitored, although adjustments to heater and fans are usually done on a temperature basis. As the house temperature fluctuates, the controller will turn on the brooders or fans as needed. The controller operates equipment in the house including: brooders, fans, inlet machines, curtain machines, evaporative cooling systems, and lights. The controller allows house conditions to be monitored and changed remotely if required.

FEED AND WATER MANAGEMENT

Providing almost constant access to feed and water is an important factor in raising broilers. Feed is stored outside of the house in large bins. When needed, the feed is pulled into the house using an auger or chain system and distributed throughout the house. Feed pans are filled automatically as the feed moves down the house through auger tubes. During the first week, extra feed pans are provided to ensure that the young chicks learn where to find feed and to start eating. Many farms place these extra feed pans between the automatic pans where drop tubes are available to fill these pans automatically. Water is provided through an enclosed drinking system. The bird obtains water by pushing on a metal pin that will allow water to be released and consumed. Water pressure has to be monitored. Too much water pressure may prevent the chick from being able to push the pin and get water and may also result in excessive leaks. In a typical flock, the water pressure will start off low and will increase as the bird ages.

CONCLUSION

As equipment is redesigned and developed, researchers are determining how broiler housing can be heated, cooled, and built in a way that allows modern broilers to continue to reach their genetic potential using the most economical and efficient methods.

REFERENCES

1. Lacy, M. P. Broiler Management. In *Commercial Chicken Meat and Egg Production*; Bell, D. D., Weaver, W. D., Eds.; Kluwer Academic Publishers: Norwell, MA, 2002; 829–868.
2. Weaver, W. D. Poultry Housing. In *Commercial Chicken Meat and Egg Production*; Bell, D. D., Weaver, W. D., Eds.; Kluwer Academic Publishers: Norwell, MA, 2002; 101–112.

Chickens: Broiler Nutrition Management

Park W. Waldroup
University of Arkansas, Fayetteville, Arkansas, U.S.A.

INTRODUCTION

The modern broiler has been genetically selected for rapid gains and efficient utilization of nutrients. Broilers are capable of thriving on widely varied types of diets, but do best on diets composed of low-fiber grains and highly digestible protein sources. They can be successfully grown in many different geographical areas to provide low-cost complete protein. Many different feedstuffs can be used to prepare diets for broilers. Broiler diets in the United States are based principally upon maize as an energy source and soybean meal as a source of amino acids. Grain sorghum and wheat are used as partial replacement for maize in areas where they are produced. Animal by-products such as meat and bone meal and poultry by-product meal typically make up approximately 5% of most broiler diets to supply both protein and minerals. Few other protein sources are utilized in poultry diets in the United States, but alternatives such as canola meal, sunflower meal, lupins, and some other legumes are utilized in countries where soybean production is minimal or infeasible. Most of these alternative protein sources are lower in amino acid digestibility than soybean meal, and often contain antinutritive factors that may limit the quantity used in broiler diets. Nutritionists should be familiar with the physical and nutritional attributes of feeds common to their region. Some sources of this information include Ensminger and Olentine[1] and Ewing.[2]

Broilers are normally allowed to consume their diets ad libitum, although in some instances, they are control-fed to minimize metabolic problems associated with rapid growth. Most diets are fed in pelleted form to encourage greater feed consumption and to minimize feed wastage. Broilers are grown to various ages or weights for different types of products, from birds weighing approximately 1 kg to be sold whole, to birds weighing 4 to 5 kg, grown for deboning of meat. They may be grown with males and females fed separately or combined as straight-run flocks. Although females tend to have lower requirements for most nutrients than males, the differences are minimal and typically not sufficient to warrant different formulations. The National Research Council[3] provides nutrient recommendations for broilers; however, these are based on minimum requirements with no allowances for variation in species, gender, or other factors. Recommendations for commercial usage are given by Leeson and Summers[4] and by Waldroup.[5]

DIETARY ENERGY

Because chickens primarily consume feed to satisfy their energy needs, most nutrients are adjusted to maintain a certain ratio to dietary energy. Approximately 70% of the cost of a broiler diet is associated with providing the energy needs, so establishing the most economical energy level of the diet is important. Factors that affect this include the grain source used and the availability of supplemental fats and oils. Maize contains more energy than other cereal grains due to its lower content of crude fiber and higher levels of oil. The availability of inedible fats and oils from animal rendering and processing of vegetable oils for human consumption enables their use in most U.S. broiler diets at levels ranging from 2% to 5%. Broiler diets in the United States range from approximately 3000 to 3300 ME kcal/kg. Nutritionists should evaluate price and availability of feedstuffs and develop diets containing energy levels that are appropriate for local conditions.

PROTEIN AND AMINO ACID NEEDS OF BROILERS

The need for crude protein reflects a need for the amino acids needed by the broiler. Some of these amino acids, considered as nutritionally indispensable, must be present in the diet in adequate amounts. Others, considered as nutritionally dispensable, can be synthesized from other closely related amino acids or from structurally related fats or carbohydrates through the process known as transamination. Although there is not a specific requirement for crude protein per se, sufficient protein must be present to support a nitrogen pool for synthesis of the dispensable amino acids. At the present time, it is not possible to suggest a minimum crude protein level that will sustain adequate performance in broilers of different ages.

Encyclopedia of Animal Science
DOI: 10.1081/E-EAS 120019526

Broilers must receive a well-balanced mixture of amino acids to sustain their genetic capability of rapid growth. This is usually provided as a mixture of intact protein supplements and synthetic amino acids. Soybean meal is almost universally considered the premier protein source for broiler diets. Amino acids commonly used in broiler diets include methionine and lysine. Threonine and tryptophan are also available, but their usage is less common.

MINERAL NEEDS OF BROILERS

Calcium and phosphorus make up about half of the total mineral needs. Calcium and phosphorus have been historically linked almost from the beginnings of nutrition as a science. The interrelationship of the two is widely documented and is generally given consideration when expressing requirements for either mineral. Calcium is one of the cheapest minerals to provide, and the tendency is often to overfortify. Excesses can be detrimental to the chicken as excess calcium forms complexes with phosphorus in the intestine that may inhibit P digestion. The ratio of calcium to phosphorus should not be allowed to become extreme. Excesses of calcium may also compete with zinc, magnesium, and manganese. Since these minerals are usually found in only small quantities, excesses of calcium may easily become antagonistic to these minerals, resulting in apparent deficiencies.

Supplemental sources of calcium include ground limestone and crushed marine shells. The limestone should be low in magnesium, as dolomitic limestones may cause diarrhea, although a certain amount can be tolerated. Oyster shell is similar in calcium content to ground limestone. Most phosphorus supplements also contain high levels of calcium that are highly digestible by chickens.

The primary role of phosphorus in poultry nutrition is for proper bone formation in growing animals. Phosphorus is also needed in a number of other roles, such as in energy metabolism, but the needs for these functions are small in relation to bone development.

Phosphorus from plant sources is poorly digested. Phytate phosphorus is an organic complex found in plants that includes phosphorus. On the average, about 70% of the phosphorus in plants is in this form. It is highly indigestible by monogastric animals and therefore is of limited use as a phosphate source. In order to break this molecule, the enzyme phytase is required. This enzyme is lacking or limited in monogastric animals. However, phytase enzyme is available for supplementing diets to release a portion of the bound phosphorus.

The majority of the phosphorus provided to the chicken is produced from phosphate rock. Most phosphate deposits contain high levels of fluorine, which can be toxic to animals. The rock is generally processed to remove much of the fluorine. The two most common phosphate supplements used in broiler diets are defluorinated phosphate and dicalcium phosphate. In some areas, phosphate deposits with low levels of fluorine are found and are often used without processing. Quite often, the biological value of such phosphates is lower than that of the processed phosphates, but in certain areas, they may be more economical to use or may be the only sources available.

Sodium, chloride, and potassium function together as primary determinants of the acid–base balance of the body and in maintenance of osmotic pressure between the intracellular and extracellular fluids. The relationship between these three is important and must be kept in proper balance, although no one agrees completely on what this balance should be. It is not generally considered necessary to supplement diets with potassium. Sodium and chloride are typically provided by the addition of salt.

Electrolyte balance refers to the balance between the positive and negative ions in the body. This has been calculated in different ways, the most common using the levels of sodium, chloride, and potassium to calculate electrolyte balance. One common formula used is as follows:

$$DEB \ (meq/kg) = (\%Na \times 434.98) + (\%K \times 255.74)$$
$$- (\%Cl \times 282.06)$$

While no specific values are recommended, most starter diets will contain a DEB of 200 to 250 meq/kg, grower diets from 180 to 200 meq/kg, and finisher diets from 150 to 180 meq/kg. There is little evidence to indicate that levels other than these might improve or detract from performance.

Trace minerals are usually fully supplemented due to their relatively low cost, the need to provide a safety factor, the variability in composition of plants due to differences in geographical locations and fertilization rates, and the tendency for many to be bound by organic complexes and poorly digested. Most premixes would provide the entire needs for manganese, zinc, iron, copper, iodine, and selenium. In the United States, copper is often supplemented in levels far exceeding its nutritional needs. These high levels of copper have come under attack by environmentalists, and may also contribute to the development of gizzard erosion, where the lining of the gizzard is inflamed and irritated.

In general, trace minerals in the form of oxides and carbonates are less digestible, while sulfates or chlorides are more highly digestible. Organic chelates of various minerals are usually more biologically available; however, they are also considerably more expensive. Because many vitamins are subject to oxidation, mixing trace minerals and vitamins in a concentrated premix should be avoided to ensure adequate vitamin stability.

VITAMIN NEEDS OF BROILERS

Vitamins are found in a wide variety of feed ingredients. However, most of the rich natural sources of vitamins such as wheat bran or alfalfa meal have been virtually eliminated from poultry feeds in favor of more concentrated but less vitamin-rich ingredients such as whole cereal grains (corn or sorghum) and processed protein sources such as soybean meal. Animal proteins such as fish meal or meat-and-bone meal may contribute significant amounts of vitamins. Vitamins are economically produced by chemical synthesis or fermentation, and poultry feeds are typically fortified with vitamin mixes that provide all of the required vitamins in sufficient amounts with little reliance placed upon the vitamins provided by the natural ingredients. Because vitamins are relatively inexpensive in relation to the total cost of the diet, most are provided well in excess of the anticipated needs of the animal.

CONCLUSION

Nutrient needs of broilers have been thoroughly researched and widely available. Many common feed ingredients can be used to provide these nutrients to manufacture broiler feed. Broilers can be successfully grown on many types of diets, provided the nutritional needs are provided. Many ingredients contain factors that may limit performance of broilers and must be considered in formulating broiler diets.

REFERENCES

1. Ensminger, M.E.; Olentine, C.G., Jr. *Feeds and Nutrition*, 1st Ed.; Ensminger Publishing Company: Clovis, CA, 1978.
2. Ewing, W.N. *The FEEDS Directory*; Context Publications: Leicestershire, England, 1997.
3. National Research Council. *Nutrient Requirements of Poultry*, 9th Rev. Ed.; National Academy Press: Washington, DC, 1994.
4. Leeson, S.; Summers, J.D. *Nutrition of the Chicken*, 4th Ed.; University Books: Guelph, Ontario, Canada, 2001.
5. Waldroup, P.W. Dietary Nutrient Allowances for Poultry. In *Feedstuffs Reference Issue*; Miller Publishing Company: Minneapolis, 2003; Vol. 75 (38), 42–49.

Chickens: Broiler Reproduction Management

Veerle Bruggeman
Eddy Decuypere
Okanlawon Onagbesan
K.U. Leuven, Leuven, Belgium

INTRODUCTION

Generations of selection for body weight, breast filet weight, and feed efficiency have produced the modern broiler strain, with a high meat yield and a high rate of growth but with poor, declining reproductive performance in the female if feeding is not restricted. Presently, severe feed restriction—especially during the rearing period and to a lesser extent during lay—is necessary to improve reproduction and to maximize the number of hatchable eggs in heavy-broiler breeder lines. This improved reproduction can be attributed to changes in the functionality of the reproductive axis (ovary-hypothalamus-pituitary). Feed restriction is also inevitable in order to counteract the occurrence of overweight and several pathologies. This article will give an overview of the current knowledge of the effects of feed restriction on reproductive physiology and concomitantly, the repercussions on welfare in these birds.

FUNDAMENTAL PRINCIPLES UNDERLYING FEED RESTRICTION

The control of growth rate in broiler breeder males and females is one of the most important management tools to ensure the best reproductive performance.[1] In females, three key points are essential. First, the rate of growth must be predetermined so that the desired body weight is attained a few weeks before onset of lay. The desired body weight is established by giving the birds a certain amount of food, which is at some ages more than 50% restriction compared to their unrestricted counterparts (Fig. 1). Second, it is important to synchronize growth and sexual maturity. Reaching sexual maturity is not accomplished just by gaining weight, but the carcass, muscle, and non-reproductive visceral tissues must have grown prior to the onset of the development of the reproductive tissue. Third, an accurate feeding, based on production rate, is necessary at the start of and throughout the laying period.[2]

Not only the level, but also the timing and duration of feed restriction could be important in controlling reproductive performance in broiler breeder females. Results from Bruggeman et al.[3] have shown the existence of critical periods during rearing in which feeding levels have repercussions on different reproductive parameters (Fig. 2). Male broiler breeders that have a very high growth potential also have to follow prescribed growth curves, taking into account the size and maturity of the females at the age of sexual maturity in order to optimize mating and to reduce aggressive behavior toward the females. It is recommended to rear the male broiler breeders separately from the females to control their feed intake. A rearing program focused on the proper weight difference between males and females and an adequate social structure in the flock is essential for optimal performance.

THE PHYSIOLOGICAL EFFECTS OF FEED RESTRICTION ON REPRODUCTION IN FEMALE BREEDERS

Reproductive processes in females are the result of controlled interaction between the hypothalamus-pituitary and the ovary and can be influenced by environmental, selection, or nutritional effects.

A well-described effect of feed restriction in broiler breeder females is the reduction of ovary weight, the number of yellow follicles during lay, and the incidence of erratic ovipositions, defective eggs, and multiple ovulations.[4–6] Unrestricted access to feed leads to a low egg production rate and fewer settable eggs for incubation.[6] There is evidence that the observed disturbances in follicular growth, differentiation, and ovulation in animals fed ad libitum could be attributed to changes in the steroid-producing capacity and in the sensitivity of the follicles to locally produced growth factors (e.g., insulin-like growth factors, bone morphogenic proteins, transforming growth factor, etc.) in interaction with each other and with gonadotrophins. Moreover, selection for growth rate or body leanness may have changed ovarian gene expression for growth factors and their receptors.[7]

Besides these changes at the ovarian level, changes in the concentrations and/or pulsatility of luteinizing hormone (LH) and follicle-stimulating hormone (FSH) may

Encyclopedia of Animal Science
DOI: 10.1081/E-EAS 120019529

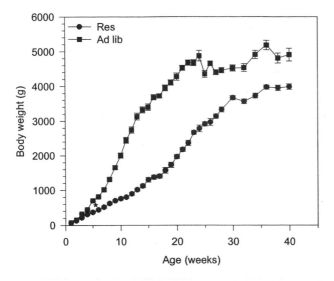

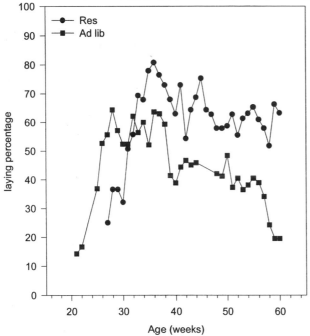

Fig. 1 Body weight curves (top) and laying curves (bottom) of feed-restricted (res) and unrestricted (ad lib) broiler breeder females (Hybro G). (Data from Bruggeman, 1998.)

be important factors explaining the alterations in follicular development and ovulation between broiler breeders fed different amounts of feed. Plasma LH/FSH ratio was increased by restricted feeding.[8] Moreover, the sensitivity of the pituitary to luteinizing hormone releasing hormone (LHRH) as well as to ovarian feedback factors (steroids, inhibin) is influenced by the nutritional level. After sexual maturation and establishment of lay, the long-term feed-restricted animals showed the highest responsiveness to both LHRH-1 and ovarian factors,

compared to animals fed ad libitum. It is possible that this increased sensitivity at the hypothalamic-pituitary level in feed-restricted animals contributes to the difference in laying performance between ad libitum-fed and restricted broiler breeder females.[9] In several studies, no significant improvement in fertility or hatchability due to feed restriction could be observed. Duration of fertility, however, appears to be significantly lower in hens fed ad libitum, probably due to sperm storage difficulties. Most of the problems concerning embryo viability and hatchability are related to the production of eggs with reduced eggshell quality. Such eggs exhibit an increased incidence of embryonic mortality. Double-yolked eggs represent a further loss, due to the poor embryo viability in multiple-yolked eggs.

WELFARE VERSUS REPRODUCTION IN BROILER BREEDERS

Welfare of broiler breeders has been questioned, in light of the severity of food restriction increasing every year, with a proportional increase in growth performances of the progeny obtained by genetic selection.[10] Physiological stress is associated with restricted feeding on the one hand and the excessive body weight for ad libitum-fed broiler breeders on the other hand. Both are questionable according to several welfare parameters.[11] Unrestricted animals are overweight and display several pathologies (leg breakages, ascites development, cardiac failures) leading to unnecessary suffering or death. Although severe feed restriction prevents these syndromes, thereby improving welfare, it has been said that feed restriction is cruel because animals cannot eat to satisfy their hunger. The dilemma facing the broiler breeder industry is thus a production/welfare paradox. There is a need to balance those problems inherent to excess intake against those that accompany severe feed restriction.

CONCLUSION: FUTURE OBJECTIVES IN BROILER REPRODUCTION MANAGEMENT

The foregoing discussion leads to the main question: Can the growth requirement of broiler breeder hens be allied with good reproductive performance, good health, and welfare, either by a feed restriction program which does not cause undue hunger, or by innovative genetic selection? Several data in literature illustrate that growth and reproduction are mutually exclusive in selection goals, suggesting that there is a causal negative biological relation. If that is true, then one has to make choices in

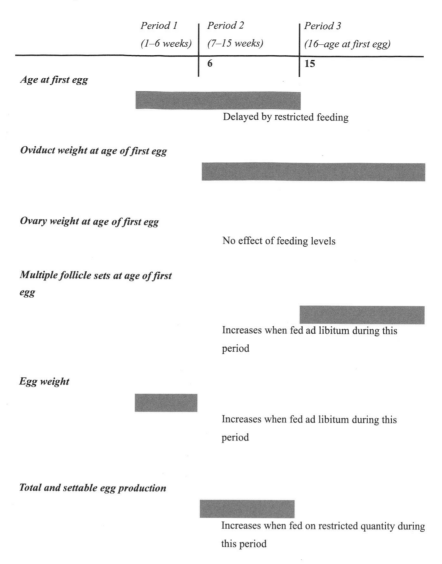

Fig. 2 Schematic presentation of important periods during the rearing and prebreeding period in the determination of reproductive performance in broiler breeder females. (From Bruggeman, 1998.)

future broiler breeder management. The following choices are proposed.

1. Continue the intense selection of broilers, with the known consequences of the need for severe feed restriction of the breeders. This becomes difficult to defend when taking into account the animal welfare policy in some societies. In this case, it is feasible to develop new feeding regimens/diets more adapted to the animals' needs, thereby improving welfare in combination with acceptable egg production. This can possibly be achieved by diminishing the duration[2] or the intensity of feed restriction. Energy restriction can be realized by the introduction of diets with energy dilution. Whether these feeding strategies/diets have repercussions on egg production is hardly looked at, but there will be a search for the optimal balance welfare/growth and reproduction goals.

2. Change selection goals in the broiler industry, thereby diminishing the need for severe feed restriction in breeders by selection, but without deterioration of the quality demands of the broiler. The introduction of new genetic lines of broiler breeder females that would tolerate ad libitum feeding could be a good alternative to counteract this welfare problem. The increasing production of slower-growing Label chickens (France), for example, has led to a practice of mating a heavy broiler cockerel with a slow-growing Label breeder hen. The resulting broiler reaches market weight 10–12 days later than a standard broiler. Another alternative is the dwarf broiler breeder hens, which seem to maintain a relatively

good reproductive fitness even with ad libitum feed allowances during growth.[12,13] The presence of the dwarf gene (*dw*) suggests that its presence may reduce the need for feed restriction in the breeder while allowing the production of fast-growing offspring. However, one has to bear in mind that this divergent selection leads to an unnatural biological situation in which natural mating can become very difficult because of the extreme size differences between male and female. The production of broilers depends on artificial insemination in such cases, as in the turkey industry. It can be questioned, from an ethical point of view, if this might affect the integrity of the animal as a population.

ACKNOWLEDGMENTS

Veerle Bruggeman is a postdoctoral fellow of the Fund for Scientific Research (Flanders, Belgium).

REFERENCES

1. Decuypere, E.; Bruggeman, V.; Barbato, G.F.; Buyse, J. Growth and Reproduction Problems Associated with Selection for Increased Broiler Meat Production. In *Poultry Genetics, Breeding and Technology*; Muir, W.M., Aggrey, S.E., Eds.; CABI Publishing: Wallingford, 2003; 13–28.

2. Costa, M.J. Fundamental principles of broiler breeders nutrition and the design of feeding programs. World Poult. Sci. **1981**, *37*, 177–192.

3. Bruggeman, V.; Onagbesan, O.; D'Hondt, E.; Buys, N.; Safi, M.; Vanmontfort, D.; Berghman, L.; Vandesande, F.; Decuypere, E. Effects of timing and duration of feed restriction during rearing on reproductive characteristics in broiler breeder females. Poult. Sci. **1999**, *78*, 1424–1434.

4. Hocking, P.M. Effects of body weight at sexual maturity and the degree and age of restriction during rearing on the ovarian follicular hierarchy of broiler breeder females. Br. Poult. Sci. **1993**, *34*, 793–801.

5. Hocking, P.M.; Waddington, D.; Walker, M.A.; Gilbert, A.B. Control of the development of the follicular hierarchy in broiler breeder pullets by food restriction during rearing. Br. Poult. Sci. **1989**, *30*, 161–174.

6. Yu, M.W.; Robinson, F.E.; Charles, R.G.; Weingardt, R. Effect of feed allowance during rearing and breeding on female broiler breeders. 2. Ovarian morphology and production. Poult. Sci. **1992**, *71*, 1750–1761.

7. Onagbesan, O.; Decuypere, E.; Leenstra, F.; Ehlhardt, D.A. Differential effects of amount of feeding on cell proliferation and progesterone production in response to gonadotrophins and insulin-like growth factor-I by ovarian granulosa cells of broiler breeder chickens selected for fatness or leanness. J. Reprod. Fertil. **1999**, *116*, 73–85.

8. Bruggeman, V. The Effect of Level and Timing of Food Restriction on Growth and Reproductive Characteristics and Their Endocrine Control in Broiler Breeder Females. PhD Thesis; Katholieke Universiteit Leuven, 1998.

9. Bruggeman, V.; Onagbesan, O.; Vanmontfort, D.; Berghman, L.; Verhoeven, G.; Decuypere, E. Effect of long-term food restriction on pituitary sensitivity to cLHRH-1 in broiler breeder females. J. Reprod. Fertil. **1998**, *114*, 267–276.

10. Karunajeewa, H. A review of current poultry feeding systems and their potential acceptability to animal welfarists. World's Poult. Sci. J. **1987**, *43*, 20–32.

11. Hocking, P.M.; Maxwell, M.H.; Mitchell, M.A. Welfare assessment of broiler breeder and layer females subjected to food restriction and limited access to water during rearing. Br. Poult. Sci. **1993**, *34*, 443–458.

12. Hocking, P.M.; Gilbert, A.B.; Walker, M.; Waddington, D. Ovarian follicular structure of White Leghorns fed ad libitum and dwarf and normal broiler breeders fed ad libitum or restricted until point of lay. Br. Poult. Sci. **1987**, *28*, 493–506.

13. Triyuwanta; Leterrier, C.; Brillard, J.P.; Nys, Y. Maternal body weight and feed allowance of breeders affect performance of dwarf broiler breeders and tibial ossification of their progeny. Poult. Sci. **1992**, *71*, 244–254.

Chickens: Layer Health Management

Eric Gingerich

University of Pennsylvania School of Veterinary Medicine, Kennett Square, Pennsylvania, U.S.A.

INTRODUCTION

Optimizing the health of layer flocks is essential for profitable egg production. Most producers equate layer health with infectious disease prevention and control, but the noninfectious production diseases are becoming increasingly important. True flock health management involves interaction among the disciplines of immunization, preventive medication, nutrition, environment control, and flock best-management practices.

RESOURCES

Numerous resources are available to the egg producer today for assistance in managing layer health. The primary breeder is a good resource for management guides, and their staff of veterinarians for health advice.[1,2] Vaccine supplier companies not only supply high-quality biologics but also supply technical expertise in applying the biologics. Many large egg-producing companies retain consulting veterinarians or hire a staff veterinarian. A qualified nutritionist is an essential player on the team. Finally, a good relationship with your diagnostic laboratory is required to be able to aid in monitoring flock health, and it can be a valuable asset in disease prevention programs.

LAYER STRAIN SELECTION

The strain of bird selected will bring in genetic characteristics that may aid in controlling certain diseases. For example, some strains show reduced problems with bacterial infections, cannibalism in high light-intensity situations, and Marek's disease mortality during growing.

PULLET-GROWING PROGRAM

Vaccinations given during the pullet program are the backbone of the layer health program. These programs should contain vaccines against diseases that the pullets will be exposed to during lay.[3] Consideration needs to be given to past disease exposure in the pullet-growing house, diseases present in the region to which the pullets will be moved, and whether the pullets are being moved to a multi-age complex that has a higher degree of disease exposure (such as to *Mycoplasma gallisepticum* (Mg), *Salmonella enteritidis* (Se), variant infectious bronchitis (IB) strains, etc.). Professional advice from a competent poultry veterinarian with knowledge of the disease exposure situation, vaccines available, proper timing of vaccinations, and appropriate routes of administration should be sought. An example of a vaccination program used for pullets going to a complex with high risk of exposure to infectious laryngotracheitis (ILT), Mg, Se, fowl pox, and variant IB is given in Table 1. Vaccine company representatives and consulting veterinarians should be involved to assist the persons vaccinating the flocks with proper techniques and to review these procedures on a routine basis.

Management practices used during growing can affect layer health as well. Improper beak trimming can lead to poor uniformity, increased cannibalism, and increased feather loss during lay. Poor feathering is a component of the increase in mortality seen toward the end of lay, with peckout mortality and bacterial infections commonly seen. The use of a lighting schedule that leads to excessive egg size will lead to problems in later lay due to poor shell quality (often blamed on respiratory disease), excessive feather loss, and increased peckout/prolapse mortality (reproductive tract damage).

MONITORING

Serology testing on a routine basis is used to determine the effectiveness of vaccinations at the point-of-lay, to determine exposure for diseases not included in the vaccination program (avian influenza or Mg in an Mg-negative unit), and to follow changes in titers during lay for such diseases as Mg in a positive unit, Newcastle disease (ND), and infectious bronchitis (IB).

Evaluation of the pox vaccination process is performed seven days after pox vaccination by checking for the "take" at the site of pox vaccine inoculation of at least 100 birds per vaccinator. Visually monitoring inactivated vaccines with added dye at the site of injection is also a

Encyclopedia of Animal Science
DOI: 10.1081/E-EAS 120019533

Table 1 Example pullet vaccination program

Age (days)	Disease	Vaccine	Route
0	MD[a]	HVT–Rispens	SQ[b]
18	ND-IB[c]	B1–Mass–Conn–Ark	VCS[d]
	IBD[e]	Intermediate	VCS
28	IBD	Intermediate	VCS
35	ND-IB	B1–Mass–Conn–Ark	VCS
49	AE-Pox[f]	Calnek AE–Fowl and Pigeon pox	WW[g]
	ILT[h]	CEO[i]	ED[j]
63	ND-IB	LaSota–Mass Connaught–Mass Holland	CS[k]
70	MG[l]	F-strain	CS
91	ND-IB-Se[m]	Inactivated	Inject IM[n] or SQ
	ILT	CEO	ED

[a]MD = Marek's disease.
[b]SQ = Subcutaneous.
[c]ND-IB = Newcastle–Infectious bronchitis.
[d]VCS = Very coarse spray, 100 micron.
[e]IBD = Infectious bursal disease.
[f]AE-Pox = Avian encephalomyelitis–Fowl pox.
[g]WW = Wing web application.
[h]ILT = Infectious laryngotracheitis.
[i]CEO = Chick embryo origin.
[j]ED = Eyedrop application.
[k]CS = Coarse spray, 50 micron.
[l]MG = *Mycoplasma gallisepticum*.
[m]ND-IB-SE = Newcastle–Infectious bronchitis–*Salmonella enteritidis*.
[n]IM = Intramuscularly.

good means of monitoring the administration of these vaccines. As with serology, the vaccine supplier can be of great help in setting up these types of monitoring programs.

Routine necropsy of fresh dead birds is an overlooked method of monitoring layer health. Many astute producers have trained flock supervisors or use local diagnostic lab veterinarians to perform necropsies on a sampling of fresh dead birds from each flock once a month. Another valuable method is listening for respiratory noise in flocks after the lights have gone off for the night.

Sampling manure for detection of Se infection of layers is essential in order to know flock and house status. Typically, a plan for sampling chick boxes at delivery and manure samples at approximately 12 weeks of age, 30 weeks, 45 weeks, and post-molt is performed, checking the samples for Se.[4] This information is then used to plan for the vaccination of pullets, and for cleaning and disinfection (C&D) programs.

LAYER NUTRITION

A sound nutrition program is needed to aid flock's ability to respond to vaccinations and to reduce the effects of disease agent challenge. Proper nutrient levels at each stage of growing and production are required for proper growth, feathering, egg production, shell quality, egg size, immune response, etc. A deficiency of phosphorus at any stage of life or excess calcium prior to sexual maturity leads directly to urolithiasis/visceral gout caused by high urine pH. A deficiency of calcium during lay leads directly to mortality caused by calcium depletion. Poor protein nutrition over time will lead to layers with inadequate feather cover at the end of lay, resulting in nervousness and excessive mortality resulting from peckout/prolapse and bacterial infections.

The nutritionist should be the part of the management team who reviews flock results routinely and is kept abreast of abnormalities involving feathering, shell quality, bone strength, and mortality due to peckouts and gout.

LAYER FLOCK MANAGEMENT

Several layer flock management practices impact layer health. Dead birds left in cages longer than one day will expose the live layers to high levels of bacteria. Composting dead birds in the pits of high-rise layer housing or maintaining a dead bird grinder in the live bird area also has been associated with an increase in bacterial infection of layers. The management of light intensity will aid in controlling peckout/prolapse mortality. Additional feedings given during hot weather will benefit birds by reducing the incidence of calcium depletion.

Proper pest control management (for rodents and flies) minimizes exposure to *E. coli* and Se. Manure management in high-rise housing storage pits is key to reduced fly breeding. Provisions are needed for drying the manure and for moving the dry manure between the manure piles to the top of the pile. An increasing number of pullet and layer units now remove manure from the house daily, or every other day, to a storage unit outside in order to control flies. Optimum rodent control involves constant vigilance in placing barriers between the layer house environment and the rodents on the outside, and in removing areas conducive to rodent nesting. Chemical baiting is also a part of the control program, but it cannot be relied on alone and needs to be considered a minor part of the entire program.

BIOSECURITY AND SANITATION

Biosecurity programs that prevent the introduction of avian pathogens are an all-important aspect of layer health management, but one that is often not routinely reviewed or given its proper share of capital input. High-risk activities that require attention to details of equipment sanitation, providing people with clean clothing and footwear, and/or setting up physical decontamination areas. These activities include bird moving (point-of-lay pullets, spent fowl, fill-in birds), egg handling materials (pallets, reused egg flats), vaccination crews, beak-trimming crews, welfare auditing, veterinary visits, flock supervisor visits, repair person visits, and so forth.

Proper cleaning and disinfection of pullet houses, usually with dry cleaning followed by wet washing and disinfection, are required for Marek's disease prevention. Decontamination of layer houses between flocks is also important to reduce exposure to disease agents, including Se, from the previous flock.[5] Water line cleaning using citric acid followed by chlorine sanitation,[6] both between flocks and during lay, is an underused tool to aid in reducing bacterial infections by reducing exposure to bacteria that cause the intestinal microflora balance to become upset or that infect the birds directly with disease-causing bacteria.

PREVENTIVE MEDICATIONS

Preventive medications are used routinely for preventing coccidiosis (coccidiostats) and necrotic enteritis (Bacitracin and/or probiotics) in litter floor growing houses.

Table 2 Preventive medication programs for *Mycoplasma gallisepticum* control

Antibiotic	Level	Program
Tylosin	20–30 g/ton	Continuous feeding through peak
Chlortetracycline	200 g/ton	1 week each month
Oxytetracycline	200 g/ton	1 week each month
Erythromycin	100 g/ton	1 week each month

Even though the use of cage growing has greatly minimized the use of coccidiostats and antibiotics, some cage units that have had coccidiosis in the past also use coccidiostats for selected times during growing. Although vaccination is the most common method of preventing Mg, some producers use government-approved antibiotics for all or part of the lay cycle in order to prevent this disease (Table 2).

ENVIRONMENT MANAGEMENT

The environment to which birds are exposed—light intensity, dust, atmospheric ammonia, high temperature, low temperature, feed availability, water availability, space allotments, etc.—significantly affects layer health and productivity. Poor productivity due to environmental problems is often mistakenly believed to be infectious disease-related. Detailed record keeping of environment-related inputs is essential for troubleshooting in these cases. For example, a very commonly seen situation in chain feeder-fed houses is the difference in feed availability and quality near the source of the feed and at the end of the feeder. This difference results in marked mortality increases and egg production losses in the cages near the end of the feeder line.

Microclimates in small areas of a house are often responsible for poor egg production or an increase in mortality. For example, air inlets that are not open sufficiently result in warmer, poorly ventilated zones. Light coming in from fans without light traps in the pit of a high-rise house will result in a higher rate of mortality from peckouts in the affected rows of cages.

CONCLUSION

Maintaining healthy layer flocks requires attention to programs involving vaccinations, preventive medications, monitoring for diseases, isolating flocks from disease exposure, sanitation, and so forth. Using a team approach to layer health management is the key to success in utilizing resources such as consulting veterinarians, nutritionists, diagnostic labs, vaccine company representatives, and primary breeder personnel.

REFERENCES

1. *Hy-Line Variety W-36 Commercial Management Guide 2003–2005*; Hy-Line International: West Des Moines, IA, 2003.
2. *Bovans White Management Guide, 2002–2003,* North American Ed.; Centurion Poultry, Inc.: Lexington, GA, 2002.
3. Cutler, G.J. Vaccines and Vaccination. In *Commercial Chicken Meat and Egg Production,* 5th Ed.; Bell, D.D., Weaver, W.D., Eds.; Kluwer Academic Publishers: Norwell, MA, 2002; 451–461.
4. Davison, S.A.; Dunn, P.A.; Henzler, D.J.; Knabel, S.J.; Patterson, P.H.; Schwartz, J.H. Monitor the Environment. In *Preharvest HACCP in the Table Egg Industry*; Penn State College of Agricultural Sciences: University Park, PA, 1997; 18–19.
5. Shane, S.M. Decontamination of Housing and Equipment. In *Biosecurity in the Poultry Industry*; Shane, S.M., Halvorson, D., Hill, D., Villegas, P., Wages, D., Eds.; American Association of Avian Pathologists: Kennett Square, PA, 1995.
6. Vaillancourt, J.; Stringham, M. Biosecurity Programs-Layers-Sanitation-Facilities-Water Lines. In *Poultry Disease Risk Management: Practical Biosecurity Resources CD*; U.S. Poultry and Egg Association: Tucker, GA, 2003.

Chickens: Layer Housing

Michael C. Appleby
The Humane Society of the United States, Washington, D.C., U.S.A.

INTRODUCTION

For commercial egg production in developed countries, the majority of hens are placed in cage houses at point-of-lay (about 16 weeks old, shortly before sexual maturity). However, an increasing proportion is kept in noncage systems, either in houses or on free range. Small-scale farmyard and household flocks survive mostly on a noncommercial basis, and in developing countries. Choice of system affects both the economic performance and the welfare of the birds.

HOUSING

Housing is usually provided, for protection and inspection of stock and for control of temperature, humidity, and light. Decisions about housing depend on many factors, including climate. Closed houses enable the environment around the birds to be modified, which ordinarily results in increased food conversion efficiency as well as labor reduction and worker comfort. Open housing has fewer requirements for ventilation and is more common in warm climates.

CAGES

Laying cages typically house from three to eight hens. Feed is delivered to a trough in front of the cage by a chain, and water is supplied by a nipple line or trough line through the cages. In conventional cages, eggs are laid on the sloping wire floor and roll out onto a conveyor belt for collection. Cages are usually arranged in tiers. These are vertically stacked—with feces removed by a belt or a scraped shelf between the tiers—or arranged stepwise, so that feces fall into a pit. The large number of cages in one house is called a battery of cages, and laying cages are often called battery cages. It is common to have 20,000 birds per house in Europe and 60,000 or more per house in the United States. In the European Union (EU), there has been a statutory minimum space allowance of 85 in^2 (550 cm^2) per bird since 2003. In the United States most producers are moving toward an allowance of 67 in^2 (430 cm^2) by 2008, on a voluntary basis. In other coun-tries, allowances vary from about 47 in^2 (300 cm^2) per bird, upward.

High-density housing means relatively low capital cost per bird, and cages have other economic advantages, such as reduction of labor and reduced feed intake because of increased house temperature. Working conditions for operatives are often better than with other systems; dust and ammonia are usually less prevalent. Cages also prevent some behavioral problems of hens. Certain aspects of behavior are controlled, such as egg-laying; there is no need for nest boxes. In addition, social problems associated with large group size, such as aggression and major outbreaks of cannibalism, are reduced. Beak trimming is therefore largely unnecessary, but is still widely practiced.

Reduction of aggression and cannibalism are also beneficial for the birds, and there are additional advantages for hen welfare, notably the separation of birds from their feces and from litter, thus reducing disease and parasitic infections. However, the use of conventional cages has become increasingly controversial, because there are also disadvantages for welfare. Space restriction limits movement and behavior such as wing-flapping, and the lack of appropriate stimuli such as loose material curbs other behavior (e.g., nesting, pecking, scratching). There are also physical effects. Standing on thin wire causes foot damage, and wire cage fronts cause feather abrasion during feeding. Other faults in design sometimes cause birds to become trapped and suffer injury or death. Modern cages have simplified fronts with horizontal bars and often have solid cage sides that reduce feather damage. Injuries are also less prevalent. However, following a report from the Scientific Veterinary Committee,[1] the EU passed a directive that will phase out conventional cages by 2012.[2]

The design of cages for laying hens has been changed often to improve economic performance. More recently, there have also been modifications specifically to ameliorate welfare problems. Perches have negligible cost and encourage normal roosting behavior. An abrasive strip behind the feed trough can reduce the overgrowth of claws. More radically, enriched cages offer increased area and height compared to conventional cages, and also provide a perch, a nest box, and a litter area. Following large-scale adoption of such cages in Sweden, results from

Encyclopedia of Animal Science
DOI: 10.1081/E-EAS 120019534

commercial flocks are now becoming available. Behavior is more varied than in conventional cages, physical condition is improved, and there has been no cannibalism reported. However, egg production costs are higher, partly because of capital costs and partly because more eggs are downgraded. The EU Directive[2] requires that by 2012 all laying cages shall be enriched, providing 116 in^2 (750 cm^2) per hen, a nest, a littered area for scratching and pecking, a perch, and a claw-shortening device.

FREE RANGE

The term free range is generally understood by consumers to mean that hens have access to pasture. This is mandatory in the EU (Table 1), but not elsewhere. Problems associated with such access are damage to the ground and buildup of disease. In early forms of free range, these problems were avoided by using small, movable houses. Highly labor-intensive, that approach was adapted by incorporating fixed housing big enough for birds to be fed inside. They also obtain some nutrition from the outdoor area, particularly on pasture. However, a similar arrangement without vegetation is adopted in some conditions that cannot provide it, for example in organic egg production in some parts of the United States. In any case, consumption of provided feed is actually higher on range than in housing, at least in temperate countries, because of increased activity and lower temperature.

One possible arrangement is to have a house surrounded by several areas of land, with pop-holes for the birds to reach each area in rotation. If one area is used permanently, stocking density must be kept low, but in large commercial flocks only a minority of birds

Table 1 Criteria defined by the European Union for labeling of eggs

Label	Criteria
Free range	Continuous daytime access to ground mainly covered with vegetation Maximum 400 hens/acre (1000 hens/hectare)
Semi-intensive	Continuous daytime access to ground mainly covered with vegetation Maximum 1600 hens/acre (4000 hens/hectare)
Deep litter	Maximum 6 hens/yd^2 (7 hens/m^2) A third of floor covered with litter; part of floor for droppings collection
Perchery or barn	Maximum 21 birds per yd^2 (25 hens/m^2) Perches, 6 in (15 cm) for each hen

(Data from Ref. [3].)

actually go outside. This is partly because cover is rarely provided, despite the fact that chickens evolved in jungles and are cautious of potential predators. Conditions in the house are typical of other floor-housed systems, with feeders, drinkers, and nest boxes for flock sizes varying from several hundred to several thousand. Behavior is more varied than in cages, but as in all noncage systems there is a risk of cannibalism, so birds are usually beak-trimmed.

FLOOR HOUSING

Several systems are available that allow birds the run of a house, but without access to the outdoors. Some have attempted to use wholly slatted or wire floors, but these result in many behavioral problems including floor laying, cannibalism, and hysteria. Strawyards are often converted from existing farm buildings, partially open and therefore having natural light and ventilation, with straw as litter. Deep-litter houses use wood shavings or other material such as sand, corncobs, or peanut hulls as litter and they are usually more fully enclosed. With automatic ventilation, this allows more precise temperature control. In many cases, natural light is also excluded to allow the use of photoperiods shorter than day length. For this reason, deep litter is often used for the rearing of poultry, even if they are to be housed in a different system later.

In any litter-based system, birds defecate on the litter. Under good conditions, feces are dispersed—partly by hens pecking and scratching—dry out, and are broken down by bacterial action, allowing the litter to remain friable. If the litter becomes wet, packed solid, or both, however, unpleasant conditions develop, including high ammonia. Foot damage and disease are likely. Management of nesting is also important—early in the laying period to ensure that hens are laying in nest boxes rather than on the floor, and later to identify and discourage broodiness. Various methods of automatic egg collection from nests are possible. Feeders are either pans supplied by augers, or troughs supplied by a chain, while water is provided in a nipple line or in bell-shaped, gravity-fed drinkers.

Stocking density can be higher if part of the floor area is slats or wire mesh, so that fewer droppings accumulate in the litter. Drinkers placed over the slats reduce the risk of wet litter. However, sale of eggs as deep-litter eggs in the EU limits stocking density to 6 birds per yd^2 (7 per m^2), with at least a third of the floor as litter (Table 1). Other systems increase the density of birds in the house by using multiple levels. The aviary uses tiers of slats or mesh to increase the use of vertical space in the house. Drinkers are placed over slats and feeders are widely distributed. Nest boxes are made as accessible as possible, but floor laying is sometimes a problem. Various arrangements of tiers have allowed experimental stocking densities of up to 19 birds per yd^2 (22 per m^2) of floor space. Group size is commonly about 1000 birds. The perchery provides perches on a frame so that birds can jump up or down. Percheries that provide litter generally have good results, but EU requirements for perchery eggs allow up to 21 birds per yd^2 (25 per m^2) and do not include a provision for litter (Table 1). Without litter, birds do not use the floor fully, and the minimal requirement of 6 in (15 cm) of perch space per bird does not provide complete freedom of movement. Commercial farms applying these standards have encountered problems such as cannibalism and nonlaying birds occupying nest boxes.

The tiered wire floor system developed in The Netherlands resembles a cage house with the partitions removed. There are rows of narrow tiers, with passages in between the rows, and a manure belt under each tier. Nest boxes are against the wall, perches are mounted over the top tier, and feed and water are supplied at all other levels except the floor, which is covered with litter. This and other variants of aviaries and percheries are almost universal in Switzerland, the only country in which laying cages have been banned. Another development in Switzerland has been the combination of these systems with either free range or a terrace along the side of the house, with open-mesh walls. With relatively small flocks, free-range birds use the outside area extensively, and terraces are also well used.

CONCLUSION

Chickens are adaptable and can be productive in many housing systems. An emphasis on technical development and cost reduction has led to cages as the most common form of housing, but this occurred at a time when effects of behavioral restriction were not understood. Systems allowing more behavioral freedom are now increasing. Economics will continue to be the most important consideration in choice of system, but an increasing economic factor is the possibility of higher prices for noncage eggs (see Eggs: Marketing elsewhere in this encyclopedia), taking hen welfare into account.

ARTICLES OF FURTHER INTEREST

Chickens: Behavior Management and Well-Being, p. 202
Chickens: Layer Health Management, p. 215
Chickens: Layer Nutrition Management, p. 222
Chickens: Layer Reproduction Management, p. 225
Eggs: Marketing, p. 311

REFERENCES

1. Scientific Veterinary Committee. *Report on the Welfare of Laying Hens*; Commission of the European Communities Directorate-General for Agriculture: Brussels, Belgium, 1996.
2. Commission of the European Communities. Council Directive 1999/74/EC laying down minimum standards for the protection of laying hens. Off. J. Euro. Communities August 3, 1999, 203, 53–57.
3. Commission of the European Communities. Amendment 1943/85 to Regulation 95/69, also amended by 927/69 and 2502171. Off. J. Euro. Communities July 13, 1985.

Chickens: Layer Nutrition Management

Robert H. Harms
University of Florida, Gainesville, Florida, U.S.A.

INTRODUCTION

As established by Bell and Weaver in 2002, ''during the past two centuries more than 300 breeds and varieties of chickens have been developed, however, few have survived commercialization and are used by modern chicken breeders.'' Commercially, laying hens are kept for the production of table eggs, and broiler breeder hens are kept to produce eggs for hatching baby chicks to grow for meat (broilers).

In order for hens to maintain maximum performance, they must receive a certain amount of each nutrient each day. Earlier, many producers offered their hens three or more ingredients in separate feeders. Hens had these feeds before them at all times. However, other producers felt they could do a better job meeting hens' needs by regulating the amount of grain and concentrate they were allowed each day.

As a result of much research, it was possible to establish the hen's requirement for each nutrient. With this knowledge, it is now possible for the nutritionist to combine various feedstuffs into one mash, which contains all of the nutrients that are needed. The mash feed gave good performance, and the mash–grain system of feeding was no longer used.

SUGGESTED DAILY NUTRIENT REQUIREMENTS

The National Research Council,[1] a committee of poultry nutritionists, has published suggested daily requirements for commercial layers and broiler feeder hens (Table 1). The requirements for the commercial layers are reported as a percentage of the diet when the hen consumed 100 grams of feed. For this article, the requirements have been changed to the daily intake. This makes it possible to compare the requirements of hens that are used for two different purposes. All of the requirements are higher for the broiler breeder hen than for the commercial egg layer.

The laying hen does not have a requirement for crude protein per se. She needs 22 amino acids, but requires specific amounts of the 10 listed in Table 1 to be present in the feed. However, there should be sufficient crude protein in the feed to ensure an adequate supply of nonessential amino acids.

Synthetic Amino Acids Routinely Used

The protein content of the feed can be reduced when synthetic amino acids are used, and they are routinely used in feed for commercial egg layers. Five amino acids are commercially available. A daily intake of 15 grams of protein is suggested for the commercial egg layer. However, a lower level is used in the commercial industry when the feed is formulated to meet the hen's amino acid requirement. Supplemental methionine has been used routinely since the early 1960s.

Considerably less research has been conducted with the broiler breeder hen than with the egg layer. Therefore, the NRC[1] recommends that the breeder feed contain 19.5% protein. Prior to 1977, the National Research Council[1] suggested requirements be expressed as a percentage of the diet. However, in 1977, they suggested a daily intake based on a feed consumption of 100 grams per day.

In 1978, a program was developed to formulate a feed to meet the daily requirements of the laying hen.[2] Recommendations were for a daily intake of 610 mg of sulfur amino acids and 730 mg of lysine. These researchers conducted many experiments on the energy and amino acid requirements of the commercial egg layer, and they developed a new formula for calculating the percentage of each amino acid needed for each flock of hens.[3]

Formula for Calculating Flock Requirement

Information needed for this calculation is shown in Table 2. Other measurements needed can be calculated: egg mass (EM), energy intake (EI), and energy/gram of egg mass.

Following is the formula to calculate the percentage of methionine needed in the feed. The percentage of other amino acids can be calculated by substituting their constants for the methionine constant, which is 5.4. Lysine has a constant of 12.2, and tryptophan has a constant of 3.2.

$$\frac{5.4}{\text{EI/EM}} \times \text{EI} \div \text{FI} = \text{percent needed in diet}$$

Encyclopedia of Animal Science
DOI: 10.1081/E-EAS 120019535

Table 1 Daily nutrient requirements of commercial egg layer and broiler breeder hens

| Nutrient | Unit[a] | Daily intake | |
		Commercial egg layers	Broiler breeder hen
Protein	g	15.0	19.5
Arginine	mg	750	1,110
Histidine	mg	170	205
Isoleucine	mg	650	850
Leucine	mg	850	1,250
Lysine	mg	690	765
Methionine	mg	300	450
Phenylalanine	mg	470	610
Threonine	mg	470	720
Tryptophan	mg	160	190
Valine	mg	700	750
Calcium	g	3.25	4.0
Nonphytate phosphorus	mg	250	350
Sodium	mg	150	150
Chloride	mg	130	185

[a]Requirements have been changed from % to mg for comparison between hens.
(Requirements for trace minerals and vitamins are given in Ref. 1.)

$$\frac{5.4}{4.941} \times 273 \div 95269 = 0.310\%$$

High Intake of Calcium Needed

A daily intake of 3.25 and 4.0% calcium is recommended for the commercial egg layer and broiler breeder hen, respectively.[4] This high intake of calcium is necessary for the hen to form a strong eggshell. The hen gets most of its calcium from the feed. However, a large amount of calcium during shell formation comes from medullary bone.

Cracked eggs as a result of thin shells is often a problem. Approximately one-half of the calcium used comes from the bone and the other half comes from the feed. The eggshell is formed throughout the night and the hen's body becomes calcium deficient. A procedure for feeding the hen at midnight has been found to be beneficial for improving eggshell quality.[5]

It has been suggested[4] that one-half to two-thirds of the dietary calcium supplement should be in the form of large-flaked oyster shell or coarse limestone (>1.0 mm; average 2.5 mm diameter). However, not all nutritionists agree that this management procedure is beneficial. One of the ingredients should be offered to the hen if the feed does not contain sufficient calcium.

Sodium Bicarbonate Improves Eggshells

The substitution of sodium biocarbonate ($NaHCO_3$) for a portion of the salt (NaCl) is often beneficial for improving eggshell strength. Many experiments were conducted to measure the potential benefits of this practice. It was assumed that the CO_3 from the $NaHCO_3$ was useful in deposition of calcium ($CaCO_3$) in the eggshell. However, it was found that sodium reduced the plasma phosphorus and was responsible for improving eggshells.[6]

Phosphorus Level Is Reduced as Hen Ages

The National Research Council[4] recommends that the commercial egg layer have a daily intake of 250 mg of nonphytate phosphorus. They recommend 350 mg intake for the broiler breeder hen, but indicate that adequate data are not available to support this recommendation.

Most nutritionists formulate the feed for a commercial egg layer to furnish considerably more than the

Table 2 Measurement for calculation of the percentage of methionine needed in the feed

Measurements needed	Unit	Assumed value
Feed intake FI	lb	0.21 (95,269 g mg)
Dietary energy ME	lb/kg	2,860
Egg production EP	%	85.00
Egg weight EW	g	65.00
Methionine/g egg mass	(mg)	5.4[a]
Egg mass EM	(EP × EW)	55.25
Energy intake EI	(ME ÷ FI)	273
Energy/g egg mass	(EI/EM)	4.941

[a]This is the requirement based on previous experimental data.

recommended 250 mg. The Florida researchers[5] recommended a decreasing intake of 650, 550, and 450 mg of total phosphorus as the hen aged. The highest level of phosphorus was recommended for the first 16 weeks of lay, for prevention of cage layer fatigue. Lowering the phosphorus after 53 weeks of lay is for the improvement of eggshell quality. Recently, the trend has been to feed lower levels of phosphorus. This is a result of the emphasis on decreasing the level of phosphorus in the environment.

ENERGY REQUIREMENTS DIFFER FOR LAYER AND BROILER BREEDERS

The commercial egg layer has been selected to efficiently produce eggs. Therefore, it eats feed to meet its daily energy requirement. Factors such as temperature, energy content of the feed, breed as strain of the hen, and rate of egg production affect this requirement. The energy-to-amino acid (methionine) ratio in the Harms-Faria formula[3] makes corrections for these differences. The hen adjusts her feed intake to compensate for differences in energy content of the diet. There is a 1% increase in feed intake for each 14 kCal per pound decrease in ME content of the diet.[7] The broiler breeder does not have the ability to control feed intake for efficient egg production. Therefore, her feed intake (energy) must be controlled to control body weight. She must be weighed at regular intervals to attain this goal.

Manipulation of Egg Weight by Dietary Changes

The addition of fat to the diet will increase egg weight.[8] Corn oil and soybean oil are slightly superior to other fats for this purpose. It is very beneficial to increase egg weight with young hens because the price of large eggs is greater than medium eggs. When eggs become larger than desired, the fat can be removed from the feed and egg weight will be reduced.

The hen requires more energy as egg weight is increased. This increases the cost of producing eggs when they weigh more than desired. Reduction of the amino acid content of the diet may be used for lowering these egg weights. This requires accurate records on feed intake, egg weight, and rate of lay.

YOLK COLOR IS AFFECTED BY CAROTENOIDS

For many years, the color of the egg yolk was determined by naturally occurring carotenoids furnished by alfalfa and yellow corn. Other sources of pigment were later obtained from marigold flowers. In 1957, pure carotenoid substances were synthesized. The use of beta-apo-8[1] carotenoid produced a pleasing yellow color, but canthaxanthin produced an orange-to-red color that was not acceptable. It was reported[9] that different combinations of these compounds could be used to produce any desired color.[9] These researchers suggested that desired yolk color could be produced by blending feeds with known xanthophyl concentrations.

SUMMARY

The feed for laying hens should be formulated to meet their daily nutrient requirements as suggested by the National Research Council.[1] A formula has been developed to calculate the percentage of each amino acid needed in the hens' feed.[3] Synthetic amino acids are routinely used in hen feeds.

The feed should contain adequate amounts of calcium, phosphorus, vitamins, and trace minerals (Table 1).

REFERENCES

1. Bell, D.D.; Weaver, W.D. *Commercial Egg Production*; Kluven Academic Publishers: Norwell, MA 02061, 2002.
2. National Research Council. *Nutrient Requirements of Poultry*, 9th Rev. Ed.; National Academy Press: Washington, DC, 1994.
3. Harms, R.H.; Douglas, C.R.; Christmas, R.B.; Damron, B.L.; Miles, R.D. Feeding commercial layers for maximum performance. Feedstuffs **1978**, *50* (8), 23–24.
4. Harms, R.H.; Faria, D.E. Energy and amino acids in layers: time to evaluate. Feed Manage. **2001**, *52* (10), 28–30.
5. Harms, R.H.; Douglas, C.R.; Sloan, D.R. Midnight feeding of commercial laying hens can improve eggshell quality. J. Appl. Poultry Res. **1996**, *5*, 1–5.
6. Miles, R.D.; Harms, R.H. Relationship between egg specific gravity and plasma phosphorus from hens fed different dietary calcium, phosphorus and sodium levels. Poultry Sci. **1982**, *61*, 175–177.
7. Hill, F.W.; Anderson, D.L.; Dansky, L.M. Studies of the energy requirements of chickens. The effect of dietary level on the rate and gross efficiency of egg production. Poultry Sci. **1956**, *35*, 1037–1042.
8. Harms, R.H.; Sloan, D.R. Manipulating egg weight through management and nutrition. Feed Manage. **2003**, *53* (10).
9. Fletcher, D.L.; Harms, R.H.; Janky, D.M. Yolk color characteristics, xanthophyll availability and a model system for predicting egg yolk color using beta-apo-8[1] carotenal and xanthaxanthin. Poultry Sci. **1978**, *57*, 624–629.

Chickens: Layer Reproduction Management

Kenneth E. Anderson
North Carolina State University, Raleigh, North Carolina, U.S.A.

INTRODUCTION

Management needs for layers have been constantly changing as a result of the genetic selection for improved productivity practiced by the egg-type poultry breeding companies. Productivity changes are well documented in strain performance reports from layer random sample tests and management reports. Changing physiological needs for optimal reproduction have been met by improvements in health care, housing, and nutrition. Layer reproductive management can be controlled during the course of physiological development through the use of pullet and layer phase lighting programs, body weight-management programs, and environmental temperature control.

LIGHT MANAGEMENT

A good light-management program is important for maximization of laying hen productivity, since it is a means of controlling the hen's behavior, metabolism, physical activity, productivity, and egg size by advancing or retarding the onset of egg production.[1] Lighting program recommendations vary slightly depending on house type, season, latitude of the farm, and layer breed, but there are components that are common to all. These components will determine the lighting program components of the rearing and laying periods, including the pattern of light and dark periods, intensity, and bird age at stimulation. Regardless of the house type, the light duration should not increase during the first 14 weeks of the pullet flock's life. In fact, pullets should be grown on decreasing day lengths (Fig. 1).

Three components of a lighting program can influence the light threshold, which is the intensity or duration of light perceived by the pullet. The first component is the light intensity. Pullets should be reared in light intensities ranging from 0.5 ft candle (fc) (5 lux) to 1 fc (10 lux). The second component, the wavelength of the light source (photons), is important for the ability of the pullet to perceive the light intensity. Different light sources used in today's poultry houses emit light of differing photon outputs, which impacts the intensity perceived by the hen.[2] Therefore, to understand and equalize these components of light ensure that the birds are receiving the proper light intensity. The third component, duration of the light period, is designed to optimize the physiological development of the pullet during the rearing period prior to the onset of egg production. The sexual maturity of the pullets is delayed by restricting the duration of the light period to below a threshold of 11–12 hours of light. Pullets must then be exposed to increased day lengths during the latter stage of the rearing period to stimulate ovary and oviduct development. When the pullet's body weight meets the target for the strain, the maximum day length must be increased past the threshold of 14 hours to stimulate the onset of reproduction and ovulation by 18 weeks (Fig. 2). The hen is usually limited to a maximum day length of 16 to 17 hours, depending on the laying house type and the latitude, which determines the longest, day length. The maximum day length used must be as long as the longest natural day length for the area, including one-half hour before sunrise and one-half hour after sunset on June 21, for northern latitudes. Day length must not decrease during the laying phases, or the hens will react by reducing or stopping production.

The use of molting as a management tool also includes the use of a specific lighting program to take the birds out of and then return them to production. Generally, the day length is reduced to 8 hours at the initiation of the molt, resulting in the cessation of production. Regardless of the molting program, the utilization of increased day length followed by an immediate reduction in day length facilitates the cessation of egg production and initiation of the resting period.

BODY WEIGHT MANAGEMENT

Body weight management comes into play at two critical periods during the life of a flock of laying hens, specifically the rearing and the molt periods. During the rearing period it is important to manage the nutrition, vaccination, beak trimming, house ventilation, and general management program so that the pullets meet the recommended body weight for the strain.[3] With the modern layer strains this process can be management-intensive, because it is not recommended to feed-restrict

Encyclopedia of Animal Science
DOI: 10.1081/E-EAS 120019536

225

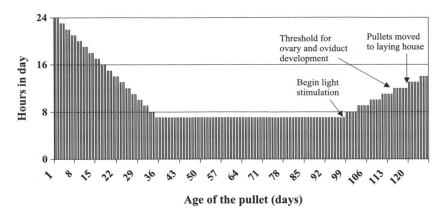

Fig. 1 Step-down/step-up lighting program for replacement pullets in light facilities. (Figure courtesy of Ref. [3].) (*View this art in color at www.dekker.com.*)

the pullets during the rearing period. Therefore, random samples of pullets should be weighed each week to ensure that body weight targets are met throughout the growing period.

Body weight is generally controlled through changes in diet formulation, altering the duration of feeding phases during the pullet-rearing period, or modifications in the lighting program (intensity and day-length), thereby controlling the protein and energy intake. The third factor that affects growth rate is ambient temperature. Low temperatures will cause overeating, and high temperatures can cause reduced consumption of nutrients. Maintaining a thermal neutral temperature (55–75°F) after the initial brooding period usually results in the best growth rate and productivity of layer flocks. Continuous monitoring of pullet body weights is important, because a dietary or management change to control body weight should be made quickly to maintain the flock's recommended average hen weight.

The impact of a dietary or management change may not manifest itself until 3 to 4 weeks later. Thus, one needs to be familiar with the strain characteristics and have an understanding of how pullets grow in the facilities being used. Another component of body weight is the uniformity of pullet body weights within the flock. A uniform flock (high percentage of the pullet weights falling within ±10% of the mean weight) is one of the best indicators of pullet quality, and flocks with good uniformity have a greater probability of meeting their genetic potential for egg production and feed conversion. Crowding, stress, improper feeder and waterer space allocations, improper nutrition, and disease are some of the factors that can have a negative impact on uniformity.

Molting is the second critical period of body weight management for laying hens. Molting is used as a management tool in the egg industry to extend the productive life of the laying hens over a longer period of time, or to improve egg production and quality during

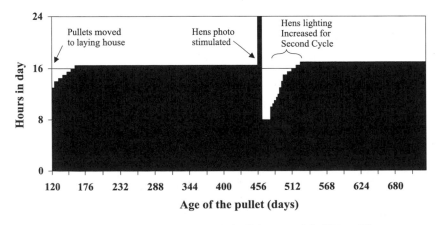

Fig. 2 Step-up lighting program for laying hens, including the molt, in light control facilities. (Figure courtesy of Ref. [3].) (*View this art in color at www.dekker.com.*)

Table 1 Ambient temperature influence on heat stress

55° to 75°F (13° to 24°C)	Thermal neutral zone: the temperature range in which the bird does not need to alter its basic metabolic rate or behavior to maintain its body temperature.
65° to 75°F (18° to 24°C)	Ideal temperature range.
75° to 85°F (24° to 29°C)	A slight reduction in feed consumption can be expected, but if nutrient intake is adequate, production efficiency is good. Egg size may be reduced and shell quality may suffer as temperatures reach the top of this range.
85° to 90°F (29° to 32°C)	Feed consumption falls further. Weight gains are lower. Egg size and shell quality deteriorate. Egg production usually suffers. Cooling procedures should be started before this temperature range is reached.
90° to 95°F (32° to 35°C)	Feed consumption continues to drop. There is some danger of heat prostration among layers, especially the heavier birds and those in full production. At these temperatures, cooling procedures must be carried out.
95° to 100°F (35° to 38°C)	Heat prostration is probable. Emergency measures may be needed. Egg production and feed consumption are severely reduced. Water consumption escalates.
Over 100°F (38°C)	Emergency measures are needed to cool birds. Survival is the concern at these temperatures.

(Table courtesy of Ref. [8].)

periods of high demand.[4] In addition, molting improves the overall health of the flock.[5] The key to a successful molting program is the rapid cessation of egg production and a uniform body weight loss during the molt. Body weight loss and subsequent performance of the flock are dependent upon the strain of the birds being molted. The various commercial laying stocks respond differently to the amount of body weight loss between 25 and 35% that ensures optimal production in the second cycle. If the weight loss is in excess of 35%, mortality may increase beyond acceptable limits and the productivity of the flock may be impaired.

TEMPERATURE CONTROL

The layer industry uses air exchange and air velocity in designing ventilation systems to control temperature. In addition, the thermal neutral zone upper limit has been expanded to 85°F (29°C) in older flocks that are producing heavier eggs (Table 1). This higher temperature means that the hens consume less feed and require less energy to maintain their body temperature and productivity. Precise environmental temperature control enhances the hens' ability to regulate sensible and insensible heat loss and cope with the higher temperatures used by

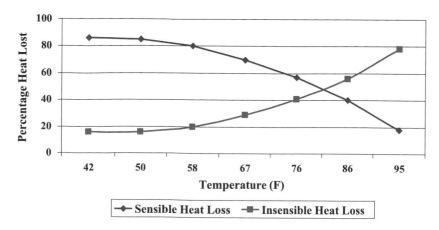

Fig. 3 Sensible (conductance) and insensible (evaporative) heat loss from birds as environmental temperatures increase. (Figure courtesy of Ref. [8].) (*View this art in color at www.dekker.com.*)

producers.[6] Heat loss by the birds gradually shifts from sensible (conductance) heat loss during the cool seasons to insensible (evaporative), as the ambient environmental temperatures increase in the summer (Fig. 3). Air exchanges regulate temperature, humidity, dust, and ammonia throughout the year to keep the hen in the range of sensible heat loss mechanisms. This provides for improvements in feed conversions since the hen requires fewer calories for body temperature homeostasis, thereby releasing energy for egg production. Air velocity is important during the hot season, because environmental temperatures can exceed 85°F (29°C). Insensible heat loss methods require more energy input by the hen because of panting, resulting in depressed feed consumption, reduced egg size, and subsequently reduced production. However, air velocity increases the sensible heat loss capabilities of the hen via a wind chill effect, which helps maintain the balance between sensible and insensible heat loss. The development of highly nutrient-dense diets has been key for the utilization of higher environmental temperatures, using the upper limits of sensible heat loss methods so the birds can optimize feed conversion.

CONCLUSION

Good management is important for the changing laying hen's reproduction as documented in management reports.[5,7,8] Light, body weight, and environmental management components have the potential to control the hen's growth, behavior, metabolism, physical activity, productivity, egg size, as well as advancing or retarding the onset of egg production. Light programs, temperature control, and body weight control all interact during the rearing and the molt periods in the life of a flock of laying hens. The poultry industry continues to push the upper limits of environmental temperatures, which impacts the growth, productivity, and house environment. This is done to enhance the hen's ability to utilize feeds, nutrients, and energy, thereby enhancing subsequent hen welfare and production performance.

REFERENCES

1. Wineland, M.J. Fundamentals of Managing Light for Poultry. In *Commercial Chicken Meat and Egg Production*, 5th Ed.; Bell, D.D., Weaver, W.D., Eds.; Kluwer Academic Publishers: Norwell, MA, 2002; 129–148.
2. Wineland, M.J.; Siopes, T.D. A comparison of light intensity measurements of different light sources. J. Appl. Poult. Res. **1992**, *1*, 287–290.
3. Bell, D.D. Cage Management for Raising Replacement Pullets. In *Commercial Chicken Meat and Egg Production*, 5th Ed.; Bell, D.D., Weaver, W.D., Eds.; Kluwer Academic Publishers: Norwell, MA, 2002; 993–1000.
4. Carey, J.B.; Brake, J.T. Induced Molting of Commercial Layers. In *Poultry Science and Technology Guide*; North Carolina State University, Agricultural Extension Service, Dept. of Poultry Science: Raleigh, NC, 1989; Vol. 30.
5. Anderson, K.E.; Carter, T.A. Hot Weather Management of Poultry. In *Poultry Science and Technology Guide*; North Carolina Cooperative Extension Service: Raleigh, NC, 1993; Vol. 30.
6. Anderson, K.E. *Final Report of the Thirty Fourth North Carolina Layer Performance and Management Test: Production Report*; North Carolina State University, North Carolina Cooperative Extension Service, Dept. of Poultry Science: Raleigh, NC, 2002; Vol. 34, No. 4.
7. Martin, G.A. *Report of the First North Carolina Random Sample Egg Laying Test*; North Carolina State University, Agricultural Extension Service, Dept. of Poultry Science: Raleigh, NC, 1960; Vol. 1, No. 4.
8. Carey, J.B. *Final Report of the Twenty-Sixth North Carolina Layer Performance and Management Test*; North Carolina State University, Agricultural Extension Service, Dept. of Poultry Science: Raleigh, NC, 1987; Vol. 26, No. 4.

Colostrum

P. T. Sangild
Royal Veterinary and Agricultural University, Frederiksberg, Denmark

R. J. Xu
University of Hong Kong, Hong Kong, China

INTRODUCTION

Before birth, the fetus is well protected by the maternal placenta, which delivers all essential nutrients to the fetus but blocks the transfer of most harmful substances. At birth, this protection ends abruptly and the newborn must absorb essential nutrients from milk. At the same time, the newborn encounters numerous harmful antigens and microorganisms from its new environment. Fortunately, the mother continues to provide the newborn some protection via milk secretion from the mammary glands, particularly via the first milk, colostrum. This fluid provides the newborn not only essential nutrients, but also a specific intake of various bioactive substances that facilitate the adaptation of the newborn to life outside the mother. This article summarizes the composition and biological effects of colostrum based mainly on data from the pig. The information would apply also for other large farm-animal species (e.g., cattle, sheep, horse), but may differ from that of species not entirely dependent on colostrum ingestion for neonatal adaptation and transfer of passive immunity from mother to offspring.

COLOSTRUM COMPOSITION

The initiation of mammary secretion (lactogenesis) consists of two stages.[1] The first stage takes place before birth and is characterized by accumulation of yellow, viscous, serumlike colostrum in the mammary glands. The second stage of lactogenesis takes place at or shortly after birth and is characterized by active synthesis of lactose in the mammary glands. Different secretory mechanisms of colostrum and milk are reflected in their chemical compositions (Tables 1 and 2).

Although wide species differences in colostrum composition exist, colostrum is generally more nutrient-dense and richer in bioactive compounds than mature milk. As shown in Table 1, colostrum contains much more protein than milk. The protein in colostrum consists mainly of immunoglobulins (Table 2). The immunoglobulins are further divided into three subgroups, i.e., Immunoglobulin G (IgG), Immunoglobulin A (IgA), and Immunoglobulin M (IgM). In colostrum, IgG is the predominant immunoglobulin, whereas in milk IgA is the predominant immunoglobulin. In addition to immunoglobulins, colostrum contains various anti-infection agents (e.g., lactoferrin, lysozyme, lactoperoxidase, live lymphocytes, and oligosaccharides), digestive enzymes (e.g., lipase and amylase), hormones (e.g., insulin and cortisol), growth factors [e.g., epidermal growth factor (EGF), insulin-like growth factor I (IGF-I), insulin-like growth factor II (IGF-II), transforming growth factor (TGF)-β1, and TGF-β2], and other bioactive peptides. More detailed analyses of colostrum composition can be found in the references listed at the end of this article.

EFFECTS OF COLOSTRAL IMMUNOGLOBULINS AND ANTI-INFECTIOUS AGENTS

The immune defense is immature in newborn animals, which depend on passive immunization from their mothers. Transmission of passive immunity from mother to young varies among different species (Table 3). In certain species (e.g., primates and rabbits) passive immunity is passed from the mother to the young through the placenta before birth. However, in most farm-animal species (e.g., cattle, sheep, pig, and horse), the newborn depends on the intestinal transmission of colostral immunoglobulins and other immunity-modulating factors for passive immune protection. Besides immunoglobulins, colostrum contains neutrophils, lymphocytes, cytokines, nucleotides, and various growth factors, and these colostrum-borne immune factors may affect the development of the immune system in the suckling young.

The ability of intestinal cells to take up macromolecules by endocytosis and to transport these molecules intact across the epithelium into the bloodstream is one of the most striking and unique features of the developing

Encyclopedia of Animal Science
DOI: 10.1081/E-EAS 120019537

Table 1 Nutrient composition of swine colostrum[a] and milk[b]

Nutritient composition (per 100 ml)	Colostrum	Milk
Total dry matter (g)	24.8	18.7
Total protein (g)	15.1	5.5
Casein (g)	1.3	2.6
Whey (g)	13.7	2.9
Lactose (g)	3.4	5.3
Total fat (g)	5.9	7.6
Palmitic acid (16:0, g)	2.0	2.8
Palmitoleic acid (16:1, g)	0.3	0.6
Stearic acid (18:0, g)	0.4	0.5
Oleic acid (18:1, g)	2.2	2.5
Linoleic acid (18:2, g)	0.7	0.8
Vitamin A (µg)	170	100
Vitamin D (µg)	1.5	0.9
Vitamin E (µg)	380	260
Vitamin K (µg)	9.5	9.2
Vitamin C (mg)	7.2	4.7
Total ash (g)	0.7	0.9
Calcium (mg)	71	184
Phosphorus (mg)	105	139
Potassium (mg)	113	82
Magnesium (mg)	8	10
Sodium (mg)	71	43

[a]Immediately after birth.
[b]2–4 weeks postpartum.
(Data adapted from Ref. 1.)

intestine in large farm-animal species.[3] The endocytosis of macromolecules by the developing intestine is facilitated by species-specific and nutrient-independent factors in colostrum. The endocytotic capacity of the developing intestine in most farm-animal species reaches a maximum at the time of birth or a few days before

Table 2 Some bioactive compounds in swine colostrum and milk

Bioactive compounds (per 100 ml)	Colostrum	Milk
Serum albumin (g)	1.46	0.45
IgG (g)	8.9	0.1
IgA (g)	2.0	0.6
IgM (g)	0.85	0.15
Lactoferrin (mg)	120	40
EGF (µg)	157	19
IGF-I (µg)	40	1
IGF-II (µg)	29	2
Insulin (µg)	1.5	0.2
TGF-β1 (µg)	4.3	0.2
TGF-β2 (µg)	2.0	0.4

(Data adapted from Ref. 1.)

Table 3 Species differences in passive immunity transmission from mother to young in some mammals

Species	Before birth via placenta	After birth via the gut
Horse, pig, ox, goat, sheep	0	+++ (12–24 h)
Wallaby	0	+++ (180 d)
Dog, cat	+	++ (1–2 d)
Mouse	+	++ (16 d)
Rat	+	++ (20 d)
Guinea pig, human, monkey	+++	0

0 = no transfer; +, ++, +++ = variable degree of transfer.
(Data modified from Ref. 2.)

birth.[3] At this time, the uptake of macromolecules by the newborn animal does not merely result from a degree of intestinal immaturity but reflects a specific maturational process.

The ability to absorb macromolecules ceases within the first day or two after birth by a process known as intestinal closure. In some species (e.g., rat, mouse, ferret), intestinal closure is delayed until several weeks after birth. In humans, only the fetal small intestine has the characteristics required for the uptake of intact immunoglobulins. The signals to induce gut closure vary among species and may involve colostral and systemic factors, as well as the maturity of the gut epithelium itself.

Immunoglobulin G in colostrum provides to the newborn systemic protection against bacterial and viral infections. Newborn animals fed colostrum generally have better growth performance and survival rates than counterparts fed artificial milk replacer.[3,4] Colostrum from the same species provides stronger immunological protection than colostrum from different species.[4] Because antigen specificity of immunoglobulins determines the degree of protection, it is not surprising that immunoglobulins obtained from one species cannot provide notable passive immunity against pathogens in another species. However, experimental evidence indicates that colostrum contains nutrients and bioactive compounds other than immunoglobulins to stimulate gut maturation and disease resistance in newborn animals. The shift from IgG dominance in colostrum to IgA dominance in milk reflects the change in the need of the neonatal animal, as passive immunization through intestinal absorption of immunoglobulins gives way to local immune protection within the gastrointestinal tract. IgA is linked to a glycoprotein and secreted into milk as an assembled molecule, secretory IgA. One of the major functions of secretory IgA is to block the adhesion of microbial pathogens onto the intestinal epithelial surface. Another important function of secretoty IgA is to bind and neutralize bacterial toxins and food antigens.

Secretory IgA in milk is important to the suckling young, as adequate endogenous production of secretory IgA does not occur until later in life.

Lactoferrin with bactericidal activity is another important anti-infectious agent in colostrum. It suppresses bacterial growth through competition for iron; the latter is an important nutrient for enteric bacteria. Lactoferrin also binds directly to bacterial surfaces, causing damage to the cell wall and eventually cell death. In addition to the antibiotic effect, milkborne lactoferrin may also facilitate iron absorption via a receptor-mediated mechanism. High-affinity lactoferrin-binding sites have been detected on the brush border membrane of the epithelial cells along the small intestine in newborn animals. Bacteriostatic effects have also been reported for lysozyme and lactoperoxidase, which are present in colostrum. Colostrumborne cytokines (e.g., TGF-β) may also play an important role in modulating immune function in the neonatal gut. Oral administration of TGF-β in neonatal animals inhibits immune response to oral challenge with antigens. It is believed that colostrumborne TGF-β facilitates oral food tolerance in suckling animals. Furthermore, colostrum contains live leukocytes including neutrophils and macrophages, which are capable of phagocytosis and can produce host resistance factors, such as lysozyme, lactoferrin, and complement components. Lymphocytes found in colostrum consist primarily of T cells with specific surface markers. Such T cells with specific memory are thought to be one of the mechanisms whereby a suckling neonate benefits from its mother's immunological experience.

EFFECTS OF COLOSTRAL GROWTH FACTORS

The small intestine of a newborn grows at an enormous rate (with an increase in weight of 50–80% over 1–2 days) following the onset of suckling.[3] Although such rapid increase in intestinal tissue mass is largely due to the transient retention of colostral immunoglobulins, there is evidence to show that the growth is partially stimulated by colostrumborne growth factors.[5,6] Oral administration of EGF or IGF stimulates intestinal epithelial cell proliferation in neonatal animals. In addition to the trophic effect, colostrumborne growth factors also affect intestinal functions, including digestive enzyme activity and nutrient absorption. The effects of colostrumborne growth factors are particularly pronounced in immature or growth-retarded newborn animals. In addition, colostrum or colostrumborne growth factors may have beneficial effects on the traumatized or diseased gut in older animals.[7] Hence, it has been reported that oral administration of colostral extract or EGF minimizes intestinal tissue damage and reduces bacterial translocation in rotavirus-infected animals.

CONCLUSION

Colostrum differs from milk both chemically and functionally. It provides to the suckling young not only essential nutrients, but also various bioactive substances. These substances protect the suckling young from various infectious agents and also modulate gastrointestinal growth and functional maturation. Many studies have documented the importance of colostrum ingestion for the growth, health, and survival of newborn animals. There is potential for therapeutic application of colostrum, colostral extracts, or colostrumborne growth factors in the treatment of patients with traumatized or diseased digestive systems in both humans and farm animals.

REFERENCES

1. Xu, R.J. Composition of Porcine Milk. In *The Neonatal Pig: Gastrointestinal Physiology and Nutrition*; Xu, R.J., Cranwell, P.D., Eds.; Nottingham University Press: United Kingdom, 2003; 213–246.
2. Brambell, F.W.R. *The Transmission of Passive Immunity from Mother to Young*; Elsevier: New York, 1970.
3. Sangild, P.T. Uptake of colostral immunoglobulins by the compromised newborn farm animal. Acta Vet. Scand. **2003**, *98* (suppl.), 1–18.
4. Gomez, G.G.; Phillips, O.; Goforth, R.A. Effect of immunoglobulin source on survival, growth and hematological and immunological variables in pigs. J. Anim. Sci. **1998**, *76*, 1–7.
5. Sangild, P.T. Transitions in the Life of the Gut at Birth. In *Digestive Physiology of Pigs*; Lindberg, J.E., Odle, B., Eds.; CAB International: Wallingford, United Kingdom, 2001; 3–17.
6. Xu, R.J.; Sangild, P.T.; Zhang, Y.Q.; Zhang, S.H. Bioactive Compounds in Colostrum and Milk and Their Effects on Intestinal Development in Neonatal Pigs. In *Biology of the Small Intestine in Growing Animals*; Zabielski, R., Lesnewski, V., Weström, B.R., Pierzynowski, S.R., Eds.; Elsevier: Amsterdam, 2002; 169–192.
7. Playford, R.J.; Macdonald, C.E.; Johnson, W.S. Colostrum and milk-derived peptide growth factors for the treatment of gastrointestinal disorders. Am. J. Clin. Nutr. **2000**, *72*, 5–14.

Competition for Land Use: Agricultural/Urban Interface

Charles W. Abdalla
The Pennsylvania State University, University Park, Pennsylvania, U.S.A.

INTRODUCTION

The agricultural–urban interface is the boundary between rural/agricultural and urban/suburban areas. In rapidly changing areas, competition for land can produce land use patterns at this interface that result in costly conflicts and policy dilemmas. The factors underlying the urbanization and development process are well understood. Numerous public and private strategies are available to prevent or reduce rural–urban conflict. Despite these efforts, agricultural/rural issues remain. With industrialization of the food system, they have become a more critical public policy issue.

COMPETITION FOR LAND USE IN THE UNITED STATES

Evidence of urbanization and the competition for farmland in the United States can be gleaned from the National Resource Inventory (NRI). For the five years prior to 1997, about 11.2 million acres of land were converted to urban uses, with about 3.2 million of that being prime farmland. The urbanization of land is concentrated in a relatively few states. More than 50% of the converted land was in Texas (894K acres), Georgia (852K), Florida (553K), California (553K), Pennsylvania (545K), North Carolina (507K), Tennessee (401K), Ohio (365K), Michigan (364K), South Carolina (362K), and Virginia (344K).[1]

Each year about 645,000 acres of prime farmland are being developed. More than 50% of this conversion is occurring in the top ten states. Texas leads the nation in annual prime farmland conversion with 67,000 acres, followed by Ohio (42K) North Carolina (34K), and Illinois (32K). While the NRI data shows that considerable farmland is being converted to developed uses each year, it does not reflect that development breaks land into fragmented units that may be uneconomic to farm. One indicator of the fragmentation problem is the significant growth in residential/lifestyle farms. These farms represent 40% of total farms in the 1998 Census of Agriculture. While important to land use patterns in many states, they account for 6% of total sales. For these farms, off-farm employment is critical to income stability. Growth in these farm types means interaction between farmers and nonfarmers at the rural–urban interface. More farmers depend on outside jobs and more urbanites have direct contact with farming.[1] This type of farming—and the accompanying rural–urban interface issues—may become more important.

URBANIZATION AND SPRAWL

Population expansion into rural areas is known as urbanization. This process uses agricultural, forest, and other lands. The quantity and rate of conversion of these rural areas into urban land uses affect many national, state, and local concerns, including adequacy of food and fiber production, economic development, environmental quality, public infrastructure, open-space amenities, rural lifestyles and ethnic patterns, and natural ecosystems.[2]

Uncontrolled urban development at the edges of cities and rural areas has been termed sprawl. Most definitions of sprawl include dispersed low-density development that uses a lot of land; geographic separation of work, home, schools, shopping, etc.; and almost complete dependence on the automobile for transportation.[3] Recently, concerns about negative consequences of sprawl have grown considerably. These concerns include public infrastructure costs, hidden costs of public services not included in residential taxes, property value impacts, traffic congestion, longer commutes, environmental impacts, changes in community structure, and quality of life.[4]

The processes underlying urbanization and the resulting development patterns at the rural–urban interface are well understood. Changes in land use are the final product of many forces affecting millions of decisions by homeowners, businesses, and government. The fundamental drivers of these decisions and, hence, land use change are population growth, household formation, and economic development.[3]

Observers of urbanization over the last decade have noted two distinctive kinds of urban development. In one case, existing urban areas continue to grow into surrounding rural areas. In another, large-lot housing developments are being built in areas beyond the rural–urban fringe.[3] Both kinds of development influence the amount and productivity of farmland. At this point there is

Encyclopedia of Animal Science
DOI: 10.1081/E-EAS 120019538

no threat that insufficient land will be available nationally for food and fiber production.[3,4] However, high-value or speciality crops in some areas may be vulnerable as urbanization continues. Also, farming can adapt in rapidly urbanizing areas, but producers often must change the mix of products they offer in order to survive.[3]

Urbanization provides benefits and costs to rural areas. A key factor affecting competition for land at the rural–urban fringe is citizens' preferences to live in lower-density areas and cheaper homes located within reasonable commutes from their jobs. Unplanned development imposes direct costs in terms of higher infrastructure and public service costs and adverse impacts on the environment and community structure, in addition to indirect costs of the forgone uses of the developed land.[3]

INDUSTRIALIZATION OF AGRICULTURE

Current controversies at the rural–urban interface are a result of ongoing changes in the U.S. food and agricultural system brought about by industrialization.[4–6] Industrialization is driven by firms seeking profits available through lowering their costs by adoption of new technologies for farm production and through marketing and greater specialization. At the farm level, these changing technological and economic factors are telling farmers to either "get big or get out."[6] The industrialization of U.S. agriculture is bringing about much change and giving rise to new concerns. In animal agriculture, the concentration of animals on fewer, larger farms and new marketing arrangements are changing the scale and location of farming.[5] Larger animal production units are increasingly leading to conflicts between producers and neighbors, and communities are faced with many possible environmental or nuisance (e.g., noise, odors) threats.[7]

In addition to the potential costs from industrialization, there are benefits of agriculture to local communities. The substitution of off-farm for on-farm inputs (e.g., feed, labor) may mean that agriculture in some areas provides less benefit to the local economy in terms of employment and farm-related purchases. Also, some amenities, such as open space valued by neighbors, may be lost as production intensifies. Industrialization may raise a host of other social issues, such as conditions or earnings of workers and concerns stemming from changes in farm ownership and stewardship.

While the costs of industrialized agriculture tend to be focused on the local neighborhood and community, the benefits (lower prices to consumers from use of new technologies) are spread more diffusely. This uneven benefit-cost distribution is one explanation of why Not-In-My-Backyard (NIMBY) groups have formed to oppose the siting of large-scale animal facilities.[6] Public

concerns over environmental issues may be only a pretext for underlying concerns related to other issues. Given the range of economic, environmental, and social concerns that are inherent in these conflicts, holistic, multidisciplinary approaches to addressing them are appropriate. In addition, proactive approaches are likely to be preferable due to the high costs of conflict.[8]

ADDRESSING URBAN–RURAL INTERFACE ISSUES

Market Failure and Public Policy

Many issues at the agricultural/rural–urban interface can be seen as a market failure, and therefore a justification can be made for government intervention to adjust the market to yield outcomes in line with society's preferences. The failure of markets often is in the form of third-party effects of business and consumer decisions. Consumers continue to demand low-density residential housing in suburbanizing areas without anticipating the direct and indirect costs of sprawl.[3] Similarly, industrialization of animal agriculture has produced spillover effects in terms of water quality impacts on neighbors and communities and residents that are not factored into prices and the decisions of private entities about expanding these operations.[5] When citizens are concerned about the unsatisfactory performance outcomes, the existence of market failure is a rationale for development of new public policies.

Public Policy Approaches

The boundary between rural/agricultural and urban/suburban areas can exist as a smooth transitional area where land uses blend well with one another, or it can be a jagged, disjointed, ill-defined edge where such land uses do not coexist easily.[1] The nature of the interface is in large part a function of public policy decisions about land use. A critical higher-order policy choice concerns which governmental jurisdiction has control over rural–urban interface issues. That is, what are the relative roles of federal, state, and local jurisdictions in addressing rural–urban interface issues? The performance outcomes will differ depending on which jurisdiction has authority to make decisions concerning these issues.[9] The purpose here is not to describe the policy issues and options available. See Refs. 1 and 3 for a description of federal policy issues and options related to the rural–urban interface.

Four different philosophical positions and strategies for addressing public issues at the agricultural/rural–urban interface can be identified; 1) reestablish the free market; 2) protect farmland and open space; 3) redevelop central cities; and 4) manage growth at the rural–urban fringe.[4]

CONCLUSION

Competition for land in rapidly developing regions can lead to land use patterns at the rural–urban interface that result in costly conflicts and policy dilemmas. Land use incompatibility problems and conflicts can be generally categorized as arising from two basic sources. The first is urban-to-rural migration, where new rural residents bring with them expectations and unfamiliarity with farming and rural life.[1] In the second case, industrialization of farming practices or marketing methods have changed farming technologies or business practices, leading to new third-party effects such as water degradation, noise, or odors.[5] In reality, land use problems are more complex than either of these two cases. Therefore, it is useful to take a broader approach to identify the true dimensions of the problem before intervening.[8] A number of different public policy strategies are available to prevent or reduce rural–urban conflict. Despite the availability of these tools, agricultural/rural issues remain, and with the advent of a more industrialized food system a critical public policy issue has emerged in many regions of the United States.[5,6]

ARTICLE OF FURTHER INTEREST

Policy Issues: Local/State Land Use Regulation, p. 719

REFERENCES

1. Libby, L.W.; Dicks, M.R. *Rural–Urban Interface Issues and Farmland Protection. The 2002 Farm Bill: Policy Options and Consequences*; Outlaw, J.L., Smith, E.G., Eds.; Farm Foundation: Oak Brook, IL, September 2001. Publication No. 2001–01.
2. Vesterby, M. Urbanization. In *The Encyclopedia of Rural America*; Goreham, G.A., Ed.; ABC-CLIO Inc.: Santa Barbara, CA, 1997; pp 403–406, 755–759.
3. Heimlich, R.E.; Anderson, D. *Development at the Urban Fringe and Beyond. Agricultural Economics Report No. 803*; USDA Economic Research Service: Washington, DC, 2001.
4. Edelman, M.A.; Roe, J.; Patton, D.B. *Land Use Conflict: When City and Country Clash*; Farm Foundation, National Public Policy Education Committee: Oak Brook, IL, 1999.
5. Abdalla, C.W. The industrialization of agriculture: Implications for public concern and environmental consequences of intensive livestock operations. Penn State J. Environ. Law **Summer 2002**, *10* (2), 175–191.
6. Abdalla, C.W.; Edelman, M.; Foster, H.; Patton, D.; Socolow, A.; Weber, B. *Land Use at the Rural–Urban Fringe. Land Use and Rural–Urban Interface Task Force*; Farm Foundation, 1997.
7. Abdalla, C.; Becker, J.C.; Cook-Huffman, C.; Gray, B.; Hanke, R.; Welsh, N. Community conflicts over intensive livestock operations: How and why do such conflicts escalate? Drake J. Agric. Law **2002**, *7* (1), Spring.
8. Abdalla, C.W.; Kelsey, T.W. Breaking the impasse: Helping communities cope with change at the rural–urban interface. J. Soil Water Conserv. **Nov./Dec. 1996**, *51*, 462–466.
9. Abdalla, C.W.; Shaffer, J.D. Politics and markets in the articulation of preferences for attributes of the rapidly changing food and agricultural sectors: Framing the issues. J. Agric. Appl. Econ. **July 1997**, *29* (1), 57–71.

Conjugated Linoleic Acid

Dale E. Bauman
Adam L. Lock
Cornell University, Ithaca, New York, U.S.A.

INTRODUCTION

Many foods contain microcomponents that have beneficial effects beyond those associated with their traditional nutrient content. These are often referred to as functional foods. One such component in foods derived from ruminants is conjugated linoleic acid (CLA). The initial discovery of a functional food role was in the 1980s when M. Pariza and colleagues identified CLA as the antimutigen present in cooked beef.[1] Subsequent studies with animal models demonstrated that synthetically produced CLA was a potent anticarcinogen.

The major dietary sources of CLA are foods derived from ruminants, with about 70% and 25% coming from dairy products and red meat, respectively.[2] CLA is a fatty acid, and thus is present in milk fat and intramuscular fat. Polyunsaturated fatty acids (PUFA) typically have a methylene group between the double bonds (e.g., see linoleic acid in Fig. 1). However, in the case of CLA, the double bonds are conjugated, or adjacent to each other. The most studied isomers are *cis*-9, *trans*-11 and *trans*-10, *cis*-12 (Fig. 1). First identified in 1977 by P. Parodi, *cis*-9, *trans*-11 is the major CLA isomer, representing about 75–90% of the total CLA in ruminant fat.[2] However, many isomers of CLA are found in trace amounts and these differ by position of the double-bond pair (e.g., 7–9, 8–10, 9–11, 10–12) or geometric orientation of the double-bond pair (*cis–trans*, *trans–cis*, *cis–cis*, and *trans–trans*). The isomer form of CLA can affect its biological activity and the presence of multiple isomers presents an analytical challenge. Frequently, quantifying CLA isomers and related fatty acids requires a combination of analytical methods.

ORIGIN OF CLA IN RUMINANT FAT

The presence of CLA in ruminant milk and meat is related to rumen fermentation. The rumen contains many types of bacteria, and a portion converts dietary PUFA to saturated fatty acids. This process is referred to as biohydrogenation and is the basis for the greater content of saturated fat in ruminants compared to nonruminants. The most common plant PUFA consumed by ruminants are linoleic and

linolenic acids, and their biohydrogenation is shown in Fig. 2. *Cis*-9, *trans*-11 CLA is an intermediate formed during the biohydrogenation of linoleic acid, whereas *trans*-11 18:1 (vaccenic acid; VA) is an intermediate from both linoleic and linolenic acids.[3]

Initially it was assumed that the CLA in milk fat and body fat of ruminants originated from incomplete biohydrogenation in the rumen. However, studies revealed that CLA represented only a transitory product during biohydrogenation, and VA was the major intermediate that accumulated in the rumen.[3] This led to more extensive investigations and it was discovered that *cis*-9, *trans*-11 CLA in milk and meat fat originates mainly from endogenous synthesis by the animal's own tissues; only a minor portion comes from production in the rumen.[4] The substrate used to form this CLA isomer is VA, produced as an intermediate during rumen biohydrogenation; the enzyme that catalyzes the reaction is Δ^9-desaturase (Fig. 2). Endogenous synthesis occurs primarily in the mammary gland during lactation and in adipocytes during the growth phase.[4]

The second most prevalent CLA isomer in ruminant fat is *trans*-7, *cis*-9 CLA (~5–10% of total CLA) and this also arises from endogenous synthesis involving Δ^9-desaturase with the precursor being *trans*-7 18:1 produced in the rumen. Other individual CLA isomers originate from rumen production and are present in only trace amounts in milk and body fat.[4]

FACTORS AFFECTING CLA CONTENT OF FOODS

Processing has little effect on CLA; thus, its content in food products is related to the concentration in the original milk and meat fat.[2] Most investigations of factors that influence CLA have examined milk fat synthesis in the dairy cow.

Diet is the most significant factor affecting the CLA in ruminant fat and the concentration can be increased several-fold by dietary means.[5,6] Increasing the dietary supply of 18-carbon PUFA substrates by addition of seeds or plant oils high in linoleic and/or linolenic acids (e.g., soybeans or sunflowers) results in an increase in rumen

Encyclopedia of Animal Science
DOI: 10.1081/E-EAS 120019539

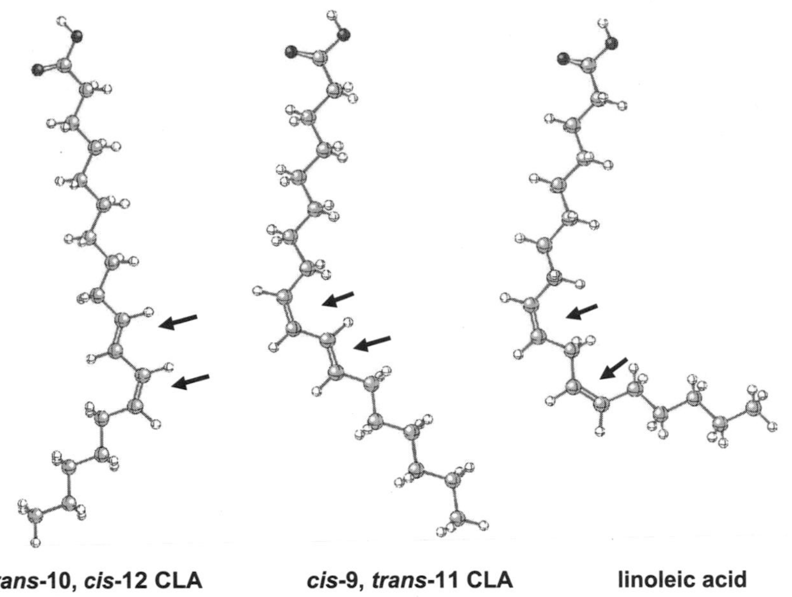

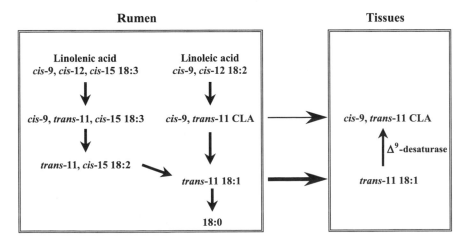

Fig. 1 Structures of two isomers of conjugated linoleic acid (CLA) and linoleic acid (*cis*-9, *cis*-12 18:2). Arrows indicate double-bond position. (From Ref. 5.) (*View this art in color at www.dekker.com.*)

output of VA, and to a lesser extent CLA, which allows for greater endogenous synthesis of CLA. Dietary factors that affect rumen bacteria involved in biohydrogenation, either directly or indirectly via changes in rumen environment, can also affect the CLA content of ruminant fat. In general, no single bacterium carries out the complete biohydrogenation process; rather, one group carries out the steps to convert linoleic and linolenic acids to VA and then another bacteria group carries out the final step to form stearic acid.[3] Alterations in the rumen environment can differentially affect these two groups so that the rates and extent of biohydrogenation are altered.

In particular, increasing the forage/concentrate ratio increases the CLA concentration by this means.

A combination of dietary supply of PUFA and modification of the rumen environment can be especially effective to increase the CLA content of ruminant fat. Dietary supplements of fish oil and grazing pasture are two examples. Fresh pasture results in a two- to three-fold increase in the CLA content of milk fat, but the effect diminishes as the pasture matures. Increases in CLA observed with fish oils and feeding fresh pasture cannot be fully explained in terms of their PUFA content. Therefore, other factors or components of these feeds must affect

Fig. 2 Pathways for the biosynthesis of *cis*-9, *trans*-11 conjugated linoleic acid (CLA) in ruminants. (From Ref. 4.)

rumen bacteria involved in biohydrogenation, thereby promoting rumen production of VA and CLA. Dietary supplements of CLA or VA can also be used to enhance the CLA content of ruminant fat. To be effective, these must be protected from rumen biohydrogenation, and dose-dependent increases in milk fat CLA content have been achieved.

Physiological factors that affect milk-fat content of CLA have also been examined, and differences among individuals are particularly striking.[4] Even when diet and other physiological variables are similar, there is still a three-fold range among individuals in the milk fat concentration of CLA. The CLA-desaturase index is a proxy for Δ^9-desaturase that is based on the relationship between substrate and product for endogenous synthesis of CLA, and it also varies about three-fold among cows regardless of diet. To a large extent, milk fat differences in CLA content and CLA desaturase index among individuals are maintained throughout lactation and across dietary shifts. This suggests a genetic basis related to rumen output of VA (and to a lesser extent CLA) or the enzyme Δ^9-desaturase. Examination of other physiological factors has established that milk fat content of CLA and CLA-desaturase index has little relation to milk or milk fat yield. Further, parity, stage of lactation, and breed have minimal effects when compared to the variation among individuals or the effect of diet.

BIOLOGICAL EFFECTS OF CLA

In vivo and in vitro investigations with animal/cell models established that CLA was anticarcinogenic for several types of cancer. As research expanded to other biomedical models, a range of additional positive health benefits were identified including antidiabetogenicity, antiatherogenicity, immunomodulation, antiobesity, and modulation of bone growth.[7,8] Early work utilized preparations of mixed CLA isomers. More recently, relatively pure preparations of cis-9, trans-11 and trans-10, cis-12

Table 1 Effect of natural and synthetic conjugated linoleic acid (CLA) on tumor development in a rat model of mammary carcinogenesis

Treatment group	Tumor incidence	Tumor number
Control	28/30 (93%)	92
Synthetic cis-9, trans-11 CLA	16/30 (53%)	46
VA/CLA-enriched butter	15/30 (50%)	43

(Data from Ref. 9.)

Table 2 Effect of supplements of trans-10, cis-12 conjugated linoleic acid (CLA) on milk fat yield in lactating cows[a] and backfat thickness in growing pigs[b]

trans-10, cis-12 CLA (g/kg dietary dry matter)	Fat variable
Lactating Cows	Milk Fat (g/day)
0.00	772
0.16	579 (−25%)
0.78	383 (−50%)
Growing Pigs	Backfat Thickness (mm)
0.00	21.0
0.93	16.9 (−20%)
1.86	14.6 (−30%)

[a]Data from Ref. 10.
[b]Data from Ref. 11.

isomers have been available, and results indicate they differ in biological activity.

Investigations of the anticancer effect have established that cis-9, trans-11 CLA is anticarcinogenic. In fact, both CLA and VA found in ruminant fat are anticarcinogenic, the latter presumably because it can be converted to CLA via endogenous synthesis. Ip et al.[9] demonstrated that dietary consumption of VA/CLA-enriched butter was effective in reducing the incidence of tumors in a rat model of mammary carcinogenesis (Table 1). These results are among the first to demonstrate that a naturally produced anticarcinogen, consumed as a component of a natural food, is effective in reducing cancer.

Trans-10, cis-12 CLA is a potent inhibitor of milk-fat synthesis in dairy cows (Table 2). This effect is specific for milk fat, and its mechanism involves coordinated reductions in mammary enzymes involved in milk fat synthesis. Effects of trans-10, cis-12 CLA are reversed when supplementation ceases, and the potential to use dietary supplements as a management tool in dairy production is being examined. The ability to selectively reduce milk fat yield could reduce energy demands during times when nutrient intake is inadequate, such as during environmental stress or in the transition period at parturition.[4] In dairy cows, certain dietary conditions also cause a reduction in milk fat, referred to as milk-fat depression (MFD). This is related to unique fatty acid intermediates formed during biohydrogenation, and rumen production of trans-10, cis-12 CLA and its metabolite trans-10 18:1 is increased during diet-induced MFD. Thus, MFD represents a natural situation in which fat synthesis is reduced as a consequence of a diet-induced increase in this specific CLA isomer.

Trans-10, cis-12 CLA has also been shown to reduce body fat accretion in a number of species including pigs (Table 2), although the effective dose is several-fold greater than that needed to affect milk fat. Thus, there is interest in animal agriculture in the potential use of this CLA isomer in the growth period to reduce carcass fat and improve the efficiency of nutrient use.

CONCLUSION

Diet is the major determinant of the CLA content of ruminant fat, and there is substantial variation among individuals. *Cis-9, trans-*11 CLA is the major isomer and it originates primarily via endogenous synthesis involving Δ^9-desaturase. This CLA isomer is anticarcinogenic and is a functional food component of ruminant-derived products. *Trans-*10, *cis-*12 CLA inhibits fat synthesis, and as a dietary supplement has potential as a management tool in lactation and growth.

REFERENCES

1. Pariza, M.W. The Biological Activities of Conjugated Linoleic Acid. In *Advances in Conjugated Linoleic Acid Research*; Yurawecz, M.P., Mossoba, M.M., Kramer, J.K.G., Pariza, M.W., Nelson, G., Eds.; AOCS Press: Champaign, IL, 1999; Vol. 1, 12–20.

2. Parodi, P. Conjugated Linoleic Acid in Food. In *Advances in Conjugated Linoleic Acid Research*; Sebedio, J.-L., Christie, W.W., Adlof, R.O., Eds.; AOCS Press: Champaign, IL, 2003; Vol. 2, 101–122.

3. Harfoot, C.G.; Hazlewood, G.P. Lipid Metabolism in the Rumen. In *The Rumen Microbial Ecosystem,* 2nd Ed.; Hobson, P.N., Stewart, D.S., Eds.; Chapman & Hall: London, 1997; 382–426.

4. Bauman, D.E.; Corl, B.A.; Peterson, D.G. The Biology of Conjugated Linoleic Acid in Ruminants. In *Advances in Conjugated Linoleic Acid Research*; Sebedio, J.-L., Christie, W.W., Adlof, R.O., Eds.; AOCS Press: Champaign, IL, 2003; Vol. 2, 146–173.

5. Bauman, D.E.; Baumgard, L.H.; Corl, B.A.; Griinari, J.M. Conjugated Linoleic Acid (CLA) and the Dairy Cow. In *Recent Advances in Animal Nutrition 2001*; Garnsworthy, P.C., Wiseman, J., Eds.; Nottingham University Press: Nottingham, UK, 2001; 221–250.

6. Stanton, C.; Murphy, J.; McGrath, E.; Devery, R. Animal Feeding Strategies for Conjugated Linoleic Acid Enrichment of Milk. In *Advances in Conjugated Linoleic Acid Research*; Sebedio, J.-L., Christie, W.W., Adlof, R.O., Eds.; AOCS Press: Champaign, IL, 2003; Vol. 2, 123–145.

7. Belury, M.A. Dietary conjugated linoleic acid in health: Physiological effects and mechanisms of action. Annu. Rev. Nutr. **2002**, *22*, 505–531.

8. Whigham, L.D.; Cook, M.E.; Atkinson, R.L. Conjugated linoleic acid: Implications for human health. Pharmacol. Res. **2000**, *42*, 503–510.

9. Ip, C.; Banni, S.; Angioni, E.; Carta, G.; McGinley, J.; Thompson, H.J.; Barbano, D.; Bauman, D. Conjugated linoleic acid-enriched butter fat alters mammary gland morphogenesis and reduces cancer risk in rats. J. Nutr. **1999**, *129*, 2135–2142.

10. Baumgard, L.H.; Sangster, J.K.; Bauman, D.E. Milk fat synthesis in dairy cows is progressively reduced by increasing supplemental amounts of *trans-*10, *cis-*12 conjugated linoleic acid (CLA). J. Nutr. **2001**, *131*, 1764–1769.

11. Ostrowska, E.; Muralitharan, M.; Cross, R.F.; Bauman, D.E.; Dunshea, F.R. Dietary conjugated linoleic acids increase lean tissue and decrease fat deposition in growing pigs. J. Nutr. **1999**, *129*, 2037–2042.

Contributions to Society: Biomedical Research Models

Harry J. Mersmann
USDA/ARS Children's Nutrition Research Center, Houston, Texas, U.S.A.

INTRODUCTION

Over the last century, biomedical research has produced phenomenal numbers of accomplishments with translation into many pragmatic medical uses. Thus, treatment of viral and bacterial diseases, surgical remedy of inherited or acquired maladies, pharmaceutical treatment of malfunctioning physiological processes, and nutritional or pharmaceutical treatment or prophylaxis for disease or malfunction of environmental, genetic, or unknown etiology have each progressed to a highly scientific form of medical practice. Essentially all biomedical research requires animal models. It is not feasible and is many times unethical to perform exploratory research on humans. Progress in the science and art of medical practice is and will continue to be dependent on the use of appropriate animal models. Given considerable knowledge about a particular biological phenomenon, some animal experiments can be replaced with cell-culture studies or computer simulation. However, because of limited knowledge, it will be many years before these simpler systems will suffice. Furthermore, the complexity and strong tendency to achieve homeostasis in the intact animal make extrapolation from simulation and experiments in vitro difficult.

BACKGROUND

During the first half of the 20th century, biomedical research relied on only a few animal models. The basic biomedical sciences—biochemistry, nutrition, pharmacology, physiology, etc.—used the rat as the primary model. Mice were used occasionally, and other species were used in specialized fields, e.g., dogs in cardiovascular research and pigeon breast muscle for study of skeletal muscle biochemistry. Selection of a particular species as an animal model was usually based on convenience, e.g., animal availability (pound dogs) or cost and ease of care (rats). Initially, there was minimal knowledge about the models or of human function, so the appropriateness of the model was not considered. As the knowledge base for models and humans increased, primarily during the latter half of the 20th century, questions arose regarding the applicability of particular long-standing models to

humans. If the model animal has a major anatomical, biochemical, or physiological difference from the human, then extrapolation of results from the model to humans becomes questionable. Over time, knowledge about other species has accrued so that alternative models may be considered. In the last 30 to 40 years, the biochemistry, nutrition, and physiology of species raised for human food production have been extensively investigated. Consequently, some agricultural species are being used in biomedical research because they are excellent models for humans. For example, the pig is generally a better cardiovascular model than the dog, the classical model species. Some details of human biology extrapolated from classical models are incorrect, and in many cases the newer models are more similar to humans. Nevertheless, the acquisition of the current incredible knowledge base about human biology was possible primarily because of the classical models, e.g., the rat and the dog.

Currently, the mouse is a popular model, not because it is an excellent human model, but because it provides a tool to study specific gene function. Transgenic mice overexpress a particular gene and in some cases overexpress the gene in particular organs. Control of the timing of gene function and tissue-specific expression is becoming feasible, so gene function during development or aging can be examined. In knockout models, specific genes are modified so that they do not function. Mice are also advantageous because they are small, require little special care, and are fecund with a continuous and short breeding cycle. There are transgenic cattle, pigs, and sheep that have special uses in the biomedical community, e.g., production of a specific human protein for use in human medicine. However, the size of these species restricts their general use.

PORCINE MODELS

The pig is extensively used as a biomedical model because of a great number of anatomical and physiological similarities to the human,[1] e.g., the cardiovascular/respiratory system, the skin, much of the digestive system, and immunological and excretory function. The pig's nutritional requirements are generally comparable to the human's and pigs are one of the few omnivorous species,

Encyclopedia of Animal Science
DOI: 10.1081/E-EAS 120019540

as is the human. The pig is docile except for reproductively active males and females with a litter. The size of the full-grown domestic pig is a disadvantage regarding housing in a biomedical facility. However, the sizes of the newborn and the neonate are advantageous as models for nutritional biochemistry and particularly for the physiology of developing systems. Several strains of minipigs have been developed. The Yucatan minipig is especially small and can be an appropriate model for chronic studies. Although not an accurate appraisal of the increasing use of pigs in biomedical research, a search of PubMed for the words pig, swine, porcine, and Sus (excluding guinea pig) in the title indicates 870 references in 1966, 1225 in 1970, 1420 in 1980, 2179 in 1990, and 2603 in 2000.

Compilation of information regarding the pig as a biomedical model was pioneered by Leo Bustad in 1966.[2] This effort was continued by Mike Tumbleson in 1986[3] and 1996.[4] These compendia represent the proceedings of extensive symposia. There are other collections of articles about the pig as a biomedical model,[5–7] as well. A recent book, *Biology of the Domestic Pig*, assembles information about anatomical/physiological systems in the pig, including its use as a biomedical model.[8] Also, there are bibliographies for literature about the use of swine in biomedical research.[9,10]

Probably the most extensive use of pigs as models has been in the cardiovascular field. The literature is summarized in the cited references above and in a specialized reference work.[11] Pigs are available in sizes comparable to humans, e.g., 70–100 kg to approximate human adults or 1–5 or more kg to approximate neonates or children. The coronary circulation is quite similar to the human's, making the pig an appropriate model. Pigs are very susceptible to atherosclerotic disease when fed diets high in saturated fat and cholesterol, and pigs can be fed diets of composition comparable to human diets. There have been successful genetic selections for abnormal cholesterol or variation in lipoprotein metabolism and also for obesity in swine. In addition, swine have been used as models by inducing cardiovascular disease with biological or chemical agents or by the use of physical manipulation, e.g., total or partial occlusion of specific blood vessels.

Another extensive use of the pig as a model is in the area of nutrition, including neonatal nutrition.[12,13] If given colostrum, the newborn pig does not need to suckle and can be fed specific diets with quantity control using either nipple-type delivery systems or by teaching the pig to drink/eat from a bowl. In the latter case, the pig can eat solid food within a few days. The pig has been used extensively to study the postnatal development of the digestive system. The anatomy and physiology of the porcine stomach and small intestine are similar to the human's, but the spiral colon in the pig is much longer than the human colon and the pig has a predominant cecum, not a feature of the human large intestine. The metabolism of amino acids, carbohydrates, and fats by various organs has been studied in pigs. This fundamental research has been augmented by dietary manipulation of the pig to study the effects of specific nutrients on metabolic function.

Swine have been used as surgical models for many years. M. Michael Swindle has been a major advocate for porcine surgical models, both for teaching purposes and for experimental surgery.[14] The many anatomical similarities of pigs and humans make this use appropriate. Pigs can also be fitted with a variety of arterial, venous, and gut catheters to deliver drugs, metabolites, or nutrients to specific organs or to sample blood being delivered to or coming from a particular organ.

OTHER SPECIES

A number of agricultural species have been used for research into various types of tumors.[1] Cattle and horses have limited use as models because their size makes housing difficult in a biomedical facility. Horses are used as models for asthma and for exercise and reproductive physiology.[1] The alimentary function of the rumen and the dependence on the products of microbial digestion give rise to specialized metabolic functions in ruminants. Consequently, ruminants usually are not used as metabolic models for the human. Calves have been used for specialized cardiovascular surgical studies, e.g., development of artificial hearts. Sheep are of a size manageable in most biomedical facilities. Sheep have been used as models for a number of disease states,[1] but perhaps the greatest use has been to study metabolism during pregnancy.[15] Sheep have one or two fetuses and are large enough that catheters may be placed in veins and arteries to sample blood traversing to and from the fetus, the placenta, and the dam. Metabolic observations must, of course, be tempered by the fact that the sheep is a ruminant and the anatomy of the placenta is different from the human's. The possibility of Q-fever in sheep precludes its use in some biomedical facilities.

CONCLUSIONS

Biomedical research is dependent on animal models. The classical animal models were and still are rodent models. Mice are particularly relevant today because of the capacity for genetic manipulation. Large animals have always been used for specialized purposes, e.g., the dog as a cardiovascular model. Of the agricultural species, the pig is the most prevalent model. Much of its anatomy, nutrition, and physiology are similar to the human's, making it the most appropriate model for many aspects of biomedical research. Sheep have also been used but are limited as models because of the specialized nutrition and metabolism dependent on the rumen. Regardless of the extent of use, species are unique and extrapolation across species must be qualified.

REFERENCES

1. Lewis, S.M.; Carraway, J.H. Large animal models of human disease. Lab Anim. **1992**, *21*, 22–29.
2. *Swine in Biomedical Research*; Bustad, L.K., McClellan, R.O., Eds.; Pacific Northwest Laboratory: Richland, WA, 1966.
3. *Swine in Biomedical Research*; Tumbleson, M.E., Ed.; Plenum Press: New York, NY, 1986; Vols. 1, 2, and 3.
4. *Advances in Swine in Biomedical Research*; Tumbleson, M.E., Schook, L.B., Eds.; Plenum Press: New York, NY, 1996; Vols. 1 and 2.
5. Use of miniature swine in research. Bustad, L.K., Crowder, C., Eds. Lab. Anim. Care, **1968**, *18*, 97–126.
6. Swine in biomedical research. Baker, H.J., Eds.; Lab. Anim. Sci. **1986**, *36*, 337–472.
7. Dodds, W.J. The pig model for biomedical research. Fed. Proc. **1982**, *41*, 247–256.
8. *Biology of the Domestic Pig*; Pond, W.G., Mersmann, H.J., Eds.; Cornell University Press: Ithaca, NY, 2001.
9. *Animal Models in Biomedical Research: Swine*, Special Reference Briefs: SRB 94–01; U.S Department of Agriculture, Agricultural Research Service, National Agricultural Library, Animal Welfare Information Center: Beltsville MD, 1993.
10. *Information Resources for Swine in Biomedical Research—1990–2000*, U.S. Department of Agriculture, Agricultural Research Service, National Agricultural Library, Animal Welfare Information Center: Beltsville, MD, 2000.
11. *Swine in Cardiovascular Research*; Stanton, H.C., Mersmann, H.J., Eds.; CRC Press, Inc.: Boca Raton, FL, 1986; Vols. 1 and 2.
12. Moughan, P.J.; Birtles, M.J.; Cranwell, P.D.; Smith, W.C.; Pedraza, M. The piglet as a model animal for studying aspects of digestion and absorption in milk-fed human infants. World Rev. Nutr. Diet. **1992**, *67*, 40–113.
13. Miller, E.R.; Ullrey, D.E. The pig as a model for human nutrition. Ann. Rev. Nutr. **1987**, *7*, 361–382.
14. Swindle, M.M. *Surgery, Anesthesia, and Experimental Techniques in Swine*; Iowa State University Press: Ames, IA, 1998.
15. Kitchen, H. Sheep as animal models in biomedical research. JAVMA **1977**, *170*, 615–619.

Contributions to Society: Companions and Pleasure

Duane E. Ullrey
Okemos, Michigan, U.S.A.

INTRODUCTION

The pleasurable associations of animals and man had their beginnings in domestication. Man's initial impetus may have been to acquire food more predictably, but these animals were more than a tasty meal. They became a needed and enriching component of human society.

BACKGROUND

Historical Origins of Domestic Animals

The role of animals as companions to man probably began with domestication of the dog from wolflike ancestors some 10,000 to 15,000 years ago.[1] A docile wolf pup, orphaned when its mother was killed, may have been carried back to camp by a human hunter.[2] If it wasn't eaten, and became habituated to its adoptive family, it possibly survived by scavenging for food within the settlement. Over generations, this close association with people, and increasing evidence of tameability and trainability, produced a mutually beneficial relationship.[3] The primitive dog was provided food and shelter, and its master acquired a hunting companion that could track and capture game. Further, the evolution of behavioral postures, such as tail-wagging and soliciting play, nurtured the indulgences that so closely link modern man and his dog.

The domestication of other animals, such as cattle, sheep, and goats, soon followed. Although they provided hides, wool, and hair for clothing, meat and milk for food, and draft power, they didn't provide the companionship, special pride of ownership, and societal dominance engendered by the horse. Horse domestication is believed to have begun in Scythia (in the area of present-day Ukraine), somewhat before 3500 B.C. By 670 B.C., mounted horsemen on the steppes of Eurasia were imposing figures, eight feet tall and seemingly at one with their steeds. The Scythian cavalry, equipped with swords, lances, or bows and arrows, readily vanquished foes that were afoot, and dominated great tracts of land for centuries.[4] Their horses were reminiscent of Arabians but were somewhat smaller. The first deliberate horse breeding is believed to have started in Persia, in the 1st millennium B.C., and

resulted in the development of both light and heavy breeds.[5]

Cats, too, were domesticated several thousand years ago—perhaps around 2000–1000 B.C.—and were kept in temples in ancient Egypt as religious symbols. They were ultimately deified, and hundreds of mummified cats have been found in Egyptian tombs.[6] A cat buried with a human about 9,500 years ago has been found recently in Cyprus, demonstrating an even earlier relationship with man.[7] Domestication generally presumes that breeding takes place under human control. This is true for some domestic cats, but as noted by Mason,[8] "the majority make their own arrangements." As a consequence, distinctions that identify particular breeds tend to disappear in the feral population.

ANIMAL COMPANIONS TODAY

Dogs, Cats, and Horses

The list of species of contemporary animal companions is a long one, but there is little question that dogs and cats are the predominant pets in U.S. households. According to the Pet Food Institute (Washington, DC; www.petfoodinstitute.org), there were approximately 60 million pet dogs and 75 million pet cats in 2002. The American Kennel Club (Raleigh, NC; www.akc.org) recognizes 150 breeds of dogs, although others have proposed that as many as 400 dog breeds inhabit the world.[3] The AKC assigns these breeds to the following groups, based on the uses for which the breeds were originally developed: sporting, hound, working, terrier, toy, nonsporting, herding, and miscellaneous. The Cat Fanciers' Association (Manasquan, NJ; www.cfainc.org) recognizes 41 breeds of cats, varying particularly in size and shape of body and head, color, color patterns, length and texture of hair, shape and color of eyes, and length and shape of ears and tail. The American Horse Council (Washington, DC; www.horsecouncil.org) reported there were 6.9 million horses in the United States in 2000, and the International Museum of the Horse at the Kentucky Horse Park in Lexington, KY (www.imh.org) lists 130 breeds of light- and heavyweight horses, worldwide.

Encyclopedia of Animal Science
DOI: 10.1081/E-EAS 120019541

Distinctive breeds of dogs did not appear until about 3000–4000 years ago.[3] Dogs resembling greyhounds were depicted on Egyptian and west Asian pottery and paintings, and greyhounds may be one of the oldest foundation breeds. The origins and evolution of unique breed characteristics are mostly obscure but were certainly influenced by physical appearance, innate capabilities, and behavior. The development of working and herding dogs illustrates this point.[9]

Sled-dog teams were composed of a variety of breeds at the first All-Alaska Sweepstakes race in Nome in 1908. Dog sizes were more uniform by 1911, but colors and morphology still resembled their ancestral breeds. Hybridization with Siberian huskies, and further selection, led to sled-racing dogs that ran fast on groomed trails without tiring, and behaved themselves as members of a team. In 1925, sled-dog teams brought serum to the diphtheria-stricken town of Nome through hurricane-force winds and −50° temperatures. The final team in the relay was led by Balto. He and his six teammates retired to Cleveland, OH, and when Balto died, his body was mounted and exhibited at the Cleveland Museum of Natural History (www.cmnh.org) as a reminder of his role in the gallant 675-mile race against death.

Livestock-guarding dogs were selected to be attentive, protective, and trustworthy (not predatory) in their responsibilities. Herding dogs were selected to conduct livestock from one location to another, taking advantage of species-characteristic behavior. Sheep-herding dogs exhibit controlled predatory behavior, projecting an intense threatening gaze, a stalk, and a directed chase (but no biting). Cattle-herding dogs also exhibit controlled predatory behavior, but may nip at the heels of herd animals to encourage or direct movement.

Other breeds of dogs have been selected for hunting, service, or simply as companions. Behavioral traits of potential usefulness to prospective pet owners when choosing dog breeds have been defined in order of declining reliability as measures of selection.[10] These include excitability, general activity, snapping at children, excessive barking, playfulness, response to obedience training, watchdog barking, aggression to other dogs, dominance over owner, territorial defense, demands for affection, destructiveness, and ease of housebreaking. Of course, susceptibilities to health problems, such as allergies and hip dysplasia, also need to be considered.

The cat is territorial, at least partly nocturnal, and a solitary hunter. By offering food, affection, and comfort, humans persuade cats to share their territory.[11] However, nearly any domestic cat can survive on its own, particularly when living on a farm or in an area where rodents and birds might be caught for food. Although there are identifiable breeds (such as Siamese, Persian, Abyssinian, Manx, and 37 others) whose matings are controlled by humans for purposes of show and sale, the majority of domestic cats throughout the world are striped tabbies, blotched tabbies, black, or sex-linked orange. They all accept affection to a degree, but the choice to do so is generally theirs.

It is ironic that the horse, which is such a popular companion to people in the United States, was extirpated in North America at the end of the Ice Age, about 8000 to 10,000 years ago. This was due, perhaps, to ecological change and conversion of grasslands to forests, and to intense hunting pressure by Paleolithic humans. Horses were reintroduced into the Americas by European conquistadores and explorers in the 16th century. They were ridden, used for draft, and sometimes eaten. Arabians were a founder breed for many warm-blooded horses, including the Thoroughbred and Standardbred. Light-horse breeds developed in America include the Standardbred, Quarter Horse, Morgan, Paint, Pinto, Tennessee Walking Horse, American Saddlebred, and Appaloosa. The cold-blooded breeds originated from the heavy military horses of the Middle Ages, and include the Percheron, Belgian, Shire, Clydesdale, and Suffolk.[5] Although some horses are used regularly work cattle on ranches, or for transportation or farm work by the Amish, most U.S. horses are used for recreation. Such uses include racing, trail riding, rodeos, and exhibitions where conformity to breed standards and rider skills are judged.

Other Animal Companions

A remarkable number of other species are kept as pets, providing companionship and pleasure. Some are relatively large, such as llamas and pot-bellied pigs. Others are small, such as ferrets, gerbils, guinea pigs, hamsters, mice, rabbits, and rats. Angelfish, barbs, catfish, cichlids, danios, eels, goldfish, gouramis, koi, loaches, mollies, oscars, pacus, sharks, swordtails, tetras, and zebra fish are found in personal aquariums. Reptile and amphibian pets include anoles, basilisk and bearded dragons, chameleons, chuckwallas, frogs, geckos, iguanas, other lizards, newts, skinks, snakes, toads, tortoises, treefrogs, and turtles. Over 12 million feathered pets are found in the United States, including canaries, cockatiels, cockatoos, conures, doves, fancy poultry, finches, lories, lovebirds, macaws, parakeets, parrots, and pigeons.[12] Despite public health concerns about zoonotic diseases and advice that wild animals should not be chosen as pets,[13] nondomestic animals such as prairie dogs have been sold by pet stores and at swap meets. In June of 2003, humans became infected with monkeypox after handling sick prairie dogs that apparently contracted this orthopox virus from Gambian giant rats, rope squirrels, dormice, or other small wild mammals imported from Africa.[14]

CONCLUSIONS

Dogs and cats are numerically the most important pet animal species found in U.S. households. Dogs may be asked to perform service, but dogs and cats also bring pleasure by providing companionship and affection in a reciprocal relationship benefiting both animals and humans. Horses that once participated so nobly in the work of farms and ranches now mostly provide recreational opportunities in the suburbs. Other pets are found among the South American camelids, Southeast Asian swine, various rodents, rabbits, reptiles, amphibians, fish, and birds. Wild animals are not recommended as pets because of their limited tractability, poor adaptability to confinement, and the dangers of zoonotic disease.

REFERENCES

1. Price, E.O. *Animal Domestication and Behavior*; CABI Publishing: New York, 2002.
2. Reed, C.A. The Beginnings of Animal Domestication. In *Evolution of Domestic Animals*; Mason, I.L., Ed.; Longman Group Limited: London, 1984; 1–6.
3. Clutton-Brock, J. Origins of the Dog: Domestication and Early History. In *The Domestic Dog: Its Evolution, Behavior and Interactions with People*; Serpell, J., Ed.; Cambridge University Press: Cambridge, UK, 1995; 7–20.
4. Trippett, F. *The Emergence of Man: The First Horsemen*; Time-Life Books: New York, 1974.
5. Bökönyi, S. Horse. In *Evolution of Domestic Animals*; Mason, I.L., Ed.; Longman Group Limited: London, 1984; 163–173.
6. Robinson, R. Cat. In *Evolution of Domestic Animals*; Mason, I.L., Ed.; Longman Group Limited: London, 1984; 217–225.
7. Vigne, J.-D.; Guilaine, J.; Debue, K.; Haye, L.; Gerard, P. Early taming of the cat in cyprus. Science **2004**, *304*, 259.
8. Preface. In *Evolution of Domestic Animals*; Mason, I.L., Ed.; Longman Group Limited: London, 1984; vii pp.
9. Coppinger, R.; Schneider, R. Evolution of Working Dogs. In *The Domestic Dog: Its Evolution, Behavior and Interactions with People*; Serpell, J., Ed.; Cambridge University Press: Cambridge, UK, 1995; 20–47.
10. Hart, B.L. Analysing Breed and Gender Differences in Behavior. In *The Domestic Dog: Its Evolution, Behavior and Interactions with People*; Serpell, J., Ed.; Cambridge University Press: Cambridge, UK, 1995; 65–77.
11. Clutton-Brock, J. *A Natural History of Domesticated Mammals,* 2nd Ed.; Cambridge University Press: Cambridge, UK, 1999.
12. Ullrey, D.E.; Bernard, J. Other Animals, Other Uses, Other Opportunities. In *Introduction to Animal Science*; Pond, W.G., Pond, K.R., Eds.; John Wiley & Sons, Inc.: New York, 1999; 553–583.
13. *The Emergence of Zoonotic Diseases*; Burroughs, T., Knobler, S., Lederberg, J., Eds.; Institute of Medicine, National Academy Press: Washington, DC, 2002.
14. Centers for Disease Control and Prevention. Atlanta, GA.

Contributions to Society: Conversion of Feed to Food

Eric Bradford
University of California, Davis, California, U.S.A.

INTRODUCTION

Meat, milk, and eggs produced by domestic animals have long represented important parts of the diets of many people. Conversion rates of the feed consumed by animals to human food are less than 100% due to losses during animal digestion and metabolism. This apparent inefficiency has led some to conclude that a reduction in the production and consumption of animal source foods would result in more food available for direct consumption by humans, and would thus help alleviate global problems of hunger and malnutrition. This view overlooks two important facts. First, much of the feed consumed by food-producing animals is not edible by humans and would not contribute to human food supply if not fed to animals. Second, animal source foods provide a safe, convenient, and palatable means of providing a number of essential nutrients, and the addition of such foods to diets composed primarily of cereals has well-documented nutritional benefits, especially for children. Also, demand for meat, milk, eggs, and fish is increasing rapidly in developing countries, a trend forecast to continue, and the production of animal source foods adds to the variety of human diets, providing a margin of safety from a nutritional perspective and adding to dietary variety.

FEEDS USED AND CONVERSION RATES

The feeds utilized by food-producing animals include forages from nonarable lands, cultivated forages, crop residues such as straw, and a wide range of food- and fiber-processing by-products. Some of the feeds used and estimated global amounts (million metric tons or MMT) fed in a recent year include straws from wheat, maize, rice, and barley (652); oil meals (116); brans (106); and bagasse (80). Information on these and many other by-product feeds are summarized in Ref. [3]. Forages, crop residues, and many of the by-products are human-inedible materials, while some of the oilmeals are potentially human-edible. These products vary widely in feeding value. Crop residues and by-products such as sugar cane bagasse provide energy, but are deficient in protein, while oilmeals are high in both energy and protein.

The conversion of human-inedible materials to human food by animals clearly adds to food supply. However, livestock are also fed cereal grains that could be consumed directly as human food. Currently, 600–700 MMT per year—approximately one-third of total global cereal grain production—is fed to animals. The proportion is higher in countries such as the United States and lower in developing countries. Feeding grain can reduce human food supply. The net effect of food animal production on human food supply therefore depends on the relative amounts of human-inedible and human-edible materials consumed, as well as on actual conversion rates. It has been estimated that, globally, 74 MMT of human-edible protein is fed to livestock, which produce 54 MMT of human food protein.[4] This gives an input/output ratio of 1.4:1, or an efficiency of about 70%. The biological value of animal protein, a measure reflecting digestibility and essential amino acid content and balance, is on average 1.4 times that of plant protein, suggesting no loss of human food protein value from livestock production.

Actual conversion rates are affected by product produced and level of technology involved in the production system, and particularly by the two related factors of type of digestive system and type of diet. Ruminant species, including cattle, sheep, goats, and buffaloes, typically have lower conversion rates, i.e., produce less product per unit of total feed intake than monogastric species such as pigs and poultry, but the diets of ruminant species on average contain a much higher proportion (often 100%) of human-inedible feeds. This is possible because of the four-compartment ruminant stomach, including the large rumen where microbial digestion takes place. Rumen microorganisms break down plant materials with high fiber content that monogastric animals (including humans) cannot digest, providing energy for the ruminant host. The microorganisms also synthesize essential amino acids from nonessential amino acids and nonprotein nitrogen, contributing to the protein nutrition of the host animal and of consumers of foods from these animals. Additionally, the rumen microflora synthesize some essential B vitamins and detoxify compounds such as gossypol in cottonseed, which are toxic to monogastric animals. As a result of these functions, ruminant animals are able to convert large amounts of human-inedible materials into nutritionally valuable human food.

Encyclopedia of Animal Science
DOI: 10.1081/E-EAS 120019549

Ruminant animals such as dairy cows and feedlot steers are often fed cereal grains and protein supplements as well, with the proportions of these in the diet determined largely by relative prices of different feeds. The inclusion of feeds that are higher in energy and protein and more digestible than many forages and by-products can markedly increase animal performance such as milk yield or growth rate. Thus, their inclusion in ruminant diets reduces the number of animals required for a given amount of meat or milk, with economic and environmental benefits. Also, the inclusion of some of these feeds in ruminant rations can lead to increased utilization of the nutrients in forages and by-products in those rations, by providing a more nutritionally balanced diet.

Pigs and poultry also consume some human-inedible materials such as milling by-products and damaged grains, but on average, their diets include much higher proportions of human-edible grains and protein supplements than ruminant diets. Pigs and poultry also have higher reproduction rates than ruminants, i.e., they produce more progeny per breeding animal and thus, fewer breeding animals are required for a given number of offspring marketed. This, along with the higher nutrient density diets, results in pigs and poultry having much better conversion rates than ruminants, based on total feed intake. However, when comparisons of output/input ratios are based on human-edible inputs, the differences between ruminants and nonruminants largely disappear and their ranking may be reversed.

Estimated conversion rates based on total and human-edible feed inputs for different species of animals, products, and production systems are summarized in Table 1.[5] These results show that, on the basis of total feed inputs, ruminant meat production is relatively inefficient, but those returns per unit of human-edible input can be higher for ruminants than for pigs or poultry. In some cases, the return is more than one unit of human food per unit of human-edible input. This is notably true for dairy production, where output/human-edible input ratios exceed 1.0 for all systems studied. This reflects the fact that milk production is a relatively efficient process as well as that much of the diet of these ruminants is human-inedible material. For beef production, the values of 7:1 to 12: 1 (conversion rates of 8 to 14%) sometimes cited as grain/meat ratios[6] are based on total feed rather than grain inputs, and on only the feedlot period, and thus are incorrect.

These data indicate that conversion rates in general are higher for U.S. livestock production than for other countries, reflecting use of more grain in rations and greater application of technology in the United States. The very high conversion rates for human edible inputs for ruminants in other countries reflect the fact that little grain or protein supplement is fed. One consequence is lower productivity, e.g., slower growth rates or lower milk production, resulting in lower output/total input ratios and larger numbers of animals kept for a given amount of product.

Another relevant point is that the primary food grains, wheat and rice, have lower yields than the primary feed grain, maize. Estimates of the numbers of people that could be fed with the grain now fed to livestock involve the implicit assumption that for each unit of grain not fed to animals, one unit would be available as human food. However, a systematic reduction over time in feeding of grain to livestock would undoubtedly result in a shift in grain crops grown, primarily from maize to wheat, resulting in a substantial reduction in total cereal grain

Table 1 Conversion rates of dietary energy and protein to human food energy and protein

Product	Countries	Energy		Protein	
		Total input	Human-edible input	Total input	Human-edible input
Beef	U.S.A.	.07	.65	.08	1.19
Beef	3 countries[a]	.05	7.63	.03	5.69
Pig meat	U.S.A.	.21	.31	.19	.29
Pig meat	5 countries[b]	.16	.40	.10	.33
Poultry meat	U.S.A.	.19	.28	.31	.62
Poultry meat	5 countries[b]	.19	.50	.32	1.29
Eggs	U.S.A.	.17	.24	.24	.36
Eggs	5 countries[b]	.13	.26	.16	.45
Milk	U.S.A.	.25	1.07	.21	2.08
Milk	3 countries[a]	.19	3.05	.15	5.67

[a]Argentina, Mexico, South Korea.
[b]Argentina, Mexico, South Korea, Egypt, Kenya.
(Data from Ref. [5].)

supply.[5] Also, feed grains represent an important buffer for temporary food grain shortages.

POTENTIAL FOR INCREASED EFFICIENCY

The potential for improving conversion rates of feed to food is an important issue affecting future food supply and particularly the ability to meet the projected increased demand for animal source foods.[2] Large improvements have occurred in recent decades due to science-based technologies. Between 1957 and 1991, growth rate of broiler chickens is estimated to have increased more than threefold, while feed required per unit of gain decreased by an estimated 35%.[7] In the United States, average milk yield per cow has more than doubled in the past 50 years, resulting in a marked increase in system efficiency. Global data on feed grain use and meat, milk, and egg production indicate an improvement of about 15% in conversion rates in the decade from the 1980s to 1990s, in both developed and developing countries.[5] The gap in conversion rates for total feed inputs between developed and developing countries, shown in Table 1, indicates a large potential for further increases in conversion rates in countries where current rates are low, as improved technologies are implemented. These include improved genetics, health care, management, and nutrition. Improvements in both the extent and efficiency of utilization of human-inedible materials as animal feed will also contribute.

CONCLUSIONS

The processes of digestion and metabolism result in losses of energy and protein in feed consumed by animals kept for the production of meat, milk, and eggs. However, food animals convert a wide variety of human-inedible materials into human food. The net effect on human food supply varies according to species, product, production system, and relative amounts of human-edible and human-inedible inputs; on a global basis, the plus and minus factors appear to be nearly in balance. The nutritional properties of animal source foods and their contributions to dietary palatability and variety as well as other factors appear to favor continued inclusion of livestock in food-producing systems. Efficiency of conversion of feed to food has increased significantly in recent years, and there appears to be good potential for further increases.

REFERENCES

1. Neumann, C.; Harris, D.M.; Rogers, L.M. Contribution of animal source foods in improving diet quality and function in children in the developing world. Nutr. Res. **2002**, *22*, 193–220.
2. Delgado, C.; Rosegrant, M.; Steinfeld, H.; Ehui, C.; Courbois, C. *Livestock to 2020: The Next Food Revolution*; Food, Agriculture and the Environment Discussion Paper No. 28, International Food Policy Research Institute: Washington, DC, 1999.
3. Fadel, J.G. Quantitative analysis of selected plant by-product feedstuffs, a global perspective. Anim. Feed Sci. Technol. **1999**, *79*, 255–268.
4. Steinfeld, H.; de Haan, C.; Blackburn, H. *Livestock–Environment Interactions: Issues and Options*; Report of a Study Coordinated by FAO, USAID and World Bank, 1997; 115 pp. (FAO, Rome).
5. CAST. *Animal Agriculture and Global Food Supply*; Report No. 135, Council for Agricultural Science and Technology: Ames, IA, 1999; 92 pp.
6. Waggoner, P.E. Food, Feed and Land. In *Food, Feed and Land: The Good Life, Justice and Global Stewardship*; Crockett, D.A., Linden, T., Eds.; Rowan and Littlefield Publishers: Lanham, MD, 1998; 69–94.
7. Havenstein, G.B.; Ferket, P.R.; Scheideler, S.E.; Larson, B.T. Growth, livability and feed conversion of 1957 vs. 1991 broilers when fed "typical" 1957 and 1991 broiler diets. Poultry Sci. **1994**, *73* (12), 1785–1794.

Contributions to Society: Draft and Transport

R. Anne Pearson
University of Edinburgh, Centre for Tropical Veterinary Medicine, Scotland, U.K.

INTRODUCTION

Animals have been used for work throughout the centuries, starting soon after cultivation began. Despite the increase in mechanization and use of motorized forms of power throughout the world over the last century, many people today still rely on animal power to complement human labor in agriculture and transport.

USE OF ANIMALS FOR WORK

Cattle are the most commonly used animals for work throughout the world. Water buffalo are also used in the humid tropics, and donkeys, horses, and camels in the semiarid areas. Draft animals are maintained over a wide range of agro-ecological zones, but are particularly common on small mixed farms where rain-fed crops are grown mainly for food production. Draft animals and humans provide an estimated 80% of the power input on third-world farms. This is largely because on farms where size and scale of enterprise rule out mechanical power, animal power is the only means the farmers have of cultivating land, other than use of family labor.

Although draft animals make their greatest contribution in agriculture, they also have an important role in transport. It has been estimated that about 20% of the population of the world relies largely on animal transport of goods. Animal carts and sledges are used to transport goods and people in rural areas, especially where roads are unsuitable for motor vehicles. Animal power reduces the drudgery of many of the household activities such as water and fuel collection. Where wheeled vehicles cannot be used, such as in mountainous areas where roads are absent or poorly developed, pack animals may be used to transport goods. Working animals, particularly in North Africa and Asia, make a considerable and important contribution to the urban economy, being used to transport produce within the urban areas. Many of the people owning and using these animals are landless people, to whom the animal represents the main way of earning a living.

Draft animals are also used in the timber industry and to power stationary equipment such as water pumps, sugar cane crushers, and grinding mills. Less widespread is their use in the movement of materials in small-scale building projects and road, dam, and reservoir construction within rural areas.

NUMBERS OF ANIMALS USED FOR WORK

It is impossible to obtain precise information on the numbers of animals used for work purposes in the world. Most countries maintain statistics on livestock numbers, but for ruminants they do not identify use for draft separately from use for beef or milk. In many places, the large ruminants are multipurpose. Most donkeys and mules kept in developing countries are used for work. At least 60% of the horses kept in the tropics are kept for draft work.

SKILL LEVELS IN SOCIETIES CURRENTLY RELYING ON ANIMAL POWER

In some areas of the world, draft animals are part of the traditional way of cultivating the land. For instance, in Ethiopia, Egypt, India, Nepal, Southeast Asia, North Africa, and in most of Latin America, people are accustomed to training and managing their draft animals. Implements are readily available locally, usually made from local materials, with a local system to repair and replace them.

In other areas of the world, draft animal power is a more recent technology in cultivation and crop production. For instance, until recently in West Africa and much of sub-Saharan Africa, animal diseases prevented the keeping of animals in many areas, and the traditional methods of cultivating the land used manual labor only. It is only within the last century that many people have made use of draft animals on their farms in these areas, following availability of drugs (Fig. 1). Because of the relative newness of the technology, the support infrastructure might not be available locally. As a result, the animals and implements available are expensive, and they involve considerable investment by the farmers before they can see the benefits and the drawbacks for themselves. Often, implements are imported or manufactured by companies selling a range of agricultural

Encyclopedia of Animal Science
DOI: 10.1081/E-EAS 120019543

Fig. 1 Training oxen on a course in Seroti, Uganda. (Photo courtesy of R.A. Pearson.) (*View this art in color at www.dekker.com.*)

equipment. Although spares may be available, the manufacturers or retailers can be some distance from the farm, and so repairs cannot be done in situ in the fields, as they often can be in more traditional systems.

A lack of skill can often be seen where working animals are used in transport enterprises in urban areas. In these operations, while some users have a long experience of working with animals, others have little experience in livestock keeping. Equids tend to be favored over ruminants for their greater speed in urban transport. The horse or donkey is used to provide a daily income, rather as a vehicle would be, and may be regarded as an expendable item by some, with little care given to working practices or its management. Cattle, buffalo, and camels generally fare better, largely due to their resale value for meat. Thus, it is not surprising that the nongovernmental organizations (NGOs) and animal charities often voice welfare concerns for the working horse and donkey.

OUTPUTS FROM WORKING ANIMALS

The output from draft animals as a contribution to the community is more difficult to assess than that from beef or dairy animals. Draft force, speed, work, and power have all been used to assess output of draft animals. Area plowed or cultivated and distance traveled or load carried in transport are outputs that can be measured fairly easily. Less immediate, perhaps, is the yield of the crop their draft animals have helped to produce.

The amount of work an animal can do will depend on the speed at which it works and the draft force generated. For a particular draft force, it is the speed that will determine the power output of the animal, i.e., the rate at which the animal does the work. Therefore, these parameters are all closely related. Various aspects of the animal, the implement, the environment, and the operator all interact to determine the amount of work done in a day.

NUTRIENT REQUIREMENTS OF WORKING ANIMALS

Researchers have determined the nutrient requirements of working animals. Ruminants have received the most attention.[1] However, interest in the performance of working horses and donkeys has increased in recent years and their requirements are now more fully understood.[2] The main requirement for work is energy. Extra requirements for protein, minerals, and vitamins for work are small and can usually be met by the increase in food given to meet the additional energy requirements. Energy requirement during a working day is more closely related to distance covered than to the draft force required to pull the implement or cart. Hence, animals doing light work such as pulling a cart can expend more energy in a day than animals doing heavy work such as plowing. Even when oxen are working for 6–7 hours a day, their total energy expenditure on a working day is rarely more than two times maintenance requirements. Horses and donkeys can exceed a requirement of $2 \times$ maintenance in a working day, but this is usually only when they are working steadily for six or more hours per day.

CONSTRAINTS TO PERFORMANCE

Many studies of the husbandry and use of working animals have been undertaken over the last 20 years.[3–5] As well as determining their capabilities, it is important to examine the constraints that can limit the contribution that working animals can make. High ambient temperature and disease[3] are well-known constraints to performance. However, the constraint most often identified by working animal owners is nutrition. The main problem is how best to meet the nutritional requirements for work with the feed resources available. Location and season determine which feeds are given to draft animals.

For most of the year, draft animals consume poor-quality forage diets that have a high cell wall content, low nitrogen content, and poor digestibility. The ME content of these diets is rarely more than 9 MJ metabolizable energy (ME)/kg and crude protein of 90 g/kg dry matter (DM). Research studies have shown that any increase in rate of eating or improvement in digestibility on working days, which result from increased energy demand during working periods, are not sufficient to meet the additional energy requirement for most types of work when animals are fed such diets. In practice, most draft animal farmers expect their animals to lose weight during the working season unless the diet is supplemented with better-quality feed. The start of the cropping season, when draft animals are required to do the most work, is usually the time when food stocks are at their lowest, particularly in areas that have a long dry or cold season. This further exacerbates the problem of feeding for work.

The need for supplementation is greatest when animals are multipurpose, being also required to maintain weight (if they are to be ultimately sold for meat), or if they are cows used for work and also required to produce a calf.

Various strategies are available to improve feed supply to draft animals, dependent upon the financial resources of the owner. They are discussed in other entries of this encyclopedia. The benefits of these techniques are well researched and widely reported, but adoption by draft animal farmers is often poor.

CONCLUSION

Continued mechanization of agricultural practices will occur where it is economically feasible, and draft animals will be replaced on those farms that can justify maintenance and use of two- or four-wheeled tractor power. On steep, inaccessible, or terraced hillsides, and on mixed farms where farm size and scale of crop production are small, animal power is still a better option than motorized power to supplement manual labor. On small farms of less than 3 ha, animal power can compete economically with gasoline-fueled tractors. Farmers using animal power will have to cope with competition for their land from a growing human population and increasing pressure on natural resources. This is likely to lead to the cultivation of more marginal land and greater use of animals for multiple purposes (e.g., work and milk or

work and meat). Cropping of marginal land will require more attention to soil and water conservation and animal-drawn tillage techniques. Reduction of grazing land may require more farmers to move to a cut-and-carry system of managing their work animals. With the need to use resources more efficiently, it is important to recognize that animal energy can be harnessed to provide several income-generating activities for the smallholder farmer outside of their use in the production of food and cash crops. More versatile, and therefore more frequent, use of animal power is an ideal way to spread the maintenance costs. A resting draft animal still uses resources, unlike a resting tractor. Hence, broader use of animal power in the areas where it is found should also be encouraged.

REFERENCES

1. Lawrence, P.R.; Pearson, R.A. Feeding Standards For Cattle Used for Work. In *Centre for Tropical Veterinary Medicine*; Scotland, UK, 1991. ISBN 0-907146-082.
2. Perez, R.; Valenzuela, S.; Merino, V. Energetic requirements and physiological adaptation of draught horses to ploughing work. Animal Sci. **1996**, *63*, 343–351.
3. Pearson, R.A.; Zerbini, E.; Lawrence, P.R. Recent advances in research on draught animals. Animal Sci. **1999**, *68*, 1–17.
4. Empowering Farmers with Animal Traction, Proceedings of the Workshop of the Animal Traction Network for Eastern and Southern Africa (ATNESA), Mpumalanga, South Africa, Sept. 20–24, 1999; Kaumbutho, P., Pearson, R.A., Simalenga, T.S., Eds.; SANAT: South Africa, 2000. ISBN 0-907146-10-4.
5. Working Animals in Agriculture and Transport. A Collection of Some Current Research and Development Observations. In *EAAP Technical Series No 6*; Pearson, R.A., Lhoste, P., Saastamoinen, M., Martin Rosset, W., Eds.; Wageningen Academic Publishers: The Netherlands, 2003; 209.

Contributions to Society: Improved Animal Source Foods

Travis J. Knight
Donald C. Beitz
Iowa State University, Ames, Iowa, U.S.A.

INTRODUCTION

Foods derived from animals contribute significantly to total nutrient intake in the United States and throughout the world. Animal-derived foods are a primary source for vitamin B_{12}, vitamin B_6, riboflavin, niacin, zinc, phosphorus, and calcium for the U.S. population. Nearly 70% of dietary protein and nearly 40% of dietary calories are of animal origin. All dietary cholesterol and about three-fourths of saturated fatty acids in the typical U.S. diet are also of animal origin. These last two constituents have caused significant concern on the part of nutritionists and consumers alike and have stimulated a movement toward the redesigning of animal-derived foods.

CONSUMER CONCERNS

The approach of this article is to focus on redesigning animal-derived foods to meet the ideals and habits of the modern consumer. Consumers are changing their dietary eating habits as determined by surveys conducted by the International Food Marketing Institute (FMI) (www.fmi.org). Ninety-three percent of people surveyed in the United States in an FMI survey in 2000 said they would be making dietary changes. These changes include increases in fruit and vegetable consumption, decreases in total meat and red meat consumption, slight increases in poultry and white meat consumption, slight decreases in dairy product consumption, increases in fish consumption, and increases in low-fat and skim-milk products. Fat and cholesterol top the nutritional concerns, with 46% and 17% of consumers being concerned about these components, respectively. But consumers select foods based on taste, nutrition, and product safety. Ease of preparation will probably increase as an emphasis for consumers as our society becomes busier.

NUTRITION RECOMMENDATIONS

Consumer ideals and habits are shaped by their exposure to reports prepared by governmental agencies and private associations. These include groups such as the U.S. Department of Agriculture (USDA), which published the *Food Guide Pyramid* (www.nal.usda.gov/fnic/Fpyr/pyramid.html) and the *Dietary Guidelines for Americans* (www.usda.gov/cnpp/Pubs/DG2000/Index.htm), the American Cancer Society's *Guidelines in Diet, Nutrition, and Cancer Prevention* (www2.cancer.org/), the American Heart Association's *Dietary Guidelines* (www.americanheart.org/Heart_and_Stroke_A_Z_Guide/dietg.html), the American Institute of Cancer Research's *Simple Steps to Prevent Cancer* (www.aicr.org/stp.htm), and the National Institutes of Health (NIH) National Cholesterol Education Program's *Therapeutic Lifestyle Changes* (www.nhlbi.nih.gov/chd/lifestyles.htm). In general, these publications encourage a plant-based, high-fiber diet that is low in total and animal fat and that includes five to nine servings of fruits and vegetables per day.

WHY REDESIGN ANIMAL-DERIVED FOOD?

In redesigning meat, milk, and eggs, we want to improve healthfulness by decreasing content of total fat and cholesterol and by increasing the ratio of unsaturated to saturated fatty acids. We should increase the consistency of tenderness of meat, especially beef, and improve its stability including both resistance to rancidity and bacteriostatic properties. We should look for ways to decrease food cost to the consumer while increasing the yield for the producer. Also, the consumer has requested quick and easy food preparation. Finally, environmental issues including a decrease in nitrogen and phosphorus waste in animal production systems should be addressed. Historically, it was probably the concern for fats, fatty acids, and cholesterol that occurred in the late '70s that initiated this trend toward redesigning animal-derived food. To continue this trend, it is timely for the animal food industry to take advantage of the current emphasis and popularity of functional foods and nutraceuticals and make some favorable changes to ensure healthful diets in the future.

Encyclopedia of Animal Science
DOI: 10.1081/E-EAS 120019544

Ideal Composition of Animal-Derived Food

If scientists and producers redesign animal foods, they need a target or end point in mind. The following discussion provides examples of improved and idealized animal products that may be of interest and usefulness in the near future.

Improved Milk

When milk is evaluated as a nutrient source, there are several facts and opinions that we need to consider when thinking about redesigning milk. Some of the facts about milk include: It is a nutritious and tasty food; it is high in fat, especially triacylglycerol; it is rich in saturated fatty acids; it is rich in CLA compared with other foods; it is a good source of calcium and an excellent source of dietary protein; and it causes intolerances for some individuals. Key features to incorporate into redesigned milk include making its fat contain an ideal fatty acid composition, converting lactose to its constituent sugars, increasing the solids in skim milk for better mouth feel, increasing the iron content, lessening the total fat content, and using milk as a carrier for specific nutrients. In 1989, a group of nutritionists, food scientists, animal scientists, producers, and processors proposed that the ideal milk fat is one in which the saturated fatty acids were decreased by being moved to the monounsaturated fatty acid category with a slight increase in the amount of polyunsaturated fatty acids (Fig. 1). These considerations did not take into account processing issues, but rather focused solely on the idealized fatty acid composition from a human health perspective.

One way of evaluating the healthfulness of the fatty acid composition of foods is by grouping the constituent fatty acids and calculating an atherogenic index (AI). The AI is calculated by summing the concentration of saturated fatty acids (omitting stearic acid) and four times the concentration of C-14 and using that sum as the numerator that is divided by the sum of unsaturated fatty acids in the product.[2] To illustrate the potential of producing a more idealized milk by genetic means, milk

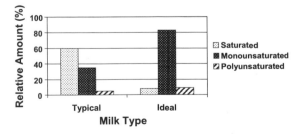

Fig. 1 Idealized milk fat. (Data are adapted from Ref. [1].)

Table 1 Variation in atherogenic index (AI) and fatty acid composition of milk

Measurement	Low 5%[a]	Mid 5%[b]	High 5%[b]
AI	**1.06**	**2.30**	**3.31**
Fatty acid		(wt. %)	
14:0	5.2	10.7	12.6
16:0	25.3	28.0	36.2
18:0	14.4	13.9	9.7
18:1	37.8	25.8	20.3
18:2	3.3	3.0	2.3

[a]Low 5% refers to the 5% of cows within a 180-cow herd that had the lowest AI.
[b]Mid 5% and high 5% refer to the 5% of cows with mid and high AIs. (Data from Ref. [3].)

samples with a low, medium, and high AI from a Holstein herd are described in Table 1. With the AI ranging from 1.06 to 3.31, we observed a wide variation in fatty acid composition of individual milks. When the largest and smallest AIs of milk samples are compared with other foods, the milk with the smallest AI fits in the range of AIs for margarine. On the other hand, the greatest AI for milk does not approach that of coconut oil (AI = 15.9), which is at the atherogenic extreme of common foods and food components.

A specific group of fatty acids that are enriched in ruminant-derived foods is CLA. Conjugated linoleic acid has been touted as a nutraceutical for several reasons because it benefits human health. For example, a study conducted by Ip et al.[4] clearly demonstrates that CLA, when incorporated into butter by preharvest or postharvest means, decreases tumor incidence in rats.

IMPROVED RED MEATS

With meat, our goal is to optimize taste and tenderness, minimize fat content, impart a healthful fatty acid composition, and develop a more stabilized color. Several niche markets have been established in which beef from pasture-fed cattle has a two- to fourfold increase in CLA content. An example of incorporating a nutraceutical into meat is the feeding of supplemental vitamin E to pigs and beef cattle to improve color stability and nutritional value and to increase meat shelf life.

Another example of a preharvest treatment is to improve tenderness of beef by feeding high doses of vitamin D_3 near the time of harvest. When 5×10^6 IU of vitamin D_3 was fed per day, the shear force, as measured by the Warner-Bratzler test, significantly decreased at 7 and 14 days postmortem, which is indicative of an increased tenderness.[5] The hydroxylated product of vitamin D_3, 25-hydroxy vitamin D_3, also seems to improve tenderness. Although neither practice currently is approved, use of 25-hydroxy vitamin D_3 seems promising for use in future beef production systems.

IMPROVED EGGS

We may define the ideal egg as an egg that is free of cholesterol and pathogens and that contains the desired nutraceuticals of interest. An improved egg may be one containing less cholesterol and a more ideal fatty acid composition. One improved egg that was introduced in the marketplace is the EggsPlus® egg. Because of dietary manipulation of the hens, including flax seed feeding, EggsPlus® eggs have double the typical amount of omega-6 polyunsaturated fatty acids and markedly more linolenic and docosahexaenoic acids, which are both omega-3 polyunsaturated fatty acids. The polyunsaturated fatty acid (w-6 and w-3) content of these eggs is triple that of traditional eggs.

OVERVIEW OF METHODS TO REDESIGN ANIMAL-DERIVED FOODS

Figure 2 summarizes approaches that could be utilized to improve animal-derived foods. Among the traditional feeding and breeding methods, some are preharvest and some are postharvest techniques (Fig. 2). Preharvest techniques include feeding animals compounds such as vitamin E, omega-3 fatty acids, or CLA. Postharvest techniques available for modifying animal-derived foods include such procedures as calcium infusion or electro-stimulation of animal carcasses to improve tenderness, the addition of vitamin D to milk, which has been done for

years, and irradiation of animal-derived foods, which is increasing in popularity and acceptance.

When genetic modification is considered, preharvest systems would include genetically altering animals or gut microbes to provide specific actions of interest, while postharvest techniques could include modifying food-processing microbes by using genetic engineering to optimize the contents of nutraceuticals in products. Two examples of preharvest genetic modification include either knocked out (deleted) genes or inserted genes. Specific examples of genetic modifications could include knocking out the triacylglycerol synthetase gene (clearly an extreme example) so that the cow would produce skim milk or the genetic addition of lactase to the secretory cells of the mammary gland, which is an experiment that already has been conducted in a mouse, to produce a lactose-decreased or a lactose-free milk.

CONCLUSION

In addition to providing satisfaction to the consumer, foods from animals are a major contributor of energy, macronutrients, and micronutrients in the American diet. Because of human health concerns of constituents like saturated fatty acids and cholesterol, animal scientists and food processors must continue to redesign animal-derived foods to meet demands of consumers. In addition to traditional nutritional, management, breeding, and processing methods, scientists have new molecular biological techniques to accomplish the goal of redesigning foods for human health and longevity.

REFERENCES

1. O'Donnell, J.A. Milk fat technologies and markets: A summary of the Wisconsin Milk Marketing Board 1988 Milk Fat Roundtable. J. Dairy Sci. **1989**, *72*, 3109–3119.
2. Ulbright, T.L.V.; Southgate, D.A.T. Coronary heart disease: Seven dietary factors. Lancet **1991**, *338*, 985–992.
3. Chen, S.; Bobe, G.; Zimmerman, S.; Hammond, E.G.; Luhman, C.M.; Boylston, T.D.; Freeman, A.E.; Beitz, D.C. Physical and sensory properties of dairy products from cows with various milk fatty acid compositions. J. Agric. Food Chem. **2004**, *in press.*
4. Ip, C.; Banni, S.; Angioni, E.; Carta, G.; McGinley, J.; Thompson, H.J.; Barbano, D.; Bauman, D. Conjugated linoleic acid-enriched butter fat alters mammary gland morphogenesis and reduces cancer risk in rats. J. Nutr. **1999**, *129*, 2135–2142.
5. Montgomery, J.L.; Parrish, F.C.; Beitz, D.C.; Horst, R.L.; Huff-Lonergan, E.J.; Trenkle, A.H. The use of vitamin D_3 to improve beef tenderness. J. Anim. Sci. **2000**, *78*, 2615–2621.

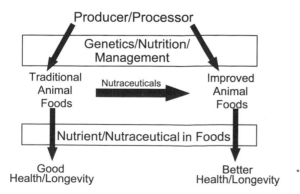

Fig. 2 Summary of redesigning animal foods.

Contributions to Society: Manure-Fertilizer/Fuel, Developed Countries

J. Mark Powell
U.S. Dairy Forage Research Center, Madison, Wisconsin, U.S.A.

INTRODUCTION

Manure provides essential and secondary nutrients for crop production, increases soil organic matter levels, and enhances soil physical properties and overall soil quality. Manure also contains energy that can be converted into fuel. This article addresses potential agronomic benefits and pollution hazards associated with land application of manure, followed by a brief discussion of the increasing attractiveness of using manure as fertilizer and energy in the current era of high energy costs.

MANURE AS A FERTILIZER FOR CROP PRODUCTION

In the United States, animal agriculture accounts for approximately $100 billion annually, or half of all farm sales. The manure produced by dairy and beef cattle, poultry, and swine contains vast amounts of nitrogen and phosphorus (Table 1) that in some regions can be land-applied at agronomic rates on farms where it is produced.[2] Nitrogen (N) is the most limiting nutrient to cereal crop production, so the fertilizer value of manure is usually equated to its ability to provide N to a succeeding crop. Manure N availability for use by crops is highly influenced by its ammonium content (Fig. 1), which depends on the amount of urine N conserved. Organic N in feces and bedding is more slowly available than urine N, and continues to mineralize and be available for crop uptake years after application. If and when manure is incorporated also affects the availability of manure N to crops.

Two approaches are commonly used to estimate the fertilizer N value of manure: 1) apparent manure N recovery by crops (i.e., the difference method, or difference in crop N uptake in plots that received and did not receive manure); and 2) comparison of crop response with approximately equivalent rates of commercial fertilizer (i.e., the fertilizer equivalence approach). A ''decay series'' is developed that predicts the proportion of manure N available the first, second, and third year after application. Beegle et al.[4] summarized the results of approximately 90 trials conducted between 1931 and 2002 across a wide range of soils and environmental conditions and found that first year manure N availabilities were remarkably consistent within animal species and averaged 36% for dairy, 32% for beef, 27% for sheep, 51% for poultry, and 62% for swine. However, averages tend to obscure within-study variability. For example, using the difference method and the fertilizer equivalent approach, Muñoz et al.[5] estimated that corn N uptake during the first year after dairy manure application ranged from −60% of applied N (a negative value obtained when crop N uptake in nonmanure control plots is greater than manure-amended plots) to 148% (values >100% obtained when crop N uptake exceeds N additions). The use of manure labeled with the stable isotope ^{15}N provides a more direct and less variable measure of manure N availability to crops.[5]

Manure applications provide crop yields comparable or superior to yields with inorganic fertilizer. The beneficial effects of manure are due not only to nutrients, but also to improvements in soil organic matter content (SOM), soil structure, and tilth. Improvements in infiltration, soil aggregation, and bulk density due to manure application can reduce runoff and erosion. SOM enhancement due to manure increases soil cation exchange and buffering capacities, which enables manure-amended soils to retain nutrients (and chemicals such as pesticides) for longer periods of time. SOM increases carbon sequestration in soils, which mitigates the effects of rising atmospheric CO_2 levels on global climate. However, manure may also provide soluble carbon and nitrates, which can enhance N_2O emissions from soil and contribute to global warming.

LIMITATIONS TO USING MANURE AS A FERTILIZER

Effective recycling of manure nutrients through crops presents many challenges. For example, to achieve analytical results with a 95% confidence interval with a 10% probable error for manure N content, 1, 55, and 17 subsamples are required for dairy compost, chicken manure, and stockpiled beef manure, respectively.[6]

Encyclopedia of Animal Science
DOI: 10.1081/E-EAS 120019545

Another factor that inhibits good manure management is the large difference in the N:P ratio of manure vs. the N:P requirements of crops. Applying sufficient manure to meet crop N requirements usually results in excessive P application, which can increase the hazard of soil P buildup and loss in runoff. The N:P ratio of manure can be aligned to the N:P requirements of crops by removing unnecessary mineral P supplements from animals' diets and through conservation of manure N.

The proximity of the site where manure is produced and crops are grown is key to managing manure for its agronomic benefits. During the early to mid part of the last century, crops and livestock were operationally and functionally linked enterprises. Most feed was home-grown and N provided by legumes and manure sustained crop yields. The introduction of inexpensive fertilizers and inexpensive transport costs allowed crops to be grown in one location and livestock produced in another. On many farms, manure became an undesirable by-product and any connotation of its intrinsic fertilizer value was replaced with a "waste" mentality.[7] Specialization in livestock is most pronounced in the feedlot cattle, swine, and poultry industries. Especially since the mid-1980s, the average herd size on U.S. dairy farms has grown markedly, and milk production is becoming concentrated on the largest farms. The trend toward fewer and larger farms for all livestock types has heightened public concern about pollution.

When mismanaged, manure has the potential to pollute air, land, and water resources. Over the past decade, environmental policy has focused on ways to improve manure management and arrest the buildup of soil test P, runoff, and the pollution of lakes, streams, and other surface water bodies. Emerging environmental policy is aimed at abating the emission of air pollutants from animal agriculture.

Major pathways of manure N losses are emissions of the gases NH_3, N_2O, and N_2, and the leaching of NO_3.

Table 1 Manure nitrogen and phosphorus available for application to cropland in the United States, 1997

Animal type	Manure nitrogen	Manure phosphorus
	1,000 Mg	
Dairy cattle	288.2	110.6
Feedlot beef cattle	176.8	115.2
Other cattle	59.2	49.1
Poultry	552.8	251.2
Swine	124.3	125.5
Total	1,201.3	651.6

(From Ref. 1.)

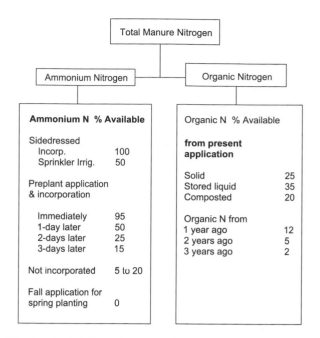

Fig. 1 Availability of manure N for crop uptake. (From Ref. 3.)

Ammonia losses range from 30% to 40% of total N excreted. Nitrate losses typically range from 10% to 30% and denitrification 2% to 5% of total N applied. High nitrate leaching contaminates groundwater and increases losses of N via denitrification. Although denitrification may constitute only a small percentage of applied manure N, N_2O contributes to global warming and ozone depletion. The highly interactive nature of manure N transformations and pathways of N loss necessitate that manure management be based on an understanding of the trade-offs involved in conservation of one N form and concomitant increases in other N losses (Table 2). For example, manure injection into soil to reduce ammonia loss (and improve air quality) may increase nitrate leaching (and reduce ground water quality) and increase denitrification (greenhouse gas formation).

NUTRIENT MANAGEMENT PLANNING

Nutrient loss from agriculture, as well as from natural ecosystems, is inevitable. A continuous challenge is to enhance nutrient use by crops and livestock and minimize nutrient loss through good management. Animal nutrition, field, whole-farm, and landscape models have been developed to improve nutrient management on crop–livestock farms. While of great use in predicting biophysical outcomes (e.g., feed nutrient use by livestock and excretion in manure, fertilizer and manure nutrient

Table 2 Qualitative comparisons of major N loss pathways for manure application under various management regimes and environmental conditions

Manure management				Nitrogen loss processes		
Rate	Time	Placement	Soil drainage	Ammonia	Denitrification	Leaching
Placement comparisons						
Med.	Spring	Surface	Well	High	Low	Med.
Med.	Spring	Incorporated	Well	Low	Med.	Med.
Med.	Spring	Injected	Well	Low	Med.	Med.
Soil drainage comparisons						
Med.	Spring	Incorporated	Excess	Low	Low	High
Med.	Spring	Incorporated	Poor	Low	High	Med.
Application rate comparisons						
Low	Spring	Incorporated	Poor	Low	Low	Low
Med.	Spring	Incorporated	Poor	Low	Med.	Med.
High	Spring	Incorporated	Poor	Low	Med.	High
Time of year comparison						
Med.	Fall	Surface	Well	High	Low	High
Med.	Winter	Surface	Well	Med.	Low	High
Med.	Spring	Surface	Well	High	Low	Med.
Med.	Summer	Surface	Well	High	Med.	Med.

(From Ref. 8.)

use by crops, soil nutrient buildup and loss), most models do not address social and economic factors that influence farmers' ability and willingness to adopt alternative practices. A manure management plan must be practical to be effective. A slightly imperfect, less comprehensive, but practical plan will almost always provide more desired results than a more complicated one that is not practical to implement.[9]

MANURE, FUEL PRODUCTION, AND USE

A principal strategy to facilitate manure management has been to improve manure handling and storage. Most dairy and swine manure is now flushed from housing, and manure is stored in outside lagoons. The widespread expansion of flush and lagoon systems was premised on labor efficiency and the notion that storage would facilitate calculation of manure nutrients available and allow for land application during favorable weather conditions and close to crop nutrient demands. However, anaerobic manure lagoons accounted for approximately 7% of the global methane emissions in 1991,[10] a figure that has likely increased substantially. Covered lagoons, complete mix digester systems, and plug-flow digester systems can capture methane that can be converted into energy and used for electricity production, heating, and cooling. The cost effectiveness of methane recovery and energy conversion is becoming increasingly attractive in

areas where livestock concentrations, and therefore the supply of manure, is high enough to produce sufficient energy competitive with classical energy sources.

The use of manure as a substitute for fertilizer N may become more attractive as energy costs increase. Natural gas is used to produce a large fraction of fertilizer N, and natural gas accounts for 75–90% of the cost of making anhydrous ammonia. Conserving manure N may be of much greater importance as energy costs continue to escalate. Furthermore, it will reduce carbon dioxide (greenhouse gas) generation during the manufacture of N fertilizer.

CONCLUSION

Manure benefits crop production through its fertilizer value and enhancement of soil physical properties and overall soil quality. The fertilizer N value of manure depends on the conservation of urine N. Approximately 25–35% of the N contained in manure of ruminant livestock (beef and dairy cattle, sheep) is available to the plant the season following application vs. 50–60% for poultry and swine. As livestock and crop production become more specialized, it becomes more difficult to conserve manure nutrients and recycle them through crops. Manure N losses via ammonia volatilization, nitrate leaching, and denitrification, and manure P losses in runoff are the principal pollution concerns. The economics of practices that enhance manure's fertilizer value, and capture of methane during manure storage may become increasingly attractive in the current era of high energy costs.

ACKNOWLEDGMENT

Dedicated to the late Dr. Les Lanyon, from whom I learned much.

REFERENCES

1. USDA-ERS. *United States Department of Agriculture-Economic Research Service.* www.ers.usda.gov/data/manure. (accessed June 2004).
2. Gollehon, N.; Caswell, M.; Ribaudo, M.; Kellogg, R.; Lander, C.; Letson, D. *Confined Animal Production and Manure Nutrients*; Agriculture Information Bulletin No. 771, Resource Economics Division, Economic Research Service, U.S. Department of Agriculture, 2001.
3. NRCS. *USDA-Natural Resources Conservation Service. CORE4 Conservation Practices Training Guide*; 1999.
4. Beegle, D.B.; Kelling, K.A.; Schmitt, M.A. Nitrogen from Animal Manures. In *Nitrogen in Agricultural Soils*; American Society of Agronomy Monograph, American Society of Agronomy: Madison, WI, Vol. x, *in press*.
5. Muñoz, G.R.; Kelling, K.A.; Powell, J.M.; Speth, P.E. Comparison of estimates of first-year dairy manure N availability or recovery using ^{15}N and other techniques. J. Environ. Qual. **2004**, *33*, 719–727.
6. Ivensen, K.V.; Davis, J.G.; Vigil, M.F. *Variability of Manure Nutrient Content and Impact on Manure Sampling Protocol*; Agronomy Abstracts, American Society of Agronomy: Madison, Winconsin, 1997; 239.
7. Nowak, P.; Shepard, R.; Madison, F. Farmers and Manure Management: A Critical Analysis. In *Animal Waste Utilization: Effective Use of Manure as a Soil Resource*; Hatfield, J.L., Stewart, B.A., Eds.; Ann Arbor Press: Chelsea, Michigan, 1998; 1–32.
8. Meisinger, J.J.; Jokela, W.E. Ammonia Volatilization from Dairy and Poultry Manure. In *Managing Nutrients and Pathogens from Animal Agriculture*; Natural Resource, Agriculture, and Engineering Service (NRARS): Cooperative Extension, 152 Riley-Robb Hall, Ithaca, NY, 2000; 334–354.
9. Risse, L.M.; Cabrera, M.L.; Franzluebbers, A.J.; Gaskin, J.W.; Gilley, J.E.; Killorn, R.; Radcliffe, D.E.; Tollner, W.E.; Zhang, H. Land Application of Manure for Beneficial Reuse. In *National Center for Animal Manure and Waste Management. Summary of White Papers*; 2001. http://www.cals.ncsu.edu:8050/waste_mgt/natlcenter/summary.pdf (accessed June 2004).
10. Roos, K.F. Profitable Alternatives for Regulatory Impacts on Livestock Waste Management. In *National Livestock, Poultry and Aquaculture Waste Management*; Balke, J., Donald, J., Magette, W., Eds.; American Society of Agricultural Engineers: St. Joseph, Michigan, 1992; 89–99.

Contributions to Society: Slaughter By-Products

John A. Marchello
Elaine V. Marchello
University of Arizona, Tucson, Arizona, U.S.A.

INTRODUCTION

Meat animal by-products are produced by several different entities in the meat industry—slaughterhouses, meat processors, fabricators (both wholesale and retail), and rendering plants.

The red meat industry in the United States defines a by-product as everything, except the carcass, that comes from food animals (cattle, sheep, swine, and goat). Animal by-products can be classified as edible or inedible, and are often referred to as offal.

HIDES AND SKINS

Humans have used animal hides and skins for clothing, shelters, and containers since prehistoric times. Hides represent a significant portion of the live animal's weight, ranging from 4 to 11%, and are considered to be the most valuable by-products coming from meat animals. Hides from cattle and pigs and pelts from sheep and goats provide many different finished products—leather goods, rawhide, athletic equipment, cosmetic products, edible gelatin, glue, and regenerated collagen.[1] To avoid bacterial or enzymatic decomposition, salt is used for curing, then the hides are tanned to form leather.

Gelatin is made from fresh hides or edible bones by a three-step process: noncollagenous material removal, hydrolysis, and drying. Gelatin's uses include: jellied desserts; stabilizing frozen desserts and ice cream; as a protective colloid for ice cream, cream pies, and yogurt; capsule coverings; binding agents for medicated tablets; sterile surgery sponges; protective ointments; as an emulsifier for emulsions and foams; and in cosmetics and silk screen printing.

Collagen from hides and skins is used as an emulsion in meat products, wherein it can be converted into a dough that is extruded into various-diameter edible or inedible sausage casings. These casings are widely used because they are shelf-stable and similar to natural casings.[2]

Pigskin is similar to human skin and is used for dressing burns and skin ulcers. Body hair and inner-ear hair from cattle is used for air filters, artist brushes, carpet pads, upholstery stuffing, felt, and textiles. Wool is a good source of lanolin and provides a durable fabric for various types of clothing and upholstery.

MEAT ANIMAL GLANDS AND ORGANS

Animal organs and glands offer a diversity of flavors, textures, and nutritional values. Traditions, culture, and religion play a big role in how these glands and organs are used for food. Many of these variety meats are exported to foreign countries for consumption.

The organs and glands used for human food include heart, kidneys, liver, spleen, tongue, pancreas, thymus, cattle and sheep stomachs, testes, and the stomachs and uteri of pigs.[2]

Brains and spinal cords are now considered inedible because of BSE (bovine spongiform encephalopathy, or Mad Cow Disease). Lungs are considered inedible because they are a filtering mechanism of inhaled air, but they are used in pet foods.

Hearts are used as table meat or in ground meat products, but must be listed separately on the label.

Kidneys are trimmed of blood vessels and ureters and can be prepared in a variety of ways. Liver is the most widely used organ meat. It is used in processed meats, such as liver sausage and liver pate. Livers from lambs, veal calves, and baby beef (3–9 mos.) are preferred because they have mild flavor and finer texture. The tongue, sweetbreads (thymus), and oxtail are sold as fresh items.[2]

Ruminant animals (cattle, sheep, and goats) have four stomach compartments: rumen, reticulum, abomasum, and omasum. The rumen and reticulum are most often used for food and are processed at slaughter by washing, scalding, and bleaching. They can be eaten after cooking or used in processed meats, or they can be sewn to form a casing and stuffed with various types of meat.

Meat animal intestines are cleaned and packed in a salt brine and used for sausage casings. The diameter of these natural casings dictates the size and shape of the sausage product, such as a wiener or a bologna.

Edible cattle udders are sliced, washed free of milk, and cooked by frying or boiling. Spleens are minced and used as flavoring agents, or in pies or processed meats.

Encyclopedia of Animal Science
DOI: 10.1081/E-EAS 120019548

Consumable uteri come from nonpregnant pigs and are poached or boiled.

Hormones are secreted by endocrine glands and tissues including the liver, lungs, pituitary, thyroid, pancreas, stomach, parathyroid, kidney, and adrenal, and the ovary at various stages. These glands and tissues are collected from healthy animals, sent to pharmaceutical companies for processing, and are used as medicines.

The inner portion of the adrenal gland (medulla) secretes epinephrine and norepinephrine. These substances are used to stop hemorrhaging, to stimulate heart action, and to overcome shock. Steroids from the cortex (outer part) regulate the utilization of nutrients such as fat, carbohydrate, minerals, and water. Steroids removed from cattle, pig, and sheep adrenal glands are used as anti-inflammatory agents and for treatment of asthma and shock.[3]

Brains, nervous tissues, and spinal cords are a good source of cholesterol, which is used in the synthesizing of vitamin D_3 and as an emulsifier in cosmetics. Melatonin is extracted from the pineal gland and may aid the treatment of schizophrenia and insomnia.

The pituitary gland produces growth hormone, thyroid stimulating hormone, mammary stimulating hormone, and adrenocortical stimulating hormone. These hormones control growth and metabolism, and regulate the activity of other endocrine glands. Adrenocortical stimulating hormone is the main hormone extracted from the pituitary and is used in the treatment of rheumatism, arthritis, eye inflammation, and multiple myeloma.[2]

The liver of cattle and pigs provides a good source of vitamin B_{12}. Heparin can be extracted from the liver, small intestine, and lungs. It is an anticoagulant to prolong the clotting time of blood and to prevent blood clotting during surgery.

Progesterone and estrogen are extracted from pig ovaries and are used in the treatment of hormone imbalances in women. Relaxin, extracted from the ovaries of pregnant sows, is used to assist with childbirth.

The pancreas of meat animals, especially from pigs, provides a good source of insulin used in diabetic therapy. However, the use of animal insulin is diminishing because insulin can be artificially synthesized. Two proteolytic enzymes, chymotrypsin and trypsin, may be extracted from the pancreas and used to improve healing after injury or surgery.

In addition to sausage casings, intestines from sheep and calves (under 9 mos.) are used to make catgut, the material used for internal surgical sutures.

TALLOW AND LARD

Another important by-product is animal fat. Lard is the fat rendered from hogs, whereas tallow is a harder fat rendered from cattle and sheep. Both have been used extensively for deep-fat frying, but this use has declined due to consumer health concerns and the increased use of vegetable oils. Furthermore, edible tallow and lard are used in the manufacturing of margarine and shortening.

Tallow provides a beneficial and wide array of products such as various soaps. Oleic acid (18 carbon fatty acid) is extracted from tallow and is used to make lubricants, textiles, shampoo, emulsifiers, and cleansing cream. It is an excellent source of glycerin and is used to manufacture inks, glues, solvents, antifreeze, and explosives. Stearic acid (18 carbon saturated fatty acid) is used in rubber tire manufacturing to provide a means of cooling the rubber when driving, and it is also used in lubricants for airplanes and cars. Linoleic acid (omega 6 fatty acid) is used to make certain lubricants and paints.[2]

MEAT ANIMAL BLOOD

Blood may be used for human food as long as it comes from healthy animals approved for human consumption. It is utilized to manufacture blood sausage, blood pudding, biscuits and bread, and nonfood items such as fertilizer and binders. Industrially, it is used in adhesives, insecticides, fungicides, and cosmetics, as well as in the manufacture of paper, plywood, fiber, plastics, and glue, and as a foaming agent in fire extinguishers.

USE OF BLOOD PLASMA IN FOODS

Blood is used in food as an emulsifier, stabilizer, color additive, and for nutritional components. Separate blood fractions, including plasma (the largest fraction), albumin, fibrogen, fibrinolysin, serotonin, and immunoglobulins, can be used for chemical and medical purposes.[3]

Purified bovine albumin is used in testing for the Rh blood factor in humans, as a stabilizer for vaccines, and in antibiotic sensitivity tests. Cattle blood is also a good source of superoxide dismutase, which is used to treat ischemia, osteorarthritis, and other types of inflammation.[3]

PET FOODS AND TREATS

Many of the by-products are processed to provide various types of foods that are used not only as treats and training tools for dogs and cats, but also for the main diet of these animals and others. Many zoos utilize by-products to formulate diets for their carnivores, and beef bones provide a tasty treat for the large animals. Some of the more commonly used by-products include raw, cooked, and smoked bones and cooked products coming from heart, liver, kidney, tendons, and muscle.[2]

ORGAN TRANSPLANTS

Certain organs, especially from pigs, have been successfully transplanted in humans. The number of people waiting for transplant organs is very large, but the use of animal organs remains questionable, not only because of the possible rejection by the recipient but also because of the ethical considerations.

CONCLUSION

Products coming from meat animal by-products have a profound effect on the everyday life of the average U.S. citizen. They provide clotting items, sporting equipment, and items that stabilize certain foods. They also can enhance the nutritional quality of these foods. The pharmaceutical industry relies heavily on by-products to produce items that are used for medical purposes or to assist in chemical reactions that produce products that can benefit humans, from both health and aesthetic standpoints.

By-products provide a number of variety meats for human consumption or for the manufacturing of value added food items, which again benefit the consumer nutritionally. Animal fats, whether edible or inedible, provide a vast array of items that are also beneficial. Some of these products are consumed directly and some are used in the manufacturing of various nonfood items that are used daily by a large majority of the U.S. population.

Without meat animal by-products, the health, nutrition, and lifestyle of the average U.S. citizen would be greatly different, and the life expectancy of our population could be adversely affected. Therefore, by-products from the meat industry are necessary for both the common as well as the affluent lifestyle that we in the United States enjoy today.

REFERENCES

1.　Taylor, R.E.; Field, T.G. *Scientific Farm Animal Production*, 8th Ed.; Pearson-Prentice Hall: New Jersey, 2004; 132–137.
2.　Liu, D.-C. *Better Utilization of By-Products from the Meat Industry*. http://www.agnet.org/library/article/eb515.html (accessed 2/4/2004).
3.　Marchello, J.A. *Meat Animal By-Products, Meat Animal Composition Manual*; Department of Animal Sciences, University of Arizona: Tucson, AZ, 2003; 220–225.

Dairy Cattle: Behavior Management and State of Being

Stanley E. Curtis
University of Illinois, Urbana, Illinois, U.S.A.

INTRODUCTION

Consensus has it that the state of being of dairy cattle, among agricultural animal species, is overall the highest. This has been viewed as being due to the closeness between keeper and animal, resulting simply from the frequent close contacts at daily milking times. In contemporary dairy cattle husbandry systems, however, that contact differs quantitatively and qualitatively from what it formerly was, and these differences have been construed as having compromised the wellness of dairy cattle.

ANIMAL STATE OF BEING

Animal state of being is determined by any homeokinetic response the environment requires and the extent to which the animal is coping.

When readily adapting, the animal is well. When having some difficulty, it is fair. When frankly unable to cope, it is ill. In reality, environments that make animals fair or ill are not uncommon. But it is our moral responsibility to minimize such occasions and correct them to the extent possible.

An environmental adaptation refers to any behavioral, functional, immune, or structural trait that favors an animal's fitness—its ability to survive and reproduce under given (especially adverse) conditions. When an animal successfully keeps or regains control of its bodily integrity and psychic stability, it is said to have coped.

BEHAVIORAL MANAGEMENT OF DAIRY CATTLE

Only a handful of the thousands of avian and mammalian species on earth have been kept for agricultural purposes. These select species share a few traits in common that equipped them to be especially strong candidates to play such a role in human civilization. Among these are several behavioral traits that have made these animals fit for being kept by humans. Many wild progenitors of modern domesticated cattle were huge, terrific creatures, able to inflict great physical harm on human beings. Through both natural and artificial genetic selection as well as supportive husbandry practices, the conformational, synthetic/productive, and temperamental traits of dairy cattle have been shaped to well serve the needs of humankind.

Genetic strains of cattle kept primarily to yield milk for human consumption have been developed so that today's dairy cattle are unique in their behavior among cattle in general: relatively gentle; catholic feed preferences; amenable to close confinement/restraint and living in large, management-imposed groups; relatively indifferent to early separation of calf from cow; and so on. Behavior of dairy cattle in modern production systems has been thoroughly explored elsewhere.[1]

STATE-OF-BEING ISSUES FOR DAIRY CATTLE

Several issues have arisen about the state of being of dairy cattle in agricultural production systems. A review of the status of these matters as of 2004 follows.

Absence of Suckling

Calves weaned shortly after birth and kept singly are deprived of the opportunity to suckle. There is evidence that this is stressful to the calf and can have psychological consequences later. Offering the calf some object for nonnutritive suckling can largely circumvent this problem.

Accommodating Individual Needs

Large herds managed intensively offer the possibility of establishing subherds that can be managed so as to more closely fulfill each individual cow's specific requirements in terms of nutrition, observation, and so on.

Body-Condition Score

Cows in poor body condition are most likely to become nonambulatory. Body condition of dairy cattle usually is scored according to a comprehensive 5-point system.[2] At least 90% of cows at a farm should have a body-condition score of 2 or 3.

Encyclopedia of Animal Science
DOI: 10.1081/E-EAS 120019551

Calf Housing

The most widely recommended and adopted calf-housing system in climates ranging from desert to tundra is an individual hut, an open side facing away from the prevailing wind, with a small fenced pen. Bedding and wind and snow breaks may be employed as needed. The health, growth, and state of being of calves in such housing are, in general, superior to those in other kinds of accommodation.

Care of Newborn Bull Calves

Surplus bull calves should be cared for just as are heifer calves to be saved for replacement purposes. They should: receive an adequate dose of colostrum; not be transported until several days postnatum, when they are able to withstand the rigors of transportation; be transported as short a distance as possible, not from place to place to place, during the fragile first week after birth.

Castration

Surplus bull calves that are expected to be kept until they become yearlings should be castrated on safety grounds. Castration should be accomplished while calves are young. It is considered a standard agricultural practice, and ordinarily is accomplished without anesthesia because the procedure is considered relatively simple and so as to circumvent problems associated with anesthesia.

Cow Longevity

The herd life of a dairy cow is a lowly heritable trait. The total husbandry system determines the useful life of a cow in a dairy herd. The fact that cow longevity has declined over the years suggests that, although genetic merit for milk yield has continuously risen for many decades, necessary adjustments in nongenetic aspects of husbandry have not kept pace, and that overall cow state of being has decreased.

Dehorning

Dairy cows and bulls use their horns as tools of aggression. Cattle horns threaten the safety of group-mates and caretakers alike. Kept cattle should not have horns. In the interest of minimizing stress and residual effects, careful dehorning by any of several appropriate methods of horned individuals should be done when the animal is no more than 4 months of age. Local anesthesia should be employed for older cattle. Polled bulls may be used to sire naturally polled calves, but this approach has not been widely adopted.

Euthanasia

Appropriate methods of euthanasia include gunshot and captive bolt, among others. The American Association of Bovine Practitioners issues and updates guidelines.

Free Stalls versus Tie (Stanchion) Stalls for Cows

Fifty years ago, keeping cows in tie or stanchion stalls during inclement weather and seasons was considered to be humanely protective, but no longer. However, although free stalls can offer several advantages relative to tie stalls in terms of cow state of being, each free-stall design and each farm is unique, and animal state of being may be compromised in certain cases. Needed resources (feed, water, and so on) must be adequately accessible to all cows in common areas; there must be an adequate number of stalls; the free stalls must be designed and maintained so as to comfortably and cleanly accommodate the cows.

Flooring

Regardless of composition, floor surfaces on which cows and bulls must stand and walk should have a friction coefficient that minimizes slippage at the same time as it minimizes abrasion, and it should be kept as dry as possible. Broken legs can result from slips, injured feet from being abraded. Once an animal has slipped on a given floor, it will try to avoid that floor and will not exhibit normal social behavior.

Identification

Good management practice requires individual identification of dairy cattle. Today, means of identification other than hot-iron or freeze branding—e.g., metal or plastic ear tags or neck-chain tags—are recommended.

Lameness

Lameness can result from a variety of situations. Any fraction of cows walking with an obvious limp that exceeds 10% indicates a compromise of animal state of being.

Nonambulatory Cattle

Cows become nonambulatory for a variety of reasons. The leading correlate of not being able to get up and walk is a lack of vigor that also is signaled by a body-condition score lower than 2.

Pasturing

Letting gestating and lactating cows graze on pasture has apparent advantages in terms of freedom of movement. It also has several drawbacks in terms of cow state of being: insect pests; being spooked and hassled by feral and wild canines; bloat; high energy expenditure sometimes associated with walking; toxic plants and soils; inadequate shelter from inclement weather, both summer and winter; and inadequate nutritional value of the pasture (especially for high-producing cows anytime or any cow around the time of peak lactation).

Reduction of Quality and Quantity of Individual Attention

Although milk yield per cow in the United States has tripled from what it was in 1950, labor per cow is around a third today of what it was then. This is due to changes in genetics, nutrition, milking facilities and procedures, and materials handling. But correlations between milk yield, cow health, and improved management techniques are highly positive, while those between herd size and cow state of being are neutral. New technology has freed progressive dairymen to devote more time to animal care per se.

Select Safety Factors

Sharp edges and protrusions in the cattle facility's construction members can injure cows, sometimes so as to reduce state of being and milk yield.

Separating Cow and Calf

So long as the newborn calf receives an adequate dose of colostrum, it can be separated from its dam during the first 24 postnatal hours without risking psychological harm. In most cases, cow–calf bonding has occurred by 48 hours postnatum, and weaning any time after this is more stressful.

"Super Cows"

Genetically superior cows fed and cared for so as to promote very high productive performance are very fragile creatures in many ways. They are more likely to develop digestive and metabolic upsets, to suffer mastitis and other health problems, and to have more reproductive maladies. Such cows do require special care and management, and when they do not receive it, these cows' wellness is in jeopardy.

Tail Docking

In many herds, the tails of dairy cows are docked with the aim of increasing sanitary conditions at milking time, especially in milking facilities in which the milker approaches the cow's udder from the rear. As of now, there is no scientific justification for the practice,[3] and it is not recommended.

Transportation

The state of being of dairy cattle is often reduced while the animals are being transported.[4] This is especially so for low-body-condition-score, sick, or injured animals.

CONCLUSION

Many changes have occurred in the biology and technology of milk production by dairy cows during the past half-century. Some of them have had implications for dairy cattle state of being. These issues have been and are being seriously addressed by scientists and milk producers alike.[5–8] Overall, the state of being of dairy cattle nowadays is better than it was 50 years ago.

ARTICLE OF FURTHER INTEREST

Adaptation and Stress: Animal State of Being, p. 1

REFERENCES

1. Albright, J.L.; Arave, C.W. *The Behaviour of Cattle*; CAB International: Wallingford, UK, 1997.
2. Keown, J.F. *How to Body Condition Score Dairy Animals*, NebGuide G-90-997-A; University of Nebraska-Lincoln, 1991.
3. Stull, C.L.; Payne, M.A.; Perry, S.L.; Hullinger, P.J. Evaluation of the scientific justification for tail docking in dairy cattle. J. Dairy Sci. **2002**, *220*, 1298–1303.
4. *Livestock Handling and Transport*, 2nd Ed.; Grandin, T., Ed.; CAB International: Wallingford, UK, 2000.
5. Arave, C.W.; Albright, J.L. *Dairy [Cattle Welfare]*. Online at http://ars.sdstate.edu/animaliss/dairy.html.
6. Grandin, T. *Outline of Cow Welfare Critical Control Points for Dairies (Revised September 2002)*. Online at http://www.grandin.com/cow.welfare.ccp.html.
7. Guither, H.D.; Curtis, S.E. Welfare of Animals, Political and Management Issues. In *Encyclopedia of Dairy Sciences*; Roginski, H., Fuquay, J.W., Fox, P.W., Eds.; Academic Press: New York, 2003.
8. Stookey, J.M. Is intensive dairy production compatible with animal welfare? Adv. Dairy Technol. **1994**, *6*, 208–219.

Dairy Cattle: Breeding and Genetics

H. Duane Norman
Suzanne M. Hubbard
United States Department of Agriculture, Agricultural Research Service, Beltsville, Maryland, U.S.A.

INTRODUCTION

For thousands of years, the dairy cow has been a valuable producer of food for humans and animals. Animal breeding began when owners tried to mate the best to the best; however, deciding which animals were best requires considerable insight. As genetic principles were discovered, animal breeding became a science rather than an art. Early cattle may have given less than 4 liters of milk per day; some herds now average 40 liters per cow per day, and a few individual cows have averaged over 80 liters per day for an entire year. Although much has been learned about how to feed and manage dairy cows to obtain larger quantities of milk, current yield efficiency would not have been achieved unless concurrent progress had been made in concentrating those genes that are favorable for sustained, high milk production.

GENETIC IMPROVEMENT

Five factors are primarily responsible for the exceptional genetic improvement achieved by domestic dairy cattle: 1) permanent unique identification (ID), 2) parentage recording, 3) recording of milk yield and other traits of economic importance, 4) artificial insemination (AI), and 5) statistically advanced genetic evaluation systems. Ironically, effective management of any less than all five factors produces little genetic improvement.

Identification

Systems for dairy cattle ID have evolved from being unique to the farm to being unique internationally. Although fewer than five characters or digits were needed to be unique within a herd, today's international dairy industry requires a 19-character ID number: 3-letter country code, 3-letter breed code, 1-letter gender code, and 12-digit animal number. Global ID has come at a price; larger ID numbers contribute to more data entry errors. Electronic ID tags and readers are sometimes used to assist dairy farmers in managing feeding, milking, breeding, and health care of individual cows with the data

transferred to an on-farm computer. In some countries, unique ID for each animal is mandatory.

Parentage (Pedigree)

Genetic improvement was slow before breeders began to summarize and use performance information from bulls' daughters. Proper recording of sire ID was required for this advance and has been used throughout the last century in selection decisions. Proper recording of dam ID was encouraged during that period, but with less successful results during early years. As genetic principles became better understood, accurate estimates of dams' genetic merit became more important. Cows of high genetic merit were designated as elite and usually were mated to top sires to provide young bulls for progeny-test programs of AI organizations. In countries that require unique ID for each animal, the sire, dam, and birth date sometimes are known for nearly 100% of animals. Genetic evaluation systems today have sophisticated statistical models that can include information from many or all known pedigree relationships.

Performance Recording

Little genetic improvement can be achieved without objective measurement of traits targeted for improvement. Countries vary considerably in percentage of cows that are in milk-recording programs. In the United States, slightly less than 50% of dairy cows are enrolled in a dairy records management program that supplies performance records to the national database, and parentage of only about 65% of those cows is known.

The first traits to be evaluated nationally in the United States were milk and butterfat yield and percentage. During the 1970s, national evaluation of protein yield and percentage, conformation traits, and calving ease (dystocia) began.[1] Evaluations for longevity (productive life) and mastitis resistance (somatic cell score) became available during the 1990s. The most recent trait to be evaluated by the U.S. Department of Agriculture is daughter pregnancy rate, which is a measure of cow fertility.

Encyclopedia of Animal Science
DOI: 10.1081/E-EAS 120019552

Artificial Insemination

Because some dilution of semen can provide nearly as high a conception rate as the original collected sample, 100 progeny or more can result from a single ejaculate. In addition, semen can be frozen and kept for decades without any serious compromise to fertility. The ability to extend and freeze semen without decreasing its fertility facilitates progeny testing early in a bull's life. A progeny test involves obtaining dozens of daughters of a bull and allowing those daughters to calve and be milked so that their performance can be examined and a determination made on whether the bull is transmitting favorable traits to his offspring. After distribution of semen for a progeny test, most bulls are held in waiting until the outcome of the progeny test. Progeny testing many bulls provides an opportunity to select from among them, to keep only the best, and to use those few bulls to produce several thousand daughters and, in some cases, millions of granddaughters. Characteristics of U.S. progeny-test programs were recently documented by Norman et al.[2] Percentage of dairy animals that result from AI in the United States is nearly 80%; that percentage varies considerably among countries.

Genetic Evaluation Systems

Accurate methods for evaluating genetic merit of bulls and cows for economically important traits are needed to identify those animals that are best suited to be parents of the next generation. The degree of system sophistication needed depends partially on effectiveness of the sampling program in randomizing bull daughters across herds that represent various management levels. If randomization is

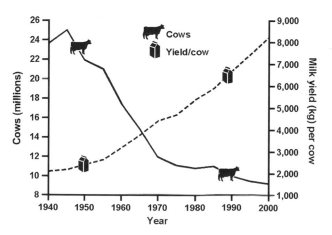

Fig. 1 Numbers of U.S. cows and mean milk yield by year. (*Source*: Animal Improvement Programs Laboratory, Agricultural Research Service, U.S. Department of Agriculture, Beltsville, MD; http://aipl.arsusda.gov [accessed Sept 2003].)

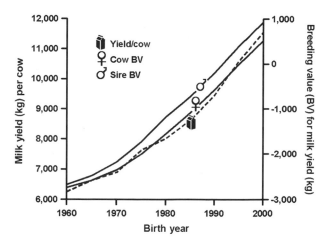

Fig. 2 Mean milk yield, genetic merit (breeding value), and sire genetic merit of U.S. Holstein cows with national genetic evaluations by birth year. (*Source*: Animal Improvement Programs Laboratory, Agricultural Research Service, U.S. Department of Agriculture, Beltsville, MD; http://aipl.arsusda. gov [accessed Sept 2003].)

equitable for all bulls, less sophisticated procedures are needed. In the United States, methodology for national evaluations has progressed from daughter-dam comparison (1936) to herdmate comparison (1960) to modified contemporary comparison (1974) and finally, to an animal model (1989).[1] The most recent development in genetic evaluation systems is the use of test-day models, which have been adopted by several countries. Because test-day models account better for environmental effects and variations in testing schemes, they can provide more accurate estimates of genetic merit than do lactation models; however, test-day models are statistically more difficult and computationally more intensive.[3] Once evaluations are released to the dairy industry, dairy farmers have an opportunity to select among the best bulls for their needs and to purchase semen marketed by AI organizations. Mating decisions for specific animals can be based on estimated genetic merit for individual traits or selection indexes that combine traits of economic interest.

Other Factors

Dairy farmers continue to make additional genetic improvement by culling within the herd. Herd replacements often allow a turnover of about 30% of milking animals per year. Some culling decisions are under the manager's voluntary control, but others may be driven by fitness traits that limit the animal's ability to remain profitable and stay in the herd. A cow must be capable of timely pregnancies so that a new lactation can begin and

Table 1 Relative emphasis of traits in selection indexes from countries with large Holstein populations

Trait	Australia (APR)	Canada (LPI)	Denmark (S-I)	France (ISU)	Germany (RZG)	Italy (PFT)	Netherlands (DPS)	New Zealand (BW)	Spain (ICO)	Sweden (TMI)	United Kingdom (PLI)	United States (NMS)
Protein	36	43	21	35	36	42	35	34	32	21	57	33
Fat	12	14	10	10	9	12	8	13	12	4	11	22
Milk	-19		-3				-14	-17	12	-4	-19	
Protein (%)				2	4	3			3			
Fat (%)				2	1	2						
Longevity	9	8	6	13	25	8	12	8	3	6	15	11
Somatic cell score (mastitis)	5	3	15	13	5	10	11		3	12		-9
Fertility	8		9	13	1		7	10		10		7
Other diseases			2							3		
Udder traits		17	9	8	6	13			16	12		7
Feet and legs		11	5	1	4	6	3		10	9		4
Size	-4	4	2	2	2			-18				-3
Dairy character					2							
Rump				1	1							
Final score			2			4			9			
Calving traits			6		4		10			12		-4
Growth (meat)			4							6		
Temperament	4		2							3		
Milking speed	3	<1	6									

(*Source:* VanRaden, P.M.; Animal Improvement Programs Laboratory, Agricultural Research Service, U.S. Department of Agriculture, Beltsville, MD; 2003.)

must remain free of chronic diseases and conditions such as mastitis and lameness so that lactation can be maintained.

Supplemental breeding techniques also can help to increase genetic gains. Embryo transfer has increased the number of offspring possible from individual cows and helped to assure that potential bull dams will produce a son. Nucleus herds allow direct comparison of elite females, but they have had limited use as an alternative to traditional AI progeny testing. Cloning technologies (embryo splitting, nuclear transfer, and adult cloning) also can produce some genetic gains, but their commercial use has been limited because of cost.[4] Use of sexed semen to produce offspring of a desired gender is possible, but reduced conception rates and higher production costs may limit widespread use. Producing more females would allow a farmer to increase within-herd genetic gains.

GENETIC PROGRESS

Practical success of genetic improvement procedures is evident in the U.S. dairy population. As cow numbers decreased, yield per cow increased (Fig. 1), in part because of improved genetic capacity for efficient dairy production, as indicated by similar trends in the genetic merit of dairy bulls and cows (Fig. 2).

Because of increased efficiency achieved through genetic programs, competition for sales of genetic material has increased. Higher productivity of North American breeds, particularly Holstein, in the 1980s[5] has led to U.S. semen exports of more than $50 million per year. As a result, the international dairy population is much more related, and population sizes of many local breeds were reduced, in a few cases to the point of extinction. As selection methods intensified, concern about level of inbreeding has increased, and interest in crossbreeding has been growing to alleviate this concern and to capture the known benefits of heterosis.

INTERNATIONAL EVALUATIONS

Increasing global trade in semen, embryos, and livestock resulted in a need for accurate comparisons of animal performance both within and across countries. However, such comparisons are made difficult by different genetic evaluation methods, breeding objectives, and management environments. In 1983, the International Bull Evaluation Service (Interbull) was established as a nonprofit organization for promoting development and standardization of international genetic evaluations of cattle.[6] Currently, Interbull provides evaluations for bulls from more than 28 populations for milk, fat, and protein yields; 23

populations for 19 conformation traits; and 21 populations for udder health traits.

SELECTION INDEXES

Nearly all dairy countries that calculate genetic evaluations for different traits produce an overall economic index in which traits are combined according to economic value. Past decisions on whether to allow animals to be parents have been made based on independent examination of each trait. Today's indexes for countries (Table 1) differ in the traits included and values assigned to each.[7]

CONCLUSION

Animal ID that includes pedigree information, routine recording of performance traits, widespread use of AI, and development of state-of-the-art statistical models and evaluation systems has led to rapid genetic gains in traits of economic importance for dairy cattle during the past 100 years. The resulting improvement in production efficiency allows dairy products to be produced with fewer cattle, thereby reducing adverse environmental impacts and conserving natural resources. Increased genetic merit of dairy populations has resulted in a global marketplace for germplasm and live animals.

REFERENCES

1. VanRaden, P.M. *History of USDA Dairy Evaluations*; 2003. http://aipl.arsusda.gov/aipl/history/hist_eval.htm (accessed Sept 2003).
2. Norman, H.D.; Powell, R.L.; Wright, J.R.; Sattler, C.G. Timeliness and effectiveness of progeny testing through artificial insemination. J. Dairy Sci. **2003**, *84* (8), 1899–1912.
3. Wiggans, G.R. Issues in defining a genetic evaluation model. Inter. Bull Eval. Serv. Bull **2001**, *26*, 8–12.
4. Norman, H.D.; Lawlor, T.J.; Wright, J.R.; Powell, R.L. Performance of Holstein clones in the United States. J. Dairy Sci. **2004**, *87* (3), 729–738.
5. Jasiorowski, H.A.; Stolzman, M.; Reklewski, Z. *The International Friesian Strain Comparison Trial, a World Perspective*; Food and Agriculture Organization of the United Nations: Rome, Italy, 1988.
6. International Bull Evaluation Service. *Interbull Summary*; 1999. http://www-interbull.slu.se/summary/framesida-summary.htm (accessed Sept 2003).
7. VanRaden, P.M. Selection of dairy cattle for lifetime profit. Proceedings of the 7th World Congress on Genetics Applied to Livestock Production, Montpellier, France, Aug 19–23, 2002; **2002**; *29*, 127–130.

Dairy Cattle: Health Management

James D. Ferguson
University of Pennsylvania, Kennett Square, Pennsylvania, U.S.A.

INTRODUCTION

Health care in dairy herds has evolved over the years and will continue to evolve in the future. Health programs need to ensure animal health, food safety, environmental, and farm profitability.

HISTORICAL BACKGROUND

Rinderpest and foot and mouth disease caused the loss of over 200 million cattle across Europe and Britain in the 16th to 18th centuries.[1] In Italy and England, individuals recognized the infectious nature of the diseases and stopped the epidemics by slaughtering cattle on infected premises and quarantining animal movement.[1] However, epidemics continued to sweep over Europe because no organized body existed to codify these individuals' recommendations.

In the 16th and 17th centuries, farriers and so-called ox leeches provided animal health care to livestock farms. These individuals had no formal training, yet some developed remarkable skills. Two notable books were *The Book of Husbandry* (1523) by John Fitzherbert in England and *The Herdsman's Mate* (1673) by Michael Harward of Chesire, England.[1] These authors described fairly sophisticated surgical and obstetrical procedures, several diseases and their treatment, and sound cattle management practices of the day.[1] These texts represented attempts to codify a system of animal health care and management for livestock farms, but formal training programs in schools of veterinary medicine and government regulation of animal disease lay in the future.

By the middle of the 18th century it was recognized that studying animal disease made good sense economically and politically, because animal disease could provide a good model of human disease. As a result, the first veterinary school was established in Lyon, France in 1761.[1] By 1800 there were 19 schools in Europe.[1] In 1862 the first veterinary college was established in North America, in Ontario, Canada.[1] Government regulatory agencies were developed in the late 19th century, such as the U.S. Bureau of Animal Industry in 1884, whose mission was to control and eradicate animal diseases associated with serious economic losses.[1] By the early 20th century, animal health care to livestock farms was a profession. Veterinary health programs evolved from this history, which was based on the host-pathogen philosophy of disease.

TRADITIONAL VETERINARY HEALTH PROGRAMS

Traditional health care programs are based on the veterinarian providing services to diagnose and treat diseases, recommend vaccination and anthelmintic programs, perform basic surgeries, test for reportable diseases, and perform rectal palpation for pregnancy diagnosis and breeding examination of cows.[2-4] These services are not much different from those described by Hawarth in 1673. Only technical expertise and knowledge are greater. Veterinarians report that the most frequent activities in cattle practice are physical exam, disease diagnosis and treatment, castration and dehorning, and advice on vaccination and anthelmintic programs (Table 1).[3,4] Producers request service as they see problems in the herd.

Traditional veterinary programs are based on the epidemic concept of disease.[5] Disease is caused by a specific agent (bacteria, virus, or other infectious agent) or a specific factor (deficiency, toxicity, irritant, genetic defect).[2] Treatment is specific for the agent, and prevention is synonymous with eliminating the agent from the herd.[2,5] Significant disease conditions have been eliminated from dairy farms based on this concept of disease. Surveillance programs for specific organisms are based on epidemic models of disease (e.g., *Mycobacterium bovis*, *Brucella abortus*). Vaccination and prepurchase health examinations and tests are designed to prevent epidemic disease problems. Surveillance, testing, vaccination, and monitoring are important components of herd health programs to control epidemic diseases on dairy farms.[2-4]

CHALLENGES TO TRADITIONAL VETERINARY PROGRAMS

With the control of epidemic diseases, endemic diseases have emerged as the main health problem. These

Encyclopedia of Animal Science
DOI: 10.1081/E-EAS 120019553

Table 1 Percentage of veterinarians reporting on services they provide to cattle farms on a monthly to weekly basis

>75%	50–75%	25–50%	20–25%	<20%
Individual animal service				
Injections (IV, IM, SC)	Treat metritis	Repair/open teat	Rumenocentesis	Rumenotomy
Treatment (PO, IMM)	Treat mastitis	Episiotomy	Toggle DA	Ultrasound
Physical exam	Examine hoof	Eye flap	Amputate digit	Adominocentesis
Breeding exam—cow	Omentopexy/	Sample milk for	Artificial	Transfaunation
Treat pneumonia	abomasopexy	bacteriologic culture	insemination	Rectovaginal
Treat diarrhea	Breeding exam—bull	Skin biopsy		tear repair
Treat bloat	Cesarean section	Fetotomy		Intestinal
Castration	Remove	Uterine detorsion		anastomosis
Dehorning	supernumerary teats	Fecal exam quantitative		Radiology
Obstetrics	Subconjunctival	Excise foot fibroma		
Uterine prolapse	eye injections	CMT test		
Vaginal prolapse		Urinalysis		
Necropsy		CBC		
Fecal flotation		Fracture splint		
Tattooing		More invasive clinical		
Wound management		chemistry tests of		
Venipuncture		body fuids		
Epidural anesthesia				
Herd-level service				
Vaccination program	Body condition scoring	Cont mastitis	Economic analysis	Advice on
Anthelmintic program	Sanitation/hygiene prgm	Cont nutrition pblm	Ration formulation	waste disposal
Cont resp pblm	Estrus synchronization	TB testing	Financial advice	Milking machine
Cont diarrhea pblm	Cont infertility pblm	Advice on milk replacer	Assess feed particles	evaluation
Cont off-feed pblm	Cont abortion pblm	SMSCC analysis	Assess milking tech.	
	Client education	Advise on feed additives		
	Dev insecticide prgm	Assess heifer growth		
	Residue avoidance prgm	Use of computer records		
		Use of spreadsheets		
		Assess DHIA records		
		Assess housing/		
		ventilation		
		Ration analysis		
		Forage sample for testing		
		Bulk tank milk analysis		
		Advise on grazing		
		Assess an intervention		
		Advise on genetics		

IV = intravenous, IM = intramuscular, SC = subcutaneous, PO = per os, IMM = intramammary, Treat = treatment, Prgm = program, Pblm = problem, Cont = control, Dev = develop, TB = tuberculosis, DHIA = Dairy Herd Improvement Association, CMT = California Mastitis Test, CBC = complete blood count, Tech = technique, DA = displaced abomasum.
(From Refs. 3 and 4.)

disease conditions include mastitis, metritis, foot infections, pneumonia, enteritis, and noninfectious metabolic conditions. Infectious endemic diseases are caused by agents normally found in the environment and host population.[5] Host–environment–pathogen interactions influence disease incidence.[5] The presence of the agent alone is not sufficient to cause disease. Disease occurs when multiple factors upset the balance in animal resist-

ance and organism pathogenicity. Environmental factors contribute to upset this balance. Factors that influence endemic disease include seasonal conditions, nutrition, ventilation, hygiene, pathogen buildup, milking practices, and general husbandry.

Metabolic conditions constitute a significant proportion of endemic health problems in a dairy herd.[6–8] These conditions are associated with parturition.[6–8] Risk factors that contribute to metabolic conditions include body condition, nutrition in both the nonlactating and lactating periods, age of the cow, and stage of lactation.[6–8]

Endemic disease and metabolic conditions may affect 30% to 60% of animals calving on an annual basis. Animals may be affected by more than one problem, and an animal may experience repeated bouts of the same problem within a lactation.[6,7] Subclinical forms of endemic and metabolic conditions may not be apparent, but they may reduce production and reproduction. Total eradication of endemic disease conditions is unlikely because control is complicated by host–management–environment interactions. Typically, veterinarians and producers need to reach a consensus on acceptable incidence rates of these diseases within a herd.

Endemic disease problems on dairy farms have led to pressures to change the approach to disease control in dairy herds. First, identification of the pathogenic factor is insufficient to control the disease. Therefore, testing to identify the organism has less value than in epidemic disease situations. Second, management and environment play significant roles in influencing disease rates. Consequently, veterinarians must evaluate management and environment, not just the cow, to identify factors influencing disease rates. Third, communication skills are critical to inform and motivate the dairy producer to change management and environment practices in order to reduce the incidence of disease. The veterinarian must have a thorough knowledge of animal husbandry, epidemiology, and communication to effectively work with dairy producers to control these diseases.[5,10]

Dairy producers are looking for cheaper solutions to health care for endemic disease. Whereas in traditional programs calling a veterinarian to diagnose and treat an epidemic problem was valued, calling a veterinarian to treat an endemic problem has less perceived value. Producers recognize these conditions with fairly high accuracy because they see them often and usually know what treatments will be appropriate. Early identification of a case, appropriate treatment, and residue avoidance are critical aspects in the control of endemic disease conditions and often do not require the veterinarian to be the primary animal health care provider.

Veterinarians are under pressure either to provide cheaper diagnostic treatment services for endemic cases or to train herd personnel to diagnose and treat these cases. The veterinarian needs to evaluate interventions and success of outcomes, and to monitor the incidence of cases. Care must be taken that should a new disease emerge in the herd, the veterinarian is notified and appropriate steps are taken to ensure it is not a pandemic disease or a zoonotic disease risk.

MANAGEMENT AND ECONOMICS

Management inefficiencies may contribute to significant financial losses in a herd. Diagnosing and repairing management inefficiencies and making recommendations to adopt technologies that can improve farm profit have been referred to as "production medicine."[9] Twenty-five to 30% of veterinarians are providing this service[5,9] (Table 1). The patient is herd management, not the individual cow.[9]

Services that primarily focus on herd management include ration formulation, economic analysis of management interventions, financial advising, and assessment of parlor efficiency (Table 1). A number of practitioners (25% to 50%) report that they look at production records, use computer records and advice on feed supplements, assess housing and ventilation, examine heifer growth, and use spreadsheets on a monthly basis[3,4] (Table 1). Skills needed for a production medicine program are knowledge based; services are analytical and less technical. This change can be uncomfortable for the practicing veterinarian because it requires new training to acquire analytical skills and a change in the philosophy of medicine.

Extension agents are advocating that management teams be established to help meet strategic goals on dairy farms.[10] Veterinarians are recognized as important members of these teams. Goals must be established by farm owners, and team members must have an altruistic vision to develop strategies to meet those goals. The veterinarian can be a key facilitator to help team development by incorporating team-building skills into veterinary training.

BEYOND THE HERD

Emerging issues for dairy farmers include environmental pathogen and nutrient pollution, animal welfare, and food safety. State agencies are encouraging veterinarians to work with clients to ensure meat and milk quality. Some veterinarians have become certified nutrient management specialists. Veterinarians can work with clients and society to define, encourage, and ensure animal welfare practices in dairy herds.

CONCLUSION

Health programs to dairy farms have evolved over time. Efforts of practicing veterinarians, governmental agencies, and producers have controlled significant health problems. Endemic disease conditions continue to be a problem on dairy farms. Understanding interactions of nutrition–housing–management and infectious agents will help improve animal health in the future. Health programs have expanded to consider farm health, the environment health, food safety, and animal welfare.

REFERENCES

1. Dunlop, R.H.; Williams, D.J. Chapter 16. Logic in the Control of Plague and the Understanding of Diseases. Chapter 17. Toward a Scientific Basis for Comparative Medicine. Chapter 18. The Launching of European Veterinary Education. Chapter 19. An Increasing Demand for Veterinary Schools. In *Veterinary Medicine. An Illustrated History*; Mosby-Year Book, Inc.: New York, 1996; 277–349.

2. Radostits, O.M.; Blood, D.C.; Gay, C.C. *Veterinary Medicine. A Textbook of the Diseases of Cattle, Sheep, Pigs, Goats, and Horses*, 8th Ed.; Bailliere Tindall: Philadelphia, PA, 1994.

3. Morin, D.E.; Constable, P.D.; Troutt, H.F.; Johnson, A.L. Individual animal medicine and animal production skills expected of entry-level veterinarians in bovine practice. J. Am. Vet. Med. Assoc. **2002**, *221*, 959–968.

4. Morin, D.E.; Constable, P.D.; Troutt, H.F.; Johnson, A.L. Surgery, anesthesia, and restraint skills expected of entry-level veterinarians in bovine practice. J. Am. Vet. Med. Assoc. **2002**, *221*, 969–974.

5. Brand, A.; Guard, C.L. Chapter 1.1 Principles of Herd Health and Production Management Programs. In *Herd Health and Production Management in Dairy Practice*; Brand, A., Noordhuizen, J.P.T.M., Schukken, Y.H., Eds.; Wageningen Press: Wageningen, Netherlands, 1996; 3–14.

6. Curtis, C.R. Path analysis of dry period nutrition, postpartum metabolic and reproductive disorders, and mastitis in Holstein cows. J. Dairy Sci. **1985**, *68*, 2347.

7. Erb, H.N.; Grohn, Y.T. Epidemiology of metabolic disorders in the periparturient dairy cow. J. Dairy Sci. **1988**, *71*, 2557–2571.

8. Gearhart, M.A.; Curtis, C.R.; Erb, H.N.; Smith, R.D.; Sniffen, C.J.; Chase, L.E.; Cooper, M.D. Relationship of changes in condition score to cow health in Holsteins. J. Dairy Sci. **1990**, *73*, 3132.

9. Van Der Leek, M.L.; Kelbert, D.P.; Donovan, G.A. Dairy Cow Production Medicine. In *Current Veterinary Therapy 3. Food Animal Practice*; Howard, J.L., Ed.; W.B. Saunders Comp.: Phialdelphia, PA, 1993; 142–147.

10. Weinand, D.; Conlin, B.J. Impacts of dairy diagnostic teams on herd performance. J. Dairy Sci. **2002**, *86*, 1849–1857.

Dairy Cattle: Nutrition Management

L. E. Chase
Cornell University, Ithaca, New York, U.S.A.

INTRODUCTION

The modern dairy cow is a marvel of nutrient metabolism and metabolic efficiency. Due to a combination of genetic selection, advances in nutrition, and improved management practices, these cows have the potential to produce >90 kg of milk per day. The average milk production for Holsteins in the United States on DHI test in 2003 was 9830 kg of milk in a 305-day lactation.[1] Individual dairy cows have produced in excess of 30,000 kg of milk in lactation. A dairy cow producing 45 kg of milk per day may consume 25–27 kg of diet dry matter per day. To support this level of milk production, the 3–3.5 kg of glucose and 2.2 kg of lactose must be synthesized daily by the cow. An emerging concern is to design nutrition programs that permit cows to attain their genetic capability for milk production while providing profit for the dairy manager, maintaining animal health, and decreasing nutrient excretion to the environment.

NUTRIENT USE EFFICIENCY

There is a relationship between level of milk production, nutrient intake, and the partition of nutrients between maintenance and milk production. Table 1 contains data on this relationship for milk production levels of 20–60 kg. As milk production increases, a greater proportion of the total nutrient intake is used to synthesize milk. This is due to the fact that maintenance is a fixed cost that does not vary with level of milk production. Dairy cows producing >50 kg per day are partitioning 70–75% of their total nutrient intake toward milk production.

NUTRIENT REQUIREMENTS

The base document for nutrient requirements used by nutritionists is the 2001 Dairy NRC publication.[2] A group of scientists appointed by the Committee on Animal Nutrition, National Research Council, periodically updates the available information. Significant new information in the current edition includes the following:

- A computer model to assist in diet evaluation.
- A summative equation approach to predict the energy content of feedstuffs.
- Metabolizable protein (MP) replaces the crude protein (CP) system.
- A discussion on amino acids.
- Mineral bioavailability factors for different classes of feeds and mineral supplements.
- A section on nutrition and the environment.
- An expanded discussion of carbohydrates.

One of the most important concepts defined in this publication is that feed nutrient values are not static, but change with level of feed intake and rate of passage. The Dairy NRC model was used to examine feed nutrient values for dairy cows producing 35 or 55 kg of milk per day. The same total mixed ration (TMR) was fed in this example. A 680-kg dairy cow producing 35 kg of milk per day had a predicted dry matter intake (DMI) of 23.6 kg. The net energy (NE)-l value for the TMR was 1.67 Mcal/kg of dry matter (DM). Rumen degradable protein (RDP) was 9.9% of total DM. The cow producing 55 kg of milk had a predicted DMI of 30.2 kg. The TMR had an NE-l value of 1.58 Mcal/kg of DM. RDP was 9.6% of total DM. In this example, the same TMR had a 5% lower energy value when fed to the higher-producing cow.

ENERGY

The energy content of a feed or forage has been most commonly estimated using regression equations based on acid detergent fiber (ADF). The 2001 Dairy NRC[2] has adopted a summative equation approach to determine feed TDN (total digestible nutrients) at 1× maintenance. The components used in this equation are the truly digestible nonfiber carbohydrate (NFC), CP, fatty acids, and neutral detergent fiber (NDF) components of the feed. The digestible energy (DE), metabolizable energy (ME), and

Encyclopedia of Animal Science
DOI: 10.1081/E-EAS 120019555

Table 1 Daily nutrient requirements and partition of nutrient use

Milk, kg/day	NE-l required, Mcal/day[a]	% of NE-l intake used for maintenance	MP required, g/day[b]	% of MP intake used for maintenance
20	24.5	43.7	1,579	43.3
30	31.4	34.0	2,129	36.9
40	38.3	27.9	2,679	33.1
50	45.2	23.7	3,230	30.7
60	52.1	20.5	3,678	27.0

[a]Net energy lactation.
[b]Metabolizable protein.
(Adapted from Ref. 2.)

net energy (NE) values for feeds are calculated from the TDN 1 × values using a series of equations.

PROTEIN

The implementation of the MP system to replace CP was a major step forward in terms of biology and nutrition. The NRC committee used a large number of research papers to evaluate the relationship between CP and milk production.[2] In this large data set, CP accounted for <30% of the differences observed in milk production. This is due mainly to the inability of the CP system to account for differences in protein fractions contained in feeds. Two feeds may have the same level of CP, but vary in the proportion in the RDP and RUP (rumen undegradable protein). This difference in the RDP and RUP fractions will result in a different milk production potential.

MP is the sum of microbial CP (MCP), RUP, and endogenous CP. One definition of MP is that it consists of the true protein that is digested in the intestine plus the amino acids (AA) absorbed in the intestine. The absorbed amino acids are the precursors used for synthesis of protein in the cow. Lysine and methionine appear to be the most limiting essential amino acids in dairy cattle. Even though the exact AA requirements have not been defined for dairy cattle, it is suggested that expressing requirements as a percentage of MP is the best current way to describe AAs in rations. The optimum values from literature data are 7.2% for lysine and 2.4% for methionine as a percentage of MP.[2] It is difficult to attain these levels in practical rations without the use of protected amino acids. A more practical approach is to target lysine at 6.6% of MP and methionine as 2.2%.[3] It is suggested that the target ratio of lysine:methionine is 3:1.

The protein fractions in feeds have also been divided into A, B, and C fractions.[2] Fraction A is the percent of the total CP that is in the nonprotein nitrogen (NPN) fraction. This fraction is assumed to be very rapidly available in the rumen. Fraction C is the portion of the CP that is undegradable in the rumen. Fraction B is the total CP minus that present in the A and C fractions. Tables in the Dairy NRC contain the protein A, B, and C fractions for most common feeds.[2]

CARBOHYDRATES

The carbohydrate constituents of feeds can be divided into the fiber and nonfiber fractions. ADF and NDF are the most common terms used to describe the fiber fractions. NDF is becoming the most commonly used term in nutrition programming and ration evaluation. NFC is the term used to describe the nonfiber carbohydrate fraction when determined by calculation. NFC can be defined as 100 − (CP + Ash + Fat + NDF).

NDF is used to characterize the fiber content of feeds and forages. NDF includes the hemicellulose fraction that is not in the ADF fraction. The particle size and digestibility of the NDF fraction also need to be considered. A review paper examined the effect of NDF digestibility (NDFD) on DMI and milk production.[4] These authors concluded that a 1-unit increase in NDFD was related to a change of +0.17 kg of DMI and +0.25 kg of 4% fat-corrected milk production. This relationship may not hold in all situations, but provides a good starting point to quantify the importance of fiber digestibility.

Forage particle size can also have an impact on DMI, chewing activity, and rumen function. The term peNDF (physically effective NDF) is used as an index of particle size. This system has been described.[5] One method of determining the peNDF value of a feed is measuring the proportion of feed particles that are retained on a 1.18-mm screen after vertical shaking. Chewing activity decreases with smaller particle size feeds.

The NFC fraction of a feed is not uniform. This fraction can include sugar, starch, fructans, beta-glucans, and other compounds. The calculated NFC value will also include fermentation acids.

MINERALS

The shift to defining mineral absorption coefficients (AC) by feed class and type of mineral supplement was a step forward in the 2001 Dairy NRC.[2] Previous NRC publications had assigned AC values by mineral rather than feed type. Calcium can be used as an example. The AC in the 1989 Dairy NRC[4] was 0.38 for calcium and did not vary by source. The 2001 Dairy NRC uses an AC of 30% for forages and 60% for concentrate feeds.[2] The AC value also varies from 30% to 95% from different mineral sources. A similar approach is used for other minerals.

NUTRITION AND THE ENVIRONMENT

Nutrient management is an issue in many parts of the world. In the United States, nitrogen (N) and phosphorus (P) are the nutrients currently regulated. A full lactation study was done, examining different protein feeding strategies for dairy cows.[6] Milk production was similar among three treatments, even though total N intake was 25 kg less and manure N excretion decreased 21 kg on one of the treatments. A 3-lactation study found that decreasing P from 0.47% to 0.39% of the total diet did not affect milk production.[7] A 5-year field study in a commercial dairy herd reported a 17% decrease in manure N excretion even though animal numbers increased by 33%.[8] P excretion decreased by 28% during this same period. Milk production per cow increased by about 9% during this same time. These results indicate that there are opportunities to reduce nutrient excretion to the environment in dairy herds without decreasing milk production.

CONCLUSION

Dairy cattle nutrition management practices continue to evolve as both the potential productivity of the dairy cow increases and additional research information becomes available. The 2001 Dairy NRC publication is an excellent resource for individuals working with dairy cattle nutrition. The provision of a CD with a diet evaluation program is also an asset.

REFERENCES

1. http://aipl.arsusda.gov. (accessed February, 2004).
2. National Research Council. *Nutrient Requirements of Dairy Cattle*, 7th Rev. Ed.; National Academy Press: Washington, DC, 2001. (www.nap.edu).
3. Schwab, C.G.; Ordway, R.S.; Whitehouse, N.L. Amino Acid Balancing in the Context of the MP and RUP Requirements, Proc. Florida Ruminant Nutr. Symposium, Gainesville, FL, 2004; 10–25.
4. Oba, M.; Allen, M.S. Evaluation of the importance of the digestibility of neutral detergent fiber from forage: Effects on dry matter intake and milk yield of dairy cows. J. Dairy Sci. **1999**, *82*, 589–596.
5. Mertens, D.R. Creating a system for meeting the fiber requirements of dairy cows. J. Dairy Sci. **1997**, *80*, 1463–1481.
6. Wu, Z.; Satter, L.D. Milk production during the complete lactation of dairy cows fed diets containing different amounts of protein. J. Dairy Sci. **2000**, *83*, 1042–1051.
7. Wu, Z.; Satter, L.D.; Blohowiak, A.J.; Stauffacher, R.H.; Wilcox, J.H. Milk production, estimated phosphorus excretion, and bone characteristics of dairy cows fed different amounts of phosphorus for two or three years. J. Dairy Sci. **2001**, *84*, 1738–1748.
8. Tylutki, T.P.; Fox, D.G.; McMahon, M. Implementation of the CuNMPS: Development and Evaluation of Alternatives, Proc. Cornell Nutr. Conf., Syracuse, NY, 2002; 57–69.

Dairy Cattle: Reproduction Management

W. W. Thatcher
University of Florida, Gainesville, Florida, U.S.A.

INTRODUCTION

Reproductive management of lactating dairy cows involves integrating the best dairy management practices, beginning with the dry cow and extending into the postpartum period, so that lactating cows are reproductively competent when systems for controlled breeding are initiated at the designated voluntary waiting period. Transition management from the dry period to lactation is critical because occurrences of metabolic and reproductive disorders following parturition are associated with subsequent lower fertility. Proper dietary formulation (e.g., anionic diets and fat feeding) and bunk management are important to regulate dry matter intake and changes in body condition to optimize onset of estrous cycles, detection of estrus, and embryonic survival. Heat abatement systems can partially alleviate seasonal heat stress periods of infertility. Herd reproductive efficiency is a major component leading to the economic success of the commercial dairy. Protocols have been developed to manipulate the ovary for timed artificial insemination (TAI) and to resynchronize TAI for cows that do not conceive.

TIMED ARTIFICIAL INSEMINATION PROTOCOLS

With the ability to synchronize ovarian follicular wave development coupled with $PGF_{2\alpha}$ to induce regression of the corpus luteum (CL), it was possible to implement a precise synchronization of ovulation permitting a TAI with acceptable conception rates at first service.

Ovsynch®

The Ovsynch® protocol is a breeding strategy to reduce the need for estrus detection. The protocol is composed of an injection of GnRH to induce ovulation of the dominant follicle and synchronize new emergence of a follicle wave. Seven days later, $PGF_{2\alpha}$ is given to regress the original and/or the newly formed CL and is followed 48 h later with a second injection of GnRH to induce a synchronized ovulation between 24 and 34 h. A TAI is

carried out at 12 to 16 h after the second GnRH injection (Fig. 1). This protocol has been implemented successfully worldwide as a strategy for TAI at the first postpartum service, as well as for reinsemination of nonpregnant cows. Although the Ovsynch® protocol allows for TAI without the need for estrus detection, approximately 10 to 15% of the cows will display signs of estrus during the protocol, and they should be inseminated promptly if maximum pregnancy rate (PR) is to be achieved (Fig. 1).

When lactating dairy cows were assigned randomly to either the Ovsynch® protocol or inseminated based on estrus detection with periodic use of $PGF_{2\alpha}$,[1] median days postpartum to first insemination (54 vs. 83) and days postpartum to pregnancy (99 vs. 118) were less for cows in Ovsynch® compared to cows inseminated following estrus detection. When measuring PR, the Ovsynch® protocol for a first service TAI was as effective as inseminating cows at detected estrus following a synchronization protocol of GnRH and $PGF_{2\alpha}$ given 7 days apart.[2]

Presynch-Ovsynch®

Response to the Ovsynch® protocol is optimized when cows ovulate after the first GnRH injection of the protocol and when a responsive CL is present at the moment of the $PGF_{2\alpha}$ treatment. Ovulation after the first GnRH injection and initiation of a new follicular wave should improve PR because a follicle with a reduced period of dominance is induced to ovulate. Furthermore, initiating the Ovsynch® protocol prior to day 12 of the estrous cycle should minimize the number of cows that come into estrus prior to the second GnRH injection and ovulate prior to the completion of the protocol.

A presynchronization protocol was developed[3] to optimize the Ovsynch® protocol by giving two injections of $PGF_{2\alpha}$ 14 days apart, with the second injection given 12 days before initiating the Ovsynch® protocol (Fig. 2). The Presynch-Ovsynch® protocol increased PR by 18% (i.e., 25 to 43%) in cyclic cows. Success of the Ovsynch® protocol is dependent on whether lactating cows are anestrus (22% PR) or cycling (42% PR). If anestrous cows ovulate after the first and second GnRH injections of the Ovsynch® protocol, PR appeared to be normal (e.g., 39%). Intravaginal inserts of progesterone administered as

Encyclopedia of Animal Science
DOI: 10.1081/E-EAS 120019556

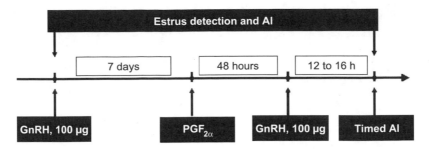

Fig. 1 Ovsynch® protocol for timed AI.

part of the Ovsynch® protocol (i.e., between GnRH and PGF$_{2\alpha}$ injections) also may benefit anestrous animals. Future protocols for further optimization of fertility likely will involve an initiation of follicular turnover via either induction of ovulation (i.e., GnRH) or follicular atresia (i.e., estrogens) in all cows, and maintenance of luteal phase progesterone concentrations with an intravaginal insert until induced CL regression.

Presynch-Heatsynch

An alternative strategy to control the time of ovulation is the ability of exogenous estradiol to induce ovulation in a low-progesterone environment during late diestrus and proestrus. Estradiol cypionate (ECP), an esterified form of estradiol-17β, can be used as part of a TAI protocol. Lactating cows are presynchronized with two injections of PGF$_{2\alpha}$ given 14 days apart with Heatsynch beginning 14 days after the second injection of PGF$_{2\alpha}$. Cows are then injected with GnRH followed by PGF$_{2\alpha}$ 7 days later. The ECP (1 mg, i.m.) is injected 24 h after PGF$_{2\alpha}$, and cows are inseminated 48 h later (Fig. 3). Pregnancy rates did not

differ between Heatsynch (35.1%) and Ovsynch® (37.1%) protocols.[4] Cows detected in estrus after ECP had a higher fertility than those not detected in estrus before the TAI. Cows in estrus during the first 36 h after ECP injection should be inseminated at detected estrus, and all remaining cows inseminated at 48 h. The elevation of estradiol following ECP injection appears to compensate for a lactational-induced deficiency in estradiol concentrations, and cows expressing estrus are fertile. If cows are anovulatory, the Heatsynch protocol may not be as effective as the GnRH-based Ovsynch® protocol in which GnRH causes the direct secretion of LH. Greater uterine tone, ease of insemination, and occurrence of estrus with the use of the Heatsynch protocol are well received by inseminators.

RESYNCHRONIZED TIMED INSEMINATIONS

Only 30 to 45% of inseminated cows are pregnant at 40 d after insemination, and nonpregnant cows need to be reinseminated as quickly as possible. Strategies to accomplish this can be rather aggressive with resynchronization of

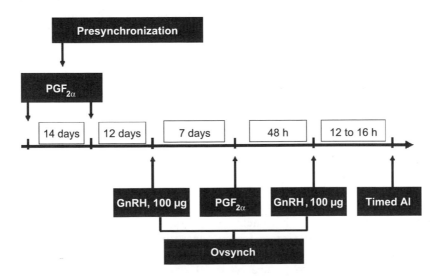

Fig. 2 Presynch/Ovsynch® protocol for timed AI at the first postpartum service.

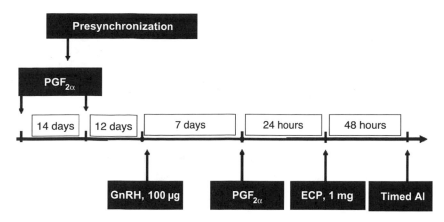

Fig. 3 Presynch/Heatsynch protocol for timed AI.

follicle development prior to an early ultrasonographic pregnancy diagnosis, as part of a TAI protocol for nonpregnant cows.

Ovsynch® Initiated 7 Days Prior to Pregnancy Diagnosis

A study was conducted to determine the effects of resynchronization with GnRH beginning on day 21 after insemination on PR and losses of pregnancy to the first service in lactating dairy cows.[5] On day 21 after a prior insemination, cows in the resynchronization group received an injection of GnRH, whereas the control group received no treatment. Pregnancy was diagnosed by ultrasound on day 28. Nonpregnant cows on day 28 received a PGF$_{2\alpha}$ injection followed by GnRH on day 30 and TAI on day 31. In contrast, nonpregnant cows of the control group initiated the Ovsynch® protocol at day 28

and were TAI 10 days later on day 38 after the previous service. For resynchronized and control cows, PR at days 28 (33.1 vs. 33.6%) and 42 (27.0 vs. 26.8%) after the initial insemination did not differ. Administration of GnRH on day 21 after insemination had no effect on the losses of pregnancy between resynchronized and control groups from 28 to 42 d (17.9%) after the first insemination. Pregnancy rate after the resynchronization period was similar for both groups and averaged 29.4%. The resynchronization and control groups were reinseminated at 31 and 38 days after the previous service.

Initiation of Ovsynch® and Heatsynch at 23 Days After AI

Based on the distribution of intervals to estrus in nonpregnant cows that returned to estrus following a previous insemination (Fig. 4), it is feasible to inject

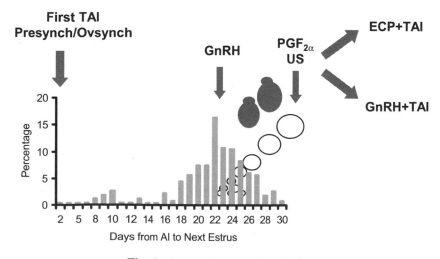

Fig. 4 Strategy for resynchronization.

GnRH at day 23 (i.e., 22–24 days) after insemination to synchronize the follicular wave and ensure that a PGF$_{2\alpha}$-responsive CL is present at day 30. Cows diagnosed nonpregnant at ultrasound on day 30 receive PGF$_{2\alpha}$, and ovulation is synchronized with either ECP or GnRH (Fig. 4). The timing of the Ovsynch® protocol is standard with the ovulatory dose of GnRH given 48 h after injection of PGF$_{2\alpha}$ and a TAI at approximately 16 h after GnRH. Our experience with ECP for resynchronization is such that ECP (1 mg) is given 24 h after injection of PGF$_{2\alpha}$, and all cows are TAI at approximately 36 h after injection of ECP. Results evaluating 593 nonpregnant cows indicate the following distribution of cows according to stages of the estrous cycle at the time of pregnancy diagnosis: diestrus 75%, metestrus 5.8%, proestrus 9.6%, ovarian cysts 7.9%, and anestrus 1.6%.[6] For the 445 diestrus cows, PR for resynchronization was 28.6% (63/220) for cows subjected to PGF-ECP-TAI and 25.8% (58/225) for cows subjected to PGF-GnRH-TAI. Pregnancy losses between days 30 and 55 averaged 11.8% and did not differ between groups. Choosing the proper stage to initiate the protocol with GnRH (e.g., day 23) takes advantage of the reoccurring follicular wave and CL to reduce the time for reinsemination (Fig. 4). Reinsemination of nonpregnant cows occurred at approximately 32 days after the first service. Future cow-side pregnancy tests may allow detection of nonpregnant cows at an early stage (e.g., day 23) so that resynchronization protocols can be initiated only in cows known to be nonpregnant.

CONCLUSION

Manipulation of ovarian function permits implementation of TAI protocols to optimize service rates with little adverse effect on PR and losses. These protocols will benefit herds with low estrus detection rates. Resynchronization protocols with early pregnancy diagnosis should optimize reproductive efficiency in all herds.

REFERENCES

1. Pursley, J.R.; Kosorok, M.R.; Wiltbank, M.C. Reproductive management of lactating dairy cows using synchronization of ovulation. J. Dairy Sci. **1997**, *80*, 301–306.
2. Burke, J.M.; De la Sota, R.L.; Risco, C.A.; Staples, C.R.; Schmitt, E.J-P.; Thatcher, W.W. Evaluation of timed insemination using a gonadotropin-releasing hormone agonist in lactating dairy cows. J. Dairy Sci. **1996**, *79*, 1385–1393.
3. Moreira, F.; Orlandi, C.; Risco, C.A.; Mattos, R.; Lopes, F.; Thatcher, W.W. Effects of presynchronization and bovine somatotropin on pregnancy rates to a timed artificial insemination protocol in lactating dairy cows. J. Dairy Sci. **2001**, *84*, 1646–1659.
4. Pancarci, S.M.; Jordan, E.R.; Risco, C.A.; Schouten, M.J.; Lopes, F.L.; Moreira, F.; Thatcher, W.W. Use of estradiol cypionate in a pre-synchronized timed artificial insemination program for lactating dairy cows. J. Dairy Sci. **2002**, *85*, 122–131.
5. Chebel, R.C.; Santos, J.E.P.; Cerri, R.L.A.; Galvão, K.N.; Juchem, S.O.; Thatcher, W.W. Effect of resynchronization with GnRH on day 21 after artificial insemination on pregnancy rate and pregnancy loss in lactating dairy cows. Theriogenology **2003**, *60*, 1389–1399.
6. Bartolome, J.A.; Sozzi, A.; McHale, J.; Swift, K.; Kelbert, D.; Archbald, L.F.; Thatcher, W.W. Resynchronization of ovulation and timed insemination in lactating dairy cows using the Ovsynch and Heatsynch protocols initiated 7 days before pregnancy diagnosis on day 30 by ultrasonography. Reprod. Fertil. Dev. **2004**, *16*, 126–127. (Abstract).

Deer and Elk

James E. Knight
Montana State University, Bozeman, Montana, U.S.A.

D

INTRODUCTION

Deer and elk are the most popular big game animals in North America. New Zealand and Scandinavian countries have important deer and elk industries. In addition to their economic and social value as game animals, their beauty and grace make them valuable as watchable wildlife for the nonhunting public as well. White-tailed deer arc found throughout the United States in brushy bottoms and wooded areas. Mule deer inhabit the rolling plains and mountains of the West. The majestic elk, often considered a western species, has now been reintroduced to historic ranges in the East.

DEER

White-tailed deer (*Odocoileus virginianus*) and mule deer (*Odocoileus hemionus*) fawns are born in late May and June after a gestation period of approximately 202 days.[1] Fawns weigh 7–8 pounds when born and their weight may double in the first two weeks of life. Twins are the normal litter size, but triplets are not uncommon. Does can breed at 6–7 months, but most breed for the first time at 18 months old. Mature bucks can weigh 200 to 300 pounds, with females weighing 25–40% less. During fall, after antlers harden, bucks begin sparring and forming a dominance hierarchy that will determine who breeds does during the November–December rut. Although bucks mark their area with scrapes, they do not really defend a territory. They rub small trees with their antlers to establish visual signposts, and they also cstablish olfactory signposts by urinating in pawed-out areas and by rubbing twigs with scent from their glands. Deer have four sets of external glands. All four hooves have a gland between the splits. The metatarsal gland is located on the outside of the hind leg above the hoof. The tarsal gland is located inside the rear leg at the hock. Both sexes, including fawns, urinate on the tarsal gland. The preorbital gland is located on the inside corner of each eye. Bucks will usually rub a twig above a scrape with the preorbital gland.

A buck will tend a doe for 1–3 days before her heat period and 2 or 3 days afterward. The doe is in heat (estrus) for 24 hours. If she fails to conceive, she will come into heat a couple of times again at 28-day intervals.

White-tailed bucks are more aggressive toward each other than are mule deer.

After the rut, deer of both sexes and all ages are intermingled. Unlike mule deer, whitetails will often winter in the same area where they spent the other seasons if food and shelter are sufficient. In some areas, whitetails will yard up, staying within a couple acres of cover rather than expose themselves to wind and more extreme weather.

ELK

A Rocky Mountain elk (*Cervus elaphus nelsoni*) is an impressive animal. Bull weights average 700 pounds, whereas cows are about 345 pounds.[2] The majestic antlers of a bull elk can weigh more than 40 pounds.

Elk calves are born in late May and June after a gestation period of about 250 days. The newborn calf weighs almost 30 pounds and is usually a single, with twins occurring less than 1% of the time. Cow elk can be productive breeders for more than 14 years. Yearling cows do not usually breed, and when they do, calf survival is lower than in older cows.

In August, bull antlers complete their growth and the bulls begin thrashing trees to remove the velvet. They begin sparring, and dominance is being established among bulls by late August. When bugling and harem formation begin, the priority of the bull is to keep subdominant bulls away from his harem of 15–20 cows. The peak of the rut, or breeding, is early October in most areas. Almost all cows are bred within a 3-week period.

During the rut, cows and calves continue feeding to build condition for the demands of winter. By early fall, calves could survive independent of their mother, but they continue to stay with the herd. Although the bull seems to control the herd during the rut, it is an older cow that decides when and where the herd goes to avoid real or perceived danger.

DEER AND ELK ANTLERS

Deer and elk antlers are true bone, with the velvet that envelops the growing antler being a modified extension of normal skin of the head. The growing antler is the

Encyclopedia of Animal Science
DOI: 10.1081/E-EAS 120019440

fastest-growing postnatal bone known. The antlers grow from permanent bony structures, on the skull called pedicles. When antlers are shed, a small segment of the outer portion of the pedicle is lost. This shortens the outer, more than the inner, length of the pedicle, which causes the antler beams to have a greater and greater spread each year.

Antler growth begins when blood testosterone concentrations increase, just as greatly reduced testosterone levels trigger antler shedding. Length of daylight influences changes in testosterone level. Elk antlers in mature bulls begin to regrow as soon as they are shed in February or March.

Deer antlers are shed earlier and scab over for a couple of months before regrowth begins. Antlers of mature bull elk weigh 40–50 pounds, but deer antlers usually weigh less than 10 pounds each.

DEER AND ELK HABITAT AND NUTRITION

Deer and elk depend on their habitat for sustenance and production.[3] The quality of that habitat is a direct reflection on the quality of the herd. Competition directly affects the ability of deer and elk to capitalize on the quality of habitat. It is important to understand that competition occurs only when a commodity is limited. The mere presence of other animals does not mean competition is occurring, but when other animals, both wild and domestic, are trying to get the same scarce resource, the benefits of quality habitat will not be realized. Deer are selective feeders. Whereas cattle have a broad, flat muzzle that allows them to clip a large swath of grass, deer have a pointed muzzle that allows them to pick selected forage. This ability allows deer to pick forbs from among grass or to nip or strip specific buds, leaves, or twigs from a shrub. In this way, a deer can select food that is more palatable or higher in nutrition.[4] Elk are between deer and cattle when it comes to selective feeding. The muzzle of an elk, while not as pointed as that of a deer, allows more selective feeding than what cattle can do. Elk will generally eat grass, but they will select forbs if they are available. Elk are primarily grazers and secondarily browsers. Unlike most ruminant grazers, the nutritional needs of elk require that they have higher-quality food than can be obtained through nonselective grazing on grass or grasslike forage. Forbs are the diet components that best allow elk to address their nutritional needs.

Deer and elk are ruminants. They have a four-chambered stomach through which food passes during various stages of digestion. The first chamber, the rumen, contains great quantities of bacteria and protozoa (microflora) that reduce plant materials to nutritional materials. The protozoa are very specialized. Some are able to break down one plant species, while others break down another plant species.

Protein

Young deer require 16–20% (dry weight) of their diet as crude protein. Although deer can maintain themselves on diets as low as 8% protein, pregnant and lactating does and bucks growing antlers need the much higher protein level of the growing deer. Elk need 6–7% crude protein in their diet for maintenance, 13–16% for growth, and as much as 20% to maximize weight gain. An advantage of the deer and elk digestive system is that, even though forage protein may vary throughout the year, microbial protein found in the rumen remains of good quality.

Energy

Elk and deer expend energy to digest food, to move, to grow, and to reproduce. Additional energy is expended during cold temperatures to stay warm. To maintain condition, all energy must be derived from food eaten each day. When sufficient food is not eaten, such as during rut or severe winter weather, most of the energy must come from body fat.

Vitamin Requirements

Ruminants have no need for a dietary source of vitamin C. Vitamin E is attained through consumption of green forage and storage of the vitamin. Vitamin D has a precursor in the body that is activated by the sun. Other vitamins are synthesized within the rumen. Nutritional deficiencies encountered by deer and elk can be traced to energy, nitrogen, or minerals, but not to vitamins.

Mineral Requirements

Minerals are necessary for the growth, development, and metabolism of deer and elk. Calcium, phosphorus, sodium, and selenium are usually the minerals of most interest. Because calcium is so important to bones and teeth, it is critical. Calcium can be transported from the bones during times when demand exceeds intake. This may happen during early antler development or during pregnancy and lactation. However, calcium is usually at adequate levels in vegetation.

Phosphorus is important for healthy bones, teeth, and red blood cells. It also aids in the transportation of nutrients throughout the body. In some situations, supplements of phosphorus may be very important. Fertilizing with phosphorus will also increase the amount of phosphorus available in vegetation.

Sodium affects the regulation of pH and plays a role in the transmission of nerve impulses. Deer and elk may use salt blocks or natural salt licks, or drink brackish water, when vegetation is inadequate in sodium. Many types of forage are low in sodium.

Selenium is often espoused as a supplemental mineral that will enhance antlers. However, selenium at too high a level can be toxic. Selenium is required at very low dietary levels. If selenium is absent from the diet, muscular dystrophy can occur.

Other minerals such as potassium, chlorine, magnesium, sulfur, iron, iodine, and copper are very important, but are adequately obtained by deer and elk in common forage plants. Trace minerals such as cobalt, zinc, and manganese are also reported to be at adequate levels in forage.

Water Requirements

Deer and elk drink water when it is available, but can go for periods of time without free water. Snow during the winter will suffice as a source of moisture. In late spring, summer, and fall, free water is important for maintaining a favorable water balance, even though deer and elk can get some of their required water from succulent vegetation.

CONCLUSION

Although similar in many ways, elk and deer have many unique differences. There are also unique differences between the two species of deer. In addition to the physiological differences, each species has evolved to prosper in a particular habitat niche. Understanding how reproduction and survival strategies differ between these cousins makes the grandeur and impressiveness of deer and elk even more spectacular.

REFERENCES

1. Anderson, A.E. Morphological and Physiological Characteristics. In *Mule and Black-tailed Deer of North America*; Wallmo, O.C., Ed.; University of Nebraska Press: Lincoln, 1981; 27–98.
2. Bubenik, A.B. Physiology. In *Elk of North America*; Thomas, J.W., Toweill, D.E., Eds.; Stackpole Books: Harrisburg, PA, 1982; 125–180.
3. Boyd, R.J. American Elk. In *Big Game of North America*; Schmodt, J.L., Gilbert, D.L., Eds.; Stackpole Books: Harrisburg, PA, 1978; 11–30.
4. Short, J.J.; Knight, J.E. Fall grazing affects big game forage on rough fescue grasslands. J. Range Manage. **2003**, *56*, 213–217.

Digesta Processing and Fermentation

Jong-Tseng Yen
United States Department of Agriculture, Agricultural Research Service, Clay Center, Nebraska, U.S.A.

INTRODUCTION

Digestion process involves both the physical and chemical breakdown of feed particles into basic units for absorption. The physical breakdown reduces the size of feed particles for easier movement of digesta through the gastrointestinal tract, as well as increases the surface area of feed particles for better access to digestive enzymes and greater chemical breakdown.

PHYSICAL PROCESSING OF INGESTED FEED

Mastication and Deglutition

The first physical processing of feed eaten by the animal is mastication in the mouth. Mastication uses teeth and is carried out to varying degrees by different species of the animal. The domestic fowl has no teeth, and uses its beak and muscular stomach (gizzard) to mechanically break down ingested feed. The duration of mastication is short in fresh-eating carnivores compared with plant-eating herbivores. Mastication forms a bolus of feed mixed with saliva. Through deglutition, the bolus is conveyed from the mouth to the stomach of nonruminant animals, the rumen of ruminant animals, or the avian crop, which is a dilatation of the esophagus and serves as a feed storage.

Rumination and Reticulorumen Motility

Ruminants regurgitate and remasticate their feed. A complete cycle of rumination consists of four phases: 1) regurgitation; 2) remastication; 3) reinsalivation; and 4) redeglutition. After the regurgitated bolus reaches the mouth, its liquid is squeezed and swallowed. Remastication and reinsalivation take place simultaneously. Remastication is thorough and the number of chews given to each bolus varies depending on diet. Redeglutition occurs at an appropriate time, and the next cycle of rumination starts in about five seconds. Daily rumination is spread into evenly distributed periods. The total duration of daily rumination varies with species and diet. The coarser the diet, the longer daily rumination lasts.

To maintain rumen fermentation, actively fermenting materials should remain in the rumen and unfermentable residue must be passed on to the abomasum. Reticulorumen motility and gravity stratify and segregate ruminal digest, and create the selective flow of particulate matter out of the rumen. Functional specific gravity further determines the flow rate of particulate matter through the zones of the reticulorumen.

Physical Processing in the Stomach

The stomach receives and stores the ingested feed in the fundus and mixes the feed with gastric secretion in the corpus. The antrum controls the propulsion of gastric contents to pass the pyloric sphincter into the duodenum. Liquid leaves the stomach at a faster rate than solid materials, so solid materials can have sufficient time for solubilization and preliminary digestion.

To ensure adequate intestinal digestion, gastric emptying is delayed by both duodenal osmoreceptors responding to hypertonic contents and duodenal H^+ receptors responding to high H^+ concentration. Gastric emptying is also delayed by cholecystokinin released from duodenal mucosa in response to lipids entering the duodenum and by gastric inhibitory polypeptide released from jejunal mucosa responding to lipids and carbohydrate.

Movements of Digesta in the Intestine

Through movements such as peristalsis and segmental contractions, the small intestine controls the flow of its contents. So, digesta are mixed properly in the lumen, dietary nutrients are adequately digested, and products of digested nutrients are maximally absorbed in the small intestine. Microbial digestion and the reabsorption of water and electrolytes in the large intestine require more time than the digestion and absorption in the small intestine. In the pig and the horse, digesta first enter the cecum and then flow into the colon. No retrograde movement of contents from the proximal colon to the cecum occurs. A pacemaker located in the midcolon generates slow waves and allows digesta to be retained for longer times in the proximal colon for adequate microbial digestion. Additional stationary segmental contractions in the proximal colon further slow the transit of digesta in the

Encyclopedia of Animal Science
DOI: 10.1081/E-EAS 120019558

pig. The motility of the cecum and colon serves to retain materials for fermentation and to separate particles based on size. For the ruminant, most of the digesta first enter the colon, but some of this retrogrades into the cecum. In the dog, an aboral mass movement generated near the ileocolic junction can empty digesta in the large intestine over long distances with very little force. The aboral movement in the cat starts much lower in the colon. In the fowl, a pair of ceca locates in the junction of the small and large intestine. Not all digesta enter the ceca. Urine that enters the colon from the cloaca may pass into the ceca via antiperistalsis, which occurs continuously.

FERMENTATION

Fermentative digestion in the ruminant occurs in the forestomachs. No anatomically distinct forestomachs exist in the nonruminant herbivorous horse and omnivorous pig. In these species, however, there is a nonglandular region of the proximal stomach in which some fermentative digestion can take place. In the ruminant, the fermentative digestion occurs before the glandular digestion. So, the microbial bodies themselves eventually are digested and absorbed by the animal. Considerable fermentation also occurs in the large intestine of the horse and the pig. However, the fermentative processes come about after the glandular digestion, and only the fermentation products (not the microbial bodies) are available for absorption by the host. In the carnivore, the digestive processes are virtually complete in the small intestine, and the colon is short, nonsacculated, and the cecum is relatively undeveloped. Therefore, fermentative digestion is of little nutritional significance in the dog and cat.

Digestion and Absorption of Nutrients in Forestomachs of the Ruminant

Fermentation occurring in the rumen and reticulum is achieved through the microbial enzymes produced by anaerobic bacteria, protozoa, and fungi. On the basis of substrates that are fermented, at least 28 functioning groups of bacterial species inhabit the rumen. Total bacterial numbers in the forestomach or hindgut range from 10^{10} to 10^{11} cells per gram of digesta. The fermentation products of most carbohydrates are short-chain volatile fatty acids (VFA), carbon dioxide, and methane. Most of these fermentation products are absorbed from the rumen before the digesta reaches the duodenum. The microorganisms of the rumen also hydrolyze proteins to peptides and amino acids (AA). These peptides and AA are absorbed into the microbial cell bodies and utilized for the formation of microbial

protein or further degraded for the production of energy through fermentation. Many rumen microbes can also use ammonia as a primary source of nitrogen for nitrogenous cell constituents. The ammonia can be derived from dietary protein, urea from saliva, or urea from rumen wall diffusion. Rumen microbes hydrolyze triglycerides to glycerol and fatty acids. The glycerol is fermented further to propionic acid and absorbed. The fatty acids pass into the duodenum for further digestion. Rumen microbes can also hydrogenate some unsaturated fatty acids to saturated fatty acids.

Forestomach fermentation, which uses plant cell wall efficiently, can potentially lead to certain nutrient deficiencies in the host because of microbial use and alteration of these nutrients in the rumen. The metabolic activities in the rumen result in production of VFA (also termed short-chain fatty acids, SCFA). The primary VFA are acetic, propionic, and butyric acids. Other quantitatively minor but metabolically important VFA are iso-butyric, valeric, and isovaleric acids. Methane is produced from CO_2 reduction in metabolic activities leading to the production of acetate and butyrate, but not propionate. The recent isolation of a new CO_2-using acetogen from bovine rumen contents suggests that it is possible to replace the methanogenic microbial community of the rumen with a community that converts CO_2 and H_2 to acetate rather than CH_4.

The forestomach epithelium absorbs nearly all VFA and allows only small amounts to escape into the lower digestive tract. The absorption of VFA aids in maintaining rumen pH by removing acid and also by generating base. About 60–80% of energy needs by the ruminant derive from the absorbed VFA. Some acetate is completely oxidized within epithelial cells and the remainder absorbed unchanged. Most propionate is absorbed, with a small portion being converted to lactate by the epithelial cells. All butyrate is essentially changed to β-hydroxybutyrate following absorption.

Hindgut Digestion and Absorption

Nutrients not digested in the small intestine pass into the large intestine where they are digested and fermented by the hindgut microflora. In general, the types of substrate and fermentative patterns of the hindgut appear to be similar to those in the forestomach of the ruminant. Like the rumen, the cecum and colon of the horse also have an extensive urea recycling for the formation of microbial protein. Unlike that in the pig, glandular digestion of carbohydrate in the horse is not too efficient, and considerable amounts of starch and sugars reach the cecum. The end-products of hindgut fermentation are VFA. The molecular mechanisms of VFA absorption in the hindgut are identical to those in the rumen. The horse derives as much as 75% of its energy requirement from absorbed VFA, and the pig can use absorbed VFA to meet up to 25% of maintenance energy need. Hindgut fermentation offers little use as a source of energy to the dog and the cat, but it decreases the effective osmotic pressure of the large intestine and allows the reabsorption of water.

Similar to the forestomach of ruminants, the hindgut of horses and pigs receives from the ileum substantial quantities of fluid, rich in bicarbonate buffer, for anaerobic microbial fermentation. Colonic mucosa also secretes fluid containing sodium, bicarbonate, and chloride in response to high concentrations of VFA in the lumen. This secretory response, in combination with the ileal secretion, is responsible for buffering luminal contents. Large amounts of water also enter the hindgut from the blood through the mucosa when active VFA production is taking place.

It should be noted that hindgut fermentation occurs in ruminants too, because they have a fairly extensive hindgut. In avian species, microbial fermentation of cellulose occurs in the ceca and is of greater importance for the energy needs in some wild fowls. A nitrogen source for the microbes associated with cellulose fermentation is uric acid in the urine, which passes from the cloaca through the colon and into the ceca.

CONCLUSION

This article describes physical processing of digesta and more detailed fermentative processes of digestion. Infor-mation regarding chemical digestion of ingested feed is presented in "Digestion and Absorption of Nutrients," elsewhere in this encyclopedia.[1] The information provided in this article is extracted from several textbooks on physiology of domestic animals[2–4] and a monograph on physiology of the vertebrate digestive system.[5] The total release of CH_4 from domestic animals and the decay of animal wastes accounts for 30% of the total anthropogenic CH_4 source. Conversion of ruminal CO_2 to acetate instead of CH_4 would decrease the undesirable CH_4 emission associated with livestock operations and simultaneously increase the yield of gut acetate as a source of energy for the ruminant. Elimination or min-imization of rumen CH_4 production should be a goal of major animal nutrition research programs.

REFERENCES

1. Yen, J.T. *Digestion and Absorption of Nutrients*. EAS, 2005.
2. Reece, W.O. *Physiology of Domestic Animals*, 2nd Ed.; Lippincott Williams & Wilkins: Philadelphia, PA, 1997.
3. Swenson, M.J.; Reece, W.O. *Dukes' Physiology of Domestic Animals*, 11th Ed.; Comstock Publishing Associates/ Cornell University Press: Ithaca, NY, 1993.
4. Cunningham, J.G. *Textbook of Veterinary Physiology*; W. B. Saunders Co.: Philadelphia, PA, 1992.
5. Stevens, C.E.; Hume, I.D. *Comparative Physiology of the Vertebrate Digestive System*, 2nd Ed.; Cambridge University Press: Cambridge, UK, 1996.

Digestion and Absorption of Nutrients

Jong-Tseng Yen
*United States Department of Agriculture, Agricultural Research Service,
Clay Center, Nebraska, U.S.A.*

INTRODUCTION

Animals obtain nutrients from feed to maintain their body functions. Proteins, fats, and complex carbohydrates in feed must be broken down through physical and chemical means into simple units. The simple units are transported across the intestinal epithelium to provide energy and building blocks for the body and its secretions. The process of breaking down complex nutrients into more basic units is called digestion. The process of transporting the basic units, minerals, vitamins, and water across the intestinal epithelium is called absorption. The two processes occur within the digestive tract. On the basis of eating habits, animals are classified as carnivores, herbivores, or omnivores. Carnivores, such as the dog and cat, are flesh-eating animals, and herbivores, like cattle and the horse, are plant-eating animals. Omnivores, such as the pig, feed on both flesh and plants.

GLANDULAR DIGESTION AND NUTRIENT ABSORPTION

For the omnivorous pig and chicken, as well as the carnivorous dog and cat, digestion of their diet is an orderly process involving a large number of digestive enzymes secreted by various glands of the animals. The sources of major digestive enzymes, and their substrates, catalytic functions, and products have been summarized.[1]

Carbohydrate Digestion and Absorption

Dietary carbohydrates include monosaccharides, disaccharides, and polysaccharides. Starch is a glucose-containing polysaccharide. Amylose, which constitutes 10 to 20% of dietary starch, is a long, straight chain of α-1, 4-glucosyl units. Amylopectin, which composes 80 to 90% of dietary starch, also has the straight chain, but with some α-1, 6-branching linkages. Glycogen is similar to amylopectin with more branching linkages. Amylopectin and amylose are of plant origin, whereas glycogen is of

animal origin. Dietary fiber (nonstarch polysaccharides) is 50 to 80% cellulose, 20% hemicellulose, and 10 to 50% lignin.

Ingested starch is first attacked by salivary α-amylase in the mouth. Because the optimal pH of this enzyme is 6.7, its activity is inhibited by the acidic gastric juice when food enters the stomach. In the lumen of the small intestine, both the salivary and the pancreatic α-amylase act on starch. The hydrolytic products are a mixture of oligosaccharides: maltose (disaccharide), maltotriose (trisaccharide), and α-dextrins. These products of luminal carbohydrate digestion cannot be absorbed by the mucosa, but must be further degraded into monosaccharides through mucosal (membranous) digestion. Specific carbohydrases for mucosal digestion are produced by epithelial cells, bound to surface membrane, and transported to the tip of the brush border. Some of these membrane-bound enzymes have more than one substrate: α-dextrinase (isomaltase) and maltase hydrolyze maltose, maltotriose, and α-dextrins into glucose. Sucrase breaks down sucrose into glucose and fructose, as well as maltose and maltotriose into glucose. Lactase hydrolyzes lactose to glucose and galactose. Trehalase breaks down trehalose, a α-1, 1-linked dimer of glucose, into two molecules of glucose.

Glucose, galactose, and fructose are absorbed by the mature enterocytes lining the upper third of the intestinal villi. Absorption takes place in the duodenum and jejunum and is usually complete before the chyme arrives at the ileum. Glucose and galactose are initially transported into the enterocyte against their concentration gradient by a Na^+-dependent glucose transporter located in the apical brush border and then released into the blood by a facilitated sugar transporter (GLUT 2) located on the basolateral membrane. Fructose is passively absorbed by a Na^+-independent brush border fructose transporter and then released out of the enterocyte into the blood by GLUT 2. Because of the simultaneous active transport of Na^+, the absorption of glucose and galactose is very rapid and efficient compared with that of fructose, which is determined by its concentration gradient from gut to blood. The monosaccharides absorbed into the blood of intestinal capillaries are drained into the portal vein. In ruminants with well-developed rumen, most of ingested

Encyclopedia of Animal Science
DOI: 10.1081/E-EAS 120019557

starch is digested and absorbed as fermentative products in the forestomach. Typically, very little monosaccharides are released and absorbed in the small intestine.

Digestion and Absorption of Proteins

Protein digestion starts in the stomach and lasts one to two hours. Gastric mucosa secretes, in the form of inactive proenzymes, three proteases: pepsin A (pepsin II), pepsin B (parapepsin I), and gastricsin (pepsin I). The inactive pepsinogens and progastricsin are activated by gastric hydrochloric acid. Gastricsin and pepsins hydrolyze the bonds between aromatic amino acids and a second amino acid to yield polypeptides of very diverse size. Chymosin (rennin), a milk-clotting enzyme with limited general proteolytic activity, is found in the stomach of young animals. The gastric proteases have two pH optima, one at pH 2 and the other near 3.5. When the chyme enters the duodenum and mixes with the alkaline bile, pancreatic juice, and duodenal secretions, the pH of the chyme rises to 6.5. Because this pH is out of their optimal range, the proteolytic activity of the gastric proteases is thus terminated in the duodenum.

The macromolecular proteins and polypeptides formed by the gastric digestion are hydrolyzed in the lumen and on the mucosal surface of the small intestine. The pancreas secretes two groups of inactive proenzymes into the duodenum. One group acts at interior peptide bonds in the peptide molecules and is called endopeptidases: trypsinogen, chymotrypsinogen, and proelastase. The other group hydrolyzes the amino acids at the carboxyl and amino ends of the polypeptides and is termed exopeptidases: procarboxypeptidases A and B. Trypsinogen is activated to trypsin in the duodenum by enterokinase, a duodenal brush border enzyme. The trypsin then activates more trypsinogen autocatalytically and the other pancreatic proenzymes. Luminal digestion produces amino acids and considerable amounts of oligopeptides. Further hydrolysis of oligopeptides occurs at the mucosal membrane by a wide array of brush border and cytoplasmic peptidases in the enterocyte. Oligopeptides of more than three amino acids are broken down extracellularly by brush border peptidases. Tripeptides and dipeptides are hydrolyzed by both brush border and cytoplasmic peptidases or are absorbed intact and transported into circulation.

The products of luminal and mucosal digestion of protein are transported across the brush border membrane and into the enterocytes by specialized transport mechanisms. There are two Na^+-independent facilitated transport systems for neutral amino acids and cationic or basic amino acids. At least four different Na^+-dependent active systems exist to transport most neutral amino acids, proline and hydroxyproline, phenylalanine and methionine, and two acidic amino acids. Cysteine and cystine are taken up by a different Na^+-dependent system. A substantial amount of protein is absorbed into the enterocytes as intact dipeptides or tripeptides. The peptide transport process is distinct from transport systems for free amino acids.[2] The absorbed amino acids are transported out of enterocytes by two Na^+-dependent and three Na^+-independent transport systems and enter the hepatic portal blood. Considerable amounts of dipeptides and tripeptides also enter the portal blood.

Fat Digestion and Absorption

Dietary fats are composed primarily of water-insoluble triglycerides, some phospholipids, sterols, and sterol esters. Fat digestion is initiated in the stomach, where fats are warmed to body temperature, and subjected to intense mixing, agitating, and sieving action of the distal stomach. Fat globules are broken up into droplets and pass into the small intestine for further emulsification and eventual enzymatic hydrolysis. Although fat digestion is mainly dependent on pancreatic enzymes secreted into the duodenum, gastric lipase also plays a major role in the hydrolysis of triglycerides in the stomach of young animals.

Digestion of triglycerides in the lumen of the small intestine involves the emulsification of lipid droplets released from the stomach by bile acids and phospholipids, the hydrolysis of emulsified particles by the combined action of pancreatic lipase and colipase as well as cholesterol esterase and phospholipase, and the formation of micelles that are small water-soluble aggregations of bile acids and the end-products of lipid digestion (fatty acids, monoglycerides, and so forth). The micelles diffuse through the gut lumen to the brush border of the mucosal cells and allow the lipids to diffuse across the apical membrane of the enterocyte and into the cell. Inside the enterocyte, the long-chain monoglycerides are reesterified with the long-chain fatty acids to diglycerides, which are further esterified to triglycerides. The resynthesized triglycerides are then associated with cholesterol, cholesterol esters, phospholipids, and various apoproteins to form chylomicrons, which are in turn transported across the intestine and into the lymph. The short-chain fatty acids, however, pass directly into the portal blood without being esterified. In the fowl, the products of fat digestion are absorbed directly into the blood rather than the lymph in the mammal.

FERMENTATIVE DIGESTION AND NUTRIENT ABSORPTION

The herbivore depends primarily on roughages. No cell wall material of roughages is subject to hydrolysis by mammalian glandular digestive enzymes. The herbivore uses fermentative digestion to break down cell wall material by the action of bacteria and other microorganisms. In the omnivore and the carnivore, fermentative digestion also occurs in the large intestine for carbohydrates and proteins that are not digested by mammalian enzymes in the small intestine.

More information on fermentation and nutrient absorption in the ruminant forestomachs, and in the hindgut of the horse, the pig, and the fowl is provided in the article, "Digesta Processing and Fermentation," elsewhere in this encyclopedia.[3]

ABSORPTION OF WATER, ELECTROLYTES, MINERALS, AND VITAMINS

Animal intestine is presented daily with large amounts of ingested fluid and endogenous secretions. The endogenous secretions are particularly voluminous in herbivorous animals. The volume of the secretory fluid in omnivores and carnivores, although generally not as large as that in herbivores, is still substantial and can be affected greatly by the type of diet.

Little water moves across the rumen by the way of mucosa. Sodium is actively absorbed from the rumen, whereas chloride is passively absorbed. Potassium is actively secreted into rumen. The rumen wall is relatively impermeable to calcium, magnesium, and phosphate. In nonruminants, only small amounts of water enter the stomach through gastric mucosa. The absorption sites in the small intestine differ depending on the species. Most of this absorption occurs in the small intestine in a strict carnivore. In the horse and pig, the absorption of water and ions is shifted from the small to large intestine as microbial digestion develops. Nevertheless, the small intestine still absorbs large amounts of water and salt, and the majority of minerals and fat- and water-soluble vitamins. Water-soluble vitamins are absorbed rapidly.

Absorption of fat-soluble vitamins, however, is affected by fat absorption. Most vitamins are absorbed in the upper small intestine, but vitamin B_{12} is absorbed in the ileum.

CONCLUSION

This article provides a brief review of digestion and absorption of nutrients. Comparisons of the digestive system among various farm animals are provided in "GI tract: Anatomical and functional comparison."[4] A detailed description of the pig's digestive system has been published.[5] A monograph[6] has also discussed comparative anatomy and physiology of the digestive system in major groups of vertebrates. The two major challenges facing animal agriculture are manure disposal and odor control. These environmental concerns are created primarily by the inefficiency in digestion, absorption, and metabolism of dietary nutrients by the animal and oversupply of nutrients in the diet to maximize individual animal performance. To be environmentally friendly and socially responsible, animal research should be directed toward improving digestive and metabolic efficiency of dietary nutrient utilization by the animal, optimizing the accretion of wholesome, nutritious, and tasteful animal products, and minimizing nutrient excretion and odor emission.

REFERENCES

1. Ganong, W.F. *Review of Medical Physiology*, 19th Ed.; Appleton & Lange: Stamford, CN, 1999.
2. Leibach, F.H.; Ganapathy, V. Peptide transporters in the intestine and the kidney. Annu. Rev. Nutr. **1996**, *16*, 99–119.
3. Yen, J.T. *Digesta Processing and Fermentation*; EAS, 2004.
4. Moran, E.T., Jr. *GI Tract: Anatomical and Functional Comparisons*; EAS, 2004.
5. Yen, J.T. Digestive System. In *Biology of the Domestic Pig*; Pond, W.G., Mersmann, H.J., Eds.; Cornell Univ. Press: Ithaca, NY, 2001; 390–453.
6. Stevens, C.E.; Hume, I.D. *Comparative Physiology of the Vertebrate Digestive System*, 2nd Ed.; Cambridge University Press: Cambridge, UK, 1996.

Disease Resistance: Genetics

Stephen C. Bishop
Roslin Institute (Edinburgh), Roslin, Midlothian, U.K.

INTRODUCTION

For many infectious diseases, host resistance may be improved by genetic means, i.e., by breeding for enhanced resistance. This is possible because genetic differences exist between host animals in their resistance to infection, or in the disease impact that infection causes, at many levels. Most obviously, diseases are usually restricted to one or a small number of host species. Additionally, within a species, differences are often seen between breeds in resistance to a specific disease and between individuals within a breed. This article considers the nature and mechanisms underlying variation in disease resistance, reasons why this variation exists despite natural selection, exploitation of this genetic variation for controlling diseases, and future trends in disease genetics.

THE NATURE OF (GENETIC) DISEASE RESISTANCE

Evidence for host genetic variation in aspects of disease resistance has been documented for more than 50 diseases, in all major domestic livestock species. Almost certainly there is genetic variation in resistance to many more diseases. However, the term disease resistance is used to mean many different things and definitions are important to avoid confusion. Infection may be defined as the colonization of a host by organisms such as viruses, bacteria, protozoa, helminths, and ectoparasites, whereas disease describes the pathogenic consequence of infection. Disease resistance is used generically to cover resistance to infection, i.e., a host's ability to moderate the pathogen or parasite life cycle, and also resistance to the disease consequence of infection. Sometimes tolerance is used to describe a host's ability to withstand pathogenic effects of infection.

Genetic variation in disease resistance may, sometimes, be due predominantly to allelic variation at a single gene. Examples include resistance to various forms of *Escherichia coli* diarrhoea in pigs and the PrP gene, which is associated with resistance of sheep to scrapie. In other cases, variation in resistance may be due to the combined effects of allelic variation at several or many genes, e.g., nematode resistance in grazing ruminants and mastitis resistance in dairy cattle and sheep. Additionally, although resistance and tolerance are sometimes qualitative phenomena, more often they are quantitative traits, i.e., they show continuous variation from one extreme to the other. Continuous variation is expected when resistance is due to the combined effects of several genes, along with environmental effects.

Many processes may control resistance or tolerance. For example:

- The host may have an appropriately targeted immune response, enabling it to successfully combat an infection or avoid pathogenic effects of disease.
- The host may have nonimmune response genes that preclude infection, or limit infection in target organs.
- The host may have physical attributes that make infection difficult, e.g., the role of skin thickness in helping to confer resistance to ticks.
- The host may have behavioral attributes that enable it to avoid infection. An example is the hygienic behavior of honeybees that helps in their defense against diseases such as American Foulbrood and Chalkbrood.

EXAMPLES

Examples of genetic variation in disease resistance span all major livestock species and pathogen types. The strength of evidence varies from anecdotal to precise, and from population-level descriptions to causative genes. Some examples are classified by host species and pathogen type in Table 1, most of which are summarized in dedicated texts.[1,2]

Of the diseases in Table 1, precise effects have been ascribed to specific genes for only a small number of cases, such as the receptor genes coding for resistance to neonatal (F4) and postweaning (F18) *E. coli* diarrhoea in pigs;[3] MHC effects associated with resistance to Marek's disease[4] and dermatophilosis in cattle;[5] and scrapie, where genetic variation in susceptibility is predominantly due to variability at PrP gene codons 136, 154, and 171.[6] More usually, genetic variation in resistance to the diseases shown in Table 1 is described at the breed level, by within-breed variation, as quantified by the heritability

Encyclopedia of Animal Science
DOI: 10.1081/E-EAS 120019566

Table 1 Examples of diseases for which there is documented or strong anecdotal evidence of genetic variation in host resistance or tolerance

| Host species | Pathogen or parasite type | | | |
	Prion and virus	Bacteria	Protozoa	Helminth and ectoparasite
Chickens	Marek's disease	*E. coli*	Coccidiosis	*Ascaridia galli*
	Infectious laryngotracheitis	Pullorum		
	Avian leucosis	Fowl typhoid		
	Infectious bursal disease	Salmonellosis		
	Avian infectious bronchitis	Campylobacter		
	Rous sarcoma			
	Newcastle disease			
Pigs	African swine fever	Neonatal diarrhoea		
	Foot-and-mouth disease	Postweaning diarrhoea		
	Atrophic rhinitis			
	Pseudorabies			
Cattle	BSE	Paratuberculosis	Trypanosomosis	Helminthosis[a]
	Foot-and-mouth disease	Mastitis	*Theileria annulata*	Ticks
	Bovine leukemia	Bovine tuberculosis	*Theileria segenti*	
		Salmonellosis	*Theileria parva*	
		Dermatophilosis	Babesia	
		Cowdriosis		
		Brucellosis		
Sheep	Scrapie	Footrot	Trypanosomosis	Helminthosis[a]
		Mastitis		Liver fluke
		Paratuberculosis		Flystrike
		Dermatophilosis		
		Salmonellosis		
		Cowdriosis		

[a]Host resistance to many species of nematode helminths has been described.

of an indicator trait, or by quantitative trait loci (QTL) that imply the existence of genes influencing resistance in specific chromosomal regions. For cases such as foot-and-mouth disease and African swine fever, the evidence is anecdotal, arising from field observations following epidemics.

WHY DOES GENETIC VARIATION EXIST FOR DISEASE RESISTANCE?

It is often asked why natural selection doesn't eliminate genetic variation for disease resistance. Complex host–parasite interactions guide the evolution of both hosts and parasites, and are one of the major reasons for the maintenance of genetic variation in natural populations.[7] Combining genetic theory and epidemiology gives insight into why genetic variation in resistance persists. First, selection pressures, especially those for disease resistance, will differ across time and environments. Second, natural selection will not make populations completely resistant to infection; as natural selection moves a host population toward resistance, the selection pressure for resistance decreases. A certain proportion of susceptible animals can

be carried without exposing the population as a whole to risks of epidemics.[8] Once the number of genetically susceptible animals falls below this level, selection pressure for resistance ceases. Thirdly, modern domestic livestock populations have been selected for other characteristics, with disease impacts masked by non-genetic control measures.

EXPLOITATION

The primary use of genetic variation in resistance is for breeding animals for enhanced resistance to specific diseases. Whereas breeding will produce permanent benefits, it may be slower and logistically more complicated than other disease control measures, and often will only be considered when other strategies are unsatisfactory. In general, breeding will be justified if: 1) there is a disease of major importance; 2) current control strategies are not adequate, sustainable, or cost-effective; and 3) available animals do not cope with these disease challenges. A successful breeding strategy should cost-effectively reduce the impact of the disease, i.e., alter disease epidemiology, in a reasonable time period.

Breeding strategies vary in sophistication. For example, choosing the appropriate breed for the environment may be the major requirement. In tropical production systems, this may mean choosing a resistant local breed ahead of an apparently more productive exotic breed that does not have resistance attributes necessary to survive local disease challenges. Appropriate within-breed selection strategies will depend on the disease. Phenotypic indicator traits following natural infection will be useful when there are nonacute endemic infections, such as nematode infections, mastitis, or tick infestations. Genetic progress may be boosted, or infectious challenges avoided, if genetic markers of resistance are available. Epidemic diseases, or those with severe impacts upon the animal, will generally require genetic markers for breeding purposes. The effectiveness of marker-based selection will depend on the proportion of variation in resistance accounted for by known allelic variation at the resistance gene(s).

Genetic variation in resistance has been exploited for several diseases. For Marek's disease, genetic strategies have been successfully used for many years, in the face of an evolving pathogen, to assist in disease control. Many national dairy cattle breeding schemes now include mastitis resistance in their breeding goal, with the aim of limiting increases in mastitis impact arising as a consequence of increasing milk production. Individual sheep breeders in New Zealand, Australia, and the United Kingdom now select for nematode resistance to improve performance and decrease treatment requirements. Furthermore, sheep industries in Western Europe are currently selecting on PrP genotype to minimize the risk of TSEs. Beef cattle industries in several countries have altered breed choice to reduce the impact of tick infestations. Many other examples of deliberate and natural selection exist.

As with all disease control strategies, pathogen or parasite evolution is a risk. This risk will generally be minimized by combining complementary control strategies, e.g., by using genetics along with appropriate interventions or biosecurity measures.

FUTURE TRENDS

The utilization and elucidation of genes underlying genetic variation in resistance will continue to increase. Pressures due to many factors—e.g., economics, legislation, decreasing effectiveness of current intervention strategies, food safety, and zoonotic concerns—will force breeders to consider genetic solutions to a wider range of diseases. At the same time, through a combination of genome mapping and functional genomics, researchers will elucidate genes underlying differences in resistance.

These technologies, along with an understanding of the epidemiological impact of increasing resistance, should provide breeders with the required tools to increase genetic resistance to a variety of diseases.

CONCLUSIONS

Genetics offers a means of increasing the resistance of animals to a variety of infectious diseases, either through increasing resistance to infection or increasing resistance to the pathogenic consequences of infection, i.e., disease. Opportunities exist across all major domestic species, for diseases caused by all major types of pathogens. Genetic variation in resistance may be exploited through appropriate breed choice, by selecting on the host's response to infection, or by using genetic markers, thus avoiding the need for infectious challenge.

Opportunities for genetically improving disease resistance will increase as our understanding of genes underlying resistance increases. Simultaneously, breeders will be forced to consider alternative and complementary disease control measures. Together, these factors will lead to greater emphasis on disease resistance in breeding programs.

REFERENCES

1. Axford, R.F.E.; Bishop, S.C.; Nicholas, F.W.; Owen, J.B. *Breeding for Disease Resistance in Farm Animals*, 2nd Ed.; CABI Publishing, 2000.
2. Office International des Epizooties Genetic resistance to animal diseases. Rev. Sci. Tech. **1998**, *17* (1).
3. Edfors-Lilja, I.; Wallgren, P. *Escherichia coli* and *Salmonella* Diarrhoea in Pigs. In *Breeding for Disease Resistance*, 2nd Ed.; Axford, R.F.E., Bishop, S.C., Nicholas, F.W., Owen, J.B., Eds.; CABI Publishing, 2000; 253–267.
4. Bacon, L.D. Influence of the major histocompatability complex on disease resistance and productivity. Poultry Sci. **1987**, *66*, 802–811.
5. Maillard, J.C.; Chantal, I.; Berthier, D.; Stachursky, F.; Elsen, J.M. Molecular markers of genetic resistance and susceptibility to bovine dermatophilosis. Arch. Tierz. (Archives of Animal Breeding) **1987**, *42*, S93–S96. (2003).
6. Hunter, N. Transmissible Spongiform Encephalopathies. In *Breeding for Disease Resistance*, 2nd Ed.; Axford, R.F.E., Bishop, S.C., Nicholas, F.W., Owen, J.B., Eds.; CABI Publishing, 2000; 325–339.
7. Khibnik, A.I.; Kondrashov, A.S. Three mechanisms of Red Queen dynamics. Proc. R. Soc. Lond., B Biol. Sci. **1997**, *264*, 1049–1056.
8. MacKenzie, K.; Bishop, S.C. A discrete-time epidemiological model to quantify selection for disease resistance. Anim. Sci. **1999**, *69*, 543–552.

Diseases: Metabolic Disorders of Ruminants

Joan H. Eisemann
North Carolina State University, Raleigh, North Carolina, U.S.A.

INTRODUCTION

Metabolic diseases or disorders result from an imbalance between dietary supply of specific nutrients and the high demand of the nutrients for productive purposes. Production may proceed using body stores, however, an imbalance occurs when there is an inability of tissues to adapt to the increased requirement in conjunction with either a decreased or limited intake. Two nutrients that have elaborate homeostatic mechanisms to maintain relatively stable plasma concentrations are glucose and calcium. There are several common disorders that relate, in part, to metabolism of these two nutrients.

DISORDERS RELATED TO CARBOHYDRATE AND LIPID METABOLISM

Ketosis

Ketosis is defined as a metabolic disorder in which the level of ketone bodies in body fluids is greatly elevated. Ketosis can occur in any animal under conditions of starvation; however, it is most common in ruminants due to their dependence on gluconeogenesis to meet glucose needs. In ruminants, ketone bodies (β–hydroxybutyrate and acetoacetate) are a product of normal metabolism by the liver and ruminal epithelium when animals are in positive energy balance. Acetoacetate is the parent ketone, however, normally most is reduced to β–hydroxybutyrate. Acetone is produced from acetoacetate as a result of spontaneous decarboxylation.[1] Peripheral tissues use β–hydroxybutyrate and acetoacetate to provide an immediate source of energy or to synthesize long-chain fatty acids for storage. Under conditions of negative energy balance, fat mobilization from adipose tissue increases, leading to an increase in circulating concentration of nonesterified fatty acids (NEFA), an increase in ketone body production by liver, and an increase in ketone bodies in the blood (Fig. 1). In liver, entry of NEFA into the mitochondria is regulated by carnitine palmitoyl transferase I (CPTI). Hypoglycemia results in an increase in the activity of CPTI and increased flux of NEFA into the mitochondria.[2] Increased partition of NEFA to ketone body formation rather than oxidation could be due to a relative deficiency of oxaloacetate. In ketosis, the amount of acetoacetate and acetone increase relative to β–hydroxybutyrate. Both of these compounds are toxic to the central nervous system.[1]

Ketosis is associated with both negative energy balance and hypoglycemia. In dairy cows, ketosis occurs most commonly in the first 3–8 weeks of lactation. At this stage of lactation, the cow is in negative energy balance, insulin concentration is decreased, glucagon concentration is increased, hormone-sensitive lipase activity is increased, and there is increased mobilization of NEFA. At the same time, the cow may be hypoglycemic due to an insufficient rate of gluconeogenesis relative to the amount of glucose needed by the mammary gland, for synthesis of lactose and the glycerol portion of milk fat, as well as glucose needs of other body tissues. In ewes and does, the condition is most commonly associated with the last month of gestation in females carrying twins. Intake declines and the rate of gluconeogenesis is not adequate to meet the demands of fetal tissues as well as glucose needs of other body tissues.[3] Cows with clinical ketosis will decrease feed intake and milk production, but may spontaneously recover from the disease. In ewes and does, the condition is often fatal. They may recover if birth occurs or if lambs or kids are removed by cesarean section.[1]

Presence of ketone bodies in urine or milk are signs of ketosis. Diagnosis is difficult prior to observation of clinical signs. Serum concentrations of β–hydroxybutyrate from 1.2–1.4 mM have been suggested to indicate subclinical ketosis. Milk tests can also be used to measure acetone and acetoacetate or β–hydroxybutyrate.[4] Treatments include intravenous administration of glucose, feeding glucose precursors such as propylene glycol, administration of glucocorticoid hormones, and use of methanogenic inhibitors. Propylene glycol, which is not fermented and is converted to pyruvate after absorption, may be administered as a drench or included in the grain mix. Administration of glucocorticoid hormones such as dexamethasone will promote increased gluconeogenesis from amino acids. Methanogenic inhibitors such as chloral hydrate can also be used to increase propionate production in the rumen and consequently increase gluconeogenic precursors.[1,4]

Encyclopedia of Animal Science
DOI: 10.1081/E-EAS 120019569

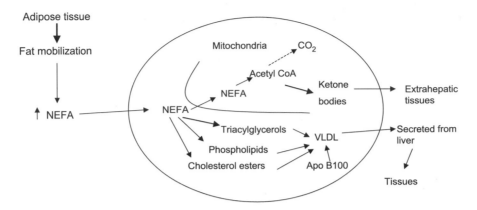

Fig. 1 Potential pathways of nonesterified fatty acid (NEFA) metabolism in liver. In conditions of undernutrition, fat is mobilized from adipose tissue, resulting in increased NEFA concentration in plasma and increased NEFA uptake by liver. In ketosis, there is an increase in the proportion of acetyl CoA converted to ketone bodies. Fatty liver arises as the formation of triacylglycerols from NEFA increases without a corresponding increase in secretion of very low-density lipoproteins (VLDL).

Fatty Liver in Ruminants

The fat content of liver is normally less than 5% of the wet weight. Fatty liver is the condition arising from the progressive infiltration of fat into the liver lobule. Fat content in the liver may increase to 30% of wet weight. Fatty liver is often associated with conditions of undernutrition such as ketosis due to the central role of the liver in the metabolism of fat (Fig. 1). During undernutrition, increased release of NEFA from adipose tissue results in increased uptake of NEFA by liver. In the liver, NEFA can enter the mitochondria for conversion to acetyl CoA and either formation of ketone bodies or complete oxidation. The NEFA that do not enter the mitochondria can be esterified to form phospholipids, cholesterol esters, and triacylglycerols. With adequate glucose availability, CPTI activity is decreased and NEFA are esterified, forming triacylglycerol (TAG).[2] These esterified compounds must be combined with apoproteins and incorporated into very low-density lipoproteins (VLDL) for export from the liver. Hepatic apoB-100 concentration, a component of VLDL, is decreased in cows with ketosis and fatty liver.[5]

In dairy cows, fatty liver is present in early lactation in conjunction with hypoglycemia and negative energy balance. However, evaluation of liver biopsies from cows around calving showed that liver triglyceride content peaked around calving. By day 1 postpartum, approximately half of the cows had more than 15% liver triglyceride. The association of fatty liver with ketosis may be due to impaired gluconeogenic capacity in the liver in conjunction with fatty infiltration.[6] In fatty liver, TAG synthesis in the liver increases and transport of fat in lipoprotein out of the liver decreases. In general, the ability of ruminants to secrete VLDL is lower

than that of other species. Decreased secretion may be due to inadequate synthesis of the protein portion of the lipoprotein.

Treatment strategies are designed to decrease lipid mobilization, increase NEFA oxidation, or increase VLDL secretion. Feeding rumen-protected methionine and administration of propylene glycol prepartum or after calving have been used to help decrease hepatic TAG accumulation.[7] Recent research evaluating the effect of a two-week glucagon infusion on TAG content of liver showed a decrease in TAG content from 12.9 to 4.7% following treatment. Glucagon therapy may have practical application if developmental challenges are solved.[8]

DISORDERS RELATED TO CALCIUM AND PHOSPHORUS METABOLISM

Parturient Paresis

Onset of lactation results in a large increase in demand for calcium. Although mechanisms in the body exist for maintenance of calcium homeostasis, some degree of hypocalcemia is common around parturition.[9] If plasma calcium becomes too low to support nerve and muscle function, the condition of parturient paresis or milk fever results. This disease is most common in high-producing dairy cows. It is associated with the rapid loss of calcium due to formation of colostrum. For example, a cow producing 10 L of colostrum loses about 23 g of calcium in a single milking. This is about nine times as much calcium as is present in the plasma pool.[10] Replacement calcium must come from intestinal absorption or bone resorption. Calcium treatments, such as intravenous infusion of a solution of calcium borogluconate, are used immediately postcalving to keep the cow alive until the homeostatic system has time to adapt.

In response to hypocalcemia, the body produces parathyroid hormone (PTH) and 1,25-dihydroxyvitamin D_3. The effect of PTH is to increase calcium reabsorption at the kidneys and also to increase resorption of bone. In addition, PTH increases the production of $1,25\text{-}(OH)_2 D_3$ by the kidney. The effects of $1,25\text{-}(OH)_2 D_3$ are to synergize with PTH to promote resorption of calcium from bone and to increase the active transport of calcium in the intestinal epithelium.[10]

Jersey cows are more susceptible than Holstein cows, which may be due to fewer intestinal receptors for $1,25\text{-}(OH)_2 D_3$. Incidence also increases with age, which may be due to both increased milk production in older cows and decreased effectiveness of homeostatic regulatory mechanisms.[10]

The current focus of prevention is on the dietary cation–anion difference in conjunction with knowledge of the homeostatic system for Ca. Feeding inorganic acids reduced the incidence of milk fever. The cation–anion difference (CAD) of diets has an impact on acid–base status. Addition of anionic salts to the diet reduces blood and urine pH and is associated with decreased incidence of milk fever. This is likely due to increased responsiveness of tissues to PTH during metabolic acidosis. Reducing cations in the diet can also have the same effect. Most emphasis has been placed on decreasing dietary potassium.[10]

Oral administration of calcium salts enhances the passive absorption of calcium from the gastrointestinal tract. A $CaCl_2$ paste given at calving and shortly thereafter reduced the incidence of milk fever. In addition to increasing calcium absorption, it also reduces blood pH. An alternative is calcium propionate, which does not have an acidifying effect.[10]

CONCLUSION

Ketosis, fatty liver, and parturient paresis are metabolic disorders that occur around the periparturient period in lactating cows. They are associated with the high demands of the mammary gland or fetal tissue for nutrients and an inability of the maternal system to adapt. Application of

knowledge of the underlying metabolic controls has lead to strategies for both prevention and treatment. Further investigation should result in more effective strategies in the future.

REFERENCES

1. Bergman, E.N. Disorders of Fat and Carbohydrate Metabolism. In *Duke's Physiology of Domestic Animals*, 11th Ed.; Cornell University Press: Ithaca, NY, 1993; 492–502.
2. Herdt, T.H. Ruminant Adaptation to Negative Energy Balance. Influences on the Etiology of Ketosis and Fatty Liver. In *The Veterinary Clinics of North America Food Animal Practice. Metabolic Disorders of Ruminants*; Herdt, T.H., Ed.; W.B. Saunders Company: Philadelphia, 2000; Vol. 16, 215–230.
3. Rook, J.S. Pregnancy Toxemia of Ewes, Does, and Beef Cows. In *The Veterinary Clinics of North America Food Animal Practice. Metabolic Disorders of Ruminants*; Herdt, T.H., Ed.; W.B. Saunders Company: Philadelphia, 2000; Vol. 16, 293–317.
4. Duffield, T. Subclinical Ketosis in Lactating Dairy Cattle. In *The Veterinary Clinics of North America Food Animal Practice. Metabolic Disorders of Ruminants*; Herdt, T.H., Ed.; W.B. Saunders Company: Philadelphia, 2000; Vol. 16, 231–253.
5. Katoh, N. Relevance of apolipoproteins in the development of fatty liver and fatty liver-related peripartum diseases in dairy cows. J. Vet. Med. Sci. **2002**, *64*, 293–307.
6. Grummer, R.R. Etiology of lipid-related metabolic disorders in periparturient dairy cows. J. Dairy Sci. **1993**, *76*, 3882–3896.
7. Buchart, D.; Gruffat, D.; Durand, D. Lipid absorption and hepatic metabolism in ruminants. Proc. Nutr. Soc. **1996**, *55*, 39–47.
8. Hippen, A.R. Glucagon as a Potential Therapy for Ketosis and Fatty Liver. In *The Veterinary Clinics of North America Food Animal Practice. Metabolic Disorders of Ruminants*; Herdt, T.H., Ed.; W.B. Saunders Company: Philadelphia, 2000; Vol. 16, 267–282.
9. Goff, J.P.; Horst, R.L. Physiological changes at parturition and their relationship to metabolic disorders. J. Dairy Sci. **1997**, *80*, 1260–1268.
10. Horst, R.L.; Goff, J.P.; Reinhardt, T.A.; Buxton, D.R. Strategies for preventing milk fever in dairy cattle. J. Dairy Sci. **1997**, *80*, 1269–1280.

Domestication of Animals

Elizabeth A. Branford Oltenacu
Cornell University, Ithaca, New York, U.S.A.

INTRODUCTION

Domestication, the intimate relationship between humans and other species, has proven to be the most successful evolutionary strategy for survival in a world dominated by the human species. Wild species that compete with humans, e.g., for land use, are increasingly threatened. Those that move closer to humans in a commensal relationship are more secure in numbers, despite their frequent treatment as pests, yet are unlikely to become domestic because the mutual benefits of domestication are lacking from the human perspective. For true domestication, there must be advantages for both humans and the second species in the partnership, and specific behavioral characteristics that facilitate the relationship. Domestication is not simply a feature of history; it is a dynamic relationship that determines the long-term survival of species living close to the constant environmental manipulations of humans. Understanding the characteristics that facilitated domestication is the key to developing successful modern management systems.

DEFINITION

Domestication is the process by which a population of animals becomes adapted to living in an environment controlled by humans. It is achieved through a combination of genetic change over many generations and environmentally induced developmental events (learning) reoccurring during each generation.[1]

HISTORY

Until the end of the last Ice Age about 10,000 years ago, humans lived a hunter-gatherer lifestyle. The only species with which they developed a domestic relationship were those that shared such a nomadic existence. Most notably, it was the wolf that, in all probability, learned the advantages of scavenging around humans, while humans took advantage of the hunting skills of the wolf pack. The relationship produced the domestic dog, whose history traces back at least 15,000 years. Another ancient domesticate is the reindeer, a nomadic species that roamed with humans in northern climates, and whose unusual (for a cervid species) social behaviors allowed domestication to develop.

As the ice sheets retreated, new land areas opened up and were exploited and colonized by the weeds of the plant and animal kingdoms—those species that were adaptable and hardy and could thrive in novel environments. Humans were part of this expansion and developed ever-closer relationships with those they hunted, especially sheep, goats, and gazelles. Sheep and goats progressed to full domestication around 9000 years ago, but gazelles, whose first response to alarm is to flee before halting to investigate the cause, did not prove capable of living closely with humans. Despite their great importance to humans for meat, they could never be fully domesticated.

Around 8000 years ago, somewhere in the Middle East, a domestication occurred that changed the face of the earth forever—humans began to domesticate plants. The production and storage of small grains demanded that the hunter-gatherers take up a more settled existence. The cultivation of highly desirable foodstuffs in concentrated areas attracted opportunistic crop robber species, much as it still attracts wild elephants in Africa and Asia today. Humans had to learn how to live in close proximity with crop robbers like cattle and swine. The simplest solution was to kill the wildest and most aggressive for meat, while coming to an agreement with the rest. As human digestive systems are not designed to utilize the roughage portion of grain crops, sharing with other species was feasible. Natural selection of social, adaptable species of relatively phlegmatic temperament thus brought humans and these species into close contact; primitive artificial selection by humans emphasized the docility that allowed full domestication to take place. Cattle and pigs were domesticated soon after settled agriculture began.

As settled agriculture progressed, so did domestication. Between 4000 and 6000 years ago, large species such as llamas in South America, horses in Central Asia, and water buffalo in South Asia were domesticated. They not only provided food, fiber, hides, and bone for human use, but were sources of power to cultivate the land and transport goods, and of manure to fertilize the soil. Animal domestication enhanced the productivity of plant domestication.

Encyclopedia of Animal Science
DOI: 10.1081/E-EAS 120019571

The storage of grain attracted rodents, which in turn attracted cats. The mutual benefits of easy prey for the cats and pest control for humans led to cat domestication in North Africa around 4000 years ago. The relationship between humans and cats has always been an unusual domestication as cats retained a single major function (hunting) that did not depend on a hierarchical social structure for its success.

Domestications of other small mammals such as rabbits and cavies all occurred in the last 2000 years. Those species originally had important functions as food animals, but modern domestications have focused primarily on the pet trade. Domestication is not limited to mammals, however. Around 5000 years ago, silk moths were domesticated in East Asia and honeybees in North Africa. Chickens were domesticated about 8000 years ago, birds such as geese and ducks around 3000 years later. The earliest fish domestication was that of the carp, domesticated in Asia around 3000 years ago. A rare example of a recent domestication of a nonpet species is the ostrich. Domestication for feathers and meat began in the 19th century in Africa, and this species is now kept in many parts of the world. Full discussion of a wide range of species domestications can be found.[2] Most domestication occurred in Eurasia and North Africa, but the Americas produced domestic turkeys around 1000 years ago, in addition to mammals (e.g., llamas) domesticated earlier. In general, the Eurasian landmass, because of its size, harbored more domesticable species, and its east–west axis allowed their widespread distribution as humans migrated.[3]

BEHAVIORAL ASPECTS

An understanding of the behavioral profile of species that were successfully domesticated leads to more knowledgeable management and handling of these animals today. Humans worldwide have captured the young of a huge range of species and kept them as pets, but this is not enough for domestication to occur. If it were, cheetahs, bears, and gazelles, to name but a few, would be domestic species. But much more beyond the taming of young animals is needed for full domestication.

In addition to the adaptability and hardiness already discussed, successful domestication virtually demands social behaviors based on a hierarchical structure within social groups. Individuals recognize each other and their status within the group, and have signaling systems that indicate dominance and submission, thus minimizing aggression and producing a stable society. Human managers become a part of that society and take the roles of dominant and leader individuals. This process is facilitated by behaviors that encourage bonding between parent and offspring and between peers in adult groups.

Behaviorally, the docile, dependent nature of domestic animals is characteristic of juveniles.[4] Even as mature adults, domestic animals retain such traits. They are also curious about novelty and willing to associate with individuals of other species. Typically, such behaviors are seen in the young of many wild species, but are lost with maturity. This group of juvenile behaviors was favored by domestication as it made animals much easier to manage. It is believed that selection favoring docile, dependent individuals led to genetic change in the rate of development so that domestic species began to reach sexual maturity before they fully completed their behavioral development. Hence, their behavior retains juvenile characteristics, a process referred to as neoteny.

The final stage in full domestication is a selective breeding program. For its success, reproductive behaviors that do not rely on tight pair bonds are desirable, as selected males are used to breed many females. Historically, it was desirable to keep fewer mature males as they tend to be more aggressive and difficult to manage. Modern systems often depend on artificial insemination, so important behaviors include ones that signify reproductive status and can be interpreted by human managers.

MODERN ISSUES

Domestication requires effort on the part of both species in the relationship, so there must be mutual benefits for it to succeed. For the human partner, there have been many uses for domestic animals, including food, work, manure, protection, sport, religious symbolism, and companionship. From the perspective of other species, the relationship with humans has provided food, shelter, and protection for much less energy expenditure than that demanded by a wild existence.

Modern intensive housing systems are relatively simple and unstimulating in contrast to the complex physical and social environments in which animals were domesticated. Animals no longer need to spend significant parts of their daily time budgets searching for and consuming their feed, so behavioral abnormalities and stereotypic behaviors develop, often based on normal feeding behaviors. It is only in the last 50 years or so that animal agriculture has reached such a large scale that the exaggerated demands of some animal production systems create welfare concerns based on observations of unusual animal behaviors. The rapid changes in management and housing systems in such a short time period have outstripped the ability of even these highly adaptable domestic species to cope. The importance of behavioral genetics in ensuring the continued success of animal agriculture is increasingly recognized.[5] Domestication incorporates genetic change as each species further adapts to the domestic relationship through continuing selection, but the adaptation process needs time to succeed.

CONCLUSION

The tendency for modern, large-scale animal production systems to change faster than species can adapt is the major challenge for domestication today. As humans become more aware of the biological similarities of all domestic species, and the psychological capabilities of domestic animals, ethical issues gain a higher profile. Abandoning a relationship that has been thousands of years in the making and that has been a major influence on human health and society is not an option. Domestication remains a dynamic, high-profile aspect of human life.

REFERENCES

1. Price, E.O. *Animal Domestication and Behavior*; CABI Publishing: Wallingford, UK, 2002.
2. Clutton-Brock, J. *A Natural History of Domesticated Mammals*; Cambridge University Press: Cambridge, UK, 1999.
3. Diamond, J. *Guns, Germs, and Steel: The Fates of Human Societies*; W.W. Norton & Company: New York, 1997.
4. Budiansky, S. *The Covenant of the Wild: Why Animals Chose Domestication*; Yale University Press: New Haven, USA, 1999.
5. *Genetics and the Behavior of Domestic Animals*; Grandin, T., Ed.; Academic Press: San Diego, 1998.

Ducks: Health Management

D

Tirath S. Sandhu
Cornell University Duck Research Laboratory, Eastport, New York, U.S.A.

INTRODUCTION

In general, ducks have fewer health problems than other domestic poultry. In commercial duck operations, significant improvements have been made in housing, nutrition, biosecurity, sanitation, and health management. Still, health problems are common, especially those due to bacterial infections. In addition to good management and sanitation, a planned vaccination program is vital to prevent diseases and raise healthy ducks. When a disease occurs in young ducklings, as in the case with duck virus hepatitis and Muscovy duck parvovirus infection, ducklings are protected through maternal immunity by vaccination of the parent flocks. The antibodies transferred through the egg yolk provide protection in progeny up to two to three weeks of age. Antimicrobial therapy with those drugs that are approved can reduce or even prevent losses due to bacterial diseases.

VIRAL DISEASES

Important viral diseases of ducks are duck virus hepatitis, duck virus enteritis, Muscovy duck parvoviral infection, and avian influenza. Other viruses such as Newcastle disease virus, reticuloendothelial virus, adenovirus, and reovirus have been isolated sporadically, but these do not cause serious health problems in ducks.

Duck virus hepatitis is a highly contagious viral infection of young ducklings characterized by rapid onset and high mortality. It is caused by three different viruses.[1] Type I is highly pathogenic and occurs worldwide except in Australia. All domestic ducklings are susceptible, with the exception of Muscovies. Pekin ducklings below three weeks of age are highly susceptible. Affected ducklings develop spasmodic convulsions of the legs and die in a typical position with their heads drawn backward. The disease is transmitted through oral and respiratory routes. Prevention is achieved by vaccination of breeder ducks or susceptible one-day-old ducklings with a live attenuated virus vaccine (Table 1). Because the disease occurs in young ducklings, vaccination of parent flocks provides adequate protection through maternal immunity. Susceptible ducklings originating from unvaccinated and unexposed parent flocks can also be

vaccinated with the same vaccine. In an outbreak, mortality can be reduced or prevented by treatment with duck virus hepatitis yolk antibody preparation (Table 1) that provides protection for 2–3 weeks.

Duck virus enteritis, also called duck plague, is an acute and highly contagious disease of ducks, geese, and swans.[2] It is caused by a herpes virus. It occurs worldwide except in Australia. Birds of all ages are susceptible. Muscovy ducks are highly susceptible. Transmission is through ingestion of contaminated feed and water. Sick birds show signs of listlessness, photophobia, and diarrhea. Duck virus enteritis is predominantly a disease of mature birds. Gross lesions include tissue hemorrhages, eruptive lesions in the gastrointestinal tract, and atrophy of lymphoid organs. Although tentative diagnosis can be made from history, signs, and lesions, definitive diagnosis should include virus isolation and identification. Recently, polymerase chain reaction (PCR) has been developed for a rapid diagnosis. Immunization with a chicken embryo-adapted live virus vaccine (Table 1) has been extensively used for prevention and control. The vaccine is administered to ducks over two weeks of age.

Parvovirus causes a serious disease in Muscovy duckling and goslings.[3] Pekin ducks are resistant to parvoviral infection. The disease is transmitted by direct or indirect contact with diseased birds. Also, vertical transmission occurs through the egg, resulting in hatchery infections. Affected birds exhibit anorexia, eye discharge, muscular weakness, and diarrhea. Diagnosis is confirmed by virus isolation and identification. Since the disease can be transmitted through the egg, the source of ducklings should be from parvovirus-free breeder flocks. The disease can be prevented by passive immunization of ducklings with a hyperimmune antiserum. Immunization of breeder ducks with a live attenuated or killed virus vaccine provides adequate protection in progeny through maternal immunity. Live or killed virus vaccine can also be used for immunization of susceptible ducklings.

Avian influenza virus does not cause a serious health problem, but infected ducks may become carriers and transmit the disease to chickens and turkeys. Ducks grown on range or semi-range are exposed to avian influenza through intermingling with wild waterfowl and other birds that may be carriers. Occasionally, mild sinusitis and sneezing may be observed in affected ducklings. Certain

Encyclopedia of Animal Science
DOI: 10.1081/E-EAS 120019576

Table 1 Vaccines, bacterins, and other biological products used in ducks[a]

Vaccine/bacterin	Live/killed	Administration/age
Duck virus hepatitis vaccine (type I)	Live, attenuated virus	Breeder ducks: S/C at 16, 20, 24 weeks of age, and thereafter every three months Ducklings (susceptible): S/C at one day of age
Duck virus enteritis vaccine	Live, attenuated virus	Breeder ducks: S/C at selection and revaccination yearly Ducklings: S/C over two weeks of age, may require revaccination
Riemerella anatipestifer vacccine	Live, avirulent (serotypes 1, 2, and 5)	Ducklings: Aerosol spray at one day of age
Riemerella anatipestifer bacterin	Killed (serotypes 1, 2, and 5)	Ducklings: S/C at two and three weeks of age
E. coli-Riemerella anatipestifer bacterin	Killed (*E. coli* serotype O78, and RA serotypes 1, 2, and 5)	Ducklings: S/C at two and three weeks of age
Duck virus hepatitis yolk antibody (type I)	Antibody preparation	Ducklings: S/C for production of passive immunity

[a]International Duck Research Cooperative, Inc., 192 Old Country Road, Eastport, New York, USA.
S/C = Subcutaneously in the neck.
RA = *Riemerella anatipestifer*.

antigenic types (H5 and H7) cause a serious disease in chickens and turkeys. Raising ducks in confinement appears to prevent exposure to avian influenza virus. No vaccine is available for use in ducks. Sanitation and biosecurity should be emphasized.

BACTERIAL DISEASES

Major bacterial diseases of ducks are *Riemerella anatipestifer* infection, avian cholera, colibacillosis, and salmonellosis. Occasionally, erysipelas, chlamydiosis, streptococcosis, staphylococcosis, boltulism, and clostridial infections have been reported in ducks.

Riemerella anatipestifer (previously called *Pasteurella anatipestifer*) infection is a major health problem of ducklings.[4] It causes serious economic losses to the duck industry due to mortality, weight reduction, and condemnation. Ducklings, one to 10 weeks of age, are highly susceptible. Affected ducklings exhibit listlessness, incoordination, convulsions of head and neck, ataxia, and torticollis. At least 20 different serotypes of *Riemerella anatipestifer* have been reported worldwide; no significant cross-protection has been observed between different serotypes. Diagnosis should be made based on history, signs, lesions, bacterial isolation, and identification. The disease is transmitted through the respiratory route and cuts in the skin. Treatment with novobiocin, penicillin, enrofloxacin, and sulfadimethoxine-ormetoprim is effective to some extent. Live and inactivated vaccines have been used successfully for immunization of ducklings

(Table 1). Because there is little or no cross-protection between different serotypes, an ideal vaccine should be effective against predominant serotypes to provide broad-spectrum protection.

Avian cholera is a contagious septicemic disease of ducks and other poultry caused by *Pasteurella multocida*. Birds show anorexia, mucus discharge from the mouth, and diarrhea. Mature birds are more susceptible than young ducklings. Bacterial isolation and identification should confirm diagnosis. Treatment with antibiotics and sulfa drugs is very effective. Killed bacterial vaccines have been used for prevention.

Collibacillosis is a common infection of all poultry including ducks. It is caused by *Escherichia coli*. *E. coli* is responsible for a variety of health problems in ducks and other poultry. It causes low hatchability, due to embryonic mortality, and omphalitis in young ducklings, due to yolk sac infection. Colisepticemia usually occurs in older and breeder ducks. The disease often occurs due to unsanitary conditions. Isolation and identification of the causative bacteria are critical to confirm diagnosis. Chlortetracycline, enrofloxacin, and sulfadimethoxine-ormetoprim have been shown to reduce mortality. Killed vaccines have also been used for prevention.

Salmonellosis or paratyphoid infections in ducks and other poultry are caused by various serotypes of salmonella. Predominant serotypes isolated from ducks are *Salmonella enteritidis* and *Salmonella typhimurium*.[5] The disease is contracted by ingestion of contaminated feed or water and by vertical transmission through the eggs. Young ducklings under three weeks of age suffer from acute intestinal infection. Treatment with chlortetracycline or sulfadimethoxine-ormetoprim in feed for the first two weeks of age is practiced on most duck farms. Serological monitoring of breeding flocks through testing and elimination of carriers is highly recommended for control. Proper management of breeder ducks along with sanitation of hatching eggs and incubators is also helpful in reducing shell surface contamination.

Aspergillosis caused by *Aspergillus fumigatus* can result in high mortality in young ducklings. Most often, the source of infection is contaminated litter or feed. Contamination of hatching eggs and the hatchery environment has been reported to cause embryonic mortality and hatchability problems. Elimination of the source of infection and proper sanitation of hatching eggs are recommended.

Ducklings are also highly susceptible to aflatoxins that may be present in feed grains, especially corn. Aflatoxicosis may cause low productivity, higher mortality, and immunosuppression that may lower immune response to vaccines. Feed grains should be tested for aflatoxins before inclusion in duck rations.

CONCLUSION

Duck health management is practiced by raising ducks in a healthy environment. This means adequate housing, nutritionally balanced feed, strict biosecurity, and good sanitation and planned vaccination program. Diseases that affect young ducklings such as duck virus hepatitis and Muscovy duck parvoviral infection are effectively controlled through maternal immunity by vaccination of breeder flocks. Raising ducklings obtained from disease-free breeder flocks can prevent diseases that are transmitted through the eggs, such as salmonellosis and Muscovy duck parvovirus infection. Health monitoring through serological testing and periodic examination of normal mortality is vital to keep close surveillance on health problems. Antimicrobial therapy is very helpful in reducing or even preventing mortality in the event of an outbreak due to a bacterial disease.

ACKNOWLEDGMENTS

The author sincerely thanks Dr. William F. Dean for critical review of the manuscript.

REFERENCES

1. Woolcock, P.R. Duck Hepatitis. In *Diseases of Poultry,* 11th Ed.; Saif, Y.M., Barnes, H.J., Glisson, J.R., Fadly, A.M., McDougald, L.R., Swayne, D.E., Eds.; Iowa State Press: Ames, 2003; 343–354.
2. Sandhu, T.S.; Shawky, S.A. Duck Virus Enteritis (Duck Plague). In *Diseases of Poultry*, 11th Ed.; Saif, Y.M., Barnes, H.J., Glisson, J.R., Fadly, A.M., McDougald, L.R., Swayne, D.E., Eds.; Iowa State Press: Ames, 2003; 354–363.
3. Gough, R.E. Goose Parvovirus Infection. In *Diseases of Poultry*, 11th Ed.; Saif, Y.M., Barnes, H.J., Glisson, J.R., Fadly, A.M., McDougald, L.R., Swayne, D.E., Eds.; Iowa State Press: Ames, 2003; 367–374.
4. Sandhu, T.S. *Riemerella anatipestifer* Infection. In *Diseases of Poultry*, 11th Ed.; Saif, Y.M., Barnes, H.J., Glisson, J.R., Fadly, A.M., McDougald, L.R., Swayne, D.E., Eds.; Iowa State Press: Ames, 2003; 676–682.
5. Dougherty, E., III. The pathology of paratyphoid infection in the White Pekin duck, particularly the lesions in the central nervous system. Avian Dis. **1961**, *5* (4), 415–430.

Ducks: Nutrition Management

J. David Latshaw
The Ohio State University, Columbus, Ohio, U.S.A.

INTRODUCTION

Many sizes and colors of ducks are available. They are usually arranged into classes by weight. Ducks in the heavy class weigh from 3.64 to as much as 5.90 kilograms (kg) when mature. In the commercial duck industry, these are used for the production of meat. Ducks in the medium class weigh from 2.72 to 3.63 kg, and those in the light class weigh 1.82 to 2.72 kg. Ducks in the light class may be used commercially for egg production. Bantam ducks generally weigh about 0.91 kg. All ducks need the same nutrients, although the concentration of nutrients that is needed may vary. The need for nutrients is affected mostly by the stage of a duck's life. When it is growing, it needs a higher concentration of nutrients than when it is mature. When a female is laying eggs for a long time, a duck needs a better quality diet than when it is not. This article will give a general presentation of the nutrition of ducks.

SUPPLYING FEED AND WATER

Ducklings that are one-day old are fairly easy to start on feed and water. Starter feed should be given as pellets, 320 or 480 mm in diameter, or crumbles (Fig. 1). The pellets are placed in the bottom of a box or feeder that is no more than 3.85 cm deep. In order for ducks to shovel the pellets with their bill, the feeder should be at least 7.6 cm wide.[1] Ducks don't require much feeder space because they can eat a lot of pellets quickly. Even mature ducks probably need 7.6 cm or less of feeder space per bird, except when breeders are given limited amounts of feed each day. Otherwise, enough feed should be provided so that there is feed in the feeder most of the day. Feeders should be appropriate for the size of the duck, and they should be positioned at a level that the duck can eat without raising or lowering its head very much. Larger ducks can eat pellets that are 635 or 952 mm in diameter.

Watering ducks is also relatively easy. Any container should provide water that is at least 1.25 cm deep, unless a nipple waterer is used. The container must be slightly wider than the duck's bill, so the duck has access to the water. Any appropriate trough or pan can be used. Ducks should have water available to them at all times, and the waterers should be kept clean. When feeding, ducks like to alternate between feeding and drinking. The area between feed and water locations becomes wet and dirty. With larger numbers of ducks, houses are designed to decrease this problem by building a wire grate over a gutter or drain. The waterer is positioned over the grate so most of the water that is spilled will fall into the drain. It is not necessary for ducks to swim; however, occasional swimming will improve feather quality.

A GENERAL DIVISION OF FOODS, FEEDS, OR INGREDIENTS

Food or feed is the source of materials that an animal's body needs to grow or to replace what it is using each day. In order to gain some information about what is in a feed or an ingredient, a procedure is followed that separates all feeds into six different parts or fractions. These are moisture or water, crude protein, crude fat, crude fiber, ash or mineral, and nitrogen-free extract. Results of some of these analyses are found on feed tags or food labels. All of these fractions are determined by using relatively simple chemical procedures. Information gained from these procedures is called the proximate analysis.

All feeds contain some moisture. The usual amount is from 8 to 10%. If the percentage of moisture is too high, feeds will spoil by getting moldy. This happens if feeds have approximately 15% or more moisture. Animals can use moisture from the feed as a source of water for their body, which is about two-thirds water. If animals are on pasture, the fresh plants that they eat will have a much higher water content, as much as 80 or 90%. In order for the animals to meet their needs for water, they must have a source of clean water. Animals that don't get enough water will become dehydrated. This will affect their health and may cause death in extreme conditions.

Waterfowl eat foods or feeds that contain a high percentage of carbohydrates. Two fractions of the proximate analysis, nitrogen-free extract (NFE) and crude fiber, give information about carbohydrates. Most of the NFE in feed ingredients is starch, but sugars are also part of this fraction. Manufactured duck feeds have most of their carbohydrates as NFE and only a small proportion as fiber. Cereal grains make up a large proportion of a complete feed, and grains are high in NFE. Flour is an

Encyclopedia of Animal Science
DOI: 10.1081/E-EAS 120019578

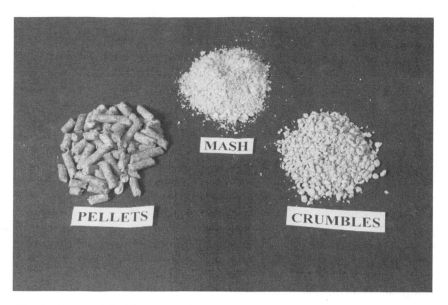

Fig. 1 Forms of duckling starter feed. (*View this art in color at www.dekker.com.*)

example of an ingredient that is very high in NFE because other fractions of the proximate analysis were removed while making it. The average composition of feed ingredients can be found in the National Research Council publication for poultry.[2] Waterfowl can digest most of the NFE in feeds, but little of the fiber can be digested. If waterfowl are eating whole plants while on pasture, their diet will contain more fiber than they would usually get with complete feeds. Alfalfa meal is more similar to pasture plants than to cereal grains.

Digested carbohydrates are the main fuel source for the body. Glucose (sugar) is the main carbohydrate that results from digestion. The use of glucose for fuel might be compared to a fire that is burning wood. The fire consumes wood and gives off heat. In a related way, an animal's body consumes glucose and gives off heat. The way an animal's body uses fuel does not release heat as quickly or it would destroy itself, but the fact that birds maintain a body temperature of approximately 41°C is evidence of heat production.

Fat that is in feeds can also be digested and used for energy. Most feeds contain less than 4% fat. If ingredients are used that increase the dietary fat by several percent, waterfowl can digest the additional fat.

Protein in feeds is digested to amino acids. Growing birds use the amino acids to make muscle and other body proteins. Females laying eggs use amino acids to make protein that is in the egg. Mature males also need some amino acids to replace protein in their body that is used during maintenance and for some specialized functions. As a result, waterfowl that are making a lot of their own

protein need slightly more protein in their feed than waterfowl that are not making as much protein.

DIETS FOR DUCKS

The composition of feed that is appropriate for ducks at different stages of their life is shown in Table 1. Feed for ducks is usually in the form of pellets, although it may be in the form of crumbles for very young ducks. When ducks

Table 1 Composition (%) of diets for ducks at different stages of their life

Ingredient	1–14 Days	15–50 Days	Breeders
Corn	62.9	77.9	73.7
Soybean meal (48.5%)	34.4	19.4	18.1
Dicalcium phosphate	1.5	1.1	1.1
Limestone	0.6	1.0	6.5
Salt	0.4	0.4	0.4
Vitamin and trace mineral mix[a]	0.2	0.2	0.2
Calculated content			
Protein (%)	22.0	16.0	15.0
Calcium (%)	0.65	0.60	2.75
Nonphytate phosphorus (%)	0.40	0.30	0.30

[a]Use a mix appropriate for the diet and follow manufacturer's instructions for use.

start to lay eggs, they need a feed with enough calcium to make the eggshells. For mature ducks that are not laying eggs, all of the limestone except for 1.0% can be replaced by corn. If ducks are becoming too fat, the amount of feed given each day should be limited to the amount needed for the ducks to maintain the proper weight.

The diets in Table 1 show that carbohydrates fill most of the volume in the diet and provide energy to waterfowl. Soybean meal varies in proportion to the percentage of protein that is needed. If waterfowl eat feed that is too low in protein, they will not get enough amino acids to make body protein that is needed for rapid growth. As a result, ducks will grow slower and mature females will lay fewer eggs. Only the concentrations of methionine[3] and lysine[4] that are needed in the diet have actually been determined. But feeding more than the required protein will not improve their growth and health.

Small amounts of ingredients other than corn and soybean meal are needed to make a balanced feed. Dicalcium phosphate provides additional calcium and phosphorus, while limestone provides only calcium. Both calcium and phosphorus are needed to make strong bones. Without enough of these minerals, bones become rubbery, a condition known as rickets. A mineral that is supplemented by salt is sodium. Without enough sodium, a bird's growth is stunted.

CONCLUSION

All ducks need the same nutrients from their feed, but in different proportions. The largest proportion of the feed is needed to supply energy, with most of the energy coming from carbohydrates. Fat and protein can also supply energy. A special function of protein is to provide amino acids that can be used to build duck protein for growth or egg production. Ducks fed an adequate amount of a nutritionally balanced diet will grow and reproduce normally. A deficiency of one or more nutrients results in poor growth and reproductive performance.

REFERENCES

1. Scott, M.L.; Dean, W.F. *Nutrition and Management of Ducks*; M.L. Scott of Ithaca: Ithaca, NY, 1991.
2. National Research Council. *Nutrient Requirements of Poultry*; National Academy Press: Washington, DC, 1994.
3. Elkin, R.G.; Stewart, T.S.; Rogler, J.C. Methionine requirement of male white Pekin ducklings. Poult. Sci. **1986**, *65*, 1771–1776.
4. Bons, A.; Timmler, R.; Jeroch, H. Lysine requirement of growing male Pekin ducks. Br. Poult. Sci. **2002**, *43*, 677–686.

Ecology and Environment: Issues

John A. Milne
The Macaulay Institute, Aberdeen, U.K.

INTRODUCTION

The impact of domesticated livestock on the functioning of ecosystems is the focus of this article. Historically, there have always been positive and negative impacts on the functioning of ecosystems, particularly those that include humans, but the extent of the impacts has increased as human and livestock populations have increased. In the last century, the application of science to animal production systems, together with an increase in the demand for food and other products from livestock, has led to an intensification of livestock systems.

Intensification has been particularly the case for pigs and poultry and, to an increasing extent, for dairy cow systems. This has led to impacts on the functioning of ecosystems containing soil as a component, and on aquatic ecosystems mainly through the housing of livestock in large numbers and the need to dispose of excreta. Intensification of dairy, beef, and sheep grazing systems, particularly in Europe, has led to the increased use of nitrogenous fertilizers, which has also led to impacts on ecosystems. Increases in the numbers of grazing beef cattle, sheep, and goats; changes in the socioeconomics of pastoral systems; and the exploitation of new grazing areas have led to reductions in plant and animal biodiversity in many parts of the world in the last century. These pressures on the environment will continue to increase as the demand for animal products is stimulated by increases in the wealth of developing countries. Regulation will continue to develop as an important tool in the control of livestock systems in watershed and ecosystem management. For this regulation to be effective, there must be a greater understanding of the functioning of grazed ecosystems.

AIR AND WATER QUALITY

A major impact on air quality is the quantity of methane produced by ruminant livestock and wild herbivores (80–100 m tonnes per year) and its contribution to greenhouse gas emissions and the effect that this may have on global warming and ecosystems. Wild herbivores have been estimated to produce 4–8% of this methane.[1] The amount produced is a function of the numbers of ruminant livestock, their size, level of productivity, and type of diet, with low-quality roughage diets producing proportionately more. Approaches to reducing methane production through changes in diet, manipulating the rumen flora, and the administration of chemicals or drugs are being advocated, but are unlikely to have application to those ruminant livestock that are extensively managed.[2] Local effects on air quality can occur through ammonia production from manure from housed pig, poultry, and ruminant livestock and from the release of ammonia from feces and urine in intensively managed grazing systems where high levels of nitrogenous fertilizer are applied. The impacts are on increasing the concentration of NO_x gases in the atmosphere, which contributes to the acidification and nitrification of soils and water, and hence impacts the productivity of ecosystems. As a result of increases in such gases in the atmosphere, changes in the composition of plant communities has occurred, for example, in the Netherlands,[3] and a loss of fish species from waters through acidification has occurred in many countries of the northern hemisphere.[4] In the European Community, regulation is being put in place to reduce such impacts on ecosystems.

Water quality is mainly affected by the movement of nutrients from manure sites, through the application of manure to soils as a fertilizer and the application of mineral fertilizers to crops used for livestock into rivers and streams. There are also issues relating to additives to feeds and silage effluent. The impact can result in nutrient saturation in soils and eutrophication of water courses, leading to major changes in aquatic ecology. A number of approaches have been adopted to attempt to minimize these impacts on water quality, including the appropriate positioning of housing for livestock and the building of manure systems that minimize the risk of contamination, and the disposal of manure to land in ways that reduce the likelihood of nutrients reaching water courses.[5] Because there is a mixture of point-source (housing) and diffuse pollution (disposal to land), approaches are now being taken to manage the problem at the level of the watershed. Targets are set for concentrations of pollutants in water; these are monitored and, by joint action, adhered to

Encyclopedia of Animal Science
DOI: 10.1081/E-EAS 120019580

through a combination of best practice guidelines and regulation. An example is the Water Framework Directive of the Europe Commission.

IMPACTS OF GRAZING

Pastoral agriculture occupies around 20% of the land surface of the world and is the predominant form of land use in some of its more fragile ecosystems, particularly in nontemperate regions. In the past 20 years, understanding of the key processes that influence plant–ruminant relationships in grazed ecosystems has increased greatly, but their development into management systems to manage the impacts of grazing, trampling, and excretal return of nutrients has been slow.[6] The reasons for this are complex, but there is an urgent need not only to develop management systems to protect pastoral resources against uncontrolled increases in stocking density in the context of potential climate change, but also to ensure that the appropriate stocking density and mix of livestock species is used to meet the objectives of the system. Ruminant livestock have the potential to increase as well as decrease ecosystem services.

In temperate regions, intensively managed systems have been developed that use simple grass and grass-legume pastures and where only one livestock species is present. These pastures can withstand high grazing pressures without reducing their productivity. In these pastures, uncertainties of weather or variation in soil quality can be buffered by the use of fertilizers and supplementary feeding. Such systems have low plant diversity and, particularly in Europe, this has led to the need to develop more extensive forms of management, sometimes using combinations of livestock species, to meet multiple objectives, including biodiversity objectives, from pastoral resources. This trend is likely to continue and will require a greater understanding of grazing behavior at larger spatial scales than currently exists.

In Mediterranean regions of the Old World, high stocking densities of particularly sheep and goats have existed for several thousand years. Such ecosystems are often considered degraded, and are believed to provide a sufficient range of ecosystem services, but there is a counterargument that they have reached a sustainable equilibrium.[7] In other parts of the Mediterranean Old World, reductions in grazing livestock numbers have occurred because of social changes and this has led to scrub encroachment and increased summer fire risk. These issues will require resolution for other Mediterranean climatic regions in the world in the future.

In the semiarid and arid regions, pressures on land for the growing of crops, reduction in the prevalence of systems where livestock are moved from site to site as in Africa and Asia, and economic pressures elsewhere in the world have led to increases in grazing pressures of many pastoral resources. In combination with the stochastic nature of rainfall, the greater grazing pressures associated with the socioeconomic changes noted earlier are likely to cause a greater incidence of discontinuous shifts in plant species composition, which often leads to a reduction in the value of the resource for livestock.[8] Issues of stability and resilience of these ecosystems to the impacts of livestock are central issues that have yet to be fully understood.

CONCLUSION

As understanding has increased and the intensity of management of livestock has also increased, there is now a greater awareness of the negative impacts of livestock on the delivery of ecosystem services. A broader systems approach to the development of new livestock systems, often combined with a stronger regulatory framework in the developed counties of the world, is now being taken. Such an approach takes into account the effects of livestock systems on terrestrial and aquatic ecosystems, the productivity of grazed ecosystems, and issues of biodiversity. As understanding of ecosystem processes develops, it will be possible to be more precise in setting the context within which livestock systems can operate. In the context of rangelands, an excellent synthesis of these issues has recently been published.[9]

ARTICLE OF FURTHER INTEREST

Environmental Pollutants, p. 338

REFERENCES

1. Crutzen, P.J.; Aselmann, I.; Seiler, W. Methane production by domestic animals, wild ruminants, other herbiverous fauna and humans. Tellus **1986**, *38B*, 271–284.
2. Howden, S.M.; Rewyenga, P.J. Methane emissions from Australian livestock: Implications of the Kyoto Protocol. Australian Journal of Agricultural Research **1999**, *50*, 1285–1291.
3. Heil, G.W.; Aerts, R. General Introduction. In *Heathlands– Pattern and Process in a Changing Environment*; Aerts, R.,

Heil, G.W., Eds.; Kluwer Academic Press: Dordrecht, The Netherlands, 1993; 1–24.

4. Ormerod, S.J.; Gee, A.S. Chemical and Ecological Evidence on the Acidification of Welsh Lakes and Rivers. In *Acid Waters in Wales*; Edwards, R.W., Gee, A.S., Stoner, J.H., Eds.; Kluwer Academic Publishers: Dordrecht, The Netherlands, 1990; 11–25.

5. Jarvis, S.C.; Wilkins, R.J.; Pain, B.F. Opportunities for reducing the environmental impact of dairy farm managements: A systems approach. Grass Forage Sci. **1996**, *51*, 21–31.

6. Illius, A.W.; Hodgson, J. *The Ecology and Management of Grazing Systems*; CAB International: Wallingford, UK, 1996.

7. Perevolotsky, A.; Seligman, N.G. Role of grazing in Mediterranean rangeland ecosystems. Bioscience **1998**, *48*, 1007–1017.

8. Walker, B. Rangeland ecology: Understanding and managing change. Ambio **1993**, *22*, 80–87.

9. Grice, A.C.; Hodgkinson, K.C. *Global Rangelands—Progress and Prospects*; CABI Publishing: Wallingford, UK, 2002.

Egg Products: Retail, Catering and Food Service Products

Gideon Zeidler
University of California, Riverside, California, U.S.A.

INTRODUCTION

Eggs were highly appreciated far beyond their nutritional contribution since early times. In different societies, they became symbols of fertility, rejuvenation, and the entering of springtime. They became part of religious rituals and inspiration to art and folklore. As a result, numerous traditional dishes and their variations were developed in many regions and societies around the world. The rapid pace of life strongly changed eating habits. Eating out surpassed supermarket and food outlet sales. A huge number of ready-to-cook and ready-to-eat products are displayed at food markets, department stores, and gas stations. Furthermore, the global communication and increased global travel opened people's palate to ethnic dishes from all over the world. As a result, large numbers of egg dishes, egg products, and egg-containing products are available everywhere.

THE VARIOUS TYPES OF EGG PRODUCT

Many retail, foodservice, restaurant, and catering egg products are available today in freshly made, chilled, frozen, and dry forms as well as in ready-to-cook and ready-to-eat products. More and more U.S. national brands are seen on retail shelves.

Upscale restaurants and catering services make numerous egg products such as omelets, deviled eggs, waffles, and blinzes fresh on-site or on the same day. This approach opens the door for many popular egg dishes in huge numbers or variations to be served.

WHOLE EGG PRODUCTS

1. *Hard-cooked eggs* are made by placing the egg in vertical position in cold water and bringing it to a boil. Then the eggs are simmered for about 10 minutes, rapidly cooled down, and peeled manually or mechanically by machines, which today have a capacity for up to 70,000 eggs/hour (Fig. 1). Products are sold with or without peel in liquid-containing packages in dry plastic that is either flexible or rigid. These packages contain as few as 2 eggs up to 5 gallon drums for institutional use.

2. *Egg salads* is chopped hard-cooked eggs mixed with mayonnaise and chives (many variations), sold in retail as is or in sandwiches as well as in mass feeding outlets and restaurants.

3. *Sliced eggs* are round hard-cooked egg slices as well as quartered or smaller chunks, used mainly for garnishing salads.

4. *Egg log* is commercially produced as a 10-inch-long hard-cooked geometrical egg cylinder. It is used mainly for garnishing with uniform slices with no waste.

5. *Deviled eggs* are hard-cooked eggs sliced into two longitudinal halves. The yolks are taken out, mashed, and mixed with mayonnaise and spices, returned back to the albumen cavity, and spread with paprika. Popular in parties, catering, and as bar snacks (many variations).

6. *Folded omelets* are the most popular egg dish in the United States. They are available in retail, catering, and restaurants, mostly in plain, cheese, and Western or Denver omelets (ham, onion, and cheese). However, hundreds of versions are known. Omelets are made from liquid eggs and water mix, which coagulates flat in a pan. A mixture of desired ingredients (meat, variety, mushroom, seafood, and various vegetables) is placed in the center, lightly cooked, and the coagulated egg is then folded.

7. *Flat omelets* are popular in Europe where the filling mix is embedded in the coagulated egg. Fritata is the Italian version (ham, onion, and Parmesan cheese), and tortilla (potato base) is the Spanish version.

8. *Scrambled eggs* originated in England although the French dispute it. They are made from well-beaten eggs and milk (7:3 ratio), salt, and pepper. The French variant uses cream and butter. Many variations exist using different ingredient combinations such as cheeses, mushrooms, ham, shrimp, and a variety of vegetables. The mix is fried gently in a heavy pan. They are commercially available in retail, catering, and restaurants (Fig. 2).

9. *French toast* is a popular breakfast dish made by soaking various types of breads in seasoned liquid

Encyclopedia of Animal Science
DOI: 10.1081/E-EAS 120039672

Fig. 1 Hard-cooked egg products. (Photo courtesy of Papeti Corp., now part of Michael Foods.)

Fig. 3 Retail frozen waffles, french toast, and scrambled eggs.

egg mixture and frying in a pan. They are commercially available in ready-to-eat frozen form and distributed nationally in the United States (Fig. 3).

10. *Batters* are composed of beaten eggs, flour, and liquid (water, milk, or a combination of the two). Common additives are salt, pepper, sugar, spices, and baking powder. Batters provide distinguishing organoleptic characteristics to fried or baked foods

and thousands of formulas exist. Many of these formulas, such as Kentucky Fried Chickens, are kept secret. Many commercial products are available in ready-to-cook, dry, frozen, or chilled versions. Ready-to-eat foods that contain batter are also available in retail, fast food, restaurants, and institution feeding outlets. Many batters are made for specific food products such as pancakes, waffles, and Yorkshire pudding.

11. *Pancakes* are beaten eggs and flour batter with many other additives. Pancakes are universally popular and many counties or regions have their own version and specific name. They are commercially available in ready-to-cook or ready-to-eat forms. The French have crepes suzette, the Russian Blinis, the Jewish Blintzes, the Chinese egg rolls, the German Pfrankuchen, and the Mexican egg-containing tostado, tortilla, and tacos. These products are completely different from each other and vary from sweet to savory, prepared on a griddle or fried, eaten hot or cold, as breakfast item, dinner, or late-night snack. In the United States pancakes were brought to New England by the settlers and are eaten hot with maple syrup and butter. Many regional versions exist such as San Francisco sourdough pancakes.

12. *Waffles* are a mixture of beaten eggs, flour, and liquid such as water or milk and flavoring products, which are made by using a very hot waffle iron. The finished products can be toasted or reheated. Many regional variations exist such as the pecan waffle made in the South. Waffles are commercially available as ready-to-eat (frozen) and ready-to-cook in liquid or dry forms (Fig. 3).

13. *Bakery products* use eggs to tremendously improve organoleptic characteristics of breads, pastries, cookies, and dough products such as noodles, pasta, and dough-filled products such as Russian pirogen, quiches, and others. Eggs provide improved texture

Fig. 2 Frozen scrambled egg breakfasts.

Fig. 4   Frozen breakfast burritos.

Fig. 5   Retail mayonnaise products in Australia.

due to egg-white coagulation and volume due to the aeration property of egg whites. The yolk provides better water-holding capacity, which results in moist products, and strong emulsifying capabilities due to large quantities of phospholipids and lecithin. Shiny crust color due to Maillard reaction and distinctive flavor are also yolk advantages. As a result, the bakery and pasta industries are the largest buyer of eggs, mostly in the form of industrial whole eggs, egg whites, or egg yolks.

The bakery products can be divided into two major groups:

a.   *Baked products* such as breads, cakes, pies, cookies, large portion of the pastries, and savory filled products, such as pockets. One of the most famous cakes, the pound cake, was originally made from one pound of eggs, one pound of butter, one pound of flour, and one pound of sugar and flavoring.
b.   *Cooked products* such as egg noodles and egg pasta.
c.   *Many other foods* exist such as precooked crusts, which are filled with fresh ingredients such as fresh fruit, pies, and tarts (fresh strawberry pie, fresh blueberry-tart).

14.   *Egg-filled products* include breakfast pockets, pita pockets, egg calzone, egg knishes, egg burritos, egg pizza, that showed up commercially in the 1990s and are widely available (Fig. 4).
15.   *Baked puddings* originated in England and spread to all parts of the British Empire. Many puddings were developed and the first American cookbook (41 pages) includes the recipes for 21 of them.[6] Today, the rice pudding and the bread pudding are highly appreciated and are available as retail catering and restaurant versions.

EGG YOLK–BASED PRODUCTS

Products such as mayonnaise, sauces, and salad dressings are commercially produced in very large volumes. A large number of variations are regionally produced as specialty items.

1.   *Mayonnaise* is made by mixing yolks with salt, dry mustard, and lemon juices (or vinegar) before whisking or blending in oil in a ratio of 1:7 (yolk mixture:oil) to make a stable emulsion (Fig. 5). Due to *Salmonella enteritis* (SE), a possible food poisoning threat, the egg yolks are pasteurized or cooked before utilization. However, when mayonnaise is made at home or in specialty restaurants, no cooking is done to obtain superior flavor. Acidifying with lemon juice just reduces the risk. *Aioli* is the French version (from Provance) of mayonnaise, in which garlic and extra virgin olive oils are used. Egg cooking sauces, salad dressings, dips, and spreads are variations of mayonnaise and are made under the same principles. Egg-containing *sauces, salad dressings, dips,* and *spreads*

Fig. 6   Frozen quiches.

Fig. 7 Chilled egg substitute made from egg whites.

are variations of mayonnaise and are made under the same principles.

2. *Custards* are known from Roman times. This product group is sweet and moist. The tender gel is made from egg yolks, sugar, milk or cream, and flavors such as vanilla, chocolate, or fruit. The most famous custards, the French crème caramel and the Spanish flan, are available in many countries in restaurant and retail. *Quiches* are unsweetened baked custard pies with filling made from egg yolks, eggs, milk, and cheese (Fig. 6). The most famous one, quiche Lorraine, came from Alsace in northeastern France.

3. *Ice cream:* Eggs have limited use in ice cream and they are used mainly in the French vanilla ice cream and chocolate ice creams, which are commercially available in large volume. Many low-volume specialty ice creams also use eggs.

EGG WHITE–BASED PRODUCTS

The foaming capability of egg albumen is the fundamental characteristic of this product group. They are used mainly in baked products prepared at 350–400°F or in foamy

drinks and desserts. They are available commercially in ready-to-cook or ready-to-eat forms.

1. *Angel cake* is made from egg whites, flour, and sugar. The egg whites and sugar are beaten until solidified and the flour is then added. The mixture is poured into a baking pan. No leavening agents are used. This cake is also used as a test model for measuring foam strength in relation to cake volume.

2. *Confectionery*: The first egg confectionery had to wait until sugar was brought from the New World. In 1550, marzipan was developed in Milan, Italy by beating egg whites with sugar. Meringues were invented in France and were widely distributed after Luis XIV made it a royal dish. Nougats (egg whites, gelatin, vegetable oils, and dried coconut and other fruit), marshmallows, and other similar products are commercially available. The incredible emulsification and water-holding capabilities of the egg yolk were well used in chocolate-type confections in earlier times; however, cheaper soy phospholipids and leuiting thin replaced most of the eggs in chocolate confections. Eggs are still used in some specialty products such as chocolate truffles.

3. *Meringues* are made with aerated egg whites with finely ground sugar.

Fig. 8 The young egg and chicken seller (Italy).

4. *Soufflés* are made from egg yolks and thick white sauce (Béchamel) made from flour, butter, milk, or cream. Various seasoned purees of vegetables, meats, or seafood are added together with aerated egg whites, which provide the desired volume and texture. The mix is baked in individual cups and the baking is finished when the product rises above the rim.

5. *Egg substitutes* are made in order to provide liquid egg without cholesterol. They are made mainly from egg whites, so the amount of fat is also very low. They are available in retail and institutional packages in frozen or chilled form (Fig. 7).

CONCLUSION

Large numbers and varieties of egg and egg-containing products are now available in retail, foodservice, and catering outlets. Many products are large-volume national brands or even global brands such as Kraft Mayonnaise and McDonald Egg McMuffin. Other egg products are relatively small-volume regional ethnic or specialty items. Catering has a major role in developing these items.

The love of eggs as a food item, egg-containing food products, and inspiration to the arts (Fig. 8) and culture is still a strong driving force for the utilization of eggs in many ways.

REFERENCES

1. Maguelonne, T.S. *History of Foods, Eggs Their Uses and Customs*; Barnes and Noble Books: New York, 1987; 355–362. (translated from French).
2. Bell, D.D.; Weaver, W.D., Jr. *Commercial Chicken Meat and Egg Production*, 5th Ed.; Kluwer Academic Publishers, 2002.
3. Stadelman, W.F.; Coterill, O.J. *Egg Science and Technology*, 4th Ed.; Food Products Press, 1995.
4. Zeidler, G. Egg Product Development: How Far Do We Need to Go? *Egg Industry*; Jan/Feb 1994; 7–14.
5. Zeidler, G. Old and new in the traditional appreciation of eggs. World Poultry-Misset **1997**, *13* (1), 22–25.
6. Simmons, A. *American Cookery 1796*; Oxford University Press, 1985. Fascimice edition.

Eggs: Marketing

Donald D. Bell
University of California, Riverside, California, U.S.A.

INTRODUCTION

Marketing is defined as the transfer of a product from a seller to a buyer. In egg marketing, this may be as simple as the sale of a dozen eggs from a production farm to a neighboring resident or as complex as selling a shipload of eggs transported halfway around the world, processed, and sold with all the associated regulations and certificates of quality and food safety assurances. Countries establish their own marketing systems based on the demands of the public and the costs of such requirements. Consumers of eggs in Third World countries are more concerned with whether they can afford a product than whether the eggs had been produced and processed under a long list of regulations, which collectively adds to the cost of the product. On the other hand, consumers in industrialized nations demand that eggs meet all the specifications for quality, size, and food safety, and price becomes less of a limiting factor relative to their consumption.

The marketing of eggs throughout the world is complex and varies because of local customs, the prices of competing protein foods, the availability of refrigeration, the proximity of production areas to consumer marketplaces, the existence and nature of regulatory agencies, and the ability of the consumer to pay for multiple price markups. Various aspects of marketing that are recognized as critical in the United States, for example, are not even considered in many regions of the world. Because of the major differences in marketing methods between countries, the emphasis of this article will concentrate on practices used in the United States.

MARKETING DEFINED—IN THE BROADER SENSE

Most people define egg marketing as the physical action of trading eggs for a fee between a producer/packer and either a wholesaler or retailer.[1] Marketing, though, also includes a long list of associated activities including, but not limited to: processing (cleaning, grading, sizing, and packaging), regulatory supervision, buying and selling (at several levels), transportation, balancing of surpluses with deficits, price discovery, price reporting, promotion/advertising, and egg export/import issues.[2]

Two examples are given here to illustrate the broad definition of marketing. In the first example, the first transfer of ownership is from the pure producer to a processor in another location. Eggs are sold unprocessed directly from the chicken house or farm cooler and transferred on plastic or pulp fiber filler flats (30 eggs per flat). In most cases, payment is based on the egg weight distribution determined in the processor plant, with different prices for each weight/grade category. The payment received, therefore, represents a blend of sizes and is termed a nest run or farm selling price.

In the second example, the first sale is for producers/packers who produce and pack (process) their own eggs in an in-line system. Eggs are gathered on conveyor belts, which take the eggs directly to the processing plant for sizing, grading, and packaging. The first transfer of ownership is in the form of graded and packaged products. Payment in this case includes the cost of processing, packaging, and transportation, which is approximately 20 to 25 cents per dozen more than the unprocessed egg price for comparable egg weight classes. This price is considered to be the wholesale price of eggs—more than the farm price, but less than the retail or consumer price.

PRODUCTS

Eggs are sold in many forms, both in the shell and with the shell removed.[3] In a 1996 survey of egg products found in 81 supermarkets located in 28 cities throughout the United States, the average store displayed 8–9 shell egg products (white, brown, and specialty eggs of different sizes) and 5 liquid or frozen products. It is currently estimated that 5–6% of all eggs sold in the United States are brown shelled.

Specialty eggs, a recent growth item for the egg industry (currently 3–4% of all eggs sold in the United States at the retail level) include eggs produced by modifying the diet of the flock (65% of the total), eggs produced by hens under welfare conditions (floor or free-range conditions) (22% of the total), fertile eggs (7% of the total), and organic eggs (from hens fed rations with ingredients that were grown without pesticides, fungicides, herbicides, or commercial fertilizers—other restrictions may apply) (7% of the total).[4]

Encyclopedia of Animal Science
DOI: 10.1081/E-EAS 120019585

RETAILING, INSTITUTIONAL, AND BREAKER MARKETING

The American Egg Board estimates that approximately 55% of the U.S. production of table eggs is marketed to the consumer through various retail store groups, mostly through supermarket chains with stores located in multiple states. Smaller independent grocery stores and convenience stores make up the remainder.[5]

Prices in supermarkets tend to be more stable than farm or wholesale prices due to less frequent responses to market changes. Supermarkets in different regions have distinctly different markup policies for eggs.

Institutional marketing (sales to restaurants, hospitals, schools, etc.) accounts for about 14% of total table egg sales. These are noncartoned eggs (loose) packaged in half-case (15 dozen) or full-case (30 dozen) cardboard containers.

Eggs for the breaker market (used for further processed products) are estimated to be about 30% of the total (2000). Much of the production of broken-out eggs is located in the Midwest region of the United States where egg production costs are the lowest. Specialized farms break 100% of their production for this use.

EXPORTING OF BROKEN-OUT AND SHELL (TABLE) EGGS

The United States exported the equivalent of almost 50 million dozen eggs in the broken-out form in 2002.[6] This represents about 0.8% of the nation's production. Leading destinations included Canada, Japan, Korea, and Mexico. Another 48 million dozen were exported as eggs in the shell to destinations such as Hong Kong and Canada. Combined, total exports of eggs for human consumption in 2002 amounted to about 1.6% of total U.S. egg production.

GRADING AND SIZE REGULATIONS

''Grading aids orderly marketing by reducing waste, confusion, and uncertainty with respect to quality values. The egg production pattern and the marketing system in the United States are such that interstate trading and shipment occur constantly and in large volume. This situation creates a need for uniform standards throughout the country so that marketing may be facilitated and the efficiency of distribution increased.''[7]

Grading is defined as the classifying of eggs by size and quality into comparable units according to established standards, which include various internal and external quality characteristics. The grading of eggs for sale is a requirement of federal and state laws. Federal laws apply for eggs in interstate commerce, whereas state laws regulate intrastate sales. Regulations also include labeling and advertising requirements relative to size and quality of the product.

Eggs are graded for size into six classes ranging from very small eggs (pee wee and small), through the midrange weights (medium and large), to the largest sizes (extra large and jumbo). Weight requirements describe the minimum weight for one dozen eggs with tolerances for individual egg weights less than the average weight for the dozen. State and federal definitions require large eggs to have minimum one-dozen weights of 24 ounces. Other sizes are in three-ounce increments above or below the definition for large eggs—from 15 to 30 ounces per dozen.

Eggs are also graded for quality (AA, A, B). This involves either human candling or a combination of candling and electronic methods (cracked egg, stain/dirty, and blood spot detection). Egg characteristics considered in grading for quality include: shape, soundness and cleanliness of the shell, air cell size, yolk shape and shadow, and freedom from internal defects.

PACKAGING AND LABELING

Eggs are usually placed in their final container as part of the processing operation. Traditionally, the consumer package is the one-dozen pulp fiber or polystyrene foam container. These, in turn, are placed in either 15-dozen wire baskets, or 15- or 30-dozen corrugated cardboard cases for transport.

Other packaging includes single or multiple plastic over-wrapped filler flats with 30 eggs per flat, 6- and 18-egg cartons, and multiple filler flat units placed in cardboard sleeves. Size and grade labels must meet the letter-size restrictions of the regulations. Other labeling requirements include all or some of the following: source, nutritional information, food safety requirements, and sell-by dates.

PROMOTION, ADVERTISING, AND RESEARCH

Eggs are commonly branded with either the store's name or the packer's logo. Relatively few eggs are nationally branded, with the exception of several brands of specialty eggs. Advertising on a short-term basis is primarily the responsibility of the retailer with financial assistance from the supplier. Such advertising (typically in newspapers and flyers) is usually associated with a sale (eggs sold at a substantial reduction in price from the usual price for that store or chain).

The American Egg Board (AEB)[8] is the egg industry's broad linkage to the consumer in promoting egg consumption through media advertisements. Funding of its activities is from a nationally legislated checkoff of all egg producers with more than 75,000 hens. In 2002, AEB spent $18 million in various promotional activities. Almost $10 million was spent on advertising, $3.3 million on nutrition programs, $1.7 million for industry and market development, and $1 million for food service programs. In addition, AEB funds and operates the Egg Nutrition Center, which promotes research on eggs.

TRANSPORTATION

Unprocessed eggs must be transported to the processing plant; processed eggs must be delivered to nearby warehouses or retail stores; surplus eggs must be transported to adjoining states or distant markets; and egg for export must be shipped overseas. Nearby delivery costs are variable because of differences in lot sizes, while interstate costs are more standardized because of more competition.

Local direct deliveries may cost 15 to 25 cents or more per dozen due to the profile of purchases, the quantity of eggs per drop-off, the number of stops per truckload, smaller truckloads, and slower local traffic. On the other hand, transportation costs from surplus to deficit egg-producing states (for example, Iowa to California) are in the 10 to 12 cents per dozen range ($2250 to $2500 per truckload for 750 to 800 30-dozen egg cases).

Costs for transporting liquid eggs are usually less (estimated to be 7 to 8 cents per dozen) because tanker trucks utilize space more efficiently (liquid vs. in the shell), 100% of the weight is product as opposed to only 90% for eggs in the shell (10% shell), and no pallets or containers are required. Loading and unloading is also less labor intensive.

CONCLUSIONS

Egg marketing is unique because of the perishability of the product and therefore, the relatively short interval of time available between production and consumption. In addition, major sites of production and consumption are commonly at great distances from one another, which necessitates major transportation costs and delay. Integrating the various elements of production, processing, and marketing is essential to keeping the consumer satisfied with the quality and price of the product.

REFERENCES

1. Anonymous. *Marketing—The Yearbook of Agriculture*; USDA, 1954.
2. Egg and Egg Products. In *ASHRAE Handbook: Refrigeration*; Owen, M.S., Ed.; American Society of Heating, Refrigerating and Air Conditioning Engineers, Inc.: Atlanta, GA, 2002; 20.1–20.14.
3. Koelkebeck, K.W.; Bell, D.D.; Carey, J.B.; Anderson, K.E.; Darre, M.J. Egg marketing in national supermarkets: Products, packaging, and prices—Part 3. Poultry Sci. **2001**, *80*, 396–400.
4. Patterson, P.H.; Koelkebeck, K.W.; Bell, D.D.; Carey, J.B.; Anderson, K.E.; Darre, M.J. Egg marketing in national supermarkets: Specialty eggs—Part 2. Poultry Sci. **2001**, *80*, 390–395.
5. Bell, D.D.; Patterson, P.H.; Koelkebeck, K.W.; Anderson, K.E.; Darre, M.J.; Carey, J.B.; Kuney, D.R.; Zeidler, G. Egg marketing in national supermarkets: Egg quality—Part 1; Poultry Sci. **2001**, *80*, 383–389.
6. Anonymous. *U.S. Trade Data Collection*; USDA, Foreign Agricultural Service, 2003. Table Eggs and Egg Products.
7. Anonymous. USDA Egg Grading Manual—Agricultural Handbook No. 75. In *Agricultural Marketing Service*; United States Dept. of Agriculture: Washington, DC, 2000.
8. Anonymous. *American Egg Board Annual Report*; 2002. Park Ridge, IL 60068.

Eggs: Pricing

Donald D. Bell
University of California, Riverside, California, U.S.A.

INTRODUCTION

Table eggs are priced at the farm as unprocessed eggs, at the processing plant as a wholesale packaged product, and in the retail outlet as a consumer product. In addition to these different levels, eggs are available in many other forms and container sizes. As a result, the determination of typical price levels for each class is critical to the orderly exchange of products and the stability of the marketplace.

PRICE DISCOVERY AND REPORTING

Ideally, egg price determination requires an active buyer and seller willing to trade eggs at a negotiated price.[1-3] In order for a transaction to be made, both must be willing to adjust their prices—downward (seller) and upward (buyer). Most sales or purchases of eggs are based on an agreed upon purchase price relative to one of several nationally published price reports. Such purchases are passive in nature and do not meet the criteria of an actively negotiated price. The determination of today's egg prices is a complex procedure because it involves so many transactions of so many different products of differing size, quality, and delivery specifications in different regions of the country.

Market reporters must measure the collective nature of such transactions and determine whether the information available is sufficient to justify an overall report that prices are up or down, thereby setting the stage for market adjustments across the nation. There is a fine line between reporting events that have already occurred and reporting a price that will become the base price for the coming few days or weeks.

In the United States, two principal reporting systems survey sales, inventories, and other factors relative to the state of the egg market. These are: 1) Urner Barry Publications Inc., a private company that specializes in the daily reporting of prices for various food products; and 2) The United States Department of Agriculture's (USDA) Agricultural Marketing Service (AMS). Both groups conduct daily interviews of major participants in the egg industry's trading arena. Both verify their findings by obtaining information from both parties in a transaction.

Reported prices, however, are subject to considerable differences in interpretation. They are meant to represent actual sales, but through the years, discounts and other costs have crept into the quote and today, the quotes (for the major sizes within regions) are considered benchmark prices only and the real prices are much below the quotation. The industry, therefore, trades eggs in relation to the quote and not necessarily at the quote.

BALANCING PRODUCTION AND NEEDS

A major component of the price reporter's conclusions is based on active sales, which are documented by organizations such as The Egg Clearinghouse, Inc. (ECI) with offices in Dover, New Hampshire.[4] The Egg Clearinghouse serves the needs of companies with excess eggs and companies who need eggs. In 2002, ECI facilitated the sale of approximately six million cases (30 dozen each), which represents 3% of the total U.S. production (205 million cases).

Offers to sell and bids to buy are matched at ECI headquarters to assure both buyers and sellers that all conditions of the trade are agreeable. This includes detailed definitions of some 40 different shell egg and broken-out egg products relative to quality and product characteristics, transportation costs, time of delivery, and other factors essential to the success of the transaction.

FACTORS THAT AFFECT EGG PRICES

Egg prices vary for a variety of reasons including their level in the marketplace, their unique characteristics, and the time of the year.[5] Table 1 lists many of the factors associated with price variation and examples of each.

EGG PRICING AT DIFFERENT LEVELS IN THE MARKETPLACE

Farm prices are the lowest prices and these vary according to their size. In most cases, the farmer receives the same price for all sizes large and above, and lower prices for

Encyclopedia of Animal Science
DOI: 10.1081/E-EAS 120026115

Table 1 Factors associated with egg price variation

Factor	Examples
Level in the marketplace	Farm nest run, processed, wholesale, retail (consumer)
Quotation system	Urner Barry, USDA
Number of price changes per year	35–75 times per year—fewer on the West Coast, more in the remainder of the country
Product characteristics	Size, grade, color, specialty, shell/liquid
Seasonal cycles	Summer—low prices, winter—high prices
Price spread between sizes	Summer—large differences, winter—low differences
National flock size (annual changes)	Large flock—low prices, small flock—high prices
Regional	Lower prices in surplus production states, higher prices in deficit states
Size of package	6, 12, 18, 30, 60, 180, 360 eggs per container
Media attention	Bad press—reduction in demand and lower prices. Good press—high demand and higher prices
Retail outlet	Retailers have unique markup policies for similar products
Delivery of product	Processor dock, warehouse delivery, individual store assortment of products
Associated services	Discounts, credit, shelf space purchases, sales and advertising allowances, store returns

medium, small, and undergrade eggs. In recent years (1999–2003), U.S. egg prices at the farm level have averaged between 45–50 cents per dozen for large unprocessed eggs. Corresponding values for medium and small eggs were 33–38 and 15–20 cents per dozen, respectively. Undergrade eggs (for breaking) were priced at 25–30 cents per dozen. The average annual price for the blend of all egg sizes is usually five cents per dozen less than the price for large eggs or 40–45 cents per dozen, but this varies with the season as price differences between the sizes change.

Wholesale egg prices include processing, packaging, and often delivery. Current industry studies estimate these added costs to be 20–25 cents per dozen. Thus, the total cost of product at this stage is estimated to be between 65–75 cents per dozen for large eggs. Costs vary according to the type of delivery (store vs. warehouse), breakdown of pallets (one size per pallet vs. multiple sizes and products), packaging costs, and the efficiency of the processing plant.

Retail prices differ between the type of product, the type of store (supermarket, small independent, and convenience), the pricing policy of the individual company, and between regions. In a 1996 survey of 81 supermarkets in 28 U.S. cities,[1] prices averaged $1.35 per dozen for white eggs, $1.54 per dozen for brown eggs, $2.09 per dozen for specialty eggs, and $3.48 per dozen (equivalent) for frozen or liquid eggs. Prices in individual states ranged from $1.05 to $1.83 per dozen large white eggs. A California survey in 1998 compared the type of

store and egg prices for large white eggs. Farm store prices averaged $1.10 per dozen, supermarkets averaged $1.75 per dozen, and warehouse stores averaged $.72 per dozen.

Market quotations theoretically represent prices at the wholesale level, but actual sales are at significantly lower levels because certain costs associated with the sale are not included (See earlier discussion of price discovery and reporting). As described, these prices are used only as benchmarks to measure the change in the market and for passive pricing. They do not represent actual sales or purchases at the prices published.

SEASONAL AND ANNUAL ECONOMIC CYCLES

Egg prices, and therefore egg profitability, follow consistent seasonal patterns. During the 1998 to 2002 period, Urner Barry Midwest egg prices for large eggs ranged from 6.6% above the annual average price for large eggs during October through March to 6.6% below the annual average price during April through September. This represents a plus or minus five cents per dozen range from the annual price. Individual months vary more than twice this amount. Interestingly, the higher prices were during the winter months when layer numbers are higher, whereas the lower prices were during the summer months when layer numbers are lower. This is the exact opposite of the annual relationship between high layer counts and low prices and low layer counts and high egg prices. This illustrates the marked differences in consumer demand between the two seasons.

Annual prices are also subject to cycles, but these are 4–5 years in length. Within a 5-year period, egg prices are usually high for 1 year, intermediate for 2 years, and low for 2 years. This reflects changes in layer populations and the time required to adjust the nation's flock size to correct overproduction.

UNIQUE PURCHASING SYSTEMS

The majority of eggs are purchased and sold in relationship to the reported prices discussed earlier. In general, prices during the last decade have been relatively low and profits were practically nonexistent. This means the purchaser was frequently buying eggs below production costs. Even though costs to the buyer were minimized, monthly price changes, often as much as 15 cents per dozen, can raise havoc with budgets and cash flow. For this reason, the industry is interested in cost-plus pricing systems, which can provide more stable egg prices and cash flow for both the buyer and seller.[6]

Traditional contractual arrangements generally state the relationship of prices relative to market quotations and the nature of added services. New arrangements are meant to stabilize prices and cash flow, to relate them to mutually agreed upon cost factors (published feed prices), and to allow both parties to have reasonable returns for their investments and efforts. Such arrangements can work

if both parties will look at the contract's effectiveness over a 3–4 year period.

CONCLUSIONS

Fifty years ago, egg marketing in the United States included buying and selling at the farm, an intermediate packer/processor, possibly a broker/handler, and the retailer. Today, trading is commonly limited to only two transactions—producer/packer to retailer and retailer to consumer. In this process, costs have been controlled and prices to the consumer have been minimized.

REFERENCES

1. Bell, D.D. *U.S. Farm Gate and Consumer Egg Prices and Egg Quality at the Retail Market*; International Egg Commission: Capetown, South Africa, Sept. 14, 1998.
2. Anonymous. *Monthly and Annual Price Reviews*; Urner Barry Publications Inc.: Tom's River, NJ, 2003.
3. Anonymous. *USDA Egg Market News Report*; U.S. Department of Agriculture, Agricultural Marketing Service, Market News Branch: Washington, DC, 2003.
4. Anonymous. *Membership Policies, Trading Procedures*; Egg Clearinghouse, Inc.: Dover, NH, 1995.
5. Bell, D.D. *Volatility of Egg Prices at the Farm and Wholesale Levels*; Misc. publication, University of California, 2003.
6. Bell, D.D. *Pricing Options For Table Eggs at Wholesale Levels in the Marketplace*; Misc. publication, University of California, 2002.

Eggs: Processing, Inspection, and Grading

Patricia A. Curtis
Auburn University, Auburn, Alabama, U.S.A.

INTRODUCTION

Numerous production and processing changes have occurred within the commercial egg industry over the past 20 years. Clearly, egg producers and processors feel that the quality of eggs being delivered to consumers in the United States is at an all-time high. Although not common, *Salmonella enteritidis* (SE) outbreaks essentially redefined consumer's views of egg quality. Prior to SE, egg quality was defined by consumers in physical and visual terms (e.g., size of the air cell, color of the yolk, height of the albumen), but the potential SE contamination has focused consumer attention on microbiological safety of eggs. Producers and processors work together to produce high quality and safe eggs for the consumer. Each step in the process of getting eggs from the farm to the consumer is briefly discussed in this article.

INCOMING EGGS

Eggs can be produced in either an off-line or in-line facility. An off-line processing facility obtains its eggs from one or more laying operations. The eggs are picked up from the laying operations on a regular basis and brought to the processing facility for cleaning, inspection, and packaging.

Although it is well known that dirty or soiled eggs are undesirable, shell eggs can acquire bacteria from every surface they contact.[1] Egg temperature is also important to maintain quality and control any SE that might be present. While the temperature of the incoming eggs will vary from season to season and from operation to operation, off-line processing plants (where eggs are brought in from off-site premises) can expect initial internal egg temperatures of 17 to 20°C. Although preprocessing coolers are generally held between 10 and 16°C, egg temperatures decline only slightly. Eggs are transported to the processing room and left until they are placed on the processing line.

In an in-line operation, the laying facility is attached to the processing facility. The eggs are automatically collected on belts that convey them into the processing facility. In in-line processing plants, internal egg temperatures generally range from 31 to 36°C when they reach the processing area. Egg temperature at processing is very important because U.S. Department of Agriculture (USDA) regulations require that wash water temperature be at 32°C or higher, or at least 11°C warmer than the highest egg temperature, and this temperature must be maintained throughout the cleaning cycle.

EGG WASHER

Egg cleaning during washing is related to wash water temperature, water quality characteristics (i.e., hardness, pH), detergent type and concentration, and defoamer. Chlorine or quaternary ammonium sanitizing compounds may be used as part of the replacement water, provided they are compatible with the detergent. Only potable water may be used to wash eggs and certificate to this effect is required by USDA.[2] It is also important to ensure that the iron content of the wash water be <2 ppm since the rate and extent of bacterial growth during storage are favored by washing eggs in water with >2 ppm iron. The USDA suggests that water with an iron content in excess of 2 ppm should not be used unless deironized.[3] Iron contamination may also influence microbial growth following penetration of shell membranes. As bacteria grow in an iron-rich environment, they can produce metabolic products that allow microorganisms to penetrate and diffuse into the albumen, making it a more favorable medium for growth of the microorganisms.[4] The addition of excess iron via wash water apparently allows microorganisms to readily satisfy their iron requirements and, in turn, to grow more easily in albumen.

Regulations also require that wash water be changed every four hours or more often if needed to maintain sanitary conditions. In addition, when the difference between wash water temperature and egg temperature is ≥22°C, thermal checks and cracks increase, allowing surface microbes greater access to the interior of the egg.

Encyclopedia of Animal Science
DOI: 10.1081/E-EAS 120019583

Contact between wash water and eggs during processing causes internal egg temperature to increase. Although blow drying following washing causes a slight decrease, internal egg temperature generally rises throughout the process and can continue to rise for up to six hours after eggs are placed in a cooler.[5]

According to USDA regulations, eggs cannot be immersed at any time. However, eggs may be prewet to soften any adhering materials prior to washing by spraying with a continuous flow of water over the eggs in a manner that permits the water to drain away. The temperature of the spray water must be similar to that of the wash water.

Although wash water temperature must be a minimum of 32°C, most processors use wash water much hotter. A survey by Anderson et al.[5] found North Carolina processors use wash water temperatures that range from 46° to 49°C. In 1955, Hillerman[6] reported that wash water maintained at 46°C would increase internal egg temperature by 0.2°C/second of washing.

Alkaline cleaning formulations produce an initial pH in the wash water near 11 and wash water pH during operation is usually in the range of 10 to 11, which is unfavorable for growth of most bacteria.[7] Alkaline pH has also been reported to increase the sensitivity of Salmonella to heat.[8,9] Kinner and Moats[10] found that at pH 10 and 11, bacterial counts always decreased regardless of water temperature. Laird et al.,[11] however, indicated that current processing practices are not sufficient to prevent the potential contamination of washed eggs with Listeria monocytogenes.

Defoamers play an important role in egg washing. When defoamers are not dispensed properly, the foam in the wash tanks accumulates and eventually overflows from the tank. When the foam spills from the tanks, it can interfere with the water level detector, in addition to affecting water temperature and pH.

Washing, drying, and candling unit operations are generally continuous operations. Eggs detected as dirties at candling must not be soaked in water for cleaning. Soaking in water for as little as one to three minutes can facilitate microbial penetration through the egg's shell.

RINSE, DRY, AND PACKAGE

After leaving the washer, eggs are rinsed in hot water. Rinse water containing chlorine or quaternary ammonium sanitizers may be used, provided they are compatible with the washing compound. Iodine sanitizing rinses may not be used.

Eggs are then blown dry with ambient air, at which point the surface temperature of the egg reaches approximately 35°C. Anderson et al.[5] found that the internal temperature of eggs continues to rise due to the high shell surface temperatures as well as candling lights. Five minutes after the eggs were processed, their internal temperature was seven to eight degrees above their initial temperature.

Shell eggs may be coated with mineral oil to slow the aging process, provided operations are conducted in a manner to avoid contamination of the product. Processing oil that has been previously used and that has become contaminated can be filtered and heat-treated to 82°C for three minutes prior to reuse.

STORAGE

Washed eggs are blown dry, candled (eggs with blood spots or cracked shells are removed), sized (small, medium, large, extra large, and jumbo), and packaged in cartons or flats. Cartons or flats are placed in cases and cases are palletized. Efficient packaging procedures such as these all but ensure that internal egg temperature increases due to processing will be maintained for several days. In fact, industry surveys have suggested as much as a week is required to dissipate temperature increases due to processing when these packaging procedures are employed.[5]

Federal law requires eggs be stored at an ambient temperature of 7°C. Researchers have found that the growth rate of SE in eggs is directly proportional to the temperature at which the eggs are stored. It has also been found that holding eggs at 4 to 7°C reduces the heat resistance of SE. Thus, it has been suggested that not only does refrigeration reduce the level of microbial multiplication in shell eggs, but it lowers the temperature at which the organism is killed during cooking.

Humidity in the storage environment is important both in maintaining egg weight and preventing microbial growth. Storage relative humidity of ≤60% can cause weight loss and a corresponding increase in air cell size. However, storage in a relative humidity of ≥80% can promote microbial growth.

CONCLUSIONS

Egg temperature (initial and throughout processing and storage) and wash water pH and temperature play key roles in reducing microbial growth in shell eggs. Eggs should be gathered, cleaned, packaged, and cooled as soon as possible to maintain their safety and high quality.

REFERENCES

1. Board, R.G.; Tranter, H.S. The Microbiology of Eggs. In *Egg Science and Technology*, 4th Ed.; Stadelman, W.J., Cotterill, O.J., Eds.; The Haworth Press: Binghamton, NY, 1995; 81–104.
2. USDA. Regulations Governing the Grading of Shell Eggs and United States Standards, Grades and Weight Classes for Shell Eggs. In *7CFR Part 56*; 1991.
3. Baker, R.C.; Bruce, C. Effects of Processing of the Microbiology of Eggs. In *Microbiology of the Avian Egg*; Board, R.G., Fuller, R., Eds.; Chapman & Hall: London, 1994; 155–173.
4. Garibaldi, J.A.; Bayne, H.G. The effect of iron on the Pseudomonas spoilage of experimentally infected shell eggs. Poultry Sci. **1960**, *39*, 1517–1520.
5. Anderson, K.E.; Jones, F.T.; Curtis, P.A. Legislation ignores technology. Egg Ind. October **1992**, 11–13.
6. Hillerman, J.P. Quick cooling for better eggs. Pac. Poultry Manage. **1955**, 18–20.
7. Moats, W.A. Egg washing—A review. J. Food Prot. **1978**, *41* (11), 919–925.
8. Anellis, A.; Lubas, J.; Rayman, M.M. Heat resistance in liquid eggs of some strains of the genus *Salmonela*. Food Res. **1954**, *19*, 377–395.
9. Cotterill, O.J. Equivalent pasteurization temperatures to kill *Salmonella* in liquid egg white at various pH levels. Poultry Sci. **1968**, *47*, 354–365.
10. Kinner, J.A.; Moats, W.A. Effect of temperature, pH and detergent on survival of bacteria associated with shell eggs. Poultry Sci. **1981**, *60*, 761–767.
11. Laird, J.M.; Bartlett, F.M.; McKellar, R.C. Survival of Listeria monocytogenes in egg wash water. Int. J. Food Microbiol. **1991**, *12*, 115–122.

Egg Products: Industrial Egg Products

Gideon Zeidler
University of California, Riverside, California, U.S.A.

INTRODUCTION

Shell eggs are highly perishable products. Shelf life of high-quality products is about 2 weeks if stored in a cool, dark place and about 1 month if refrigerated. When eggs age, chemical and physical changes occur. Moisture and CO_2 escape through the porous shell, and the pH increases and changes from acidic to alkaline. The air cell expands in size and the albumen becomes flat and watery, and less desired flavor and odors may develop. If left for a long period of time, the egg contents could dry up, especially at high storage temperatures. Under certain circumstances, the egg will rot. In order to extend shelf life and preserve quality, several methods of preservation were developed by the 19th century. This article chronicles preservation methods and development of currently available industrial egg products.

EARLY EGG PRESERVATION METHODS

Among preservation methods are the following:[1]

1. *Brine preservation.* Fresh eggs were fully immersed in brine and lime solution and remain edible for 2–3 years.
2. *Gum arabic coating.* Newly laid eggs were dipped in a thick solution of gum Arabic to create a coating and then packed in powdered charcoal. The coating was washed away before eggs were used.
3. *Packaging in salt.* Fresh eggs were placed layer by layer in a large box, small end down, and covered with salt. The full boxes were placed in a dark, cool place.
4. *Dipping in lard.* During the times of Louis V, extended shelf life of shell eggs was achieved by dipping them in lard.

The first industrial method of preservation, egg drying, was developed in the late 19th century and until the 1930s, it was the only method available. When refrigeration became common in the 1930s, freezing egg products, whole eggs, yolks, and whites became a common method of preservation. However, a major development in industrial egg products came in the last decade of the 20th century when the ultrapasteurization of eggs was developed and provided user-friendly chilled liquid products. This product line became the preferred product line for the food industry.[2]

EGG PRODUCTS FROM BREAKING OPERATIONS

Egg-breaking operations were established in order to open an outlet for surplus eggs, small eggs, cracked eggs, and dirty eggs and to provide relatively long–shelf life products for bakers and confectioners who were the main users until World War II (WWII). Today, the entire production of some farms is fully directed to egg breaking. In other egg farms, most of the medium eggs are also directed to breaking, and larger eggs are sent to the fresh egg market. Prior to 1940, breaking operations accounted for 5–6% of U.S. egg production. They were more common in the Midwest where mainly frozen products were produced. During and after WWII, large quantities of dry products were needed to feed the troops and for emergency feeding programs for European populations. Twelve large drying facilities were erected in the Midwest and operated around the clock. Fast egg-breaking machines were developed to meet the volumes of production needed. Egg-breaking production jumped to 9.0% in 1960, 24.4% in 1992, and stabilized around 30% in 2003.

Retail outlets generally have a small number of egg products, but many food products that contain eggs. Typical retail food products are mayonnaise, salad dressing, pasta, noodles, quiches, bakery products, and eggnog. Other egg products such as deviled eggs, Scott eggs, frozen omelets, egg patties, and scrambled eggs are prepared mainly for fast food and institutional feeding establishments, catering, hotels, and restaurants. Products such as noncholesterol egg substitutes and liquid scrambled egg mix are made for both retail and institutional markets.

Egg products are classified into four groups according to the American Egg Board Guidelines.[2]

1. Frozen egg products
2. Refrigerated egg products

Encyclopedia of Animal Science
DOI: 10.1081/E-EAS 120039673

Table 1 Commonly available chilled, frozen, and dry forms of further-processed egg products

Liquid products	Dry products
Pasteurized whole eggs (HTST)	White flaked egg whites
Ultrapasteurized whole eggs (UHT)	Golden flaked egg whites
Whole eggs with salt	Flaked egg whites (granular)
Whole eggs with corn syrup	Flaked egg whites (powdered)
Whole eggs with sugar	Nonwhipping spray dried egg whites
Whole eggs with added yolks	Whipping spray dried egg whites
Whole eggs with added yolks and corn syrup	Neutral pH spray dried egg whites
Blends of yolks and whites	Egg whites for foaming
Blends of yolks and whites and salt	Instant egg whites with sugar
Blends of yolks and whites and sugar or corn syrup	
Egg yolk	
Egg yolks with salt	
Egg yolks with sugar	
Egg whites	
Whole eggs with corn syrup	
Whole eggs with added yolk and corn syrup	
Whole eggs with corn syrup	
Whole eggs with added whites	

3. Dried egg products
4. Specialty egg products (mostly in ready-to-cook or ready-to-eat forms)

Commonly available industrial egg products are shown in Table 1 and their usage in food products is shown in Table 2.

The extensive use of eggs as an ingredient is due to their unique functional properties, which greatly contribute to the characteristics of foods. The contribution of the functional properties of eggs to various food products is summarized in Table 3.

Frozen Egg Products

Chilled or frozen eggs, yolks, and whites are currently the major high-volume products of egg-breaking plants. These and other products are described subsequently. They usually are frozen in various carton sizes, plastic bags, 30-lb plastic cans, or 55-gal drums. Freezing is usually accomplished by air blasts at temperatures ranging from -10 to $-40°F$. Pasteurized products designated for freezing must be frozen solid or cooled to a temperature of at least $10°F$ within 60 h after pasteurization. Newer

freezing techniques for products containing cooked white (deviled eggs or egg logs) include individual quick freezing at very low temperatures (to $-240°F$).

Defrosting of frozen eggs is inflexible and inconvenient; eggs may be defrosted at $35°C$ in approved metal tanks within 40 to 48 h. If defrosted at higher temperatures (up to $50°F$), the time cannot exceed 24 h. The long defrosting period is one of the main drawbacks for frozen egg utilization in industrial production.

Frozen Stabilized Egg Products

The addition of certain food ingredients to yolk products before freezing prevents coagulation during thawing. 10% salt is added to yolks used in mayonnaise and salad dressings, and 10% sugar is added to yolks used in baking, ice cream, and confectionery manufacturing. Whole-egg products also contain salt or sugar according to finished product specifications. Egg whites are not fortified with salt or sugar, however, as they do not gel during defrosting.

UHT Products (Ultra Heat Treatment)

The development of the ultrapasteurized chilled liquid products revolutionized the utilization of eggs in the food

Table 2 Further-processed egg products most commonly used in commercial foods

Egg product	Food uses
Whole egg	
• Liquid	Egg noodles, bakery and pastry, ice cream
• Salted	Mayonnaise, sauces
• Powder	Bakery and pastry, egg noodles (depending on local legislation), stuffing for pasta, premix for bakery and ice cream
Yolk	
• Liquid	Bakery and pastry, ice cream, egg noodles
• Sugared	Bakery and pastry, ice cream
• Frozen or deep frozen	Ice cream, pastry
• Powder	Bakery and pastry, premix for bakery, pastry, and ice cream
Albumen	
• Liquid	Ice cream, bakery and pastry, confectionery (meringue, torrone)
• Powder	Premix for ice cream and pastry, premix for soups and batters
• Crystallized	Confectionery (meringue, torrone)

Table 3 Functional properties of eggs and their contributions to various food products

Function	Description	Application
Adhesive properties	Adheres ingredients such as seeds and grains to food products	Health bars, variety breads, snacks
Aeration and structure improvement	Creates foam in products, resulting in lighter and airier products	• Meringues
Binding	Holds together food products	• Mousses
		• Snack foods
		• Prepared entrees
Browning	Provides desirable brown color to baked products	• Rolls and buns
		• Variety breads
Clarification	Egg whites inhibit enzymatic browning and discoloration in beverages	• Wines
		• Juices
Coagulation	Egg whites and yolks convert liquids into a solid state	• Cakes and frostings
		• Sauces
Coating	Locks in flavor and aroma	• Baked goods
		• Snacks
Color	Contributes yellow color to many foods	• Baked products
		• Noodles
		• Custards
Crystallization control	Prevents crystallization of sugar and promotes smoothness of chocolate	• Confections
Emulsification	Phospholipids and lipoproteins serve as surface-active agents allowing emulsions such as oil and water	• Salad dressings
		• Sauces
Finish/gloss	Used universally in baking to improve product appearance Egg wash gives surface gloss and shine	• Sweet breads
		• Cookies
		• Frostings
Flavor	Carries and melds some flavors, improves others, and imparts desirable egg flavor	• Custards
		• Confections
Freezability	Improves texture and acceptibility of products through freeze/thaw cycle	• Frozen doughs
		• Microwavable foods
Humectancy	Holds moisture in food products to help increase shelf life	• Variety breads
		• Rolls
Insulation	Keeps products from turning soggy	• Breads
		• Frozen doughs
Mouth-feel improvement	Provides substantial body to foods	• Variety breads
		• Sweet goods
		• Puddings
pH	Stable pH	• Will not disrupt food product formulations.
Shelf-life extension	Keeps starch molecules moist and maintains fresh formulations	• Commercial bread
Tenderization	Tenderizes foods naturally, giving a soft surface feel	• Soft breads
		• Rolls
Texture improvement	Firms up the texture of food products and provides crumb improvement	• Rolls
		• Light foods
Thickening	Thickens sauces and gravies and adds body to achieve product improvement	• Sauces
		• Toppings
		• Prepared foods

(From Ref. 2.)

industry[3] (Fig. 1). Today, most of the relatively short-shelf life egg products are available in chilled form. UHT development was initially aimed at producing nonrefrigerated sterile milk with superior palpability by replacing conventional sterilization at 250°F for about 12 to 20 min, with sterilization at 275°F for 3 to 5 seconds.

UHT treatment of liquid eggs is more complicated, as egg proteins are more sensitive to heat treatment and cannot be sterilized. Therefore, UHT liquid eggs must be kept under refrigeration. Ultrapasteurized, aseptically filled, chilled, whole-liquid egg product is now available in packages from 1 to 200 lb to institutional food establishments,

Fig. 1 Ultrapasteurization system for liquid eggs (Italy).

restaurants, and for the food industry (Fig. 2). Egg whites are available in retail outlets; however, liquid whole eggs are not.

Egg Substitutes

In order to satisfy the demand for low-cholesterol egg products, substitutes are made from egg white, which does not contain cholesterol. The yolk is replaced with vegetable oil, food coloring, gums, and nonfat dry milk. Recent formulations have reduced the fat content to almost zero. These products are packaged in cardboard containers and sold frozen or chilled in numerous formula variations in retail outlets and restaurants.[4]

DRY EGG PRODUCTS

Spray drying is the most commonly used method for egg dehydration. However, other methods are used for specific products such as scrambled eggs, which are made by freeze-drying, and egg white products, which are usually made by pan-drying to produce a flakelike product. The products are packaged into fiber drums lined with vapor-retarding liners. The moisture level in dehydrated products is usually around 5% or less.[5]

Whole-egg and yolk products naturally contain some reducing sugars. In order to extend the shelf life of these products and to prevent color change through the browning (Maillard) reaction, the glucose in the eggs is

Fig. 2 Ultrapasteurized, aseptically filled, chilled liquid eggs in restaurant packaging.

Fig. 3 Drum and bags of dried egg products.

Fig. 4   Bagged dry egg powder warehouse (Brazil).

removed by baker's yeast. Yeast consumes the glucose within 2 to 3 h at 86°F. The liquid is then pasteurized in continuous heat exchanges at 142°F for 4 min and dried. Whole-egg and yolk powder have excellent emulsifying, binding, and heat-coagulating properties, whereas egg white possesses whipping capabilities.

Liquid eggs can be combined before drying with other ingredients such as milk and other dairy products, sucrose, corn syrup, and other carbohydrates. Standard egg products are commonly used by food processors; however, many egg products are custom-made to specific customer requirements. Common refrigerated, frozen, or dry egg products are summarized in Table 2. Dry egg products are packaged in moisture-proof bags or drums (Figs. 3 and 4).

CONCLUSION

The rapid expansion of the food and food-service industry, which already surpassed the retail markets, constantly demands more industrial egg products and more sophistication of egg products in recent years. Industrial egg product rates stabilized at around 30% of all egg produced; however, it is expected to increase in the future.

REFERENCES

1. Beezley, R.A.; Gregory, A.R.; Chabuson, A. Eggs and Fifty Ways to Cook Them. In *The National Course in Home Economics*; National School of Home Economic Pub., 1917; 175–186.
2. American Egg Board. *Egg Products—Reference Guide*; 1998.
3. Swartzel, K.R.; Ball, H.R., Jr.; Samimi, M.H.H. Method for the ultrapasteurization of liquid whole egg products. U.S. Patents, 4,808,425. (1989) 4,967,959, (1990) and 4,994,291.
4. Bell, D.D.; Weaver, W.D., Jr. *Commercial Chicken Meat and Egg Production*, 5th Ed.; Kluwer Academic Pub., 2002.
5. Stadelman, W.F.; Cotterill, O.F. *Egg Science and Technology*, 4th Ed.; Food product Press, 1995.

Eggs: Shell Egg Products

Gideon Zeidler
University of California, Riverside, California, U.S.A.

INTRODUCTION

Eggs were a prized food since prehistoric times far before the domestication of the chickens and other birds. Eggs were gathered from nests of many avian species and considered a delicacy.[1]

The majority of edible eggs produced around the world today are laid by chickens. Intensive breeding has yielded systems that lay up to 300 eggs year-round, distinguishing the chicken from all other avian species. Duck eggs are popular in China, as they are used to produce the 100-year-old eggs (century eggs) and the salted eggs. These eggs are produced in small quantities in the West to cater to ethnic communities and for export to Asia.

Fresh or canned quail eggs are produced also in small commercial quantities in numerous countries such as India, Thailand, France, Israel, and the United States and can be found in supermarkets as specialty items. Fresh duck, goose, and turkey eggs are often found in farmers markets.

IMPORTANT MARKET EGG CHARACTERISTICS

Eggshell Color

Shell eggs are produced and marketed by shell colors.[2] White and brown are the dominant colors. However, light green, light blue, and pink shell colors are also produced, mainly by Araucana chickens for farmers markets. Brown shell eggs are preferred in many countries in Europe and the Far East and in parts of the northeastern United States. White shell eggs are preferred in the rest of the United States and in numerous other countries. Both egg types are produced all over the world. Although there are no major differences in the nutritional profile and organoleptic characteristics, each eggshell color has its uncompromised fans.

Yolk Color

Europeans traditionally prefer deep orange yolks, whereas North Americans prefer light- to medium-yellow yolks. Yolk color can be achieved by various feed ingredients such as corn, corn meal, and alfalfa meal, depending on the quantities in the feed. Artificial colorants added to the feed can produce colors such as orange, red, or green at different intensities. The usage of artificial colors is not allowed in the United States.

Egg Quality Standards

The Egg Products Inspection Act of 1970 in the United States requires that all eggs moving in interstate commerce be graded for size and quality.[2,3] Cracked or dirty eggs may be sold directly to consumers only on the farm or at an authorized processing plant. Loss eggs (inedible eggs) such as leakers (broken shell and broken membranes), eggs with blood and meat spots, rots, or eggs with developed embryos may not be used for human consumption, but may be used in pet foods. Shell eggs for intrastate commerce are not regulated by the USDA unless they are part of the USDA's shield program, which is voluntary. Most states, however, have egg-grading laws or regulations very similar or identical to those of the USDA. The U.S. egg weight classes for consumers are shown in Table 1. The table shows that the minimum weight must be achieved for 12-egg cartons as well as for 30-dozen cases.

The USDA standards for quality of individual shell eggs are shown in Table 2. The quality of shell eggs is judged by external appearance and by internal appearance, as seen by candling.

The quality of shell eggs begins to decline immediately after the egg is laid. Water loss from the egg causes an increase in the size of the air cell. The dissipation of carbon dioxide migration from the egg results in an increase in albumen pH and a decrease in vitelline membrane strength. Today, supermarkets sell mostly AA shell eggs. However, as it is not mandatory for producers to participate in the USDA program, their product does not have to show the quality standard and USDA shield. Products that do not have these are seen more in discount stores.

In the United States, shell egg shelf life is 30 days from the packaging date. At 30 days, if retested, all eggs will receive much lower grades. Rapid cooling of shell eggs followed by refrigeration at 41°F to 45°F has been found to dramatically extend shell egg quality. By U.S. law, eggs should be stored and transported at a minimum temperature of 45°F. European Union countries and their followers

Encyclopedia of Animal Science
DOI: 10.1081/E-EAS 120019582

Table 1 United States standards for quality of shell eggs[a]

Quality factor	AA Quality	A Quality	B Quality
Shell	Clean	Clean	Clean to slightly stained[b]
	Unbroken	Unbroken	Unbroken
	Practically normal	Practically normal	Abnormal
Air cell	1/8 in. or less in depth	3/16 in. or less in depth	Over 3/16 in. in depth
	Unlimited movement and free or bubbly	Unlimited movement and free or bubbly	Unlimited movement and free or bubbly
White	Clear	Clear	Weak and watery
	Firm	Reasonably firm	Small blood and meat spots present[c]
Yolk	Outline slightly defined	Outline fairly well-defined	Outline plainly visible
	Practically free from defects	Practically free from defects	Enlarged and flattened
			Clearly visible germ development, but not blood
			Other serious defects

[a]For eggs with dirty or broken shells, the standards of quality provide for two additional qualities:
1. Dirty, unbroken (dirt or foreign material adheres, prominent stains, moderate stained areas in excess of B quality).
2. Broken or cracked shell, membranes intact, not leaking. (Leaker has broken or cracked shell and membranes; contents are leaking or free to leak.)
[b]Moderately stained areas permitted (1/32 of surface if localized, or 1/16 if scattered).
[c]If they are small (aggregating not more than 1/8 in. in diameter).
From Ref. 4.

do not require egg refrigeration, but specify a shorter expiration date.

Specialty Shell Eggs Production

Shell eggs are still a commodity item. They are packaged in simple and low-cost fiber or plastic cartons or flats that rarely have a brand name. These are sold at a low price, which strongly fluctuates with a small surplus or shortage of eggs. In countries where eggs are protected and prices are higher, sophisticated packages can be found, which can also cater to specific target groups. For example, a dozen eggs in clear packages wherein two eggs are chocolate eggs was developed to target children in Austria. In order to get out of the commodity market, several higher-priced specialty items were developed,

which currently hold up to 7% of the shell egg market in France and a lower market share in the United States and many other countries.

Shell Eggs Marketed by Weight and Unit

Most retail shell eggs are sold by the unit with weight constraints. The most common unit is a dozen eggs. However, quantities of 4, 6, 8, 18, 20, or 30 eggs are also available, packaged in cartons or flats. The U.S. classes for shell eggs are shown in Table 1.

In recent years, more eggs are directed to breaking operations for out-of-the-shell egg products. As a result, peewee, small, and most of the medium eggs have been eliminated from supermarket shelves. Some retail outlets sell loose egg mix, which contains all egg sizes. The consumer chooses the desired mix and pays by weight. The major shell egg specialty categories are described subsequently.

Free range

In this production, hens are kept on floor spaces and must have access to a large yard where they can walk and stretch their wings. In France, where this concept was developed, more requirements are imposed: minimum space requirements (square ft per hen) indoors as well as outdoors; no artificial lighting; no pesticide usage indoors or outdoors; and no more than 2 weeks shelf life of

Table 2 United States egg weight classes for consumer grades

Size or weight class	Minimum net weight per dozen, oz	Minimum net weight per 30-dozen case, lb	Minimum weight for individual eggs, oz
Jumbo	30	56.0	2.42
Extra large	27	50.5	2.17
Large	24	45.0	1.92
Medium	21	39.5	1.67
Small	18	34.0	1.42
Peewee	15	28.0	

Fig. 1 Designer eggs rich in omega-3 fatty acids (Australia).

products. In the United States, only access to an outdoor yard is required.

Cageless hen houses

Numerous EU countries are now converting to a cageless system without access to an outdoor yard. Hens are raised on the floor with laying chambers, which is a costly method compared to cages.

Designer eggs

Such production is based on the fact that the fat-soluble component fed to chickens can accumulate in the yolk. The most commercially successful shell egg product is the one fortified with omega-3 fatty acids (Fig. 1). This nutraceutical is found in deep-sea fatty fish such as salmon, tuna, and mackerel and in plants such as flaxseed. Eggs enriched with vitamin E up to 6% of daily recommendation are also available in the market.

Organic eggs

Organic eggs are produced by feeding chicken grains and other plant-origin ingredients that are produced without pesticides, fungicides, herbicides, or organic fertilizers (Fig. 2). Animal by-products such as meat-and-bone meal are also prohibited from being fed. As a result, egg flavor is improved due to the elimination of rancid components developed in the animal by-products during processing and storage. Off flavors and odors tend to accumulate in the yolk.

Fertile eggs

Fertile eggs are eggs produced in cageless houses where hens and roosters share the floor (Fig. 3).

Shell Eggs Produced by Different Processing Methods

In the United States, eggs are moved directly from the hen houses on conveyors into the processing equipment (in-line) or by crates (off-line) from older houses or from other farms. The eggs are then washed and dried. External defects (cracks, dirt, weak or abnormal shell) or internal defects (meat or blood spots) are removed by candling equipment, which is now almost fully automated. The eggs are then weighed, separated according to weight groups, packaged, and sent to cold storage. Later, refrigerated vehicles distribute them. In the EU and their followers, shell eggs are not washed. Eggs that have any contact with water are sent to a breaking operation. Furthermore, the EU does not refrigerate their eggs. As a result, products from one processing system cannot be sold legally in a country using the other system.

Pasteurized Shell Eggs

Such eggs are produced to eliminate the risk of ovarian *Salmonella enteritidis* (S.E.), which are located inside the egg, if inspected. However, due to the high cost of the processing and the low level of ovarian S.E., the availability of these eggs is still very limited.

Rapidly Cooled Eggs

Technology was developed to drastically reduce the risk of ovarian S.E. by rapidly lowering the internal egg temperature from 100 to 41°F. Another benefit of this procedure is significant shelf-life extension and quality preservation. These eggs are not in commercial production yet, mainly because currently the USDA does not require the monitoring of internal egg temperature or cooling rate, as it does other animal products.

Fig. 2 Organic eggs.

Fig. 3 Fertile eggs.

Fig. 4 Canned, hard-cooked quail eggs.

Canned Eggs

Hard-boiled eggs are canned in water. Chicken and quail eggs are commonly available (Fig. 4).

CONCLUSION

Due to successful breeding, shell eggs are abundant year-round products that hold an important role in human nutrition; however, the commodity nature of the majority of shell eggs consumed creates a major problem for producers. Constantly improving the efficiency of egg production as well as creating exciting new shell products is a vital strength of this industry.

REFERENCES

1. Pennington, M.E.; Platt, F.L.; Snyder, C.G. *Eggs*; Progress Pub: Chicago, 1933.
2. Bell, D.D.; Weaver, W.D., Jr. *Commercial Chicken Meat and Egg Production*, 5th Ed.; Kluwer Academic Publishers, 2002.
3. Stadelman, W.F.; Coterill, O.J. *Egg Science and Technology*, 4th Ed.; Food Products Press, 1995.
4. *Federal Register, CFR7, Part 56, USDA Agriculture Handbook No 75*; May 1, 1991; 18.

Embryo Transfer in Farm Animals

John F. Hasler

AB Technology, Pullman, Washington, U.S.A.

INTRODUCTION

Embryo transfer is one step in the process of removing one or more embryos from the reproductive tract of a donor female and transferring them to one or more recipient females. Embryos also can be produced in the laboratory via techniques such as in vitro fertilization (IVF) or more sophisticated technologies such as cloning or production of transgenic embryos. These technologies are of little value without adding the embryo transfer step. Embryo transfer has been used extensively in farm animals including cattle, horses, sheep, goats, and pigs and, to a lesser extent, in buffaloes and most species of camelids. Embryo transfer also has been successful in domestic dogs and cats and in virtually all species of laboratory rodents and primates. Lastly, a limited amount of embryo transfer has been successful in numerous wild mammals. However, availability of suitable recipients for rare or endangered species has limited this application of the technology. This article will focus on embryo transfer in farm animals.

BACKGROUND

The first successful embryo transfers were conducted in 1890 in rabbits at Cambridge, England.[1] Subsequently, there were only a few reports of embryo transfers in any species until the first calf was born in 1951. Commercial embryo transfer in farm animals started with cattle in North America in the early 1970s. The primary economic driving factor was the high prices being paid for various breeds of so-called exotic beef cattle imported in small numbers from Europe. Recently, it was estimated that approximately 1 out of every 300 dairy calves born in North America is from embryo transfer.[2]

Embryo transfer is usually used to increase the number of genetic offspring that a donor female can produce in a given unit of time, because recipients gestate the pregnancies to term. On the average, dairy cattle in North America produce only about three calves in their lifetime. Under some circumstances, with repeated superovulation, individual donor cows have produced more than 100 offspring in 2 to 3 years.

EMBRYO TRANSFER INDUSTRY

The exact size of the embryo transfer industry is difficult to determine, but it is truly international in scope. The International Embryo Transfer Industry (IETS) conducts an annual assessment of the number of embryos recovered and transferred worldwide. A summary of the results for 2002 is shown in Table 1.[3] Clearly, cattle represent the greatest amount of commercial activity, and the largest portion of the industry is centered in North America.

SUPEROVULATION

Embryos can be recovered from donor females following a normal estrous cycle that does not involve any hormonal stimulation. However, this limits the potential number of embryos available, especially in cattle. Consequently, in most cases, donors are superovulated, defined as treatment of a female with gonadotropins so that more ova than normal are ovulated. The most common gonadotropin employed is follicle-stimulating hormone (FSH), which is derived from either porcine or ovine pituitary glands. Regulation of the estrous cycle of the donor with prostaglandin F2α and progesterone usually is done concurrently with superovulation. Superovulated cattle usually are inseminated artificially and produce approximately 10 ova, of which 6 are viable embryos. The range of responses, however, is very large in all species; cattle on rare occasions produce as many as 100 ova, yielding 70 or more viable embryos. In contrast, the mare has proven quite difficult to superovulate, although recently a commercially available equine pituitary extract has proven moderately effective in increasing ovulation rates.

EMBRYO RECOVERY

Embryos were recovered from cattle by midventral surgery in the early days of the commercial industry. Nonsurgical recovery utilizing flexible Foley catheters replaced surgery in cattle in the late 1970s. With this technique, the uterus is repeatedly irrigated about a week after estrus, using media composed primarily of NaCl under gravity flow. In most cases, the outflow is directed

Encyclopedia of Animal Science
DOI: 10.1081/E-EAS 120019586

Table 1 Collection of embryos from domestic farm animals in different regions of the world in 2002

| Region | Number of recoveries (Number of embryos) | | | | |
	Cattle	Horses	Sheep	Goats	Pigs
Africa	1,968 (12,641)	59 (48)	NA[a]	NA	NA
Asia	17,557 (120,951)	NA	NA	NA	30 (505)
Europe	18,294 (102,996)	115 (74)	NA	NA	NA
N. America	42,238 (265,175)	10,000[b]	164 (749)	151 (1,360)	NA
S. America	14,189 (90,572)	9,600[b] (5,520)	NA	NA	NA
Oceania	7,149 (37,352)	60 (45)	NA	NA	NA
Total	101,665 (629,687)	19,953 (10,762)	NA (110,496)[c]	NA (17,921)[c]	30 (505)

[a]Not available.
[b]Partially estimated.
[c]Based partially on imported frozen embryos.
(From Ref. 3.)

through a filter, trapping the embryos. Equine embryos are recovered similarly. Laparoscopic surgical recovery of embryos, with the donor under intravenous anesthesia, is the primary method in swine, sheep, and goats.

EVALUATION OF EMBRYOS

Preimplantation embryos from all domestic farm animals are microscopic in size, ranging from 150 to 300 microns in diameter. Due to their density, they sink rapidly to the bottom of their container, usually a petri dish, and are identified and evaluated with a stereomicroscope at 10 to 50× magnifications. Embryos can be maintained in a variety of holding/culture media for periods of up to 24 hours.

EMBRYO TRANSFER

Embryos are transferred into surrogate cattle and horses by nonsurgical methods similar to artificial insemination. Most transfers into sheep, goats, and pigs are via a surgical approach similar to that used for embryo recoveries. It is important that estrous cycles of surrogates be closely synchronized within ±24 hours of the age of the embryo.

FREEZING

Cryopreservation of embryos plus storage in liquid nitrogen (−196°C) has several important advantages. First, it eliminates the immediate need for recipients that are closely synchronized in estrus with the donor at the time of embryo recovery. Frozen embryos can be thawed when recipient(s) of suitable breed, size, and estrous synchrony are available. Also, freezing allows

convenient movement of embryos over long distances, including internationally, and, in contrast to the transport of live animals, virtually eliminates the chances of transporting infectious microbes.[4] Also, their surrogate mothers endow calves resulting from embryo transfer with significant immunity to local infectious microbes, via colostrum.

Currently, ethylene glycol is usually used as a cryoprotectant, and embryos are transferred immediately following thawing. Embryos of most farm animals can be frozen with high survival rates, but pig embryos have proven very difficult to freeze successfully, and there is currently no commercially practical protocol. Equine embryos less than 300 microns in diameter survive cryopreservation reasonably well, but only small numbers are frozen commercially. Horse embryos are frequently chilled to 4°C and transported for periods of 12 to 24 hours before transfer into suitable surrogates.

MICROMANIPULATION

One application of micromanipulation is splitting of embryos into two half- or demi-embryos. This technique has limited commercial value in pigs, sheep, and goats and has been successful in horses in only a few cases. Splitting has been used commercially on a small scale in cattle since the mid 1980s, because more calves are produced due to doubling the number of embryos. Of course, identical twins result if both halves go to term. The technique has probably not become more widely used because it requires a high degree of skill. The equipment used for splitting embryos is also used by some commercial cattle practitioners to remove embryo biopsies consisting of a few cells for determination of sex, using the polymerase chain reaction.

IN VITRO FERTILIZATION

Most donors of embryos are inseminated, so fertilization occurs in vivo. With in vitro fertilization (IVF), sperm are added to the oocytes in a test tube or petri dish. Usually, the processes of in vitro maturation, fertilization, and culture go together. IVF has been successful in all farm animals, but it has proven especially difficult in horses and has been commercially applied most frequently to cattle, especially to females with infertility problems.[5] To obtain oocytes from cows or mares, a long needle is inserted into the ovary through the vaginal wall in the same way that oocytes are recovered from infertile women for IVF. Ultrasonography is used to guide the needle so oocytes can be aspirated from ovarian follicles. An often used, alternative approach is to obtain oocytes from slaughterhouse ovaries to produce relatively inexpensive IVF-derived embryos for research, specific export markets, and for getting dairy cattle pregnant in heat-stressed environments.

CLONING AND TRANSGENICS

Domestic sheep, represented by the now-famous Dolly, were the first mammalian species to be cloned by the nuclear transfer of somatic cells of an adult donor animal. All the other farm animal species covered by this article have subsequently been cloned, with the most recent success being the cloning of one horse and three mules in 2003. Several companies in North America operate commercial cattle cloning programs, and hundreds of clones have been born. However, as of early 2004, the U.S. Food and Drug Administration had not yet made a ruling regarding the safety of cloned animals for human consumption. As a consequence, commercial cloning of cattle has slowed considerably.

Animals carrying foreign genes, or transgenics, have been produced from cattle, sheep, goats, and pigs. A number of commercial enterprises have produced hundreds to thousands of transgenic goats, sheep, and pigs. Goals for these transgenics include increased disease resistance, improved feed efficiency and growth characteristics, and modifications in milk composition. There are also large commercial programs to make genetically engineered farm animals that produce pharmaceutical products, and even industrial products, in their milk.

RESEARCH

Embryo transfer has been used for studying reproductive mechanisms such as the intrauterine spacing and migration of pig embryos, embryo–uterine interactions in several species, and aging of the reproductive tract. A significant amount of research is being conducted in the areas of superovulation, embryo freezing, IVF, interspecific embryo transfer, and cloning.

CONCLUSION

Embryo transfer, whether thought of as a single step or a process including superovulation and embryo recovery and storage, is an important research tool. In addition, there are numerous commercial applications of embryo transfer. The process is more complicated and expensive than artificial insemination, so it usually is used to amplify reproductive rates of the top few percent of genetically valuable females.

REFERENCES

1. Hasler, J.F. The current status and future of commercial embryo transfer in cattle. Anim. Reprod. Sci. **2003**, *79* (3–4), 245–264.
2. Seidel, G.E., Jr.; Elsden, R.P.; Hasler, J.F. *Embryo Transfer in Dairy Cattle*; W.D. Hoard & Sons Company: Fort Atkinson, 2003.
3. Thibier, M. A contrasted year for the world activity of the animal embryo transfer industry. Embryo Transfer Newsl. **2003**, *20* (4), 13–19.
4. Wrathall, A.E.; Sutmöller, P. Potential of Embryo Transfer for Control Transmission of Disease. In *Manual of the International Embryo Transfer Society*, 3rd Ed.; Stringfellow, D.A., Seidel, S.M., Eds.; IETS: Savoy, 1998; 17–44.
5. Hasler, J.F. The current status of oocyte recovery, in vitro embryo production, and embryo transfer in domestic animals, with an emphasis on the bovine. J. Anim. Sci. **1998**, *76* (Suppl. 3), 52–74.

Environment: Accommodations for Animals

Donald C. Lay, Jr.
United States Department of Agriculture, Agricultural Research Service,
Livestock Behavior Research Unit, West Lafayette, Indiana, U.S.A.

INTRODUCTION

All domesticated animals evolved in an environment that was very different from that in which they are currently housed. Thus, livestock and poultry have environmental needs that were shaped by evolution. The characteristic of sheep to graze while goats browse was shaped through evolution, and these characteristics dictate what these two different species need in relation to both foraging behavior and dietary nutrients. It is critical to keep this basic principle in mind when designing animal environments because although an animal's inherent needs are able to change, these changes can only occur over thousands of years. Our rapid progression of developing animal agriculture practices means that the environment in which we keep livestock is altered at a much quicker pace than these animals are able to evolve. Therefore, sound management practices dictate that we strive to create a match between the nature of our livestock and that environment in which we house them.

WHY ACCOMMODATE?

The first question that needs to be addressed is: Why should we accommodate the needs of livestock? The idea that livestock are for our use, and therefore, it is they that must accommodate to our needs, is flawed simply because often livestock are unable to accommodate. This inability to accommodate is due to characteristics that are hard-wired, innate, or instinctual. These words mean that livestock have needs that are determined by their genetic makeup, thus they can not be altered.

It is in the best interest of producers to accommodate livestock because when the animal's environment and its needs are not matched, animal productivity can decrease and animal health can suffer. The effects on productivity and health are largely due to animals entering a state of distress. Stress can occur when an animal's needs or desires are not met. The animal enters a state of distress when its body tries to cope with stress by altering both physiologic and behavioral parameters, but these adaptations are not able to meet its needs. The severity of the stressor and the productivity measure being affected will determine to what extent productivity is decreased.

Although decreased productivity can be a measure of a mismatch between an animal and its environment, a lack of impaired productivity does not mean that the animal's needs are being satisfied.

Not accommodating livestock needs, which thus results in distress, can also impair animal health. When animals enter a state of distress, their bodies attempt to cope with this stress by increasing glucose availability, altering blood flow, and altering behavior. The hormones responsible for these alterations, often termed stress hormones, can impair the immune system and other functions of the body such as reproduction. Glucocorticoids are key hormones in the stress response. When an animal is stressed, a cascade of events, starting in the hypothalamus and culminating at the cortex of the adrenal gland, causes the release of glucocorticoids, which are then able to increase glucose availability in order for the animal to effectively respond to the stressor. However, glucocorticoids are also known to be immunosuppressive. Thus, chronic exposure to stress (for example, due to crowding) can allow the animal to succumb to pathogens in the environment, becoming sick and possibly dying. In addition, glucocorticoids are also known to inhibit leutinizing hormone (LH) from the anterior pituitary gland. This hormone is the key for ovulation in females and the production of androgens in males. Farms with low reproductive rates or excessive health-related problems should determine appropriate accommodations to alleviate distress.

An additional reason to meet accommodations of livestock is simply for ethical reasons. If we place animals in situations where there is a mismatch between their inherent natures and their present environment, yet they still produce at a profitable level, we still have a moral obligation to ensure the animals are not suffering unnecessarily. Basic human values dictate that animals must not be subjected to cruel and inhumane treatment. Reasons of profit cannot obviate these rights. Our challenge then is to determine when an animal's adjustments to accommodate to an environment are extraordinary to the point that the animal is subjected to inhumane treatment.

The following paragraphs are an introduction and summary of key areas that must be evaluated when considering accommodations for livestock. More specific information can be found in the following three articles,

Encyclopedia of Animal Science
DOI: 10.1081/E-EAS 120019588

elsewhere in this encyclopedia: 1) Environment: Effects on Animal Health; 2) Environment: Fulfilling Behavioral Needs; and 3) Environment: Fulfilling Physical Needs. In addition, Ewing, Lay, Eberhard[1] and Moberg and Mench[2] are two books that provide a more comprehensive discussion of these topics.

PHYSICAL REQUIREMENTS

Current agricultural practices maintain livestock in some form of confinement, ranging in size and complexity from a pasture to a small pen not much bigger than the animal itself. These diverse environments each have similar areas of concern that need to be evaluated to determine to what extent livestock must be accommodated. These areas of concern are related to space allocation, thermal environment, air quality, and lighting level, to name a few. Determination of how much space animals need is a very difficult task. The question that needs to be answered is, given that we provide livestock with water and food, how much space is required to optimize the health and well-being of the animal? For instance, a recent review by a scientific committee[3] evaluating space requirements of laying hens found that hens should be given 1.4 times more space than the current industry average. This recommendation was predominantly based on mortality and eggs laid per hen. However, the committee also considered the ability of the hens to rest, turn around, and feed at the same time. Currently, space recommendations for livestock are based on the amount of space that provides optimal growth and health (not maximal), given economics of production facilities and herd size. Typical space recommendations for livestock in research can be found in the Ag Guide.[4]

When considering space requirements, it is important that not only quantity of space be considered, but quality of space as well. Quality issues deal with such characteristics as: 1) complexity, such as a multiroomed space vs. a fully open space; 2) floor substrate, such as concrete vs. straw; and 3) behavior-specific areas, such as a wallow area or a dust-bathing area vs. these areas being absent.

The thermal environment is also an important component of the physical environment that must meet the needs of livestock. Meeting this need in an outdoor system is often difficult, but can be accomplished with the provision of shade or wallows for cooling cattle and hogs and by providing dry, sheltered areas in winter. Because dairy cows are easily affected by excessive heat load, many farms are accommodating cows by installing cooling fans and misters in their loafing sheds. To meet the thermal demands of piglets, which require a thermal environment about 15°–20°F greater than their dam, heat lamps are placed beside the sow.

Other physical factors such as air quality and the amount of provided light are also important to meet the animal's needs. With intensive livestock production comes intensive concentration of animal waste. This waste produces toxic gases such as ammonia, which can adversely affect animal health. Air quality and ventilation must be closely monitored. Often, simply increasing the number of air exchanges in the facility can address this need and decrease both animal and human health concerns.

SOCIAL REQUIREMENTS

Assessing physical space requirements is comparatively easy as compared to assessing the social requirements of livestock. This is due to our inability to fully understand the complexity of social interactions and animal communication. All livestock species are gregarious. A significant amount of work has been conducted on optimal group size for livestock. To date, no clear recommendation exists. The complex nature of groups created by the total number in the group, complexity of the space, genetic composition, gender composition, etc. all contribute to social interactions and whether the social needs of the animals are being met. Some signs that the animals needs are not being met, either socially or physically are performance of abnormal behavior, poor productivity, excessive injury, excessive cull rates, and poor reproductive rates. For example, Deen and Xue[5] found that farm cull rates increased from 8 to 14% between the years 1996 and 1998. At the same time, Geiger, Irwin, and Pretzer[6] found that muscular-skeletal problems, gastrointestinal problems, and reproductive failure were the main causes for death in the sow herd. These data indicate a mismatch between swine and their environment, but whether the mismatch is due mainly to the physical or social environment is not yet clear.

BEHAVIORAL REQUIREMENTS

Behavioral requirements are even more difficult to assess than either physical or social requirements. The idea of behavioral needs is not new; most would agree that animals may have a need to scratch in response to an itch, or to urinate in response to a full bladder. The idea is more difficult to grasp when we consider things such as the need of a horse to graze if all its nutrients are provided. And, do sows need to build a nest if a nest is already provided? It is clear that horses do have a need to graze. Horses provided with all their required nutrients, but not allowed to graze will find substitute foraging activity. Sows, too, would appear to have a need to build a nest, because sows placed in barren environments will perform vacuum activities, by going through the motions of rooting at the bare floor and grabbing the bars of the pen as farrowing approaches. Thus, it is apparent that livestock have behavioral needs, although less is understood of these needs and what the prevention of the performance of specific behaviors means to the physical or psychological well-being of the animal. Jensen and Toates[7] provide a thorough discussion of behavioral needs.

CONCLUSION

Ensuring that livestock are housed appropriately to meet their needs is a basic requirement of producers to ensure animal health, productivity, and to meet our social ethic. Instances in which the conditions of the environment do not meet the needs of the animal create a mismatch, which can cause unnecessary distress to livestock. To date, agricultural science has been efficient at defining the physical and dietary needs of livestock. Research continues and needs to progress much further in defining the social and behavioral needs of livestock. The key to

identifying these needs in the future will be advances in neuroscience and behavior that provide a clear understanding of livestock cognition.

REFERENCES

1. Ewing, S.A.; Lay, D.C.; Eberhard, V.B. *Farm Animal Well-Being*; Prentice Hall, 1999.
2. Moberg, G.P.; Mench, J.A. *The Biology of Animal Stress*; CABI Publishing, 2000.
3. UEP Scientific Advisory Committee on Animal Welfare. *Recommendations for UEP Animal Welfare Guidelines*; United Egg Producers: Atlanta, GA, 2000.
4. *Guide for the Care and Use of Agricultural Animals in Agricultural Research and Teaching*; Federation of Animal Science Societies, 1999.
5. Deen, J.; Xue, J. Sow Mortality in the US: An Industry-Wide Perspective, Allen D. Leman Swine Conference, 1999; 91–94.
6. Geiger, J.O.; Irwin, C.; Pretzer, S. Assessing Sow Mortality, Allen D. Leman Swine Conference, 1999; 84–87.
7. Jensen, P.; Toates, F.M. Who needs 'behavioral needs'? Motivational aspects of the needs of animals. Appl. Anim. Behav. Sci. **1993**, *37*, 161–181.

Environment: Effects on Animal Health

Donald C. Lay, Jr.
USDA-ARS-Livestock Behavior Research Unit, West Lafayette, Indiana, U.S.A.

INTRODUCTION

The health status of livestock is influenced by many factors, including prenatal development, neonatal care, genetic disposition, and the environment in which the animal is housed. Managing environmental influences to maximize the health status of livestock is critical to both animal productivity and animal well-being. A major influence of the health status of livestock is how each individual animal is able to cope with the environment in which it is housed. The inability to cope with potential stressors in an environment predisposes livestock to succumb to disease by suppressing their ability to combat pathogens. Even in the best housing systems, livestock can be subjected to stress, and each housing system offers its own challenges to livestock and managers. For example, pasture systems may decrease stress by allowing livestock more space to escape aggression. However, this same system can place livestock under both heat stress and cold stress. In addition, two individuals managed in the same system can perceive the situation entirely differently—one perceives the environment as stressful while the other does not perceive it as stressful. Therefore, it is important to manage each system and each animal on an individual basis to optimize the health of livestock.

RESPONSE TO STRESS

Every environment can expose livestock to some type of stressor. These stressors can be thermal, physical, and social. How the animal is able to cope with these potential stressors depends on the species abilities, for instance, swine can not sweat. Similarly, past experiences are important for coping in situations that may involve confrontations between individuals. When livestock are exposed to a stressor, the body automatically initiates a stress response. Stress responses are characterized by a behavioral response as well as a physiological response. The first behavioral response is simply for the animal to remove itself from the stressor, to move away. However, often this is not possible, such as when livestock are exposed to heat stress or to a pen mate that is aggressive. If unable to escape the stressor, a chronic physiologic stress response is maintained. Physiologically, the stress response is characterized by activation of the sympatho-adrenal axis (SA) and the hypothalamic-pituitary-adrenal axis (HPA) (see Fig. 1). The SA axis is activated immediately upon being exposed to a stressor and is the body's short-term response. This response is characterized by activation of the sympathetic nervous system, which stimulates the adrenal medulla to secrete epinephrine (also called adrenaline) into the circulation. Epinephrine is responsible for increasing blood flow and pressure in the body by increasing heart rate and vasoconstriction. This increase in blood flow allows the body to deliver more oxygen and energy (glucose) to muscle and brain tissue, thereby allowing the animal to react to the stressor (often termed the fight-or-flight response.[1] Activation of the HPA axis is used to maintain a physiologic status that enables the animal to continue to respond to the stressor. This axis is characterized by the release of corticotropic-releasing hormone (CRH) from the hypothalamus, which then causes the release of adrenocorticotropic hormone (ACTH) from the anterior pituitary gland. ACTH is then released into the circulation to cause the release of glucocorticoids from the adrenal cortex. Glucocorticoids increase the availability of energy to the muscles and brain by facilitating glucose availability in the circulation. Thus, the stress response[2,3] is critical for livestock to cope with stressful situations.

However, several products of the stress response can cause the immune system to be suppressed. Glucocorticoids, CRH, and epinephrine have all been shown to alter immune function and typically are considered immuno-suppressive. For example, glucocorticoids are known to suppress the function of lymphocytes, macrophages, natural killer cells, and neutrophils. Some of these immune cells, for instance, lymphocytes and macrophages, have receptors for glucocorticoids and/or catecholamines (i.e., epinephrine), which allow these compounds to have direct effects on the immune system. Other parameters of the immune system are altered indirectly when the stress hormones cause lymphocytes and macrophages to have an altered expression of cytokine release. A more in-depth review of the stress response on immune function can be found under "Immune System: Stress Effects," and in several reviews.[4–6]

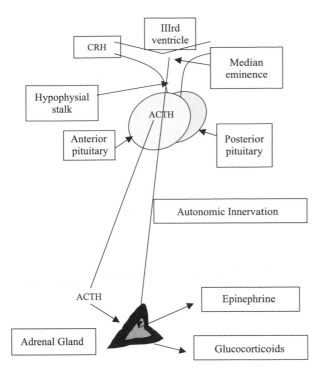

Fig. 1 The hypothalamic-pituitary-adrenal (HPA) axis and the sympatho-adrenal (SA) axis are activated in response to a stressor. CRH, corticotropic-releasing hormone; ACTH, adrenocorticotropic hormone. CRH causes the release of ACTH, which causes the release of glucocorticoids from the cortex of the adrenal gland (the HPA response). Sympathetic activation of the autonomic nervous system causes the release of epinephrine from the medulla of the adrenal gland (the SA response). (*View this art in color at www.dekker.com.*)

THERMAL CHALLENGES

Thermal challenges, either hot or cold, are common to all animals. Typically, these challenges to homeostasis are nonconsequential. The body's physiologic mechanisms respond appropriately by either evoking mechanisms to create heat, such as increasing metabolism, or to decrease heat load by sweating or diverting blood flow. Behavioral adjustments are made in concert with the physiologic mechanisms. Swine will seek a wallow during periods of elevated temperatures to cause evaporative cooling (swine must use an external water source because they do not sweat), while cattle will seek shade and may stand in water to cool themselves. The inability of livestock to appropriately warm or cool themselves has severe consequences on health. Mortality and morbidity due to hypothermia and hyperthermia can be high. Typically, livestock are most susceptible to these conditions when being transported. Wind chill will greatly reduce the ability of livestock to maintain body temperature during

cold, wet weather. Similarly, overcrowding trucks with animals destined to slaughter when ambient temperatures are high will easily cause a percentage of the animals to "go down," or die during transit. Another area of concern for hypothermia and hyperthermia is in feedlot cattle. Due to the weight and condition of these animals, heat waves can easily claim the lives of a significant number of cattle. During winter months, a lack of attention to keeping the feedlot dry will result in losing cattle from hypothermia because as the hair on the cattle becomes more matted, it loses its ability to insulate. Losses due to hypo- and hyperthermia result from the inability of the stress response to maintain homeostatic conditions in the body.

Environmental conditions relative to thermal environment are critical for newborn livestock. Piglets and chicks require a thermal environment approximately 15 degrees warmer than their dam. This is due to their inability to generate adequate heat as compared to other neonatal livestock. Calves and sheep possess brown adipose tissue at birth. Brown adipose tissue has a high content of mitochondria, which allows the neonates to generate body heat. However, piglets and chicks lack this type of adipose tissue and thus must rely on the warmth of their dam and external heat sources (a heat lamp is commonly used in production) to maintain their body temperature. The inability of neonates to maintain body temperature quickly leads to hypothermia and death.

HOUSING

Parasites, bacteria, and viruses offer a significant health concern in all livestock production systems. Because all livestock are housed in groups, pathogens are easily transmitted from one animal to the next. Control of many pathogens is enhanced by housing livestock in concrete and metal buildings, which allows for complete sanitation of the environment. Features such as slatted flooring, which allows feces to drop through the floor and away from the livestock, enhance control of parasites. Intensive housing systems that individually house animals, such as veal calves and sows, also aid in our ability to treat livestock that become infected. Individual treatment of poultry is not practical due to large groupings. When necessary, entire flocks are treated. It is significantly more challenging to control pathogen infestation in extensive systems such as pastures. However, such systems benefit from the extensive conditions because: 1) pathogen load is less because of a greater area of distribution and sunlight kills many pathogens; 2) direct contact is less and thus, fewer pathogens are passed directly to herd mates; and 3) 100% open air flow does not allow airborne pathogens to accumulate and thus decreases the stocks' exposure. Common management practices that help reduce pathogen exposure in extensive systems are rotational movement of dairy calf hutches to clean ground to allow any pathogens to be destroyed, and rotational movement of grazing livestock between pastures.

Housing that requires livestock to spend significant amounts of time on hard flooring can cause both lameness and skin lesions. Lameness is a common reason that sows and dairy cows must be culled from the herd. Wet floors in dairy facilities acerbate this problem because cows that slip may cause serious injury to joints and musculature. Skin lesions in sows mainly occur during lactation when sows lose body weight. Less fat cover allows pressure sores to develop from lying on the floor. These sores then rupture, and once they are established, they are extremely difficult to heal.

The group size in which livestock are kept can also have effects on their health. Some of these reasons are those discussed earlier, relating to pathogen exposure. Other effects on health are due to stress from group competition. Anytime animals are grouped, they will compete for any resource that is limited. In production agriculture, all animals being fed to produce meat or milk are not being limited in feed or water, but limitations can occur due to limited access. Limited access to the feeder or water will cause increased aggression, which in turn will activate the stress response. Broiler breeders and sows are limit-fed and thus, a high degree of aggression can be seen when they are housed in groups. Those animals lying intermediate in the dominance hierarchy tend to be more stressed than either those at the top or bottom.

CONCLUSIONS

Environmental conditions under which we keep livestock have significant effects on animal health. Some environmental characteristics have direct effects on animal health, such as conditions that cause injury or allow pathogens to be easily spread. Other characteristics of the environment have indirect effects on animal health by causing the animal to enter a state of distress, which then predisposes it to succumb to disease. Each livestock species has specific environmental needs to optimize healthful conditions. It is most important to realize that even individuals within the same group may have needs that are different than that of its herd mates. Meeting individual needs is critical to maintaining healthy herds and flocks. Sainsbury[7] provides more in-depth information on the effects of the environment and animal health.

REFERENCES

1. Selye, H. The evolution of the stress concept. Am. Sci. **1973**, *61*, 692.
2. Moberg, G.P.; Mench, J.A. *The Biology of Animal Stress*; CABI Publishing, 2000.
3. Balm, P.H.M. *Stress Physiology in Animals*; Sheffield Academic Press, 1999.
4. Black, P.H. Central nervous system-immune system interactions: Psychoneuroendocrinology of stress and its immune consequences. Antimicrob. Agents Chemother. **1994**, *38*, 1–6.
5. Marsland, A.L.; Bachen, E.A.; Cohen, S.; Rabin, B.; Manuck, S.B. Stress, immune reactivity and susceptibility to infectious disease. Physiol. Behav. **2002**, *77*, 711–716.
6. Kehrli, M.E.; Burton, J.L.; Nonnecke, B.J.; Lee, E.K. Effects of stress on leukocyte trafficking and immune responses: Implications for vaccination. Adv. Vet. Med. **1999**, *41*, 61–81.
7. Sainsbury, D. *Animal Health*; Blackwell Science, 1998.

FURTHER READING

Ewing, S.A.; Lay, D.C.; Eberhard, V.B. *Farm Animal Well-Being*; Prentice Hall, 1999.

Environmental Pollutants

J. L. Hatfield
United States Department of Agriculture, Agricultural Research Service, Ames, Iowa, U.S.A.

INTRODUCTION

Animal production systems have been considered sources of environmental pollution. The complexity of this problem of animal production and environmental impacts exists because of two factors: 1) the diversity among and within species production systems; and 2) the range of environmental endpoints affected through animal production.

ANIMAL PRODUCTION SYSTEMS AND ENVIRONMENTAL QUALITY

To fully understand environmental issues, the animal production system has be to dissected into phases, e.g., housing, manure storage, and manure application, and environmental endpoints, e.g., water, soil, or air quality. We can consider the flow of manure through a swine operation as typical animal production and then the linkage to environmental quality can be seen as a series of environmental consequences (Fig. 1). These effects can be altered by the diet of the animal, changing nitrogen excretion, and carbohydrate composition of the manure. The linkages that exist between diet and environmental quality have been demonstrated and remain a viable part of the management options for improving environmental quality.

Environmental quality endpoints occur within the soil, water, or air surrounding animal production facilities (Table 1). These are potential impacts from all phases of animal production; however, air quality emanates from all phases, whereas soil and water quality spring from the manure storage and application phases. These impacts vary with production systems. For example, broiler production in houses does not impact water or soil quality until manure and bedding are moved onto the land for application. In contrast, a beef or dairy feedlot could create a water quality problem from the housing phase, because these animals are in an open feedlot subject to surface runoff during large rainfall events.

Environmental impacts of confined animal feeding operations (CAFOs) in Hamilton County, Iowa, evaluated by Jackson et al. revealed the potential to create nutrient loading too high for the ecosystem to assimilate.[2] Potential outcomes of large nutrient loadings are increased rates of ammonia volatilization, suppression of biological nitrogen fixation, and increased rates of nitrate leaching and runoff from manured soils. Current regulations require individual CAFOs to account for N utilization on cropland, but there is no assessment of these impacts at the regional, local, or watershed scale. Upon completing their analysis, they suggested five policy recommendations: 1) increase research and outreach on alternative production systems to those using liquid-based manure systems; 2) increase regulatory scrutiny of current system and require a public comment period on manure management plans; 3) increase research on nutrient management methods; 4) establish statewide zoning regulations for the density of animal units regardless of size; and 5) increase the diversity of crops on the landscape in order to utilize manure nutrients more effectively.[2] Environmental concerns are becoming a dominant force in shaping management practices for animal production, and manure storage and application. These forces will create changes in how we blend production systems and environmental quality.

Evidence that animal operations create an environmental problem has become a concern among producers and the rural and urban community. Recordings of fish kills in streams where excess manure has created high ammonia levels cause a public concern about the environmental consequences of animal operations. Application of manure onto the soil surface or smells from animal operations create a perception that animal production systems are an environmental problem. These issues define the role of various environmental pollutants from animal agriculture.

SOIL QUALITY

Environmental quality concerns related to soil management are primarily related to N and P levels in the soil. Manure is a valuable resource as a soil amendment that can actually reduce environmental quality problems by increasing water infiltration and water storage in the soil profile. Environmental quality problems result from

Encyclopedia of Animal Science
DOI: 10.1081/E-EAS 120019592

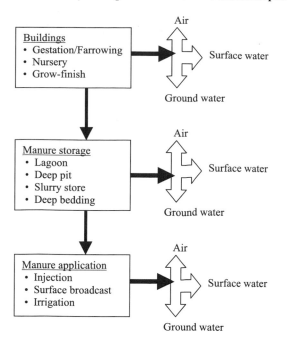

Fig. 1 Flow of manure through a swine production operation and the environmental endpoints at each phase. (Adopted from Ref. [1].)

manure added to soil when there is surface runoff that moves either ammonia or P into streams. This topic is covered in a related article on nutrient management/soil and water quality.

WATER QUALITY

Water quality problems result from movement of nutrients from manure moving into nearby waters from either the production site, manure storage, or manure application site. Water quality problems are associated primarily with manure storage or application and can be either nutrients or pathogens (Table 1). Leakage from manure storage systems has been assumed to be a source of water quality problems; however, Ham demonstrated on several lagoons in Kansas that seepage from swine lagoons ranged from 200 to 5000 kg ha^{-1} yr^{-1}, while in beef cattle feedlots, the seepage rate averaged 385 kg ha^{-1} yr^{-1}.[3] In spite of these seepage rates, the concentrations of organic-N, ammonium-N, and phosphorus were at background levels at 3 m below the lagoon. Management of manure storage systems to reduce the risk of water movement from overflowing manure storage systems will greatly reduce the risk of environmental pollution.

AIR QUALITY

Air quality derived from animal production systems includes ammonia, volatile organic compounds, methane, nitrous oxide, hydrogen sulfide, pathogens, and particulates. Differences among animal operations are greatest in the emissions; however, ammonia is probably the most common and most significant air quality parameter. Particulates and odor are major concerns from animal production units. Variation in emission rates within animal

Table 1 Phases of animal production and potential environmental quality endpoints from each production phase

Production phase	Soil	Water	Air
Buildings	None	Minimal	Ammonia
			Particulates
			Methane
			Nitrous oxide
			Volatile organic compounds
			Pathogens
Manure storage	Nitrate	Nitrate	Ammonia
	Ammonia	Ammonia	Methane
	Pathogens	Pathogens	Nitrous oxide
	Phosphorus	Phosphorus	Volatile organic compounds
			Pathogens
Manure application	Nitrate	Nitrate	Ammonia
	Ammonia	Ammonia	Particulates
	Pathogens	Pathogens	Methane
	Phosphorus	Phosphorus	Nitrous oxide
			Volatile organic compounds
			Pathogens

Table 2 Nitrogen lost from various types of manure handling and storage systems

System	Nitrogen lost (%)
Solid manure	
Daily scrape and haul	20 to 35
Manure pack	20 to 40
Open lot	40 to 55
Liquid manure	
Deep pit within building[a]	15 to 30
Slurry tank above-ground[a]	10 to 30
Earthen or concrete basin	20 to 40
Anaerobic lagoon	70 to 85

[a]Includes losses due to agitation. (From Ref. [10].)

species and across locations creates a problem in being able to make general statements about the impact of different management systems on air quality.

One of the measurements of air quality is the emission rate of a given gas per animal per day. In Europe, estimates of ammonia loss in free-stall dairy barns typically range between 20–45 g NH_3 per cow per day or approximately 5–10% of excreted N. Ammonia loss from tie-stall barns ranges between 5–27 g per cow per day.[4] Annual ammonia emissions are related to factors such as housing and bedding type, frequency of manure removal, ventilation, and seasonal differences in weather. Hutchings et al. estimated that 10% of excreted N is volatilized from a free-stall barn under North European conditions on an annual basis.[5] For beef feedlots, the ammonia loss is often expressed as a concentration per unit volume (g m^{-3}), which makes it difficult to compare among species unless sufficient detail is given to relate the air volume to a specific animal number. Hutchinson et al. reported a range of concentrations from 290 to 1200 µg m^{-3} for beef feedlots.[6] Concentrations of ammonia adjacent to a swine production unit in Iowa ranged between 50 and 1000 µg m^{-3} (Hatfield and Pfeiffer, 2003, unpublished data). Arogo et al. reviewed the current literature on ammonia emissions from swine production and concluded that the range was 2.3 to 7.6 kg NH_3-N yr^{-1} animal^{-1}, with the variation being attributed to housing, manure management, and climate.[7] Emissions from poultry operations are often expressed as a fraction of N excreted, and it has been estimated that between 15 to 65% of the N excreted is lost as ammonia.[8] Poultry production in the United States has been estimated to contribute up to 27% of total U.S. ammonia emissions.[9] Ammonia emissions from animal production are one of the major sources of environmental impact. Management techniques to reduce ammonia loss need to be developed and implemented on farms.

Ammonia losses from animal production systems are only part of the puzzle. The differences among manure storage systems are quite large and represent significant losses of N into the environment (Table 2). Losses of N from manure may be either as ammonia or other forms of nitrogen gas.

Particulates emitted from animal facilities show extreme variation within and among animal species. Hydrogen sulfide is commonly associated with swine production and is a human nuisance problem rather than an environmental problem. Likewise, the emission of volatile organic compounds (VOCs) from animal operations is responsible for the odors that emanate from livestock production. Zahn et al. provided one of the first classifications of swine production systems for the types and concentrations of VOCs emitted from various production phases.[11]

CONCLUSIONS

Managing animal production systems to reduce environmental impacts is most difficult for air quality. Water and soil quality responses to animal production can be managed through planning and understanding the risk of spills, overapplication, or improper use of manure. Escape of gaseous or particulate material into the atmosphere from all phases of animal production is more difficult to quantify, and the current body of knowledge contains a wide variation in the observed values of all gases. To address this problem will require the development of tools that can more accurately measure the concentrations of all of the gases in the atmosphere and couple these measurements with greatly enhanced atmospheric transport models so that a more accurate emission model can be developed.

ARTICLE OF FURTHER INTEREST

Nutrient Management: Water Quality/Use, p. 667

REFERENCES

1. Hatfield, J.L. Minimizing the Environmental Impact of the Swine Industry. Proceedings of the 17th IPVS Congress, Ames, IA, 2002; 95–104.
2. Jackson, L.L.; Keeney, D.R.; Gilbert, E.M. Swine manure management plans in North-Central Iowa: Nutrient loading and policy implications. J. Soil Water Conserv. **2000**, *55*, 205–211.

3. Ham, J.M. Seepage losses from animal waste lagoons: A summary of a four-year investigation in Kansas. Trans. ASAE **2002**, *45*, 983–992.

4. Monteny, G.J.; Erisman, J.W. Ammonia emission from dairy cow buildings: A review of measurement techniques, influencing factors and possibilities for reduction. Neth. J. Agric. Sci. **1998**, *46*, 225–247.

5. Hutchings, N.J.; Sommer, S.G.; Anderson, J.M.; Asman, W.A.H. A detailed ammonia emission inventory for Denmark. Atmos. Environ. **2001**, *35*, 1959–1968.

6. Hutchinson, G.L.; Mosier, A.R.; Andre, C.E. Ammonia and amine emissions from a large cattle feedlot. J. Environ. Qual. **1982**, *11*, 288–293.

7. Arogo, J.; Westerman, P.W.; Heber, A.J. A review of ammonia emissions from confined swine feeding operations. Trans. ASAE **2003**, *46*, 805–817.

8. Bouwman, A.F.; Van Der hoek, K.W. Scenarios of animal waste production and fertilizer use and associated ammonia emission for the developing countries. Atmos. Environ. **1997**, *31*, 4095–4102.

9. Battye, R.; Battye, W.; Overcash, C.; Fudge, S. *Development and Selection of Ammonia Emission Factors: Final Report. EC/R Inc. Durham, N.C.*, EPA Contract Report #68-D3-0034; U.S. EPA: Research Triangle Park, NC, 1994; 111.

10. MWPS (MidWest Plan Service). *Manure Storages*; Manure Management System Series. MWPS-18, Section 2, MidWest Plan Service, Iowa State University: Ames, IA 2001; 50011-3080.

11. Zahn, J.A.; Hatfield, J.L.; Laird, D.A.; Hart, T.T.; Do, Y.S.; DiSpirito, A.A. Functional classification of swine manure management systems based on solution-phase chemical and gas emission characteristics. J. Environ. Qual. **2001**, *30*, 635–647.

Estrous Cycle: Cattle, Sheep, Goat

Keith Inskeep
West Virginia University, Morgantown, West Virginia, U.S.A.

INTRODUCTION

Estrous cycles have two ovarian phases, luteal and follicular. The luteal phase is longer and is dominated by progesterone, secreted by the corpus luteum. After luteal regression, the follicular phase is relatively short, two to four days. Rapidly increasing secretion of estradiol, by the largest follicle(s), initiates the luteinizing hormone (LH) surge from the anterior pituitary. Ovulation occurs 24 to 27 hours after the LH surge. The hormonal relationships during the luteal and follicular phases in an example animal, the cow, will be presented in the discussion below. Most breeds of sheep and goats are seasonally polyestrus. Cycle length is marked by behavioral estrus, which occurs at average intervals of 21 to 22 days (range 17 to 24) in cows, 16 to 17 days in ewes, and 19 to 21 days in does (goat breeds vary).

LUTEAL PHASE

The corpus luteum is the dominant structure during most of the estrous cycle. The luteal phase is measured from ovulation until regression of the corpus luteum (luteolysis). Following ovulation, the corpus luteum forms from the ruptured follicle and can be observed until day three as a corpus hemorrhagicum. About day three to five, the corpus luteum loses its bloody appearance, increases in size, and produces sufficient progesterone to be detected in peripheral circulation.[1] By approximately midcycle, the corpus luteum reaches maximum size and secretion of progesterone (Fig. 1).

Roles of Progesterone

Progesterone has two major regulatory functions. First, progesterone controls the release of LH. High concentrations of progesterone reduce frequency of secretion of pulses of gonadotropin releasing hormone (GnRH) from the hypothalamus. Frequency of secretion of pulses of LH from the anterior pituitary gland is thus reduced, and the surge of LH and subsequent ovulation are prevented. In the cow, 37% of the variance in frequency of pulses of LH and 38% of the variance in concentrations of estradiol-17β are accounted for by concentrations of progesterone.[2]

Second, progesterone establishes the capacity of the endometrium to secrete prostaglandin $F_2\alpha$ ($PGF_2\alpha$) and regulates the timing of initial increases in secretion of $PGF_2\alpha$ for luteolysis. Increases usually begin around day 11 of the cycle in the ewe and around day 14 in the doe and cow (Fig. 1). Progesterone also modulates episodic secretion of $PGF_2\alpha$, keeping it at midrange values until luteal regression has begun. With decreasing concentrations of progesterone, greater secretion of $PGF_2\alpha$ by the uterus and the corpus luteum[3] completes luteal regression. Maximal secretion of $PGF_2\alpha$ occurs after luteal secretion of progesterone has ceased (Fig. 1).

Follicular Growth During the Luteal Phase

Early stages of ovarian follicular development are not dependent upon gonadotropins; a pulse of follicle stimulating hormone (FSH) initiates growth of a cohort of tertiary follicles[4,5] and is required for growth from approximately a diameter (mm) of 2 to 4 (ewe) or 4 to 9 (cow). Frequent pulses of LH are necessary for development beyond about 4 or 9 mm, respectively. As follicles grow, they secrete increasing amounts of estradiol-17β and inhibin. Each hormone has negative feedback effects upon secretion of FSH (estradiol limits secretion of GnRH, and inhibin reduces responsiveness of the anterior pituitary to GnRH). As FSH becomes limiting, the dominant follicle becomes more reliant on LH.[4] Pulses of LH maintain growth of dominant follicles until either ovulation or atresia. During continued progesterone dominance, increased secretion of estradiol and inhibin by the growing follicle causes a gradual decrease in FSH. Further, pulse frequencies of LH (kept low by progesterone) become limiting and the dominant follicle becomes atretic. Estradiol and inhibin then decrease, allowing a short-lived increase in FSH that recruits a new cohort of follicles.[4,5]

Waves of follicular growth occur sequentially, with one follicle of a cohort becoming largest (dominant) every seven to 10 days in the cow (Refs. [5] and [6]; Fig. 2), or one to three follicles every three to four days in most breeds of ewe or doe.[7,8] Numbers of follicular waves during the estrous cycle vary by species and breed. British and continental breeds of beef and dairy cows usually have two to three follicular waves.[5,6] However, two to

Encyclopedia of Animal Science
DOI: 10.1081/E-EAS 120019593

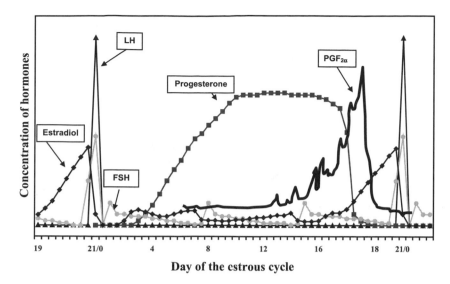

Fig. 1 Hormonal patterns during the bovine estrous cycle. (Drawn by Darron L. Smith and Keith Inskeep.) (*View this art in color at www.dekker.com.*)

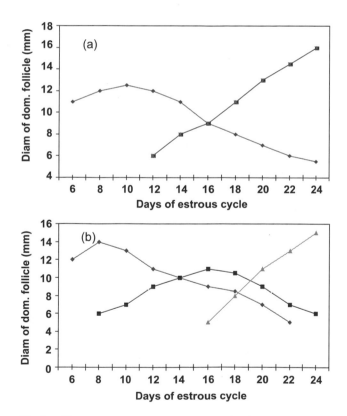

Fig. 2 Observed patterns of development for the largest follicle during the bovine estrous cycle. Shown are the average diameters of the first (◇–◇), second (□–□), and third (Δ–Δ) sequentially largest follicles in cows that had (a) two or (b) three waves of follicular development, respectively. (From Ref. [6].) (*View this art in color at www.dekker.com.*)

four follicular waves may be seen in Brahman cattle and approximately four may be typical in ewes and does.[7,8] Follicular waves are less well-defined in ewes and does.[7,8] Largest follicles show less dominance over smaller ones or recruitment of new ones in ewes than in cows. Thus, in ewes, ovulatory follicles may arise from different cohorts, as early as day nine or as late as day 15.

FOLLICULAR PHASE

As luteolysis proceeds, decreasing progesterone reduces negative feedback on pulsatile secretion of LH by the anterior pituitary. Increased frequency of pulses of LH promotes final maturation of the dominant follicle. During the follicular phase, LH reaches higher concentrations than in the luteal phase, because of removal of negative feedback from progesterone on the hypothalamus.

Dominant follicles, as they grow, secrete increasing concentrations of estradiol-17β and inhibin, so that FSH declines during the follicular phase, but estradiol does not limit pulse frequency of LH. Behavioral estrus (seeking out and standing to be mounted by a male) and a preovulatory surge of LH and FSH occur when the dominant follicle(s) reach adequate size and secretion of estradiol-17β reaches threshold. Follicular diameters of approximately 10 mm in the cow and 4 mm in the ewe are required for ovulation. Cows show homosexual mounting behavior, but this is not seen in ewes and seldom in does. At the preovulatory surge of LH, concentrations of estradiol-17β abruptly decline, and a secondary surge of FSH occurs on the day of ovulation (recruiting a new cohort of follicles into the growing pool).

SUBNORMAL LUTEAL PHASE

During a subnormal luteal phase, defined by low secretion of progesterone, there is a sustained increase in frequency of pulses of LH from the anterior pituitary. Increased LH stimulates continued growth and persistence of the largest follicle, with greater secretion of estradiol-17β. Fertility is compromised by ovulation of a persistent dominant follicle.

When a persistent follicle ovulates, the oocyte is likely at a later stage of maturation. Although the oocyte is fertilizable, the resultant zygote often experiences retarded development and early embryonic death (between the 2- and 16-cell stages) in the cow. The effect might not occur in the ewe. In lactating dairy cows, low concentrations of progesterone (2.1 to 2.3 ng/ml) before estrus altered endometrial morphology during the subsequent cycle and increased secretion of the major metabolite of $PGF_2\alpha$, in response to oxytocin on day 15 of that cycle. These effects could decrease fertility even though the original oocyte was healthy.

SHORT LUTEAL PHASES

Ruminants usually have a short luteal phase following first ovulation or first estrus at puberty or after parturition. In goats, short luteal phases are a problem in animals that are superovulated in preparation for embryo transfer. Premature uterine secretion of $PGF_2\alpha$ is responsible for the short luteal phase in both cows and ewes.[1,2,9] Pretreatment of anestrous cows with a progestogen usually results in formation of a corpus luteum with a normal functional life span, in response to weaning or injection of gonadotropins, and increased numbers of receptors for progesterone in the uterus on day five after estrus. Upregulation of uterine progesterone receptors appears essential to normal timing of secretion of $PGF_2\alpha$. Understanding the function of progesterone in normalizing length of the estrous cycle has enabled development of methods to initiate normal cycles in anestrous cows, with normal fertility when cows are bred at the induced estrus.[9]

CONCLUSIONS

The ruminant estrous cycle depends on a complex interplay of hormones from the hypothalamus, pituitary, ovaries, and uterus, as well as changes in ovarian structures and in behavior. During the luteal phase of the cycle, the corpus luteum is the dominant ovarian structure and the secretion of progesterone is critical to fertility. Progesterone regulates frequency of pulses of LH, through negative feedback on the hypothalamus, and also prevents an LH surge. In addition, progesterone programs uterine secretion of $PGF_2\alpha$, which times initiation of luteolysis. Follicles are stimulated by FSH; some are selected to continue growth and become dependent upon LH. Luteolysis removes negative feedback by progesterone on LH, allowing ovulation. High concentrations of progesterone lead to timely atresia of older follicles. However, if concentrations of progesterone are low, an increase in frequency of pulses of LH allows development of a persistent dominant follicle, increased secretion of estradiol-17β, and, if that follicle ovulates, fertility may be decreased.

REFERENCES

1. Niswender, G.D.; Juengel, J.J.; Silva, P.J.; Rollyson, M.K.; McIntush, E.W. Mechanisms controlling the function and life span of the corpus luteum. Physiol. Rev. **2000**, *80* (1), 1–29.
2. Inskeep, E.K. Factors that Affect Embryonic Survival in the Cow: Application of Technology to Improve Calf Crop. In *Factors Affecting Calf Crop: Biotechnology of Reproduction*; Fields, M.J., Sand, R.S., Yelich, J.V., Eds.; CRC Press: Boca Raton, FL, 2002; 255–279.
3. Griffeth, R.J.; Nett, T.M.; Burns, P.D.; Escudero, J.M.; Inskeep, E.K.; Niswender, G.D. Is luteal production of $PGF_2\alpha$ required for luteolysis? Biol. Reprod. **2002**, *66* (Suppl. 1), 287. (Abstr.).
4. Scaramuzzi, R.J.; Adams, N.R.; Baird, D.T.; Campbell, B.K.; Downing, J.A.; Findlay, J.K.; Henderson, K.M.; Martin, G.B.; McNatty, K.P.; McNeilly, A.S.; Tsonis, C.G. A model for follicle selection and the determination of ovulation rate in the ewe. Reprod. Fertil. Dev. **1993**, *5* (5), 459–478.
5. Ginther, O.J.; Wiltbank, M.C.; Fricke, P.M.; Gibbons, J.R.; Kot, K. Selection of the dominant follicle in cattle. Biol. Reprod. **1996**, *55* (6), 1187–1194.
6. Ahmad, N.; Townsend, E.C.; Dailey, R.A.; Inskeep, E.K. Relationships of hormonal patterns and fertility to occurrence of two or three waves of ovarian follicles, before and after breeding, in beef cows and heifers. Anim. Reprod. Sci. **1997**, *49* (1), 13–28.
7. Ginther, O.J.; Kot, K.; Wiltbank, M.C. Associations between emergence of follicular waves and fluctuations in FSH concentrations during the estrous cycle in ewes. Theriogenology **1995**, *43* (3), 687–703.
8. Ginther, O.J.; Kot, K. Follicular dynamics during the ovulatory season in goats. Theriogenology **1994**, *42* (6), 987–1001.
9. Inskeep, E.K. Factors that affect fertility during oestrous cycles with short or normal luteal phases in postpartum cows. J. Reprod. Fertil. **1995**, (Suppl. 49), 493–503.

Estrous Cycle: Mare, Sow

Rodney D. Geisert
Steven R. Cooper
Oklahoma State University, Stillwater, Oklahoma, U.S.A.

INTRODUCTION

Following the initiation of puberty (onset of the first ovulatory estrus), the female will exhibit distinct periods of receptivity and nonreceptivity to approaches for mating by the male. In domestic farm animals, the estrous cycle is defined as the number of days from initiation of behavioral estrus expression to onset of a subsequent estrus. Mares and sows are both polyestrous (exhibit repeated estrous cycles). However, unlike the sow that can exhibit cycles throughout the year, the mare is a seasonal breeder that initiates estrus activity as day length increases during the early spring, usually becoming anestrus (no estrus expression) as day length decreases following the summer solstice. Length of the estrous cycle in both the sow and mare averages 19–22 days. Cycle length in the mare can also be affected by type (pony, horse, donkey) and time of year, as length of the estrous cycle tends to be longer in winter and early spring compared to late spring and summer.[2] Estrous cycle of the mare and sow is characterized by four distinct stages called proestrus, estrus, metestrus, and diestrus. Classifications of the stages are based on ovarian, hormonal, and behavioral changes that occur during the estrous cycle.

STAGES OF THE ESTROUS CYCLE

Proestrus—Concentration of progesterone in the blood declines to its lowest level following luteolysis (regression) of the corpora lutea (pl) in the sow or the single corpus luteum (CL) in the mare.[1–3] With regression and transformation of the corpus luteum to nonfunctional corpus albicans on the ovary, systemic blood concentration of progesterone declines, the block to final follicle growth is removed, and the Graafian follicle(s) is permitted to enlarge through stimulation by rising systemic concentrations of follicle-stimulating hormone (FSH) and luteinizing hormone (LH) from the anterior pituitary (Fig. 1).

In the sow, a cohort of 10 to 25 antral (fluid-filled) follicles (2–5-mm diameter) continues to develop to ovulatory size[4] while a 25–30-mm dominant follicle continues to enlarge toward the ovulation fossa of the mare's ovary.[2] Gonadotropin (FSH and LH) stimulation triggers production of estrogen from the recruited follicles that initiate a transition in the female's behavior from a nonreceptive to receptive state to mounting (copulation) by the male.

With uterine release of the luteolysin, prostaglandin $F_{2\alpha}$ ($PGF_{2\alpha}$) corpora lutea usually undergo regression shortly after day 15 of the sow's estrous cycle[5] and estrogen production by the many developing follicles increases (Fig. 1). Prior to initiation of estrus (standing for mounting by male), the sow's vulva may become swollen and red, she may increase activity, reduce appetite, vocalize (estrual grunts), display increased interest in the male, and attempt to mount other females, but will not stand for mounting herself.

Proestrus in the mare occurs following uterine release of $PGF_{2\alpha}$ to regress the corpus luteum on approximately day 18 of the estrous cycle. With the approach of estrus, the mare may tend to seek the stallion, but not display outward signs of estrous behavior. A nonreceptive mare may display various repelling behaviors to the stallion such as pinning back her ears, kicking, rapidly switching tail, biting, pawing, and squealing.[2,3]

Estrus—Concentration of estrogen peaks either shortly before or after the initiation of behavioral estrus expression (Fig. 1). Increased production of estrogen from the multiple 7–8-mm follicles of the sow and 45–50-mm follicle of the mare triggers the preovulatory surge of LH and FSH. Specifically, release of LH induces enzymes to break down the follicle wall and induces ovulation of the oocyte(s).

Expression estrus in pigs averages 24 to 48 h in gilts and 24 to 96 h in sows.[6] The sow's behavioral estrus is characterized by taking a rigged sawhorse-like stance when mounted or having back pressure applied (Fig. 2A). Her ears become erect and she is basically immobile following the tactile stimulation (see video at www.ansi.okstate.edu/resource-room/reprod/all/videos/). This standing heat response is more evident in the presence of a boar as stimuli such as boar chanting, tactile nudging, and smell elicit a much stronger expression of estrus in the female. Placing back pressure on the sow will elicit the standing response; however, only approximately 50% of

Encyclopedia of Animal Science
DOI: 10.1081/E-EAS 120021382

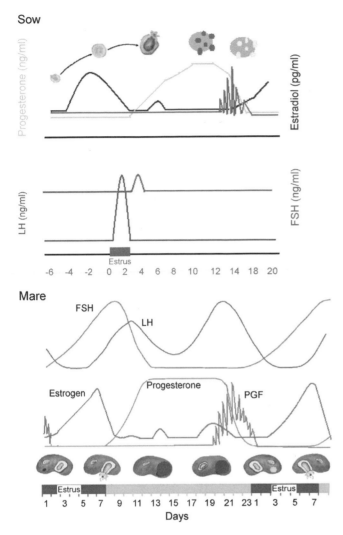

Fig. 1 Representation of the hormonal changes for the endocrine hormones during the estrous cycle of the sow and mare (day zero is the first day estrus is expressed). (Hormonal profiles adapted from Refs. [2,3,5,7].) (*View this art in color at www.dekker.com.*)

the females will respond to back pressure alone in the absence of a boar. During estrus, elevated concentrations of estrogen cause the cervix to become very rigid and the long uterine horns to be tightly coiled. Multiple follicles of the sow ovulate over a 1 to 3 h period about 30–35 h after the peak of the LH surge. The LH surge may occur before, during, or after first detection of behavioral estrus, with peak release occurring approximately 12 h from its initial rise. Ovulation usually occurs approximately 70% of the way through estrus. Because the length of estrus is quite variable, determination of the exact time ovulation will occur from initiation of estrus is not a very accurate method to predict time of AI.[6]

Length of the mare's estrus is variable and dependent upon the time of the breeding season. Average length of the mare's estrus is five to seven days, but can range from two to 12 days.[2,3] During estrus, estrogen continues to increase temporally, with the sustained rise (prolonged surge) of LH and FSH during estrus (Fig. 1), and the cervix becomes soft and flat (opposite of the sow). The developing dominant Graafian follicle grows at a rate of about 3 mm/day,[2] reaching a diameter of approximately 40–50 mm prior to ovulation (Fig. 2D). Prolonged length of estrus and LH surge allows the preovulatory follicle to grow toward the ovulation fossa (Fig. 2C). Because the layers (cortex and medulla) of a mare's ovary are inverted compared to other species (thick connective tissue layer of medulla is on the outside), the ovulation fossa is the only site on the ovary that the follicle can release the oocyte. Detection of estrus in the mare is determined through evaluation of behavioral responses following daily exposure to the stallion (teasing). During estrus, the mare displays strong behavioral characteristics of posturing, clitoral winking, and receptivity to teasing by the stallion. Posturing of mare during teasing with a stallion consists of raising her tail and bending her hind legs (squatting) to lower her hindquarters (Fig. 2B). Frequent urination is associated with the squatting response to presence of a stallion. During estrus, the mare displays clitoral winking through the many rhythmic contractions of labia that expose and project the clitoris. A majority of ovulations in the mare occur within two days before the end of estrus expression. Appraisal of estrus and closeness to the time of ovulation on the breeding farm is based on palpation, ultrasonography, and teasing scores (see Table 1) that are utilized to indicate the mare's relative estrous behavior and the level of receptivity to the stallion (see video at www.ansi.okstate.edu/resource-room/reprod/all/videos/). The length of estrus expression and intensity of behavior varies greatly among mares. Some mares display very subtle signs of estrus, requiring palpation and/or ultrasonography to optimize time of breeding.

Metestrus—Following ovulation of the follicle(s), blood concentrations of estrogen and LH decline rapidly and there is a secondary surge release of FSH caused by the loss of negative feedback of the hormone inhibin (origin Graafian follicle).[1] Rise in FSH following ovulation recruits ovarian follicles into the developing pool for future estrous cycles. After ovulation, the Graafian follicle collapses and blood and lymph seep into the follicle cavity, forming the structure called the corpus hemorrhagicum. Ovulation can be detected with ultrasonography and/or palpation of the ovary. Metestrus is a very short period of the estrous cycle (one to two days), during which the granulosa and thecal cells of the follicle differentiate into progesterone-secreting luteal

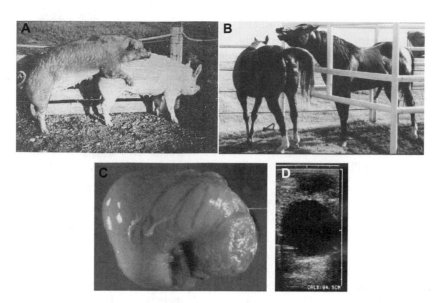

Fig. 2 Typical display of behavioral estrus (standing heat) in the sow (A) and mare (B). Photograph of a mare's ovary (C), containing a large Graafian follicle and displaying location of the ovulation fossa. Ultrasonograph of a large (45-mm) mare preovulatory follicle during estrus (D). (*View this art in color at www.dekker.com.*)

cells. With growth and expansion of the luteal cells, a functional corpus luteum forms and the first rise in plasma progesterone marks the start of diestrus. Both the sow and mare become rapidly unreceptive to the male following the decline of estrogen and increase in plasma progesterone.

Diestrus—With formation of the corpora lutea, concentration of progesterone increases from day three to peak concentrations on day 12 of the sow's estrous cycle. Duration of diestrus is 10 to 12 days. Although tonic release of LH is necessary to support the corpora lutea after day 12 of the estrous cycle, elevated concentrations of progesterone suppress the LH surge and prevent estrus and ovulation. During diestrus, the sow is unreceptive to mounting by the boar. Following 10 to 12 days of progesterone stimulation, the endometrium of the uterus releases the luteolysin $PGF_{2\alpha}$ into the uterine vasculature to initiate luteolysis of the corpora lutea on day 15 of the estrous cycle.[5] With regression of the corpora lutea and decline of progesterone, follicle growth occurs and behavioral patterns of proestrus return.

Diestrus in the mare is initiated with the first increase in progesterone on day nine of the estrous cycle. Progesterone concentrations peak on day 12 and remain elevated until day 18 of the estrous cycle.[2] Duration of diestrus is 14 to 15 days in length, during which the mare will be unreceptive to the stallion. The mare will show disinterest in the stallion (teaser), ears will be back, and she may strike, kick, and squeal in the presence of the male. Uterine release of $PGF_{2\alpha}$ occurs 17 to 19 days after the initiation of estrus expression. Because of the variable length of estrus, the day of ovulation is considered day zero of diestrus on the breeding farm. Thus, luteolysis would occur on days 12 to 15 of diestrus (postovulation). With CL regression, progesterone concentrations decline, follicles grow, and proestrus is initiated.

Table 1 Teasing scores for estrous detection in the mare

Tease score	Description
1	Resistant to the stallion (kicking, striking, and squealing)
2	Indifferent (no interest in stallion)
3	Some interest in stallion (stands for teasing without raising tail, winking, or squatting)
4	Responds to teasing by stallion (displays estrus behavior by winking vulva, raising tail, and urinating)
5	Intense expression of estrus behavior (profuse urination, winking vulva, and squatting)

CONCLUSION

Knowledge of the endocrine changes during the estrous cycle of the sow and mare allows an understanding of the behavioral patterns during the various stages of the estrous cycle. With regression of the CL and decline of progesterone, estrogen from maturing Graafian follicles promotes the physical and behavioral expression patterns that are utilized to determine the proper timing of breeding. A complete understanding of characteristics for typical estrous behavior in the sow and mare is especially important when utilizing artificial insemination (AI). Utilization of ultrasonography has assisted in determining the time of ovulation in the mare. Research continues to explore methods to accurately predict or induce ovulation for optimal breeding.

REFERENCES

1. Senger, P.L. *Pathways to Pregnancy and Parturition*, 2nd Ed.; Current Conception, Inc.: Pullman, WA, 2000.
2. Ginther, O.J. *Reproductive Biology of the Mare*, 2nd Ed.; Equiservices: Crossplains, WI, 1992.
3. Daels, P.F.; Hughes, J.P. The Normal Estrous Cycle. In *Equine Reproduction*; McKinnon, A.O., Voss, J.L., Eds.; Williams & Wilkins: Media, PA, 1993; 121–131.
4. Hunter, M.G.; Wiesak, T. Evidence for and Implications of Follicular Heterogeneity in Pigs. In *Control of Pig Reproduction III*; Cole, D.J.A., Foxcroft, G.R., Weir, B.J., Eds.; The Journals of Reproduction and Fertility Ltd.: Cambridge, UK, 1990; 163–177.
5. Moeljono, M.P.E.; Thatcher, W.W.; Bazer, F.W.; Frank, M.; Owens, L.J.; Wilcox, C.J. A study of prostaglandin $F_{2\alpha}$ as the luteolysin in swine: II. Characterization and comparison of prostaglandin F, estrogen and progestin concentrations in utero-ovarian vein plasma of nonpregnant gilts. Prostaglandins **1977**, *14*, 543–555.
6. Soede, N.M.; Kemp, B. Expression of oestrus and timing of ovulation in pigs. J. Reprod. Fertil. Suppl. **1997**, *52*, 91–103.
7. Foxcroft, G.R.; Van De Wiel, D.F.M. *Endocrine Control of the Oestrous Cycle*; Cole, D.J.A., Foxcroft, G.R., Eds.; Butterworths: London, 1982; 161–177.

Estrus Synchronization: Cattle

Jeffrey S. Stevenson
Duane L. Davis
Kansas State University, Manhattan, Kansas, U.S.A.

INTRODUCTION

Controlling estrous cycles (day 0=onset of estrus) by synchronizing estrus facilitates artificial insemination (AI) or natural service of a high percentage of breeding age or postpartum females. As a result, it also facilitates promulgation of superior genetics of progeny-tested sires of economic worth for continued livestock improvement. Some methods are also used to delay or prevent estrus in females, induce puberty, or initiate estrous cycles in postpartum or seasonally anestrous females.

Various hormones have been tested to control the estrous cycle of domestic farm species. These include compounds that: 1) lyse the corpus luteum (CL); 2) artificially elongate the luteal phase via feeding, drenching, or injecting a progestin, or administering intravaginal sponges or inserts, or body implants that deliver a progestin; 3) induce ovulation using gonadotropins; or 4) induce ovulation using combinations of several hormones.

PROGESTINS

Progesterone is secreted by the CL and prevents estrus (sexual receptivity). When an exogenous progestin is administered for a period longer than the luteal phase of the estrous cycle (cow: 14–15 days), the CL regresses spontaneously and estrus is prevented by the exogenous progestin until treatment ends. In females whose CL regresses before progestin withdrawal, ovarian follicles continue to grow. One follicle often reaches greater than normal diameters (known as persistent follicle)[1] because the dose of progestin is inadequately low in many of the market-available progestins. Upon progestin withdrawal, oocytes shed from a persistent follicle usually are fertilized, but most embryos fail to develop, resulting in compromised fertility.

If the progestin treatment is shorter in duration, some females may have a functional CL upon progestin withdrawal and estrus will be delayed until after luteolysis occurs. Although a shorter duration of treatment is less effective in synchronizing estrus, fertility is less compromised because persistent follicles are not formed during progestin treatment.

PROGESTIN–ESTROGEN COMBINATIONS

Administration of an estrogen during metestrus (days 1–3) or early diestrus (days 4–8) generally induces premature regression of the CL. As a result, combining a short-duration (approximately 7–9 days) progestin treatment with an estrogen given at the beginning of progestin treatment improves synchrony without compromising fertility. Treatment with estrogen can ovulate, luteinize, or induce atresia of a large or dominant follicle, thus preventing formation of a persistent follicle.

PROSTAGLANDIN $F_{2\alpha}$ AND ANALOGUES

The best known luteolysin in farm animals is $PGF_{2\alpha}$. It induces luteolysis when administered by intramuscular injection or when placed into the uterus, as early as four to six days after ovulation. Therefore, $PGF_{2\alpha}$ has been used widely in estrus-synchronization programs for cattle.

A single injection of $PGF_{2\alpha}$ regresses the CL in approximately 50–60% of randomly cycling females. The CL is not responsive until after days 5–6 of the cycle. The percentage of females actually detected in estrus during five days after a single injection includes any in the responsive portion of the luteal phase at the time of injection plus those in the follicular phase that are coming into estrus spontaneously. If a second injection of $PGF_{2\alpha}$ is given 10 to 14 days after the first injection, females responding to the first injection (those recently in estrus and now in the luteal phase of their cycles) are responsive to the second injection and the remainder (those not responsive to the first injection) have a functional CL that is now responsive to $PGF_{2\alpha}$. Theoretically, estrus in all females may be synchronized after the second of two injections. Limitations to this theoretical potential include skills of those detecting estrus, luteolytic failure, or inadequate follicular development at the time of treatment. Prepubertal or early postpartum females without a functional CL are not

Encyclopedia of Animal Science
DOI: 10.1081/E-EAS 120019594

affected by $PGF_{2\alpha}$ treatment. The estrus that occurs after one or two injections is equally fertile.

PROGESTIN–PROSTAGLANDIN F$_{2\alpha}$ COMBINATIONS

Injecting $PGF_{2\alpha}$ at the end of a short-duration (7 days) progestin treatment allows estrus in nearly all females to be synchronized during a shorter treatment period. Administering progestin for approximately seven days allows any female in estrus or metestrus at the outset to advance to the luteal phase before $PGF_{2\alpha}$ is administered. Expression of estrus is prevented in the remaining females that are in proestrus or late diestrus by the progestin treatment, and those in the luteal phase respond to the injection of $PGF_{2\alpha}$. Therefore, the combination of both hormones shortens the overall period of treatment and generally allows normal fertility.[3]

GnRH OR ESTROGEN–PROGESTIN– PROSTAGLANDIN F$_{2\alpha}$ COMBINATIONS

Creating persistent follicles is a particular problem when using progestins. Persistence occurs because the exogenous dose of progestin is inadequate to inhibit normal LH pulse secretion as effectively as progesterone secreted by the CL or because greater rates of metabolism reduce biologically available progestin in lactating dairy cattle with high feed intakes. Gonadotropins or GnRH address the problem of follicle persistence by pharmacologically releasing sufficient LH to induce ovulation of LH-dependent follicles that are present at the onset of progestin treatment. As a consequence, a new follicular wave emerges and a mature follicle ovulates when progestin is withdrawn and the CL is lysed by $PGF_{2\alpha}$.[2]

A common regimen in cattle includes an injection of GnRH at the onset of progestin treatment and the injection of $PGF_{2\alpha}$ either one day before or on the day of progestin withdrawal.[3] The initial GnRH injection may produce the first postpartum ovulation, resulting in a shortened luteal phase or short cycle. The progestin primes the uterus of the anestrous cow, so when ovulation occurs, the life span of the first CL is nearly normal.[2]

For cows undergoing normal estrous cycles, the progestin is likely unnecessary and can be deleted.[4] Subsequent to luteolysis induced by $PGF_{2\alpha}$, ovulation occurs spontaneously or can be induced by an injection of estrogen or a second injection of GnRH to accommodate insemination by appointment (timed AI [TAI]).

PROTOCOLS

Examples of more common estrus-synchronization protocols are illustrated (Fig. 1). Feeding an orally active progestin (melengestrol acetate, MGA) for 14 days synchronizes estrus (see [1] in Fig. 1). Most females show estrus within two to six days after withdrawing MGA from the diet. However, this estrus is infertile in those females whose CL regressed during the progestin treatment and in which a persistent follicle formed. In practice, this first estrus is passed over and females are given an injection of $PGF_{2\alpha}$ 17 to 19 days after MGA withdrawal. To gain better control of follicular development, GnRH may be injected seven days before $PGF_{2\alpha}$. Insemination is based on detected estrus, which usually occurs between two and five days after $PGF_{2\alpha}$. An option of inseminating any noninseminated females at 72 h after $PGF_{2\alpha}$ is possible, but conception rates are usually 60–75% of those achieved after observed estrus, or a one TAI at 48 to 72 h after $PGF_{2\alpha}$ plus a second GnRH injection to ensure that ovulation occurs. Use of MGA is not approved for lactating dairy cows in the United States.

Applying an intravaginal insert that contains progesterone, in combination with an injection of $PGF_{2\alpha}$, effectively synchronizes estrus in a short-term, seven-day period (see [2] in Fig. 1). Injection of $PGF_{2\alpha}$ can occur 24 h before or at insert removal. Inseminations occur after detected estrus or by appointment at 48 to 66 h after insert removal.

A less expensive protocol (see [3] in Fig. 1) includes detection of estrus and insemination of any estrual female during six days. On the seventh day, $PGF_{2\alpha}$ is injected in any noninseminated female to induce luteolysis and estrus for subsequent insemination.

Another protocol involves giving two injections of $PGF_{2\alpha}$ 14 days apart. One can inseminate females in estrus after the second of two injections (see [4] in Fig. 1) or inseminate estrual females after the first injection (see [5] in Fig. 1) and administer a second injection only to noninseminated females. Timing of inseminations without regard to detected estrus at 72 to 80 h after the second $PGF_{2\alpha}$ injection often results in conception rates less than those for females inseminated after detected estrus.

A newer protocol (see [6] in Fig. 1) combines GnRH to induce release of follicle-stimulating hormone (FSH) and luteinizing hormone (LH) plus injection of $PGF_{2\alpha}$ seven days later. The GnRH injection better controls follicular development in some females and synchronizes it with luteolysis that follows $PGF_{2\alpha}$. About 15% of females show estrus within 24 h of $PGF_{2\alpha}$, and therefore, for optimal results, detection of estrus should begin 24 h before $PGF_{2\alpha}$.

An alternative (see [7] in Fig. 1) to the previous protocol allows for a single TAI after the injection of

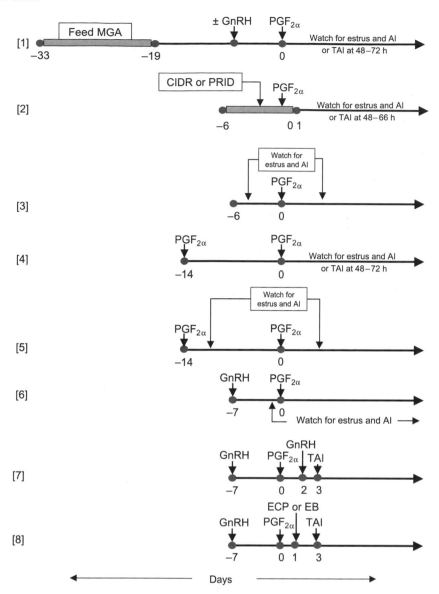

Fig. 1 Protocols used to synchronize estrus or ovulation in cattle. CIDR=controlled internal drug release (intravaginal insert that releases progesterone); EB=estradiol benzoate; ECP=estradiol cypionate; GnRH=gonadotropin-releasing hormone; MGA=melengestrol acetate; $PGF_{2\alpha}$=prostaglandin $F_{2\alpha}$; PRID=progesterone-releasing intravaginal device; TAI=timed artificial insemination. (*View this art in color at www.dekker.com.*)

$PGF_{2\alpha}$.[4] One gives a second injection of GnRH to all females at about 48 h after $PGF_{2\alpha}$ and then inseminates 0–24 h later. If estrus occurs before $PGF_{2\alpha}$ or the second GnRH injection, one should inseminate the female and discontinue the remaining protocol. To maximize pregnancy rates, inseminate after detected estrus until all remaining females are inseminated between zero and 24 h after the second GnRH injection (given 48 h after $PGF_{2\alpha}$).

An alternative to the preceding protocol replaces GnRH with estrogen (estradiol benzoate or estradiol cypionate) at 24 h after $PGF_{2\alpha}$ to induce behavioral estrus and the LH surge before AI, or in the absence of estrus, one TAI at 36 to 48 h after estrogen (see [8] in Fig. 1).

CONCLUSIONS

During the last decade, proven techniques were discovered to synchronize estrus and ovulation in cattle. Using both GnRH and $PGF_{2\alpha}$, with or without progestin treatment, combines control of follicular growth[3,5] and luteal function. These protocols allow for TAI in cattle with fertility often equal to that achieved at natural estrus.[3,4]

ARTICLES OF FURTHER INTEREST

Beef Cattle: Reproduction Management, p. 88
Dairy Cattle: Reproduction Management, p. 275
Estrus Synchronization: Horses, Pigs, Sheep, and Goats, p. 353

REFERENCES

1. Ireland, J.J.; Mihm, M.; Austin, E.; Diskin, M.G.; Roche, J.F. Historical perspective of turnover of dominant follicles during the bovine estrous cycle: Key concepts, studies, advancements, and terms. J. Dairy Sci. **2000**, *83* (7), 1648–1658.
2. Thompson, K.E.; Stevenson, J.S.; Lamb, G.C.; Grieger, D.M.; Loest, C.A. Follicular, hormonal, and pregnancy responses of early postpartum suckled beef cows to GnRH, norgestomet, and prostaglandin $F_{2\alpha}$. J. Anim. Sci. **1999**, *77* (7), 1823–1832.
3. Stevenson, J.S.; Lamb, G.C.; Johnson, S.K.; Medina-Britos, M.A.; Grieger, D.M.; Harmoney, K.R.; Cartmill, J.A.; El-Zarkouny, S.Z.; Dahlen, C.R.; Marple, T.J. Supplemental norgestomet, progesterone, or melengestrol acetate increases pregnancy rates in suckled beef cows after timed inseminations. J. Anim. Sci. **2003**, *81* (3), 571–586.
4. Stevenson, J.S. Reproductive management of dairy cows in high milk-producing herds. J. Dairy Sci. **2001**, *84* (E. Suppl.), E128–E143.
5. Driancourt, M.A. Regulation of ovarian follicular dynamics in farm animals. Implications for manipulation of reproduction. Theriogenology **2001**, *55* (6), 1211–1239.

Estrus Synchronization: Horses, Pigs, Sheep, and Goats

Duane L. Davis
Jeffrey S. Stevenson
Kansas State University, Manhattan, Kansas, U.S.A.

INTRODUCTION

Controlling the time of estrus facilitates several management goals. It is desirable to have females in estrus at certain times to provide maximum use of intensive pork production facilities, to schedule breeding of mares to stallions, and as a part of artificial insemination (AI) programs. The general approaches for all species are outlined elsewhere in this encyclopedia. These are: 1) lysing the corpus luteum or corpora lutea (CL); 2) artificially extending the luteal phase by administering a progestin; 3) inducing follicle growth and ovulation using gonadotropins; or 4) using combination protocols. However, differences in the reproductive physiology of the various livestock species require unique estrus-synchronization protocols for each species. Furthermore, before animals are treated, the regulations governing use of each drug in the country or jurisdiction should be determined.

HORSE

Mares respond to $PGF_{2\alpha}$ products with CL regression,[1] but only after the CL has formed and the mare is in diestrus (i.e., day 5 after ovulation). For mares, day 0 is ovulation rather than onset of estrus, as in other species. Duration of estrus is variable, and ovulation does not occur until the last one or two days of estrus; therefore, it is not practical to determine the timing of $PGF_{2\alpha}$ administration based on the onset of estrus. Treatment of mares with responsive CL generally results in estrus in two to four days and ovulation in eight to 12 days.

The orally active progestin, altrenogest (Regumate®), is effective for regulating the estrous cycle of mares.[2] Mares having regular cycles should be fed altrenogest daily for 15 consecutive days (see [1] in Fig. 1). Altrenogest may be administered by adding it to a concentrate mix or by direct placement on the posterior of the mare's tongue using a syringe. Estrus is expected an average of five days after the last altrenogest treatment and ovulation occurs near the end of estrus.

Either luteolytic or progestin methods can be combined with human chorionic gonadotropin (hCG) or with a gonadotropin hormone releasing hormone (GnRH) implant (Ovuplant®) to control timing of ovulation.[3,4] These products are generally administered when a follicle sufficiently large (30 to 35 mm) is detected. Ovulation is expected 24 to 48 h later and mating or insemination is recommended 12 to 24 h before ovulation.

PIG

Gilts often reach puberty just before the beginning of breeding. Gilts that are near spontaneous puberty may respond to daily exposure to a boar and be in estrus in four to 10 days. A gonadotropin, either eCG (500 to 1200 IU) or PG600® (200 IU hCG + 400 IU PMSG) may also be injected to induce puberty and the peak response in estrus is generally five to six days after injection.

Suckling by the litter prevents resumption of estrous cycles and is widely used to synchronize estrus in sows. Suckling usually inhibits estrus during at least the first four weeks after farrowing and may be effective as long as six weeks. Most sows return to estrus between three and seven days after their litter is weaned. Gonadotropins may be administered at weaning or 24 h after weaning, to further regulate the follicular phase and increase the percent of sows promptly returning to estrus.

Once estrous cycles are initiated, they can be modified in a variety of ways. Many of the synthetic progestins used for synchronizing estrus in other species result in a high incidence of follicular cysts and infertility in pigs. A progestin that is effective in pigs is altrenogest. The dose for gilts is 15 mg per day mixed in the diet or top-dressed. A 14- to 18-day feeding period produces good synchrony of estrus[5] (see [1] in Fig. 1). Altrenogest synchronizes estrus when treatment has continued beyond the time of spontaneous luteolysis in all females in the group. With small groups and when the date of last estrus is known, it may be possible to shorten the treatment period by delaying treatment until the first gilt or sow reaches day 14 of her cycle.

Encyclopedia of Animal Science
DOI: 10.1081/E-EAS 120024369

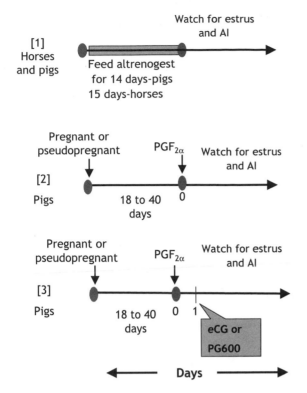

Fig. 1 Protocols to synchronize estrus or ovulation in horses and pigs. PGF$_{2\alpha}$=prostaglandin F$_{2\alpha}$; eCG=equine chorionic gonadotropin; PG600$^{®}$=400 IU eCG + 200 IU human chorionic gonadotropin. (*View this art in color at www.dekker.com.*)

Technology for shortening the porcine cycle has not been developed because the CL of pigs are not responsive to known luteolytic agents until at least day 12 of the cycle.[6] Another approach is to interrupt estrous cycles by first establishing pregnancy[7] or pseudopregnancy.[8] The latter is accomplished by administering an estrogen on days 11 to 15 to mimic the pregnancy recognition signal. In early pregnancy (or pseudopregnancy), the CL become responsive to PGF$_{2\alpha}$ and luteolysis can be induced with exogenous PGF$_{2\alpha}$ (see [2] in Fig. 1). A single dose of PGF$_{2\alpha}$ may be given, or two doses eight to 12 h apart may be more effective. This approach can be combined with gonadotropic hormones to increase ovulation rate and/or control the time of ovulation (see [3] in Fig. 1). For example, pregnant females may be given PGF$_{2\alpha}$ to regress the CL of pregnancy, followed 24 h later with an injection of gonadotropin, either eCG (500 to 1200 IU) or PG600. Inseminations may be based on detected estrus. Further control of ovulation timing is possible by administering hCG (500 to 750 IU) at 72 to 84 h after the gonadotropin treatment. Ovulation is expected 40 to 44 h after hCG and inseminations eight to 16 h before ovulation are most effective.

SHEEP

Sheep are seasonal breeders and the occurrence of estrus can be controlled by altering the photoperiod, stimulation by presence of a ram, and by various hormones.[9]

Ewes in seasonal anestrus may come to estrus in response to extended day length (~16 h) by supplementing light for 30 or more days followed by 60 days or more of 16 h of darkness per day to mimic the seasonal changes normally entraining cyclicity (see [1] in Fig. 2). This treatment is more effective when females are exposed to progestin treatments or teasers (intact males or androgen-treated, castrated males or females) near the end of the program. Exposure to novel teasers generally results in LH production and ovulation without estrus within a few days followed by normal estrus and ovulation in 18 to 24 days. Success is greater in breeds that are less seasonal in their breeding patterns. In fact, stimulation of less seasonal breeds with ram or teaser exposure without photoperiod manipulation may be highly effective.

As in other species, PGF$_{2\alpha}$ or its analogues are only effective for rescheduling estrus when CL are present and therefore should be used to synchronize estrus in cycling

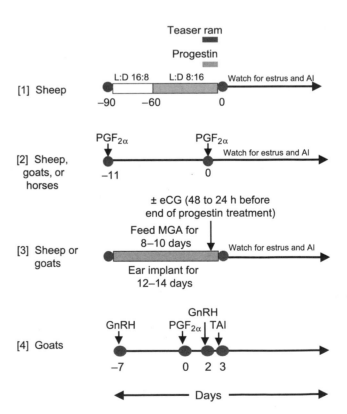

Fig. 2 Protocols to synchronize estrus or ovulation in sheep and goats. eCG=equine chorionic gonadotropin; GnRH=gonadotropin-releasing hormone; MGA=melengestrol acetate; PGF$_{2\alpha}$=prostaglandin F$_{2\alpha}$; TAI=timed artificial insemination. (*View this art in color at www.dekker.com.*)

females during the normal breeding season. Estrus usually occurs within 36 to 48 h after $PGF_{2\alpha}$. Flocks can be syn chronized by administering two injections of $PGF_{2\alpha}$ 11 days apart (see [2] in Fig. 2). Estrus usually occurs within 36 to 48 h after the second $PGF_{2\alpha}$ injection. Other protocols used in cattle, such as administering GnRH seven days before $PGF_{2\alpha}$, may have merit in ewes.

Hormonal synchronization of estrus in sheep may be accomplished by administration of progestin (feeding oral active progestins, providing intravaginal sponges or inserts containing progestin or progesterone, or ear implants containing norgestomet) plus injections of eCG near or at the end of progestin treatment (see [3] in Fig. 2). Feeding the orally active progestin melengestrol acetate (0.25 mg per female per day) for 8–10 days produces similar synchrony to ear implants containing norgestomet (3 mg per female) administered for 12 to 14 days. Estrus generally occurs 24 to 56 h after progestin withdrawal.

GOATS

Hormonal manipulations of the doe include administration of a progestin for nine to 20 days combined with an injection of eCG either 48 h before, or at progestin withdrawal (see [3] in Fig. 2).[10] During the breeding season, progestin treatments < 16 days are combined with $PGF_{2\alpha}$ to ensure luteolysis occurs before or at progestin withdrawal. Availability of progestin sources for synchronizing estrus varies among countries and includes intravaginal sponges containing fluorogestone acetate or medroxyprogesterone acetate, and intravaginal inserts containing progesterone. If a progestin is not available, use of GnRH preceding $PGF_{2\alpha}$ is a reasonable approach in does, such as is done in cattle (see [4] in Fig. 2).

CONCLUSION

Several management techniques and pharmacological agents have been developed to schedule estrus in female livestock. There are physiological differences between species that limit the use of many of these techniques and drugs to the species for which they were developed. There also are governmental regulations that vary by country and species. Application of estrus synchronization programs should begin with an evaluation of available tools and the regulations applicable to the species and country.

ARTICLES OF FURTHER INTEREST

Estrus Synchronization: Cattle, p. 349
Horses: Reproduction Management, p. 536
Sheep: Reproduction Management, p. 803
Swine: Reproductive Management, p. 831

REFERENCES

1. Allen, W.R.; Rowson, L.E.A. Control of the mare's oestrus cycle by prostaglandins. J. Reprod. Fertil. **1973**, *33* (3), 539–543.
2. Squires, E.L.; Heesemann, C.P.; Webel, S.K.; Shideler, R.K.; Voss, J.L. Relationship of altrenogest to ovarian activity, hormone concentrations and fertility of mares. J. Anim. Sci. **1983**, *56* (4), 901–910.
3. Meinert, C.; Silva, J.F.; Kroetz, I.; Klug, E.; Trigg, T.E.; Hoppen, H.O.; Jochle, W. Advancing the time of ovulation in the mare with a short-term implant releasing the GnRH analogue deslorelin. Equine Vet. J. **1993**, *25* (1), 65–68.
4. Loy, R.G.; Hughes, J.P. The effects of human chorionic gonadotrophin on ovulation, length of estrus, and fertility in the mare. Cornell Vet. **1966**, *56* (1), 41–50.
5. Stevenson, J.S.; Davis, D.L. Estrous synchronization and fertility in gilts after 14- or 18-day feeding of altrenogest beginning at estrus or diestrus. J. Anim. Sci. **1982**, *55* (1), 119–123.
6. Guthrie, H.D.; Polge, C. Treatment of pregnant gilts with a prostaglandin analogue, Cloprostenol, to control oestrus and fertility. J. Reprod. Fertil. **1978**, *52* (2), 271–273.
7. Meeker, D.L.; Rothschild, M.R.; Christian, L.L. Breed differences in return to estrus after PGF2 alpha-induced abortions in swine. J. Anim. Sci. **1985**, *61* (2), 354–357.
8. Zavy, M.T.; Geisert, R.D.; Buchanan, D.S.; Norton, S.A. Estrogen-induced pseudopregnancy in gilts: Its use in estrus synchronization and subsequent influence on litter response. Theriogenology **1988**, *30* (4), 721–731.
9. Sharkey, S.; Callan, R.J.; Mortimer, R.; Kimberling, C. Reproductive techniques in sheep. Vet. Clin. North Am., Food Anim. Pract. **2001**, *17* (2), 420–435.
10. Bretzlaff, K.N.; Romano, J.E. Advanced reproductive techniques in goats. Vet. Clin. North Am., Food Anim. Pract. **2001**, *17* (2), 421–455.

Farm Animal Welfare: Philosophical Aspects

Paul B. Thompson
Michigan State University, East Lansing, Michigan, U.S.A.

INTRODUCTION

Traditionally thought of as part of the art of husbandry, the welfare of farm animals has become a critical area of livestock production and animal science. The notion of welfare is derived from economics and utilitarian philosophy. Its application to animal production reflects that heritage. Developing and applying measures of welfare continue to require philosophically based assumptions, working principles, and judgments.

WELFARE ETHICS AND ANIMAL AGRICULTURE

Welfare is a normative or evaluative term indicating how well or poorly a creature does (e.g., fares) in a given situation or setting. The term became especially important in the British utilitarian tradition of ethics and social thought made famous by Jeremy Bentham (1748–1832) and John Stuart Mill (1806–1873), by which conduct was evaluated in light of its impact on human welfare. Many approaches in ethics hold that human conduct must abide by predetermined constraints. In contrast, utilitarian ethics claim that actions or policies are justified only if they have the best possible impact on the happiness or satisfaction (e.g., welfare) of affected parties, without regard to whether conduct conforms to legal, religious, and customary rules and codes. As early as 1789, Bentham argued that the concept of welfare applied to both human beings and nonhuman animals capable of suffering.

For a utilitarian, ethics demands that one anticipate the benefits and harms to everyone affected for each of one's options, and then choose the option producing the greatest good for the greatest number. Utilitarianism gave rise to the field of welfare economics, which developed economic tools for evaluating the costs and benefits of alternative social policies, especially those intended to secure the well-being of indigent people (hence the popular meaning of the word welfare).

Welfare Economics

Attempts to measure or quantify welfare are subject to a number of difficult conceptual and methodological prob-

lems, even when the problem is confined to human beings. Economists have argued that market prices provide a measure of the relative value that human beings place on goods (such as food, automobiles, or entertainment) that are easily bought and sold, but concede that other goods (such as health, environmental quality, or community) resist the mechanisms of ordinary economic exchange. Providing such goods may require a degree of cooperative effort that borders on coercion. Furthermore, some people may be effectively excluded from participating in market exchange (either by inequities in law or poverty), and the impact that an activity or good has on their welfare will not be reflected in the market price. Goods having an impact on welfare that is not reflected by market price are referred to as externalities in welfare economics.

The identification, conceptualization, and quantification of health, environmental, or social externalities can be confusing, contentious, and inherently philosophical. Additional philosophical difficulties arise when one attempts to sum or compare impacts on welfare accruing to different parties. Kenneth Arrow (b. 1921) proved an impossibility theorem, showing that it is mathematically impossible to derive an optimal social welfare function (that is, a calculation of the greatest good for society as a whole) from measurements of the welfare of individuals.[1] For these reasons, welfare economics remains one of the most philosophical areas of modern economic theory.[2] Many of these issues carry over to any attempt to understand the welfare of animals.

Application to Farm Animals

The externality model applies to the welfare of farm animals. Historically, farm animals have been held as chattel by producers. Concern for the welfare of farm animals has traditionally been understood as a personal ethical responsibility of individual owners. However, as the livestock industries have become highly competitive, producers are under increasing pressure to utilize the most cost-effective methods for raising and handling animals. Although some adverse effects on livestock affect producer profitability, those that do not affect profitability represent costs that are borne by animals, rather than being internalized in those production costs that are eventually passed on to consumers. These external costs—costs

Encyclopedia of Animal Science
DOI: 10.1081/E-EAS 120019596

above and beyond those reflected in the normal profitability of livestock farming—represent the basic problem of farm animal welfare. How should these external costs be understood, and what responses are appropriate?

The model for answering these questions that has been most widely adopted in the animal sciences has been to utilize a blend of standard veterinary health indicators, physiological stress measures, behavioral studies, and cognitive performance measures to form an estimate of how animals are faring in a given setting. This approach to animal welfare has been applied to develop comparative estimates of farm animal welfare relative to alternative housing and production methods, including cage and pen size, water and feed mechanisms, gestation stalls, and the use of methods for production practices such as beak trimming, milking, and molting (see Animal Welfare Science). Once such measures were available, one would then use them to reflect costs borne by animals in a given production system, and these costs could, in principle, be compared to costs and benefits that would be borne by humans in the form of higher production cost and increased food prices.[3,4] This general model follows the basic outline of utilitarian ethics in that each production option is evaluated in terms of its expected impact on the welfare of affected parties (human and animal), and then the option producing the greatest good is the one seen as ethically justified.

Philosophical Difficulties

Historically, animal welfare scientists have not always agreed on how to prioritize the indicators listed earlier. The use of multiple indicators to determine welfare also leads to an analogue of Arrow's impossibility theorem: Since improvements in one parameter can be correlated with declining measurements in another, there may be no way to create a consistent cardinal ordering of animal welfare under a variety of different production regimes. Another problem associated with comparing production systems is that situational features such as climate and especially husbandry practices may have more impact on the welfare of animals than do the production systems that have been tested empirically. Hence, whereas animal welfare science provides a basis for understanding how animals fare in production settings, well-known problems are associated with summing and comparing individual welfare measurements. As such, like welfare economics, animal welfare is likely to remain dependent on philosophical value judgments.

The classic utilitarian response to externalities has been regulations that require producers to mitigate harm to others. This allows the cost of mitigation to be inter-nalized and reflected in the cost of producing goods. However, many animal producers continue to see animal welfare as a personal ethical responsibility and see government intervention in their operations as a form of interference. It may thus be necessary to interpret farm animal welfare as one among several elements that would need to be addressed in a complete approach to animal ethics. Ethical responsibilities associated with traditional notions of stewardship of animals might provide a useful complement to welfare-based approaches to animal ethics.[5,6] Advocacy groups have often argued that a rights approach, stressing constraints on producer behavior, might be required.

Animal Rights

Some would argue that if the problem consists in the fact that animal interests are external to decision making in animal agriculture, the most direct legal response is to provide an actionable basis for advocates to intervene in policy and production practices. Recognizing animal rights as the basis for human's ethical responsibility to animals provides philosophical support for legal action on behalf of animals. Animal rights philosophy has been advocated by Tom Regan (b. 1938), who argues that the utilitarian arguments in Peter Singer's (b. 1946) widely read book[7] do not provide a strong enough basis for protecting animal interests.[8]

Effective legal rights allow affected parties (or their representatives) recourse against harms or costs that are inflicted on them by others. Once such rights are in place, affected parties may enter into negotiations for compensation, allowing formerly external costs to be reflected in normal economic activity. Animal rights may thus represent an alternative response to the problem of external costs to animal welfare. This intervention might take the form of government regulation of animal production, or the creation of new legal standing that would allow court cases to be brought on animals' behalf.[9]

It is not clear how such an approach would be operationalized as a response to problems in farm animal welfare. One question concerns who would be entitled to represent the interests in a legal or regulatory proceeding. If animal advocates were to take on this role, there would be a considerable shift in the property rights traditionally held by producers, and the economic repercussions of this shift might be considerable. Furthermore, the rhetorical use of animal rights as a catch-phrase representing an extreme position on the human use of animals may serve as an additional political barrier to any use of rights reform as a strategy for addressing farm animal welfare. As such, an animal rights approach represents at best one among many possible responses to resolving the problem of farm animal welfare, rather than a clear alternative to utilitarianism.

may result in innovative approaches to problems in measuring animal welfare.

CONCLUSION

Animal welfare can be understood as an external cost borne by animals and not reflected in the prices paid by food consumers in the industrial food system. Animal scientists have developed a utilitarian approach to this problem by utilizing animal welfare science to quantify the costs to animals, whereas some animal advocates prefer a rights approach. However, neither of these approaches escapes the need for judgment and assumptions about how to frame problems and interpret values.

At present there is no widely accepted or noncontroversial philosophical approach to augmenting scientific studies of animal welfare, nor is there a clear way to resolve conflicts between utilitarian and rights-based approaches. Pragmatic ethics calls for systematic articulation, discussion, and debate over uneliminable subjective, interpretive, and judgmental assumptions. Articulation of assumptions and opportunity to challenge and debate them at least offer the possibility of consensus solutions and

REFERENCES

1. Arrow, K. *Social Choice and Individual Values*. Wiley and Co: New York, 1951.
2. Sen, A.K. *On Ethics and Economics*. Oxford U. Press: Oxford, 1987.
3. Rollin, B.E. *Farm Animal Welfare*. Iowa State U. Press: Ames, 1995.
4. Appleby, M.C. *What Should We Do About Animal Welfare?*. Blackwell Science: Oxford, UK, 1999.
5. Fraser, D. Animal ethics and animal welfare science: Bridging the two cultures. Appl. Anim. Behav. Sci. **1999**, *65*, 171–189.
6. Thompson, P.B. Getting Pragmatic About Farm Animal Welfare. In *Animal Pragmatism: Rethinking Human-Nonhuman Relationships*. McKenna, E., Light, A., Eds.; Indiana U. Press: Bloomington, IN, 2004. Forthcoming.
7. Singer, P. *Animal Liberation*. Avon Books: New York, 1977.
8. Regan, T. *The Case for Animal Rights*. U. California Press: Berkeley, 1986.
9. Wise, S.M. *Rattling the Cage: Toward Legal Rights for Animals*. Perseus Press: Cambridge, MA, 2000.

Feed Quality: External Flow Markers

Alexander N. Hristov
University of Idaho, Moscow, Idaho, U.S.A.

F

INTRODUCTION

Tracers or markers are used to study digestion, intake, or pool sizes and kinetics of digesta fractions in specific organs or the entire digestive tract of farm animals. Digesta kinetic analyses are integral parts of animal nutrition research. Nutrients (and symbiotic microbial mass) are associated and leave digestive compartments with the fluid or the solid digesta phases. Thus, the rate of flow of digesta dictates, in the large part, nutrient availability for growth and production. This entry will briefly discuss the most common external markers used in animal nutrition research with particular emphasis on ruminant nutrition.

FLUID AND PARTICULATE EXTERNAL MARKERS

In general terms, a tracer is *a detectable substance added to a chemical, biological, or physical system to follow its process or to study distribution of the substance in the system.*[1] An external marker is a substance that is either not present or present in minute concentration in the diet. An ideal marker must: (a) not be absorbed throughout the digestive tract; (b) not affect or be affected by digestive processes, including microbial fermentation; (c) follow the kinetics of and not separate from the material/digesta phase it is to mark; and (d) have a specific and sensitive method of analysis.[2] Detailed reviews on marker use in animal nutrition have been published.[2–5] Passage rate and residence time of digesta can be determined from a given meal to which a unique marker has been applied. Therefore, external markers and pulse dosing are the techniques of choice when digesta flow characteristics are studied.

Fluid Markers

Digesta, particularly ruminal contents, is not a homogenous entity. Digesta phases have different composition and flow characteristics, which necessitates a compartmental approach and the use of separate markers for as many digesta pools as can be reliably distinguished by physical or chemical means. With ruminal contents, the most common approach is fractionation into fluid and solid phases. The fluid phase includes not only solutes, but also small feed particles, which are densely populated with microbial cells and obey the kinetics of the fluid. Fluid markers should behave as ideal solutes and have a molecular weight high enough not to be absorbed throughout the digestive tract. A number of fluid markers have been proposed and employed with varying success.

Polyethylene glycol (PEG) with a molecular weight of 1000 Da or greater (usually 4000 Da) has been extensively, and relatively successfully, used as a solute marker. Studies with rabbits and sheep, however, showed incomplete (95%) recovery in digesta and feces. Reports also indicated that PEG was not completely associated with water in beet pulp tissues, can be precipitated by dietary tannins, and binds to particulate matter if digesta is frozen. PEG is assayed by turbidimetry.

Complexes of cobalt (Co) and chromium (Cr) with ethylenediamine tetraacetic acid (EDTA)[6,7] occupy larger fluid space in the rumen and have practically replaced PEG as fluid markers. Similar to PEG, both chelates are slightly absorbed (at approximately 5%) through the rumen wall. Adsorption of Cr-EDTA to particulate matter has been reported at low concentrations and is affected by osmotic pressure in the rumen, which could lead to overestimation of water flow. Co–EDTA is prepared as the sodium or lithium (Li) salt of the monovalent Co–EDTA anion. Both compounds are readily soluble in water, relatively easy to prepare with a yield of approximately 90% (the Li salt in the case of Co–EDTA), and are stable on drying. A common practice is to use Li/Co–EDTA as a fluid and Cr-mordanted fiber as a solid marker (see the following discussion). Cobalt and Cr are routinely analyzed by atomic absorption spectrophotometry, neutron activation, or plasma emission spectroscopy.

Particulate Markers

Compared to solute markers, particulate digesta markers are considerably less reliable. Problems related to recovery, migration, representativeness of labeled fraction kinetics, and effect on digestion and the ruminal ecosystem make the choice of particulate marker a difficult one. Stained feed particles and synthetic organic materials such as plastic and rubber pieces, cotton knots,

Encyclopedia of Animal Science
DOI: 10.1081/E-EAS 120027391

charcoal, and others have been used as solid markers in the past. Lack of reliable quantitative assays, different physical properties (specific gravity and size) than those of the particulate digesta fractions in the case of nonfeed materials, and uncertainty as to what extent particle kinetics represent the kinetics of the fraction they are intended to label have rendered these techniques of little value in animal nutrition research.

A variety of heavy metals and rare earth elements, particularly those forming strong bonds with feed/digesta particles, have been successfully employed as particulate markers. An important prerequisite is that these elements are either not present or present in minimal concentration in soil and plants. Metal oxides (Cr and titanium) have been proposed as digestibility markers. Chromium sesquioxide (Cr_2O_3) is one of the most commonly used digestibility markers, but it is an unreliable passage marker because its physical properties and flow kinetics have little resemblance to the flow characteristics of any digesta fraction.[2] Chromium forms strong ligands with plant cell wall constituents, and Cr-mordanted fiber is used as a particulate flow marker.[7] Nonfiber substances are removed before binding in order to improve retention of Cr on the cell wall matrix. Concentration of Cr, however, dramatically increases the density and reduces digestibility of the labeled particles. It is recommended that the Cr concentration be reduced to 10 g/kg hay (or 23 g/kg feed pellets) in order to minimize the effect of the heavy metal on particle density.[4] Particle size of the Cr-mordanted fiber can also significantly affect the rate of passage.

Other metals such as ruthenium (Ru) and hafnium (Hf) have been proposed as particulate markers. Ruthenium is usually used in the form of Ru–phenanthroline (Ru–phe or ^{103}Ru–phe) in low concentration, which reportedly does not adversely affect microbial fermentation in the rumen.[8] Ruthenium has a strong affinity for particulate matter, but no specific affinity for binding to fiber fractions, and a very high rate of recovery in the digestive tract. Hafnium has strong binding properties, is resistant to displacement at low pH,[9] and can be a suitable particulate flow marker (specifically for the more acidic segments of the gastrointestinal tract) if applied at low concentrations in order to minimize the effect on particle density and digestibility.

Various rare earth elements (cerium, europium, ytterbium, terbium, samarium, lutetium, lanthanum, samarium, neodymium, dysprosium, erbium) have been used as particulate markers. These elements are inert, indigestible, and, if feed/digesta samples are properly labeled (and within the normal pH range for ruminal digesta), are relatively resistant to displacement from the treated material.[5] Dissociation in the acidic, postruminal

sites is of little importance in digesta flow studies. The number of acid-resistant binding sites for rare earths on feedstuffs is low (2 to 30 mg rare earth/g DM) and should not be exceeded.[9]

Relatively large amounts of feed have to be labeled in order to achieve sufficiently high marker concentrations in digesta.[5] The strength of binding will depend on the application method used. Simple spraying will saturate both strong and weak binding sites and will result in significant marker migration in the rumen. A strong relationship between gastrointestinal mean residence time of La, Yb, and Tb and potentially indigestible fiber was established for cottonseed-based diets.[10] The most commonly used rare earths give similar digesta kinetic estimates and can be used to label different particles[11] or dietary ingredients. Ytterbium is perhaps the element of choice since it is relatively inexpensive, has a low analytical detection limit, and forms strong complexes with feed particles. Rare earths can be assayed by neutron activation analysis, plasma emission spectroscopy, and flameless atomic absorption spectroscopy.

Even-chain n-alkanes occur in low concentrations in plants and were used as particulate phase markers delivered by various techniques (in most cases, with cellulose as a carrier), i.e., gelatin capsules, impregnated filter paper, or grass particles, or by being sprayed onto the forage. Recovery in the feces of the most commonly used external alkane marker (dotriacontane, C_{32}) was around 87%.[4]

Internal markers flow with undigested feed residues and do not affect particle digestion kinetics, but they are not unique to a given meal and can be used as flow markers only with rumen evacuation or slaughter techniques. Indigestible fractions of plant cell walls can be intrinsically labeled with stable or radioactive isotopes of carbon (C)[12] or with ^{15}N (ADF-^{15}N)[13] and used as particulate flow markers. Both C and N are incorporated in indigestible as well as digestible fractions, and care must be taken to remove potentially digestible C or N before analysis.

CONCLUSIONS

Flow kinetics of the digesta fluid phase can be reliably determined using EDTA complexes of Cr or Co. A number of solid external markers have been utilized with variable success in animal nutrition research. Mordanting fiber with heavy metals can potentially affect digestion and flow characteristics of the labeled material. When properly used, rare earth elements are the particulate marker of choice. Intrinsic labeling of forage plant cell walls with stable isotopes, particularly ^{15}N, provides the advantage of being unique to a given meal without the negative impact on particle density and digestion associated with the most common external markers.

REFERENCES

1. Tracer. *Encyclopædia Britannica*; Encyclopædia Britannica Premium Service, Dec. 20, 2003. <http://www.britannica.com/eb/article?eu=75027>.

2. Owens, F.N.; Hanson, C.F. External and internal markers for appraising the site and extent of digestion in ruminants. J. Dairy Sci. **1992**, *75* (9), 2605–2617.

3. Kotb, A.R.; Luckey, T.D. Markers in nutrition. Nutr. Abstr. Rev. **1972**, *42* (3), 813–845.

4. Marais, J.P. Use of Markers. In *Farm Animal Metabolism and Nutrition*; D'Mello, J.P.F., Ed.; CABI Publishing: Wallingford, UK, 2000; 255–277.

5. Ellis, W.C.; Matis, J.H.; Hill, T.M.; Murphy, M.R. Methodology for Estimating Digestion and Passage Kinetics of Forages. In *Forage Quality, Evaluation and Utilization*; Fahey, G.C., Jr., Collins, M., Mertens, D.R., Moser, L.E., Eds.; American Society of Agronomy: Madison, WI, USA, 1994; 682–756.

6. Downes, A.M.; McDonald, I.W. The chromium-51 complex of ethylenediamine tetraacetic acid as a solute rumen marker. Brit. J. Nutr. **1964**, *18* (1), 153–162.

7. Uden, P.; Colucci, P.E.; Van Soest, P.J. Investigation of chromium, cerium and cobalt as markers in digesta. Rate of passage studies. J. Sci. Food Agric. **1980**, *31* (7), 625–632.

8. Tan, T.N.; Weston, H.; Hogan, J.P. Use of ^{103}Ru-labelled tris (1,10-phenanthroline) ruthenium (II) chloride as a marker in digestion studies with sheep. Int. J. Appl. Radiat. Isot. **1971**, *22* (5), 301–308.

9. Worley, R.; Clearfield, A.; Ellis, W.C. Binding affinity and capacities for ytterbium (3+) and hafnium (4+) by chemical entities of plant tissue fragments. J. Anim. Sci. **2002**, *80* (12), 3307–3314.

10. Ellis, W.C.; Wylie, M.J.; Matis, J.H. Validity of specifically applied rare earth elements and compartmental models for estimating flux of undigested plant tissue residues through the gastrointestinal tract of ruminants. J. Anim. Sci. **2002**, *80* (10), 2753–2758.

11. Hristov, A.N.; Ahvenjarvi, S.; Huhtanen, P.; McAllister, T.A. Composition and digestive tract retention time of ruminal particles with functional specific gravity greater or less than 1.02. J. Anim. Sci. **2003**, *81* (10), 2639–2648.

12. Smith, L.W. A review of the use of intrinsically ^{14}C and rare earth-labeled neutral detergent fiber to estimate particle digestion and passage. J. Anim. Sci. **1989**, *67* (8), 2123–2128.

13. Huhtanen, P.; Hristov, A.N. Estimating passage kinetics using fiber-bound ^{15}N as an internal marker. Anim. Feed Sci. Technol. **2001**, *94* (1–2), 29–41.

Feed Quality: Natural Plant Markers—Alkanes

Hugh Dove
CSIRO Plant Industry, Canberra, Australia

Robert W. Mayes
Macaulay Institute Aberdeen, U.K.

INTRODUCTION

The measurement of diet composition and total intake of grazing animals has always been difficult and error-prone, mainly because of limitations in the available techniques. A relatively recent development has been the use of plant wax compounds, especially the saturated hydrocarbons (alkanes), as fecal marker compounds that can be measured in dietary components and feces, and that permit more accurate estimates of diet composition and intake.

THE CONCEPT OF FECAL MARKERS

Fecal markers can be defined as substances of dietary origin found in the feces (often referred to as internal markers) or substances that are absent from the diet (or present in very small amounts), but which are given by oral dosing (external markers). An ideal marker is one that: 1) is completely recovered in the feces; 2) is chemically discrete and accurately quantifiable; 3) is inert, with no effect on digestion or passage through the gut and no toxic effect; and 4) is physically similar to the contents of the digestive tract.[1,2] To date, no ideal marker has been found; the suitability of existing markers depends on the purpose to which they are put.

Main Uses of Fecal Markers

The fecal output (FO) of an animal depends on its intake (I) and the proportion of this that remains undigested. This proportion can be calculated as $(1-D)$, where D is the digestibility of the diet (D). In mathematical terms:

$$FO = I \times (1 - D)$$

Rearranging this relationship provides the major approach to estimating intake:

$$I = FO/(1 - D)$$

External markers have been used for many years to determine FO. They are given as an oral dose once or twice daily, or in the form of a controlled-release device, which is dosed once and then resides in the digestive tract, releasing a known daily dose of marker. The FO is estimated from the dilution of the marker dose in feces.

Indigestible substances in the diet can also be used as fecal markers. In this case, they are functioning as internal markers. The increase in the fecal concentration of marker relative to the concentration in the diet provides an estimate of digestibility (D), which, in the previous equation, also allows the estimation of intake.

Many dietary substances have been evaluated as digestibility markers, and none has proved wholly successful. Consequently, digestibility has routinely been determined using laboratory procedures imitating the process of digestion (in vitro digestibility).

ALKANES AS NATURAL PLANT MARKERS

Plant wax compounds offer major advantages as possible fecal markers. They are a readily analyzed, normal part of the diet, and are relatively inert, with no adverse effects at normal intakes. Moreover, the patterns of the different plant-wax compounds differ between plant species, providing a means of identifying the species composition of the diet. Previous fecal markers have not permitted this.

Plant Wax Components

Almost all higher plants have, on their outer surfaces, a layer of epicuticular wax containing a complex mixture of aliphatic lipids. The major components of plant wax are listed in Table 1; most classes of compounds are present as mixtures of individual compounds with differing carbon chain length. Only the alkanes, wax esters, and the long-chain fatty acids and alcohols will be discussed in detail.

Hydrocarbons

Hydrocarbons are present in the cuticular wax of most plants, mainly as mixtures of *n*-alkanes, but are rarely the

Encyclopedia of Animal Science
DOI: 10.1081/E-EAS 120027390

Table 1 Major components of plant epicuticular wax

Component	Remarks
Hydrocarbons	Saturated straight-chain hydrocarbons (*n*-alkanes) and branched-chain alkanes; unsaturated hydrocarbons (alkenes). Predominantly odd-numbered carbon chains
Wax esters	Esters of long-chain fatty acids and fatty alcohols (mainly even-numbered carbon chains C32–C64)
Free long-chain fatty alcohols	Predominantly even-numbered carbon chains
Free long-chain fatty acids	Predominantly even-numbered carbon chains
Long-chain fatty aldehydes and ketones	Quantitative analytical procedure not yet established
β-diketones	Quantitative analytical procedure not yet established
Sterols[a]	Potentially difficult to separate from alcohols

[a]Not part of plant wax, but extracted together with plant wax components.

major component of plant wax. Their carbon chain lengths range from C21 to C37, with over 90% by weight having odd-numbered carbon chains. In pasture plants, C29, C31, and C33 predominate. Alkanes are easily analyzed and relatively inert, and thus have received the most attention as potential fecal markers.

Wax Esters, Fatty Acids, and Alcohols

Wax esters arise from linkages between long-chain fatty acids and alcohols, and are usually the main components of cuticular wax. Free (unesterified) long-chain fatty acids and alcohols are also usually present. Existing procedures for analyzing plant wax markers hydrolyze wax esters into their component fatty acids and alcohols, and thus quantify total fatty acids and alcohols. The esters, free fatty acids, and alcohols have therefore not yet been evaluated as markers. The relatively high fecal recoveries

of fatty acids and alcohols, plus their wide variation in pattern between plants species means that the compounds have great potential to complement *n*-alkanes as diet composition markers.

USING *n*-ALKANES TO ESTIMATE DIET COMPOSITION

Cuticular wax alkane patterns differ markedly between plant species (Table 2). The fecal alkane pattern will therefore closely reflect the combination of plant species consumed by the animal and can be used to estimate this, with one proviso: While the fecal recovery of alkanes is high, it is not complete and generally increases with increasing carbon chain length.[3] Before relating fecal alkane patterns to those in the dietary components, it is therefore necessary to correct for differential recoveries of individual alkanes.[1,3]

Table 2 Patterns of the major *n*-alkanes in a selection of pasture and browse species consumed by livestock

Plant species	Alkane (mg/kg dry matter)				
	C25	C27	C29	C31	C33
Grasses					
Perennial ryegrass (*Lolium perenne*)	6	25	122	208	117
Cocksfoot (*Dactylis glomerata*)	–	20	38	58	21
Deschampia cespitosa	17	43	384	657	95
Legumes					
White clover (*Trifolium repens*)	–	29	92	67	6
Subterranean clover (*T. subterraneum*)	4	16	250	74	10
Alfalfa (*Medicago sativa*)	–	36	202	324	21
Browse species					
Mulga (*Acacia aneura*)	226	119	126	1197	1646
Willow (*Salix* sp.)	38	162	74	63	19
Juniper (*Juniperus communis*)	5	9	23	73	477

Several mathematical packages are available for calculating diet composition from alkane patterns in feces and the plant species on offer. In general, these return very similar results.[1] In controlled comparisons with relatively simple mixtures (<5 species), alkane-based diet compositions have shown excellent agreement with known diet compositions.[1,3] However, as the number of species to be separated approaches the number of available alkanes, it becomes increasingly difficult to reliably estimate diet composition; the number of dietary components cannot exceed the number of available markers. The use of long-chain alcohols and fatty acids, in addition to n-alkanes, will probably help to overcome this limitation and allow more species to be discriminated.

A point to note is that many supplementary feeds also contain alkanes, or can be labeled with them. The proportion of supplement in the total intake can thus be estimated by treating it as one of the species in the diet.[1]

USING n-ALKANES TO ESTIMATE DIGESTIBILITY AND INTAKE

Together with diet composition and the nutrient content of the dietary components, the total intake of the animal and whole-diet digestibility determine the intake of nutrients and are thus key determinants of the productivity of grazing livestock. To determine digestibility, fecal and dietary concentrations of a natural alkane (e.g., C31 or C33) can be used as an internal marker, as described earlier; corrections for incomplete fecal recovery would be necessary. If the animals are also dosed with an even-chain alkane (e.g., C32) as an external marker to determine fecal output, intake can also be estimated. As with the digestibility marker, the fecal output estimate would be biased unless a fecal recovery correction were applied. However, the conceptual leap that permitted the use of alkanes to estimate intake was the realization that if the fecal recoveries of the dosed and natural alkane are the same, unbiased estimates of intake can be obtained without fecal recovery corrections;[4] the biases in the digestibility and fecal output estimates will cancel out. Furthermore, it is not necessary for the dosed alkane to be absent from the diet. Comparative studies indoors have demonstrated that dosed C32 alkane and natural C33 alkane had very similar fecal recoveries, resulting in very close agreement between actual intake and that estimated using these alkanes.[1,3] The combination of dosed (even-chain) alkanes and natural (odd-chain) alkanes has now become a standard method for estimating intake, and a single-dose device providing an accurate daily dose of alkane is commercially available for ruminant livestock.

OTHER USES OF ALKANE MARKERS

Natural alkanes are part of the plant material and remain attached to it during transit through the digestive tract. This means they could be used as markers for estimating the flow of digesta in different parts of the tract. The passage rate of material through the gut could also be determined from the levels of radioactively labeled alkanes, in a series of feces samples taken after a single feed of labeled plant material.

CONCLUSION

Experiments have shown that plant wax alkanes permit an accurate estimate of total diet digestibility and intake, plus an estimate of the species composition of the diet. It thus becomes possible to define the nutrient intake of the grazing animal with much greater accuracy, and also to define those parts of the plant biomass preferred by the animals. This has ramifications for the sustainability of the system, by identifying plants at risk of overgrazing, and also for plant breeding, by indicating which plants the animals prefer. Similarly, since the proportion of supplement in the total intake can be defined, the interaction between supplement and herbage can be quantified much better, with major ramifications for the management of supplementary feeding, one of the largest discretionary costs in grazing systems.

REFERENCES

1. Mayes, R.W.; Dove, H. Measurement of dietary nutrient intake in free-ranging mammalian herbivores. Nutr. Res. Rev. **2000**, *13* (1), 107–138.
2. Kotb, A.R.; Luckey, T.D. Markers in nutrition. Nutr. Abs. Rev. **1972**, *42* (3), 813–845.
3. Dove, H.; Mayes, R.W. Plant wax components: A new approach to estimating intake and diet composition in herbivores. J. Nutr. **1996**, *126* (1), 13–26.
4. Mayes, R.W.; Lamb, C.S.; Colgrove, P.M. The use of dosed and herbage n-alkanes as markers for the determination of herbage intake. J. Agric. Sci., Camb. **1986**, *107* (1), 161–170.

Feed Quality: Natural Plant Markers—Indigestible Fiber

William C. Ellis
J. H. Matis
Texas A&M University, College Station, Texas, U.S.A.

H. Lippke
Texas Agricultural Experiment Station, Uvade, Texas, U.S.A.

INTRODUCTION

Plant fiber (NDF) is the major source of potentially digested nutrients for ruminants, and variations in NDF digestibility are a major factor determining feed quality, especially that of foragers. The NDF consists of two conceptual entities: potentially digestible NDF (PDF) and indigestible NDF (IDF). Being indigestible, the level of IDF in the feed is an important predictor of feed quality, albeit negative. Thus, digestibility of PDF determines the digestibility of NDF. Additionally, IDF is nutritionally important as an indigestible natural plant marker intrinsic to the feed that can be used to estimate digestibility of PDF and other analytically definable feed entities. Because of the dynamic physical and chemical interactions involved in ruminal microbial digestion (hydrolysis) of PDF, one must distinguish between conceptual and analytically definable entities of PDF and IDF in their application to ruminant nutrition.

INDIGESTIBLE FIBER (IDF)

Fiber is commonly determined as the dry matter (DM), or preferably the organic matter (OM), insoluble after extraction with a neutral detergent solvent. The NDF consists of the structural carbohydrates cellulose and hemicelluloses and potentially indigestible entities such as lignin and lignified structural carbohydrates. Conceptually, NDF can be divided into PDF and IDF. Analytically, IDF is estimated by fitting kinetic models[1,2] that describe the disappearance of NDF over digestion time. The IDF is estimated as the undigested NDF remaining when no further disappearance of NDF is detectable by the kinetic model. Alternatively, IDF is analytically defined as the undigested NDF remaining after exposure to agents of digestion for a sufficient time (6–10 days) to approximate complete digestion of PDF.[3] The PDF is analytically defined as the difference between NDF and IDF. Thus, by

difference, the quantitative estimation and utility of both IDF and PDF are inseparable.

CHEMICAL AND PHYSICAL DIGESTION OF NDF

Chemical digestion (hydrolysis) of PDF is achieved by enzymes associated with the microbial cells of fibrolytic microbes. These enzymes physically attach to and hydrolyze specific plant tissue surfaces of PDF.[4] Digestion of PDF is via erosion from the surface attachment site. Therefore, rate and extent of digestion of PDF are functions of 1) the microbially accessible surface area of plant tissue fragments;[5] 2) the abundance of PDF on such surfaces; 3) the rate of exposure of new surface levels of PDF by ruminative mastication;[6] and 4) an adequate ruminal flux of ruminal degraded protein (RDP) for growth of the fibrolytics.

Newly ingested fragments have intrinsic buoyancy due to the structure of large fragments of ingestive mastication. Intrinsic buoyancy of vascular tissues within the relatively large fragments of ingestive mastication is the initial force that positions younger fragments of ingestive mastication into flow paths involving ruminative mastication. With microbial colonization and residence time in the lag-rumination pool, aging fragments undergo age-dependent changes in their masticated size, rate of exposure of new surfaces of microbially accessible PDF ($_{ma}$PDF), and fermentation-based buoyancy. Collective changes of ruminative mastication, fermentation-based buoyancy, and mass action competition among fragments of similar buoyancy constrain ruminal escape of individual fragments until fragments' surface level $_{ma}$PDF is extensively digested (mean of $90\pm5\%$) (Fig. 1A) and fragments are physically masticated to relatively small fragments. We propose[7,8] that the fractional rate of digestion of $_{ma}$PDF provides the fermentation-based buoyancy gradients that constrain the fractional rate of escape of IDF from the rumen (Fig. 1B).

Encyclopedia of Animal Science
DOI: 10.1081/E-EAS 120019601

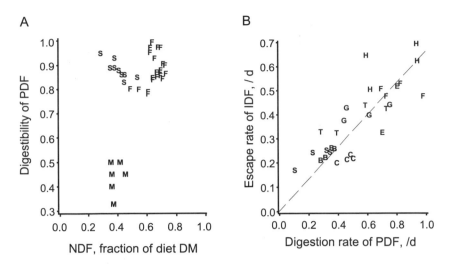

Fig. 1 A. Digestibility of microbially accessible, potentially digestible PDF is relatively complete for forages fed to cattle (F) and to lactating dairy cows (S), but not for mixed concentrate-forage diets (M). B. Variations in digestion rate of PDF are postulated as causal of a positive relationship with the escape rate of IDF—a relationship that results in relatively complete digestion of microbial accessible PDF (A). Relatively low digestibility of PDF from mixed concentrate-forage diets (M) is postulated due to inadequate RDP for the fibrolytic bacterial ecosystem.

FRAGMENT SIZE AND ESTIMATION OF IDF AND PDF

Being digested, it is obvious that digested NDF must define $_{ma}$PDF, and ruminative mastication is the process that determines the rate of exposure of $_{ma}$PDF. Ruminative mastication is incapable of completely exposing the total mass of fragments. Consequently, considerable micro-bially inaccessible PDF remains within the mass of fragments escaping the rumen. The range in mean size of fragments entering the rumen is relatively large and highly variable among feeds (1405 to 6494 μm). In contrast, the mean size of fragments escaping the rumen is on the order of 240 to 360 μm.[9] Thus, on the order of 4.6 to 21% (300 μm/1405 μm and 300 μm/6494 μm, respectively) of the mass of ingestively masticated fragments escape the

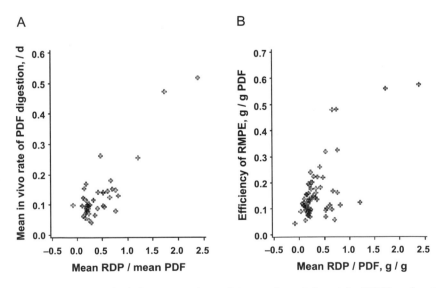

Fig. 2 Positive relationships between ruminal flux proportions of rumen degraded protein (RDP) and potentially digestible NDF (PDF) and rate of in vivo digestion of PDF (A), and the efficiency of ruminal microbial protein efflux (RMPE) (B) suggest that RDP drives the growth rate of the fibrolytic bacterial ecosystem and the consequent rate of digestion of PDF and growth of the total ruminal bacterial ecosystem.

rumen as fragments ≤ 300 µm. The ratio of $_{ma}PDF/_{mi}IDF$ presumably differs for different size distributions of fragments produced in the laboratory mill-ground feed versus fragments escaping the rumen. Thus, the 5–10% indigestibility for analytically defined PDF (Fig. 1A) could easily be accounted for by differences in mean size of ground feed versus ruminal escaping fragments. Grinding feed samples to pass 1- or 2-mm screens of the laboratory mills traditionally used may not mimic the distribution of fragments produced by ruminative mastication.

The importance of ruminative mastication is indicated by differences observed between in vivo and non-in vitro methods for estimating the rate of digestion of $_{ma}PDF$. Mean in vivo rate of digestion of PDF (inclusive of effects of ruminative rumination) consistently exceeds (1.3- to 4.4-fold) rate estimates obtained by in vitro or in situ methods (which exclude effects of ruminative mastication) obtained with feed samples ground to pass 1- or 2-mm screens.

A number of analytical pitfalls are associated with the gravimetric estimation of NDF and its constituents, IDF and PDF. Problems of physical loss of matter due to the typical 30- to 50-µm porosity of in situ bags[10] are a major problem. Rather than a gravimetric ''by-difference'' method as currently used, a more direct estimation of the specific carbohydrates of conceptual NDF is needed—a specific colorimetric procedure, for example. Use of a specific, heat-stable amylase to remove starch and adequate washing to remove neutral detergent-solubilized matter are commonly unrecognized problems.

NUTRITION OF FIBROLYTIC BACTERIAL ECOSYSTEMS

The fibrolytic bacterial ecosystem is unique in its essential growth requirement for short-chained fatty acids derived from RDP. Thus, if not constrained by the exposure rate of $_{ma}PDF$, the rate of $_{ma}PDF$ digestion may be limited by ruminal flux proportions of RDP/PDF (Fig. 2A). Mean rate of in vivo digestion of PDF and synthesis of RMPE appear to be progressively associated with increasing proportions of RDP/$_{ma}PDF$, well beyond levels of dietary CP commonly considered to be adequate (Figs. 2A and 2B).

REGULATION OF RUMINAL KINETICS

The National Research Council (NRC)[11] has indicated the need for a kinetic model of ruminant digestion involving rates of digestion and ruminal escape of feed fragments. The current NRC model[11] assumes that digestion and escape rates are singular attributes of the feed. In contrast, we propose[6,12–14] that ruminal kinetics are the result of complex interactions among the ruminants' nutritional status, the physical aspects of ruminative mastication, and nutritional attributes of the feed by rumen microbial interactions involving RDP, $_{ma}PDF$, and IDF.

Lippke[15] observed that digestible organic matter intake from forage and, consequently, live-weight gains by forage-fed ruminants could be accurately accounted for by considering the chemically extracted correlate of IDF, acid detergent fiber, and crude protein. Live-weight gains could be estimated more accurately than digestibility and intake rate—differences that reflect the importance of net flux of nutrients from the rumen and specific constraints of $_{mi}IDF$ upon the intake rate of NDF and the rate of and efficiency of digestion of $_{ma}PDF$.

CONCLUSION

The IDF is a nutritionally important component of the diet of ruminants, in that it is a major component and is a marker of the indigestibility of the diet. Its nutritional utility appears to have been unappreciated, as it is not frequently estimated and reported. Existing information from forage-fed ruminants suggests that $_{ma}PDF$ is essentially completely digested, so that the digestibility of NDF can be estimated from knowledge of IDF and $_{ma}PDF$. The importance of rate of ruminative mastication in determining rate of exposure of new surfaces of $_{ma}PDF$ is stressed. That topic and the amino acid nutrition of fibrolytic bacterial ecosystems are proposed as potentially fruitful areas for future research.

REFERENCES

1. Waldo, D.R.; Smith, L.W.; Cox, E.L. Model of cellulose disappearance from the rumen. J. Dairy Sci. **1972**, *55*, 25–129.
2. Weimer, P.J.; Lopez-Guisa, J.M.; French, A.D. Effect of cellulose fine structure on kinetics of its digestion by mixed ruminal microorganisms in vitro. Appl. Environ. Microbiol. **1990**, *56*, 2421–2429.
3. Lippke, H.; Ellis, W.C.; Jacobs, B.F. Recovery of indigestible fiber from feces of sheep and cattle on forage diets. J. Dairy Sci. **1986**, *69*, 403–412.
4. Akin, D.E.; Amos, H.E. Rumen bacterial degradation of forage cell walls investigated by electron microscopy. Appl. Microbiol. **1975**, *29*, 692–701.
5. Weimer, J.P. Why don't ruminal bacterial digest cellulose faster? J. Dairy Sci. **1996**, *79*, 1496–1502.
6. Ellis, W.C.M.; Wylie, J.; Dennis Herd, H.; Lippke, J.; Matis, H.; Poppi, D.P. The Nutritional Regulation of Feed Intake by Ruminants. Proceedings of the Sixth International Symposium on the Nutrition of Herbivores, Merida,

Yucatan, Mexico, October 19–24, 2003; Herrera-Camacho, J., Sandoval-Castro, C.A., Eds.; Tropical and Subtropical Agroecosystems; University Autonoma de Yucatan: Mexico, 2003; 355–359.

7. Ellis, W.C.; Poppi, D.; Matis, J.H. Feed Intake in Ruminants: Kinetic Aspects. In *Farm Animal Metabolism and Nutrition: Critical Reviews*; D'Mello, J.P.F., Ed.; Commonwealth Agricultural Bureaux International: Oxon, UK, 2000; 335–363.

8. Ellis, W.C.; Poppi, D.P.; Matis, J.H.; Lippke, H.; Hill, T.M.; Rouquette, F.M., Jr. Dietary-Digestive-Metabolic Interactions Determining the Nutritive Potential of Ruminant Diets. Proc. 5th Int. Symposium on the Nutrition of Herbivores, Jung, H.J.G., Fahey, G.C., Jr., Eds.; Am. Soc. Anim. Sci., Savoy, IL; 1999; 423–481.

9. Deswysen, A.G.; Pond, K.R.; Rivera-Villareal, E.; Ellis, W.C. Effects of time of day and monensin upon the distribution of different size particles within digestive tract site of heifers fed corn silage. J. Anim. Sci. **1988**, *67*, 1773–1783.

10. Van Hellen, R.W.; Ellis, W.C. Sample container porosities for rumen in situ studies. J. Anim. Sci. **1976**, *44*, 141–146.

11. NRC. *Nutrient Requirements of Dairy Cattle*; National Academy Press: Washington, DC, 2001.

12. Ellis, W.C.; Matis, J.H.; Dennis Herd, H.; Lippke; Rouquette, F.M., Jr.; Poppi, D.P.; Wallace, R.J. A role for rumen degraded protein in regulating intake rate of digested fiber. J. Anim. Sci. **2001**, *79* (Supplement 1), 365.

13. Ellis, W.C.; Dennis Herd; Matis, J.H.; Lippke, H.; Rouquette, F.M., Jr.; Poppi, D.P.; Wallace, R.J. A role for ruminally degraded protein in determining yield and efficiency of rumen microbial protein efflux. J. Anim. Sci. **2001**, *79* (Supplement 1), 365.

14. Ellis, W.C.; Matis, J.H. A role for rumen microbial protein synthesis in regulating ruminal turnover. J. Anim. Sci. **2001**, *79* (Supplement 1), 289.

15. Lippke, H. Forage characteristics related to intake, digestibility and gain by ruminants. J. Anim. Sci. **1980**, *50*, 952–961.

Feed Supplements: Antibiotics

Gary L. Cromwell
University of Kentucky, Lexington, Kentucky, U.S.A.

INTRODUCTION

Antibiotics and chemotherapeutics belong to a class of compounds that suppress or inhibit the growth of microorganisms. These compounds are commonly referred to as antimicrobial agents. Antibiotics are naturally occurring substances produced by yeasts, molds, and other microorganisms, whereas chemotherapeutics are chemically synthesized substances with activity similar to that of antibiotics. In addition, certain mineral elements (copper and zinc) have antimicrobial properties when included at high levels in diets for certain classes of animals.

ANTIMICROBIAL USE IN ANIMAL FEEDS

Antibiotics were first discovered by Sir Alexander Fleming in 1928. However, it was not until more than 20 years later, in 1949, that animal scientists discovered that feeding a fermentation media to chickens and pigs stimulated growth.[1] Subsequently, an antibiotic (chlortetracycline) was isolated from the media and given the name aureomycin.

Within a few years after this discovery, the use of antibiotics in animal feeding programs was readily adopted by the livestock and poultry industries. Over the past 50 years, antibiotics and other antimicrobial agents have been widely used in swine and poultry feeds and, to a lesser extent, in beef and dairy feeds. These agents are commonly used at low (subtherapeutic) levels in feeds to enhance growth rate and efficiency of feed utilization in swine and poultry, to reduce mortality and morbidity in young pigs and dairy calves, to improve reproductive performance in swine, and to reduce liver abscesses in feedlot cattle. Antibiotics are also used at moderate to high levels (prophylaxis) for the prevention of disease in exposed animals, and at high (therapeutic) levels to treat diseases in animals.

Although many antibiotics have been discovered over the past six decades, relatively few have been approved by the Food and Drug Administration (FDA) for use in animal feeds. For example, only 12 antibiotics and five chemotherapeutics are approved by the FDA for inclusion in swine feeds.[2] These include the antibiotics apramycin, bacitracin (two forms), bambermycins, chlortetracycline,

lincomycin, neomycin, oxytetracycline, penicillin, tiamulin, tylosin, and virginiamycin, and the chemotherapeutics arsanilic acid, carbadox, roxarsone, sulfamethazine, and sulfathazole. Certain ones of these antimicrobial agents are approved for combination usage (e.g., chlortetracycline, sulfamethazine, and penicillin; tylosin and sulfamethazine; neomycin and oxytetracycline), whereas certain others can only be fed alone and not with other agents. Usage is permitted only at levels approved by the FDA.[2] All of the chemotherapeutics approved for swine require withdrawal from the feed for specific periods of time before marketing the animal, but most of the antibiotics do not require withdrawal except when fed at certain therapeutic levels.[2]

ANTIMICROBIALS AS GROWTH PROMOTERS

The growth-promoting effects of antibiotics and other antibacterial agents have been documented in most species of food-producing animals. Because antibiotics are used to a greater extent in the swine industry than in other animal industries, this article will focus on the benefits of antibiotic use in swine.

The efficacy of antibiotics in improving the rate and efficiency of growth in pigs is well documented in numerous research studies.[3–7] Hays[3] summarized data from 1194 experiments conducted in the United States from 1950 to 1985 and found that in studies with weanling pigs from 7- to 25-kg body weight, antibiotics improved growth rate by an average of 16.4% and reduced the amount of feed required per unit of gain by 6.9%. In studies with growing pigs from 17- to 49-kg body weight, antibiotics improved growth rate by 10.6% and feed efficiency by 4.5%.[3] In growing finishing pigs from 24 to 89 kg, growth rate was improved by 4.2% and feed efficiency by 2.2% when antibiotics were fed.[3] These results were derived mostly from experiments conducted at research stations where the environment is less stressful, pens are cleaner, and the disease load of the pigs is generally less than on typical swine farms. Thus, the responses to antibiotics under farm conditions may be twice as great as those occurring in research station environments.[6,7]

Encyclopedia of Animal Science
DOI: 10.1081/E-EAS 120019604

Even though some antibiotics have now been used for more than 50 years, they seem to be as effective as they were in the early years following their discovery. A comparison of data from the first 28 years of antibiotic usage[3,4] and during the following 8 years[5] indicated that the overall effectiveness of antibiotics did not diminish.

Antibiotic usage in swine feeds has been shown to reduce mortality and morbidity, particularly in young pigs. A summary of 67 field trials conducted over a 22-year period indicates that antibiotics reduced mortality by one-half (from 4.3 to 2.0%) in young pigs.[6,7] The reduction in mortality was even greater under high-disease conditions and environmental stress (15.6 versus 3.1%).[6,7]

The mineral element copper has antibiotic-like properties when present at high levels (100–250 ppm) in diets for swine, especially young pigs.[8] The growth responses are similar in magnitude to those resulting from the feeding of antibiotics. Interestingly, the responses to copper and antibiotics seem to be additive in young pigs; that is, copper is efficacious in both the presence and absence of antibiotics (and vice versa). Dietary zinc as zinc oxide at high levels (2000 to 3000 ppm) also has been found to stimulate growth performance in young pigs.[9]

ANTIMICROBIALS AND REPRODUCTIVE EFFICIENCY

Antibiotics are not as commonly used in diets for breeding animals as for growing pigs, but they have been shown to be quite effective when fed during certain stages of the reproductive cycle, such as at the time of breeding. Based on a summary of nine studies involving 1931 sows, feeding a high level of an absorbable antibiotic before and after breeding improved conception rate by 7% and improved litter size by one-half pig at the subsequent farrowing.[6] A summary of 13 studies (2338 litters) showed a slight improvement in survival and weaning weights of nursing pigs when antibiotics were included in the prefarrowing and lactation diet.[6] Long-term withdrawal of antibiotics from a swine herd was found to be associated with a marked reduction in reproductive performance.[10]

MECHANISMS OF GROWTH PROMOTION BY ANTIMICROBIALS

The mechanisms by which antibiotics and other antimicrobial agents stimulate growth in animals are not completely understood. There are probably several modes of action that involve metabolic, nutritional, and disease control effects.[3,4,6,7] Gut wall thickness and the entire

mass of the digestive tract (which has a high energy requirement) are reduced when antibiotics are fed. In addition, antibiotics suppress those microorganisms that are responsible for nonspecific, subclinical disease, thereby allowing pigs to respond more closely to their genetic potential. Evidence for the disease control mechanism includes the facts that young pigs (which are more susceptible to diseases than older animals) respond more to antibiotics than older pigs, that responses to antibiotics are greater in pigs carrying a high disease load compared with healthy pigs, and that responses to antibiotics are greater in a dirty environment compared to a clean one.

SAFETY OF ANTIMICROBIALS

Not long after the antibiotics were discovered and accepted into feeding programs for livestock and poultry, questions were raised relative to their safety. Many of those concerns continue today. The most pressing concern is whether the widespread usage of antibiotics in animal feeds contributes to a reservoir of drug-resistant enteric bacteria that are capable of transferring their resistance to pathogenic bacteria, thereby causing a potential public health hazard.[11,12]

Although transfer of antibiotic-resistant plasmids (R-plasmids) occurs rapidly in vitro, the extent to which it occurs in the animal, and between animal bacteria and human bacteria, is not well documented. Animal bacteria do not colonize very effectively in humans unless extremely large doses are consumed, and even then they are transient.[13]

In 1988, the National Academy of Science's Institute of Medicine was asked by the FDA to conduct an independent review of the human health consequences and make a quantitative risk assessment associated with the use of penicillin and tetracyclines at subtherapeutic levels in animal feeds. The committee was unable to find a substantive body of direct evidence that established the existence of a definite health hazard in humans that could be associated with the use of subtherapeutic concentrations of these antibiotics in animal feeds.[14] Other groups of scientists have extensively reviewed the published data and concluded that there is no evidence of human health being compromised by subtherapeutic antimicrobial usage in animals.[4,15]

The question of whether antimicrobial resistance constitutes a significant threat to human health will likely continue to be debated in the scientific community as well as in the political arena. Antibiotics for growth promotion have already been banned in several countries in Europe, and a ban on certain, if not all, antibiotics for growth promotion has been proposed for the United States. Even a complete ban would likely have little effect on antibiotic resistance levels or patterns, according to some long-term, antibiotic withdrawal studies.[10] Three years after the European ban on growth-promoting antibiotics, there was little effect on resistance levels in humans, whereas the health of pigs and chickens markedly deteriorated.[16]

Monitoring and surveillance of microbial resistance in animals and humans has continued for many years with no animal-to-human infection path being clearly delineated. While the incidence of antimicrobial resistance in the human population is high, the amounts and patterns of resistance have not changed substantially.[17] Many would argue that the high incidence of antimicrobial resistance in humans is mainly a result of antibiotics that are prescribed directly for human use, because well over half of the antibiotics produced in the United States are used in human medicine.[15]

CONCLUSIONS

Numerous studies conducted over the past 50 years have shown that antibiotics and certain other antimicrobial agents are effective growth performance enhancers when included in animal feeds. Although antimicrobial agents have been fed for more than 50 years to billions of animals, there is still no convincing evidence of unfavorable health problems in humans that have been associated with the feeding of growth promotion levels of antibiotics to food-producing animals.[18]

REFERENCES

1. Stokstad, E.L.R.; Jukes, T.H.; Pierce, J.; Page, A.C., Jr.; Franklin, A.L. The multiple nature of the animal protein factor. J. Biol. Chem. **1949**, *180*, 647.
2. *Feed Additive Compendium*; The Miller Publishing Co.: Minnetonka, MN, 2004.
3. Hays, V.W. *Effectiveness of Feed Additive Usage of Antibacterial Agents in Swine and Poultry Production*; Office of Technology U.S. Assessment, Congress: Washington, DC, 1977. (Edited version: V.W. Hays, The Hays Report. Rachelle Laboratories, Inc., Long Beach, CA. 1981).
4. Council for Agricultural Science and Technology. *Antibiotics in Animal Feeds*; Ames, IA, 1981. Report No. 88.
5. Zimmerman, D.R. Role of subtherapeutic antimicrobials in animal production. J. Anim. Sci. **1986**, *62* (Suppl. 3), 6–17.
6. Cromwell, G.L. Antimicrobial and Promicrobial Agents in Swine Nutrition. In *Swine Nutrition*; Lewis, A.J., Southern, L.L., Eds.; Marcel Dekker: New York, NY, 2001; 401–426.
7. Cromwell, G.L. Why and how antibiotics are used in swine production. Anim. Biotech. **2002**, *13*, 7–27.
8. Cromwell, G.L. Copper as a Nutrient for Animals. In *Handbook of Copper Compounds and Applications*; Richardson, H.W., Ed.; Marcel Dekker, Inc.: New York, 1977; 177–202.
9. Hahn, J.D.; Baker, D.H. Growth and plasma zinc responses of young pigs fed pharmacologic levels of zinc. J. Anim. Sci. **1993**, *71*, 3030.
10. Langlois, B.E.; Dawson, K.A.; Cromwell, G.L.; Stahly, T.S. Antibiotic resistance in pigs following a 13 year ban. J. Anim. Sci. **1986**, *62* (Suppl. 3), 18–32.
11. Falkow, S. *Infectious Multiple Drug Resistance*; Pion Ltd.: London, 1975.
12. Linton, A.H. Antibiotics, Animals and Man—An Appraisal of a Contentious Subject. In *Antibiotics and Antibiosis in Agriculture*; Woodbine, M., Ed.; Butterworths: Woburn, MA, 1977; 315–343.
13. Smith, H.W. Transfer of antibiotic resistance from animal and human strains of 14 strains of *Escherichia coli* to resistant *E. coli* in the alimentary tract of man. Lancet **1969**, *1*, 1174–1176.
14. Institute of Medicine. *Human Health Risks with the Subtherapeutic Use of Penicillin or Tetracycline in Animal Feed*; Institute of Medicine, National Academy of Sciences. National Academy Press: Washington, DC, 1988.
15. National Research Council. *The Use of Drugs in Food Animals: Benefits and Risks*; National Academy Press: Washington, DC, 1999.
16. Casewell, M.; Friis, C.; Marco, E.; McMullin, P.; Phillips, I. The European ban on growth-promoting antibiotics and emerging consequences for human and animal health. J. Antimicrob. Chem. **2003**, *52*, 159–161.
17. Lorian, V. Antibiotic sensitivity patterns of human pathogens in American hospitals. J. Anim. Sci. **1986**, *62* (Suppl. 3), 49–55.
18. National Research Council. Nonnutritive Feed Additives. In *Nutrient Requirements of Swine*; National Academy Press: Washington, DC, 1998; 97–102.

Feed Supplements: Crystalline Vitamins

Trygve L. Veum
University of Missouri, Columbia, Missouri, U.S.A.

INTRODUCTION

Vitamins are essential organic compounds required in minute amounts in the diets of humans and animals for normal metabolic function. Vitamins are involved in over 30 metabolic reactions at the cellular level involving carbohydrate, fat, and protein metabolism. All complete feeds made for livestock in confinement are fortified with crystalline or synthetic sources of vitamins. Crystalline vitamins supplement the natural vitamin content of feed ingredients (mainly grains) that are known to be deficient in diet formulations. However, not all the vitamins required metabolically by livestock are provided in a vitamin supplement or premix because: 1) The feed ingredients may contain adequate bioavailable amounts of one or more vitamins or their precursors; 2) the microflora in the digestive tract of adult animals may synthesize adequate amounts under normal conditions; 3) dietary antibiotics may alter the intestinal microflora and their synthesis of vitamins; and 4) the vitamin is synthesized by body tissues. In the latter case, Vitamin C (ascorbic acid) is synthesized in body tissues of most animals, but not in humans (primates) or guinea pigs. The chemistry and commercial synthesis of all the vitamins required for supplementation in human and animal nutrition is well known.

Manufacturers of crystalline vitamins provide guaranteed amounts of vitamins in concentrated supplements known as premixes. The fat-soluble vitamins A, D, E, and K require dietary fat for their absorption from the small intestine. When vitamins A and D (not vitamins E and K) are consumed in great excess, they accumulate in body tissues and eventually produce toxicity. The B vitamins—the water-soluble vitamins—are not stored in body tissues and need to be provided continuously to maximize metabolic efficiency and prevent vitamin deficiencies.

CRYSTALLINE VITAMINS IN ANIMAL NUTRITION

The chemical and physical vitamin product forms available for use in animal nutrition are presented in Table 1.

Only minor changes have occurred in vitamin production and use since 1978.[1] The fat-soluble vitamins used to fortify poultry and swine feeds include vitamins A, D, E, and K. Vitamin A, D, and E requirements are expressed as International Units (IU) per kilogram of diet. Poultry require Vitamin D_3 because D_2 is poorly utilized.[2] Vitamin K and the B vitamin requirements are expressed as an amount per kilogram of diet. Vitamins E and C—and to a limited extent, vitamin A and β-carotene—also function physiologically as antioxidants.[3–5]

For poultry housed in intensive production systems, meal (mash) diets are usually supplemented with vitamins A, D_3, E, K, riboflavin, niacin, pantothenic acid, B_{12}, and choline.[3] Supplementation levels usually meet or exceed the requirements for poultry.[2] The major ingredients in grain–oilseed meal diets usually provide adequate quantities of biotin, folacin, thiamine, and vitamin B_6 (pyridoxine). There is less intestinal synthesis of vitamin K in poultry than in other animal species because of their shorter intestinal tract and faster transit time.[3]

For growing–finishing swine raised in confinement, grain–oilseed meal diets are supplemented with vitamins A, D, E, riboflavin, niacin, pantothenic acid, and vitamin B_{12}.[3] Vitamin K is frequently added because of the common occurrence of mold toxins in cereal grains, a factor that compromises the blood-clotting mechanism and reduces intestinal synthesis in swine. Supplementation levels usually meet or exceed the requirements for swine.[6] Grain–soybean meal diets for growing–finishing swine may be adequate in choline, whereas diets for weanling pigs may require choline supplementation. In addition to the vitamins required by growing–finishing pigs, sow reproductive performance is improved by adding choline and folic acid to the vitamin premix.[7] Feed manufacturers may also add vitamin B_6 and small amounts of biotin to swine diets, although most research do not indicate a need for these vitamins in practical diets.[3] Swine raised outdoors with exposure to sunlight require less supplementation of all vitamins, particularly vitamin D.[8]

Ruminants have physiological requirements for all the vitamins. However, a diet consisting of high-quality forage may provide all the fat- and water-soluble vitamins required as dietary sources (β-carotene as the vitamin A

Encyclopedia of Animal Science
DOI: 10.1081/E-EAS 120019605

Table 1 Product forms of vitamins and applications in animal nutrition

| Vitamin | Product form | | Applications |
	Chemical	Physical	
A	Acetate, palmitate, or propionate	Gelatin beadlets; dry dilutions	Dry feeds
		Spray-dried powders	Water-dispersible vitamin products
		Liquid concentrates	Liquid feed supplements
D_2 or D_3[a]	Cholecalciferol (D_3) or ergocalciferol (D_2)	Gelatin beadlets (with vitamin A)	Dry feeds
		Spray- or drum-dried powders	Dry feeds; water-dispersible vitamin products
		Liquid concentrates (with vitamin A)	Liquid feed supplements
E	d- or dl-α-tocopheryl acetate	Adsorbate powders; dry dilution; oils	Feeds
		Spray-dried powders	Water-dispersible vitamin products; feeds
		Liquid concentrates	Liquid feed supplements
K	Menadione (K_3); MSB (menadione sodium bisulfite), MSBC (menadione sodium bisulfite complex), or MPB (menadione dimethyl pyrimidinol bisulfite)	Dry dilutions	Dry feeds
		Water-dispersible powders	Water-dispersible products
Thiamin (B_1)	Thiamin mononitrate	Crystalline; dry dilutions	Feeds
	Thiamin hydrochloride	Crystalline; dry dilutions	Feeds; water-dispersible vitamin products
Riboflavin (B_2)	Riboflavin: chemically synthesized crystalline product; fermentation product	High-potency powder; spray-dried powders	Feeds; water-dispersible vitamin products
	Riboflavin-5′-phosphate sodium	Crystalline	Water-dispersible vitamin products
Niacin	Niacin, niacinamide (nicotinic acid)	Crystalline	Feeds; water-dispersible vitamin products
		Dry dilutions	Feeds
Pyridoxine (B_6)	Pyridoxine hydrochloride	Crystalline	Feeds; water-dispersible vitamin products
Pantothenic acid	Calcium d- or dl-pantotenate	Spray-dried powders	Feeds; water-dispersible vitamin products
		Dry dilutions	Feeds
	Calcium dl-pantothenate calcium chloride complex	Powder	Feeds
Biotin	d-Biotin	Crystalline; spray-dried powders	Feeds; water-dispersible vitamin products
		Dry dilutions	Feeds
Folic acid	Folic acid	Crystalline; spray-dried powders	Feeds; water-dispersible vitamin products
		Dry dilutions	Feeds
B_{12}	Vitamin B_{12} (cyanocobalamin): crystalline product from fermentation	Dry dilutions	Feeds
	Chemically synthesized crystalline product	Water-soluble dilutions	Water-dispersible vitamin products
C	Ascorbic acid	Coated products	Feeds
		Crystalline	Water-dispersible vitamin products
Choline	Choline chloride	25–60% dry powders; 70% liquid	Feeds
	Choline bitartrate	Water-soluble powders	Water-dispersible vitamin products

[a]Poultry require vitamin D_3 because D_2 is poorly utilized by poultry.[2] Both D_2 and D_3 are utilized by swine, although D_3 is more toxic in excess than D_2.[6]

(From Refs. 1 and 11.)

precursor) for adult ruminants when some of the forage has been sun-cured to provide vitamin D_2.[9,10] Also, healthy rumen microflorae synthesize all the B vitamins. Calves fed milk do not need vitamin supplementation, although milk replacers should be fortified with the required vitamins.[10] Ruminants fed high percentages of concentrate feed in intensive production, such as high-producing (lactating) dairy cows and feedlot cattle, may benefit from supplementation with vitamins A, D, and E.[10,11] Lactating dairy cows may also benefit from added niacin, choline, and thiamine.[9]

Bioavailability and Stability

The bioavailability and stability of natural and crystalline vitamins is affected by exposure to heat, ultraviolet (UV) light, moisture, pH (acids or bases), and trace minerals.[3,4,11,12] Crystalline vitamin A stability has been improved with technology in the production process by incorporating the vitamin into a small beadlet of stable fat or gelatin. For vitamins A and E, esters are more stable than the alcohol forms.[12] Vitamin stability in premixes and complete feeds may also be enhanced by adding natural antioxidants or synthetic antioxidants such as ethoxyquin, butylated hydroxytoluene (BHT), or butylated hydroxyanisole (BHA).[4,12] Pelleting, a processing method commonly used in the swine industry, is destructive to most vitamins because it produces friction (abrasion), pressure, heat, and moisture. Pelleting may increase the bioavailability of niacin and biotin.[3,4] Extrusion is more destructive than pelleting because it produces higher moisture, pressure, heat, and redox reactions.[11,12] Extrusion is widely used in the pet food industry. Higher concentrations of vitamins are normally added to pelleted or extruded diets to compensate for the increased losses in vitamin activity.

Deficiency and Toxicity Symptoms

Deficiency and toxicity symptoms of the vitamins in humans and animals have been reviewed.[7,8,13,14] Vitamins with the highest potential for toxicity are vitamins A and D, and choline as choline chloride. In each case, increasing the amount to about 10 times the requirement may produce toxicity symptoms, whereas vitamin E is tolerated at levels up to 100 times the requirement.[8] Niacin, riboflavin, and pantothenic acid are tolerated at dietary levels of 10 to 20 times the requirement. Vitamin K, vitamin C, thiamine, and folic acid are tolerated at extremely high levels (>1000 times the requirement).[9]

Vitamin Premixes

Vitamin premixes are custom formulated to meet the desired requirements for growth or reproduction, and are blended with carrier materials to produce a batch mix. Premixes are formulated so that only small amounts (5–10 pounds) are added to 1 ton of complete feed. Rice hulls are widely used as a carrier because they are less destructive than most cereal grains and by-product feeds. Ground limestone is often added to increase flowability and density; however, the amount used should be stated on the premix label in order to account for the added calcium in diet formulation.[3,12] Vitamins should not be premixed with trace minerals because the latter will enhance vitamin oxidation. Important physiochemical and handling properties of vitamin premixes and the carriers used are chargeability (electrostaticity), compression, hygroscopicity, lumping, and flowability.[12]

CONCLUSION

Vitamins are essential organic compounds that are required in the diets of humans and animals for normal metabolic function. Feed ingredients contain some natural vitamins, although the natural vitamins vary in bioavailability and lack stability. However, economical sources of crystalline or synthetic vitamins are commercially available with high bioavailability and good stability when used and stored properly. These include all the fat- and water-soluble vitamins required for supplementation of human and animal diets.

REFERENCES

1. Adams, C.R. Vitamin Product Forms for Animal Feeds. In *Vitamin Nutrition Update—Seminar Series 2, RCD 5483/1078*; Hoffman-LaRoche Inc.: Nutley, NJ, 1978.
2. NRC. *Nutrient Requirements of Poultry*, 9th Ed.; National Academy Press: Washington, DC, 1994.
3. McDowell, L.R. *Vitamins in Animal and Human Nutrition*, 2nd Ed.; Iowa State Univ. Press: Ames, IA, 2000.
4. Combs, G.F., Jr. *The Vitamins: Fundamental Aspects in Nutrition and Health*, 2nd Ed.; Academic Press: New York, 1998.
5. Basu, T.K.; Dickerson, J.W. *Vitamins in Human Health and Disease*; CAB International: Wallingford, U.K., 1996.
6. NRC. *Nutrient Requirements of Swine*, 10th Ed.; National Academy Press: Washington, DC, 1998.
7. Dove, C.R.; Cook, D.A. Water-Soluble Vitamins in Swine Nutrition. In *Swine Nutrition*, 2nd Ed.; Lewis, A.J., Southern, L., Eds.; CRC Press LLC: New York, 2001; 315–355.

8. NRC. *Vitamin Tolerance of Animals*; National Academy Press: Washington, DC, 1987.

9. NRC. *Nutrient Requirements of Dairy Cattle*, 6th Ed.; National Academy Press: Washington, DC, 1989.

10. NRC. *Nutrient Requirements of Beef Cattle*, 7th Ed.; National Academy Press: Washington, DC, 1996.

11. Hoffman-LaRoche Inc. Vitamin Nutrition for Swine. In *Animal Nutrition*; Hoffman-LaRoche Inc.: Nutley, NJ, 1991.

12. BASF. Vitamins—One of the Most Important Discoveries of the Century. In *Animal Nutrition*; BASF Corp.: Mount Olive, NJ, 2000. Documentation DC 0002.

13. Rucker, R.B.; Suttie, J.W.; McCormick, D.B.; Machlin, L.J. *Handbook of Vitamins*, 3rd Ed.; Marcel Dekker, Inc.: New York, 2001.

14. Puls, R. *Vitamin Levels in Animal Health: Diagnostic Data and Bibliographies*; Sherpa International: Clearbrook, BC, Canada, 1994.

Feed Supplements: Enzymes, Probiotics, Yeasts

C. Jamie Newbold
University of Wales, Aberystwyth, U.K.

Kevin Hillman
Scottish Agricultural College, Aberdeen, U.K.

INTRODUCTION

The use of microbial feed additives [probiotics or direct-fed microbials (DFM)] and enzymes in animal diets is not new. In 1924, Eckles and Williams published a report on the use of yeast as a supplementary feed for lactating cows,[1] while in 1947, Møllgaard reported improvements in health and skeletal formation in pigs with impaired mineral absorption supplemented with lactic acid bacillus.[2] However, it is only in the last two decades that a clear consensus has started to develop on how addition of such additives to the diet might stimulate productivity in farm animals.

PROBIOTICS FOR NONRUMINANT ANIMALS

The original application of probiotics in the nonruminant animal was as prophylactics for the prevention of intestinal disease, although they have also found application as treatments to accelerate the reestablishment of the intestinal microflora after illness or antibiotic treatment.[3] They are generally of limited use in the treatment of active infection. The probiotic is defined as a live microbial supplement that enhances gut health or improves gut function. However, wider-ranging improvements on health and growth in nonruminant animals have been reported. These effects are outside the original intention of the probiotic principle, but may arise naturally as a consequence of improved intestinal function. As the intestine constitutes an enormous drain on the energy and protein resources of any animal,[4] any improvement in the efficiency of this organ will have noticeable effects on the overall health and growth of the animal. Many studies have demonstrated that probiotic preparations are capable of producing improvements in growth and in feed-conversion efficiency comparable to those obtained with antibiotic growth promoters when applied to pigs, although the beneficial effects are generally most marked in the first few weeks after weaning. However, the improvements obtained with probiotics have been found to be less consistent than those obtained with antibiotics when applied to both pigs and poultry.[5]

The principal bacterial genera applied as probiotics for nonruminant animals are *Lactobacillus*, *Streptococcus*, and *Bacillus*. Generally, those species isolated from intestinal contents or faecal materials are the most effective. Yeast-based probiotics do not appear to provide significant benefits to the intestinal function of the pig, although there are indications that yeasts may have some influence on microbial fermentation in the caeca of hens. Overall, the application of probiotics in the nonruminant has proved effective in improving intestinal health, although the response of individual animals can be variable. Improvements in growth are highly variable and probably occur as a consequence of improved intestinal efficiency.

ENZYME ADDITIVES FOR NONRUMINANT ANIMALS

In the nonruminant diet, enzymes are used more as a feed treatment than as a supplement. Their purpose, principally, is to degrade indigestible or antinutritional factors (such as protease inhibitors) within the feed, to improve digestibility of poor-quality feed, or to remove inhibitors of digestion. Improvements to health are brought about by the removal of these antinutrients and by rendering poorly digestible carbohydrates into a form that is digested in the ileum, resulting in a reduction in fermentable substrate entering the large intestine. Although the enzyme may be added to the feed rather than applied as a pretreatment, the principle is the same. The enzymes act on components of the feed, not on the digestive processes of the animal or on its microflora.

Nonstarch polysaccharides (NSP), such as xylans and glucans in poultry feeds, can cause poor digestibility, resulting in sticky litter and hock burn in the birds. These problems have been successfully treated with xylanases and glucanases in the feed.[6] In pigs, the hexose-based NSP (glucans) are broken down by microbial action in the

Encyclopedia of Animal Science
DOI: 10.1081/E-EAS 120023509

small intestine and therefore do not cause problems, although xylans can pass undigested into the large intestine. Wheat-based diets contain proportionately higher quantities of pentosan-based NSP such as xylan, and supplementation of these diets with xylanases is associated with a reduced incidence of nonspecific colitis in pigs. There are few problems associated with barley-based diets for pigs, and enzyme supplementation shows little improvement in the pigs on these diets.

Further applications include the use of phytases to increase the availability of phosphorus in the diet and the removal of protease inhibitors, particularly in high-soya diets. To date, enzymes are much more widely used in poultry than in pig diets, although their application for pigs is increasing.

PROBIOTICS FOR RUMINANTS

Bacterial Additives

Bacterial cultures from both ruminal and nonruminal sources, either alone or in combination with fungal extracts, have been used to stimulate rumen development in young animals. Only a few studies have documented positive effects of feeding bacterial probiotics to adult ruminants, principally *Lactobacillus acidophilus*, and it is not clear to what extent these benefits arise from effects in the rumen or from effects in the lower gut as described earlier.[7]

Fungal Additives

Yeast culture

Yeast cultures based on *Saccharomyces cerevisiae* are widely used in ruminant diets. Typically added to the diet of cattle at between 4 and 100 g/d, available products vary widely in both the strain of *S. cerevisiae* used and the number and viability of yeast cells present. Not all strains of the yeast are capable of stimulating digestion in the rumen. These differences are not related to the number of viable yeast cells in the preparations, although their ability to stimulate rumen fermentation may be related to dif-

ferences in metabolic activity.[8] Milk yield increased by an average of 4.5% and liveweight gain in growing adult cattle by 7.5% in response to yeast addition. However, responses were diet- and animal-dependent, with greater response reported in early lactation and in animals fed high-concentrate diets.[8] There is general agreement that production responses are the result of the action of the yeast within the rumen. An increase in the number of total culturable bacteria that can be recovered from the rumen would appear to be one of the most consistently reported responses to yeast addition. The increased bacterial count seems to be central to the action of the yeast (Fig. 1), driving both an increased rate of fiber degradation in the rumen and an increased flow of microbial protein from the rumen. What remains contentious is how small amounts of yeast in the diet can stimulate microbial numbers in the rumen. A number of possible modes of action have been proposed, including provision of vitamins or other stimulatory nutrients to the rumen microbial population, but to date, the only proposed mode of action that has been investigated in depth is the suggestion that yeast might scavenge oxygen from the rumen, promoting the growth of anaerobic bacteria therein.[8]

Other fungi

In addition to *S. cerevisiae*, products based on other fungi have also been described. Although preparations based on *Aspergillus niger*, *Penicillium* sp., and *Trichoderma harianum*—and even the ruminal fungus *Neocallimastix frontalis*—have been used experimentally, the only commercial products known to us are based on *Aspergillus oryzae* (AO). Production responses to AO are generally similar to those seen with *S. cerevisiae* and are certainly as variable.[8] Like *S. cerevisiae*, AO stimulates microbial numbers in the rumen. It has been suggested that vitamins and other nutrients in AO stimulate bacterial activity in the rumen in a manner similar to that postulated for *S. cerevisiae*. However, unlike *S. cerevisiae*, AO did not stimulate oxygen uptake by rumen fluid.[8] The wide range of polysaccharidase enzymes produced by *Aspergillus* spp. has led to the suggestion that enzymatic attack of plant fibers by *Aspergillus* may be an important factor in the stimulation of forage degradation in the rumen when AO was fed.[8]

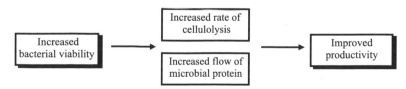

Fig. 1 The central role of an increase in bacterial numbers in the rumen in driving production responses to fungal addition.

ENZYME ADDITIVES FOR RUMINANTS

In addition to microbial preparations and fermentation extracts, there is an increasing interest in the use of concentrated enzyme products in ruminants. The majority of commercial products are extracted from *Trichoderma* spp, although products from other fungal or bacterial species have been reported.[9] Production responses have been reported in both beef and dairy cattle, with an average increase in milk yield of 4% over 16 published trials, but responses are highly variable, possibly reflecting both differences in the products and the diets fed.[9] Enzymes are added to supplement fibrolytic activity in the rumen, stimulating dry matter degradation and thus, indirectly, microbial numbers. Effects are thought to be both preingestive and in intraruminal. Free enzymes can survive in an active form for a surprising length of time, but there is evidence to suggest that the products are more effective if they are allowed time to form a stable enzyme feed association prior to feeding.[9]

CONCLUSION

Responses to microbial feed additives and enzymes in farm animals are often small and often highly variable. Much of this variability is due to differences between products; even the same microbial strain grown under different conditions will have different effects. However, as progress is made in defining the mode of action of these additives, predicting dietary situations in which they may be beneficial should be possible. Indeed, as we learn more about the mode of action of the current products, strategies for the development of new additives with enhanced and more reliable activities could be devised.

REFERENCES

1. Eckles, C.H.; Williams, V.M.; Wilbur, J.W.; Palmer, L.S.; Harshaw, H.M. Yeast as a supplementary feed for calves. J. Dairy Sci. **1924**, *7*, 421–439.
2. Møllgaard, H. Resorption af calcium og fosforsyre. Bertning fra forsøgslab. **1947**, *228*, 1–55.
3. Fuller, R. History and Development of Probiotics. In *Probiotics—The Scientific Basis*; Fuller, R., Ed.; Chapman and Hall: London, 1992; 1–8.
4. Edmunds, B.K.; Buttery, P.J.; Fisher, C. Protein and Energy Metabolism in the Growing Pig. In *Energy Metabolism*; Mount, L.E., Ed.; Butterworths: London, 1980; 129–133.
5. Thomke, S.; Elwinger, K. Growth promotants in feeding pigs and poultry III: Alternatives to antibiotic growth promotants. Annales de Zootechnie **1998**, *47*, 245–271.
6. Pettersson, D.; Aman, P. Enzyme supplementation of a poultry diet containing rye and wheat. Br. J. Nutr. **1989**, *62*, 139–149.
7. Kung, L., Jr. Developments in Rumen Fermentation-Commercial Applications. In *Recent Advances in Animal Nutrition 2001*; Garnsworthy, P.C., Wiseman, J., Eds.; Nottingham University Press, 2001; 281–295.
8. Newbold, C.J. Microbial Feed Additives for Ruminants. In *Biotechnology in Animal Feeds and Animal Feeding*; Wallace, R.J., Chesson, A., Eds.; VCH: Weinheim, 1995; 259–278.
9. Beauchemin, K.A.; Morgavi, D.P.; McAllister, T.A.; Yang, W.Z.; Rode, L.M. The Use of Enzymes in Ruminant Diets. In *Recent Advances in Animal Nutrition 2001*; Garnsworthy, P.C., Wiseman, J., Eds.; Nottingham University Press, 2001; 297–322.

Feed Supplements: Mineral Salts

Lee R. McDowell
University of Florida, Gainesville, Florida, U.S.A.

INTRODUCTION

Mineral deficiencies are reported for almost all regions of the world,[1,2] with mineral supplementation required for successful livestock and poultry production. The first step in feeding farm animals supplemental minerals is to have knowledge of both element requirements (e.g., National Research Council series *Nutrient Requirements of Domestic Animals*, National Academy Press, 2101 Constitution Avenue NW, Washington, DC) and tolerance[3] for the various classes of animals and poultry. In the United States, rules and regulations governing the registration, distribution, and ingredients of supplements, including mineral premixes, are published by the Association of American Feed Control Officials (AAFCO), Inc. (Consumer Protection Division, Charleston, WV). All mineral supplements sold must abide by controls set forth by this commission. As an example, ammonium sulfate must contain not less than certain levels of N and S, but also not more than 75 ppm As and 30 ppm Pb.

Other information of use to mineral manufacturers are the *Feed Industry Redbook* (Communications Marketing, Inc., Edina, MN) and the *Feedstuffs Yearbook*.[4] These publications provide formulation, purchasing, distribution, and nutritional information of ingredients and serve as directories of suppliers of ingredients.

The National Feed Ingredients Association (NFIA, West Des Moines, IA) has published a minerals ingredient handbook. For commonly used mineral salts, there is information on the AAFCO definition, general description (e.g., bulk density, water solubility, appearance, typical sieve analysis, analysis of primary element, and other elements), handling and storage recommendations, precautions, and analyses procedures. Most mineral sources recommend storing mineral salts in a cool, dry, and ventilated area.

COMPOSITION OF MINERAL SUPPLEMENTS

The percentage of mineral elements in some sources commonly used in mineral supplements as well as bioavailability and comparative values are shown in Table 1. Great variability in mineral content among the same mineral salts has been shown. Also, mineral supplements contain variable amounts of elements other than those of primary interest. The amounts of these additional elements depend on the geological origin of the ore and processing that it undergoes. Two Mn oxides contained from 15 to 61% Mn, with the 15% source containing 23% Fe.[5] A dicalcium–monocalcium phosphate included at 1% of the diet would provide 50 to 100% of the ruminant's requirement for Co and all of the Fe needs for poultry, ruminants, and most classes of swine.

Likewise, domestic animals can receive potentially toxic minerals from various sources. Lead and As levels in Mn oxide sources varied from 660 to 2180 ppm and 119 to 1400 ppm, respectively.[5] Zinc oxide could contain 3% Pb, 149 ppm As, and 1290 ppm Cd. A phosphate source could contain 1400 ppm V.[6] This concentration would exceed the maximum tolerable level of 10 ppm for poultry when fed at 1% of the diet.

When discussing quality of mineral supplements, they must be described in terms of analytical values and in terms of physical and/or sensory characteristics. The color, odor, texture, and test weight of the various mineral sources are important. Mixing properties and compatibilities of different ore ingredients are essential. Palatability is an important consideration for mineral mixtures offered free-choice to grazing livestock, but of negligible importance for mineral mixtures included in palatable concentrate diets. The ultimate judgment of ingredient quality requires laboratory testing and analysis (e.g., quality control). It is important to be reasonably certain that laboratory analyses are reliable and that there are continuous analyses of ingredients and complete mixtures.

PROVIDING SUPPLEMENTAL MINERALS FOR LIVESTOCK

For many classes of livestock including swine, poultry, feedlot cattle, and dairy cows, mineral supplements are incorporated into concentrate diets, which generally ensures that animals receive required minerals. However,

Encyclopedia of Animal Science
DOI: 10.1081/E-EAS 120019606

Table 1 Percentage of mineral element and relative bioavailability[a]

Element	Source compound	Element in compound (%)	Bioavailability	Comparative values (%)[b]
Calcium	Calcium carbonate	40.0	Intermediate	100
	Calcium chloride	36.0	High	125
	Defluorinated rock phosphate	29.2 (19.9–35.7)	Intermediate	105
	Dicalcium phosphate	23.2	High	110
	Dolomitic limestone	22.3	Intermediate	–
	Ground limestone	38.5	Intermediate	90
	Monocalcium phosphate	16.2	High	130
	Steamed bonemeal	29.0 (23–37)	High	135
	Soft phosphate	18.0	Low	–
	Tricalcium phosphate	31.0–34.0	–	–
Chlorine	Sodium chloride	60.0	High	100
	Ammonium chloride	65.0	High	95
	Potassium chloride	47.0	High	95
Cobalt	Cobalt sulfate	21.0	High	100
	Cobalt carbonate	46.0–55.0	High	98
	Cobalt chloride	24.7	High	–
	Cobalt glucoheptonate	4.0	Intermediate	85
	Cobaltous oxide	70.0	Low	50
Copper	Cupric sulfate	25.0	High	100
	Copper lysine	10.0	High	100
	Copper proteinate	8.5–10.0	High	105
	Cupric carbonate	53.0	High	120[c]
	Cupric chloride	37.2	High	115
	Cupric chloride—tribasic	56.0	High	110
	Cupric nitrate	33.9	Intermediate	–
	Cupric oxide	80.0	Low	30[d]
Iodine	Potassium iodide, stabilized	69.0	High	100
	Calcium iodate	63.5	High	95
	Cuprous iodide	66.6	High	–
	Ethylenediamine dihydroiodide	80.0	High[e]	105
	Pentacalcium orthoperiodate	28.0	High	100
Iron	Ferrous sulfate	20.0–30.0	High	100
	Ferrous carbonate	36.0–42.0	Low[d]	10–85[f]
	Iron methionine	15.0	High	90
	Iron oxide	46.0–60.0	Unavailable	5
Magnesium	Magnesium sulfate	9.8–17.0	High	100
	Magnesite	29.0	Low	2
	Magnesium carbonate	21.0–28.0	High	–
	Magnesium chloride	12.0	High	100
	Magnesium hydroxide	30.0–40.0	Intermediate	60
	Magnesium oxide	54.0–60.0	Intermediate	75
	Potassium and magnesium sulfate	11.0	High	–
Manganese	Manganous sulfate	27.0	High	100
	Manganese carbonate	43.0	Low	30
	Manganese dioxide	36.0	Low	35
	Manganese methionine	15.0	High	125
	Manganese proteinate	10.0	High	110
	Manganous oxide	52.0–62.0	Intermediate	75

(Continued)

Table 1 Percentage of mineral element and relative bioavailability[a] (*Continued*)

Element	Source compound	Element in compound (%)	Bioavailability	Comparative values (%)[b]
Phosphorus	Sodium phosphate	21.0–25.0	High	100
	Calcium phosphate-dibasic	18.5	High	95
	Calcium phosphate-monobasic	18.6–21.0	High	100
	Defluorinated rock phosphate	13.3 (8.7–21.0)	High	90
	Phosphoric acid	23.0–25.0	High	100
	Potassium phosphate	22.8	–	100
	Soft phosphate	9.0	Low	40
	Steamed bonemeal	12.6 (8–18)	High	95
	Tricalcium phosphate	18.0	–	–
Potassium	Potassium chloride	50.0	High	–
	Potassium sulfate	41.0	High	–
	Potassium and magnesium sulfate	18.0	High	–
Selenium	Sodium selenite	45.6	High	100
	Sodium selenate	40.0	High	100
	Selenium yeast	0.1–0.2	High	120
Sodium	Sodium chloride	40.0	High	100
	Sodium bicarbonate	27.0	High	95
Sulfur	Sodium sulfate	10.0	High	100
	Ammonium sulfate	24.0	High	95
	Anhydrous sodium sulfate	22.0	–	–
	Calcium sulfate (gypsum)	12.0–20.1	High	100
	DL-Methionine	20.0	High	100
	Potassium sulfate	18.0	High	–
	Potassium and magnesium sulfate	22.0	High	–
	Sulfur, flowers of	96.0	Low	55
Zinc	Zinc sulfate	22.0–36.0	High	100
	Zinc basic chloride	55.0	High	105
	Zinc carbonate	52.0	Intermediate	85
	Zine chloride	48.0	High	105
	Zinc methionine	4.0–10.0	High	105
	Zinc oxide	46.0–73.0	High	95[g]
	Zinc proteinate	9.0–14.0	High	130

[a]From Ellis et al. (1988). Most recent updates provided by Ref. 5 and Pamela H. Miles (personal communications, 2002).

[b]Bioavailability percentages computed by Pamela H. Miles (personal communications, 2002). Percentages are not absolute, but rather relative comparisons using the source designated as 100 as the standard. Comparative values are estimated for both monogastric and ruminant species, unless otherwise stated.

[c]Value is for ruminant, 65% for chick.

[d]Value is for ruminant, 0% for chick.

[e]Some liberation of free iodine when mixed with trace minerals.

[f]Some samples are fairly high in availability, but not as available as ferrous sulfate.

[g]Value is for ruminant, 55% for chick.

for grazing livestock to which concentrate feeds cannot be fed economically, it is necessary to rely on both indirect and direct methods of providing minerals. Animals that do not receive concentrates are less likely to receive an adequate mineral supply; free-choice mineral mixtures provided to grazing livestock are much less palatable than are concentrates and are often consumed irregularly. The consumption of mineral mixtures free-choice is highly variable and has no relationship to mineral require-ments.[7] Factors that affect the consumption of mineral mixtures have been listed[1,2] and are as follows:

- Soil fertility and forage type consumed.
- Season of year.
- Available energy-protein supplements.
- Individual requirements.
- Salt content in drinking water.
- Palatability of mineral mixture.

Table 2 Characteristics of a good, complete, free-choice cattle mineral supplement

An acceptable complete cattle mineral supplement should be as follows:

1. Final mixture containing a minimum of 6–8% total P. In areas where forages are consistently lower than 0.20% P, mineral supplements in the 8–10% phosphorus range are preferred.
2. Calcium–phosphorus ratio, not substantially over 2:1.
3. Provide a significant proportion (i.e., about 50%) of the trace mineral requirements for Co, Cu, I, Mn, and Zn.[a] In known trace-mineral–deficient regions, 100% of specific trace minerals should be provided.
4. Composed of high-quality mineral salts that provide the best biologically available forms of each mineral element and avoidance of minimal inclusion of mineral salts containing toxic elements. As an example, phosphates containing high F should be either avoided or formulated so that breeding cattle would receive no more than 30–50 ppm F in the total diet. Fertilizer or untreated phosphates could be used to only a limited extent for feedlot cattle.
5. Formulated to be sufficiently palatable to allow close-to-adequate consumption in relation to requirements.
6. Backed by a reputable manufacturer with quality control guarantees as to accuracy of mineral supplement label.
7. An acceptable particle size that will allow adequate mixing without smaller size particles settling out.
8. Formulated for the area involved, the level of animal productivity, the environment (temperature, humidity, etc.) in which it will be fed, and is as economical as possible in providing the mineral elements used.

[a]For most regions, it would be appropriate to include Se, unless toxicity problems have been observed. Iron should be included in temperate region mixtures, but often both Fe and Mn can be eliminated for acid soil regions. In certain areas where parasitism is a problem, Fe supplementation may be beneficial.

- Availability of fresh mineral supplies.
- Physical form of minerals.
- Exposure time, previous experience, and social interaction.

BIOLOGICAL AVAILABILITY OF MINERAL SOURCES

General Considerations

Biological availability may be defined as that portion of the mineral that can be used by the animal to meet its bodily needs. The bioavailability and percentage of mineral elements in some sources commonly used in mineral supplements are shown in Table 1.

SELECTING AND EVALUATING FREE-CHOICE MINERAL SUPPLEMENTS

As low-cost insurance to provide adequate mineral nutrition, modified complete mineral supplements should be available free-choice to grazing livestock. A modified complete mineral mixture usually includes salt, a low fluoride–phosphorus source, Ca, Co, Cu, Mn, I, and Zn. Except where selenosis is a problem, most free-choice supplements should contain Se. Magnesium, K, S, or additional elements can also be incorporated into a mineral supplement or can be included at a later date as new information suggests a need. Table 2 lists the characteristics of a modified complete mineral supplement.[1,2] To

evaluate a free-choice mineral supplement, it is necessary to have an approximation of: 1) requirements of animal class; 2) relative biological availability of the mineral sources; 3) approximate daily intake per head of the mineral mixture and total dry matter that is anticipated for the target animals; and 4) concentration of the essential minerals in the free-choice mixture.

MANUFACTURE OF MINERAL MIXES

Mineral elements exist in many chemical forms including sulfates, carbonates, chlorides, oxides, and organic forms (e.g., amino acid complexes). The form chosen for use should depend on its biological value, cost, availability in the area, its stability and effect in the type of diet used, and other functions. A particular expertise is required to produce mineral blocks. If the block is too hard, consumption will be reduced; if not hard enough, the product will crumble. Safe, biologically available and palatable forms of the minerals, at a fair price, allow both the user and manufacturer to realize a profit from their use.

CONCLUSION

Inadequate mineral nutrition severely limits livestock production. Typical livestock diets frequently contain inadequate concentrations of required minerals. The most efficient method of providing supplemental minerals is through the use of mineral supplements combined with concentrates. This system cannot be used with grazing ruminants that receive few concentrates. Often, grazing livestock receive minerals as a free-choice complete mixture. Mineral supplements need to be compared and evaluated in relation to composition of elements, bioavailability, source of toxic elements, palatability, and mixing properties. Mineral manufacturers are responsible for providing quality control products.

REFERENCES

1. McDowell, L.R. *Minerals in Animal and Human Nutrition*, 2nd Ed.; Elsevier: London, 2003.

2. McDowell, L.R. *Minerals for Grazing Ruminants in Tropical Regions*, 3rd Ed.; University of Florida: Gainesville, FL, 1997.

3. NRC. Mineral Tolerance of Domestic Animals. In *National Academy of Sciences-National Research Council*; National Academy Press: Washington, D.C., 1980.

4. Feedstuffs. Feedstuffs Ref. Issue **2002**, *74* (28), 1–196.

5. Ammerman, C.B.; Baker, D.H.; Lewis, A.K. *Bioavailability of Nutrients for Animals*; Academic Press: San Diego, 1995.

6. Berg, L.R. Evidence of vanadium toxicity resulting from the use of certain commercial phosphorus supplements in chick rations. Poultry Sci. **1963**, *42*, 766.

7. McDowell, L.R. *Nutrition of Grazing Ruminants in Warm Climates*; Academic Press: New York, 1985.

Feed Toxicants

Dan L. Brown
Cornell University, Ithaca, New York, U.S.A.

INTRODUCTION

Feed toxicants are naturally occurring compounds that are: 1) intrinsic components of a plant (such as the cardiac glycosides in oleander); 2) produced by organisms living in the feed (such as aflatoxins produced by a mold) or taken up from the environment; or 3) placed in the feed in a deliberate effort to improve it (such as copper added to salt supplements).

OVERVIEW

Natural feed toxicants are found in every bag of feed and in every pasture, but usually at doses far too small to do harm to animals that eat them in moderation. Plants produce these compounds to protect themselves against herbivory and attack by microorganisms. Without these chemicals, toxic to the plants' enemies, wild plants could not survive and domestic crops would require such large amounts of insecticide, fungicide, bird netting, etc., that raising feed would be economically prohibitive. Many feed toxicants may even be beneficial at moderate doses, and in the case of certain potentially toxic nutrients (e.g., vitamin A and selenium), are absolutely required for normal growth and production.

Protection of animals from feed toxicants cannot be focused on complete abolition of feed toxicants, since this would be too expensive, if not impossible. Instead, livestock protection and the safety of animal source foods depend on ensuring that the total load and identity of plant toxicants is appropriate for a given species, breed, and physiological state. This requires an awareness of the nature of feed toxins and animal responses generally and the specific feed toxicants that are most important for any given location. Although globalization of feed components increases the breadth of toxicant awareness needed, feed toxicants are still mostly regional problem, particularly for feeds taken by animals themselves as browse, pasture, or locally harvested forage (Figs. 1 and 2).

INTRINSIC FEED TOXICANTS

Cyanogens

While all plants make a little cyanide, and animals all have ways of detoxifying significant amounts of that deadly compound, some plants make cyanide-releasing compounds in sufficient concentrations to cause illness and death. Members of the *Prunus* (such as wild cherries and peaches), *Sorghum* (Johnson grass, Sudan grass, etc.), and *Lotus* (trefoil) genera can cause cyanide poisoning under certain circumstances. Since the cyanide is released by enzymatic action from a cyanogenic glycoside, cell damage from frost or wilting is usually required to cause sudden death. Typically, acute poisoning results when a downed tree or large branch brings enough wilting leaves into a pasture to provide such a lethal dose. In addition, grazing or green chop feeding after freezing of Sudan grass or Johnson grass can kill as well.

Heart Poisons

A variety of compounds that interfere with sodium or potassium flow through membranes in the heart are found in the yew (*Taxus*), oleander (*Nerium*), western milkweeds (*Asclepias*), and dogbane (*Apocynum*). This causes the heart to slow and stop during diastole (relaxing phase of the heart beat) in severe cases.

Hepatotoxins

A wide variety of feed toxins specifically attack the liver. Usual symptoms of liver damage such as jaundice (or, icterus) and elevated liver enzymes in the blood may be present, but usually the first symptoms noticed are severe damage to the skin on exposure to sunlight. Liver damage can become fairly advanced before stock owners notice their animals are behaving as if they are ill, so blood may not be drawn or the color of membranes assessed in the early stages. But when the liver has been damaged,

Encyclopedia of Animal Science
DOI: 10.1081/E-EAS 120019608

chlorophyll and related plant pigments cannot be completely catabolized, and some of the intermediate breakdown products build up in the blood. These fragments capture energy from sunlight and release it in such a way that overlying skin tissue is damaged and may develop into serious sores, sloughing off and leaving the animal open to infection. This secondary photosensitization is observed after liver damage caused by the ingestion of pyrrolizadine alkaloids from groundsel (*Senecio*), alsike clover (in horses), and *Lantana camara*. The latter plant, an escaped ornamental, has been responsible for the deaths of thousands of Ethiopian cattle.[1]

Primary photosensitization can also occur without liver damage when plants such as buckwheat and St. Johnswort (or, Klammath weed) are consumed in sunny climates, since they contain compounds that trap light energy and cause skin damage in the presence of an intact liver.

Reproductive Toxins

Limb-shortening birth defects caused by the maternal ingestion of quinolizidine alkaloid-rich lupines have been seen in cattle, goats, and dogs that consumed milk from intoxicated goats, and it is possible that at least one human case can be attributed to this as well. Low-alkaloid lupines has been developed as animal feed to overcome this limitation. Cyclopia (large single eyes) and related craniofacial defects have been observed in sheep consuming *Veratrum californicum*.

A variety of legumes including subterranean clover produce isoflavones that can interact with estrogen receptors, resulting in feminization of male stock, abnormal development in females, and severely disrupted breeding cycles.

Fig. 1 Yew leaves, seed and aril (*Taxus baccata*). (*View this art in color at www.dekker.com.*)

Fig. 2 Oleander (*Nerium oleander*). (*View this art in color at www.dekker.com.*)

FEED TOXICANTS FROM ORGANISMS IN FEED OR THE ENVIRONMENT

Mycotoxins

Aflatoxins are produced by molds growing in corn, peanuts, and other grain and pulse crops. This widespread toxicant can cause reduced feed intake and both acute and chronic liver damage. Highly carcinogenic, this is one of the few important natural toxins that can pass into animal products in sufficient amounts to threaten human health. Zearalenone, which is produced by a different mold in corn, is a powerful estrogen analogue that can cause feminization of male animals and disruption of reproduction in females.

Ergot grows not only on rye grain, but also in rye grass, and is related to a fungus that grows in fescue as well. Chemicals released by this fungus cause feed intake to be reduced, problems with abortion, reduced milk production, gangrene at the joints, nervous symptoms, and skin necrosis.

Oxidant Toxins

Nitrate is accumulated in a variety of plants (corn, sorghum family, pigweed, etc.) when grown on nitrogen-rich soils (fertilized, bedding ground, manure piles). Nitrate can be converted to nitrite in an animal's body and results in darkened red blood cells that cannot carry oxygen well. Eventually, this oxidative onslaught will cause red cell destruction, anemia, and sometimes death.

Some intrinsic toxins also act through oxidation. For example, compounds found in maple leaves (not just red maple!) can have effects on horses similar to those caused by nitrates, and at sufficiently high levels (such as found in oak buds as an exclusive diet), oxidants such as pyrogallol formed from gallic acid can injure cattle.

FEED ADDITIVES AND NUTRIENTS

Copper is added to feeds and trace mineral salts intended for poultry, swine, and even cattle at levels that are often toxic for sheep. Exact requirements for and tolerance of copper depend on the zinc, molybdenum, and sulfur content of the feed; thus, an awareness of all of these factors is needed if copper supplementation of sheep is contemplated. Vitamin D may be added to animal diets (especially for those kept indoors in confinement), and decimal errors in the rate of addition can result in toxicity. Likewise, selenium has a narrow range of deficiency/sufficiency/toxicity and such small amounts need be added that errors are quite possible, especially when small batches of feed are being supplemented with the element. Ionophores such as monensin improve feed utilization, reduce methane production in ruminants, and prevent coccidiosis in a variety of livestock. But even the 33 ppm found in cattle feed may be fatal to horses, causing heart failure. Equestrians diverting grain mixes from cattle or sheep fattening rations to feed their horses need to be made aware of this.

REFERENCE

1. Shiferaw, B. Observation on *Lantana camara* poisoning in cattle of pastoralists of Eastern Ethiopia. EVA Proc. **2002**, *16*, 94–102.

ADDITIONAL READINGS

Canadian Poisonous Plants Information System: http://www.cbif.gc.ca/pls/pp/poison?p_x=px.

Cornell University Poisonous Plants Informational Database: http://www.ansci.cornell.edu/plants/index.html.

Natural Toxicants in Feeds, Forages, and Poisonous Plants, 2nd Ed.; Cheeke, P.R., Ed.; Interstate Publisher, Inc.: Danville, IL, 1998.

Poisonous Plants of California; Fuller, T.C., McClintock, E., Eds.; University of California Press: Berkeley, CA, 1986. [Although the reader may not live in California, most U.S. toxic plants can].

University of Pennsylvania's Poisonous Plants Home Page: http://cal.nbc.upenn.edu/poison/.

Venomous Animals and Poisonous Plants; Foster, S., Caras, R., Eds.; Houghton Mifflin Company: Boston, Massachusetts, 1994. [A Peterson Field Guide—The poisonous animals are a bonus.]

Feedstuffs: High-Energy Sources

Trygve L. Veum
University of Missouri, Columbia, Missouri, U.S.A.

INTRODUCTION

High-energy feeds are concentrate feeds that contain maximums of 20% crude fiber and 20% crude protein, and a minimum of 2646 kcal of digestible energy (DE) per kg of air-dry diet (or a minimum of 60% total digestible nutrients), plus a high amount of one or more nutrients that will enhance nutritional adequacy.

Cereal grains are the primary high-energy ingredients fed to livestock worldwide because of their extensive production, high digestible carbohydrate content, and economical cost. Cereal grains are the major ingredients in poultry and swine diets and concentrate feeds fed to ruminants. High-concentrate diets based on cereal grains also supply adequate amounts of essential fatty acids because cereal grains contain 2% to 4% oil. However, by-product fat sources are commonly added to cereal grain-based diets to increase energy density. Alternative high-energy feedstuffs may consist of cull or surplus sugar beets and potatoes in temperate regions; and bananas, cane sugar molasses, cassava (tapioca), and sweet potatoes in tropical and subtropical regions. The minerals supplied by high-energy feedstuffs should be accounted for in diet formulation. The vitamin content (or vitamin precursor content) is usually considered in ruminant diet formulation, whereas it is usually ignored in nonruminant diet formulation.

HIGH-ENERGY FEEDSTUFFS FOR LIVESTOCK

Cereal Grains

Cereal grains are seeds produced by plants of the grass family Gramineae for animal feed and human food. Corn, wheat, and the coarse grains—barley, oats, and sorghum—are used for animal feed, whereas very little rice or rye are used for animal feed.[1,2] Nutrient composition values for feedstuffs fed to livestock are provided in comprehensive publications[3,4] and in the nutrient requirement publications for each livestock species.[5–8] Book values provide useful estimates of feedstuff nutrient composition. However, nutrient composition of cereal grains may vary from one region or year to the next because of differences in plant genetics or environment (e.g., soil fertility and rainfall).[9] With the continued development of new trait-related and genetically modified grains, it may be prudent to obtain analytical nutrient composition values for current feedstuffs to increase the validity of the data used in diet formulation. Laboratories must be selected with care, however, because the analytical variability between laboratories may be as great or greater than the variability within ingredients.[10] The feeding values of the commonly fed cereal grains are discussed subsequently, excluding rice, which is grown almost exclusively for human consumption.

Corn (*Zea mays*), also called maize, is native to the American continent and is the most important feed grain in the regions of the world where the soil, temperature, and rainfall are suitable for growth. Corn can produce more energy per acre than any other cereal grain because it has a C4 photosynthetic pathway that utilizes solar energy more efficiently than C3 plants.[2] There are several types of corn, but dent yellow corn is the primary type grown for feed. Corn has the highest metabolizable energy (ME) in Mcal/kg [89% dry matter (DM)] compared with all other grains, with values that range from 3.03 for ruminants to 3.30 and 3.38 for swine and poultry, respectively.[3] The main energy-yielding fraction is the starchy endosperm consisting of amylose (about 25%) and amylopectin (about 75%). Corn contains about 4% oil, of which the fatty acid composition is about 50% linoleic acid.[5,6] Corn hybrids have been developed that have higher contents of oil or lysine (Opaque-2), or a lower content of phytic acid. Feeding low-phytic acid corn hybrids will reduce phosphorus and other mineral excretion in poultry and swine manure.[11,12]

Grain sorghum (*Sorghum vulgare*) includes several varieties, of which milo is the most important as a feed grain in the United States. Milo is more resistant to heat and drought than most grain crops. It may be grown on a variety of soil types, and is usually grown where the environmental conditions are too harsh for corn. Compared with corn at 100%, the ME feeding value of milo ranges from 96% when ground for nonruminants to 99% when steam flaked for ruminants. A higher tannin content (dark seed color) lowers nutrient digestibility.[1,2]

Barley (*Hordeum vulgare*) is well adapted for growing seasons that are too short for corn production in the cooler

Encyclopedia of Animal Science
DOI: 10.1081/E-EAS 120019609

regions of United States, Canada, and Europe. There are many types of barley that are grown for livestock feed or to make malt for beer production. Compared with corn, barley contains more protein and amino acids, but is lower in fat and higher in fiber. Barley contains beta-glucans, water-soluble carbohydrates that are poorly digested by poultry and weanling swine.[2,9] Feeding low-phytic acid barley will reduce the excretion of phosphorus and other minerals in poultry and swine manure.[13,14] Compared with corn at 100%, the ME feeding values of barley are 75%, 89%, and 96%, respectively, for poultry, swine, and ruminants.

Wheat (*Triticum* spp.) is grown primarily for human consumption, and ranks first in world grain production. Wheat is higher in protein and lower in fat than corn. Wheat should not be finely ground for nonruminant diets fed as a meal to avoid sticky diet problems that reduce consumption. Dry- or steam-rolling increases the feeding value for feedlot cattle, although lactic acidosis is more common in cattle fed wheat than corn. Compared with corn at 100%, the ME feeding value of wheat is about 95%, 97%, and 100%, respectively, for poultry, swine, and ruminants.[1,2]

Oats (*Avena sativa*) are of minor importance as a livestock feed because they are higher in fiber and lower in energy than other grains. The energy yield per acre is also low, making oats less profitable to grow. However, oats have the highest protein content of the grains, and hull-less oat cultivars are available that have a higher energy content than hulled oats. Compared with corn at 100%, the ME feeding values of hulled oats are 75%, 80%, and 87% for poultry, swine, and ruminants, respectively.[1,2]

Rye (*Secale cereale*) is cold-tolerant and will grow at high altitudes in northern climates. It will also grow in acid soils with low fertility. However, rye is susceptible to ergot infection, and contains pentosans that reduce the feeding value for poultry. Compared with corn at 100%, rye has ME feeding values of 79%, 89%, and 96% for poultry, swine, and ruminants, respectively.[1,2]

Triticale, a grain derived by crossing durum wheat and rye, has poor palatability similar to rye, whereas the energy value is closer to that of wheat. Compared with corn at 100%, the ME feeding value is 92% for poultry and swine, and 96% for ruminants.[1,2]

Other High-Energy Feeds

Cassava (*Manihot esculenta*), also called tapioca, is a tropical root crop grown for human food and livestock feed. The roots are high in starch and should be processed (chopped, macerated, or cooked) before feeding to allow the plant enzymes to convert cyanogenic glycosides to hydrocyanide (prussic acid), most of which will volatilize as free cyanide. Processed cassava may be fed fresh or sun-dried to produce cassava meal.[1,2,15]

Potatoes (*Solanum tuberosum*) and sweet potatoes (*Ipomoea batatas*) are grown extensively in the temperate and the tropical/subtropical regions of the world, respectively, for human consumption. Cull potatoes and by-products of either variety are used as livestock feed. Specific high-yielding potato varieties that produce twice the energy yield per acre compared with cereal grains are grown for livestock feed in Europe. However, raw potatoes must be cooked to destroy the trypsin and chymotrypsin inhibitors before consumption or feeding.[1,2]

Molasses is a liquid sugar by-product derived from sugar cane, sugar beet, citrus fruit, and corn starch (glucose) processing that is used in ruminant diets to increase DM intake. The energy value for ruminants is equal to that of a good quality grain when the amount added to the diets does not exceed 10%.[1] Table sugar (sucrose) is usually not fed to livestock, because of its cost, although it can be an excellent source of energy for most livestock, except for baby pigs that lack adequate intestinal sucrase production.[16]

Fats and Oils

Digestible fat provides 2.25 times more digestible energy than carbohydrate, and is added to livestock diets at 1% to 5% to increase energy density. Higher additions of fat may cause diet handling or pellet quality problems, such as bridging in the storage bins and feeders, or crumbling pellets, respectively. Animal fats and animal–vegetable blends are usually the most economical sources of fat, but they must be heated to liquefy prior to mixing the diet. Vegetable oils are liquids at room temperature, although they usually are too expensive for use in animal feeds. Nonruminants can be fed diets high in fat when the diet is formulated to keep the ratio of energy to other nutrients balanced. Any fat source used should be a high-quality product that is stabilized with an antioxidant such as ethoxyquin (santoquin), butylated hydroxyanisole (BHA), or butylated hydroxytoluene (BHT) to prevent rancidity. Ruminants are less tolerant to added dietary fat than nonruminants, although feeding high-fat soybeans or cottonseed to lactating dairy cows increases the milk fat percentage.[1,2]

CONCLUSION

Cereal grains are excellent high-energy feedstuffs for livestock that supply energy primarily as digestible carbohydrates, plus a small amount of energy as natural oil. Alternative high-energy feedstuffs may be fed, depending on availability and cost. By-product sources of fat are commonly added to livestock diets to increase the energy density of the diet.

REFERENCES

1. Kellems, R.O.; Church, D.C. *Livestock Feeds and Feeding*, 4th Ed.; Prentice Hall: Upper Saddle River, NJ, 1998.
2. Cheeke, P.R. *Applied Animal Nutrition*, 2nd Ed.; Prentice Hall: Upper Saddle River, NJ, 1999.
3. NRC. *U.S.–Canadian Tables of Feed Composition*, 3rd Ed.; National Academy Press: Washington, DC, 1982.
4. NRC. *Atlas of Nutritional Data on United States and Canadian Feeds*; National Academy Press: Washington, DC, 1971.
5. NRC. *Nutrient Requirements of Poultry*, 9th Ed.; National Academy Press: Washington, DC, 1994.
6. NRC. *Nutrient Requirements of Swine*, 10th Ed.; National Academy Press: Washington, DC, 1998.
7. NRC. *Nutrient Requirements of Beef Cattle*, 7th Ed.; National Academy Press: Washington, DC, 1996.
8. NRC. *Nutrient Requirements of Dairy Cattle*, 6th Ed.; National Academy Press: Washington, DC, 1989.
9. Sauber, T.E.; Owens, F.N. Cereal Grains and By-products for Swine. In *Swine Nutrition*, 2nd Ed.; Lewis, A.J., Southern, L.L., Eds.; CRC Press LLC: New York, 2001; 785–802.
10. Cromwell, G.L.; Calvert, C.C.; Cline, T.R.; Crenshaw, J.D.; Crenshaw, T.D.; Easter, R.A.; Ewan, R.C.; Hamilton, C.R.; Hill, G.M.; Lewis, A.J.; Mahan, D.C.; Miller, E.R.; Nelssen, J.L.; Pettigrew, J.E.; Tribble, L.F.; Veum, T.L.; Yen, J.T. Variability among sources and laboratories in nutrient analyses of corn and soybean meal. J. Anim. Sci. **1999**, *77* (12), 3262–3273.
11. Li, Y.C.; Ledoux, D.R.; Veum, T.L.; Raboy, V.; Ertl, D.S. Effects of low phytic acid corn on phosphorus utilization, performance, and bone mineralization in broiler chicks. Poultry Sci. **2000**, *79* (10), 1444–1450.
12. Veum, T.L.; Ledoux, D.R.; Raboy, V.; Ertl, D.S. Low phytic acid corn improves nutrient utilization for growing pigs. J. Anim. Sci. **2001**, *79* (11), 2873–2880.
13. Li, Y.C.; Ledoux, D.R.; Veum, T.L.; Zyla, K. Low phytic acid barley improves performance, bone mineralization and phosphorus retention in turkey poults. J. Appl. Poultry Res. **2001**, *10* (2), 178–185.
14. Veum, T.L.; Ledoux, D.R.; Bollinger, D.W.; Raboy, V. Low-phytic acid barley improves calcium and phosphorus utilization in growing pigs. J. Anim. Sci. **2002**, *80* (10), 2663–2670.
15. Myer, R.O.; Brendemuhl, J.H. Miscellaneous Feedstuffs. In *Swine Nutrition*, 2nd Ed.; Lewis, A.J., Southern, L.L., Eds.; CRC Press LLC: New York, 2001; 839–864.
16. Veum, T.L.; Odle, J. Feeding Neonatal Pigs. In *Swine Nutrition*, 2nd Ed.; Lewis, A.J., Southern, L.L., Eds.; CRC Press LLC: New York, 2001; 671–690.

Feedstuffs: Nonconventional Energy Sources

R. O. Myer
University of Florida, NFREC Marianna, Florida, U.S.A.

INTRODUCTION

The cereal grains (corn, oats, barley, and grain sorghum) are the most widely used energy feedstuffs for livestock and poultry rations. However, there is a wide range of nonconventional or alternative energy feedstuffs available that can be utilized for livestock and poultry feeding. With feed representing the largest single cost item in most livestock and poultry operations, alternative feedstuffs can provide needed dietary energy often at a lower cost than traditional energy feedstuffs.

Energy feedstuffs typically are high in carbohydrates and low in protein, less than 20% crude protein on a moisture-free basis. Energy feedstuffs can be divided into two major groups—concentrates and roughages. Concentrates are low in crude fiber concentration (less than 18%) and are suitable for all livestock and poultry. Roughages are high in crude fiber (more than 18% on a moisture-free basis) and are best suited for ruminant animals (cattle, sheep) and horses. Energy is not a nutrient; however, energy feeds are high in carbohydrates (starch, sugar, cellulose, etc.), which are used by the animal to supply energy for various metabolic functions.

SOURCES OF ALTERNATIVE ENERGY FEEDSTUFFS

Many of the alternative energy feedstuffs that can be utilized are by-products (or co-products), waste products, and residues from the food and feed processing, food preparation, and food service industries. Example industries include grain milling, brewing and distillation, sugar refining, baking, fruit and vegetable processing, meat, poultry, milk and egg processing, seafood processing, prepared food manufacturing, and retail food outlets. Other alternatives include feedstuffs that are not commonly fed to livestock and poultry but that may be fed during times of low prices or surpluses or during shortages of traditional feedstuffs. Alternative feedstuffs may also include those available in many areas that can be economical substitutes for traditional feedstuffs not available locally. Various residues from crop production are also viable alternatives.

Livestock and poultry provide a practical outlet for many alternative feedstuffs that are not suited for human consumption. Some of these products have been used in livestock and poultry feeding for so long and extensively that they are almost as common as the cereal grains. More than 40 million tons of by-product feedstuffs are used annually in animal feeds in the United States.[1] The list of alternative energy feedstuffs is very long. Only a handful will be mentioned. For the common by-product feedstuffs, the reader is referred to the articles on by-product feeds of plant origin and of animal origin in this encyclopedia. For a more complete listing, the reader is referred to publications by Ensminger et al.[2,3] and the National Research Council (NRC).[4] In addition, the publication *Feedstuffs Magazine,* in its yearly reference issue, has a long listing, along with estimated nutrient compositions of alternative feedstuffs.[5]

EXAMPLES OF ALTERNATIVE FEEDSTUFFS

The processing of cereal grains for human consumption results in the largest amount of by-products available for the feeding of livestock and poultry. Nearly 10% of the corn grown in the United States is processed for the production of starch, sugar (syrup), oil, grits, meal, hominy, and breakfast foods.[6] The by-products—primary corn gluten feed and hominy feed—are fed to livestock. In the milling of wheat for flour, about 28% of the wheat is fed by-product, primarily wheat middlings.[2] Other by-products include wet and dried brewers grains from the brewing industry, distillers dried grains from the distillation industry, molasses from sugar production, wet and dry citrus pulp from citrus juice processing, soyhulls from soybean processing, dried bakery waste from the baking industry, and so on.

Most of the wheat grown worldwide is for human consumption. However, some wheat is fed to livestock and poultry, in particular when prices are low. In addition, off-grade wheat is typically fed. As such, about 20% of the crop is fed to livestock and poultry.[2] Some by-products, such as whole cottonseed, a by-product of cotton ginning, can be a good source of both energy and protein for livestock feeding.

Encyclopedia of Animal Science
DOI: 10.1081/E EAS 120019610

FAT AS AN ALTERNATIVE ENERGY FEEDSTUFF

The rendering industry in the United States produces approximately 9 billion pounds of fat each year from by-products of the meat packing industry and from spent cooking oils from restaurants and supermarkets.[7] Much of this fat is used in animal feeding. Fat is a concentrated source of energy, having more than twice the calorie density as carbohydrates, and can thus be an easy way to boost the energy concentration of a ration. Fat can be utilized in rations of all livestock and poultry with some limitations. Recommended maximum diet levels (DM basis) are 10% for nonruminants and 6% for ruminants.[2]

CONSIDERATIONS IN USING ALTERNATIVE FEEDSTUFFS

Although alternative feedstuffs may offer an opportunity to reduce feed costs, they can present many challenges in their use. For one, many alternative feedstuffs are infrequently available. Composition of an alternative feedstuff can vary considerably. Many alternatives are very perishable, especially high-moisture products. Many alternative feeds can contain toxic substances, disease organisms, and other contaminants. The alternative should not be fed unless the deleterious factor(s) can be eliminated or neutralized inexpensively. In addition, alternatives may require special handling, processing, and storage.

Accurate identification of alternative feedstuff is important, as there is a large database of information on alternative feeds, some of which have already been mentioned. The Association of American Feed Control Officials[8] gives detailed descriptions and nomenclature of many feedstuffs and this listing is updated annually.

Some alternative feedstuffs are illegal to feed to some species (i.e., meat and bone meal from ruminants to ruminants) and some are regulated (i.e., feeding of kitchen waste and plate scraps to pigs—for further information, refer to Westendorf[9]). Also, some pesticides used in crop production may not be cleared for feeding to livestock, even as part of crop residue.

NONCONVENTIONAL ALTERNATIVE FEEDSTUFFS

In addition to the more conventional by-products mentioned earlier, many other possible by-products and waste products can be and are fed. In most instances, these are by-products from the food processing and food preparation industries. Examples include cannery waste, damaged or expired foods, surplus foods, and off-spec food and food ingredients, etc. To identify those materials offering potential as a feedstuff, one should attempt to answer the following:[10] 1) Does it have potential nutritional value for livestock and poultry? 2) Is it likely to be palatable and acceptable to the animals? 3) Does it contain contaminants? 4) Does it contain toxic substances or chemical residues? 5) What is the amount and seasonality of production? 6) What are the handling and storage considerations?

NUTRIENT COMPOSITION

As mentioned earlier, the nutrient composition of many alternative energy feedstuffs can vary considerably. In fact, the variation is generally greater than that typically encountered for the cereal grains. The best advice is to analyze the feedstuff for its nutrient composition before purchasing and feeding, especially if it is intended to feed a large amount. Published composition tables (e.g., NRC,[4] *Feedstuffs Magazine* yearly reference issue) can also be utilized, but be aware that these tables report only averages based on information available at the time of their publication. The desirable nutrient information would include contents of energy (DE, ME, TDN, NE_m, NE_g, and NE_l), crude protein (or amino acids for nonruminants), fiber (CF, ADF, and NDF), crude fat, Ca, P, Na, Cl, ash, and moisture. Minimum information would include contents of moisture, and of protein, P, and energy, which are usually the most costly components of a typical livestock ration.

DETERMINING THE ECONOMIC VALUE OF AN ALTERNATIVE FEEDSTUFF

The degree to which alternative energy feedstuffs are used in livestock or poultry rations is obviously dependent on the cost of the alternative. Typically, this cost is related to the price of traditional energy feedstuffs, in particular, corn.

The major costs in a typical ration are ingredients that provide energy and protein. The value for an alternative can be estimated by considering its energy and protein contents relative to those in traditional feedstuffs such as corn and soybean meal,[11] taking into consideration extra costs associated with special handling, storage, processing, etc.

CONCLUSION

Nonconventional energy feedstuffs are often an economical source of energy, and in many instances can also be a significant source of protein and other important nutrients for livestock and poultry rations. In the future, the variety and quantity of by-products and edible wastes are expected to increase, while disposal options for many of these wastes, such as landfills, will become more limited and costly. Thus, the role of livestock and poultry in recycling and adding value to many of these by-products and wastes will become increasingly important not only to decrease feed costs but also as a viable waste management option.

REFERENCES

1. Fadel, J.G.; Asmus, J.N. Production, Geographical Distribution, and Environmental Impact of By-Products. In *Alternative Feeds for Livestock and Poultry*, Proceedings of the 3rd National Symposium, Kansas City, MO, USA, Nov. 4–5, 2003; Eastridge, M., Ed.; Animal Sci. Dept., Ohio State Univ.: Columbus, OH, USA, 2003; 1–14.
2. Ensminger, M.E.; Oldfield, J.E.; Heinemann, W.W. Grains/High Energy Feeds. In *Feeds and Feeding*, 2nd Ed.; Ensiminger, M., Oldfield, J., Heinemann, W., Eds.; Ensminger Publishing Co.: Clovis, CA, USA, 1990; 363–392.
3. Ensminger, M.E.; Oldfield, J.E.; Heinemann, W.W. By-Product Feeds/Crop Residues. In *Feed and Feeding*, 2nd Ed.; Ensiminger, M., Oldfield, J., Heinemann, W., Eds.; Ensminger Publishing Co.: Clovis, CA, USA, 1990; 433–490.
4. NRC. *United States—Canadian Tables of Feed Composition*, 3rd Ed.; National Academy Press: Washington, DC, USA, 1982.
5. Waller, J.C. Byproducts and Unusual Feedstuffs. In *Feedstuffs Reference Issue*; Miller Publishing Co.: Minnetonka, MN, USA, 2002; Vol. 74 (28),18–22.
6. Weigel, J.C. Wet Corn Milling: The Industry. In *Alternative Feeds for Dairy and Beef Cattle*, Proceedings of the National Invitational Symposium, St. Louis, MO, USA, Sept. 22–24, 1991; Jordan, R., Ed.; Coop. Ext. Serv., Univ. of Missouri: Columbia, MO, USA, 1991; 1–3.
7. Hamilton, C.R. Future of Feeding Animal By-Products. In *Alternative Feeds for Livestock and Poultry*, Proceedings of the 3rd National Symposium, Kansas City, MO, USA, Nov. 4–5, 2003; Eastridge, M., Ed.; Animal Sci. Dept., Ohio State Univ.: Columbus, OH, USA, 2003; 221–237.
8. AAFCO. *Official Publication*; Association of American Feed Control Officials: P.O. Box 470, Oxford, IN, USA, 2002.
9. Westendorf, M.L. Food Waste as Swine Feed. In *Food Waste to Animal Feed*; Westendorf, M., Ed.; Iowa State University Press: Ames, IA, USA, 2000; 69–90.
10. Harpster, H.W. Case Studies in Utilization Food Processing By-Products as Cattle and Hog Feed. In *Food Waste to Animal Feed*; Westendorf, M., Ed.; Iowa State University Press: Ames, IA, USA, 2000; 145–162.
11. St-Pierre, N.R. Establishing an Economical Value for By-Product Feeds. In *Alternative Feeds for Livestock and Poultry*, Proceedings of the 3rd National Symposium, Kansas City, MO, USA, Nov. 4–5, 2003; Eastridge, M., Ed.; Animal Sci. Dept., Ohio State Univ: Columbus, OH, USA, 2003; 203–215.

Feedstuffs: Protein Sources

Lee I. Chiba
Auburn University, Auburn, Alabama, U.S.A.

INTRODUCTION

Efficient utilization of protein sources can improve profitability of animal enterprises, minimize adverse impacts on water pollution and odorous emissions, and reduce competition with humans for quality sources of protein, thus contributing greatly to successful and sustainable food animal production. The objective of this article is to review briefly protein sources used for animal and poultry production.

PROTEIN SOURCES IN GENERAL

Amino Acids and Protein Quality

Animals do not have a protein requirement per se. Instead, they need a sufficient amount of each indispensable amino acid (AA) and an adequate N supply to synthesize dispensable AA. For ruminants, the dietary needs are a combination of nourishing microorganisms and supplying adequate, indispensable AA to the gut. Although protein quality can be an indication of nutritional value for nonruminant species, the value of a protein source for ruminants is more complex because of microbial fermentation. For rapidly growing ruminants and productive dairy cows, microbial proteins may not be adequate. To present additional AA to the abomasum or the small intestine, some of the protein in feed must escape microbial degradation in the rumen and be digested by the animal.

Protein Sources

Many protein sources can be used for food animal production. (See Table 1 for the world production of major protein meals in recent years.[1,2]) They have, however, different feeding values because of a multitude of factors.[3] The composition of selected protein sources is presented in Tables 2 and 3. Although protein supplements are defined as those feedstuffs containing 20% or more crude protein (CP),[4] some with less CP are included. For complete information on the composition, readers are referred to National Research Council (NRC) and other publications.[5–9] Similarly, more detailed information on major protein sources has been presented

recently,[3] and there are excellent reviews on protein supplements.[4,10,11]

FEEDING STRATEGY AND DIET FORMULATION

Optimum Feeding Strategy

To maximize economic efficiency and minimize adverse impacts on the environment, it would be advantageous to supply indispensable nutrients as close as possible to meeting but not exceeding the requirements. Two concepts that may contribute to such optimum feeding strategies for nonruminant species are ideal protein and formulation of diets based on available AA.[3] Similarly, metabolizable protein is used for ruminants,[6,8] even though absorbed and available AA are not synonymous, and it is assumed that an ideal pattern of absorbed AA also exists for ruminants.[8]

Ideal Protein

Ideal protein can be described operationally as protein that cannot be improved by any substitution of a quantity of one AA for the same quantity of another. Any departure from a desirable pattern of AA can result in, among other things, a reduced efficiency of AA utilization and a concomitant increase in N excretion. Although the efficiency of AA utilization in commercial food animal production can be enhanced in several ways,[3] using various protein sources with complementary AA compositions or supplementing diets with crystalline AA to simulate the ideal pattern would be more practical means to incorporate this concept.

Amino Acid Availability

Expressing the requirement and formulating diets based on the available nutrient would be more effective in satisfying the animal's needs precisely. Currently, however, there seems to be insufficient information on the nutritive value of feedstuffs and no agreement on how to address the availability issue in practice. Nevertheless, formulation of diets based on available AA should be an

Encyclopedia of Animal Science
DOI: 10.1081/E-EAS 120019612

Table 1 World production of major protein meals (million metric tons)

Protein meal	Year					
	1996/97	1997/98	1998/99	1999/00	2000/01	2001/02[a]
Soybean meal	91.02	99.15	107.81	107.38	116.57	125.32
Canola meal	18.13	18.44	19.55	22.30	21.33	20.29
Cottonseed meal	11.90	11.78	11.38	11.44	11.29	12.08
Sunflower seed meal	10.07	9.55	10.50	10.72	9.40	8.49
Fish meal	6.64	4.80	5.57	6.28	5.74	5.72
Peanut meal	6.01	5.41	5.76	5.28	5.52	6.12
Palm kernel meal	2.70	2.68	2.94	3.32	3.62	3.80
Copra meal	1.97	1.74	1.40	1.77	1.88	1.66
Total	148.44	153.54	164.92	168.49	175.35	183.47

[a]Preliminary data.
(From Refs. 1 and 2.)

improvement over formulation on a total basis. Further progress must be made in developing procedures to describe a true nutritional value of feedstuffs. Apparent ileal digestibility of indispensable AA, which provides some indication of AA availability, in common protein sources has been presented.[5,7]

PLANT PROTEIN SOURCES

Oilseed Meals

Oilseed production has increased from 261 million metric tons in 1996/1997 to 324 million metric tons in 2001/2002.[1,2] Rapeseed, peanut, safflower, sesame seed, soybean, and sunflower are grown primarily for oil production. Nutritionally superior rapeseed cultivars are tradenamed "Acanola." Cottonseed is a by-product of cotton production, and its oil is used for food and other purposes. Linseed is now mostly grown for industrial oil production. Today, the residues of oil production or oilseed meals are the major protein sources used for food animal production. Soybean is clearly the prominent oilseed produced in the world,[1,2] and soybean meal accounted for 68.1% of the world production of protein meals in 2001/2002 (Table 1).

Moderate heating is necessary to inactivate antinutritional factors present in oilseed meals, but overheating can greatly reduce the lysine availability. Oilseed meals are generally high in CP, and its content is usually standardized before marketing by dilution, usually with hulls. Most oilseed meals are low in lysine, but soybean meal is an exception. The extent of dehulling affects the CP and fiber contents, whereas the oil extraction method influences the ether extract content. Oilseed meals are generally low in Ca and relatively high in P. However, P is mostly present as phytate P, which is not utilized well by nonruminant species. Oilseed meals contain low-to-moderate concentrations of the B vitamins and are low in carotene and vitamin E.

Other Plant Protein Sources

Alfalfa is one of the most popular forage crops grown throughout the world and has good AA balance. It is a good source of most vitamins and many minerals, except P. Coconut is widely distributed in the tropics, and copra, its dry kernel, is used for coconut oil production. The remaining residue or copra meal is low in CP content and is a poor source of AA. Corn gluten feed is the residue remaining after removal of the larger part of the starch, gluten, and germ, and it contains the bran. Corn gluten meal is the residue remaining after removal of the larger part of the starch, germ, and bran. They are satisfactory protein sources for ruminants, but not for nonruminant species because of their AA balance.

ANIMAL PROTEIN SOURCES

General

For many years, animal by-products from the meat-, poultry-, and fish-processing industries have been used as a source of protein for food animal production. In general, animal protein sources contain highly digestible protein and their AA pattern is often similar to dietary needs. They are also an excellent source of many vitamins and minerals. Animal protein sources are, however, more variable than plant sources in terms of the nutrient content and quality because of the source of raw materials and heat processing used for dehydration and sterilization. Since the first diagnosis in the mid 1980s, there has been

Table 2 Composition of selected protein sources (% or Mcal/kg for ME and NE, data on DM basis)

Protein source	DM	CP	Ru UP	ME (Sw)	MEn (Po)	NEm (Ru)	NEg (Ru)	Eth Ex	Ca	P
Alfalfa meal, dehy, 17% CP	91.5	18.9	36.3	1.79	1.30	1.31	0.74	2.8	1.55	0.26
Alfalfa meal, dehy, 20% CP	92.0	21.5	–	2.05	1.77	–	–	3.8	1.78	0.30
Blood meal, conventional	91.7	89.8	74.2	2.55	3.01	2.00	1.34	1.6	0.42	0.34
Blood meal, spray/ring-dried	93.0	95.5	–	3.17	3.68	–	–	1.2	0.44	0.32
Canola meal, mech ext	86.2	39.4	31.2	–	–	1.74	1.13	4.4	0.73	1.15
Canola meal, sol ext	91.5	40.2	–	2.93	2.15	–	–	4.0	0.72	1.19
Copra meal, sol ext	92.0	22.3	–	2.79	1.66	–	–	2.8	0.18	0.67
Corn gluten feed, dried	89.9	23.7	27.0	2.89	1.94	1.91	1.27	3.4	0.21	0.94
Corn gluten meal, 60% CP	88.7	66.8	69.2	4.26	4.13	2.37	1.66	2.8	0.06	0.56
Cottonseed meal, mech ext	92.5	45.0	–	2.92	2.49	–	–	5.4	0.25	1.12
Cottonseed meal, sol ext	90.2	45.8	43.8	2.57	2.67	1.82	1.20	1.8	0.19	1.14
Feather meal, hydrolyzed	93.2	88.9	63.8	2.67	2.54	1.93	1.29	6.1	0.56	0.58
Fish meal, herring, mech ext	93.0	75.5	–	3.51	3.43	–	–	10.3	2.52	1.86
Fish meal, menhad, mech ext	91.7	67.3	62.5	3.65	3.07	2.09	1.41	10.4	5.50	3.16
Fish solubles, dried	92.0	69.5	–	3.31	3.08	–	–	9.1	0.97	1.57
Linseed meal, sol ext	90.2	35.0	48.0	3.01	–	1.48	1.10	1.9	0.42	0.88
Meat-and-bone meal, rend	93.3	54.6	54.8	2.39	2.31	1.71	1.09	11.0	10.81	5.19
Meat meal, rend	93.4	58.1	44.4	2.76	2.39	1.98	1.32	11.0	8.79	4.28
Milk, skim, dried	96.0	36.0	–	3.87	–	–	–	0.9	1.36	1.04
Peanut meal, mech ext	91.0	46.8	–	3.87	2.78	–	–	7.6	0.18	0.63
Peanut meal, sol ext	92.2	53.3	11.2	3.53	2.39	2.00	1.35	1.6	0.24	0.67
Plasma protein, spray-dried	91.0	85.7	–	–	–	–	–	2.2	0.16	1.88
Poult by-product meal, rend	93.0	66.7	–	3.08	3.17	–	–	13.8	4.01	2.21
Safflower meal, dehu, sol ext	92.0	46.5	–	3.16	2.09	–	–	1.4	0.39	1.41
Safflower meal, sol ext	92.5	26.6	31.2	2.36	1.30	1.27	0.70	1.8	0.37	0.78
Sesame meal, mech ext	93.0	46.5	–	3.26	2.38	–	–	7.5	2.09	1.39
Soybean meal, dehu, sol ext	89.9	53.6	36.7	3.76	2.71	2.26	1.57	1.7	0.33	0.72
Soybean meal, sol ext	89.1	49.6	29.5	3.57	2.51	2.18	1.50	1.4	0.37	0.72
Soybean protein iso/conc	92.5	91.8	–	3.87	3.76	–	–	0.5	0.09	0.78
Soybeans, heat-processed	90.3	41.1	34.3	4.10	3.67	2.54	1.80	19.7	0.27	0.65
Sunflower meal, dehu, sol ext	92.8	47.1	20.0	2.94	2.49	1.47	0.88	3.0	0.42	1.06
Sunflower meal, sol ext	90.7	31.2	13.9	2.03	1.71	1.49	0.92	1.4	0.37	1.00
Whey, dried	94.5	13.3	–	3.32	2.04	–	–	0.9	0.91	0.78
Whey, low lactose, dried	93.5	18.0	–	3.03	2.30	–	–	1.1	2.11	1.25
Yeast, brewer's, dried	93.0	48.5	–	3.25	2.14	–	–	1.5	0.15	1.53
Yeast, torula, dehy	93.0	50.3	–	2.97	2.32	–	–	2.6	0.62	1.72

(From Refs. 5–9.) ME = metabolizable energy; NE = net energy; DM = dry matter; CP = crude protein; Ru UP = ruminal undegradable protein, % CP; ME (Sw) = ME for swine; MEn (Po) = N-corrected ME for poultry; NEm & NEg (Ru) = NE for maintenance & growth for ruminants; Eth Ex = ether extract; dehy = dehydrated; mech ext = mechanically extracted; sol ext = solvent extracted; menhad = menhaden; rend = rendered; Poult = poultry; dehu = dehulled; iso/conc = isolate/concentrate. Dash = no available data.

some impact of bovine spongiform encephalopathy (BSE) on the food animal industries in many countries. In light of BSE, regulations on the use of some animal protein sources may differ depending on the country, species, or product, and they are subject to change.

Blood Products and Meat By-Product Meals

Blood meal produced by conventional vat cooking and drying has poor palatability and low lysine availability. Spray-drying and flash-drying procedures have improved the quality of blood meal. Blood meals are generally a poor source of vitamins and minerals, except Fe. The plasma fraction of blood yields a fine, light-tan powder with high protein content. Spray-dried plasma protein is palatable and may have a positive effect on the immune system of young pigs. Meat meal and meat-and-bone meal are produced from carcass, trimming, condemned carcasses and livers, offal, and bones. Meat meal can be distinguished from meat-and-bone meal based on P content. If the product contains more than 4.4% P, it is considered meat-and-bone meal.

Table 3 Amino acid composition of selected protein sources (%, data on DM basis)[a]

Protein source	Arg	His	Ile	Leu	Lys	Met+Cys	Phe+Tyr	Thr	Trp	Val
Alfalfa meal, dehy, 17% CP	0.77	0.51	0.74	1.31	0.81	0.47	1.65	0.77	0.26	0.93
Alfalfa meal, dehy, 20% CP	1.00	0.39	0.97	1.47	0.97	0.63	1.62	0.86	0.37	1.10
Blood meal, conventional	3.81	4.68	1.01	11.73	7.69	1.72	8.38	3.93	1.30	7.82
Blood meal, spray/ring dried	3.94	5.72	1.09	11.90	8.25	2.24	9.14	4.14	1.53	7.83
Canola meal, mech ext[a]	2.77	1.11	1.52	2.68	2.23	1.75	–	1.75	0.58	1.87
Canola meal, sol ext	2.35	1.04	1.53	2.77	2.20	1.77	2.79	1.70	0.49	1.96
Copra meal, sol ext	2.37	0.41	0.75	1.38	0.59	0.65	1.49	0.68	0.17	1.08
Corn gluten feed, dried	1.15	0.77	0.73	2.15	0.70	0.99	1.50	0.91	0.10	1.15
Corn gluten meal, 60% CP	2.12	1.40	2.78	11.41	1.16	2.89	7.73	2.30	0.38	3.15
Cottonseed meal, mech ext	4.66	1.18	1.41	2.53	1.75	1.35	3.51	1.43	0.56	1.95
Cottonseed meal, sol ext	5.11	1.26	1.46	2.71	1.93	1.39	3.77	1.50	0.55	2.00
Feather meal, hydrolyzed	6.01	1.01	4.17	7.37	2.34	5.18	6.89	4.10	0.59	6.34
Fish meal, herring, mech ext	4.42	1.75	3.30	5.73	5.88	3.00	5.38	3.28	0.85	3.96
Fish meal, menhad, mech ext	4.00	1.74	2.65	4.74	5.08	2.48	4.67	2.78	0.63	3.16
Fish solubles, dried	2.97	1.86	1.91	3.17	3.33	1.71	2.23	1.50	0.47	2.26
Linseed meal, sol ext[b]	3.09	0.71	1.63	2.14	1.30	1.23	2.88	1.31	0.54	1.81
Meat and bone meal, rend	3.61	1.01	1.54	3.35	2.74	1.37	3.05	1.79	0.30	2.36
Meat meal, rend	3.93	1.31	1.71	3.83	3.25	1.51	3.28	1.99	0.39	2.66
Milk, skim, dried	1.29	1.09	1.95	3.82	2.98	0.64	1.91	1.69	0.53	2.43
Peanut meal, mech ext	5.02	1.03	1.47	2.86	1.51	1.14	3.96	1.20	0.44	1.78
Peanut meal, sol ext	5.65	1.16	1.81	3.15	1.74	1.30	4.53	1.37	0.52	2.09
Plasma protein, spray dried	5.00	2.80	2.98	8.36	7.52	1.86	4.37	5.19	1.49	5.43
Poult by-product meal, rend	4.24	1.25	2.25	4.24	3.45	2.01	4.19	2.34	0.46	2.89
Safflower meal, dehu, sol ext	3.93	1.16	1.77	2.74	1.33	1.49	3.21	1.40	0.62	2.53
Safflower meal, sol ext	2.49	0.69	1.25	1.95	1.04	1.05	2.05	1.03	0.41	1.58
Sesame meal, mech ext	5.13	1.06	1.60	2.91	1.03	2.11	3.60	1.53	0.62	2.02
Soybean meal, dehu, sol ext	3.87	1.42	2.38	4.12	3.33	1.56	4.73	2.07	0.78	2.50
Soybean meal, sol ext	3.58	1.31	2.22	3.83	3.10	1.46	4.46	1.94	0.76	2.32
Soybean protein iso/conc	7.34	2.36	4.79	7.16	5.82	1.89	8.02	3.50	1.03	4.66
Soybeans, heat processed	2.88	1.09	1.76	3.05	2.48	1.20	3.48	1.56	0.55	1.85
Sunflower meal, dehu, sol ext	3.11	0.97	1.55	2.45	1.31	1.57	2.83	1.41	0.46	1.88
Sunflower meal, sol ext	2.58	0.67	1.27	1.91	1.11	1.15	1.73	1.16	0.46	1.71
Whey, dried	0.32	0.22	0.76	1.21	0.99	0.49	0.63	0.86	0.20	0.68
Whey, low lactose, dried	0.64	0.31	1.10	1.58	1.59	1.07	1.07	1.08	0.29	1.06
Yeast, brewers, dried	2.37	1.16	2.31	3.40	3.47	1.31	3.59	2.29	0.57	2.54
Yeast, torula, dehy	2.73	1.34	2.90	3.67	3.91	1.40	4.88	2.63	0.55	2.96

[a](From Refs. [6,8].)

[b](From Refs. [7,8].)

(From Refs. [5,7], unless otherwise indicated.) See Table 2 for the dry matter (DM) content. Dehy=dehydrated; CP=crude protein; mech ext=mechanically extracted; sol ext=solvent extracted; menhad=menhaden; rend=rendered; Poult=poultry; dehu=dehulled; iso/conc=isolate/concentrate. Dash=no available data.

Poultry, Marine, and Milk Products

Poultry feathers are virtually indigestible in their natural state, and disulfide bonds in feather keratin must be destroyed before the protein can be used by animals. The most widely used product is hydrolyzed feather meal, which is deficient in methionine, lysine, histidine, and tryptophan. Poultry by-product meal consists of the ground, rendered, clean parts of slaughtered poultry, exclusive of feathers. Fish meals are produced from fish caught specifically for making meals or from the residues remaining after processing fish mostly for human consumption. Dried fish solubles are by-products of the canning and oil-production industries. After centrifuging to remove the oil, the remaining fraction can be dried to make the product. Dried skim milk and dried whey have been used for young animals. Most of the fat and fat-soluble vitamins are removed in the skim milk, and whey is the part of milk that separates from the curd during cheese manufacturing. They are low in fat-soluble vitamins A and D.

OTHER PROTEIN SOURCES

Yeast products, such as brewer's and Torula dried yeast, contain high-quality protein and are an excellent source of B vitamins. The most often used nonprotein N for animals with a functioning rumen is urea, which is hydrolyzed and then ammonia can be incorporated into AA and proteins by rumen microbes. Dried poultry litter from caged layers or broiler operations is not suitable for nonruminant species, but can be used as a source of N for ruminants in some situations. Crystalline lysine and methionine have been used by the pig and poultry industries for some time, and threonine and tryptophan are now commercially available. There is potential to replace all the intact protein supplement with crystalline AA, even though current research findings indicate some limitations to this approach. Other protein sources can be used for food animal production: Readers are referred to, among others, the aforementioned NRC publications[5–8] and reviews.[3–4,9–11]

CONCLUSION

Many protein sources can be used for food animal production, but they have different feeding values because of a multitude of factors such as the nutrient content, palatability, antinutritional factors, and bioavailability. Consideration of the ideal protein concept and AA availability would be important in developing environmentally friendly, optimum feeding strategies. Efficient utilization of protein sources can contribute greatly to successful and sustainable food-animal production.

REFERENCES

1. USDA. *Oilseeds: World Market and Trade, December 2000*; Foreign Agricultural Service, USDA: Washington, DC, 2000. http://www.fas.usda.gov/oilseeds/circular/2003/00-12/toc.htm (accessed March 2003).
2. USDA. *Oilseeds: World Market and Trade, March 2003*; Foreign Agricultural Service, USDA: Washington, DC, 2003. http://www.fas.usda.gov/oilseeds/circular/2003/03-03/toc.htm (accessed March 2003).
3. Chiba, L.I. Protein Supplements. In *Swine Nutrition*, 2nd Ed.; Lewis, A.J., Southern, L.L., Eds.; CRC Press: Boca Raton, 2001; 803–837.
4. Church, D.C.; Kellems, R.O. Supplemental Protein Sources. In *Livestock Feeds and Feeding*; Kellems, R.O., Church, D.C., Eds.; Prentice Hall: Upper Saddle River, 1998; 135–163.
5. NRC. *Nutrient Requirements of Poultry*, 9th Ed.; National Academy Press: Washington, DC, 1994.
6. NRC. *Nutrient Requirements of Beef Cattle*, 7th Ed.; National Academy Press: Washington, DC, 1996.
7. NRC. *Nutrient Requirements of Swine*, 10th Ed.; National Academy Press: Washington, DC, 1998.
8. NRC. *Nutrient Requirements of Dairy Cattle*, 7th Ed.; National Academy Press: Washington, DC, 2001.
9. Dale, N. Ingredient analysis table: 2001 edition. Feedstuffs **2001**, *73* (29), 28–37.
10. Aherne, F.X.; Kennelly, J.J. Oilseed Meals for Livestock Feeding. In *Recent Developments in Pig Nutrition*; Cole, D.J.A., Haresign, W., Eds.; Butterworths: London, 1985; 278–315.
11. Thacker, P.A., Kirkwood, R.N., Eds.; *Nontraditional Feed Sources for Use in Swine Production*; Butterworths: Boston, 1990.

Female Reproduction: Anatomy and Physiology

Fuller W. Bazer
Thomas E. Spencer
Texas A&M University, College Station, Texas, U.S.A.

Rodney D. Geisert
Oklahoma State University, Stillwater, Oklahoma, U.S.A.

INTRODUCTION

The female reproductive system includes ovaries that produce sex steroids and protein hormones that act on the hypothalamic-pituitary axis and the uterus for regulation of the estrous or menstrual cycle and pregnancy.[1] This article provides basic information on mammalian and avian reproductive tracts.

MAMMALIAN FEMALE REPRODUCTIVE TRACT

The following Web site can be accessed for viewing of videos of the female anatomy of several mammalian species: http://www.ansi.okstate.edu/resource-room/ reprod/all/videos/. A schematic illustration of the female reproductive tract in cattle is presented in Fig. 1.

Development

The Müllerian (paramesonephric) duct and the urogenital sinus give rise to the female reproductive tract. The ovaries develop from the urogenital ridge and contain primordial germ cells which will differentiate into oocytes that mature to ova and are ovulated. The anterior vagina, derived from the urogenital sinus, differs histologically from the posterior vagina and the vestibule. The hymen forms at the site of fusion of the Müllerian duct and the urogenital sinus. The oviducts, uterus, and cervix develop during fetal life into endometrial and myometrial layers, but complete differentiation of the endometrium occurs only after birth, during the neonatal period with timing depending on species. The glands of the uterus differentiate and develop only after birth. The inner circular and outer longitudinal layers of smooth muscle of the myometrium differentiate during late fetal and/or early neonatal periods.

Genetic Regulation

The following genes affect development and differentiation of the female reproductive tract:

Wnt genes

Wnt genes are homologous to wingless. A *Drosophila* segment polarity gene encodes a secreted molecule implicated in patterning and establishment of cell boundaries during embryogenesis.

Wnt-7a. The Wnt gene guides the development of the anterior–posterior axis in the female reproductive tract.[2]

Hox genes

Homeobox genes encode transcription factors that regulate genetic cascades for developmental destinies of cells.

Hoxa-10. Homeobox genes are required for urogenital duct patterning and uterine development.[3]

Hoxa-11. Lack of gene expression results in sterility in males and females, and complete fetal resorption during early pregnancy.[4]

Estrogen receptor (ER) and progesterone receptor (PR)

Female mice lacking ERα and PR have defects in adult reproductive tract functions that involve the ovary and/or the uterus.

Ovary

Mammalian ovaries are bilateral, round structures surrounded by the infundibulum, which is a part of the oviduct, and is attached to the dorsal wall of the peritoneal

Encyclopedia of Animal Science
DOI: 10.1081/E-EAS 120019614

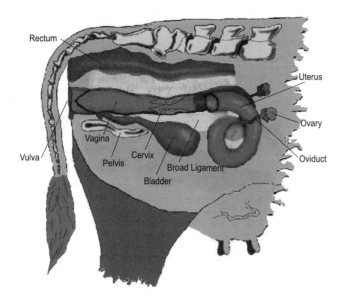

Fig. 1 Schematic illustration of the female reproductive tract in cattle. (*View this art in color at www.dekker.com.*)

cavity by the mesovarium, part of the broad ligament supporting the reproductive system (Fig. 2).

Histology of the ovary

The layers of cells/tissues of the ovary include:

Germinal Epithelium. This simple squamous or low cuboidal-type epithelium covers the free surface of the ovary.

Tunica Albuginea. This dense connective tissue beneath the germinal epithelium supports the structure of the ovary.

Cortex. This outer connective tissue of the ovary contains follicles.

Medulla. This inner connective tissue is highly vascularized and innervated, but lacks follicles except in equids.

Follicles. These structures within the ovary contain an ovum and cells responsible for steroidogenesis, which develop through the following stages:

Primary follicles: spheroidal primary oocytes about 45 μm in diameter surrounded by a single layer of follicle cells that separate the oocyte from adjacent interstitial tissue.

Secondary and tertiary follicles: growing follicles with multiple layers of cells from differentiation of follicle cells into granulosa cells surrounding the ovum; increased size of the oocyte nucleus and mitochondria; formation of the zona pellucida around the primary oocyte; and development of an antrum in tertiary follicles.

Mature Graafian follicles: These large, blister-like structures have an antrum filled with follicular fluid; theca interna and theca externa layers; prominent cumulus oophorus and corona radiata cells attached to the ovum; and the zona pellucida surrounding the vitelline

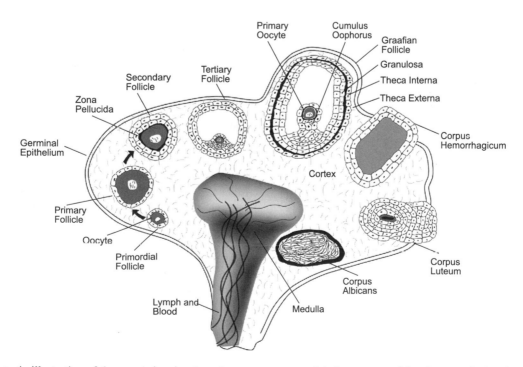

Fig. 2 Schematic illustration of the ovary showing the primary structures and their sequence of development during the ovarian cycle.

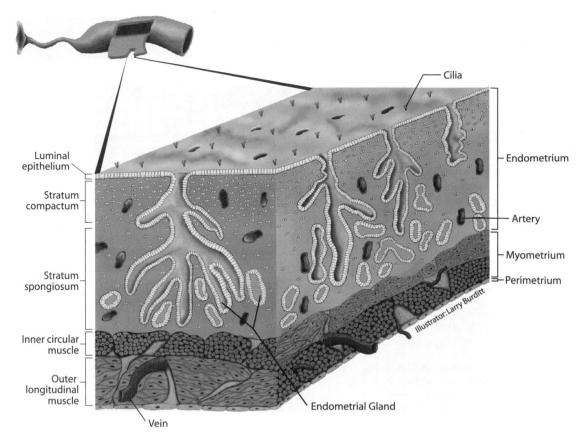

Fig. 3 Schematic illustration of the uterine wall of domestic animals. (*View this art in color at www.dekker.com.*)

membrane of the ovum. These follicles produce estrogens that induce an ovulatory surge of luteinizing hormone (LH) for ovulation and release of the ovum into the oviduct. Following ovulation, granulosa and theca cells form transitional structures on the ovary known as: 1) the corpus hemorrhagicum (CH), a newly ruptured follicle containing a blood clot and proliferating granulosa and theca cells; 2) the corpus luteum (CL), with yellow body or solid glandular structure formed through hyperplasia and hypertrophy of granulosa and theca cells (one CL forms from each ovulated follicle to secrete progesterone, the hormone required for pregnancy); and 3) the corpus albicans (CA), the white body or connective tissue remains of the CL that regress due to effects of luteolytic prostaglandin $F_{2\alpha}$ if pregnancy is not established.

Oviducts (Fallopian Tubes)

Oviducts are paired tubular structures that include: 1) the infundibulum, the membranous funnel-shaped end of each oviduct, lined with ciliated columnar epithelium, that directs ova into the ampulla; 2) the ampulla, the ovarian end of the oviduct, lined with ciliated columnar epithelial cells, that transports ova to the ampullary–isthmic junction;

3) the isthmus, the straight and rigid portion of the oviduct lined primarily with secretory columnar epithelium; and 4) the ampullary–isthmic junction, the site of fertilization.

Histology of the oviduct

The layers of tissue from the lumen include: 1) the endometrium (epithelial mucosa)—ciliated or secretory columnar epithelia; 2) the lamina propria, the mucous membrane beneath the endometrium and separating it from the myometrium; 3) the myometrium, the inner circular and outer longitudinal layers of smooth muscle; 4) the perimetrium, the outer serosal layer of the oviduct; and 5) the mesosalpinx, the portion of the broad ligament that supports the oviducts.

Functions of the oviduct

Oviduct functions include:

Infundibulum aids in freeing ova from follicles and directing them into the ampulla.
Ciliated cells of fimbria move ovum into ampulla.
Site of sperm capacitation.

Site of fertilization of ova.

Site of embryonic development for the first 48 to 72 hours of pregnancy, except in equids.

Nutrition for developing embryo prior to entry into the uterus.

Tubo-Uterine Junction (Uterotubal Junction)

The valve-like structure at the junction of the oviduct and the uterus has various morphologies among species and serves to regulate sperm numbers within the oviduct, prevent movement of uterine fluids into the oviduct, and prevent premature entry of embryos into the uterus.

Uterus

The uterus has two uterine horns connected by a common uterine body in most animals, but only a uterine body in most primates. Uteri, based on morphology, are of the following types:

Duplex

Two cervices, no uterine body, and two uterine horns completely separated from each other, in rats, mice, and rabbits.

Bicornuate

One cervix, short uterine body, and prominent uterine horns, in swine.

Bipartite

One cervix, prominent uterine body, and two uterine horns, in bitch, cow, goat, ewe, and mare.

Simplex

One cervix, highly developed uterine body, and no uterine horns, in humans and in nonhuman primates.

Histology of the uterus

The uterus has the following tissue layers from lumen to serosa (Fig. 3):

Endometrium. This layer includes:

Epithelia: simple columnar epithelium, mostly secretory, but with some ciliated cells around the openings of uterine glands. The luminal epithelium lines the uterine lumen and the glandular epithelium forms glands that are highly secretory during the luteal phase of the estrous or menstrual cycle and pregnancy.

Stroma: fibroblasts surrounding basal aspects of luminal and glandular epithelia.

Caruncles: specialized aglandular endometrial structures in ruminants for attachment of the placenta.

Myometrium. Inner circular and outer longitudinal layers of smooth muscle.

Perimetrium. Serosa or connective tissue lining the outside of the uterus.

Mesometrium. The portion of the broad ligament that supports the uterus.

Functions of the uterus

The uterus serves as the:

Site for conceptus (embryo/fetus and associated extra-embryonic placental membranes) development from early cleavage stages, implantation, and placentation to term.

Organ for secretion and/or transport of proteins, lipids, carbohydrates, and ions for histotrophic nutrition of the conceptus.

Site of placental development for hematotrophic nutrition of the fetus through transfer of nutrients to the fetal circulation via the placenta.

Transporter of sperm.

Organ for peristalsis for expulsion of the fetus at the end of pregnancy.

Organ for secretion of prostaglandin $F_{2\alpha}$ to induce luteolysis in nonpregnant females.

Cervix

The cervix connects the uterine body and the vagina. In ruminants, the cervix contains connective tissue ridges called annular rings, but the mare has none, and in pigs they are interwinding and interdigitating. The internal and external os cervix are the anterior and posterior openings of the cervix.

Histology of the cervix

Structures of the cervic include: 1) the endometrium—columnar epithelium and goblet cells that secrete mucus; 2) the myometrium—smooth muscle cells, not in distinct layers; and 3) connective tissue—dense fibrous tissue forming interlocking annular rings.

Functions of the cervix

The cervix serves: 1) as the site of semen deposition and sperm transport in some species; 2) as a barrier to

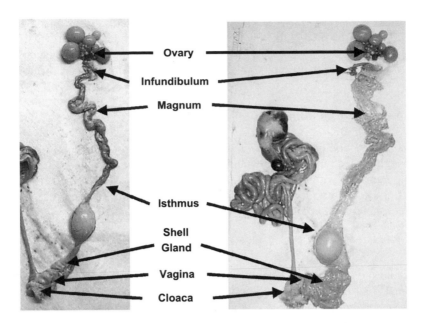

Fig. 4 Gross anatomical aspects of the avian female reproductive tract. (*View this art in color at www.dekker.com.*)

transport of abnormal sperm; 3) as the site for maximum sperm longevity; 4) to seal the cervix with a mucus plug during pregnancy to prevent uterine contamination; and 5) to dilate during parturition to allow the birth process.

Vagina

The vagina is the most posterior portion of the female reproductive system and includes the: 1) anterior vagina—extends from the external os cervix to anterior to the urethral opening; and 2) vestibule—extends from the urethral opening to the most posterior part of the vulva.

Histology of the vagina

Structures of the vagina include: 1) the endometrium—epithelium is low cuboidal in the luteal phase and stratified squamous during the follicular phase of the estrous or menstrual cycle; and 2) the myometrium, with an inner circular layer (smooth muscle; not well developed) and an outer circular layer (smooth muscle; very thin and poorly developed).

Functions of the vagina

The vagina serves: 1) as site of semen deposition in most species; 2) as part of the birth canal; 3) as site of production of pheromones that attract the male for mating; and 4) to maintain bactericidal and bacteriostatic secretions that aid in preventing infection of the reproductive tract.

Other Anatomical Structures

Hymen

The hymen is the thin connective tissue membrane that forms a border between the anterior vagina and the vestibule anterior to the urethral opening. It is seldom intact by the time a female reaches puberty.

Urethral orifice

The urethral orifice is the opening of the urethra on the ventral surface of the vestibule.

Suburethral diverticulum

The suburethral diverticulum is a blind pouch beneath the urethral orifice.

Clitoris

The clitoris is the homologue of the penis, located on the ventral surface of the vestibule.

Vulva

The external genitalia of the female reproductive tract are the vulva, which includes the labia minora (inner folds of tissue of the vulva) and the labia majora (the most prominent outer folds of skin).

AVIAN FEMALE REPRODUCTIVE TRACT

(http://www.ansi.okstate.edu/resource-room/reprod/all/videos/). The gross anatomical aspects of the avian female reproductive tract are presented in Fig. 4.

Ovary

The right ovary is rudimentary, whereas the functional left ovary has two lobes located ventral to the kidneys within the peritoneal cavity.[5]

Histology of the ovary

The ovary has a vascular medulla surrounded by the cortex and covered by the tunica albuginea with its dense capillary network. The germinal epithelium is a layer of cuboidal to columnar cells attached to the tunica albuginea. The ovary has ovarian follicles in one of five stages of development: 1) primary follicles; 2) growing follicles; 3) mature follicles; 4) discharged or ovulated follicles; and 5) atretic follicles. The ovum has a nucleus and cytoplasm surrounded by a vitelline membrane and the zona pellucida. Granulosa cells surround the zona pellucida and are separated from theca interna cells by a basement membrane. The theca interna cells merge into the stroma of the ovarian cortex.

Functions of the ovary

The ovary is the site for maturation and ovulation of ova and production of both estrogen and progesterone by granulosa and theca cells of preovulatory and postovulatory follicles.

Reproductive Tract/Oviduct

The tract is about 80 cm long, suspended by folds of peritoneum, and composed of distinct anatomical and functional regions.

Infundibulum

The ovarian end of the oviduct receives and retains the ovum for about 15 minutes while chalazae are formed.

Magnum

The magnum (35 to 40 cm in length) is where the albumen is secreted and deposited about the yolk during a 3-hour period.

Isthmus

The isthmus, between the magnum and shell gland, secretes albumen and soft shell membranes around the ovum over a period of about 75 minutes.

Shell gland

The shell gland, an expanded 10- to 12-cm-long organ, provides the hard calciferous shell over a period of 18 to 22 hours.

Vagina

The vagina is 7 to 10 cm long and secretes a mucus-like material that coats the egg during its one-minute transit to the opening of the vagina in the cloaca.

Histology of the oviduct

The oviduct consists of the serosa, inner circular and outer layers of smooth muscle, connective tissue supporting blood vessels and nerves, and mucosa. The mucosa is highly folded with numerous glands that produce various secretions including albumen, components of the soft shell, and other molecules that make up the egg. The mucosa includes both ciliated and secretory epitheilia.

CONCLUSIONS

This article describes the anatomy and general functions of the mammalian and the avian female reproductive tracts as the source of ova and sex steroids. This information will prepare the reader for other readings on pregnancy, oocyte maturation, fertilization, pregnancy recognition signals, uterine secretions, implantation, placentation, and parturition.

REFERENCES

1. Senger, P.L. *Pathways to Pregnancy and Parturition*, 2nd Ed.; Current Conception, Inc.: Pullman, WA, 2000.
2. Kitajewski, J.; Sassoon, D. The emergence of molecular gynecology: Homeobox and Wnt genes in the female reproductive tract. Bioessays **2000**, *22*, 902–910.
3. Benson, G.V.; Lim, H.; Paria, B.C.; Satokata, I.; Dey, S.K.; Mass, R.L. Mechanisms of reduced fertility in Hoxa-10 mutant mice: Uterine homeosis and loss of maternal Hoxa-10 expression. Development **1996**, *122*, 2687–2696.
4. Gendron, R.L.; Paradis, H.; Hsieh-Li, H.M.; Lee, D.W.; Potter, S.S.; Markoff, E. Abnormal uterine stromal and glandular function associated with maternal reproductive defects in Hoxa-11 null mice. Biol. Reprod. **1997**, *56*, 1097–1105.
5. Horton-Smith, C.; Amoroso, E.C. *Physiology of the Domestic Fowl*; Oliver and Boyd: Edinburgh, 1966.

Female Reproduction: Endocrine System

Janice Bahr

University of Illinois, Urbana, Illinois, U.S.A.

INTRODUCTION

Success in production of domestic animals depends heavily on the female to produce numerous young. For high reproductive efficiency, it is important to know the time of puberty and what factors can be manipulated to cause early onset of puberty without jeopardizing subsequent reproductive performance and to be familiar with hormonal changes during the estrous cycle of domestic animals and during the ovulatory cycle of poultry. In mammals, the expression of estrus is an outward indicator of pending ovulation. Knowledge of the temporal relationship between estrus and ovulation is essential to ensure optimum fertilization. The reproductive cycle of animals is influenced by photoperiod (day length), temperature, nutrition, pheromones, and stress. These factors, managed correctly, can have positive influences on reproductive efficiency. Finally, knowledge of the length of a productive breeding period is essential because reproductive efficiency decreases with age. This article provides an overview of the endocrinology of female reproduction of the pig, cow, sheep, goat, and chicken.

COMPONENTS OF THE FEMALE REPRODUCTIVE SYSTEM

Hypothalamus

The basic components of the female reproductive system are the hypothalamus, the pituitary, and the ovary. The hypothalamus, located at the base of the brain, is "grand central station," where internal and external signals are translated into chemical messages, called releasing or inhibiting factors. The key releasing factor for reproduction is gonadotropin-releasing hormone (GnRH), which when released in defined pulses causes the secretion of luteinizing hormone (LH) and in some cases follicle-stimulating hormone (FSH) by the anterior pituitary gland. A key inhibiting factor is dopamine, which inhibits the secretion of prolactin by the anterior pituitary gland.

Pituitary Gland

The pituitary gland consists of anterior, intermediate, and posterior lobes. The anterior pituitary gland has a vascular connection with the hypothalamus called the hypophyseal portal system, which transports releasing and inhibiting factors from the hypothalamus to the anterior pituitary. The anterior pituitary is also regulated by steroid hormones, as well as activin and inhibin secreted by the ovary. In contrast, the posterior pituitary gland is a neural extension of the hypothalamus containing nerve terminals that release oxytocin and vasopressin. The former hormone has a key role in uterine contractions, parturition, and milk let-down.

Ovary

The third major component of the female reproductive system is the ovary. During pregnancy or incubation (poultry), numerous oocytes are laid down in the cortex of the ovary. The number of available oocytes for the lifetime of a female is determined before birth or hatching (birds). During the pre- and postpubertal period, many oocytes begin to mature but become atretic due to a lack of a supportive hormonal environment. Only a very small percentage of oocytes with the surrounding follicular layers ever reach full maturity and ovulate. After ovulation in mammals, the granulosa and theca layers undergo morphological and biochemical differentiation and become a corpus luteum (CL). The CL secretes copious amounts of progesterone and is dependent on LH in most species. Eventually, prostaglandin $F_{2\alpha}$ ($PGF_{2\alpha}$), produced by the uterus, causes structural and functional regression of the CL.

NEGATIVE AND POSITIVE FEEDBACK SYSTEMS

The female reproductive system is tightly regulated through negative and positive feedback systems. Negative

Encyclopedia of Animal Science
DOI: 10.1081/E-EAS 120019615

feedback systems predominate and maintain a steady hormonal milieu. Ovarian steroids and inhibin, also produced by the ovary, negatively feedback to the hypothalamus and the anterior pituitary and control secretion of FSH and LH. However, an exception to this negative feedback system is the positive feedback system that operates during the period immediately preceding ovulation and triggers the LH surge. Under the influence of ever-increasing blood concentrations of estradiol 17-β produced by the rapidly growing ovarian follicles, the pulses of GnRH increase in frequency and amplitude, triggering a similar increase in LH secretion from the anterior pituitary gland. In poultry, rapidly increasing secretion of progesterone from the largest preovulatory follicle increases the secretion of GnRH and the subsequent increase in LH secretion. When this preovulatory LH surge reaches adequate concentrations in the blood, ovulation occurs. The number of follicles ovulating varies among species. The preovulatory surge of LH is terminated because estradiol-17β or progesterone secretion in the case of poultry subsides due to a lack of response of the ovarian follicles to LH.

EXTERNAL EFFECTORS

Photoperiod

External effectors of reproduction include photoperiod (day length), pheromones, temperature, nutrition, and stress. Responses to these effectors are communicated to the hypothalamus, where the secretion of releasing and inhibiting hormones, specifically GnRH and dopamine, is controlled. Photoperiod affects reproduction in all mammals and birds. However, some animals (e.g., sheep, goats, and poultry) are extremely sensitive to changes in day length. The annual initiation of the estrous cycle in sheep and goats is dependent on decreasing day length so that sheep and goats are called short-day breeders. Poultry need 14–17 hours of daylight for maximum egg production.

Pheromones

Pheromones are chemicals released by one animal that are detected by another animal and bring about a reproductive change in that animal. Dependency on pheromones varies with species and is found in mammals but not birds. Pheromones from males can reduce the age at which puberty occurs and induce estrus in females. Likewise pheromones from females communicate to the male that

the female is receptive for mating. Pheromones can also influence reproductive behavior within the same sex.

Temperature

Temperature is another regulator of reproduction. In most cases, temperature, especially hot temperature, can have a negative influence on overall reproductive efficiency.

Nutrition

Adequate nutrition is essential for high reproductive efficiency. Inadequate nutrition prior to puberty can delay the onset of puberty. Lack of adequate energy during lactation can delay the return of the female to estrus after weaning the offspring. Hypothalamic neurons can sense the level of nutrition and through hormones, such as neuropeptide Y and possibly leptin, can alter the secretion of GnRH from the hypothalamus.

Stress

Finally, stress—which usually will elevate glucocorticoids—has a negative impact on reproduction. Stress can result in sickness, loss of weight, and other related phenomena, and reduced reproductive efficiency.

ESTROUS CYCLES

The estrous cycle in mammals encompasses hormonal changes associated with the development of a Graafian follicle(s), ovulation, and CL formation. In domestic mammals (e.g., pig, cow, sheep, and goats) day 0 of the estrous cycle is defined as the first day the female is sexually receptive. The cycle consists of a follicular phase and a luteal phase (Fig. 1).[1] The follicular phase is short, occurring several days before estrus, and is dominated by increasing concentrations of estradiol-17β being produced by the rapidly growing ovarian follicles. The luteal phase is longer and is dominated by progesterone secreted by the CL. The ovulatory cycle of poultry has only a follicular phase and is terminated by ovulation of the largest preovulatory follicle, which is oviposited (laid) about 24 hours later.

Pig

The pig reaches puberty at age 6–9 months.[2,3] Its estrous cycle is 21 days in length. During the latter part of the

Phases of the Estrous Cycle

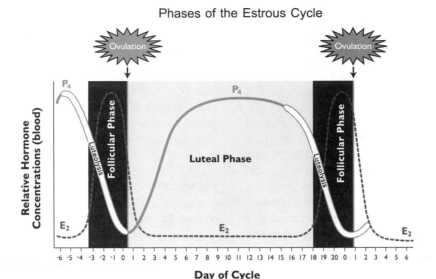

Fig. 1 Phases of the estrous cycle. The follicular phase begins after luteolysis, which causes a decline in progesterone. Gonadotropins (FSH and LH) are therefore produced that stimulate follicles to produce estrogen (E_2). The follicular phase is dominated by E_2 produced by ovarian follicles. The follicular phase ends at ovulation. Estrus is designated as day 0. The luteal phase begins after ovulation and includes the development of corpora lutea that produce progesterone (P_4). The luteal phase also includes luteolysis, brought about by prostaglandin $F_{2\alpha}$. (From *Pathways to Pregnancy and Parturition*—2nd Edition, with permission from Current Concepts, Inc., Pullman, WA.) (*View this art in color at www.dekker.com.*)

estrous cycle, rapidly growing ovarian follicles secrete large amounts of estradiol-17β about 48 hours prior to the LH surge. The pig displays estrus for 48–72 hours with ovulation occurring at the end of estrus or about 36 hours after onset. The LH surge peaks at the time of estrus and returns to basal levels about 10 hours later. FSH increases about 2–3 days after the initation of estrus and then decreases due to an increase of inhibin secretion from ovarian follicles. Following ovulation, a CL forms and progesterone secretion reaches its maximum around day 12 of the cycle and decreases after day 15. This decrease is due to episodic releases of $PGF_{2\alpha}$ from the uterus that cause the demise of the CL.

Cow

The cow reaches puberty at 10–12 months of age.[4] Its estrous cycle is 21 days in length. The follicular phase of the estrous cycle is 3–5 days, during which time multiple follicles begin developing, but only one Graafian follicle will develop to become the ovulatory follicles. During the luteal phase duration of 17–18 days, predominated by progesterone, there are 2–3 waves of follicular growth. Only as progesterone is decreasing does one of these follicles proceed to the final stages of maturation. The other follicles become atretic. The cow displays estrus for 12 to 24 hours with ovulation occurring about 30 hours after the onset of estrus.

Sheep and Goats

Sheep and goats reach puberty at 6–8 months of age. However, this time can range from 5–12 months depending on the time of year the animal is born.[5] They have an estrous cycle 16–17 days in length. The follicular phase, several days in length, is the time of rapid follicular growth. Estrus is displayed for about 24 to 36 hours. LH surge is coincident with the onset of estrus, and ovulation occurs about 30 hours after onset of estrus. Following ovulation, a CL forms and is functional until days 14–15,

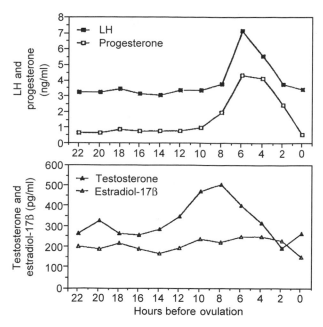

Fig. 2 Concentrations of LH, progesterone, testosterone, and estradiol-17β in blood of chickens during the ovulatory cycle. (Values from Ref. 7.)

when increased episodic releases of PGF2α from the uterus cause the demise of the CL.

Chicken

Chickens have only a follicular phase, called the ovulatory cycle.[6] The ovulatory cycle is 24–26 hours in length, determined mainly by the age of the chicken, with older chickens having longer ovulatory cycles. The LH surge, induced by rapidly increasing concentrations of progesterone produced by the granulosa cells of the largest follicle, occurs 4–6 hours before ovulation (Fig. 2).[7] After the follicle that ovulated the preceding day is oviposited (laid), ovulation of the largest follicle occurs

15–45 minutes later. Therefore, time of ovulation is determined by noting the time of oviposition.

CONCLUSION

Whereas there is a certain amount of variation in the reproductive endocrinology among female domestic mammals—and certainly between chickens and mammals—similar endocrine mechanisms regulate the female reproductive cycle. The differences reflect the various reproductive strategies used by animal species over the years. Future research needs to investigate how the reproductive system can function at an optimum level as animals are produced in more intense and restricted environments and are fed new feedstuffs, and as demands for animal products increase.

REFERENCES

1. Senger, P.L. *The Estrous Cylce-Terminology and Basic Concepts. Pathways to Pregnancy and Parturition*, 1st Rev. Ed.; Current Conceptions, Inc.: Pullman, WA, 1999; 116–128.
2. Cole, D.J.A.; Foxcroft, G.R.; Weir, B.J. Control of pig reproduction III. J. Reprod. Fertil. **1990**, (Suppl. 40).
3. Ford, S.F. Control of pig reproduction V. J. Reprod. Fertil. **1997**, (Supplement 52).
4. Lucy, M.C.; Savio, J.D.; Badinga, L.; De La Sota, R.L.; Thatcher, W.W. Factors that affect ovarian follicular dynamics in cattle. J. Anim. Sci. **1992**, *70*, 3615–3626.
5. Bindon, B.M.; Piper, L.R. The reproductive biology of prolific sheep breeds. Oxf. Rev. Reprod. Biol. **1986**, *8*, 414–451.
6. Johnson, A.J. Reproduction in the Female. In *Avian Physiologym*, 5th Ed.; Academic Press: New York, 2000; 569–596.
7. Bahr, J.M.; Johnson, P.A. Reproduction in Poultry. In *Reproduction in Domestic Animals*, 4th Ed.; Academic Press: New York, 1991; 555–575.

Female Reproduction: Maternal–Fetal Relationship

Alan W. Bell
Cornell University, Ithaca, New York, U.S.A.

INTRODUCTION

The mammalian fetus depends absolutely on its mother for its supply of oxygen and nutrients, and for disposal of heat and chemical excreta. It is largely insulated from the external thermal environment by its location in the uterus, the temperature of which is regulated by maternal systems. To an extent that diminishes with advancing gestation, it is also insulated from variations in maternal nutrient supply by the mother's ability to mobilize endogenous nutrient reserves and other maternal adaptations. However, in preparation for postnatal life, the fetus must develop an independent ability to respond appropriately to external stimuli that are delivered via the maternal system. Thus, as term approaches, fetal homeostatic mechanisms mature and the intimacy of the maternal–fetal relationship becomes increasingly apparent for some—but by no means all—maternal and fetal variables, as indicated by the degree of temporal association between maternal and fetal responses. This article will focus on key elements of the maternal–fetal relationship in late pregnancy. Most examples will be from experiments on sheep, the first and most commonly used species for studies of fetal physiology and metabolism in vivo in the conscious intact animal.

EXPERIMENTAL APPROACHES

Much insight into the maternal–fetal relationship was gained from acute experiments on anesthetized pregnant ewes by Joseph Barcroft and his successors during the first half of the 20th century.[1] However, assessment of normal fetal responses to changes in maternal physiology and metabolism did not become possible until the 1960s when Barron's group developed surgical and experimental techniques for chronic vascular catheterization and instrumentation of the sheep fetus in conscious intact ewes.[2] Simultaneous measurement of uterine and umbilical blood flows and concentrations of gases, nutrients, and metabolites in relevant arteries and veins allowed quantitative assessment of net exchanges of these materials between the maternal and fetal circulations. Net metabolism in nonfetal (predominantly placental) conceptus tissues was calculated as the difference between net

uterine and net umbilical exchange of a substrate (Fig. 1). Application of isotope dilution tracer techniques added further precision to the measurement of maternal–fetal exchanges and, by enabling measurement of rates of maternal production and utilization of nutrients, provided a means of estimating the partition of nutrients between maternal and conceptus tissues[3] (Fig. 1).

These experimental approaches to investigation of maternal–fetal relationships have been applied most extensively to sheep, but have also been used successfully in other farm animal species, including cattle, horses, and pigs.[4]

METABOLIC AND ENDOCRINE RELATIONSHIPS

Maternal and Fetal Nutrient Concentrations

The earliest applications of techniques for chronic catheterization of fetal blood vessels included simultaneous measurement of maternal and fetal blood concentrations of gases, nutrients, and metabolites under different nutritional and physiological conditions. It soon became apparent that for some important nutrients, such as glucose, fetal concentration closely parallels maternal concentration with a gradient favoring continuous transfer from dam to fetus in sheep, cattle, horses, and pigs[4] (Fig. 2). For other vital nutrients, such as amino acids and calcium, relations between maternal and fetal concentrations are much less apparent. For calcium and many amino acids, fetal concentration is persistently greater than maternal concentration. Under normal conditions, maternal and fetal blood oxygen tensions and concentrations and acid–base status are tightly regulated, and a strong, positive maternal–fetal oxygen gradient is maintained. However, maternal hypoxemia induced naturally by altitude or artificially in hypobaric chambers is associated with development of fetal hypoxemia and acidemia.[2]

Partition of Maternal Nutrient Supply Between Maternal and Conceptus Tissues

The progressive gestational increases in fetal and placental demand for nutrients results in the consumption

Encyclopedia of Animal Science
DOI: 10.1081/E-EAS 120019616

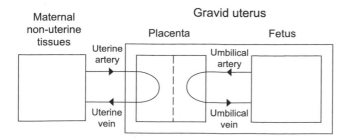

Fig. 1 Schematic representation of the pregnant ewe and its conceptus, illustrating the approach to estimating the partition of nutrients in vivo.

of a progressively greater fraction of the maternal nutrient supply by conceptus tissues. Thus, as term approaches, the gravid uterus consumes 30–50% of maternal glucose supply in well-fed ewes, depending on fetal number and maternal nutrition.[3] Maternal glucose production increases concomitantly through increased voluntary feed intake, if diet quantity and quality allow, and increased mobilization of endogenous glucogenic precursors. However, the rate of increase in maternal production lags behind the rate of increase in conceptus consumption. Accordingly, the fetus becomes increasingly sensitive to changes in maternal glucose supply as gestation advances.

Partition between maternal and conceptus tissues of other important nutrients, including amino acids, is less well-described. However, we have estimated that net consumption by the gravid uterus accounts for 60–70% of the protein absorbed by well-fed ewes carrying twins in late pregnancy.[5]

Maternal and Fetal Endocrine Relationships

During late gestation, fetal endocrine systems rapidly mature, and fetal concentrations of most important hormones are regulated independently of those of the mother. This separation is enabled by placental impermeability to most maternal protein and steroid hormones. Nevertheless, the dam can indirectly influence the endocrine status of her fetus(es) in several ways. Examples include the tendency for maternal and fetal insulinemia to be associated through the independent responses of the maternal and fetal pancreas to parallel changes in blood glucose concentrations, and the association between maternal and fetal thyroid hormone concentrations commonly mediated by maternal iodine status.

Other fetal endocrine systems are essentially uninfluenced by the dam during late pregnancy, including the somatotropic and adrenocorticotropic axes. In sheep (and presumably in other large domestic animal species) the somatotropic axis does not become fully engaged until

soon after birth and is characterized by very high plasma concentrations of growth hormone and low levels of insulin-like growth factor (IGF) I during fetal life.[6] Circulating levels of IGF-II are much higher in the fetus than in the dam, related to the relatively high expression of this growth factor in multiple fetal tissues.

Fetal adrenal responsiveness to ACTH accelerates dramatically as term approaches, and the resulting exponential increase in fetal cortisol concentrations, independent of maternal levels, is a key factor in induction of the cascade of events leading to parturition.[7]

PLACENTAL INFLUENCES ON MATERNAL–FETAL COMMUNICATION

Placental Nutrient Transport

Major functions of the placenta, comprising transport of nutrients and excreta, production of hormones and other bioactive signaling molecules, and immune protection of the fetus, are discussed elsewhere in this encyclopedia. The selective ability of the placenta to transport nutrients from maternal to fetal circulations is an important aspect of maternal–fetal communication. Ultimately, maternal–fetal nutrient transfer is determined by the complex integration of fetal demand and is dictated by genetic capacity for growth, placental transport capacity, and maternal nutrient supply, which are regulated in an interdependent manner. For example, moderate maternal undernutrition and reduction in glucose supply can lead to upregulation of placental capacity for glucose transport, whereas more severe nutrient deprivation decreases both placental transport capacity and fetal demand for energy substrates such as glucose.[8]

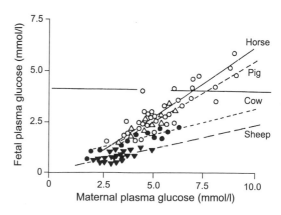

Fig. 2 Relations between fetal and maternal arterial concentrations of plasma glucose in sheep (▼), cow (●), pig (△), and horse (○) during late gestation. (Reproduced from Ref. [4] with permission of the publisher.)

Differences among the molecular mechanisms for nutrient transport account for different patterns of association between maternal and fetal nutrient concentrations. Placental glucose transport is accomplished by facilitated diffusion through actions of the glucose transporter molecules GLUT1 and GLUT3.[8] It is therefore not surprising that this concentration-dependent process results in strong association between maternal and fetal glucose concentrations[4] (Fig. 2). In contrast, maternal–fetal transfer of calcium and most amino acids is achieved by active transport, which explains how it is possible both for fetal concentrations of these nutrients to exceed those of the dam and for the general lack of correlation between maternal and fetal concentrations.[8] Placental transfer of oxygen is influenced more by a combination of uterine and umbilical blood flows and by maternal and fetal hemoglobin concentrations than by placental diffusion characteristics. Nevertheless, the adaptability of the system is such that, in the sheep, placental blood flows must be reduced substantially ($\geq 50\%$) before clear decreases in fetal oxygenation occur.[2]

Influence of Placental Hormones

Placental production and release of hormones into maternal and fetal circulations represent another powerful means of maternal–fetal communication that is responsive to changes in maternal and fetal physiological and metabolic status. For example, increased placental expression and release of placental lactogen during maternal undernutrition is thought to at least partly mediate metabolic adaptations that promote glucose-sparing and fatty-acid mobilization and utilization in maternal insulin-responsive tissues. It is equally likely that placental hormones directly or indirectly modulate fetal metabolic and growth processes, as indicated in recent observations of fetal growth retardation in mice with placenta-specific deletion of the IGF-II gene.[9]

CONCLUSIONS

Communication between the mammalian fetus and its mother is achieved through the transport and endocrine functions of the placenta, facilitated by the intimate association of uterine and umbilical microvasculature. Placental functions are, in turn, modulated by integration of signals from both maternal and fetal systems. Fetal nutrition depends absolutely on placental transfer of vital nutrients, and is therefore influenced by maternal nutritional status. However, the placenta effectively shields the fetus from direct influences of maternal hormones and immune cytokines, allowing independent development of fetal endocrine and immune systems. Also, placental constraint of fetal access to maternal nutrients ensures that unbridled fetal growth is less likely to compromise maternal metabolic health during late pregnancy or lead to serious difficulties during parturition.

ARTICLES OF FURTHER INTEREST

Placenta: Functions, p. 712
Pregnancy: Maternal Response, p. 748

REFERENCES

1. Dawes, G.S. *Foetal and Neonatal Physiology; A Comparative Study of the Changes at Birth*; Year Book Medical Publishers: Chicago, IL, 1968; 1–247.
2. Battaglia, F.C.; Meschia, G. *An Introduction to Fetal Physiology*; Academic Press: Orlando, FL, 1986; 1–245.
3. Bell, A.W. Pregnancy and Fetal Metabolism. In *Quantitative Aspects of Ruminant Digestion and Metabolism*; Forbes, J.M., France, J., Eds.; CAB International: Wallingford, England, 1993; 405–431.
4. Fowden, A.L. Comparative aspects of fetal carbohydrate metabolism. Equine Vet. J. Suppl. **1997**, *24*, 19–25.
5. McNeill, D.M.; Slepetis, R.; Ehrhardt, R.A.; Smith, D.M.; Bell, A.W. Protein requirements of sheep in late pregnancy: Partitioning of nitrogen between gravid uterus and maternal tissues. J. Anim. Sci. **1997**, *75*, 809–816.
6. Gluckman, P.D.; Pinal, C.S. Maternal-placental-fetal interactions in the endocrine regulation of fetal growth: Role of the somatotrophic axis. Endocrine **2002**, *19*, 81–89.
7. Fowden, A.L.; Li, J.; Forhead, A.L. Glucocorticoids and the preparation for life after birth: Are there long-term consequences of the life insurance? Proc. Nutr. Soc. **1998**, *57*, 113–122.
8. Bell, A.W.; Ehrhardt, R.A. Regulation of placental nutrient transport and implications for fetal growth. Nutr. Res. Rev. **2002**, *15*, 211–230.
9. Constancia, M.; Hemberger, M.; Hughes, J.; Dean, W.; Ferguson-Smith, A.; Fundele, R.; Stewart, F.; Kelsey, G.; Fowden, A.; Sibley, C.; Reik, W. Placental-specific IGF-II is a major modulator of placental and fetal growth. Nature **2002**, *417*, 945–948.

Fertilization

S. E. Echternkamp
*United States Department of Agriculture, Agriculture Research Service,
Clay Center, Nebraska, U.S.A.*

INTRODUCTION

Fertilization is the process by which mammalian male (spermatozoon) and female (oocyte or ovum) haploid gametes unite to produce a totipotent diploid zygote that develops into a genetically distinct individual. The fertilization process is composed of a series of sequential steps: 1) sperm capacitation; 2) binding of capacitated sperm to the zona pellucida (ZP); 3) acrosome reaction; 4) sperm penetration of ZP; 5) fusion of spermatozoon and ovum (egg); 6) egg activation; and 7) establishment of the embryonic genome. Descriptions of the molecular and physiological mechanisms for most fertilization events are incomplete and limited primarily to laboratory animals, and for some processes (e.g., intercellular fusion of gametes) are primarily hypothetical.

SPERM CAPACITATION

Mammalian spermatozoa are composed of a head and a tail region. The head, surrounded by a plasma membrane, contains the apical acrosome (enlarged lysosome with outer and inner acrosomal membrane), nucleus (haploid complement of genomic DNA bound to sperm-specific histones), and postnuclear cap. The tail region includes the midpiece (densely packed, helical array of mitochondria that produce ATP), principal piece (self-powered flagellum with $9+2$ array of microtubules), and terminal piece. Freshly ejaculated mammalian sperm are incapable of fertilizing ova but acquire functional competence through capacitation. Only capacitated sperm can penetrate the cumulus oophorus, bind to the ZP, and undergo the acrosome reaction.

Capacitation is a poorly defined maturational process that occurs in sperm during migration through the female uterus and into the oviducts, and includes a series of intracellular and membranal changes that remodel the plasma membrane surface and increase its fluidity. Capacitation is likely mediated by soluble factors secreted by the female reproductive tract, by the presence or removal of proteins in seminal plasma (e.g., human antifertility factor), and/or by removal of decapacitation

factors on the sperm surface; identification of such proteins varies among species. The molecular process includes an initial cholesterol efflux and lowering of the cholesterol/phospholipid ratio in the plasma membrane followed by removal of glycoproteins from the sperm cell surface, tyrosine phosphorylation of plasma membrane proteins, an increase in intracellular pH, increase in bicarbonate and Ca^{2+} ion concentrations, and membrane hyperpolarization. Such intracellular and membrane changes facilitate binding of sperm to the ZP and induction of the acrosome reaction. Capacitated sperm detach from the epithelium of oviductal ampulla; express a transient hyperactive, frenzied, dancing motion; and either are attracted by substances from the ovulating follicle or ovum or are lost into the peritoneal cavity via the oviductal infundibulum.

OVULATION

The ovum is released from the Graafian follicle at ovulation, captured by the infundibulum of the oviduct, and transported to the ampullar–isthmus junction (site of fertilization). The oocyte/ovum (Fig. 1) is surrounded by the ZP, a viscoelastic, spherical, extracellular matrix composed of three glycoproteins: ZP1, ZP2, and ZP3 in rodents and humans (homologous to ZPB, ZPA, and ZPC in pigs). These glycoproteins are synthesized by the oocyte in rodents or by cells of primary and secondary preantral ovarian follicles in species with a thicker ZP (e.g., cattle and pigs). The murine ZP is an arrangement of repeating filaments of ZP2 and ZP3 units joined by intermittent cross-linking by ZP1. In addition to being structural components, ZP3 and ZP2 are associated with gamete recognition and receptor–ligand binding between the egg extracellular matrix and sperm. Glycoprotein ZP3 is the primary receptor for binding of the egg to acrosome-intact sperm, leading to initiation of signal transduction events of the acrosome reaction; ZP2 is a secondary receptor and binds to proteins within the matrix of the inner acrosomal membrane of acrosome-reacted sperm.

Outside the ZP are multiple layers of specialized granulosa cells embedded in a mucopolysaccharide matrix

Encyclopedia of Animal Science
DOI: 10.1081/E-EAS 120019617

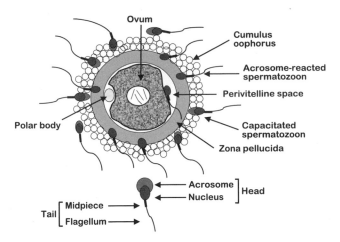

Fig. 1 Diagram of mammalian fertilization. (*View this art in color at www.dekker.com.*)

(cumulus oophorus). The cumulus oophorus occurs only in mammals with a placenta, and is lost shortly after ovulation in some mammals (e.g., cattle, pigs, and sheep) but remains attached to the ZP for several hours in other species. Speculation is that the ovum and/or its cumulus cells secrete attractants for capacitated sperm. Penetration of the cumulus oophorus by capacitated sperm is assisted by hyaluronidases (e.g., PH-20) on the sperm surface.

SPERM ACROSOME REACTION

Binding to the ZP initiates the acrosome reaction and exocytosis, which enables the spermatozoon to penetrate the ZP. The reaction is initiated in acrosome-intact murine sperm by *O*-linked oligosaccharides of ZP3 binding to protein ligands in the anterior head of the spermatozoon. In other species, it is unclear whether *O*-linked or *N*-linked oligosaccharides are the sperm-binding component, and ZPB (e.g., pigs), rather than ZP3, is the primary binding protein. Binding to the ZP induces activation of cyclic AMP/protein kinase A and protein kinase C. Protein kinase A together with inositol *tris*-phosphate activates calcium channels in the outer acrosomal membrane. Depletion of calcium in the acrosome activates a store-operated calcium entry mechanism in the plasma membrane that increases cytosolic calcium and enables contact and fusion of the plasma membrane with the outer acrosomal membrane at multiple sites, leading to membrane vesiculation and release of the acrosome's contents. Release of acrosomal contents exposes the equatorial segment and the inner acrosomal membrane and enables secondary binding to ZP2, which orientates the thrusting spermatozoon for ZP penetration.

SPERM PENETRATION OF ZONA PELLUCIDA

Sperm penetration of the ZP and entrance into the perivitelline space are likely achieved by a combination of enzymatic cleavage of the glycoprotein filaments around the spermatozoon and enhanced forward mechanical thrusting by hyperactive beating of the tail or ratcheting movement of the spermatozoon. Possible digestive enzymes include those released during acrosomal exocytosis (e.g., nonacrosin proteases, serine protease homologues, and glycosidases), a variant of acrosin, or novel enzymes (e.g., hydrolases). For years, acrosin was considered to be the primary proteolytic enzyme to digest the ZP, but results show that acrosin-knockout mice are fertile, and proacrosin/acrosin is associated with inner acrosome membrane-mediated sperm binding to the ZP (e.g., ZP2). In boar spermatozoa, the major role of acrosin is to regulate release of acrosomal matrix proteins during exocytosis, and proacrosin-binding protein is in the acrosome matrix.

EGG ACTIVATION

Upon entering the perivitelline space, the spermatozoon attaches to the ovum plasma membrane (oolemma) and, through a series of complex molecular interactions, the membranes of the two gametes fuse to form a diploid cell. Initial attachment of the spermatozoon inner acrosomal membrane is followed by firm adhesion of the equatorial segment and the posterior head to the oolemma. In several mammals, adhesion is mediated by disintegrin domains of ADAM (acronym for disintegrin and metalloprotease domain) and cysteine-rich secretory proteins (CRISP) on the sperm membrane interacting with integrins, tetraspanins, integrin-associated proteins, and unidentified molecules on the ovum membrane. Fertilin α (ADAM 1), fertilin β (ADAM 2), and cyritestin (ADAM 3) undergo proteolytic processing between the metalloprotease and disintegrin domains so that only disintegrin domains, cysteine-rich domains, and EGF-like repeats remain on the sperm surface. Fertilin α and β form heterodimers in bovine, guinea pig, and mouse sperm that attach to the α and β ligand-binding sites of ova integrins; however, fertilin α and cyritestin are not essential for binding of human sperm. Integrins are a family of heterodimeric cell adhesion molecules that includes 18 α and 8 β subunits that combine to produce 24 integrins. Epididymal CRISP proteins are detected on the postacrosomal region of the head and on the midpiece and principal piece of the tail of rat, mouse, horse, human, and rhesus monkey sperm. However, the mechanism by which CRISP proteins participate in gamete membrane interactions is unknown.

Tetraspanin CD9 appears to be a component of the multimeric molecular complex as ova from CD9 knockout mice do not undergo sperm–oolemma fusion. Sperm attachment may also require tail motility, but it decreases or stops within seconds after sperm–oolemma fusion.

Proposed molecular mechanisms for the fusion process are primarily hypothetical. The ovum engulfs the spermatozoon through a process similar to phagocytosis, beginning with the inner acrosomal membrane and eventually incorporating the tail. Fusion of the spermatozoon and the ovum plasma membrane causes formation of a fusion pore and, ultimately, incorporation of one membrane into the other, followed by incorporation of the paternal cytoplasm and DNA, the sperm centriole, and a sperm factor(s) (e.g., glucosamine-6-phosphate isomerase), which initiates egg activation. An early event in egg activation is an increase in cytosolic calcium that induces resumption of meiosis, exocytosis of the cortical granules, and the vitelline block. Release of the cortical granule contents (e.g., mucopolysaccharides, proteases, plasminogen activator, acid phosphatase, and peroxidase) increases the volume of the perivitelline space, modifies or hardens the ZP, and degrades sperm-binding proteins to prevent fusion of the ovum plasma membrane with additional sperm (i.e., polyspermy, a lethal condition). Release of calcium stores in the endoplasmic reticulum is induced by inositol 1,4,5-*tris*-phosphate binding to its receptor. The inositol 1,4,5-*tris*-phosphate may be induced either by a sperm phospholipase C stimulatory factor or by stimulation of egg phospholipase C through signal transduction pathways.

Subsequent egg activation responses include recruitment of maternal mRNAs for translational changes in protein syntheses. Resumption of the cell cycle begins with a second meiotic division, followed by extrusion of the second polar body and formation of the female pronucleus a few hours after gamete fusion. Similarly, the nucleus of the spermatozoon is decondensed and transformed into a male pronucleus. Both maternal chromatin and male pronuclear development are regulated by common egg cytoplasmic cell-cycle regulatory factors through a series of transformations that restore the transcriptional competence of the inactive gamete chromatin.

Spatial organization of the microtubule arrays in a cell is largely dependent on the centrosome contributed by the spermatozoon in most primate and animal species, except mice. The centrosome consists of two centrioles and pericentriolar material, and is responsible for nucleation of the microtubules and formation of the mitotic spindle between opposed pronuclei. At fusion, the sperm tail is incorporated into the ooplasm, and its centriolar region forms the sperm aster. While the sperm head is decondensing, the aster guides the female pronucleus toward the male pronucleus and increases in size as the two pronuclei migrate toward the center of the egg. The centriole duplicates during the pronuclear stage, and syngamy centrioles are found at opposite poles of the first cleavage. Migration of the pronuclei into their juxtaposition is followed by breakdown of the pronuclear envelope, giving rise to a group of chromosomes for the ensuing cell division. Subsequently, maternally and paternally derived chromosomes intermix to establish the embryonic diploid genome and initiate embryogenesis.

CONCLUSION

Fertilization is a complex system encompassing a series of physiological and biochemical events performed in a well-orchestrated plan to create a new genetically unique individual. In-depth reviews of the fertilization processes have been published previously.[1–5] Fertilization rates for competent sperm and ova are >95%; however, 25% to 30% of the resulting embryos die within 5 to 15 days after fertilization. The contributions of genomic, gametogenic, and fertilization anomalies, and of maternal deficiencies to this early embryonic mortality are subject to debate. Of primary importance in understanding gamete fertilization is its application to successful artificial insemination, in vitro fertilization, and gamete and species preservation. Fertilization rates and embryonic survival are substantially lower for in vitro methods, but research in humans and animals to improve the methodology has provided information for several fertilization processes, especially sperm capacitation. However, information on many of the molecular and physiological mechanisms is limited or unknown, and has been obtained primarily in rodents, zona-free hamster oocytes, and sea urchins.

REFERENCES

1. Evans, J.P. The molecular basis of sperm–oocyte membrane interactions during mammalian fertilization. Hum. Reprod. Updat. **2002**, *8* (4), 297–311.
2. Evans, J.P.; Florman, H.M. The state of the union: The cell biology of fertilization. Nat. Cell Biol. **2002**, *4* (Suppl 1), s57–63.
3. *Fertilization*; Hardy, D.M., Ed.; Academic Press: San Diego, 2002.
4. Saacke, R.G.; Dalton, J.C.; Nadir, S.; Bame, J.; Nebel, R.L. Spermatozoal Characteristics Important to Sperm Transport, Fertilization and Early Embryonic Development. In *Gametes: Development and Function*; Lauria, A., Gandolfi, F., Enne, G., Gianaroli, L., Eds.; Serono Symp.: Milano, 1998; 320–335.
5. Yanagimachi, R. Mammalian Fertilization. In *The Physiology of Reproduction*; Knobil, E., Neill, J.D., Eds.; Raven Press: New York, 1994; 189–317.

Fiber-Producing Animals

Margaret Merchant
Macaulay Institute, Aberdeen, U.K.

INTRODUCTION

As a proportion of global fiber production (including synthetics and cotton), animal fiber production accounts for less than 10% of manufactured goods and is declining. However, it remains vital to those communities living in pastoral areas, with few other options for generating income. It may be the sole output, or a by-product of animals providing food or transport. It is produced in a range of environments, from extensive pastoral systems to intensive, highly specialized systems focused on the production of very high quality fiber. This article briefly describes fiber growth, the main commercial fibers produced, their origins, and production systems.

Animal fibers vary in physical characteristics, permitting a wide range of end uses (from apparel and furnishings to insulation and brushes). However, apart from silk, all animal fiber is produced by structures called hair follicles in the skin of mammals.

HAIR FOLLICLES

Hair follicles develop in the skin during fetal life. Primary follicles, which form first, are generally larger, have an associated sweat gland and erector muscle, and produce longer, coarser fibers called guard hairs. The smaller, secondary follicles generally produce shorter, finer fibers forming the undercoat or down. Animals with two distinct layers to the coat are double-coated (Table 1). Skin follicles undergo cycles of active fiber growth and molting. In most species, the cycles are synchronized, primarily by day length, to provide a pelage appropriate to climatic conditions. Genetic selection of fiber-producing animals, such as the Merino sheep and the Angora goat, has increased the total number of follicles, reduced the differences between primary and secondary follicles (producing a uniform single fleece), and increased the length of the growing period to what is, effectively, continuous fiber growth.

All hair fibers are formed from long, spindle-shaped cortical cells lying parallel to the fiber axis and surrounded by a flattened sheath of cuticle cells.[1] Within the cortical cells, the protein keratin forms a complex system of helical fibrils, embedded in a nonhelical matrix. The number and physical arrangement of the cells affect the fiber diameter, medullation (hollow core), and smoothness of the cuticle, which are characteristic of different animal fibers and have a major influence on their mechanical properties.

HARVESTING ANIMAL FIBER

Wild animals molt their pelage, usually once annually in spring, and the fiber can be gathered where it falls. Domestic species that molt may be harvested by plucking or combing, but those that do not must be shorn.[2] Shearing is skilled and physically demanding work, even with the development of machine-operated shears. Research to reduce the cost and effort in harvesting wool has focused on chemical defleecing and robotic shearing, but neither method is yet in practical use. Chemical defleecing using a natural plant extract, Lagodendron® (Societe Proval, 75012 Paris), is used in the harvesting of angora fiber from rabbits kept in intensive systems in France.

FIBER PRODUCTION FROM DIFFERENT ANIMALS

The five main keratinous fibers used in the production of textiles are wool, mohair, angora, cashmere, and alpaca. Basic details of their production and of some of the rarer fibers are listed in Table 1.

Globally, the dominant animal fiber produced is wool. Grown by many different breeds of sheep, often as a by-product of meat or milk, wool varies in type with a mean fiber diameter ranging from 12 to 50 μm. It can be divided into three broad categories: merino wool (≤ 24.5 μm), crossbred wool (24.6 to 32.5 μm), and carpet wool (≥ 32.6 μm). About 50% of all wool traded is merino wool, grown predominantly in extensive grazing systems.

Mohair and cashmere are produced by goats in extensive pastoral systems, although where meat production is important, stubbles and cereal by-products may also be provided. Angora goats (producing mohair) are usually kept in hotter, drier conditions than cashmere goats. The two types interbreed freely, but their coat types are quite distinct and the crossbred fleece (cashgora) has little commercial value. Mohair forms a single, uniform, generally white fleece of wavy, lustrous fibers. The

Encyclopedia of Animal Science
DOI: 10.1081/E-EAS 120019619

Table 1 Fiber-producing animals

Species	Fiber	Global production k tons/year	Major regions of production in descending order	Coat type	Range in mean fiber diameter[1] μm	Range in yield per animal[a] kg/year	Commercial colors	Usual method of harvest
Sheep (genus *Ovis*)	Wool	1,500	Australia, New Zealand, China	Single/rarely double	12–50	1–10	White + others	Shear annually
Goat (*Capra hircus aegarus*)	Mohair	10	S. Africa, U.S.A., S. America	Single	23–46	4–10	White	Shear twice annually
Goat (*Capra hircus laniger*)	Cashmere	5	China, Mongolia, Iran, Afghanistan	Double	12–19	0.05–0.50	White, fawn gray, brown	Comb or shear annually
Alpaca (*Llama pacos*)	Alpaca	4.5	S. America	Single	20–40	3.0–5.0	White, brown, black, gray	Shear annually
Llama (*Llama glama*)	Llama	2.5	S. America	Double	30–40	2.0–5.0	White, brown, black, gray	Shear annually
Guanaco (*Llama hunchus*)	Guanaco	>0.01	S. America	Double	13–16	0.50–0.95[b]	Golden brown	Shear occasionally
Vicuña (*Vicugna vicugna*)	Vicuña	0.005	S. America	Double	12–15	0.08–0.25[b]	Golden brown	Shear occasionally
Rabbit (*Oryctolagus cuniculus*)	Angora	3	China, S. America, Eastern Europe	Three fiber types	11–15	0.4–1.4	White	Pluck or shear × 4 annually
Bactrian camel (*Camelus bactrianus*)	Camelhair	4.5	Northern China, Mongolia	Double	18–24	3.5–6.0	Reddish brown, rarely white	Gather or comb annually
Yak (*Bos phoephagus grunniens*)	Yak	1.0	Himalayan region	Double	15–20	0.1–0.2	Brown, fawn, gray, white	Comb annually
Musk ox (*Ovibos moschatus*)	Qiviut	>0.003	N. America	Double	11–20	0.9–2.5	Light to dark brown	Gather or comb annually

[a]Whole coat in single-coated animals, undercoat in double-coated animals.
[b]Yield per harvest.
(From Refs. 3 and 4.)

presence of kemp fibers grown by primary follicles is a serious fault. Cashmere is the downy undercoat of double-coated goats and is separated from the coarse outer guard hairs before processing. Several breeds have been developed specifically for cashmere production, but cashmere may be harvested from other breeds that have a well-defined undercoat under 19 μm. Fine cashmere grown in India is known as pashmina, but this term has also been applied, confusingly, to mixtures of cashmere and silk.

Angora fiber is grown by the Angora rabbit. The coat comprises three types of fiber, all medullated: guide hairs, guard hairs, and down, in the ratio 1:4:60.[5] Rigid kemp fibers give the yarn its characteristically fluffy appearance. Length and cleanliness are the most important traits, commercially. Production systems are intensive. High levels of food intake, particularly protein, are required.

The alpaca is one of four types of camelid found predominantly in South America. There are two distinct breeds of alpaca: the Huacaya, which has short, crimped staples, and the less-common Suri, which produces ringlets of wavy, silky fiber (the preferred type). Smaller amounts of fiber, used in the manufacture of coarse blankets and socks, are produced by the llama. Traditional pastoral systems of production are still found in the high-altitude grasslands of the Andes. The guanaco and vicuña are both wild. The vicuña was hunted to the verge of extinction for its very fine undercoat, but efforts today are centered on sustainable harvesting (chaku), with capture and shearing followed by safe release.

Camel hair comes mainly from the two-humped Bactrian camel, a multipurpose animal providing meat, milk, hides, and transport in desert areas. It has a double coat, the undercoat being sold for fine textile production and the coarser fiber being used to make felt for local use. Yaks have a similar multipurpose role in high-altitude regions across Central Asia and into China.

Two very rare and very fine fibers are qiviut, the undercoat of the musk ox found in arctic conditions in northern America and the USSR, and shahtoosh, the undercoat of the wild Tibetan antelope found in herds at high altitude on the Chang Tang plateau of northern Tibet. Both of these animals have been hunted close to extinction, but they are making a managed return backed by international law.

SILK

About 75,000 tons of silk is produced annually worldwide. Silk forms a continuous filament (up to 1600 meters in length) composed of two strands of a macromolecular protein, fibroin, bound together by the protein sericin. It is spun by the larval stage of moths (silkworms) in the formation of their cocoons. Wild silk (tussah) is spun by silkworms (*Antheraea pernyi*) that have fed on oak leaves. Mulberry silk is produced, mainly in China, by domesticated silkworms (*Bombyx mori*) that have fed on mulberry leaves. Genetic selection has left the domesticated silkworm totally dependent on man for its survival, requiring intensive husbandry. Once the cocoons have been formed, the chrysalides are killed, the gum that binds the filament is softened, and the silk is removed in a process called reeling.

CONCLUSION

Animal fibers are produced by a wide range of species found across all continents except Antarctica. Some of these species have been exported to other continents, and rare fibers may now be grown far from their traditional origins—cashmere, for example, now grown in small quantities in Europe.

Animal fiber accounts for a small proportion of world textile fiber production, and even with improved genetic selection and animal husbandry techniques, it is unlikely to increase. It is now regarded as a luxury commodity because of its high quality (fineness, softness, warmth, and handle), its rarity, and its exotic image. Because of this, it commands a high unit price, which covers the difficulties of production and harvesting, often in remote locations. However, expectations for quality of the raw product continue to rise, and only those systems focused on maintaining and improving fiber quality will remain financially viable in the long term.

ARTICLES OF FURTHER INTEREST

Camelids, p. 187
Yak, p. 898

REFERENCES

1. Ryder, M.L. *Hair. The Institute of Biology's Studies in Biology*; Edward Arnold: London, 1973; 41.
2. Petrie, O.J. *Harvesting of Textile Animal Fibres. FAO Agricultural Services Bulletin*; FAO: Rome, 1995; 122.
3. *Silk, Mohair, Cashmere and Other Luxury Fibres*; Franck, R.R., Ed.; Woodhead Publishing Ltd.: Cambridge, 2001.
4. Watkins, P.; Brown, A. *Luxury Fibres. Rare Materials for Higher Added Value. Special Report No 2633*; Economic Intelligence Unit: London, 1992.
5. Lebas, F.; Coudert, P.; de Rochambeau, H.; Thébault, R.G. *The Rabbit—Husbandry, Health and Production. Animal Production and Health Series*; FOA: Rome, 1997; 21.

Forages: Grasses

D. J. R. Cherney
J. H. Cherney
Cornell University, Ithaca, New York, U.S.A.

INTRODUCTION

Grasses, belonging to the botanical family Poaceae (or Gramineae), furnish the bulk of feed used for domestic animals worldwide. Grasses include sod crops and the cereals. One of the most ubiquitous of flowering plants, grasses are distributed all over the world. There are about 10,000 species of grasses grouped into 650 to 785 genera.

Grasses, like legumes, are made up of proteins, lipids, sugars, minerals, and structural carbohydrates (hemicellulose, cellulose, and lignin). These structural carbohydrates, which give grasses their rigidity, cannot be digested by mammalian enzymes. Microflora in the foregut (ruminants) or hindgut (equids) of herbivores convert hemicellulose and cellulose (β-linked polysaccharides) into products that can be utilized by the herbivores, thus giving them a particular ecological advantage. Many factors influence grass feeding value, including species and variety, maturity, fertility, environment, and postharvest management. Grass serves as the major nutrient source for domestic herbivores, and is increasingly important to the animal producer for soil erosion control, improvement of soil structure, waste management, and water protection.

STRUCTURE AND MORPHOLOGY

While grasses vary considerably in their growth habits and habitats and may be perennial or annual, they share some things in common.[1] Almost all grasses are herbaceous. The seed contains an embryo with one cotyledon, as opposed to legumes with two monocotyledons. The cotyledon of all grass seedlings remains below the soil upon emergence.

The basic organs of grasses are leaves, stems, and roots (Fig. 1). Specially modified stems and leaves constitute the inflorescence and fruits. Leaves are attached to the stem, one at each node, alternately in two rows on opposite sides of the stem. Leaf blades are typically flat, narrow, and parallel-veined.[1]

Grass stems have two distinctive forms.[1] The terminal meristem in seedlings and vegetative growth tends to be close to ground and enclosed in a whorl of folded leaf sheaths. This is an adaptive mechanism that makes it more difficult for the meristem, sitting atop nodes and unelongated internodes, to be grazed or cut. Once flowering begins, the terminal meristem differentiates into the inflorescence, and the internodes elongate. It is advantageous to the plant for this process to occur quickly, resulting in a relatively short harvest window to achieve high-quality forage. Elongated stems of flowering grass plants are clearly differentiated into nodes (joints) and internodes. Joints are always solid; internodes are usually hollow, but may be pithy or solid.

Established grasses have a fibrous or adventitious root system, which varies among species in depth and distribution. Adventitious roots are heavily branched, particularly in the upper soil horizon, making grasses particularly well-suited for soil conservation purposes and for efficient uptake of surface-applied fertilizer. The adventitious root system can make grasses more susceptible to drought than legumes. Warm-season grasses, however, typically have fewer roots, which are larger in diameter and grow to a deeper depth than those of cool-season grasses, thus increasing their drought tolerance.

PHOTOSYNTHETIC PATHWAYS

There are two main photosynthetic pathways in grasses. In C_3 (cool-season) grasses, the first measurable product of photosynthesis is a 3-carbon compound, 3-phosphoglycerate.[2] In C_4 (warm-season) grasses, 4-carbon intermediaries, such as malate or aspartate, are formed. Associated with C_3 photorespiration is a leaf anatomy that has many more mesophyll cells and less lignified vascular bundles than that associated with C_4 photorespiration. Thus, C_3 grasses generally have a higher nutritive value than C_4 grasses in terms of protein, sugars, and starches. Most C_3 grasses can fix CO_2 at temperatures near freezing, with net photosynthesis being maximized at 20 to 25°C and decreasing above 30°C. Photosynthesis at full solar radiation

Encyclopedia of Animal Science
DOI: 10.1081/E-EAS 120019621

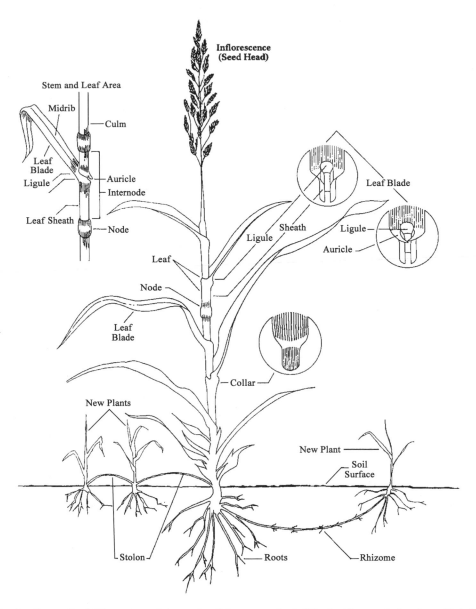

Fig. 1 Generalized illustration of the parts of the grass plant. (Used with permission from Ref. 10.)

is reduced. This means that C_3 grasses are ideally suited for the temperate regions of the world. The C_4 grasses have a higher biomass production per unit of water used than C_3 grasses and are often deeper-rooted than C_3 grasses. Because of their anatomy, C_4 grasses tend to produce more biomass per unit of fertilizer (nitrogen, N) than C_3 grasses, but this results in lower N content for C_4 grasses. At full sun, photosynthesis of C_4 grasses is nearly double that of C_3 grasses. Photosynthesis of C_4 plants is low at temperatures less than 10°C, increasing to a maximum between 35 and 40°C, and decreasing above 40°C because of protein destabilization.[2] These factors make C_4 grasses well adapted to hot, dry climates.

GRASS VALUE

Much of the world's land is poorly suited to growing legumes because of low pH or poorly drained soils, making the use of grasses under these conditions the most viable economic alternative. Perennial grass also can remove over twice the nitrogen/acre compared to corn, making perennial grasses attractive choices for nutrient management, regardless of soil conditions.[3]

From a nutritional standpoint, however, perennial grasses often are less preferred than perennial legumes. Perennial grasses generally contain more fiber than legumes, resulting in lower dry matter intake and consequently lower production if used as the major feed source in the diet.

Grass feeding value can be defined as its capacity to promote animal production or performance.[4] Animal performance is a function of nutrient intake and availability, nutrient concentration, digestibility, and metabolic efficiency.[5] Intake, digestibility, and efficiency of utilization are characteristics of forages that determine animal performance, with variation in intake accounting for 60 to 90% of the variation in digestible energy or dry matter intake.[6]

Understanding biological mechanisms that affect forage digestion in relation to chemical analyses is critical for accurate prediction of animal response to a diet.[7] Lignin is the chemical constituent most often identified as limiting fiber digestibility.[8] Lignin is indigestible by ruminants or microbes, and inhibits the digestion of hemicellulose, probably accounting for its close association with digestibility. Notwithstanding this association, every species has a different relationship between lignin content of dry matter and dry matter digestibility.[9]

GRASS MANAGEMENT

Periodic soil testing, followed by liming if pH is too low, and fertilization according to results of the soil test are the most important practices of grass management. No other management practice has been shown to have more impact on long-term meat or milk production.[10] Fields used for pasture should be tested every two to three years, but those fields used for silage or hay production should be tested every year. Liming, the addition of limestone or other basic amendments to the soil, is necessary in many areas to raise soil pH, depending on the grass species present. Although there is variation among species, grasses generally grow best when pH levels are between 6.0 and 7.0, in part because phosphorus (P) and essential micronutrients are most available at these pHs. The major nutrients required by grasses are nitrogen (N), P, and potassium (K). N, needed by grass plants to carry on photosynthesis, produces the largest growth response in grass and is needed in relatively large quantities, because, unlike legumes, grasses cannot fix their own nitrogen. P and N have important roles in water quality issues, contributing to eutrification (P) of water sources and high nitrate levels in water (N). It is imperative to manage these nutrients for the optimum benefit of the grass and the environment. Other nutrients are required in lesser amounts, but these are less likely to limit crop growth.

Two primary factors to consider when selecting perennial forage species and varieties are persistence and heading date (inflorescence emergence). Grasses vary in their tolerance to soil acidity and moisture extremes, so they must be selected for the environment in which they will be grown. Maturity is the single most important factor controlling forage quality in grasses, assuming no antiquality components, because of the strong negative relationship between maturity and digestibility. Awareness of heading date allows for harvest to occur at optimum maturity. Because heading dates among grass species and varieties within species can vary greatly, selecting several varieties and/or species can spread out the spring harvest window.

CONCLUSIONS

Grasses furnish the bulk of the feed used for domestic herbivores worldwide. Much of the world's land is poorly suited to growing legumes because of low pH or poorly drained soils, making the use of grasses under these conditions the most viable economic alternative. From a nutritional standpoint, however, perennial grasses often are less preferred than perennial legumes. Perennial grasses generally contain more fiber than legumes, resulting in lower dry matter intake and consequently lower production if used as the major feed source in the diet. Selecting forages for persistence, managing for timely harvest, and proper preservation technique can ensure high nutritive value.

ARTICLE OF FURTHER INTEREST

Forages: Legumes, p. 421

REFERENCES

1. Moser, L.E.; Nelson, C.J. Structure and Morphology of Grasses. In *Forages: An Introduction to Grassland Agriculture*, 6th Ed.; Barnes, R.F., Nelson, C.J., Collins, M., Moore, K.J., Eds.; Iowa State University Press: Ames, IA, 2003; Vol. 1, 25–50.
2. MacAdam, J.W.; Nelson, C.J. Physiology of Forage Plants. In *Forages: An Introduction to Grassland Agriculture*, 6th Ed.; Barnes, R.F., Nelson, C.J., Collins, M., Moore, K.J., Eds.; Iowa State University Press: Ames, IA, 2003; Vol. 1, 73–97.
3. Cherney, J.H.; Cherney, D.J.R. *Grass for Dairy Cattle*;

Cherney, J.H., Cherney, D.J.R., Eds.; CAB International: Oxon, UK, 1998.

4. Cherney, D.J.R.; Mertens, D.R. Modelling Grass Utilization for Dairy Cows. In *Grass for Dairy Cattle*; Cherney, J.H., Cherney, D.J.R., Eds.; CAB International: Oxon, UK, 1998; 351–371.

5. Beever, D.E.; Offer, N.; Gill, M. The Feeding Value of Grass and Grass Products. In *Grass—Its Production and Utilization*; Hopkins, A., Ed.; Blackwell Science: Oxford, UK, 2000; 140–195.

6. Mertens, D.R. Regulation of Forage Intake. In *Forage Quality, Evaluation, and Utilization*; Fahey, G.C., Collins, M., Mertens, D.R., Moser, L.E., Eds.; American Society of Agronomy: Madison, WI, 1994; 450–493.

7. Van Soest, P.J. Cell Wall Matrix Interactions and Degradation—Session Synopsis. In *Forage Cell Wall Structure and Digestibility*; Jung, H.G., Buxton, D.R., Hatfield, R.D., Ralph, J., Eds.; ASA-CSSA-SSSA: Madison, WI, 1993; 377–395.

8. Buxton, D.R.; Mertens, D.R. Quality-Related Characteristics of Forages. In *Forages Vol. II. The Science of Grassland Agriculture*, 5th Ed.; Barnes, R.F., Miller, D.A., Nelson, C.J., Eds.; Iowa State University Press: Ames, IA, 1995; 83–96.

9. Sullivan, J.T. A rapid method for the determination of acid-insoluble lignin in forages and its relation to digestibility. J. Anim. Sci. **1959**, *18*, 1292–1298.

10. Ball, D.M.; Hoveland, C.S.; Lacefield, G.D. *Southern Forages*, 3rd Ed.; Potash and Phosphate Institute: Norcross, GA, 2002.

Forages: Legumes

J. H. Cherney
D. J. R. Cherney
Cornell University, Ithaca, New York, U.S.A.

INTRODUCTION

Legumes belong to the plant family Fabaceae, the bean family, and characteristically have a legume or pod fruit. Most legumes are also characterized by their ability to form root nodules that contain symbiotic nitrogen-fixing bacteria. Legumes are valued for their high forage quality, as well as for their use as green manure crops, but require more intensive management than grasses. Animal agriculture in the future must have high-quality forage crops that also maintain or improve environmental quality, and most legumes fit these criteria. There are about 12,000 species of legumes grouped into more than 500 genera. The most common genera from a temperate forage standpoint are *Medicago* (lucerne or alfalfa), *Trifolium* (clovers), and *Lotus* (trefoils). Woody legumes are used as browse by ruminants.

Legumes are not only a source of forage for domesticated animals, but also an excellent source of nutrients for native wildlife. Legumes such as birdsfoot trefoil (*Lotus corniculatus* L.) are used extensively for mined-land reclamation, revegetation, and other soil stabilizing situations. Their popular use for stabilization and revegetation of roadsides has been curtailed, however, because the forage attracts wildlife to the roadside. Some annual legumes, such as cowpea (*Vigna unguiculata* L. Walp.) (also known as southern pea and blackeye pea), can be used as a forage crop, but are primarily used as vegetables or grain crops in tropical and subtropical regions of the world.

STRUCTURE AND MORPHOLOGY

Legumes may be annual, biennial, or perennial. Some typical legumes and their relative attributes are shown in Table 1. Biennial legumes, such as sweet clover (*Melilotus* spp.), grow vegetatively during the seeding year, produce seed the year after seeding, and then die. Some short-lived perennial legumes are referred to as effective biennials, for example, red clover (*Trifolium pratense* L.), a perennial that often does not survive for more than two growing seasons. Legume seed contains an embryo with two seed leaves or cotyledons (dicots) that may stay

below ground or emerge, depending on the legume species. Many perennial legumes undergo contractile growth six to eight weeks after cotyledon emergence.[5] The first stem node holding the cotyledons is pulled down below the soil surface, providing increased winter hardiness for the developing crown that contains axillary buds for regrowth.

Legumes develop multiple stems with a variety of leaf shapes (Fig. 1), and stems may have a terminal or lateral inflorescence. They produce seed in a pod but are also capable of asexual reproduction by stolons or rhizomes. Stolons are horizontal stems above the soil surface and rhizomes are horizontal stems below the soil surface. Both have nodes and buds that are capable of producing a clone of the original plant.

Most common legumes develop a prominent or branched taproot (Fig. 1), which can be relatively shallow or may penetrate up to several meters deep, in the case of alfalfa or crownvetch (*Securigera varia* L.). A deep taproot gives legumes a competitive advantage over grasses when surface soil moisture is limiting. Taproots are used as a food storage organ for generating regrowth, especially important in the case of alfalfa.

BIOLOGICAL DINITROGEN FIXATION

Symbiotic dinitrogen (N_2) fixation is a mutually beneficial relationship that has evolved between many legumes and rhizobia soil bacteria. Free-living rhizobia bacteria infect the legume roots, which concurrently are developing structures to house the bacteria. Within these oxygen-limiting structures, or nodules, rhizobia are capable of fixing atmospheric N_2, providing the plant with an adequate supply of reduced nitrogen.

FORAGE MANAGEMENT

Harvest management of legumes is planned to optimize forage quality and to maximize the life of the perennial stand.[7] Optimum forage quality depends on the class of livestock utilizing the forage. The number of harvests or

Encyclopedia of Animal Science
DOI: 10.1081/E-EAS 120019622

Table 1 Characteristics of some typical forage legumes

Scientific name	Common name	Plant lifespan	Tolerance to low soil fertility	Tolerance to soil acidity	Tolerance to drought	Tolerance to wet soils	Cold hardiness	Bloat potential	Ease of establishment
Aeschynomene americana L.	Aeschynomene (or American joint vetch)	Annual	Moderate	Moderate	Low	High	None	No	Moderate
Medicago sativa L.	Alfalfa	Perennial	Low	Low	Very high	Very low	Very high	Yes	Easy
Trifolium hybridum L.	Alsike clover	Perennial	Moderate	Moderate	Low	Very high	High	Yes	Easy
Alysicarpus vaginalis (L.) DC.	Alyceclover	Annual	Low	Moderate	Moderate	Low	None	No	Moderate
Kummerowia striata (Thunb.) Schindler	Annual (or Japanese) Lespedeza	Annual	Very high	High	Moderate	Moderate–high	None	No	Very easy
Lotus corniculatus L.	Birdsfoot trefoil	Perennial	High	High	Moderate	Moderate	Moderate	No	Moderate
Desmodium heterocarpon (L.) DC.	Carpon desmodium	Perennial	Moderate–high	Moderate–high	Low–moderate	Moderate–high	Very low	No	Difficult
Astragalus cicer L.	Cicer milkvetch	Perennial	High	Moderate	High	Moderate	Very high	No	Moderate
Securigera varia (L.) Lassen	Crownvetch	Perennial	High	Moderate	Moderate	Low	Moderate	No	Moderate
Trifolium ambiguum Bieb.	Kura clover	Perennial	Moderate	Moderate	Moderate	Moderate	Very high	Yes	Difficult
Trifolium repens (pratense) L.	Red clover	Perennial	Moderate	Moderate	Moderate	Low	High	Yes	Very easy
Arachis glabrata Benth. Var. *glabrata*	Rhizoma peanut	Perennial	Moderate–high	Moderate–high	Low	Low	Low	No	Difficult
Onobrychis viciifolia Scop.	Sainfoin	Perennial	High	Low	Very high	Very low	High	No	Moderate
Lespedeza cuneata (Dum. Cours.) G. Don	Sericea Lespedeza	Perennial	High	High	High	Low	Moderate	No	Moderate
Glycine max (L.) Merr.	Soybean	Annual	Low	Low	High	Low	None	Yes	Easy
Stylosanthes guianensis (Aubl.) Sw. var. *guianensis*	Stylo	Perennial	Moderate–high	Moderate–high	Moderate–high	Moderate	Very low	No	Moderate
Melilotus albus (*Melilotus alba*) Medik.	Sweetclover	Biennial	High	Low	Very high	Very low	Very high	Yes	Easy
Trifolium repens L.	White clover	Perennial	Moderate	Moderate	Very low	Moderate	High	Yes	Easy

(Adapted from Refs. 1–4.)

Some typical legume leaf types:

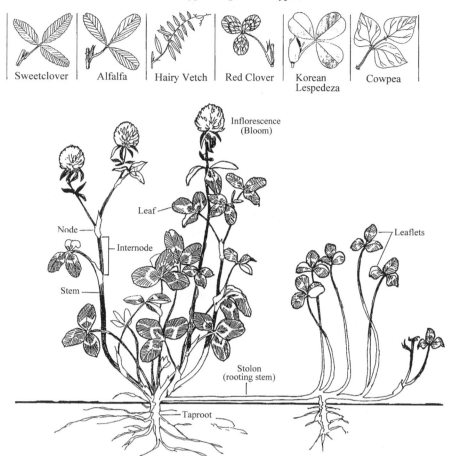

Fig. 1 Characteristics of some forage legumes. (From Ref. 6.)

grazing cycles per year ranges from 1 in colder climates to as high as 10 in irrigated warmer climates.[8]

diet, particularly in regions that can support only low-quality tropical grasses.[10]

Legume Persistence

A higher level of intensive management is usually necessary to maintain legumes in a stand, compared to the effort required to maintain grasses.[9] Individual legume plants may be relatively short-lived, but legume species can persist in stands by vegetative reproduction, using rhizomes or stolons, or by natural reseeding.[4]

All legumes are C$_3$ plants, so named because the first product of photosynthesis is a 3-carbon compound. This means that legumes can compete with C$_3$ grasses in temperate zones but do not compete well with C$_4$ grasses in tropical and subtropical regions. Because legumes are relatively short-lived, it is important to match legume species to the appropriate soil conditions to maximize stand life. Most forage legumes are grown in mixtures with grasses to improve the nutritive value of the animal's

FORAGE QUALITY

Legumes often have higher crude protein content than grasses because of their symbiotic relationship with nitrogen-fixing rhizobia, which reduces the legumes' dependence on fertilizer nitrogen. Lignin content, which reduces the extent of digestion in ruminants, is comparatively higher in legumes than in grass. A high rate of fiber digestion, coupled with lower overall fiber, results in high passage rates and increased animal productivity for legumes, compared to most grasses. While legumes are generally considered high-quality forage, there are serious antiquality factors associated with some legumes (Table 2), in addition to the potential for inducing bloat, summarized in Table 1. These factors are not always detrimental, and in some cases can be beneficial. For example, at moderate

Table 2 Antiquality factors in forage legumes

Antiquality factor	Example species	Clinical symptoms	Possible consequences
Coumarin	Sweetclover	Susceptibility to hemorrhaging	Fatal for cattle
Mimosine	Leucaena	Loss of hair, goiter	Poor growth in ruminants
Phytates	Soybean	Skin lesions	Poor growth
Phytoestrogens	Red clover	Reproductive problems	Permanent infertility
Saponins	Alfalfa	None	Productivity decline in swine and poultry
Slaframine	Red clover	Profuse salivation	Diarrhea and abortion
Tannins	Birdsfoot trefoil	Reduced feed intake	Reduced animal performance
Toxic amino acids	Flatpea	Trembling and incoordination	Fatal for sheep
Trypsin inhibitors	Cowpea	None	Growth depression in swine and poultry
Unknown	Alsike clover	Jaundice, neurological disturbances	Fatal for horses
Unknown	Cicer milkvetch	Photosensitization, sunburned skin	Poor growth in cattle

(Adapted from Ref. 11.)

concentrations, tannins slow the breakdown of proteins in the rumen and improve protein utilization.

CONCLUSIONS

Legumes are highly nutritious forage plants that are capable of fixing their own supply of nitrogen, with the assistance of rhizobia bacteria. Most legumes support higher animal productivity than grasses, but there are antiquality factors in some legume species that can be fatal to livestock. Legumes are a major contributor to livestock production in temperate regions, but less important in warmer climates because they are not as well suited to such climates as are C_4 grasses. Persistence of perennial legumes requires intensive management and varies with each legume species.

ARTICLES OF FURTHER INTEREST

Forages: Grasses, p. 417
Forages: Shrubs and Forbs, p. 425

REFERENCES

1. Duke, J.A. *Handbook of Legumes of World Economic Importance*; Plenum Press: New York, 1981.
2. FAO. *Grassland Index*. http://www.fao.org/ag/AGP/AGPC/doc/Gbase/mainmenu.htm (accessed June 2004).
3. McGraw, R.L.; Nelson, C.J. Legumes for Northern Areas. In *Forages: An Introduction to Grassland Agriculture*, 6th Ed.; Barnes, R.F., Nelson, C.J., Collins, M., Moore, K.J., Eds.; Iowa State University Press: Ames, IA, 2003; Vol. 1, 171–190.
4. Sollenberger, L.E.; Collins, M. Legumes for Southern Areas. In *Forages: An Introduction to Grassland Agriculture*, 6th Ed.; Barnes, R.F., Nelson, C.J., Collins, M., Moore, K.J., Eds.; Iowa State University Press: Ames, IA, 2003; Vol. 1, 191–213.
5. Mitchell, R.B.; Nelson, C.J. Structure and Morphology of Legumes and Other Forbs. In *Forages: An Introduction to Grassland Agriculture*, 6th Ed.; Barnes, R.F., Nelson, C.J., Collins, M., Moore, K.J., Eds.; Iowa State University Press: Ames, IA, 2003; Vol. 1, 51–72.
6. Ball, D.M.; Hoveland, C.S.; Lacefield, G.D. *Southern Forages*, 3rd Ed.; Potash & Phosphate Institute: Norcross, GA, 2002.
7. Sheaffer, C.C.; Lacefield, G.D; Marble, V.L. Cutting Schedules and Stands. In *Alfalfa and Alfalfa Improvement*; Hansen, A.A., Barnes, D.K., Hill, R.R., Jr., Eds.; American Society of Agronomy, Crop Science Society of America, and Soil Science Society of America: Madison, WI, 1988; 411–437.
8. Humphreys, L.R. Diversity and Productivity of Tropical Legumes. In *Tropical Legumes in Animal Nutrition*; D'Mello, J.P.F., Devendra, C., Eds.; CAB International, Wallingford: Oxon, United Kingdom, 1995; 1–21.
9. Cherney, J.H.; Cherney, D.J.R. Legume Forage Quality. In *Quality Improvement in Field Crops*; Basra, A.S., Randhawa, L.S., Eds.; Food Products Press: Binghamton, NY, 2002; 261–284.
10. Barnes, D.K.; Sheaffer, C.C. Alfalfa. In *Forages: An Introduction to Grassland Agriculture*, 5th Ed.; Barnes, R.F., Miller, D.A., Nelson, C.J., Eds.; Iowa State University Press: Ames, IA, 1995; Vol. 1, 205–216.
11. Cheeke, P.R. *Natural Toxicants in Feeds*; Forages, and Poisonous Plants Interstate Publishers, Inc.: Danville, IL, 1998.

Forages: Shrubs and Forbs

D. J. R. Cherney
J. H. Cherney
Cornell University, Ithaca, New York, U.S.A.

INTRODUCTION

Shrubs and forbs are of utmost importance in parts of the world where there is an arid or semiarid environment and where inadequate feeds constrain animal production and survival. They are considered of limited economic importance, however, to animal production systems in much of North America and Europe, where there are improved pastures and hay fields. In Northern Africa, 60–70% of rangeland production and 40% of total animal feed is browse. There are some 200,000 hectares of cultivated forage trees and shrubs in Australia, with three species—Leucaena (*Leucaena leucocephala*), Tagasaste (*Chamaecytisus proliferous*), and Saltbush (*Atriplex* spp.)—accounting for most of this acreage. Shrubs and forbs make up the principal component of the diets of goats throughout Asia, Africa, the Near East, and Latin America.

FORBS AND SHRUBS AS COMPONENTS OF NATURAL ECOSYSTEMS

Forbs and shrubs are often important components of natural ecosystems and grasslands. It is important to preserve and maintain the genetic and ecological integrity of these ecosystems, because plant diversity promotes stability during climatic extremes. Social and economic pressures in many areas of the world are leading to conversion of these lands into high-value cash crops. Using such lands for pasture or hay for livestock can provide economic benefit for the area while maintaining the integrity of the grassland.[1]

Forbs and shrubs also contribute to special niche markets, allowing for value-added agricultural products, even where improved pastures are possible. An example is the Hyblean region of southeastern Italy.[2] Here pastures typically contain 30–40 plant species, with grasses and legumes being only a small component. Cheese produced in this region, Ragusano cheese, was traditionally made from milk of cows grazing in these pastures. As herds moved to total mixed rations and diets based on monoculture to increase milk yields, cheese

quality declined. It is believed that the flavor compounds in the forbs consumed on pasture were responsible for the unique flavor attributes of Ragusano cheese.[2]

FORBS

Forbs are generally defined as herbaceous broadleaf plants, including brassicas and legumes. Forbs exist in pastures and rangelands, contributing to yield, species diversity, nutrients for livestock, and food and habitat for wildlife. Forbs are generally opportunists and are usually not a management objective in temperate regions,[3] although some have important economic niches. Forbs may be annual, biannual, or perennial. Most of the naturally occurring poisonous plants are forbs.[4] They differ greatly in palatability and nutritive value.

The Asteraceae family is the largest plant family of forbs. It contains over 1500 genera with more than 19,000 species. These species include aster, dandelion, chicory (*Cichorium intybus* L.), artichoke, and sunflower. Another class of forbs, the Cruciferae, or mustard family, has about 300 genera and 3000 species, including turnip and kale. A few of these species are economically important in the United States.

Chicory is a perennial herb of the family Asteraceae that shows potential for use in grazing. Chicory produces leafy growth that can be higher in nutritive value than alfalfa if properly managed. Chicory has a relatively deep taproot, which makes it drought-tolerant. It requires nitrogen fertilization for maximum yield.

Brassicas are annual crops with high digestibility (75–90%) and high crude protein content (18–25%), provided nitrogen fertilization is adequate.[5] Because of high digestibility and very low fiber content, forage brassicas could be considered concentrates rather than forages and should probably be fed as supplements. Unlike that of many other forage crops, the dry matter digestibility of brassicas does not decrease markedly with advancing maturity. They can be used as insurance against summer drought or to extend the grazing season into November and December. Intensive management is necessary to prevent stem production, which markedly decreases

Encyclopedia of Animal Science
DOI: 10.1081/E-EAS 120019620

palatability.[5] Forage brassicas are seldom used for dairy cattle, however, because they can cause an off flavor in milk. Some species can be managed to reduce off flavors in milk, although caution must be used.

SHRUBS AND TREES

Shrubs are defined as any low-growing, woody plant that produces multiple stems. Leguminous trees are included

in this category. Leucaena is the most widely used multi-purpose tree legume in the tropics.[6] It is used as a high-quality livestock forage, fuelwood, and construction timber, and for soil stabilization and improving soil fertility. The nutritive value of Leucaena is good where it is used, and livestock production is increased over conventional pastures. Rate of adoption has been low-to-moderate due to the high cost of establishment, the high rate of establishment failure due to weed competition and insect predation, the low returns on beef production in

Table 1 Forage quality of selected species of forage shrubs and forbs

Forage class and species	Forage constituent		
	% NDF	% CP	% IVDMD
Shrubs			
Artemisia tridentate (Big sagebrush)[a]	40.3	8.5	61.3
Atriplex nummularia (Oldman saltbush)[b]	41.2	20	71.5
C. proliferus (Tagasaste)[b]	39.9	19.6	64.9
Cytisus maderiensis (Broom)[b]	38.3	19.3	68.1
Leucaena esculenta-paiculata (Leucaena)[b]	42.1	18	42.4
L. leucocephala (Leucaena)[b]	40.8	21.6	49.1
Leucaena pulverulenta (Leucaena)[b]	47.1	16.7	38.9
Teline stenopetala (Leafy broom)[b]	39.9	20.2	—
Forbs			
Astragalus filipes (Threadstalk milkvetch)[a]	52.5	17.7	54.8
Achillea millefolium (Common yarrow)[a]	33.0	8.6	80.5
Anthemis arvensis (Corn chamomile)[c]	27.4	26.4	73
Berteroa incana (L.) (Hoary alyssum)[d]	42.3	14.4	76.2
Beta maritima (Wild beet)[c]	29.5	33.9	77
Borago officinalis (Borage)[c]	26.2	24.4	69
Calendula arvensis (Field marigold)[c]	19.7	34.1	79
Carduus corymbosus (Thistle)[c]	30.6	18.3	75
C. intybus (Chicory)[c]	43.7	11.8	76
Cirsium arvense (L.) (Canada Thistle)[d]	32.1	18.6	78.1
Crepis accuminata (Western yarrow)[a]	30.9	8.5	81.8
Crysanthemum coronarium (Crown daisy)[c]	31.4	50.8	73
Diplotaxis erucoides (White wall rocket)[c]	14.8	26.9	28.7
Helianthus tuberosus L. (Jerusalem artichoke)[d]	29.3	19.3	81.4
Lepidium perfoliatum (Clasping pepperwort)[a]	51.8	9.9	54.8
Lithospermum ruderale (Western gromwell)[a]	30.2	10.5	73.5
Notabasis syriaca (Prickly thistle)[c]	34.2	28.5	72
Polygonum coccineum (Swamp smartweed)[d]	35.0	21.8	57.6
Rumex crispus L. (Curly dock)[d]	32.8	17.4	64.4
Silene alba (Mill.) (White campion)[d]	45.9	15.4	74.7
Sinapsis arvensis (Wild mustard or charlock)[c]	20.0	27.9	81
Sonchus oleraceus (Common sowthistle)[c]	27.3	26.6	79
Sonchus arvnesis L. (Perennial sowthistle)[d]	26.7	21.4	79.2
Taraxacum officinale (Dandelion)[d]	32.8	13.2	76.7
Urospermum dalechampii (Pennywort)[c]	27.8	12.6	72

NDF=neutral detergent fiber; CP=crude protein; IVDMD=in vitro dry matter digestibility.
[a](From Ref. [7].)
[b]Leaf material only. (From Ref. 6.)
[c]Early vegetative to mid-bloom. (From Ref. 8.)
[d]Second harvest, early to mid-June. (From Ref. 9.)

relation to grain feeding, and the low levels of skills among graziers.[6]

Acacia is another forage shrub that has a significant role in animal production systems. These shrubs have been used historically as maintenance feed during droughts and periods of seasonal feed shortage in arid and semiarid zones. The seed pods of these woody shrubs are highly nutritious and serve as excellent supplement for grazing animals.

NUTRITIONAL VALUE OF FORBS AND SHRUBS

The nutritional value of forage shrubs and forbs is variable, but can be high (Table 1). In many cases, the nutritional value of these species is high in comparison to tropical grasses. Because of this, forage shrub and forb species often work well as supplements in tropical areas. In temperate areas, the nutritional value of forbs can be competitive with alfalfa.[9] When considering management of these species, we need to consider not only forage quality, but other factors as well. Yield is often lower with forb species than with improved temperate grasses. In addition, there is wide variation in palatability and acceptability of forb species, which would affect a species' feeding value.[9]

Many forbs and shrubs contain materials that are deleterious to livestock. Some, such as Acacia and Leucaena, are rich in tannins, which can cause palatability problems. Tannins also bind proteins, which is deleterious when protein levels are low, but potentially beneficial at some level when protein levels and solubility are high. Species may contain cyanogens, saponins, nonprotein amino acids (such as mimosine), alkaloids, oxalates, or phytohaemagglutins, which have various deleterious effects on animals. In some cases, such as mimosine, ruminal microorganisms can adapt so that the toxic agent becomes ineffective. In other cases, limiting the amount of material eaten by the animal is sufficient to control deleterious effects.

MANAGEMENT

In improved pastures many forbs and shrubs are considered weeds, as these species tend to be opportunists. Proper pasture management can help control unwanted pasture species, including controlled grazing with goats. In some cases, eradicating the unwanted forbs and shrubs reduces pasture phytomass, because the forb species have not competed with preferred species, but rather have filled a void vacated by loss of preferred species.[9] Proper

management will require knowledge of the forb or shrub nutritive value, as well as any possible deleterious effects.

Caution is required when introducing new forage forb or shrub species to a given area where they can make an economic impact, because many of these species are opportunists. There are numerous documented cases where introduced exotic species have become noxious weed problems.[10] The honey locust tree (*Gleditsia tricanthos*) in Australia and dandelion (*T. officinale* Wigg) and mutiflora rose (*Rosa multiflora* Thunb. Ex Murr.) in the United States are just a few examples of unintended consequences. A prudent approach to shrub research might be to develop native plants as livestock resources, mitigating the possibility of introducing a serious environmental weed.[6]

Larkin et al.[11] noted low natural variation in high-tannin tropical leguminous tree species. He further suggested that there would be a limited ability to alter tannin content through natural selection. He suggested that transgenics would be the best method of lowering tannin content in these species. Poppi et al.[12] suggested that proper grazing management and the use of nutritional supplements would be as effective as high-tech manipulation of lignin and carbohydrate content in tropical shrub species.

CONCLUSION

Shrubs and forbs are forage plants that contribute significantly to the nutrition of herbivores in parts of the world with an arid or semiarid environment, and where inadequate feeds constrain animal production and survival. They are also capable of making significant niche contributions in more temperate areas. Nutritional value is variable, but can be quite high. Substantial improvement in nutritive value can be obtained through proper management and feeding. In some cases, such as high-tannin species, the use of transgenics may be necessary to improve nutritive value.

ARTICLE OF FURTHER INTEREST

Forages: Legumes, p. 421

REFERENCES

1. Mikhailova, E.A.; Bryant, R.B.; Cherney, D.J.R.; Post, C.J.; Vassenev, I.I. Botanical composition, soil and forage properties under different management regimes in Russian grasslands. J. Agric. Ecosyst. Environ. **2000**, *80*, 213–226.

2. Carpino, S.; Licitra, G.; Van Soest, P.J. Selection of forage species by dairy cattle on complex Sicilian pasture. Anim. Feed Sci. Tech. **2003**, *105*, 205–214.

3. Mitchell, R.B.; Nelson, C.J. Structure and Morphology of Legumes and Other Forbs. In *Forages: An Introduction to Grassland Agriculture*, 6th Ed.; Barnes, R.F., Nelson, C.J., Collins, M., Moore, K.J., Eds.; Iowa State University Press: Ames, IA, 2003; Vol. 1, 51–72.

4. Smith, D.H.; Collins, M. *Forages: An Introduction to Grassland Agriculture*, 6th Ed.; Barnes, R.F., Nelson, C.J., Collins, M., Moore, K.J., Eds.; Iowa State University Press: Ames, IA, 2003; Vol. 1, 215–236.

5. Cherney, D.J.R. Forages for Dairy Cattle: Economical Alternatives to Alfalfa, Grass, and Corn. In *1998 Tri-State Dairy Nutrition Conference*, Proceedings, Fort Wayne, IN, April 21–22, 1998; Eastridge, M.L., Ed.; The Ohio State University: Columbus, OH, 1998; 35–50.

6. Lefroy, E.C. *Forage Trees and Shrubs in Australia: A Report for the RIRDC/L & W*; Australia/FWPRDC Joint Venture Agroforestry Program. Rural Industries Research and Development Corporation: Kingston, ACT, Australia, 2002; 1–69. RIRDC Publication No. 02/039.

7. Fajemisin, B.; Ganskoppp, D.; Cruz, R.; Vavra, M. Potential for wood plant control by Spanish goats in the sagebrush steppe. Small Ruminant Res. **1996**, *20*, 99–107.

8. Licitra, G.; Carpino, S.; Schadt, I.; Avondo, M.; Barresi, S. Forage quality of native pastures in a Mediterranean area. Anim. Feed Sci. Technol. **2000**, *69*, 315–328.

9. Marten, G.C.; Sheaffer, C.C.; Wyse, D.L. Forage nutritive value and, palatability of perennial weeds. Agron. J. **1987**, *79*, 980–986.

10. Low, T. Tropical pasture plants as weeds. Tropic. Grasslands **1997**, *31*, 337–343.

11. Larkin, P.J.; Tanner, G.J.; Joseph, R.G.; Kelman, W.M. Modifying Condensed Tannin Content in Plants. In *XVIII International Grassland Congress*, Winnipeg Mannitoba and Saskatoon, Saskatchewan, June 8–19, 1997; Buchanan-Smith, J.G., Bailey, L.D., McCaughey, P., Eds.; Guelph, Ontario, Canada, 1999; 167–178. Session 8.

12. Poppi, D.P; McLenna, S.R.; Bediye, S.; deVega, A.; Zorrilla-Rios, J. Forage Quality: Strategies for Increasing Nutritive Value of Forages, In *XVIII International Grassland Congress*, Winnipeg Mannitoba and Saskatoon, Saskatchewan, June 8–19, 1997; Buchanan-Smith, J.G., Bailey, L.D., McCaughey, P., Eds.; Guelph: Ontario, Canada, 1999; 307–322. Session 17.

Fur and Mink

Simon Ward
Fur Commission USA, Paranaque, Philippines

James Oldfield
Oregon State University, Corvallis, Oregon, U.S.A.

INTRODUCTION

From prehistoric times to the present, fur has been the preeminent clothing choice in cold climates, mainly for its insulating qualities but also for its beauty and sense of luxury. Since the mid-20th century its importance has been diminished by the advent of cheaper synthetics, but the rise of fur farming as an alternative to the trapping of wild animals has helped keep the cost of fur down and ensure its continued accessibility. Although most furbearing species are still caught in the wild, most furs now derive from domesticated mink and, to a lesser extent, fox.

BACKGROUND INFORMATION

The farming of furbearers began in Canada and Russia in the late 19th century, and by the early 20th century had become a serious business in the United States. Two other important producers in the history of fur farming, Scandinavia and Britain, did not see their industries take off until the 1930s.

Production focused heavily on fox until the 1940s, when fashion leaned toward slimmer styles that favored mink. Since that time, mink production has grown steadily while fox production has declined.

Mink production today is dominated by Scandinavian countries, with the United States, Russia, and China also making important contributions. Pelts sold worldwide in 2003 totaled over 34 million, of which some 35% came from Denmark, 13% from China, and 7–8% each from the Netherlands, Russia, and the United States.

MODERN MINK FARMS

In common with livestock operations generally, today's mink farms tend to be larger than their predecessors. Although most are still operated by individual families, a modern farm typically has a thousand or more breeding stock.

The vast majority of farms are found in temperate regions since the climate favors fur growth. After some early attempts to raise mink outdoors, a system of housing has evolved in which the animals occupy rows of wire cages in large sheds with open sides for maximum ventilation (Fig. 1). Yet, even in these facilities, spells of hot weather can result in the loss of animals, so sprinkler systems are often installed for added cooling.

Wide aisles between the rows allow access by motorized feed carts that pump wet feed mixes onto the tops of the wire cages. Droppings are gathered regularly from beneath the cages and either applied directly to agricultural land as fertilizer or collected in waste lagoons for later application.

GENETICS AND BREEDING

The first domesticated mink were developed from wild animals caught in northerly parts of North America. These were dark brown to black in color, with a lighter underfur. Through selective breeding on farms, the coats have darkened to the point that today's so-called standard mink are almost jet-black.

From time to time, strikingly different pelt colors caused by genetic mutations are found among litters of newborn kits, and farmers may select them for further breeding. As a result, today's mink population includes a variety of exotic color phases such as silver-blue, "sapphire" (a very light bluish-gray), "pastel" (a brown color phase), and albino (white).[1] Breeding such phases can be difficult, however, and farmers often refer to studies on mink heredity by such experts as Dr. Richard Shackelford of the University of Wisconsin/Madison to increase their chances of success.

As with any livestock operation, a key to success is the selection of breeding stock. The process begins with close examination of the latest kit crop. Each animal is ranked according to a grading system, and the rankings are stored on computer. The farmer then decides how many of each sex he or she needs for breeding and selects these based on their rankings.

Color is an important criterion in selecting breeders, but other traits are considered too, such as size, vitality,

Encyclopedia of Animal Science
DOI: 10.1081/E-EAS 120019623

Fig. 1 Modern mink farms raise their animals in clean, airy, and well-lit sheds. (*View this art in color at www.dekker.com.*)

number of kits per litter, and freedom from disease. To speed up selection, farmers sometimes start by concentrating on one trait, such as color, before proceeding to the next. Many farmers also use what is called the index method to aid selection. This allows them to combine several traits, perhaps with different weightings, into a single index figure that is then used to rank the animals.

In early spring, cages are fitted with nest boxes filled with warm bedding such as shredded paper or grass straw, and breeding cards, containing information from the selection process, are hung over the cages. Prior to mating, males and females are often kept in separate parts of the shed, and females are generally restricted in their feed for a few weeks to keep them in active condition.

The males are then introduced to their chosen mates, with a mature male typically servicing 5–10 females and a kit male servicing 4–5. It is particularly important to ensure the males are fertile, and this may be done by extracting fluid from a female's vagina right after mating and examining it to determine the number of live, active sperm.

DIET AND NUTRITION

Feed represents the single largest expense in mink production, so the feeding program is crucial to a farm's profitability. Because of significant differences in the nutritional needs of mink from those of other domesticated animals, mink farmers have been unable to rely on information gathered for other species in developing diet formulations, and have had to do a lot of work for themselves.

As carnivores, mink require a diet derived primarily from animal sources, be they meat, fish, poultry, or dairy. Many mink farms base their feed programs on expired produce originally intended for humans, or on by-products collected from packing plants. The food producers also benefit because the amount of waste they must dispose of is reduced.

Diet formulations are dictated to a great extent by the length of the mink's digestive tract, the shortest of any domesticated species. Food can pass through a mink in as little as 2.5 hours, compared with about 72 hours for cattle, which means their diet must be highly digestible. The major nutritional needs of mink, like other species, are protein and energy, but the quantities and form in which they are ingested demand special attention.

A mink's protein needs are high because, in addition to providing for growth and maintenance of body tissues, it must also provide for fur production. Accordingly, proteins fed to mink should be of high biological value, supplying a good mix of the essential amino acids. Muscle tissues require considerable lysine and methionine, while fur production needs methionine, arginine, and cystine. Quality protein can be derived from eggs, fish and meat products, and dairy products such as cheese. Conventional mink diets contain such protein sources in a fresh state, often purchased in bulk and placed in cold storage until they are needed.

Most farm animals obtain their energy from carbohydrates, but mink use them to a much lesser extent, deriving most of their energy from dietary fats and oils. Such feedstuffs, however, must be stored correctly or they will

Fig. 2 The color and quality of a mink's pelt are good indicators of its health and diet. The pelt at left shows graying and banding of the fur, indicating the presence of avidin in the diet. The pelt at center has been parted to show a condition known as "cotton fur," a deficiency in melanin formation absent in normal mink (right). (*View this art in color at www.dekker.com.*)

oxidize and turn rancid. Vegetable oils are not too problematic because they usually contain sufficient vitamin E, an antioxidant, to retard the onset of rancidity. Fish oils, however, are high in unsaturated fatty acids, which are easily oxidized, and lack the protective levels of vitamin E.

Supplementary minerals and vitamins can be supplied naturally as components of a mink's diet, or added in synthetic form. Minerals such as calcium and phosphorus, for example, can be derived either from bone-in products, such as whole fish, or by adding dicalcium phosphate to the feed. Most of the vitamin requirements, meanwhile, can be met by using so-called "protective feeds." One of the most popular of these is liver, usually from beef cattle or chickens, and many farmers include liver in amounts of 5% or even 10% of the diet as a safety measure.

Mink farmers usually calculate dietary requirements for chemical nutrients based on the published works of animal nutritionists.[2,3] They then set about gathering appropriate raw materials at the best prices, often showing great ingenuity in formulating diets from a wide range of feeds and by-products. Sometimes farmers form feed cooperatives to achieve economies of scale, and take delivery every other day or so of however much feed they need.

In the quest for diet formulations that are both nutritious and economical, inevitably some diet-related problems have been identified in mink (Fig. 2). One example is "cotton fur," a bleached-out and consequently worthless fur condition, which has been linked to the presence in the diet of a substance that interferes with iron metabolism. Found in some fish such as hake, this substance prevents the formation of melanin, a dark fur pigment. Another is "fur graying" caused by the presence in the diet of avidin, found particularly in turkey eggs, which creates a deficiency of the B vitamin biotin. The U.S. fur industry has formed the Mink Farmers' Research Foundation, which sponsors research to solve and advise on such problems.

In recent years, considerable effort has been expended on developing dry feeds for mink that meet the requirements for both growth and furring. The incentive here is to reduce the cold storage costs associated with fresh feed, and many farms now use dried, pelleted feeds at some time of the year.

CONCLUSION

Mink farming differs in major ways from other kinds of livestock production due to the distinct needs of these carnivores and also the nature of the end product. Raising an animal for its fur involves considerations not shared by producers of meat, milk, or eggs.

Yet successful mink farmers also follow rules common to all livestock producers. The finest furs come about only by selecting animals with the best genes, and then providing proper nutrition and high standards of animal welfare.

REFERENCES

1. Ness, N.; Einarson, E.; Lohi, O. *Beautiful Fur Animals and their Colour Genetics*; SCIENTIFUR: Hillerod, Denmark, 1988.
2. Ensminger, M.; Oldfield, J.; Heineman, W. *Feeds and Nutrition*, 2nd Ed.; Ensminger Publishing: Clovis, CA, 1990; 1145–1168.
3. *Nutrient Requirements of Mink and Foxes*, 2nd Revised Ed.; National Research Council, National Academy of Sciences: Washington, DC, 1982; 72.

Future of Animal Agriculture: Demand for Animal Products

Christopher L. Delgado
International Food Policy Research Institute (IFPRI), Washington, D.C., U.S.A.
International Livestock Research Institute (ILRI), Nairobi, Kenya

INTRODUCTION

From the beginning of the 1970s to the mid-1990s, meat consumption in developing countries increased by 70 million metric tons (mmt), almost triple the increase in developed countries, and consumption of milk by 105 mmt of liquid milk equivalents (LME), more than twice the increase that occurred in developed countries. The market value of that increase in meat and milk consumption totaled approximately $155 billion (1990 US$), more than twice the market value of increased cereals consumption under the better-known Green Revolution in wheat, rice, and maize. The population growth, urbanization, and income growth that fueled the increase in meat and milk consumption are expected to continue well into the new millennium.

THE LIVESTOCK REVOLUTION

These changes create a veritable Livestock Revolution propelled by demand.[1] People in developing countries are increasing their consumption from the very low levels of the past, and they have a long way to go before coming near developed country averages. In developing countries, people consumed an annual average in 1996–1998 of 25 kg/capita meat and 44 kg/capita milk, one-third the meat and one-fifth the milk consumed by people in developed countries. Nevertheless, the caloric contribution per capita of meat, milk, and eggs in developing countries in the late 1990s was still only a quarter that of the same absolute figure for developed countries and, at 10%, accounted for only half the share of calories from animal sources observed in the developed countries.[1] For present purposes, developed countries include Western Europe and Scandinavia, North America, Eastern Europe and the former Soviet Union, Japan, Malta, Israel, and South Africa. All others are classified as developing countries.

Per capita consumption is rising fastest in regions where urbanization and rapid income growth result in people adding variety to their diets. Across countries, per capita consumption is significantly determined by average per capita income, and aggregate consumption grows fastest where rapid population growth augments income and urban growth.[2] Since the early 1980s, total meat and milk consumption grew at 6 and 4% per year, respectively, throughout the developing world (Table 1). In East and Southeast Asia—where income grew at 4–8% per year between the early 1980s and 1998, population at 2–3% per year, and urbanization at 4–6% per year—meat consumption grew between 4 and 8% per year.[1]

China plays a dominant role on the meat side. The share of the world's milk consumption rose from 34 to 44%. Pork and poultry accounted for 76% of the large net consumption increase of meat in developing countries from 1982–1984 to 1996–1998. Conversely, both per capita and aggregate milk and meat consumption stagnated in the developed world, where saturation levels of consumption have been reached and population growth is small. Whether these trends will continue was explored in 1998 with the International Food Policy Research Institute's (IFPRI) International Model for Policy Analysis of Agricultural Commodities and Trade (IMPACT), a global food model.[4,5]

RISING CONSUMPTION OF MEAT AND MILK TO 2020

The IMPACT model projects developing countries aggregate consumption growth rates of meat and milk separately to be 3.0 and 2.9% per year, respectively, over the 1996/1998 to 2020 period, compared to 0.8 and 0.6%, respectively, in the developed countries. Aggregate meat consumption in developing countries is projected to grow by 106 mmt between the late 1990s and 2020, whereas the corresponding figure for developed countries is 19 mmt (Table 2). Similarly, additional milk consumption of 32 mmt of liquid milk equivalents (LME) in the developed countries will be dwarfed by the additional consumption of 177 mmt in developing countries.

In the developing countries, 71% of the additions to meat consumption are from pork and poultry; in the developed countries, the comparable figure is 74%. Poultry consumption in developing countries is projected to grow at 3.9% per annum through 2020, followed by

Encyclopedia of Animal Science
DOI: 10.1081/E-EAS 120019628

Table 1 Per capita meat and milk consumption[a] by region, 1983 and 1997

	Meat[b]		Milk[c]	
	1983[d]	1997	1983	1997
Region		(kg)		
China	16[e]	43	3	8
Other East Asia	22	31	15	19
India	4	4	46	62
Other South Asia	6	9	47	63
Southeast Asia	11	18	10	12
Latin America	40	54	93	112
WANA[f]	20	21	86	73
Sub-Saharan Africa	10	10	32	30
Developing world	14	25	35	43
Developed world	74	75	195	194
United States	107	120	237	257
World	30	36	76	77

[a]Consumption is direct use as food, uncooked weight, bone-in.
[b]Beef, pigmeat, sheep and goat meat, and poultry.
[c]Includes cow and buffalo milk and milk products used as human food, in liquid milk equivalents.
[d]Dates are three-year moving averages centered on the year shown.
[e]Values are three-year moving averages centered on the year shown, calculated from data in FAO 2002.
[f]Western Asia and North Africa.
(From Ref. 3.)

beef at 2.9% and pork at 2.4%. In the developed countries, poultry consumption is projected to grow at 1.5% per annum through 2020, with other meats growing at 0.5% or less (Table 2). As the growth rates in Table 3 suggest, high growth in consumption is spread throughout the developing world and is in no way limited to China, India, and Brazil, although the sheer size and vigor of those countries will mean that they will continue to increase their dominance of world markets for livestock products.

Real beef prices fell by a factor of three from 1970/1972 to 1996/1998. IMPACT projects the expected change in real prices to 2020, relative to 1996/1998. The overall picture for 2020 is a noticeable decline for wheat and rice (8 and 11%, respectively), a similar decline for milk (8%), more modest decreases for meats (3%), and stability or slight increases for feedgrains (+11 and −4% for maize and soybeans, respectively).[1] The Livestock Revolution will also cushion, if not prevent, the further fall in real global livestock prices.

CONCLUSIONS

The demand-driven future of animal agriculture includes both opportunities and perils. The principal conclusion of the most recent projections is to confirm the view that the

Table 2 Food consumption trends of various livestock products projected to the year 2020[a,b]

		Total consumption			Per capita consumption	
	Projected growth of consumption 1997–2020 (%/year)	1997[c]	2020	% of world total 2020 (%)	1997[c]	2020
Region		(million mt)			(kg)	
Developed world						
Beef	0.5	30	34	40	23	25
Pork	0.4	36	39	33	28	29
Poultry	1.5	28	39	36	22	29
Meat	0.8	98	117	35	75	87
Milk	0.6	251	286	43	194	210
Developing world						
Beef	2.9	27	52	61	6	9
Pork	2.4	47	81	67	10	13
Poultry	3.9	29	70	64	7	11
Meat	3.0	111	217	65	25	36
Milk	2.9	194	375	57	43	62

[a]See notes to Table 1 for definitions.
[b]The 2020 projections are from the July 2002 version of the IMPACT model.
[c]Total and per capita consumption for 1997 are calculated from FAO 2002 and are three-year moving averages centered on 1997.
(From Refs. 3 and 5.)

Table 3 Projected food consumption trends of meat and milk, 1997–2020[a,b]

Region	Projected annual growth 1997[c]–2020		Total consumption in 2020		Per capita consumption in 2020	
	Meat[d]	Milk	Meat	Milk	Meat	Milk
	(%/year)		(million mt)		(kg)	
China	3.1	3.8	107	24	73	16
India	3.5	3.5	10	133	8	105
Other East Asia	3.2	2.5	5	2	54	29
Other South Asia	3.5	3.1	7	42	13	82
Southeast Asia	3.4	3.0	19	12	30	19
All of Latin America	2.5	1.9	46	85	70	130
Brazil alone	2.4	1.8	20	30	94	145
WANA[e]	2.7	2.3	13	42	26	82
Sub-Saharan Africa	3.2	3.3	11	35	12	37
Developing world	3.0	2.9	217	375	36	62
Developed world	0.8	0.6	117	286	86	210
World	2.1	1.7	334	660	45	89

[a]See Table 1 for product definitions.
[b]Projections are from the July 2002 version of IMPACT.
[c]1997 is the average of 1996–1998.
[d]Total and per capita meat consumption for 1997 are annual averages of 1996 to 1998 values.
[e]Western Asia and North Africa.
(From Refs. 3 and 5.)

Livestock Revolution in developing countries will continue at least until 2020 and will increasingly drive world markets for meat, milk, and feed grains. Whether it is a good thing is not the issue; it is a phenomenon that will occur. Meat and milk production increases in developing countries will largely match the big consumption increases, and meat exports from Latin America to Asia will soar.

Even so, for the large majority of people in developing countries, consumption levels will remain very low, at 36 kg of meat per capita on average in 2020 (compared to 87 kg per capita in the developed countries as a whole). Average consumption in poor rural areas will surely be much lower than this, and especially for poor people. Protein and micronutrient deficiencies, which tend to disappear with increased consumption of livestock products, will likely remain widespread in developing countries.

The rapidly growing demand for livestock products in developing countries is a rare opportunity for smallholder farmers to benefit from a rapidly growing market, and for their families to have a viable source of much-needed micronutrients and dense calories. The worst thing that agencies targeted to poverty reduction and rural development can do is to cease public investments that facilitate

sustainable small-operator forms of market-oriented livestock production. Lack of action will not stop the Livestock Revolution, but by abandoning the field to big industrial farming operations concentrated around large cities, it will help ensure that the form it takes is less favorable for poverty alleviation, better nutrition, and health.

ACKNOWLEDGMENTS

This article draws on fruitful collaboration over several years with Mark Rosegrant of IFPRI, creator of the IMPACT global food model. Greater detail on the results of that collaboration can be found in Refs. 1 and 6, and in the IMPACT model.[4,5]

REFERENCES

1. Delgado, C. A food revolution: Rising consumption of meat and milk in developing countries. J. Nutri. **2003, Nov.,** *133* (11 Supplement II).
2. Cranfield, J.A.L.; Hertel, T.W.; Eales, J.S.; Preckel, P.V.

Changes in the structure of global food demand. Am. J. Agric. Econ. **1998**, *80*, 1042–1050.

3. Food and Agriculture Organization of the United Nations. *FAOSTAT Statistical Database*; FAO. http://faostat.fao.org/default.htm (accessed various months, 2002).

4. Rosegrant, M.W.; Praisner, M.; Meijer, S.; Witcover, J. *Global Food Projections to 2020: Emerging Trends and Alternative Futures*; International Food Policy Research Institute: Washington, DC, 2001.

5. Rosegrant, M.; Meijer, S.; Cline, S. *International Model for Policy Analysis of Agricultural Commodities and Trade (IMPACT): Model Description*; International Food Policy Research Institute: Washington, D.C., 2002. http://www.ifpri.org/themes/impact/impactmodel.pdf. Accessed June 2003.

6. Delgado, C.; Rosegrant, M.; Steinfeld, H.; Ehui, S.; Courbois, C. Livestock to 2020: The Next Food Revolution. In *Food, Agriculture, and the Environment Discussion Paper 28*; International Food Policy Research Institute: Washington, DC, 1999.

Future of Animal Agriculture: Market Strategies

Wayne D. Purcell
Virginia Tech, Blacksburg, Virginia, U.S.A.

INTRODUCTION

Animal agriculture is moving from commodity products to consumer-driven product lines. As part of the transformation, the historical price-driven systems are being replaced by contracts, vertical alliances, and other forms of nonprice coordination and quality control. It is likely that the moves away from a price-driven marketplace will continue. Market strategies will have to change. The objective here is to explain why the transformation is occurring and to suggest strategies for the future.

ECONOMIC SETTING OF ANIMAL AGRICULTURE

Animal agriculture is a textbook illustration of an atomistic economic setting. There are many small producers at the farm level in cattle, hogs, and sheep. The individual producer is a price taker and has no ability to command a price that ensures costs will be covered. In recent research, the average per-head profit for cattle feeding activities during the 1990s was estimated at −$4.27.[1] Profits at the cow-calf level are variable, ranging in recent decades from $80 per cow in 1990–1991 to −$75 in 1996.[2]

Returns to producers will be variable as cycles run their course, even if demand is constant. Since the late 1970s, demand has not been constant. Demand for beef declined each year from 1980 through 1998, and demand for pork declined through 1995 (demand indices at www.aaec.vt.edu/rilp). Most researchers attribute the declines to a divergence between the fresh product offering and changing consumer preferences.[3] Price signals to prompt changes in what producers offer have not worked. Important product attributes such as tenderness in beef have not been incorporated into the quality grades. The pricing system cannot motivate needed genetic and management changes at the producer level when important product attributes are not identified. The beef and pork sectors produced commodity product during the 1980s and into the 1990s and demand languished.

Conversely, the poultry sector grew during the 1980s and 1990s as investments were attracted by profit opportunities. The reduction in per-capita consumption of beef from 94.5 lb in 1976 to 67.4 lb in 2002 was more than offset by chicken, where per-capita consumption increased from 46.9 lb in 1980 to 93.8 lb in 2002. Cattle and hog producers were forced out of business. The beef cow inventory declined from 45.7 million head in 1975 to 32.4 million head in 1990 and was 32.9 million on January 1, 2003. The breeding herd in hogs was 9.6 million head in 1978 and declined to 6.0 million head as of December 1, 2002.

Significant increases in production per breeding animal in beef and pork were not enough to maintain market share. If the demand problems had continued, the beef and pork sectors would have been even smaller in 2003. Fortunately, the demand declines have been halted by moving to a new business model. Processors have made massive investments in product and market development since the mid-1990s. Following the demand lows in 1995 for pork and in 1998 for beef, the cumulative increases in demand have been 9.78% and 8.26% for beef and pork, respectively. Tables 1 and 2 show demand indices for beef and pork.

The transformation of the supply chain away from commodity products and its related demand improvement have improved the economic outlook for every participant and especially the livestock producer. Producers suffer the most when processors see no reason to make investments in new product offerings. Check-off programs are too small to prompt change on the scale needed. It is the transformation from a commodity orientation to a consumer orientation that will be the primary determinant of the economic future of the animal industry.

TRANSFORMATION TO MARKET DRIVEN

As Table 1 shows, the demand problems were especially acute in beef. Figure 1 provides another perspective, showing per-capita consumption of beef and inflation-adjusted retail prices of Choice beef from 1975 through 2002. During the 1970s, 1980s, and into the 1990s, the trend in both series was down, and there are consecutive years in which both the price and consumption declined. If price and per-capita consumption are both declining,

Encyclopedia of Animal Science
DOI: 10.1081/E-EAS 120019631

Table 1 Demand index for beef, 1980–2002

Year	Per-capita consumption	Deflated price (cents/lb)	Constant demand price	Index (1980=100)	Index (1998=100)[a]
1980	76.6	283.5	–	100.00	198.89
1981	78.3	258.2	274.13	94.19	187.40
1982	77.1	247.0	280.71	87.99	175.00
1983	78.6	235.0	272.40	86.27	171.57
1984	78.5	227.3	271.82	83.26	165.62
1985	79.3	212.7	268.59	79.19	157.56
1986	78.9	206.9	270.78	76.41	152.02
1987	73.9	209.8	298.35	70.32	139.92
1988	72.7	211.6	304.99	69.38	138.00
1989	69.0	214.2	325.38	65.83	130.95
1990	67.8	214.5	332.04	64.60	128.53
1991	66.6	212.0	338.71	62.59	124.50
1992	66.2	203.3	340.94	59.63	118.65
1993	64.6	203.1	349.69	58.08	115.52
1994	66.3	190.9	340.41	56.08	111.59
1995	66.6	186.6	338.78	55.08	109.58
1996	67.2	178.6	335.40	53.25	105.95
1997	65.7	174.2	343.79	50.67	100.81
1998	66.7	170.0	338.17	**50.27**	100.00
1999	67.5	173.4	333.85	51.94	103.33
2000	67.6	178.1	333.08	53.47	106.35
2001	66.2	190.7	340.96	55.93	111.29
2002	67.5	184.3	333.82	55.21	**109.78**

[a]By rescaling the index to 1998=100, the 9.78% improvement since the demand bottom in 1998 can be read directly from the 2002 index value.

Table 2 Demand index for pork, 1980–2002

Year	Per-capita consumption	Deflated price (cents/lb)	Constant demand price	Index (1980=100)	Index (1995=100)[a]
1980	57.3	1.79	1.79	100.00	151.43
1981	54.7	1.77	1.91	92.78	140.50
1982	49.1	1.92	2.17	88.53	134.07
1983	51.7	1.80	2.05	87.90	133.11
1984	51.5	1.65	2.06	80.18	121.42
1985	51.9	1.59	2.04	78.01	118.13
1986	49.0	1.72	2.18	79.06	119.72
1987	49.2	1.75	2.16	80.92	122.54
1988	52.5	1.64	2.02	81.34	123.17
1989	52.0	1.56	2.04	76.46	115.78
1990	49.8	1.72	2.15	80.08	121.27
1991	50.2	1.65	2.12	77.66	117.60
1992	52.8	1.50	2.01	74.77	113.22
1993	51.9	1.45	2.05	70.83	107.26
1994	52.5	1.41	2.01	70.16	106.24
1995	51.8	1.35	2.04	**66.04**	100.00
1996	48.4	1.49	2.21	67.51	102.23
1997	47.9	1.53	2.24	68.45	103.66
1998	51.5	1.49	2.06	72.21	109.35
1999	52.7	1.45	2.00	72.49	109.78
2000	51.2	1.50	2.07	72.31	109.51
2001	50.2	1.52	2.12	71.67	108.53
2002	51.4	1.48	2.07	71.50	**108.26**

[a]By rescaling the index to 1995=100, the 8.26% improvement since the demand bottom in 1995 can be read directly from the 2002 index value.

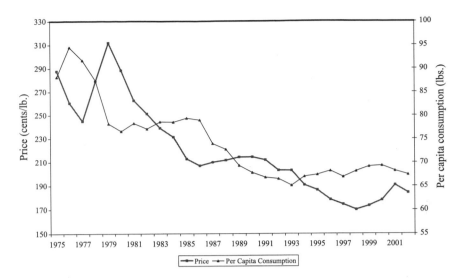

Fig. 1 Inflation-adjusted retail price (CPI, 1982–1984=100) and per-capita consumption for beef, 1975–2002. (*From:* Livestock Marketing Information Center (LMIC), www.lmic.info.) (*View this art in color at www.dekker.com.*)

demand is decreasing. The situation was similar if less dramatic in pork, but was significantly different for chicken. A comparable plot for chicken would show consecutive years in which both price and per-capita consumption were increasing.[4]

Changes to move toward a consumer-friendly product offering for beef and pork were essential. Investments in the product offering had lagged for nearly two decades in the face of a commodity orientation and the continued absence of the levels of coordination and quality control that processors and retailers needed to offer branded fresh beef and pork. Investments in new products have surged since the mid-1990s, but the moves to contracts, vertical alliances, and vertical integration to get the coordination and quality control necessary to prompt those investments have been controversial.

The historical price-driven system used price signals to coordinate production with consumer preferences. Adversarial relationships between participants along the supply chain constrained the level of coordination achieved, however. Packers who can only buy slaughter cattle or slaughter hogs of variable quality do not see reasons to invest in new products. The quality control needed for branded product lines looked impossible to achieve and the animal industry drifted for two decades.

In the 1990s, processors discovered that consumers would pay significant premiums for branded and quality-assured product offerings. Major pork processors such as Smithfield Foods, Inc., moved to common genetics in company-owned and contract production facilities. Taking advantage of a level of quality control that had not been possible when buying slaughter hogs in the traditional open market, Smithfield has introduced an

array of branded products and is active in the quality-conscious Japanese market.

Larger producers who started vertical beef or pork alliances to avoid selling at average prices approve of the new nonprice systems. But independent livestock producers sometimes feel they are being denied access to the marketplace and they wonder about the competitiveness of bids for cattle or hogs. The U.S. Department of Agriculture was petitioned for rule changes that would have banned most types of contract buying in livestock.[5] In 2002, an amendment to farm bill legislation would have prevented packers from owning, producing, or controlling the production of livestock. Legislation calling for a similar set of regulations was introduced in the 2003 Congressional session.

As we look back, the price-driven system had little chance to survive as a coordinating mechanism. The quality grades in beef and pork were never changed to allow effective price signals that communicate needed changes and incentives for those changes to the producer. Producers of uniformly fed cattle or slaughter hogs using outdated genetics face the unwelcome specter of having cattle or hogs that are uniformly wrong compared to the needs of new branded and quality-assured product lines.

LOOKING AHEAD TO NEW MARKET STRATEGIES

The transformation away from the historical price-driven system is likely to continue. The economic reasons to move toward a consumer-friendly product offering are grounded in significant profit opportunities. Nonprice types of coordination that provide the raw material needed to support branded consumer product lines are growing in popularity with retailers, processors, and some producers. The research literature shows that when a participant in an organized group effort such as a vertical alliance makes investments in technology that is use-specific, the traditional pricing system may not be adequate as a governance system.[6] Investments in genetics, scanning technology, and technology to inject tenderness are clearly investments in use-specific technologies. In the presence of such new investments, governance systems will change and market strategies will have to change as well.

CONCLUSIONS

The marketing strategies of the future in animal agriculture will be different. Consumers will demand that their needs be met in terms of product form, product offerings, consistency, quality, and convenience in preparation, and they will be willing to pay premiums for the right products. Quality-controlled, quality-assured, and branded fresh meat lines will continue to replace commodity products, and the new products will be mainstays of the animal industry of the future.

If nonprice means of coordination such as contract, vertical alliances, and vertical integration are required to prompt the needed investments, those nonprice means of coordination are likely to grow in importance. Consumers will be helped by revised product offerings consistent with changed lifestyles, and profits are always more likely at the producer level when the consumer is well served.

In the new market strategies, genetic selection will focus on livestock to meet the needs of a consumer-driven supply chain. Producers of superior livestock will earn

premiums through alliances or price grids in contracts with buyers. Investments in technology will be made within governance systems that specify performance standards for everyone involved. Packers will seek arrangements to eliminate the quantity and quality variations in the historical price-driven systems in efforts to reduce their costs of operation and to ensure access to the livestock that support consumer-driven product lines. Selling most slaughter cattle, regardless of quality, at essentially the same price during a brief marketing window each week will disappear. Producers' marketing strategies will focus on market access, on valuations that reflect the true value of their livestock, and on sharing in the profits that can be earned when consumers are well served.

REFERENCES

1. Purcell, W.D.; Hudson, W.T. Risk sharing and compensation guides for managers and members of vertical beef alliances. Rev. Agric. Econ. **2003**, *25* (1), 44–65.
2. *Livestock Marketing Information Center (LMIC)*. www.lmic.info, (accessed June 23, 2003).
3. Schroeder, T.C.; Marsh, T.L.; Mintert, J. *Beef Demand Determinants. Report Prepared for the Joint Evaluation Advisory Committee, National Cattlemen's Beef Association*; Kansas State University, 2000; 61 pp.
4. Purcell, W.D. Measures of changes in demand for beef, pork, and chicken, 1975–2000. Res. Inst. Livest. Pricing Res. Bull. **2000**, *4*, 32 pp.
5. *Petition for Rulemaking: Packer Livestock Procurement Practices*; GIPSA, USDA, October 12, 1996.
6. Boehlje, J.; Schrader, L.F. The Industrialization of Agriculture: Questions of Coordination. In *The Industrialization of Agriculture*; Royer, J.S., Rogers, R.C., Eds.; The Ipswich Book Company: U.K., 1988; 3–26.

Future of Animal Agriculture: Urban/Rural Agriculture Ecosystems

Maurice Lenuel Eastridge
The Ohio State University, Columbus, Ohio, U.S.A.

INTRODUCTION

The age of the agrarian society in the United States has long passed, but the volume of food needed to feed the world population continues to increase. Less than 2% of the U.S. population is presently engaged in food production; thus, the number of farms has decreased, the size (acres or number of animals) per farm has increased, and the performance of each productive unit (land, crop, or animal) continues to make improvement. This advancement in productive capacity is made possible by advancement in genetics, new technology in production and harvesting, and more specialized management skills. The economics of this food production continues to be challenged, resulting in globalization of the food production system and increased size of operations to increase total profitability. The increased size of operations is driven by limited margins per production unit, thus causing farm owners to increase the number of producing units to achieve a targeted income.

In the midst of these changes in agriculture, the increase in spendable income and the desire to work in an urban setting and live in a rural setting have resulted in movement of people from cities—even from the suburban areas—to residential developments in more rural locations with increased area of land per resident. The interface issues between urban and rural sometimes occur between cities and commercial agriculture, but the issues are more common between rural residential developments and commercial agriculture. These residential developments occur with zoning regulations set by townships instead of by city zoning boards and are usually established with fewer restrictions. Agriculture in some areas is exempt from zoning, but increased focus on environmental preservation is beginning to change this. The future of animal agriculture is being affected by the issues that arise between the commercial food operation and community residents.

URBAN AND RURAL INTERFACE

The term urban and rural interface is frequently uttered in communities today. The idea of an interface is that a common boundary is being shared by two or more groups with different identities. The urban and rural interface would imply that the boundary is being shared between a city, which has the purpose of sustaining commercial businesses, governmental offices, and high-density residential housing, and the dwellers in the country who have taken on the responsibility of food production for the population. And although this interface sometimes occurs, the more frequent interface is rural-to-rural residents, with the identity differences being those in commercial food production versus those with public jobs who live in the country in low-density housing (Fig. 1). In some cases the interface is rural-to-rural, in that the identity difference is small- versus large-scale food production operations.

The primary issues that surface in the urban and rural interface are environmental effects and quality of life. Water quality and availability are the primary environmental issues. The concern with water quality is caused by the risk of contamination from manure storage and the land application of manure. The availability of water is a concern related to the amount of water consumed by the livestock and the water used for cleaning the facilities or product (e.g., egg washing). The level of risk for impacts to the water supply depends on the specific site. The odor from food animal operations is viewed by some as both an environmental and a quality of life issue: There are environmental risks from airborne particles, and the quality of life is affected by the repulsive nature of the odor. These aspects have also led to concerns about property values in proximity to animal operations. Other quality of life issues include road damage due to heavy equipment, mud on roads from farm equipment, slow-moving equipment on the local roads, loud noises (e.g., from tractors or drying equipment) during all hours of the day from farm operations, and dust from crop harvesting or animal operations.

FOOD PRODUCTION AND LAND USE

Location of food production in the world is affected by people and land resources. The suitability of the land for

Encyclopedia of Animal Science
DOI: 10.1081/E-EAS 120019636

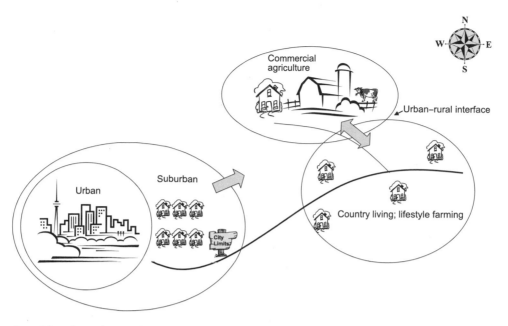

Fig. 1 Urban and rural interface: the coexistence of the human population and commercial food animal production. (*View this art in color at www.dekker.com.*)

food production is very important, and the availability of technology to people in developed countries is key to production of food for the population in the country and for export. Public policies and cultural traditions also impact the food production system. Over 50% of the land area is used for agricultural production in Argentina, Australia, China, New Zealand, and the United Kingdom, but land area per person ranges from 0.7 ha/person (China) to 40 ha/person (Australia), with each having a population growth of about 1.0 to 1.2% (Table 1). In

contrast, Canada and Japan have 7.5 and 13.8% of the land in agricultural production, with population densities of 32.1 and 0.3 ha/person, respectively. Yet the reasons for the percentage of land in agricultural production differ. Much of Canada's land is not productive because it is in the extreme northern climate, and much of Japan's land is used for housing in that densely populated country. However, the Netherlands and the United Kingdom have a similar human population per land area to that of Japan, yet the Netherlands and the United Kingdom have more

Table 1 Human population, total land area, and agricultural land area in selected countries for 2001

Country	Population[a] (× 1000)	Population[a] growth (%)	Land area[b] (× 1000 ha)	Land area (ha/person)	Agricultural land area[b] (× 1000 ha)	Agricultural land area (% of land area)
Argentina	37,488	1.3	278,040	7.4	177,000	63.7
Australia	19,338	1.2	774,122	40.0	455,500	58.9
Brazil	172,559	1.4	854,740	5.0	263,465	30.8
Canada	31,015	1.0	997,061	32.1	74,880	7.5
China	1,284,972	1.0	959,805	0.7	555,276	57.9
Japan	127,335	0.3	37,780	0.3	5,199	13.8
Netherlands	15,930	0.6	4,153	0.3	1,931	46.5
New Zealand	3,808	1.1	27,053	7.1	117,235	63.7
United Kingdom	59,542	0.3	24,291	0.4	16,954	69.8
United States	285,926	1.0	962,909	3.4	411,259	42.7

[a]From Ref. 1.
[b]From Ref. 2.

Table 2 Population (× 1000) of primary food animals, animal units (AU; × 1000), and hectares of agricultural land area (ALA) per AU in selected countries for 2002

Country	All cattle	Dairy cows	Sheep	Goats	Pigs	Chickens	Ducks	Geese	Turkeys	Horses	Animal units[a] (AU)	ha ALA/AU
Argentina	50,669	2,300	14,000	3,550	4,250	110,500	2,350	135	2,850	3,650	64,519	2.74
Australia	30,500	2,120	113,000	310	2,912	93,000	540	–	1,400	220	53,154	8.57
Brazil	176,000	15,600	15,000	9,800	30,000	1,050,000	3,500	–	13,000	5,900	225,345	1.17
Canada	13,700	1,084	994	30	14,367	160,000	1,150	300	5,900	385	19,990	3.75
China	106,175	5,134	136,972	161,492	464,695	3,923,600	661,250	215,000	250	8,262	306,874	1.81
Japan	4,564	1,219	11	35	9,612	283,102	–	–	3	20	10,384	0.50
Netherlands	4,050	1,486	1,300	215	13,000	98,000	1,020	–	1,523	122	9,589	0.20
New Zealand	9,633	3,749	43,142	183	358	13,000	170	65	70	78	21,793	5.38
United Kingdom	10,343	2,222	35,832	–	5,588	155,800	4,000	100	8,500	184	21,916	0.77
United States	96,700	9,135	6,685	1,250	59,074	1,940,000	6,650	–	88,000	5,300	148,654	2.77

[a]Calculated based on estimated dry matter excreted per day using the beef animal as the base, with body weight (kg) and the coefficient for each species, respectively, being: cattle (less dairy cows), 500.0 and 1.000; dairy cows, 545.0 and 2.310; sheep, 45.0 and 0.160; pigs, 70.0 and 0.170; chickens, 1.1 and 0.009; ducks, 1.6 and 0.014; geese, 4.5 and 0.040; turkeys, 6.0 and 0.024; and horses, 455.0 and 1.700, respectively.
(From Ref. 2.)

land devoted to agricultural production than Japan. Increased environmental regulations in both countries and animal welfare guidelines in the United Kingdom are having major impacts on food animal production. These changes are driven somewhat by cultural views and the limited land base to support the presence of food animals, with the Netherlands and the United Kingdom having less than one hectare of agricultural land per animal unit (Table 2).

Sufficient land base is needed for food animal production, not only directly for the animals but also for growing the crops to feed the animals and to which manure can be applied for fertilizer. Alternative uses of manure, instead of providing nutrients for crop production, include energy generation from methane production and composting for use in agronomic or ornamental horticulture, although these systems are in various stages of development and acceptance. Countries with high concentrations of animals per hectare of agricultural land are going to be faced with continued pressure from the urban and rural interface. Yet the concentration of animals within a country is not the only factor that gives rise to these pressures. For example, the United States has 2.77 ha per animal unit, and many hectares of agricultural land have been idled in recent years by governmental programs to control production of grain. Consequently, a lot of available land for agriculture has not been in use.

The concern over food animal production varies by state within the United States due to the availability of water resources, the human population of the state, the cultural acceptance of agriculture, and the accepted meaning of a family farm. Within a state, these aspects can vary even within a community. In some areas, animal density is actually much lower than 20 years ago, but urban–rural pressures are intense. Therefore, the interface oftentimes becomes a local community issue because of the concentration of animals within a community and the demand for resources. Who was there first—the animal production facility or the resident community? Was the new animal production unit begun by someone from the local community or by someone outside the local community (e.g., from another state or country)—"Can they be trusted?" If the animal operation already in existence is expanding, "Are they accepted in the community?"

BEING A GOOD NEIGHBOR

Minimizing the challenges of the urban and rural interface can be aided if the individuals sharing this common boundary agree to be good neighbors.[3–5] This attitude is needed by both the farmers and the rural residents. Each party needs to make efforts to get to know each other, to keep their properties neat and clean (i.e., take pride in an attractive community), to accept that they are a community, and to develop respect for each other. The farmer needs to take the responsibility for sharing good will in the community, promptly cleaning up spills on the roads, using management practices to minimize environmental risks, and providing opportunities for the residents to understand their production enterprise and the food production system. Rural residents need to take the responsibility to ask questions about the agricultural enterprise, to not trespass on the farmer's property, and to know the proper manner in which to file complaints about an animal operation. Realtors and communities are working together in some areas to educate people about country living before they purchase a house in a rural community.[6]

CONCLUSION

Food production is essential to the world's population of people, and where food animal production occurs it will continue to be determined by the economic viability in the area and the production efficiency that can be attained. We have focused for many years on these two aspects as the foundation for the future of animal agriculture. However, with increased concentration of animals per operation to attain economic viability, environmental risks have increased. This has given rise to increased environmental standards for food animal production in order to preserve the environment. Sustaining the environment is critical for the future of food animal production.

An ever-arising force affecting the future of animal agriculture is social acceptance. Increased social pressure arises from the environmental risks, perceived concerns with quality of life in the community, the notion that a large-scale operation is not a family farm, and the perception that animal well-being is less in a large-scale operation. Social pressure has been intense, even in some areas that have fewer animals per land area than 20 years ago. Although the population may prefer that food be produced locally and at low cost,[7] the reality of the economic forces resulting in larger animal operations may not even enter their mind as a trade-off. Fewer people have agrarian backgrounds, yet more of them desire to live in the country. The increased presence of low-density housing in rural areas and the increased size of animal production operations will continue to cause challenges in the urban and rural interface. In some communities, it is the social acceptance of animal agriculture that will determine the continued presence of animal agriculture, even if the land and economics are not limiting. These social issues also will direct some of the changes in public policy that affect land use,[8] from preserving open space in rural areas to bringing agricultural enterprises more in line with what is expected from other commercial businesses.

REFERENCES

1. UNICEF. **2003**. http://www.unicef.org/statistics.
2. Food and Agriculture Organization of the United Nations. FAOSTAT, agriculture data. **2003**. http://faostat.fao.org.
3. Ohio Livestock Environmental Assurance Program. *Building Positive Neighbor Relations*; Ohio Livestock Coalition: Columbus, OH.
4. *The Code of Country Living: A Look at the Realities of Living in the Countryside of Rural Illinois*; Illinois Farm Bureau: Bloomington, IL, 1999.
5. *Good Neighbor Relations: Advice and Tips from Farmers*; The Pennsylvania State University: University Park, PA, 1997.
6. *If You Are Thinking About Moving to The Country ... You May Want to Consider This*; Ottawa County Planning Department: West Olive, MI, 2003.
7. Davis, G.; Smith, M.B.; Tucker, M. *Ohioans' Perceptions of Agricultural Land Use and the Environment*; Department of Human and Community Resource Development, The Ohio State University: Columbus, 2002. http://www.ag.ohio-state.edu/~hcrd/staff/AgEnPollReport.pdf.
8. Libby, L.W. *Rural Land Use Problems and Policy Options: Overview from a U.S. Perspective*; The Ohio State University: Columbus, 2002. http://aede.osu.edu/programs/Swank/pdfs/rural_land.pdf.

GI Tract: Anatomical and Functional Comparisons

Edwin T. Moran, Jr.
Auburn University, Auburn, Alabama, U.S.A.

INTRODUCTION

The gastrointestinal (GI) tract provides nutrients to support the body and all its activities. Essentially six functions exist, with the effectiveness of each one being reliant on its predecessor. From beginning to end, these are food seeking, oral evaluation, gastric preparation for digestion, small intestinal recovery of nutrients, large intestinal action on indigesta, and waste evacuation.

GASTROINTESTINAL SYSTEM DIFFERENCES

Gastrointestinal systems differ largely with respect to the presence of a meaningful symbiotic microbial population and its location. Simple-stomached animals (Figs. 1A and B) do not have an extensive microbial population to greatly alter nutrient recovery, whereas ruminants (Fig. 1C) and nonruminant herbivores (Fig. 1D) support symbiotic populations prior to and after formal digestion by the small intestine, respectively. All GI systems accomplish the same sequence of events but are anatomically and functionally modified to accommodate predominating food and microbial populations.

FOOD SEEKING

Food seeking combines sight, smell, and hearing, which are largely evolutionary adaptations to improve survival. All senses are generally employed, but each animal may be more dependent on one than on the others. Pigs are heavily dependent on olfactory acuity but visually weak, whereas fowl are to the converse. The subterranean location of predominant food likely predisposed the pig to a keen sense of smell, whereas feedstuffs at diverse locations above ground probably led fowl to have extraordinary visual capacity. Farm mammals have extensive nasal scrolling that is well endowed with olfactory sensitivity compared to a severe limitation in both respects with fowl. Mammals also have the ability to generate a bucopharangeal seal and ''sniff,'' thereby accentuating olfactory acuity, whereas fowl do not.

SENSORY EVALUATION

Sensory evaluation predominates in the oral cavity once food is prehended. Evaluation by mammals represents a complex of texture, taste, and aroma that generally arises during mastication.[2] Teeth and a mobile tongue aid prehension by mammals, followed by mastication in a warm mouth lubricated by blends of viscous and serous types of saliva that optimize sensory detection. Ruminants masticate extensively and make considerable demand on serous saliva, particularly from the parotid gland. Fowl have an oral cavity that differs markedly from mammals. Their eyes provide acute depth perception to accurately retrieve particulates, but food size is limited by the absence of teeth, a rigid beak, and fixed oral dimension. Beak manipulations using an inflexible tongue coat the oral mass with viscous saliva to lubricate swallowing. Fowl appear to depend on mechanoreceptors, because few chemoreceptors and a poor environment for solute detection exist for oral evaluation.[3] Land mammals generally have extensive numbers of taste buds for evaluation that are reinforced by the olfaction of volatiles passing from oral to nasal cavity. Mammals generate a bucopharangyl pressure with swallowing that supplements peristalsis in propelling both solids and fluids down the esophagus. However, absence of this seal and pressure in fowl necessitates the use of gravity to consume fluids.

FOOD SWALLOWING

Food swallowing initiates formal entry into the GI tract, followed by involuntary control until defecation. Four basic layers appear in the wall, from the esophagus through to the rectal canal, but their expression may change with location and among animals. Mucosa has direct contact with lumen contents, and its appearance markedly changes with function. Underlying submucosa generally provides a network of blood vessels, lymphatics, and nerves to support mucosal activity. Bolus movement is accomplished by two layers of muscle that are held together by a final serosa that contains connective tissue. Circular-oriented fibers are positioned on the lumen side and function either to peristaltically move the bolus or to contract in place and mix by segmentation. Overlying

Encyclopedia of Animal Science
DOI: 10.1081/E-EAS 120019638

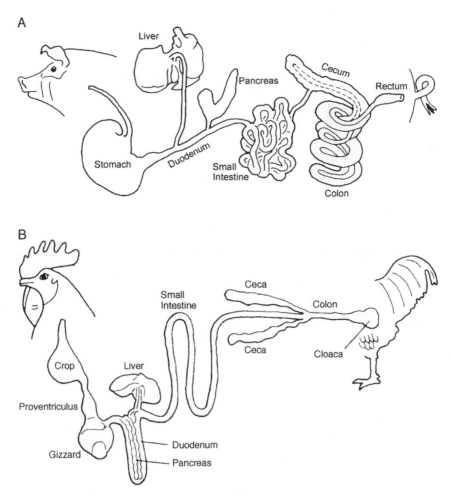

Fig. 1 Schematic GI systems of (A,B) simple-stomached (pig and chicken), (C) ruminant (cow), and (D) nonruminant herbivore (horse) animals. The anatomical differences most obvious are those that accommodate symbiotic microbial populations. Simple-stomached animals are limited in this respect, and mammals employ an extensive colon, whereas two ceca are predominant in fowl. Ruminants acquire their microbial population prior to formal digestion, which improves overall nutrient access, whereas in nonruminant herbivores microbial action on indigesta occurs in the small intestine to enhance energy recovery. (Reconstructed using diagrams from Ref. 1.) (*View this art in color at www.dekker.com.*)

longitudinal fibers are positioned around the circumference and provide stabilization of the circular fibers during contraction. Coordination of motility and other routine activities is accomplished by a complex of nerves, known as the intramural plexus, located within and between each layer. Autonomic and central nervous system inputs occur as necessary to maintain synchrony with the body at large.

GASTRIC DIGESTION

Gastric digestion alters food to improve its overall compatibility with water, to enhance the subsequent rate of enzyme action and nutrient recovery by the small intestine. Consumed food is initially stored, and then gastric juice is added and mixed into the mass for enzyme

modification. Food storage occurs at the end of the esophagus and/or in the cardiac area of the mammal's stomach. The crop is an outpocketing midway down the fowl esophagus that provides storage. Ruminants have a specialized esophageal area compartmentalized into rumen, reticulum, and omasum. Bacteria and protozoa anerobically ferment feed in the rumen to greatly expand their numbers while producing by-product volatile fatty acids (VFAs). Additional microbial mass provides protein and vitamins for eventual recovery in the small intestine, whereas VFAs are largely removed prior to and during gastric digestion. The reticulum acts to move swallowed food into the rumen for microbial action as well as to remove spent contents for entry into the omasum. Passage between the omasal leaves acts to decrease liquid and particulate size before access to the abomasum, or "true" stomach.

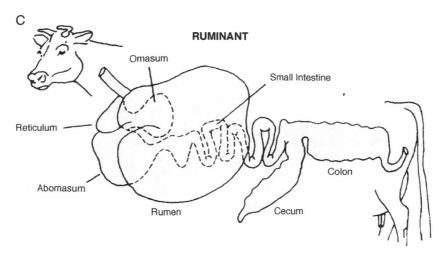

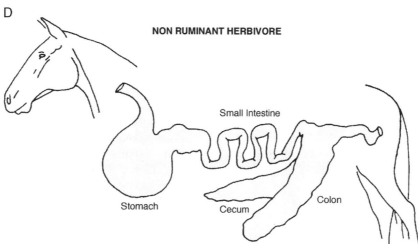

Fig. 1 (*Continued.*)

Gastric juice is a composite of hydrochloric acid and pepsin. Production and release occur in the gastric gland or fundic area of simple-stomached mammals, in the abomasum of ruminants, and in the proventriculus of fowl. Motility progressively conveys lumen contents from storage past gastric glands and then facilitates mixing for enzyme action in the antrum of the stomach and abomasum. Peristalsis also conveys food from the fowl's crop for a brief stop in the proventriculus to acquire gastric juice before subsequent mixing in the gizzard. Circular muscle associated with the gizzard is emphasized to support intense contractions for grinding, while a tough koilin mucosa endures digestive and physical stresses.

SMALL INTESTINE

The small intestine is divided into duodenum, jejunum, and ileum, in that order from the end of gastric digestion through to entry into the large intestine. Proportions of small, relative to large, intestine vary extensively with simple-stomached mammals; carnivores have the most and nonruminant herbivores the least.[4] Mammals release an array of enzymes from the pancreas together with bile from the gall bladder at the beginning of the duodenum, while accompanying bicarbonate acts to neutralize contents and initiate digestion. Slow peristalsis of the composite is interdispersed by segmentation through the duodenum. Nutrient digestion then gathers momentum, and rapid absorption occurs through the jejunum before diminishing along the ileum. In fowl, pancreatic enzymes and bile enter at the distal end of the duodenum, and then peristaltic refluxing back and forth along its length mixes the contents to initiate digestion before continuing though the jejunum and ileum in the same to-and-fro manner.

Convection of lumen contents by motility is complemented by a mucosa having villi to expand the contact area. Mucosal anatomy is remarkably similar among animals. Muscle fibers extending from the base into each villus also foster movement to enhance surface exchange. Enterocytes on each villus arise from their mitotic origin at the base, known as the crypt of Lieberkuhn, and become competent at digestion and absorption once beyond midpoint.[5] Microvilli located on the surface of mature enterocytes are coated wih mucus from adjacent goblet cells to create an unstirred water layer that is stabilized by a fibrous glycocalyx projecting from their ends. Enzymes immobilized on microvilli encounter digestion products diffusing into the unstirred water layer. Resulting products are immediately capable of absortion and are then transferred through the basolateral membrane to an underlying vascular system, for rapid removal and maintainance of a concentration gradient. In mammals, lymphatics convey absorbed fat as chlomicrons from the mucosa, whereas fowl form very low density lipoproteins that enter the portal system. Distinct lymphatic vessels are absent in fowl.

LARGE INTESTINE

The large intestine of mammals comprises the colon, cecum, and rectum.[6] Cecum and colon have longitudinal fibers in the muscle layer, gathered from their equal distribution at the circumference into bundles to appear as three bands (tenae coli). In turn, contractions of the circular fibers without overhead stabilization create out-pocketings (haustrae) of circular fibers between bands. The ileocolonic sphincter opens only with transfer of indigesta from the small to the large intestine. A low-profile mucosa well covered with mucus aids in providing anaerobic conditions for an extensive microbial population. Gentle motility concentrates solutes and fine particulates in the haustrae, where microbial action on complex polysaccharides leads to VFA production and absorption. Coarse fiber collects in the lumen core and rapidly moves to the rectum. In simple-stomached mammals and ruminants, the colon forms coils that dominate the large intestine, whereas in nonruminant herbivores indigesta enter into an accentuated cecum and are retained in the haustrae before movement through the colon.

Fowl have a large intestinal system that drastically differs from mammals. No haustrae exist in the muscle layer, and two large ceca are connected to a small colon. Each cecum has a small entrance protected by villi that restrict entry to fluid and fines. These microbiologically labile materials are segregated from coarse fiber and forced into both ceca by reverse peristalsis originating at the cloaca. In mammals, coarse fiber collects in the rectum to a critical mass before evacuation. However, the cloaca in fowl not only has a coprodeum for such storage but a separate urodeum for urine. Reverse peristalsis moves urine through the colon to facilitate indigesta segregation for ceca entry while the mucosa actively resorbs salt and water. Microbial action on ceca contents yields volatile fatty acids similar to those in the mammal's cecum–colon. Fecal excreta from mammals are a combination of coarse fiber in the core, with haustrae residue appearing on the surface as nodules. Coprodeum excreta are voided from fowl as a fibrous mass covered with a uric acid white cap that accrues with urine dehydration. Ceca excreta are separately voided as a viscous mass and may be eaten by the fowl to provide considerable nutrition, particularly vitamins.

CONCLUSION

In summary, all animals must find food, orally evaluate it, and then digest it and recover nutrients before evacuation. Simple-stomached farm animals have limited resources to assimilate food, and therefore require high-quality feed-stuffs in order to perform favorably. Additional capacity for digestion and synthesis by ruminants, provided by an expansive symbiotic microflora at the front of the GI system, reduces contraints on feedstuff sources. Nonruminant herbivores employ similar microbes after formal nutrient recovery, and fermentive activity largely improves energy access. Coping with genetic alterations to feedstuffs, enzyme supplements that improve digestive capacity, threats from food pathogens, and excreta pollution with intensive production requires that producers understand the functioning of the GI system.

REFERENCES

1. Moran, E.T., Jr. *Comparative Nutrition of Fowl and Swine—The Gastrointestinal Systems*; Published by E.T. Moran: Guelph, Canada, 1982.
2. Bickel, H. *Palatability and Flavor Use in Animal Feeds*; Verlag Paul Parey: Hamburg, Germany, 1980.
3. Toyoshima, K. Chemoreceptive and mechanoreceptive paraneurons in the tongue. Arch. Histol. Cytol. **1989**, *4* (Suppl.), 383–388.
4. Snipes, R.L.; Snipes, H. Quantitative investigation of the intestines in eight species of domestic mammals. Z. Säughtierkunde **1997**, *62* (2), 359–371.
5. Pacha, J. Development of intestinal transport function. Physiol. Rev. **2000**, *80* (2), 1633–1667.
6. Kirchgessner, M. *Digestive Physiology of the Hind Gut. Fortschr.Tierphysiol. Tiernahrg*; Beihft 22. Verlag Paul Parey: Hamburg, Germany, 1991.

GI Tract: Animal/Microbial Symbiosis

James E. Wells
Vincent H. Varel
United States Department of Agriculture, Agricultural Research Service,
Clay Center, Nebraska, U.S.A.

INTRODUCTION

The gastrointestinal tract is indispensable for an animal's well-being. Food is consumed through the mouth and digested by host enzymes in the stomach and small intestine, and nutrients are extracted and absorbed in the small and large intestines. In this nutrient-rich environment, microorganisms can colonize and grow, and as a result, numerous interactions or symbioses between microorganisms and the animal exist that impact the health and well-being of the host animal.

Symbiosis is defined biologically as "the living together in more or less intimate association or even close union of two dissimilar organisms" and this, in a broad sense, includes pathogens. Thus, symbiosis is living together, irrespective of potential harm or benefit, and living together is no more apparent than in the animal gastrointestinal system. This symbiosis can be relatively defined by the degree of benefit to one or both partners within the association, as well as by the closeness of the association.

GASTROINTESTINAL ECOSYSTEM

Microorganisms within the gastrointestinal system are predominantly strict anaerobes, the study of these bacteria was greatly limited until culture techniques capable of excluding oxygen were developed.[1] Prior to the 1940s, theories of microbial fermentations of fiber contributing energy to the host abounded, but little direct evidence was found. Since that time, microbiologists have refined the culture techniques and conditions to support the growth of numerous gastrointestinal bacteria. Additional works with nutritionists and physiologists have identified more specific interactions between the host and microbes.

The gastrointestinal tract begins at the mouth and ends at the anus and is colonized with bacteria in nearly its entirety. The system contains over 400 species of microorganisms and the gastrointestinal microbial cells outnumber the animal cells nearly 10:1. This diverse, dynamic population of bacteria in the gastrointestinal system is referred to as the microflora or microbiota. The specific species (or strains of species) of microorganisms can vary with animal host, diet, and environment, but in general the predominant species are associated with a limited number of bacterial genera.

Parasitic or pathogenic microorganisms incur a cost on the host and have been studied more extensively. The mutualistic microorganisms generate a benefit to the host. If the interaction is not parasitic or mutualistic, it is then considered to be commensal. However, animal/microbe interactions are difficult to define and study; thus, most interactions are considered commensal. The Vin diagram (Fig. 1) best indicates the complexity of these animal/microbe interactions.

PARASITISM

When symbiosis confers benefit to one organism at the cost of the other (i.e., the host), the relationship is often viewed as being parasitic.[2] Many parasites, such as the parasitic protozoa *Entamoeba*, can persist as a common inhabitant of the gastrointestinal system. These inhabitants compete for nutrients and impair production, but seldom generate acute symptoms associated with disease. When symptoms of disease are observed, the organism is then considered to be pathogenic. Typically, pathogenic microbes are thought to be transient inhabitants, but disruption of the ecosystem can provide opportunity for indigenous microbes to overwhelm the host.

The host has several mechanisms to prevent infection of the gastrointestinal tract. Acid secretion by the stomach, intestinal motility and secretions, and the indigenous flora are deterrents to pathogen colonization. Nonetheless, microbes have adapted and evolved to overcome or, in some cases, take advantage of the preventive mechanisms. Specialized immune cells (Peyer's patch) in the intestine secrete antibodies to protect the body against toxins and potential pathogens, but some pathogenic

Encyclopedia of Animal Science
DOI: 10.1081/E-EAS 120019639

449

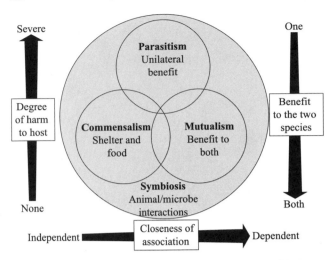

Fig. 1 Vin diagram showing interrelationships of various symbioses and the relationship to the host. (Adapted from Ref. 4.) (*View this art in color at www.dekker.com.*)

bacteria can bind and invade these specialized immune cells.

Zoonotic pathogens are a problem in animal production. These microorganisms may be commonly found in animals without any apparent disease, and yet are potentially disease-causing to humans. *Salmonella, Campylobacteria, Shigella, Enterococcus,* and the *Escherichia coli* Shiga toxin-producing strains are all potential pathogens to humans and are commonly associated with animal waste.[3] As a result, potential for fecal adulteration of meats and the possible contamination of water and food supplies from land application of animal waste are burdening issues of food safety and animal production.

MUTUALISM

Most examples of mutalistic interactions in animals demonstrate a positive gain for the host. Farm animals

require nutrients for growth and most examples of mutualism are based on synthesis of nutrients by the microflora. The specific benefit to the host is dependent on the animal's gastrointestinal anatomy (Table 1). Many herbivores have specialized digestive systems to harness the ability of the microflora to degrade indigestible feeds and supply the host with volatile fatty acids, which the animal can utilize for energy. In addition, amino acids and vitamins may be synthesized by the microflora and may be utilized by the animal host.

Ruminant animals such as deer, sheep, and cattle have a large pregastric compartment called the rumen that can account for 15% of the gastrointestinal system.[1] Microbial enzymes, in contrast to mammalian enzymes, can digest cellulose. Under anaerobic conditions, the microbes generate volatile fatty acids as end products of fermentation. The rumen environment is adapted for microbial fermentations, and this interaction allows these animal species to utilize the complex carbohydrates and nonamino-nitrogen for energy and protein needs. Ruminants complement microbial activity by regurgitating (rumination), which permits additional chewing of the large feed particles (bolus). Movement of muscles in the rumen wall allows for the continuous mixing of rumen contents to maintain digestion by microbes and absorption of volatile fatty acids by the host. The volatile fatty acids, acetate, propionate, and butyrate, can contribute up to 80% of the animal's energy needs.

In all animals, some microbial fermentation occurs in the colon or large intestine. The extent of fermentation and energy contribution to the host is highly variable, but typically correlated with the transit time of digesta through the intestine. Some herbivores, such as horses, rabbits, and chickens, utilize postgastric compartmentalization (e.g., cecum) to derive additional energy from the diet by means of microbial fermentations. In these species, the energy contribution from microbial fermentation in the cecum is much less than in the rumen.

In addition to energy from the microbial fermentation of cellulose, amino acids can be derived from microbial

Table 1 Examples of gastrointestinal adaptations of animals to benefit from the presence of microorganisms

Animal	Dietary classification	Gastrointestinal adaptation	Host benefit
Cattle, sheep, goats	Herbivore	Ruminant (pregastric adaptation)	Fermentation of cellulose, protein, vitamins
Swine, rodents, humans	Omnivore	Simple stomach with elongated colon (postgastric adaptation)	Fermentation, vitamin K
Horses, rabbits	Herbivore	Hindgut fermenter (postgastric adaptation)	Fermentation of cellulose, some vitamins

activity. In ruminants, microbial cells ($\sim$50% protein) amass from fermentation and pass out of the rumen into the stomach and small intestine. Microbes thus serve as a protein source for the ruminant animal and can contribute over 50% of the animal's protein needs. Postgastric fermenters do not benefit appreciably from microbial biosynthesis because fermentation is beyond the sites of digestion and absorption. Some animals, such as rabbits, practice copraphagy to circumvent limitations associated with postgastric fermentation. However, recent work with pigs has shown that bacteria in the small intestine may contribute 10% of a young pig's lysine dietary requirement and a majority of a grown pig's lysine dietary requirement.[4]

Ruminant animals typically do not require vitamin supplementation to their diet. In particular, the B vitamins are synthesized by the rumen microflora, often in excess of the animal's requirement. Fermentation in the lower gastrointestinal system also generates vitamins, but absorption in the lower gut is limited.[5] Germ-free animals appear to require more B vitamins in the diet, suggesting some intestinal synthesis and absorption of these vitamins. In most animals, vitamin K appears to be a microbial product absorbed from the intestine and colon, since germ-free rodents require supplementation of this vitamin and normally raised animals do not.

COMMENSALISM

By convention, most of the gastrointestinal microorganisms are viewed as commensal. These microbes establish niches and benefit from the host environment, but appear to contribute little to the host. However, this view may be in error. As our understanding of biology and its complexities changes, so does our understanding of biological interactions and the assessment of commensal bacteria. Establishment of the commensal population is affected by host factors and the population typically recovers after a perturbation (i.e., antibiotic treatment).

Numerous studies with simple-stomach animals such as swine and rats reared in germ-free environments (without the gastrointestinal microflora) suggest that microorganisms are not essential for the animal's survival, but they are beneficial. In laboratory rats as a model, animals raised germ-free need to consume significantly more calories than conventionally raised animals to maintain their body weight.[6] Mutualistic bacteria can contribute some energy, amino acids, and/or vitamins (discussed earlier), but the commensal bacteria appear to stimulate development of the gastrointestinal capillary system and intestinal villi.[7]

A healthy commensal population colonizes the gastrointestinal tract and, as a result, competitively excludes transient pathogens. The presence of commensal bacteria helps fortify the gastrointestinal barrier, regulate postnatal maturation, affect nutrient uptake and metabolism, and aid in the processing of xenobiotics.[8] More important, commensal bacteria appear to communicate with specialized cells (Paneth cells) in the intestine to elicit the production by the host of antimicrobial factors called angiogenins, which that can help shape the microflora composition.[9]

Not all examples of commensal bacterial interactions are advantageous to the host. Some *Clostridium* species can transform secreted bile acids to form secondary products that may impact nutrient digestion and absorption. Metabolism of feedstuff components can generate toxic products that affect animal performance and health.

CONCLUSIONS

Bacteria are ubiquitous in nature and have an impact on animal health, growth, and development. Within the gastrointestinal system, animals have established relationships with bacteria that appear to benefit both in many cases. Scientists are just starting to understand the complexities of these relationships and their implications. In the future, better formulation of animal diets and supplementation may enhance these relationships.

ARTICLES OF FURTHER INTEREST

REFERENCES

1. Hungate, R.E. *The Rumen and Its Microbes*; Academic Press: New York, NY, 1966.
2. Mims, C.A.; Playfair, J.H.L.; Roitt, I.M.; Wakelin, D.; Williams, R. *Medical Microbiology*; Mosby: London, 1993.
3. Swartz, M.N. Human diseases caused by foodborne

pathogens of animal origin. Clin. Infect. Dis. **2002**, *34* (Suppl. 3), S111–S122.

4. Torrallardona, D.; Harris, C.I.; Fuller, M.F. Pigs' gastrointestinal microflora provide them with essential amino acids. J. Nutr. **2003**, *133*, 1127–1131.

5. Hooper, L.V.; Midtvedt, T.; Gordon, J.I. How host microbial interactions shape the nutrient environment of the mammalian intestine. Annu. Rev. Nutr. **2002**, *22*, 283–307.

6. Wostmann, B.S.; Larkin, C.; Moriarty, A.; Bruckner-Kardoss, E. Dietary intake, energy metabolism, and excretory losses of adult male germfree Wistar rats. Lab. Anim. Sci. **1983**, *33*, 46–50.

7. Stappenbeck, T.S.; Hooper, L.V.; Gordon, J.I. Developmental regulation of intestinal angiogenesis by indigenous microbes via Paneth cells. Proc. Natl. Acad. Sci. U. S. A. **2002**, *A99*, 15451–15455.

8. Hooper, L.V.; Wong, M.H.; Thelin, A.; Hansson, L.; Falk, P.F.; Gordon, J.I. Molecular analysis of commensal host-microbial relationships in the intestine. Science **2001**, *291*, 881–884.

9. Hooper, L.V.; Stappenbeck, T.S.; Hong, C.V.; Gordon, J.I. Angiogenins: A new class of microbicidal proteins involved in innate immunity. Nat. Immun. **2003**, *4*, 269–273.

Geese

Michael N. Romanov
Michigan State University, East Lansing, Michigan, U.S.A.

G

INTRODUCTION

Geese are one of the most ancient poultry species, domesticated about 3000–2500 B.C. There are currently several different goose production techniques, some of them known from time immemorial: 1) force-feeding for fat liver (Egypt, 2686–2181 B.C.); 2) selection for extremely large body size, exceeding that of modern Toulouse geese (Egypt, 600 B.C.–200 A.D.); and 3) feather plucking, introduced by ancient Egyptians and Romans. Commercial goose breeding today is dispersed as almost cosmopolitan. The majority of world goose flocks are concentrated in Asia, predominantly in China. In Europe, especially eastern Europe, we observe plentiful goose breed diversity (Fig. 1). The main goose products are raw and processed foodstuffs (meat, fat liver, and goose fat) and down and feathers for stuffing.

PRODUCTION

Over the last half-century, selective breeding programs and improved feeds and management have contributed to the tremendous growth in commercial goose production. During the period 1961–2002, the world production of goose meat increased from 149,717 to 2,073,016 metric tons.[1] Yet, goose today takes only fourth place after chicken, turkey, and duck among poultry species, contributing 2.8% of total poultry meat output.[2] Goose meat production in developing countries exceeds that of developed countries, and in such a top market as the United States, goose meat products are merely marginal. In 2002, China had stocks of 215,000,000 live geese and produced the lion's share (92%) of goose meat in the world—1,926,150 metric tons, most of it (>99%) for internal consumption. According to Food and Agriculture Organization of the United Nations (FAO) statistics,[4] other leaders in world goose production are Egypt, Hungary, Romania, Madagascar, and Russia.

A recognized goose delicacy is fattened liver, or foie gras. Today, foie gras is chiefly made in France, Hungary, Poland, Israel, Canada, and the United States. Although in the 1950s foie gras in France was exclusively produced from geese, current production consists of 94% from ducks and only 6% from geese.[3] In 2003, the largest goose liver operation in Asia was in China, with an annual processing volume of 2.5 million geese. World annual consumption of this product can reach 15,000 tons at the price of US$40–50/kg.[4] The World Society for the Protection of Animals leads a campaign against the force-feeding of geese and ducks, and the practice has been banned in Denmark, Germany, Poland, the United Kingdom, Switzerland, and Israel.

Goose down and feathers are commonly used for pillows, mattresses, comforters, furniture upholstery, and outerwear linings. World production is estimated to be in the thousands of tons, most of which originates in China, Hungary, and Poland, although Canadian white goose feathers are among the best.

BIOLOGY

The wild ancestors of domestic geese belong to genus *Anser*. Most European breeds are derived from Graylag Goose (*A. anser*) and most Asiatic breeds derive from Swan Goose (*A. cygnoides*).

Geese have a body weight of 6–8 kg and lay 40–60 eggs per female (90–110 eggs in the Chinese breed). They lay one of the largest eggs (up to 200 g) and have the longest life span (20–25 years) among all poultry species. Profitable biological features are the greatest growth intensity among poultry and utilization of large amounts of green forage.[5] By 60–70 days of age, goslings weigh 4 kg. Compared with other poultry meat, goose meat contains the minimum level of moisture and maximum level of dry matter. The protein content in goose meat is greater than in pork and mutton. The energy content of goose meat is 29–66% greater than that of pork, beef, or mutton; 30–63% greater than that of other poultry meat; and 2.1 times greater than that of chicken meat. One female can produce 40–45 goslings per year, totaling 160–180 kg of meat, up to 70–80 kg of fat, and 20–25 kg of fat liver. The high content of fat in goose meat does not reduce its quality but, on the contrary, brings it delicacy, sappiness, and pleasant taste and odor (due to its low melting point, 26–34°C), as well as marmoreal color. One goose can produce 25–50 g of down and 95–130 g of feathers.

Encyclopedia of Animal Science
DOI: 10.1081/E-EAS 120019645

Fig. 1 A flock of Russian geese. (Courtesy of Annette Gün-therodt, Beberstedt, Germany.) (*View this art in color at www. dekker.com.*)

Based on economic implications, reproduction in geese possessing large body size is of great concern, and maximizing the number of day-old offspring produced is a primary target. Increases in the output of day-old goslings reflect improvements in selection, food quality, management, incubation technology, and health.[6]

BREEDING AND GENETICS

Genetic differences between and within breeds and strains are the basis for artificial selection in geese.[5] In commercial crossing, dam strains are selected for reproductive efficiency and sire strains for meat traits. Geese species are less variable compared to other poultry species. Long-term selection strategies including family selection and progeny testing systems are used. Heterosis (vigor induced by crossbreeding) for most traits was found to head in an undesirable direction; therefore it is necessary to test for heterosis effects in crossbreeding geese strains. However, one can take advantage of other crossbreeding effects such as maternal or sex-linked gene traits. An average annual increase in egg production of almost one egg, average annual improvements of 1% in fertility, and an increase of one-day-old gosling per year were reported as the result of 15-year selection in Hungarian Upgraded and Gray Landaise geese.[6]

An important feature in a number of goose breeds and synthetic lines is the possibility of autosexing in day-old purebred goslings based on phenotypic differences in their down color. Producing the color-sexing crosses of geese is a unique way to utilize sex-linked genes and to concurrently acquire maternal or sex-linked gene traits in the crossbred progeny during intensive production.

The goose genome is much less studied than the chicken genome. Implementation of novel DNA research approaches has begun in domestic and wild geese. Other promising prospects would open with successful quantitative trait loci detection and implementation of marker-assisted selection. Progress in and results from other avian species (especially chicken) would be helpful to compensate for the present deficiency of specific markers and other molecular tools in geese.[5]

NUTRITION AND FEEDING

A valuable feature of geese is their ability to consume green forage and other inexpensive crop ingredients. The intake of 5–7 kg green forage or 1.1–1.3 kg grass meal yields a 1-kg gain in weight. Reduction in protein content in diets without negative impact on productivity permits the utilization of locally available feed resources.[5] The semi-intensive system of fattening geese that includes cut green forage has a positive influence on feed utilization, higher content of meat in the carcass, and reduced fat. In contrast, when crude fiber intake is increased appreciably, a decline in goose performance can be observed due to decreased metabolizable energy and feed conversion.

MANAGEMENT SYSTEMS

Management systems applied to breeding and producing geese are generally of two types: intensive (in premises) and extensive (on pasture; Fig. 1). Preference for either type depends on the existing breeding and production traditions and on the objectives for raising birds.[5] At present geese are raised by using: 1) deep litter, free range, cages, or slats; 2) short daylight, diminishing light intensity, or fluorescent light; and 3) one or two cycles of lay.

Geese are not fastidious with regard to management conditions. For raising young birds, supplementary heating is necessary during the first 3–4 weeks only. Adults do not require on-premise heating and can be on pasture almost the whole year. An environmentally friendly free-range technology for keeping geese involves serial grazing, electric fencing, and avoiding both seeding of plants rejected by geese and fertilizer application.

Because geese have relatively few offspring per dam, caused by low laying intensity and short laying persistency, they can be exploited for more than one laying period. Geese cling to photorefractivity in the summer months, so it is difficult to induce summer egg production. Limitation of daylight to about 10 hours prolongs laying persistency and increases the number of hatching eggs. Artificial insemination is preferable for intensive management systems, and artificial incubation has practically replaced natural incubation as a method of securing goslings for replacement of parent stock and for meat production.

CONCLUSION

Further progress in goose production will depend on new tendencies in world market development and diversification, and will rely on advances in selection and management utilizing goose biological and economic features. Integration of genetic, nutritional, reproductive and management approaches—all of which are necessary for more complete utilization of goose genetic potential and adjustment to specific production systems—will aid sustainable production of a variety of healthy and high-quality goose products.

ARTICLES OF FURTHER INTEREST

REFERENCES

1. FAO. *FAOSTAT Agriculture Database*; Agriculture Production Domain; FAO: Rome, Italy. http://apps.fao.org/page/collections?subset=agriculture (accessed October 2003).
2. Bilgili, S.F. Poultry Products and Processing Worldwide. In *Business Briefing: FoodTech*; Business Briefings Ltd.: London, UK, June 2002. CD-ROM, Reference Section, Reference 2; http://www.bbriefings.com/businessbriefing/pdf/foodtech2002/reference/ref2.pdf (accessed October 2003).
3. GAIA. *Welfare Aspects of the Production of Foie Gras in Ducks and Geese: Report of the Scientific Committee on Animal Health and Animal Welfare*; GAIA: Brussels, Belgium, 16 December 1998. http://www.gaia.be/nl/rapport/foiegras02.html. (accessed October 2003).
4. ChinaFeed.Info. *Asia Largest Goose Liver Production Base Set up at Beihai City of Guangxi Province, China [9/4/2003]*; The Information Centre of China Feed Industry Association & Titan Technology Development Ltd.: Hong Kong, China, 2003. http://www.chinafeed.info/newpage1.asp?recno=894 (accessed October 2003).
5. Romanov, M.N. Goose production efficiency as influenced by genotype, nutrition and production systems. World's Poult. Sci. J. 1999, 55 (3); 281–294.
6. Kozák, J.; Bódi, L.; Janan, J.; Ács, I.; Karsai, M. Improvements in the reproductive characteristics of Hungarian Upgraded and Grey Landes geese in Hungary. World's Poult. Sci. J. **1997**, *53* (2), 197–201.

Gene Action, Types of

David S. Buchanan
Oklahoma State University, Stillwater, Oklahoma, U.S.A.

INTRODUCTION

Genes carry the information necessary for organisms to develop and function. They come in pairs, one from each parent. These pairs of genes have effect both as pairs and individually. Additionally, different pairs of genes may interact with each other. The ways these effects occur are referred to as gene action.

DOMINANT–RECESSIVE

The most familiar gene action is the simple dominant–recessive relationship. Examples in livestock include black–red in Angus and polled–horned in Herefords. Many genetic anomalies, such as dwarfism or hydrocephalus, are recessive, whereas the normal condition is dominant. This type of gene action is outlined here:

RR—black
Rr—black
rr—red

PP—polled
Pp—polled
pp—horned

DD—normal
Dd—normal
dd—dwarf

The distinguishing characteristic is that the heterozygote has the same phenotype as one of the homozygotes.

CODOMINANCE

There are instances in which a pair of genes does not have a clear dominant–recessive relationship. If the heterozygote has some of the features of both of the homozygotes, it is called codominance. The best known example in livestock is coat color in Shorthorns. This type of gene action is outlined here:

RR—red
Rr—roan
rr—white

EPISTASIS

There are also instances when two or more gene pairs interact with one another. One common example is the inclusion of the scurred condition along with polled vs. horned in cattle. Scurs are horn tissue on the skin, but not fastened to the skull. Inheritance of horns is at a different locus (gene location) than are scurs. The gene action is outlined here:

Genotype		Gender	
Poll–horn	*Scur*	*Male*	*Female*
PP, Pp	SS	Scurs	Scurs
PP, Pp	Ss	Scurs	Polled
PP, Pp	ss	Polled	Polled
pp	SS, Ss, ss	Horns	Horns

The scur locus is expressed only in an animal that is polled. There is an interaction between two loci such that one locus is expressed only when the other locus is arranged in a specific manner. This is also an example of sex-influenced inheritance. Scurs are dominant in males but recessive in females.

QUANTITATIVE GENE ACTION

The previously described types of gene action were all controlling characteristics that were qualitative (able to be classified). Many economically important traits in livestock are quantitative (able to be measured), such as weaning weight, egg production, milk production, or litter size. Quantitative traits are normally controlled by many pairs of genes, each with relatively small effect. They are also affected by the environment. This can be described with a simple model:

$$P = G + E$$
Phenotype = Genotype + Environment

The genotype part of this model is the result of the sum of all the gene pairs that affect the trait. The gene action for the various gene pairs follows patterns that are quite similar to those involved in qualitative traits.

Encyclopedia of Animal Science
DOI: 10.1081/E-EAS 120019646

The following examples illustrate types of gene action for single gene pairs. In each case, an uppercase allele contributes 2 units to the trait in question. This is referred to as the additive effect. When an uppercase allele is present, there is a +2 and when two uppercase alleles are present there is a +4. The other examples illustrate different degrees of dominance. In the purely additive example, there is no other effect than that of the individual alleles. However, in this example of complete dominance, there is an additional +2 for the heterozygote to make the heterozygote equal to the best homozygote. In partial dominance, there is an additional +1 in the heterozygote, and the heterozygote is intermediate between the homozygotes, but not exactly at the halfway point. Overdominance is the most extreme type of dominance. In this example, there is an additional +4 in the heterozygote. The heterozygote is actually outside of the range of the two homozygotes. Quantitative genetic theory is predicated on the idea that each gene pair that influences a quantitative trait behaves in a manner that is similar to one of these pictures. Alleles have an additive effect and for many gene pairs there is also a dominance effect. In addition, gene pairs influencing quantitative traits may also interact in a manner that gives rise to epistatic effects.

AA—+4	BB—+4	CC—+4	DD—+4
Aa—+2	Bb—+4	Cc—+3	Dd +6
aa—+0	bb—+0	cc—+0	dd—+0
Additive	Complete Dominance	Partial Dominance	Overdominance

With the inclusion of the concepts of additive, dominance, and epistatic effects, our model can be extended:

$$P = G + E$$
$$P = A + D + I + E$$

Phenotype = Additive effects + Dominance effects + Epistatic effects + Environment

The symbol I is used for epistatic effects to indicate interaction (and because E already signifies ''environment'').

HERITABILITY

Additive effects are tied to individual alleles, which are passed from parent to offspring. Dominance and epistatic effects arise from combinations of alleles and are not passed from parent to offspring because each gamete contains only one member of each gene pair. The additive effects are therefore of special interest as we consider how genetic improvement is made from generation to generation. The model can be altered to represent the amount of variability in the phenotypes of a group of animals with the statistical concept of variance:

$$Var (P) = Var (A) + Var (D) + Var (I) + Var (E)$$

This suggests that the observed variance in the phenotypes of a group of animals is created by underlying variance in the genes they possess (additive effects), the ways those genes are arranged (dominance and epistatic effects), and the environments in which they exist. It is probably important to point out that we are talking about a group of animals that exist together in the same place and time. Environment, in this context, does not mean Montana vs. Oklahoma or some other extreme environmental difference. It is the environmental variation that exists within a group of animals because of seemingly small differences in environment experienced by individual animals. There may be differences, for example, among a group of calves in the same pasture that arise from differences in date of birth, where they tended to stay in the pasture, the pathogen load to which they were exposed, or the quality of the grass. These small differences in environmental quality all contribute to the overall Var (E).

Only the additive effects are important in determining how genetic improvement is passed from parent to offspring. The proportion of the phenotypic variance that is due to additive effects (Var (A)/Var (P)) should, therefore, be an indicator of the expected rate of genetic improvement arising from selection of superior parents. This ratio is called the heritability (symbolized h^2).

Estimates of heritability[1–5] suggest that traits associated with reproduction (e.g., calving interval, litter size, etc.) tend to be minimally heritable ($h^2 < 0.2$). Traits associated with growth (e.g., weaning weight, average daily gain, etc.) tend to be moderately heritable ($0.2 < h^2 < 0.4$), and traits associated with carcass merit (e.g., backfat thickness, rib eye area, etc.) tend to be highly heritable ($0.4 < h^2 < 0.6$). Highly heritable traits are those that are influenced chiefly by additive effects, whereas minimally heritable traits are those influenced mainly by nonadditive effects. Minimally heritable traits are also influenced more heavily by environmental effects, although variation in all quantitative traits has a substantial environmental component, as suggested by the fact that very few quantitative traits have heritability in excess of 0.5.

GENOTYPE × ENVIRONMENT INTERACTION

The phenotypic model described earlier includes independent genetic and environmental effects. It has also been shown that genotype and environment may interact.[6] Relative to each other, genotypes may respond differently in different environments. The classic example in large farm animals involves the fact that Brahman cattle are adapted to warm, humid climates, whereas breeds such as Hereford or Angus are adapted to more temperate climates. Those adaptations would lead the British breeds to perform better than the Brahman in the Midwest, and the Brahman would be expected to perform better in the Gulf Coast area. Genotype interactions may be important, not only in breed utilization for different climates, but also in (inter)national genetic evaluation programs. There may be reason to develop different ranking of sires to be used in different regions or countries.

HETEROSIS

Heterosis is the advantage of crossbred individuals over the average of purebreds from the breeds used in the cross. Heterosis arises because dominance effects frequently create a situation in which the heterozygote is superior to the average of the two homozygotes. The examples of gene action illustrate this. If a trait is controlled by many pairs of genes in which there is dominance, then we would expect an advantage for crossbred animals, relative to the average of the purebreds that formed the cross. Because, as seen previously, minimally heritable traits are generally influenced by dominance effects, such traits may be expected to show evidence of large amounts of heterosis. Such a pattern has been observed.[1,4,7] Minimally heritable traits, such as those involved with reproduction or livability, tend to also show a large advantage for crossbreds over purebreds. Similarly, there is little heterosis for traits associated with carcass merit where heritability tends to be high. Besides the contributions of dominance and heterozygosity, epistasis also affects the amount of observed heterosis. Different types of epistasis

may cause the actual heterosis to be larger or smaller than expected due simply to heterozygocity.

CONCLUSION

Variation in animals is controlled, in part, by genetics. Effects of genes and gene combinations influence how genetic tools are used to improve efficiency of production. Additive effects—those that provide value to individual genes—contribute to the effectiveness of selection. However, dominance effects—those that result from certain gene combinations that influence performance over and above the additive effects of the genes—contribute to the concepts of inbreeding depression and heterosis and, thus, to the use of inbreeding and crossbreeding.

REFERENCES

1. Bourdon, R.M. *Understanding Animal Breeding*, 2nd Ed.; Prentice Hall: Upper Saddle River, NJ, 2000; pp. 161–172, 371–384.
2. Fogarty, N.M. Genetic parameters for live weight, fat and muscle measurements, wool production and reproduction in sheep: A review. Anim. Breed. Abstr. **1995**, *63* (3), 101–143.
3. Koots, K.R.; Gibson, J.P.; Smith, C.; Wilton, J.W. Analyses of published genetic parameter estimates for beef production traits. 1. Heritability. Anim. Breed. Abstr. **1994**, *62* (5), 309–338.
4. Legates, J.E.; Warwick, E.J. *Breeding and Improvement of Farm Animals*, 8th Ed.; McGraw-Hill: New York, 1990; pp. 136–149, 242–259.
5. Tolley, E.A.; Notter, D.R.; Marlowe, T.J. A review of the inheritance of racing performance in horses. Anim. Breed. Abstr. **1985**, *53* (3), 163–185.
6. Dickerson, G.E. Implications of genetic–environmental interaction in animal breeding. Anim. Prod. **1962**, *4*, 47.
7. Johnson, R.K. *Heterosis and Breed Effects in Swine*, NC Reg. Pub 262: 1980.

Gene Mapping

Gary Alan Rohrer
United States Department of Agriculture, Agricultural Research Service, Clay Center, Nebraska, U.S.A.

INTRODUCTION

Gene mapping is the science of determining the location of a gene in a species' genome. The genome of most mammalian species is composed of approximately 3 billion bases of deoxyribonucleic acid (DNA) contained in 18–35 separate linear molecules (chromosomes). Mammals are diploid organisms, so each cell possesses two copies of the genome in the nucleus, one copy that was contributed by the father and the other copy by the mother.

BACKGROUND INFORMATION

A common analogy is that a gene map is the "road map of life." Road maps are a depiction of long segments of concrete known as roads and locations on the roads that represent cities. While the units of measure for a road map are often in miles or kilometers, different units of measurement are used for gene maps based on the type of map that is presented. Two types of gene maps commonly used in genetics are genetic maps (or linkage maps) and physical maps. Both maps depict the linear order of genes located on a chromosome. The concepts of gene mapping presented are located in most college genetics text books.[1]

DEFINITION OF A GENETIC MAP

A genetic map is the linear alignment of genes or segments of DNA as they reside on a chromosome. Position in a genetic map is based on units of recombination. Gamete formation requires diploid cells to produce haploid gamete cells through the process of meiosis. In the early stage of meiosis, the paternally derived chromosome will align next to its maternally derived counterpart. Once the chromosomes are tightly paired, the maternal and paternal chromosomes will break somewhat randomly at the same position and be fused to the other chromosome in a phenomenon known as recombination (Fig. 1). Recombination produces more unique combinations of gametes and increased genetic variation.

For investigators to be able to differentiate between maternally and paternally derived chromosomes, small variations in the DNA sequence need to be present. Assays that can visualize these differences are developed forming a polymorphic marker (marker with different forms). Investigators determine how alleles (forms of a gene) at different markers segregate in gamete formation. If the alleles at two different markers segregate independently, they are considered unlinked and are located on different chromosomes or far apart on the same chromosome. However, if the alleles tend to cosegregate, then the two markers are located in close proximity to each other. Their distance is measured in units of recombination known as centimorgans (cM). One centimorgan is equivalent to 1% recombination. Rather than gametes being analyzed, progeny are often evaluated and the results of two separate meioses, one maternal and one paternal, can be studied simultaneously.

EXAMPLE OF A GENETIC MAP

Fig. 1 depicts a meiotic event where the animal is typed for two different markers (A and B loci). The paternally derived chromosome contained alleles A1 and B1 and the maternally derived chromosome contained alleles A2 and B2. Based on the genotypes of the gametes (offspring), it is determined that the A and B loci are 20 cM apart.

Numerous types of genetic markers exist. The first used were phenotypes such as coat color or pattern, eye color, etc. The first biochemical markers relied upon protein polymorphisms or erythrocyte antigen markers. Then DNA-based markers were developed, such as restriction fragment length polymorphisms (RFLP), microsatellite markers, and single nucleotide polymorphisms (SNP).

DEFINITION OF A PHYSICAL MAP

A physical map is the linear alignment of genes or segments of DNA as they reside on a chromosome in positions based on units of DNA nucleotides or chromosomal

Encyclopedia of Animal Science
DOI: 10.1081/E-EAS 120019649

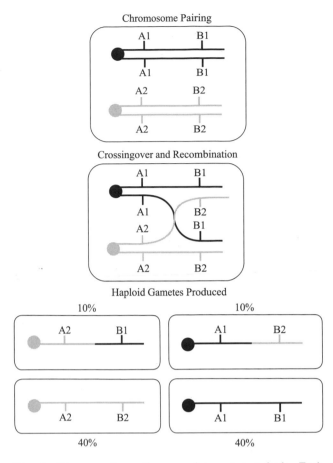

Chromosome Pairing

Crossingover and Recombination

Haploid Gametes Produced

10%   10%

40%   40%

Fig. 1 Diagram of a cell prepared to enter meiosis. Each chromosome has been replicated but the sister chromatids are still attached at the centromere. The black chromosome was contributed by the father and contains the A1 and B1 alleles at marker loci A and B, respectively. Likewise, the mother contributed the gray chromosome with marker alleles A2 and B2. The maternal and paternal chromosomes pair at the beginning of meiosis. Next, one paternal chromatid crosses over one maternal chromatid, the two chromosomes break at the point of the crossover, and the segments are then fused to the other chromatid. After two cycles of cell division, four haploid gametes are produced. Two of the gametes are identical to a gamete contributed by one of the parents (parental gametes) and two gametes have one allele from the maternal chromosome and one allele from the paternal chromosome (recombinant gametes). After observation of many gametes, the percentage of recombinant gametes is determined to be 20% (10% contain A2 and B1 alleles and 10% contain A1 and B2 alleles), indicating that these two markers are located 20 centimorgans apart.

bands. The resolution of a physical map depends on the technique used and the status of available information for the species of interest.

The first techniques developed could only assign genes to chromosomes; in situ hybridization technology permit-

ted assignments to specific chromosome bands, and now for the human and mouse genomes, assignments can be based on the actual number of base pairs.

TYPES OF PHYSICAL MAPPING TECHNIQUES

The first technology used in physical mapping took advantage of cell lines derived from animals with identified chromosomal abnormalities (monosomics, trisomics, or chromosomal translocations). The next technology utilized the results of fusing cells from the species of interest with rodent cell lines. A small portion of the fused cells proved to be viable and retained segments of the species of interest's genome (often whole chromosomes). Individual somatic cell hybrid lines were then characterized to determine which foreign chromosomes were present in each line. A panel of somatic cell hybrid lines was then developed, and chromosomal assignments were determined based on a gene's presence or absence in each of the lines of the panel.

The resolution of a somatic cell hybrid panel is greatly enhanced by irradiating the cells from the species of interest prior to fusion. Radiation-induced fragmentation of the genome is similar to what occurs during recombination, except that the amount of fragmentation is directly proportional to the dosage of radiation and the breakages are more random. With high doses of radiation, markers within 30,000 bases can be accurately ordered.

Another commonly used technology in physical mapping relies on visualizing a labeled segment of DNA that was hybridized to metaphase chromosomes fixed to glass microscope slides (in situ hybridization). The use of highly sensitive fluorescent-labeled DNA probes allows scientists to assign the segment of DNA to specific bands on chromosomes. These techniques are refined with multicolor fluorescent probes and by using less condensed chromosomes.

Ultimately, the highest resolution physical map uses base pairs as its unit of measurement. This type of map can be obtained by two different technologies. The first utilizes a map built of contiguous overlapping clones containing inserts of hundreds of thousands of bases. These maps most often are based on bacterial artificial chromosome (BAC) clones that have been ''fingerprinted'' by digesting each clone with a restriction endonuclease, sizing each fragment produced, and then analyzing fragment sizes to develop a contiguous BAC map. With the knowledge of which BAC clones contain which genes, the distance in bases between two genes can be determined. However, once a genome has been completely

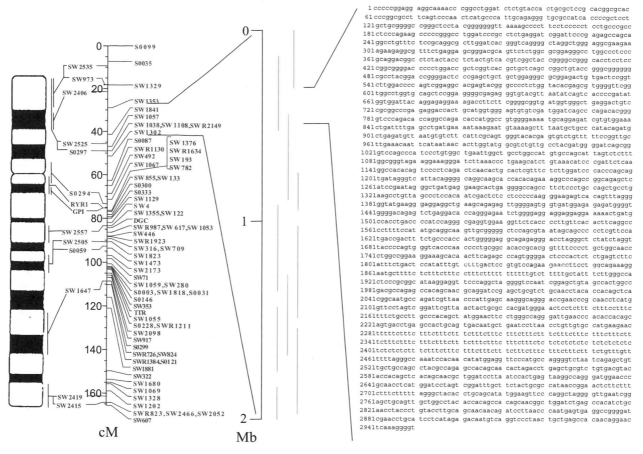

Fig. 2 This diagram represents a comprehensive map of pig chromosome 6. At the far left is a diagram of the banded metaphase chromosome. The lines attaching markers to the chromosome diagram indicate these markers were physically assigned to that region of chromosome 6 by in situ hybridization. The scaled vertical bar labeled cM is the genetic map for chromosome 6 in centimorgans (cM). The next scaled bar (labeled Mb) represents a physical map based on overlapping BAC clones of the genetic map spanning 42 to 52 cM. Markers were positioned based on presence or absence in each of the BAC clones. This physical map is based on millions of bases or megabases (Mb). Finally, a 3,060-base region containing the microsatellite marker SW1057 has the complete sequence displayed. (*View this art in color at www.dekker.com.*)

sequenced, this information can be determined by simple sequence comparisons to the genomic sequence.

COMPREHENSIVE GENOMIC MAPS

Physical and genetic maps can be combined to form comprehensive maps if enough genes or markers have been placed on both maps. Comprehensive maps would not be necessary if there was a perfect correlation between the two different units of measure for the maps. While the linear order of markers should be the same on both maps, distances between genes may not be similar. Recombination does not occur at the same frequency throughout a chromosome. In general, recombination is suppressed near centromeres and is more frequent at telomeric ends of chromosomes. For most mammalian species, 1 centimorgan is approximately equal to 1 million base pairs. Fig. 2 presents a representation of pig chromosome 6 displaying the genetic map with some markers assigned to chromosomal bands by in situ hybridization; a segment of this chromosome has a BAC contig map developed, and a smaller segment of the chromosome is completely sequenced.

CONCLUSIONS

Due to the rapid evolution of gene mapping technologies, many of the earlier technologies that had provided valuable information to researchers in the past are now obsolete. Once a species' genome has been sequenced, the quickest and easiest method to ''map'' a gene or segment of DNA is to know the sequence of bases of the DNA segment and then use sequence comparison software to determine the gene's location in the genome. Genetic maps are still necessary to map the chromosomal location of genes that affect quantitative traits; the technique is known as quantitative trait loci mapping (QTL mapping).

There are many useful resources available on the internet for further information. A site developed by Cornell University (http://www.ansci.cornell.edu/usdagen/usdamain.html) explains these genetic concepts and also presents some interesting examples. The most current genetic maps for cattle and pigs can be viewed at (http://www.marc.usda.gov), and the most current physical map for the pig can be found at (http://www.toulouse.inra.fr/lgc/pig/cyto/cyto.htm). Unfortunately, livestock gene mapping has not yet reached the stage of human gene mapping. For viewing the human genome sequence data, the following two sites are suggested (http://genome.ucsc.edu/ and http://www.ncbi.nlm.nih.gov/mapview/map_search.cgi).

REFERENCE

1. Gardner, E.J.; Snustad, D.P. Linkage, Crossingover, and Chromosome Mapping. In *Principles of Genetics*, 7th Ed.; John Wiley & Sons, Inc.: New York, 1984; 147–192.

Genetics: Mendelian

David S. Buchanan
Oklahoma State University, Stillwater, Oklahoma, U.S.A.

G

INTRODUCTION

Gregor Mendel was a member of a monastery in the mid-19th century in what is now the Czech Republic. In addition to his work at the monastery, he conducted a series of experiments with the ordinary garden pea that would, years after his death, spark a scientific revolution that is still reverberating through fields as diverse as medicine and food production. Mendel conducted his research using seven characteristics of the plants, the pods, and the seeds. He was, in several ways, fortunate in his choice of experimental material and characteristics. He was able to achieve clear results that would probably not have happened had he chosen differently. Following several years of meticulous work, he delivered two lectures in 1865 to the Natural History Society of Brünn and, in 1866, wrote a lengthy paper presenting his results. His conclusions lay dormant, despite his communication with some of the leading scientists of the time, until three scientists, Hugo deVries, Carl Correns, and Erich von Tschermak, working independently in 1900, discovered the concepts and performed the necessary research to confirm the results. By the close of the 20th century, the entire human genome had been mapped, making the 20th century, quite literally, the century of genetics.

THE ORGANIZATION OF THE EXPERIMENTS

In his lengthy paper of 1866,[1] Mendel described the design and the results of his experiments. He chose the ordinary garden pea as his primary experimental material. Peas had the virtues of having several simple, easily separated traits, were naturally self-fertilizing although they could be crossed, and true-breeding varieties could be established. They were also very prolific so that large experimental populations could be developed quickly. The basic design of the experiments is described in many basic textbooks of genetics.[2–5]

Some definitions are appropriate:

Phenotype—observable properties of an organism
Genotype—genetic makeup of an organism
Gene—determinant of a characteristic of an organism
Allele—alternative form of a gene

Homozygous—individual that received the same allele from each parents for a particular gene
Heterozygous—individual that received different alleles from its two parents for a particular gene
Dominant—allele that is expressed either in the homozygous or the heterozygous state
Recessive—allele that is expressed only in the homozygous state
True-breeding—parents and offspring consistently display the same phenotype generation after generation
Parental generation—experimental generation that starts with true-breeding parents
F_1 generation—offspring experimental generation resulting from mating of parental strains
F_2 generation—offspring experimental generation resulting from mating of members of the F_1 generation
Hybrid—cross between true-breeding parents
Monohybrid—cross between true-breeding parents that differ for one characteristic
Gamete—reproductive cell that contains one member of each gene pair in the parent

Mendel chose seven characteristics, each with a clear dominant—recessive relationship. These were (dominant allele listed first):

Seed shape—smooth vs. wrinkled
Seed color—yellow vs. green
Flower color—purple vs. white
Pod shape—inflated vs. constricted
Pod color—green vs. yellow
Flower position—axial vs. terminal
Plant height—tall vs. short

Mendel's basic experiments started with true-breeding parents. These were mated in hybrid crosses and Mendel carefully counted the offspring. Several of the experiments resulted in thousands of observations.

THE PRINCIPLE OF SEGREGATION

The first experiments were monohybrid crosses. True-breeding parents that differed in only one of the seven characteristics were mated. Plants from a true-breeding

Encyclopedia of Animal Science
DOI: 10.1081/E-EAS 120019650

Table 1 Expected results of an experiment to illustrate the principle of segregation

		Parent 1	Parent 2	Offspring
Parental generation	Phenotype	Smooth seed	Wrinkled seed	
	Genotype	SS	ss	
	Gametes produced	All S	All s	
F_1 generation	Offspring			All Ss (all smooth seed)
	Phenotype	Smooth seed	Smooth seed	
	Genotype	Ss	Ss	
	Gametes produced	$\frac{1}{2}$ S: $\frac{1}{2}$ s	$>\frac{1}{2}$ S: $\frac{1}{2}$ s	
F_2 generation	Offspring	Obtained by multiplying the frequencies and combining the alleles in the gametes		$\frac{1}{4}$ SS: $\frac{1}{2}$ Ss: $\frac{1}{4}$ ss (3/4 smooth seed: $\frac{1}{4}$ wrinkled seed)

smooth-seeded line were mated with plants from a true-breeding wrinkled-seeded line. The offspring (F_1) were all smooth-seeded. However, when the F_1 plants were self-fertilized, they produced 5474 smooth seeds and 1850 wrinkled seeds. Mendel recognized that this was close to a 3:1 ratio. He repeated this experiment with each of the other six characteristics and, in each case, the results were close to a 3:1 ratio. He concluded, from these results, that there was a genetic determinant that existed in pairs, one from each parent. We now refer to this genetic determinant as a gene. The true-breeding parents had two copies of the same gene and the F_1 offspring had one allele from each parent. The dominant (smooth) allele masked

the recessive (wrinkled) allele in the F_1. The F_2 individuals could be divided into those that showed the recessive allele (received the recessive allele from both parents) and those that showed the dominant allele (either received the dominant allele from both parents, or the dominant allele from one parent and the recessive allele from the other parent). Offspring receive genes from parents via the gametes.

From this Mendel deduced the principle of segregation. This principle states that the two members of a gene pair segregate (separate) from each other during the formation of gametes. As a result, half of the gametes carry one member of each gene pair and the other half carry the

Table 2 Expected results of an experiment to illustrate the principle of independent assortment

		Parent 1	Parent 2	Offspring
Parental generation	Phenotype	Smooth yellow seed	Wrinkled green seed	
	Genotype	SSYY	ssyy	
	Gametes produced	All SY	All sy	
F_1 generation	Offspring			All SsYy (all smooth yellow seed)
	Phenotype	Smooth yellow seed	Smooth yellow seed	
	Genotype	SsYy	SsYy	
	Gametes produced	$\frac{1}{4}$ SY: $\frac{1}{4}$ Sy: $\frac{1}{4}$ sY: $\frac{1}{4}$ sy	$\frac{1}{4}$ SY: $\frac{1}{4}$ Sy: $\frac{1}{4}$ sY: $\frac{1}{4}$ sy	
F_2 generation	Offspring	Obtained by multiplying the frequencies and combining the alleles in the gametes		1/16 SSYY:1/8 SSYy:1/16 Ssyy: 1/8 SsYY:1/4 SsYy:1/8 Ssyy: 1/16 ssYY:1/8 ssYy:1/16 ssyy (9/16 smooth yellow:3/16 smooth green:3/16 wrinkled yellow:1/16 wrinkled green)

other member of each gene pair. This is illustrated in Table 1.

THE PRINCIPLE OF INDEPENDENT ASSORTMENT

After Mendel reached his conclusions concerning mono-hybrid crosses, he continued his research by looking at two traits at a time. Crosses involving true-breeding parents that differ in two traits are called dihybrid crosses. He mated peas that produced smooth yellow seeds with those that produced wrinkled green seeds. As expected, the F_1 generation contained only plants that produced smooth yellow (both dominant) seeds. When the F_1 plants were self-fertilized, they produced 315 smooth yellow seeds, 108 smooth green seeds, 101 wrinkled yellow seeds, and 32 wrinkled green seeds. He recognized that these results were close to a 9:3:3:1 ratio. This was simply a multiple of the 3:1 ratio produced in the F_2 generation of the monohybrid crosses. The pattern is illustrated in Table 2.

From these results, along with further experiments with other combinations of traits, Mendel was able to deduce the principle of independent assortment. This principle states that the segregation of genes for one gene pair is independent of (does not influence) the segregation of genes for any other gene pair.

One of the places in which Mendel was fortunate was that the genes for the seven traits he chose were not in proximity to one another on the chromosomes. Of course, since Mendel was unaware of the concept of the chromosome, he would not have had any way to understand this. The principle of independent assortment does not apply to genes that are near one another on the chromosomes. The degree to which two genes do not obey this principle is affected by their proximity to each other. Failure to abide by the principle is used as the basis for forming genetic maps.

APPLICATIONS OF MENDELIAN GENETICS IN LIVESTOCK

These principles may be used to predict the results of matings for traits affected by single gene pairs. For example, polled is dominant to horned in cattle. Matings of heterozygous polled individuals are expected to produce 3/4 polled and 1/4 horned offspring. If combined with black (dominant) vs. red (recessive) matings of heterozygous polled, black cattle are expected to produce 9/16 polled black, 3/16 polled red, 3/16 horned black, and 1/16 horned red.

Additionally, these principles may be used to develop test crosses to evaluate individuals suspected of being carriers (heterozygous) for lethal or deleterious conditions. For example, a bull that is suspected of being a carrier for dwarfism (recessive) could be mated to a group of 10 cows that are known to be carriers. The probability of 10 normal calves, if the bull is a carrier, would be $(3/4)^{10}=0.056$. This is low enough that the bull's owner could state, with a reasonably high degree of confidence, that the bull is not a carrier. Of course, a single dwarf calf would be all it takes to demonstrate that he is a carrier.

It must be remembered that these basic principles also apply to the genetic background for performance traits such as growth rate, egg production, racing speed, or backfat thickness. Such traits may be influenced by hundreds of gene pairs but these genes are also discrete and come in pairs, one from each parent. Even though the effect of any one gene pair may not be clearly observed, the gene pairs do exist and behave according to Mendel's principles.

CONCLUSION

Mendel was brilliant and was at least 30 years ahead of his time. His principles of segregation and independent assortment laid the groundwork for a revolution in science that spanned the 20th century. Whether the topic is genetic evaluation of sires, genome mapping, crossbreeding systems, or any other genetic concept, the appropriate theory still starts with Mendel's basic principles.

REFERENCES

1. Mendel, G. *Experiments in Plant Hybridization*; Proceedings of the Natural History Society, 1866; 3–47.
2. Hartl, D.L.; Jones, E.W. *Genetics: Analysis of Genes and Genomes*, 5th Ed.; Jones and Bartlett: Sudbury, MA, 2001; 134–148.
3. Klug, W.S.; Cummings, M.R. *Concepts of Genetics*, 7th Ed.; Prentice Hall—Pearson Education, Inc.: Upper Saddle River, NJ, 2003; 19–44.
4. Russell, P.J. *iGenetics*; Benjamin Cummings: San Francisco, 2002; 9–24.
5. Snustad, D.P.; Simmons, M.J. *Principles of Genetics*, 2nd Ed.; John Wiley & Sons, Inc.: New York, 2000; 23–40.

Genetics: Molecular

Dan Nonneman
Timothy P. L. Smith
United States Department of Agriculture, Agricultural Research Service, Clay Center, Nebraska, U.S.A.

INTRODUCTION

Molecular genetics is the study of molecules important for biological inheritance. Advances in molecular genetics allow more accurate identification and selection of superior animals, diagnosis and treatment of inherited disorders, and a clearer understanding of biological processes that dictate inherited traits. Traditionally, animal breeders have made genetic progress by using phenotypic information on available animals for selection of breeding stock. Breeding goals may involve a combination of traits, and mass selection for these traits can be difficult. Experimental and statistical methods have been developed that separate environmental from genetic effects to better define quantitative traits and to identify chromosomal positions of loci affecting those traits (called quantitative trait loci, or QTL). The ultimate goal is to identify DNA sequence variations having effects on important phenotypes, understand the biology of phenotypic differences, and develop schemes that use this information to direct breeding decisions using marker-assisted selection. The mid-1990s saw the first genetic linkage maps for chicken, cattle, and swine and the concept of incorporating marker-assisted selection for production traits and disease resistance in livestock species. Development of detailed comparative maps has facilitated application of information from the human genome to accelerate the discovery of genes (or chromosomal regions) involved in phenotypic differences. Since that time, several instances of causal genetic variations or mutations in livestock that alter phenotype have been identified at the molecular level.

BIOLOGY OF MOLECULAR GENETICS

Biological effects are primarily initiated from genomic DNA and mediated through expression of gene products, either RNA or protein. Genes are composed of exons (protein-coding regions), introns (noncoding regions spliced out of the mRNA), and regulatory regions. Gene discovery has progressed with the sequencing of large numbers of expressed sequences (ESTs) representing mRNAs of genes. Trait differences are inherited due to

variation or mutation of the parent DNA molecule, and these effects are transmitted to the RNA transcripts that code for mature proteins. Nucleotide variations that can affect expression include single nucleotide polymorphisms (SNPs; previously identified as restriction fragment length polymorphisms, or RFLPs), small insertions or deletions (indels), or variation that encompasses larger portions of genomic DNA. Variation in an RNA transcript can affect the protein code directly as a change in the coding template or a change in efficiency of initiation, transcription, stability of the message, or correct splicing of exonic sequences that code for the translated protein. Changes in the protein's amino acid sequence can affect protein function, folding, or posttranslational modifications. Sequence variation in regulatory regions of genes containing promoters, enhancers, or repressors (very short transcription factor-binding sites) can alter timing, location, or levels of expression. Inheritance of variation can be manifested as measurable traits, biochemical deficiencies, or developmental abnormalities. Mode of inheritance is usually crucial to understanding the molecular genetics of a particular phenotype, i.e., whether the trait is inherited as a recessive, dominant, additive, or sex-linked trait. Deficiencies are usually easiest to study because we can rely on knowledge of biochemistry to determine defects in metabolic pathways. Developmental defects are more difficult to study because phenotype may be determined during very short and specific stages during development. Quantitative traits are assumed to be under the control of many genes and require specific approaches to detect genomic regions that contribute to an overall phenotype. Linkage analysis is one common approach used to guide the molecular genetic study of inherited traits by identifying positional candidate genes.

IDENTIFICATION OF MYOSTATIN AS THE *MH* LOCUS IN CATTLE

One example where molecular genetics identified causal mutations of an extreme phenotype is the elucidation of double-muscling in cattle.[1] For nearly 200 years, the muscular hypertrophy (mh) syndrome called double-

Encyclopedia of Animal Science
DOI: 10.1081/E-EAS 10.1081/E-EAS-120019651

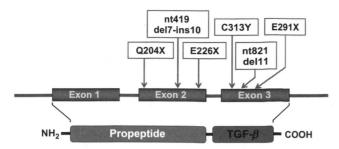

Fig. 1 Diagram of myostatin mutations that cause double-muscling in cattle. Abbreviations for the amino acid change and the position in the coding region are shown by arrows. Six of the known mutations are 1) Q204X, which changes a glutamine to a termination signal; 2) E226X and 3) E291X, which change a glutamic acid to a stop codon; 4) nucleotide 419 in exon 2, deletion of 7, and insertion of 10 nucleotides (nt419del7ins10); 5) nt821deletion11 in exon 3 of Belgian Blue cattle, which alters the coding sequence and results in premature stop codons; and 6) C313Y, which changes a cysteine to a tyrosine residue in Piedmontese cattle, changing the coding sequence and again resulting in a premature stop codon. A model showing location of domain structures is shown in Fig. 2. (Adapted from Ref. 1.). (*View this art in color at www.dekker.com.*)

musculature has captured the attention of geneticists and livestock breeders. Affected cattle exhibit bulging musculature of the shoulders and hindquarters and are extremely efficient in production of lean, tender meat. A major drawback to this phenotype is higher birth weights and a consequent increase of dystocia, frequently requiring veterinary assistance during calving. A single autosomal recessive pattern of inheritance is characteristic of the phenotype, and "carrier" animals are intermediate in growth and body composition. The genetic map was used to show that the locus lies at the centromeric end of bovine chromosome 2.[2] In 1997, a group at John Hopkins University investigating members of the TGF-β family of growth factors discovered that targeted gene-knockout of myostatin (GDF-8) in mice led to a dramatic muscle-specific growth similar to that of double-muscled cattle.[3] Researchers then independently determined that myostatin mapped to the mh locus[4] and identified nucleotide changes in Belgian Blue and Asturiana de los Valles cattle that effectively "knockout" or cause loss of function mutations of the myostatin gene.[5] A surprisingly large number of different allelic forms of myostatin exist in several breeds of cattle, and body composition varies by individual, breed, and sex.[1,5] Six disruptive mutations have been discovered in this relatively small gene and several other polymorphisms exist that do not change the amino acid code or have an apparent affect on the function of the gene or phenotype (Fig. 1). Although the defect in myostatin was first presumed to have a common

origin and mutation, it is now thought that this is not the case, since several haplotypes have been identified.[5] Now that specific allelic variants have been characterized, efforts to select and produce animals with highly desirable phenotypes, i.e., greater yields of leaner meat and reduced dystocia, can be implemented by breeders. The discovery of mutations in myostatin that cause double-muscling was the first successful identification of a gene causing an extreme and economically exploitable phenotype in cattle.

CLONING THE RN⁻ LOCUS IN PIGS

The first successful demonstration of positional cloning in a farm animal was the discovery of the Rendement Napole (RN⁻) allele in Hampshire pigs. "Positional cloning" refers to identification of a mutation with no knowledge other than its approximate position in the genome. The RN (a measure of cooked weight to fresh weight) locus contains a dominant mutation with large effects on meat quality and processing yield. Affected animals have low ultimate muscle pH 24 hours after slaughter, reduced water-holding capacity, and reduced yield of cured, cooked product.[6] These effects are caused by a large

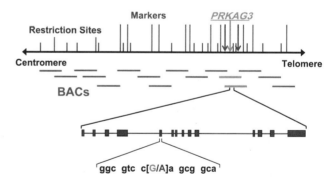

Fig. 2 Diagram of the strategy used to positionally clone the mutation for Rendement Napole (RN⁻). Using DNA markers (red vertical lines), a contiguous alignment of large-insert genomic clones called Bacterial Artificial Chromosomes (BACs; purple horizontal bars) were identified that cover the genomic region where the mutation most likely resided. These BACs were positioned by markers they contained and by a restriction enzyme map of the individual BACs (restriction sites shown as blue vertical lines). The gene responsible, PKRAG3 (green arrow), was identified in two overlapping BACs by position between the two flanking markers (red arrows) closest to the RN⁻ mutation. The exonic organization of the gene and the position and sequence of the mutation is shown below the genome. The "G" (green) is the normal allele and the "A" (red) is the mutated allele that causes the sequence to code for a glutamine instead of arginine. (Adapted from Ref. [7].) (*View this art in color at www.dekker.com.*)

($\sim$70%) increase in muscle glycogen without other pathological effects. The RN$^-$ allele has been found only in Hampshire pigs and probably increased in frequency due to favorable effects on growth rate and meat content of the carcass. The RN$^-$ mutation was mapped to porcine chromosome 15, and the pig/human comparative map indicated the corresponding human gene that lies on chromosome 2.[6] The discovery of the specific underlying mutation used the arduous approach of constructing a complete physical map of the genomic region by screening a large-insert swine genomic library for clones carrying genes that map to the target region of human chromosome 2 (Fig. 2). New probes were designed from these clones to rescreen the library and develop a series of overlapping clones that span the region containing the RN$^-$ mutation. This "contig" of clones spanned over 2 million base pairs and was used to generate genetic markers to narrow the position of the mutation and identify clones that most likely contained the gene. These clones were sequenced to reveal the gene content, which resulted in matches to three known RNA transcripts. Only one of these transcripts, AMP-activated protein kinase (AMPK) γ-subunit (PRKAG), appeared to be a reasonable candidate for RN$^-$ effects.[7] AMPK is composed of three subunits: a catalytic α-subunit and 2 regulatory subunits, β and γ. AMPK is activated by an increase in AMP, stimulates ATP-producing pathways, and inactivates glycogen synthase, the key regulatory enzyme of glycogen synthesis. Complete sequencing of the cDNA of this gene determined it was a novel AMPK γ-subunit designated PRKAG3.[7] Screening of several rn$^+$ and RN$^-$ pigs of different breeds revealed that a mutation in a functional domain of the protein (Fig. 2) was exclusively associated with RN$^-$, but not normal rn$^+$ animals from Hampshire or other breeds, consistent with the idea that RN$^-$ originated with the Hampshire breed. Since the discovery of the RN$^-$ mutation in the PRKAG3 gene, other polymorphisms have been identified in PRKAG3 in commercial lines, some of which are associated with glycogen content and meat quality. This is another example where additional alleles of genes involved in major mutations have a significant affect on quantitative trait variation in livestock.

CONCLUSIONS

The application of molecular genetics to the selection of superior animals used for production shows promise for traits affecting meat quality and production, repro-

ductive efficiency, and disease resistance. As we develop faster and more accurate ways to measure phenotype and genotype and the ability to integrate these with further knowledge of livestock genomes, the dissection of molecular variation causing desirable traits will be unraveled.

ARTICLES OF FURTHER INTEREST

Gene Mapping, p. 459
Genetics: Mendelian, p. 463
Genomics, p. 469
Molecular Biology: Animal, p. 653
Myostatin: Physiology and Applications, p. 661
Proteins, p. 757
Quantitative Trait Loci (QTL), p. 760
Selection: Marker Assisted, p. 781

REFERENCES

1. Arnold, H.; Della-Fera, M.A.; Baile, C.A. Review of myostatin history, physiology and applications. Int. Arch. Biosci. **2001**, *2001*, 1014–1022.
2. Charlier, C.; Coppieters, W.; Farnir, F.; Grobet, L.; Leroy, P.L.; Michaux, C.; Mni, M.; Schwers, A.; Vanmanshoven, P.; Hanset, R.; Georges, M. The mh gene causing double-muscling in cattle maps to bovine chromosome 2. Mamm. Genome **1995**, *6*, 788–792.
3. McPherron, A.C.; Lawler, A.M.; Lee, S.J. Regulation of skeletal muscle mass in mice by a new TGF-beta superfamily member. Nature **1997**, *387*, 83–90.
4. Smith, T.P.; Lopez-Corrales, N.L.; Kappes, S.M.; Sonstegard, T.S. Myostatin maps to the interval containing the bovine mh locus. Mamm. Genome **1997**, *8*, 742–744.
5. Grobet, L.; Martin, L.J.; Poncelet, D.; Pirottin, D.; Brouwers, B.; Riquet, J.; Schoeberlein, A.; Dunner, S.; Menissier, F.; Massabanda, J.; Fries, R.; Hanset, R.; Georges, M. A deletion in the bovine myostatin gene causes the double-muscled phenotype in cattle. Nature Genet. **1997**, *17*, 71–74.
6. Mariani, P.; Lundstrom, K.; Gustafsson, U.; Enfalt, A.C.; Juneja, R.K.; Andersson, L. A major locus (RN) affecting muscle glycogen content is located on pig chromosome 15. Mamm. Genome **1996**, *7*, 52–54.
7. Milan, D.; Jeon, J.T.; Looft, C.; Amarger, V.; Robic, A.; Thelander, M.; Rogel-Gaillard, C.; Paul, S.; Iannuccelli, N.; Rask, L.; Ronne, H.; Lundstrom, K.; Reinsch, N.; Gellin, J.; Kalm, E.; Roy, P.L.; Chardon, P.; Andersson, L. A mutation in PRKAG3 associated with excess glycogen content in pig skeletal muscle. Science **2000**, *288* (5469), 1248–1251.

Genomics

Gary Alan Rohrer
United States Department of Agriculture, Agricultural Research Service, Clay Center, Nebraska, U.S.A.

INTRODUCTION

Genomics is the science involving the study of the nucleotide sequence and organization of an organism's DNA in its entirety, otherwise known as its genome. A useful analogy of genomics is that of looking at an entire forest, rather than at individual trees. Genomics is more a thought process than a science and truly came to fruition when high throughput genetic technologies and powerful computer algorithms were developed. Typically, genomic approaches assume that nothing about the genome is known a priori and hence require the results of previous experiments to drive the direction of future genetic research.

FIELDS OF GENOMIC RESEARCH

The term "genomics" was coined by T. H. Roderick in 1986 when a journal by the same name was launched.[1] Three fields of genomic research described by McKusick[1] are structural genomics, comparative genomics, and functional genomics.

DEFINITION OF STRUCTURAL GENOMICS

Structural genomics is the study of the structure of a genome. The structure is composed of DNA nucleotides arranged in chromosomes. Within the sequence of nucleotides are ones that have specific functions, whether the function be regulatory, protein encoding, providing attachment sites for proteins, or just separating other functional DNA segments. The ultimate structural genomics end point would be the complete sequence of the genome. The term structural genomics is less commonly used today than comparative or functional genomics.

DEFINITION OF COMPARATIVE GENOMICS

Comparative genomics is the study of similarities between genomes of different species. Comparative genomics reveals the changes made in genomes during evolution and provides insight into the molecular features and mechanisms responsible for the evolution of all life forms. The resolution possible for a comparative genome map relies on the type of reagents available for the species being studied. The pig–human comparative map includes one of the most elegant uses of fluorescent in situ hybridization (FISH) in a livestock species.[2] Researchers[2] used entire single human chromosomes labeled with a fluorescent dye as probes on pig metaphase chromosome spreads. Once this was accomplished, entire single pig chromosomes could be used as probes and hybridized to human metaphase chromosome spreads. The bidirectional FISH study provided a detailed comparison of the pig and human genomes. The results of this study are continually refined and available on the web site (http://www.toulouse.inra.fr/lgc/pig/compare/compare.htm). This study was possible only because the necessary whole chromosome libraries were available for both species. Unfortunately, this methodology is unable to determine conservation of gene order within conserved syntenic chromosomal segments.

The highest-resolution comparative map compares the sequences of the entire genomes of different species. To date, in mammals, this is possible only for a comparison between the human, mouse and rat genomes. However, there are plans to sequence the genomes of several other animal species including chicken and dog. Two additional livestock species (pig and cow) have been placed in the high priority category for genome sequencing by the National Genome Research Institute (http://www.genome.gov/). Until complete genome sequences for livestock species are available, comparative genomics can be conducted by computerized (virtual) mapping using conserved synteny of large segments of the target animal's sequence against the human, mouse, or rat genome sequence. This is essentially one of the projects the National Institute of Health's Intramural Sequencing Center is currently studying (http://www.nisc.nih.gov/).

This large-scale comparison of conserved genomic sequence is a powerful method to identify DNA sequences with specific functions, preserved throughout the evolutionary process. Thus, modern day comparative genomic research is critical to the state of the art of functional genomics studies.

Encyclopedia of Animal Science
DOI: 10.1081/E-EAS 120019653

469

DEFINITION OF FUNCTIONAL GENOMICS

Functional genomics is the science of determining the effects that segments of the genome or genes have on biological processes. Functional genomics is amenable to the study of gene expression for virtually all genes in the genome (thus the term genomics). However, it could be argued that the term applies to other types of "functions." A broader definition of functional genomics suggests that there are at least three strategic approaches at the genome level that describe functional genomics. The first approach uses genomic scans to identify loci affecting phenotypes of interest. A second approach monitors gene expression on a genome-wide scale (micro arrays), and the third is the use of genomic sequence comparisons across species to identify functional DNA elements.

Genome Scans

The approach of scanning the entire genome of animals with evenly spaced, highly informative, genetically linked single-locus markers in a segregating population to identify segments of the genome associated with differences in phenotypes has been successful in localizing genes that cause genetic defects (especially in humans[3]). This approach has identified locations in the genome that affect quantitative traits (traits such as growth rate or body composition; quantitative trait loci, QTL). However, determining the causal gene and DNA variation for these phenotypic differences is much more difficult.[4] Results of a genome scan are used to identify genes located in the region whose function is necessary for the phenotype being studied (positional candidate gene). Positional candidate genes are evaluated for variation in DNA sequence that causes the observed effect on performance. If the positional candidate gene approach does not yield the causative variation, then potentially, the entire region of the genome is sequenced and the sequence data are evaluated for putative causative variation. After the causative variation is identified, the function of the variation as well as any pleiotropic effects that the gene may possess can be determined.

Micro Arrays

A truly genomic approach to evaluating gene expression is to observe the expression of all genes in the genome. Unfortunately, this is possible only for a limited number of species, and for mammalian species there are currently more genes than can fit on standard matrices. One of the species for which all of the reagents are available is yeast (*Saccharomyces cerevisiae*). The genome of *S. cerevisiae* has been completely sequenced and all of the potentially expressed transcripts determined. All of the transcripts for *S. cerevisiae* (approximately 6220 transcripts) will fit on most expression array media (nylon membranes or glass slides). One of the first gene expression functional genomic studies in yeast determined the genes differentially expressed due to heat shock,[5] and since that time numerous other studies have been conducted to evaluate differences in expression due to growth conditions[6] or stage of cell cycle.[7]

Functional Elements

As diagrammed by Frazer et al.,[8] genome sequence comparisons between multiple species varying in genetic distance provide tremendous insight into conserved genetic elements residing within a genome. In general, highly conserved segments of DNA across distant species are indicative of a DNA segment with a critical function. At the other end of the spectrum, sequences that are unique to a species most likely contain DNA elements that confer species uniqueness or prevent interspecific hybridization. Once conserved DNA elements are identified, then a variety of approaches can be used to determine the function of the conserved element.

CONCLUSIONS

While only 16 years old, the term and field of genomics is a mainstay in current research programs. High-throughput data collection and powerful computers are enabling scientists to take more holistic views toward research pertaining to genetics. Almost all research tools used in genomics are the same procedures implemented in genetic research, just on a much larger scale. Comparative mapping and gene expression can be conducted on a gene-by-gene basis, and sequence comparisons can be performed with only short segments of DNA. What really makes an approach a genomic approach is the magnitude of the study or the proportion of the genome being evaluated.

Eventually, researchers will have the reagents/resources necessary to conduct whole genome studies for most economically important species. More mammalian species will have their genomes sequenced, and researchers working with species for which the genome is not sequenced will often be able to use reagents from closely related species to facilitate their research.

The rate at which data are collected is currently creating bottlenecks at the data management and analysis steps. However, as computers become more powerful and statistical algorithms more sophisticated, many of these bottlenecks will probably be alleviated. Then the rate-limiting step will be data collection or formulation of new research hypotheses.

ARTICLE OF FURTHER INTEREST

Gene Mapping, p. 459

REFERENCES

1. McKusick, V. Genomics: Structural and functional studies of genomes. Genomics **1997**, *45*, 244–249.
2. Goureau, A.; Yerle, M.; Schmitz, A.; Riquet, J.; Milan, D.; Pinton, P.; Frelat, G.; Gellin, J. Human and porcine correspondence of chromosome segments using bidirectional chromosome painting. Genomics **1996**, *36*, 252–262.
3. Risch, N.J. Searching for genetic determinants in the new millennium. Nature **2000**, *405*, 847–856.
4. Darvasi, A.; Pisante'-Shalom, A. Complexities in the genetic dissection of quantitative trait loci. Trends Genet. **2002**, *18*, 489–491.
5. Lashkari, D.A.; DeRisi, J.L.; McCusker, J.H.; Namath, A.F.; Gentile, C.; Hwang, S.Y.; Brown, P.O.; Davis, R.W. Yeast microarrays for genome wide parallel genetic and gene expression analysis. Proc. Natl. Acad. Sci. **1997**, *94*, 13057–13062.
6. ter Linde, J.J.; Liang, H.; Davis, R.W.; Steensma, H.Y.; van Dijken, J.P.; Pronk, J.T. Genome-wide transcriptional analysis of aerobic and anaerobic chemostat cultures of *Saccharomyces cerevisiae*. J. Bacteriol. **1999**, *181*, 7409–7413.
7. Cho, R.J.; Campbell, M.J.; Winzeler, E.A.; Steinmetz, L.; Conway, A.; Wodicka, L.; Wolfsberg, T.G.; Gabrielian, A.E.; Landsman, D.; Lockhart, D.J.; Davis, R.W. A genome-wide transcriptional analysis of the mitotic cell cycle. Mol. Cell. **1998**, *2*, 65–73.
8. Frazer, K.A.; Elnitski, L.; Church, D.M.; Dubchak, I.; Hardison, R.C. Cross-species sequence comparisons: A review of methods and available resources. Genome Res. **2003**, *13*, 1–12.

Goat Meat: Carcass Composition/Quality

Jeffrey W. Savell
David A. King
Texas A&M University, College Station, Texas, U.S.A.

INTRODUCTION

Goat meat is a significant source of protein for people throughout the world. Despite the importance of goats as a food source, relatively limited research data are available on the quality and cutability of goat carcasses. This is partially attributable to goat production being managed less intensively than other species in economically developed countries. However, several factors have been identified that affect the cutability of carcasses and the palatability of meat from those carcasses. Among those are breed type, diet, and market class. These factors will be reviewed as they affect the composition and lean meat quality of goat carcasses.

CARCASS COMPOSITION

Numerous breeds of goats are utilized throughout the world for various purposes. Breeds are generally classified as dairy or fiber-producing breeds. Those breeds that do not fit either of these categories are considered to be meat producers. However, dairy and fiber breeds also are used for meat production. In the United States, meat-producing goats are distinguished from milk or fiber goats and are generally referred to as Spanish goats. Recent importation of the South African Boer goat has dramatically altered the breeding systems used in meat goat production. Boer × Spanish goats have heavier live and carcass weights, higher carcass and leg conformation scores, and greater adjusted fat thicknesses than Spanish goats when fed a concentrate-based diet to a constant age.[1] However, on a constant carcass weight basis, differences in fat thickness are not observed.[1] Additionally, no differences have been noted in the percentage of fat, lean, or bone between the two breed types. Differences between these breed types appear to be due to the increased frame size of the Boer × Spanish goats compared to Spanish goats. In support of this conclusion, Boer × Spanish and Spanish goat carcasses do not differ in the percentage of knife-separable lean or fat, despite the greater carcass weights and higher leg conformation scores in the Boer × Spanish carcasses.[2]

Angora goats are bred primarily for fiber production, but are often marketed as meat animals as well. Comparisons between Angora and Spanish goats found that Spanish goats had heavier carcass weights, larger longissimus muscle areas, higher leg conformation scores, and greater internal fat.[3] Additionally, carcasses of both breeds are lighter and less muscular than lamb carcasses. At a constant age, Angora carcasses are lighter and have smaller longissimus muscle areas compared to Boer × Spanish carcasses.[2] Furthermore, Angora carcasses have a lower percentage of knife-separable lean and a higher percentage of fat than Boer × Spanish and Spanish carcasses.

Genetics determine the animal's potential for lean meat production. However, limited nutrition will determine the extent to which this potential is expressed. Goat production is generally less intensive than the production of other species; the majority of goats are raised under pasture conditions or are fed forage-based diets. Under these conditions, growth will likely be restricted and less fat deposition will occur. Concentrate feeding increases the percentage of the carcass comprising lean tissue and fat, while decreasing the percentage of bone.[1] Concentrate-fed goats also have heavier live and carcass weights, much larger longissimus muscle areas, higher conformation scores, and greater subcutaneous fat and body wall thicknesses.

Different breed types respond differently to production systems.[1] Boer × Spanish goats fed concentrates are generally larger, more muscular, and fatter than their Spanish counterparts. However, no differences due to breed type are detected when the goats are raised under pasture conditions. It is evident that while some breeds may have superior genetic potential, limited nutritional resources can prevent these advantages from being expressed.

As animals age, the proportions of fat, lean, and bone found in the carcass will change. Goats are traditionally marketed at different end-points, ranging from very young animals used for cabrito to aged animals at the end of their reproductive life. Young, intact males have higher conformation scores and greater fat thickness compared to aged females.[3] Additionally, young intact Spanish males have higher percentages of dissectible lean from the

Encyclopedia of Animal Science
DOI: 10.1081/E-EAS 120019654

rack than aged animals. Young intact Angora males have more fat in that subprimal area compared to their aged counterparts. In contrast, other research reported no differences in knife-separable lean, fat, or bone in goats harvested at live weights between 14 and 22 kg, compared to goats harvested at live weights that were between 30 and 35 kg.[4]

MEAT QUALITY

Product appearance is important to consumers making purchasing decisions. However, the palatability of meat products ultimately determines the final level of customer satisfaction. Using the results of sensory analysis to predict the consumer acceptance of goat meat is difficult, because thresholds of acceptability of flavors unique to goats differ among ethnic groups. Consumer sensory panelists from the United States score lamb and goat samples lower for overall palatability than panelists from Asia, South America, and the Middle East.[5] Cultural influences have a profound influence on an individual's affinity for goat meat.

The lean quality of goat meat also is affected by breed type, diet, and marketing class. Comparisons of Boer × Spanish, Spanish, Spanish × Angora, and Angora goats found no differences due to breed type in lean color, surface discoloration, or overall appearance during simulated retail display.[2] In contrast, Boer × Saanen produced meat that was less red than meat from feral and Saanen × feral kids.[4]

Sensory panelists gave meat from Boer goats higher scores for goaty aroma, goaty flavor, and aroma intensity than meat from South African indigenous goats. Additionally, Boer goat meat was juicier and greasier than meat from indigenous goats.[6] Sensory analysis revealed no differences in the flavor of meat from kids from six breed combinations.[4] However, meat from Boer × Feral kids was more tender than meat from Boer × Saanen and feral kids. Boer × feral kids received higher overall acceptability ratings than meat from Saanen × feral kids. Spanish and Angora goat meat did not differ in tenderness.[3]

Age at marketing strongly impacts the palatability of goat meat.[7] Meat from aged animals has more intense flavor, is less juicy, and is tougher than other age classes. Carcasses of very young animals (4 mo of age) are tougher than 6-mo-old or yearling animals. This is likely due to the rapid chilling of very small trim carcasses causing a cold-shortened condition. Animals harvested at 6 mo of age received optimal ratings for flavor, juiciness, and tenderness.[7] In contrast, some studies have found no differences in tenderness between young intact males and

aged females,[3,5] although aged females received higher flavor intensity scores.[5] Kids harvested at live weights between 14 and 22 kg received higher overall acceptability scores than those harvested at 30–35 kg.[4] However, differences in flavor, tenderness, and juiciness were not detected.

Concentrate feeding will impact the eating quality of goat meat by affecting tenderness and flavor. However, comparisons of concentrate- and forage-fed goats of varying ages found that concentrate feeding did not result in extensive subcutaneous fat deposition or improve carcass quality. Additionally, carcass fatness did not affect sensory ratings.[6]

CONCLUSION

Goat meat will continue to be a principal source of protein for people throughout the world. Breed type, diet, and age at marketing have significant effects on carcass yields. However, the relationships between these factors and palatability are less clear. As the market for goat meat grows in economically developed countries, the amount of research data available will likely increase and help elucidate production systems that best meet consumer demands.

REFERENCES

1. Oman, J.S.; Waldron, D.F.; Griffin, D.B.; Savell, J.W. Effect of breed-type and feeding regimen on goat carcass traits. J. Anim. Sci. **1999**, *77*, 3128–3215.
2. Oman, J.S.; Waldron, D.F.; Griffin, D.B.; Savell, J.W. Carcass traits and retail display-life of chops from different goat breed types. J. Anim. Sci. **2000**, *78*, 1262–1266.
3. Riley, R.R.; Savell, J.W.; Johnson, D.D.; Smith, G.C.; Shelton, M. Carcass grades, rack composition and tenderness of sheep and goats as influenced by market class and breed. Small Rumin. Res. **1989**, *2*, 273–280.
4. Dhanda, J.S.; Taylor, D.G.; Murray, P.J. Part 1. Growth, carcass and meat quality parameters of male goats: Effects of genotype and liveweight at slaughter. Small Rumin. Res. **2003**, *50*, 57–66.
5. Griffin, C.L.; Orcutt, M.W.; Riley, R.R.; Smith, G.C.; Savell, J.W.; Shelton, M. Evaluation of palatability of lamb, mutton, and chevon by sensory panels of various cultural backgrounds. Small Rumin. Res. **1992**, *8*, 67–74.
6. Tshabalala, P.A.; Strydom, P.E.; Webb, E.C.; de Kock, H.L. Meat quality of designated South African indigenous goat and sheep breeds. Meat Sci. **2003**, *65*, 563–570.
7. Smith, G.C.; Carpenter, Z.L.; Shelton, M. Effect of age and quality level on the palatability of goat meat. J. Anim. Sci. **1978**, *46* (5), 1220–1235.

Goat Milk: Composition, Characteristics

Young W. Park
Fort Valley State University, Fort Valley, Georgia, U.S.A.

INTRODUCTION

Goats produce only about 2% of the world's total annual milk supply.[1] However, their global contribution to the nutritional and economic well-being of humanity is tremendous. Worldwide, more people drink the milk of goats than the milk of any other single species. Goat milk differs from cow or human milk in having higher digestibility of protein and fat, alkalinity, buffering capacity, and certain therapeutic values in medicine and human nutrition. Goat milk and its products are important daily food sources of protein, phosphate, and calcium in developing countries where cow milk is unavailable. Goat milk and cow milk contain substantially higher protein and ash, but lower lactose, than human milk. Specific constituents and physicochemical properties differ between goat and cow milks.

Interest in dairy goats and goat milk products is a part of the recent trend in health food demand and consumption in several developed countries.[2] Goat milk is also of great importance to infants and patients who suffer from cow milk allergy. Such unique properties of goat milk contribute to the sustainability of the dairy goat industry.

NUTRIENT COMPOSITION OF GOAT MILK

Basic Composition

Goat milk is similar to cow milk in its basic composition. Caprine milk, on the average, contains 12.2% total solids, consisting of 3.8% fat, 3.5% protein, 4.1% lactose, and 0.8% ash (Table 1). It has more fat, protein, and ash and less lactose than cow milk. Goat milk contains slightly less total casein, but higher nonprotein nitrogen than the cow counterpart. Goat milk and cow milk have 3 to 4 times greater levels of protein and ash than human milk. Total solids and caloric values of goat, cow, and human milks are similar.[3–5]

Lipids

Fat content of goat milk across breeds ranges from 2.45 to 7.76%. Average diameters of fat globules for goat, cow, buffalo, and sheep milks are reported as 3.49, 4.55, 5.92, and 3.30 μm, respectively.[3,4] Smaller fat globules make a better dispersion and a more homogeneous mixture of fat in goat milk, providing a greater surface area of fat for enhanced digestive action by lipases.[4–6]

Goat milk fat contains 97–99% free lipids (of which about 97% is triglycerides) and 1–3% bound lipids (about 47% neutral and 53% polar lipids).[7] Goat milk fat has significantly higher levels of short- and medium-chain-length fatty acids (MCT) (C4:0–C14:0) than cow and human milks. This property has been utilized for treatment of a variety of fat malabsorption problems in patients.[3–6,8]

Protein

There are five principal proteins in goat milk: α_{s2}-casein (α_{s2}-CN), β-casein (β-CN), κ-casein (κ-CN), β-lactoglobulin (β-Lg), and α-lactalbumin (α-La).[3–5] β-casein is the major casein fraction in goat milk, whereas α_{s1}-casein is the major one in cow milk. Differences in amino acid composition between casein fractions of goat milk are much greater than differences between species (goat versus cow).[4] The α-caseins contain greater aspartate, lysine, and tyrosine than β-casein, whereas the latter has higher leucine, proline, and valine than the former.[4] Casein micelles of goat milk are less solvated, are less heat stable, and lose β-casein more readily than bovine micelles.[9]

Commonalities in the overall amino acid pattern were reported among the milks of many species.[10] The most abundant amino acids were glutamate (plus glutamine, 20%), proline (10%), and leucine (10%). Among the three most abundant amino acids, goat and other nonprimate milk contained greater glutamate and proline and lower leucine than human milk. For sulfur-containing amino acids, cystine was higher and methionine was lower in primate milks than in goat and other nonprimate milks.[10]

Carbohydrates

The major carbohydrate of goat milk is lactose, which is about 0.2–0.5% less than in cow milk.[5,11] Lactose is a disaccharide made up of a glucose and a galactose molecule and is synthesized in the mammary gland. Milks of most of the lower mammalian species have a higher

Encyclopedia of Animal Science
DOI: 10.1081/E-EAS 120019655

Table 1 Average concentrations (per 100 g) of basic nutrients, minerals, and vitamins in goat milk compared with those in cow and human milks

Constituents	Goat	Cow	Human
Basic nutrients			
Fat (g)	3.8	3.6	4.0
Protein (g)	3.5	3.3	1.2
Lactose (g)	4.1	4.6	6.9
Ash (g)	0.8	0.7	0.2
Total solids (g)	12.2	12.3	12.3
Calories (cal)	70	69	68
Minerals			
Ca (mg)	134	122	33
P (mg)	141	119	43
Mg (mg)	16	12	4
K (mg)	181	152	55
Na (mg)	41	58	15
Cl (mg)	150	100	60
S (mg)	2.89	–	–
Fe (mg)	0.07	0.08	0.20
Cu (mg)	0.05	0.06	0.06
Mn (mg)	0.032	0.02	0.07
Zn (mg)	0.56	0.53	0.38
I (mg)	0.022	0.021	0.007
Se (µg)	1.33	0.96	1.52
Vitamins			
Vitamin A (I.U.)	185	126	190
Vitamin D (I.U.)	2.3	2.0	1.4
Thiamine (mg)	0.068	0.045	0.017
Riboflavin (mg)	0.21	0.16	0.02
Niacin (mg)	0.27	0.08	0.17
Pantothenic acid (mg)	0.31	0.32	0.20
Vitamin B_6 (mg)	0.046	0.042	0.011
Folic acid (µg)	1.0	5.0	5.5
Biotin (µg)	1.5	2.0	0.4
Vitamin B_{12} (µg)	0.065	0.357	0.03
Vitamin C (mg)	1.29	0.94	5.00

(From Refs. 3,4,11, and 12.)

content of fat and a lower content of lactose than goat milk.[3] Cow milk contains minor levels of monosaccharides and oligosaccharides, but their presence in goat milk is not known.[5]

MINERALS AND VITAMINS IN GOAT MILK

Minerals

Goat milk contains about 134 mg Ca and 141 mg P/100 g (Table 1). Human milk contains only one-fourth to one-sixth of these mineral amounts. Goat milk has higher

calcium, phosphorus, potassium, magnesium, and chlorine, but lower sodium and sulfur contents, than cow milk[3,4,12] (Table 1).

There is a close inverse relationship between lactose content and the molar sum of sodium and potassium contents of goat and other species' milks.[4,12] Chloride is positively correlated with potassium and negatively with lactose, but sodium is not significantly correlated with K, Cl, and lactose. Concentrations of trace minerals are affected by diet, breed, animal, and stages of lactation.[12] The average mineral content of goat milk is higher than that of cow milk. However, goat milk has a lower degree of hydration, and has an inverse relationship between the mineralization of the micelle and its hydration.[13]

Vitamins

Goat milk has a higher amount of vitamin A than cow milk. Caprine milk is whiter than bovine milk because goats convert all β-carotene into vitamin A in the milk. Goat milk supplies adequate amounts of vitamin A and niacin, and an excess of thiamin, riboflavin, and pantothenate, for a human infant (Table 1). A human infant fed solely on goat milk is oversupplied with protein, Ca, P, vitamin A, thiamin, riboflavin, niacin, and pantothenate in relation to the Food and Agriculture Organization and World Health Organization (FAO-WHO) requirements.[4] Vitamin B levels in goat and cow milks are a result of rumen synthesis, and are somewhat independent of diet.[3]

Goat milk, however, is deficient in folic acid and vitamin B_{12} compared to cow milk.[3,4,6] Cow milk has 5 times more folate and vitamin B_{12} than goat milk, and folate is necessary for the synthesis of hemoglobin.[4,6] Goat milk and cow milk are equally deficient in pyridoxine (B_6) and vitamins C and D, and these vitamins must be supplemented from other food sources.[4]

MINOR CONSTITUENTS IN GOAT MILK

The lactoferrin, transferrin, and prolactin contents of goat milk are comparable to those of cow milk. Human milk contains more than 2 mg lactoferrin/ml, which is 10–100-fold higher than in goat milk. The high level of folate-binding protein in goat milk lowers the available level of folic acid in this milk (Table 2).

The amount of immunoglobulin IgG type in both goat and cow milk is much higher than in human milk, whereas human milk contains greater levels of IgA and IgM immunoglobulins than either goat or cow milk (Table 2).

Table 2 Caseins, minor proteins, and enzyme contents of goat milk compared with those of cow and human milks

Proteins	Goat	Cow	Human
Protein (%)	3.5	3.3	1.2
Total casein (g/100 ml)	2.11	2.70	0.40
α_{s1} (% of total casein)	5.6	38.0	–
α_{s2} (% of total casein)	19.2	12.0	–
β (% of total casein)	54.8	36.0	60–70
κ (% of total casein)	20.4	14.0	7.0
Whey protein (%) (albumin and globulin)	0.6	0.6	0.7
Nonprotein N (%)	0.4	0.2	0.5
Lactoferrin (µg/ml)	20–200	20–200	<2,000
Transferrin (µg/ml)	20–200	20–200	50<
Prolactin (µg/ml)	44	50	40–160
Folate-binding protein (µg/ml)	12	8	–
Immunoglobulin			
IgA (milk: µg/ml)	30–80	140	1,000
IgA (colostrum: mg/ml)	0.9–2.4	3.9	17.35
IgM (milk: µg/ml)	10–40	50	100
IgM (colostrum: mg/ml)	1.6–5.2	4.2	1.59
IgG (milk: µg/ml)	100–400	590	40
IgG (colostrum: mg/ml)	50–60	47.6	0.43
Lysozyme (µg/100 ml)	25	10–35	4–40
Ribonuclease (µg/100 ml)	425	1,000–2,000	10–20
Xanthine oxidase (µl O_2/h/ml)	19–113	120	–

(From Refs. 4,7,9, and 13.)

Concentrations of lysozyme, ribonuclease, and xanthine oxidase in goat, cow, and human milks are highly variable among and within species (Table 2). Xanthine oxidase activity of goat milk is less than 10% of that of cow milk.[5] Goat milk contains less lipase and alkaline phosphatase than cow milk.[3,5]

VARIATIONS IN GOAT MILK COMPOSITION

The composition and yield of goat milk and milks of other species vary with breed, animals within breed, environmental conditions, feeding and management conditions, season, locality, and stage of lactation.[3,4,12,14] High variability in goat milk composition between different seasons and genotypes has also been noted.[4,5] The casein composition of goat milk is influenced by genetic polymorphism on the casein loci. The allele frequencies at the α_{s1}-casein locus vary with breed.[15]

CONCLUSION

Although goat milk is similar to cow milk in its basic composition, the significance of goat milk and its prod-

ucts in human nutrition and well-being can never be underestimated. Goat milk products provide essential nutrients in human diet, as well as income sources for the survival of mankind in ecosystems of many parts of the world. The contribution of dairy goat products is also greatly valued by those who have cow milk allergy and other nutritional diseases.

REFERENCES

1. FAO. *Production Yearbook*; FAO, United Nations, 1988; Vol. 42, 241.
2. Park, Y.W. Nutrient profiles of commercial goat milk cheeses manufactured in the United States. J. Dairy Sci. **1990**, *73*, 3059.
3. Haenlein, G.F.W.; Caccese, R. Goat Milk Versus Cow Milk. In *Extension Goat Handbook*; Haenlein, G.F.W., Ace, D.L., Eds.; USDA Publ.: Washington, DC, 1984; 1. E-1.
4. Jenness, R. Composition and characteristics of goat milk: Review 1968–1979. J. Dairy Sci. **1980**, *63*, 1605.
5. Chandan, R.C.; Attaie, R.; Shahani, K.M. *Nutritional Aspects of Goat Milk and Its Products*; Proc. V. Intl. Conf. Goats, 1992; Vol. II, 399. New Delhi, India, Part II.
6. Park, Y.W. Hypo-allergenic and therapeutic significance of goat milk. Small Rumin. Res. **1994**, *14*, 151.

7. Cerbulis, J.; Parks, O.W.; Farrell, H.M. Composition and distribution of lipids of goats milk. J. Dairy Sci. **1982**, *65*, 2301.

8. Jensen, R.G.; Ferris, A.N.; Lammi-Keefe, C.J.; Henderson, R.A. Lipids of bovine and human milks: A comparison. J. Dairy Sci. **1990**, *73*, 223.

9. Juàrez, M.; Ramos, M. Physico-chemical characteristics of goat milk as distinct from those of cow milk. Intl. Dairy Bull. **1986**, *202*, 54.

10. Davis, T.A.; Nguyen, H.V.; Garcia-Bravo, R.; Florotto, M.L.; Jackson, E.M.; Lewis, D.S.; Lee, D.R.; Reeds, P.J. Amino acid composition of human milk is not unique. J. Nutr. **1994**, *124*, 1126.

11. Posati, L.P.; Orr, M.L. *Composition of Foods*; Agric. Handbook, ARS, USDA: Washington, DC, 1976; Vol. 8-1.

12. Park, Y.W.; Chukwu, H.I. Trace mineral concentrations in goat milk from French-Alpine and Anglo-Nubian breeds during the first 5 months of lactation. J. Food Composit. Anal. **1989**, *2*, 161.

13. Remeuf, F.; Lenoir, J. Relationship between the physico-chemical characteristics of goat's milk and its rennet-ability. Intl. Dairy Bull. **1986**, *202*, 68.

14. Park, Y.W. Relative buffering capacity of goat milk, cow milk, soy-based infant formulas, and commercial non-prescription antiacid drugs. J. Dairy Sci. **1991**, *74*, 3326.

15. Moioli, B.; Pilla, F.; Tripaldi, C. Detection of milk protein genetic polymerphisms in order to improve dairy traits in sheep and goats: A review. Small Rum. Res. **1998**, *27*, 185–195.

Goat Milk Products: Quality, Composition, Processing, Marketing

Young W. Park
Fort Valley State University, Fort Valley, Georgia, U.S.A.

INTRODUCTION

Through utilization of manufacturing cheeses and other products, goat milk has played an important role in many parts of the world.[1] Large-scale industrialization of the dairy goat sector in many countries is limited due to the low level of milk production, approximately 50 kg per doe per lactation annually.[2]

Goat milk products include fluid products (low fat, fortified, or flavored); fermented products such as cheese, buttermilk, or yogurt; frozen products such as ice cream or frozen yogurt; and butter, as well as condensed and dried products. However, cheese, which is produced and consumed in large quantities around the world, is the only dairy goat product having significant research data.

PRODUCTION OF QUALITY GOAT MILK

Fresh goat milk is a white, opaque liquid with a slightly sweet taste and practically no odor.[3] Milk drawn from the lacteal glands is highly perishable. It is adversely affected by improper practices of feeding, handling of animals and milk during and after milking, and of its cooling and transportation, pasteurization, processing, packaging, and processing equipment.[3,4] High-quality goat milk must contain no pathogens or foreign substances, such as antibiotics, antiseptics, or pesticide residues,[3,5] and it is indistinguishable in taste and odor from quality cow's milk.

Pasteurization and protection from sunlight or UV light control oxidized and ''goaty'' flavors. Goaty flavor is attributable to caproic, caprylic, and capric acids, which are present at high levels in goat milk fat and subject to release from fat globule membranes by lipases if improper milking and processing are practiced.[3,6]

REQUIREMENTS FOR GRADE A GOAT MILK AND ITS PRODUCTS

In the United States, the regulations for production, processing, and marketing of milk are described in the federal government (FDA) publication called the Grade A Pasteurized Milk Ordinance (PMO). Each state health department establishes its minimum regulations for Grade A milk from these standards,[4] and may adopt more stringent standards than those of the PMO. For example, a state may set its somatic cell count (SCC) standard at 750,000 cells per mL, whereas the PMO standard is 1 million per mL.

Although goat milk contains a naturally higher SCC than cow milk, due to the apocrine secretion process, the same regulations are enforced for the milk of both species. It is common to find a high SCC in goat milk when actual numbers of leucocytes are relatively low.[7] Dairy goat farmers have pursued this problem of SCC legal thresholds.[7]

Many states have an annotated code, wherein a permit from the state regulatory agency is required to: 1) bring, send, or receive a milk product into the state for sale; 2) offer a milk product for sale; 3) give a milk product away; or 4) store a milk product.[4,7,8]

Milk, by FDA standards, contains a minimum of 3.25% fat and 8.25% milk solids not fat (MSNF), which is the sum of the protein, lactose, and minerals. Table 1 shows the nutrient composition of goat milk products in the United States. Notable variations in nutrient composition have been reported (Table 1).[3,8–11]

PROCESSING GOAT MILK AND TYPES OF DAIRY GOAT PRODUCTS

Standardization of milk composition is essential to ensure the uniformity and legality of the finished dairy goat products. General manufacturing conditions for various cultured goat products are listed in Table 2.

Beverage Milk

A low-fat beverage milk is processed and adjusted to 2% fat and 10.5% MSNF before it is high-temperature, short-time (HTST) pasteurized, homogenized, and packaged in 946-mL containers.[6]

Encyclopedia of Animal Science
DOI: 10.1081/E-EAS 120024343

Table 1 Basic nutrient contents (%) of commercial U.S. goat milk products (wet basis)

Goat milk product	Total solids X̄	Total solids SD	Protein X̄	Protein SD	Fat X̄	Fat SD	Carbohydrates X̄	Carbohydrates SD	Ash X̄	Ash SD
Fluid Milk										
Report 1[a]	11.3	0.05	2.92	0.09	3.40	0.10	4.15	0.13	0.79	0.01
USDA[b]	13.0	0.15	3.56	0.03	4.14	0.05	4.45	–	0.82	0.01
Evaporated Milk										
Report 1[a]	20.85	0.05	6.11	0.33	6.75	0.05	6.56	0.53	1.43	0.10
USDA[c]	25.86	0.08	6.81	0.03	7.56	0.01	10.04	–	1.55	0.02
Powdered Milk										
Report 1[a]	94.1	0.56	27.0	0.45	28.2	1.35	32.0	0.33	6.77	0.15
USDA[d]	97.5	0.13	26.3	0.18	26.9	0.25	38.4	–	6.08	0.09
Yogurt[e]										
Plain	11.5	2.56	3.99	0.12	2.25	0.13	4.49	0.56	0.82	0.02
Blueberry	17.7	2.34	3.37	0.13	1.18	0.17	12.6	2.72	0.86	0.09
Cheese[f]										
Soft										
Plain	40.2	6.81	18.9	5.26	22.5	4.37	–	–	1.74	0.97
Herb	40.9	2.11	17.3	2.26	21.8	2.13	–	–	1.60	0.61
Hard										
Cheddar	58.3	1.76	30.3	0.56	26.6	1.13	1.40	–	3.60	0.13
Blue	74.1	1.62	20.2	0.35	31.8	1.06	–	–	3.32	0.36

X̄=Mean; SD=Standard deviation.
[a](Report 1 from Ref. 8.)
[b](From Ref. 9.)
[c](From Ref. 9; evaporated cow milk data from Ref. 10.)
[d](From Ref. 9.)
[e](From Ref. 10.)
[f](From Ref. 11.)

Table 2 Manufacturing conditions for cultured goat milk products

Products	Milk type	Culture microorganism	Type of inoculum	Rate of inoculation (%)	Incubation Temp. °F(°C)	Incubation Time (hr)	Stop incubation at pH	Stop incubation at %TA
Acidophilus	Skim or low fat	*Lactobacillus acidophilus*	Bulk start	0.5	100–111 (37–44)	18–24	3.8	1.0
Buttermilk	Skim or low fat	*S. lactis* *S. cremoris*	Bulk start or direct set	0.5–1.0 as directed	72 (22)	14–16	4.5	0.8
		L. citrovorum *S. diacetilactis*			72 (22)	12–16	4.5	0.8
Sour dip	Half-n-half (11% fat)	Same as for buttermilk[a]	Bulk start or direct set[a]	1.0	72 (22)[a]	14–16	4.8[a]	0.7[a]
Yogurt	Skim or low fat	*S. thermophilus* *L. bulgaricus*	Individual cultures or direct set	1.25 each or as directed	114 (45.6)	5–6	4.2	0.9
Kefir	Whole	*S. kefir* *T. kefir* *L. caucasicus* *S. lactis*	Kefir grains	As directed	72 (22) followed by 50 (10)	12 24–72	4.5	0.8

[a]Same conditions for sour dip and sour cream; sour cream as 18% fat.
(From Refs. 12 and 14.)

Cheese

Cheeses hold the greatest economic value among all manufactured goat milk products. *Agricultural Handbook No. 54* of the U.S. Department of Agriculture[13] describes over 400 varieties of goat cheese and lists over 800 names of cheeses, many of which are made from goat milk or combinations of goat with cow, ewe, or buffalo milk.[11] The general procedures of cheese manufacturing are: 1) standardizing the milk; 2) setting the temperature; 3) adding starter cultures; 4) adding rennet; 5) cutting curds; 6) cooking; 7) draining whey; 8) salting; 9) hooping; 10) pressing; 11) packaging; and 12) aging.[3,12] Soft cheeses are made by natural draining without pressing.

Buttermilk

Buttermilk is usually made from skim milk (less than 0.5% fat) using the by-product from churning butter out of sour cream. Yogurt is made from whole milk (3.25% fat), low-fat milk (0.5 to 2.5% fat), or skim milk. Sour cream must contain 18% fat in most states.[14] Acidophilus milk can be made by the activity of *L. acidophilus*, which is capable of converting a greater proportion of the lactose to lactic acid (2%).

Kefir

Kefir is an acidic, slightly foamy product made from pasteurized and fat-standardized or decreamed goat milk that has passed through a combined acidic and alcoholic fermentation of symbiotic lactic acid bacteria and yeast kefir grains.[12] The finished product, kefir, contains 0.6–0.8% lactic acid and 0.5–1.0% alcohol.

Yogurt

Yogurt, one of the major cultured products, may be made from skim, low-fat, or whole milk. It is made essentially the same way as buttermilk, but a different combination of microorganisms is cultured at a higher incubation temperature. Goat yogurt is softer and less viscous, and often lacks the typical flavor of cow yogurt.[6,15]

Frozen Products

Ice cream and frozen yogurt are manufactured from goat milk. The three flavor formulations of goat ice cream are French vanilla, chocolate, and premium white mixes.[6]

Evaporated and Powdered Products

Evaporated and powdered goat milk are manufactured and marketed in the United States.[8] Evaporation is usually done under reduced pressure, primarily to allow boiling at a lower temperature to prevent heat damage. Powdered products available include whole milk, skim milk, whey, and infant foods.

Other Products

Ghee is an Indian clarified butterfat product manufactured by fermenting whole milk into curd and churning out the butter, followed by heat clarification at 105–145°C.[12] Additional goat milk products made in India include chhana, khoa, and paneer (a cheese). Chhana is an acid- and heat-coagulated milk product, and a chhana-based sweet is made by kneading chhana and cooking it in sugar syrup over medium heat. Khoa is a heat-desiccated indigenous milk product used for various sweets.

MARKETING GOAT MILK PRODUCTS AND ITS CHALLENGES

The most important quality standard for goat milk is acceptable, attractive milk odor and taste. Two formidable barriers exist in marketing goat milk products: 1) negative public perception of goaty flavor; and 2) seasonal milk production, which prevents year-round uniform marketing. To overcome these problems and achieve a sustainable dairy goat industry, effective strategies have to be sought.

Technological approaches are needed to resolve the seasonal milk supply, such as ultrafiltration of milk, freezing and storage of curds, spray-drying, and production of mixed-milk cheeses. Ultrafiltration was used for the production of retentate (very high-fat and -protein liquid) to make the precheese fraction that is subsequently made into cheese.[5,6] Goat cheeses can be made during off-season using the ultrafiltered, spray-dried retentate, which can be reconstituted into cheese and stored frozen for later use.[5,12]

Key factors for successful marketing of dairy goat products include: 1) consumer perception of safety and nutrition; 2) quality of flavor, body texture, and appearance; 3) availability of specialty types; 4) attractiveness of packaging; 5) relative price of products; and 6) establishment of proper distribution and marketing channels.[5]

CONCLUSION

Various goat products, including fluid, fermented, frozen, condensed, and dehydrated milk products, are produced in many countries. Cheese is the most important goat dairy commodity, traded in large quantities among and within nations. There is high variation in nutritional, chemical, and rheological compositions between and within goat products, due to the multiplicity of manufacturing procedures, localities, animals, and management factors. Technological advances are required for a uniform supply of goat products. Promotion of consumer perception, identification of proper distribution and marketing channels, and development of specialty-type goat products are crucial for establishment of a successful and profitable dairy goat industry.

REFERENCES

1. Juàrez, M.; Ramos, M. Physico-chemical characteristics of goat milk as distinct from those of cow milk. Int. Dairy Bull. **1986**, *202*, 54.
2. *FAO Production Yearbook*; Food Agr. Organ., UN: Rome, Italy, 1996–1997.
3. Le Jaouen, J.C. *The Fabrication of Farmstead Goat Cheese*; Cheesemaker's Journal, 1987; 45–121. Ashfield, MA.
4. Peters, R.R. Proper milk handling. Dairy Goat J. **1990**, *68* (4), 223–227.
5. Kosikowski, F.V. Requirements for the acceptance and marketing of goat milk cheese. Dairy Goat J. **1986**, *64*, 462.
6. Loewenstein, M.; Speck, S.J.; Barnhart, H.M.; Frank, J.F. Research on goat milk products: A review. J. Dairy Sci. **1980**, *63*, 1631.
7. Kapture, J. Somatic counts don't tell whole mastitis story with goat milk. Dairy Goat Guide **1980**, *3* (Dec), 9.
8. Park, Y.W. Comparison of mineral and cholesterol composition of different commercial goat milk products manufactured in USA. Small Rumin. Res. **2000**, *37*, 115–124.
9. Posati, L.P.; Orr, M.L. *Composition of Foods*; Agric. Handbook No. 8-1, ARS, USDA: Washington, DC, 1976.
10. Park, Y.W. Basic nutrient and mineral composition of commercial goat milk yogurt produced in the U.S. Small Rumin. Res. **1994**, *13*, 63–70.
11. Park, Y.W. Nutrient profiles of commercial goat milk cheeses manufactured in the United States. J. Dairy Sci. **1990**, *73*, 3059.
12. Kosikowski, F.V. *Cheese and Fermented Milk Foods*, 2nd Ed.; Edwards Brothers, Inc.: Ann Arbor, MI, 1977; 90.
13. Sanders, G.P. *Cheese Varieties and Descriptions*; USDA Agric. Handbook No. 54, USDA, 1969. Washington, D.C.
14. Loewenstein, M.; Frank, J.F.; Barnhart, H.M.; Speck, S.J. Cultured Products Made from Goat Milk. In *Extension Goat Handbook*; Haenlein, G.F.W., Ace, D.L., Eds.; USDA Publ.: Washington, DC, 1984; 1. E-5.
15. Remeuf, F. *Physico-chemical Properties of Goat Milk in Relation to Processing Characteristics*; Nat'l Symp. Dairy Goat Prod. Marketing, Oklahoma City, OK, Aug. 12–15, 1992; 98–111.

Goats: Behavior, Stress, and Management

G. Kannan
Fort Valley State University, Fort Valley, Georgia, U.S.A.

INTRODUCTION

Goats are raised throughout the world for milk, meat, fiber, biomedical research, and companionship. Goat milk is known for its hypoallergenic properties and easy digestibility. Certain breeds of goats yield some of the most valued fibers in the world. In addition, goats are useful in pasture management and brush control. Goat meat is a major source of animal protein throughout the world, particularly in Asia and Africa. In the United States, the importance of goats as meat animals has increased in the recent years. However, meat goat marketing systems are still not fully organized, which makes the management of meat goats prior to harvesting a challenge. Management practices that improve well-being of goats invariably result in better productivity, although scientific data available regarding these aspects are limited.

CONFINED ENVIRONMENT

Heat stress is of concern in goats, particularly under intensive management situations. Reduction in feed intake and productivity are commonly observed in goats subjected to heat stress.[1] Feedlotting is not a common practice in the meat goat industry due to difficulties with disease management and a lack of economic viability. However, Flint and Murray[2] emphasized the importance of intensive management programs as one of the strategies to improving goat meat production. Under intensive conditions, environmental enrichment increases growth rate in goats, but does not affect feed intake or agonistic behavior.[2] Agonistic behavior indicates combative or submissive responses to each other in animals. Stress responses in goats are not influenced by stocking density when they are held in pens without feed,[3] although agonistic encounters are frequent in high-density groups.[2]

SOCIAL INTERACTION

Almost immediately after birth (<48 h), goat kids are capable of sensing changes in their social environment.[4]

Goats are highly social animals and tend to be together, particularly when they sense danger or are moved from their home range. However, it is common for a few goats to break away from the herd when cornered. Goats use head butts to establish dominance hierarchy, and a dominant goat often butts the sides of subordinate ones. Physical injuries such as bruising may increase in horned goats under crowded conditions, resulting in elevated blood creatine kinase (CK) activities.[3] Dominance hierarchy in goats primarily depends on body weight and horn size. Interestingly, an individual with the largest number of relatives in the group tends to be the dominant one in the Jamunapari breed of goats.[5] Kannan et al.[6] observed a spike in CK activity in goats, when measured after 7 h of holding in pens, as a result of a higher frequency of agonistic encounters during the initial hours of holding.

SOCIAL ISOLATION

Isolation of goats from their social group can cause increased emotional stress or fearfulness, as reflected by elevated cortisol concentrations.[6] Plasma cortisol concentration is a reliable indicator of stress in goats. To study the responses to social isolation in goats, Kannan et al.[6] conducted an experiment in which individual does were blood-sampled after imposing one of three isolation treatments: a 15-min isolation with no visual contact with other does (I); a 15-min isolation with visual contact (IV); or no isolation (control, C). The stress levels, as indicated by plasma cortisol concentrations, were higher in the I group compared to the IV and C groups. Cortisol concentrations in the IV and C groups were not significantly different (Fig. 1).

Social isolation also causes stress in sheep. However, based on social interactions initiated per unit time and on the behaviors exhibited when socially isolated, goats are more social than sheep.[7] Although plasma glucose and nonesterified fatty acid (NEFA) concentrations were not influenced by handling treatment, the trends were similar to that of cortisol (Fig. 1). Plasma NEFA concentrations increase in goats as a result of stress, probably due to epinephrine-induced lipolysis. Goats can be easily conditioned to routine laboratory procedures such as isolation

Encyclopedia of Animal Science
DOI: 10.1081/E-EAS 120019656

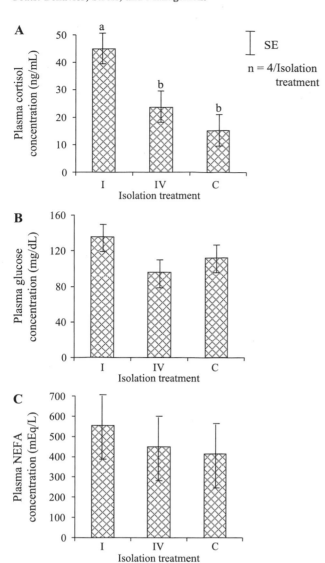

Fig. 1 Effect of isolation treatment (isolation with no visual contact with other goats, I; isolation with visual contact with other goats, IV; control, C) on (A) plasma cortisol, (B) plasma glucose, and (C) plasma nonesterified fatty acid (NEFA) concentrations in Spanish does. Bars with different letters are significantly different ($P<0.05$) by LSD. (Modified from Ref. 6.) (*View this art in color at www.dekker.com.*)

and blood sampling by using a restraint device and a rewards program, because they can remember positive encounters very well.[8]

TRANSPORTATION STRESS

Goats intended for meat production are frequently transported long distances in the United States. Transportation includes not only physical stress, but also emotional stress caused by loading and unloading, noise, vibration, and social disruption. Loading onto the transport trailer increases stress in goats, and transportation further increases physiological stress responses.[3]

The pattern of decline in stress responses in Spanish goats after a 2.5-hour transportation is depicted in Fig. 2. In this study, stocking density during transportation did not influence the physiological stress responses measured. Although the cortisol concentrations decreased within 1 h after transportation, plasma glucose concentrations remained elevated until 2 h after transportation and started declining around 3 h after transportation.[3] If the stressor is severe enough, the elevation of plasma cortisol is followed by an elevation of plasma glucose,[9] probably as a result of the breakdown of liver glycogen. The elevation of plasma CK activity noticed after transportation (Fig. 2) is due to physical stress and injuries such as bruising. After Spanish goats encounter a physical stressor, their plasma CK activity increases after a lag time of about 2 h.[3]

NUTRITIONAL STRESS

Pasture management is of great importance in maintaining a healthy productive herd, although goats are known to survive on vegetation too rough for other livestock. Undernourishment in goats makes them prone to diseases, particularly nematode infections. Meat goats are normally housed without feed in slaughter plant holding pens prior to harvesting, primarily to reduce fecal contamination of carcasses. Holding at the slaughter facility for limited periods also helps goats recover from transportation stress prior to slaughter.[3] However, prolonged feed deprivation, social disruption, and the novelty of environment that accompany preslaughter holding may increase stress responses and metabolic changes. Feed deprivation has been reported to increase plasma cortisol concentration in Spanish goats.[3] Despite certain advantages, feed deprivation in slaughter goats may result in the reduction of live and carcass weights, which is of economic significance.

STRESS AND HEALTH

Differential leukocyte count is of particular importance in evaluating prolonged effects of stress in goats. Lymphocyte percent decreases and neutrophil percent increases as a result of stress in goats.[3] It is not clear whether changes in leukocyte profiles could have an adverse effect on disease resistance in goats, although mortalities due to respiratory infections are common after prolonged journeys under unfavorable conditions. The major causes

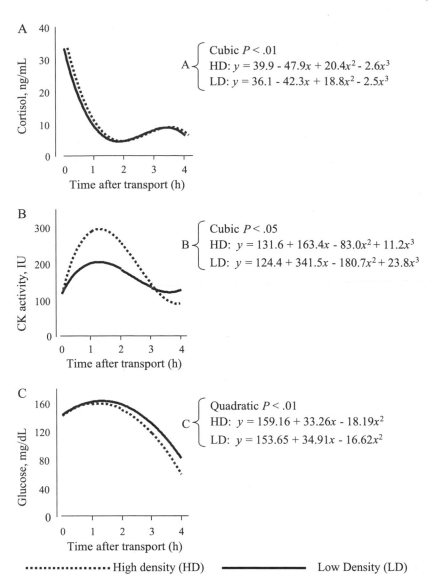

Fig. 2 Regression curves showing (A) cubic trends in plasma cortisol concentrations, (B) cubic trends in plasma creatine kinase activities (CK), and (C) quadratic trends in plasma glucose concentrations with time after transportation in Spanish goats. (Modified from Ref. 3.) (*View this art in color at www.dekker.com.*)

of mortalities in goats under feedlot conditions are salmonellosis and bronchopneumonia.[2] Glucocorticoids that are released during stress are known to suppress the immune system. There is evidence that increasing antioxidant status in goats can have beneficial effects on their immune function, particularly during stress.[10]

Common health problems in goats include coccidiosis and gastrointestinal nematodes (GIN). Parasite management is particularly challenging, because goats quickly develop resistance to common anthelmintics and become reinfected easily when they overgraze the same pasture. However, GIN load does not seem to influence plasma cortisol and glucose concentrations in goats.

STRESS AND MUSCLE METABOLISM

Preslaughter stress in animals causes release of catecholamines and depletion of muscle glycogen, which influence the extent of postmortem glycolysis and pH decline in muscles. Severe stress in goats prior to harvesting may result in inferior meat quality. Short-term preslaughter stress causes reduction in muscle glycogen levels in young goats, but not in older ones (Fig. 3), although increases in circulating cortisol and glucose concentrations are noticeably less in young goats compared to older ones.[11] Muscle glycogen concentrations and pH values during the immediate postmortem period may indicate the

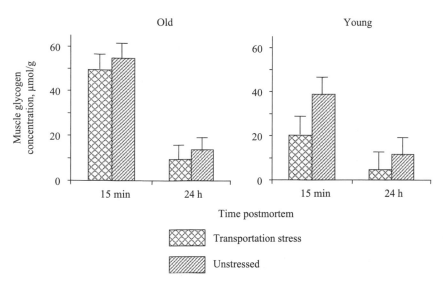

Fig. 3 Effects of short-term preslaughter transportation stress on glycogen concentrations (stressor treatment, $P<0.05$; age of goat, $P<0.01$) in longissimus muscle samples from male goat carcasses ($n=14$ per stress treatment at each sampling time). (Modified from Ref. [11].) (*View this art in color at www.dekker.com.*)

intensity of preslaughter stress the animals may have gone through.

CONCLUSIONS

Understanding the social dynamics of a herd and the behavioral repertoire of individual goats is the key to improving animal well-being and productivity. Conditioning goats with positive reinforcement for routine laboratory procedures will facilitate easy handling with minimum animal stress. Environmental enrichment with cost-effective materials may improve welfare and productivity of goats in intensive management conditions. Goats are highly social animals; therefore, isolating an individual animal from its group will increase stress levels, particularly if it is not able to maintain visual contacts with other goats. Long journeys under adverse weather conditions not only increase stress in goats, but also increase economic losses due to live-weight loss, susceptibility to infections, and mortality. Dietary antioxidant supplementation may help goats combat the negative effects of corticosteroid release on immune function during stress. Mixing different social groups, combined with feed deprivation, is likely to increase agonistic encounters and bruising in goats. Preslaughter stress in goats also depletes muscle glycogen levels and can negatively affect meat quality.

REFERENCES

1. Lu, C.D. Effects of heat stress on goat production. Small Rumin. Res. **1989**, *2*, 151–162.

2. Flint, M.; Murray, P.J. Lot-fed goats—The advantages of using an enriched environment. Austr. J. Exp. Agric. **2001**, *41*, 473–476.

3. Kannan, G.; Terrill, T.H.; Kouakou, B.; Gazal, O.S.; Gelaye, S.; Amoah, E.A.; Samake, S. Transportation of goats: Effects on physiological stress responses and live weight loss. J. Anim. Sci. **2000**, *78*, 1450–1457.

4. Lickliter, R.E.; Heron, J.R. Recognition of mother by newborn goats. Appl. Anim. Behav. Sci. **1984**, *12*, 187–192.

5. Rout, P.K.; Mandal, A.; Singh, L.B.; Roy, R. Studies on behavioral patterns in Jamunapari goats. Small Rumin. Res. **2002**, *43*, 185–188.

6. Kannan, G.; Terrill, T.H.; Kouakou, B.; Gelaye, S.; Amoah, E.A. Simulated preslaughter holding and isolation effects on stress responses and live weight shrinkage in meat goats. J. Anim. Sci. **2002**, *80*, 1771–1780.

7. Price, E.O.; Thos, J. Behavioral responses to short-term social isolation in sheep and goats. Appl. Anim. Ethol. **1980**, *6*, 331–339.

8. Lager, K. Apparatus and technique for conditioning goats to repeated blood collection. Lab. Anim. **1998**, *27* (3), 38–42.

9. Sanhouri, A.A.; Jones, R.S.; Dobson, H. Effects of xylazine on the stress response to transport in male goats. Br. Vet. J. **1992**, *148*, 119–128.

10. Kannan, G.; Terrill, T.H.; Kouakou, B.; Galipalli, S.; Saker, K.E.; Kircher, R.A.; Gelaye, S.; Gadiyaram, K.M. Physiological responses, immune function, and live weight shrinkage due to simulated preslaughter stress in goats fed a diet (Tasco) containing seaweed extract. J. Anim. Sci. **2002**, *80* (1), 293.

11. Kannan, G.; Kouakou, B.; Terrill, T.; Gelaye, S. Endocrine, blood metabolite, and meat quality changes in goats as influenced by short-term, preslaughter stress. J. Anim. Sci. **2003**, *81*, 1499–1507.

Goats: Breeding and Genetics

Jackson M. Dzakuma
Prairie View A&M University, Prairie View, Texas, U.S.A.

INTRODUCTION

Goats generally have a seasonal breeding cycle. The shortening hours of daylight bring about the estrous cycle in the doe. Gestation is approximately 150 days, with births occurring as the temperature becomes warmer and food more plentiful. In tropical climates goats tend to be fertile year-round. A breeding ratio of one buck to 15–20 does is recommended depending on the physical condition and age of the buck.

GENETICS

The diploid chromosome number in the goat is 60. A gene is the unit of heredity occupying a particular position (locus) on a chromosome. Alleles are different forms of a gene occupying a given locus. When alleles are the same, they are homozygous, and if different, they are heterozygous for the trait. There can be several alleles for any locus, but only two alleles can be present in any one individual (zygote). Most characters of economic importance in goats (growth rate, milk production, prolificacy, fertility) are influenced by large numbers of genes (quantitative) instead of single genes (qualitative). These characters are measurable and vary among breeds and among individuals within breeds. For such traits it is appropriate to consider the sum of the average effect of all genes (additive genetic effect) influencing the trait.

A gene does not have the same effect (value) in all individuals in which it occurs. The effect of a particular allele may differ according to the identity of the other allele at the same locus (known as dominance) and also depends on which alleles are found at other loci (epistasis). Dominance and epistasis are nonlinear genetic effects that mask the expression of the additive genetic variation. The variation within a herd can be partitioned into environmental and additive genetic variance. An animal's breeding value is its additive genetic value, and its variance constitutes the additive genetic variance. The heritability (h^2) of a trait is that proportion of the total variance that is due to additive genetic variance, and is used to predict the probable response to selection for quantitative characters.[1]

Mendelian Inheritance in Goats

There are several genetic disorders associated with characteristics found in goats, which are caused by single genes. These are summarized in Tables 1 and 2. The autosomal dominant polled gene P, causes hornlessness and its recessive (p) causes sexual abnormality in goats.[1,2] The absence of wattles and the absence of ears have been shown to be recessive characters.[2] Coat color may be important in skin and hair production (e.g., in the Red Sokoto and Cashmere goats). The order of dominance in coat color is white, red, fawn or chamois, and black, and the wild-type face pattern found in Toggenburgs is dominant to the reversed pattern known as badger face.[3]

Traditionally, genetic crosses have been used to determine the presence of alleles that code for a particular phenotype. In qualitative inheritance, only one pair of genes or a single locus is involved. Most inheritance involves multiple genes or quantitative trait loci (QTL).[4] Recent advances in molecular genetic analyses—restriction fragment length polymorphism analyses (RFLP), randomly amplified polymorphic DNA (RAPD), simple sequence repeat (SSR) microsatellites, amplification fragment length polymorphism (AFLP), and single nucleotide polymorphism (SNP) analyses—have allowed the development of a variety of DNA-based markers. With sufficiently dense genetic maps, entire genomes can be scanned for genes associated with QTL.[5] Once a QTL has been identified, populations can be tested quickly and easily for the frequency of alleles and associated phenotypes.

The Tennessee Stiff-legged or the Myotonic goat has a condition called myotonia congenita. By the sequencing of the genes of affected and nonaffected goats, a single nucleotide polymorphism that caused an amino acid change in the CIC-1 protein was found.[6] This change reduced the effectiveness of the channel to remove chloride ions. Through molecular genotyping for the CIC-1 gene, Sayre et al.[7] have identified a positive association with the single nucleotide polymorphism and the myotonia phenotype. The identification of this genotype/phenotype relationship allows for an easy test for the presence of myotonia in goats and may allow for more extensive analyses of the effects of myotonia on carcass and performance traits.

Encyclopedia of Animal Science
DOI: 10.1081/E-EAS 120025008

Table 1 Cause and effect of qualitative characters in goats

Dominant phenotypes		Recessive phenotype	Effect
PP	Pp		Polledness, due to dominant autosomal gene P.
		pp	The P gene has a recessive masculinizing effect with complete penetrance in females and incomplete penetrance in males.[1,2]
WW	Ww		Presence of wattles. Does with wattles were 13% more prolific than ww does.[2] Note: polled females with wattles (PPPp+WWWw) were 25.6% more prolific than the average.[2]
		ww	Absence of wattles.
EE	Ee		Presence of long or normal ears.
		ee	Absence of ears, or "gopher ears." The American La Mancha breed.[2]
CC			White coat color (Saanen).
	Cc		Roan, red, or chamoisee coat color (Saanen).
		cc	Black or dark coat color.

(From Refs. 1 and 2.)

Sayre et al.[7] discussed in detail genotyping methodologies and strategies, marker analyses, and lactation-related genes in goats. Using various sequencing methods and protein analyses, alleles in caseins and beta-lactoglobulins have been identified. Once the different alleles were identified, PCR-RFLP procedures were used to determine differences in phenotype associated with the presence of the various alleles. Differences in goat milk casein have been implicated as a possible explanation for an apparent lower allergic response to goat milk consumption compared to cow milk. A discussion on scrapie resistivity/susceptibility and identification using genotyping protocol is also provided.[7]

Genetic identification/relationship

The domestic goat (*Capra hircus*) may have evolved from the bezoar (*Capra aegagrus*). Differences in the cytochrome *b* gene of mitochondrial DNA were used to cluster the bezoar and domestic goat together, while the markhor (*Capra falconeri*) was clustered separately.[8] Further, the genetic diversity of several breeds of goats in several locations has been determined. Variations in allele frequencies in red blood cell groups and blood proteins were used to determine the genetic distance between breeds in France.[9] In Switzerland, PCR amplification of 20 bovine microsatellites on 20–40 unrelated animals per

Table 2 Mode of action of gene P according to genetic sex and genotypes

	Genotypes	
PP (polled homozygote)	**Pp (polled heterozygote)**	**pp (horned)**
Genetic females (Karyotype XX)		
All sterile	All fertile	All fertile
Sterile females	Advantage of prolificacy of polled Pp	
Hermaphrodites	goats (6–7%) over horned goats	
Pseudomales with testicular hypoplasia	Favorable maternal effect of polled Pp mothers on weight of their kids (5–6%) higher, from 1 to 7 months	
Genetic males (Karyotype XY)		
(1-b) fertile males	All fertile	All fertile
b males with obstructed epididymal ducts	Males partly or completely sterile	
unilateral and bilateral blocking		
Coefficient of hyperprolificacy of fertile homozygous		
males PP vs. polled Pp and horned pp males, r=1.080		

(From Ref. 2.)

breed revealed that all Swiss goat breeds were closely related and there was significant distance between these breeds and the ibex, bezoar, and Creole breeds.[10]

Quantitative Inheritance

Selection implies a differential reproductive rate. Some animals are allowed to reproduce extensively, some limitedly, and some not at all. We select superior animals, hoping that at least some of the mean superiority of the parents will be demonstrated by the offspring. The h^2 is used to predict genetic progress between the selected and nonselected populations and should be appropriately used to make predictions in the environment within which it was calculated. The genotype of an individual is determined at fertilization, but the estimate of h^2 that is used to predict the genotype is influenced by temporary environmental effects, interactions between genotype and environment, and other factors, including age.

Goats contribute significantly to the food resources of the world. Producers around the world will continue to seek genetics that they believe will increase their financial value and their existing genetic resources. The traditional mating systems—pure breeding, artificial insemination (AI, which has been used in dairy goats), crossbreeding, development of synthetics, and variations thereof—have been used with some success in developing countries.[11] Genetic progress in goat breeding will be realized when these mating systems are used judiciously, by matching goat genotypes with the environments and in tandem with modern genetic tools. Further readings on topics discussed are provided in Refs. [1–3,8].

CONCLUSION

Genetic progress in applying traditional mating systems has been slow. Molecular genetic techniques will allow identification and use of single genes with major effects in goat breeding. For the effects of identified major genes to be manifested in goat populations, they will have to be applied through quantitative breeding schemes. The future of goat breeding will depend heavily on all areas discussed. The discovery of various gene alleles for compounds regulating economically important traits will improve breeders' ability to manage and select goats tailored for the producers' market, with optimum potential income.

REFERENCES

1. Devendra, C.; Burns, M. *Goat Production in the Tropics*; Commonwealth Agricultural Bureaux, 1983; 183 pp.
2. Ricordeau, G. Genetics: Breeding Plans. In *Goat Production*; Gall, C., Ed.; Academic Press: London, 1981; 111–169.
3. Berge, S. Geitefarger. [Color in Goats]. In *Meldinger fra Norges Landbrukshogskole*; 1966; Vol. 45 (3), 24 pp. Anim. Breed Abstr. 35: 501.
4. Womack, J.E. The cattle gene map. ILAR J. **1998**, *39*, 153–159.
5. O'Brien, S.J.; Menotti-Raymond, M.; Murphy, W.J.; Nash, W.G.; Wienberg, J.; Stanyon, R.; Copeland, N.G.; Jenkins, N.A.; Womack, J.E.; Marshall-Graves, J.A. The promise of comparative genomics in mammals. Science **1999**, *286*, 458–481.
6. Beck, C.L.; Fahlke, C.; George, A.L., Jr. Molecular basis for decreased muscle chloride conductance in the Myotonic goat. Proc. Natl. Acad. Sci. **1996**, *93*, 11248–11252.
7. Sayre, B.L.; Tritschler, J.P.; Minouna, J.H. Adding to the Knowledge and Practice of Goat Production Through Molecular Genotyping. In *Proc. Scientific Conf. Goats*; Dzakuma, J.M., Risch, E., Johnson, B.M., Eds.; Prairie View A&M University: Prairie View, TX, 2002; 19–33.
8. Mannen, H.; Nagata, Y.; Tsuji, S. Mitochondrial DNA reveal that domestic goats (*Capra hircus*) are genetically affected by two subspecies of bezoar (*Capra aegagrus*). Biochem. Genet. **2001**, *39*, 145–154.
9. Pepin, L.; Nguyen, T.C. Blood groups and protein polymorphism in five goat breeds (*Capra hircus*). Anim. Genet. **1994**, *25*, 333–336.
10. Saitbekova, N.; Gaillard, C.; Oberxer-Ruff, G.; Dolf, G. Genetic diversity in Swiss goat breeds based on microsatellite analysis. Anim. Genet. **1999**, *30*, 36–41.
11. Rewe, T.O.; Ogore, P.B.; Kahi, A.K. Integrated Goat Production Projects in Kenya: Impact on Genetic Improvement, Proc. 7th World Congr. Genet. Livest. Prod., Montpellier, France, 2002. Comm #25-19.
12. *Goat Production*; Gall, C., Ed.; Academic Press: London, 1981; 619 pp.

Goats: Breeds

Jackson M. Dzakuma
Barbara McBride Johnson
Prairie View A&M University, Prairie View, Texas, U.S.A.

INTRODUCTION

The goat (*Capra hircus*) was domesticated in mountainous areas of southwestern Asia in the 7th to 9th centuries B.C. The goat was the earliest domesticated agricultural animal, and it has made a significant impact on the supply of meat and fiber for the world economy.

BREEDS

A breed is an interbreeding population within a livestock species. There are several breeds of goats. The literature is replete with references to their origins[1,2] and their descriptions,[3–6] and Mason[7] has provided a dictionary listing different goat breeds or types. The agriculturalist might prefer a classification based on products such as meat, milk, fiber, and skin. All goats, however, produce these products to a greater or lesser extent. International conferences on goats have been held since 1982 (Tucson, Arizona, 1982;[8] Brasilia, Brazil, 1987;[9] New Delhi, India, 1992;[10] Beijing, China, 1996;[11] Tours, France, 2000[12]). Conference proceedings provide invaluable resources on goat production from around the world. The October 1980 issue of the *Journal of Dairy Science* [Vol. 63(10)] was devoted to dairy goats. The International Goat Research Center at Prairie View A&M University recently hosted a scientific conference on goats that consolidated current goat research knowledge.[13]

Meat Breeds

Boer goat

The Boer goat of South Africa was derived principally from Hottentot stock that inhabited the semiarid country north of the Cape Peninsula.[3] It tends to show the Roman nose and long ears of the Nubian, weighing up to 90 kg for bucks and 60 kg for does. Since the 1920s, much effort has gone into improvement through selective breeding for meat production. There is a preferred color pattern of reddish-brown head and neck, with white body and legs.[6]

The Boer goat was introduced into the United States in 1993. The growth and carcass characteristics of the Boer were appreciated by goat producers and, as a result, many producers started grading up their stock to the Boer. This has resulted in the decline in numbers of purebred Spanish, Angora, and Tennessee Stiff-Legged goats.

Spanish goat

The term Spanish goat is used in the southwestern United States to refer to a goat maintained primarily for meat production from brush or browse on ranges of the Edwards Plateau of Texas.[3] Most Spanish goats are of the same origin as the Mexican Criollo but show Nubian and Toggenburg influences. They are variable in appearance and performance, as most have evolved by natural selection.[5] The Criollo breed is of Spanish origin, being derived from goats introduced by traders in the 16th century, and is widely scattered in Central America. It is mainly black or brown in color with scimitar (convex)-shaped horns. The average height at the shoulders is 75 cm for males and 65 cm for females, and live weight is 40–60 kg.

Tennessee Stiff-Legged goat

The Tennessee Stiff-Legged breed, sometimes called the Tennessee wooden-leg, nervous goat, scared goat, fainting goat, fall-down goat, or myotonic goat, was reportedly first brought to Texas from Giles County in central Tennessee.[14] Mason[7] lists the breed as imported from Asia, possibly India, in the early 1800s. The breed has a condition called myotonia congenita. This disease state is not detrimental to the production of this breed, which is known for its heavy muscling (Fig. 1). Lipicky and Bryant[15] have implicated the role of the chloride channel-1 (CIC-1) gene in the disorder.

Dairy Breeds

Alpine or the French Alpine

The Alpine breed originated in the French Alps and has since been transplanted to many places in the world. The Alpine comes in a wide variety of colors and patterns.[3,7]

Encyclopedia of Animal Science
DOI: 10.1081/E-EAS 120019657

Fig. 1 Tennessee Stiff-Legged or Myotonic goats. This breed is threatened.

Nubian

The Nubian breed is of North African origin. The more common type referred to as the Anglo Nubian had its origin in Great Britain when domestic does of Swiss origin were mated to bucks imported from Africa and India. Through selective breeding, the modern Anglo Nubian was produced. The Nubian looks different from all other breeds, having short, sleek hair, long drooping ears, and a Roman nose. The Nubian does not give as much milk (average 660 kg/yr; Table 1) as the Swiss breeds; however, it produces milk with the highest butterfat content. It tends to be meatier than the Swiss breeds. Colors vary and include a uniquely spotted type similar to the Appaloosa horse.[3]

Saanen

The Saanen breed is derived from the Saanen Valley in Canton Berne, Switzerland. In the 1890s, several thousand heads were taken out of this valley and spread throughout Europe. The Saanen is one of the largest of the Swiss breeds. The hair is white or cream in color. The ears are erect, and the nose is straight or dished slightly. Both bucks and does may have beards, but the buck beards are fuller. Saanens have been acclaimed widely for their milking ability.[3]

Toggenburg

The Toggenburg breed also originated in the Swiss Alps and is the oldest officially recognized breed of dairy goats. Does are shorter and more compact than in other breeds. They are angular and show considerable width and depth. The ears are erect, the muzzle is deep and wide, and the nose is dished. Beards and tassels are common.[6] The color is a shade of brown with white lining on the ears, white facial stripes, white legs, and a white triangle at the base of the tail.

La Mancha

The American La Mancha is the youngest breed and the only totally American dairy breed, with the registry started in 1959. Short-eared Spanish goats living in herds on the West Coast were bred to top sires of other breeds in the 1920s and 1930s. The original breeders envisioned a thrifty milk goat, compact like the Toggenburg, but very broad in the chest with deep open ribbing. The head should be broad with a powerful muzzle and a flat face with "gopher ears," i.e., nonexistent or very short.[3]

Oberhasli

Oberhasli is a medium-sized, vigorous breed. These goats originated in Switzerland and are also known as Oberhasli-Brienz (from Bernese, Oberland, Switzerland).[7] The correct markings are chamoisee, with pure black acceptable in does. A few Oberhasli were imported into the United States as early as 1906 but were considered part of the Alpines until 1980. Shelton[3] described one of the color patterns of the Alpine breed as chamoisee, a blackish or brownish body with black feet and legs, a black dorsal stripe, and often a black face.

Table 1 Production and phenotypic characteristics of U.S. dairy breeds

Breed	No. of herds (does)[a]	Avg. yearly milk production[a] (kg)	Doe mature weight[b] (kg)	Doe height at shoulders[b] (cm)
Alpine	79 (1,860)	920	61	76
Nubian	93 (1,118)	660	64	76
Saanen	38 (797)	865	64	76
Toggenburg	26 (334)	860	55	66
La Mancha	37 (674)	772	59	71
Oberhasli	14 (152)	720	55	71

[a]Based on 2002 USDA DHI herd records. (www.aipl.arsusda.gov.)
[b]Minimum breed standards per ADGA. (www.adga.org.)

Fig. 2 Angora goats. This breed is threatened.

Fiber

The predominant fiber-producing goat in the United States is the Angora or mohair goat. It is lop-eared and spirally horned in both sexes. The fleece has been developed by an increase in the number of the secondary fibers and a reduction in the diameter and medullation of the primary fibers (Fig. 2). The breed originated in the dry plateau of Central Anatolia (Turkey) and takes its name from Ankara. It accounts for about one-quarter of the goats in Turkey.[5,6] Angora goats were imported into the United States from Turkey during 1849–1976 and from South Africa in 1925–1926. They are confined to the Edwards Plateau in Texas. The Angora goat is a small animal, shoulder height about 54 cm and average body weight about 27 kg. The color is almost always white, with a fleece of long white lustrous ringlets. They are annual breeders, usually producing a single kid.

OTHER WORLD GENETIC RESOURCES

There is a vast array of goat genetic resources in the world.[3–7] Some of these goats are used elsewhere in the world for meat production: The Pygmy, actually called the West African Dwarf or Fouta Djallon goat, is adapted to humid tropical environments and is resistant to trypanosomiasis. It has been recognized as a breed in the United States, where it is used as a pet or a laboratory animal.[3] The Galla or Somali goat in East Africa is also used for meat. The Damascus and the Black Bedouin goats in the Middle East are used for milk production. The Jamnapari or Etawah goat in India and Southeast Asia is used for both meat and milk production, as are the Nubian Sahel, in arid sub-Saharan Africa, and the Bhuj of Northeast Brazil. The skins on the Red Sokoto or Maradi breed, maintained pure in the Sokoto province of Nigeria, are very valuable in the production of Morocco leather, and also contribute meat to the poor. The Mubende of Uganda and the Black Bengal of Northeast India and Bangladesh also contribute skins and meat. Some goats are used exclusively for fiber: The Pashmina or Cashmere Goats, found predominantly in mountainous areas (altitudes 3000–5000 m) of Central Asia, produce the fine "down" fiber. This list is by no means exhaustive. The available goat genetic resources of the world are worth noting so that goat breeders can mold breeds and populations within breeds to meet the array of human needs.[16]

CONCLUSION

Brief introductions to some goat breeds have been given. The classification of goats is based on products such as meat, milk, fiber, and the skins they produce. The following web sites provide useful information on goats: www.aipl.arsusda.gov and www.sheepandgoat.com/breeds.html.

REFERENCES

1. Zeuner, F.E. *A History of Domesticated Animals*; Hutchinson: London, 1963; 560.
2. Epstein, H. *The Origin of Domestic Animals of Africa*; Africana Publishing Corporation: New York, 1971; Vol. 1 & 2. Revised in collaboration with I. L. Mason, Vol. I: xii+573pp, Vol. II: xi+719 pp.
3. Shelton, M. Reproduction and breeding of goats. J. Dairy Sci. **1978**, *61*, 994–1010.
4. *Goat Production*; Gall, C., Ed.; Academic Press: London, 1981; 111–169.
5. Mason, I.L. Breeds. In *Goat Production*; Gall, C., Ed.; Academic Press: London, 1981; 57–110.
6. Devendra, C.; Burns, M. *Goat Production in the Tropics*; Commonwealth Agricultural Bureaux, 1983; 183.
7. Mason, I.L. *A World Dictionary of Livestock Breeds, Types and Varieties*, 4th Ed.; CAB International, 1996; 91–114.
8. International Goat Association. Proc. III Intl. Conf. Goat Prod. & Disease, Tucson, Arizona, 1987.
9. International Goat Association. Proc. IV Intl. Conf. Goats, Brasilia, Brazil, 1987.
10. International Goat Association. Proc. V Intl. Conf Goats, New Delhi, India, 1992.
11. International Goat Association. Proc. VI Intl. Conf. Goats, Beijing, China, 1996.
12. International Goat Association. Proc. VII Intl. Conf Goats, Tours, France, 2000.
13. Proc. Scientific Conf. on Goats. Prairie View A&M University, Prairie View, Texas; Dzakuma, J.M., Risch, E., Johnson, B.M., Eds.; 2002; 232.
14. Lush, J.L. Nervous goats. J. Heredity **1930**, *21*, 243–247.
15. Lipicky, R.J.; Bryant, S.H. Sodium, potassium, and chloride fluxes from normal goats and goats with hereditary myotonia. J. Gen. Physiol. **1996**, *50*, 89–111.
16. Blackburn, H.D. Conservation of Goat Genetic Resources. In *Proc. Scientific Conf. on Goats*; Dzakuma, J.M., Risch, E., Johnson, B.M., Eds.; Prairie View A&M University, Prairie View, Texas, 2002; 7–18.

Goats: Health Management

Lionel J. Dawson

Oklahoma State University, Stillwater, Oklahoma, U.S.A.

INTRODUCTION

Herd health programs are usually tailored to fit individual herds. They depend on the herd size and the production goals of the owner. Past management practices contribute significantly to disease problems. Goat husbandry is very labor-intensive, and most people who maintain herds earn their living away from the farm. The majority of the diseases associated with goats could be prevented with good management, with emphasis on a good vaccination program and biosecurity. Control of common infections and metabolic diseases of goats is addressed in this article.

VACCINATION

Basic vaccination programs for goats include vaccinations against *Clostriduim perfringens* types C and D and *Clostridium tetani*.[1,3,6] There are multivalent clostridial vaccines, including those against black leg, malignant edema, and bacillary hemoglobinuria, used in goats. These are unusual diseases in goats, and vaccination to prevent them is usually not economically justified. Vaccines against contagious ecthyma, caseous lymphadenitis, and *Chlamydia* are incorporated in the vaccination program if there is a need in that particular herd.[1–3,5]

INFECTIOUS DISEASES

Infectious diseases of goats are addressed in detail elsewhere.[1–8] Prominent infectious diseases of goats include caseous lymphadenitis, tetanus, enterotoxemia, caprine arthritis encephalitis (CAE), contagious ecthyma (sore mouth), Johne's disease, and pinkeye. Causative agents, diagnoses, and control measures for each of these infectious diseases are summarized in Table 1. Vaccination schedules are described in Table 2.

Abortions in Goats Due to Infectious Agents

The most common causes of infectious abortions are *Toxoplasma, Chlamydia, Salmonella, Brucella melitensis, Listeria, Leptospira,* and *Coxiella.* Transmission is mainly through ingestion of the microorganisms or oocysts through feed and water, inhalation, conjunctiva, skin, and mucosal abrasions. Q-fever caused by *Coxiella burnetti* can be spread through tick bites. Most of the abortions are midterm to late term.[10] Methods for preventing and controlling infectious abortions in goats are summarized in Table 1.

COMMON METABOLIC DISEASES

Metabolic diseases of goats are addressed in detail elsewhere.[1,3–5,7] Common metabolic diseases of goats include acidosis, parturient paresis (hypocalcemia, milk fever), polioencephalomalacia, pregnancy toxemia (ketosis), and floppy kid syndrome. Causes, diagnosis, and control measures for each of these diseases are summarized in Table 3.

CONCLUSION

The goal of a herd health program is to improve the goat herd's productivity through general husbandry, nutritional management, parasite control, vaccination, and environmental management. The level of management determines the success and sustainability of an operation. The majority of goat diseases can be prevented with good nutritional and herd health management.

REFERENCES

1. Smith, M.C.; Sherman, D.M. *Goat Medicine*; Lea and Febiger: Malvern, PA, 1994.
2. Olcott, M.B. Caprine Herd Health. In *Proceedings of Goat Field Day*; Langston University, 1995.
3. Pugh, D.G. *Sheep and Goat Medicine*; WB Saunders: Philadelphia, 2002.
4. Dawson, L.J. General Care of Goats. In *Proceedings of Goat Field Day*; Langston University, 1998.
5. Mobini, S. Herd Health Management Practices for Goats. In *Proceedings of Goat Field Day*; Langston University, 1999.
6. Dawson, L.J. Caprine Herd Health Program. In *Proceedings of Goat Field Day*; Langston University, 2001.
7. Smith, M.C. Small Ruminants for the Mixed Animal

Encyclopedia of Animal Science
DOI: 10.1081/E-EAS 120019658

Table 1 Causative agents, clinical signs, diagnosis, and control measures for infectious diseases of goats

Cause	Clinical signs	Diagnosis	Control
Caseous lymphadenitis is caused by *Corynebacterium pseudotuberculosis*.	Peripheral swelling of the superficial lymph nodes. Internal lymph nodes and organs could be involved. Decreased body weight and milk production, lower reproductive efficiency	Presence of a firm to a slightly fluctuant swelling in the location of the lymph nodes	Separate and isolate the affected animals. Proper sanitation of the pens, feeders, water troughs, and equipment. Use individual hypodermic needles. Purchase animals from a noninfected herd. Replacement animals need to be quarantined for at least 60 days. Kids from infected animals should be removed at birth, raised separately on milk replacers or pasteurized milk. Cull animals with multiple abscesses, chronic respiratory disease, and wasting disease. Vaccination could be considered if other methods have failed
Tetanus is caused by *C. tetani*, which produces spores. These spores release toxin, which affects the nervous system.	Stiffness, difficulty in moving or walking, "saw horse" stance, easily excited to touch or noise, "lock jaw" or difficulty in opening the mouth, salivation, food accumulated in the mouth, prolapse of the third eyelid, seizures or convulse periodically, and later death	Clinical signs, presence of deep wounds or history of castration, disbudding, kidding, etc. Confirm the diagnosis by sending tissues or blood to the lab.	Vaccination, surgical procedures such as castration should be carried out in a clean and hygienic manner. Wounds should be kept clean. Proper sanitation of the pens, lots, feeders, etc.
Enterotoxemia is caused by *C. perfringens* types C and D, which produce toxins.	Type C affects very young kids and adults with blood-tinged diarrhea, anemia, and later death. Type D affects young kids and is mainly seen as sudden death. Rise in temperature, abdominal pain, depressed, laying down, convulsions, paddling, head thrown straight over the back, and later death. May not have diarrhea. Chronic form seen in the adults; they experience listlessness, off feed, weight loss, intermittent episodes of pasty or loose feces, and milk production down if lactating	Clinical signs, necropsy, isolating the toxin, impression smears from the intestine, and improvement with intravenous antitoxin	Vaccination

Disease and cause	Clinical signs	Diagnosis	Management
Caprine arthritis encephalitis is caused by a retro virus.	Young kids: ataxic and weak in the rear legs. Cannot get up and later die from affecting the nervous system. Adults: swollen joints, arthritis, and contracted joints. Udder gets hard with no mastitis, and decrease in milk production	Clinical signs, serology, and necropsy	Test and cull. Remove the kids from their affected mother. Heat-treat the colostrum. Raise the kids on pasteurized milk or milk replacer. Kids should be separated from the adults at birth
Contagious ecthyma, or sore mouth, is caused by a parapox virus.	Thick scabby sores are seen on the lips, gums, face, ears, coronary band, scrotum, teats, or vulva	Clinical signs, electron microscopy, or immunologic techniques to demonstrate antigen in the scabs	Vaccine is a live virus vaccine
Johne's disease is caused by a bacterium Mycobacterium paratuberculosis.	Loss of weight, rough hair coat, decrease in milk production, may or may not have diarrhea. Usually seen in animals 3 to 5 years old	Clinical signs, fecal culture, serology, and lymph node biopsy	Proper sanitation and management of the kidding pens is very essential. Kids removed immediately after kidding and raised on heat-treated colostrum, pasteurized milk, or milk replacer. Blood test every 6 months and remove the affected animals. Kids should not commingle with the adults until they have kidded. In Norway, this disease has been controlled by vaccination
Infectious kerato conjunctivitis, or pinkeye, in goats is caused by Mycoplasma conjunctivae or Chlamydia psittaci.	Acute onset, watery eyes, redness of the eye, swelling of the eyelids, photophobia, cloudy cornea with later forming ulcers	Clinical signs	Prevent dusty environment and feed. Proper isolation and quarantine measures for your replacements
Abortions in goats due to infectious agents: Toxoplasma gondii; C. psittaci; Salmonellosis (Salmonella typhimurium and Salmonella dublin); Brucella melitensis; Listeria monocytogenes; Leptospirosis (Leptospira icterohaemorrhagiae, L. grippotyphosa, L. pomona).	Abortions, still births, and birth of weak infected kids. Systemic effects may be seen in the doe with salmonellosis, brucellosis, listeria, and leptospirosis	Abortion, serology, and histopathology of the fetus and placenta	Proper sanitation, rodent control, clean feed and water supply. Isolating pregnant animals. Avoid overcrowding and stressing of the does. Prevent exposure to barn cats. Do not feed spoiled and poorly fermented silage. Vaccinate for Chlamydia; B. melitensis is controlled by test and slaughter policy

Table 2 Vaccination schedule for infectious diseases of goats

Period	Time to vaccinate	Disease/causative agent	Booster
Kids	2, 4, and 8 weeks	*C. perfringens* C&D *C. tetani*—toxoid	Annual
Kids	4 to 6 weeks	Contagious ecthyma (if a herd problem)	Annual or 2 months before the show season
Kids	8 and 12 weeks	Caseous lymphadenitis	Annual
Prebreeding			
Doe	30 days prior to breeding	*Chlamydia* (abortions)	Annual
Bucks	30 days prior to breeding	*C. perfringens* C & D *C. tetani*—toxoid	Annual
Gestation			
Doe	30 days prior to kidding	*C. perfringens* C & D *C. tetani*—toxoid	Annual

Table 3 Causes, clinical signs, diagnosis, and control measures for metabolic diseases of goats

Disease	Cause	Clinical signs	Diagnosis	Control
Acidosis	Increased grain in the diet	Depressed, off feed, bloat, grinding teeth, diarrhea, and dehydration	Clinical signs. Rumen pH drops below 5	Gradual increase of grain in the diet
Milk fever	Hypocalcemia	Mild bloat, off feed, ataxia, down, hypothermia, "S-" curved neck, pupils dilated, and muscle twitching	Close to or 1–3 weeks after kidding. Mainly seen in dairy goats. Response to intravenous calcium therapy	Proper nutrition during the dry period. Cation/anion [(Na+K)/(cl+S)] balance during the last month of pregnancy
Polioencephalomalacia	Thiamine deficiency or low availability of thiamine	Loss of appetite, depressed, no rumen motility, head pressing, aimless walking, blindness, muscle tremors, and hyperexcitable	Symptoms. Response to thiamine treatment	Proper nutrition, good quality roughage, less stress, low sulfates in the ration, and early diagnosis
Pregnancy toxemia	Low-energy diet or low availability of energy during the last trimester of pregnancy	Weak, depressed, poor muscle tone, and down	Symptoms. Does carrying multiple fetuses	Proper nutrition and increased energy intake during the last 6 weeks of pregnancy
Floppy kid syndrome	Metabolic acidosis Cause unknown.	Depressed, weak, ataxic, and cannot suckle	Response to bicarbonate orally or i.v.	Supportive care. Correction of electrolyte imbalance

Practitioners. In *Proceedings of the 70th Western Veterinary Conference*, 1998.
8. Piontkowski, M.D.; Shivvers, D.W. Evaluation of a commercially available vaccine against *Corynebacterium pseudotuberculosis* for use in sheep. JAVMA **1998**, *212* (11), 1765–1768.

9. Bowen, J.S. A Practitioner's Approach to Caprine Arthritis Encephalitis. In *Proceedings of Goat Field Day*; Langston University, 1995.
10. Dawson, L.J. Infectious Abortions in Goats. In *Goat Newsletter*; E (kika) de la Garza Institute for Goat Research: Spring, 2002.

Goats: Nutrition Management

Tilahun Sahlu
Arthur Goetsch
Langston University, Langston, Oklahoma, U.S.A.

INTRODUCTION

Currently, two widely used goat nutrition management recommendations are those of the National Research Council (NRC) and the Agriculture and Food Research Council (AFRC). However, those recommendations were, in most instances, obtained by averaging determinations from a relatively small number of reports or extrapolated from experimentation with other ruminant species. Hence, recently a large database of treatment mean observations from available goat feeding and nutrition reports in the literature was constructed and used to develop equations for prediction of energy and protein requirements by regression analyses. This work is described in a special issue of the journal, *Small Ruminant Research* (Volume 53, Number 3), published by Elsevier Science, and some findings are highlighted here.

ENERGY

Recently Determined Requirement Recommendations

Metabolizable energy (ME) requirements of nonlactating goats were determined by regressing ME intake (MEI) against body weight (BW) change or average daily gain (ADG). Requirements of ME for maintenance (ME_m) and gain (ME_g) of suckling goats were 485 kJ/kg $BW^{0.75}$ and 13.4 kJ/g ADG, respectively.[3] The ME_m values were 489, 580, and 489 kJ/kg $BW^{0.75}$ and the ME_g values were 23.1, 23.1, and 19.8 kJ/g ADG for growing meat (~50% Boer), dairy (selected for milk production), and indigenous or local goats, respectively.[3] The ME_m and ME_g for mature goats (indigenous and dairy) were 462 kJ/kg $BW^{0.75}$ and 28.5 kJ/kg $BW^{0.75}$, respectively.[3] Because ME_m for growing goats was similar between meat and indigenous (from weaning to 1.5 years of age) goats and ME_g for mature goats did not differ between indigenous and dairy goats, Sahlu et al.[4] suggested an ME_m of 462 kJ/kg $BW^{0.75}$ and an ME_g of 28.5 kJ/kg $BW^{0.75}$ for mature meat goats. The ME_m of mature Angora goats from multiple regression analysis (0 tissue gain and clean fiber

growth) was 473 kJ/kg $BW^{0.75}$; ME requirements of Angora goats for tissue gain and clean fiber growth were 37.2 and 157 kJ/g, respectively.[5] Based on previous findings,[3] Luo et al.[5] suggested that for growing Angora goats, an ME_m 5% greater than that for mature Angoras could be assumed. These estimates are pertinent to animals on constant planes of nutrition near maintenance or above, in a thermoneutral confinement environment, and without a significant parasite burden. In addition, because it was not possible to determine expressions for different genders, Sahlu et al.[4] suggested that, based on NRC recommendations,[6] the aforementioned ME_m could be decreased by 7.5% for wethers and doelings and increased by 7.5% for intact males.

A factorial approach was used to determine ME requirements for lactation by goats via two methods.[7] For one of the methods used, estimates of ME_m from a companion study[3] for dairy (501.3 kJ/kg $BW^{0.75}$) and other goat biotypes (422.7 kJ/kg $BW^{0.75}$) were derived by adjusting ME_m of growing goats for the difference between mature and growing goats. When BW increased, ME intake was adjusted for tissue accretion (efficiency = 0.75) to derive dietary ME used in milk secretion (ME_{l-d}). Milk yield was corrected to 4% fat [FCM; MJ/kg = 1.4694 + (0.4025 × % milk fat)]. For does decreasing in BW, FCM from the diet (FCM_d) was estimated by adjusting for use of mobilized tissue energy (23.9 kJ/g; efficiency = 0.84). Based on a no-intercept regression (ME_{l-d} against FCM_d), ME_{l-d} was 5224 kJ/kg FCM, corresponding to efficiency of ME use for lactation of 0.59.

Other Considerations

Sahlu et al.[4] proposed a system to predict the grazing activity energy cost based on variables that could be reasonably well assessed in the field (i.e., grazing plus walking time, diet quality, distance traveled, and terrain) that might be refined by future research. Goats are raised in many different environments, necessitating consideration of effects of acclimatization and cold and heat stress on ME_m. Effects of acclimatization may relate to indications that desert goats have lower ME_m relative to goats in other environments.[8] Although there has been less

Encyclopedia of Animal Science
DOI: 10.1081/E-EAS 120019659

research of environmental effects on nutritional needs of goats compared with cattle or sheep, the same general principles should apply.

Energy requirements of goats in the last one-third of pregnancy have not been thoroughly characterized. Thus, it is suggested that approaches such as those of AFRC[2] and Sahlu et al.,[4] based on energy needs of sheep, be employed. Doelings kidding at 1 year of age require more energy during lactation than older does for continual growth and development. To account for this need, Sahlu et al.[4] suggested the use of the mature goat ME_g of 28.5 kJ/g ADG.[3] As discussed by Nsahlai et al.,[7] it is likely that ME_m is not constant throughout lactation, but insufficient data with goats are currently available to recommend an adjustment.

PROTEIN

Recently Determined Requirement Recommendations

Based on the aforementioned database of treatment mean observations, metabolizable protein (MP) requirements of goats were estimated. To do so, the sum of ruminal outflow of feed and microbial protein digested in the small intestine (MPI) was predicted with an approach similar to that of AFRC[2] and NRC (Ref. 6, Level 1). However, because ruminal digesta passage rates in goats, relative to other ruminant species, have not been well characterized, and also passage rates vary with level of feed intake, extents of ruminal digestion of soluble and insoluble true protein potentially digested in the rumen were based on ruminal digesta passage rates (e.g., retention time) and rates of protein degradation. Fluid passage rate was determined as a function of particulate passage rate from an equation derived for cattle,[9] and particulate passage rate was estimated from an ARC[10] equation with the independent variable of level of feed intake relative to ME_m.

The MP for maintenance (MP_m) of non-Angora goats was calculated as the sum of metabolic fecal (2.67% of DM intake for diets not containing appreciable browse),[11] endogenous urinary (1.031 g/kg $BW^{0.75}$)[12] and scurf crude protein (CP) losses (0.2 g/kg $BW^{0.6}$, based on beef cattle data)[13] assuming an efficiency of MP use for maintenance protein of 1.0. To determine MP available for use in lactation (MP_l), MPI was adjusted for BW change assuming a tissue protein concentration of 14.3% and efficiency of MP use for gain of 0.59.[2] A no-intercept regression of MP_l against milk protein yield resulted in an MP requirement of 1.45 g/g milk protein, equivalent to a milk protein efficiency of 0.69.[14]

Based on linear regression of MPI against ADG, MP_m was 3.07 g/kg $BW^{0.75}$ for growing non-Angora goats; the MP requirement for gain (MP_g) was 0.290 g/g ADG for dairy and indigenous goats and 0.404 g/g ADG for meat goats.[15] The MP_m of growing and mature Angora goats from multiple regression analysis (0 tissue gain and clean fiber growth) was 3.35 g/kg $BW^{0.75}$, and MP requirements for tissue gain and clean fiber growth were 0.281 and 1.65 g/g, respectively.[5]

A factor that may limit use of MP requirements by livestock producers is lack of familiarity with MP relative to CP. However, the NRC[6] stated that the efficiency of conversion of CP to MP ranges from 0.64 to 0.80 for diets with 100% ruminally degraded CP to 100% ruminally undegraded CP, which should allow reasonable estimates of CP needs.

Other Considerations

Accuracy of MP requirement expressions may be enhanced by research with goats concerning most important factors influencing MPI, notably feedstuff CP degradation properties, fluid and particulate passage rates, and ruminally fermentable energy (RFE) concentrations in feedstuffs. Another consideration in need of attention is consumption of plants with antiquality factors, such as condensed tannins, that may impact behavior of feedstuff constituents in the digestive tract as well as maintenance protein and energy losses.

Goats appear capable of recycling relatively high amounts of nitrogen;[2] therefore, research should be conducted to determine dietary CP levels and the ratios of CP:RFE below which ruminal availability of nitrogenous compounds, rather than RFE, limit microbial growth. Finally, accuracy of ME_g and MP_g determined by regressions against ADG is influenced by tissue concentrations of energy and protein, respectively, indicating the desirability of study of the composition of tissue accreted by goats as well as mobilized.

MINERALS AND VITAMINS

Minerals and vitamins are as important in the production of goats as they are for other ruminant species. Nonetheless, as noted earlier for energy and protein, not a great deal of research has been conducted in this area with goats. The most recent thorough summary of mineral nutrition of goats is that of the AFRC.[2] For vitamins, the AFRC[2] suggested that requirement recommendations for cattle and sheep be employed rather than the use of the few available feeding trials with goats.

CONCLUSION

Recently derived recommendations of energy and protein requirements of goats, in conjunction with appropriate adjustments for particular conditions, may lead to nutrition management appropriate for desired levels and efficiencies of production by goats. Future research is required to develop more accurate nutrient requirement recommendations unique to goats.

ACKNOWLEDGMENTS

The authors acknowledge the contributions of Jun Luo, Ignatius Nsahlai, John Moore, Michael Galyean, Calvin Ferrell, Fredric Owens, and Zelpha Johnson. In addition, appreciation is expressed to the USDA 1890 Institution Capacity Building Grant Program for support (Project Number 98-38814-6214).

REFERENCES

1. NRC. *Nutrient Requirements of Goats: Angora, Dairy, and Meat Goats in Temperate and Tropical Countries*; National Academy Press: Washington, DC, 1981.
2. AFRC. *The Nutrition of Goats*; CAB International: New York, NY, 1998.
3. Luo, J.; Goetsch, A.L.; Sahlu, T.; Nsahlai, I.V.; Johnson, Z.B.; Moore, J.E.; Galyean, M.L.; Owens, F.N.; Ferrell, C.L. Prediction of metabolizable energy requirements for maintenance and gain of preweaning, growing, and mature goats. Small Rum. Res. **2004**, *in press.*
4. Sahlu, T.; Goetsch, A.L.; Luo, J.; Nsahlai, I.V.; Moore, J.E.; Galyean, M.L.; Owens, F.N.; Ferrell, C.L.; Johnson, Z.B. Estimates of energy and protein requirements of goats: Developed expressions, other considerations and future research. Small Rum. Res. **2004**, *in press.*
5. Luo, J.; Goetsch, A.L.; Nsahlai, I.V.; Sahlu, T.; Ferrell, C.L.; Owens, F.N.; Galyean, M.L.; Moore, J.E.; Johnson, Z.B. Prediction of metabolizable energy and protein requirements for maintenance, gain and fiber growth of Angora goats. Small Rum. Res. **2004**, *in press.*
6. NRC. *Nutrient Requirements of Beef Cattle, Update 2000*; National Academy Press: Washington, DC, 2000.
7. Nsahlai, I.V.; Goetsch, A.L.; Luo, J.; Moore, J.E.; Johnson, Z.B.; Sahlu, T.; Ferrell, C.L.; Galyean, M.L.; Owens, F.N. Energy requirements for lactation of goats. Small Rum. Res. **2004**, *in press.*
8. Silanikove, N. The physiological basis of adaptation in goats to harsh environments. Small Rum. Res. **2000**, *35*, 181–194.
9. Nsahlai, I.V.; Bryant, M.J.; Umunna, N.N. The utilisation of barley straw by steers: Effects of replacing urea with protein, source of protein and quantity of rumen degradable nitrogen on straw degradation, liquid and particle passage rates and intake. J. Appl. Anim. Res. **1999**, *16*, 129–146.
10. ARC. *The Nutrient Requirements of Ruminant Livestock*; Commonwealth Agricultural Bureaux: Slough, UK, 1980.
11. Moore, J.E.; Goetsch, A.L.; Luo, J.; Owens, F.N.; Galyean, M.L.; Johnson, Z.B.; Sahlu, T.; Ferrell, C.L. Prediction of fecal crude protein excretion of goats. Small Rum. Res. **2004**, *in press.*
12. Luo, J.; Goetsch, A.L.; Moore, J.E.; Johnson, Z.B.; Sahlu, T.; Ferrell, C.L.; Galyean, M.L.; Owens, F.N. Prediction of endogenous urinary nitrogen of goats. Small Rum. Res. **2004**, *in press.*
13. NRC. *Nutrient Requirements of Beef Cattle*, 6th Ed.; National Academy Press: Washington, DC, 1984.
14. Nsahlai, I.V.; Goetsch, A.L.; Luo, J.; Johnson, Z.B.; Moore, J.E.; Sahlu, T.; Ferrell, C.L.; Galyean, M.L.; Owens, F.N. Metabolizable protein requirements of lactating goats. Small Rum. Res. **2004**, *in press.*
15. Luo, J.; Goetsch, A.L; Nsahlai, I.V.; Johnson, Z.B.; Sahlu, T.; Moore, J.E.; Ferrell, C.L.; Galyean, M.L.; Owens, F.N. Protein requirements of growing goats. Small Rum. Res. **2004**, *in press.*

Grazing Practices, Soil Conservation

Thomas L. Thurow
University of Wyoming, Laramie, Wyoming, U.S.A.

INTRODUCTION

Maintenance of the soil resource is an essential element of sustainable grazing practices because the water and nutrients stored in the soil are the foundation for the production potential of the site. The type and depth of soil are a reflection of the environment in which it was formed. Large herbivores were part of most ecosystems prior to human settlement; therefore, the presence of the existing soil resource implies that grazing practices can be compatible with soil conservation. Indeed, nutrient cycling and maintenance of desirable forage composition can be enhanced by grazing practices if the use patterns are compatible with sustaining the ecological equilibrium necessary for conserving the soil resource.

Regardless of the type of grazing system that is implemented, the relationship between large herbivores and soil conservation can be anticipated by understanding the degree to which the grazing practice alters the structural characteristics of the soil (erodibility) and the amount of kinetic energy acting on the soil (erosivity). The erodibility of a soil, within a similar soil texture, varies with the organic matter content and the biological activity within the soil. The erosivity of the site is influenced by direct raindrop impact on bare soil, runoff, wind speed at the soil surface, and hoof impact. These factors that influence the erodibility and erosivity of a site can all be altered by the degree to which grazing practices affect the species composition of the vegetation community and the amount of cover that it provides.

INFLUENCE OF GRAZING ON ERODIBILITY

Soil structure is the arrangement of soil particles and intervening pore spaces. The degree to which soil particles are bound to each other (aggregation), and the stability of those aggregates when subjected to kinetic energy (associated with water, wind, and physical impacts caused by animals and machinery) determine the susceptibility of soil particles to being detached and transported off the site. The formation of soil aggregates is aided by any action that mixes the soil, thereby promoting contact between decomposing organic matter and inorganic soil particles. Soil mixing occurs as a result of burrowing by

microorganisms, insects, and mammals; root growth; wetting and drying; freezing and thawing; and soil churning by hooves or farm implements.

Herbivory has the potential to influence the composition of the vegetation community and the amount of organic matter returned to the soil. Regardless of the type of grazing system, moderate or light grazing has little impact on the vegetation community, soil structure, and erosion.[1] Heavy grazing usually results in a decrease in organic matter being available for enhancement of soil structure. Furthermore, bunchgrasses tend to be harmed by heavy grazing, which leads to an increase in short grasses or annuals (which usually results in a long-term decrease in soil organic matter, structure, and microbial activity).[2,3]

INFLUENCE OF GRAZING ON EROSIVITY

Direct Raindrop Impact on Bare Ground

Bare ground is exposed soil that is susceptible to unimpeded raindrop impact. Direct raindrop impact on soil represents the greatest erosive force on grazing land;[4] cover of standing vegetation and plant litter is therefore vital for dissipating the erosive energy of raindrops. Cover and soil structure tend to be greatest under trees and shrubs, followed in decreasing order by bunchgrass, shortgrass, and annuals. The interrill (splash) erosion rate follows the same pattern, being lowest under trees and shrubs and highest under shortgrass and annuals.[5] Grazing practices that increase the amount of bare ground or contribute to a shift in species composition toward dominance of shortgrass species or annuals result in an increased incidence of interrill erosion.

A common indicator of interrill or wind erosion are pedestals of soil under impermeable cover such as rocks or plants that appear elevated over the rest of the terrain. Some of the particles that are detached by raindrop impact clog the pore spaces in the soil. This is a common way that soil crusts are formed. Crusts cause a significant reduction of water movement into the soil, thereby substantially increasing runoff.

Encyclopedia of Animal Science
DOI: 10.1081/E-EAS 120019661

Runoff

The degree to which sediment is detached and transported by runoff is strongly correlated with obstructions on the soil surface that reduce the kinetic energy of runoff by diverting, and thereby slowing, overland flow. Litter and substantial obstructions such as the bunchgrass growth form are strongly correlated with reduced ability to transport sediment. Runoff and the associated erosive energy can also be reduced by maintaining/enhancing the rate of water movement into the soil through grazing practices that maintain cover and enhance soil structure.

Wind Speed at Soil Surface

Reduction of cover and standing crop increases the exposure of soil to the erosive force of wind. If grazing intensity causes a reduction in cover, or if soil structure is poor, the potential for soil detachment and transport by wind increases. This is especially a concern on arid sites because another precondition for wind erosion is that the soil be dry.

Hoof Impact

Treading effects on erosion at a particular site depend on the soil type, soil water content, and the intensity of livestock use, with most severe impacts occurring when the soil is wet, the herbaceous canopy has been grazed to less than 20 mm in height, and the stocking rate is high.[6] Compacted trails, usually manifest as an array of radial paths leading to areas to which livestock must return frequently, result in concentrated runoff, which can eventually create gullies. Common causes of path formation are poor distribution of limiting resources (such as water) or regular movement through gates associated with an intensive rotational grazing system. Another source of compacted trails are tracks formed by repeated passage of vehicles across hilly range and pasture lands. Since these tracks/roads are often poorly (if at all) designed or maintained, they can become a serious source of runoff-induced erosion.

Another way livestock trampling increases the erosion risk is by churning dry soil to dust, which increases the susceptibility of soil particles to wind and water erosion. Trampling a crusted soil can produce the benefits of incorporating mulch and seeds into the soil. However, temporarily breaking soil crusts by trampling does not reduce runoff or erosion risk because the impact of falling raindrops reseals the soil surface after several minutes. Soil crusting problems can ultimately be overcome only through enhancing soil structure by improving vegetation cover and facilitating an increase in soil organic matter.

LONG-TERM DEGRADATION PATTERNS

The ability of the soil to store moisture and nutrients strongly influences the annual production potential of a site. If erosion significantly reduces topsoil depth, there is some danger that a self-generating cycle of degradation will begin, whereby grazing reduces the cover and organic matter on the site, resulting in less water and fewer nutrients being retained for use by plants. This also causes the microclimate to deteriorate, leading to a decrease in soil-enhancing microorganism activity and a harsher environment for germination. In such a situation, plant density is reduced and less forage is produced, leading to the remaining plants receiving greater focus by grazing animals. These factors further accelerate runoff and erosion. This can eventually lead to the diminution or destruction of the biological production potential of the land and can also reduce the potential magnitude of future benefits associated with introduction of improved livestock breeds or technological innovation.[7]

One way in which loss of biological production potential is frequently manifest is in the context of a drought paradox: Ranchers perceive that drought frequency and severity have increased over time, but the climatic data show no significant change in long-term precipitation amount or pattern. This apparent paradox can often be attributed to erosion and the concomitant loss of soil moisture storage capacity, which results in the remaining topsoil drying out sooner and more frequently.[8] The risk of grazing practices interacting with drought to accelerate erosion is often increased because of the lag time associated with destocking in response to the lower plant productivity/livestock carrying capacity caused by the drought.

Soil loss cannot be effectively restored through management since topsoil formation occurs at the rate of 1 cm formed every 100–400 years. By the time a self-generating degradation cycle becomes obvious, it may be too late to implement economically viable conservation options. Early recognition of a developing degradation pattern requires knowledge of grazing land ecology because the first signs of an impending erosion problem almost invariably are manifest by changes in plant community characteristics and subtle changes in surface soil structure.[7,9]

CONCLUSION

The impact of grazing practices on soil conservation can be anticipated by the degree to which livestock influence the erodibility of the soil and the erosive energy acting on the soil. Erodibility can be increased by sustained heavy grazing pressure, causing a significant reduction of organic matter being returned to the soil, thereby limiting the key ingredient required for formation and maintenance of soil structure. Erosivity can be increased by heavy grazing pressure, altering the species composition and cover of the plant community in a manner that increases the unimpeded impact of raindrops, runoff, and wind on the soil. Erosivity can also be increased by trampling in a matter that breaks aggregates at the soil surface or increases soil compaction.

In general, light or moderate grazing pressure does not alter either the erodibility or erosivity of a site, regardless of the grazing system employed. However, there can be great cumulative damage to the site production potential, even if the moderate grazing rate target is only occasionally exceeded, for seasons or years during which accelerated erosion of topsoil is likely to occur. Drought and market risk management planning and policy therefore pose the greatest challenge associated with keeping grazing practices compatible with long-term sustainability objectives that require conservation of the soil.

REFERENCES

1. Holechek, J.L.; Gomez, H.; Molinar, F.; Galt, D. Grazing studies: What we've learned. Rangelands **1999**, *21*, 12–16.

2. Archer, S.; Smeins, F.E. Ecosystem-Level Processes. In *Grazing Management: An Ecological Perspective*; Heitschmidt, R.K., Stuth, J.W., Eds.; Timber Press: Portland, Oregon, 1991; 109–139.

3. Blackburn, W.H.; Pierson, F.B.; Hanson, C.L.; Thurow, T.L.; Hanson, A.L. The spatial and temporal influences of vegetation on surface soil factors in semiarid rangelands. Transc. ASAE **1992**, *35*, 479–486.

4. Hudson, N. *Soil Conservation*; Cornell University Press: Ithaca, New York, 1981.

5. Thurow, T.; Blackburn, W.; Taylor, C.A., Jr. Hydrologic characteristics of vegetation types as affected by livestock grazing systems, Edwards Plateau, Texas. J. Range Manag. **1986**, *39*, 505–509.

6. Russell, J.R.; Betteridge, K.; Costall, D.A.; Mackay, A.D. Cattle treading effects on sediment loss and water infiltration. J. Range Mange. **2001**, *54*, 184–190.

7. Thurow, T.L. Hydrology and Erosion. In *Grazing Management: An Ecological Perspective*; Heitschmidt, R.K., Stuth, J.W., Eds.; Timber Press: Portland, 1991; 141–160.

8. Thurow, T.L.; Taylor, C.A., Jr. Viewpoint: The role of drought in range management. J. Range Manag. **1999**, *52*, 413–419.

9. Pellant, M.; Shaver, P.; Pyke, D.A.; Herrick, J.E. *Interpreting Indicators of Rangeland Health*; U.S. Bureau of Land Management: Denver, Colorado, 2000. Publ. 1734-6.

Growth and Development: Avian Embryos

Vern L. Christensen
North Carolina State University, Raleigh, North Carolina, U.S.A.

INTRODUCTION

Currently, nearly one-third to one-fifth of the growth-out period of poultry is spent in ovo, yet little is known about the growth of poultry embryos. Birds are most suitable for such studies because of the available life-history information comparing the relationships between structure and function and the environment. Moreover, the cleidoic egg allows easy access to embryos under controlled conditions.

BACKGROUND INFORMATION

Ricklefs[1] described mathematically derived growth curves fitted to compare embryonic growth among avian species. He concluded that embryonic growth across avian species is similar and that the greatest contributors to its variation are egg weight and length of the incubation period. Ricklefs and Starck[2] assert that avian growth and development is a successful model system for comparative study of the evolutionary diversification and the adaptive modification of patterns of growth and maturation.

Classifications of avian development utilize the pattern of altricial versus precocial as the standard, but the pattern is continuous rather than discrete and many intermediate forms or grades exist.[3] Altriciality and precociality are based on neonate maturity at hatching.[3] Altricial hatchlings require more maternal care than precocial; thus, embryo tissues need to function at different times of development.[4,5]

EGG WEIGHT

Egg weight and length of the incubation period are the major determinants of avian embryonic growth and the developmental state of the neonate.[2] Precocial birds lay larger eggs relative to adult body size than do altricial species,[6,7] and they take longer to hatch.[8] Portmann[8] argued that altricial and precocial species progress through the same developmental stages, but that altricial chicks hatch relatively earlier in this progression than precocial. Indeed, the major difference in the weight of altricial and precocial embryos and neonates is water. More water than dry matter would indicate less tissue

growth and maturity. Extremely large birds such as the ostrich lay large eggs with variable lengths of incubation that can hatch anywhere from 43 to 49 days of incubation,[9] suggesting great plasticity in the length of incubation at the extremes of egg size.

When differences in egg size and incubation period are taken into account, the slopes of growth curves of embryos do not differ between altricial and precocial species.[1] Embryonic growth would then appear to be an evolutionarily conserved trait, and most variation in egg size may be related to adult size. Larger birds lay larger eggs with longer incubation periods. Smaller birds exhibit slower growth and more rapid maturation. Therefore, regardless of the developmental state of the neonate, differences among egg sizes are accommodated primarily by the uniform acceleration or deceleration of growth rate over most of the developmental period. In other words, egg size and incubation period seem to be closely related and inseparable biologically.

LENGTH OF THE INCUBATION PERIOD

Divergence in the length of the incubation period among species occurs late in embryogenesis when different species need different lengths of time to pass through maturational stages. Indeed, only precocial species exhibit an extended plateau in oxygen consumption immediately prior to hatching[10] as well as increased thyroid and adrenal hormones in circulation.[11,12] It has been suggested that both the plateau in oxygen uptake[13] and the thyroid and adrenal hormones[12] are associated with the maturational processes at hatching.

The availability of oxygen may constrain growth during development[14] when gas exchange is limited by the gas conductance[10] and the plateau stage. Ar and Rahn[15] suggested that eggshell conductance, the functional characteristic of an eggshell, might also be the determinant of the length of the incubation period and embryonic growth as well. Three conditions are determined by the eggshell conductance and were proposed to induce hatching. First, the incubating egg should lose approximately 15% of its initial mass as water vapor. Second, the fractional concentration of carbon dioxide in the air space of eggs should have increased from 0.25% to

Encyclopedia of Animal Science
DOI: 10.1081/E-EAS 120019663

6%. Third, the relative fractional concentration of oxygen should have declined from 20.9% to 14%. Eggshell conductance establishes these conditions at a precise time in development that initiates tissue maturation and the hatching response, thus determining the length of the developmental period. Therefore, despite differences in egg size and incubation periods that may exist among species, gas tensions determined by the ratio of metabolic rate to diffusive gas conductance across the pores of the eggshell may be the primary determinant of the length of the incubation period. It has been postulated that the gas tensions in the airspace of the egg may constitute an adequate stimulus to cause pipping and terminate the embryonic developmental period.[16] These differences may exist to ensure that tissues mature properly during the plateau stage in oxygen consumption at the termination of embryonic development by ensuring the proper length of the incubation period.

Selection of poultry species for improved reproduction results in a decrease in egg weight and eggshell conductance and a prolonging of the length of the incubation period.[17,18] Conversely, selection for increased adult growth increases egg weight, decreases eggshell conductance, and prolongs the length of the developmental period.[17,19] When growth was measured relative to egg size, selection for improved reproduction increased the weight of hatchlings relative to egg weight, but selection for growth did not. Thus, within a species, plasticity in embryonic growth exists but may also have impact upon the survival rates of embryos in the eggs with varied lengths of incubation periods.

NUTRIENT LIMITATIONS

Limiting nutrients to the embryo is a possible intrinsic factor that may be limiting to growth capacity of avian embryos.[20] The supply of yolk or the mechanism providing yolk to the developing embryos may limit embryonic growth, particularly late in development. Early in development, embryos in both large and small eggs have ample yolk because of equal access to nutrients. Late in development, the acquisition of yolk is dependent upon the surface area covered by the yolk sac membrane. Large eggs have larger yolks than small eggs, thus providing more nutrients, but the surface covering the yolk increases according to the surface law. The absorptive surface of the yolk sac membrane covering the yolk, calculated as the yolk volume to the two-thirds power, declines in large eggs.[2] Thus, larger eggs have larger yolks, and the surface area and the vascularity of the yolk sac membrane available for nutrient assimilation decreases compared to smaller eggs.

GROWTH AND MATURATION OF VITAL ORGANS

Another factor that may limit the overall growth of the avian embryo is the possibility that the growth of critical individual organs may limit the overall growth of the embryo.[4] The upper limit of growth of any of several tissues could set upper limits to the growth of the embryo as a whole. A good example of such an organ would be the brain and nervous system, which are some of the initial tissues formed early in embryogenesis and, relative to other tissues, grow to immense size during the embryonic period relative to the body and other tissues.[2,4] Lilja and Olsson[4] divided organs by their supply and demand functions. Demand tissue growth (breast, wings, legs, and feathers) compared to supply tissue growth (esophagus, proventriculus, gizzard, intestines, heart, and liver) is accelerated in avian embryos whose parents have been selected for rapid growth. Thus, growth of embryonic organs in larger eggs from larger adults may be disproportional and lead to overall growth-limiting functions.

The maturation of organs into functional entities may also limit overall embryonic growth.[21] Glycogen acquisition by individual organs is a requisite process to survive the plateau stage in oxygen consumption. Organs must have adequate nutrients for anaerobic metabolism to support them through the hypoxia and hypercapnia of hatching.[13] Selection for reproduction has decreased the amount of glycogen found in vital tissues compared to unselected controls.[22] Similarly, selection for rapid growth has also depressed the acquisition of glycogen prior to the plateau stage in oxygen uptake. Thus, the ability of individual organs to continue their maturation and function late in development may be impaired by the lack of nutrients for vital organs.

CONCLUSIONS

Avian embryo growth is determined primarily by egg size and the length of the incubation period; however, other variables may play roles in determining the maturity of the hatchling. Oxygen and nutrient availability, vital organ maturation, and genetic expression of sequences for egg production or rates of growth may be modulators.

REFERENCES

1. Ricklefs, R.E. Comparative analysis of avian embryonic growth. J. Exp. Zool. 1987, 1 (Suppl. 1), 309–323.
2. Ricklefs, R.E.; Starck, M.J. Embryonic Growth and Development. In Avian Growth and Development; Oxford University Press: New York, NY, 1998; 31–58.

3. Nice, M.M. Development of behavior in precocial birds. Trans. Linn. Soc. N.Y. **1962**, *8*, 1–211.

4. Lilja, C.; Olsson, U. Changes in embryonic development associated with long-term selection for high growth rate in Japanese quail. Growth **1987**, *51*, 301–308.

5. Fan, Y.K.; Croom, J.; Christensen, V.L.; Black, B.L.; Bird, A.R.; Daniel, L.R.; McBride, B.; Eisen, E.J. Jejunal glucose uptake and oxygen consumption in turkey poults selected for rapid growth. Poult. Sci. **1997**, *76*, 1738–1745.

6. Rahn, H.; Paganelli, C.V.; Ar, A. Relation of avian egg weight to body weight. Auk **1975**, *92*, 750–765.

7. Sotherland, P.R.; Rahn, H. On the composition of bird eggs. Condor **1987**, *89*, 48–65.

8. Portmann, A. Die Postembryonale Entwicklung der Vogel als Evolutionsproblem. In *Acta XI Congress of International Ornithologists*; Basel, 1955; 138–151.

9. Christensen, V.L.; Davis, G.S.; Lucore, L.A. Eggshell conductance and other functional qualities of ostrich eggs. Poult. Sci. **1996**, *75*, 1404–1410.

10. Dietz, M.W.; van Kampen, M.; van Griensven, M.J.M.; van Mourik, S. Daily energy budgets of avian embryos: The paradox of the plateau phase in egg metabolic rate. Physiol. Zool. **1998**, *71*, 147–156.

11. McNabb, F.M.A. Peripheral thyroid hormone dynamics in precocial and altricial avian development. Am. Zool. **1988**, *28*, 427–440.

12. McNabb, F.M.A.L.; Lyons, J.; Hughes, T.E. Free thyroid hormones in latricial (ring doves) vs. precocial (Japanese quail) development. Endocrinology **1984**, *115*, 133–2136.

13. Rahn, H. Gas exchange of avian eggs with special reference to turkey eggs. Poult. Sci. **1981**, *60*, 1971–1980.

14. Metcalf, J.; McCutcheon, I.E.; Francisco, D.L.; Metzenberg, A.B.; Welsh, J.E. Oxygen availability and growth of the chick embryo. Resp. Physiol. **1981**, *46*, 81–88.

15. Ar, A.; Rahn, H. Interdependence of Gas Conductance, Incubation Length, and Weight of the Avian Egg. In *Respiratory Function in Birds, Adult and Embryonic*; Piiper, J., Ed.; Springer Verlag: Berlin, 1978; 227–236.

16. Visschedijk, A.H.J. The air space and embryonic respiration. 2. The times of pipping and hatching as influenced by an artificially changed permeability of the shell over the airspace. Br. Poult. Sci. **1968**, *9*, 185–196.

17. Christensen, V.L.; Nestor, K.E. Changes in functional qualities of turkey eggshells in strains selected for increased egg production and growth. Poult. Sci. **1994**, *73*, 1458–1464.

18. Christensen, V.L.; Noble, D.O.; Nestor, K.E. Influence of selection for increased body weight, egg production, and shank width on the length of the incubation period of turkeys. Poult. Sci. **2000**, *79*, 613–618.

19. McNabb, F.M.A.; Dunnington, E.A.; Siegel, P.B.; Suvarna, S. Perinatal thyroid hormones and hepatic 5′deiodinase in relation to hatching time in weight-selected chickens. Poult. Sci. **1993**, *72*, 1764–1771.

20. Carey, C.; Rahn, H.; Parisi, P. Calories, water lipid, and yolk in avian eggs. Condor **1980**, *82*, 335–343.

21. Lilja, C.; Marks, H.L. Changes in organ growth pattern associated with long-term selection for high growth rate in quail. Growth Dev. Aging **1991**, *55*, 219–224.

22. Christensen, V.L.; Donaldson, W.E.; Nestor, K.E. Embryonic viability and metabolism in turkey lines selected for egg production or growth. Poult. Sci. **1993**, *72*, 829–838.

Growth and Development: Cell Differentiation

Sylvia P. Poulos
Gary J. Hausman
United States Department of Agriculture, Agricultural Research Service, Athens, Georgia, U.S.A.

INTRODUCTION

Tissue mass is maintained by coordinated regulation of cellular processes, including proliferation, differentiation, and apoptosis. Changes in these processes occur during normal growth and development throughout an animal's lifetime beginning in the embryo. Irregularities in these processes can result in abnormalities, such as double muscling or bone dysplasia. A cell's ultimate phenotype is expressed as cellular structure, shape, and function and is determined during differentiation. Transgenic animals, in which expression of specific genes has been altered, have been especially helpful in determining gene functions in vivo, whereas in vitro studies have been useful in determining these roles in more controlled environments.[1]

TRANSCRIPTIONAL CONTROL OF CELL DIFFERENTIATION

Studies have shown that both internal and external factors can regulate differentiation by mediating gene and protein expression. External compounds, such as growth factors, pharmaceutical agents, lipids, hormones, etc., influence cell differentiation through cascades that culminate in transcription factor activation followed by gene transcription.[2] This may be followed by translation of the gene product into a protein that induces the cell's phenotypic change. For example, thiazolidinediones are PPAR ligands that induce the transcription factor PPAR-γ2, which induces adipocyte differentiation and protein production, including adipocyte lipid-binding protein (aP2) and leptin. Transforming growth factor (TGF) and bone morphogenic proteins (BMP) are examples of growth factors that induce transcription factors and alter gene expression in various cell types in domestic animals (Table 1). Sma- and Mad-related proteins (Smads) are activated by both the TGF and BMP superfamilies and have roles in the differentiation of several cell types.[3] Although some transcription factors, such as Jak/STAT, regulate similar processes in all cell types, it should be noted that transcription factors can have cell-specific effects. For example, CEBPs play roles in the differentiation of adipocytes, epithelial cells, and neutrophils.

Transcription factors in the MyoD muscle regulatory factor (MRF) family are responsible for muscle development and, when expressed, can induce myogenesis in nonmyogenic cell types.[4] Avian, bovine, and porcine studies have shown that MyoD and myogenin expression precede myotube formation. Muscle from double-muscled cattle expresses higher levels of MyoD and myostatin reflecting the importance of these factors in inhibiting proliferation. The interaction of various transcription factors is also key in regulating cell differentiation as shown by the myostatin-induced Smad3 phosphorylation and interaction with MyoD, which inhibits differentiation in cultured cells. Myostatin is also a potent inhibitor of Pax-3 and Myf-5, which are associated with proliferation, whereas follistatin promotes Pax3-enhanced proliferation in muscle. Alternatively, some transcription factors are involved in cellular processes other than terminal differentiation.

THE ROLE OF EXTRACELLULAR MATRIX PROTEINS

Many cells are coated by a layer of extracellular matrix (ECM) called the basement membrane (BM).[5] The BM is composed of two layers: an internal basal lamina (BL) linked to the plasma membrane and an external, fibrillar reticular layer. Several important ECM functions include providing substrates for cell adhesion and migration and presenting key growth factors to regulate cell growth and differentiation. ECM consists of two classes of macromolecules (Table 2). First, proteoglycans are molecules that can bind, concentrate, and present marginally soluble molecules to the cell and effectively modulate growth factor distribution and activities.[6] Proteoglycans are glycosaminoglycans that are covalently linked to protein and include perlecan, agrin, HSPG, decorin, and fibromodulin. The second class is made up of fibrous proteins that include the structural proteins collagens, elastin, and fibrillin, and the adhesive proteins laminin and fibronectin.

Collagens are the most abundant fibrous proteins in the ECM. Of the 20 collagens identified, types I, II, V, and XI are the predominant ones (Table 2).[7] Type I is the most

Encyclopedia of Animal Science
DOI: 10.1081/E-EAS 120019664
Published 2005 by Marcel Dekker, Inc. All rights reserved.

505

Table 1 Select transcription factors involved in cell differentiation of domestic animals[a,b]

Transcription factor	Preadipocytes/ adipocytes	Myoblast/muscle cells	Endothelial cells	Chondrocytes/ osteoblasts
CEBP	CEBP-α and CEBP-δ increase with adipogenesis while CEBP-β remains constant (P).			
PPAR	PPAR-γ induces adipogenesis (P, O) and increases with adipogenesis. PPAR-γ agonist induces UCP1 expression in SV cells (Rb).	PPAR-γ agonists induce adipogenesis in fibroblast like cells from skeletal muscle (B).		
Smad		TGF-β treatment induces Smad-2 translocation in corneal myofibroblasts (Rb). Smad-3 translocation is decreased in myofibroblasts compared to fibroblasts (P).	TGF-β induces Smad-1/5 and Smad-2/3 phosphorylation and BMP-6 induces Smad-5 phosphorylation in BAEC, BCEC, and BMEC. Smad-2/3 overexpression activates PDGF-B promoter and may mediate TGF-β response in BAEC cells.	TGF-β induces PTHrP via Smad signaling to regulate the differentiation rate of chondrocytes (A). Retinoic acid increases embryonic chondrocyte differentiation via BMP-2-induced Smad (A). Nuclear translocation of Smad-1 and -7 induces differentiation of articular chondrocytes, whereas Smad-6 inhibits differentiation (B).
Id		Id-2 increases with muscle atrophy following weight-induced muscle hypertrophy (A).	BAEC migration and tube formation is induced via SMAD-activated Id-1 expression.	
Pax		Ectopic BMP-2 expression in cardiac mesoderm inhibits Pax-3 expression and impairs somite formation (A). Pax-3 and Paraxis activities are upstream of MyoD in developing embryos (A).		

[a]A, avian; B, bovine; BAEC, bovine aortic endothelial cells; BCEC, bovine corneal endothelial cells; BMEC, bovine microvascular endothelial cells; CEBP, CAAT Enhancer Binding Protein; Id, Inhibitor of Differentiation; O, ovine; P, porcine; PDGF, Platelet-Derived Growth Factor; PPAR, Peroxisome Proliferator Activating Receptor; PTHrP, Parathyroid Hormone-Related Protein; Rb, rabbit; Smad, Sma-, and Mad-related proteins; TGF; Transforming Growth Factor.

[b]MyoD family muscle regulatory factor (MRF) transcription factors are only expressed in muscle tissue and are not included in the table but are discussed in the text.

Table 2 Developmental studies of ECM components representing porcine (P), bovine (B), and avian (A) species[a]

ECM components[b]	Preadipocytes/ adipocytes	Chondrocytes/ osteoblasts	Myoblasts /muscle cells
Collagens	IM (B): types I–VI identified. V and VI remodeling important for differentiation. SQ (P): no influence of types I and IV substrata but IV expressed with differentiation.	Predominance of types I6II, IX6X (A); I6 II6 X, IX (B); I6II (P) associated with differentiation. Type II influences calcification (A) and TGF-β response via integrin signaling (B). Types I and II substrata differentially influence integrin expression (P).	Types I, III, V, and VI localized in perimysium and endomysium, IV only in endomysium and no change in localization with age (B). Type I localization associated with satellite cell myogenesis (A). Types I, III, and IV expressed in embryo (A).
Laminins	Expressed with differentiation (B,P) and substrata induces morphological differentiation (P).		Early expression in embryo (A). No change in localization with age after localization in endomysium (A,B).
Fibronectin	Decreases with differentiation (B,P) and no influence of substrata (P).	Increased and then constant expression with differentiation indicate involvement in initial attachment of early osteoblasts to pericellular matrix (A).	Decreased expression and reduced binding associated with myoblast fusion (A). Localized in fetal and embryonic connective tissue (A,B).
Integrins		β1 modulates response to TGF-β; β 3/BSP adhesion-mediated signaling influences differentiation (B). Estrogen increases β3 expression (A). ECM influences α1 and α2 differentially (P).	α subunit ratios, cytoplasmic domains, and growth factor synergy influence myogenesis (A). α5 is critical adhesion plaque component (A). α1 is laminin/type IV collagen receptor (A).
PGs and MMPs		Age and differentiation dependent changes in PG amounts, composition, and structures that include aggrecans, biglycans, and decorin (A,B). BMP-7 enhances PG synthesis (B). MMP-3 proteolysis required for differentiation with matrix mineralization (B).	Growth- or differentiation-dependent changes in amounts and size of HS, HSPG, DSPG, CSPG, and glycogenin (A,B). HSPG localizes around myotubes with development (A). Developmental shift from versicon to decorin PGs (A). Decorin associated with perimysial fibrillogenesis and TGF-β signaling pathway (A).

[a]BMP, bone morphogenetic protein; BSP, bone sialoprotein; CSPG, chondroitin sulfate proteoglycan; DSPG, dermatan sulfate proteoglycan; HS, heparin sulfate; HSPG, heparin sulfate proteoglycan; IM, intramuscular; MMPs, matrix metalloproteinases; PGs, proteoglycan; SQ, subcutaneous; TGF-β, transforming growth factor beta.
[b]Complete ECM substrata induce morphological differentiation of preadipocytes (P), endothelial cells (A,B), and epithelial cells (B) and are used in myoblast and satellite cell studies (P).

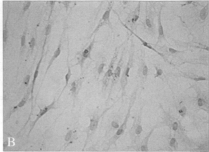

Fig. 1 Myotube formation is strongly influenced by laminin (A) but is not influenced by fibronectin (B).

abundant, whereas type IV collagen has a more flexible structure and forms a meshlike structure. There are 12 laminin isoforms, each of which is a heterotrimer of alpha, beta, and gamma subunits.[8] Laminin and type IV

collagen, the major components of BL, are signaling molecules that activate signal-transducing receptors in the membrane. Fibronectin and laminin are directly involved in cell sorting and cell differentiation (Fig. 1). BL

Table 3 Proteomic and genomic techniques are useful in studying the regulation of cell differentiation[a]

	Technology
Gene identification and quantitative expression analysis	
SAGE	Unique 14 base-pair DNA tag used to identify gene and relative abundance.
DNA array	Immobilized DNA sequences spotted on a slide/chip recognize and hybridize complementary DNA in sample. Relative abundance is determined using fluorescent tagged samples.
SNP analysis	DNA sequences compared between two individuals to reveal sequence variation.
Protein identification and quantitative expression analysis	
2D gels with MS	Proteins separated by molecular weight and pI. Peptide sequences identified.
ICAT	Proteins are labeled, digested, and analyzed using microcapillary liquid chromatography and MS.
Gene cloning	Convert computed sequence data into molecules that are produced and characterized.
Protein arrays	Analogous to DNA arrays. Polyclonal antibodies generated, spotted, and used to identify protein targets and protein expression.
Protein interaction determination	
In vitro protein interaction analysis	Study protein signaling pathways by identifying binding domains, ligands, and binding affinity. Determine protein interactions and pathway characterization.
Cell map/subcellular proteomics	Biochemical fractionation of subcellular material precedes protein identification. Pathway characterization by identifying location, orientation, and movement of proteins.
Multipole coupling spectroscopy	Measure frequency-dependent dielectric properties. Signal transduction in whole cells, direct detection of pathway function.
Protein structure analysis	
De novo structure	Experimental determination using crystallography and/or NMR spectroscopy. Predictive structures can also be determined.
Post-translational modification	MS including TOF, MALDI, PSD, and IMAC. Limited by the nature of protein modification.
Protein function determination	
Mutagenesis	Site-directed alteration of gene to investigate phenotypic changes from altered protein expression.

[a]SNP, single nucleotide polymorphism; SAGE, serial analysis of gene expression; MS, mass spectroscopy; ICAT, isotope-coded affinity tags; NMR, nuclear magnetic resonance; TOF, time of flight; MALDI, matrix-assisted laser desorption/ionization; PSD, post source decay; IMAC, immobilized metal affinity chromatography.

components not only orchestrate morphogenesis directly but also regulate development by presentation of morphogenic, mitogenic, and trophic factors.

Integrins are cell-surface receptors responsible for cell attachment to extracellular matrices and to other cells (Table 2).[9] They effectively link the ECM to the cytoskeleton and play an important role in controlling various steps in the signaling pathways that regulate processes, such as differentiation, proliferation, and cell migration. The integrin family consists of 24 receptors assembled from combinations of 18 alpha and 18 beta chains. Matrix metalloproteinases (MMPs) are responsible for ECM breakdown and remodeling associated with morphogenesis and cell differentiation. Sixteen MMPs and several tissue inhibitors of MMPs have been identified.

CONCLUSION

Cell differentiation is an integral part of tissue growth and homeostasis. Although this process is often specific to a particular cell type, transcription factors, growth factors, extracellular matrices, and external compounds are key partners in the regulation of cell differentiation. The continued development and refinement of genomic and proteomic techniques will aid in understanding this process (Table 3).[10] Understanding the regulation of cell differentiation can lead to strategies aimed at improving health, performance, and production in animals.

REFERENCES

1. Valet, P.; Tavernier, G.; Castan-Laurell, I.; Saulnier-Blache, J.S.; Langin, D. Understanding adipose tissue development from transgenic animal models. J. Lipid Res. **2002**, *43* (6), 835–860.
2. Oikawa, T.; Yamada, T. Molecular biology of the Ets family of transcription factors. Gene **2003**, *303*, 11–34.
3. Lutz, M.; Knaus, P. Integration of the TGF-beta pathway into the cellular signaling network. Cell Signal. **2002**, *14* (12), 977–988.
4. Pownall, M.E.; Gustafsson, M.K.; Emerson, C.P., Jr. Myogenic regulatory factors and the specification of muscle progenitors in vertebrate embryos. Annu. Rev. Cell Dev. Biol. **2002**, *18*, 747–783.
5. Sanes, J.R. The basement membrane/basal lamina of skeletal muscle. J. Biol. Chem. **2003**, *278* (15), 12601–12604.
6. Kresse, H.; Schonherr, E. Proteoglycans of the extracellular matrix and growth control. J. Cell. Physiol. **2001**, *189* (3), 266–274.
7. Ghosh, A.K. Factors involved in the regulation of type I collagen gene expression: Implication in fibrosis. Exp. Biol. Medicine (Maywood.) **2002**, *227* (5), 301–314.
8. Colognato, H.; Yurchenco, P.D. Form and function: The laminin family of heterotrimers. Dev. Dyn. **2000**, *218* (2), 213–234.
9. van der Flier, A.; Sonnenberg, A. Function and interactions of integrins. Cell Tissue Res. **2001**, *305* (3), 285–298.
10. Richards, J.; LeNaour, F.; Hanash, S.; Beretta, L. Integrated genomic and proteomic analysis of signaling pathways in dendritic cell differentiation and maturation. Ann. N. Y. Acad. Sci. **2002**, *975*, 91–100.

Growth and Development: Mammalian Fetus

Robert A. Merkel
Matthew E. Doumit
Michigan State University, East Lansing, Michigan, U.S.A.

INTRODUCTION

Prenatal development of mammals can be divided into ovum, embryonic, and fetal phases. The fetal phase represents over 80% of the prenatal period, and extends from the embryonic phase until birth. The fetal period begins when the specific species becomes identifiable. At the onset of the fetal phase, organs and systems are identifiable, but varying extents of tissue differentiation and development occur during the fetal period. The majority of the prenatal increase in body size and maturation of tissues and organs characterizes the fetal phase.

FETAL GROWTH

Rapid growth of the fetal body occurs during the last trimester of pregnancy in domestic animal species (Fig. 1). Components of the fetal body exhibit differential growth and development, and the relative development of specific body portions and systems is species dependent. In general, growth rates of tissues and regions of the body peak in a regular sequence, which begins during fetal development, and continue through postnatal life.[1] Although the brain, limbs, and some internal organs have little function in utero, they are required to be functional at birth. Growth of some vital organs, such as the heart, liver, and kidney, generally parallels fetal weight gain, whereas the lungs and spleen have been shown to stop growing late in gestation.[2] Fetal growth of the head and brain of all species is proportionally greater than that of other body regions. Additionally, the legs of those species that nurse while standing undergo relatively greater fetal growth and are more highly developed than those of species that nurse dams that are lying down. This accounts for the disproportionately large head and long legs of newborn animals of species such as cattle, sheep, and horses. In many cases, development and growth of one tissue is dependent upon that of others. For example, skin or hide development is stimulated by whole body growth, just as skeletal muscles grow in length at a rate proportional to growth of the long bones with which they are associated.

The nature of fetal growth is somewhat tissue-specific, but typically begins as hyperplasic growth (increase in cell number), which is followed by cellular hypertrophy (increase in cell size). Accumulation of extracellular material such as collagen coincides with the cellular growth of a tissue. The following discussion will focus on fetal development and growth of bone, skeletal muscle, and adipose tissue, which are critical to the function of agricultural species and the composition and quality of the products derived from these species.

Bone

Fetal bone formation occurs by either endochondral ossification (i.e., from a cartilage template) or by intramembranous ossification (i.e., without a cartilage precursor). Most mammalian fetal bone is formed via endochondral ossification, but intramembranous ossification forms bones of the skull. The fetal skull is developed when osteoblasts in connective tissue begin producing collagen fibers and bone matrix. The osteoblasts ultimately differentiate into osteocytes and produce bone. The cartilage template of the axial and appendicular skeleton formed during the embryonic phase is gradually replaced by ossification of the cartilage model. The chondrocytes die as the cartilage matrix becomes ossified by activity of chondrocytes themselves, as well as by osteoblasts and osteocytes of developing bone. Ossification of the diaphysis (shaft) of long bones begins in the center and progresses toward each end to form compact bone. Ossification of the epiphysis (head) of long bones and in the axial skeleton is less extensive, resulting in spongy bone. At birth, most of the cartilage has been replaced by bone.[3] However, cartilage remains in the intervertebral disks, dorsal surfaces of the vertical processes of vertebrae, articular surfaces, and the epiphyseal plate of long bones.

Skeletal Muscle

More than 600 skeletal muscles arise from myoblasts, which originate from mesodermal cells located in pairs of somites that flank the developing notochord and neural tube. Of the three germ layers in the early embryo, the paraxial mesoderm gives rise to somites. A somite may be subdivided into the dorsomedial (epaxial) domain, which

Encyclopedia of Animal Science
DOI: 10.1081/E-EAS 120019666

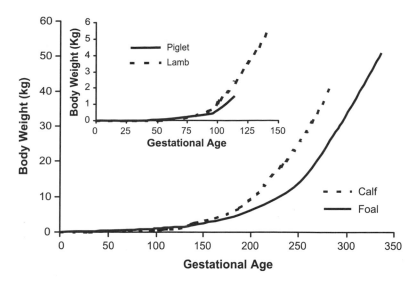

Fig. 1 Pattern of weight change for equine, bovine, ovine, and porcine fetuses. The fetal period represents approximately the last 80–85% of the gestational time period.

generates the muscles of the back, and the ventrolateral (hypaxial) domain, which gives rise to the abdominal, intercostal, and limb musculature. Distinct classes of proliferative myoblasts are present during embryonic, fetal, and adult skeletal muscle development.[3] Ultimately, these myoblasts undergo terminal differentiation, which involves both permanent withdrawal from the cell cycle and expression of muscle-specific genes. Differentiation is followed by fusion of myoblasts to form multinucleated myotubes, or immature muscle fibers. Primary myotubes represent the first muscle fibers to form, and provide a scaffolding upon which other myoblasts align and fuse to form secondary myotubes. The process of secondary myotube, or muscle fiber, formation persists for most of the fetal period. Essentially all muscle fiber formation occurs prenatally in domestic animal species.[4] Small muscles will have fewer muscle fibers than large muscles within an animal, but the number of muscle fibers also varies by species, genotype, and fetal nutrient availability. Individual muscle fibers are encased in a collagenous matrix referred to as endomysium. The complement of secondary muscle fibers surrounding each primary muscle fiber represents a fasciculus, or muscle fiber bundle, which is surrounded by a connective tissue border called perimysium. The connective tissue border surrounding the entire developing muscle is the epimysium. Connective tissue septa of muscle are contiguous with the dense connective tissue of tendons, which attach muscle to bone. Similar partitioning of individual cells and clusters of cells by connective tissue septa contributes to the organization and support of most organs.

Myotubes synthesize and accumulate muscle proteins, which are assembled into highly organized contractile structures referred to as myofibrils. During maturation of myotubes into muscle fibers, centrally located nuclei migrate to the periphery of muscle cells as myofibrils assemble and form a centrally located contractile apparatus. Muscle fiber growth is achieved primarily by increased fiber length and diameter, and this coincides with an increase in myofibril content. Myofibrils increase in length by addition of sarcomeres to the ends of myofibrils, and in number by longitudinal splitting. Growth in skeletal muscle fiber length accompanies bone growth and typically precedes extensive increases in muscle fiber diameter, which do not occur until the last trimester of gestation.

Adipose Tissue

Adipose tissue (fat) is deposited in various locations, called depots, in the mammalian body. The major depots include internal body fat associated with the gastrointestinal tract, heart, and kidneys, and subcutaneous, intermuscular and intramuscular fat. The relative amount of each depot varies with species, breed, frame size, and gender. During fetal growth, proliferative fat cells, i.e., preadipocytes (adipoblasts), arise from mesenchymal cells. These cells differentiate into immature adipocytes, but they accumulate little fat prior to the perinatal period.[5] Even though adipose tissue is late developing, some fat is laid down prior to birth. Pigs, lambs, calves, and foals have only 1–3% fat at birth,[6] which is primarily found in the body cavity. Another deposit laid down during late fetal development is brown fat found externally over the scapula area and in the thoracic cavity of some species, but not in the pig. It serves as a readily available source for heat generation in neonatal mammals.[3]

Factors Affecting Fetal Growth

Numerous factors influence the growth of the fetus. The fetus derives nutrients from the maternal plasma through the placenta. Mothers on a high plane of nutrition give birth to larger offspring than those with nutritional limitations. Any restriction of blood supply to the placenta and fetus will hinder fetal growth. When competition for available maternal nutrients becomes greater, such as when a multiparous animal produces a larger than average litter, the placenta is generally smaller and the average birthweight more variable than when a litter of average size is produced.[1] Growth of a fetus in a region of the uterine horn with restricted blood supply may result in a runt, which is much smaller than its littermates at birth. Skeletal muscles are particularly small in growth-retarded animals, whereas the brain of the runt is nearly as large as that of its littermates.[6] Since fewer muscle fibers form during fetal development of runts compared to larger littermates, runts tend to grow slower, become fatter, and remain lighter muscled postnatally than offspring of normal birthweight.[3]

The size of the fetus is also controlled by the size of the dam, which may be even more important than nutrition of the dam. Reciprocal crosses between large Shire horses and Shetland ponies, in which the size of the foal follows that of the dam, have demonstrated this. The size of the dam's uterus limits the size of the placenta and subsequently the nutrition and size of the foal.[1]

In addition to maternal nutrition and obvious genetic factors associated with breed or body frame size, fetal development of specific tissues is regulated by a variety of endocrine and local growth factors. Perhaps the dominant fetal growth regulator in late gestation is insulin-like growth factor-1 (IGF-1), which is produced by the fetal liver and other tissues.[7] Fetal IGF-I promotes fetal substrate uptake and inhibits tissue catabolic pathways. In contrast to regulation of IGF-1 by growth hormone during postnatal life, fetal IGF-1 is stimulated by fetal insulin, which is predominantly controlled by fetal glucose concentration. Thus, fetal IGF-1 is sensitive to maternal nutrition, and reduction in fetal growth due to nutrient restriction is associated with reduced fetal IGF-1.

The importance of local growth factors on fetal development is highlighted by the discovery of myostatin,

a member of the transforming growth factor-beta superfamily. Myostatin is an inhibitor of skeletal muscle development, and defects in this growth factor lead to increases in myoblast proliferation and subsequent increases in muscle fiber number that characterize the double-muscled condition of cattle. This again illustrates the important effects of fetal development on postnatal growth.

CONCLUSION

Fetal tissue development and growth occupy most of the prenatal period, although most of the increase in fetal body weight occurs during the last trimester of gestation. Fetal tissues grow by cellular hyperplasia and hypertrophy, and cell differentiation within tissues and organs enables distinct functional requirements of those tissues to be achieved. Fetal tissue growth is orchestrated by complex interactions among genetic and environmental factors that not only determine the viability of the offspring at birth, but also influence the growth and functional characteristics of the postnatal animal.

REFERENCES

1. *Hammond's Farm Animals*, 5th Ed.; Hammond, J., Bowman, J.C., Robinson, T.J., Eds.; Edward Arnold: London, England, 1983.
2. Ullrey, D.E.; Sprague, J.I.; Becker, D.E.; Miller, E.R. Growth of the swine fetus. J. Anim. Sci. **1965**, *24*, 711–717.
3. Gerrard, D.E.; Grant, A.L. *Principles of Animal Growth and Development*; Kendall/Hunt Publishing Company: Dubuque, Iowa, 2003.
4. Robelin, J.; Lacourt, A.; Bechet, D.; Ferrara, M.; Briand, Y.; Geay, Y. Muscle differentiation in the bovine fetus: A histological and histochemical approach. Growth Dev. Aging **1991**, *55*, 151–160.
5. Martin, R.J.; Hausman, G.J.; Hausman, D.B. Regulation of adipose cell development in utero. Proc. Soc. Exp. Biol. Med. **1998**, *219* (3), 200–210.
6. Widdowson, E.M.; Lister, D. Nutritional Control of Growth. In *Growth Regulation in Farm Animals, Advances in Meat Research*; Pearson, A.M., Dutson, T.R., Eds.; Elsevier Applied Science: London, 1991; Vol. 7.
7. Gluckman, P.D.; Pinal, C.S. Regulation of fetal growth by the somatotropic axis. J. Nutr. **2003**, *133*, 1741–1746.

Growth and Development: Postnatal

Matthew E. Doumit
Robert A. Merkel
Michigan State University, East Lansing, Michigan, U.S.A.

G

INTRODUCTION

Postnatal growth of animals varies among species, breed, gender, and genotype. Nutrition, climatic conditions, and exogenous growth promoters are among the many environmental and management factors influencing body weight gain and nutrient partitioning. Body weight gain reflects the summation of individual tissue growth, which generally follows a predictable sequence that reflects the prioritization of nutrients based on tissue function.

POSTNATAL GROWTH

When raised under ideal conditions, domestic animals exhibit a sigmoidal pattern of weight gain. Rate of gain and final mature weight are influenced by a multitude of factors, such as species, breed, genotype, gender, or the use of exogenous growth promotants. When compared at the same body weight, animals that are heavier at maturity (e.g., large frame vs. small frame or males vs. females) generally grow faster (Fig. 1), contain more bone and protein, and have less fat than animals that mature at a smaller size.[1] The amount of energy needed to maintain an animal body increases with the size of the animal. The inflection point of the growth curve, where growth begins to slow, reflects a decreasing proportion of the nutrients consumed that are used for growth.[2] This typically coincides with rapid accumulation of fat in animals maintained on a high level of nutrition.

Increases in body weight reflect different patterns of growth of each organ. Most internal organs approach their mature weight long before final body weight is reached, and are considered early maturing.[1] Of the other major body tissues, bone is earlier developing than muscle, and muscle develops prior to extensive fat deposition (Fig. 2). Growth of a tissue is influenced by functional demands, e.g., the extent of bone mineralization depends on both body weight and functional demand placed on the bone. Similarly, bone growth in length determines growth in length of associated muscles, but muscle diameter is associated with the force that is demanded of a muscle. Muscles used for locomotion, such as the hindlimb biceps femoris, have larger-diameter muscle fibers and more connective tissue than postural muscles, e.g., the psoas major. The following discussion will highlight the cellular aspects of postnatal bone, skeletal muscle, and adipose tissue accretion. These tissues compose the majority of body mass in all domestic animal species.

Bone Growth

Postnatal growth in length of long bones of the appendicular skeleton precedes growth in diameter. Growth in length involves both cartilage and bone cells. Chondroblasts continue to proliferate at the growth plate adjacent to the epiphysis to maintain this cartilage plate throughout the growth period. Chondroblasts produce cartilage matrix materials but gradually differentiate into chondrocytes, which produce and maintain mature matrix. As more chondroblasts arise, and accompanying newly synthesized matrix accumulates, mature matrix and chondrocytes begin to abut the diaphysis. Chondrocytes eventually die as a result of their initiation of the ossification process, which prevents diffusion of nutrients to cartilage cells. Ossification of cartilage results in invasion of capillaries, osteoblasts, and, ultimately, osteocytes to further bone formation adjacent to the diaphysis, thus extending its length.[3,4] While a growth plate is present at both the proximal and the distal ends of long bones, the extent of growth is not the same at each end. The differential growth rate varies among bones of an animal, e.g., in some bones the proximal end predominates and in others the distal end does.

Long bone growth in diameter occurs as osteoblasts proliferate along the outer surface of the diaphysis beneath the periosteum surrounding the diaphysis. Deposition of bone on the outer diaphyseal surface is appositional growth. It results from activity of osteoblasts and osteocytes laying down compact bone, thereby increasing bone density and strength. Simultaneously, mononuclear precursors of osteoclasts originate in the diaphyseal

Encyclopedia of Animal Science
DOI: 10.1081/E-EAS 120030461

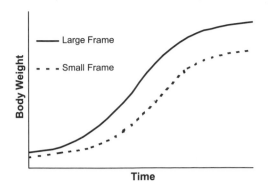

Fig. 1 Idealized growth curves for large- and small-framed animals within a species.

marrow of the medullary cavity.[3,4] Fusion of mononucleated precursors forms multinucleated osteoclasts, which are responsible for bone resorption. Osteoclastic resorptive activity increases the size of the medullary cavity. Thus, long bone growth involves the highly coordinated activity of osteoblasts, osteocytes, and osteoclasts. During growth, bone formation exceeds resorption.

Onset of puberty initiates closure of the cartilage growth plate as sex hormones begin to increase. Estrogen is more effective than testosterone in initiating ossification. The earlier onset of puberty in females accounts for their smaller frame size. Castration of either males or females results in further growth in length of long bones compared with gonadally intact animals. However, closure of the growth plate of castrates eventually occurs via the action of other hormones. Complete ossification of the growth plate results in cessation of long bone growth in length. Appositional growth to increase diameter continues as added weight and other stresses require stronger, more compact bone. Remodeling of bone occurs throughout the life of the animal and is accomplished by the combined activity of the three bone cell types.[3,4]

Increases in size of the skull and axial skeleton postnatally occur by appositional growth. Osteoblasts proliferate from precursor cells located adjacent to existing bone beneath the periosteum. Osteoblasts produce matrix materials, which are deposited on the bone surfaces, thereby increasing their size and density. Osteoblasts differentiate into osteocytes to produce more mature bone matrix materials consistent with the maturation of the animal. Bones of the axial skeleton exhibit a posterior–anterior gradient in maturation.[4]

Skeletal Muscle Growth

Postnatal skeletal muscle growth coincides with rapid body growth, and requires both DNA and protein accumu-

lation. Muscle fiber (myofiber) number is established prenatally, but nuclei within the sarcolemma do not synthesize DNA. Nevertheless, skeletal muscle DNA accretion generally parallels myofiber hypertrophy and muscular animals have greater muscle DNA than less muscular animals. Postnatal accumulation of myofiber DNA results from the activity of satellite cells, which are located between the sarcolemma and the basement membrane of myofibers. Satellite cells proliferate, differentiate, and fuse with preexisting myofibers, thereby contributing their DNA. Each myofiber nucleus is capable of supporting a finite cell volume. Since over 80% of skeletal muscle DNA of most species accumulates postnatally, satellite cell incorporation is obligatory for normal myofiber growth.[4]

Protein accumulation in all tissues occurs when protein synthesis exceeds degradation. In skeletal muscle, fractional protein accretion, synthesis, and degradation rates are high in young animals and decline in older animals.[5] Myofiber growth in length and diameter is achieved by increases in myofibrillar proteins. Myofibrils increase in length by addition of sarcomeres. Addition of myofilaments and longitudinal splitting of myofibrils increase myofibril diameter and number, respectively. Growth in skeletal muscle length accompanies bone growth and precedes extensive increases in muscle diameter.

Adipose Tissue Deposition

In early stages of adipose tissue development, vascularization of connective tissue increases markedly and lobules (i.e., aggregations of preadipocytes) are formed.

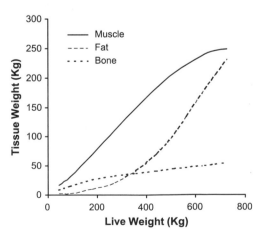

Fig. 2 Accretion of bone, muscle, and fat during postnatal live weight gain of cattle.

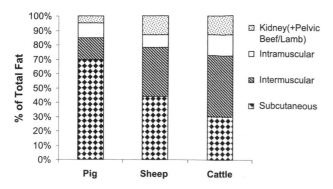

Fig. 3 Distribution of fat in various depots of pigs, sheep, and cattle.

As adipogenesis proceeds, the lobules give rise to large lobes of proliferating preadipocytes, which are associated with an extensive capillary network within a connective tissue sheath. The preadipocytes differentiate into immature adipocytes and accumulate lipid droplets (multilocular lipid). When lipid droplets become so numerous as to abut one another, they coalesce to form one large lipid globule (unilocular lipid), which characterizes mature adipocytes.[4] These adipogenic events apply to all depots, but the rate and extent of development differs among depots, genders, and species (Fig. 3). The brown fat present at birth gives way to white adipose tissue during the first few weeks postnatally.

Preadipocytes are <20 μm in diameter, while mature adipocytes normally average from 120 to 150 μm in diameter, but have been found to be as large as 300 μm in diameter in very obese animals.[4] When adipocytes accumulate lipid so as to reach their average size, recruitment of new preadipocytes occurs. The newly recruited preadipocytes add further to the overall fatness of an animal.

Fat in adipose tissue of mammals is derived from dietary fatty acids present in the blood as triglycerides, as well as from de novo fatty acid synthesis and esterification to form triglycerides in adipose tissue depots. Triglyceride formation is called lipogenesis and it accounts for the bulk of the lipid present in adipocytes. Fatty acids are removed from triglycerides by enzymes within the adipocyte, pass into capillaries, and are carried to tissues where they provide energy. The process of fatty acid mobilization is called lipolysis. During fattening, lipogenesis exceeds lipolysis. However, lipolysis exceeds lipogenesis when the energy demand for maintenance and activity exceeds the dietary energy intake.[4]

Notable among the factors affecting fat deposition are the sex hormones. Estrogen increases deposition, while androgens limit fat deposition. Hence, females are fatter than males. Castration markedly increases fat deposition of both genders.

Factors Affecting Postnatal Growth

The proportion of dietary energy used for maintenance of body temperature and tissue mass influences body weight gain. Temperature extremes reduce the growth rate of animals due to additional energy expended to reduce or increase body temperature, or decreased appetite to reduce heat generated in digestion. Because of their larger surface area-to-volume ratio and lack of insulation, young animals have a higher critical temperature than older animals.[2]

Postnatal growth is dependent upon food intake. Appetite is regulated by nerve centers in the hypothalamus, which is influenced by leptin from adipose tissue and by insulin.[6] The quantity and availability of dietary nutrients influence growth rate and body composition. Rapidly growing, muscular genotypes have greater amino acid requirements for maximal growth than slower-growing, less muscular animals of the same species.

Animals on a high plane of nutrition have greater organ weights, which increase energy expenditure. Increased energy expenditure is also associated with high lean genotypes. When feed is restricted to animals, organ weights and maintenance requirements decrease. Animals with restricted feed intake typically exhibit compensatory gain when shifted to a higher plane of nutrition because a higher proportion of dietary nutrients are available for tissue gain.[7]

Estrogenic and androgenic steroids are commonly used as growth promoters for cattle in the United States.[8] These steroids increase food intake, rate of body weight gain, and efficiency of growth, and the effects of estrogens and androgens are additive. Androgenic implants increase skeletal muscle and reduce fat accretion. More recently, ractopamine, a beta-adrenergic agonist, has been approved for finishing pigs and cattle. This compound increases animal growth rate, efficiency, and muscularity.

CONCLUSION

Postnatal body growth of animals follows a sigmoidal curve that reflects the differential growth of bone, muscle, and fat. Absolute rate of postnatal growth is species dependent, and is influenced by breed, body frame size, gender, nutrition, and environment. Understanding of food intake regulation and factors controlling expression of growth-related genes is rapidly improving. This information will enhance efforts to improve animal growth and body composition.

REFERENCES

1. Black, J.L. Animal growth and its regulation. J. Anim. Sci. **1988**, *66* (3), 1–22.
2. *Hammond's Farm Animals*, 5th Ed.; Hammond, J., Bowman, J.C., Robinson, T.J., Eds.; Edward Arnold: London, England, 1983.
3. Lawrence, T.L.J.; Fowler, V.R. *Growth of Farm Animals*; CAB International: New York, 1997.
4. Gerrard, D.E.; Grant, A.L. *Principles of Animal Growth and Development*; Kendall/Hunt Publishing Company: Dubuque, IA, 2003.
5. Bergen, W.G.; Merkel, R.A. Protein Accretion. In *Growth Regulation in Farm Animals*; Pearson, A.M., Dutson, T.R., Eds.; Advances in Meat Research; Elsevier Applied Science: London, 1991; Vol. 7.
6. Hogg, B.W. Compensatory Growth in Ruminants. In *Growth Regulation in Farm Animals*; Pearson, A.M., Dutson, T.R., Eds.; Advances in Meat Research; Elsevier Applied Science: London, 1991; Vol. 7.
7. Schwartz, M.W.; Woods, S.C.; Porte, D.; Seeley, R.J.; Baskin, D.G. Central nervous system control of food intake. Nature **2000**, *404*, 661–671.
8. Hancock, D.L.; Wagner, J.F.; Anderson, D.B. Effects of Estrogens and Androgens on Animal Growth. In *Growth Regulation in Farm Animals*; Pearson, A.M., Dutson, T.R., Eds.; Advances in Meat Research; Elsevier Applied Science: London, 1991; Vol. 7.

Hormones: Anabolic Agents

Hugh Galbraith
University of Aberdeen, Aberdeen, U.K.

INTRODUCTION

Growth in animals is well known to be influenced by a range of endogenous anabolic compounds that promote commercially desirable greater lean tissue deposition and reduced fat in body tissues. These compounds, which act directly or indirectly to alter anabolic or catabolic processes, include protein hormones and growth factors and steroidal androgens and estrogens. Of these only androgenic and estrogenic compounds along with certain progestagens have been approved for commercial application in farm animals. This long-standing practice now mainly applies to beef production in North American countries. In contrast, the European Union has applied the "precautionary principle" and prohibited both the use of these preparations internally and importation of meat from treated animals from external countries. This prohibition is frequently questioned on the grounds of the small amounts of residues consumed in beef in relation to endogenous quantities in humans and those determined as safe by toxicological methodology. This review will consider, for the anabolic agents in commercial use, application and responses in practice, mode of action, residues, and contemporary issues relating to risk assessment for human consumers and the general environment.

APPLICATION, PROPERTIES, AND CONSUMER ISSUES

Commercial Preparations, Hormone Delivery, Responses, and Mode of Action

The anabolic preparations available in the United States[1] contain naturally occurring testosterone (T) and its propionate ester, estradiol-17β (E) and its benzoate ester, progesterone (Pr), and the xenobiotic compounds trenbolone acetate (TA), zeranol (Z), and melengestrol acetate (MGA). Active ingredients may be further characterized as estrogens (E is a steroid hormone synthesized mainly in gonadal tissues; Z is a resorcylic acid lactone derivative of the nonsteroidal fungal estrogen zearalenone), steroidal androgens (T is a hormone synthesized in gonads and adrenal cortex with potential for conversion to estrogens; TA with effects produced mainly by its active metabolite

trenbolone-17βOH, exhibits both androgenic and anticorticosteroid properties), and progestagens (naturally occurring steroid Pr; synthetic steroidal compound MGA). Formulations containing single, or certain combinations of, ingredients are applied as impregnated silastic rubber implants or compressed pellets under the skin of the upper surface of the ear, or for MGA, inclusion in the diet.

The relative quantities of active ingredients (up to 43.9 mg for E and 200 mg for T, TA, and Pr) in implants[1] reflect amounts required to produce effects in vivo. These result in variably circulating concentrations of total E in the range of 5 to 80 pg/ml with those for T, TA, and Pr in excess of 250 pg/ml.[2] Typical improvements in growth, feed conversion efficiency, and carcass leanness have been summarized[2] in the range of 10 to 30%, 5 to 15%, and 5 to 8%, respectively, with greatest effects occurring in steers in the relative absence of endogenous sex hormones. Smaller responses occur in postpubertal heifers and bulls.[3] Estrogens are considered to have the greatest anabolic activity with potentiation by androgens and in particular when combined with trenbolone acetate. For implants, the growth responses are affected by rates and quantities of systemic uptake of hormonal compounds from the implant, their transport by carrier proteins such as sex hormone binding globulin or serum albumin, and the diffusion of free forms into target cells. These events precede interaction with specific members of the steroid nuclear hormone family of receptor transcription factors for estrogens, androgens, and progestagens and associated chaperone proteins.[4–6] These ligand-bound steroid receptors form activated, usually dimer, complexes that along with co-activators bind to specific nuclear hormone response elements. Depending on recognition sites, these may activate or repress DNA expression to affect gene transcription and translation directly in skeletal muscle or adipose cells or indirectly by stimulating expression of other hormonal compounds, such as IGF-I with suppression of thyroid or corticosteroid hormone function.[2] Although poorly understood, changes in these messaging systems are considerable to produce alterations in the balance of anabolism and catabolism of protein and fat. Synthesis of protein may be influenced directly at a gene level, with catabolism mediated by proteolysis, such as produced by lysosome, ubiquitin, and/or proteasome-dependent pathways.[7]

Encyclopedia of Animal Science
DOI: 10.1081/E-EAS 120023508

The maintenance of activity of hormonal preparations is determined by continued availability from the implant and by retention in tissues in the active form. These, along with metabolized and variably inactivated forms, contribute to the presence of residues in meat postmortem. Metabolic inactivation is effected predominantly by liver CYP450 systems with elimination, for example, following hydroxylation or sulphation in urine or if more lipophilic via bile, with the additional possibility of reabsorption.[4] An issue of increasing contemporary importance is persistence in the environment of excreted compounds, including the nonabsorbed fraction for MGA, and subsequent re-entry to the water or food chain.[8]

Assessment of Risk to Human Consumers

For human beings, consumption of meat containing hormones and their residues involves absorption from digested products, systemic transport in blood (usually protein-bound), metabolism, and excretion in urine and feces with retention in some body tissues.[4] Important issues include the physiological status of human consumers, concentrations and production rates of endogenous sex hormones, sensitivity of prepubertal children, and short- and long-term effects of embryonic and fetal exposure in utero. Xenobiotic hormones that do not occur naturally in animals require consideration in the context of absolute quantities.

The acceptability of meat from animals treated with veterinary drugs is determined by the Codex Alimentarius,[9] frequently utilizing information from the Joint Food and Agriculture Organization of the United Nations (FAO)/World Health Organization (WHO) expert Committee on Food Additives (JECFA). Current methodology estimates: 1) the acceptable daily intake (ADI) of residues based on intake of standard portions of food ingredients and 2) the maximum residue limit in tissues (MRL), which restricts intake to less than the ADI. Values for ADI are derived from toxicological studies that determine the maximum quantity to produce no effect (NOEL) and incorporate a safety factor that effectively reduces the NOEL value usually by 100- to 1000-fold. The end points of toxicological evaluation for compounds with sex hormone activity are usually receptor-mediated biochemical or physiological processes that are unlikely to be appropriate to assess non–receptor-mediated effects.[4] Differences in the affinities of estrogenic ligands for estrogenic receptors ER-α and ER-β also make inappropriate the assessment of risk based on the summation of all estrogens in the diet.[4]

Specific tolerances for residues in uncooked edible beef tissues are published by the U.S. Food and Drug Administration (USFDA)[10] and, with some differences in values for ADI and MRL separately, by JECFA and Codex Alimentarius (e.g., Ref. [9]). Examples of these, derived using contemporary methodology and based on estimated intakes by adult human consumers, are shown consistently to be less than 20% of ADI (Table 1). MRLs have been defined as unnecessary for naturally occurring hormonal preparations implanted according to good veterinary practice, as residues are considered safe for human consumers.[9] This recommendation is at variance with the permanent ban on E and its esters by the European Commission (EC), mainly on the grounds that E is a total carcinogen.[11] This conclusion derives from epidemiology and evidence of cancer induction following nuclear free-radical damage by certain catechol metabolites in cell and laboratory animal test systems, and proliferative cancer promotion in ER-receptive cells. Opposing views highlight the low bioavailability of E and its small contribution as a proportion of total E synthesis in human consumers, including prepubertal children.[4] Possible carcinogen status has been applied to T, because of its convertibility to estrogens, and to Pr.[4] Variable results have been obtained for genotoxicity and carcinogenicity of TA and Z and their metabolites.[4] The European Commission[11] has recently continued the previous temporary ban on T, Pr, TA, Z, and MGA.

Table 1 Values for maximum ADI of residues in standard portions of beef from hormone-implanted cattle[a]; estimated intake of extractable residues as percentage of ADI; MRL[b]

	Anabolic agent				
	E	**T**	**Pr**	**TA**	**Z**
ADI	3.5	140	2100	1.4	35
Intake as % ADI	1.5	0.04	0.008	15	0.48
MRL	Unnecessary	Unnecessary	Unnecessary	2 (muscle)	2 (muscle)
				10 (liver)	10 (liver)

[a]ADI: μg/70 kg body weight.
[b]MRL: μg/kg tissue.
(From Refs. 4,9,11.)

CONCLUSIONS

The hormonal anabolic preparations currently used provide an effective means of increasing the efficiency of beef production. However, knowledge of their precise mode of action at molecular and supramolecular levels remains incomplete. Major disadvantages include their broad-based effects on nonmeat tissues and potential for adverse biological activity of residues. Concerns about misuse may be addressed by systems for random testing and traceability of source of beef product. Current methods for assessing risk for human consumers, for example, in determining non–receptor-mediated effects, appear inadequate. The absorption from meat of naturally occurring hormones that produce systemic concentrations considerably less than those present endogenously presents a limited hazard. However, for these and xenobiotics, what is needed is quantitative risk assessment based on the "molecular materiality" of the additional residue intake and utilizing principles of quantitative chemical and biological stoichiometry to assess responses in biological test systems.[4]

A continuing focus on the contribution of excretory sex hormone products to human and animal health appears relevant in the context of justification of agricultural practices in human society.

REFERENCES

1. Code of Federal Regulations. Title 21. Food and Drugs. Part 522. Implantation or injectable dose form new animal drugs. http://www.access.gpo.gov/nara/cfr/waisidx_03/21cfr522_03.html (accessed July 2003).

2. Preston, R.L. Hormone containing growth promoting implants in farmed livestock. Advance Drug Delivery Reviews **1999**, *38*, 123–138.

3. Galbraith, H.; Topps, J.H. Effect of hormones on growth and body composition of animals. Nutrition Abstract and Reviews **1981**, *51B*, 521–540.

4. Galbraith, H. Hormones in international meat production: Biological, sociological and consumer issues. Nutrition Abstract and Reviews **2002**, *15*, 293–314.

5. Taylor, P.M.; Brameld, J.M. Mechanisms of Regulation and Transcription. In *Protein Metabolism and Nutrition*; Lobley, G.E., White, A., MacRae, J.C., Eds.; Wageningen Pers: Wageningen, 1999; 25–50.

6. Meyer, H.H.D. Biochemistry and physiology of anabolic hormones used for improvement of meat production. APMIS, **2001**, *109*, 1–8.

7. Attaix, D.; Combaret, L.; Taillandiet, D. Mechanisms and Regulation in Protein Degradation. In *Protein Metabolism and Nutrition*; Lobley, G.E., White, A., MacRae, J.C., Eds.; Wageningen Pers: Wageningen, 1999; 51–67.

8. Anderson, A.-M., Grigor, K., Meyts, E.R.-De., Letters, H., Eds.; Hormones and Endocrine Disrupters in Food and Water. APMIS, Acta Pathol. Microbiol. Immunol. Scand., 2001; Vol. 109 (Supplementary No. 103).

9. Codex Alimentarius Commission. FAO/WHO Food Standards. http://www.codexalimentarius.net (with links: accessed July 2003).

10. Code of Federal Regulations. Title 21. Food and Drugs. Part 556. Tolerances for residues in new animal drugs in food. http://www.access.gpo.gov/nara/cfr/waisidx–03/21cfr556–03.html.

11. The European Commission. Food and Feed Safety. Hormones in Meat. http://europa.eu.int/comm/food/food/chemicalsafety/contaminants/hormones/index_en.htm (with links: accessed April 2004).

Hormones: Protein

John Klindt
United States Department of Agriculture, Agricultural Research Service,
Clay Center, Nebraska, U.S.A.

INTRODUCTION

Hormones are produced and released from endocrine glands directly into the bloodstream and transported to distant tissues. They direct physiological processes to maintain homeostasis and direct growth, development, and reproduction. Hormone secretion is regulated by genetic and environmental inputs and constant negative and positive feedback control by metabolites, neurotransmitters, and other hormones. Protein hormones are polymers of amino acids that effect their actions through binding to cell-surface receptors.

DEFINITIONS

Classically, hormones are described as substances that are produced and secreted from one organ and that travel via the circulation to other organs to direct physiological processes. The endocrine system is often described as a hierarchical system with instructions flowing from the central nervous system as neurotransmitters through the hypothalamus and/or the pituitary gland to peripheral organs and tissues. In actuality, the endocrine system has many points of information input, both from within the animal and from the environment, and feedback loops producing a highly integrated interactive system that maintains fine control over homeostasis and productive processes. Greater elucidation of endocrine regulation has revealed hormone action on nearby cells without transport through the circulatory system. These actions, without bloodstream transport, are classified as paracrine, affecting cells of a different type than those that produced them, and autocrine, affecting cells of the same type as those that produced them.

Naturally occurring protein hormones are peptide polymers of L-amino acids. Biologically active analogues of naturally occurring hormones containing D-amino acids have been synthesized. Amino acid polymers of less than 100 amino acids are generally considered peptides and larger polymers are considered proteins. Protein hormones are polar compounds that affect target tissues by binding to specific cell-surface receptors, initiating a cascade of intracellular signals directing specific pathways.

HYPOTHALAMUS

The hypothalamus is a region of the brain that produces hormones released by the posterior pituitary gland and releasing peptides that regulate the anterior pituitary gland. There are five hypothalamic-releasing hormones. Gonadotropin-releasing hormone (GnRH, LHRH, FSHRH) stimulates secretion of luteotropin (luteinizing hormone, LH) and follitropin (follicle-stimulating hormone, FSH). Corticotropin-releasing hormone (CRF) stimulates proopiomelanocortin (POMC) gene expression, and thus, corticotropin (adrenocorticotropic hormone, ACTH) secretion. Thyrotropin-releasing hormone (TRH) stimulates thyrotropin (thyroid-stimulating hormone, TSH) secretion. Secretion of growth hormone is controlled by the stimulatory action of growth hormone-releasing hormone (GRH) and the inhibitory action of somatostatin (SRIH).

PITUITARY GLAND

The pituitary gland, the hypophysis, is a small structure at the base of the brain composed of two glands—the adenohypophysis and neurohypophysis—that control homeostasis, growth, and reproduction. Hormones of the neurohypophysis, or posterior pituitary gland, vasopressin, vasotocin and oxytocin, are produced as prohormones in the hypothalamus and are transported via neural axons to the neurohypophysis. There they are stored, processed, and released into the circulation. Vasopressin or antidiuretic hormone (ADH) stimulates blood vessel constriction and water resorption by kidneys and enhances corticotropin (ACTH) secretion from the anterior pituitary. Vasotocin and vasopressin are structurally and functionally similar. Oxytocin acts on the uterus to stimulate contractions and mammary glands to induce milk ejection.

Encyclopedia of Animal Science
DOI: 10.1081/E-EAS 120019674
Published 2005 by Marcel Dekker, Inc. All rights reserved.

The adenohypophysis, or anterior pituitary gland, produces and secretes ACTH, GH, LH, FSH, TSH, prolactin (PRL), melanocyte-stimulating hormone (MSH), β-endorphin, and β-lipoprotein. ACTH, MSH, and β-endorphin are cleavage products of POMC gene regulated by CRH. ACTH stimulates glucocorticoid synthesis in the adrenal cortex in response to stress. GH has actions in growth and development, immune development, reproduction, and lactation. GH is under dual hypothalamic regulation, GRH and SRIH. LH and FSH are regulated by GnRH. LH is the regulator of testosterone production by Leydig cells in testes and the stimulus for ovulation and maintenance of corpora lutea in ovaries. Ovarian follicle recruitment and development and testicular Sertoli cell function are dependent upon FSH. TSH regulates synthesis and release of thyroxine (T_4) from the thyroid. Thyroxine is converted to biologically active triiodothyronine (T_3), which regulates oxidation of fats, proteins, and carbohydrates in the liver, kidneys, heart, and muscle, and thus regulates basal metabolism. TSH, LH, and FSH are dimeric glycoproteins sharing a common α subunit. PRL has roles in maintenance of corpora lutea and lactation. Consensus PRL-release inhibiting factor is dopamine but no specific PRL-releasing factor has been identified.

PERIPHERAL ENDOCRINE ORGANS

Of peripheral sources of protein hormones, the pancreas, the source of insulin and glucagon, has received the most emphasis. Deficiency of insulin action, due to lack of or response to insulin, results in diabetes. Insulin is produced by pancreatic islets of Langerhans. Cells within the islets also secrete glucagon, SRIH, pancreatic polypeptide, and amylin. Cellular uptake of glucose and amino acids is stimulated by insulin. Insulin and glucagon act in concert in the liver to maintain energetic and glucose homeostasis. Increased blood concentrations of insulin result in reduced blood concentrations of glucose. Low blood glucose induces secretion of pancreatic glucagon, which activates hepatic gluconeogenesis.

Insulin is a member of a family of structurally similar hormones that comprise two peptide chains bound together by disulfide bonds. Other members of this hormone family are insulin-like growth factor (IGF)-I, IGF-II, relaxin, and nerve growth factor (NGF). Relaxin is produced by late pregnant corpora lutea and its principal action in mammals is to soften the cervix and pelvic ligaments in preparation for parturition. IGF-I and IGF-II have endocrine, paracrine, and autocrine actions, are produced by a plethora of tissues, respond to GH stimulation, and are generally considered anabolic. IGF-I and -II can exert insulin-like endocrine effects on blood glucose in sufficient doses. Most IGF in the circulation are bound to specific binding proteins (IGFBP) that modify their biological activity and clearance. While IGF-I is important in postnatal growth, evidence from exogenous administration[1] and transgenic studies has not established whether actions are endocrine, paracrine, and autocrine. IGF-II is important for fetal growth and has a role in myoblast differentiation.

The gastrointestinal (GI) tract is a set of tissues with numerous secretory activities. Among the protein hormones produced by the GI tissues are secretin, gastrin, motilin, cholecystokinin, glucose-dependent intestinal polypeptide, galanin, vasoactive intestinal polypeptide, gastric inhibitory peptide, neurotensin, TRH, SRIH, glicentin, and ghrelin. Some GI hormones influence aspects of digestive tract function including motility, blood flow, and excretory functions. Others coordinate digestive processes with systemic metabolic and anabolic processes.

Liver is a major organ of the endocrine system. It is a site of glucagon and insulin action and produces IGF, IGFBP, and hormone-binding globulins. Hormone-binding globulins are important in the transport of steroid hormones.

Many tissues produce and receive hormonal signals. The heart produces atrial natriuretic hormones; lungs produce vasoactive intestinal peptide, SRIH, and substance-P; the thymus produces thymulin and thymosins; the spleen produces splenin; kidneys produce renin, erythropoietin, and angiotensins; platelets produce growth factors, e.g., platelet-derived growth factor (PDGF), hepatocyte growth factor, and others; macrophages produce interleukins and interferons; and muscle produces IGF.

Adipocytes are targets of many hormones and secretors of the hormones leptin, resistin, and adipsin, as well as sites where energy is stored as fat. Leptin has satiety effects and has received much attention as a potential treatment for obesity. Blood concentrations of leptin correlate with fatness and may be means by which adipocytes communicate information about body condition to higher centers, suppressing appetite and stimulating reproductive processes. Exogenous leptin has positive actions on some reproductive processes.

REPRODUCTIVE HORMONES

LH, FSH, and, in some species, PRL are considered pituitary gland regulators of gonadal function. However, the entire endocrine system, through maintenance of metabolic balance, impacts reproductive activity. Gonads respond to and produce protein and steroid hormones. Ovarian follicles and Sertoli cells of the testes produce inhibin and activin. Pituitary activin has positive influences, and gonadal inhibin has negative influences on

FSH secretion from the pituitary gland. These hormones act to influence secretion of FSH and may allow specific regulation of both LH and FSH with a single releasing hormone, GnRH. Castration removes gonadal steroids and results in increased circulating concentrations of LH and FSH and, in boars, decreased insulin and IGF-I. Placenta of pregnant animals are sources of many hormones. Most hormonal proteins are produced in some concentration in placenta. Placental lactogen (somatommotropin, PL) is produced by trophoblast cells of many species, but not sows. Circulating PL concentrations rise in midpregnancy and remain elevated until parturition. PL has GH- and PRL-like activity. Pregnant mares serum gonadotropin (PMSG) is a highly glycosylated protein with primarily FSH-like activity and long half-life in circulation. Human trophoblast cells produce human chorionic gonadotropin (hCG) that has LH-like activity.

SEX EFFECTS

Endocrine functions are often sexually dimorphic, different in males and females. Programming of sexual dimorphism begins with embryonic expression of the sex-determining gene (SRY) in males and secretion of Müllerian-inhibiting hormone (anti-Müllerian hormone, MIH), prevents development of internal reproductive tracts, of females. Among sexually dimorphic characteristics of protein hormone secretion are GH secretory pattern, serum concentrations of IGF-I and IGF-II, and serum concentrations of glucose and insulin; concentrations of insulin and glucose are greater in boars than in gilts or barrows. Castrated males, the primary meat animal of many species, differ hormonally from intact males in many aspects.

FETAL ENDOCRINOLOGY

Most of the hormones produced in postnatal animals are produced in the fetus. Timing of appearance of individual hormones in fetal circulation is hormone-specific. Most hormones have the same actions in the fetus and postnatal animal, but their effectiveness is often reduced. Hormones of the anterior pituitary gland attain maximal concentrations in the fetus near the middle of the last third of pregnancy and then decline with development of feedback systems. While the endocrine system develops and becomes competent during fetal life, hormonal secretion is less dynamic, or episodic, than postnatally, possibly a reflection of the constancy of the intrauterine environment.

USES OF PROTEIN HORMONES IN ANIMAL PRODUCTION

So many physiological functions are regulated, at least in part, by protein hormones that their potential for use in animal production is enormous. A problem with use of protein hormones is administration. Protein hormones have short half-lives in circulation, less than 20 minutes. Thus, continuous administration of exogenous protein hormones is generally most effective. Injections in aqueous and slow-release depot preparations and osmotic pumps implanted subcutaneously have been efficacious. Transgenic animals have been developed, but technology is not perfected. In 1993, recombinant bovine GH (bST, Posilac®, Monsanto) in a slow release depot preparation was approved for enhancement of milk production in dairy cows in the United States. Use of species-specific recombinant GH has been investigated in beef cattle and swine to improve efficiency and carcass composition. Porcine GH, which is approved in Australia (Reprocin®, Alpharma), improves efficiency of body weight gain 10 to 15% and produces carcasses with more lean and less fat. PMSG has been used to stimulate Graafian follicle growth on the ovary, and either GnRH or hCG are used to induce ovulation in estrous induction and synchronization protocols. There is limited use of FSH in place of PMSG and LH in place of hCG. PG600® (Intervet) is a combination of PMSG and hCG sold in every pig-producing country for induction of estrus in gilts and sows. Immunoneutralization of GnRH to reduce boar taint, an androgen in meat from boars that results in an objectionable odor upon cooking, is approved in Australia (Improvac®, CSL Ltd.).

CONCLUSION

Protein hormones are involved in the regulation of all physiological processes in animals, functioning as stimulatory and inhibitory regulators. Identification and enumeration of protein hormones and elucidation of their functions and regulation is ongoing. With full understanding of their regulation and actions and development of recombinant and transgenic technologies, protein hormones may be harnessed to provide greater control over productive processes in livestock.

REFERENCE

1. Klindt, J.; Yen, J.T.; Buonomo, F.C.; Roberts, A.J.; Wise, T. Growth, body composition, and endocrine responses to chronic administration of insulin-like growth factor I and(or) porcine growth hormone in pigs. J. Anim. Sci. **1998**, *76*, 2368–2381.

Hormones: Steroid

Olga U. Bolden-Tiller
The University of Texas-M. D. Anderson Cancer Center, Houston, Texas, U.S.A.

Michael F. Smith
University of Missouri, Columbia, Missouri, U.S.A.

INTRODUCTION

Hormones are chemical messengers (steroids, prostaglandins, and protein/peptides) involved in cellular signaling from point A to B within a physiological system (endocrine, paracrine, autocrine, and/or intracrine communication). To date, numerous hormones, including steroid hormones, have been characterized biochemically. Steroids are required for a plethora of mammalian biological functions, ranging from organogenesis during development to the regulation of metabolic pathways and the proliferation of reproductive/mammary tissues. Steroids consist of six classes—progestins, estrogens, androgens, mineralocorticoids, glucocorticoids, and vitamin D. This article focuses on the structure, synthesis, and physiological mechanism of action of steroids.

STEROID HORMONES: STRUCTURE AND ORIGIN

Steroid hormones have a common molecular nucleus, composed of four rings designated A, B, C, and D, that serves as the molecular backbone (Fig. 1, cholesterol structure). All steroids originate from cholesterol after a series of complex enzymatic conversions (Fig. 1). Therefore, cholesterol availability and transport, as well as the expression and activity of steroidogenic enzymes, are required for optimal steroid biosynthesis (Fig. 1).[1,2]

Availability and Transport of Circulating Cholesterol

Free cholesterol is the precursor for all steroid hormones, but free cholesterol is typically not found within steroidogenic cells. Cholesterol transport involves protein–protein interactions and is critical for steroid biosynthesis. Most of the cholesterol is provided by low-density lipoproteins (LDL) or high-density lipoproteins (HDL), although small amounts of cholesterol are produced by de novo synthesis. The LDL/HDL cholesterol complexes bind to specific membrane receptors and are subsequently internalized and transported to the lysosomes, where cholesterol is released from the complex. Free cholesterol is converted to cholesterol esters by acyl coenzyme A:cholesterol acyltransferase and stored as lipid droplets until used for steroid biosynthesis.[3] Cholesterol esterase hydrolyzes cholesterol esters, thereby liberating stored cholesterol.[3]

Translocation of Cholesterol

Cholesterol is translocated through the cytoplasm to the mitochondria via the cytoskeleton. Sterol carrier protein-2 is also thought to be involved in cholesterol transport. Once cholesterol reaches the mitochondria, it is actively transported into the inner mitochondrial membrane, where steroidogenesis begins. The transport of cholesterol into the inner mitochondrial membranc is the rate-limiting step in steroid biosynthesis, as it appears to be more tightly regulated than the subsequent steps in the process.[4]

Steroidogenic acute regulatory protein (StAR), peripheral-type benzodiazepene receptor (PBR), and endozepine are involved in the movement of cholesterol into the mitochondria. At the cytoplasmic–mitochondrial interface, cholesterol is bound by StAR, which actively transports it from the cytoplasm to the outer mitochondrial membrane. Peripheral-type benzodiazepene receptors located in the outer mitochondrial membrane are associated with the movement of cholesterol to the inner mitochondrial membrane, where the cholesterol is converted to pregnenolone. Endozepine, the ligand for PBR, facilitates the uptake of cholesterol into the inner mitochondrial membrane. The role of endozepine in this process is not understood, but it is thought to be associated with the ability of PBR to transport cholesterol and the exchange of cholesterol from StAR to PBR at the interface of the inner and outer mitochondrial membranes.[4]

Steroidogenesis

The conversion of cholesterol to various steroids is dependent upon a number of biochemical conversions. This section highlights the biosynthesis of steroid

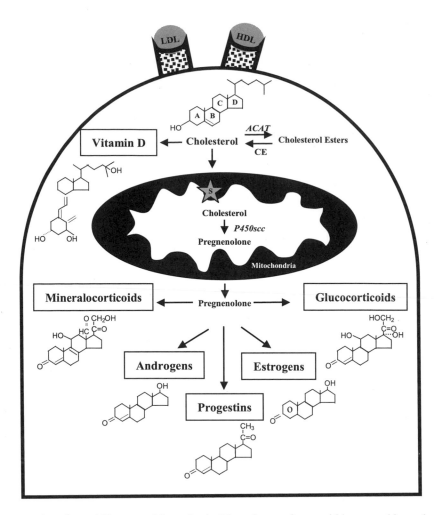

Fig. 1 Schematic representation of steroid hormone biosynthesis. The substrate for steroid hormone biosynthesis is cholesterol, which is derived from low-density lipoproteins (LDL), high-density lipoproteins (HDL), hydrolysis of cholesterol stored in lipid droplets, or de novo synthesis. Free cholesterol is transported to the mitochondria, from where it is next transported to the inner mitochondrial membrane via steroidogenic acute regulatory protein (S) along with peripheral-type benzodiazepene receptor and endozepine (not shown). Once cholesterol arrives at the inner mitochondrial membrane, it is cleaved by cytochrome P450 side-chain cleavage enzyme ($P450_{scc}$) to form pregnenolone, which is transported into the cytoplasm and converted by specific steroidogenic enzymes. Structures shown: progestin=progesterone; androgen=testosterone; glucocorticoid=cortisol; mineralocorticoid=aldosterone; estrogen=estradiol; vitamin D=1,25-dihydroxyvitamin D_3; ACAT=acyl coenzyme A:cholesterol acyltransferase; CE=cholesterol esterase. (From Ref. 2.)

hormones from cholesterol, with particular emphasis on the initial enzyme in the cascade: cytochrome P450 side-chain cleavage enzyme ($P450_{scc}$; Fig. 1).

Once cholesterol arrives at the inner mitochondrial membrane, it is cleaved by $P450_{scc}$, an enzyme complex found only in that membrane, to form pregnenolone, an intermediate product that is subsequently converted into various steroid hormones by enzymatic reactions at the level of the smooth endoplasmic reticulum. An exception to that pathway is seen in the vitamin D family, which is synthesized directly from cholesterol without conversion to pregnenolone (Fig. 1). After synthesis, steroids are secreted into the bloodstream. Because steroids are not water-soluble, they must be bound to a carrier protein to be transported to specific target tissues.[2]

CHARACTERIZATION OF STEROID RECEPTORS

Steroid hormones initiate cellular responses in target organs primarily via specific intracellular proteins referred to as receptors. The bulk of these receptors have been localized to genomic and cytosolic compartments of the cell.

Steroid Receptor Structure

Steroid receptors belong to the nuclear receptor super-family, one of the largest families of transcription factors, including receptors for estrogen, progesterone, thyroid hormone, vitamin D, retinoids, and orphan receptors, for which the ligands are not known.[5] Genes encoding members of the nuclear receptor superfamily consist of a single polypeptide chain that can be divided into several domains—the amino-terminal domain (A/B), the DNA-binding domain (DBD, C), the hinge region (D), the ligand-binding domain (LBD, E), and the C-terminal domain (F) (Fig. 2).[2,5,6] The N-terminal domain is a highly variable region, containing at least one activation function (discussed subsequently), whereas the DBD is a conserved region (60–95%). The DBD contains two zinc fingers that form cysteine repeats, which are involved in the interactions between the receptor dimer and DNA at the steroid response element (SRE). For each receptor, this region is completely conserved among mammalian species and highly homologous to the DBD of other steroid receptors. The variable hinge region is located between the DBD and the LBD and is critical for interaction between the receptor and heat shock proteins (hsp), which modulate steroid receptor activation and inactivation. The hinge region also plays a role in nuclear translocation. The LBD is conserved among the related steroid receptors, including the progesterone receptor, estrogen receptor, glucocorticoid receptor, and mineralocorticoid receptor. This region is responsible for ligand binding, which initiates conformational changes of the receptor that are necessary for proper signal transduction,

as well as interactions between the steroid receptor and the hsp. The C-terminal domain, like the N-terminal domain, is variable and contains one of the activation functions (discussed subsequently).[6]

Hormone Action

In plasma, steroids dissociate from the carrier protein and diffuse through the plasma membrane into the nucleus. Several mechanisms have been identified by which steroids and their receptors may cause cellular responses. These mechanisms appear to be hormone-, receptor-, and cell-specific, and they include ligand-dependent and -independent activation of intracellular receptors in addition to the activation of a putative membrane-bound receptor.

Traditional steroid signaling

The effects of steroids are primarily mediated by their receptors, acting as steroid-activated transcription factors to regulate the expression of a variety of genes. In the absence of ligand, steroid receptors are functionally inactive. These receptors exist in complexes that include one or more receptor molecules, a dimer of the 90-kDa hsp, and a monomer of the 70-kDa hsp. Once bound to the steroid, the receptor dissociates from each of the hsp and undergoes a conformational change that results in posttranslational modifications (Fig. 3). The steroid receptor complex subsequently binds to DNA at SREs within the regulatory regions of target genes. The steroid receptor–DNA complex interacts with general transcriptional machinery including cofactors, coactivators, or corepressors, resulting in the positive or negative regulation of target gene transcription. Newly synthesized mRNA leaves the nucleus and undergoes translation, which will ultimately result in a biological response by that cell or other cells.[2,6,7]

Novel steroid signaling

In addition to the traditional genomic receptor, functional membrane-bound receptors have been identified for progesterone and estrogen, suggesting the possibility of nongenomic mechanisms of action.[8] Similar findings have been reported for estrogen for which the cell membrane and genomic receptors originate from a single transcript.[8] The rapid, nongenomic effects of steroids appear to be transmitted by nongenomic membrane receptors. Investigators postulate that the activity of these receptors is associated with an influx of intracellular Ca+, suggesting that a membrane receptor or a fragment of one is involved in nongenomic signaling for some steroids.[9] The mechanism is unclear however.

In addition to the ligand-induced actions described previously, some steroid receptors, such as those for

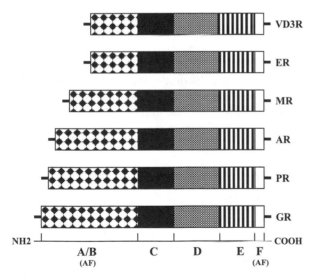

Fig. 2 Schematic representation of the steroid hormone receptor genes. A single individual gene encodes each steroid receptor. The gene has several features that are common among members of the nuclear receptor superfamily: 1) a highly variable amino-terminal domain (A/B); 2) the DNA-binding domain (C); 3) the hinge domain (D); 4) the ligand-binding domain (E), and the carboxyl-terminal domain (F). The A/B and F domains contain activation functions (AF) that are responsible for regulating steroid hormone-mediated transactivation. VD3R = vitamin D_3 receptor; ER = estrogen receptor; MR = mineralocorticoid receptor; AR = androgen receptor; PR = progesterone receptor; GR = glucocorticoid receptor. (From Ref. 5.)

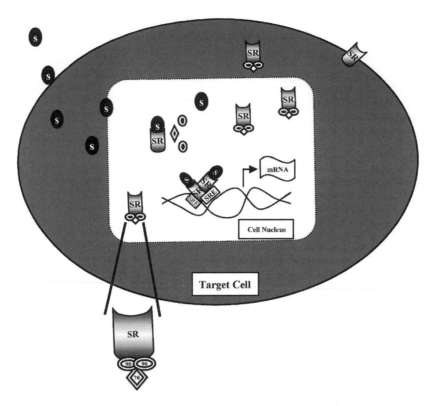

Fig. 3 Steroid-dependent gene transactivation. Steroid hormones (S) diffuse through the plasma membrane and bind to specific intracellular proteins called receptors (SR) that are found primarily within the nucleus of target cells, although minute amounts have been localized elsewhere within the cell. Binding of the hormone induces conformational changes in the receptor, resulting in the release of heat shock proteins (70 and 90) from the receptor. The steroid receptor complexes dimerize and bind to specific sites on the DNA, called the steroid response elements (SRE), resulting in the regulation of target gene transcription (mRNA). (From Ref. 7.)

progesterone, can be activated in the absence of the ligand by phosphorylation pathways that modulate the interaction of these receptors with cofactors.[10] In this model, steroid receptor coactivators, such as the steroid receptor coactivator-1 (SRC-1), are activated after phosphorylation is induced by neurotransmitters. The activated coactivator recruits the receptors, forming a hyperphosphorylated transcriptional complex that binds to the SRE in the absence of the steroid. This interaction regulates the transcription of target genes.[11]

Regulation of transcriptional activity

The mechanism for steroid receptor-mediated regulation of target genes involves specific transactivation domains referred to as activation functions, the number of which varies depending on the particular steroid receptor. The availability of the activation domains is modulated by conformational changes induced by steroids and their analogues. In general, agonists induce changes in receptor structure that promote interactions with coactivators, thereby increasing transcription. On the other hand, some agonists and some antagonists induce changes in recep-

tor structure that facilitate receptor interactions with corepressors, thus inhibiting transcription.[10] However, antagonists generally inhibit transcriptional activity by occupying the receptor, thus preventing the steroid from binding.[7]

CONCLUSION

Cholesterol is the precursor for the steroid hormone family, which can be divided into six classes. The members of each class are similar structurally and in their mechanism of action. Steroids are responsible for regulating numerous processes within the body that are necessary for normal biological function.

REFERENCES

1. McKenna, N.J.; O'Malley, B.W. Minireview: Nuclear receptor coactivators—An update. Endocrinology **2002**, *143* (7), 2461–2465.

2. Norman, A.W.; Litwack, G. Steroid Hormones. In *Hormones*; Academic Press: San Diego, CA, 1997; 49–82. NY.

3. Niswender, G.D.; Nett, T.M. Corpus Luteum and its Control in Infraprimate Species. In *The Physiology of Reproduction*; Knobil, E., Neill, J.D., Eds.; Raven Press: New York, NY, 1994; 781–816.

4. Niswender, G.D. Molecular control of luteal secretion of progesterone. Reproduction **2002**, *123* (3), 333–339.

5. Tsai, M.J.; O'Malley, B.W. Molecular mechanisms of action of steroid/thyroid receptor superfamily members. Annu. Rev. Biochem. **1994**, *63*, 451–486.

6. Beato, M.; Herrlich, P.; Schutz, G. Steroid hormone receptors: Many actors in search of a plot. Cell **1995**, *83* (6), 851–857.

7. Senger, P.L. Regulation of Reproduction—Nerves, Hormones and Target Tissues. In *Pathways to Pregnancy and Parturition*; Current Conceptions, Inc.: Pullman, WA, 1998; 78–98. NY.

8. Razandi, M.; Pedram, A.; Greene, G.L.; Levin, E.R. Cell membrane and nuclear estrogen receptors (ERs) originate from a single transcript: Studies of ERalpha and ERbeta expressed in Chinese hamster ovary cells. Mol. Endocrinol. **1999**, *13* (2), 307–319.

9. Falkenstein, E.; Heck, M.; Gerdes, D.; Grube, D.; Christ, M.; Weigel, M.; Buddhikot, M.; Meizel, S.; Wehling, M. Specific progesterone binding to a membrane protein and related nongenomic effects on Ca^{2+}—fluxes in sperm. Endocrinology **1999**, *140* (12), 5999–6002.

10. Conneely, O.M. Perspective: Female steroid hormone action. Endocrinology **2001**, *142* (6), 2194–2199.

11. Auger, A.P. Ligand-independent activation of progestin receptors: Relevance for female sexual behaviour. Reproduction **2001**, *122* (6), 847–855.

Horse: Nutrition Management

Harold F. Hintz
Cornell University, Ithaca, New York, U.S.A.

INTRODUCTION

Proper nutrition and nutrition management are critical for the performance and health of the horse. Simple nutrient deficiencies are much less common now than 40 years ago, but colic, founder, and obesity are among the most common problems of horses today. All three can be related to nutrition and nutrition management.

NUTRITION MANAGEMENT GUIDELINES

Guidelines for horse nutrition management include the following:

1. Parasite control is essential for the horse to properly utilize food.
2. Maintenance of dental health.
3. Adequate clean water.
4. Feed adjusted to need. The nutrient requirements are influenced by factors such as age, function of horse, temperament, type of work, physiological state, state of health, environmental temperature, and genetics. Energy intake should be adjusted according to body weight and body condition. Scales and body condition scoring are important tools and should be used to evaluate adequacy of energy intake. Obesity can increase the risk of several metabolic problems and cause excess stress on the musculo-skeletal system.
5. A balanced diet. The diet must provide appropriate amounts of energy, amino acids, vitamins, and minerals.
6. Grain, fed in small amounts per meal. As discussed below, large meals can cause serious digestive upsets.
7. Severe changes in the diet should be made gradually to allow bacteria to adapt to the new diet without causing digestive and metabolic upsets.
8. A diet without adequate fiber and an excess of starch predisposes a horse to several problems including colic, founder, gastric ulcers, and increased feeding vices.
9. Accurate weights are necessary to evaluate a feeding program. Feed by weight, not by volume. Density of feeds can vary significantly. A coffee can of one grain may provide twice as much energy as a coffee can of another. Avoid dusty or moldy feed. Horses are very susceptible to respiratory disease because of allergies to dust from feed. Horses are more susceptible to mold toxins in feed than are ruminants.
10. There is no one best feed or diet. A wide variety of ingredients can be used in horse rations if the diets are properly formulated and processed.

DIGESTIVE FUNCTION

The horse is a nonruminant herbivore that can effectively utilize diets containing a high content of fiber. The ruminant utilizes fibrous feeds because of fermentation of the fiber by the microflora in the rumen, which is anterior to the small intestine, whereas the horse utilizes fiber due to the action of microflora in the hindgut (cecum and colon), which is posterior to the small intestine. The small intestine is the primary site of protein digestion. It is also the primary site for amino acid, vitamin, and mineral absorption. Thus, the ruminant can utilize organic nutrients produced by the microflora because they can be prepared for absorption in the small intestine. The horse makes only limited use of the amino acids and B vitamins produced by the microflora of the hindgut because they are not effectively absorbed from the hind gut.

Coprophagy (eating of feces) would enable the horse to utilize the amino acids and B vitamins but it is less common in mature horses than foals. The incidence of coprophagy may be increased by feeding low protein diets.[1] The mechanism that triggers a low-protein diet to increase coprophagy in horses is not known. Low-fiber diets and boredom have also been reported to increase the incidence of coprophagy. The disadvantages of coprophagy include abhorrence by horse owners and increased risk of infestation of the horse by parasites.

The microflora of the hindgut convert fiber and other fermentable material in feeds to volatile fatty acids (VFA), particularly acetate, propionate, and butyrate, which are absorbed from the hindgut. VFA can be the major source of energy for horses. Some fermentation may occur in the distal small intestine but the magnitude and importance of this still needs to be determined.

Bacteria are the primary organisms in the hindgut. Protozoa may be present in only about half of the horses

Encyclopedia of Animal Science
DOI: 10.1081/E-EAS 120019684

and apparently are not essential for the normal gut environment (Dawson, K. 2001. Personal communication). Anaerobic fungi may also be present and may help digest fiber but the importance of the fungi is unknown (Dawson, K. 2001. Personal communication).

One of the most important principles of horse nutrition management is that the horse must be fed in a manner that maintains a healthy population of appropriate microflora in the hindgut.

Rapid changes in diet, particularly a significant increase of the intake of soluble carbohydrates such as starch (carbohydrate overload) can have dire effects. When large amounts of grain are fed at one time, the enzymes in the small intestine are inadequate to digest all the starch. The starch then goes to the hindgut where it is rapidly fermented. The fermentation causes a decrease in pH and thus stimulates the growth of *Lactobacillus* spp., resulting in lactic acidosis.

A horse fed a hay diet is likely to have a pH greater than 7 in the hindgut. Carbohydrate overload can decrease the pH to below 6. A pH of 6 is considered to be sub-clinical acidosis and a pH below 6 can greatly increase the risk of clinical conditions such as colic and founder.[2]

Appropriate management practices can be used to decrease the incidence of carbohydrate overload. Roughage diets with vitamin and mineral supplements, as needed, can be adequate for horses at maintenance. Growing horses, working horses, and mares in late gestation or lactation usually require additional energy in a more concentrated form such as grain. As earlier mentioned in the guidelines, the horse fed large amounts of grain should be fed often, in small amounts. A common rule of thumb is to give no more than 4 to 5 pounds of grain per feeding.

Because grains can differ significantly in starch content, a rule of thumb based on the amount of starch in the diet could be more precise than one based on just the weight of grains. Limits of 2 to 4 g of starch/kg body weight have been suggested. However, the type of starch can also influence site of digestion. Oat starch is much more readily digested in the small intestine than the starch in corn and barley because of the difference in the crystalline starch granules.[3] Processing can also increase the rate of starch digestion in the small intestine. Fine-grinding or heat treatments such as popping or micronizing can increase the amount of starch from corn and barley digested in the small intestine.[4]

Some of the grain can be replaced by oils and fat, which contain more than twice the energy per unit of weight but do not disturb the environment of the hindgut as drastically as does starch. The diet should contain adequate fiber in order to maintain an effective environment in the hindgut, to prevent equine gastric ulcers, and to decrease the incidence of vices such as wood chewing. The ratio of roughage to concentrates should be

considered. The National Research Council[5] did not establish a requirement for fiber but suggests that horses be fed a minimum of 1% of body weight or dry matter from hay or pasture per day. A common rule of thumb is to feed at least 1 to 2% of dry matter as hay or pasture depending on the function of the horse.

The fiber content of hay and pasture can vary greatly due to date of harvest (the older the plant at harvest, the greater the fiber), type of plant, and harvesting conditions. For example, late-cut, sun-cured timothy hay may contain 69% neutral detergent fiber (dry matter basis), whereas early-cut alfalfa hay would contain approximately 39% neutral detergent fiber (dry matter basis). Some authors prefer to recommend a fiber content for the entire ration. For example, Wolter[6] recommended that diets contain at least 17% cellulose, 20% neutral detergent fiber, or 12% acid detergent fiber. But not all fibers are equal, nor are all soluble carbohydrates. Hoffman et al.[7] recommended that fermentable carbohydrate be partitioned into resistant starches, soluble fiber (gums, mucilages, pectins, and algae polsaccharides), insoluble fiber (hemicellulose, cellulose, and lignins-cellulose), and hydrolyzable carbohydrate (hexoses, disaccharides, oligosaccharide, and nonresistant starches).

VALUE OF PASTURE

Good quality pasture is an excellent basis for a feeding program. The old saying that "Dr. Green is an excellent veterinarian" is still true. Proper use of pasture provides a much higher level of such antioxidants as vitamin E and carotene than are present in hay. Pasture can reduce the incidence of colic, ulcers, signs of respiratory diseases (due to decreased mold and dust), and abnormal behaviors.

Of course pasture is not a perfect diet. Excessive intake of lush pasture can cause founder because of the high content of soluble carbohydrates. Pasture may be lacking in certain minerals depending on the content of the soil. Soils in many areas of the United States may contain low levels of selenium, zinc, or copper. Toxins may be present in the cultivated plants or in weeds. For example, the USDA found 61.6% of the samples of tall fescue tested positive for the endophyte, *Neotyphodium coenophalium*.[8] Compounds produced by the endophyte adversely affect reproduction.

Pasture can also be a source of parasite infestation. Prompt removal of feces will greatly reduce the parasite load and improve pasture utilization. Horses normally will not graze near fecal piles, although they will if pasture is in short supply.

The diet must contain all required nutrients in reasonable amounts. Ration evaluation should be conducted periodically. Fortunately, the widespread use of commercial rations has greatly decreased the incidence of simple nutrient deficiencies. Nutrients of particular concern when evaluating rations include energy, protein, calcium, phosphorus, zinc, copper, iodine, selenium, and vitamins A and E.

CONCLUSIONS

Proper nutritional management is required to promote health performance of the horse. Three key management points are: 1) maintain an appropriate intestinal environment; 2) monitor the body condition of the horse; and 3) evaluate the ration for nutritional completeness.

REFERENCES

1. Schurg, W.A.; Frei, D.L.; Cheeke, P.R.; Holtan, D.W. Utilization of whole corn plant pellets by horses and rabbits. J. Anim. Sci. **1977**, *45* (6), 1317–1321.

2. Radicke, S.; Kienzle, E.; Meyer, H. Preileal Apparent Digestibility of Oats and Corn Starch and Consequences for Caecal Metabolism. Proc. 12th Equine Nutrtion Physiol Soc Symp, 1991, 43–48.

3. Meyer, H.; Radicke, S.; Kienzle, E.; Wilkes, S.; Kleffken, D. Investigations on preileal digestion of starch from grain, potato and manioc in horses. Zentralbl. Veterinarmed., A **1995**, *42*, 371–381.

4. Potter, G.D.; Arnold, F.F.; Householder, D.D.; Hansen, D.H.; Brown, K.M. Digestion of starch in the small or large intestine of the equine. Pferdeheilkunde **1992**, *1*, 107–111.

5. National Research Council. *Nutrient Requirements of Horses*; National Academy Press: Washington, DC, 1989.

6. Wolter, R. Fibre in the feeding of horses. Practique Vet. Equine **1993**, *25*, 45–59. as abstracted in Nutr. Abstr. Rev. **1993**, *63*, 605.

7. Hoffman, R.M.; Wilson, J.A.; Kronfeld, D.S.; Copper, W.; Lawrence, L.A.; Sklan, D.; Harris, P.A. Hydrolyzable carbohydrates in pasture, hay, and horse feeds: direct assay and seasonal variation. J. Anim. Sci. **2001**, *79*, 500–506.

8. USDA. *Baseline Reference of 1988 Equine Health and Management*; USDA:APHIS:VS, CEAH. National Animal Health Monitoring System: Fort Collins, CO, 1999.

Horses: Behavior Management and Well-Being

Katherine Albro Houpt
Cornell University, Ithaca, New York, U.S.A.

INTRODUCTION

Horses are charismatic megavertebrates whose images are seen frequently in art and advertising. They are seldom used for work except in some developing countries, but are the main source of power for crop production by Amish farmers in North America. Five million or so horses live in the United States and are used for sport and recreation. A knowledge of their behavior makes it possible for us to manage them humanely and in accordance with their evolutionary history.

GRAZING

Horses are found in many different environments, but the one in which they evolved ranges from forest dwellers to plains grazers in the Miocene. They were last seen in the wild on the grassland plains of Eurasia. Feral horses in that type of environment, or domestic horses kept in pastures, spend the majority of their time grazing.[1] Grazing is a behavior that consists of not only eating, but also selecting the patch on which to graze and the plants within that patch to harvest. Once selected, the horse must prehend the plant, usually by grasping it with his prehensile upper lip, ripping the plant from its roots with his incisors, then masticating the plant with his heavily ridged molars, and finally swallowing. After a few mouthfuls, the horse will take a few steps and select new plants. This behavioral pattern of slowly moving (several kilometers per day) and chewing (about 40,000 times per day) can be considered optimal for the horse's foot and gastrointestinal health. Horses salivate only when they are chewing. Saliva contains sodium bicarbonate, so every one of those chewing movements delivers a few milliliters of sodium bicarbonate solution to the stomach. Every step pushes blood out of the hoof and allows fresh blood to enter.

This behavior pattern must be compared to that of the typical modern domestic horse. He lives in a box stall and is fed a minimal amount of hay and maximal amount of grain. He is turned out (usually alone) into a paddock (usually grassless) for a variable period of time and ridden (usually at speed), depending on the recreational purpose of the owner. The most valuable horses are kept in this manner and their welfare is probably the poorest as indicated by the rate of stereotypic behavior displayed and the rate of gastrointestinal problems (colic) and lamenesses reported. The stalled horse will spend 20% or less of his time eating. He may compensate somewhat for the absence of grazing by foraging through the bedding of his stall, sometimes eating the wood shavings that are typical bedding for horses. If wooden surfaces are available, he may chew them. This behavior is not a response to confinement, but rather a response to lack of dietary roughage, i.e., chewing time. Provision of free-choice hay, a bale a day for a 500-kilogram horse, increases the eating time of a stalled horse to approximately that of the grazing horse. The hay-fed horse may chew enough, but he does not move as frequently, nor does he have equine companions.

ABNORMAL BEHAVIORS

A horse behavior that is a response to confinement is weaving. The horse walks in place, usually at the door of his stall. The horse is not just rocking from side to side, but is actually walking in place. Weaving is apparently a ritualized escape attempt. The horse is trying to escape from his stall *and* join other horses. We know this because a view of other horses or a mirror decreases weaving.[2] A related behavior is stall walking, in which the horse circles his stall again and again. This behavior is more common in endurance horses than in dressage or jumping horses.

A behavior unique to horses is cribbing. Cribbing involves grasping a horizontal surface with the teeth, arching the neck and swallowing air with an audible grunt. The behavior begins when the foal is weaned, particularly if the foal has been weaned into a stall and fed concentrates. Foals left on pasture when their mothers are removed are less likely to begin to crib. Cribbing occurs mostly in the period just after grain is consumed, apparently in response to some component of a grain and molasses mixture (sweet feed), and can occupy 10 to 60%

Encyclopedia of Animal Science
DOI: 10.1081/E-EAS 120019679

of the horse's day. The behavior is displayed by 5% of horses, especially certain breeds and during certain activities. Thoroughbreds are the breed most likely to crib. Risk factors are being used as a dressage horse, as a three-day event performer, as a jumper, or as a race horse. The behavior is not learned by observing other horses, but there is a familial factor—relatives of cribbers are more likely to crib. Various methods are used to eliminate cribbing, but a collar that prevents the horse from arching his neck to crib is the most effective. Surgical treatment is not very effective, and muzzles seem more frustrating than the collars. Nothing needs be done to prevent the horse from cribbing unless he experiences gas colic as a result. The behavior may help the horse cope with its unnatural environment or may even add buffering substances to his stomach and intestines by adding some saliva with every cribbing bite. Provision of a chest-high cribbing bar prevents damage to fences or stall furnishings. Horses pull very hard when they flex their necks; they can move 100 kg with each cribbing motion.

SOCIAL STRUCTURE

One reason for the various aberrant behaviors of the stalled horse is the difference between their natural social organization and modern equine management. The social organization of feral horses—as well as of true wild horses, Przewalski's horses, or takhi—is a harem group consisting of a stallion, several mares, and their juvenile offspring. These groups are called bands, and the bands in a given geographic area are called a herd. Bands are rarely larger than 10 adult animals. The band is always together (always within visual contact), and each horse is rarely more than 10 meters from another horse. The stallion is the most peripheral member of the group. The proximity of the band members functions to protect the individual horse from predators. Ten pairs of eyes and ears are better than one at detecting an approaching wolf or mountain lion.

EXERCISE

Many of the uses to which we put horses involve galloping—racing, hunting foxes, chasing calves, or jumping fences. In an undisturbed situation, horses rarely move faster than a walk. Galloping is reserved for fleeing from prey. Given a choice, horses don't exercise at speed. They do like to leave their stalls, but if they are not with another horse, they choose to return to their stalls in 15 minutes. They will gallop, buck, and sometimes roll when first released from stall confinement, and will spend more time in these activities if they have been confined for long periods.

FOAL DEVELOPMENT

Foals are precocious newborns. They rise within an hour or so of birth and can walk and gallop shortly thereafter. They follow their mother, who threatens any other horse that approaches her foal, so they don't have the opportunity to follow another horse. Foals must find the udder and ingest colostrum within a few hours of birth in order to acquire passive immunity that will last until they can manufacture their own antibodies. Foals suckle every 15 minutes for the first week of life and the rate decreases slowly as they mature. By six months, they still suckle hourly, although they are now grazing almost half of the time. During the first few months, foals lie down and sleep frequently. Even as two-year-olds, they spend more time recumbent than adults. When the foal lies down, the mother stands beside it, although as the foal grows older, she will be farther and farther away. Both fillies and colts leave their mother's band when they are between two and three years old. The colts usually join a bachelor band, a group of other immature males (Fig. 1). They harass band stallions and their mares, and may eventually acquire mares, which are usually kept by the dominant bachelor as the nucleus of his own band. Occasionally more than one stallion will accompany mares; one stallion, the dominant one, breeds the mares while the other wards off other stallions. Fillies may join an established band or join other youngsters.

COMMUNICATION

Horses, when content, are quiet animals. Almost the only vocalization one should hear in a well-managed stable is a low-decibel nicker, which is an approach call given by a mare to her foal and by any horse to a human who feeds it. The whinny or neigh is a separation call, commonly given by horses that are separated from their group and usually

Fig. 1 Two stallions fighting. (*View this art in color at www.dekker.com.*)

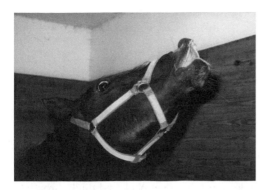

Fig. 2 The flehmen or lipcurl response. This movement allows nonvolatile substances, such as urine, to run down the horse's lip into its nostril, where it enters a special organ—the vomeronasal organ—that detects socially and sexually significant substances. (*View this art in color at www.dekker.com.*)

agitated. When two strange horses meet, they stand nostril to nostril, sniffing one another's breath. Then one or both will squeal, a loud, high-pitched sound. They may also strike out with a forelimb at the same time. These are aggressive actions and can be the prelude to a fight. The aggressive horse pins its ears flat to its head and lunges toward the victim.[3] The more aggressive the threat, the more likely that the horse will show its teeth. Aggression can escalate to biting. Before kicking, a horse usually lashes its tail and then may kick with one or both hind limbs. Frightened horses show the whites of their eyes, turn their ears to the side, and clamp their tails close to their rumps. When playing or very excited, they hold their tails straight up.[3] Frustrated horses snort and paw the ground. They may twist their necks. Horses also communicate by odor (Fig. 2).

SLEEP

Horses can sleep standing up or lying down because of the arrangement of the ligaments and tendons in their limbs, which allows them to stand with little expenditure of energy. When resting, a horse usually flexes its hind limb on one side and closes or half-closes its eyes. In this way, it can rest, doze, or even enter one stage of sleep, but the deepest stage of sleep—REM or rapid eye movement sleep, in which people (and probably horses) dream—can only begin when the horse lies down. He can lie down on his sternum or chest like a cat, by resting his muzzle on the ground, or he can lie on his side. In these positions, he can relax his muscles completely.

CONCLUSION

The behavior of horses is as fascinating and worthy of study as that of any endangered or wild species. An understanding of how horses communicate with one another and how they live in natural condition allows us to handle them safely and ensure their welfare, even under modern stabling conditions.

REFERENCES

1. Houpt, K.A. *Domestic Animal Behavior for Veterinarians and Animal Scientists*, 3rd Ed.; Iowa State University Press, 1998.
2. Mills, D.; Nankervis, K. *Equine Behavior: Principles and Practice*; Iowa State University Press.
3. McDonnell, S. *Understanding Horse Behavior*; Horse Health Care Library, 2002.

Horses: Breeds/Breeding/Genetics

Rebecca K. Splan
Virginia Tech, Blacksburg, Virginia, U.S.A.

INTRODUCTION

Horses and humans have enjoyed a long and unique relationship through history. This partnership has existed for nearly 6000 years.[1] Originally considered only a source of food, the domestic horse (*Equus caballus*) now serves man in more ways than any other domesticated species. Around the world, the horses of today are used for transportation, draft, recreation, warfare, companionship, and, of course, food. Within the recreation sector alone, horses are engaged in hundreds of activities, from racing to the Olympic Games to pleasure riding. Horses are now found in almost every country in the world and have become a major force in many economies. Horses generate more than $25 billion annually in goods and services in the United States alone. Their large geographical distribution and myriad phenotypes, from the large Shire to the tiny Shetland pony, serve as a testament to the selection pressures horses have undergone through the ages, shaping them according to human needs and desires. Modern advances in quantitative and molecular genetics allow man to mold the horse quickly and accurately.

HORSE BREEDS

A breed is defined as a group of animals similar enough in form or function to be distinguished from other groups, and which, when bred together, reproduce this consistent phenotype. Granted, this can be a rather nebulous definition, especially when a breed is still in the formative stages. Most of the more than 395 horse breeds in existence today have a recorded history of less than 20–30 generations, and periodic or continual introduction of animals from outside the breed often occurs. Very few breeds have been formed in strict isolation, or without the influence of other breeds over time. A description of all breeds is beyond the scope of this article, but it is important to note that breeds may generally fall into one of three basic groups: draft breeds, light breeds, and ponies.

Draft breeds, also known as coldbloods, have traditionally been bred for heavy harness or agricultural work. The prototype draft horse developed in the forests of Northern Europe. They are characterized by large size, both absolutely—often standing 17 hands high (hh), or more—and proportionally (a greater circumference of bones and joints relative to smaller riding horses). Characteristics also associated with draft horses include a convex facial profile; small eye; long distance from eye to muzzle; short, high-set neck and thick throatlatch; short back; steep croup; short pasterns; and large hooves. Popular modern draft breeds include the Percheron, Belgian, Clydesdale, Shire, and Suffolk Punch.

The next group is the light breeds. This includes most breeds found worldwide. Some breeds in this category may include heavier horses, which at one point may have included horses used for harness or agricultural work, but which are now bred for riding purposes, such as the warmblood breeds. Also included in this group are the breeds bred for pleasure riding or driving. Generally, horses in this category range from 14.2 hh to 17 hh, weigh between 850 and 1500 lbs., and come in a wide variety of shapes. Many breeds, such as the Quarter Horse, Saddlebred, Tennessee Walking Horse, Morgan, Appaloosa, and Paint Horse, were originally bred for specific purposes, but have since become very versatile in their usage. Most can trace their roots at least in part to the Thoroughbred or Arabian, two breeds classified as hotbloods.

Ponies make up the third group. Ponies are classified as 14.2 hh or smaller. Ponies vary widely in their conformation and usage, and they generally developed where environmental conditions were harsh and vegetation relatively scarce. Most modern pony breeds descend from the original European Celtic pony, although a number of breeds share roots with the Caspian pony. Modern ponies have often been crossed with light horse breeds for improved refinement and rideability. Common pony breeds include the mountain and moorland breeds of the Welsh, Shetland, Connemara, Fell, Dales, Exmoor, and Dartmoor regions of the United Kingdom and Ireland. Other popular breeds include the Pony of the Americas and the Hackney. While typically thought of as a child's mount, ponies are enjoyed by people of all ages and routinely compete in all the same events as their larger cousins.

HORSE BREEDING AND GENETICS

Whereas the horse has been shaped by human hands for centuries, scientific principles have only recently been

Encyclopedia of Animal Science
DOI: 10.1081/E-EAS 120019680

applied to horse breeding. Great success has been made to reduce the racing times of Swedish trotters and improve traits such as type, conformation and dressage, and jumping ability in a number of European warmblood breeds, using application of these advanced mathematical breeding techniques.[2] While these methods have been used to generate tremendous progress in other species (e.g., to improve milk production in dairy cattle or increase litter size in swine), horse breeders have been slow to embrace modern methodology. This is in part due to the lack of a specified breeding goal for many breeds, as well as a reduced willingness of horse breeders to accept strict selection and culling schemes and employ organized performance testing of horses at a young age. However, more and more breeds have begun to use molecular and quantitative advances to make genetic improvement.

Molecular Genetics

Great advances have been made in recent years with respect to incorporation of information from molecular genetics. Genes for a number of equine diseases have been discovered, and tests are now available to breeders to determine an animal's genotype for such conditions as hyperkalemic periodic paralysis, severe combined immunodeficiency syndrome, and lethal white overo syndrome. Further, many coat color genes have now been mapped to the equine genome. Discovery of major genes for performance traits in horses has been slow, however, so advancements in these traits are currently accomplished by employing quantitative breeding principles.

Selection and Modern Horse Breeding

Horses don't come with barcodes. There are few obvious outward signs of true genetic merit, even to the experienced horseman. The phenotype that can be measured is a function of genetic and environmental effects. A mediocre horse with good training, or one that has been campaigned strategically, can appear better than he actually is, while an incredibly talented mount may find himself in an environment in which he will never have the opportunity to fulfill his potential. However, selection for physical attributes such as beauty of the head, height at the withers, or many conformational traits may be easier than for performance ability, as these traits generally have a lower environmental component.

The term heritability describes how much of a population's variation for a trait is due to environmental factors, and how much is due to the summed effects of genes responsible for the trait in question. The fraction of total variation due to genetic effects is defined as heritability, and is expressed as a number between 0 and 1. It is important for breeders to remember that heritability is a population parameter, and is not concerned with individual horses or individual genes. Numerous genes influence most performance traits. Money earned by a racehorse, for example, is not due to the effects of a single gene. More than likely, superior racing performance is due to many genes working together to enhance aspects of racing ability such as lung capacity, desire to win, bone strength, metabolic efficiency, and more.

Heritabilites for conformation traits are generally moderate to high,[3] as are those for gait characteristics.[4] Performance traits, such as racing, dressage, or jumping ability, generally have low heritabilities.[4] For the breeder, a trait with high heritability means that by using animals who excel for that trait, progress will be made rapidly. If heritability is low, however, progress may be better made by enhancing management, because much of the total variation is due to environmental effects rather than to genetic effects.

Also of importance when breeding horses are genetic correlations between and among traits. When breeders select for one trait, other traits may be desirably or undesirably associated. If breeders attempt to select for two negatively correlated traits, genetic progress may be hindered, depending on the strength of the association.

CONCLUSION

The long partnership forged between horses and humans is evident in the myriad of phenotypes now observable in horse breeds. This partnership continues to be shaped today through further genetic manipulation. Although long- and short-term breeding goals may differ widely across breeds and disciplines, all horse breeders can maximize genetic progress by practicing effective selection and making appropriate mating decisions.

REFERENCES

1. Budiansky, S. *The Nature of Horses*; The Free Press: New York, 1997.
2. Arnason, T.; Van Vleck, L.D. Genetic Improvement of the Horse. In *The Genetics of the Horse*; Bowling, A.T., Ruvinsky, A., Eds.; CAB International: Wallingford, 2000; 473–497.
3. Saastamoinen, M.T.; Barrey, E. Genetics of Conformation, Locomotion and Physiological Traits. In *The Genetics of the Horse*; Bowling, A.T., Ruvinsky, A., Eds.; CAB International: Wallingford, 2000; 439–471.
4. Ricard, A.; Bruns, E.; Cunningham, E.P. Genetics of Performance Traits. In *The Genetics of the Horse*; Bowling, A.T., Ruvinsky, A., Eds.; CAB International: Wallingford, 2000; 411–438.

Horses: Reproduction Management

Martha M. Vogelsang
Texas A&M University, College Station, Texas, U.S.A.

INTRODUCTION

Horse breeding today is a relatively intensely managed equine activity. Breeding is conducted primarily through hand-mating or artificial insemination (AI) programs. Even amateur horse owners need to know basic physiology related to the estrous cycle of the mare to optimize chances for conception. The goals of this article are to: 1) present the fundamental concepts for management of the stallion and mare for successful breeding; and 2) give a brief overview of management practices related to foaling.

Horses have long been perceived to have lower reproductive efficiency than other domestic livestock. It is apparent that mismanagement rather than inherently low fertility may be the cause of poor reproductive performance. The mare's long gestation ($\sim$340 days) requires almost immediate rebreeding if annual foal production is the goal. Given this parameter, poor management and breeding techniques and unforeseen health problems can very quickly decrease reproductive efficiency.

STALLION MANAGEMENT

Housing facilities play a role in reproductive management. Stallions should be maintained where they have visual and vocal social, but not tactile, contact with other horses. With the exception of pasture breeding, the stallion should be housed in a stall or paddock by himself. He needs exercise, whether free or controlled, on a regular schedule. Stallions that do not get enough exercise may develop vices that lead to problems in the breeding shed. As important as housing are the facilities where breeding is performed. Stallions are creatures of habit and perform more consistently if this activity is conducted in the same place at each breeding or semen collection.

Nutritionists recommend that the stallion be fed to maintain adequate body condition (Body Condition Score of 6–7)[1] (Fig. 1). Those with a full book of mares may be breeding twice a day several days per week in a hand-mating program. Teasing mares along with breeding leads to increased energy requirements for the stallion during the breeding season. Preventive health care is essential. Immunization against infectious disease and regular deworming are the basis of a good health program.

Prior to each breeding season, the stallion should receive a breeding soundness examination (BSE). Most equine veterinary clinics can perform this service, providing valuable information on semen quality and the number of bookings the stallion can handle. The BSE is useful in estimating the stallion's potential fertility. In addition, the BSE characterizes the semen parameters necessary for establishing a breeding schedule for the stallion.

The stallion performs more consistently when maintained on a regular schedule during the breeding season. Semen collection three times per week (or every other day) yields the highest number of sperm for use in AI with the fewest number of collections.[2] In a hand-mating program, the stallion may be required to service mares on a more frequent basis. Provided that the stallion has normal semen characteristics, libido may be the most limiting factor in determining his breeding schedule.

MARE MANAGEMENT

Housing

Broodmares are maintained in a wide variety of housing situations. From individual stalls and paddocks to large multimare pastures, housing for the broodmare should minimize stress and exposure to extreme environmental conditions, should provide for adequate exercise, and should be constructed so that there is little chance of injury to either mares or foals. Most important, selection of housing for a mare should attempt to maintain the type of housing to which she is accustomed or to gradually get her acclimated to a more suitable environment. Abrupt changes in housing increase stress that may be detrimental to reproductive performance.

Nutrition

Mares fed to maintain adequate body condition have a higher level of reproductive success than those kept in a lower state of body condition.[3] Parameters including

Encyclopedia of Animal Science
DOI: 10.1081/E-EAS 120019685

length of time to first ovulation, pregnancy rate, and pregnancy maintenance are all enhanced in mares on an optimal nutritional program. Mares that are thin (Body Condition Score of 4 or less) generally have lower reproductive efficiency. The Body Condition Scoring system developed at Texas A&M University[4] has proven to be a reliable tool for horse breeders in determining the nutritional status and needed changes to optimize the reproductive performance of the mare that is in sound reproductive health.

Immunization and Deworming Schedule

Mare owners should maintain a rigorous preventive health care program that keeps their mares in the best physical condition for gestation and lactation. Preventive immunization and deworming schedules vary in the mare depending on her reproductive status. Most importantly, the pregnant mare should receive vaccinations for infectious diseases during the last 60 days of gestation. This results in an adequate antibody titer in the mare's colostrum that will provide passive immunity for the foal when it nurses (important because there is no active transfer of immunity across placental membranes). Specific diseases the broodmare should be immunized against include tetanus, encephalomyelitis, rhinopneumonitis, and influenza, but mare owners should seek the advice of a veterinarian familiar with diseases endemic to their locale. Treatment of broodmares with anthelmintics prior to parturition helps to decrease parasite infestation in the foal.[5]

Breeding Soundness Examination (BSE)

For mares entering the breeding season as maidens or in a barren state, it may be beneficial to have a BSE conducted by a veterinarian. Components of a BSE may include visual inspection of the external genitalia, vagina, and cervix; examination of the internal reproductive tract (cervix, uterus, and ovaries) by palpation and/or ultrasonography; uterine cytology and culture; endometrial biopsy; and uterine endoscopy. Reproductive history of the mare should also be a part of the BSE. Generally, maiden mares are not subjected to extensive BSEs, whereas barren mares usually require diagnosis of potential problems contributing to their lack of reproductive success.

BREEDING MANAGEMENT

Primarily for economic reasons, mares are bred to have their foals during the months of January through May (Northern Hemisphere). However, horses are long-day breeders that have optimal reproductive success from April through July. The equine reproductive cycle is entrained to daylength (photoperiod); therefore, estrus can be induced earlier in the year by using an artificially lengthened photoperiod. The daily schedule should provide approximately 16 hours of light (natural plus artificial) and 8 hours of darkness. This schedule should begin around the first of December, allowing time for the mare to go through the transitional phase and enter the first ovulatory cycle in mid-to-late February. The artificial lighting program should continue until the mare is determined to be safe in foal. Artificial lighting programs are sometimes used with gestating mares to ensure a return to cyclicity after foaling. Stallion owners may also consider an artificial photoperiod if the majority of their stallion's book will be bred early in the breeding season, but this is not recommended if most of his mares will be bred later (April–June).

Exogenous hormonal treatments may be beneficial in managing the reproductive cycle of the mare. The most frequently used treatments are prostaglandin (for shortening the luteal phase between ovulations), human chorionic gonadotropin (for ensuring ovulation of a large preovulatory follicle), and progestins (for preventing estrus or for early pregnancy maintenance).

Time of breeding is determined by evaluation of the following criteria: 1) intensity of estrus (Fig. 2); 2) patency of the cervix; 3) uterine environment; and 4) follicular status. All of these criteria are indicative of the mare's physiologic readiness for breeding. They provide a checklist for the breeder to ensure that the mare is inseminated at the optimal time for conception. Mares that do not meet these criteria may not be candidates for breeding.

The method of breeding plays a significant role in the timing of insemination of the mare. When multiple inseminations are possible, initial inseminations tend to be made slightly earlier during estrus. The interval between inseminations in the mare should be 48 hours, the length of time that spermatozoa remain viable within the female reproductive tract. For hand-mating or if semen is limited, timing the insemination as close to ovulation as possible is paramount to the success of breeding. Conception rates in the mare are increased when sperm are within the female reproductive tract prior to ovulation,[6] providing adequate time for capacitation. For situations in which only one insemination or breeding is possible, it is important to use all information available to optimize chances for conception and to inseminate close enough to ovulation that only one insemination is necessary.

A significant factor related to successful artificial insemination is the number of motile spermatozoa used

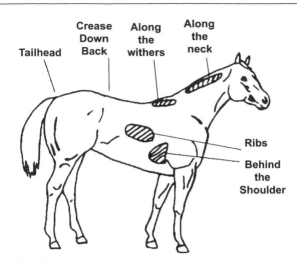

Score	Description

1   **Poor.** The horse is extremely emaciated. Spinous processes (backbone), ribs, and tailhead project prominently. Bone structure of the withers, shoulders, and neck easily noticeable. No fatty tissue can be felt anywhere.

2   **Very Thin.** Horse is emaciated. Slight fat covering over base of spinous processes and transverse processes of lumbar vertebrae feels rounder. Spinous processes, ribs, hips, and tailhead are prominent. Withers, shoulders, and neck structures faintly discernable.

3   **Thin.** The spinous processes stand out, but fat covers them to midpoint. Very slight fat cover can be felt over the ribs, but the spinous processes and ribs are easily discernable. The tailhead is prominent, but individual vertebrae cannot be seen. Hips are visible but appear rounded. The withers, shoulders, and neck are accentuated.

4   **Moderately Thin.** The horse has a negative crease along its back, and the outline of the ribs can just be seen. Fat can be felt around the tailhead. Hip bones cannot be seen, and the withers, neck, and shoulders do not look obviously thin.

5   **Moderate.** The back is level. Ribs cannot be seen but can be easily felt. Fat around the tailhead feels slightly spongy. The withers look rounded, and the shoulder and neck blend smoothly into the body.

6   **Moderate to Fleshy.** There may be a slight crease down the back. Fat around the tailhead feels soft, and fat over the ribs feels spongy. There are small fat deposits along the sides of the withers, behind the shoulders, and along the sides of the neck.

7   **Fleshy.** There may be a crease down the back. Individual ribs can be felt, but there is noticeable fat between the ribs. Fat around the tailhead is soft. Fat is noticeable at the withers, the neck, and behind the shoulders.

8   **Fat.** The horse has a crease down the back. Spaces between the ribs are filled with fat so that the ribs are difficult to feel. The area along the withers is filled with fat, and fat around the tailhead feels very soft. The space behind the shoulders is filled in flush, and some fat is deposited along the inner buttocks. There is noticeable thickening of neck.

9   **Extremely Fat.** The crease down the back is very obvious. Fat appears in patches over the ribs, and there is bulging fat around the tailhead, withers, shoulders, and neck. Fat along the inner buttocks may rub together, and the flank is filled in flush.

Fig. 2 During estrus, the mare demonstrates a number of signs indicating that she is receptive to the sexual behavior of the stallion. (*View this art in color at www.dekker.com.*)

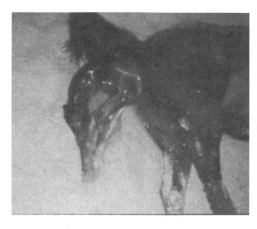

Fig. 3 Stage II of the foaling process, during which the foal is pushed out of the mare's uterus front feet and head first. (*View this art in color at www.dekker.com.*)

for breeding. Traditionally, the minimum insemination dose using fresh semen has been 500×10^6 sperm cells. The number is doubled when the semen has been preserved in a cooled environment (1 billion). Samper[7] stated that there was no consensus on the minimum number of progressively motile sperm when using frozen semen due to the wide variation in freezing success among stallions. He did indicate that insemination doses ranging from $600-800 \times 10^6$ sperm with 30–35% motility seemed to provide the highest pregnancy rates.

FOALING

Reproduction management of horses also includes the foaling process, which is closely related to breeding because of the short postpartum interval before beginning the next gestation. The normal gestation length for horses is 340 days, with a range of 330–350 days.

Parturition occurs in three stages. Stage I is a preparatory stage for delivery and usually goes unnoticed, except for waxing of the teats. Stage II begins when the waterbag (allantois) ruptures. Stage II is the actual delivery of the foal and lasts approximately 20 minutes. If delivery takes longer, veterinary assistance should be sought. A key to a fairly normal delivery is the position of the emerging foal. The front feet should protrude through the vulva, one slightly behind the other. The muzzle should appear resting on the cannon bones or knees (Fig. 3). If this order of emergence is not observed, the foal may be malpositioned and normal delivery may not be possible. Mares seldom experience dystocia (only 2–3%). When they do, however, they require assistance immediately to prevent potential loss of foal and/or dam.

Stage III of parturition is the passage of the placenta. It usually occurs within 30 minutes to 1 hour, but may take several hours. Again, if this stage is prolonged, veterinary care may be required.

Within 30 minutes, the foal may be able to stand. Nursing should be accomplished within 2 hours. Routine neonatal care includes treatment of the navel stump, administration of tetanus antitoxin, administration of an enema, and testing the foal's immunoglobulin G (IgG) levels 12 hours after it has consumed colostrum. Foals do not receive any type of immunity from the dam before birth and must receive colostrum that is rich in antibodies for protection from disease. On-the-farm kits are available that can provide qualitative assessment of the foal's IgG levels.

Mares typically have a fertile estrus 7–15 days postpartum. Some breeders will choose to breed on this cycle, while others will use hormonal treatments (prostaglandin) to short cycle or will wait until the next normal cycle (around 30 days postpartum). With the long gestation of the horse, breeding must occur fairly soon after foaling in order to produce offspring every year.

CONCLUSION

This article provides information on normal reproductive management concepts and procedures. Current practices in management of the stallion and broodmare, the use of photoperiod and hormone treatments for efficient reproduction, breeding schedules differentiating the use of hand-mating vs. AI, and basic foaling management have been described. Other entries in this encyclopedia

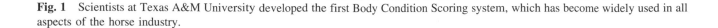

Fig. 1 Scientists at Texas A&M University developed the first Body Condition Scoring system, which has become widely used in all aspects of the horse industry.

should be consulted for other aspects of horse production and management.

REFERENCES

1. Gibbs, P.G. Stallion Nutrition. In *The Veterinarian's Practical Reference to Equine Nutrition*; Purina Mills & The American Assoc. of Eq. Practicioners: St. Louis, 1997; 33–37.
2. Pickett, B.W.; Sullivan, J.J.; Seidel, G.E. Reproductive physiology of the stallion. V. Effect of frequency of ejaculation on seminal characteristics and spermatozoal output. J. Anim. Sci. **1975**, *40*, 917–923.
3. Henneke, D.R.; Potter, G.D.p; Kreider, J.L. Body condition during pregnancy and lactation and reproductive efficiency of mares. Theriogenology **1984**, *21*, 897.
4. Henneke, D.R.; Potter, G.D.; Kreider, J.L.; Yeates, B.F. A scoring system for comparing body condition in horses. Equine Vet. J. **1983**, *15*, 371–373.
5. Card, C.E. Management of the Pregnant Mare. In *Equine Breeding Management and Artificial Insemination*; W.B. Saunders Company: Philadelphia, 2000; 253.
6. Brinsko, S.P.; Varner, D.D. Artificial Insemination. In *Equine Reproduction*; McKinnon, A.O., Voss, J.L., Eds.; Lea & Febiger: Philadelphia, 1993; 793.
7. Samper, J.C. Artificial Insemination. In *Equine Breeding Management and Artificial Insemination*; W.B. Saunders Company: Philadelphia, 2000; 126.

Immune System: Nutrition Effects

Rodney W. Johnson
University of Illinois, Urbana, Illinois, U.S.A.

Jeffery Escobar
Baylor College of Medicine, Houston, Texas, U.S.A.

INTRODUCTION

The National Research Council (NRC) nutrient require-ments for animals can be defined as nutrient levels adequate to permit the maintenance of normal health and productivity. Failure to provide a diet that fulfills the minimal requirements established by the NRC for any nutrient will ultimately immunocompromise the animal and render it more susceptible to infectious disease. Because nutrient requirements to support optimal produc-tivity are well defined, marked deficiencies in protein, amino acids, or trace nutrients are not likely to occur in animals reared in commercial situations. However, the nutrient requirements for optimal productivity may not equal those for optimal immunity because the NRC requirements have been determined from experiments conducted in laboratory situations where infectious disease is minimal. Thus, an important issue that has been the focus of nutritional immunology research is whether specific nutrients fed at or above NRC-recom-mended levels could be used to modulate the animal's immune system in a beneficial manner.

THE IMMUNE SYSTEM

The cells of the immune system and their responses to infection are obviously complex, but can be partitioned into two separate but interacting components—those that provide innate immunity and those that provide acquired (or adaptive) immunity (Fig. 1). Both components are influenced by nutrition (Table 1).

The component of the immune system that protects the host animal but does not distinguish one pathogen from another provides innate immunity. For example, macro-phages recognize pathogens using relatively indiscrimi-nant receptors. They ingest and degrade microorganisms, and provide important signals (e.g., cytokines) that orchestrate other aspects of the immune response. The innate immune system is inherent and the capacity of it to respond does not change or improve from the first encounter with a particular pathogen to the second encounter. Neutrophils and natural killer (NK) cells are also important for innate immunity.

Acquired immunity is a highly specific response to a specific pathogen that is acquired over time due to previous exposure to that same pathogen or through vaccination. Fully differentiated B lymphocytes (i.e., plasma cells) se-crete pathogen-specific antibodies, whereas T lymphocytes use discrete receptors to recognize and kill infected cells or activate other cells of the immune system. The initial exposure to a pathogen produces lymphocytes with immu-nological memory so that if the pathogen is encountered a second time, a rapid response is initiated and the pathogen is eliminated before visible signs of infection appear.

IMMUNOMODULATORY EFFECTS OF NUTRIENTS

Amino Acids

Numerous amino acids have important roles in proper immune function, but methionine, arginine, and glutamine seem to be the ones that are required in the greatest quantities during an immune response. Methionine is the first limiting amino acid in most poultry diets and is the second or third limiting amino acid in barley and wheat-based swine diets, making it a primary concern for mar-ginal deficiency. Chicks may require a greater quantity of methionine to maximize humoral and cell-mediated im-munity, but the idea that animals may require methionine for immune function at levels above those that support maximal growth is not entirely agreed upon.

Arginine is considered a semiessential amino acid for humans and other mammals because it is synthesized from other amino acids via the urea cycle. However, exogenous arginine is required for growth in young animals and in various stress situations (e.g., sepsis, trauma) to optimize growth and minimize nitrogen excretion. Arginine is a direct precursor of nitric oxide (NO), a potent cytotoxic agent produced by macrophages and neutrophils to kill bacteria.

Although glutamine is not an indispensable amino acid for growth of animals, it may be conditionally essential

Encyclopedia of Animal Science
DOI: 10.1081/E-EAS 120019687

541

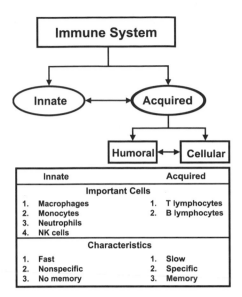

Fig. 1 The immune system can be partitioned into two separate but interacting components—that which provides innate immunity and that which provides acquired immunity. Both innate and acquired immunity can be modulated by nutrition.

in times of immune system activation. Glutamine is essential for the normal functioning of macrophages and lymphocytes during an immune response. The requirement for glutamine in these cells is due to the increased metabolic activity following stimulation by an infectious pathogen. Accelerated metabolism is necessary to facilitate cell division and the secretion of antibodies and cytokines—all processes that require amino acids and energy. Glutamine is a primary carrier of nitrogen in the blood, and its concentration is generally maintained within a relatively small range. However, during catabolic states like sepsis, there is an increased demand for glutamine as a substrate for cells of the immune system.

Lipids

High-fat diets reduce lymphocyte proliferation compared to low-fat diets, but the precise effects depend on the amount and type of fat. There are two major classes of polyunsaturated fatty acids (PUFAs)—the n-6 and the n-3 families. Linoleic acid is the precursor of the n-6 family, and is found in plant oils, including corn and soybean oil. In animals, linoleic acid is converted to arachidonic acid, which can account for 25% of the total fatty acids in the plasma membranes of immune cells. The amount of arachidonic acid in the plasma membrane of immune cells is important because it is the precursor of several prostaglandins and leukotrienes that have potent inflammatory effects. The precursor of the n-3 PUFAs is α-linolenic acid, which in animal tissues is converted to eicosapentaenoic and docosahexaenoic acids. As op-

posed to n-6 PUFAs, which are inflammatory, n-3 PUFAs are anti-inflammatory.

Diets rich in n-3 PUFAs decrease inflammation in at least two ways. First, diets rich in n-3 PUFAs increase membrane levels of eicosapentaenoic and docosahexaenoic acids at the expense of arachidonic acid. Thus, when immune cells are stimulated, there is less arachidonic acid available to generate prostaglandins and leukotrienes, which are inflammatory in nature. Second, eicosapentaenoic acid is a substrate for the same enzymes that metabolize arachidonic acid. However, the products of eicosapentaenoic acid metabolism are less inflammatory than those derived from arachidonic acid.

Although it may be useful to consume high levels of n-3 PUFAs to decrease inflammation associated with autoimmune and neoplastic disease, or to reduce the risk of heart disease, these conditions are not especially relevant to food-animal production, and the immunosuppression may render animals more susceptible to infectious disease. Thus, inclusion of fish or other n-3 PUFA-rich oils in animal diets should be approached with caution to avoid increased incidence of infections.

Zinc

Zinc (Zn) is a component of at least 300 enzymes, and inadequate intake of Zn renders animals severely immunodeficient and highly susceptible to infection. Both innate and acquired immunity are inhibited by Zn deficiency. Some studies suggest that the Zn required for optimum immunity is higher than that for optimum productivity. For example, in humans daily Zn supplementation reduced the incidence and duration of diarrhea and reduced the incidence of acute and lower respiratory infections. Furthermore, strains of mice that are genetically susceptible to infection by a certain pathogen can be made resistant by consuming a Zn-enriched diet. However, adverse effects of Zn excess on lymphocyte proliferation and chemotaxis and phagocytosis of neutrophils are

Table 1 Several nutrients with well-documented immunomodulatory effects

Nutrient	Reference	Primary immunological function
Arginine	[1]	Nitric oxide production
Glutamine	[1]	Primary nitrogen carrier in blood
n-6 PUFAs	[2]	Promote inflammation
n-3 PUFAs	[2]	Inhibit inflammation
Vitamin E and Selenium	[3]	Enhance humoral and cell-mediated immunity and inhibit inflammatory cytokine production

possible, and beneficial immunological effects of excess Zn have not been clearly demonstrated in livestock.

Iron and Copper

The effect of iron (Fe) on immunocompetence is not as clear as that of Zn; however, generally speaking, an imbalance in Fe intake—either too much or too little—decreases immunity. One of the acute responses induced by infection is hypoferremia. The inflammatory cytokines released by activated macrophages cause Fe to be sequestered. Because Fe is a rate-limiting nutrient for the growth of several pathogenic microorganisms, its removal from blood and temporary storage in compartments that are not accessible to pathogens is considered part of the host defense. Iron-binding proteins chelate the most Fe; however, supplementation can saturate these proteins, leaving excess Fe available to pathogens.

Copper (Cu) status is determined primarily by the plasma concentration of the acute-phase protein ceruloplasmin. The inflammatory cytokines induce synthesis of ceruloplasmin. Therefore, whereas infection decreases circulating Fe, it increases circulating Cu. The increase in plasma Cu may be to enhance lymphocyte responses because Cu deficiency reduces production of IL-2—a cytokine that acts in an autocrine manner to promote T-cell proliferation. To our best knowledge, there have been no studies clearly demonstrating that the Cu required for optimum immunity is higher than that for optimum production.

Vitamin E and Selenium

The primary role of vitamin E in nutrition is to protect cell membranes from peroxidative damage, whereas Se is an integral component of glutathione peroxidase. Vitamin E and Se also play an active role in the host's response to infection. Vitamin-E and Se supplementation in excess of minimal requirements may increase both innate and acquired immunity and offer protection against certain pathogens such as influenza. However, feeding a vitamin E level 50 times the NRC requirement did not afford pigs protection from the effects of porcine reproductive and respiratory syndrome virus infection on growth performance, cytokine production, or certain hematological traits (e.g., white blood cell counts). Nonetheless, vitamin E reduces the production of certain inflammatory cytokines and inhibits some behavioral signs of sickness. Thus, in certain instances vitamin-E supplementation may be beneficial.

Vitamin A

Vitamin-A deficiency severely compromises the integrity of mucosal epithelial cells in the respiratory, gastrointestinal, and uterine tracts. In the respiratory tract, ciliated columnar epithelium with mucus and goblet cells traps and removes inhaled microorganisms. In animals deficient in vitamin A, ciliated epithelial cells are replaced by stratified, keratinized epithelium, and there is a decrease in mucin. Similarly, in the small intestine, vitamin-A deficiency results in a loss of microvilli, goblet cells, and mucin. Other effects of vitamin-A deficiency on innate immunity include changes in epidermal keratins that disrupt skin barrier function; defects in chemotaxis, adhesion, phagocytosis, and the ability to produce reactive oxygen species in neutrophils; decreased number of NK cells and cytotoxicity; and a decrease in the expression of the receptor that recognizes Gram-negative bacteria as well as the secretion of inflammatory cytokines by macrophages and monocytes.

An adequate level of vitamin A is also necessary to support acquired immunity. The growth and activation of B cells require retinol. Pigs deficient in vitamin A synthesize less than one-tenth of the amount of antibody produced by pigs fed vitamin A–fortified diets. Infection with *Trichinella spiralisa* normally induces a strong T helper type 2-like response (i.e., high levels of parasite-specific IgG and production of IL-4, IL-5, and IL-10), but in vitamin-A deficiency an inappropriately strong T helper type 1–like response (i.e., production of interferon-γ and IL-12) is induced.

CONCLUSION

The nutrient requirements determined to support optimal productivity of healthy animals may fall short of those needed to promote optimal immune responses in animals challenged by infectious disease. It may be possible to develop diets that promote optimal immune responses. What is considered optimal may change from one production system to another, or even within a system, depending on the disease environment at a given time. The goal should not always be to minimize the immune response, for in certain environments this would result in increased incidence of infection. Similarly, the goal should not always be to maximize the immune response because an overzealous response to nonpathogenic stimuli can be counterproductive.

REFERENCES

1. Johnson, R.W.; Escobar, J.; Webel, D.M. Nutrition and Immunology of Swine. In *Swine Nutrition*, 2nd Ed.; Lewis, A.J., Southern, L.L., Eds.; CRC Press LLC: Boca Raton, 2001; 545– 562.
2. Calder, P.C.; Grimble, R.F. Polyunsaturated fatty acids, inflammation and immunity. Eur. J. Clin. Nutr. **2002**, *56* (Suppl 3), S14–S19.
3. Meydani, S.N.; Beharka, A.A. Recent developments in vitamin E and immune response. Nutr. Rev. **1998**, *56*, S49–S58.

Immune System: Stress Effects

Susan D. Eicher
United States Department of Agriculture, Agricultural Research Service, West Lafayette, Indiana, U.S.A.

Jeanne L. Burton
Michigan State University, East Lansing, Michigan, U.S.A.

INTRODUCTION

Stress has been difficult to define because of its dual function in life. It can be a positive influence that satisfies a need for excitement (environmental enrichment) or a negative influence that interferes with homeostasis and life functions. The latter is referred to as a state of distress. Our use of stress will refer to this darker side of stress. The interaction between stress and the immune system is a conundrum because of the negative impact that stress can have on immune functions, and because active immune responses can be stressors in and of themselves. Stress can also activate or suppress immune responses depending on the degree and persistence of the stressor; the species, age, sex, and genetics of the subject; and the immune cells that are the targets of the stress. Not all stressors result in the same immune response, such as isolation compared to restraint stress. But, in general, most psychological and environmental stressors lead to impaired immune functions, especially those that regulate inflammatory and cytotoxic responses. The deleterious effects of stress are readily observed at an early gene expression level in cells of the innate (not requiring prior exposure to foreign antigen) and adaptive (requiring prior exposure to foreign antigen) immune systems. Thus, stress-immune interactions usually have significant physiological consequences even before behavioral or gross pathogenic changes are observed.

TWO MAJOR PATHWAYS OF THE STRESS RESPONSE

The degree to which homeostasis becomes unbalanced and leads to distress[1] is largely influenced by the impact of stress hormones on target cells. Glucocorticoids (primarily cortisol in farm animals) are the main effector endpoints of the neuroendocrine response to stressors,[2] and result from activation of the hypothalamus-pituitary-adrenal (HPA) axis (Fig. 1). Systemic cortisol concentrations increase several minutes after a perceived threat and can last for a number of hours and recur in waves if the threat (stressor) is not removed. The well-known anti-inflammatory and immunosuppressive effects of cortisol may serve as physiological downregulators of initiated immune responses following infection or tissue damage.[3] However, contemporary management stressors that significantly and repeatedly activate the HPA axis in otherwise healthy animals cause pronounced changes in immune cell physiology, leading to disease susceptibility and clinical pathology.

Another pathway that mediates stress responses in animals is the sympatho-adrenal axis (Fig. 1). Activation of this neurotransmitter axis results in release of adrenergic hormones (mainly the catecholamines, adrenaline, and noradrenaline) from the medullae of the adrenal glands and from nerves that innervate lymphoid tissues and blood vessels. Catecholamine secretion occurs seconds following perceived threats, enabling rapid increases in heart and respiration rate and constriction of small blood vessels in peripheral tissues to increase blood flow to the brain, liver, and muscles, and enhancing awareness and athletic prowess to facilitate the fight-or-flight response.[4] However, like HPA axis activation, catecholamine responses may be inappropriate and harmful to immunity and health in the context of exposure to recurring or chronic stressors.

TWO ARMS OF THE IMMUNE SYSTEM AFFECTED BY STRESS

Molecules such as cytokines, chemokines, adhesion molecules, major histocompatability complexes (MHC), and antibodies link the innate and adaptive arms of the immune system (Fig. 2). The innate immune system provides the first line of immune defense and is composed primarily of neutrophils, macrophages, and dendritic cells. Under nonstress conditions, these professional phagocytes gain rapid entry into infected tissues to clear pathogens by receptor-mediated phagocytosis, leading to the production of free radicals and the release of enzymes that kill the ingested microorganisms. The adaptive immune system is primarily composed of B and T

Encyclopedia of Animal Science
DOI: 10.1081/E-EAS 120019688

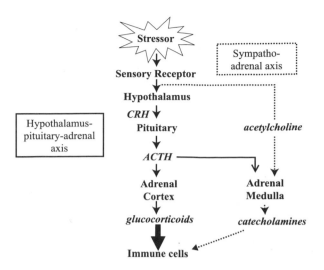

Fig. 1 Environmental and psychological stressors activate the hypothalamus-pituitary-adrenal (HPA) axis and sympatho-adrenal axis.

lymphocytes, which require prior exposure to pathogens for immune activation. The B lymphocytes (B cells) produce and secrete antibodies, which are particularly effective in protecting animals against extracellular pathogens. The T lymphocytes are made up of several subpopulations. Helper T cells of the type I class (T_HI) participate in inflammatory, cytotoxic, and some antibody responses. Helper T cells of the type II class (T_HII) facilitate primarily antibody-mediated responses. Cytotoxic T cells (T_C) and their innate counterparts, the natural

killer (NK) cells, lyse and kill host cells infected with intracellular viruses and bacteria. Less well-defined gamma delta-T cells ($\gamma\delta$ T cells) appear to have tissue healing and immune-modulating roles that vary in significance across species.

STRESS AFFECTS GENE EXPRESSION IN IMMUNE CELLS

Glucocorticoids (GC) such as cortisol act by regulating expression of multiple GC-sensitive genes and thus the expression of proteins that determine the phenotype and function of cells responsible for coordinating the body's response to stress. Gene expression regulation results from the binding of GC to its receptor (GR), found primarily in the cytoplasm of target cells, with subsequent translocation of the hormone-activated GR into the nucleus. It is here that GR has its major effects on gene expression, by interacting either directly (GR-DNA binding, as shown in Fig. 3) or indirectly (GR-other protein-DNA binding; not shown) with regulatory DNA in and around GC-sensitive genes. Glucocorticoids both induce and inhibit the expression of sensitive target genes, depending on the gene and the target cell affected. Thus, blood cortisol concentrations resulting from a stress response can have pronounced effects on immunity through altered expression of hundreds of immune cell genes.

Phagocytic cells, T_HI cells, and $\gamma\delta$ T cells seem to be particularly sensitive to the potent anti-inflammatory and immunosuppressive properties of stress cortisol, which:

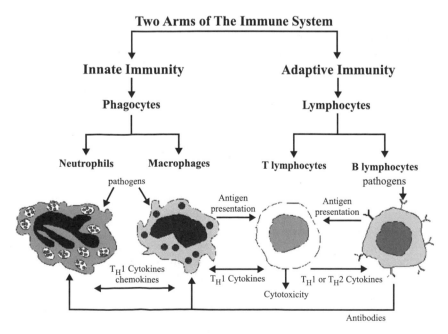

Fig. 2 Two arms of the immune system are affected by stress.

Glucocorticoid Sensitive Cell

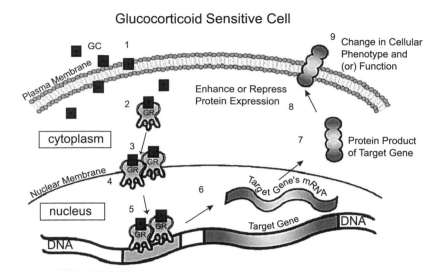

Fig. 3 Immune cells respond to stress by expressing cytoplasmic receptors (GR) for glucocorticoids (GC) such as cortisol. Cortisol readily crosses the plasma membrane of cells (step 1) and binds tightly with GR (step 2). This activates GRs to dimerize with another hormone-bound receptor (step 3), enabling them to translocate into the cell's nucleus (step 4), where they interact directly (shown in step 5) or indirectly (through interaction with other transcription factors; not shown) with promoters of GC-responsive genes. This interaction with promoter DNA enables GR to influence transcription of the target gene, either inducing (step 6) or suppressing (not shown) expression of mRNA for the gene. When mRNA abundance is increased or decreased by GR, increased abundance or reduced availability of protein encoded by the affected gene (steps 7 and 8) can alter the phenotype and thus the function of the cell (step 9).

1) downregulates the expression of multiple chemokines responsible for recruitment of innate immune cells into infected tissue; 2) inhibits expression of leukocyte adhesion molecules responsible for migration of circulating innate immune cells into infected tissues and adaptive immune cells into inflamed lymph nodes; 3) alters the expression of apoptosis genes in most immune cells, thereby changing their numbers in primary and secondary lymphoid tissues and blood; 4) inhibits expression of key pro-inflammatory cytokines, upsetting the balance of T_HI-based inflammatory/cytotoxic responses in favor of T_HII-based antibody responses; and 5) downregulates MHC II expression on key antigen presenting cells (macrophages, dendritic cells) normally responsible for alerting T_HI cells to an infection.[5]

More immediate immune regulation is induced by stress through the actions of catacholamines. In addition to circulating catacholamines secreted by the adrenal medullae in response to stress (Fig. 1), sympathetic nerve fibers from the central nervous system innervate primary and secondary lymphoid tissues providing direct "hits" of these neurotransmitters to developing B and T cells. Blood vessels are also innervated, so stress catacholamines influence the trafficking of leukocytes between lymphoid compartments and peripheral tissues by influencing gene expression in vascular endothelial cells. The most common of these in stressed farm animals are increased circulating neutrophil numbers, which drive

similar increases in blood neutrophil:lymphocyte ratios. Variable decreases in blood T_H:T_C cell ratios are also observed in stressed animals, but these ratios may be more responsive to cortisol than to catacholamines. Adrenoreceptors for the catacholamines are expressed by each of these immune cells and may be partly responsible for the acute alterations in lymphoid tissue cellularity, leukocyte trafficking patterns, and cytokine and antibody networks observed in some stressed animals.[4–7] Compared to glucocorticoids, however, relatively little information is available on molecular mechanisms used by catacholamines to change leukocyte biology and immune responses.

STRESS EFFECTS ON THE IMMUNE RESPONSE

Given that stress hormones modify expression patterns of hundreds of immune genes, it is reasonable to speculate that stress also has complex and pleiotropic effects on disease resistance through its effects on innate and adaptive immune responses. Several examples can be cited to substantiate this speculation. One is that glucocorticoids interfere with activation of adaptive immune responses, including those to vaccinations,[8] via their negative effects on MHC expression, cytokine expression, and the T_H:T_C ratio in blood. In addition, the combined actions of catacholamines and glucocorticoids on adhesion molecule expression by vascular endothelial cells and circulating neutrophils prevents this first line of immune defense from gaining access to infected tissues, leaving animals susceptible to diseases caused by opportunistic pathogens. The macrophage barrier to infection in peripheral tissues is also compromised during stress because glucocorticoids inhibit expression of key inflammatory molecules, including prostaglandins, chemokines, cytokines, and free radicals, which normally clear pathogens, initiate neutrophil recruitment to the site, and activate appropriate adaptive immune responses. Glucocorticoids also dramatically reduce circulating numbers of $\gamma\delta$ T cells in ruminants and alter the expression of key apoptosis genes to induce death in developing T cells and longevity in circulating neutrophils. This partly accounts for the altered tissue and circulating cell numbers during stress. Some degree of species specificity is evident in responses of the immune system to stress.[9] However, these changes in leukocyte numbers and their altered ability to communicate with each other through chemokines, cytokines, adhesion molecules, MHC complexes, and other inflammatory mediators occur in most farm animals when blood glucocorticoids and catacholamine concentrations increase, leaving stressed animals at risk for diseases caused by bacteria, virus, and parasites.

CONCLUSION

Whereas endocrine factors that link the stress and immune systems are beginning to be elucidated, phenotypic responses of the whole immune system to stress are not well understood and are often unpredictable.[10] Past studies in the animal sciences have mostly focused on measuring altered proportions of blood leukocytes as potential biological indicators of physiological stress and disease susceptibility. However, most of the indicators studied have been used with little biological justification. Rather, indicators such as the ratios of $T_H:T_C$ lymphocytes or neutrophil:lympocyte in blood have been used because researchers have the technology to perform such measurements and can show impressive changes in them due to imposed stressors. Whereas these measurements may indicate that changes are occurring in the animals, they are incomplete and not diagnostic of the overall immunophysiological response to stress. Part of the current lack of ability to prevent stress-related disease in farm animals is our lack of basic knowledge about what stress hormones do to leukocytes at the molecular level. Future prevention and treatment of stress-related infectious diseases will undoubtedly require that animal science researchers move beyond the study of isolated cellular phenomena to more holistic studies of genome-level changes that occur in

specific leukocytes in response to glucocorticoids, catacholamines, and other stress mediators and explain the cells' dysfunctions.

ACKNOWLEDGMENTS

The authors extend thanks to Sally Madsen and Jennifer Jacob for contributing to the development of Figs. 2 and 3.

ARTICLES OF FURTHER INTEREST

Environment: Effects on Animal Health, p. 335
Molecular Biology: Animal, p. 653

REFERENCES

1. Moberg, G.P. Biological Response to Stress: Implications for Animal Welfare. In *The Biology of Animal Stress Basic Principles and Implications for Animal Welfare*; Moberg, G.P., Mench, J.A., Eds.; CABI Publishing: New York, 2000; 1–21.
2. Eskandari, F.; Sternberg, E.M. Neural-immune interactions in health and disease. Ann. N. Y. Acad. Sci. **2002**, *966*, 20–27.
3. O'Connor, T.M.; O'Halloran, D.J.; Shanahan, F. The stress response and the hypothalamic-pituitary-adrenal axis: From molecule to melancholia. Q. J. Med. **2000**, *93*, 323–333.
4. Kohm, A.P.; Sanders, V.M. Norepinephrine and beta 2-adrenergic receptor stimulation regulate CD4+T and B lymphocyte function in vitro and in vivo. Pharmacol. Rev. **2001**, *53* (4), 487–525.
5. Burton, J.L.; Erskine, R.J. Mastitis and immunity: Some new ideas for an old disease. Veterinary Clinics of North America. Food Anim. Pract. **2003**, *19*, 1–45.
6. Elenkov, I.J.; Wilder, R.L.; Chrousos, G.P.; Vizi, E.S. The sympathetic nerve—An integrative interface between two supersystems: The brain and the immune system. Pharmacol. Rev. **2000**, *52* (4), 595–638.
7. Bergmann, M.; Sautner, T. Immunomodulatory effects of vasoactive catecholamines. Wien. Klin. Wochenschr. **2002**, *114* (17–18), 752–761.
8. Kehrli, M.E.; Burton, J.L.; Nonnecke, B.J.; Lee, E.K. Effects of stress on leukocyte trafficking and immune responses: Implications for vaccination. Adv. Vet. Med. **1999**, *41*, 61–81.
9. Webster, J.I.; Tonelli, L.; Sternberg, E.M. Neuroendocrine regulation of immunity. Annu. Rev. Immunol. **2003**, *20*, 125–163.
10. Blecha, F. Immune System Response to Stress. In *The Biology of Animal Stress Basic Principles and Implications for Animal Welfare*; Moberg, G.P., Mench, J.A., Eds.; CABI Publishing: New York, 2000; 111–121.

Immunity: Acquired

Joan K. Lunney
Max J. Paape
Douglas D. Bannerman
United States Department of Agriculture, Agricultural Research Service, Beltsville, Maryland, U.S.A.

INTRODUCTION

Higher species have the evolutionary benefit of an immune system that comprises both innate and acquired components. Whereas the innate immune system confers initial protection, the acquired immune system provides a second line of defense against infectious organisms.[1,2] The acquired immune system is activated once macrophages, dendritic cells, and other antigen-presenting cells (APCs) process foreign antigens (i.e., the products derived from infectious organisms, tumors, vaccines, etc.) Many APCs also transport the foreign antigen into regional immune lymph nodes.[3] APCs initiate adaptive immune responses by interacting with different populations of T and B cells.

IMMUNE CELL SUBSETS AND MARKERS

Table 1 outlines the differences between the innate and the adaptive, or acquired, immune response. Figure 1 shows some of the blood cell subsets involved in immune responses. Immune cell subsets are designated by their cluster of differentiation (CD) antigen markers, recognized by monoclonal antibodies (e.g., CD4+ T helper cells, CD25+ activation antigen, CD1+ dendritic cells, CD172+ macrophages).[a] T cells express the CD3 antigen and the T cell receptor (TCR). B cells produce immunoglobulins (Igs); some express them on their surface as part of the B cell receptor (BCR). The variant antigen-binding T and B cell receptors—the TCR and Ig—are complex; in the genome they are encoded as sets of gene segments coding for variable and constant regions.[2,3] To have an active TCR or Ig expressed,

multiple gene rearrangements must take place in each individual cell. Each TCR has two antigen-binding polypeptides—the TCR alpha and beta or gamma and delta gene complexes. The γδTCR+ T cells and αβTCR+ T cells are active in innate and adaptive immune responses, respectively. Each Ig also has four antigen-binding polypeptides, two heavy and two light chains.[4]b There are different Ig isotypes defined by their heavy chains (e.g., IgA, IgM, IgD, IgE, and multiple IgG isotypes) on B cells or in blood and mucosal secretions. The diversity of TCR and Ig expression adds to immune diversity, enabling the acquired immune system to respond to a broad array of immune molecules.

IMMUNE SYSTEM DEVELOPMENT

As it matures, the fetus develops its immune organs. Lymphocytes are generated in the primary lymphoid organs: the bone marrow, thymus, and intestinal Peyer's patches.[2,3] T and B lymphocytes from these tissues then start circulating and eventually localize in peripheral or secondary immune tissues, where adaptive, or acquired, immune responses take place. Effective immune responses require immune cells to be localized in secondary lymphoid organs. The neonate requires time for its immune tissues to become mature. Because of their lack of immune system development, neonates are typically more susceptible than older animals to respiratory or intestinal infections. Probiotics have been developed to assist in maturing the intestinal immune tissues. Cytokines and chemokines serve as lymphoid tissue hormones and help to regulate immune system development and differentiation.[5]

Once a foreign antigen (i.e., an antigen produced from infectious microbes or vaccine preparations) enters the body, it is encountered by an APC—a dendritic cell or macrophage—and is transported to the local lymphoid

---

[a]The Veterinary Immunology Committee of International Union of Immunological Societies (VIC-IUIS) maintains a series of websites for immune reagent information. (Pig website: http://eis.bris.ac.uk/~lvkh/welpig.htm; cattle: www.iah.bbsrc.ac.uk/leucocyte/bovsite.html; horses: www.vetmed.wisc.edu/research/eirh; other websites are under development.) The Human Leucocyte Differentiation Antigens (HLDA8) Animal Homologues Workshop (www.hlda8.org) is underway to expand the CD markers and species tested for cross reaction of anti-human CD markers on other species cells.

[b]The VIC-IUIS Comparative Immunoglobulin Workshop [CIgW] Committee maintains a website on immunoglobulins, Fc-receptors and their genes for veterinary species (http://www.medicine.uiowa.edu/cigw/).

Encyclopedia of Animal Science
DOI: 10.1081/E-EAS 120019689

Table 1 Comparison of innate immunity to acquired, or adaptive, immunity

	Innate immunity	Acquired (adaptive) immunity
Timing	Immediate maximal response	Lag time before maximal response
Specificity	Broad antigen specificity	Narrow antigen specificity
	Antigen independent	Antigen dependent
Memory	None	Positive immunologic memory
		Enhanced recall responses
Receptor	Fixed in genome	Encoded in germline, but rearrangement required
Expression	Fixed for cell	Regulated for each cell
Effector proteins	Antimicrobial peptides	Cytokines, chemokines
	Acute phase proteins, complement	Immunoglobulin (Ig) antibodies
	Cytokines, chemokines	Perforins, granzymes
Effector cells	Monocytes, macrophages	APC: dendritic cells, macrophages
	Granulocytes, neutrophils	T and B cells
	Natural killer (NK) cells	Regulatory cell subsets

organ, the lymph node, spleen, or specialized lymphoid tissues in the gut or respiratory sites. In these secondary lymphoid sites the foreign antigen is presented by APCs to T and B cells and an acquired immune response is initiated. Many immune cells excrete a broad range of cytokines and chemokines, such as the interferons (IFNs) and interleukins (ILs), that activate the immune system and encourage cells to migrate and localize to the area of infection or tumor growth.[5]

MAJOR HISTOCOMPATIBILITY COMPLEX (MHC) ANTIGENS

The major histocompatibility complex (MHC) antigens—or the swine, dog or bovine leukocyte antigens (SLA, DLA or BoLA)—are highly polymorphic, cell-surface antigens involved in antigen presentation.[4]c Class I MHC antigens are expressed on most cells, whereas class II MHC antigens are preferentially expressed on APC. The MHC genes are localized close together in the genome. Animals are usually MHC heterozygous, having two alleles at each of the multiple classes I and II genes.[3,4] Each animal expresses several class I MHC molecules, each of which is highly polymorphic. Class II genes are encoded by several linked loci, the DR and DQ alpha and beta genes. This wide diversity of MHC antigens is thought to be needed to handle the enormous number of foreign antigens that an animal encounters.

---

cThe international ImMunoGeneTics project (IMGT) maintains the HLA website and its IMGT/HLA Sequence Database. A related IPD/MHC sequence database website (http://www.ebi.ac.uk/ipd/mhc/index.html) will be used for MHC sequences of veterinary species.

INITIATION OF ADAPTIVE T CELL IMMUNITY

Innate immune responses help to control and eliminate infectious organisms, yet they are not always completely effective. However, even if the innate response is not fully protective, it results in the activation of the adaptive immune response. Numerous innate signals (e.g., Toll-like receptor (TLR) signaling, chemokines, and cytokines) attract immune cells to the local tissues where they are activated, causing the more complex, adaptive immune response. To stimulate adaptive immunity, foreign antigens must first be processed into peptide fragments by APC; the resulting fragments associate with MHC class I or II antigens and are presented to the TCR. In most cases, class I MHC binds internally processed foreign antigens, such as cell-processed viral or parasite peptides, whereas MHC class II presents externally generated peptides, such as vaccine peptides (Table 2). CD8+ T cells respond to class I MHC presented foreign antigens; CD4+ T cells respond to class II MHC.[2,3]

The way in which the animal's immune system initially reacts to an infectious pathogen is critical; it determines whether a protective, or an ineffective, or even a pathogenic, immune response will be mounted. The intensity of the response to foreign antigen peptides is dependent on the strength of immunostimulation. This is determined by the immunogenicity of the foreign peptide and the strength of the MHC-antigen complex, as well as on the frequency of TCRs that recognize that complex.[2,3]

POLARIZATION OF T CELL CYTOKINE RESPONSES

Cytokines are secreted by immune cells and can either stimulate or suppress the activity of immune cells and alter each cell's pattern of cytokine expression.[5] They

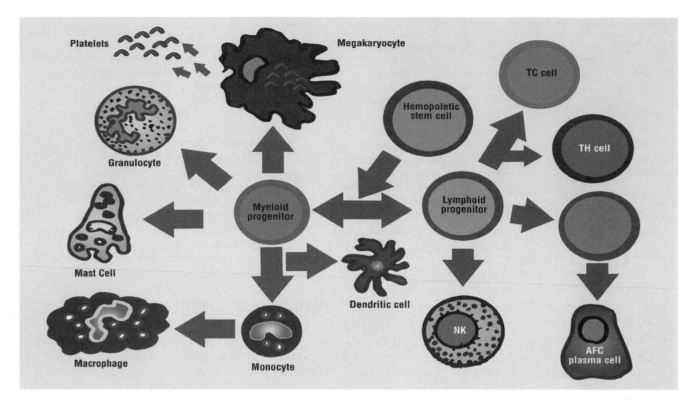

Fig. 1 Cells regulating immune responses. Blood immune cells. Immune cells that circulate in blood are shown. All immune cells in the blood, the hematopoietic cells, are derived from bone marrow stem cells. These hematopoietic stem cells give rise to two main lineages: one for lymphoid cells (lymphoid progenitor) and one for myeloid cells (myeloid progenitor). The common lymphoid progenitor will differentiate into either T cells or B cells depending on the tissue to which it travels (homes). In mammals, T cells develop in the thymus while B cells develop in the fetal liver and bone marrow. Pigs use special areas of their intestines, termed the Peyer's patches, for B cell maturation. B cells produce the antibodies so crucial to immune and vaccine responses. To produce antibodies, B cells must become antibody-forming cells (AFC), or plasma cells. Innate immune responses are carried out by natural killer (NK) cells that also derive from the common lymphoid progenitor cell. The myeloid cells differentiate into the committed cells on the left. The platelets help blood to clot and thus heal injured tissue. Three other myeloid-derived cell types, the monocyte, macrophage and dendritic cells are critical in helping the immune system recognize what is foreign, and thus stimulating specific immune system responses. Finally, the "granulocytes", a term used for eosinophils, neutrophils and basophils, have specialized functions, e.g., neutrophils will use antibodies to trap and kill invading bacteria. (Picture used with permission of National Hog Farmer.) Adapted from http://www.ed.sc.edu:85/book/immunol-sta.htm. Courtesy of Department of Pathology & Microbiology, University of South Carolina School of Medicine, Columbia, SC. (*View this art in color at www.dekker.com.*)

regulate a broad range of actions resulting in antigen-specific immune responses, alterations in levels of other cytokines, chemokine secretion, Ig production and isotype maturation, eosinophil and mast cell recruitment and activation, and cytotoxic T cell generation.[3] To counteract these mediators of host defense, certain infectious organisms actually encode their own cytokine modulators or receptor-blocking proteins.

Once activated, CD4+ T cells produce specific sets of cytokine signals. CD4+ T helper 1 (Th1) cells express the cytokine IFN-γ, which is essential for effective antiviral and bacterial responses (Table 2). In many

species Th1 responses are amplified by the release of IL-12. Th1 cytokines activate macrophages and natural killer cells in response to internally processed antigens. CD4+ Th2 cells stimulate a different set of cytokines, including IL-4, IL-5, and IL-13 in response to external peptides. These Th2 cytokines increase mast cell and eosinophil numbers and activities and stimulate B cells to switch to IgA and IgE production, thus enhancing inflammatory and allergic responses.

Cytotoxic CD8+ T cells interact with infected cells or tumor cells via antigen presented by class I MHC. Cell conjugates stimulate TCR-encoded recognition processes.

Table 2 T cell subsets and their adaptive immune responses

| T cell type[a] | T helper (Th) cells | | Regulatory T cells (Treg) | Cytotoxic T cells (CTL) | |
	Th1 CD4	Th2 CD4	Treg		
Major CD marker	CD4+	CD4+	CD4+CD25+	CD8+	CD4+
Cell location of microbe/ processed antigen	Intracellular microbe	Extracellular microbe		Intracellularly processed antigen	Extracellularly processed antigen
Dominant cytokines/ proteins	IFN-γ, IL-12	IL-4, IL-13	IL-10, TGFβ	Perforins, granzymes	Perforins, granzymes
MHC/SLA	Class II	Class II	Class II	Class I	Class II
Size antigenic peptide	6–8 amino acids	6–8 amino acids		9–12 amino acids	6–8 amino acids

[a]CD8+ cytokine-secreting cells are noted as type I and type II cells, as they express IFN-γ, IL-12 or IL-4, IL-13, respectively.

CD8+ T cells can stimulate cytokine production similar to that by CD4+ T cells; they can also lyse infected cells. Lysis occurs by cytolytic processes, by signaling through death receptors and apoptotic pathways, or by stimulating release of enzymes (granzymes, perforins) from specialized organelles, thus resulting in degradation of the infected target cell.[2,3] Tumors and some viruses suppress immunity by causing infected cells to downregulate MHC expression or by secreting cytokines that modulate effector responses.

CONCLUSION: UTILITY OF ACQUIRED IMMUNE RESPONSES

Acquired immune responses ultimately determine whether an infectious organism will be controlled and disease prevented.[3,6] Vaccines enhance immunity by altering the acquired immune response. Much research is now aimed at biotherapeutics that alter the balance between Th1 and Th2 cytokine responses. Because cytokines set the direction and amplify the intensity of specific antipathogen and vaccine immune responses, setting the direction of the early specific acquired immune response will help determine whether effective immunity will develop. Indeed, the ability to turn cytokine responses on and off quickly will determine how efficiently an animal controls the infection process.

REFERENCES

1. Bannerman, D.D.; Paape, M.J.; Lunney, J.K. Immunity: Innate. In *Encyclopedia of Animal Science*; Pond, W.G., Bell, A.W., Eds.; Marcel Dekker, Inc.: New York, 2004.
2. Janeway, C.A.; Travers, P.; Walport, M.; Shlomchik, M. *Immunobiology: The Immune System in Health and Disease*, 5th Ed.; Garland Publishing: New York, 2001.
3. Paul, W. *Fundamental Immunology*; Lippincott-Raven: New York, 2003.
4. Lunney, J.K.; Butler, J.E. Immunogenetics. In *Genetics of the Pig*; Rothschild, M.F., Ruvinsky, A., Eds.; CAB Intnl.: Wallingford, UK, 1998; 163–197.
5. Thomson, A.; Lotze, M. *The Cytokine Handbook*, 4th Ed.; Academic Press: New York, 2003.
6. Tizard, I. *Veterinary Immunology: An Introduction*, 6th Ed.; Elsevier Science: Amsterdam, the Netherlands, 2000; 482 pp.

Immunity: Innate

Douglas D. Bannerman
Max J. Paape
Joan K. Lunney
United States Department of Agriculture, Agricultural Research Service, Beltsville, Maryland, U.S.A.

INTRODUCTION

The ability of pathogens to establish a successful infection is mediated by both intrinsic properties of the pathogen itself and the ability of the host to respond to the invading organism. The immune system is responsible for responding to and protecting against infectious agents and comprises innate and adaptive components. The innate immune system represents the first line of defense in the host response to infection. Unlike the adaptive (acquired) immune response, which requires several days to generate effector lymphocytes in the numbers necessary to mount an effective immune response, the innate immune system is poised to immediately recognize and respond to the earliest stages of infection. Whereas the adaptive immune system of an organism acquires over time the ability to readily respond to highly specific antigens found on previously encountered pathogens, the innate immune system is able to respond to pathogens that have not been previously or repeatedly encountered. Thus, differences in the time needed to respond to a pathogen, the requirement for host memory, and the effector cells and molecules involved in the response all distinguish innate immunity from that of adaptive immunity.

PATHOGEN RECOGNITION

The inherent capability of the innate immune system to respond to a vast number of pathogens is mediated by its ability to recognize highly conserved motifs shared by diverse pathogens.[1–3] Examples of these motifs—commonly referred to as pathogen-associated molecular patterns (PAMPs)—include the bacterial cell wall components, lipopolysaccharide (LPS), peptidoglycan (PGN), and lipoteichoic acid (LTA), as well as unmethylated cytosine phosphate guanine (CpG) residues present in the DNA of lower microorganisms.[2] Because these PAMPs are commonly expressed by pathogenic organisms, but not by the host, the innate immune system is capable of differentiating self from nonself. Further, the ability to recognize common PAMPs on distinct pathogens enables the innate immune system to respond to vast numbers of infectious agents with only a limited repertoire of host recognition elements.

Innate recognition of PAMPs is mediated by evolutionarily conserved pattern recognition receptors (PRRs) and molecules (PRMs) expressed by a variety of cell types, including endothelial and epithelial cells, neutrophils, and cells of monocytic lineage.[1–3] The specificity of a given PRR is identical among all cells of one type (e.g., macrophages) that display that given PRR.[1] Toll-like receptors (TLRs) comprise a family of PRRs that are capable of recognizing distinct PAMPs. At least 10 members of the TLR family have been identified in mammals.[4] Each member is capable of recognizing a distinct PAMP. For example, TLR-2 and TLR-4 recognize the bacterial cell wall constituents LTA and LPS, respectively.

HOST CELL RESPONSES

Following PRR recognition of its cognate PAMP, cellular activation of effector cells of the innate immune system, including neutrophils and macrophages, often leads to the generation of an inflammatory response that is elicited, in part, by cytokine production.[5] Proinflammatory cytokines, such as TNF-α and IL-1β, are potent inducers of the acute-phase response, fever, and vascular endothelial activation. This latter event of endothelial activation in combination with PRR-mediated generation of the chemoattractant IL-8, facilitates neutrophil recruitment to the site of infection. Upregulation of other cytokines, such as IL-6 and IL-12, following PRR activation contributes to the adaptive immune response by stimulating lymphocyte proliferation and differentiation.

In addition to cytokines, PRR-mediated cell activation elicits cellular production of toxic oxygen radicals and proteases (which have direct bactericidal effects), as well as the generation of lipid mediators of inflammation, including platelet-activating factor (PAF) and the arachidonic acid metabolites, prostaglandins, leukotrienes, and thromboxanes.[5,6] Cell activation can further result in the release of antimicrobial peptides, including the well-characterized defensins and larger antimicrobial

Encyclopedia of Animal Science
DOI: 10.1081/E-EAS 120029997

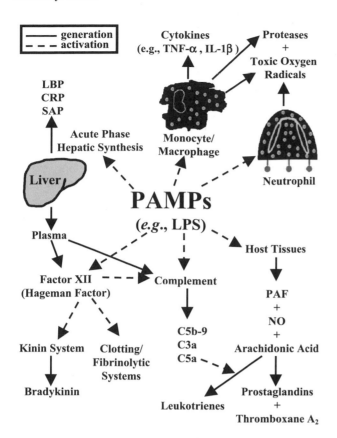

Fig. 1 Effector mechanisms of the innate immune response. Innate immune recognition of pathogen-associated molecular patterns (PAMPs) such as the Gram-negative bacterial wall constituent, lipopolysaccharide (LPS), activates multiple host mediator systems that promote inflammation and the generation of antimicrobial agents. Activation of Factor XII (Hageman Factor) leads to the induction of kallikrein-kinin, clotting, and fibrinolytic systems as well as the activation of complement. Activation of these systems results in the generation of anaphylotoxins, including bradykinin and complement cleavage products (e.g., C3a, C5a, C5b-9), which are highly proinflammatory. Priming and activation of macrophages and neutrophils enhance their release of proteases, toxic oxygen radicals, and proinflammatory cytokines (e.g., interleukin-1β (IL-1β) and tumor necrosis factor-α (TNF-α)). Host tissue activation leads to the production of platelet-activating factor (PAF), nitric oxide (NO), and lipid-derived mediators of inflammation (e.g., prostaglandins, leukotrienes, and thromboxanes). Host innate recognition of invasive pathogens stimulates an acute-phase response characterized by increased hepatic synthesis of proteins involved in both detection and clearance of infectious agents, including serum amyloid proteins (SAP), LPS-binding protein (LBP), and C-reactive protein (CRP).

proteins such as bactericidal-permeability increasing protein (BPI).[2] Both defensins and BPI are directly bactericidal. In addition, defensins can induce cytokine production, whereas BPI is an opsonin that facilitates bacterial clearance.

INNATE IMMUNE EFFECTOR MOLECULES

Although PAMP-binding to cell surface PRRs is a central mode of cell activation, the activity of effector cells involved in the innate immune response is also influenced by pattern recognition molecules (PRMs).[2] These secreted proteins include mannose-binding proteins (MBP), C-reactive protein (CRP), LPS-binding protein (LBP), and complement. Hepatic synthesis of CRP and LBP is up-regulated during the acute-phase response to infection and is stimulated by LPS, TNF-α, IL-1β, and IL-6.[2,6] CRP recognition of bacterial cell wall lipopolysaccharides leads to the activation of complement, a set of serum proteins with enzymatic activity that are directly bactericidal and promote inflammation. Complement activation results in the generation of products that enhance effector cell recognition and phagocytosis of infectious microorganisms. MBP recognition of bacterial cell surface carbohydrate residues similarly initiates complement activation. Another acute-phase response protein, LBP, is a lipid transfer molecule that facilitates the transfer of bacterial LPS to membrane-bound CD14 found on the surface of macrophages and neutrophils. LPS-CD14 complexes subsequently interact with TLR-4, leading to cell activation. Although CD14 is capable of binding to LPS in an LBP-independent manner, LBP enhances this interaction, and thus greatly enhances host innate detection of LPS present on Gram-negative bacteria.

Innate recognition of PAMPs initiates a series of events that contribute to the development of inflammation through cytokine production and the generation of lipid mediators. The initiation of one event can trigger multiple cascades leading to amplification of the inflammatory response (Fig. 1). For example, LPS activation of the liver-derived protein Factor XII (Hageman Factor) activates both the coagulation and fibrinolytic systems, and products generated by these systems promote a proinflammatory state.[5] Factor XII–mediated activation of the kinin system leads to the generation of kalikreins that can feed back to activate Factor XII. Further, activation of Factor XII can lead to the generation of complement products that, in turn, promote the production of leukotrienes. The complex interaction between these pathways culminates in the development of a highly proinflammatory state that enhances host innate immune responses to infectious pathogens.

INNATE IMMUNE EFFECTOR CELLS

The primary effector cells of the innate immune response are neutrophils and macrophages.[5,7] Resident tissue macrophages are one of the first cells to detect and become activated by the presence of an infectious agent. Once the pathogen is detected, macrophages and other host tissue cells release chemical messengers called chemoattractants that cause the directed migration of neutrophils to the site of infection. Potent chemoattractants for neutrophils include leukotriene B4, IL-1, IL-2, and IL-8. Other proteins generated during inflammation, such as the complement cleavage product C5a, also attract neutrophils. Migration of neutrophils into tissues provides the first immunological line of defense against bacteria that penetrate the physical barrier of the skin. Neutrophils express a number of functionally important receptors on their surface, including L-selectin and β2-integrin adhesion molecules, both of which facilitate neutrophil-binding to and migration through the vascular wall. Membrane receptors for the Fc component of the IgG_2 and IgM classes of immunoglobulins and complement component C3b mediate neutrophil phagocytosis of invading bacteria.

The most prominent characteristic of the neutrophil is the multilobulated nucleus. The multilobulated nucleus is important because it allows the PMN to line up its nuclear lobes in a thin line, allowing for rapid migration between endothelial cells. Macrophages, on the other hand, have a large horseshoe-shaped nucleus that makes migration between endothelial cells more difficult. Thus, the PMN is the first newly migrated phagocytic cell to arrive at an infection site. Activated macrophages and neutrophils are both sources of proinflammatory cytokines, as well as bactericidal proteases and toxic oxygen radicals. As mentioned earlier, neutrophils are also a primary source of defensins and BPI, both of which are directly bactericidal.

The first events in the process of phagocytosis are contact and recognition between the phagocyte and bacterium.[7] Opsonins, including antibodies and complement components, facilitate phagocyte recognition and engulfment of the bacterium. In the absence of specific opsonins, neutrophils are able to bind and ingest certain species of bacteria. After contact and recognition, pseudopods form around the microbe. Fusion of the engulfing pseudopods results in the formation of a phagocytic vacuole or phagosome. Cytoplasmic granules migrate toward the phagosome where the membrane surrounding the granules fuses with the internalized plasma membrane that lines the phagosome, creating the phagolysosome. As a result of this, bactericidal contents of the granule are then emptied into the phagolysosome where digestion of the microbe occurs.

CONCLUSION

Innate immunity represents an ancient and highly conserved means by which the host can defend itself against pathogens that have penetrated the physical barriers of the skin and other tissues. The ability of the innate immune system to respond immediately to invading pathogens, as well as respond to a broad variety of infectious agents with a limited repertoire of receptors and molecules, delineates this system from that of adaptive immunity. Thus, the innate immune system serves as the initial mode by which the host defends itself from potentially injurious pathogens.

REFERENCES

1. Medzhitov, R.; Janeway, C. Innate immunity. N. Engl. J. Med. **2000**, *343* (5), 338–344.
2. Uthaisangsook, S.; Day, N.K.; Bahna, S.L.; Good, R.A.; Haraguchi, S. Innate immunity and its role in infections. Ann. Allergy, Asthma, & Immun. **2002**, *88* (3), 253–264.
3. Lunney, J.K.; Paape, M.J.; Bannerman, D.D. Immunity: Acquired. In *Encyclopedia of Animal Science*; Pond, W.G., Bell, A.W., Eds.; Marcel Dekker Inc.: New York, 2004.
4. Holger, H.; Lien, E. Toll-like receptors and their function in innate and adaptive immunity. Int. Arch. Allergy Immunol. **2003**, *130* (3), 180–192.
5. Janeway, C.A.; Travers, P.; Walport, M.; Shlomchik, M. Innate Immunity. In *Immunobiology: The Immune System in Health and Disease*, 5th Ed.; Garland Publishing: New York, 2001; 35–91.
6. Collins, T. Acute and Chronic Inflammation. In *Robbins Pathologic Basis of Disease*, 6th Ed.; Cotran, R.S., Kumar, V., Collins, T., Eds.; W.B. Saunders Company: Philadelphia, 1999; 50–88.
7. Paape, M.J.; Bannerman, D.D.; Zhao, X.; Lee, J.-W. The bovine neutrophil: Structure and function in blood and milk. Vet. Res. **2003**, *34* (5), 597–627.

Implantation

Fuller W. Bazer
Robert C. Burghardt
Greg A. Johnson
Texas A&M University, College Station, Texas, U.S.A.

INTRODUCTION

Implantation is attachment of trophectoderm (Tr) of the developing conceptus (the embryo and associated extraembryonic membranes) to the luminal epithelium (LE) of the uterus. This highly synchronized event requires reciprocal secretory and physical interactions between the conceptus and uterine endometrium during a restricted period known as the window of receptivity. The receptive state is established by critical levels of progesterone and estrogen that regulate locally produced cytokines, growth factors, homeobox transcription factors, and cyclooxygenase-derived prostaglandins through autocrine and paracrine pathways. Initiation of endometrial receptivity also depends upon silencing expression of progesterone receptors (PR) in uterine LE and superficial gland epithelia, although PRs continue to be expressed in stroma and myometrium. Effects of progesterone on PR-negative epithelial cells appear to be mediated by various stromal cell-derived growth factors that function as progestamedins.

The initial interactions between apical uterine LE and Tr surfaces begin with sequential phases (i.e., nonadhesive or prereceptive, apposition, and attachment) and conclude with development of a placenta that supports fetal development throughout pregnancy. During the early phases of implantation, secretory products of both uterine glands (histotroph) and conceptus Tr exert a mutual influence. Histotroph provides nutritional support for conceptus development, which in turn promotes secretion of hormones and cytokines, including the signal for maternal recognition of pregnancy, which is obligatory to prolong progesterone production by the corpus luteum (CL) and maintain pregnancy.

MATERNAL RECOGNITION OF PREGNANCY

Maintenance of pregnancy in mammals requires the continued integrity of the CL beyond its normal cyclic lifespan for progesterone production to support secretory functions of the endometrium that sustain early embryonic development, implantation, and placentation.[1–3] Maternal recognition of pregnancy signals between the conceptus and maternal system[3] are luteotrophic if they directly promote luteal function, or antiluteolytic if they prevent uterine release of luteolytic prostaglandin F_2, which would cause CL regression. Chorionic gonadotrophin is the luteotrophic signal that acts directly on the CL of primates, as is mating-induced release of prolactin and placental lactogens in rodents. In domestic animals, antiluteolytic signals from the conceptus include estrogen and prolactin in pigs, interferon-tau in ruminants, and an undetermined factor(s) in horses.[4]

IMPLANTATION STRATEGIES

Implantation may be noninvasive (central) or invasive (interstitial or eccentric), depending on whether or not Tr invades through uterine LE into the stroma. Implantation in domestic animals differs from that of rodents and primates where the conceptus enters a receptive uterus and almost immediately attaches to uterine LE. Domestic animals have a prolonged preimplantation period (the prereceptive phase) in which the developing conceptus migrates throughout the uterine lumen (Fig. 1A). Equine embryos remain spherical and contained within a capsule prior to attachment, whereas pig and ruminant conceptuses shed the zona pellucida (hatching) and transform morphologically from a spherical to a filamentous structure. Preattachment conceptus development is accompanied by differentiation of the Tr layer that secretes the pregnancy recognition signal.

Considerable variability exists among species relative to histogenesis and organization of the placenta (the structure derived from both fetal membranes and maternal tissues). Despite differences in duration of the preimplantation period and degree of conceptus invasiveness, initial stages of apposition and attachment are common across species. During these events, maternal-conceptus crosstalk is extensive and receptivity results from the acquisition of ligands and receptors facilitating apposition and adhesion, as well as from loss of antiadhesive components at the maternal-conceptus interface that

Encyclopedia of Animal Science
DOI: 10.1081/E-EAS 120019690

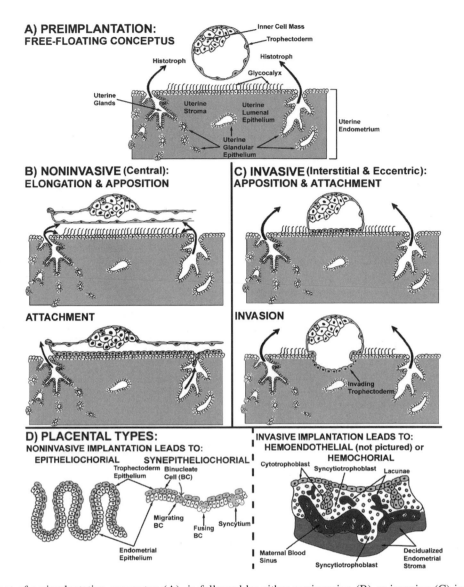

Fig. 1 Development of preimplantation conceptus (A), is followed by either noninvasive (B) or invasive (C) implantation and then either noninvasive or invasive type of placenta (D).

sterically prevent this interaction. The functional changes in uterine LE include a decrease in the apical glycocalyx, cytoskeletal remodeling of LE, and loss of polarity. The initial stages depicted in Fig. 1 compare conceptus/maternal interactions in domestic animals (noninvasive implantation, Fig. 1B) with those of rodents, carnivores, and primates (invasive implantation, Fig. 1C). Differences in the extent of trophoblast (gives rise to chorion) interaction with maternal tissues among species are illustrated in Fig. 1D, which depicts the interface between maternal and fetal cells, giving rise to placental structures. For example, intimate contact between chorion derived from Tr and an intact LE is maintained in pigs throughout pregnancy (epitheliochorial placenta, Fig. 1D, left panel). Because the chorion is continuously in contact with uterine LE, this is referred to as a diffuse placenta. Ruminant conceptuses form binucleate Tr cells, which invade and fuse with uterine LE to form multinucleated cells or a syncytium (synepitheliochorial placenta, Fig. 1D, middle panel). Binucleate Tr cells and the syncytium derived from binucleate cell migration are the source of placental lactogen.[5] In both epitheliochorial and synepitheliochorial placentation, the conceptus remains within the uterine lumen throughout gestation. In contrast to the diffuse porcine placenta, attachment of chorioallantois in ruminants occurs at discrete sites along the uterine wall called caruncles that are oval elevations of endometrial mucosa devoid of uterine glands. Contact between chorioallantois and caruncles leads to development of highly convoluted placental villous structures termed cotyledons. The resultant structure, consisting of maternal caruncles and placental cotyledons, is the placentome.

Carnivores, rodents, and primates exhibit invasive implanation where the blastocyst invades and implants deeply into the endometrial stoma and the uterine LE is restored over the site of implantation. During initial contact, the trophoblast layer is highly proliferative and undergoes syncytial formation to form a syncytiotrophoblast cell layer that develops stable adhesion with uterine LE followed by penetration of syncyiotrophoblasts into the uterine wall to establish extensive contacts with maternal vasculature. Loss of maternal vascular endothelial cells results in the formation of maternal blood sinusoids in the hemochorial placentae of higher primates and rodents (Fig. 1D, right panel), whereas the hemoendothelial placentae of carnivores (not shown) retain the endothelial layer. Mononuclear cytotrophoblasts underlie syncytiotrophoblasts, and these cells migrate out of the trophoblast layer.

RECEPTIVITY AND IMPLANTATION ADHESION CASCADE

Initial conceptus attachment requires loss of antiadhesive components, mainly mucins, contained in the glycocalyx of LE that sterically inhibit attachment.[1] The mucin, MUC1, exists as both an intrinsic transmembrane mucin and an alternatively spliced, secreted variant. Both forms are localized to the apical uterine LE to provide a barrier to attachment, but are generally reduced during the receptive phase (mice, pig, sheep) or locally at the site of blastocyst attachment (human, rabbit) due to activation of cell-surface proteases.

Unmasking adhesion molecules on the LE surface permits initial low-affinity contacts with Tr that are subsequently combined with or replaced by more stable adhesive interactions. In invasive implantation, these initial interactions precede a repertoire of trophoblast interactions with maternal extracellular matrix (ECM) and stromal cell populations encountered following intrusion beyond the LE.[6,7] Initial adhesion is mediated by molecules that contribute low affinity but specific carbohydrate ligand-binding, including selectins and galectins. Other molecules that have been implicated in implantation adhesion events include heparan sulfate proteoglycan, heparin-binding EGF-like growth factors, cadherins, and CD44. Low-affinity interactions are followed by stable adhesion.[6,7] In all mammals investigated, integrins expressed on blastocysts and uterine LE and their ECM ligands appear to be the dominant contributors to stable implantation adhesion systems by virtue of their roles in adhesion, migration, invasion,

cytoskeletal organization, and bidirectional signaling.[8] In humans, expression of $\alpha_v\beta_3$ and $\alpha_4\beta_1$ integrins increases in LE during the window of implantation.[7] These and other integrins identified at both maternal and conceptus interfaces along with integrin-binding matrix proteins such as fibronectin, oncofetal fibronectin, vitronectin, osteopontin (OPN), laminin, and the latency-associated peptide linked to transforming growth factor-(TGF-)beta are critical in both noninvasive and invasive implanting species.[8,9] These and other ECM constituents may function as bridging ligands for stable adhesion between apically expressed maternal and fetal integrins.

Global gene profiling using high-density microarray technology has identified genes that either increase or decrease during the window of implantation. Comparison of endometrial tissue between late proliferative phase and secretory phase human endometria identified 323 genes that increase and over 370 genes that decrease by at least twofold.[10] Modulated genes include cell-surface proteins/receptors, ECM molecules, secretory proteins, immune modulators/cytokines, cytoskeletal proteins, transporters, and transcription factors, as well as proteins involved in cholesterol trafficking, prostaglandin biosynthesis, detoxification, cell-cycle regulation, signal transduction, and other cellular functions. About 20% of the changes were attributed to genes encoding cell-surface receptors, adhesion and ECM proteins, and growth factors,[10] including markers of uterine receptivity in humans such as glycodelin and OPN, stromal cell-specific insulin growth factor-binding proteins-1 and -2, prostaglandin E_2 receptor, IL-15 and TGF-type II receptor for which expression increased.[10] Notably, OPN expression from uterine glands increased 12-fold at the receptive phase in women[10] and up to 60-fold during pregnancy in rats,[11] suggesting a direct role in embryo-uterine interactions. Similar microarray studies are addressing uterine gene expression in early bovine pregnancy.[12]

DECIDUALIZATION

Invasive implantation triggers endometrial stromal responses collectively identified as decidualization. The endometrium is transformed by hyperplasia and hypertrophy of stromal cells, secretion of prolactin and ECM proteins, OPN, laminin and fibronectin, the invasion by numerous immune cells, and formation of cell–cell contacts.[13] Decidualized stroma produces many endocrine and paracrine factors not present in nondecidualized cells[14] and controls trophoblast invasion during implantation by generating a local cytokine environment that promotes trophoblast attachment.[15] Varying degrees of decidualization occur in all implanting species with the most extensive stomal transformation occurring with the invasive implantation of rodents and primates, moderate transformation occurring in synepitheliochorial sheep, and only minor changes occurring in the epitheliochorial pig.[16]

CONCLUSIONS

Implantation involves the complexity of the steroid-dependent regulation of uterine receptivity and many classes of molecules that are modulated during initial conceptus-uterine LE interactions. Subsequent cellular interactions involve epithelial-stromal communication to limit invasiveness, establish relationships between conceptus and maternal vasculature, and numerous other functions essential to successful development of the conceptus.

REFERENCES

1. Carson, D.D.; Bagchi, I.; Dey, S.K.; Enders, A.C.; Fazleabas, A.T.; Lessey, B.A.; Yoshinaga, K. Embryo implantation. Dev. Biol. **2000**, *223* (2), 217–237.
2. Paria, B.C.; Reese, J.; Das, S.K.; Dey, S.K. Deciphering the cross-talk of implantation: Advances and challenges. Science **2002**, *296* (5576), 2185–2188.
3. Spencer, T.E.; Bazer, F.W. Biology of progesterone action during pregnancy recognition and maintenance of pregnancy. Front. Biosci. **2002**, *7*, d1879–d1898.
4. Roberts, R.M.; Xie, S.; Mathialagan, N. Maternal recognition of pregnancy. Biol. Reprod. **1996**, *54* (2), 294–302.
5. Wooding, F.B.; Morgan, G.; Forsyth, I.A.; Butcher, G.; Hutchings, A.; Billingsley, S.A.; Gluckman, P.D. Light and electron microscopic studies of cellular localization of oPL with monoclonal and polyclonal antibodies. J. Histochem. Cytochem. **1992**, *40* (7), 1001–1009.
6. Kimber, S.J.; Spanswick, C. Blastocyst implantation: The adhesion cascade. Semin. Cell. Dev. Biol. **2000**, *11* (2), 77–92.
7. Lessey, B.A. Adhesion molecules and implantation. J. Reprod. Immunol. **2002**, *55* (1–2), 101–112.
8. Burghardt, R.C.; Johnson, G.A.; Jaeger, L.A.; Ka, H.; Garlow, J.E.; Spencer, T.E.; Bazer, F.W. Integrins and extracellular matrix proteins at the maternal-fetal interface in domestic animals. Cells Tissues Organs **2002**, *172* (3), 202–217.
9. Johnson, G.A.; Burghardt, R.C.; Joyce, M.M.; Spencer, T.E.; Bazer, F.W.; Gray, C.A; Pfarrer, C. Osteopontin is synthesized by uterine glands and a 45-kDa cleavage fragment is localized at the uterine-placental interface throughout ovine pregnancy. Biol. Reprod. **2003**, *69* (1), 92–98.
10. Carson, D.D.; Lagow, E.; Thathiah, A.; Al-Shami, R.; Farach-Carson, M.C.; Vernon, M.; Yuan, L.; Fritz, M.A.; Lessey, B. Changes in gene expression during the early to mid-luteal (receptive phase) transition in human endometrium detected by high-density microarray screening. Mol. Hum. Reprod. **2002**, *8* (9), 871–879.
11. Girotti, M.; Zingg, H.H. Gene expression profiling of rat uterus at different stages of parturition. Endocrinology **2003**, *144* (6), 2254–2265.
12. Ishiwata, H.; Katsuma, S.; Kizaki, K.; Patel, O.V.; Nakano, H.; Takashi, T.; Imai, K.; Hirasawa, A.; Shiojima, S.; Ikawam, H.; Suzuki, Y.; Tsujimoto, G.; Izaike, Y.; Todoroki, J.; Hashizume, K. Characterization of gene expression profiles in early bovine pregnancy using a custom cDNA microarray. Mol. Reprod. Dev. **2003**, *65* (1), 9–18.
13. Loke, Y.W.; King, A. Human Implantation. In *Cell Biology and Immunology*; University Press: Cambridge, 1995; 1.
14. Brar, A.K.; Handwerger, S.; Kessler, C.A.; Aronow, B.J. Gene induction and categorical reprogramming during in vitro human endometrial fibroblast decidualization. Physiol. Genomics **2001**, *7* (2), 135–148.
15. Kliman, H.J. Uteroplacental blood flow. The story of decidualization, menstruation, and trophoblast invasion. Am. J. Pathol. **2000**, *157* (6), 1759–1768.
16. Johnson, G.A.; Burghardt, R.C.; Joyce, M.M.; Spencer, T.E.; Bazer, F.W.; Pfarrer, C.; Gray, C.A. Osteopontin expression in uterine stroma indicates a decidualization-like differentiation during ovine pregnancy. Biol. Reprod. **2003**, *68* (6), 1951–1958.

International Animal Germplasm Exchange

Harvey Blackburn
United States Department of Agriculture, Agricultural Research Service,
Fort Collins, Colorado, U.S.A.

INTRODUCTION

The exchange of animal genetic resources has resulted in major increases in livestock productivity and/or increased market acceptability of livestock products. In the Americas the importation of livestock species and breeds from Europe, Asia, and Africa has made significant contributions to the vitality of the livestock sector. As producers within countries have developed their animal genetic resources, there has been an impetus from breeders in other countries to want to explore how those breeds or strains produce in their own production system. Such explorations have over time proved to be beneficial in altering livestock productivity. For example, during the 1970s and 1980s, numerous cattle breeds were imported into the United States from continental Europe, Latin America, and Africa. Many of the imported cattle breeds played a significant role in U.S. livestock production (e.g., Charolais, Simmental, Limousin). Other key examples are the U.S. Holstein in its role as a global breed for milk production, and the impact the South African Boer goat has had on the U.S. meat goat sector. All these examples underscore the importance of being able to exchange genetic resources. It is anticipated that as the livestock industry and consumer demands change, there will be a need to develop new genetic combinations to address those needs. These new genetic combinations will be developed from existing genetic resources within countries or acquired from other countries.

CURRENT LEVELS OF U.S. TRADE

Improved animal performance is the primary impetus for trade. Some of the factors taken under consideration when deciding whether or not to import include: the potential to increase level of productivity, presence of a unique characteristic that is not present in indigenous populations (e.g., high ovulation rate), and ability to efficiently produce in a particular production system.

In terms of cash revenues the international exchange of animal germplasm is not large. U.S. imports and exports combined are less than 0.5% of the beef and dairy industries' annual cash receipts. Table 1 provides the level and value of imports and exports from the United States. The trade in semen composes the largest segment of germplasm trade. However, cash values do not account for the impact that exported or imported germplasm has on long term productivity (or national economic activity), which could be quite large. The future value of genetic resources is a key element in the valuation of genetic resources and may play an important role in bilateral and multilateral trade agreements.

Ownership of traded germplasm is diverse, ranging from individual breeders, artificial insemination companies, national and multinational breeding companies, and governments. As a result, germplasm is being exchanged for a wide variety of purposes (e.g., research and altered productivity). Regardless of the trader the same phytosanitary and multilateral and bilateral trade agreements control the movement and exchange of germplasm.

GOVERNING TRADE

Trade Regulations

Regulation of international trade in animal germplasm is based on animal health issues and national socioeconomic policies. Animal health regulations have been formulated at national and international levels to prevent the spread of diseases between animal populations either within a country or between countries. Generally, countries have a set of phytosanitary regulations focusing on important diseases. For example, a country may want to bar the importation of semen from a country that is endemic with foot and mouth disease. Nonphytosanitary trade regulations are primarily focused upon decreasing consumer costs for animal products or protecting the economic viability of a country's livestock sector.

The World Trade Organization (WTO) has had a significant impact on how germplasm is traded between countries. The WTO has linked trade (monetary issues) with health issues. This is an essential element for the facilitation of international trade. To ensure disease risk is minimized and to assist in preventing nontariff barriers to trade, the WTO developed the Agreement on Sanitary and Phytosanitary (SPS) Measures. The purpose of this

Encyclopedia of Animal Science
DOI: 10.1081/E-EAS 120023814
Published 2005 by Marcel Dekker, Inc. All rights reserved.

Table 1 U.S. exports and imports of semen or embryos in 2002

Germplasm type and species group	Export quantity	Export value, $	Import quantity	Import value, $
Semen				
Bovine	6,366,272	47,470,000		
Dairy			1,544,857	8,157,000
Beef			1,754,142	7,635,000
Other	9,021	372,000	13,229	476,000
Embryos				
Dairy cattle	3,888	2,483,000	60	20,000
Beef cattle	3,125	1,091,000	283	141,000
Chickens				
Broiler & layer	5,709,425	11,704,395	2,439,078	1,858,146
Total value ($)		63,120,395		18,287,146

(From USDA—Foreign Agriculture Service, www.fas.usda.gov/ustrdscripts/USReport.exe, accessed 9–9–2003.)

agreement is to allow Members "to adopt and enforce measures necessary to protect human, animal or plant life health, subject to the requirement that measures are not applied in a manner which would constitute a means of arbitrary or unjustifiable discrimination between Members where the same conditions prevail or a disguised restriction on international trade."[1] The WTO has designated the Office of International Epizootics (OIE) as the reference organization for animal health and zoonoses. Since 1960 the OIE has developed and altered over time the Terrestrial Animal Health Code, the objective of which is to prevent the spread of animal diseases, while facilitating international trade in live animals, semen, embryos, and animal products.[2] It is through the Terrestrial Animal Health Code that the OIE contributes to the global trade in animal germplasm. Because the OIE is a body consisting of member countries, it provides a forum for discussing and modifying the Terrestrial Animal Health Code; member countries have input as to the content of the health code.

Convention on Biological Diversity

In addition to the agreements formed under the WTO, a large number of countries are signatories to the Convention on Biological Diversity (CBD). The objectives of the CBD are:[3]

Conservation of biological diversity, the sustainable use of its components and the fair and equitable sharing of the benefits arising out of the utilization of genetic resources, including by appropriate access to genetic resources and by appropriate transfer of relevant technologies, taking into account all rights over those resources and to technologies, and by appropriate funding.

There are several aspects of the CBD that impact the exchange of animal genetic resources. These include the consideration that farm animal genetic resources are part of a country's natural resources and that states have sovereign rights over such resources, and thus the

Table 2 State of cryopreservation by species to facilitate germplasm exchange

Species	Status of cryopreserving semen	Success of postthaw utilization of cryopreserved semen	Status of cryopreserving embryos	Success of postthaw utilization of cryopreserved embryos
Cattle	Routine & efficient	Very high	Routine & efficient	High
Swine	Feasible	Low–Moderate	Feasible	Very low
Sheep	Feasible	Low–Moderate	Feasible	Moderate
Goat	Feasible	Moderate	Feasible	Moderate
Chicken	Feasible	Low	Not possible	–
Turkey	Not possible	–	Not possible	–

authority to determine access to genetic resources. Each contracting party shall endeavor to create conditions to facilitate access to genetic resources. A key element in the CBD is language aimed at sharing in a fair and equitable way the benefits arising from commercial and other utilization of genetic resources. It is unclear at this time the ramifications that the CBD will have on the exchange of animal genetic resources.

TECHNICAL ASPECTS

Several technical aspects need to be in place to facilitate international exchange of genetic resources. The ability to move germplasm either as cryopreserved semen or as embryos significantly increases the ease by which germplasm can be moved. Cryopreservation of sperm is feasible for most livestock species (Table 2), whereas embryos are a less reliable form of preservation. For most species, cryopreservation procedures have not been optimized and such an effort would facilitate the efficiency of germplasm exchange. For nonruminant species, considerable efforts are needed to improve cryopreservation of embryos. Although cryopreservation of germplasm facilitates international trade, it does not alleviate the need to follow health testing protocols that the importing and exporting countries have. Across species, there are technologies that enable health officials to test germplasm directly or blood samples from the imported or exported animal.

International genetic evaluations that estimate breeding values across countries provide another mechanism that can facilitate international trade. Such an approach provides a multinational evaluation of an individual animal's performance; it has also been shown that the predicted accuracy of the evaluation is increased by utilization of performance data from multiple countries. Therefore, it is possible for breeders to globally identify sires with desired performance levels. This capability has the potential to allow a wide range of producers in different countries access to genetic resources that rapidly alter performance. Conversely it may also speed a reduction in genetic diversity.

CONCLUSIONS

The international exchange of animal genetic resources has had a large and significant impact on global livestock production. In general, the exchange of germplasm has been positive in increasing the economic viability of national livestock industries. However, a negative aspect to this type of trade is that it tends to decrease genetic diversity of major production species and in some instances displaces some indigenous livestock breeds. But this breed substitution is not simply a function of importation of different germplasm. Rather, the imported germplasm is better able to meet consumer demands and increase production efficiency. To counter the reduction in genetic diversity and breed substitution, nations can establish national genetic conservation programs that will enable better management of genetic diversity and the conservation of breed variation.

Technically, increasing international germplasm trade requires improved cryopreservation protocols across species, refinement of health tests, sharing of performance information for genetic evaluation, and mechanisms to help value the financial worth of the commodity being traded. From a nonbiological perspective, artificial trade barriers must be removed and a willingness of governments is needed to allow the livestock sector to explore the full utilization of genetic resources.

REFERENCES

1. World Trade Organization (WTO). *The WTO Agreement on the Application of Sanitary and Phytosanitary Measures (SPS Agreement)*; Geneva, WTO: Switzerland, 1994.
2. Office of International Epizootics (OIE). *Terrestrial Animal Health Code*, 12th Ed; World Organization for Animal Health: Paris, 2003.
3. United Nations Environmental Programme. *Convention on Biological Diversity*; United Nations Environmental Programme: New York, 1992.

Lactation, Land Mammals, Species Comparisons

Olav T. Oftedal
Smithsonian Institution, Washington, D.C., U.S.A.

INTRODUCTION

Lactation is a diagnostic trait of all mammals, involving the synthesis of a nutrient-rich secretion by specialized mammary glands. The many similarities among living mammals in mammary gland development, regulation, and ultrastructure, as well as in secretory mechanisms and types of milk constituents, indicate that lactation has a single evolutionary origin. However, there are diverse lactation patterns among living mammals, involving differences in the duration and intensity of lactation, as well as differences in suckling frequency, milk composition, and milk yield. In this article, aspects of milk secretion and yield that underlie species differences will be discussed, and some of the variation seen among major orders of land mammals will be mentioned.

ORIGIN OF LACTATION

Lactation was well established before the divergence in the late Jurassic and/or early Cretaceous periods of the monotremes (such as echidnas and the platypus), marsupials (such as opossums and kangaroos), and eutherians (such as mice, sheep, and humans).[1] Lactation appears to be an ancient trait that first appeared more than 200 million years ago, perhaps as a source of moisture for incubated eggs.[2]

MILK SECRETION

Lactation involves the production of milk by epithelial cells that line the expanded terminal ends, or alveoli, of an intricate system of ducts. Milk is formed as a mixture of two primary phases: an aqueous phase (including water, electrolytes, proteins, and sugars) released from small vesicles that migrate to the cell surface, and a lipid phase that forms by the coalescence of lipid droplets and is released from the cells as membrane-bound fat globules.[3,4] Most constituents are synthesized within the epithelial cells themselves, but some are transported from blood across the mammary epithelial cells or pass into milk by extracellular routes. Differences in the rates of secretion of the different phases, as well as in the rates of synthesis and/or transport of particular constituents, result in wide variation in milk composition.

Mammary glands do not attain structural or physiological maturity until the onset of reproduction, and thereafter undergo cyclical proliferation and regression. Milk secretion begins shortly before parturition (or egg-laying in monotremes), and is substantially upregulated in the postnatal period. Milk production usually rises to a peak in well-fed mammals and then declines as the offspring switch to solid foods. In some mammals, such as many species of true seals, milk production appears to remain at high levels until the young are abruptly weaned.

MILK ENERGY OUTPUT

Although a general relationship exists between peak milk yield (or milk energy output) and maternal metabolic body size (body mass$^{0.75}$),[5,6] there are large differences in peak production among species independent of metabolic body size. In terrestrial mammals, species with large litters, such as rats, dogs, and pigs, have peak milk energy outputs per maternal metabolic size that are two to three times those of ungulates with one young (Table 1). The peak energy outputs of most primates are even lower. The highest daily outputs of milk energy are found among seals. The hooded seal appears to be the mammalian champion: Its daily milk energy output is four times that of a pig, 11 times that of a horse, and 27 times that of a human, relative to metabolic size.

Among terrestrial mammals, milk energy outputs are higher for species with large litters, reflecting the greater energy demands of additional offspring. This effect can be accounted for by expressing milk energy output relative to litter metabolic mass (litter size × offspring mass$^{0.83}$).[6] Among terrestrial mammals, milk energy output expressed in this way varies from about 0.71 to 1.11 (Table 1). However, much higher values have been observed in seals with very short lactations.

Mammals with long lactations tend to have higher total energy outputs over the lactation period, presumably because they supply the maintenance requirements of suckling young for a longer time. Some species, such as seals and dogs, opt for a short, intensive lactation with high peak energetic costs, while others, such as horses and

Encyclopedia of Animal Science
DOI: 10.1081/E-EAS 120019696

Table 1 Milk and energy outputs at midlactation in terrestrial mammals

Species	Litter size	Lactation length	Maternal mass (kg)	Peak (d after birth)	N	Milk yield (kg/d)	Energy output, EO (MJ/d)	EO per maternal MBS[a] (MJ/kg$^{0.75}$/d)	EO per litter MBS[a] (MJ/kg$^{0.83}$/d)
Human	1	6–36 mo	57	60–120	5	1.05	3.03	0.15	0.72
Baboon	1	12–18 mo	16.7	120	4–8	0.40	1.34	0.16	0.85
Reindeer	1	5 mo	107	21–28	3	1.59	11.05	0.33	1.19
Horse	1	11–12 mo	515	39	5	17.6	37.21	0.35	0.88
Dorcas gazelle	1	3 mo	20.6	30–60	4	0.56	3.59	0.37	0.88
Black-tailed deer	2	3–4 mo	49.8	28	6	1.26	9.28	0.49	0.98
Sheep	2	4–6 mo	52.6	17	5	2.47	11.47	0.59	1.05
Mink	5	8–10 wk	0.96	20	6	0.12	0.59	0.60	0.89
Striped skunk	5	8–16 wk	2.22	31	5	0.15	1.24	0.69	1.05
Greater spear-nosed bat[b]	1	11 wk	0.077	30–45	13	0.015	0.11	0.76	1.00
Rabbit	7	4 wk	4.40	21	5	0.27	2.32	0.77	1.01
Dog	5	6–8 wk	12.7	26	5	1.05	6.45	0.96	1.11
Brown rat	8	4 wk	0.20	14	?	0.041	0.24	1.01	0.89
Pig	9	3–4 mo	120	24	44	7.16	37.34	1.03	0.88

[a]MBS = metabolic body size (mass$^{0.75}$ in adults; mass$^{0.83}$ in suckling young). (From: Refs. 6 and 7.)
[b]Species binomial: *Phyllostomus hastatus*.

humans, have evolved long, extensive lactations with lower peaks but large overall energy costs.

LACTATION PATTERNS AMONG ORDERS

Monotremata

Monotremes (echidnas, platypus) lay shelled eggs that are incubated for 10–12 days; the young hatch at an extremely undeveloped state.[8] Initially, the mammary glands are simple tubules that produce dilute milk, but as the secretory cells proliferate, they organize into alveoli within discreet mammary lobules. Each lobule drains via a duct onto the skin surface adjacent to an enlarged mammary hair. Milk oozing onto the skin is sucked up by the young. The milk becomes increasingly concentrated over the course of the 6-month lactation. In late lactation, suckling echidnas consume milk equivalent to 10% of body weight at once-daily nursing bouts.[8] As in other mammals with long intersuckling intervals, the milk is high in fat (ca. 30%) in midlactation.

Marsupialia

Marsupial young are both very small (0.004–0.93 g) and very altricial (immature) at birth. Survival after birth depends on successful attachment to a nipple, which swells in size to fill the mouth, forming a seal. The nipples and attached young may be within a pouch, as in kangaroos and wallabies, but many pouchless species (including opossums) carry their young dangling from the nipples when traveling. Both the nipples and mammary glands increase in size as the young mature, and the milk, which was quite dilute at birth, becomes increasingly rich in fat, protein, and sugars, especially oligosaccharides. An important developmental milestone is the time of teat detachment, which initiates a period of rapid change in milk composition as fat and protein increase but sugars decline markedly.[9] Some marsupials, such as kangaroos and wallabies, give birth while an older young is still suckling. The neonate attaches to a nipple that produces dilute secretion, while the older "joey" continues to ingest late lactation milk of very different composition.

Rodentia and Lagomorpha (Rodents, Rabbits and Hares)

In both rodents and rabbits, newborn young range from relatively small and altricial, such as many species of mice, rats, hamsters, and domestic rabbits, to large and precocial (well-developed), such as spiny mice, guinea pigs, porcupines, and hares. The milks of species with altricial young tend to be high in water and low in energy, and their young may be unable to eat solid food for 10 days or more. By contrast, the highly precocial guinea pig begins to eat solid foods within a few days of birth, and can be weaned as early as one week of age. Altricial rodents may initially remain attached to nipples for extended periods, obtaining small amounts of milk at frequent intervals. However, in rabbits the young are nursed infrequently, only once or twice a day, at which time they ingest highly concentrated milk (Table 1).

Chiroptera (Bats)

Lactating bats must provide milk until the young are able to fly on their own, i.e., until bone growth and mineralization are largely complete. Bats have small litters (one to two young), provide a large amount of milk to each young,[7] wean them at a high proportion (ca. 55–90%) of adult mass, and appear to be sensitive to availability of calcium for milk synthesis.[10] Many species of bats produce relatively concentrated milks, particularly species such as the Mexican free-tailed bat that forage over great distances between nursing bouts.

Primates

Many monkeys and apes, like humans, have an extensive rather than intensive lactation: They give birth to single young that nurse frequently on a dilute, low-energy milk for many months to several years. However, marmosets and tamarins rear twins during a lactation period of just a few months. Among prosimian primates, some species such as lemurs (*Eulemur* spp.) carry their young and nurse frequently, while others, such as bushbabies (*Otolemur* spp.), leave their young in nests and return to nurse at intervals. The former produce dilute milks like most monkeys and apes, but the latter provide more energy-dense milks for their young.

Ungulates (Artiodactyla, Perissodactyla) and Proboscidea (Elephants)

Most ungulates (including ruminants, horses, and rhinos) produce precocial offspring that rely solely on milk for the first week or more of life, and then are gradually weaned onto solid foods over a prolonged period of many months to several years. In wild ruminants, peak milk production is not high (Table 1). Although African elephant calves eat solids by 3 months of age, they may continue to suckle for 2–8 years. The extent to which milk is important to calf nutrition in such extended lactations is not known.

Carnivora

In most carnivores, the mother nurses and rears her litter by herself, but in wolves, African hunting dogs, dholes, and some mongooses, other pack members assist by bringing food to the mother and to older pups. This assistance permits the female to produce large amounts of milk for a large litter, as in domestic dogs (Table 1). At the other extreme, some bears lactate during hibernation, providing small amounts of milk to altricial cubs even though the mother is fasting. Milk yields increase when mother and cubs emerge from the den and the mother can begin to eat and drink.

CONCLUSION

Despite general similarity in the process of milk secretion, almost all other aspects of lactation vary tremendously among land mammals. There is large variation in developmental state of suckling young, postnatal growth rate, suckling frequency, milk composition, milk yield, lactation energetics, size at weaning, and overall duration of lactation.

ARTICLES OF FURTHER INTEREST

Lactation, Marine Mammals, Species Comparisons,
    p. 565
Milk Composition, Species Comparisons, p. 625

REFERENCES

1. Oftedal, O.T. The mammary gland and its origin during synapsid evolution. J. Mammary Gland Biol. Neoplasia **2002**, *7*, 225–252.
2. Oftedal, O.T. The origin of lactation as a water source for parchment-shelled eggs. J. Mammary Gland Biol. Neoplasia **2002**, *7*, 253–266.
3. Keenan, T.W.; Patton, S. The Structure of Milk: Implications for Sampling and Storage. A. The Milk Lipid Globule Membrane. In *Handbook of Milk Composition*; Jensen, R.G., Ed.; Academic Press: San Diego, 1995; 5–50.
4. Linzell, J.L.; Peaker, M. Mechanism of milk secretion. Physiol. Rev. **1971**, *51*, 564–597.
5. Linzell, J.L. Milk yield, energy loss in milk, and mammary gland weight in different species. Dairy Sci. Abstr. **1972**, *34*, 351–360.
6. Oftedal, O.T. Milk composition, milk yield and energy output at peak lactation: A comparative review. Symp. Zool. Soc. Lond. **1984**, *51*, 33–85.
7. Stern, A.A.; Kunz, T.H.; Studier, E.H.; Oftedal, O.T. Milk composition and lactational output in the greater spearnosed bat, *Phyllostomus hastatus*. J. Comp. Physiol. B **1997**, *167*, 389–398.
8. Griffiths, M. *The Biology of Monotremes*; Academic Press: New York, 1997.
9. Green, B.; Merchant, J.C. The Composition of Marsupial Milk. In *The Developing Marsupial. Models for Biomedical Research*; Tyndale-Biscoe, C.H., Janssens, P.A., Eds.; Springer Verlag: Berlin, 1988; 41–54.
10. Barclay, R.M.R. Does energy or calcium availability constrain reproduction by bats? Symp. Zool. Soc. Lond. **1995**, *67*, 245–258.

Lactation, Marine Mammals, Species Comparisons

Olav T. Oftedal
Smithsonian Institution, Washington, D.C., U.S.A.

L

INTRODUCTION

Members of three mammalian orders, Carnivora [carnivores, including the pinnipeds (seals and sea lions) and otters], Cetacea (dolphins and whales), and Sirenia (manatees and dugongs), live and feed at sea. In all groups, lactation entails production of a fat- and energy-rich milk, either to promote deposition in the young of an insulating layer of subcutaneous fat, or to cover high metabolic costs of life at sea. Yet there are remarkable differences in all other aspects of lactation, including duration, pattern of nursing, growth of the young, and milk and energy outputs. In this article, the unusual lactation patterns seen among the three orders of marine mammals are briefly reviewed.

CARNIVORA

The marine carnivores include three families of seals or pinnipeds—the true seals (Phocidae), fur seals and sea lions (Otariidae), and walruses (Odobenidae)—as well as marine species of otters (family Mustelidae). Polar bears (family Ursidae) are also considered marine mammals as they hunt their prey at sea.

Phocidae (True Seals)

The true seals (family Phocidae) produce large amounts of high-fat (ca. 30–60%) milk, and wean their young at a young age (4 days to 8 weeks).[1,2] During the shortest lactation of any mammal (4 days), the hooded seal provides 8 kg/d of 60%-fat milk, causing pups to increase in weight from 22 kg at birth to 45 kg at weaning.[3] Such an enormous transfer of energy to the young, whether expressed relative to the metabolic size of the mother (4.0 MJ/kg$^{0.75}$/d) or the metabolic size of the pup (14 MJ/kg$^{0.83}$/d), is unparalleled among other marine mammals (Table 1) or terrestrial mammals. This intensive lactation may have evolved to allow completion of lactation in a very short time because the pack ice on which pups are born is liable to disintegrate during storms.[3] However, most phocids have both a short lactation and a high rate of

milk energy transfer relative to other mammals (Table 1). This is an evolutionary compromise to resolve the conflict between needing to feed at sea and having to nurse out of the water, whether on land or on ice. Phocids are able to ingest and deposit large amounts of fat and protein in body reserves before giving birth, and are thus able to fast for much or all of lactation.[9] A short lactation with rapid energy transfer to the young minimizes the time that mothers must remain ashore, and thus reduces maintenance energy costs during the fast.

Otariidae (Eared Seals)

The fur seals and sea lions (family Otariidae) have resolved the conflict between marine foraging and terrestrial nursing in a strikingly different manner. Although mothers initially haul out onto land to give birth and remain ashore for 1–1.5 weeks, they then begin a series of periodic foraging trips to sea interspersed with 1–4-day nursing periods ashore. Depending on species and pupping site, the foraging trips may be of remarkable length, from less than 1 day to more than 20 days.[1,2] The mother accumulates high-fat (30–55%) milk in her mammaries while at sea,[1,8] but the pup remains at the breeding colony initially digesting milk (from the prior nursing bout) and then fasting. It is not known how lactating otariids manage to sustain milk secretion without either a suckling stimulus or milk removal during these prolonged foraging trips. The fact that otariid species with longer foraging trips produce milks higher in fat[10] suggests that mammary storage volume may be limiting. Upon the mother's return, the pup ingests large quantities of milk over several days, equivalent to 50% of body weight in some species. However, as these nursing bouts are interspersed with periods of fasting, the average daily milk energy intake by otariid pups is lower, growth is slower, and lactation is of much longer duration than in the phocids (Table 1). Across both phocids and otariids, the intensity of lactation, expressed as milk-energy output per maternal metabolic size per day, is inversely related to the duration of lactation, ranging from 0.36 MJ/kg$^{0.75}$/d in the California sea lion to 4.0 MJ/kg$^{0.75}$/d in the hooded seal (Table 1).

Encyclopedia of Animal Science
DOI: 10.1081/E-EAS 120040344

Table 1 Milk and energy outputs at midlactation in marine mammals[a]

Species[b]	Lactation length (d)	Body mass (kg)	Study period (d after birth)	N	Milk yield (kg/d)	Energy output, EO (MJ/d)	EO per maternal MBS[c] (MJ/kg$^{0.75}$/d)	EO per offspring MBS[c] (MJ/kg$^{0.83}$/d)
Cetacea—Odontoceti								
Common dolphin	~540	112	~90	–	*0.42*	*6.0*	*0.17*	*0.6*
Great sperm whale	~740	13500	~180	–	*9.0*	*12*	*0.09*	*0.3*
Cetacea–Mysticeti								
Fin whale	210	65000	~180	–	*160*	*2500*	*0.62*	*1.1*
Blue whale	210	100000	~180	–	*220*	*4000*	*0.72*	*1.3*
Pinnipedia–Otariidae								
California sea lion	330	88	30–60	13	0.73	10.2	0.36	1.3
Australian fur seal	330	80	125–147	10	0.70	13.9	0.52	1.3
Northern fur seal	120	38	~85–105	23	0.72	16.8	1.1	1.9
Antarctic fur seal	115	41	84–98	13	0.70	12.5	0.82	2.1
Pinnipedia–Phocidae								
Weddell seal	45	342	8–38	9	3.5	75	0.94	2.2
N. elephant seal	27	402	0–24	6	5.5	91	1.0	2.3
Grey seal	17	173	0–14	9	3.0	69	1.4	4.0
Harp seal	12	113	4–11	4	3.6	75	2.2	4.3
Hooded seal	4	166	0–4	7	7.5	187	4.0	14.0

[a]Measured values except those in italics, which were estimated from growth rate and mammary mass. All species have only one young. (From Refs. 1–8.)

[b]Scientific binomials provided in Refs. 1, 2, 4, and 7.

[c]MBS = metabolic body size (mass$^{0.75}$ in adults; mass$^{0.83}$ in sucking young). (From Refs. 6 and 7.)

Odobenidae (Walruses)

The walruses (family Odobenidae) have the longest lactation (2–3 years) of any pinnipeds. They differ from other pinnipeds in that the calf suckles in the water while the mother floats at the surface.[2]

Other Carnivores

Another marine carnivore, the sea otter (in the family Mustelidae), also nurses at sea: The pup suckles while the mother floats on her back. Polar bears (in the family Ursidae) give birth in snow dens and nurse their cubs during winter hibernation. After den emergence, the cubs follow their mothers out onto sea ice, but may continue to suckle for two years. All of these carnivores produce high-fat milk, but milk yields are not well documented.

CETACEA

Mysticeti (Baleen Whales)

The baleen whales (suborder Mysticeti) are filter-feeders that reach gargantuan size. At 100,000 kg or more, a fully-grown blue whale attains the largest mass of any animal. This large mass allows females to mobilize vast quantities of nutrients from body reserves during lactation.[4,9] Most of the very large species, such as gray, humpback, fin, and blue whales, migrate back and forth between high-latitude/polar regions, where they feed, and warm temperate/tropical regions, where they give birth and lactate but fast or feed little.[4] In blue and fin whales, the calves gain about 50–80 kg/d, ingest milk containing 32–35% fat, and are weaned at 6–7 months (Table 1). This short lactation, relative to body size, minimizes the time spent on breeding grounds where food resources are sparse. The amounts of milk (220 kg/d) and milk-energy (4000 MJ/d) that blue whales are estimated to produce far surpass those of other mammals, but in relation to maternal metabolic size, the daily output of milk-energy (0.72 MJ/kg$^{0.75}$/d) is not remarkable, resembling that of many terrestrial mammals.

Odontoceti (Dolphins and Toothed Whales)

Fasting and use of stored reserves is not a major component of the lactation strategy of dolphins or most other toothed whales (suborder Odontoceti). Odontocete calves typically grow slowly during a relatively long lactation period. Depending on species, the calves take first solids at 2–12 months, and nurse for 8–34 months,[4] although longer lactations may occur in bottlenose dolphins and sperm whales. Estimated daily milk energy outputs (ca. 0.1–0.2 MJ/kg$^{0.75}$/d) are very low (Table 1), similar to those seen in primates. A long period of dependence during which the young grow slowly may be important for the acquisition of hunting and social skills in these large-brained, highly social mammals, just as it is in primates.[4]

SIRENIA

The manatees and dugongs (order Sirenia) are unique among marine mammals in that they are strict herbivores. The calves suckle underwater from nipples located in the axillary region (i.e., armpit). Calves take first solids at about 3–4 months, but lactation lasts for 1–2 years. Although manatee milk is relatively high in fat (16%) and very low in carbohydrate (0.2%), milk yield has not been reported.

CONCLUSION

Marine mammals exhibit a great range of lactation strategies, from species with long lactations but low milk energy yields to species with very short lactations and very high milk-energy yields. In both phocid seals and baleen whales, females typically fast for much or all of lactation, putting an evolutionary premium on abbreviation of the lactation period. On the other hand, dolphins and toothed whales resemble primates in their low growth rates and long lactations. Lactating otariid seals alternate foraging and nursing in distinct cycles. The one consistency is that all species produce milks that are moderately to greatly enriched in fat.

ARTICLES OF FURTHER INTEREST

REFERENCES

1. Oftedal, O.T.; Boness, D.J.; Tedman, R.A. The behavior, physiology, and anatomy of lactation in the Pinnipedia. Curr. Mammal. **1987**, *1*, 175–245.
2. Boness, D.J.; Bowen, W.D. The evolution of maternal care in pinnipeds. Bioscience **1996**, *46*, 645–654.
3. Oftedal, O.T.; Bowen, W.D.; Boness, D.J. Energy transfer by lactating hooded seals and nutrient deposition in their pups during the four days from birth to weaning. Physiol. Zool. **1993**, *66*, 412–436.
4. Oftedal, O.T. Lactation in whales and dolphins: Evidence of divergence between baleen- and toothed-species. J. Mammamary Gland Biol. Neoplasia **1997**, *2*, 205–230.
5. Oftedal, O.T.; Bowen, W.D.; Boness, D.J. Lactation performance and nutrient deposition in pups of the harp seal, *Phoca groenlandica*, on ice floes off southeast Labrador. Physiol. Zool. **1996**, *69*, 635–657.
6. Arnould, J.P.Y. Lactation and the cost of pup-rearing in Antarctic fur seals. Mar. Mammal Sci. **1997**, *13*, 516–526.
7. Arnould, J.P.Y.; Hindell, M.A. Milk consumption, body composition and pre-weaning growth rates of Australian fur seal (*Arctocephalus pusillus doriferus*) pups. J. Zool. Lond. **2002**, *245*, 351–359.
8. Donohue, M.J.; Costa, D.P.; Goebel, E.; Antonelis, G.A.; Baker, J.D. Milk intake and energy expenditure of free-ranging northern fur seal, *Callorhinus ursinus*, pups. Physiol. Biochem. Zool. **2002**, *75*, 3–18.
9. Oftedal, O.T. Use of maternal reserves as a lactation strategy of large mammals. Proc. Nutr. Soc. **2000**, *59*, 99–106.
10. Ochoa-Acuòa, H.; Francis, J.M.; Oftedal, O.T. Influence of long intersuckling interval on composition of milk in the Juan Fernandez fur seal, *Arctocephalus philippi*. J. Mammal. **1999**, *80*, 758–767.

Lamb: Carcass Composition and Quality

J. D. Wood
University of Bristol, Bristol, U.K.

INTRODUCTION

Sheep meat is produced throughout the world, with areas such as the Middle East and countries such as New Zealand being major producers and consumers. Older animals, termed mutton, are popular for meat in some countries. In other countries, particularly those where most work has been published, carcass weights and ages are lower—typically 16- to 20-kg carcass weight and less than one year of age. These lighter carcasses are generally referred to as lamb, although lamb is used as a general term for sheep meat.

Lamb is often described as a fatty meat, so there is great interest in ways to change composition, i.e., reduce fat and increase muscle in the carcass and the joints/cuts that are commonly purchased. Quality characteristics important in lamb include muscle color, fat hardness, and eating quality (tenderness, juiciness, and flavor). These are influenced by factors such as breed, age, and diet and by processing. As with other meat species, carcass and meat quality in lamb can be controlled by altering the various production and processing factors.

CARCASS COMPOSITION IN LAMB

The proportions of muscle, fat, and bone in lamb carcasses are affected by breed (including selection line), sex, and diet. In comparison with beef cattle and pig carcasses, studies show that lamb carcasses are slightly fatter and contain less muscle, but the contrast is even greater in the meat at retail. This reflects the difficulty of trimming fat from small lamb cuts. In a comparison of loin steaks/chops purchased at retail, lamb had 30% fat (range 15–51%), beef 16% (7–23%), and pork 21% (4–40%).[1]

Genetic Effects on Carcass Composition: Breed and Selection

There are many different breeds of sheep in the world and in individual countries, reflecting the different environments where sheep are found—from high mountains to temperate lowland pastures, and from arid to extremely cold regions. Sheep are a natural grazing species, but in many dry countries, they are also reared on grain (concentrate) diets and in feed lots. These different environments have resulted in wide variation in body shape (conformation) and size.

In general, smaller, lighter breeds are fatter at a particular slaughter weight than the bigger, heavier breeds, reflecting differences in the stage of maturity (smaller breeds are closer to maturity). These differences are best expressed when all groups have been fed in a similar way. However, some breeds seem to depart from the general rule linking carcass composition with stage of maturity; e.g., the Soay and Texel are leaner than expected on this basis. In one study, Texel carcasses contained 60% muscle compared with 56% in the Oxford Down, whose mature weight was greater (100 kg in Oxford, 87 kg in Texel).[2]

Because carcass composition traits such as the percentages of muscle and fat are moderately heritable (typically 0.3–0.5), it is possible to select leaner animals within breeds. This is likely to be most successful where large populations can be evaluated by linking flocks on different farms. One approach is the Sire Reference Scheme, in which the same sires are evaluated on several linked farms.[3] Progress on within-breed selection for leaner carcasses could be accelerated if accurate methods for evaluating carcass composition in the live animal were widely available, for example, computed tomography (CT).

The shape of the body or carcass, termed conformation, is affected by breed type. The ewe-type breeds, noted for maternal traits, have thinner muscles and more angular carcasses (poorer conformation) than the meat-type breeds, whose carcasses are blockier. These carcasses contain more muscle at the same fat cover, so a higher price is justified when carcasses are classified for fatness and conformation. However, premiums for conformation often penalize acceptably lean carcasses from ewe-type breeds.

Conformation differences between breeds are linked to differences in how the body fat is partitioned between fat depots. The ewe-type breeds have a higher proportion in the abdominal cavity and a lower proportion subcutaneously on the carcass compared with the meat-type breeds.[4]

Encyclopedia of Animal Science
DOI: 10.1081/E-EAS 120019697

Feed/Nutritional Effects on Carcass Composition

The effects of nutritional treatments on carcass composition, within normal practical limits, are relatively small. Feeding at a high level (ad libitum) to the same body weight increases fat compared with restricted feeding, and grass-based diets produce fatter carcasses than grain-based (concentrate) diets, associated with a reduction in available protein. However, these nutritional effects are relatively small compared with breed effects. Weight is an important determinant of carcass composition, with fatness increasing significantly at higher carcass weights.

Sex Effects on Carcass Composition

As with cattle and pigs, the carcass of the entire male has a higher proportion of muscle and a lower proportion of fat than that of the castrated male. Entire males also grow faster and convert feed into meat more efficiently, these effects being due to the actions of androgens secreted from the testes. Nevertheless, castration is very common in sheep since it rules out unwanted pregnancies in flocks.

Effects of Growth Hormones on Carcass Composition

Hormonal effects are important in controlling body composition, as shown by the differences between entire males and castrates. These effects can also be achieved by exogenous administration of hormones, through implants behind the ear in the case of estrogens and androgens, and via the diet in the case of β-adrenergic agonists. Growth hormone must be given by intramuscular injection. All these materials are effective in changing body composition, although they are not allowed in the European Union because of the potential safety risk. This also applies to lamb imported into the European Union. Ralgro, a compound with estrogenic effects, is licensed for use in the United States, but is not widely used at present. It appears that the use of hormones for controlling body composition in sheep is much less common than in beef and is likely to reduce further under pressure from consumers.

LAMB MEAT QUALITY

Meat quality refers to the visual appearance, handling characteristics, and eating quality of lamb meat, i.e., those aspects that are important to processors, and to consumers when they purchase and eat lamb. Lamb has many distinctive qualities. It is relatively dark, with an ultimate pH (measured at cutting, 24 or 48 hours after slaughter) higher than beef and pork (i.e., 5.7 vs. 5.5). In these

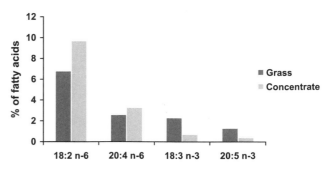

Fig. 1 Major n-6 and n-3 polyunsaturated fatty acids in semimembranous muscle from lambs fed a grass or concentrate diet (% of total fatty acids). (From Ref. 7.) (*View this art in color at www.dekker.com.*)

species, a high pH would indicate excessive preslaughter stress, causing glycogen depletion and limited lactic acid production in muscle postmortem. Sheep are apparently more resistant to preslaughter stress—for example, long-distance transportation to market[5]—so this higher ultimate pH is a natural feature and is not associated with variation in muscle color or drip loss.

Tenderness and Flavor of Lamb

Tenderness in lamb also seems to be less variable than in beef and pork and generally receives high scores from taste panelists. As with these species, tenderness can be greatly influenced during processing, especially by extending the aging (conditioning) period. This results in proteolytic breakdown of the muscle structure. Electrical stimulation is sometimes used in the early stages of processing to tenderize lamb and to prevent cold shortening during chilling. This can easily arise in the lamb carcass with its high ratio of surface area to weight. Another factor in the generally high tenderness of lamb could be intramuscular fat (marbling fat), which is higher than in beef and pork with similar carcass fat levels, but is not so visible in the meat.

The flavor of lamb is particularly distinctive. In comparison with beef and pork, this is explained by high concentrations of branched-chain fatty acids of medium-chain length, e.g., 4-methyloctanoic acid and 4-methylnonanoic acid, and perhaps by more saturated fat.[6] Skatole is also a significant factor in the flavor of lamb. Different flavors in grass-fed and grain-fed lamb have been shown in several studies.[7] This is associated with higher concentrations of n-3 (omega-3) polyunsaturated fatty acids in muscle after grass-feeding, whereas grain-fed lamb contains higher concentrations of n-6 polyunsaturated fatty acids (Fig. 1). The different oxidation products of these fatty acids produce different odors and flavors during cooking (Fig. 2). Grass-fed lamb also has

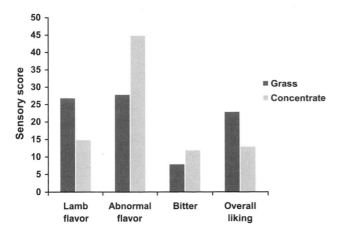

Fig. 2 Scores from University of Bristol taste panel for flavor of loin steaks from lambs fed a grass or concentrate diet (1–100 scales increasing in intensity for each characteristic). (From Ref. 7.) (*View this art in color at www.dekker.com.*)

higher concentrations of vitamin E (α-tocopherol) obtained from the grass. This prevents the fatty acids oxidizing, whereas in concentrate-fed lambs, a high level of fat oxidation may explain the different flavor.[8] It should be pointed out that in several countries where grain-feeding of lamb is more common than grass-feeding, the flavors and odors associated with this feeding practice are preferred by consumers. In one study, grass-fed lamb was preferred by a British taste panel, whereas grain-fed lamb was preferred by a Spanish taste panel.[9]

Nutritional Value and Hardness of Lamb Fat

Lamb fat has high levels of saturated fatty acids, particularly stearic acid (18:0), and a low ratio of polyunsaturated to saturated fatty acids (P:S). Values of P:S are around 0.1, whereas the recommended value for optimum nutrition is 0.4.[1] On the other hand, lamb has significant concentrations of n-3 polyunsaturated fatty acids, higher than beef, especially after grass-feeding. The ratio of n-6 to n-3 polyunsaturated fatty acids, also an important nutritional index, is therefore beneficially low in lamb. The high concentration of stearic acid is a factor in the hardness of lamb fat, which is very noticeable when the meat is eaten cold. There is a strong correlation between the concentration of stearic acid and the melting point of the lipid extracted from lamb fat, as also shown in other species.[10]

CONCLUSION

Sheep have relatively fat carcasses, although there is considerable genetic variation and fat content can be reduced by selection of leaner animals. Conformation of the carcass varies greatly between sheep breeds; too much attention is often paid to this in the grading/classification process. Lamb meat has distinctive qualities. It has a high ultimate pH and marbling fat content, and generally scores high for tenderness and flavor, with less variability than in beef and pork. Grass-feeding increases flavor intensity, which may not suit all tastes, because of relatively high levels of n-3 polyunsaturated fatty acids obtained from a grass-based diet.

ACKNOWLEDGMENTS

Much of the research at University of Bristol is funded by the U.K. Department for Environment, Food, and Rural Affairs (DEFRA) and Meat and Livestock Commission (MLC).

REFERENCES

1. Enser, M.; Hallett, K.; Hewett, B.; Fursey, G.A.J.; Wood, J.D. Fatty acid content and composition of English beef, lamb and pork at retail. Meat Sci. **1996**, *44*, 443–458.
2. Wolf, B.T.; Smith, C.; Sales, D.I. Growth and carcass composition in the crossbred progeny of six terminal sire breeds of sheep. Animal Prod. **1980**, *31*, 307–313.
3. Simm, G. *Genetic Improvement of Cattle and Sheep*; Farming Press: Ipswich, UK, 1998.
4. Wood, J.D.; MacFie, H.J.H.; Pomeroy, R.W.; Twinn, D.J. Carcass composition in four sheep breeds. The importance of type of breed and stage of maturity. Animal Prod. **1980**, *30*, 135–152.
5. Knowles, T.G. A review of the road transport of slaughter sheep. Veterinary Rec. **1998**, *143*, 212–219.
6. Wood, J.D.; Richardson, R.I.; Nute, G.R.; Fisher, A.V.; Campo, M.M.; Kasapidou, E.; Sheard, P.R.; Enser, M. Effects of fatty acids on meat quality: A review. Meat Sci. **2003**, *66*, 21–32.
7. Fisher, A.V.; Enser, M.; Richardson, R.I.; Wood, J.D.; Nute, G.R.; Kurt, E.; Sinclair, L.A.; Wilkinson, R.G. Fatty acid composition and eating quality of lamb types derived from four diverse breed x production systems. Meat Sci. **2000**, *55*, 141–147.
8. Kasapidou, E.; Wood, J.D.; Sinclair, L.D.; Wilkinson, R.G.; Enser, M. Diet and vitamin E metabolism in lambs: Effects of dietary supplementation on meat quality. Proc. 47th Congress Meat Sci. Technol. **2001**, *1*, 42–43.
9. Sanudo, C.; Enser, M.; Campo, M.M.; Nute, G.R.; Maria, G.; Sierra, I.; Wood, J.D. Fatty acid composition and sensory characteristics of lamb carcasses from Britain and Spain. Meat Sci. **2000**, *54*, 339–346.
10. Enser, M.; Wood, J.D. Effect of time of year on fatty acid composition and melting point of UK lamb. Proc. 39th Int. Congress Meat Sci. Technol. **1993**, *2*, 74.

Lamb: International Marketing

Julie Stepanek Shiflett
Juniper Economic Consulting, Byers, Colorado, U.S.A.

INTRODUCTION

Five issues shape international lamb marketing: 1) geographic supply; 2) geographic demand; 3) exchange rates; 4) trade barriers; and 5) sheep-borne animal diseases. Sheep inventories worldwide are contracting, but sheep meat (lamb and mutton) remains an important traded good for many countries. Sheep inventories worldwide fell 11% between 1992 and 2002. In the United States, white tablecloth restaurants and the growing ethnic populations from the Mediterranean and Latin America fuel lamb and mutton consumption, making the United States a net importer of lamb.

INTERNATIONAL LAMB TRADE

The world's sheep and lamb supply has been contracting. Between 1992 and 2002, world sheep inventory fell from 1157 million to 1034 million.[1] Between 1992 and 2002, sheep inventory in Australia fell by 24%, by 18% in New Zealand, by 10% in the 15 European Union (EU) countries, and by 38% in the United States.[1]

The international trade in sheep meat is dominated by Australia and New Zealand (Fig. 1). In 2001, New Zealand accounted for 39% of total international sheep meat exports and Australia followed at 35% of the total exports.[1] Ireland was a distant third with 8% of international sheep meat exports.[1] Although China had the largest sheep population in the world, 13.25% in 2002, China is not an important exporter on world markets.[1] In 2002, Australia had 11% of the world's sheep population and New Zealand had 4%. New Zealand exports roughly 90% of its lamb and mutton production, with about one-fifth, or its largest share, to the United Kingdom.

The top five importers of sheep meat by volume accounted for 45% of total international imports in 2001. France was number one with 14% of international sheep meat imports, United Kingdom at 11%, United States at 8%, Mexico at 6%, and China at 6%.[1]

SHEEP-BORNE DISEASES AND INTERNATIONAL TRADE

Sheep-borne diseases affect trade flows as each country protects its flock from real or perceived diseases in trading partner's flocks. One of the most recent epidemics affecting trade flows was the outbreak of foot and mouth disease (FMD) in the United Kingdom, Ireland, France, and The Netherlands in 2001.

The U.S. Department of Agriculture, Animal and Plant Health Inspection Service monitors trade issues related to animal or plant health. In May 2003, a case of bovine spongiform encephalopathy (BSE) was found in a Canadian cow. Shortly thereafter, the United States closed its border with Canada to sheep imports. By the end of October, the U.S. Department of Agriculture reopened the border, but with certain conditions.

UNITED STATES LAMB IMPORTS

In the United States, 99% of lamb imports come from Australia and New Zealand. Since 2000, almost 62% of lamb imports were from Australia and 38% from New Zealand. Between 1998 and 2002, smaller volumes of lamb and mutton came from Canada, Uruguay, Nicaragua, Ukraine, and Iceland.

Imports from Australia and New Zealand primarily coincide with seasonal high production periods in the United States—namely, during the Easter holidays around March and April. Most imported lamb comes in the form of fresh or chilled meat and a smaller percentage is imported frozen.

Lamb and mutton imports by volume from Australia were 31,569 metric tons (MT) in 1998, 32,201 MT in 1999, 38,727 MT in 2000, 43,995 MT in 2001, and 45,810 MT in 2002. Between January and August 2003, the total volume of lamb imports from Australia was 27,099 MT.

Lamb and mutton imports by value from Australia were $86.66 million in 1998, $95.66 million in 1999,

Encyclopedia of Animal Science
DOI: 10.1081/E-EAS 120023834

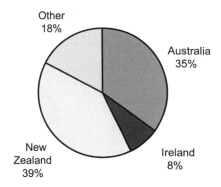

Fig. 1 Share of international fresh sheep meat exports by volume in 2001. (From United Nations, Food and Agricultural Organization, FAOSTATS, http://apps.fao.org/page/collections?subset=agriculture, accessed November 2003.) (*View this art in color at www.dekker.com.*)

$108.81 million in 2000, $139.47 million in 2001, and $152.56 million in 2002. Between January and August 2003, the total value of lamb imports from Australia was $120.69 million.

Lamb and mutton imports by volume from New Zealand were 15,354.30 MT in 1998, 14,451 in 1999, 14,980 MT in 2000, 16,660 MT in 2001, and 20,899 MT in 2002. Between January and August 2003, the total volume of lamb imports from New Zealand was 17,201 MT.

Lamb and mutton imports by value from New Zealand were $72.94 million in 1998, $77.66 million in 1999, $80.98 million in 2000, $88.57 million in 2001, and 109.67 million in 2002. Between January and August 2003, the total value of lamb imports from New Zealand was $86.83 million.

During the 1990s, lamb imports to the United States increased in volume at a rate of nearly 13% per year[2] (Fig. 2). Between 2000 and 2001, imports increased 14.42%.[2] In the ten years 1992–2001, total imported lamb volumes increased 248%, from 31 million pounds to

a little over 108 million pounds.[2] From 1992 to 2001, Australian imports increased in volume by 353%.[2] In the same period, New Zealand imports increased in volume by 216%.[2]

Favorable exchange rates coupled with strong demand can strengthen trade flows. For much of the 1990s and early 2000s, the U.S. dollar strengthened, thereby making imports to the United States relatively less expensive (Fig. 3). During this period, lamb imports increased dramatically as the U.S. market became relatively more profitable. From a four-year high in November 1996 to a three-year low in April 2001, the U.S. dollar fell by 37% against the Australian dollar, from $0.79 USD/AUD to $0.50 USD/AUD. During this period the U.S./New Zealand exchange rate fell from $0.71 USD/NZD to $0.41 USD/NZD.[3]

From mid-2001 through October 2003, the U.S. exchange rate weakened against the Australian dollar and the New Zealand dollar, making U.S. imports relatively more expensive. In January 2003, the U.S./Australian exchange rate was an average $0.58 USD/AUD, but weakened to $0.69 USD/AUD in October.[3] In January 2003, the U.S./New Zealand exchange rate was an average $0.54 USD/NZD, but weakened to $0.60 USD/NZD in October.[3]

TRADE BARRIERS

Trade barriers can affect countries' competitive advantage on world markets by determining relative profitability of different import and export markets, and thus shape trade flows. Trade barriers include tariffs and quotas, but can also include direct payment support by governments to sheep and lamb producers. One objective of the World Trade Organization (WTO) Doha Development Agenda is to increase access to agricultural markets by reducing barriers to trade such as tariffs, quotas, and other federal

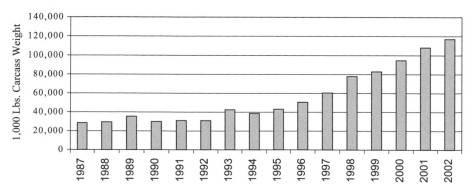

Fig. 2 U.S. lamb and mutton imports. (From U.S. Department of Agriculture, Economic Research Service, "Cumulative U.S. Meat and Livestock Trade," www.ers.usda.gov/Briefing/Poultry/Data/AnnualLivestockTable.xls, accessed November 2003.)

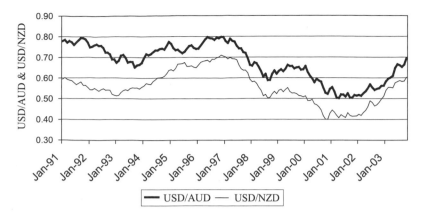

Fig. 3 Exchange rates: U.S./Australia and U.S./New Zealand. (From Pacific Exchange Rate Service, http://fx.sauder.ubc.ca/data.html, accessed November 2003.)

support to producers. The Doha agricultural trade negotiations began in early 2000 and plan for resolution by January 2005.

Support levels to agricultural sectors in the early 2000s dropped for most agricultural commodities in Western countries relative to the late 1980s. However, support for sheep meat increased in 2002. One indicator of relative agricultural support is the Percentage Producer Support Estimate (PSE). PSE is an indicator of the annual monetary value of gross transfers from consumers and taxpayers to agricultural producers. The PSE was 16% for the United States in 2000 and estimated at 15% in 2001.[4] By comparison, the PSE for Australia and New Zealand for sheep meat in 2000 was 4% and 0%, respectively.[4] The PSE in the EU was 53% for sheep meat in 2000 and estimated at 72% in 2001.[4]

Trade barriers to lamb and mutton trade can also be more transparent. Lamb and mutton imports to the United States increased steadily since the mid-1980s, but increased sharply since 1994. On October 7, 1998, the American Sheep Industry Association, Inc. and copetitioners filed a petition that increased quantities of low-priced imported lamb from Australia and New Zealand and were a substantial cause of serious injury to the U.S. lamb meat industry. As a result, the U.S. president issued Proclamation 7208 on July 7, 1999, which imposed a tariff-rate quota (TRQ) on imports of fresh, chilled, or frozen lamb meat for three years and one day.

Australia and New Zealand submitted complaints to the World Trade Organization (WTO). The United States is Australia's largest market. In May 2001, the WTO Appellate Body ruled that the United States' import restrictions on lamb meat were illegal. The United States complied with the ruling and the TRQ was removed on November 15, 2001.

The effect of the TRQ was mostly offset by weak Australian and New Zealand currencies. Imports increased under the TRQ, even with an over-quota tariff of 40% in 1999 and 32% in 2000, because the U.S. dollar appreciation occurred concurrently.[5]

UNITED STATES SHEEP AND LAMB EXPORTS

Lamb and mutton exports from the United States were 6.5 million pounds in 2001 and 7.1 million pounds in 2002. Between January and August 2003, 4.7 million pounds were exported compared to 4.4 million pounds during the same period in 2002.[6] Between 1998 and 2002, 50% of U.S. lamb and mutton exports went to Mexico by value and 41% by volume.

The United States also exports live sheep and lamb, but primarily ewes, to Mexico. In 2001, 284,435 head were exported, 322,706 head in 2002, and 89,706 head by October 2003. In August 2003, U.S. sheep exports to Mexico fell to zero after exporting close to 7,000 head of sheep in July 2003. The Government of Mexico closed its border due to concerns about scrapie requirements for slaughter sheep entering the country. By mid-September the border was reopened for wethers and slaughter ewes, but remained closed for rams.

CONCLUSION

International lamb exports are dominated by Australia and New Zealand. The largest net importers are France, the United Kingdom, and the United States. Relative exchange rates between countries, trade barriers and federal support to sheep and lamb industries, as well as sheep-borne diseases are key trade issues that can shape trade flows. It is anticipated that international sheep and lamb marketing will grow as demand in key net importing countries such as the United States increases. The U.S. sheep industry is likely to grow in coming years, but consumption is likely to continue to outpace U.S. production. In mid-2002, the American Lamb Board began the first national check-off program in the sheep industry funded by assessments on sales of sheep and lambs to help promote lamb demand.

REFERENCES

1. United Nations, Food and Agricultural Organization. *FAOSTATS*, http://apps.fao.org/page/collections?subset= agriculture (accessed November 2003).
2. U.S. Department of Agriculture, Economic Research Service. "Cumulative U.S. Meat and Livestock Trade," http://www.ers.usda.gov/Briefing/Poultry/Data/ AnnualLivestockTable.xls (accessed November 2003).
3. Pacific Exchange Rate Service. http://fx.sauder.ubc.ca/ data.html, (accessed November 2003).
4. Organisation for Economic Co-operation and Development (OECD). *Agricultural Policies and OECD Countries, Monitoring and Evaluation*; Organisation for Economic Co-operation and Development: Paris, France, 2002.
5. U.S. Department of Agriculture, Economic Research Service. *Agricultural Outlook,* "Livestock, Dairy, and Poultry, U.S. Sheep Industry Continues to Consolidate," Washington, D.C., January–February 2002.
6. U.S. Department of Agriculture, Foreign Agricultural Service. BICO Export Commodity Aggregations, from Department of Commerce, U.S. Census Bureau, Foreign Trade Statistics, Washington, D.C., November 2003.

Lamb: U.S. Marketing

Michael L. Thonney
Cornell University, Ithaca, New York, U.S.A.

INTRODUCTION

Lambs in the United States are marketed through either traditional commodity markets or value-added specialty markets. Most U.S. sheep are raised in large flocks from which lambs are sold through commodity markets as feeder lambs and then marketed from feedlots directly to major packing companies. Traditionally, these lambs are from western range flocks lambing in the spring. Lambs are weaned in the autumn and fed high-energy diets in confinement until marketed at 50 to 70 kg live weight. A growing number of lambs in flocks located near urban centers are marketed more directly to specialty markets. Customers for these specialty markets are usually recent immigrants whose food preferences include lamb and, sometimes, mutton (meat from mature sheep). The additional effort required to sell lambs in specialty markets usually results in higher prices per unit weight compared to lambs sold in commodity markets.

COMMODITY MARKETS

Most of the sheep in the United States (Table 1) are raised in large flocks in the western range states of Texas, Wyoming, California, Utah, South Dakota, Montana, Idaho, Colorado, and New Mexico.[1] Traditionally, spring-born lambs in these flocks are weaned in the fall and sorted into replacement and feeder groups. Feeder lambs are fed completely balanced, high-energy diets to reach heavy weights in feedlots also located in the west or mountain states, sometimes with partial- or full-retained ownership by the ewe flock owners. Some lambs are grown out on crop residue and other pastures prior to entering feedlots. Finished feedlot lambs are then marketed to large packing plants mainly in Texas, Colorado, Iowa, and California (Fig. 1). Some packing plant operators purchase lambs for their own feedlots to create more vertically integrated operations.

As shown in Fig. 1, a large proportion of the lambs are marketed in California, Texas, Colorado, and Oregon. One major company in California dominates the purchase of lambs west of the Rocky Mountains and also fabricates and distributes lamb carcasses purchased from overseas. Prices and market reports for commodity markets are available from the Livestock Marketing Information Center[2] and from the USDA.[3]

Per-capita consumption and real prices for lamb in the United States have declined dramatically since the second World War. Reasons for the decline in per-capita consumption may include consumer inexperience in preparing lamb, the perception that lamb is high-priced, unpleasant experiences with cold mutton by World War II veterans, and declining sheep production (thus declining product availability). Also, by the time lambs sold through traditional commodity markets have completed their stay in feedlots, they can be older and fatter than is desired by most consumers. The seasonal nature of lamb production in most of the United States has limited the availability of fresh product during some parts of the year. Lamb consumption by many Americans has been reserved for religious holidays such as Easter, Christmas, Passover, Rosh Hashana, the Feast of the Sacrifice, and the breaking of the fast of Ramadan.

SPECIALTY MARKETS

Most consumers who purchase lamb through specialty markets are recent immigrants. The 2000 census[4] showed that 28.4 million people, or about 10% of the U.S. population, were foreign-born, with half of them coming from Latin America. More than 40% of the people in New York City were born outside of the United States. In contrast with the nonimmigrant population, many immigrants have cultural backgrounds that include fresh lamb or mutton as a major part of their traditional foods and they like to know the source of the meat they purchase. A large number of sheep farmers with small flocks are located near urban centers in the United States (Table 1). Some of these farmers have begun to market USDA-inspected meat and even live animals more directly to these consumers.

A traditional approach in the East is to sell lambs and sheep through auction markets such as the one in New Holland, PA. Although USDA statistics do not provide documentation for lambs marketed in New Jersey (Fig. 1, Table 1), large numbers of lambs pass through these markets on their way to New Jersey processing plants that service Muslim, Greek, and other ethnic groups in the

Encyclopedia of Animal Science
DOI: 10.1081/E-EAS 120019698

Table 1 Sheep and marketing statistics in the United States for 2002

Time zone	State	Lamb crop[a] 1,000s	Ewes 1,000s	Lambs/ewe	Farms (1,000s)	Ewes/farm	Lambs marketed (1,000s)
Eastern	MI	53	40	1.3	1.90	21	19
	New England[b]	38	32	1.2	2.00	16	3.5
	NY	51	40	1.3	1.50	27	7
	OH	135	93	1.5	3.50	27	20
	PA	71	55	1.3	2.60	21	11
	VA	55	37	1.5	1.50	25	11.5
	WV	33	24	1.4	1.10	22	6
Central	IA	215	142	1.5	4.60	31	74
	IL	59	44	1.3	2.20	20	12
	IN	47	39	1.2	2.00	20	8.9
	KS	62	53	1.2	1.40	38	31
	MN	145	95	1.5	2.30	41	44
	MO	60	46	1.3	1.60	29	10.5
	TX	540	720	0.8	6.80	106	230
	WI	73	52	1.4	2.30	23	13.5
Mountain	AZ	40	57	0.7	0.27	211	66
	CO	200	170	1.2	1.90	89	164
	ID	240	184	1.3	1.00	184	35
	MT	315	232	1.4	1.70	136	34
	ND	100	85	1.2	1.00	85	39
	NE	80	58	1.4	1.50	39	27
	NM	125	150	0.8	0.80	188	42
	OK	46	36	1.3	1.50	24	14
	SD	325	265	1.2	2.30	115	77
	UT	275	275	1.0	1.40	196	42
	WY	340	320	1.1	0.80	400	87
Pacific	CA	285	310	0.9	2.80	111	415
	NV	62	69	0.9	0.30	230	14
	OR	150	134	1.1	3.10	43	111
	WA	56	36	1.6	1.20	30	8.5
	Other states[c]	84	87	1.0	5.3	16	23
	U.S.	4360	3980	1.1	64.20	62	1700.4

[a]Lamb crop is defined as lambs born in the eastern states and lambs docked or branded in the western states.
[b]New England includes CT, ME, MA, NH, RI, and VT.
[c]Other states include AL, AK, AR, DE, FL, GA, HI, KY, LA, MD, MS, NJ, NC, SC, and TN.
(Compiled from Ref. 1.)

New York City metropolitan area. Some farmers have adopted reproduction methods such as the Cornell STAR© system[5] to directly market fresh, young lamb year-round. Methods of direct marketing include sales of live animals directly off the farm, pooling with other farms to furnish a set number of carcasses of specific weight to ethnic butcher shops each week, and pooling with other farms to provide truckloads of fresh animals for live animal markets in large, urban areas. For example, more than 20 markets sell live sheep and goats—and the service of slaughtering them—to ethnic communities in New York City. More information on specialty markets is available from the Northeast Sheep and Goat Marketing Program[6] and from the American Sheep Industry Association.[7]

Lamb prices in the United States fluctuate seasonally, typically with higher prices during the late winter and spring. While prices through specialty markets are not higher during those times than prices of lambs marketed through commodity markets, they generally remain high throughout the year, while prices for lambs sold through commodity markets can be depressed during summer, autumn, and early winter.

CONCLUSIONS

Real lamb prices have declined for more than four decades in the United States. Sheep numbers have also declined

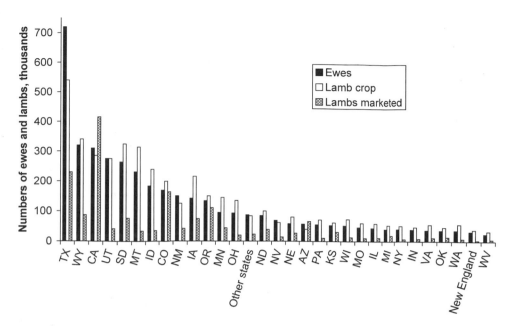

Fig. 1 Numbers of ewes and lambs (thousands) in 2002[1] ordered by number of breeding ewes within state. Lamb crop numbers represent lambs born in the eastern states and lambs docked or branded in the western states. Other states include AL, AK, AR, DE, FL, GA, HI, KY, LA, MD, MS, NJ, NC, SC, and TN. New England includes CT, ME, MA, NH, RI, and VT. The total numbers for the United States were 3.98 million ewes, 4.36 million lambs, and 1.70 million lambs marketed.

and now lamb is regarded by most consumers as a specialty meat. Producers of lambs marketed through traditional commodity channels are working toward supplying younger and leaner lambs that are better tailored to the current American pallet and commercial processors are providing more consumer-friendly products. Pockets of farmers directly supplying specialty markets have sprung up near urban centers around the United States. Because prices are consistently higher, additional efforts should be made to assist farmers in supplying these markets.

REFERENCES

1. USDA. *Sheep and Goat Statistics. USDA Economics and Statistics System*; 2003. http://jan.mannlib.cornell.edu/reports/nassr/livestock/pgg-bb/shep0103.txt.

2. Anonymous. Livestock Marketing Information Center. World Wide Web **2003**. http://www.lmic.info/.

3. USDA. USDA Weekly National Lamb Market Summary. World Wide Web **2003**. http://www.ams.usda.gov/LSMNpubs/PDF_Daily/frilamb.pdf.

4. Schmidley, A.D. *Profile of the Foreign-Born Population in the United States: 2000. U.S. Census Bureau*; Series P23-206; U.S. Government Printing Office, 2001. http://www.census.gov/prod/2002pubs/p23-206.pdf.

5. Lewis, R.M.; Notter, D.R.; Hogue, D.E.; Magee, B.H. Ewe fertility in the STAR accelerated lambing system. Journal of Animal Science **1996**, *74*, 1511–1522.

6. Thonney, M.L.; Stanton, T.L.; Melchior, R.J. Northeast Sheep and Goat Marketing Program. World Wide Web **2003**. http://www.sheepgoatmarketing.org/.

7. Anonymous. Marketing out of the MainStream. World Wide Web **2003**. http://www.sheepusa.org/marketplace/outofstream/menu.shtml.

Lipids

Harry J. Mersmann
*Unites States Department of Agriculture, Agricultural Research Service, and
Children's Nutrition Research Center, Department of Pediatrics,
Baylor College of Medicine, Houston, Texas, U.S.A.*

INTRODUCTION

The vertebrate organism ingests complex whole foods containing carbohydrates, fats or lipids, minerals, proteins, and vitamins. Digestion simplifies foods to the major components and to simpler moieties, e.g., carbohydrates to simple sugars, proteins to amino acids, and lipids to fatty acids (FAs). Digestive products are absorbed and distributed to body tissues where they are resynthesized to complex cellular components or oxidized for energy. Digestion, including that of lipids, primarily occurs in the stomach and intestine of nonruminant mammals, but in ruminants, much digestion occurs in the rumen. Absorption is concentrated in the small intestine.

Lipids are one of the major components of feeds and of vertebrate cells. Although there are exceptions, lipids are not water-soluble, i.e., they are hydrophobic. Animal lipids are generally complex structures built from FAs, e.g., phospholipids or triacylglycerol, or from the sterol nucleus (a complex set of ring structures). Plant lipids are even more complex than animal lipids.

FATTY ACIDS

The common FAs are long hydrocarbon chains, i.e., a chain of carbon atoms with accompanying hydrogen atoms and with a carboxyl group (an organic acid) at one end (Fig. 1).[1–5] The simplest FA is formic acid with one carbon atom. Acetic acid has two carbons, propionic acid has three carbons, etc. The FA components of complex lipids are long-chain FAs usually with 12 or more carbons. The most common mammalian saturated FAs (no double bonds) are palmitic acid or C16:0 (C16=number of carbons and number after the colon, i.e., 0=number of double bonds) and stearic acid or C18:0. These two FAs are concentrated in animal fats, e.g., lard and tallow.

Unsaturated FAs, containing one to six double bonds, are the other common type of animal FA (Fig. 1). Monounsaturated FAs (MUFAs) have one double bond and polyunsaturated FAs (PUFAs) have two or more double bonds. The most common MUFA is oleic acid, with 18 carbons and one double bond at the ninth carbon (C18:1). Double bonds are numbered either from the end opposite the carboxyl group (oleic acid=C18:1, n-9) or from the carboxyl group (oleic acid=C18:1Δ^9). Oleic acid is predominant in many feedstuffs and animal cells; it is concentrated in olive and canola oils making up approximately 70% of the total FA.

The common PUFAs (Fig. 1) are linoleic acid (C18:2, $\Delta^{9,12}$) and α-linolenic acid (C18:3, $\Delta^{9,12,15}$). Linoleic acid is present at high concentration in many plant oils (e.g., corn oil with >50%) and animal tissues. Linolenic acid is present at high concentration in select plant oils (e.g., linseed oil) and is at low concentration in most animal tissues. Both of these PUFAs are also important because they give rise to other FAs and to various FA derivatives (mostly oxidation products, e.g., eicosanoids) that have important regulatory functions in animal cells.

Many FAs are supplied by the diet as components of animal and plant feedstuffs. However, some animal cells synthesize FAs de novo. This complex process consists of sequential addition of 2-carbon units (C2+C2=C4+C2= C6, etc.), with the final product being C16:0. Mammalian cells synthesize FAs from glucose or acetate, predominantly in the gut, liver, and adipose tissue; in ruminants, FAs with an odd number of carbons arise from use of propionate to initiate FA synthesis. The prevalent site for de novo FA synthesis varies with species; the liver in chickens and humans, the adipose tissue in pigs, and both liver and adipose tissue in rats. Mammalian cells can also transform FAs by elongation and desaturation (Fig. 2). Elongation proceeds by sequential addition of two carbons, e.g., C16:0+C2= C18:0. Because the C2 are added at the carboxyl end, the position of the double bonds shifts, e.g., C18:2, $\Delta^{9,12}$+C2=C20:2, $\Delta^{11,14}$. There are three common mammalian desaturase enzymes that insert double bonds into specific positions in the carbon chain (Δ^9, Δ^6, and Δ^5). Linoleic acid (C18:2, n-6) is elongated and desaturated to arachidonic acid (C20:4, n-6), which is an important structural lipid, but also a precursor to many eicosanoids, e.g., prostaglandins. α-Linolenic acid (C18:3, n-3) is elongated and desaturated to other eicosanoid precursors and to eicosapentaenoic acid (C20:5, n-3) and docosahexaenoic acid (C22:6, n-3), both important structural elements in cell membranes, particularly in nervous tissue. Eicosapentaenoic acid and docosahexaenoic

Encyclopedia of Animal Science
DOI: 10.1081/E-EAS 120019701

Structure	Common name	Shorthand	Position of double bond	Source
Saturated				
$CH_3-(CH_2)_{14}-\overset{\overset{O}{\|\|}}{C}-O^-$	Palmitic acid	C16:0		Diet + synthesis
$CH_3-(CH_2)_{16}-\overset{\overset{O}{\|\|}}{C}-O^-$	Stearic acid	C18:0		Diet + synthesis
Unsaturated				
$CH_3-(CH_2)_7-CH=CH-(CH_2)_7-\overset{\overset{O}{\|\|}}{C}-O^-$	Oleic acid	C18:1	n-9 Δ^9	Diet + synthesis
$CH_3-(CH_2)_4-CH=CH-CH_2-CH=CH-(CH_2)_7-\overset{\overset{O}{\|\|}}{C}-O^-$	Linoleic acid	C18:2	n-6,9 $\Delta^{9,12}$	Diet
$CH_3-CH_2-CH=CH-CH_2-CH=CH-CH_2-CH=CH-(CH_2)_7-\overset{\overset{O}{\|\|}}{C}-O$	α–Linolenic acid	C18:3	n-3,6,9 $\Delta^{9,12,15}$	Diet

Fig. 1 Types and source of fatty acids.

acid are at relatively high concentration in fish oils. The positions for mammalian FA desaturation are limited; thus, linoleic and α-linolenic acid are required dietary components.

COMPLEX LIPIDS

Fatty acids are toxic to cells. One mechanism to sequester them is to form complex lipids.[1,2,5–7] Triacylglycerols (TAG; Fig. 3) are synthesized from FAs. The primary energy storage molecule in mammalian cells is TAG. Adipose tissue cells contain large amounts of TAG so that a large lipid droplet occupies the majority of the cell

volume. The metabolism of this cell revolves around TAG synthesis and degradation (mobilization of FA). Phospholipids (PLs; Fig. 3), another major class of FA-containing complex lipids, are principal components of cellular membranes. Compared to TAG, PLs are less hydrophobic

Elongation (add 2–carbons)

precursor	product
C16:0	C18:0
C18:1 (Δ^9)	C20:1 (Δ^{11})
C18:2 ($\Delta^{9,12}$)	C20:2 ($\Delta^{11,14}$)

Desaturation (insert double bonds)

desaturase	precursor	product	
Δ^9	C18:0	C18:1 (Δ^9)	[oleic acid]
Δ^6	C18:3 ($\Delta^{9,12,15}$)	C18:4 ($\Delta^{6,9,12,15}$)	
Δ^5	C20:3 ($\Delta^{8,11,14}$)	C20:4 ($\Delta^{5,8,11,14}$)	[arachidonic acid]

Fig. 2 Mammalian interconversion of fatty acids.

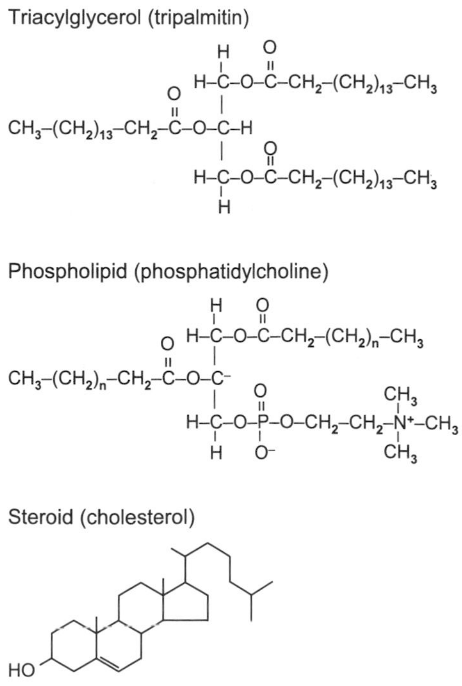

Triacylglycerol (tripalmitin)

Phospholipid (phosphatidylcholine)

Steroid (cholesterol)

Fig. 3 Complex mammalian lipids.

Diet	TAG, PL, CE
Absorb	MAG, FA, C, lysoPL, glycerol, choline, etc
Lymph	chylomicrons, VLDL
Portal blood	glycerol, choline, short FA
Arterial & Venous blood	lipoproteins (chylomicrons, VLDL, LDL, HDL, albumin)

Abbreviations: C=cholesterol, CE=cholesterol ester, FA=fatty acid, HDL=high–density lipoprotein, LDL=low–density lipoprotein, lysoPL=lysophospholipid, MAG=monoacyglycerol, PL=phospholipid, TAG=triacylglycerol, VLDL=very low density lipoprotein,

Fig. 4 Metabolism and transport of lipids.

because they contain ionic groups (a negative charge in the phosphate group and a positive charge in the nitrogenous base, e.g., choline).

The other major class of complex lipids is the steroids (Fig. 3) synthesized by plants and animals. The major animal steroid, cholesterol (C), is not made by plants but is obtained from animal feedstuffs or is synthesized de novo with the liver being the predominant site. Much of the C is stored as the ester (CE, i.e., C with an attached FA). Cholesterol is a component of cell membranes and a precursor to bile acids and steroid hormones (e.g., estrogen, testosterone, glucocorticoids, etc.).

METABOLISM AND TRANSPORT OF LIPIDS

Digestion

Complex lipids in dietary fats must be simplified or digested in the gastrointestinal tract or gut to be absorbed (Fig. 4).[1,8,9] Rumen microbes simplify the ingested feedstuffs, so that the ruminant animal absorbs many microbial products. In ruminants and nonruminants, lipase enzymes secreted by the stomach, small intestine, and pancreas digest the fat (mostly TAG, PL, and CE). The digestive tract and its contents, including the lipases, are aqueous in nature so that lipid components must be emulsified for effective lipase action and efficient absorption. Emulsification is the combination of hydrophobic (lipids) and hydrophilic (bile acids) components to make the former relatively hydrophilic. Bile acids are derivatives of C, made in the liver, and secreted in bile into the small intestine.

Absorption

The products of fat or lipid digestion are simpler molecules, e.g., monoacylglycerol (MAG=TAG with two FAs removed), FAs (removed from TAG, PL, and CE), C, lysophospholipids (PL with one FA removed), glycerol (from TAG, PL, and CE after removal of FAs), choline (from PL), etc. Enterocytes, cells lining the small intestine, absorb these molecules.[1,8,9] The enterocyte resynthesizes TAG, PL, and CE, which are secreted into the lymph; lymph enters the general circulation near the heart and bypasses the liver on the first circulatory pass. The portal circulation (the venous blood draining the viscera and with delivery directly to the liver) transports

Table 1 Lipoproteins

Type	Site of synthesis	% Protein	Total % lipid	% of Total lipid			
				TAG	PL	C+CE	FA
Chylomicrons	Gut	2	>95	88	8	4	
VLDL	Liver, gut	7	>90	56	20	23	
LDL	Plasma	20	80	13	28	58	
HDL	Plasma, gut, liver	50	55	15	45	38	
Albumin	Adipose tissue/plasma	99	1				100

Abbreviations: C=cholesterol, CE=cholesterol ester, FA=fatty acid, HDL=high-density lipoprotein, LDL=low-density lipoprotein, PL=phospholipid, TAG=triacylglycerol, VLDL=very low-density lipoprotein.
Adapted from Refs. 1 and 8.

the more hydrophilic components, e.g., glycerol, choline, and short-chain FAs.

Transport in the General Circulation

Blood serum is an aqueous environment incompatible with the hydrophobic lipid molecules.[1,8,10] Lipids are transported in lipoprotein molecules composed of several proteins and various lipid components (Table 1). Protein and lipid components are exchanged and some lipoproteins are synthesized from others. The chylomicrons are very large particles synthesized by the gut and present in lymph and the general circulation. They contain a large lipid component, mostly TAG, and little protein. The gut and the liver synthesize very low-density lipoproteins (VLDL) that also contain considerable amounts of lipid, mostly TAG and C+CE, and 10% protein. The low-density lipoproteins (LDL) are synthesized in the serum from degraded VLDL and chylomicrons. They are composed of large amounts of C+CE with 20% protein. In humans and pigs, but not all species, most of the C+CE is carried in LDL. The high-density lipoproteins (HDL) are synthesized in the serum, liver, and gut. They are composed of 45% protein, a small amount of TAG, 40% C+CE, and 45% PL. Finally, the FA is carried on albumin, a protein with multiple FA binding sites.

The lipoproteins deliver complex lipids to the tissues where they are absorbed to be used to build membranes, for storage as energy reserves or as precursors for many biologically active regulatory molecules (steroid hormones, eicosanoids, etc.). The animal cell cannot absorb intact TAG. It is digested in the intestinal tract to simpler components. In tissues that rely on FA as an oxidative substrate, e.g., cardiac and skeletal muscle and adipose, there is a specialized enzyme, lipoprotein lipase (LPL), that is secreted by these cells to cleave TAG to FAs. The LPL moves to the surface of the capillary endothelial cell, where it cleaves TAG in lipoproteins, particularly the chylomicrons and VLDL. The FAs are absorbed by the capillary endothelial cell and then pass to the underlying tissue cells.

CONCLUSIONS

Lipids are one of the major components of animal and plant cells and therefore of feedstuffs. Fats and oils contain almost exclusively lipids. Fatty acids are the basic building blocks for synthesis of the complex lipids, triacylglycerol, the major energy storage molecule, and phospholipids, major components of cellular membranes. Fatty acids may be obtained from the diet or synthesized by animal cells. Fatty acids may also be elongated and double bonds inserted to produce unsaturated fatty acids. Animal cells are limited in the position to insert double bonds so that some unsaturated fatty acids must be supplied in the diet. Fatty acids serve not only as building blocks for complex lipids, but also as a major oxidative substrate for many cells and can be precursors for regulatory molecules, e.g., eicosanoids. The other type of complex lipid is based on the steroid nucleus; in animal cells this is primarily cholesterol that is supplied in the diet and is synthesized de novo. Cholesterol is important in membrane structure and is the precursor for the sex hormones and the adrenal corticoid hormones.

REFERENCES

1. Gurr, M.I.; Harwood, J.L.; Frayn, K.N. *Lipid Biochemistry*, 5th Ed.; Blackwell Science: Malden, MA, 2002.
2. Small, D.M. Structure and Properties of Lipids. In *Biochemical and Physiological Aspects of Human Nutrition*; Stipanuk, M.H., Ed.; W.B. Saunders Company: Philadelphia, PA, 2000; 43–71.
3. *Fatty Acids in Foods and Their Health Implications*; Chow, C.K., Ed.; Marcel Dekker Inc.: New York, NY, 1992.
4. Azain, M.J. Fat in Swine Nutrition. In *Swine Nutrition*, 2nd Ed.; Lewis, A.J., Southern, L.L., Eds.; CRC Press: Boca Raton, FL, 2001; 95–105.
5. McGarry, J.D. Lipid Metabolism I: Utilization and Storage of Energy in Lipid Form. In *Biochemistry with Clinical Correlations*, 5th Ed.; Devlin, T.M., Ed.; Wiley-Liss: New York, NY, 2002; 693–725.
6. Glew, R.H. Lipid Metabolism II: Pathways of Metabolism of Special Lipids. In *Biochemistry with Clinical Correlations*, 5th Ed.; Devlin, T.M., Ed.; Wiley-Liss: New York, NY, 2002; 727–777.
7. Goodridge, A.G.; Sul, H.S. Lipid Metabolism—Synthesis and Oxidation. In *Biochemical and Physiological Aspects of Human Nutrition*; Stipanuk, M.H., Ed.; W.B. Saunders Company: Philadelphia, PA, 2000; 305–350.
8. Marinetti, G.V. *Disorders of Lipid Metabolism*; Plenum Press: New York, NY, 1990.
9. Tso, P.; Crissinger, K. Digestion and Absorption of Lipids. In *Biochemical and Physiological Aspects of Human Nutrition*; Stipanuk, M.H., Ed.; W.B. Saunders Company: Philadelphia, PA, 2000; 125–141.
10. Fielding, C.J. Lipoprotein Synthesis, Transport, and Metabolism. In *Biochemical and Physiological Aspects of Human Nutrition*; Stipanuk, M.H., Ed.; W.B. Saunders Company: Philadelphia, PA, 2000; 351–364.

Livestock Breeds

David S. Buchanan
Larry G. Burditt
Oklahoma State University, Stillwater, Oklahoma, U.S.A.

INTRODUCTION

Livestock species are divided into genetic groups called breeds. Unfortunately, a clear definition of the term breed is difficult to find. Breed might be defined as a group of animals with similar physical characteristics (such as color, horns, body type, etc). However, there are breeds that contain wide variation in such traits, while some breeds may share many characteristics. There is general agreement that the concept of a breed denotes common ancestry. However, some breed organizations choose to allow entry of animals from other breeds. An early observation was made about the definition of breed:[1] "A breed is a group of domestic animals, termed such by common consent of the breeders, a term which arose among breeders of livestock, created one might say for their own use, and no one is warranted in assigning to this word a scientific definition and in calling the breeders wrong when they deviated from the formulated definition. It is their word and the breeders' common usage is what we must accept as the correct definition." A breed has also been described as something that arises more rapidly than normal evolutionary processes would allow but more slowly than would be true in the laboratory.[2] Some breeds arise almost entirely through natural forces, whereas others are developed by human managers in a highly directed fashion. The total number of recognized breeds is probably in excess of 1000 worldwide, although some are just national derivatives of the same breed.[3] Several hundred of these breeds are illustrated in the Breeds of Livestock website maintained by the Department of Animal Science at Oklahoma State University (www.ansi.okstate.edu/breeds). Numerous breeds have also been described in other venues.[4,5]

BREED ORGANIZATIONS

Many developed countries have organizations that are devoted to the purpose of protecting purity of breeds. These "breed societies" originated in Great Britain during the early part of the 19th century and spread to other countries, most notably the United States. The size of breed societies varies from very large organiza-tions with registrations in the millions to others that register only a few hundred animals each year. Many of the larger breed associations generally provide services such as magazines, advertising and performance programs to their members. One of the functions is to preserve the breed. Breeds may be conserved due to economic, scientific, or cultural reasons.[1–6] There are also organizations, such as the American Livestock Breeds Conservancy (www.albc-usa.org), that are devoted to cataloging the status of breeds that may be at risk.

BREED HISTORY

Breeds have developed in countless different ways in places all over the world. Any attempt at trying to summarize such development is inherently limited. One approach is to examine the ways that animal agriculture in the Americas and Europe has been influenced by breeds. With only a few exceptions, such as Arabian, Barb, Holstein, or Merino, most agriculturally significant breeds have much more recent origin. Much of the current concept of breed originated in Great Britain a few hundred years ago. Breed societies were first developed there and the work of Robert Bakewell is recognized as the first truly organized attempt to improve livestock. Great Britain is the place of origin for many breeds (e.g., Hereford, Angus, Shorthorn, Ayrshire, Jersey, Dorset, Hampshire, Suffolk, Leicester, Berkshire, Large White, Tamworth, Thoroughbred). Such breeds were developed with attention paid to local production practices and, in several cases, with influence from breeders who wished to show their animals in competition with other breeders.

Numerous breeds were developed on the European continent (e.g., Brown Swiss, Simmental, Limousin, Charolais, Chianina, Maine-Anjou, Salers, Rambouillet, Landrace). The exact origin of some of these breeds is difficult to trace because they developed as local strains over a period of centuries. They became uniform in appearance due to limited initial gene pools and because breeders in a localized area desired some degree of uniformity. Several of the European beef cattle breeds have become important contributors to North American beef production in the last 50 years because they

Encyclopedia of Animal Science
DOI: 10.1081/E-EAS 120020312

possessed characteristics that were not available in the British breeds that previously dominated North American beef production.

The early Spanish explorers brought their livestock to the Americas. The animals they left behind have created their own legacy. Collectively they are referred to as the Criollo breeds. The Texas Longhorn, Spanish goat, and Mustang horse are the primary North American examples. In addition, the San Clemente goat, the Florida Cracker cattle, the Gulf Coast Native sheep, and several South American cattle breeds (e.g., Blanco Orejinegro, Romosinuano) derive from remnants left by the Spanish explorers.

Numerous breeds have their origin in the United States. This includes several breeds of swine (e.g., Chester White, Duroc, Hampshire, Spot) that were developed from breeding stock brought from Great Britain to the United States during the last part of the 19th century and the early part of the 20th century. The Brahman breed was developed from Indian cattle of the *Bos indicus* type, primarily Guzerat, Nellore, and Gir, brought to the Western Hemisphere in the 19th century. Brahman cattle have also been the basis for several breeds developed to combine the adaptive advantages of the *Bos indicus* with beef production strengths derived from British or European breeds (e.g., Santa Gertrudis, Beefmaster, Brangus, Simbrah, Braford). Numerous breeds of sheep have also been developed in the United States (e.g., Columbia, Debouillet, Katahdin, Montadale, Polypay, Targhee).

In the last half of the 20th century, closer scientific and cultural ties with many other countries opened up opportunities for bringing breeds with unique characteristics to the North America from many parts of the world. The Finnish Landrace and the Booroola Merino sheep and several Chinese swine breeds, including the Meishan and Fengjing, were imported because of their high prolificacy. Several cattle breeds from Africa (e.g., Africander, Boran, N'Dama, Nguni, Tuli) have been imported because they are tropically adapted. Some of the African cattle breeds are of the *Bos taurus* type, while others are from a grouping referred to as the Sanga cattle, which had their foundations in crosses between *Bos indicus* and *Bos taurus* cattle several centuries ago.

These different approaches to development also lead to different situations regarding the genetic makeup of breeds. Breed societies encourage and facilitate genetic improvement. Genetic improvement goals tend to differ among different breeds, which leads to differences among breeds in average genetic merit. Additionally, breed societies, necessarily, hold to pedigree barriers in order to maintain breed purity. These barriers create limited population size. This, inevitably, leads to inbreeding, which also differs among breeds and contributes to levels of heterosis when breeds are crossed.

BREED COMPARISON RESEARCH

The U.S. Department of Agriculture and various state Agricultural Experiment Stations have devoted substantial resources to genetic comparisons of breeds of beef cattle, dairy cattle, swine, and sheep during the last half of the 20th century. Published reports of these comparisons appear in numerous places in the scientific literature. Attempts to summarize much of this research have been made.[7–12] The research clearly shows that there are substantial differences between breeds, suggesting that livestock producers have a wide variety from which to choose.

BREED DEVELOPMENT

Despite the large number of diverse breeds that are available to livestock producers, there continues to be interest in developing new breeds. Each new breed is, of course, developed for somewhat unique reasons using highly individual methods. One example of breed development was that used by many of the developers of the Brahman-derivative breeds of cattle. Several of those breeds are 3/8 Brahman and 5/8 of the British or European breed. Such a breed could be developed using the following procedure:

How to build 5/8 A: 3/8 B

Step 1 A × B → 1/2 A: 1/2 B
Step 2 A × AB → 3/4 A: 1/4 B
Step 3 AB × A(AB) → 5/8 A: 3/8 B
Step 4 inter se matings.

Inter se matings are matings among individuals with common background. Although one could technically claim development of a new breed after one generation of inter se mating, generally generations of inter se matings combined with selection to establish type, color pattern, etc., would yield a result that could be called a breed. It is very important, when pursuing development of a new breed, to start with a large population of foundation animals and to keep the population size large in order to avoid damage caused by inbreeding and genetic drift.

CONCLUSION

Just as there was early unwillingness to assign a single scientific definition to the concept of breed,[1] the concept remains fairly fluid at the beginning of the 21st century. Development of new breeds is continuing. New genetic technologies may contribute to an evolving concept of breed. It is tempting to assume that the important breeds of today will continue to be important in the future. One has only to examine the history of breeds during the 20th century to see the fallacy of this assumption. Societal needs for livestock will no doubt change with time. The evolutionary pace in livestock may become even more lively.

REFERENCES

1. Lloyd-Jones, O. What is a breed? J. Heredity **1915**, *6*, 531–535.
2. Wright, S. *Evolution and the Genetics of Populations. Experimental Results and Evolutionary Deductions*; The University of Chicago Press: Chicago, 1977; Vol. 3, 526–555.
3. Mason, I.L. *A World Dictionary of Livestock Breeds, Types and Varieties*, 4th Ed.; CAB International: Wallingford, UK, 1996.
4. Briggs, H.M.; Briggs, D.M. *Modern Breeds of Livestock*, 4th Ed.; Macmillan: New York, NY, 1980.
5. Felius, M. *Cattle Breeds of the World*; Merck & Co., Inc.: Rahway, NJ, 1985.
6. Committee on Managing Global Genetic Resources. *Managing Global Genetic Resources—Livestock*; National Academy Press: Washington, DC, 1993; 21–46.
7. Buchanan, D.S.; Dolezal, S.L. Breeds of Cattle. In *The Genetics of Cattle*; Fries, R., Ruvinsky, A., Eds.; CABI Publishing: Oxon, UK, 1999; 667–696.
8. Cundiff, L.V.; Gregory, K.E.; Koch, R.M.; Dickerson, G.E. Genetic Diversity Among Cattle Breeds and Its Use to Increase Beef Production Efficiency in a Temperate Environment. In *Proc. 3rd World Cong. on Genetics Applied to Livestock Production*; Unversity of Nebraska, 1986; Vol. IX, 271–282.
9. Cundiff, L.V.; Szabo, F.; Gregory, K.E.; Koch, R.M.; Dikeman, M.E.; Crouse, J.D. Breed Comparisons in the Germplasm Evaluation Program at MARC. Proceedings Beef Improvement Federation, Asheville, NC, 1993; 124–136.
10. Dickerson, G.E. *Crossbreeding Evaluation of Finnsheep and Some US Breeds for Market Lamb Production*, NCR Pub. No. 246; 1977.
11. Johnson, R.K. *Heterosis and Breed Effects in Swine*, NC Regional Pub 262; 1980.
12. McDowell, R.E. Crossbreeding as a system of mating for dairy production. South. Coop. Ser. Bull. **1982**, *259*.

Lower Digestive Tract Microbiology

Vincent H. Varel
James E. Wells
United States Department of Agriculture, Agricultural Research Service, Clay Center, Nebraska, U.S.A.

INTRODUCTION

The lower digestive tract of animals is often referred to as the hindgut and normally denotes the large intestine, which includes the cecum, colon, and rectum. The cecum is a branch from the junction of the small intestine and colon. There is a great diversity among animals in hindgut morphology, mainly in relation to diet of the animal. Carnivores have a small hindgut and a cecum may be absent. However, herbivores, such as the horse, have a large hindgut capacity. The hindgut of nonruminant animals is the primary site for retention of food residues and endogenous substrates for microbial fermentation. Conditions in the hindgut include a constant temperature, pH between 6.5 and 7.5, and low concentrations of oxygen, thus providing an environment for 10^9 to 10^{11} microorganisms of up to 400 different species per gram of lumen contents.[2] The fermentation end products of the microorganisms—short-chain volatile fatty acids, primarily acetate, propionate, and butyrate—are absorbed throughout the hindgut and used as energy by the animal. Humans have continuously tried to influence the microbial species present in the intestinal tract with the objective to increase meat-animal production efficiency. This has occurred primarily with the use of antibiotics, prebiotics, probiotics, or other dietary additives.

COLONIZATION OF HINDGUT

The digestive tract (Table 1) is an open ecosystem; therefore any microorganism taken in with food or water has the potential to colonize the hindgut and influence the fermentation. Microorganisms remain permanent residents if they can attach to the lining of the intestine or grow at a faster rate than the rate at which the digesta flow. The microbial species found in the digestive tract are affected by the host's diet, environment, drug administration, and stress to the animal. All animals are microbially sterile at birth, but microorganisms from the animal's environment rapidly colonize the gastrointestinal tract. Lactose content of mammalian milk encourages growth of lactic acid bacteria in the intestine.[3] The lactic acid bacteria are gradually overgrown by strictly anaerobic microorganisms

as the gut lumen enlarges and the feed becomes more solid. However, the lactic acid bacteria (*Lactobacillus*) coexist with the *Bacteroides* and other strict anaerobes. Some of the common bacterial species found in the pig hindgut are listed in Table 2. Lactic acid–producing bacteria are thought to suppress other microorganisms and are now generally recognized as desirable, thus they are given as supplements (probiotics) to promote health.

Microorganisms associated with the hindgut can be divided into two groups: 1) autochthonous microorganisms are indigenous organisms that colonize a particular region of the gut early in life, multiply to high population levels soon after colonization, and remain in the gut throughout the lives of a healthy host; 2) nonautochthonous microorganisms are indigenous organisms that colonize the hindgut of animals living in a given area, but may not be present in all individuals of a given animal species.[4] Stewart[5] and Hillman[3] have recently reviewed the microorganisms found in the hindgut of the pig through the use of conventional identification techniques. More recent studies using identification of bacterial 16S rDNA genes by polymerase chain reaction, cloning, and DNA sequencing suggest that 50% or more of the microflora of the pig hindgut is unidentified.[6] This is likely true for most other animals because they have been studied much less than the pig. This suggests that the current classification systems for the major genera of microorganisms in the hindgut are inadequate. Recent studies have also demonstrated that the genetic diversity within existing taxonomic groups has been greatly underestimated. Future challenges will involve evaluating this large biodiversity and determining the link between diversity and metabolic function. Sensitive methods are needed that follow in detail, at short time intervals, the individual population changes occurring in the hindgut.

Composition of the hindgut microbiota is thought to be relatively stable. Several hundred species coexist without one or a few becoming dominant. The stability appears to be a function of inhibition of bacterial multiplication by such compounds as volatile fatty acids, hydrogen sulfide, bile salts, and bacteriocins. These bacterial inhibitors may prolong the lag phase of invading bacteria sufficiently that they are washed out of the hindgut. Competition for limiting nutrients is another method by which a balance of

Encyclopedia of Animal Science
DOI: 10.1081/E-EAS 120019702
Published 2005 by Marcel Dekker, Inc. All rights reserved.

Table 1 Classification of some animals based on gastro-intestinal anatomy

Class	Species	Dietary habit
Pregastric fermenters		
Ruminants	Cattle, sheep, deer	Grazing herbivores
	Antelope, camel	Selective herbivores
Nonruminants	Colobine monkey	Selective herbivore
	Hamster, vole	Selective herbivores
	Kangaroo, hippopotamus	Grazing and selective herbivores
Hindgut fermenters		
Cecal (rodents)	Capybara	Grazer
	Rabbit	Selective herbivore
	Rat	Omnivore
Colonic digesters		
Sacculated	Horse	Grazer
	New World monkey	Selective herbivore
	Pig, man	Omnivores
Unsacculated	Dog	Carnivore
	Cat	Carnivore

(From Ref. 1.)

microbial species is selected. The greater the number of limiting nutrients in the hindgut, the greater the diversity of the bacterial population, since each limiting nutrient will support the one bacterial species that is most efficient at using it.[2] Protozoa and fungi are also found in the

Table 2 Common bacteria in the hindgut of pigs

Bacteroides fragilis
Bacteroides thetaiotaomicron
Bacteroides uniformis
Bacteroides suis
Butyrivibrio fibrisolvens
Clostridium perfringens
Escherichia coli
Eubacterium aerofaciens
Fibrobacter succinogenes
Lactobacillus acidophilus
Lactobacillus brevis
Lactobacillus cellobiosus
Lactobacillus fermentum
Lactobacillus salivarius
Methanobrevibacter spp
Peptostreptococcus productus
Prevotella bryantii
Prevotella ruminicola
Proteus spp
Ruminococcus flavefaciens
Selenomonas ruminantium
Streptococcus bovis
Streptococcus equinus
Streptococcus faecalis
Streptococcus intestinalis
Streptococcus salivarius
Veillonella spp

hindgut of some animal species, but their occurrence is not universal and their roles are poorly understood.

MICROBIAL EFFECTS ON HOST ANIMALS

A stable intestinal microflora is inherently more resistant to pathogenic infection than an unstable one. The health of the gastrointestinal tract has a direct bearing on the growth and productivity of livestock animals, since the gut comprises the body's largest organ and represents a considerable part of the animal's protein and energy requirements.[3] Some of the benefits and negative effects of intestinal microorganisms in the intestinal tract are given in Table 3. The large mass of adherent autochthonous bacterial population is in itself an important physiological contribution to the health of the animal. It provides a

Table 3 The effects of gut microorganisms

Benefits	Negative effects
Synthesis of vitamins B and K	Production of toxic metabolites
Detoxification of food components or endogenous products	Modification of nutrients
Recovery of endogenous nitrogen	Release of toxins from nontoxic precursors
Production of digestive enzymes, e.g., bacterial amylase for starch digestion	Uptake of nutrients, e.g., amino-acids. Decreased digestibility of fat due to altering lipids and bile salts

(From Ref. 7.)

formidable barrier through which a pathogen must penetrate to establish itself. However, perturbations such as antibiotic treatment, stress, and abrupt diet modification can disrupt the adherent flora and allow a pathogen to temporarily flourish in the gastrointestinal tract.

The microbial end products of the hindgut fermentation include the short-chain fatty acids acetate, propionate, and butyrate, along with the gases methane, hydrogen, and carbon dioxide. In the young pig, the short-chain fatty acids can contribute up to 30% of the maintenance energy of the animal, while in the adult pig this may be even greater. Among other animals, large variations exist in the amount of energy derived from hindgut volatile fatty acids, with the dog and human being at the low end (<5%) and the horse at the high end (>30%). Although volatile fatty acids and vitamins synthesized in the hindgut benefit the animal, the microbes also impose a considerable burden to the animals in terms of replacement of epithelial cells, detoxification of microbial metabolites, and production of inflammatory and immunological cells. The benefits and negative effects of microbes in the hindgut are further discussed elsewhere in this encyclopedia.

MANIPULATION OF THE HINDGUT FERMENTATION

In order to maintain a healthy intestinal microflora for efficient animal growth, growth promotants, primarily in the form of antibiotics, have been therapeutically fed to livestock for several decades. This practice is suspected to be linked to development of antibiotic-resistant microorganisms. Thus, alternatives to antibiotics are being sought.[3] These include supplementary enzymes to diets, organic acids, prebiotics, and probiotics. However, many of these alternatives are viewed with skepticism because the results obtained are variable and few have been studied sufficiently to adequately explain a mode of action.

Other efforts to increase animal growth efficiency are the use of genetically modified grains and forages that contain appropriate hydrolytic enzymes in vacuoles or in the cytosol to be released after crop harvest and animal consumption. These enzymes will assist microbial enzymes in extracting nutrients for animal growth. Recent studies have also demonstrated that it is possible for transgenic mice to produce key microbial enzymes that degrade fiber or plant phosphorous more efficiently.[8] Generation of transgenic animals that secrete xylanase from the pancreas suggests that this may prove to have a dual benefit. Intestinal secretion of xylanase by swine would enhance nutrient absorption and the xylooligosaccharide products from xylanase action would enrich *Bifidobacterium* spp. in the intestine, thus providing a more favorable intestinal environment.

CONCLUSIONS

The gastrointestinal tract is the largest organ in an animal. The population of microorganisms in the tract will out number the tissue cells making up the entire body of the animal. The microflora in the hindgut are critical to the well-being of an animal and provide nutrients (volatile fatty acids, vitamins) and protection from invading pathogens that constantly enter the open ecosystem with food and water. Currently, a large proportion of hindgut microorganisms is unknown (50%). New methods and techniques are needed to identify this large mass of diverse microorganisms. Once this capability is obtained, efforts are needed to follow the changing population of microorganisms on a short-term basis. This will allow us to more fully understand the significance of the microflora in animal growth efficiency and health.

ARTICLE OF FURTHER INTEREST

GI Tract: Animal/Microbial Symbiosis, p. 449

REFERENCES

1. Van Soest, P.J. *Nutritional Ecology of the Ruminant*; Comstock Publishing Associates, Cornell University Press: Ithaca, NY, 1982; 202.
2. Hume, I.D. Fermentation in the Hindgut of Mammals. In *Gastrointestinal Microbiology*; Mackie, R.I., White, B.A., Eds.; Chapman and Hall: New York, 1997; 84–115.
3. Hillman, K. Bacteriological Aspects of the Use of Antibiotics and Their Alternatives in the Feed of Non-ruminant Animals. In *Recent Advances in Animal Nutrition*; Garnsworthy, P.C., Wiseman, J., Eds.; Nottingham University Press: UK, 2001; 107–134.
4. Ewing, W.N.; Cole, D.J.A. *The Living Gut*; Context Publication: Co Tyrone, N. Ireland, 1994.
5. Stewart, C.S. Microorganisms in Hindgut Fermentors. In *Gastrointestinal Microbiology*; Mackie, R.I., White, B.A., Isaacson, R.E., Eds.; Chapman and Hall: New York, 1997; 142–186.
6. Leser, T.D.; Amenuvor, J.Z.; Jensen, T.K.; Lindecrona, R.H.; Boye, M.; Moller, K. Culture-independent analysis of gut bacteria: The pig gastrointestinal tract revisited. Appl. Environ. Microbiol. **2002**, *68* (2), 673–690.
7. Coates, M.E. The Gut Micro-flora and Growth. In *Growth in Animals*; Lawrence, T.L.J., Ed.; Butterworths: London, 1980; 175–188.
8. Golovan, S.P.; Hayes, M.A.; Phillips, J.P.; Forsberg, C.W. Transgenic mice expressing bacterial phytase as a model for phosphorus pollution control. Nat. Biotechnol. **2001**, *19*, 429–433.

Male Reproduction: Physiological Comparisons

Robert P. Wettemann
Oklahoma State University, Stillwater, Oklahoma, U.S.A.

INTRODUCTION

Sperm production by the testes is a continuous process after puberty. Accessory glands are stimulated by male hormones and secretions of the glands compose most of the volume of semen. Size of the testes, number of sperm produced each day, volume of ejaculum, and methods to store semen for artificial insemination vary among species. Increased testicular temperatures can reduce sperm production and cause reduced fertility or infertility. This temporary reduction in fertility exists until testicular tissues return to normal and there is sufficient time for the formation and maturation of a new cycle of sperm production.

TESTICULAR DEVELOPMENT AND DESCENT

The embryonic gonad has the potential to become either a testis or an ovary. After gonadal differentiation, testes remain in the abdominal cavity until they descend into the scrotum. In cattle and sheep, testicular descent occurs in midgestation and descent occurs in late gestation in swine and horses. In contrast, testicular descent occurs postnatally in rabbits and dogs. Avian testes remain in the body cavity attached to the wall of the kidney, and the testes function at body temperature. Cryptorchidism, the retention of one or both testes in the abdominal cavity, is inherited. In most domestic mammals, the normal temperature of the testes is several degrees cooler in the scrotum compared with body temperature. The cooler environment is essential for sperm production and bilateral cryptorchid males are sterile. Temperature regulation of the testes is controlled by muscular regulation (cremaster muscle) of the distance that the testes is from the body, heat transfer from arterial blood going to the testes to cooler venous blood from the testes to reduce the temperature of testicular arterial blood, and changes in scrotal surface area and sweating.

TESTICULAR FUNCTIONS

Testes have two major functions: production of sperm and synthesis of male hormones. The endocrine function of the testes is the production of testosterone and androstenedione. These sex hormones are synthesized in the interstitial or Leydig cells. The seminiferous tubules in the testes are lined with sertoli cells that support germ cells during the production of sperm (spermatogenesis). The weight of the two testes ranges from 6 g for rabbits to 720 g for boars (Table 1). Gonadotropic hormones synthesized in the anterior pituitary gland stimulate growth and maturation of testes resulting in sexual maturation, sperm production, and ejaculation.

SPERMATOGENESIS

A blood–testis barrier prevents some compounds in blood from entering the seminiferous tubules where sperm are produced. This prevents compounds such as heavy metals and drugs from damaging sperm. Mitotic and meiotic cell divisions occur during spermatogenesis. Spermatogonia undergo several mitotic divisions to become primary spermatocytes, which undergo meiotic divisions to become secondary spermatocytes, then spermatids, and finally spermatozoa or sperm. Spermatogenesis results in a multiplication in the number of sperm produced and a reduction in the genetic material in sperm to half the amount of other cells in the body (haploid).

Spermatogenesis is a continuous process in males unless conditions are abnormal such as when heat stress increases testicular temperature. The interval required for the production of sperm from the first cell division of spermatogonia—until a spermatozoon or sperm is released into the lumen of the seminiferous tubule—varies with species. For instance, in farm animals it only requires 34 days for spermatogenesis in boars; however, 61 days are required in bulls. Compared with mammals, spermatogenesis in birds is about four times faster and about four times the number of sperm are produced per gram of testis. The duct system from the testes (efferent ducts) transports sperm to the epididymis, a long coiled tube. Length of the epididymis is about 18 meters in boars and 75 meters in stallions. Sperm cells undergo a maturation process in the epididymis during 7 to 14 days, depending on the species. Sperm that enter the epididymis are not motile or capable of fertilization until maturational changes occur in the epididymis.

Encyclopedia of Animal Science
DOI: 10.1081/E-EAS 120019704

Table 1 Testicular characteristics of farm animals

Species	Weight of both testes (g)	Daily sperm production ($\times 10^9$)	Age at puberty (mo.)[a]
Boar	720	16.2	5–8
Ram	500	9.5	4–9
Bull, beef	650	5.9	9–12
Stallion	340	5.3	12–20
Rabbit	6	0.2	3–4
Dog	32–88	0.9	6–12

[a]Sperm ejaculated.
(Compiled from the literature.)

If males have increased body temperature due to fever or exposure to hot climatic conditions, testicular temperature can increase and result in a reduction in the number of sperm produced or the production of sperm that are less fertile or infertile.[2] If bulls or boars are heat-stressed for an interval of only three days, this can cause temporary infertility. After heat stress, boars must be exposed to a cool environment for five weeks and bulls must be cool for seven weeks before normal sperm are produced and animals are fertile. Heat stress also causes infertility in birds and the effect appears to be greater in males than in females.

SEMEN

Only a small part of an ejaculate of semen is composed of sperm cells. Most of the volume of semen is from secretions of accessory glands that are stimulated by the secretion of testosterone by the testes. The major accessory glands are ampullary gland, seminal vesicle, prostate, cowers gland, coagulating gland, and preputial gland. The presence, size, and amount of secretion by the different glands vary among species. For instance, ampullary glands are large in stallions and absent in boars. Seminal vesicles are large in boars and absent in dogs. Accessory glands are absent in birds. The differences in the occurrence and size of accessory glands result in differences in volume and composition of semen.

PUBERTY

Puberty in males can be defined as the time when spermatogenesis is completed and the male has the willingness and eagerness to mount and complete service of a female. Although sperm can be ejaculated by bulls at 9 months, rams at 4 months, boars at 5 months, and stallions at 12 months of age, adequate numbers of fertile sperm for successful mating programs are not usually produced until 12, 12, 10 and 24 months of age, respectively.

EJACULATION

Movement of sperm cells from the cauda of the epididymis to the reproductive tract of the female during mating or collection of semen for artificial insemination involves an integrated sequence of events. The penis is erected, sperm and secretions from the accessory glands are moved into the ejaculatory duct, and ejaculation moves semen to the exterior of the penis. The duration of

Table 2 Composition of semen and fertility of farm animals

Species	Volume (ml)	Sperm concentration (10^9/ml)	Duration of ejaculation	Pregnancy rates with natural mating (%)
Boar	250	0.2	minutes	85–95
Ram	1	3.0	<second	80–90
Bull, beef	5	1.0	<second	65–75
Stallion	60	0.15	minutes	40–75
Rabbit	1	0.2	<second	80–90
Dog	4	0.2	minutes	—

(Adapted from Ref. 1.)

ejaculation varies with species: from a fraction of a second for bulls and rams, to several minutes for boars (Table 2). Stallions, rams, and bulls produce 5 to 10 billion sperm per day and daily sperm production of boars is about 16 billion sperm.

The volume of semen produced in an ejaculum varies with size and function of accessory glands. The average volume of an ejaculum from a bull is 5 ml, whereas boars produce 250 ml.

ARTIFICIAL INSEMINATION

Artificial insemination, or deposition of semen in the female without contact between the male and female, is a common practice in most mammalian and avian species. This was the first application of genetic technology to livestock.[3] After semen is collected from the male, it is usually processed and stored to maintain maximal fertility until it is deposited in the female. Short-term storage of semen usually occurs at ambient or cool temperature. The optimal diluent for semen and storage temperature vary with species. The limitations of maintaining fertile semen with liquid storage of semen were overcome with the discovery of methods to store semen indefinitely by cyropreservation. The techniques for cryopreservation (diluents, temperature, additives, and freezing and thawing rates) vary with species. Chicken and turkey semen can be maintained for insemination as liquid, in a suitable medium, or frozen using a cryoprotectant. Pregnancy rates obtained by insemination of females with cryopreserved semen vary with species. When beef cattle are inseminated with semen after cryopreservation, fertility is similar to that which occurs with natural mating. However, pregnancy rate is reduced 10 to 15% when sows are inseminated with frozen-thawed semen compared with natural mating. Additional research will result in new techniques to improve pregnancy rates after insemination with frozen-thawed semen.

CONCLUSIONS

Although reproductive functions of male farm animals are similar in most species, there is much variation among species. Some characteristics that vary among species are size of testes, number of sperm produced each day, age at puberty, volume of semen, and duration of ejaculation. However, in all farm animals, normal testicular temperature is several degrees cooler than body temperature and this temperature gradient is essential for production of fertile sperm. Increases in body and testicular temperature, due to health problems or heat stress, result in reduced fertility or sterility. The duration of altered fertility is variable among species and is the result of the time required for sperm cell production and maturation.

REFERENCES

1. Garner, D.L. Artificial Insemination. In *Reproduction in Domestic Animals*; Cupps, P.T. Ed.; Academic Press: New York, 1991; 251 pp.
2. Wettemann, R.P.; Wells, M.E.; Omtvedt, I.T.; Pope, C.E.; Turman, E.J. Influence of elevated ambient temperature on reproductive performance of boars. J. Anim. Sci. **1976**, *42*, 664–669.
3. Foote, R.H. The history of artificial insemination: Selected notes and notables. Am. Soc. Anim. Sci. **2002**. Available at http://asas.org/symposia/esupp2/Footehist.pdf (accessed January, 2004).

Mammals: Carnivores

Duane E. Ullrey
Michigan State University, East Lansing, Michigan, U.S.A.

INTRODUCTION

Walker's Mammals of the World assigns dogs, bears, raccoons, weasels, civets, mongooses, hyenas, and cats to the order Carnivora. This taxonomic category brings together species with phylogenetic features relevant to their evolutionary history, but has limited application to the care of animals exhibiting carnivory as defined by natural dietary habits. This article discusses mammal species both inside and outside the order Carnivora that characteristically choose their food from the animal kingdom.

NATURAL DIETARY HABITS

Carnivores derive most or all of their energy and nutrient needs from consumption of animal tissues, either by predation or scavenging.[1] We are most likely to associate carnivory with predators such as lions, tigers, and leopards, which feed primarily on terrestrial animals. However, carnivores that are specialized to feed on aquatic vertebrates (fish) and invertebrates (squid), such as dolphins, have been called piscivores.[2] Those that feed on aquatic invertebrates of limited mobility (crustaceans and clams), such as walruses, have been called crustacivores.[2] Carnivores that feed primarily on colonial insects (ants and termites), such as anteaters or pangolins, might be called myrmecivores. Those that feed on noncolonial insects or arachnids, such as tarsiers and shrews, have been called insectivores.[2] Those that feed on zooplankton, such as baleen whales, have been called plaktonivores.[2] Bats in the family Phyllostomatidae are adapted for feeding on the blood of warm-blooded vertebrates and have been called sanguivores.[2] Whatever their dietary habits, if their food consists of tissues from members of the animal kingdom, these specialized feeders—broadly defined—are known as carnivores.

Food acquisition strategies vary with species. Ancestral dogs and many of their canid relatives are considered pack hunters, allowing them to kill prey as large or larger than themselves. Surplus food remaining after a meal is sometimes hidden for later recovery and consumption. Most felids, except lions, tend to be solitary hunters. Lions and tigers are of sufficient size and strength to kill prey larger than themselves and are adapted to large but infrequent meals. Smaller wild felids, particularly those in the genus *Felis* tend to depend upon frequent predation of smaller prey. Locally abundant food resources, such as spawning salmon, may attract brown bears to a common feeding site, but there appears to be little cooperative predation. Some cetaceans cooperate in their acquisition of food. Groups of bottlenose dolphins have been observed approaching fish at opposite ends of a school of fish, or herding fish toward individuals patrolling offshore to prevent the fish from escaping.[3]

OBLIGATE VS. FACULTATIVE CARNIVORES

Animals that eat only animal prey are sometimes called strict or obligate carnivores to distinguish them from facultative carnivores that eat mostly animal prey but also consume nonanimal foods. Felids are strict carnivores and, in the wild, obtain most of their food by predation on the tissues of mammals, birds, or fish. Their domestic representative, the cat (*Felis catus*), differs in several respects in its metabolism and nutrient requirements from the domestic dog (*Canis familiaris*), a canid that is a facultative carnivore. It is presumed that these differences are an evolutionary consequence of their respective ancestral diets. The cat has a higher dietary requirement for protein because it has only a limited ability to regulate nitrogen losses in the urine— losses that are of little consequence when nitrogen (protein) intakes are high, as they would be when whole animal prey are consumed. Further, the cat is particularly sensitive to a deficiency of the essential amino acid arginine—a deficiency that results in toxic levels of ammonia in the blood but which is unlikely when whole animals are consumed. The cat also has a dietary requirement for taurine, a sulfur-containing amino acid that can be synthesized from methionine by the tissues of most other mammals after weaning. An experimental taurine deficiency results in central retinal degeneration and cardiomyopathy in the cat. Fortunately, taurine requirements of felids can be met by consuming whole animals.

Carbohydrates are rarely consumed by wild felids, and the domestic cat has evolved with the ability to derive

Encyclopedia of Animal Science
DOI: 10.1081/E-EAS 120019707

most of its needs for blood glucose from specific amino acids by gluconeogenesis. The dog, by contrast, is more omnivorous and derives most of its blood glucose from carbohydrate precursors via hepatic glycolysis.

Other differences between strict and facultative carnivores are illustrated by the inability of the cat, as compared with the dog, to meet its needs for vitamin A from provitamin A carotenoids, for niacin from tryptophan, or for arachidonic acid from linoleic acid. These needs all are met by adequate concentrations of these nutrients in the tissues of whole animals. Whether there are comparable metabolic adaptations related to food choices of obligate piscivores, crustacivores, myrmecivores, insectivores, planktonivores, or sanguivores is presently unknown.[1]

MOUTH STRUCTURE, DENTITION, AND GASTROINTESTINAL MORPHOLOGY

Mouth structure and dentition tend to be specialized to accommodate efficient capture and consumption of particular types of prey. Classical carnivores, such as lions and tigers, have well-developed incisors and carnassial teeth that facilitate effective grasping of terrestrial vertebrate prey and shearing of flesh. Simple pointed teeth for grasping and holding fish prior to swallowing are found in pinnipeds such as dolphins. The tusks of walruses are used to dislodge crustaceans from their underwater locations. Small insectivores, such as shrews, have teeth with cusped surfaces that efficiently grasp the rigid exoskeletons of insect prey. Dentition is much reduced in carnivores that consume colonial insects, such as anteaters, which have a long manipulable tongue used to catch and ingest ants and termites from tunnels and cavities. Whales that consume zooplankton have baleen rather than teeth—platelike structures that project downward from either side of the upper interior mouth surface and that trap zooplankton while allowing release of water ingested with their food.

Although the dentition of carnivores is quite diverse, the gastrointestinal systems of those species that have been studied tend to be similar and relatively simple, presumably because carnivorous diets are quite digestible. There are seldom compartments in the stomach or large intestine that delay movement of digesta and that house microorganisms that assist digestion of refractory compounds, as in herbivores. If the cecum is present, it is often small; in many species, both the small and large intestines may be rather short. Nevertheless, there are a number of distinct species differences, the functions of which are not yet understood.[4]

CONCLUSIONS

Proper care and feeding of mammalian carnivores are most logically based on natural dietary habits and specialized features of oral and gastrointestinal morphology and physiology. Obligate carnivores may have unique metabolic characteristics that influence their ability to use specific nutrient sources, thus affecting both qualitative and quantitative nutrient requirements.

REFERENCES

1. Allen, M.E.; Oftedal, O.T.; Baer, D.J. The Feeding and Nutrition of Carnivores. In *Wild Mammals in Captivity, Principles and Techniques*; Kleiman, D.G., Allen, M.E., Thompson, K.V., Lumpkin, S., Eds.; University of Chicago Press: Chicago, 1996; 139–147.
2. Eisenberg, J.F. Feeding and Foraging Categories: Some Size Constraints. In *The Mammalian Radiations: An Analysis of Trends in Evolution, Adaptation, and Behavior*; University of Chicago Press: Chicago, 1981; 247–263.
3. Nowak, R.M. *Walker's Mammals of the World*, 6th Ed.; Johns Hopkins University Press: Baltimore, 1999; Vols. 1 and 2.
4. Stevens, C.E.; Hume, I.D. *Comparative Physiology of the Vertebrate Digestive System*, 2nd Ed.; Cambridge University Press: Cambridge, UK, 1995.

Mammals: Nonruminant Herbivores

Gerald B. Huntington
North Carolina State University, Raleigh, North Carolina, U.S.A.

INTRODUCTION

Nonruminant, noncamelid, herbivorous mammals are a varied and robust group. Examples will be provided (in parentheses) throughout this article to aid in illustration of the point at hand. They range from some of the smallest mammals (mice) to the largest (elephant). They live in mountains (hyrax), prairies (zebra), trees (colobus monkey), jungles (tapir), deserts (kangaroo rat), rivers (hippopotamus), and underground (rabbit). They are solitary (hyrax) or participate in complicated social groups (mole rat). They hop (kangaroo), gallop (horse), swim (manatee), tunnel (mole rat), and fly (fruit bat). They have long gestations with single births (elephant), or short gestations of several offspring (gerbils). Many are feral, some have long histories of human domestication (horse, rabbit), and others are popular pets (mice, hamster). Their main and often exclusive source of food is plants—fruit, nectar, flower, seed, stem, leaf, root, bark, and sap. Within species, the food source can be wide and versatile (porcupine, rhinoceros), or narrow and specific (koala, panda, gibbon). Pandas are classified as carnivores, but subsist mainly on plant parts. This article discusses differences among herbivorous mammals, and explores commonalities among them and among other animals as well.

STRUCTURE AND FUNCTION OF THE GASTROINTESTINAL TRACT

Because herbivores are classified by their diet, it is pertinent to explore the specialities of their physiological machinery to prehend and digest food required to sustain life. Specifics of diet and habit interact with location of eyes, length of neck and legs, and structure of the mouth. For example, the lemur has binocular vision, a prehensile tail, and dexterous hands; the beaver is renowned for its teeth and swimming ability; the elephant's trunk and the manatee's lips are magnificent adaptations to food supply; and the sightless mole rat has incisors that function as excavators, and stubby legs to propel loosened soil to the rear of its subterranean habitat.

The wide variety of habitats and food preferences is associated with a myriad of subtle distinctions among herbivores of the shape of the teeth, tongue, and jaw, number and type of molars, presence or absence of functional canines, and the eruption of teeth during life.[1] Jaw structure, articulation with the skull, and musculature provide the fulcrum for cutting, crushing, and grinding. For example, horses have side-to-side jaw movement similar to that of ruminants to facilitate the diminution of grasses,[2] and elephants and kangaroos have front-to-back lower jaw movement to grind highly structured plant cell walls. The structure and composition of teeth with specific functions allow them to break seed coats, rupture highly lignified plant cell walls, or comminute leaves or other physical alteration of diet that predicate digestion. The hypsodont molar teeth of some herbivores are designed to be ground away, yet retain their abrasive surface.[2] The loxodont molars of elephants have pronounced enamel ridges that enhance grinding capacity.[3] Elephants slough and replace these molars several times. The incisors of rodents grow throughout life to replace teeth worn away by gnawing.[3] The diastema between incisors and molars allows space for the jaw and soft tissues of the mouth of grazing herbivores to prehend long pieces of plant material (such as leaves and stems), protrude them to the side, then shorten and ingest them at a deliberate pace. The same diastema allows other herbivores to gnaw through unwanted material (such as soil, bark, and shell) and expel the unwanted material to the side.[1,2]

Digestion and absorption of nutrients can be divided into two strategies or two main structures for the gastrointestinal tract. The strategies are: 1) rapid transit of chyme with high (fruit bat) or low (panda) extraction of nutrients; or 2) slower transit of chyme for increased extraction of nutrients (horse). The two main structures center on the: 1) pregastric (colobus); or 2) postgastric site (rabbit) of simbiotic, microbial fermentation. Within these general divisions are a myriad of subtle adaptations. Most nonruminant herbivores belong in the slower transit, postgastric fermentation category, finding survival and the opportunity to reproduce in a habitat that provides highly structured food material that benefits from microbial fermentation in the gut. In general, fluids have lower retention time than particulates (therefore faster passage rates) in the gut, but some postgastric fermenters have developed methods to selectively retain fluids.[4] The most active method to achieve selective retention is antiperistalsis in the lower gut.

Encyclopedia of Animal Science
DOI: 10.1081/E-EAS 120019709

Table 1 Diets of nonruminant and noncamelid herbivores from various orders of mammals

Order	Common names of herbivorous animals and principal diet
Carnivora	Giant panda—bamboo; Lesser (red) panda—berries, blossoms, leaves
Chiroptera	Fruit-eating bat; Nectar-feeding bat
Marsupialia	Petaurids (gliders, ring-tailed possums) and koalas—eucalyptus leaves, blossoms, shoots. Ring-tailed possum is coprophagous; Kangaroo and wallaby—grasses, shrubs; Wombat—grasses, roots, bark
Edentata (Xenarthra)	Three-toed sloth—tree leaves; Two-toed sloth, ground sloth—leaves, fruits, buds
Rodentia	Beaver—bark, leaves, coprophagy; Hamster, lemming, vole—seeds, shoots, roots, fruit; Gopher—roots, tubers, grass leaves; Squirrel—leaves, seeds, nuts; Spring hare—bulbs, corms, green shoots; Mole rat—roots, tubers, rhizomes, bulbs, coprophagy; Flying squirrel; Porcupine—bulbs, roots, berries, tree bark, thistles, leaves; Capybara; Kangaroo rat—seeds, vegetable material; Gerbil, sand rat—seeds; Cane rat; Chinchilla; Guinea pig
Primates	Lemur—leaves, flowers, coprophagy; Colobus monkey—leaves, buds, flowers, fruits; Langur—leaves, fruits, flowers; Gibbon—ripe fruit
Artiodactyla	Hippopotamus
Dermoptera	Flying lemur (colugo)—leaves, buds, flowers, fruits
Lagomorpha	Pika—leaves and stems of forbs and shrubs, grass leaves and seeds, coprophagy; Rabbit—grass, leaves, coprophagy
Perissodactyla	Horse, zebra, ass—grass; Rhinoceros—grass, stems, leaves of woody vegetation; Tapir—tree leaves, aquatic vegetation, fruit, grass
Proboscidea	Elephant—leaves, roots, bark, fruit; Hyrax—leaves, grasses, bark
Sirenia	Dugong—bottom-growing, shallow vegetation, coprophagy; Manatee—aquatic and marine vegetation, algae, coprophagy

(From Refs. 4–6.)

Table 2 Nonruminant and noncamelid herbivores from various orders of mammals

Order	Common names of herbivorous animals				
Carnivora	Giant panda	Red panda			
Chiroptera	Fruit-eating bat	Nectar-feeding bat			
Marsupialia	Ring-tailed possum	Kangaroo	Wallaby	Wombat	Koala
Edentata (Xenarthra)	Three-toed sloth	Two-toed sloth	Ground sloth		
Rodentia	Beaver	Squirrel	Gopher	Kangaroo rat	Spring hare
	Hamster	Capybara	Lemming	Gerbil	Mole rat
	Porcupine	Cane rat	Chinchilla	Guinea pig	Flying squirrel
Primates	Lemur	Colobus monkey	Langur monkey	Wooly monkey	Orangutan
	Gibbon				
Artiodactyla	Hippopotamus				
Dermoptera	Flying lemur				
Lagomorpha	Pika	Rabbit			
Perissodactyla	Horse	Zebra	Tapir	Rhinoceros	
Proboscidea	Elephant	Hyrax			
Sirenia	Dugong	Manatee			

(From Refs. 5 and 6.)

In addition to major components of the gastrointestinal tract, herbivorous mammals have in common with other mammals the usual complement of digestive enzymes, tissue structures, and nutrient transport mechanisms.[4] The stomach of herbivores has four types of gastric epithelium: stratified squamous, cardiac gland, proper gastric, and pyloric gland.[4] With the exception of the fruit bat, the stomach of herbivorous mammals is large enough and compartmentalized enough to accommodate microbial fermentation. Nonruminant herbivores with substantial pregastric fermentation include the Colobus monkey, Langur monkey, brush-tailed porcupine, hamster, three-toed sloth, and the kangaroo. Most herbivores also have sites for postgastric fermentation.[4] The site of postgastric fermentation is caudal to the small intestine and may include a large cecum (rabbit) or large proximal colon (horse, elephant). Other nonruminant herbivores with substantial postgastric fermentation include the wombat, koala, opposum, capybara, night monkey, rhinoceros, dugong, and rock hyrax.[4] The hippopotamus is unusual because it has a very complex stomach, yet a simple hindgut without a cecum and a short colon. The panda is also unusual because it has neither pregastric or postgastric fermentation, but relies on rapid transit of bamboo selected for its high-nutrient content.[4]

Fermentation in the gut is accomplished predominantly by anaerobic bacteria. Bacteria and other microbes produce short-chain fatty acids (acetate, propionate, and butyrate); these acids are absorbed and provide 8–44% of the energy required for maintenance of nonruminant, noncamelid herbivores.[4] In the case of pregastric fermenting herbivores, the animal may also gain significant nutrient supply of protein and lipids upon digestion of the microbial biomass carried with chyme (see articles on ruminants and camelids elsewhere in this encyclopedia).

Coprophagy (eating one's own feces) is a common behavior among herbivores (Table 1). Coprophagy provides these animals with important nutrients (vitamins, protein) that are produced by the simbiotic microbes in their gut. A special subgroup of coprophagic herbivores are those that produce cecotrophs, special fecal pellets formed in the cecum that have high nitrogen content (rabbits, hares, chinchillas, guinea pigs, ringtail possums, and several rodent species). Cecotrophs are excreted once or twice during a 24-hour period, and are the fecal components preferentially ingested.[4]

REPRODUCTION AND OTHER SOCIAL ACTIVITIES

The range of orders (Table 2) is consistent with the wide range of gestation times, ranging from a few days (small rodents and rabbits) to a few months (bats, beavers, sloths, hippopotamus, and primates), a year to a year and one-half (horses, zebras, manatees, and rhinoceros), to 22 months for elephants.[6] The number of neonates per gestation ranges from one (olive colobus monkey, grey gibbon, plains zebra, three-toed sloth, hippopotumus, long-nosed bat), to 14 (long-tailed mouse, guinea pig, desert cottontail, antelope ground squirrel, European beaver, nutria, hoary marmot), to 27 or more for mole rats, which can enlarge their vertebrae to increase space in the abdominal cavity to accommodate their prolificacy.[3,6] Metatherian (marsupial) species have short gestation periods similar to those for small eutherian rodents followed by several months of maturation of neonates in their mother's pouch. A female kangaroo can simultaneously support three offspring in different stages of development—a zygote in her uterus, a developing neonate on one nipple in her pouch, and a joey that spends most of its time outside the pouch, but returns periodically for suckling. The female kangaroo can arrest development of the zygote in her uterus while a previously conceived joey is nursing in her pouch. When lactation (and the associated energy demand) diminishes, development of the zygote resumes. She can also produce milk of differing composition to each nipple, one milk suited for the developing neonate and the other for the independent joey who is not yet weaned.[3]

Social structures vary from solitary lives except at mating (wombat, sloth, rhinoceros, manatee) to larger groups—usually family groups of a dozen or fewer members (beaver, colobus monkey, guinea pig) or large herds (wild asses, zebra, elephant, hippopotamus).[6] Many species are nocturnal, and some hibernate to survive cold winters. Some species are territorial (lemur, gibbon, fruit bat, tammar wallaby) and others are nonterritorial (manatee, swamp wallaby, elephant). A good example of a highly organized society is the inconspicuous and arguably inelegant mole rat.[3]

CONCLUSION

Humans routinely interact with these herbivores in a variety of formats. Domesticated species or individuals (horse, guinea pig, elephant) have long histories of providing labor, food, and entertainment for humans. Others have been hunted for their pelts, bones, or meat (beaver, hippopotumus, zebra, wild ass, manatee). Some are hunted and killed as pests (short-eared bushtail possum, common wombat, tammar wallaby, several rodent species). Many species are vectors or intermediates in parasitic or infectious diseases that affect humans (rats, mice, primates). In short, their dietary preferences place these herbivores in the middle links of food chains or ecosystems, animals designed to convert biomass from photosynthesis to biomass to be used by subsequent links in the biological systems of the earth.

REFERENCES

1. Animal Diversity Web. *The University of Michigan Museum of Zoology Website*; http://animaldiversity.ummz.umich.edu/anat/tooth_introduction.html. Accessed August 2003.
2. McNeill Alexander, R. *Animals*; Cambridge University Press: New York, 1990.
3. Attenborough, D. *The Life of Mammals*; Princeton University Press: Princeton, 2002.
4. Stevens, C.E.; Hume, I.D. *Comparative Physiology of the Vertebrate Digestive System*, 2nd Ed.; Cambridge University Press: New York, 1995.
5. Anderson, S.; Knox Jones, J., Jr. *Orders and Families of Recent Mammals of the World*; John Wiley and Sons: New York, 1984.
6. Animal Diversity Web. *The University of Michigan Museum of Zoology Website*; http://animaldiversity.ummz.umich.edu/chordata/mammalia.html. Accessed August 2003.

Mammals: Omnivores

Duane E. Ullrey
Michigan State University, East Lansing, Michigan, U.S.A.

M

INTRODUCTION

Omnivores choose food from both the animal and plant kingdoms. These choices may represent preferences, may be opportunistic, or may be dictated by seasonal and site differences in food availability. In any case, omnivores appear to be flexible in their ability to digest and metabolize nutrients from a variety of sources.

NATURAL DIETARY HABITS

When observed for a sufficient period, omnivory is clearly a combination of carnivory and herbivory. The proportions of animal and plant foods consumed by omnivorous mammals are dependent both upon species' preferences and foods available in the environment. Omnivorous species are found in taxonomic orders that include bats, marsupials, pigs, primates, rodents, and Carnivora.[1,2] However, grouping these species in an omnivorous category tends to obscure the diversity of their dietary habits. All are presumed to consume animal tissues of various types, but food selections from the plant kingdom are sometimes used to identify particular specializations. For example, bats that consume insects incidental to (or as supplements to) their principal food—nectar—may be called nectarivores. Primates feeding on insects and small vertebrates but predominantly on plant exudates may be known as gummivores. Rodents feeding on invertebrates and small vertebrates but mainly on seeds may be known as granivores. Although there seem to be no agreed-upon proportions of animal and plant foods that define a mammal as a facultative carnivore, facultative herbivore, or omnivore, it is presumed that if significant amounts of foods are chosen from both the animal and plant kingdoms, the previously mentioned specialized feeders can be classified as omnivores.[2–4] Other, less specialized consumers of animal and plant material (such as American black bears or maned wolves), are usually known simply as omnivores. The diets of American black bears (*Ursus americanus*) are commonly about 75% vegetable matter, such as berries, acorns, beechnuts, wild cherries, grass, herbs, and roots but also include insects, honey, carrion, and mammalian

prey.[1,5] The diets of maned wolves (*Chrysocyon brachyurus*) vary appreciably in their proportions of vegetable and animal matter, depending upon location, but include small rodents, birds, armadillos, invertebrates, fruit (particularly *Solanum lycocarpum*), herbs, and grass.[1,6]

GASTROINTESTINAL MORPHOLOGY AND METABOLIC ADAPTATIONS

The animal and plant foods consumed by omnivores appear to be associated with gastrointestinal structures that are generally more complex than those of carnivores, although not as complex as the compartmentalized gastrointestinal tract of the herbivore.[4] Omnivores tend to have a simple stomach, a small intestine of moderate length, and a cecum and/or colon with a structural configuration allowing some digesta retention, accommodating modest fiber digestion by microorganisms. This arrangement is found in a number of omnivores, including the domestic pig, African warthog, African bush pig, bandicoots, sugar gliders, American opossums, lorises, some lemurs, many New World monkeys, and humans. The chimpanzee, with a gastrointestinal tract similar to that of humans except for more distinct colonic haustrations, is generally considered herbivorous but has been observed hunting and eating termites, small monkeys, and duikers. The omnivorous raccoon and American black bear do not have a cecum, and there is no clear demarcation between the midgut and hindgut.[4]

Due to the variations in food availability with site and season, omnivores must be versatile in their capacity to digest carbohydrates, protein, fat, and fiber and to metabolize the nutrients and energy sources absorbed.[3] Although obligate herbivores, such as cattle, may not require starch- or sugar-digesting enzymes because energy needs can be realized by absorption of volatile fatty acids from microbial fermentation, omnivores at various times must rely on both enzymatic digestion and microbial fermentation of dietary carbohydrates. Likewise, those omnivores that have been studied require dietary supplies of essential amino acids and B-complex vitamins (and possibly vitamin K) because microbial synthesis, as

Encyclopedia of Animal Science
DOI: 10.1081/E-EAS 120019710

occurs in the ruminant, is generally insufficient to meet needs unless coprophagy is practiced. The ability of the tissues of omnivores to synthesize vitamin C varies with species and is not clearly associated with dietary preferences. Moderate amounts of dietary fiber are necessary for gastrointestinal health and normal stool formation.[3]

CONCLUSIONS

Omnivorous mammals, as a group, consume a wide variety of animal and plant foods, dependent upon preference and site and temporal availability. As a consequence, there is considerable diversity among omnivores in their ability to digest and metabolize energy and nutrient sources. This diversity is seen in oral and gastrointestinal morphology and in qualitative and quantitative nutrient requirements.

REFERENCES

1. Nowak, R.M. *Walker's Mammals of the World*, 6th Ed.; Johns Hopkins University Press: Baltimore, 1999; Vols. 1 and 2.
2. Eisenberg, J.F. Feeding and Foraging Categories: Some Size Constraints. In *The Mammalian Radiations: An Analysis of Trends in Evolution, Adaptation, and Behavior*; University of Chicago Press: Chicago, 1981; 247–263.
3. Oftedal, O.T.; Allen, M.E. The Feeding and Nutrition of Omnivores with Emphasis on Primates. In *Wild Mammals in Captivity, Principles and Techniques*; Kleiman, D.G., Allen, M.E., Thompson, K.V., Lumpkin, S., Eds.; University of Chicago Press: Chicago, 1996; 148–157.
4. Stevens, C.E.; Hume, I.D. *Comparative Physiology of the Vertebrate Digestive System*, 2nd Ed.; Cambridge University Press: Cambridge, UK, 1995.
5. Domico, T. *Bears of the World*; Facts on File: New York, 1988.
6. Redford, K.H.; Eisenberg, J.F. *Mammals of the Neotropics*; University of Chicago Press: Chicago, 1992; Vol. 2.

Mammals: Ruminants

Peter J. Van Soest
Cornell University, Ithaca, New York, U.S.A.

M

INTRODUCTION

Ruminants are a diverse group of ungulates having the common factor of chewing their cud, and all have pregastric fermentation that occurs in a rumen. All are herbivores. They include some of the most important domesticated species that contribute economically to agriculture and other uses. Important domesticated groups include cattle, sheep, goats, buffalo, reindeer, and yaks. A closely related group are the camels and camelids. Deer and antelope are the most numerous wild groups.

TAXONOMY AND CLASSIFICATION

Two suborders of the Artiodactyla are the Ruminantia, which include the true ruminants, about 155 species; and the Tylopoda, four species, which include camels and camelids (Table 1). There are four families within the Ruminantia of which the Bovidae are the most numerous. The Bovidae include cattle, sheep, goats, buffaloes, bison, and the diverse African antelope (Table 2).[1–3] Not closely related to the African antelope is the pronghorn antelope of North America. The North American pronghorn antelope is treated as a separate subfamily, Antilocapridae, but may belong in the Bovidae.[3]

The Cervidae—including deer, elk, moose, caribou, and reindeer—are the next largest family and exist in most parts of the world except subsaharan Africa, where antelopes dominate. The Giraffidae have only two species, the giraffe and the okapi. The Tragulidae are small animals, including chevrotains and mouse deer, and may be evolutionarily the most primitive.

The tylopods comprise the camels and camelids. The camels include the one-humped dromedary and the two-humped Bactrian camel. The camelids are Andean and include alpacas, llamas, vicuña, and guanacos. Alpacas and llamas are domesticated, whereas vicuña and guanacos are mostly wild.

FEEDING HABITS AND SIZE

Ruminants range in size from the pygmy Royal antelope, *Neotragus pygmaeus*, at 1–3 kg and only 25 cm (10 inches) at the shoulder, to the giraffe. A large male giraffe can be 5.5 meters (18 ft) tall and weigh 1000 kg. Body size is related to feeding behavior and digestive capacity.[1] Feeding habits (Table 2) of herbivores are classified into selectors: intermediate browsers, intermediate grazers, grazers, and bulk and roughage eaters.[4] The smaller ruminants lack digestive capacity for the slower-digesting grasses, and avoid lower-quality feed by selection of better parts. The very small antelope are largely forest dwellers and live on fruit and leaves. Browsing is selective feeding on bushes and trees. The term intermediate indicates some ability to move between browsing and grazing. The goat is an excellent example of versatility on feeding adaptation, and uses selectivity in both grazing (grass) and browsing. All of the selectors have narrow muzzles, and many have prehensile tongues that aid selection. The bulk and roughage eaters—including cattle, buffalo, and some of the larger antelope—have wider muzzles to facilitate grazing but are less efficient in selection.

EVOLUTION

The Artiodactyla (even-toed herbivores) arose in the Eocene and separated into lines leading to hippos and pigs and then tylopods and ruminants (Fig. 1). Early ruminants were small forest dwellers and began to diversify in the Oligocene. The early ruminants were small forest dwellers lacking horns. Probably in this period the stomach diversified into the ruminal compartments,[5] although fossil evidence is lacking. Fossil evidence for ruminants is limited to bones, teeth, and horns. Upper incisors are missing or reduced to aid grazing. Horns appeared as body sizes became larger. Cervid antlers are deciduous bone, whereas bovid and antilocaprid horns are bone sheathed in keratin, and likely evolved independently. The bovids arose later in the Miocene when the earth's climate became drier and grasslands appeared, allowing grazing behavior to develop.

Cattle, sheep, and goats were domesticated in neolithic times, and the process of domestication greatly altered these species. Humans selected these animals for special characteristics: docility, milk production, wool, and their ability to plow and haul. The result has been specialized

Encyclopedia of Animal Science
DOI: 10.1081/E-EAS 120019711

Table 1 Suborders of Tylopoda and Ruminantia

	No. of genera	No. of species	Examples
Tylopoda			
Camelidae	2	4	Alpaca, llama, camel
Ruminantia			
Tragulidae	2	4	Chevrotain, mouse deer
Giraffidae	2	2	Giraffe, okapi
Antilocapridae	1	1	Pronghorn
Cervidae	17	38	Caribou, deer, elk, moose
Bovidae	54	120	Antelope, bison, buffalo, cattle, gazelle, eland, goat, sheep, yak

(From Refs. 2 and 3.)

breeds, of which the genetic manipulation continues. The modern dominant breeds are on a narrow genetic base, which has spread through the developed world. Some native breeds are endangered. The largest repository of genetic diversity is in Africa. The specialized domestic types are dependent upon humans for their continued survival.[1]

NUMBERS AND USE

There are about 3400 million ruminants in the world, of which 3100 million (90%) are domestic. Cattle are about 1300 million, sheep 1200 million, goats 460 million, and buffalo 130 million. Yaks, camels, camelids, and reindeer together total less than 25 million. The majority of ruminants are in the developing world. Domestic cattle in Canada and the United States are only 6% (~90 million) of the total world cattle. Statistics for wild ruminants are less reliable. The largest populations are in Africa, where there may be 100–500 million. The rest of the world has lower estimates—around 30 million.[1]

Domestic ruminants have been associated with human societies before the dawn of history. While they are mainly used for meat and milk in North America and Europe, they provide more diverse benefits to some other parts of the world. A particular example is the sacred cows in India, where may number several hundred million. The cows provide milk that Hindus consume. They subsist on straw, other cellulosic wastes, garbage, etc., and do not compete for human food resources because 99% of arable land is in cereal crops. Manure is dried into bricks for domestic cooking fuel, which is a billion-dollar industry. They provide tillage and haulage in a country that is oil-poor. Tillage and haulage are important in other parts of Asia and Africa.[1]

Ruminants harvest plant material in rangelands and other untillable lands. This converts otherwise unusable plants into food and useful products. In most of the developing world these systems are extensive and have low efficiency. This is in contrast to the management of beef and dairy animals in North America and Europe,

Table 2 Classification of the family Bovidaea

Subfamily and tribe	Example	Feeding habit[a]
Cephalophinae		
Cephalophini (2)[b]	Duikers	Selector
Antelopinae		
Neotragini (8)	Klipspringer,	Selector
	Suni, Dik-dik,	Selector
	Royal antelope.	Selector
	Oribi	Grazer (selective)
	Steenbok	Intermediate grazer
Antelopini (7)	Gerenuk	Selector
	Gazelles	Intermediate grazer
Hippotraginae		
Hippotragini (3)	Sable and	B+R[c]
	Roan antelope	B+R
	Oryx	B+R
Reduncini (5)	Waterbuck	B+R
	Kob	B+R
	Reedbuck	B+R
Alcephalini (5)	Topi	B+R
	Wildebeest	B+R
	Hartebeest	B+R
	Impala	Intermediate grazer
Bovinae		
Tragelaphini (4)	Kudu	Selector
	Eland bushbuck	Selector
Boselaphini (2)	Nilgai	Selector—intermediate
	4-horned antelope	Selector—intermediate
Bovini (6)	Cattle, yak	B+R
	Buffalo, bison	B+R
Capriniae		
Saigini (2)	Chiru, saiga	Intermediate browser, or grazer
Rupicaprini (4)	Goral, chamois, Mountain goats[d]	Intermediate browser
Ovibovini (1)	Musk ox	Intermediate browser
Caprini (5)	Goats	Intermediate browser
	Sheep, ibex	Grazer (selective)
Antilocaprinae	Pronghorn	Intermediate grazer

[a]Classification according to Hofmann.[4]
[b]Number of genera given in parenthesis.
[c]B+R=bulk and roughage eaters.
[d]Mountain goat may belong in the Caprini.
(Taxonomy according to Refs. 2 and 3.)

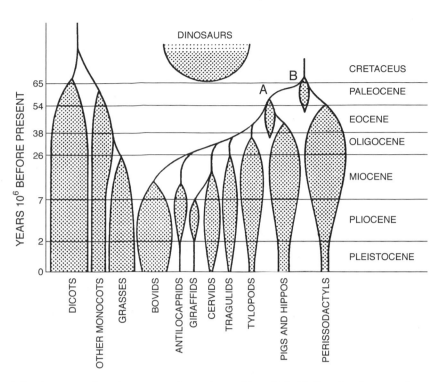

Fig. 1 Appearance and development of angiosperms and ungulates. (From Ref. 1.) Postulated ancestral groups A and B have been questioned. (From Ref. 3.)

where intensive feeding management and animal breeding have produced high levels of production.

DIGESTIVE SYSTEM

The ruminant stomach is four chambered, consisting of rumen, reticulum, omasum, and abomasum.[4] The rumen and reticulum—or the reticulorumen, as they are called—are the primary sites of fermentation. The reticulum is involved in sorting food for rumination and, with the omasum, for regulating selective passage to the abomasum, the site where gastric digestion begins. The tylopods and tragulids lack an omasum.[5] The omasum is less developed in the smaller selectors and most developed in the bulk and roughage eaters.[4]

Young ruminants are essentially monogastric when they are born, and thus dependent on amino acids and B vitamins, which as adults they receive from the ruminal fermentation. The rumen develops and grows and probably receives its organisms from the mother or other ruminants in the months after weaning from salivary slobber and fecal material.

The ruminant system is more efficient in extracting dietary energy because of selective retention, and all of the microbial products must pass through gastric digestion, whereas in a nonruminant hindgut, fermentation loses much of the microbial protein to the feces because it

is postgastric. Compared to nonruminant herbivores, ruminants can exist on smaller intakes of food through higher digestive extraction. This has played a role in herbivore evolution. Ruminants have become the dominant herbivores, replacing many nonruminant herbivores in the oligocene and pleistocene. The rumen probably evolved, in part, as a detoxification system for secondary compounds; this is important in selector and browser species. The effect is to allow the animal access to a wider range of plant foods.[1]

CONCLUSIONS

Most of the world's ruminants are domesticated and represent an important economic resource for food and other benefits for humans. The relationship between humans and domesticated ruminants goes back to prehistory, and the animals have become dependent upon humans. Their contribution derives in part from the ability to convert low-quality fibrous feeds into edible products. Wild ruminants are only about 10% of the world's total and include some endangered species.

ARTICLE OF FURTHER INTEREST

Rumen Microbiology, p. 773

REFERENCES

1. Van Soest, P.J. *Nutritional Ecology of the Ruminant*, 2nd Ed.; Cornell University Press: Ithaca, NY, 1994.
2. Mochi, U.; Carter, T.D. *Hoofed Mammals of the World*; Charles Scribner's Sons: NY, 1971.
3. Gentry, A.W.; Hooker, J.J. The Phylogeny of the Artiodactyla. In *The Phylogeny and Classification of the Tetrapods—Volume 2: Mammals*; Benton, M.J., Ed.; Systematics Association Special, Clarendon Press: Oxford, 1988; Vol. 35B, 235–272.
4. Hofmann, R.R. Evolutionary steps of ecophysiological adaptation and diversification of ruminants: A comparative view of their digestive system. Oecologia **1989**, *78*, 443–457.
5. Hume, I.D.; Warner, A.C.I. The Evolution of Fermentative Digestion. In *Digestive Physiology and Metabolism in Ruminants*; Ruckebusch, Y., Thivend, P., Eds.; M.T.P. Press Ltd.: Lancaster, England, 1980; 665.

Mammary Glands: Developmental Changes

Anthony V. Capuco
United States Department of Agriculture, Agricultural Research Service, Beltsville, Maryland, U.S.A.

Steven Ellis
Clemson University, Clemson, South Carolina, U.S.A.

INTRODUCTION

The mammary gland progresses from the accumulation of a few cells in the embryonic ectoderm to a highly arborescent tubulo-alveolar gland capable of secreting a highly nutritious product for consumption. Throughout this progression, various changes occur during each developmental stage: prenatal, prepubertal, pubertal, gestational, lactational, and mammary involution. Other articles in this encyclopedia describe hormones that regulate mammary development and lactation. However, understanding the general anatomy of the mammary gland and developmental changes that occur during the reproductive life of an animal is critical to appreciating the hormonal regulation and full productive potential of the mammary gland.

GENERAL ANATOMY

In the vast majority of mature mammals, the mammary gland is a compound tubulo-alveolar organ, although exceptions do exist (e.g., among monotremes and platypi). Milk is formed in secretory alveoli and channeled down progressively larger ducts until it reaches the gland and teat cisterns (when present). Milk is removed through the canals or galactophores of the teat or nipple. Collectively, the secretory and ductular tissue present in the mammary gland is referred to as parenchyma. The connective tissues that support the parenchyma are referred to as the stroma, which contains cellular and noncellular (e.g., collagen, elastin) elements. Cells of the stroma are primarily fibroblast; however, stroma also contains immune cells that are resident or transitory, as well as cells of blood vessels and lymphatics.

DEVELOPMENT STAGES

Prenatal Mammogenesis

The earliest stage of recognizable mammary development is the mammary streak, a pair of thickened areas of darkly stained cells on the ventral side of the embryo.[1] The next major developmental stage is the mammary line that appears as a readily discernable area of stratified cells. The mesenchyme underlying the mammary line is notably denser than that seen under the mammary streak. The mammary line defines the orderly arrangement of mammary glands in mature animals. The bovine mammary line does not extend past the umbilicus, whereas porcine and rodent mammary lines extend into the thoracic region. Thus ruminant mammary glands are located only in the inguinal region, but mammae of pigs and rodents are spaced along the ventral surface.

The mammary hillock and bud occur as the next prominent stages of embryonic mammary development. The mammary bud is a compact cluster of cells separated from the underlying mesenchyme by a well-defined basement membrane. The migration of cells that compose the mammary line results in formation of discrete epithelial buds. Cell proliferation and extension of the mammary bud result in formation of the mammary sprout. As it extends, the mammary sprout gradually invades the underlying mesenchyme. Concurrent proliferation by the mesenchyme surrounding mammary buds and sprouts causes distortion of the overlying dermis and formation of teats/nipples. At birth, the mammary gland consists of short, branching ductal elements embedded in a dense stromal matrix underlying the teat.

Prepubertal Development

Prepubertal mammary development is important to the milk-producing ability of an animal, as either excessive energy intake or under-nutrition may impair future milk yield of dairy animals.[2] In dairy cattle, the amount of mammary parenchyma increases nearly 100-fold between birth and puberty. Much of the parenchymal growth involves penetration of the unpopulated mammary fat pad. In the murine mammary gland, structures at the distal extremity of mammary ducts, known as the terminal end buds (TEB), are responsible for this parenchymal invasion. In ruminants, more arborescent structures known as terminal ductal units (TDU) are responsible for parenchymal development.[3] Proliferation of epithelial cells occurs throughout the TDU, with the greatest rates of growth at the periphery. Regardless of the specific architectural features of development, no true alveolar development occurs prepubertally. Instead, there is a progressive increase in the amount and size of ductal structures upon which alveoli will develop during pregnancy. In ruminants, ductal elongation does not reach the limits of the mammary fat pad by the onset of puberty. The teat and gland cisterns developed in concert with the rest of the milk-conducting and-storage structures in the gland. Mice lack a gland cistern and only develop relatively large milk ducts.

Changes Associated with the Estrous Cycle

The primary structural differences between pre- and postpubertal mammary glands are the extent of lateral outgrowths along the ducts and the extent of parenchymal penetration of the fat pad. In rodents, ductal branching occurs primarily after puberty. With the first few estrous cycles, ducts reach the margins of the mammary fat pad, the number of lateral outgrowths increase, and spacing between adjacent ductal outgrowths decreases. In ruminants, branching of the ducts occurs simultaneously with ductal elongation. Thus, in these species the extent of ductal elongation is the primary distinction between pre- and postpubertal mammary gland. Postpubertally, the ductal network becomes increasingly dense and displaces much of the mammary stroma. Occasionally, areas of secretory tissue develop and undergo limited differentiation during estrus, but these areas quickly de-differentiate and become quiescent as the estrous cycle progresses.

Gestational Development and Lactogenesis

Extensive mammary development occurs during gestation, at which time mammary growth is exponential and driven by hormones of pregnancy.[1,2] Epithelial development during pregnancy gives rise to true alveoli that emanate from the distal termini of ducts. The resulting structures have been likened to clusters of grapes, wherein the grapes represent alveoli and the stems represent ducts that drain these secretory units. Alveoli consist of a single layer of epithelial cells overlain and engulfed by a few myoepithelial cells and their processes. During pregnancy, mammary epithelial cells undergo extensive cytological and biochemical differentiation necessary for transition to an organ that is capable of producing copious quantities of milk during lactation.[4] The process of cellular differentiation to a secretory state is termed lactogenesis. The timing of lactogenic events differs among species, but generally some synthesis of milk protein and fat is initiated during early lactogenesis (last trimester of pregnancy), whereas synthesis of α-lactalbumin is more tightly coupled to parturition. Because α-lactalbumin is a cofactor for lactose synthetase, its synthesis is coupled to lactose synthesis. Being the primary osmotically active molecule in milk, lactose synthesis draws water into milk and accounts for the onset of copious milk secretion. These processes are hormonally regulated and timed to meet the nutritional needs of the neonate through interaction of the dam's endocrine system and fetus-placenta during pregnancy and parturition.

Lactation

Rates of cell proliferation and death, along with changes in secretory activity of mammary epithelial cells, account for the shape of the lactation curve.[5,6] In litter-bearing species such as rodents and pigs, considerable mammary growth occurs during early stages of lactation (pre-peak lactation), and may even equal the extent of mammary growth that occurred during gestation. In ruminants, the magnitude of mammary growth during lactation is more limited and appears to be restricted to the first weeks of lactation. In goats, mammary growth during lactation may equal approximately 20% of the mammary growth that occurred during gestation.[1] In dairy cows, nearly all mammary growth occurs prior to parturition, but increased milking stimuli during the first three weeks of lactation may promote postparturient proliferation of mammary epithelium.[7] Increased milk production during early lactation may be due to increased mammary growth and increasing secretory activity per cell until peak lactation. In dairy cows, increased synthetic activity per cell is typically the predominant factor. After peak milk production there is a steady and gradual decline in milk production with advancing lactation. This is due to loss of secretory cells by programmed cell death, with a smaller contribution due to declining secretory activity per cell, particularly during late lactation when concomitant pregnancy may play an important role in the decline of milk yield. Although absolute rates of cell proliferation and death during lactation appear to be very low, the balance of these processes promotes gradual cell loss, but considerable cell turnover during a long lactation.

Involution

Continued removal of milk during lactation is key to maintaining lactation. The milking stimulus elicits a neuroendocrine reflex that causes release of oxytocin from the posterior pituitary, contraction of myoepithelial cells surrounding alveoli, and ejection of milk from the alveoli into the ductal system (milk letdown).[2] In the absence of milk removal, intra-alveolar pressure builds, blood flow to the gland declines, and there is an accumulation of factors that inhibit lactation. The outcome is inhibition of milk secretion and stimulation of pathways for programmed death of epithelial cells.[8] In rodents, mammary regression is rapid and extensive.[9,10]

For dairy cows, a nonlactating period between lactations (dry period) is important for maximizing milk production in the successive lactation. During a typical dry period there is extensive turnover of secretory cells, rather than extensive involution. This is likely because cows are in the final months of gestation when milking is terminated, and mitogenic effects of the hormones of pregnancy counterbalance the death-inducing effects of milk stasis.[7] The replacement of secretory cells during the dry period may be necessary for maximizing milk production in the next lactation. By contrast, goats do not appear to require a dry period between successive lactations. The underlying basis for this is unclear, but may be associated with an ability of goats to replace mammary secretory cells during lactation. This may relate to the endocrine release of growth hormone during milking in goats, but not in cows, as growth hormone appears to enhance mammary cell turnover.[7]

CONCLUSIONS

Understanding the biology and regulation of mammary growth, development, and lactation is important for developing management schemes to maximize production efficiency and enhance animal health. The ability to promote mammary development has positive implications on milk yield for human consumption and for enhancing growth of suckling meat-producing animals. The ability to lengthen lactation and shorten the dry period can enhance lifetime milk production, with the added advantage that animals will need to produce offspring less frequently and therefore be at reduced risk of parturition-related diseases.

The mammary gland—with its postnatal development and cyclical periods of growth, lactation, and involution—provides an exciting area for biological investigation.

REFERENCES

1. Anderson, R.R. Mammary Gland. In *Lactation*; Larson, B.L., Ed.; The Iowa State University Press: Ames, IA, 1985; 3–38.
2. Akers, R.M. *Lactation and the Mammary Gland*; Iowa State Press: Ames, IA, 2002.
3. Capuco, A.V.; Ellis, S.; Wood, D.L.; Akers, R.M.; Garrett, W. Postnatal mammary ductal growth: Three-dimensional imaging of cell proliferation, effects of estrogen treatment and expression of steroid receptors in prepubertal calves. Tissue Cell **2002**, *34*, 9–20.
4. Akers, R.M.; Capuco, A.V. Lactogenesis. In *Encyclopedia of Dairy Sciences*; Roginski, H., Fuquay, J.W., Fox, P.F., Eds.; Academic Press: London, 2002; 1442–1446.
5. Capuco, A.V.; Wood, D.L.; Baldwin, R.; McLeod, K.; Paape, M.J. Mammary cell number, proliferation, and apoptosis during a bovine lactation: Relation to milk production and effect of bST. J. Dairy Sci. **2001**, *84*, 2177–2187.
6. Knight, C.H.; Peaker, M. Mammary development and regression during lactation in goats in relation to milk secretion. Q. J. Exp. Physiol. **1984**, *69*, 331–338.
7. Capuco, A.V.; Ellis, S.; Hale, S.A.; Long, E.; Erdman, R.A.; Zhao, X.; Paape, M.J. Lactation persistency: Insights from mammary cell proliferation studies. J. Anim. Sci. **2003**, *81* (Supplement 3), 18–31.
8. Wilde, C.J.; Knight, C.H.; Flint, D.J. Control of milk secretion and apoptosis during mammary involution. J. Mammary Gland Biol. Neoplasia **1999**, *4*, 129–136.
9. Capuco, A.V.; Akers, R.M. Mammary involution in dairy animals. J. Mammary Gland Biol. Neoplasia **1999**, *4*, 137–144.
10. Holst, B.D.; Hurley, W.L.; Nelson, D.R. Involution of the bovine mammary gland: Histological and ultrastructural changes. J. Dairy Sci. **1987**, *70*, 935–944.

Mathematical Models: Metabolism

C. C. Calvert
R. L. Baldwin
University of California, Davis, California, U.S.A.

INTRODUCTION

Mathematical, computer-based models of metabolism relevant to the animal sciences extend from detailed models of energy input:output relationships established with intact animals, such as those developed by early workers in nutritional energetics in the late 1800s and used in current feeding systems to compute the nutrient requirements of animals, to the detailed models of enzyme kinetics pioneered by Garfinkel and his colleagues in the 1950s. Because of this range of applications, the authors of this presentation had considerable discretion in deciding the focus of this article. We elected to forgo discussion of models of enzymes, individual metabolic pathways, and whole-animal metabolism, except by way of background, and to focus on models of the metabolisms of individual tissues in ruminant animals.

BACKGROUND INFORMATION

In the 1940s, Kleiber recognized that future improvements of equations used to estimate the nutrient requirements of domestic livestock would require advancements in our understanding of nutrient transactions in animals. This led Kleiber and his many colleagues to undertake extensive studies using radiotracers to trace the metabolisms of individual nutrients in animals. The contributions of his and other groups, along with advances in our understanding of metabolic pathways, led to the adoption of the view by many workers in the late 1960s that future models used to estimate the nutrient requirements of producing livestock should be based upon equations that explicitly capture our knowledge of enzymes and the metabolic pathways in animals. Such models, comprising equations that depict our current understanding of animal metabolism and its regulation and that are firmly based on experimental data, are now referred to as mechanistic models. Also, recognition of the dynamic of the rapid changes in metabolism that occur in animals over time and observations that the previous and current physiological and nutritional status of an animal influence metabolic patterns led to the formulation of dynamic equations.

Thus, our focus is on the development of dynamic, mechanistic models of tissue and animal metabolism.

Dynamic, mechanistic models are often developed explicitly to either evaluate the adequacy of current knowledge of the system under investigation for adequacy in the quantitative and dynamic domains, or to extend the interpretation of experimental data. In this context, failures to simulate reality indicate an inadequacy in current understanding of the system and can be used as a guide in the selection, design, and interpretation of critical experiments. Because of this, they are generally considered research models.

ADIPOSE TISSUE

The history of the application of mathematical models in the animal sciences has been reviewed.[1–4] Smith[5] developed a dynamic, mechanistic model of the metabolism of a lactating cow using the KINSYM modeling language of Garfinkel.[6] The model comprised mass action equations depicting individual metabolic processes, and was so large, unwieldy, and overparameterized that it was unstable and required excessive solution times on the computers available at that time. Several major benefits arose from the modeling effort of Smith.[5] The first was the collection and summarization of a great many data from the literature that have proven very useful to subsequent attempts to model ruminate metabolism. A number of the data summaries of Smith[5] were presented by Baldwin.[1] A problem arose during development of the data summaries that illustrates a benefit to research arising from the modeling process. They could not find data on organ and tissue weights in lactating dairy cattle in the literature. This required that these critical data be collected.[7] From this, the impact of changes in relative organ weights with changes in physiological state upon whole-animal energy requirements became apparent. This has since become a major focus in nutritional energetics.[8] This led us to our often-stated view that the modeling process aids in identification of critical experiments and that persons conducting modeling research must have the ability and resources required to collect

Encyclopedia of Animal Science
DOI: 10.1081/E-EAS 120019714

critical data.[9–11] A second benefit was identification of significant gaps in our understanding of metabolism in adipose, liver, and mammary tissues of lactating dairy cows.[1] Another benefit was the initiation of efforts directed to the development of strategies for simplification and formulation of more stable models resulting in less expensive solutions.

The most notable failure of the Smith[5] model was that milk fat percentages increased when the simulated cow was fed diets known to depress milk fat percentage. This failure clearly indicated that our knowledge and representations of adipose tissue metabolism were inadequate. This led to the conduct of a series of studies of adipose tissue metabolism.[12–15] Although we continue to have some problems with fine control of adipose tissue metabolism,[16,17] these studies led to the formation and parameterization of the adipose metabolism elements of our current models of adipose and lactating cow metabolism, in which the problem of simulating milk fat depression due to diet is resolved. As approaches to modeling animal metabolism evolved, mass action equations were replaced with Michaelis–Menten-type equations in recognition of the fact that most metabolic systems exhibit saturation kinetics and the Michaelis–Menten equation form yields more stable numerical solutions. This change impacted our experimental designs. Whereas parameterization of a mass action equation simply requires an estimate of metabolite flow through a pathway at a given substrate concentration, the full relationship between concentrations of substrates and reaction rates is essential to parameterization of equations depicting saturation kinetics. Recognition of the need for these types of data is evident in the publications of Yang and Baldwin[12,13] and Forsberg et al.[18–20] This was also recognized explicitly by Baldwin et al.[11] An advantage to a model arising from the use of Michaelis–Menten-type equations is that these yield more stable computer solutions.

The above-mentioned experimental studies of adipose, mammary, and liver metabolism aided not only parameterization, but also the formulation of tissue model applications. For example, significant interactions among substrates were observed.[12,13,18–20] Prominent among these were large increases in the rates of glucose uptake and oxidation in the presence of increasing concentrations of acetate and vice versa (see Figs. 3.5 and 12.5 in Ref. 1 for an example). This effect of increases in acetate availability on glucose metabolism was ascribed to observed increases in rates of lipogenesis, which in turn increased glucose-6-phosphate (G6P) entry to the pentose cycle to replenish $NADPH_2$ utilized. Equations representing these processes follow.

$$D_{G6P}/dT = U_{G1,G6P} - U_{G6P,Ru} - U_{G6P,F6P} + U_{F6P,G6P}$$

$$U_{G1,G6P} = V_{G1,G6P}/(1.0 + k_{G1,G6P}\{k_{INS}/[INS]\}^{eINS1}$$
$$/[G1] + [G6P]/jG6P)$$

$$U_{G6P,Ru} = V_{G6P,Ru}/(1.0 + k_{G6P,Ru}/[G6P]$$
$$+ k_{NP,Ru}/[NP])$$

$$U_{G6P,F6P} = K_{G6P,F6P} * [G6P]$$

$$U_{F6P,G6P} = K_{F6P,G6P} * [F6P]$$

where D_{G6P}/dT identifies the differential equation for glucose-6-phosphate (G6P), which upon integration tracks changes in the G6P pool and concentration of G6P or [G6P] over time. $U_{G1,G6P}$ depicts glucose transport and phosphorylation of glucose in aggregate; $V_{G1,G6P}$ is the Vmax; $k_{G1,G6P}$ is the apparent affinity for glucose, which is modified by insulin (Fig. 12.4 in Ref. 1) according to ($k_{INS}/[INS]$) the ratio of a constant and insulin concentration that has a reference value of 1.0; the exponent $eINS1$ is a steepness parameter; and [G6P]/jG6P represents the negative feedback of G6P on hexokinase. $U_{G6P,Ru}$ depicts the glucose-6-P dehydrogenase and 6-phosphogluconate dehydrogenase reactions in aggregate; $V_{G6P,Ru}$ is the Vmax, and $k_{G6P,Ru}$ and $k_{NP,Ru}$ are the affinity constants for G6P and NADP (NP), respectively. Ru codes for ribulose-5-P. $U_{G6P,F6P}$ and $U_{F6P,G6P}$ represent the reversible phosphohexoisomerase reaction and $K_{G6P,F6P}$ and $K_{F6P,G6P}$ are mass action coefficients. The key reactions of lipogenesis are:

$$U_{AcCs,Fa} = V_{AcCs,Fa}/(1.0 + k_{AcCs}/[AcCs]$$
$$+ k_{NPH,Fa}/NPH + k_{At,Fa}/At)$$

$$V_{AcCs,Fa} = 14 + V_{AcCs,Fa}/(1.0 + \{k_{ins2}/INS\}^{eINS2})$$

where $U_{AcCs,Fa}$ depicts the conversion of acetyl coenzyme A (AcCs) to fatty acids (Fa); $V_{AcCs,Fa}$ is the variable Vmax; k_{AcCs} is the affinity constant for AcCs; $k_{NPH,Fa}$ is the affinity constant for $NADPH_2$ (NPH); and $k_{At,Fa}$ is the affinity constant for ATP (At). $V_{AcCs,Fa}$ was incorporated as a state variable relatively late in the modeling process. This decision was based on observations in other species indicating that insulin causes the phosphorylation of acetyl-CoA carboxylase in adipose tissue and that the observed 30% increase in rates of lipogenesis in ruminant adipose tissue caused by insulin could not be accounted for solely by its effect on glucose transport. In this equation, $V_{AcCs,Fa}$ and k_{INS2} are scaling factors, and $eINS2$ is an exponent that defines the steepness of the insulin response.

CONCLUSIONS

This article presents a very brief and concise overview of a research program that incorporates experimental and modeling techniques to advance and integrate our understanding of animal metabolism. After introductory remarks directed at setting context and a couple definitions, focus is directed to models of tissue metabolism using ruminant adipose tissue as an example to illustrate the interplay of modeling and experimental research. Equations depicting the interesting interactions among glucose, acetate, and insulin in effecting rates of lipogenesis from acetate, glucose uptake, and pentose cycle flux are presented along with a very brief description of the data required and the reasoning underlying the equation forms adopted. The key observations are that acetate incorporation into fatty acids is highly dependent on the availability (concentration) of glucose and vice versa, and that rates of utilization of both nutrients are enhanced by insulin. The well-known effect of insulin on glucose uptake is not adequate for accurate simulations of observed responses in this ruminant adipose tissue. Thus, provision for the insulin-induced covalent modification of acetyl-CoA carboxylase to a more active form reported for adipose tissue in other species but not yet for ruminants is incorporated to enable the accurate simulations of reality that are the goal and test of research models. The key link between lipogenesis from acetate and increased glucose oxidation is clearly due to increased NADP availability drawing G6P into the pentose cycle as represented in the model.

REFERENCES

1. Baldwin, R.L. *Modeling Digestion and Metabolism*; Chapman & Hall: UK, 1995.
2. Garfinkel, D. A simulation study of the metabolism and compartmentation in brain of glutamate, aspartate, the krebs cycle and related metabolites. J. Biol. Chem. **1966**, *241*, 3918–3925.
3. Black, A.L.; Kaneko, J.J.; Smith, A.H. *A Festschrift Commemorating the Centennial Birth of Max Kleiber*; University of California: Davis, CA, 1993; 16.
4. Thornley, J.H.M.; France, J. Role of Modeling in Animal Production Research and Extension Work. In *Modeling Ruminant Digestion and Metabolism*; Baldwin, R.L., Bywater, A.C., Eds.; Department of Animal Science University of California at Davis: Davis, CA, 1984.
5. Smith, N.E. Quantitative Simulation Analyses of Ruminant Metabolic Functions: Basal; Lactation; Milk Fat Depression. Ph.D. Dissertation; University of California: Davis, CA, 1970.
6. Garfinkle, D. A machine-independent language for the simulation of complex chemical and biochemical systems. Computers Biomed. Res. **1968**, *2*, 31–45.
7. Smith, N.E.; Baldwin, R.L. Effects of breed, pregnancy, and lactation on weights of organs and tissues in dairy cattle. J. Dairy Sci. **1974**, *57*, 1055–1060.
8. Johnson, D.E.; Johnson, K.A.; Baldwin, R.L. Changes in liver and gastrointestinal tract energy demands in response to physiological workload in ruminants. J. Nutr. **1990**, *120*, 649–655.
9. Baldwin, R.L.; Koong, L.J.; Ulyatt, M.J. A dynamic model of ruminant digestion for evaluation of factors affecting nutritive value. Ag. Syst. **1977**, *2*, 255–288.
10. Baldwin R.L., Jr.; Smith, N.A. Molecular Control of Energy Metabolism. In *The Control of Metabolism*; Sink, J.D., Ed.; Pennsylvania State University Press: University Park, PA, 1974; 17–34.
11. Baldwin, R.L.; Forsberg, N.E.; Hu, C.Y. Potential for altering energy partition in the lactating cow. J. Dairy Sci. **1985**, *68*, 3394–3402.
12. Yang, Y.T.; Baldwin, R.L. Preparation and metabolism of isolated cells from bovine adipose tissue. J. Dairy Sci. **1973**, *56*, 350–365.
13. Yang, Y.T.; Baldwin, R.L. Lipolysis in isolated cow adipose cells. J. Dairy Sci. **1973**, *56*, 366–374.
14. Yang, Y.T.; Baldwin, R.L.; Garrett, W.N. Effects of dietary lipid supplementation on adipose tissue metabolism in lambs and steers. J. Anim. Sci. **1978**, *47*, 686–690.
15. Yang, Y.T.; Rohde, J.M.; Baldwin, R.L. Dietary lipid metabolism in lactating dairy cows. J. Dairy Sci. **1978**, *61*, 1400–1406.
16. McNamara, J.P.; Baldwin, R.L. Estimation of parameters describing lipid metabolism in lactation: Challenge of existing knowledge described in a model of metabolism. J. Dairy Sci. **2000**, *83*, 128–143.
17. Baldwin, R.L. History and Future of Modeling Nutrient Utilization in Farm Animals. In *Modelling Nutrient Utilization in Farm Animals*; McNamara, J.P., France, J., Beever, D.E., Eds.; CAB International: Wallingford, UK, 2000; 1–9.
18. Forsberg, N.E.; Baldwin, R.L.; Smith, N.E. Roles of acetate and its interactions with glucose and lactate in cow mammary tissue. J. Dairy Sci. **1984**, *67*, 2247–2254.
19. Forsberg, N.E.; Baldwin, R.L.; Smith, N.E. Roles of glucose and its interactions with acetate in maintenance and biosynthesis in bovine mammary tissue. J. Dairy Sci. **1985**, *68*, 2544–2549.
20. Forsberg, N.E.; Baldwin, R.L.; Smith, N.E. Roles of lactate and its interactions with acetate in maintenance and biosynthesis in bovine mammary tissue. J. Dairy Sci. **1985**, *68*, 2550–2556.

Mathematical Models: Population Dynamics

Michael D. MacNeil
United States Department of Agriculture, Agricultural Research Service, Miles City, Montana, U.S.A.

Matthew A. Cronin
ENTRIX, Inc., Anchorage, Alaska, U.S.A.

INTRODUCTION

The basic function of any model is to represent something in abstract form, simplifying the complex conditions encountered in nature. Because there are many variables that affect populations of animals, P6F0Ba model is often necessary to focus on the most important variables. A model allows the mathematical description of a population by considering a few important and estimable variables and consists of equations that represent assumptions about how a system works in nature. Solving the equations allows predictions or inferences about the natural system. Models of population dynamics have only rarely been used in animal science. However, mathematical models of population dynamics have been used in several other related areas, including human demographics, epidemiology, and wildlife management. This article reviews the basic concepts of mathematical models of population dynamics and related approaches that have been applied in the animal sciences.

POPULATION DYNAMICS

Constrained by certain basic assumptions, a mathematical model can describe salient dynamics of a population.[1] For example, a population may be considered a group of animals of the same species (i.e., potentially interbreeding) in a specific geographic location. A population can interact with others through migration (i.e., immigration and emigration), but in general, members of a population interbreed with each other more frequently than with members of other populations.[2] One of the basic assumptions in most population models is that the members of the population are subject to the same environmental conditions.

In human demographics, epidemiology, and wildlife management applications, models are frequently used to describe and predict the growth of populations. These models consider basic population parameters such as numbers of births, deaths, immigration, and emigration. An example of a simple model describing changes in population size (N) over a time interval (t) is:

$$N_{(t+1)} = N_{(t)} + B - D + I - E$$

where B is the number of births, D is the number of deaths, I is the number of immigrants, and E is the number of emigrants.[1,2] The basic assumptions of the model are simple: numbers increase due to births and immigration, and numbers decrease due to deaths and emigration. Data that could be entered into the model include estimates of births (or recruitment into the adult cohort), death (including harvest or culling), and numbers of animals moving into and out of the population.

Other mathematical models of population growth that are commonly used include those for exponential and logistic growth. Exponential models describe population growth of the type described by Thomas Malthus in his famous description of the geometric increase in population size. Exponential population models rely on estimates of the rate of population growth, which is derived from estimates of individual fecundity. In these models, as the population increases the rate of increase per individual (i.e., fecundity) remains constant, but the increasing number of individuals results in an increasing rate of population growth. In simple terms, exponential growth may be described by the model:

$$N_{(t+k)} = N_{(t)}R^k$$

where $N_{(t)}$ is the population size at time t, $N_{(t+k)}$ is the population size at time $t+k$ (say after k years or generations), and R is the rate of population growth.[1] Note that R can be positive or negative depending on whether a population is increasing or decreasing in size. The exponential model allows prediction of unrestrained population growth. Because populations are actually limited by resource availability, predictions from these models are usually accurate for only a limited amount of time, until the rate of growth decreases.

Encyclopedia of Animal Science
DOI: 10.1081/E-EAS 120019715

The logistic population growth model incorporates information about resource availability and allows for change in the rate of population growth. The standard population logistic equation is:

$$dN/dt = r_{max}N(1 - N/K)$$

where dN is the change in population number, dt is the change in time, r_{max} is the maximum rate of increase, N is the beginning population size, and K is the maximum sustainable population size or carrying capacity.[3] This model is popular in wildlife management applications, but has limitations because it has the unlikely assumption that K remains the same regardless of population size. In many situations, resource availability is dynamic and also affects K.

POPULATION GENETICS

Another common use of mathematical models is in population genetics. For example, basic assumptions of Mendelian inheritance and independent assortment allow modeling the genotypic distribution of a population following random mating without migration, mutation, or selection according to the Hardy-Weinberg equation:

$$(p + q)^2 = p^2 + 2pq + q^2$$

where p and q are frequencies in the parental generation of the A and B alleles respectively, and p^2, $2pq$, and q^2 are the frequencies in offspring of AA, AB, and BB genotypes, respectively.[4,5]

Other population genetics models have been derived that include selection, mutation, or migration rates. For example, the change in allele frequency in a mixed population due to migration from population b into population a can be estimated with:

$$q_{ab} = q_a + (q_b - q_a)m$$

where q_{ab} denotes the allele frequency in the mixed population after migration; q_a and q_b are the allele frequencies in populations a and b, respectively; and m is the fraction of individuals in the mixed population that are immigrants.[4] Additionally, the change in allele frequency due to selection against the BB genotype can be estimated with:

$$q_{(t+1)} = (q_t - sq_t^2)/(1 - sq_t^2)$$

where q_t is the allele frequency population before selection occurs, s is the coefficient of selection against the BB genotype, and $q_{(t+1)}$ is the allele frequency after selection has occurred.[4] If there is no selection against the BB genotype then $s=0$ and if the BB genotype is lethal before the age of reproduction, then $s=1$. If reproduction is compromised, but not eliminated, by the BB genotype, then $0<s<1$.

APPROACHES IN ANIMAL SCIENCES

While mathematical models of population dynamics may not be frequently used in the animal sciences, the concepts contained therein remain important. Reproduction has been frequently identified as the most important contributor to the economic success (or failure) of livestock and poultry production systems. Further, producing replacements for females that are culled is a major source of cost in many production systems. Significant resources have been invested in efforts to increase numbers of live offspring per female per year and functional longevity of breeding females. Finally, models of gene flow allow increased understanding of dissemination of genetic improvement from seedstock breeders to the commercial industries.

Increasing Reproductive Rate

Genetic improvement in reproductive rate has been a common thread through a substantial body of literature in the animal and poultry sciences. Exploiting heterosis through crossbreeding holds immediate promise for increasing reproductive success. Applications include the extensive use of multibreed composite strains for commercial production in poultry and swine, and use of systematic crossbreeding in beef cattle and sheep. The general success of crossbreeding in increasing reproductive rate results from the very substantial contribution of nonadditive gene action to the total genetic variation. Significant progress in increasing reproductive rate has also resulted from selection. Specific selection strategies vary widely among agriculturally important species, with greater progress made in species subject to intensive management and exhibiting greater variability in reproductive rate.

Age Structure of Populations

Lewis[5] and Leslie[6,7] provide classical presentations of an age-structured population, given rates for fecundity and mortality. Extension of these techniques describing the culling process as a Markov chain allows age distributions to be calculated for individuals remaining in a herd and those culled.[8] Culling criteria and, consequently, necessitated replacement rates can be evaluated systematically using this approach for a variety of genetic resources and management systems. Parameters used in describing the age structure of populations can be estimated using survival analysis techniques that overcome issues of censoring and nonnormality of longevity data.[9]

Gene Flow

Following the Leslie matrix models of population dynamics, Hill[10] developed a deterministic mode of gene flow describing how genetic gain from selection in an age-structured population spread through age classes in domestic animal populations. This approach has been used to better understand genetic gain through selection in several applications.

CONCLUSION

Mathematical models are valuable tools to increase understanding of population dynamics. In natural populations, formal applications of classical models of population dynamics provide insight into changes in census numbers and facilitate prediction of future inventories. Modeling census numbers has been less valuable in domestic animal agriculture. However, detailing factors affecting reproductive rate, survival, and gene flow have important ramifications on present and future efficiency of animal production.

REFERENCES

1. Akcakaya, H.R.; Burgman, M.A; Ginzburg, L.R. *Applied Population Ecology*; Sinauer Associates: Sunderland, MA, 1999.
2. Gotelli, N.J. *A Primer of Ecology*; Sinauer Associates: Sunderland, MA, 2001.
3. Caughley, G.; Sinclair, A.R.E. *Wildlife Ecology and Management*; Blackwell Scientific Publications: Cambridge, MA, 1994.
4. Falconer, D.S. *Introduction to Quantitative Genetics*, 3rd Ed.; John Wiley and Sons: New York, 1989.
5. Lewis, E.G. On the generation and growth of a population. Sankhya **1942**, *6*, 93–96.
6. Leslie, P.H. On the use of matrices in certain population mathematics. Biometrika **1945**, *33* (3), 183–212.
7. Leslie, P.H. Some further notes on the use of matrices in population mathematics. Biometrika **1948**, *35* (3&4), 213–245.
8. Azzam, S.M.; Azzam, A.M.; Nielsen, M.K.; Kinder, J.E. Markov chains as a shortcut method to estimate age distributions in herds of beef cattle under different culling strategies. J. Anim. Sci. **1990**, *68* (1), 5–14.
9. Ducrocq, V.; Quaas, R.L.; Pollak, E.J.; Casella, G. Length of productive life of dairy cows. 1. Justification of a Weibull mode. J. Dairy Sci. **1988**, *71* (11), 3061–3070.
10. Hill, W.G. Prediction and evaluation of response to selection with overlapping generations. Anim. Prod. **1974**, *18*, 117–139.

Mathematical Models: Production Systems

Michael D. MacNeil
United States Department of Agriculture, Agricultural Research Service, Miles City, Montana, U.S.A.

INTRODUCTION

The processes involved in producing palatable and nutritious food for people from livestock and poultry are numerous, complex, and interactive. Traditional experimentation has resulted in a tremendous quantity of detailed, but relatively fragmented, information about these processes. Integrating this information to develop best practices for application in managing agricultural production systems is a daunting task. When approached in an ad hoc manner, this integration will very possibly be flawed and the resulting management practices far from optimal. Further, experimental evaluation of the proposed practices is hampered by the fact that commitment of resource to the management strategy itself constitutes an experimental unit and sufficient replication for testing hypotheses is difficult to obtain. In attempting to overcome these problems, mathematical models have been developed and used to guide management of agricultural production systems.

BACKGROUND

The concepts and general techniques used in developing mathematical models of production systems are not new. Rather, they stem from systems analysis approaches applied to military and industrial problems almost a half century ago.[1] Forrester[2] is a classic treatise on the principles of systems analysis that remains relevant today and Spedding[3] provides an entry point to the use of systems analysis in addressing agricultural problems. Optimization and simulation are two fundamental approaches that have been applied in modeling livestock production systems. Linear programming has been a widely used optimization technique in addressing problems from ration formulation to enterprise analysis. The fundamental concept of optimization is to derive a maximum (or minimum) yield from a production system subject to existing constraints on the system. From a managerial perspective, optimization approaches may be philosophically consistent with maximizing profit or minimizing cost. However, optimization approaches have been largely superceded by simulation to describe the essential elements of a system and their relationships to each other without respect to a specific outcome. In developing and using simulation models, the concern is that each of several variables characterizing the state of the system has values within a tolerable degree of error relative to those observed in nature. Once a model has been built, it is analogous to a scientific hypothesis of the way in which the system works. The truth of this hypothesis is tested by: 1) verifying the model's ability to reproduce the data used in its construction and 2) demonstrating its ability to predict outcomes of independent trials.

Models may be organized on any of several levels depending upon their intended use.[4] Ordinarily, models of production systems are formulated at the level of process within individual animals (e.g., digestion and tissue deposition) or with a greater degree of aggregation (e.g., whole animals, herds, or flocks). The level of organization is most often related to the intended scope of the inferences to be made from the model. For instance, models to be used in planning livestock production systems as components of national economies are generally more highly aggregated than models for evaluating responses of individual animals to varying levels of ingested energy. Depending on whether or not the simulation reflects random fluctuations in component processes, models may be either stochastic or deterministic, respectively.

APPLICATIONS OF PRODUCTION SYSTEM MODELS

Numerous models of production systems have since been developed and used in a wide variety of applications relevant to livestock production systems. A number of applications of mathematical models of production systems are described briefly in order to provide insight into the potential of this technology for investigations in the animal sciences.

Planning Livestock Production in Developing Countries

Originating with the global planning exercise—Agriculture Toward 2000[5,6]—Hallam[7] initiated simulation

Encyclopedia of Animal Science
DOI: 10.1081/E-EAS 120019716

experiments to evaluate and identify potential constraints on livestock numbers, herd composition, and use of feed resources in Sudan, Pakistan, and Columbia. The approach used was modular, with representations of the complete livestock industry built up as aggregations of the models of component systems. Only within the feed accounting component was the entire industry considered simultaneously. This structure had advantages in being able to manipulate any component system or combination of component systems in isolation and of facilitating analysis of changes in the livestock sector through time. These case studies serve to highlight constraints imposed by available feed resources on livestock production in developing countries.

Disease severely limits livestock production in many developing countries. Both stochastic and deterministic models of the relationship between level of disease resistance and production under constant infection pressure were developed and used to evaluate strategies to improve resistance to trypanosomosis.[8] These models illustrate that resistance to disease will increase when selection is based only on the level of production. Further, only when heritability for resistance is low does selection on predicted production using quantitative trait loci for resistance result in greater gain for resistance and observed production than mass selection on observed production.

Nutrition

Mathematical models of nutritional requirements for all species of livestock and poultry are widely accepted and used in managing feeding systems. These models hold the promise of continued increases in efficiency of feed utilization and reductions in nutrient excretion into the environment. More highly-aggregated models, such as the National Research Council model for nutrient requirements of beef cattle,[9] provide end-users ready access to an extensive body of knowledge pertinent to the feeding of domestic animals. More mechanistic models may provide a deeper understanding of animal requirements, performance, and feed utilization.[10]

Production of ruminant livestock by grazing indigenous grasslands is thought to be one of the most sustainable of all agricultural production systems.[11] Relative to the calculation of nutrient requirements and prediction of performance in confinement, models for grazing[12] are complicated by abiotic and spatial factors affecting primary production and by foraging behavior. The increased breadth of domain opens an opportunity to address more varied questions relevant to livestock production systems, but potentially at some sacrifice in resolution.

Using Genetic Resources

Exploiting genetic differences among breeds and capturing heterosis are two fundamental tactics to improve efficiency and profitability of livestock and poultry production. The multifaceted nature of the breed utilization problem and the extensive resources needed for experimental evaluation of alternative combinations have motivated extensive use of mathematical models of herds or animals to derive recommendations.[13–15]

A logical extension of selection among breeds leads to selection among individuals within breeds. Mathematical models of production systems place individual phenotypes in the context of a production system. Partial derivatives of profit with respect to individual phenotypes provide relative economic values that can be used as weighting factors for genetic predictions in a selection index.[16,17] This strategy leads to a consistent and objective means of selection for improved profitability.

Decision Support Systems

Mathematical models coupled with databases containing necessary, but often difficult-to-access, input information and with a straightforward user-interface can provide individual producers insight into their production system that was previously unavailable. These applications of mathematical models allow individuals to pose and answer what-if questions in a matter of minutes rather than over the course of years, as would be required to address the same questions using the actual production system. Additionally, more questions can be addressed in the computer than would be feasible to pose otherwise. Using decision support systems could help producers avoid costly mistakes or missed opportunities that otherwise might not be recognized. The Decision Evaluator for the Cattle Industry (DECI) developed by the Agricultural Research Service in conjunction with the National Cattlemen's Beef Association[18] and GRAZPLAN[19] are examples of this use of mathematical models of cattle and sheep production systems.

CONCLUSION

Mathematical models are valuable tools to increase understanding of production systems. Using models, investigation of factors influencing the behavior of systems can be conducted in a more timely and comprehensive manner and at less cost than if the systems were manipulated directly.

REFERENCES

1. Stockfish, J.A. *The Intellectual Foundations of Systems Analysis*; Rand Corp.: Santa Monica, CA, 1987. Publ. No. P-7401.
2. Forrester, J.W. *Principles of Systems*; MIT Press: Cambridge, MA, 1968.
3. Spedding, C.R.W. *The Biology of Agricultural Systems*; Academic Press Inc.: New York, 1975.
4. MacNeil, M.D.; Harris, D.L. Highly aggregated simulation models. J. Anim. Sci. **1988**, *66* (10), 2517–1523.
5. FAO. *Agriculture: Toward 2000*; FAO Conference 20th Session, FAO: Rome, 1979.
6. FAO. *Agriculture: Toward 2000*; FAO: Rome, 1981.
7. Hallam, D. Livestock Development Planning: A Quantitative Framework. In *Centre for Agricultural Strategy Paper 12*; Univ. of Reading: UK, 1983.
8. van der Waaij, E.H. Breeding for Trypanotolerance in African Cattle. Doctoral Thesis; Wageningen Institute of Animal Sciences: Wageningen, The Netherlands, 2001.
9. National Research Council. *Nutrient Requirements of Beef Cattle*, 7th Revised Ed.; National Academy Press: Washington, DC, 1996.
10. Fox, D.G.; Barry, M.C.; Pitt, R.E.; Roseler, D.K.; Stone, W.C. Application of the Cornell net carbohydrate and protein model for cattle consuming forages. J. Anim. Sci. **1995**, *73* (1), 267–277.
11. Heitschmidt, R.K.; Short, R.E.; Grings, E.E. Ecosystems, sustainability, and animal agriculture. J. Anim. Sci. **1996**, *74* (6), 1395–1405.
12. Wright, J.R.; Skiles, W. *SPUR: Simulation of Production and Utilization of Rangelands. Documentation and User Guide*; USDA–ARS, 1987. ARS 63.
13. Minyard, J.A.; Dinkel, C.A. *Crossbreeding Beef Cattle: A Guide for Using Simumate*; Coop. Ext. Serv. South Dakota State Univ.: Brookings, SD, 1974.
14. Blackburn, H.D.; Cartwright, T.C. Description and validation of the Texas A&M sheep simulation model. J. Anim. Sci. **1987**, *65* (2), 373–386.
15. Sanders, J.O.; Cartwright, T.C. A general cattle production systems model. 1. Description of the model. Agric. Syst. **1979**, *4*, 217–227.
16. Barwick, S.A. B-OBJECT: A PC-Program to Derive Economic Weights for Beef Cattle. In *Design of Livestock Breeding Programs*; Fewson, D., James, J.W., Nitter, G., Kinghorn, B.P., Barwick, S.A., Graser, H.-U., Savicky, J., Eds.; Animal Genetics and Breeding Unit, The University of New England: Armidale NSW, Australia, 1993.
17. MacNeil, M.D.; Newman, S.; Enns, R.M.; Stewart-Smith, J. Relative economic values for Canadian beef production using specialized sire and dam lines. Can. J. Anim. Sci. **1994**, *74* (2), 411–417.
18. Hardin, B. DECI: Information age tool for the cattle industry. Agricultural Research **1998**, *46* (5), 16–19.
19. Donnelly, J.R.; Moore, A.D.; Freer, M. GRAZPLAN: Decision support systems for Australian grazing enterprises. I. Overview of the GRAZPLAN project and a description of the MetAcess and LambAlive DDS. Agric. Sys. **1997**, *54* (1), 57–76.

Mating Systems

Brian Kinghorn
University of New England, Armidale, Australia

INTRODUCTION

We control the selection and mating of domestic livestock in order to generate and exploit favorable genetic effects. This is an artificial process—we disrupt what may happen naturally in order to help meet our goals—and yet we can learn from the patterns of evolution of sex and mating systems that we see in natural populations.

An equal sex ratio has usually evolved, because each animal has one father and one mother. The sexes are thus, on average, equally prolific, but biology dictates that females are much more consistent. Males compete hard to generate progeny, with much more variable results. Females also compete with each other for high-quality mates to help project their genes into future generations, and the best females are more likely to attract the best males. We can observe such battles within and between the sexes throughout nature. These struggles serve the interests of genes and the animals that host them. Under domestication, the focus is shifted to agriculture and to the genes, animals, and mating systems that can best serve that purpose.

MATING SYSTEMS TO GENERATE MERIT

With the relative lack of investment by males in the raising of their progeny, they can concentrate on competing to father many progeny. This has sometimes given rise to extremely high potential fecundity in males, a situation we can exploit through mating systems that allocate many females to the few best males (Fig. 1). Assortative mating systems that allocate the best selected females to the best selected males give some benefits beyond the progeny generation, because the distribution of genetic merit is widened in the progeny generation.

We can boost the effective fecundity of males with artificial insemination. In dairy cattle, a single bull can father over a million progeny. This makes such individual bulls of critical value, and we must make every opportunity to select the best bulls. This can be done by starting in the previous generation with a mating strategy designed to produce elite young bulls, achieved by mating the very best cows in the land to the best available bulls. The

resulting young bulls are progeny-tested for their milk traits, and the very best become the new champions. This is then a two-tier mating system with four pathways for genes to flow through—the elite tier with MM (males to breed males) and FM, and the commercial or base tier with MF and FF.

Mating systems that promote the use of the same males across different farms and counties give us power to identify the average genetic merit of animals born in these different farms and countries. This means that we can make extra genetic progress by more confidently exploiting the genetic inventory that we have.

We can also boost the fecundity of females using multiple ovulation and embryo transfer (MOET). There is more potential to make gains from boosting female fecundity. If we were to double fecundity in both sexes, we would half the size of the shaded areas in Fig. 1, and it can be seen that this would give more improvement in females than in males, despite the wider distribution of male estimated breeding values (EBVs).

However, when we use MOET, the ideal mating system may change. Females become more important than they are in the four-pathway mating system. We can breed fewer females to support the same herd size, so that selection pressure can be higher. But we can also ''turn them over'' more quickly—normally a cow has to be kept for two or three mating years just to be able to replace herself in the herd, but under MOET she can be used just once, reducing generation interval and speeding up progress per year.

It turns out that with this higher fecundity in both sexes, the normal two-pathway mating system (just two classes of animal—M and F) is predicted to be more effective, with opportunistic use of elite progeny-tested sires available from existing four-pathway schemes. Generation intervals can be decreased dramatically by use of gametes from sexually immature animals (Fig. 2). Such practices have animal welfare implications that cannot be addressed here.

In Vitro Mating Systems

Novel mating systems become possible with in vitro fertilization (IVF). This happens naturally in some

Encyclopedia of Animal Science
DOI: 10.1081/E-EAS 120019717

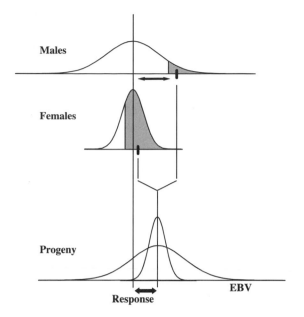

Fig. 1 Distributions of perceived genetic merit (or estimated breeding value, EBV) in male and female parents and their progeny. Selected parents are shaded. We allocate many females to each male, so that we can select fewer, more elite males. We can capitalize on this by gathering more information on males, giving more power to identify the best and worst males, as reflected in their wider genetic distribution.

animals, notably fish. We have the opportunity to mate each female with many males, as well as vice versa. One benefit is a richer pedigree structure, with maternal half-sib families as well as paternal half-sib families, increasing the accuracy of genetic evaluation. With use of surrogate mothers in mammals, we can also help avoid the confounding effects of maternal environment. These

higher accuracies help to reduce the compromises in using juvenile mating systems.

However, the key promise for juvenile mating systems is the advent of marker-assisted selection (MAS). If we can get reasonable genetic evaluations from DNA tests, then we can contemplate very juvenile systems, even to the extent of developing cycles of in vitro sexual propagation, including meiosis and zygote formation, with selection among zygotes on genetic markers. Selection among gametes on marker information would be even more powerful, together with appropriate in vitro mating systems, especially if we target the generation of specific genotypes across many loci.

Such developments are currently well out of sight. However, we will soon need mating systems to target the generation of specific genotypes across many loci in normal MAS schemes. This becomes more evident as we discover that interaction between genes is important. These mating systems will need to handle nonadditive effects; thus they relate to mating systems that exploit heterosis.

MATING SYSTEMS TO EXPLOIT HETEROSIS

In many cases, the value of an animal's genes to its progeny depends on the genes contributed by its mate. This is true for nonlinear merit traits, for which corrective mating systems can be used. However, the classic case is that the value of an animal may be higher if its mates are of a different breed, because the progeny will be more heterozygous and will exhibit heterosis.

Three types of crossbreeding system can be defined, according to the incidence of purebreds in the breed pedigree (Table 1). Fully structured mating systems can

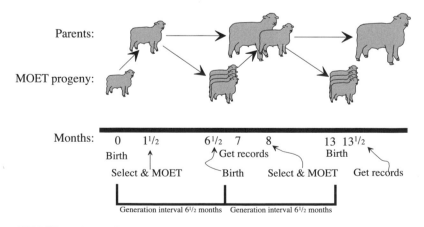

Fig. 2 A juvenile sheep MOET life cycle. To decrease generation interval so dramatically, individuals must be selected on information from the parental generation.

Table 1 Mating systems that exploit heterosis

Mating system type	Definition	Heterosis expression	Running cost	Example
Fully structured	Short path to purebreds on both sides of the pedigree	High	High	Multiple-breed crosses in poultry and pigs
Semi-structured	Short path to purebreds on male side of the pedigree	Moderate	Moderate	Rotational crosses in temperate beef
Unstructured	Short path to purebreds on neither side of the pedigree	Low	Low	Composite breeds in tropical beef

generate maximal heterosis, but with loss of structure this becomes impossible. However, more structure means more cost, because purebreds need to be maintained to feed into the system. This is more important for low-fecundity species, as a higher proportion of breeding females need to be in upstream populations.

Variations on classic crossbreeding systems can be found that fit better with the prevailing farming system. An example proposed by Andrew MacTaggart (personal communication) is shown in Fig. 3. At equilibrium, the cows in the commercial herd contain predominantly Brahman genes, even for a moderate level of within-herd female replacement. This is largely because the sires of imported heifers are pure Brahman, and their dams are part Brahman. High Brahman content makes for good mothering ability in the tough tropical environment that prevails. In contrast, the growing stock in the commercial herd typically contains mostly British genes, at a level that depends on migration rates, improving growth and product quality in slaughter stock. This system overcomes the fluctuations in breed content that affect classic rotational mating systems[1] and better exploits the specific merits of different breed types.

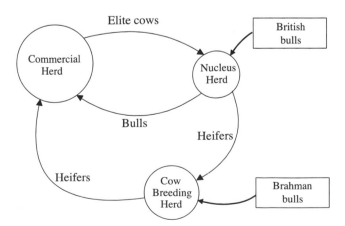

Fig. 3 A custom mating system that exploits the specific merits of different breed types.

MATING SYSTEMS TO AVOID INBREEDING

Inbreeding is the mating of relatives. Inbred animals have a certain probability of inheriting the same gene variant from each parent, identical by descent from a common ancestor. This probability is the inbreeding coefficient, F. Inbreeding causes reduced merit, expression of recessive defects, and reduction of genetic variation within lines.

The obvious way to avoid inbreeding is to avoid mating relatives. However, this is really only effective in the following generation, unless we can import unrelated stock of sufficient genetic merit on a regular basis. For the longer term, we should avoid using few animals as parents—a practice that inevitably leads to inbreeding. In some cases, such as a threatened gene pool, this is unavoidable, and the inevitable can be delayed by planning matings over a few generations to avoid mating relatives. However, this is not appropriate in genetic improvement programs, due to loss of selection differential.

There is a balance required here, as few parents give more selection differential, yet more inbreeding. The solution is to optimize the number of matings allocated to each breeding candidate to achieve a targeted combination of genetic gain and rate of inbreeding.[2] When applied, such a scheme gives more matings to animals of higher genetic merit, and to fewer related ''new blood'' animals.

TACTICAL MATING SYSTEMS

This entry has covered several motivating factors for the design of a mating system—genetic gains, heterosis, inbreeding, exploiting genetic markers, use of reproductive boosting, etc. However, many applications require simultaneous attention to several such factors, plus costs and logistical constraints. These can all be handled in a tactical mating system. Tactical means that the mating system is fully specified in terms of the actual animals available to be used. The outcome is the result of targeting all these factors in a single objective function.[3] This approach is finding increasing use in the key domestic species.

CONCLUSION

Animal breeding is implemented by choice of animals to use as parents, and the pattern of mate allocation. These simple actions aim to exploit or satisfy a wide range of issues—technical, cost, and logistical issues. Mating systems embody this selection and mate allocation, and aim to generate and exploit genetic improvement. This can be achieved either by following design rules or by

letting a tactical system set the design as it seeks the most effective outcome.

REFERENCES

1. Nicholas, F.W. *Introduction to Veterinary Genetics*, 2nd Ed.; Iowa State Press, 2003.
2. Meuwissen, T.H.E. Maximising the response of selection with a predefined rate of inbreeding. J. Anim. Sci. **1997**, *75*, 934–940.
3. Kinghorn, B.P.; Meszaros, S.A.; Vagg, R.D. Dynamic Tactical Decision Systems for Animal Breeding. In *Proceedings of the 7th World Congress on Genetics Applied to Livestock Production*; Montpellier, France, Aug 19–23, 2002; Vol. 33, 179–186. [CD-ROM communication no. 23–07. ISBN 2–7380–1052–0].

Meat Quality in Carcasses: Visual Appraisal

Mark F. Miller
Wendy C. Palmore
Texas Tech University, Lubbock, Texas, U.S.A.

INTRODUCTION

Meat quality is an important aspect of the meat industry today because it defines the total eating experience a consumer will likely have. Meat quality refers to the palatability of meat, including tenderness, juiciness, and flavor. Consumers correlate their level of acceptance of their cooked meat products with these three main factors. The relationship between consumer acceptance and meat quality makes it highly valuable to assess the quality grades of beef carcasses prior to being marketed. Therefore, the sole purpose of applying U.S. Department of Agriculture (USDA) Quality Grades is to detect quality differences that will affect the eating quality of meat from the carcasses. USDA Quality Grades are determined for carcasses based on visual appraisal of two distinct factors: physiological maturity of the carcass and intramuscular fat (marbling) contained within the ribeye. Therefore, this article will discuss the visual appraisal of these quality factors.

UNITED STATES STANDARDS FOR GRADES OF CARCASS BEEF

The USDA and its subdivisions publish the grade standards for the purpose of standardizing the USDA Quality and Yield Grades of carcasses across all marketing sectors. The standards were first developed in 1916 and have been revised and amended throughout the years based on industry and scientific opinion, in order to improve the consistency and uniformity of the grades.[1]

In June 1965, a revision was made requiring all carcasses to be ribbed prior to assessing their USDA Quality Grade.[1] Later, in October 1980, a 10-minute minimum period was required between carcass ribbing and presentation for grading to allow for more uniform and accurate grading.[1] The standards identify eight designations for USDA Quality Grade, including Prime, Choice, Select, Standard, Commercial, Utility, Cutter, and Canner.[1] Additionally, the standards recognize five maturity groups that carcasses are categorized into, including A, B, C, D, and E.[1]

MARBLING

Marbling, or intramuscular fat, is defined as flecks of fat found within the muscle that relate positively to consumer evaluations of juiciness, tenderness, and flavor.[2] Marbling significantly improves overall consumer satisfaction ratings.[3] Marbling is visually determined by evaluating the amount of flecks within the surface of the ribeye muscle where the carcass is split between the 12th and 13th ribs.[4] There are ten degrees of marbling that can be assigned to the carcass, including Very Abundant, Abundant, Moderately Abundant, Slightly Abundant, Moderate, Modest, Small, Slight, Traces, and Practically Devoid, with Very Abundant being the highest degree of marbling and Practically Devoid being the lowest degree.[4] Photographs of these marbling degrees, published by the National Cattlemen's Beef Association, serve as the standard used by the USDA for visual appraisal of marbling scores (Fig. 1).

MATURITY

The maturity of the carcass has shown to be highly correlated to tenderness of the meat upon cooking.[5] As cattle mature, they become tougher due to an increased amount of connective tissue and less soluble collagen.[5] Therefore, the maturity of the carcass is considered in determining a USDA Quality Grade. Maturity is divided into two categories: skeletal maturity and lean maturity. The more important of the two is the skeletal or bone maturity, meaning that when there is a difference between the two factors, the overall maturity score is in the direction of the bone.[1] However, in no instance may the overall maturity score vary from the skeletal maturity score by more than 100.[1]

Encyclopedia of Animal Science
DOI: 10.1081/E-EAS 120028186

619

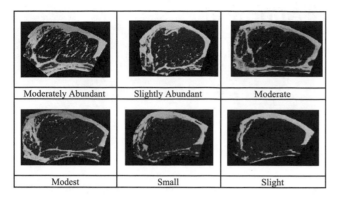

| Moderately Abundant | Slightly Abundant | Moderate |
| Modest | Small | Slight |

Fig. 1 Reproductions of the official USDA marbling photographs prepared by the National Cattlemen's Beef Association for the U.S. Department of Agriculture. (*View this art in color at www.dekker.com.*)

Skeletal Maturity

The skeletal maturity of a carcass is visually determined by the amount of ossification in the sacral, lumbar, and thoracic vertebrae of the carcass (Fig. 2).[4] Ossification is defined as the process by which cartilage progresses into bone.[4] Animals typically age from the hindquarter to the forequarter and would therefore reveal ossification in the sacral vertebrae first, and eventually in the thoracic vertebrae.[4] The five maturity groups correlate with the age of the animal as follows: A (9–30 months), B (30–42 months), C (42–72 months), D (72–96 months), and E (greater than 96 months).[4] In A-maturity, or very young carcasses, the cartilage at the ends of the thoracic vertebrae shows no ossification, the lumbar vertebrae all reveal some cartilage, and there is distinct separation in the sacral region.[1] Also, in a young animal the vertebrae appear red and porous, and the rib bones appear in a curvature configuration and still have a red tinge to them. However, as the animal ossifies or ages, the vertebral column appears very different. In more mature carcasses, ossification is notable at the ends of the thoracic vertebrae, the cartilage at the tips of the lumbar vertebrae is completely ossified, and the sacral vertebrae are completely fused, with no separation.[4] Additionally, the bone appears hard, flinty, and white.[1] Furthermore, the ribs become whiter in color and wider and flatter in appearance.[1]

Lean Maturity

The lean, or flesh, of the animal undergoes physiological changes as the animal matures, just as the skeleton does. However, the change in lean color is a more noted quality

issue with consumers because they purchase their meat products on the basis of appearance. If a steak in a supermarket is dark in color, which is different from the preferred bright, cherry-red color of beef, they will not be as likely to purchase the product. For this reason, lean maturity is an important factor in determining an overall USDA Quality Grade. In a young A-maturity carcass, the lean typically has a fine texture and is a light, youthful, cherry-red color.[1] However, as the lean matures it appears dark red in color and coarse-textured.[1] It is important to note that the U.S. standards for quality grades relating to lean maturity refer only to changes in lean color due directly to changes in maturity of the animal. This is important because a condition called "dark cutting beef" can occur, causing the meat to appear very dark in color.[4] However, this condition is due to lack of glycogen in the muscle at time of slaughter, not due to the maturity of the animal.[4] This condition does not effect the palatability of the carcass in a negative way, but actually creates a more tender, juicy product with slight soapy off-flavors. Carcasses identified as dark cutters are therefore quality-graded according to their maturity and marbling scores to obtain a USDA Quality Grade. The final quality grade may be reduced by as much as one full grade because of the reduced acceptance of dark beef by consumers.[1]

RELATIONSHIP BETWEEN MARBLING, MATURITY, AND USDA QUALITY GRADE

A USDA Quality Grade is determined by the correlation between marbling and maturity as shown in Fig. 3. For instance, only carcasses of A and B maturity are eligible for the Prime, Choice, Select, and Standard USDA Quality Grades.[4] The chart also reveals that as maturity progressively increases, carcasses must have increasingly higher degrees of marbling to continue to grade in their respective grades.

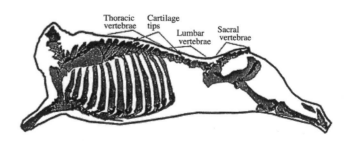

Fig. 2 Location of cartilage and vertebrae for determination of maturity. (From Ref. 4.)

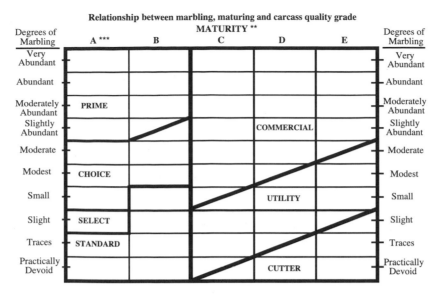

Fig. 3   Relationship between marbling, maturity, and carcass quality grade. (From Ref. [4].)

CONCLUSION

USDA Quality Grades are determined through visual appraisal of the lean and skeletal maturity of the carcass, as well as the degree of marbling. Both factors have been associated with obtaining a USDA Quality Grade because of their high correlation to tenderness, juiciness, and flavor of the meat. Consumer acceptance is of great concern in the meat industry today, consequently making the assessment of USDA Quality Grades important as well. Although many factors other than marbling and maturity (e.g., diet and genetics) might affect the overall palatability of the meat, the degree of marbling and maturity may be visually determined on the carcass without any further background information about the animal. Thus, the U.S. standards recognize marbling and maturity as the measures used to assess USDA Quality Grades.

REFERENCES

1. Anonymous. *United States Standards for Grades of Carcass Beef*; US Department of Agriculture, Agricultural Marketing Service, Livestock and Seed Division: Washington, DC, 1997; 1–16.

2. Smith, G.C. Relationship of USDA quality grades to palatability of cooked beef. J. Food Qual. **1987**, *10* (2), 269–286.

3. Savell, J.W. National consumer retail beef study: Palatability evaluations of beef loin steaks that differed in marbling. J. Food Sci. **1987**, *52* (3), 517–519.

4. Burson, D.E. *Quality and Yield Grades for Beef Carcasses*; North Central Regional Extension Publication # 357: Lincoln, NE. http://www.ianr.unl.edu/pubs/Beef/rp357.htm (accessed December 2003).

5. Fry, G. *Quality Grades*; Bovine Engineering and Consultion: Rosebud, AR. http://www.bovineengineering.com/quality_grades.html (accessed December 2003).

Meat Quality in Cattle: Live Evaluation

Mark F. Miller
Jason H. Byrd
Texas Tech University, Lubbock, Texas, U.S.A.

INTRODUCTION

Meat quality can be identified as those factors that affect the palatability of tenderness, flavor, and juiciness of meat products. Meat quality evaluations in the live animal try to predict eating quality and overall consumer satisfaction of meat products. The United States Department of Agriculture (USDA) established a set of standards commonly referred to as USDA quality grades, which predict the expected beef meat quality. These USDA quality grades take into account the amount of intramuscular fat and the overall maturity of the animal. Quality grades are administered by USDA graders after the animals have been harvested and chilled at least 18 hours. Quality grades include Prime, Choice, Select, and Standard for young cattle (A or B maturity), and Commercial and Utility for mature cattle (C, D, or E maturity). Prime and Choice are the target grades, and are used to designate beef with the highest eating qualities.

Cattle buyers are faced with the tremendous challenge of predicting these USDA quality grades on a live basis. If the quality grade of an animal is correctly estimated, then the price will be more fair for both the buyer and seller. This requires tremendous skill and a great deal of experience.

INTRAMUSCULAR FAT EVALUATION

Breed Type

One of the most influential factors that influences quality grade in cattle is breed type. Different breeds of cattle deposit fat at different rates. English cattle in general (Angus, Red Angus, Hereford, Shorthorn) deposit intramuscular fat at the fastest rate and are commonly associated with higher quality grades. Dairy breeds also tend to grade well because intramuscular fat is related to milk butterfat and total milk production. On the other hand, Exotics (Charolais, Limousin, Chianina) and *Bos indicus* cattle (Brahman, Bonsmara, Tulie) deposit low levels of marbling.

Fat Thickness

Fat thickness is the measurement of subcutaneous fat opposite the 12th rib, and relates highly to meat quality. Dairy cattle require a minimum of 0.2 inch of backfat to reach the Select grade and 0.35 inch to grade Low Choice. English cattle typically need 0.4 inch to grade Low Choice. Exotic cattle generally need 0.4 inch to grade Select, and 0.5 inch to reach Low Choice. *Bos indicus* cattle require 0.6 inch of backfat to grade Low Choice.

Muscle/Cattle Thickness

Muscle thickness and cattle thickness are other factors that greatly affect quality grade. Generally speaking, heavy-muscled cattle do not quality grade as well as light-muscled cattle. Cattle thickness is variable. If the thickness is due to fat, animals grade higher. However, if the thickness is due to muscle and not fat, then cattle thickness doesn't correlate with increased quality grade.

Trained live cattle evaluators look at many specific places on an animal's body to help correctly estimate quality grade. One of the most important places to evaluate is tail pones (fat deposits that accumulate around the tail-head of an animal) (Fig. 1B).[1] The larger the tail pones, the higher the cattle graded for English, Dairy, and Exotic cattle.[2]

Lower Quarter

Lower quarter (Fig. 1E) refers to the fat deposits along the inner thighs of the animal. Lower quarter has a positive relationship with quality grade.[2] This trait is most effective when predicting quality grade of English cattle and is the second most useful trait when all breeds are considered.

Cod/Udder Fat

Cod/udder fat (Fig. 1D) has been used to predict quality grade on live cattle. Cod fat isn't very reliable because it is too dependent on how the animal was castrated. If the

Encyclopedia of Animal Science
DOI: 10.1081/E-EAS 120019720

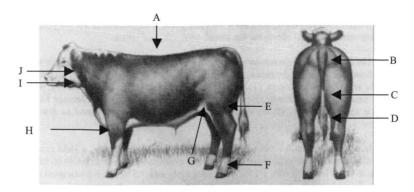

Fig. 1 A diagram showing where various live animal quality grade indicators are located: A. Turn over the top, B. tail pones, C. round creases, D. cod/udder, E. lower quarter, F. dewclaws, G. flank, H. brisket, I. jowl, J. cheeks.

animal was castrated up high on his scrotal sac, then there is no room for the fat to deposit. Also, if he was castrated at the base of the scrotum, then he will deposit lots of cod fat early on, and estimation errors can occur. This trait is highly dependent on breed type. It is most accurate on Brahman cattle, and doesn't work well in Dairy cattle.[2]

Brisket/Flank

The brisket and flank (Fig. 1G and H) are two of the most influential traits on quality grade.[1] Cattle with very full, wide briskets generally grade higher than those with sharp, angular briskets. Also, deep-flanked cattle grade higher than shallow-bodied cattle. These two areas were found to be most accurate in evaluating English and Exotic cattle.[2]

Cheeks/Jowl

Checks and jowl (Fig. 1I and J) are other factors that can be used to successfully predict quality grade.[1] As an animal reaches the Choice grade, its cheeks become very "puffy" and full. The same is true for its jowl area. Fullness of the cheeks and jowl relate to quality grade across all breeds studied.[2]

Turn Over the Top

One of the more modern places to evaluate quality grade on live cattle has been the turn over the top (Fig. 1A). This expression refers to how wide an animal is over the loin and rib, and how sharp appearing their top is. Fatter cattle will have a wide top, with a very gradual turn. Generally, cattle with a "rooftop" shape over their top will not grade as well as those with a wide turn.

Round Creases

In heifers round creases (Fig. 1C) are a useful tool for predicting meat quality.[1] As heifers begin to get fatter, the area below their vulva will fill in with fat and creases will begin to be visible. They will look like folds of skin that extend down on both sides of the animal. This trait has been found to be the most useful trait in predicting live quality grade on *Bos indicus* females.[2]

In the 1940s and 1950s, "old time" cattle buyers on the river markets used dewclaws (Fig. 1F) to predict meat quality.[1] Their consensus was that if the dewclaws pointed toward the ground, then that animal wasn't ready to be slaughtered and would not quality grade very high, but if the dewclaws pointed out or even slightly upward, then the animal was ready and would quality grade well. In today's markets, dewclaws are not given that much emphasis by current live animal evaluators. However, research does show a positive relationship between the directions of the dewclaws and quality grade, especially in Black, English-type cattle.[2]

Disposition

Disposition has long been linked to meat quality in cattle. Calmer, more docile animals have the ability to deposit marbling (intramuscular fat) at a higher level than cattle that are "excitable." Also, more docile animals tend to have fewer incidences of major carcass defects (blood splash, bruising, fiery fat, etc.) than highly excited animals. Swirl has historically been used to predict docility. Swirl refers to the swirl pattern of hair on the animal's forehead. It is said that the lower the swirl, the more docile the animal will be. The reverse is true for animals with very high swirl patterns. Docility was found to be highly related to quality grade in Exotic and *Bos indicus* type cattle.[3]

Growth Implants

Another important consideration when predicting meat quality in live cattle is whether they were implanted or nonimplanted. Growth implants are commonly placed in cattle's ears in an attempt to increase weight gain and growth. Research shows that implanting cattle can negatively affect quality grade anywhere from 0–30%. Live cattle evaluators use this information and sometimes this factor to determine quality grade if an animal is on the border between two grades.

MATURITY EVALUATION

A major factor to consider when predicting quality grade on live animals is maturity. In order for an animal to be eligible for USDA quality grades of Prime, Choice, Select, or Standard, the animal must be young (A or B maturity). Maturity is important, because as animals age, the meat greatly decreases in tenderness. Tough meat leads to consumer dissatisfaction. The following is a chart that relates maturity to age in months:

Age (months)	9–30	30–42	42–72	72–96	>96
Maturity Classification	A	B	C	D	E
	Young cattle	Young cattle	Mature cattle	Mature cattle	Mature cattle

Live maturity evaluation is very subjective in nature. Trained personnel have few tools at their disposal. However, there are a few factors that can predict age of an animal. Trained evaluators will look at an animal's tail to predict maturity. As an animal ages, its tail will grow longer and be closer to the ground. Also, the switch (cluster of hair) at the end of the tail will get very coarse in nature as an animal matures. The head is another factor to consider when predicting maturity. The head of an older animal will be proportionally larger compared to its body. Young cattle will look normal and be very proportional.

As one can conclude, live evaluation of meat quality in cattle is extremely subjective. According to Fred L. Williams, Jr. (USDA), a trained expert can expect to be correct only about 70% of the time. A person should play the law of averages to be the most accurate. Live cattle evaluation is very important in today's cattle industry. Cattle buyers make purchases according to how good or bad they believe a pen of cattle will grade. It is up to them to decide which cattle will have the greatest chance of grading the best. If they can accurately predict meat quality, then consumers should receive a tender, juicy, flavorful piece of meat that they will enjoy time and time again.

REFERENCES

1. Boggs, D.L.; Merkel, R.A.; Doumit, M.E. *An Integrated Approach to Evaluation, Grading, and Selection. Livestock and Carcasses*, 5th Ed.; Kendall/Hunt Pub.: Dubuque, IA, 1998.
2. Williams, F.L., Jr.; Miller, M.F. *Advanced Quality Grading: Slaughter Cattle*; USDA. CEV Multimedia: Lubbock, TX, 1998.
3. Grandin, T. Problems with Bruises and Dark Cutters in Slaughter Steers/Heifers. In *Improving the Consistency and Competitiveness of Beef—A Blueprint for Total Quality Management in the Fed-Beef Industry. The Final Report of the National Beef Quality Audit—1991*; 1992. Colorado State University, Ft. Collins, CO; Texas A&M University, College Station, TX.
4. Schertz, M.J. Evaluation of Quality Grade Indicators for Live Slaughter Cattle. In *A Thesis in Animal Science*; Texas Tech University, May 1999.

Milk Composition, Species Comparisons

Olav T. Oftedal
Smithsonian Institution, Washington, D.C., U.S.A.

INTRODUCTION

All mammals depend on milk as their primary source of nutrients during a phase of development. This may begin at an early developmental stage and cover a long period, as in hatchling monotremes or neonatal marsupials, or it may be a brief period following the birth of large, precocial offspring. Milk composition can change markedly during lactation, especially in monotremes and marsupials. These changes probably correlate to developmental maturation in digestive function, substrate metabolism, and requirements for tissue synthesis, but the specifics are not well understood. Milk also provides immunoglobulins and other antibacterial compounds important in protecting suckling young from infection. In this article, the major constituents of milk are discussed, both in terms of significance for the young and in relation to species differences. Examples of the milk composition of a wide variety of species are given.

MAJOR MILK CONSTITUENTS

The most abundant constituents in milk are water, lipids, proteins, and sugars.[1–3] At midlactation, the milks of domesticated and semidomesticated animals used for human consumption range in energy content from 2.1 to 6.9 kJ/g, with most at the lower end (Table 1). Among wild animals a greater range of energy content (1.8–25 kJ/g) is evident, with large differences among mammalian orders as well as among species within an order (Table 2).

Water

Water is essential to neonates for tissue growth and to replace water lost through evaporation and excretion. Milk water ranges from 90% in some zebras, rhinos, and primates to about 30% in some seals (Tables 1 and 2). High water intake may be essential for offspring of zebras and rhinos that require water for evaporative cooling in hot, arid environments. The milks consumed by hatchling monotremes and newborn marsupials are also very high in water (88–91%), which may relate to immature renal function and inability to concentrate urine. Altricial (immature) eutherian neonates also have limited ability to regulate water excretion.

Species that fast during lactation, such as hibernating bears, some seals, and some whales, produce milks that are low in water (30–65%) and thus do not impose a heavy water demand on lactating females. A low water content is also typical of mammalian species that are very small (e.g., shrews, mice), that suckle infrequently (e.g., tree shrews, rabbits), or that live in marine environments (e.g., dolphins, sea otters).

Milks that are high in water are low in energy (Tables 1 and 2), and must be produced in large volumes to meet the energetic needs of suckling young. It is remarkable that most animal milks consumed by humans, such as those of cow, goat, sheep, water buffalo, yak, camel, horse, and ass, are high in water content (82–91%; Table 2). This may reflect a preference for domestication of species that produce larger milk volumes, or it may relate to the fact that human milk is also dilute (Table 1).

Lipids

Milk fat is usually the next most abundant constituent, ranging from less than 1% in rhinos and some lemurs to 50–60% in many seals (Table 2). Milk fat is composed primarily of fatty acids esterified as triacyl glycerols (97–99% by weight) and is packaged in fat globules enveloped in cell membrane, forming a more or less stable emulsion. Given the high energy in lipids, milk fat supplies a large proportion (35–90%) of the energy in most milks, except for equids and rhinos (5–25%).[2]

High-lipid, energy-dense milks may have evolved to support a variety of functions:

- Fat deposition in subcutaneous blubber layers may be necessary for insulation in marine mammal young, such as seals and whales;
- A high energy intake may be needed to fuel high rates of metabolism, as in sea lions and sea otters;
- Mothers may need to transfer energy-dense milks quickly to their young during suckling bouts that are short and infrequent, as in rabbits and tree shrews;
- Mothers that undertake long foraging trips may need to store energy-dense milk in mammary glands between returns to the rookery, as in fur seals and some bats;
- Production of high-fat, low-sugar milk minimizes the glucose demand of lactation for fasting mothers, as in hibernating bears and fasting seals.

Encyclopedia of Animal Science
DOI: 10.1081/E-EAS 120019721

Table 1 Major constituents of milks used for human consumption

Species	Days after birth	Gross energy[a] kJ/g	Water (%)	Fat (%)	Protein[b] (%)	Sugar (%)	Protein energy %
Horse	24–54	2.1	89.5	1.3	1.9	6.9	22
Ass	30–180	2.3	89.2	1.8	1.7	6.9	18
Domestic goat	14–56	2.9	88.0	3.8	2.9[c]	4.7	22
Cow	"mature"	3.0	87.6	3.7	3.2	4.6	26
Zebu	"mature"	3.3	82.7	4.7	3.2	4.9	21
Camel (dromedary)	?	3.4	86.4	4.5	3.6	5.0	26
Bactrian camel	23–91	3.5	84.8	4.3	4.3	–	30
Human	>10	3.8	87.6	4.1	0.8	6.8	7
Water buffalo	30	4.3	83.2	6.5	4.3[c]	4.9	23
Sheep	13–35	4.6	81.8	7.3	4.1	5.0	22
Yak	?	4.6	82.7	6.5	5.8[c]	4.6	30
Eland	30–60	6.0	78.1	9.9	6.3	4.4	32
Reindeer	21–30	6.9	73.7	10.9	9.5[c]	3.4	32

[a]Energy calculated as in Ref. 2.
[b]Protein is protein nitrogen × 6.38.
[c]Protein is total nitrogen × 6.38.
(From Refs. 1–3.)

Milk fat supplies a source of essential and nonessential fatty acids that are utilized in tissue deposition and metabolism. The fatty acid composition of milk varies greatly among species, reflecting differences in maternal diet, hydrogenation of lipids during digestion, postabsorptive modification of chain length and double bonds, and de novo synthesis.[5] Ruminant milks are typically rich in short-chain and saturated fatty acids, elephant milks are particularly high in medium-chain (C8–C12) fatty acids, horse milks contain an abundance of unsaturated long-chain (C18) fatty acids, and the milks of pinnipeds (seals and sea lions) and cetaceans (whales and dolphins) are typically high in polyunsaturated, very long chain (C18–24) fatty acids.[5] Milk also contains free and esterified cholesterol as well as a variety of phospholipids and glycolipids that may function as metabolic substrates, precursors for structural materials, or protective agents in suckling young.

Proteins

Milk proteins are of central importance because they provide a source of amino acids for suckling young, and serve a variety of functions both in the mammary gland and in suckling young. At midlactation, protein ranges from about 1% to 12% among most species (Table 2), although cottontail rabbit milk may be up to 15%.[3] Protein is usually higher in milks that are rich in lipids, so that the amount of energy supplied as protein is about 20–35% in most taxa (Table 2). However, lower values appear to be characteristic of many seals and sea lions, bats, and primates (Table 2). In primates, the protein-energy percentage is correlated to rate of growth of the young, but this relationship does not hold for all mammals.[6]

The proteins in milk are divided into two categories: caseins and whey proteins.[1] The caseins are organized into large micelles suspended in milk and serve to transport much of the calcium and phosphorus that the young need. Upon ingestion and exposure to gastric secretions, the caseins precipitate in the stomach forming semisolid curds that are gradually digested. It is thought that species that nurse infrequently may have higher casein levels to retain milk constituents in the stomach for longer periods. Cow's milk is higher in casein and forms a more solid curd than does the milk of humans or pigs, which suckle frequently, but few species have been compared in this light.

The whey proteins include milk-specific proteins, such as α-lactalbumin, β-lactoglobulin, and late lactation protein, as well as more widely expressed proteins such as serum albumin, γ-globulins, and transferrin.[1,7] Some of these proteins transport trace elements or vitamins, others have enzymatic activity, and some have structural roles in the cell membranes surrounding milk fat globules. The particular set of whey proteins varies among species, and, in some marsupials, may vary according to lactation stage.

Sugars

Lactose is the predominant sugar in the milks of most eutherian mammals, including milks consumed by humans. However, the milks of some marine mammals are devoid of lactose, while a large variety of oligosaccharides are important constituents in the milks of

Table 2 Major constituents of the milks of wild mammals, demonstrating variation within and between orders[a]

Species	N	Days after birth	Gross energy[b] kj/g	Water (%)	Fat (%)	Protein[c] (%)	Sugar (%)	Protein energy %	Source[d]
Artiodactyla									
Collared peccary	4	21–48	3.8	83.8	4.2	5.1	6.2	31	3
Giraffe	12	14–109	5.3	81.5	8.4	5.2	5.3	23	DZ
Bongo	5	15–39	8.0	69.6	13.0	10.4	3.2	31	DZG
Carnivora									
Red fox	3	28–35	4.6	81.9	5.8	6.7	4.6	34	2
Giant panda	13+	77–196	8.6	68.1	15.9	8.1	3.6	22	BU
California sea lion	9	3–60	14.3	59.0	31.7	8.6[e]	0.3	15	3
Hooded seal	15	2–4	24.6	30.2	61.1	4.9	1.0	5	3
Cetacea									
Fin whale	7–9	~210	15.6	53.5	33.2	10.5	2.3	16	3
Chiroptera									
Little golden-mantled flying fox	2–5	7–11	3.8	87.3	6.1	2.1	6.0	12	9
Little brown bat	3	~13–19	8.7	72.9	15.8	8.5	4.0	23	3
Brasilian free-tailed bat	21	22–42	12.2	63.5	25.8	7.7	3.4	15	3
Marsupialia									
Queensland ringtail possum	20–23	100–120	4.3	77.0	3.0	4.5	12.5	24	3
Red-necked wallaby	8–39	226	6.2	75.0	7.2	6.8	10.9	26	3
Virginia opossum	5	~77	9.7	66	17	10	5.0	25	10
Perissodactyla									
Black rhinoceros	8	36–115	1.8	90.0	0.85	1.7	6.6	19	MCZG
Mountain zebra	7	90–360	1.9	90.0	1.0	1.6[e]	6.9	20	3
South American tapir	9	4–20	3.3	84.8	3.6	4.8	5.0	33	CZS
Primates									
Pygmy chimpanzee	9	46–126	1.9	89.6	1.1	1.0	8.0	9	MCZG
Brown lemur	6	28–74	2.1	90.4	0.9	1.3[e]	8.5	15	3
White-tufted-ear marmoset	43	10–55	3.2	86.0	3.6	2.7	7.4	19	6
Aye-aye	4	25–85	4.1	83.5	5.8	3.9	6.1	21	DUPC
Verreaux's Sifaka	3	62–97	7.2	73.4	12.6	6.8	4.8	22	DUPC
Proboscidea									
African elephant	6	60–80	3.7	82.7	5.0	4.0	5.3	24	2
Rodentia									
Naked mole rat	5	8–12	3.7	84.1	4.8	4.5	5.1	28	NZP
Guinea pig	17	3–13	4.8	81.2	6.3	6.13	5.6	30	2
House mouse	5	9–10	13.7	59.2	27.0	12.5	2.6	22	3

[a]For scientific binomials, see Ref. 4 and for data on additional species, see Refs. 2 and 3.
[b]Energy calculated as in Ref. 2.
[c]Protein is total nitrogen × 6.38.
[d]Entries without a numbered source reference are unpublished data for milk samples obtained from: BU = Beijing University, Beijing, China; CZS = Chicago Zoological Society, Chicago, IL; DUPC = Duke University Primate Center, Durham, NC; DZ = Dallas Zoo, Dallas, TX; DZG = Denver Zoological Gardens, Denver, CO; MCZG = Milwaukee County Zoological Gardens, Milwaukee, WI; NZP = National Zoological Park, Washington, DC. Analytic methods: water by oven-drying, fat by Roese-Gottlieb extraction, protein (total nitrogen × 6.38) by Kjeldahl or CHN elemental gas analysis, sugar by phenol-sulfuric acid. From Ref. 3.
[e]Protein is protein nitrogen × 6.38.

monotremes, marsupials, primates, carnivores, and other mammals.[8] At midlactation the total sugar content of milk ranges from about 0.2% to 9% in eutherian mammals (Table 2), and from 6% to 14% in marsupials.[3]

Lactose is synthesized only by mammary epithelial cells, and occurs nowhere in nature. The biochemical pathways by which lactose is synthesized, and how these may have evolved, have been much studied and debated. Molecular and genetic evidence suggest that the constituents of lactose synthetase may have an ancient origin, predating the appearance of mammals by 100 million years or more.

In suckling young, lactose is digested by an intestinal brush-border enzyme, lactase. It is less clear how and to what extent oligosaccharides are digested. One hypothesis is that oligosaccharides in human milk have antibacterial properties that are most effective if the oligosaccharides survive passage through the intestines.[8] In marsupials, oligosaccharides represent such a large proportion of energy that it is thought they must be digested, perhaps following uptake into intestinal cells by pinocytosis.

OTHER CONSTITUENTS

Species differences occur relative to other nutrients, some of which have practical importance in the feeding of infant mammals. Calcium and phosphorus levels are correlated to milk casein content, but some marine mammals have very low calcium levels and inverse calcium–phosphorus ratios. Ruminant milks are so low in iron that suckling young must obtain an environmental source (such as vegetation or dirt) to avoid iron deficiency. By contrast, mammals with very altricial young produce iron-rich milks. The very low vitamin D levels in many primate and ruminant milks may produce vitamin D deficiency if the young are not provided access to ultraviolet B light needed for vitamin D synthesis in skin. In ruminants and horses, milk consumed immediately after birth is a vital source of immunoglobulins that provide passive immunity, but in many other mammals immunoglobulins cross the placenta before birth, so milk immunoglobulins are less crucial. Milk may be an important source of enzymes, growth factors, and hormones, but variation among species is not well studied.

CONCLUSION

Milk is needed by suckling young of all species. The physiologic, digestive, and nutritional consequences of the remarkable differences among mammals in milk composition are only partially understood. Nonetheless, it is sound practice in feeding neonatal mammals to mimic the composition of mother's milk.

ACKNOWLEDGMENTS

I would like to thank collaborators who helped acquire the unpublished data in Table 2, especially Wendy Hood, Nancy Irlbeck, David Kessler, Prof. Pan, Andy Teare, and Kathy Williams.

ARTICLES OF FURTHER INTEREST

REFERENCES

1. Jenness, R. The Composition of Milk. In *Lactation: A Comprehensive Treatise*; Larson, B.L., Smith, V.R., Eds.; Academic Press: New York, 1974; Vol. 3, 3–107.
2. Oftedal, O.T. Milk composition, milk yield and energy output at peak lactation: A comparative review. Symp. Zool. Soc. Lond. **1984**, *51*, 33–85.
3. Oftedal, O.T.; Iverson, S.J. Comparative Analysis of Nonhuman Milks. A. Phylogenetic Variation in the Gross Composition of Milks. In *Handbook of Milk Composition*; Jensen, R.G., Ed.; Academic Press: San Diego, 1995; 749–789.
4. Wilson, D.E; Cole, F.R. *Common Names of Mammals of the World*; Smithsonian Institution Press: Washington, DC, 2000.
5. Iverson, S.J.; Oftedal, O.T. Comparative Analysis of Nonhuman Milks. B. Phylogenetic and Ecological Variation in the Fatty Acid Composition of Milks. In *Handbook of Milk Composition*; Jensen, R.G., Ed.; Academic Press: San Diego, 1995; 789–827.
6. Power, M.L.; Oftedal, O.T.; Tardif, S.D. Does the milk of callitrichid monkeys differ from that of larger anthropoids? Am. J. Primatol. **2002**, *56*, 117–127.
7. Lönnerdal, B.; Atkinson, S. Nitrogenous Components of Milk. A. Human Milk Proteins. In *Handbook of Milk Composition*; Jensen, R.G., Ed.; Academic Press: San Diego, 1995; 351–368.
8. Urashima, T.; Saito, T.; Nakamura, T.; Messer, M. Oligosaccharides of milk and colostrum of nonhuman mammals. Glycoconjugate J. **2001**, *18*, 357–371.
9. Hood, W.R.; Kunz, T.H.; Oftedal, O.T.; Iverson, S.J.; LeBlanc, D.; Seyjagat, J. Interspecific and intraspecific variation in proximate, mineral and fatty acid composition of milk in Old World fruit bats (Chiroptera: Pteropodidae). Physiol. Biochem. Zool. **2001**, *74*, 134–146.
10. Green, B.; Krause, W.J.; Newgrain, K. Milk composition in the North American opossum (*Didelphis virginiana*). Comp. Biochem. Physiol. **1996**, *113B*, 619–623.

Milk Synthesis

R. Michael Akers
Virginia Polytechnic Institute and State University, Blacksburg, Virginia, U.S.A.

INTRODUCTION

Copious milk secretion begins shortly after parturition and requires: 1) the prepartum proliferation of alveolar epithelial cells; 2) biochemical and structural differentiation of these cells; and 3) synthesis and secretion of milk constituents. Except for bottle-fed humans and milk replacer-fed dairy calves, the success of reproduction does not end with the birth of healthy offspring. Rather, suckling of the neonate determines survival.

Milk synthesis and secretion are biological marvel and hallmark of mammals. Milk contains proteins, carbohydrates, and fats suspended in an aqueous medium. The purposes of this article are to: 1) provide an overview of the dramatic, acute changes in secretory cell structure and function as the gland prepares for onset of copious milk secretion, and 2) describe the activity and function of the secretory cells to promote milk synthesis and secretion.

PROPERTIES OF MAMMARY SECRETIONS

The mammary gland is an unusual exocrine gland. Its product is a complex mixture, which depends on apocrine and meocrine modes of cellular secretion. Milk is stored within the lumen of the alveoli and ductular system until it is removed by the milking machine or the suckling offspring. Interestingly, suckling intervals vary widely between mammals, ranging from minutes to hours in cattle, to once daily in rabbits, to once every two days in tree shrews, or only once a week in some seals. There are species-specific changes in milk composition with stage of lactation, but milk composition is generally only moderately affected by environmental or nutritional changes.[1] Function of the mammary gland during established lactation is closely linked with a number of hormones, growth factors, and local tissue regulators, but it is difficult to ascribe a specific transport activity to a particular molecule or to determine whether effects are direct or indirect.[2–5]

Requirements for high levels of milk production are staggering. In the dairy cow, the energy requirements for milk production can approach 80% of net energy of intake. Lactose production may require 85% of available glucose. Approximately one-third of the milk produced during the first month or more of lactation is energetically accounted for by mobilization of endogenous nutrient reserves. Finely tuned coordinated interactions between all the major physiological systems are essential.

OVERVIEW OF MAMMARY STRUCTURE

During the second half of gestation, alveolar formation predominates mammogenesis as new alveoli appear and existing alveoli increase in size. Connected via a terminal duct to progressively larger ducts and ultimately to the teat or nipple, it is the epithelial cells of the many alveoli that synthesize and secrete milk. Once initiated, secreted milk is stored in the spaces of the hollow alveoli and ducts between milking and suckling episodes (Fig. 1). There is also storage of milk in the gland and teat cisterns of those animals where mammary glands are arranged into an udder (ruminants).[1]

SECRETORY CELL DIFFERENTIATION

Biochemical differentiation of the secretory cells is critical, but the alveolar cells must also acquire the structural machinery needed to synthesize, package, and secrete milk constituents. When they first appear, the cells exhibit few of the needed organelles (Fig. 2). They are characterized by a sparse cytoplasm with few polyribosomes or free ribosomes, limited rough endoplasmic reticulum, rudimentary Golgi, some isolated mitochondria, and occasional widely dispersed vesicles. Soon after the alveolar structures appear, alveolar and ductal spaces accumulate fluid and progressively increase concentrations of serum-derived proteins. Accumulated secretions result in formation of immunoglobulin-rich colostrums, which—depending on the species—may be essential for the survival of the offspring. As parturition approaches, the cells undergo a dramatic structural transformation. Cell nuclei become rounded and displaced to the basal area of the cell. Lateral and basal regions of the cell become filled with arrays of rough endoplasmic reticulum and small lipid droplets. The apical area becomes populated with swollen arrays of Golgi membranes,

Encyclopedia of Animal Science
DOI: 10.1081/E-EAS 120019722

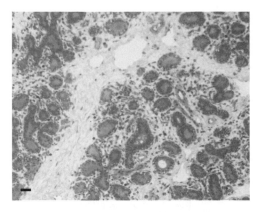

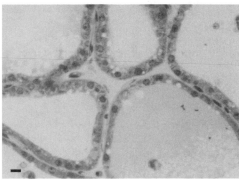

Fig. 1 Developing mammary tissue. The upper panel shows a microscopic view of a section of mammary parenchymal tissue from a nonlactating heifer about mid-gestation. Developing alveoli are evident in clusters of epithelial tissue surrounded by connective tissue (bar indicates 25 μm). The lower panel illustrates mammary tissue from a lactating cow. Notice how the entire parenchymal tissue area is occupied by closely aligned alveoli. Several alveoli cut in cross section are illustrated. Lighter-stained areas are alveolar lumena. Secretory cells form a single layer around the periphery of each alveolus. Because of accumulation of secretions within the lumenal spaces, alveoli are closely packed together with little apparent stomal or vascular tissue (bar indicates 10 μm). (*View this art in color at www. dekker.com.*)

developing secretory vesicles and small lipid droplets. Even in the light microscope, these changes are evident (Fig. 2). A lacy appearance highlights the apical region of the cell because of the abundance of secretory vesicles, in contrast to the darkly stained basal–lateral cytoplasm. The fully differentiated cell becomes polarized with the basolateral area devoted to the uptake of precursors and synthesis of proteins and lipids and the apical cytoplasm, with now abundant Golgi, devoted to posttranslational modification of proteins and packaging of proteins and lactose for secretion from the cell.

Five routes of secretion across the mammary epithelium have been described: 1) membrane route; 2) Golgi route; 3) milk fat route; 4) transcytosis; and 5) the

paracellular route. The membrane route refers to interstitial fluid—derived substances that cross the basolateral membrane, traverse the cell, and pass across the apical membrane into milk. Examples are water, urea, glucose, and some ions. To utilize the Golgi route, products are synthesized, sequestered, or packaged into secretory vesicles that bud from the stacks of Golgi membranes. These vesicles, either individually or in chains, fuse with the apical plasma membrane to release their contents to become part of milk. Examples include lactose, caseins, whey proteins, citrate, and calcium. The milk fat route refers to substances that become entrained with the budding lipid droplets as they are released from the apical cell surface to become part of milk. Actually, as the fat droplets are secreted, bits of cytoplasm can become engulfed by plasma membrane and secreted from the cell. They are especially common in the milk of goats. In transcytosis, vesicles derived from the basolateral membrane (pinocytosis or endocytosis) are transported in membrane-bound vesicles for release at the apical membrane. Finally, in the paracellular route there is

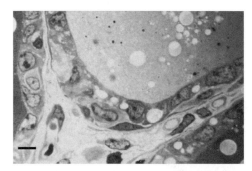

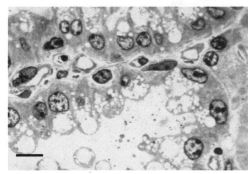

Fig. 2 Mammary tissue from a cow about two weeks prepartum is illustrated in the upper panel. Secretory cells from three alveoli are shown. At this point the cells are very poorly differentiated with little indication of secretory activity. The lower panel illustrates portions of two alveoli about one week postpartum. The secretory cells are well differentiated, basal areas of the cells are darkly stained, and apical regions have a distinct lacy appearance because of the presence of numerous secretory vesicles and lipid droplets (bars indicate 10 μm). (*View this art in color at www.dekker.com.*)

direct passage for materials in the interstitial fluids between the epithelial cells and into milk. Except in situations of disease, i.e., mastitis or failure of frequent milk removal, the paracellular route is likely of minimal importance during established lactation.[1]

Production of milk requires close coordination between biochemical pathways to supply synthesis intermediates and secretory pathways for secretion. To illustrate, the disaccharide lactose is the predominate sugar in milk. The enzyme complex necessary for lactose synthesis, membrane-bound galactosyltransferase and the whey protein α-lactalbumin, combines in the Golgi apparatus to form lactose synthetase, which serves to combine glucose and galactose and thereby form lactose. Activation of the α-lactalbumin gene occurs near parturition and heralds the onset of lactogenesis. Moreover, continuing synthesis of lactose is essential to maintain milk volume and composition. This is because lactose becomes trapped in secretory vesicles and water is osmotically drawn into the vesicles. Because the plasma membranes of the secretory and ductular cells are also impermeable to lactose, the osmolarity of the secretory vesicles is maintained in secreted milk and water remains within the lumens of the alveoli and ducts. It is generally accepted that some minimal level of lactose production is likely essential to maintain the relative fluidity of milk for efficient milk removal either by the sucking young or the milking machine. This is perhaps best illustrated by recent data for transgenic mice in which prevention of α-lactalbumin synthesis essentially prevented lactation, because sucking mice failed to survive despite the presence of milk proteins and fat in the alveolar spaces of mammary tissue of lactating mothers.

CONTROL OF MILK SYNTHESIS

As confirmed in numerous species, classical mammary explant culture studies demonstrated that the major positive regulators of differentiation of the secretory cells are glucocorticoids and prolactin.[4] Recent data support the idea that insulin-mediated effects on mammary cells in culture may actually represent effects more appropriately ascribed to the insulin-like growth factors (IGF-I and IGF-II). This is because mammary epithelial cells have specific IGF-I receptors, and insulin (especially at higher concentrations typical of culture experiments) is likely to bind to the IGF-I receptor. In general terms, glucocorticoids are most closely associated with development of rough endoplasmic reticulum and prolactin with maturation of the Golgi apparatus and appearance of secretory vesicles.[4]

Molecular techniques applied to mammary gland biology have served to solidify the idea that prolactin and glucocorticoids are primary stimulators of mammary cell differentiation. For example, both prolactin and glucocorticoid response elements are found within the promoter regions of the genes for several mammary-specific milk proteins. Similarly, induction of both mRNA and specific milk proteins in response to the addition of prolactin or glucocorticoids in isolated mammary epithelial cells indicate the importance of these hormones in lactogenesis.[2,3]

CONCLUSION

Lactogenesis—the onset of copious milk synthesis and secretion that is initiated near the time of parturition—is stimulated by the positive actions of prolactin and glucocorticoids and the removal of the negative effects of progesterone. These hormonal changes promote both biochemical and structural differentiation of the alveolar epithelial cells that are required for synthesis, cellular packaging, and secretion of milk components.

REFERENCES

1. Akers, R.M. *Lactation and the Mammary Gland*; Iowa State Press: USA, 2003.
2. Capuco, A.V.; Akers, R.M. Galactopoiesis, Effects of Hormones and Growth Factors. In *Encyclopedia of Dairy Science*; Academic Press: New York, 2002; Vol 3, 1452–1458.
3. Capuco, A.V.; Akers, R.M. Galactopoiesis, Effect of bST Treatment. In *Encyclopedia of Dairy Science*; Academic Press: New York, 2002; Vol 3, 1458–1464.
4. Tucker, H.A. Lactation and Its Hormonal Control. In *The Physiology of Reproduction*, 2nd Ed.; Knobil, E., Neill, J.D., Eds.; Raven Press Ltd.: New York, 1994; 1065–1098. Chapter 57.
5. Akers, R.M. Lactation. In *Encyclopedia of Agricultural Science*; Academic Press: New York, 1994; Vol 2, 635–643.

Milk Yield Differences

L. E. Chase
Cornell University, Ithaca, New York, U.S.A.

INTRODUCTION

Milk production is an integral component of the total life cycle of mammals. The term lactation is another term commonly used to describe this biological process. Milk production serves a number of functions. A primary function, in most species, is to provide nutrients for newborn animals. The milk produced in the first few days of lactation is called colostrum. Typically, colostrum contains a higher level of protein, fat, energy, and solids than milk produced in later lactation. Colostrum also provides a method of providing immunity to newborn animals. Milk and milk products are also utilized as a food source for humans in many parts of the world. The quantity of milk produced has increased in many species over time. These species have been genetically selected for milk yield and are managed for production of milk for sale and consumption by humans. The most common species used for this purpose are dairy cattle, goats, sheep, and water buffalo. The quantity of milk produced varies both within and among animal species.

MILK YIELD

Table 1 contains milk yield data for selected species on a total lactation length basis. This information provides averages for several breeds of dairy cattle, goats, deer, and water buffalo. The difference between the seven U.S. dairy breeds is 3189 kg of milk per lactation. There is also a large variation in herd average milk production within breed. As an example, Holstein herds in the United States may produce <7200 to >14,500 kg of milk per cow per year. Individual Holstein cows have produced in excess of 30,000 kg milk in a single lactation and >200,000 kg in total lifetime milk production. The milk yields for water buffalo in Table 1 are for animals selected and managed for producing milk. These yields are higher than would be expected for the same species in less intensively managed situations.

The production of milk requires the synthesis of large quantities of precursors by the animal. The milk of Holstein dairy cattle typically contains about 5% lactose. Thus, a dairy cow producing 45 kg of milk per day needs to synthesize about 2.25 kg of lactose on a daily basis. This cow also needs to synthesize 3–3.6 kg of glucose, 1.4–1.8 kg of microbial protein, and 1–1.2 kg of amino acids daily to support this level of milk production.

There are also milk production estimates for other animals that either have shorter lactations or are not continuously milked. Milk yield in beef cattle will vary depending on breed, genetic selection, and number of calves suckled. Reported daily milk production of Angus and Hereford beef cattle was 5.2 to 7 kg/day at peak yield.[5] Average peak milk for the Angus cows was 6.98 kg/day for the daughters of the high-EPD (expected progeny difference) bulls compared with 5.74 kg for daughters of the low-EPD Angus sires. The Hereford cows from the high-EPD bulls produced 6.07 kg/day at peak compared with 5.24 kg for the daughters of the low-EPD sires.

Milking sheep produce an average of about 3 kg/day during a 180-day lactation period.[6] These sheep are mainly of the East Friesian breed housed in large commercial flocks. Average daily milk production for ewes nursing either single or twin lambs over a 63-day lactation period ranged from 2.5 to 3.5 kg.[7]

Total milk production of sows nursing pigs was reported to vary from 7.8 to 13.8 kg/day during a 5-day period in early lactation (days 10–14).[8] Total daily yields were 8.2 to 12.4 kg for sows in late lactation (days 24–28) in the same trial. The higher yields are for sows suckling a larger number of pigs.

LACTATION LENGTH

The length of the lactation cycle varies greatly among various species of animals. A review paper indicated that lactation length can range from 4 to >900 days in various species of mammals.[8] Animals such as hooded seals, spiny rats, and elephant shrews had a 4–5-day lactation length. A lactation length of >900 days was found in some of the great apes. This same paper indicated that there was a positive relationship between adult female body mass and lactation length. This relationship is for animals not used in intensive milk production systems.

Encyclopedia of Animal Science
DOI: 10.1081/E-EAS 120019723

Table 1 Annual lactation milk yields

Animal	Lactation length (days)	Milk yield, kg	4% FCM yield, kg	Milk fat, %	Milk total protein, %	Year	Country
Dairy Cattle							
Ayrshire	305	7,016	6,899	3.88	3.33	2003	US
Brown Swiss	305	8,045	8,093	4.04	3.54	2003	US
Guernsey	305	6,665	7,195	4.53	3.53	2003	US
Holstein	305	9,830	9,314	3.65	3.21	2003	US
Jersey	305	7,144	7,808	4.62	3.76	2003	US
Milking shorthorn	305	6,444	6,125	3.67	3.28	2003	US
Red and white	305	8,979	8,534	3.67	3.16	2003	US
Normande	305	6,649	7,018	4.37	3.6	2000	France
Swedish red	305	8,378	8,717	4.27	3.41	2001	Sweden
Swedish friesian	305	9,204	9,177	3.98	3.28	2001	Sweden
Danish red	305	7,553	7,791	4.21	3.56	2002	Denmark
Goats							
Alpine	305	945	874	3.5	3.1	2003	US
LaMancha	305	765	734	3.73	3.24	2003	US
Nubian	305	679	742	4.61	3.79	2003	US
Oberhasli	305	668	642	3.74	3.07	2003	US
Saanen	305	871	811	3.54	3.07	2003	US
Toggenburg	305	840	752	3.3	3.0	2003	US
Others							
Iberian red deer	238	224	475	11.5	7.6	2000	Spain
Water buffalo	270	2,524	3,808	7.39	4.5	2002	England

(From Refs. 1–4.)

FACTORS THAT INFLUENCE MILK YIELD

Many factors influence either daily or total lactation milk yield. The two key factors that control milk yield within an animal are genetics and environment. The heritability of milk yield in dairy cattle is estimated to be 0.25 to 0.3. This implies that 25–30% of the difference in milk yield among cows is due to genetics. The remainder of the difference is related to environment. The quantity and quality of the nutrients fed will also impact both milk production and composition.

The frequency of milk removal from the udder is another factor that will influence milk yield. In nursing animals, the number of animals being suckled will also affect milk yield. Sows nursing 12 pigs produced about 50–75% more milk per day than sows nursing 6 pigs.[8] Sheep nursing twin lambs had higher milk production over a 63-day lactation period than ewes nursing single lamb.[7] Dairy cattle milked three times per day produced about 3.5 kg more milk per day than cows milked twice daily.[9]

The use of recombinant bovine somatotropin (BST) is another tool that can be used to increase milk production in dairy cattle. The results of a field study using 15 dairy herds reported daily milk production increases of 3.6 to 5.5 kg in cows receiving exogenous BST.[11] The response

to BST was greater in multiparous than primiparous cows in this study. Milk production to exogenous BST has also been reported to increase milk yield in beef cattle and goats.

There has also been interest in milking animals more frequently in the early part of the lactation cycle. A recent paper examined milking cows either three or six times daily for the first 21 days of lactation.[10] Both groups were then milked three times per day for the remainder of the lactation cycle. Peak milk yields were 57.0 and 51.1 kg per day for cows milked six or three times per day, respectively. Over the total lactation period, cows milked 6 times daily for the first 21 days produced 1118 kg more total milk.

LACTATION CURVES

The quantity of milk produced daily varies throughout the lactation period. In most animals, there will be a high, peak yield followed by a gradual decrease in daily milk production for the remainder of the lactation cycle. In dairy cattle, peak milk production occurs in the first 40–70 days of the lactation cycle for multiparous cows. The days to peak milk are usually slightly later in primiparous cattle. The decline in milk production after peak is 6–9% per month for multiparous cows, while the rate of decline for primiparous cows is 3–6%. Peak milk production in beef cattle and sheep occur at days of lactation similar to those in dairy cattle.

WHAT IS THE LIMIT FOR MILK YIELD IN DAIRY CATTLE?

One approach to this question is to examine the quantity of milk produced by world-record cows. The world record for a Holstein dairy cow is 30,805 kg in a 365-day lactation period.[11] The world record for a Jersey is 20,380 kg in a 365-day lactation.[12] Even though these are records for individual cows, they do provide an index of the potential of dairy cows for milk yield. It is probable that these records will be surpassed in the next 5 years.

CONCLUSION

Milk yield varies both within and among species due to a combination of genetic and management factors. The quantity of milk produced can be altered by the nutrient content of the diet provided. Other factors that can influence the quantity of milk produced include the number of animals suckled, frequency of milking, and BST. The biological limit for milk yield has not been defined. However, individual Holstein dairy cows have produced >30,000 lb of milk in a 365-day lactation and >200,000 kg in total lifetime milk production.

REFERENCES

1. http://aipl.arsusda.gov (accessed February 2004).
2. http://www.buffalomilk.co.uk (accessed June 2003).
3. http://www.milkproduction.com (accessed March 2003).
4. Landete-Castillejos, T.; Garcia, A.; Molina, P.; Vergara, H.; Garde, J.; Gallego, L. Milk production and composition in captive Iberian red deer (*Cervus elaphus hispanicus*): Effect of birth date. J. Anim. Sci. **2000**, *78*, 2771–2777.
5. Minick, J.A.; Buchanan, D.S.; Rupert, S.D. Milk production of crossbred daughters of high- and low-milk EPD Angus and Hereford bulls. J. Anim. Sci. **2001**, *79*, 1386–1393.
6. http://www.blacksheepcheese.com (accessed February 2004).
7. Cardellino, R.A.; Benson, M.E. Lactation curves of commercial ewes rearing lambs. J. Anim. Sci. **2002**, *80*, 23–27.
8. Auldist, D.D.; Carlson, D.; Morrish, L.; Wakeford, C.M.; King, R.H. The influence of suckling interval on milk production in sows. J. Anim. Sci. **2000**, *78*, 2026–2031.
9. Erdman, R.A.; Varner, M. Fixed yield responses to increased milking frequency. J. Dairy Sci. **1995**, *78*, 1199–1203.
10. Dahl, G.E.; Wallace, R.L.; Shanks, R.D.; Lueking, D. Hot topic: Effects of frequent milking in early lactation on milk yield and udder health. J. Dairy Sci. **2004**, *87*, 882–885.
11. Thomas, J.W.; Erdman, R.A.; Galton, D.M.; Lamb, R.C.; Arambel, M.J.; Olson, J.D.; Madsen, K.S.; Samuels, W.A.; Peel, C.J.; Green, G.A. Responses by lactating cows in commercial dairy herds to recombinant bovine somatotropin. J. Dairy Sci. **1991**, *74*, 945–964.
12. http://www.holsteinuse.com (accessed January 2004).
13. Hayssen, V. Empirical and theoretical constraints on the evolution of lactation. J. Dairy Sci. **1993**, *76*, 3213–3233.
14. http://www.usjersey.com (accessed January 2004).

Mineral Elements: Macro

Lee R. McDowell
University of Florida, Gainesville, Florida, U.S.A.

M

INTRODUCTION

All forms of living matter require inorganic elements—or minerals—for normal life processes. All animal tissues and all feeds contain inorganic or mineral elements in widely varying amounts and proportions. The mineral elements are solid, crystalline, chemical elements that cannot be decomposed or synthesized by ordinary chemical reactions. Minerals that are needed in relatively large amounts are referred to as major minerals or macrominerals. Others that are needed in very small amounts are referred to as trace minerals or microminerals. Seven mineral elements are classified as macrominerals: calcium (Ca), phosphorus (P), sodium (Na), chlorine (Cl), potassium (K), magnesium (Mg) and sulfur (S).

OVERVIEW

Ninety-six percent of body weight consists of four organically bound elements: carbon, hydrogen, oxygen, and nitrogen. The principal macrominerals account for 3.5% of body weight. The percentage of macrominerals in the human body are: Ca, 1.5; P, 1.0; K, 0.35; S, 0.25; Cl, 0.15; and Mg, 0.15.

Typically, Ca represents about 46% and P about 29% of total body minerals. K, S, Na, Cl, and Mg together account for about 25%, whereas essential trace elements constitute less than 0.3% of the total. Mineral distribution within the body's tissues is not uniform, since some tissues selectively concentrate specific elements. However, the proportions of each mineral, expressed as amount of fat-free dry body substance, are very similar among species in adult mammals and poultry.

Each organ—in accordance with its function—has a characteristic mineral composition, which again is very similar in all mammals. However, after a period of undernutrition or water deprivation, there is quite a sharp rise in the mineral content (fat-free DM). The Na, K, and Cl concentrations of the body (% of body weight) are constant during all stages of development from embryo to full development, whereas the Mg, Ca, and P contents in the embryo are only one-half of the respective concentration in the adult animal.

Bone is the primary storage site for many of the essential elements. Between 80% and 85% of the total mineral matter, or ash, of the body is located in the skeletal tissues and consists mainly of salts of Ca, P, and Mg. Thus, 99% of the total Ca, 80% to 85% of P, and some 70% of Mg occur in bone. In contrast to Ca, P, and Mg in bone, the other four macrominerals are distributed more evenly throughout the body, where they exist in a variety of functional combinations and in characteristic concentrations. These elements must be maintained within quite narrow limits if the functional and structural integrity of the tissues is to be safeguarded and health and production optimized.

REQUIREMENTS

Macromineral requirements for the major livestock species have been established by a series of national research publications.[1,2] Requirements of different livestock classes will vary depending on: 1) class of animal; 2) type of feed fed; 3) activity of animal; 4) production of animal; 5) animal age and genetics; 6) environment factors (e.g., stress); 7) mineral interrelationships; and 8) criteria of requirement needs. In relation to criteria of requirement needs, the requirement for growth, optimum immune response, and maximum bone mineralization may be quite different. For example, the levels of Ca and P that result in maximum growth rate are not necessarily adequate for maximum bone mineralization. The requirements for maximizing bone strength and bone ash content for swine are at least 0.1 percentage unit higher than the requirements for maximum rate and efficiency of gain.[3] The requirements for Ca and P are dependent on the quantities and ratio to one another as well as vitamin D. General functions, metabolism, sources, interrelationsips, and toxicities have been summarized.[2]

Unlike other nutrients, mineral elements cannot be synthesized by living organisms. Minerals have four broad functions: structural, physiological, catalytic, and hormonal or regulatory. The most obvious function of mineral elements in the body is to provide structural support (skeleton). Bone is formed through the deposition of Ca and P as hydroxyapatite into a protein matrix. Ca, P, and Mg in bones and teeth all contribute to the mechanical

Encyclopedia of Animal Science
DOI: 10.1081/E-EAS 120019724

stability. Another example of structural function is the use of Ca by birds to produce eggshells. The presence of P and S in muscle proteins further illustrates the function of structural components of body tissue for these minerals. Minerals such as P can also contribute structural stability to the molecules and membranes of which they are part.

Only small fractions of the Ca, Mg, and P and most of the Na, K, and Cl are present as electrolytes in the body fluids and soft tissues. Electrolytes present in body fluids—such as blood or cerebrospinal fluid—serve important functions in maintaining acid–base equilibrium, water balance, and osmotic pressure; they regulate membrane permeability and affect the exitability of muscles and nerves. For example, a certain balance between Ca, Na, and K in the fluid that bathes the heart muscle is essential for the normal relaxation and contraction that constitute heart beats. Profound disturbances in neuromuscular function arise in animals when Ca and Mg in the blood plasma levels fall below threshold limits.

In addition to its bone function, P participates in a multiplicity of metabolic reactions involving energy transfer. Phosphorus is also an integral part of the nucleic acids. Certain minerals have regulatory functions in that they exert some control on cell replication and differentiation; Ca, for example, influences signal transduction. Functions of minerals are interrelated and balanced against each other, and most often cannot be considered as single elements with independent and self-sufficient roles in organized bodily processes. A definite relationship between Ca and vitamin D is needed for formation of bones and teeth.[4] Na, K, Ca, P, and Cl serve individually and collectively in the body fluids.

MACROMINERAL DEFICIENCIES

Calcium and Phosphorus

Failure of normal Ca and P nutrition may occur at any time of life when the supply of these elements and the factors concerned in their assimilation, notably vitamin D, are not adequate to meet functional needs. The outstanding disease of Ca and P deficiency is rickets, a decreased concentration of Ca and P in the organic matrices of cartilage and bone. In the adult, osteomalacia (the counterpart of rickets when longitudinal bone growth has ceased) is characterized by a decreased concentration of Ca and P in the bone matrix. In young animals, outward signs of rickets include the following skeletal changes, varying somewhat with species depending on anatomy and severity: 1) weak bones, causing curving and bending of bones; 2) enlarged hock and knee joints; 3) tendency to drag hind legs; and 4) beaded ribs and deformed thorax.

Clinical signs of Ca or P deficiency are seen mainly in the young. Deficiency results in an inhibition of growth, loss of weight, and reduced or lost appetite before characteristic signs in the skeletal system become apparent. The decreased mineralization of the bones results in lameness and fractures at all ages, although during the formative stage, abnormalities of bone growth are more common.

Naturally occurring deficiencies of Ca and P in domestic animals usually develop in quite different circumstances. Phosphorus deficiency is predominantly a condition of grazing ruminants, especially cattle, whereas Ca deficiency is more a problem of hand-fed animals, especially pigs and poultry. Extensive grazing areas in the world contain forages deficient in P.[3,5] Calcium deficiency is inevitable for swine and poultry fed low-Ca, cereal grain-based diets, and for high-yielding dairy cows given concentrate diets, unless diets are appropriately supplemented.

Sodium and Chlorine (Common Salt)

Deficiencies of Cl in animals in general have been unequivocally observed only on specially purified or concentrated diets. By contrast, extensive areas of Na deficiency in livestock occur worldwide. A dietary deficiency of Na is most likely to occur: 1) in rapidly growing young animals fed cereal-based diets or forages inherently low in Na; 2) during lactation as a consequence of Na (also Cl) losses in milk; 3) in tropical or hot regions conducive to loss of NaCl in sweat and particularly hard-working animals that sweat in abundance; and 4) for pastures fertilized with K that are high in K and low in Na. For all species, the initial sign of Na and Cl deficiency is a craving for salt, demonstrated by avid licking of wood, soil, and sweat from other animals, and by overconsumption of water.

Potassium

For all species studied, reduced appetite is one of the first signs of K deficiency. With K depletion in the body, there is depressed growth, muscular weakness, stiffness, and paralysis. Continued K deficiency results in intracellular acidosis, degeneration of vital organs, and nervous disorders. Potassium loss accompanies persistent diarrhea. Young animals with diarrhea develop acidosis and a K deficit more rapidly than do mature animals. Body stores of K are small; therefore, a deficiency can occur rapidly.

Magnesium

Magnesium deficiency is manifested clinically by retarded growth, hyperirritability and tetany, peripheral vasodilation, anorexia, muscular incoordination, and convulsions.

Most practical diets contain adequate Mg to promote optimal performance. The exception is grazing ruminants and especially mature lactating cattle, which are most susceptible to Mg deficiency and/or abnormal Mg metabolism. Because of the adequacy of Mg for most species consuming typical diets, special dietary ingredients (i.e., purified diets) are used to study both requirements and deficiency in nonruminants.

Sulfur

Despite the fact that S is a key mineral in many compounds essential for life, dietary inorganic S is not necessary for the health of monogastric animals. Pigs and poultry can do quite well with only organic S (S-amino acids, thiamin, biotin, etc.) sources in their diets. The dietary requirements of S are not stated for monogastric species but, rather, the requirement for methionine. Clinical signs of deficiency for monogastric species are typical for protein efficiency (e.g., suboptimal growth) in the various monogastric species.

Outward signs of S deficiency include loss of appetite, reduced weight gain, reduced wool growth in sheep, excessive lacrimation, cloudy eyes, dullness, weakness, emaciation, and death.[1] With deficiency, wool or hair can be shed; adding S to deficient animals increased grease and clean mohair production and staple length.[6] Lameness in dairy cattle may be associated with S deficiency, as characterized by slower growing, less flexible hooves.

SUPPLEMENTATION

Farm livestock should be provided with supplemental minerals under most circumstances. The minerals most likely needed for mineral supplementation are common salt (NaCl) and Ca and P. Minerals can be provided as mineral blocks, as free-choice minerals, and as part of the overall ration mix. Minerals can also be provided via water and through increased feed mineral concentration as a result of crop fertilization with minerals.

CONCLUSION

Seven required mineral elements are classified as macro-minerals: Ca, P, Na, Cl, K, Mg, and S. Requirements of these minerals are dependent class of animal, type of feed fed, animal activity, production level, age, genetics, environment, and mineral interrelationships. Diet supplementation is needed to provide these elements, particularly Ca, P, and NaCl, to different classes of livestock.

REFERENCES

1. McDowell, L.R. *Minerals in Human Nutrition*, 2nd Ed.; Elsevier: London, GB, 2003.
2. McDowell, L.R. *Minerals in Grazing Ruminants in Tropical Regions*, 3rd Ed.; University of Florida: U.S.A., 1997.
3. NCR. Nutrient Requirements of Domestic Animals. In *Nutrient Requirements of Swine*, 10th Ed.; National Academy of Sciences - National Research Council: Washington, DC, 1998.
4. McDowell, L.R. *Vitamins in Animal and Human Nutrition*, 2nd Ed.; Iowa State University Press, 2000.
5. McDowell, L.R. *Nutrition of Grazing Ruminants in Warm Climates*; Academic Press: N.Y., 1985.
6. Qi, K.; Owens, F.N.; Lu, C.D. Effects of sulfur deficiency on performance of fiber-producing sheep and goats. Small Rumin. Res. **2000**, *14*, 302.

Mineral Elements: Micro (Trace)

Xin Gen Lei
Cornell University, Ithaca, New York, U.S.A.

Hong Yang
ADM Alliance Nutrition, Inc., Quincy, Illinois, U.S.A.

INTRODUCTION

Trace minerals are so named because they exist in the body at concentrations of <0.001% and animals require them in diets at <100 mg/kg of feed. Up to the early 1950s, only six trace elements (iron, iodine, copper, manganese, zinc, and cobalt) were identified as nutritionally essential. In 1957, selenium was added to the list. At present, another eight elements—including boron, chromium, lithium, molybdenum, nickel, silicon, tin, and vanadium— are considered occasionally beneficial or conditionally essential. Six elements—including aluminum, arsenic, cadmium, fluorine, lead, and mercury—are considered essentially toxic.[2] There is controversy as to whether elements such as arsenic and fluorine should also be classified as conditionally essential or simply as toxic. However, it is clear that copper, iodine, iron, manganese, selenium, and zinc are absolutely essential to domestic animals, and have the most practical significance. Cobalt is required by all species as a constituent of vitamin B_{12}. The chemical properties, major functions, deficiency and toxicity symptoms, requirements, maximal tolerable levels, and sources of seven trace elements are summarized in Table 1.

GENERAL FUNCTIONS

The best characterized and probably the most important function of trace elements is their catalytic roles in enzyme and hormone systems. As presented in Table 1, these elements serve as: 1) integral components of metalloenzymes such as copper, zinc, and manganese in superoxide dismutases or selenium in glutathione peroxidase; 2) activators or inhibitors of certain enzymes; and 3) structure components of hormones or their complexes such as iodine in thyroid hormones and zinc in insulin. Certain trace elements are essential components of metabolically important compounds such as iron in hemoglobin and cobalt in vitamin B_{12}. Although trace elements, similar to the macro ones, are normally detectable in bone and other organs or tissues, it is unclear whether they have any structural or electrolytic essentiality other than the aforementioned biocatalyst roles. In addition, a number of elements have been shown to be important for body immune functions, but their mechanism remains to be elucidated.

DOSE-DEPENDENT RESPONSES AND METABOLISM

Unlike other nutrients, trace elements cannot be generated in the body by de novo synthesis. Animals need to regularly ingest them from their diets or they may deplete their body store and develop deficiency (Table 1). Homeostatic regulations of trace elements in animals are largely unclear, but probably occur mainly through absorption. Specific metal transporters such as divalent metal transporter-I have been characterized. Meanwhile, urine, skin, hair, and breath also contribute to the loss of certain elements. The nutrient requirements of trace minerals by animals define the lower limits of dietary adequacy. These requirements are established by relating responses of specific biochemical indicators, growth or performance, and health to graded levels of dietary mineral concentrations. Deficiency occurs when trace element levels in diets are lower than required and animals do not receive nonoral supplementation. In contrast, excessive minerals in diets cause toxicity. The toxic levels of individual elements appear to be highly variable, ranging between 10 and 1500 times of the recommended adequate levels.[4] For some elements, dietary levels between the adequate and the toxic levels may have pharmacological effects. A good example is that high levels of copper (125–250 mg/kg of diet as sulfate) or zinc (up to 3000 mg/kg of diet as oxide) have been shown to promote growth and to help control gut pathogens. However, their effects are not additive in diets for weanling pigs,[5] and there are environmental concerns associated with such high dietary levels of metals.

Encyclopedia of Animal Science
DOI: 10.1081/E-EAS 120019725

Table 1 Chemical and nutritional properties of practically important trace elements

	Cobalt	Copper	Iodine	Iron	Manganese	Selenium	Zinc
Atomic number	27	29	53	26	25	34	30
Atomic weight	58.9	63.5	126.9	55.9	54.9	79.0	65.4
Major functions	A cofactor of vitamin B_{12}, involved in one-carbon unit metabolism	A component of metalloenzymes (cytochrome C oxidase, lysyl oxidase, superoxide dismutase, tyrosinase, etc.), involved in cellular respiration, cross-linking of connective tissues, pigmentation, integrity of central nervous system, immune function, reproduction, and lipid metabolism	A component of thyroid hormones, involved in regulation of metabolic rate, protein synthesis, reproduction, and mental development	A component of hemoglobin, myoglobin, cytochromes, and enzymes (catalase, etc.), involved in oxygen and electron transport and peroxide breakdown	A component of pyruvate carboxylase, superoxide dismutase, and glycosylamino transferases, involved in lipid and carbohydrate metabolism, cartilage development, blood clotting, antioxidation, reproduction and immune functions	A component of at least 15 enzymes such as glutathione peroxidase, involved in protecting biological membranes, proteins, and lipids from oxidative degeneration; important for thyroid hormone metabolism and reproduction; closely linked to vitamin E function	A component of >200 enzymes involved in DNA synthesis, nucleic acid, protein, lipid, carbohydrate, and vitamin metabolism; interact with insulin and other hormones; specific effect on gene expression, appetite, and skin and wound healing; essential for growth, reproduction, and immune functions
Typical deficiency signs	Similar to vitamin B_{12} deficiency: anemia, lack of appetite, poor growth, wasting away	Anemia, anoxia, ataxia, aortic rupture, bone disorders, depigmentation, loss of appetite	Goiter, myxedema, impaired reproduction, postnatal mortality, growth retardation, and integument disorders	Anemia, poor growth, pallor, rough hair coat, anoxia, fatty liver, and enlarged heart and spleen, loss of appetite	Skeletal abnormalities, perosis (chicks), ataxia, reproductive disorders, poor growth and appetite	White muscle disease (ruminants), exudative diathesis and pancreatic atrophy (chicks); liver necrosis and mulberry heart disease (pigs)	Abrupt loss of appetite and growth, parakeratosis, skeletal and reproductive disorders, reduced thymus weight

Toxicity	Reduced growth and feed intake, arthritis, gastritis, enteritis	Alkali disease (grazing animals), anorexia, hair loss, hoof separation, depression, emaciation, death	Reduced growth and appetite, anemia, stiffness of limbs and stilted gait	Anorexia, diarrhea, rickets, oliguria, diphasic shock, hypothermia, metabolic acidosis and death	Depression, anorexia, listless, eye lesions, impaired immune function, hypothermia	Nausea, vomiting, icterus, anemia, impaired growth and reproduction, paralysis, collapse and death	Anorexia, growth depression, emaciation, anemia, hyperchromemia, and debility
***Requirement*[a]**							
Cattle	30	0.1	20–40	50	0.50	10	0.1
Poultry	29–70	≤0.2	17–60	38–80	0.35	4–8	NR[b]
Swine	50–100	0.3	2–20	40–100	0.14	3–6	NR
MTL[c]							
Cattle	500	(2)	1000	1000	50	100	10
Poultry	1000	2	2000	1000	300	300	10
Swine	1000	2	400	3000	400	250	10
Sheep	300	(2)	1000	500	50	25	10
Common sources	Sulfate, oxide, and organic	Sodium selenate or selenite; Se-enriched yeast	Sulfate, oxide, and organic	Sulfate, oxide, carbonate, and organic	Calcium iodate, potassium iodide, and EDDI[d]	Sulfate, oxide, and organic	Carbonate, sulfate, chloride, and oxide (for ruminants)

[a]Requirement = Values (mg/kg of diet) are taken from NRC (National Research Council) standards.
[b]NR = No recommendations have been made by NRC. The levels in parentheses were derived by interspecies extrapolation.
[c]MTL = Maximal tolerable level (mg/kg of diet).
[d]EDDI = Ethylene diamine dihydro-iodide.

SOURCES

Trace elements are normally supplemented into animal diets as inorganic salts, primarily as oxide, sulfate, and carbonate. Bioavailability of any given element in these salts is generally high, but varies with the form of salt. Caution should be given to acid–base balance in formulating diets using various forms of trace mineral salts. Recently, a number of organic forms of trace element supplements have been developed, due to the increasing interests in improving bioavailability of trace elements to animals, in reducing their concentrations in animal excreta, and in enriching their contents in animal products for human health. According to the Association of American Feed Control Officials (AAFCO), there are five basic types of organic trace mineral complexes: metal polysaccharide complex, metal proteinate, metal amino acid complex, metal (specific amino acid) complex, and metal amino acid chelate. A limited amount of research has shown the benefit of these organic forms of trace minerals over their inorganic salts to animal nutrition and environment. However, further research is certainly warranted to confirm consistency of these benefits.

INTERACTIONS

It is well known that trace elements interact with each other, but the molecular mechanism and the physiological impacts of those interactions are far from clear. Simply speaking, different elements interact at sites of absorption, transport, metabolism, and function. A large portion of copper and zinc is presumably absorbed in the small intestine via the same protein carrier. Thus excess of zinc can induce a deficiency of copper. Mobilization of iron from storage for hemoglobin synthesis requires a copper-containing enzyme. Selenium-dependent iodothyronine 5′-deiodinase catalyzes the deiodination of thyroxine to the active 3,3′,5-triiodothyronine. As a result, selenium deficiency impairs iodine function. Meanwhile, antagonistic interactions between minerals such as selenium and arsenic or cobalt and iron can be used to alleviate the toxicity of each other.[1,3]

NEW PARADIGM

Traditionally, metabolic functions and nutrient requirements of trace elements have been studied using purified or natural diets deficient in a specific element. Because of the functional and metabolic complexity of trace elements, this conventional deficiency model does not give specific biochemical explanations to many clinical symptoms. In some cases, deficiency is not easy to produce. Recent advances in molecular biology have enabled scientists to determine the effects of trace elements on gene and protein expression, signal transduction, and metabolic functions at the molecular, cellular, and genomic levels.[6] The development of transgenic and gene-knockout animal models allows for the determination of specific functions of individual trace element–dependent or related proteins. A successful example is the use of selenium-dependent glutathione peroxidase-1 knockout mice to study the contribution of this particular enzyme to the total function of selenium.[7] These models can be applied to check the presumed functions of the established essential elements and to help in determining nutritional significance of those less well-characterized elements.

CONCLUSION

Seven trace elements have been well characterized as nutritionally essential to farm animals. The nutrient requirements of these elements by different species and their deficiency symptoms are better understood than the biochemical and molecular mechanisms for their physiological functions. Various organic complexes of trace elements have been developed to improve their bioavailability to animals and to reduce their excretion by animals to the environment.

REFERENCES

1. McDowell, L.R. *Minerals in Animals and Human Nutrition*; Academic Press: San Diego, CA, 1992.
2. Underwood, E.J.; Suttle, N.F. *The Mineral Nutrition of Livestock*, 3rd Ed.; CABI Publishing: New York, 1999.
3. Nelssen, J.L.; Miller, E.R.; Henry, S.C. Chapter 60: Nutrition, Deficiencies and Dietetics. In *Disease of Swine*; Leman, A.D., Straw, B.E., Mengeling, W.L., D'Allaire, S., Taylor, D.J., Eds.; Iowa State University Press: Ames, IA, 1992; 744–755.
4. NRC. *Mineral Tolerance of Domestic Animals*; National Academy Press, National Academy of Sciences: Washington, DC, 1980.
5. Hill, G.M.; Cromwell, G.L.; Crenshaw, T.D.; Dove, C.R.; Ewan, R.C.; Knabe, D.A.; Lewis, A.J.; Libal, G.W.; Mahan, D.C.; Shurson, G.C.; Southern, L.L.; Veum, T.L. Growth promotion effects and plasma changes from feeding high dietary concentrations of zinc and copper to weanling pigs (regional study). J. Anim. Sci. **2000**, *78*, 1010–1016.
6. O'Dell, B.L.; Sunde, R.A. *Handbook of Nutritionally Essential Mineral Elements*; Mercel Dekker, Inc.: New York, NY, 1997.
7. Lei, X.G. Chapter 19: In vivo Antioxidant Role of GPX1: Evidence From the Knockout Mice. In *Protein Sensors of Reactive Oxygen Species: Selenoproteins, Thioredoxin, Thiol Enzymes, and Proteins*; Sies, H., Packer, L., Eds.; Methods in Enzymology, Academic Press, 2002; Vol. 347, 21–225.

Mitosis and Meiosis

David S. Buchanan
Oklahoma State University, Stillwater, Oklahoma, U.S.A.

INTRODUCTION

Multicelled organisms are composed of millions—or billions—of cells. Although these cells perform numerous diverse functions, almost all of them contain the genetic information necessary for operation of the entire organism. This information is stored in deoxyribonucleic acid (DNA). The structure and organization of DNA were discovered only 50 years ago.[1]

Two unique processes must be present for these cells to contain the proper DNA. These processes are called mitosis and meiosis. Mitosis is ordinary cell division. Meiosis is the process by which sperm and egg cells are formed in a manner that allows them to join together to start a new life. Detailed descriptions of these can be found in any standard textbook on genetics.

MITOSIS

DNA is organized into genes that reside on chromosomes. In animals, the chromosomes are linear DNA-protein complexes that reside in the nucleus of cells. Each species has a characteristic number of chromosomes (Table 1).[2]

Mitosis is the process by which one cell becomes two cells. Each life begins as a single cell and billions of mitoses enable the organism to grow and mature. New cells replace those that are no longer viable or are lost. Yet each of those cells, with only a few exceptions, contains the same genetic information. The process of mitosis allows this to happen properly.

Each cell goes through a process called the cell cycle. This cycle is roughly divided into four phases that total approximately 24 hours. One of those phases is mitosis, which takes approximately one hour. The other three phases—presynthesis gap, synthesis of DNA, and postsynthesis gap—compose interphase. The key event that occurs during interphase is the replication of DNA. During this time each chromosome is precisely duplicated.

The cell goes through a very precise four-step process during mitosis. These steps are called prophase, metaphase, anaphase, and telophase (Fig. 1). During prophase the chromosomes shorten and thicken, such that they become visible by examination under a microscope. Spindle fibers begin to form at the ends of the cell and

they attach to the centromeres (point of junction between the two chromatids). The chromosomes are composed of two chromatids as they enter mitosis because they have undergone replication during interphase. During metaphase the chromosomes migrate to and line up along the central plane of the cell. Anaphase is characterized by the splitting of the centromeres and migration of the chromosomes toward the poles. This is accomplished with the assistance of the spindle fibers. The final phase is telophase, during which the cell will undergo cytokinesis (division of the cytoplasm or cell contents) to become two cells.

At this point there are two new cells where previously only one existed. The genetic material in the nucleus of the two new cells is identical. Furthermore, even if these are cells that have become specialized (muscle, nerve, skin, cardiac, etc.), each of these new cells contains all of the genetic material for the organism, not just the genetic material pertaining to the nature of the specialized cell.

MEIOSIS

In organisms that reproduce sexually, there must be a mechanism by which cells are formed that can combine to form a new member of the species. These specialized cells are called gametes. In animals, the male gamete is called the sperm and the female gamete is called the egg. Such cells must contain one member of each pair of chromosomes so that, when combined with the cell from the other parent, they will form a zygote (fertilized egg), which is the first cell of the new organism. The mechanism by which such cells are formed is called meiosis.

In animals, meiosis occurs only in those cells that are designed to produce the sperm or egg cells. Such cells exist in the testes in the male and in the ovaries of the female. These cells undergo normal mitoses until they are prepared to start a process during which they will reduce the number of chromosomes by half and produce gametes.

Meiosis involves two successive cell divisions (Fig. 2). Each division includes a prophase, metaphase, anaphase, and telophase. There is no interphase between the two divisions. Prophase I is divided into several specific

Encyclopedia of Animal Science
DOI: 10.1081/E-EAS 120019726

Table 1 Chromosome numbers of selected species

Organism	Chromosome number (2N)
Human	46
Cattle	60
Goat	60
Sheep	54
Swine	38
Chicken	78
Turkey	82
Horse	64
Donkey	62
Dog	78
Cat	38
Fruit fly	8
Mouse	40

(Adapted from Ref. 1.)

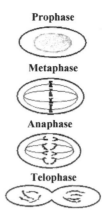

Fig. 2 Meiosis. (From Refs. 3–6.)

phases: leptotene (thin thread), during which the chromosomes start to condense; zygotene (paired thread), when the homologous chromosomes (members of the same pair) pair together (synapsis); and pachytene (thick thread), in which the homologous pairs form tetrads (each pair of chromosomes is composed of four chromatids). The genetic diversity-increasing process of crossing over (sharing of genetic material between homologous chromosomes) begins during pachytene. Finally, diplotene (double thread) is characterized by more condensation of the chromosomes and clearly distinguished chiasma (points of crossing over). Prophase I is completed when the homologous chromosomes begin to pull apart, except at the points of chiasma in a process called diakinesis. Metaphase I is characterized by the homologous pairs of chromosomes lining up along the central plane. During anaphase I the homologous chromosomes separate, but the chromatids stay together and during telophase I the

cellular material divides so that there are now two cells. At this point each of the two cells contains one replicated chromosome from each pair. The member of each homologous pair that is contained in each cell is chosen randomly. There is no interphase, and therefore no replication, prior to prophase II. Indeed, the events of telophase I and prophase II blend together so that there are not two separate pictures in Fig. 2 illustrating the two phases. During metaphase II the chromosomes line up along the metaphase plate. Anaphase II is characterized by a splitting of the centromeres and movement of the separated chromatids (now called chromosomes again) to the poles. During telophase II, the cellular material splits and daughter cells are formed. There are now four cells, each with one member of each homologous pair of chromosomes. Genetic diversity has been created by the Mendelian law of segregation, which describes the fact that the member of each pair of chromosomes that resides in the gamete is random. The principle of independent assortment describes the fact that the segregation of chromosomes for any one pair is independent of the segregation of chromosomes for any other pair and crossing over.

GAMETOGENESIS

Meiosis, when combined with additional processes to form functional gametes, is called gametogenesis (formation of gametes). In the males, this is called spermatogenesis and is referred to as oogenesis in the female. Spermatogenesis occurs continuously throughout the reproductive life of the male. Oogenesis is typically arrested during prophase I until the female begins to ovulate. At that time, oogenesis continues to develop one egg for release at each ovulation. For some species, like cattle, there is typically one ovulation each estrous cycle. Litter-bearing species may have several ovulations during

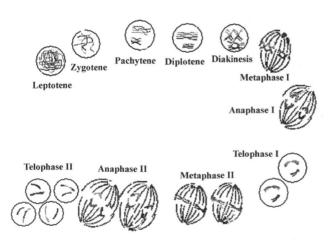

Fig. 1 The four stages of mitosis. (From Refs. 3–6.)

each estrous cycle. Each spermatogenesis results in four sperm cells that have the potential to be viable. Each oogenesis results in only one potentially viable egg cell. The other products of meiosis are called polar bodies. Polar bodies contain the chromosomes in the nucleus but little additional cytoplasm (nonnucleus cell contents). The resulting larger size means that the egg has more nutrients for the developing embryo than for the cells that become the polar bodies.

CONCLUSION

Mitosis is ubiquitous in life. The machinery for mitosis is essentially the same in almost all organisms. One cell becomes two cells. Each of those becomes two cells and so on and so on. Single-celled organisms undergo mitosis as the mechanism of reproduction, whereas multicelled organisms undergo mitosis to build bodies. In either case, the daughter cells have the same genetic material and have all the genetic material for any type of cell, even if differentiation has occurred and the cells in question now have a specific function. Species with sexual reproduction also undergo meiosis in a manner that is highly uniform across a wide range of species. In meiosis, gametes are formed that contain one member of each chromosome pair. Processes in meiosis create genetic diversity through a number of mechanisms such that no two gametes produced by any one individual contain precisely the same

genes. These mechanisms must work properly an exceptionally high proportion of the time in order for life to continue.

Mitosis and meiosis are similar processes but differ in some important ways. Mitosis involves only a single division, whereas meiosis involves two divisions. Mitosis results in two identical daughter cells, whereas meiosis results in four unique daughter cells. The daughter cells from a mitotic division contain the full complement of chromosomes, whereas the daughter cells from meiosis contain just one representative from each pair of chromosomes.

REFERENCES

1. Watson, J.D.; Crick, F.H.C. Molecular structure of nucleic acids. Nature **1953**, *171*, 737–738.
2. Hutt, F.B.; Rasmusen, B.A. *Animal Genetics*, 2nd Ed.; John Wiley & Sons Inc.: New York, 1982; 108–121.
3. Hartl, D.L.; Jones, E.W. *Genetics: Analysis of Genes and Genomes*, 5th Ed.; Jones and Bartlett: Sudbury, MA, 2001; 134–148.
4. Klug, W.S.; Cummings, M.R. *Concepts of Genetics*, 7th Ed.; Prentice Hall—Pearson Education, Inc.: Upper Saddle River, NJ, 2003; 19–44.
5. Russell, P.J. *Genetics*; Benjamin Cummings: San Francisco, 2002; 9–24.
6. Snustad, D.P.; Simmons, M.J. *Principles of Genetics*, 2nd Ed.; John Wiley & Sons, Inc.: New York, 2000; 23–40.

Mohair: Biology and Characteristics

Christopher John Lupton
Texas A&M University, San Angelo, Texas, U.S.A.

INTRODUCTION

Mohair is the white, lustrous fiber produced by the Angora goat (*capra hircus aegagrus*). Most goat breeds have double coats (to highly variable degrees), consisting of an outer coat of coarse guard hairs and a relatively short undercoat of fine down that sheds annually. The practice from early times of selecting for white, wavy, lustrous, single-coated (i.e., no coarse guard hair) fleeces that do not shed eventually resulted in the stabilization of this type of fleece and an animal that has both high priority for and high efficiency of fiber production. Only recently have nonwhite (e.g., brown and black) Angora goats become popular with specialty breeders. In spite of mohair's specialty status and historically low production, it has been the subject of many studies and research reports. Some of these were in association with wool, and much of the research added to our understanding of human hair growth, a topic that remains economically and sociologically important.

SKIN BIOLOGY

Mohair fibers are produced by cell division in primary (P) and secondary (S) follicles in the skin of Angora goats (Fig. 1). The two types of follicles are distinguished by their accessory structures. The P follicles each have a sebaceous gland, a sudoriferous (sweat) gland, and an arrector pili muscle. The S follicles have only a sebaceous gland. Some S follicles produce more than one fiber. The central P follicles are first observed on the fetal head about 40 days into pregnancy and spread across the body over the next 20 days. During this time, two more P follicles (laterals) appear on either side of the central P follicle, thus forming a trio group. After 80 days of pregnancy, S follicles associated with each trio group begin to emerge, forming a follicle group. At birth (day 149), all P follicles are fully formed and are actively producing fiber, whereas only a small but quite variable proportion of the S follicles are producing fibers. Twelve weeks after birth, most of the secondary follicles are producing fibers. The ratio of S follicles to P follicles in mature Angora goats ranges from 6 to 12:1 (compare merino sheep at 15 to 25:1). Prenatal and early postnatal nutrition affects the rate of maturation and the ultimate number of active S follicles. This number has a direct influence on the lifetime production of mohair.

Fibers produced by P follicles are coarser than those produced by S follicles. In some cases, the fiber produced in a P follicle is medullated (hollow) to varying degrees. When medullation exceeds 60% of the fiber diameter, the fiber is termed a kemp, which is a chalky white, objectionable (from a textile viewpoint) fiber that appears not to accept dyestuff. Centuries of visual selection against kemp have resulted in low levels in most commercial animals. When the degree of medullation is less than 60% of the fiber diameter, this fiber is termed a med or heterotype. Angora goats containing excessive amounts of these fibers are also discriminated against, because med and kemp production appear to be inseparable genetic traits.[2]

FIBER MORPHOLOGY

Fine mohair fibers are round in cross-section. As the fibers become coarser, the cross-section becomes more elliptical. Some kemp fibers are collapsed and have the appearance of a flattened straw. The microstructure of mohair fibers is composed predominantly of cortex, a collection of long, cigar-shaped cortical cells ($\sim 8 \times 100$ microns) lying parallel to the fiber axis that are embedded in a matrix sometimes referred to as intercellular cement (composed of lipids and sulfur-rich proteins). The cigar-shaped cortical cells are themselves composed of macrofibrils, which in turn are made up of microfibrils (low sulfur-content proteins). It has been suggested that microfibrils consist of protofibrils, which in turn are composed of three polypeptide molecules arranged in an α-helix.

Overlapping scales (about 0.4 microns in thickness) composed of cuticle cells surround the cortex, each having a free edge that points toward the tip of the fiber (Fig. 2). The scales consist of three distinct layers—the epi-, exo-, and endocuticle—and form a protective coating around the cortex. Though similar in appearance to the scales on coarse wools, scale thickness in mohair is invariably less than that of wool (0.7 to 1.0 micron, Fig. 3). This difference is the basis of a scanning electron

Encyclopedia of Animal Science
DOI: 10.1081/E-EAS 120019727

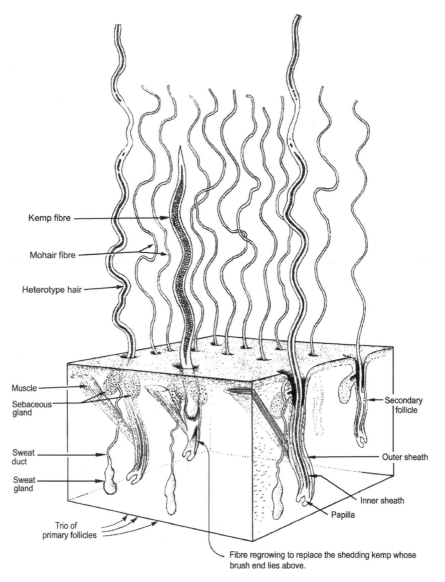

Fig. 1   Simplified drawing of adult Angora goat skin. (From Ref. 1 with permission from Elsevier.)

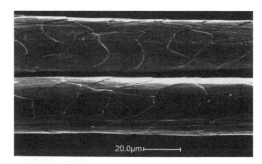

Fig. 2   Magnified image of mohair fibers obtained with a scanning electron microscope. (Courtesy of the International Wool Textile Organization.)

microscope test method for quantifying mohair and wool in textile blends.

A third component of the fiber, the medulla, is contained in some of the fibers produced by P follicles and consists of a continuous or fragmented central core composed of air-filled cell residues (Fig. 1). A bilateral arrangement of two types of cell has been reported in the cortex of wool: orthocortical and paracortical cells. Both types also exist (but randomly mixed) in mohair, but orthocortical cells predominate, especially in mohair grown by young animals. Paracortical cells have about twice the sulfur content of ortho-cells. This sulfur is contained in amino acids that cross-link adjacent peptide chains in the protein structure. Consequently, mohair has lower

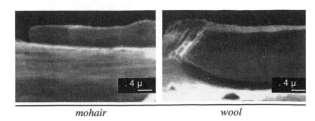

mohair   wool

Fig. 3 Scanning electron microscope images of mohair and wool scale edges showing the difference in thickness. (Courtesy of the International Wool Textile Organization.)

resistance to chemicals (e.g., acids and alkalis) but can absorb dye molecules faster than wool.

CHEMICAL COMPOSITION

Chemically, mohair, cashmere, and wool are very similar. The parent protein of the fibers is keratin, a complex mixture of proteins containing the sulfur-amino acid cystine. In the raw fleece, natural nonprotein impurities also are present. These include suint (water-soluble dried sweat secreted by the sudoriferous glands), wax (secreted by the sebaceous glands), inorganic dust and dirt, and organic vegetable matter (twigs, seeds, burrs, etc.). One objective of textile scouring and processing is to eliminate these contaminants. Moisture (up to 30%) is also associated with mohair. On a dry basis, cleansed mohair contains approximately 50% carbon, 22–25% oxygen, 16–17% nitrogen, 7% hydrogen, and 3 to 4% sulfur. The basic building blocks for keratin are 18 amino acids. Differences among the amino acid contents of adult, kid, and kemp mohair fibers have been documented.

FIBER GROWTH

Mature females (called does, ewes, or nannies) produce 2 to 2.5 kg of greasy mohair every six months. This production is under genetic and nutritional control to varying degrees. In contrast, kids (6 months and 12

Table 1 Ranges for important mohair characteristics

Clean yield (U.S. ranges; South African values are reported to be higher), %	Kids (6–12 mo)	70–76
	Young goats (18 mo)	72–78
	Mature does (≥2 yr)	74–80
Grease content, %		1–10
Suint content, %		1.5–5.0
Average fiber diameter, μm	Kids (6–12 mo)	21–29
	Young goats (18 mo)	30–34
	Mature does (≥2 yr)	32–38
	Mature bucks (≥2 yr)	32–45
Secondary/primary follicle ratio (mature animal)		6–12:1
(at birth)		2.5:1
Follicles per unit area, mm^2		10–20
Lock length (6-month), cm		7.5–15
Lock type	Ringlet, flat, intermediate, sheepy, unclassifiable	
Waves per unit length, cm^{-1}		2–7
Medullation, %		0–8
Color	White (yellow, brown, stained); brown; black	
Specific gravity		1.297–1.320
Regain at 65% rh and 21°C, %		14.5–17.5
Tenacity, cN/tex		13–17
Elongation at break, %		40–43
Work at rupture, cN/tex		2.65
Initial modulus, cN/tex		350–410

(From Refs. 2–6.)

months of age) typically yield less than 1 kg at their first shearing and between 1 and 1.5 kg at the second shearing. In a six-month period, the fiber grows to a length of 10 to 15 cm, this being a requirement for worsted (long-staple) processing.

Age, nutrition, season, sex, and reproductive status each have important effects on mohair production and properties. From birth to about four years of age, the mohair fibers become progressively coarser, after which time the average fiber diameter remains fairly constant. After four years of age, Angora does begin to produce less mohair, and some follicles stop producing altogether. Mohair production by kids and mature animals is influenced greatly by the plane of nutrition. Inadequate nutrition causes fewer, shorter, and finer fibers to be produced. Unless goats are on a very high plane of nutrition, mohair production and average fiber diameter will usually respond positively to protein supplementation. Mohair shorn in February (grown in autumn and winter) is usually shorter, finer, and less kempy than that shorn in August (grown predominantly in spring and summer). Males tend to produce more, coarser, and longer mohair than females of similar age maintained under similar conditions. Pregnant and lactating Angora does tend to produce less and finer mohair than comparable nonpregnant does.

PHYSICAL PROPERTIES

Physical properties important for marketing, textile processing, and product performance are listed in Table 1. The great versatility of mohair is due in part to its availability in a wide range of fiber diameters. The more valuable 26-micron mohair can be manufactured into fine, lightweight suitings, whereas 40-micron mohair might be used to make hard-wearing rugs, carpets, or upholstery. Several of mohair's unique or superior properties may be attributed to its relatively thin scale structure. These include high luster, smooth feel (handle), good resistance to soiling and physical abrasion, excellent soil release, and low propensity for felting. Similarly, the physical and chemical structure of the mohair cortex is responsible for superior durability, tenacity, strength, and elasticity compared to wool of similar dimensions. The predominance of orthocortical cells in mohair explains mohair's superior ability to be set in a predetermined shape (e.g., a crease in a pair of trousers) and to be dyed to deeper shades than wool, whereas the perceived brilliance of such dyeings is likely more a function of mohair's exceptional whiteness and luster. In common with wool and other animal fibers, mohair has low flammability, is subject to attack by moths, bacteria, and mildew, has excellent moisture absorption and release (important for comfort), has very good insulation properties, and blends well with other fibers.

CONCLUSION

Growth and structure of mohair have been the subjects of numerous studies and reports.[4–6] Many scientists would agree on the gross aspects of structure and chemical composition. However, the absolute physical structure of mohair fibers and the chemical composition of the many individual protein fractions and associated lipids that constitute mohair's keratin are either unknown or are the subjects of much conjecture. With declining national budgets for animal fiber research (and agricultural and textile research in general), it is doubtful these unknowns will be determined in the foreseeable future. Nevertheless, this unique and versatile fiber continues to be grown and used, and it is still quite an important commodity in specific areas of South Africa, the United States, and Turkey. With the increasing movement toward natural and organic products by (relatively) affluent consumers in developed nations, and perhaps with a favorable change in fashion, it is possible that the downward trend in mohair production could be reversed.

ARTICLES OF FURTHER INTEREST

Angora Goats: Production and Management, p. 13
Mohair: Production and Marketing, p. 649

REFERENCES

1. Ryder, M.L.; Stephenson, S.K. *Wool Growth*; Elsevier, 1968.
2. Lupton, C.J.; Pfeiffer, F.A.; Blakeman, N.E. Medullation in mohair. Small Rumin. Res. **1991**, *5*, 357–365.
3. Van der Westhuysen, J.M.; Wentzel, D.; Grobler, M.C. *Angora Goats and Mohair in South Africa*, 3rd Ed.; Mohair Board: Port Elizabeth, 1988; 258 pp.
4. Hunter, L. *Mohair: A Review of Its Properties, Processing and Applications*; CSIR Division of Textile Technology, Port Elizabeth, South Africa and International Mohair Association, Ilkley, U.K., 1993; 278 pp.
5. Hunter, L.; Hunter, E.L. Mohair. In *Silk, Mohair, Cashmere and Other Luxury Fibres*; Franck, R.R., Ed.; Woodhead Publishing Ltd.: Cambridge, England, 2001; 68–132.
6. Shelton, M. *Angora Goat and Mohair Production*; Mohair Council of America: San Angelo, 1993; 233 pp.

Mohair: Production and Marketing

Christopher John Lupton
Texas A&M University, San Angelo, Texas, U.S.A.

INTRODUCTION

Mohair is the white, lustrous fiber produced by the Angora goat (*Capra hircus aegagrus*). This unique breed of goat, thought to have originated in the Asian Himalayas, had migrated to the Ankara region of Turkey by the 13th century. The breed obtained its name from this region. The word mohair is derived from the Arabic word mukhayar, variously translated as best of selected fleece, select choice, silky-goat skin cloth, cloth of bright goat hair, and hair cloth. The spinning and textile processing of mohair was confined to Turkey until 1820, when a few bales of the raw material were exported to Europe. Mohair is a specialty animal fiber, others being cashmere, alpaca, camel, and llama hair, to name but a few. Mohair production is an important agricultural activity in South Africa, the United States, and Turkey, in regions where agricultural enterprise options are limited by harsh range conditions. In recent years, South Africa has consistently produced the most mohair, but this has not and may not always be the case. Specific climate and economic conditions, combined with current and anticipated demand for mohair, have over time caused growers to alternate between mohair production and other livestock enterprises. Production in the United States, primarily in Texas, has been declining since 1989.

THE MOHAIR INDUSTRY

Mohair constitutes ~0.01% of world textile fiber production (Table 1). World production of mohair is summarized in Table 2. In the broadest sense, the industry is made up of producers, their Angora goats (Fig. 1), and employees on the ranches and farms, as well as professional shearers, fiber handlers, and classers (for harvesting mohair), and warehouse personnel and mohair buyers (for marketing) who arrange for purchase and transfer of the fiber from the warehouse to facilities where it will be scoured and processed into yarn and fabric. Because the mohair industry (and the specialized fiber industry in general) is so fragmented, these textile processes typically involve movement of the mohair through many production areas—and often among countries—before a finished product is obtained. It would not be unusual for mohair produced in Texas to be blended with South African mohair, manufactured into fabric in one or more countries in Europe, then shipped to countries in Asia for garment manufacturing, and finally returned to the United States for sale.

SHEARING, FLEECE PREPARATION, AND MARKETING

In typical range operations, Angora goats are gathered twice a year (February and August in the Northern Hemisphere) for shearing. Animals are drafted into three major age categories—kid, young goat (18 months old), and adult, providing about 20%, 20%, and 60% by weight of the total clip, respectively—and shorn by professional shearers. Shearing facilities range from makeshift tents with plywood floors and temporary pens to custom-built shearing sheds complete with raised hardwood shearing floors and individual catch pens. In Texas, shearers use power-driven shears to first remove mohair from the belly and legs before tying all four legs. This essentially immobilizes the animal and facilitates removal of the rest of the fleece, ideally in one piece. The mohair is then moved from the shearing floor to another location, depending on the marketing philosophy of the producer.

Some owners attempt to add value to their clip at this point by removing urine- and fecal-stained portions, as well as any inferior mohair. The remaining mohair may be further differentiated by fiber diameter, staple length and structure (e.g., ringlet versus flat lock), type or amount of vegetable contamination, and estimated clean yield. This grading or classing may be accomplished by a skilled owner or an experienced classer. In this case, bags (or bales) of classed mohair are delivered to the warehouse for sale. The processes are labor-intensive and slow. Some U.S. producers concur that this extra work after shearing is not cost-effective, and they package their mohair straight from the shearing floor into burlap bags that are delivered to the warehouse as "original bag" (OB) mohair. Before processing, this mohair must be skirted and classed either at the warehouse or at the textile mill.

In South Africa, shearing is carried out using hand or power shears. Most South African growers take great

Encyclopedia of Animal Science
DOI: 10.1081/E-EAS 120034271

Table 1 World textile fiber production in 2000, million kg

Fiber	Amount
Rayon and acetate[a]	2,199
Noncellulosic fibers[b]	25,977
Cotton	19,173
Wool	1,374
Flax	671
Silk	86
Hemp (soft)	74
Mohair[c]	5.52
TOTAL	49,559.52

[a]Excluding filter tow.
[b]Excluding polyolefin.
[c]Not included in original table.
(From Refs. 1–3.)

Fig. 1 Angora goats on western Texas rangeland exhibiting the unique luster for which their mohair is famous. (Photograph courtesy of J.W. Walker.) (*View this art in color at www. dekker.com.*)

personal pride in having the entire clip skirted and classed at the ranch prior to delivery for sale. Both South Africa and the United States have official guidelines[3–5] for classing and marketing mohair. At the warehouse, the different lines may be grab-and-core-sampled and the samples objectively tested for the main value-determining characteristics: clean yield, vegetable matter content, average fiber diameter (and variability), degree of medullation, and possibly staple length and staple strength. This information may be made available to mohair buyers when they view representative opened bags or bales of mohair. Sales may be by private treaty, sealed bid, or open bid, the first method being quite common in the United States and open bid being more popular in South Africa. The buyer's representative then arranges for transportation to a scouring plant. Prices (converted to U.S. currency and weight units) paid for South African mohair in December 2003 are listed in Table 3. The lower adjusted

Texas prices reflect the high proportion of OB mohair that is marketed in the United States.

TEXTILE PROCESSING

Typically, many different producer lots are blended to constitute a processing lot. As it progresses from raw fiber to finished textile, mohair passes through a series of mechanical and aqueous treatments. A list of those processes follows.[6]

- *Opening.* This is a mechanical process designed to remove loose dirt and vegetable material prior to washing.
- *Scouring.* Raw mohair is cleaned in a scouring process that dissolves suint, emulsifies wax, and removes and suspends dirt particles. This is achieved by raking the fiber through a series of four to six large baths containing hot water and detergent, each one followed by a squeeze roller. After the final rinse bath, the mohair is again squeezed to remove excess water and then dried.
- *Carbonizing.* Mohair contaminated with excessive amounts of vegetable matter must be carbonized. This involves impregnation of the mohair with dilute sulfuric acid, followed by drying, baking, shaking, neutralizing, rewashing, and drying. Carbonizing is expensive and environmentally challenging. Only badly contaminated lots are treated in this way.
- *Processing additives.* Scoured mohair is frequently sprayed with oils and other chemicals to facilitate

Table 2 Mohair production by country in 2002

Country	Production, million kg, greasy	Percentage of world production
South Africa	4.20	63.6
United States	0.75	11.4
Lesotho	0.45	6.8
Argentina	0.30	4.6
Turkey	0.30	4.6
Australia	0.20	3.0
New Zealand	0.10	1.5
Other	0.30	4.5
TOTAL	6.60	100.0

(From Ref. 3.)

Table 3 Description, micron ranges, and prices of mohair sold on December 2, 2003

Description	Micron range	South African actual sale price, U.S. $/lb greasy	Adjusted Texas price,[a] $/lb greasy
Fine kid	<26.0	7.21	6.69
Good kid	26.0–27.9	5.12	4.67
Average kid	28.0–29.9	3.76	3.36
Young goat	30.0–31.9	2.93	2.56
Find adult	32.0–33.9	2.16	1.81
Adult	≥34.0	2.16	1.81

[a]Texas prices adjusted for typical U.S. marketing costs (commission, freight, clearance, sorting, stain loss, and clean yield) in an attempt by MCA to estimate expected prices for comparable U.S. mohair.
(From the Mohair Council of America (MCA) Newsletter, 12/2/2003.)

mechanical processing and minimize static electricity. Application of processing additives may occur before opening and possibly again before combing. The types and amounts of these compounds and procedures for adding them are closely guarded trade secrets, as are the specifics of the mechanical processes themselves.

- *Worsted processing.* Most mohair is processed on the worsted system, which involves the following processes: opening and cleaning, carding, pin-drafting, combing, pin-drafting, autoleveling, roving, ring spinning, and twisting.[7]
- *Woolen processing.* Mohair is also processed using the woolen system, which involves fewer stages of processing and produces a softer, bulkier yarn.
- *Fabric formation.* Once in yarn form, mohair can be woven, knitted, or made into rugs and carpets.
- *Dyeing.* Mohair can be dyed at almost any stage of processing (immediately after scouring or in the sliver, yarn, or fabric forms) to produce many attractive and varied effects.

Fig. 2 A multicolored lady's jacket knitted with brushed mohair yarns. (*View this art in color at www.dekker.com.*)

- *Finishing.* To stabilize and enhance their appearance, mohair fabrics are subjected to finishing processes. These may include desizing, washing, decating, drying, semidecating, brushing, and pressing.

END USES OF MOHAIR

Compared to wool, other specialty fibers, and other natural and synthetic fibers, the main distinguishing characteristics of mohair are its luster, whiteness, ability to be dyed to brilliant colors (Fig. 2), smooth handle, durability, and resistance to soiling and felting shrinkage. Traditionally, mohair was used in hand knitting yarns (~65%), men's suiting fabrics (~15%), women's woven accessories and rugs (~12%), and woven furnishings and velours (~8%). Consumption trends are changing, however, and in the United States particularly, a greater promotional emphasis is being placed on adult mohair for carpets and rugs. Often, mohair is blended with wool or synthetic fibers to either improve product performance, assist in processing, or reduce product cost. End use is greatly influenced by fashion. Hunter[6] documented 189 specific end uses for mohair.

CONCLUSION

Despite its numerous superior and unique properties, mohair production is declining. This is a result of mohair producers not being able to make a consistent, adequate income from this enterprise. This in turn is a result of competition from new fibers and textile products, shifting consumer preferences, and mohair being regarded as a fashion fiber and thus being subject to unpredictable demand. One positive aspect of decreasing supply is the general increase in consistency and quality of mohair being produced. Producer and textile processor organizations have made many attempts to increase and stabilize mohair consumption by developing and promoting products that are not subject to fashion-related uncertainties. Their efforts have met with mixed success. Use of mohair in socks, sweaters, rugs, and carpets appears to be on the increase in the United States. Also in the United States, the federal government provided a support program for mohair in the 2002 Farm Bill to assist producers. This program was designed to provide a higher and more consistent income from mohair production, just as similar programs do for wool and cotton growers. The support program is expected to stabilize U.S. production of mohair, at least for the duration of the current Farm Bill. South African production of mohair is expected to increase slowly and then stabilize, so long as current prices remain firm.

ARTICLES OF FURTHER INTEREST

Angora Goats: Production and Management, p. 13
Mohair: Biology and Characteristics, p. 645

REFERENCES

1. USDA, Economic Research Service, Market and Trade Economics Division. *Cotton and Wool: Situation and Outlook Yearbook*; November 2002; 56 pp. http://jan.mannlib.cornell.edu/reports/erssor/field/cws=bby (accessed February, 2004).
2. *Natural Fibers Information Center*: http://www.utexas.edu/depts/bbr/natfiber (accessed February, 2004).
3. *South African Classing Standards. Source: Mohair South Africa.* http://www.mohair.co.za (accessed March, 2004).
4. Hunter, L.; Hunter, E.L. Mohair. In *Silk, Mohair, Cashmere and Other Luxury Fibres*; Franck, R.R., Ed.; Woodhead Publishing Ltd.: Cambridge, UK, 2001; 68–132.
5. *Guidelines for Marketing U.S. Mohair*; Mohair Council of America: San Angelo, 1990.
6. Hunter, L. *Mohair: A Review of Its Properties, Processing and Applications*; CSIR Division of Textile Technology: Port Elizabeth, South Africa and International Mohair Association: Ilkley, U.K., 1993; 278 pp.
7. Lupton, C.J. *Wool Chapter, SID Sheep Production Handbook*, 7th Ed.; American Sheep Industry Association, Inc.: Centennial, 2003; 1042.

Molecular Biology: Animal

Guolong Zhang
Oklahoma State University, Stillwater, Oklahoma, U.S.A.

INTRODUCTION

The past two decades have brought a revolution in molecular biology research and the emergence of new techniques such as high-throughput DNA sequencing, microarray, nuclear transfer, RNA interference, and mass spectrometry-based proteomic techniques. With these new technologies it is now possible to sequence the entire genome of any animal species, carry out systematic genome-wide screens of gene functions, and manipulate (delete, mutate, overexpress, or suppress) virtually any individual gene in the genome. Such new tools are now being applied to most aspects of animal production and will undoubtedly have a profound impact on animal agriculture by improving production efficiency and sustainability, animal health, food safety, and environmental stability. This article briefly describes the major molecular techniques and their application in animal agriculture.

NEW EMERGING MOLECULAR BIOLOGY TECHNIQUES

High-Throughput DNA Sequencing

With the advent of automated DNA sequencing technology in the mid-1980s, which involves the labeling of DNA fragments with fluorescent dyes, sequencing the entire genome has become a reality, leading to the recent explosion in genomics research.[1] Following the completion of the human genome in early 2003, nearly 200 genomes of mammals, plants, insects, and microbes, as well as over 1200 viral genomes, have been sequenced so far. The dog and chicken genomes have been sequenced at a coverage of one-and-a-half and sevenfold, respectively, while the large-scale genome sequencing of other major farm animal species, including cattle, pig, horse, and aquatic species, is either in progress or will soon be initiated. Complementary DNA (cDNA) sequences, also known as expressed sequence tags (EST), from hundreds of cell/tissue-specific libraries of farm animals have also been sequenced.[2–4] The availability of such enormous amounts of genomic and cDNA sequence information will

undoubtedly facilitate the identification of genes of agricultural importance and development of new strategies for improving production efficiency of livestock.

High-Throughput Differential Gene Expression Techniques

Analysis of the changes in gene expression pattern associated with biological processes is critical to understand gene function. The recent development of powerful high-throughput differential gene expression techniques allows simultaneous detection of differential expressions of tens of thousands of genes in a single experiment[5] (Table 1). Among commonly used techniques, DNA microarray has attracted tremendous interest among biologists since its introduction in 1995.[2–5] Utilizing a simultaneous two-color hybridization scheme, DNA microarray promises sensitive, quantitative monitoring of gene expression profiles on the whole genome scale. Such a tool has been applied to farm animal research for studying reproduction, muscle development, fat deposition, nutrient utilization, and disease resistance for all major livestock species.[2–4] Hundreds of putatively important genes have been identified and their biological functions are being confirmed.

Transgenesis

Gene(s) of interest can be modified and reintroduced into animals to create new breeds with desired traits by the technique of transgenesis. The major strategies to generate transgenic animals have gone from pronuclear injection, embryonic stem cells, and nuclear transfer to the latest lentiviral delivery.[6] Nuclear transfer, a cloning technology introduced in 1996 that involves the injection of nuclei of genetically modified somatic cells into the enucleated oocytes, allows precise targeting of genomes in virtually any animal species. Transgenic animals from all major livestock species have been generated by nuclear transfer, but this technique suffers from low efficiency and high technical demands.[6] The lentiviral delivery of transgenes is extremely efficient in introducing foreign gene(s) into the germline by taking advantage of the ability of lentivirus to integrate into both dividing and

Encyclopedia of Animal Science
DOI: 10.1081/E-EAS 120019729

Table 1 Comparison of major high-throughput differential gene expression techniques

	Minimum mRNA requirement	Simultaneous comparison of >2 samples?	Simultaneous detection of >2 genes?	Detection of quantitative difference?	Require previous knowledge of mRNA or gene sequences?	Detection of unknown genes?
EST[a] sequencing	0.01–1 µg	Yes	Yes	Yes	No	Yes
cDNA-RDA	0.01–0.1 µg	No	Yes	No	No	Yes
Differential display	0.01–0.1 µg	Yes	Yes	Yes	No	Yes
SSH	0.5–1 µg	No	Yes	No	No	Yes
SAGE	1–5 µg	Yes	Yes	Yes	No	Yes
DNA microarray	0.1–1 µg	Yes	Yes	Yes	Yes	No
Real-time RT-PCR[b]	1 cell	Yes	Yes, but limited	Yes	Yes	No

[a]Abbreviations: EST, expressed sequence tag; cDNA-RDA, complementary DNA representational difference analysis; SSH, suppression subtractive hybridization; SAGE, serial analysis of gene expression; RT-PCR, reverse transcriptase PCR; mRNA, messenger RNA.
[b]Strictly speaking, real-time RT-PCR is not a high-throughput technique, but provides a highly sensitive and quantitative analysis of gene expression, and is therefore listed here for comparison.

nondividing cells.[6] Therefore, it appears to be economically possible for genetic manipulation of livestock in the future.

RNA Interference

RNA interference emerged in 1998, following an observation that the introduction of double-stranded RNA into cells induces potent and specific gene silencing.[7] It has become the method of choice for analysis of gene functions, particularly in mammalian systems. Combined with genomics data, RNA interference could allow functional determination of any gene encoded in the genome. In animal agriculture, it holds great promise for use against infections by expressing small interfering RNA to disrupt the replication of pathogens or to inhibit the expression of receptors for pathogens. In addition, germline integration of interfering RNA by the lentiviral delivery technique could generate new animal strains with enhanced disease resistance or suitable organs for xenotransplantation. Such an application is expected to be seen within 5 years.

Proteomic Techniques

All biological processes—ranging from development to reproduction, response, and infection—are ultimately dependent upon the selective expression and interactions of a complex network of proteins. Major proteomic techniques include two-dimensional polyacrylamide gel electrophoresis, yeast two-hybrid, proteome microarray,

and various formats of mass spectrometry.[8] These techniques allow detecting expression levels, interactions, posttranslational modifications, or enzymatic activities of thousands of proteins simultaneously. Most of these tools have yet to be utilized in animal agriculture, but are expected to have a significant impact in the next 5–10 years.

APPLICATION OF MOLECULAR BIOLOGY IN ANIMAL AGRICULTURE

Animal Growth and Production Efficiency

A number of genes associated with growth and productivity traits have been identified by genome-mapping approaches.[1,9] The availability of these genes provides an excellent opportunity for marker-assisted breeding[9] and genetic manipulation by transgenesis[6] to produce new breeds with desired traits. Generation of transgenic animals bearing the desired genes or gene alleles is the most straightforward approach. For example, transgenic pigs and sheep overexpressing growth hormone or growth hormone-releasing factor normally grow faster and utilize feed more efficiently than nontransgenic littermates.[6,10] Transgenesis efforts to alter milk composition, wool formation, and meat quality are currently ongoing. With the advances of new molecular techniques, particularly through genome sequencing and DNA microarray, additional genes will be identified, providing more and better targets for breeding and genetic manipulation.

Animal Health and Well-Being

Genome sequencing of veterinary and zoonotic pathogens has led to a better understanding of microbial pathogenesis and development of novel approaches for producing safer and more effective vaccines. Differential gene expression techniques are being employed for comprehensive studies of microbial pathogenesis and the mechanisms of host defense.[11] It is expected that important genes involved in microbial pathogenesis or host immune responses will be identified for all major veterinary pathogens. Enhanced disease resistance can be and has been demonstrated in farm animals by disruption of certain disease-susceptible genes (such as Prion protein and pathogen receptors) or by overexpression of immunomodulatory cytokines, microbial antigens, and immunoglobin genes specific for certain pathogens.[6,10] Transient viral delivery of such immune-responsive genes into animals at certain production stages (e.g., postweaning and onset of disease) also appears to be a viable approach. Rapid disease diagnosis and monitoring by differential expression techniques, particularly real-time polymerase chain reaction (RT-PCR), is another notable application.

Biomedical Applications

The use of transgenic farm animals as bioreactors for producing pharmaceuticals and as organ donors for transplantations in humans has attracted vast attention in the past two decades. A few therapeutic proteins, such as α-1 antitrypsin and antithrombin III, have been produced in large quantities in the milk or blood of large farm animals,[6,10] and are currently in advanced phases of clinical trials. Because of a worldwide shortage of human organs available for transplantation, pigs are being explored for their potential as organ donors. In order to reduce hyperacute rejection of pig transplants, several genes associated with this process, such as α-1,3-galactosyltransferase, have been deleted and knockout pigs generated.[6,10] Availability of such transgenic pigs is expected to have important applications in xenotransplantation. In addition, development of transgenic farm animals as experimental models for human diseases that cannot be recapitulated in rodents is another attractive and important application.

Environmental and Other Applications

Modern intensive animal production practice poses considerable stress to the environment by creating significant amounts of animal waste. Molecular strategies to reduce the pollution are also being sought. Recently, transgenic pigs expressing a bacterial phytase gene were shown to have improved uptake of organic phosphate, thus reducing the need for inorganic phosphate supplementation in feed and release of phosphorus in manure.[10] New strains of microbes have also been genetically engineered with enhanced ability to convert animal waste into less polluted material. Another potential application includes the generation of new exotic breeds of pets for leisure purposes. GloFish, a transgenic zebra fish expressing fluorescent protein, is a notable example that is currently on sale in the United States (http://www. glofish.com/).

CONCLUSION

These newly emerged molecular techniques are beginning to transform the research and practice of animal agriculture, and will be instrumental in developing profitable, environment-friendly agriculture and in meeting the demands of growing world populations. The complete genomic sequences and DNA microarrays featuring the whole genome of major farm animal species are expected to be available within the next 5–10 years. Novel approaches to enhancing animal productivity and health will be developed, and new biotherapeutics and new animal breeds with desired characteristics will be produced. In addition, transgenic farm animals hold great promise to provide much needed pharmaceuticals and immunologically suitable organs for transplantation. However, it should be kept in mind that usage of transgenic animals for the production of foods and pharmaceuticals and for xenotransplantation will require extensive characterization before release to the market. It is our scientists' responsibility to ensure the safety of genetically modified animals and animal products, and also to educate the general public for its increased acceptance of animal biotechnology.

ACKNOWLEDGMENTS

I would like to thank Drs. Wilson Pond, Joan Lunney, Rodney Geisert, and Udaya DeSilva for their thoughtful suggestions and critical review of the manuscript. I apologize for failing to refer to all primary sources due to space constraints.

REFERENCES

1. Rohrer, G. Genomics. In *Encyclopedia of Animal Science*; Pond, W.G., Bell, A.W., Eds.; Marcel Dekker, Inc.: New York, 2004.
2. Suchyta, S.P.; Sipkovsky, S.; Kruska, R.; Jeffers, A.; McNulty, A.; Coussens, M.J.; Tempelman, R.J.; Halgren,

R.G.; Saama, P.M.; Bauman, D.E.; Boisclair, Y.R.; Burton, J.L.; Collier, R.J.; DePeters, E.J.; Ferris, T.A.; Lucy, M.C.; McGuire, M.A.; Medrano, J.F.; Overton, T.R.; Smith, T.P.; Smith, G.W.; Sonstegard, T.S.; Spain, J.N.; Spiers, D.E.; Yao, J.; Coussens, P.M. Development and testing of a high-density cDNA microarray resource for cattle. Physiol. Genomics **2003**, *15* (2), 158–164.

3. Tuggle, C.K.; Green, J.A.; Fitzsimmons, C.; Woods, R.; Prather, R.S.; Malchenko, S.; Soares, B.M.; Kucaba, T.; Crouch, K.; Smith, C.; Tack, D.; Robinson, N.; O'Leary, B.; Scheetz, T.; Casavant, T.; Pomp, D.; Edeal, B.J.; Zhang, Y.; Rothschild, M.F.; Garwood, K.; Beavis, W. EST-based gene discovery in pig: Virtual expression patterns and comparative mapping to human. Mamm. Genome **2003**, *14* (8), 565–579.

4. Cogburn, L.A.; Wang, X.; Carre, W.; Rejto, L.; Porter, T.E.; Aggrey, S.E.; Simon, J. Systems-wide chicken DNA microarrays, gene expression profiling, and discovery of functional genes. Poult. Sci. **2003**, *82* (6), 939–951.

5. Liang, P.; Pardee, A.B. Analysing differential gene expression in cancer. Nat. Rev. Cancer **2003**, *3* (11), 869–876.

6. Clark, J.; Whitelaw, B. A future for transgenic livestock. Nat. Rev. Genet. **2003**, *4* (10), 825–833.

7. Hannon, G.J.; Conklin, D.S. RNA interference by short hairpin RNAs expressed in vertebrate cells. Methods Mol. Biol. **2004**, *257*, 255–266.

8. Zhu, H.; Bilgin, M.; Snyder, M. Proteomics. Annu. Rev. Biochem. **2003**, *72*, 783–812.

9. Thallman, M. Selection: Marker Assisted. In *Encyclopedia of Animal Science*; Pond, W.G., Bell, A.W., Eds.; Marcel Dekker, Inc.: New York, 2004.

10. Niemann, H.; Kues, W.A. Application of transgenesis in livestock for agriculture and biomedicine. Anim. Reprod. Sci. **2003**, *79* (3–4), 291–317.

11. Munir, S.; Kapur, V. Transcriptional analysis of the response of poultry species to respiratory pathogens. Poult. Sci. **2003**, *82* (6), 885–892.

Molecular Biology: Microbial

Harry J. Flint
Rowett Research Institute, Aberdeen, U.K.

INTRODUCTION

The powerful array of techniques that constitute molecular biology arose largely from the study of microorganisms. The ability to construct genomic DNA libraries—and cDNA libraries derived from expressed mRNA—in bacterial and fungal hosts remains a key approach for isolating genes. Dramatic technical developments, however, have now brought about a further revolution. In particular the polymerase chain reaction (PCR) allows precise amplification of DNA sequences, whereas developments in DNA sequencing, microarray, and proteomics technologies are making it more efficient to deal with whole microbial genomes rather than to search for individual genes. Molecular biology now pervades all areas of microbiology and is producing major advances in our understanding of the diversity and dynamics of the microbial ecosystems found in the animal gut, on plant surfaces, and in soils. Genes are being uncovered that define the interactions between microbes and animal hosts, notably the mechanisms involved in pathogenesis, survival, and the mutualistic relationships that allow herbivorous animals to gain energy from plant material. Molecular information underpins the quest to treat and prevent infectious diseases in animals, track and suppress microbes harbored by animals that cause disease in humans, optimize animal production, and minimize pollution.

MICROBIAL DIVERSITY

Ribosomal RNA

It has been difficult for microbiologists to know whether they can culture the full range of microorganisms present in a given habitat, but molecular approaches are now revealing the extent of previously unknown diversity. Most "culture-independent" approaches involve the sequencing of ribosomal genes that are amplified directly by PCR from environmental samples. Ribosomal genes (particularly those coding for the small subunit rRNA—16S in prokaryotes, 18S in eukaryotes) are suitable because they occur in all living organisms and contain highly conserved sequences (which are useful for such things as designing "universal" eubacterial or archaeal primers for PCR amplification) as well as regions that vary between strains and species. In soils, less than 1% of microbial rRNA sequence diversity appears to be represented by cultured species.[1] Analyses performed on the microbiota of the rumen and the pig and horse large intestine (Fig. 1) reveal enormous diversity; only 17% of eubacterial sequences recovered from the pig, and only 11% from the horse, correspond to known species.[2,3] The rapidly expanding sequence databases allow the design of probes and primers, specific to particular groupings, that are suitable for enumeration by dot blot hybridization, whole-cell fluorescent in situ hybridization (FISH), or real-time PCR.[4] Microarrays are also being developed in which panels of specific oligonucleotide probes can be used to describe the composition of microbial ecosystems.

Molecular profiling approaches such as denaturing gradient gel electrophoresis (DGGE) and terminal restriction fragment length polymorphism (T-RFLP), again usually based on amplified ribosomal sequences, are widely used to follow shifts in the composition of microbial communities. These produce bands characteristic of different DNA% G+C contents or sequences using primers that target broad phylogenetic groupings. These methods are contributing to our understanding of such topics as the impact of host variation and of diet upon the gut microflora and the impact of management practices upon soil microbial communities.

Gene Tracking

Polymerase chain reaction methods can be used to detect a variety of specific genes in environmental samples without prior cultivation and isolation of microorganisms. They have been applied particularly to virulence determinants (e.g., toxin genes) providing information on pathogen contamination in the food chain. PCR tracking of antibiotic resistance genes in the environment and in human and animal gut bacteria has implications for the debate over the impact of antibiotic use in animal husbandry, which centers on resistance to the antibiotics used in clinical and veterinary medicine.

Encyclopedia of Animal Science
DOI: 10.1081/E-EAS 120019730

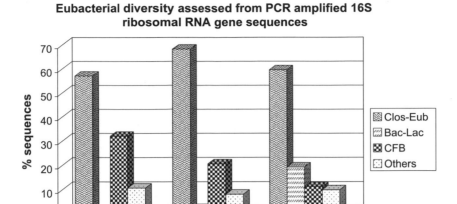

Fig. 1 Eubacterial diversity in gut samples as determined by amplification and sequencing of 16SrRNA genes. Data are from bovine rumen, horse large intestine, and pig intestine. Clos-Eub=*Clostridium/Eubacterium/Ruminococcus* relatives; Bac-Lac=*Bacillus/Lactobacillus/Streptococcus*; CFB=*Cytophaga/Flavobacterium/Bacteroides*. While independent of culture bias, it should be noted that PCR bias and rRNA gene copy number influence the apparent proportions of different types obtained by this approach. (From K. Tajima et al., 1999 cited in Ref. 4 and Refs. 2,3.)

Strain Typing

A plethora of DNA-based methods are now available that enable more precise strain identification among the better known cultivable microorganisms, especially pathogens. Many rapid typing techniques rely on PCR amplification of randomly primed sequences, repeated sequences, or on ribotyping based on ribosomal RNA sequences. Alternatively, the whole genome can be profiled after restriction enzyme cleavage into large fragments that are separated by pulsed field gel electrophoresis (PFGE).

GENOMICS

Complete Genomes

Complete microbial genomes range in size from around 1 to 8 Mb for bacteria, and from 10 to 150 Mb for eukaryotes such as yeasts and protozoa. There has been an explosion in genome sequence information that now extends to most human and many animal bacterial pathogens (Table 1).[5] One important outcome has been to identify large genetic regions, or pathogenicity

Table 1 Some examples of fully sequenced bacterial genomes

Species, strain	Chromosome (plasmid)		
	Size—base pairs	Predicted protein-coding genes	DNA % (G+C)
Streptomyces coelicolor A3(2)	8,667,507	7,825	71.1
Bacteroides thetaiotaomicron VPI5482	6,260,361 (33,038)[b]	4,779 (38)	42.8 (47.2)
Escherichia coli K12	4,639,221	4,288	50.8
Clostridium tetani E88[a]	2,799,250 (74,082)[b]	2,372 (61)	28.6 (24.5)
Bifidobacterium longum NCC2705	2,256,646	1,730	60.0
Campylobacter jejuni NCTC11168[a]	1,641,481	1,654	30.6
Mycoplasma pulmonis[a]	963,879	782	26.6

[a]Pathogenic strain.
[b]Plasmid.

islands, that make particular strains infectious. The first projects are now underway to sequence genomes of mutualistic and commensal microorganisms from the animal gut.

Microarrays and Gene Expression

New technologies allow large numbers of sequences, e.g., representing all genes from a given species, to be arrayed on glass slides (microarrays) or on membranes. Genes showing differential expression can then be identified by comparative DNA hybridization. Allied to genome sequencing and rapidly developing proteomic methods for two-dimensional separation and identification of polypeptides, this provides unprecedented power for studies on microbial gene regulation.[6]

Metagenomics

Another powerful new approach, metagenomics, involves creating gene libraries from the DNA recovered from a mixed microbial community, followed by screening for specific functions. This allows the recovery of valuable and important genes from microorganisms that may never have been cultivated.[7]

GENE TRANSFER AND GENETIC ANALYSIS

Natural Gene Transfer Mechanisms

Microorganisms, especially bacteria, frequently carry genetic elements that are capable of transfer between cells independently of the main chromosome. Such elements, which include extrachromosomal plasmids and chromosomally located conjugative transposons, possess genes that promote their own transfer by cell–cell contact (conjugation), or that allow them to be mobilized by other elements. In addition many bacteria are able to take up DNA from their environment resulting in natural genetic transformation, or may acquire genes via bacteriophage virus-mediated transduction. Such genetic exchanges play a major role in microbial evolution. Traits including antibiotic resistance, heavy metal resistance, virulence factors, adhesion properties, substrate utilization pathways, and the production of antimicrobials show evidence of natural horizontal transfer.

Genetic Analysis

Mobile genetic elements provide the basis for many molecular biology procedures, in particular, as vectors. In addition, transposons that insert randomly in the genome are used for insertional mutagenesis to identify microbial gene function. In many bacteria and fungi it is relatively straightforward to introduce and over express foreign genes through conjugal transfer or transformation, and to perform targeted gene knockouts. Refinements of these techniques allow the identification of genes that are switched on in particular environments, e.g., in mammalian host tissues (IVET, in vivo expression technology).[8] However, the lack of convenient gene transfer systems remains an obstacle to research in many less-studied species, including most anaerobes. Transformation can be induced artificially in bacteria, e.g., by electroporation, but endogenous nucleases normally present in wild-type strains tend to destroy the incoming DNA.

BIOTECHNOLOGY

Modified (mutant or genetically manipulated) strains of bacteria and fungi are used in a contained manner in the production of enzymes and other products (e.g., amino acids) used as animal feed additives or feed pretreatments. Modified microbial strains have also been considered for other applications that would require their release into the environment, e.g., as silage additives, probiotics, or for bioremediation. These latter possibilities are clearly subject to detailed risk assessments and to public acceptance. Recombinant vaccines and antibody engineering are increasingly important in the treatment and prevention of infectious diseases in animals caused by a wide range of viruses, bacteria, fungi, and protozoa. Again, genomic and proteomic approaches are helping to define new antigens, as well as possible targets for the development of new antimicrobial agents. Microbial genes continue to provide valuable proteins and enzymes for research, industry, and medicine.[9]

CONCLUSIONS

Molecular techniques are revolutionizing our understanding of the diversity and functioning of microbial ecosystems associated with the mammalian gut, soils, and wastes. These techniques provide new tools for tracking and identifying individual genes and species. Complete genome sequences are available for many human and animal pathogens and should soon become available for more nonpathogenic bacteria and eukaryotic microorganisms. The potential benefits for disease prevention, animal production, and environmental management are enormous, although many will take some time to be realized.

ACKNOWLEDGMENT

The author wishes to acknowledge the support of the Scottish Executive Environment and Rural Affairs Department.

ARTICLES OF FURTHER INTEREST

Antibiotics: Microbial Resistance, p. 39
Genetics: Molecular, p. 466
Genomics, p. 469
GI Tract: Animal/Microbial Symbiosis, p. 449
Rumen Microbiology, p. 773

REFERENCES

1. Amman, R.I.; Ludwig, W.; Schleifer, K.H. Phylogenetic identification and in situ detection of individual microbial cells without cultivation. Microbiol. Rev. **1995**, *59* (1), 143–169.
2. Leser, T.D.; Amenuvor, J.Z.; Jensen, T.K.; Lindecrona, R.H.; Boye, M.; Moller, K. Culture independent analysis of gut bacteria: The pig gastrointestinal tract revisited. Appl. Environ. Microbiol. **2002**, *68* (2), 673–690.
3. Daly, K.; Stewart, C.S.; Flint, H.J.; Shirazi-Beechey, S.P. Bacterial diversity within the equine large intestine as revealed by molecular analysis of cloned 16S rRNA genes. FEMS Microbiol. Ecol. **2001**, *38* (2–3), 141–151.
4. Tajima, K.; Aminov, R.I.; Nagamine, T.; Matsui, H.; Nakamura, M.; Benno, Y. Diet-dependent shifts in the bacterial population of the rumen revealed with real time PCR. Appl. Environ. Microbiol. **2001**, *67* (6), 2766–2774.
5. Bruggeman, H.; Baumer, S.; Fricke, W.F.; Wiezer, A.; Liesegang, H.; Decker, I.; Herzberg, C.; Martinez-Arias, R.; Merki, R.; Henne, A.; Gottshalk, G. The genome sequence of *Clostridium tetani*, the causative agent of tetanus disease. Proc. Natl. Acad. Sci. **2003**, *100* (3), 1316–1321.
6. *Functional Microbial Genomics*; Wren, B., Dorrell, N., Eds.; Methods in Microbiology; Academic Press: London, UK, 2002; Vol. 33.
7. Rondon, M.R.; August, P.R.; Betterman, A.D.; Brady, S.F.; Grossman, T.H.; Liles, M.R.; Loiacono, K.A.; Lynch, B.A.; MacNeil, I.A.; Minor, C.; Tiong, C.L.; Gilman, M.; Osborne, M.S.; Clardy, J.; Handelsman, J.; Goodman, R.M. Cloning the soil metagenome: A strategy for accessing the genetic and functional diversity of uncultured microorganisms. Appl. Environ. Microbiol. **2000**, *66* (6), 2541–2547.
8. Handfield, M.; Levesque, R.C. Strategies for isolation of in vivo expressed genes from bacteria. FEMS Microbiol. Rev. **1999**, *23* (1), 69–91.
9. Vielle, C.; Zeikus, G.J. Hyperthermophilic enzymes: Sources, uses and molecular mechanisms for thermostability. Microbiol. Mol. Biol. Rev. **2001**, *65* (1), 1–43.

Myostatin: Physiology and Applications

Clifton A. Baile
Mary Anne Della-Fera
University of Georgia, Athens, Georgia, U.S.A.

INTRODUCTION

Myostatin is a negative regulator of muscle cell growth and the loss of functional myostatin is known to cause the double-muscled phenotype in several cattle breeds and in other species. With the advent of transgenic technology, researchers have created a knockout mouse model with which to efficiently explore the biochemical pathways and influences of myostatin. Research involving this model has both agricultural and biomedical applications, such as developing methods of controlling myostatin synthesis or activity in domestic animals to produce increased muscle and decreased adipose tissue growth, and regulating myostatin levels in humans for the treatment of muscle-wasting conditions.

PHYSICAL CHARACTERISTICS OF DOUBLE-MUSCLED ANIMALS

For nearly two hundred years, the phenomenon of the double-muscled animal, a spectacular model of muscular hypertrophy, has intrigued both livestock producers and scientists. Though livestock other than cattle produce double-muscled individuals, recent characterization of the protein myostatin, a specific inhibitor of muscle cell growth, has rekindled interest in the condition.[1] Myostatin gene mutations are the genetic and biochemical basis for one form of muscular hypertrophy in the bovine and advances in biotechnology have shown new means to exploit the gene involved.

One property that sustained interest in the mutation-causing double muscling is the easily recognizable extreme phenotype of the myostatin-null individual. Myostatin knockout mice are characterized by bulging muscular development, with the most extreme hypertrophy apparent in the shoulders and hindquarters. Double-muscled cattle are even more easily discernable than their murine counterparts. The double-muscled phenotype is characterized by much higher proportions of muscle and much lower proportions of fat than conventional cattle of comparable background. These trends occur not only across breeds but across species as well.[1]

In spite of the name, a double-muscled animal has the same number of muscles as a conventional animal. Double-muscled cattle develop more muscle fibers than cattle of normal conformation, and this hyperplastic growth leads to the increased muscular development. Cellular hyperplasia is pronounced in the fetal stage of growth in double-muscled cattle, with cell number increasing at a rate nearly three times that of normal cattle. Double-muscled cattle also have significantly lower lipid content and a greater proportion of polyunsaturated fat than conventional cattle.

GENETIC BASIS OF THE DOUBLE-MUSCLED PHENOTYPE

The genetic origin of double muscling in cattle was never truly in doubt. By the end of the 1980s, the most favored theory was a single, autosomal recessive pattern. In 1997, McPherron and Lee discovered a novel gene that closely resembled other members of the transforming growth factor-β (TGF-β) superfamily and subsequent targeted mutation of the gene in mice resulted in animals with excessive muscle development very similar to the condition observed for nearly two centuries in double-muscled cattle.[1] Independent researchers subsequently established that the novel protein, myostatin, did indeed map to the muscle hypertrophy (mh) locus,[2] and defects in myostatin were shown to be responsible for the double-muscled phenotype in Belgian Blue cattle.[3,4] DNA sequencing of the myostatin gene in other breeds known to produce a large number of double-muscled animals showed that several mutations were capable of inducing the double-muscled phenotype.[4]

STRUCTURAL CHARACTERISTICS AND REGULATION OF MYOSTATIN FUNCTION

Myostatin is synthesized in myoblasts as a 375-amino acid precursor protein that is proteolytically processed to produce the biologically active myostatin protein.[5] The active protein includes a highly conserved pattern of nine

Encyclopedia of Animal Science
DOI: 10.1081/E-EAS 120022490

661

M

cysteine residues at the C-terminal end that result in intramolecular and intermolecular disulfide bridges, the so-called cysteine knot structure.[5] One of the nullifying mutations changes the fifth cysteine to tyrosine, causing the functional loss seen in the Piedmontese breed.[4] The striking effects of this one-residue alteration give some indication of the structural importance of this pattern in the mature protein function.

The secretion of myostatin has been shown to be controlled in part by T-cap, a 19-kDa sarcomeric protein important in the structural integrity of sarcomeres.[6] Once secreted, mature myostatin binds to activin type II receptors (Act RIIB), eliciting its biological functions.[7] Like TGF-β, however, myostatin exists as a large, latent complex with other proteins, including its propeptide. In vitro, the propeptide blocked myostatin binding to Act RIIB receptors, and in vivo, increased expression of the propeptide in transgenic mice resulting in increased muscle mass; thus, the propeptide acts as a myostatin inhibitor.[7] Follistatin, an inhibitor of other TGF-β family members, also appears to be a potent myostatin antagonist: Mice expressing increased levels of follistatin in muscle had dramatic increases in muscle weight.[7]

PHYSIOLOGICAL ACTIONS OF MYOSTATIN

The cell cycle is an ordered set of events culminating in cell growth and division. Following mitosis, cells progress from Gap1 (G1) to Synthesis (S), during which DNA replication occurs, then to G2, prior to the next mitotic phase (M). Myoblasts proliferate during myogenesis, then withdraw at G1 of the cell cycle and commit to form myotubes. Progression through the cell cycle and cell cycle arrest are controlled by cyclin-dependent kinase and cyclin-dependent kinase inhibitor (CDK/CKI) complexes. Myostatin is thought to control the G1 to S and G2 to M transitions of the cell cycle in myoblasts by modulating p21cip1 and Cdk2 protein levels.[5] Myostatin upregulates expression of several genes involved in proliferation and differentiation of skeletal muscle cells, including p21cip1 (a CKI), and downregulates expression of Cdk2, inactivating the Cyclin/CDK complex that allows progression from G1 to S.[5] Another CKI, p27kip, also plays a role in myostatin's regulation of muscle growth. P27kip knockout mice exhibit growth enhancement, and muscle tissue from these mice had decreased myostatin mRNA.[8] Myostatin has also been shown to decrease protein levels of MyoD and myogenin, possibly as a result of changes in their posttranscriptional regulation.[9]

Myostatin specifically affects muscle cells; however, it is expressed in other tissues, and may carry out cell cycle control functions in these tissues as well. For example, although myostatin is expressed only at low levels in adipocytes,[1] it inhibits differentiation of preadipocytes into adipocytes probably by inhibition of transcription factors.[10] Myostatin can thus be said to have a direct effect on adipogenesis in addition to its indirect effects that result from changing the ratio of muscle to adipose tissue.

Myostatin is highly expressed in embryonic and fetal stages, and although it can be primarily viewed as a growth regulator in early development, myostatin has been shown to affect adult tissue as well.[1,5,11] Overexpression of myostatin has been linked to muscle wasting, such as that seen in individuals infected with HIV.[12] Inhibition of myostatin activity may also slow the progression of muscle wasting in muscular dystrophy.[13] In addition, because myostatin decreases muscle mass, increases adipose mass, and increases blood glucose levels, myostatin-blocking antibodies are being developed for potential therapeutic use in diabetics.

CONCLUSION

Our understanding of the mechanism of myostatin function and its specific roles in development has offered researchers several potential methods to manipulate myostatin activity. Changes in myostatin function caused either by targeted mutation of the gene or pharmacological or immunological targeting of the myostatin pathway have already produced increased muscle growth and body composition alterations. The ability to identify myostatin polymorphisms that can interrupt function opens the door for widespread screening for carrier animals and breeding strategies that take advantage of naturally occurring myostatin mutations. Identification of the human myostatin gene and analysis of its expression patterns have indicated that myostatin may play a role in certain diseases characterized by cachexia or muscle wasting, including AIDS. Agents that block myostatin secretion or receptor binding and action may offer a way to turn off myostatin function in a controlled manner in adult animals. These methods may also be useful in human medicine, offering new treatment modalities for AIDS and cancer-related cachexia and for muscular dystrophy.

ACKNOWLEDGMENT

Supported in part by the Georgia Research Alliance Eminent Scholar endowment held by Clifton A. Baile.

REFERENCES

1. McPherron, A.C.; Lawler, A.M.; Lee, S.J. Regulation of skeletal muscle mass in mice by a new TGF-beta superfamily member. Nature **1997**, *387* (6628), 83–90.

2. Smith, T.P.; Lopez-Corrales, N.L.; Kappes, S.M.; Sonstegard, T.S. Myostatin maps to the interval containing the bovine mh locus. Mamm. Genome **1997**, *8* (10), 742–744.

3. McPherron, A.C.; Lee, S.J. Double muscling in cattle due to mutations in the myostatin gene. Proc. Natl. Acad. Sci. U. S. A. **1997**, *94* (23), 12457–12461.

4. Grobet, L.; Poncelet, D.; Royo, L.J.; Brouwers, B.; Pirottin, D.; Michaux, C.; Menissier, F.; Zanotti, M.; Dunner, S.; Georges, M. Molecular definition of an allelic series of mutations disrupting the myostatin function and causing double-muscling in cattle. Mamm. Genome **1998**, *9* (3), 210–213.

5. Thomas, M.; Langley, B.; Berry, C.; Sharma, M.; Kirk, S.; Bass, J.; Kambadur, R. Myostatin, a negative regulator of muscle growth, functions by inhibiting myoblast proliferation. J. Biol. Chem. **2000**, *275* (51), 40235–40243.

6. Nicholas, G.; Thomas, M.; Langley, B.; Somers, W.; Patel, K.; Kemp, C.F.; Sharma, M.; Kambadur, R. Titin-cap associates with, and regulates secretion of, Myostatin. J. Cell. Physiol. **2002**, *193* (1), 120–131.

7. Lee, S.J.; McPherron, A.C. Regulation of myostatin activity and muscle growth. Proc. Natl. Acad. Sci. U. S. A. **2001**, *98* (16), 9306–9311.

8. Lin, J.; Della-Fera, M.A.; Li, C.; Page, K.; Ho Choi, Y.; Hartzell, D.L.; Baile, C.A. P27 knockout mice: Reduced myostatin in muscle and altered adipogenesis. Biochem. Biophys. Res. Commun. **2003**, *300* (4), 938–942.

9. Joulia, D.; Bernardi, H.; Garandel, V.; Rabenoelina, F.; Vernus, B.; Cabello, G. Mechanisms involved in the inhibition of myoblast proliferation and differentiation by myostatin. Exp. Cell. Res. **2003**, *286* (2), 263–275.

10. Kim, H.S.; Liang, L.; Dean, R.G.; Hausman, D.B.; Hartzell, D.L.; Baile, C.A. Inhibition of preadipocyte differentiation by myostatin treatment in 3T3-L1 cultures. Biochem. Biophys. Res. Commun. **2001**, *281* (4), 902–906.

11. Grobet, L.; Pirottin, D.; Farnir, F.; Poncelet, D.; Royo, L.J.; Brouwers, B.; Christians, E.; Desmecht, D.; Coignoul, F.; Kahn, R.; Georges, M. Modulating skeletal muscle mass by postnatal, muscle-specific inactivation of the myostatin gene. Genesis **2003**, *35* (4), 227–238.

12. Gonzalez-Cadavid, N.F.; Taylor, W.E.; Yarasheski, K.; Sinha-Hikim, I.; Ma, K.; Ezzat, S.; Shen, R.; Lalani, R.; Asa, S.; Mamita, M.; Nair, G.; Arver, S.; Bhasin, S. Organization of the human myostatin gene and expression in healthy men and HIV-infected men with muscle wasting. Proc. Natl. Acad. Sci. U. S. A. **1998**, *95* (25), 14938–14943.

13. Khurana, T.S.; Davies, K.E. Pharmacological strategies for muscular dystrophy. Nat. Rev., Drug Discov. **2003**, *2* (5), 379–390.

Nutrient Management: Diet Modification

Terry J. Klopfenstein
University of Nebraska, Lincoln, Nebraska, U.S.A.

INTRODUCTION

Animal feeding operations are becoming more concentrated and the U.S. EPA (Environmental Protection Agency) has proposed more restrictive requirements. Great progress has been made in diet modifications designed to reduce animal excretion of nutrients. The nutrients of primary concern are nitrogen and phosphorus.

PHOSPHORUS UTILIZATION

Phosphorus (P) is an essential mineral nutrient required for bone growth and maintenance and for most body metabolic functions such as energy utilization. Phosphorus has been supplemented to animal diets in mineral form such as dicalcium phosphate produced from mined mineral deposits. Typically, phosphorus was fed above the requirement of the animals as a safety factor due to lack of confidence in the precise P requirements and supplies. P in manure can build up in soils and subsequently contaminate ground water if not properly managed. P requirements are quite different for ruminants (cattle and sheep) and nonruminants (pigs and chickens), and P is metabolized differently by ruminants.

Poultry and swine grow rapidly and therefore require high levels of P in their diets (up to .6% of diet;[1–3]). Much of the P in feed ingredients (such as corn and soybean meal) is in the form of phytate P. Swine and poultry lack the enzyme (phytase) necessary to utilize the phytate P so it appears in the manure. Inorganic P must be supplemented to meet the animal's requirements. This makes P use very inefficient (10 to 20%) and most of the P ends up in the manure. There are four technologies that producers can use to reduce P excretion.

1. Feeding to requirements. Ongoing research is helping to more precisely define P requirements for each type of production and for animal ages within each type of production. With modern technology, it is possible to formulate diets quite precisely so that P is not overfed.[1]
2. Phytase. This enzyme is produced commercially through microbial fermentations and can be added to swine or poultry diets. Phytase releases the organic P from phytate and makes it available to the animal.[4,5] Therefore, the phytate P in corn and soybeans, the primary feedstuffs in swine and poultry diets, is utilized to meet the animal's requirements, reducing the need for supplement.
3. Phase feeding. Swine and poultry grow rapidly. Bone growth is very rapid in young animals and is essentially zero in mature animals. Therefore, the requirement for P decreases as the animals grow and mature.[2,3] Phase feeding is the process of changing diets to reduce the amount of P. In the past, two or three diets may have been fed, but now the number is increasing to five or six. Phase feeding, combined with precise formulation and precise requirements, decrease dietary P and therefore manure P.[1]
4. Low phytate feeds. Genetically enhanced low-phytate corn and soybean meal are available. The total P in these feedstuffs is not necessarily lower, but the P is in the available, inorganic form rather than the organic (phytate) form.[1,6] Feeding low-phytate corn and soybeans can decrease P excretion by 50%.

Beef and dairy cattle digest and metabolize P somewhat differently than nonruminants. The microorganisms in the rumen digest the P in phytate, making the P available to the animal. Beef and dairy cattle tend to grow slower and have lower P requirements than nonruminants.[7,8] Lactating dairy cows excrete considerable amounts of P in milk so cows giving milk have higher requirements—higher requirements for higher producers.[8]

The most important issue with ruminants is to establish precise requirements and then formulate diets to meet but not exceed requirements. The requirements for lactating dairy cows is about .30% of the diet.[9] The ingredients (corn, supplemental protein, silage, alfalfa) fed to dairy cows will supply most, if not all, of this requirement.

Beef cattle in feedlots are typically fed diets high in corn grain, which contains .25 to .3% P. Recent research suggests the requirement for feedlot cattle is .12 to .14%.[10] The problem is that the ingredients in the feedlot diets (primarily corn) have nearly .3% P. There does not seem to be any practical way of reducing dietary P levels below .25% and therefore, P excretion by feedlot cattle is relatively high.

Encyclopedia of Animal Science
DOI: 10.1081/E-EAS 120019731

NITROGEN UTILIZATION

Nitrogen (N) is a part of amino acids (AA) that form proteins required by all animals; animals consume protein and AA and then excrete various forms of N. If N in manure is not managed appropriately, it can contaminate surface and ground waters (nitrate). Just as important is the volatilization of N (NH_3) from manure. The resulting NH_3 (ammonia) adds to odors and can be redeposited on cropland or environmentally sensitive areas such as lakes and streams.

Swine and poultry must be fed essential AAs to meet requirements. Because of rapid lean growth, AA requirements are high and must be met to produce optimal body weight gains and feed efficiencies.[2,3] However, if any AA is fed above the requirement, that AA will be used for energy and the N excreted.

IDEAL PROTEIN

The ideal protein is a protein with a balance of amino acids that exactly meets an animal's AA requirements.[11] By formulating diets to ideal protein content, no excess AAs are fed and N excretion is minimized. Formulation for ideal protein can be accomplished by using high-quality protein sources with good balances of AA and protein sources that complement the AA balance in corn. The greatest opportunity is to use crystalline AA to balance for AA deficiencies. Lowering the dietary protein content by two percentage points and supplementing with crystalline AA results in a 20 to 25% decrease in N excretion in swine or 30 to 40% in poultry.[12]

FEED ADDITIVES

Feed additives or feeding management systems that increase feed efficiencies also increase efficiency of N utilization. Ractopamine increases lean growth in swine and, therefore, increases N-use efficiency.[1]

PHASE FEEDING

Amino acid requirements decrease as swine and poultry grow, just as the P requirement decreases. Balancing diets to ideal protein and changing diets often as pigs or poultry grow decrease the protein fed and, therefore, the N excreted.[1]

NITROGEN FOR RUMINANTS

Cattle are unique because of the microflora in the rumen. This ability allows them to digest fiber, but does raise some challenges in protein nutrition. Protein that reaches the small intestine is a combination of microbial protein and undegraded feed protein. This protein (metabolizable protein, MP) is digested and absorbed in a manner similar to nonruminants. The growing beef animal and lactating dairy cows have two requirements that nutritionists must meet—degradable protein for the rumen microbes and undegraded protein that supplies the additional MP needed by the animal.[7,8] Only recently have these requirements been elucidated, and further refinement of requirements is needed.

The greatest opportunity for decreasing N excretion by cattle is to use the MP system to meet but not exceed requirements for degradable and undegradable protein. Phase feeding feedlot cattle and group feeding dairy cows have the potential to markedly reduce N excretion. Ammonia losses have been reduced by as much as 32% by using these technologies.[13] There is some reluctance by nutritionists to reduce levels of degradable and undegradable protein because of concern that milk or beef production will be compromised. Research indicates that will not happen, but it is more difficult to control variables in commercial production facilities.[14–16]

CONCLUSION

Phosphorus and nitrogen excretion can be reduced markedly by the use of new technologies. In the future, there will be incentives for producers and nutritionists to make use of these technologies.

REFERENCES

1. Klopfenstein, T.J.; Angel, R.; Cromwell, G.L.; Erickson, G.E.; Fox, D.G.; Parsons, C.; Satter, L.D.; Sutton, A.L. *Animal Diet Modifications to Decrease the Potential for Nitrogen and Phosphorus Pollution*; Council for Agricultural Science and Technology: Ames, IA, 2002. CAST Issue Paper Number 21.
2. National Research Council. *Nutrient Requirements of Poultry*, 9th Ed.; National Academy Press: Washington, DC, 1994.
3. National Research Council. *Nutrient Requirements of Swine*, 10th Ed.; National Academy Press: Washington, DC, 1998.
4. Kornegay, E.T.; Denbrow, D.M.; Yi, Z.; Ravindran, V. Response of broilers to graded levels of microbial phytase

added to maize–soybean meal-based diets containing three levels of non-phytate phosphorus. Br. J. Nutr. **1996**, *75*, 839–852.

5. Cromwell, G.L.; Stahly, T.S.; Coffey, R.D.; Monegue, H.J.; Randolph, J.H. Efficacy of phytase in improving the bioavailability of phosphorus in soybean meal and corn-soybean meal diets for pigs. J. Anim. Sci. **1993**, *71*, 1831–1840.

6. Cromwell, G.L.; Traylor, S.L.; White, L.A.; Xavier, E.G.; Lindemann, M.D.; Sauber, T.E.; Rice, D.W. Effects of low-phytate corn and low-oligosaccharide, low-phytate soybean meal in diets on performance, bone traits, and P excretion by growing pigs. J. Anim. Sci. **2000**, *78* (Suppl. 2), 72. (abstract).

7. National Research Council. *Nutrient Requirements of Beef Cattle*, 7th Ed.; National Academy Press: Washington, DC, 1996.

8. National Research Council. *Nutrient Requirements of Dairy Cattle*, 7th Ed.; National Academy Press: Washington, DC, 2001.

9. Wu, Z.; Satter, L.D.; Blohowiak, A.J.; Stauffacher, R.H.; Wilson, J.H. Milk production, estimated phosphorus excretion and bone characteristics of dairy cows fed different amounts of phosphorus for two or three years. J. Dairy Sci. **2001**, *84*, 1738–1748.

10. Erickson, G.E.; Klopfenstein, T.J.; Milton, C.T.; Brink, D.; Orth, M.W.; Whittet, K.M. Phosphorus requirement of finishing feedlot calves. J. Anim. Sci. **2002**, *80*, 1690–1695.

11. Baker, D.H.; Han, Y. Ideal amino acid profile for chicks during the first three weeks posthatching. Poult. Sci. **1994**, *73*, 1441–1447.

12. Allee, G.; Liu, H.; Spencer, J.D.; Touchette, K.J.; Frank, J.W. Effect of Reducing Dietary Protein Level and Adding Amino Acids on Performance and Nitrogen Excretion of Early-Finishing Barrows. In *Proceeding of the American Association of Swine Veterinarians*; American Association of Swine Veterinarians: Perry, PA, 2001; 527–533.

13. Erickson, G.E.; Klopfenstein, T.J.; Milton, C.T. Dietary Protein Effects on Nitrogen Excretion and Volatilization in Open-dirt Feedlots. In *Proceedings of the Eighth International Symposium on Animals, Agriculture and Food Processing Wastes*; ASAE Press: St. Joseph, MO, 2000; 204–297.

14. Satter, L.D.; Klopfenstein, T.J.; Erickson, G.E. The role of nutrition in reducing nutrient output from ruminants. J. Anim. Sci. **2002**, *80* (E. Suppl. 2), E143–E156.

15. Klopfenstein, T.J.; Erickson, G.E. Effects of manipulating protein and phosphorus nutrition of feedlot cattle on nutrient management and the environment. J. Anim. Sci. **2002**, *80* (E Suppl. 2), E106–E114.

16. Wang, S.J.; Fox, D.G.; Cherney, D.J.; Chase, L.E.; Tedeschi, L.O. Whole herd optimization with the Cornell net carbohydrate and protein system. III. Application of an optimization model to evaluate alternatives to reduce nitrogen and phosphorus mass balance. J. Dairy Sci. **2000**, *83*, 2160–2169.

Nutrient Management: Water Quality/Use

J. L. Hatfield
United States Department of Agriculture, Agricultural Research Service, Ames, Iowa, U.S.A.

INTRODUCTION

Animals generate a valuable source of nutrients in both organic and inorganic forms. Nutrients in manure can be a valuable soil amendment; however, if manure is misused, it can be a potential water quality problem. Water quality is a primary concern among environmental issues; manure application is the focus of this article.

MANURE NUTRIENTS

Nutrients vary among species, manure handling, and storage systems as shown in Table 1. Nutrient content is affected by species, diet, age, sex, manure storage system, and length of time in storage. Values shown in Table 1 illustrate the nutrient content in different manure storage systems but do not represent the full range of variation within a species or among manure storage systems.

These data provide an indication of the variation among species and the need for nutrient management systems to consider animal production systems and manure storage systems before making assumptions about the best management system. The goal in nutrient management is to develop a system in which manure nutrients may be applied to the soil to supply the crop needs without being a potential environmental problem.

WATER QUALITY CONCERNS

In nutrient management, water quality concerns focus on phosphorus (P) and nitrate-nitrogen (NO_3-N). Broadcast manure on the soil surface provides for potential surface runoff conditions, particularly when rain occurs shortly after application. In a 2001 study, broadcasting manure resulted in the greatest potential for surface runoff of soluble P.[2] Kleinman and Sharpley[3] compared dissolved reactive phosphorus from three manures at six rates under simulated rainfall and found that dissolved reactive phosphorus loss was related to runoff and manure application rate. Soluble P losses were a function of the type of manure, the application rate, and soil type. Broadcast manure on the soil surface increases the potential for surface runoff into nearby surface water bodies. In addition, surface runoff of manure may provide pathogens that are present in manure a pathway into nearby water bodies. There are few studies of this problem and the evidence is insufficient to provide a set of factors that contribute to pathogen movement.

Incorporation of manure into the soil greatly reduces the chances of surface runoff. Tabbara[4] showed that incorporation of manure or fertilizer 24 hours before a heavy rainfall reduced both dissolved reactive P or total P concentrations by as much as 30% to 60% depending on the nutrient source and application rate. The incorporation process moves P below the volume of soil eroded under high rainfall events. To reduce potential surface losses of P, manure should be incorporated on soils with intensive erosive rain, recent extensive tillage, or little or no surface residue. Incorporation of manure will reduce the likelihood of surface runoff of P and protect surface water from excess P levels; however, the process of incorporating manure may increase the potential for sediment loss from the soil. The development of management practices that protect soil from surface runoff will decrease potential losses of manure P into nearby water bodies.

Incorporation of manure may lead to NO_3-N leaching because nutrients placed below the surface mixing layer are in a soil volume where leaching of nutrients can occur. NO_3-N present in the manure may be moved into deeper soil layers by soil water. However, there is no evidence that this is a direct result of manure application. Incorporation of manure changes the availability of nutrients in the soil profile. Nutrients present in manure are in the organic form and the conversion into available forms is a function of biological activity and time in the soil profile. Klausner et al.[5] developed a method to estimate the decay rate for organic nutrients from dairy manure that has worked well for this species over a range of environmental conditions. One of the challenges for manure management is to determine the temporal patterns of nutrient availability from different manure types and species. Jokela[6] showed that NO_3-N levels were actually lower in soils treated with dairy manure compared to commercial fertilizer because of the slower release of NO_3-N from manure.

Nutrient patterns in manured soils can lead to potential water quality problems; however, these can be managed through a proper rate of application and incorporation.

Encyclopedia of Animal Science
DOI: 10.1081/E-EAS 120019732

Table 1 Nutrient content in solid and liquid manure for different species and manure handling systems

| | Solid manure storage | | | | Liquid manure storage | | | |
| | | Total N | P₂O₅ | K₂O | | Total N | P₂O₅ | K₂O |
Species	Dry matter %		(g/kg)		Dry matter %		(g/l)	
Beef	50	10.5	9.0	13.0	9	3.5	2.2	3.1
Dairy	21	4.5	1.5	3.0	8	3.7	1.8	2.3
Poultry	18	19.0	22.5	12.5	10	7.2	5.4	3.6
Swine	76	6.5	4.0	2.5	4	4.3	3.0	2.6

(From Ref. 1.)

Water quality problems can be reduced through relatively simple management practices that increase nutrient availability to the crop and decrease the potential for offsite movement through runoff or leaching.

EFFECT OF MANURE ON SOIL PROPERTIES RELATED TO WATER QUALITY

Addition of manure to soil causes changes in the soil properties[7,8] that reduces the likelihood of water quality problems. Water infiltration rate, soil water-holding capacity, cation exchange capacity, bulk density, organic matter, biological activity, and plant availability of nutrients are changed by manure additions. These changes required at least five years of manure additions to the soil. A positive impact on water quality is derived from increased water infiltration rates and water storage capacity. Surface runoff occurs in soils that quickly develop

a surface seal and ponding begins on the soil surface leading to the development of small rills that transport water along the surface. Manure-amended soils have a larger infiltration rate and more rainfall can enter the soil before saturation occurs. This change is not a direct effect of manure addition but a combination of increased biological activity and organic materials that create a more stable soil particle that has a higher soil water content before becoming saturated. The higher water-holding capacity of soil allows more absorption before the profile is saturated. Eghball et al.[9] concluded that the increased intensity of rainfall could cause surface runoff but changes in the soil properties from manure could offset water quality problems.

Addition of manure to soil not only changes the soil properties but also restores the soil to a higher level of soil productivity. Freeze et al.[10] found that the application of manure to eroded soil was of greater benefit than application to noneroded soils. Changes in soil

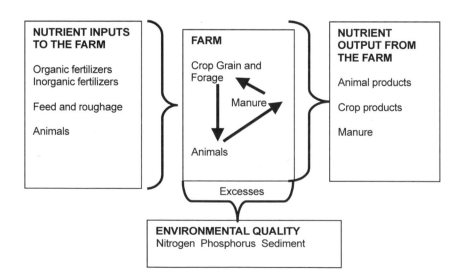

Fig. 1 Conceptual diagram of nutrient flows in the MINAS systems for the Netherlands. (Adapted from Ref. 11.)

properties are more detectable in eroded soils. These effects of manure can be realized with all sources and types of manure. Often the water quality problems that occur in agriculture are from soils that are in a degraded state and restoration of soil properties will benefit the environment.

NUTRIENT ACCOUNTING FROM MANURE SOURCES

To achieve water quality goals and manure application requires the proper amount of nutrients added to the soil to supply crop requirements. The components in a nutrient budget are rates of crop removal, change in the soil nutrient content, and amount supplied from manure. In the Netherlands, nutrient accounting systems have been developed for livestock and cropping systems. Ondersteijn et al.[11] described the mineral accounting system (MINAS) and provided a framework for nutrient accounting (Fig. 1). Manure that is produced is accounted for through the MINAS approach to ensure that both an economic and environmental quality goal is achieved. Development of nutrient management guidelines for producers to help guide their decisions can have a positive impact on environmental quality.

CONCLUSION

Nutrient management programs must have a positive impact on water quality. The challenge for producers is to understand the nutrient balance in the soil and to reduce the risk of surface runoff of manure. The challenge for science is to increase our understanding of the value of manure in the soil and in the restoration of eroded soils to a higher level of productivity. Improved methods for sampling manure to determine the nutrient content from individual farms and for manure application that incorporates manure to reduce erosion and enhance the value of

manure on soil properties will benefit livestock, crop producers, and the environment.

REFERENCES

1. MWPS (MidWest Plan Service). *Manure Storages. Manure Management System Series. MWPS-18, Section 2. MidWest Plan Service.* Iowa State University: Ames, IA, 50011-3080, 2001.
2. Zhao, S.L.; Gupta, S.C.; Huggins, D.R.; Moncrief, J.F. Tillage and nutrient source effects on surface and subsurface water quality at corn planting. J. Environ. Qual. **2001**, *30*, 998–1008.
3. Kleinman, P.J.A.; Sharpley, A.N. Effect of broadcast manure on runoff phosphorus concentrations over successive rainfall events. J. Environ. Qual. **2003**, *32*, 1072–1081.
4. Tabbara, H. Phosphorus loss to runoff water twenty-four hours after application of liquid swine manure or fertilizer. J. Environ. Qual. **2003**, *32*, 1044–1052.
5. Klausner, S.D.; Kanneganti, V.R.; Bouldin, D.R. An approach for estimating a decay series for organic nitrogen in animal manure. Agron. J. **1994**, *86*, 897–903.
6. Jokela, W.E. Nitrogen fertilizer and dairy manure effects on corn yield and soil nitrate. Soil Sci. Soc. Am. J. **1992**, *56*, 148–154.
7. Sommerfeldt, T.G.; Chang, C. Changes in soil properties under annual applications of feedlot manure and different tillage practices. Soil Sci. Soc. Am. J. **1985**, *49*, 983–987.
8. Sommerfeldt, T.G.; Chang, C. Soil-water properties as affected by twelve annual applications of cattle feedlot manure. Soil Sci. Soc. Am. J. **1987**, *51*, 7–9.
9. Eghball, B.; Gilley, J.E.; Baltensperger, D.D.; Blumenthal, J.M. Long-term manure and fertilizer application effects on phosphorus and nitrogen in runoff. Trans. ASAE **2002**, *45*, 687–694.
10. Freeze, B.S.; Webber, C.; Lindwall, C.W.; Dormaar, J.F. Risk simulation of the economics of manure application to restore eroded wheat cropland. Can. J. Soil Sci. **1993**, *87*, 267–274.
11. Ondersteijn, C.J.M.; Beldman, A.C.G.; Daatselaar, C.H.G.; Giesen, G.W.J.; Huirne, R.B.M. The Dutch mineral accounting systems and the European nitrate directive: Implications for N and P management and farm performance. Agric. Ecosyst. Environ. **2002**, *92*, 283–296.

Nutrient Requirements: Carnivores

Duane E. Ullrey
Michigan State University, East Lansing, Michigan, U.S.A.

INTRODUCTION

Carnivores, broadly defined, sustain themselves by feeding on vertebrate or invertebrate animal tissues, a practice observed in both the animal and plant kingdoms. The Venus flytrap (*Dionaea muscipula*), one of over 500 carnivorous plant species, lives in humid, acidic bogs in the Carolinas and, like most plants, acquires energy and nutrients by photosynthesis and through the roots. In this environment, nitrogen and some mineral elements are in short supply, and these needs are met by capturing insects attracted to nectar in a specialized leafy trap, functioning both as a mouth and stomach. Animals, of course, do not possess roots or the mechanisms of photosynthesis. Thus, energy and nutrient requirements of wild carnivorous animals are acquired principally by consuming vertebrate or invertebrate prey.[1,2]

Wilson[3] estimated there are about 4000 species of extant mammals, 9000 of birds, 6300 of reptiles, 4200 of amphibians, and 18,000 of fish and lower chordates. The nutrient requirements of these species are presumed to be *qualitatively* similar, but *quantitative* nutrient requirements have been defined by the National Academy of Sciences/National Research Council (NAS/NRC) only for humans and a few domesticated or captive mammals, birds, and fish. Of the species with NRC-defined requirements, the cat, mink, tarsiers, rainbow trout, and salmon are obligate carnivores. The NRC also has defined the nutrient requirements of the dog and fox, but these species appear to be facultative carnivores and may consume considerable vegetable matter.

CARNIVOROUS MAMMALS

The immediate ancestors of the domestic cat (*Felis catus*) were strictly carnivorous, and its needs have been the most thoroughly studied of any of the obligate carnivores. Although commercial diets for cats may contain vegetable matter, the nutrients and the amounts that must be present reflect a long evolutionary dependence on a strictly carnivorous diet. The cat has a simple digestive system, presumably because digestibility of natural prey tends to be high, and there is no need for extended food retention and microbial fermentation. Due to its limited ability to conserve nitrogen, the cat has a high protein requirement, and it converts only negligible amounts of tryptophan to niacin (neither ability is necessary when consuming whole prey). Requirements for blood glucose are met primarily by gluconeogenesis rather than from dietary carbohydrate, and the cat has a high requirement for arginine for disposal of nitrogen via the urea cycle. It requires taurine and arachidonic acid because of limited tissue synthesis (vertebrate prey provide adequate amounts), and it is unable to convert β-carotene (a plant provitamin) to vitamin A. Vitamin D_3 needs are met by diet because cutaneous concentrations of 7-dehydrocholesterol (provitamin D_3) are insufficient to support vitamin D photobiogenesis. Nutrient needs of the cat have been reviewed by the NRC,[4] and minimal requirements, adequate intakes, and recommended allowances have been published. The NRC-recommended allowances for growth, maintenance, late gestation, and peak lactation are presented in Table 1.

The mink (*Mustela vison*) eats small mammals, fish, frogs, crayfish, insects, worms, and birds in the wild. Like the cat, its protein requirements are high—38% of dietary dry matter (DM) from weaning to 13 weeks of age, 22–26% for adult maintenance, 38% for gestation, and 46% for lactation.[5] Whether the mink shares the other unique metabolic features of the cat has not been determined.

Tarsiers (*Tarsius* spp.) eat insects (beetles, ants, locusts, cicadas, cockroaches, mantids, moths) and sometimes small vertebrates in the wild. Although the quantitative nutrient requirements of tarsiers have not been specifically defined, estimated adequate nutrient concentrations in dietary DM have been proposed.[6] When kept in captivity, tarsiers are often provided crickets as a major food item. Because crickets and other commercially available insects tend to be deficient in certain nutrients (particularly calcium, vitamin A, and vitamin D),[7] specifically formulated diets are offered to these insects for about 48 hours before feeding them to tarsiers so that the insects plus their gut contents will be nutritionally complete.[8–10]

Other obligate carnivorous mammals include felids such as lions, tigers, leopards, cheetahs, and jaguars. Aquatic mammals such as dolphins, seals, sea lions, and walruses also are obligate carnivores, but little is known about their quantitative nutrient requirements.

Encyclopedia of Animal Science
DOI: 10.1081/E-EAS 120019733

Table 1 Recommended nutrient allowances in dietary dry matter (DM) for domestic cats consuming diets containing 4 kcal of metabolizable energy per g of DM

Nutrient	Growth	Maintenance	Late gestation	Peak lactation
Crude protein, %	22.5	20.0	21.3	30.0
Arginine, %	0.96	0.77	1.50	1.50
Histidine, %	0.33	0.26	0.43	0.71
Isoleucine, %	0.54	0.43	0.77	1.20
Methionine, %	0.44	0.17	0.50	0.60
Meth.+cystine, %	0.88	0.34	0.90	1.04
Leucine, %	1.28	1.02	1.80	2.00
Lysine, %	0.85	0.34	1.10	1.40
Phenylalanine, %	0.50	0.50	–	–
Phenyl.+tyrosine, %[a]	1.91	1.53	1.91	1.91
Threonine, %	0.65	0.52	0.89	1.08
Tryptophan, %	0.16	0.13	0.19	0.19
Valine, %	0.64	0.51	1.00	1.20
Taurine, %[b]	0.04–0.2	0.04–0.2	0.04–0.2	0.04–0.2
Total fat, %	9.0	9.0	9.0	9.0
Linoleic acid, %	0.55	0.55	0.55	0.55
α-Linolenic acid, %	0.02	–	0.02	0.02
Arachidonic acid, %	0.02	0.004	0.02	0.02
Eicosapentaenoic and docosahexaenoic acid, %	0.01	0.01	0.01	0.01
Calcium, %	0.80	0.29	1.08	1.08
Phosphorus, %	0.72	0.26	0.76	0.76
Magnesium, %	0.04	0.04	0.06	0.06
Sodium, %	0.14	0.07	0.13	0.13
Potassium, %	0.40	0.52	0.52	0.52
Chloride, %	0.09	0.10	0.20	0.20
Iron, mg/kg	80	80	80	80
Copper, g/kg	8.4	5.0	8.8	8.8
Zinc, mg/kg	75	75	60	60
Manganese, mg/kg	4.8	4.8	7.2	7.2
Selenium, mg/kg	0.4	0.4	0.4	0.4
Iodine, mg/kg	2.2	2.2	2.2	2.2
Vitamin A, IU/kg	3,550	3,550	7,500	7,500
Vitamin D$_3$, IU/kg	250	250	250	250
RRR-α-tocopherol, mg/kg	38	38	38	38
Vitamin K (menadione), mg/kg	1.0	1.0	1.0	1.0
Thiamin, mg/kg	5.5	5.6	5.5	5.5
Riboflavin, mg/kg	4.25	4.25	4.25	4.25
Pyridoxine, mg/kg	2.50	2.50	2.50	2.50
Niacin, mg/kg	42.5	42.5	42.5	42.5
Pantothenic acid, mg/kg	6.25	6.25	6.25	6.25
Folic acid, mg/kg	0.75	0.75	0.75	0.75
Biotin, μg/kg	75	75	75	75
Vitamin B$_{12}$, μg/kg	22.5	22.5	22.5	22.5
Choline, mg/kg	2,550	2,550	2,550	2,550

[a]At least twice as much phenylalanine (or phenylalanine plus tyrosine) is required for maximal black hair color as for growth.

[b]Recommended taurine allowances are lowest when diets are unprocessed (0.04% of DM) but are increased by extrusion (0.1% of DM) or canning (0.2% of DM).

(Adapted from Ref. 4, recommended allowances for growth of an 800-g kitten, maintenance or late gestation of a 4-kg adult cat, and lactation of a 4-kg queen with four kittens.)

CARNIVOROUS BIRDS

The digestive systems of obligate carnivorous birds (such as hawks and eagles), like their mammalian counterparts, do not have compartments adapted for microbial fermentation. Relatively indigestible portions of prey, such as fur, feathers, bones, fins, scales, shells, and exoskeletons, may be separated from more digestible portions by the beak prior to food ingestion. Sometimes, this separation is accomplished in the gizzard, followed by egestion of indigestible matter out of the mouth, as in owls.[11] Although the NRC[12] has defined the nutrient requirements of poultry, these species are principally herbivorous. Based on present metabolic evidence and the composition of vertebrate and invertebrate prey, it seems likely that nutrient needs of carnivorous birds are similar to those of carnivorous mammals, with adjustments for differences in reproductive strategy.

CARNIVOROUS REPTILES AND AMPHIBIANS

The long evolutionary association of snakes, crocodilians, and some lizard families with subsistence on vertebrate and invertebrate prey suggests that they are obligate carnivores. They tend to have simple gastrointestinal systems as compared to herbivorous reptiles, although there are adaptations related to the periodicity of feeding and to unique characteristics of certain food items. Tortoises are chiefly herbivorous with a few that are omnivorous. Turtles tend to be omnivorous—carnivorous as juveniles and herbivorous or omnivorous as adults— although a few species are mostly carnivorous throughout life.[13] Studies that define qualitative or quantitative needs of reptiles are few, although protein and amino acid needs of the hatchling green sea turtle (*Chelonia mydas*; carnivorous as hatchlings, herbivorous as adults) have been investigated. Some studies suggest that young red-eared slider turtles (*Trachemys scripta elegans*) and green anoles (*Anolis carolinensis*) do not have an elevated requirement for arginine (as does the cat), and addition of taurine to a diet based on plant proteins does not improve growth of young American alligators (*Alligator mississippiensis*). Also, American alligators appear to convert linoleic acid to arachidonic acid to some extent, although rates may not be optimum for maximum growth.[1] When a purified diet containing adequate tryptophan but no niacin was administered weekly by stomach tube to bull snakes (*Pituophis melanoleucus sayi*) for 132 days, no signs of deficiency were seen, suggesting that either a longer period of depletion is necessary to induce niacin deficiency or metabolic conversion of tryptophan to niacin may occur in this species.[14] Thus, if these reptiles are

indeed obligate carnivores, their nutrient needs seem to deviate from those of the cat.

Most amphibians appear to be obligate carnivores.[13] Adult frogs and toads consume invertebrates and small vertebrates, although most species are herbivorous as larvae (tadpoles) and have a long, coiled intestine permitting them to digest plant matter. At metamorphosis, the intestine is much shortened and the diet becomes strictly carnivorous. Tadpoles of a few species are carnivorous and have a much shorter gut than do herbivorous tadpoles. Salamanders and newts are carnivorous both as larvae and as adults, feeding on insects, slugs, snails, and worms. Caecilians (limbless, viviparous amphibians) prey on worms, termites, and orthopterans. Metabolic features characteristic of carnivory have not been well studied in amphibians.

CARNIVOROUS FISH

Rainbow trout (*Salmo gairdneri*) and coho salmon (*Oncorhynchus kirsutch*) have protein requirements of $\geq 40\%$ of dietary DM for maximal growth of juveniles and have an absolute requirement for arginine. They also lack the ability to synthesize niacin from tryptophan. Gluconeogenesis is important for provision of blood glucose, and essential fatty acid requirements include linoleic acid and eicosapentaenoic acid and/or docosahexaenoic acid.[15]

CONCLUSIONS

Qualitative and quantitative nutrient requirements of obligate carnivores generally appear to reflect evolutionary adaptations to the composition of ancestral diets.

REFERENCES

1. Allen, M.E.; Oftedal, O.T. The Nutrition of Carnivorous Reptiles. In *Captive Management and Conservation of Amphibians and Reptiles, Contributions to Herpetology, Vol. 11*; Murphy, J.B., Adler, K., Collins, J.T., Eds.; Society for the Study of Amphibians and Reptiles: Ithaca, NY, 1994; 71–82.

2. Allen, M.E.; Oftedal, O.T.; Baer, D.J. The Feeding and Nutrition of Carnivores. In *Wild Mammals in Captivity: Principles and Techniques*; Kleiman, D.G., Allen, M.E., Thompson, K.V., Lumpkin, S., Eds.; Univ. Chicago Press: Chicago, IL, 1996; 139–147.

3. Wilson, E. *The Diversity of Life*; Harvard Univ. Press: Cambridge, MA, 1992.

4. National Research Council. *Nutrient Requirements of Dogs*

and Cats; National Academies Press: Washington, DC, 2004.

5. National Research Council. *Nutrient Requirements of Mink and Foxes*, 2nd Rev.; National Academy Press: Washington, DC, 1982.

6. National Research Council. *Nutrient Requirements of Nonhuman Primates*, 2nd Rev. Ed.; National Academies Press: Washington, DC, 2003.

7. Finke, M.D. Complete nutrient composition of commercially raised invertebrates used as food for insectivores. Zoo Biol. **2002**, *21*, 269–285.

8. Allen, M.E.; Oftedal, O.T. Dietary manipulation of the calcium content of feed crickets. J. Zoo Wildl. Med. **1989**, *20*, 26–33.

9. Finke, M.D. Gut loading to enhance the nutrient content of insects as food for reptiles: A mathematical approach. Zoo Biol. **2003**, *22*, 147–162.

10. Roberts, M.; Kohn, F. Habitat use, foraging behavior, and activity patterns in reproducing Western tarsiers, *Tarsius bancanus*, in captivity: A management synthesis. Zoo Biol. **1993**, *12*, 217–232.

11. Klasing, K.C. *Comparative Avian Nutrition*; CAB International: New York, NY, 1998.

12. National Research Council. *Nutrient Requirements of Poultry*; National Academy Press: Washington, DC, 1994.

13. *The Encyclopedia of Reptiles and Amphibians*; Halliday, T.R., Adler, K., Eds.; Facts on File, Inc.: New York, NY, 1986.

14. Bartkiewicz, S.E.; Ullrey, D.E.; Trapp, A.L.; Ku, P.K. A preliminary study of niacin needs of the bull snake (*Pituophis melanoleucus sayi*). J. Zoo Anim. Med. **1982**, *13*, 55–58.

15. National Research Council. *Nutrient Requirements of Fish*; National Academy Press: Washington, DC, 1993.

Nutrient Requirements: Nonruminant Herbivores

Michael R. Murphy
Amy C. Norman
University of Illinois at Urbana–Champaign, Urbana, Illinois, U.S.A.

INTRODUCTION

Nonruminant herbivorous mammals include a small number of commercially important animals and a larger number of wild species.[1] Digestive strategies clearly differ among these herbivores. Mammals lack enzymes to hydrolyze a substantial portion of plant material (cell walls), but various pregastric (including ruminant) and postgastric microbial fermentation systems have evolved that enable herbivorous mammals to utilize fibrous substrates. Digestive strategy and body size data for East African nonforest herbivores indicated that ruminants dominated medium body sizes, whereas nonruminants prevailed among very large and small herbivores[2] (Fig. 1).

Our objective was to briefly review current knowledge about the nutritional requirements of nonruminant herbivores. Those for horses (*Equus caballus*) and domestic rabbits (*Oryctolagus cuniculus*) are stressed. Among commercially important and widely distributed species, horses and rabbits represent very large and small mammalian herbivores, respectively. In addition, they exemplify subgroups of postgastric fermenters that emphasize colonic (horses) or cecal (rabbits) function. More detailed information is also available on their nutritional requirements than for many other species.

HORSES

Water

Horses usually drink 2 to 3 L of water/kg of dry matter consumed. Water intake increases with lactation, exercise, and elevated temperatures by 50 to 70%, 20 to 300%, and up to 300%, respectively. Ad libitum access to fresh, clean water is recommended except after intense exercise, when horses should be allowed to drink only small amounts every 5 to 10 minutes for approximately 1 hour.[3]

Energy

Horses get most of their dietary energy from carbohydrates and lipids. Energy value is usually expressed in terms of digestible energy (DE, gross energy minus fecal energy).[4] Structural carbohydrates, such as cellulose and hemicellulose, often make up the majority of their diet[3] and are fermented by microbes in the cecum and colon to provide much of the energy required by a horse at maintenance.[4] A minimum of 12 to 15% fiber is presumed necessary to minimize incidence of colic and laminitis, but forages alone do not generally provide sufficient energy for growing, working, or lactating horses, so cereal grains are added to their diets. Cereal grains provide digestible nonstructural carbohydrate (starch).[4] Lipids may also be supplemented, providing 2.25 times the energy value of carbohydrates,[5] and 20% added fat can be included in the diet without adverse effects.[4] Diets supplemented with fat should be monitored closely for rancidity, because spoiled feed is not accepted. Supplementation with fat improves work output, reproductive performance, milk production, and foal growth, but it must be monitored closely to avoid obesity and insulin resistance.[4]

Protein

Amino acids, the building blocks of protein, are required.[4] Protein deficiency retards growth of young horses and causes tissue loss, poor coat, and abnormal hoof development in the adult. Average protein intake at maintenance is approximately 0.6 g of digestible protein/kg/day and should be increased during late gestation and early lactation. Protein requirements for working horses have not been clearly defined, but it is not considered advantageous to feed protein above the maintenance requirement. High-quality protein is essential for the growing horse, and it appears that growth is maximal when the protein-to-energy ratio is 50 and 45 g of crude protein/Mcal of DE/day for weanlings and yearlings, respectively. Lysine is the first-limiting amino acid for growing horses, and there appears to be no beneficial effect of including nonprotein nitrogen sources in practical diets for horses.[4]

Minerals and Vitamins

The major minerals needed by horses are Ca, P, Na, K, Cl, I, Fe, Cu, Zn, Mg, and Se.[4] Bone is approximately 35%

Encyclopedia of Animal Science
DOI: 10.1081/E-EAS 120019734

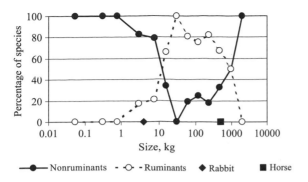

Fig. 1 The relationship between digestive strategy and body size in 186 species of East African nonforest herbivores. (Adapted from Ref. 2, with the sizes of rabbits and horses marked for comparison.) (*View this art in color at www. dekker.com.*)

Ca and 16% P. The dietary Ca:P ratio is critical for proper bone development; ratios less than 1:1 can impair Ca absorption and cause detrimental bone abnormalities in developing horses. Sodium, K, and Cl are the three major minerals involved in electrolyte balance, and it is necessary to maintain proper concentrations of each. Iodine is important for regulation of metabolism, but it should be closely monitored because horses are susceptible to iodine

toxicity. Iron is adequate in most diets, so supplementation is unnecessary, although frequently practiced.

Vitamins are often classified as fat-soluble or water-soluble. The former category includes vitamins A, D, E, and K. Vitamin A is important for good vision. Vitamin D is essential for calcium and phosphorus absorption, but rarely needs to be supplemented if animals are exposed to sunlight. Water-soluble thiamin and riboflavin are discussed in a publication of the National Research Council (NRC).[4] A deficiency of thiamin can cause a multitude of problems, but neither deficiency nor toxicity of riboflavin has been reported. Requirements for other water-soluble vitamins (niacin, pantothenic acid, pyridoxine, biotin, folacin, B12, ascorbic acid, and choline) have not been determined, but they are presumed to be required. Table 1 summarizes nutrient requirement data for horses.

RABBITS

Mature rabbits vary greatly in size, from 1 to 6 kg.[6] Therefore, their nutrient requirements are not usually specified on an amount-per-day basis, but on a dietary concentration relative to body size, or relative to metabolic body size basis.

Table 1 Estimated nutrient requirements for a 500-kg mature horse

Nutrient	Unit[a]	Growth	Maintenance	Gestation	Lactation	Work
Water	L	23–30	38–45	38–57	38–57	38–68
Energy	Mcal of digestible energy	14–19	16.5	18–19	28–24	20–33
Protein	g	720–850	656	801–866	1,427–1,048	820–1,300
Minerals						
Calcium	g	34–29	20	35–37	56–36	25–40
Phosphorus	g	19–16	18	26–28	36–22	18–29
Potassium	g	11.3–17.8	25	29.1–31.5	46–33	31.2–49.9
Magnesium	g	3.7–5.5	7.5	8.7–9.4	10.9–8.6	9.4–15.1
Sulfur	%	0.15	0.15	0.15	0.15	0.15
Sodium	%	0.1	0.1	0.1	0.1	0.3
Iron	mg/kg	50	40	50	50	40
Manganese	mg/kg	40	40	40	40	40
Zinc	mg/kg	40	40	40	40	40
Copper	mg/kg	10	10	10	10	10
Selenium	mg/kg	0.1	0.1	0.1	0.1	0.1
Iodine	mg/kg	0.1–0.6	0.1 0.6	0.1–0.6	0.1–0.6	0.1–0.6
Cobalt	mg/kg	0.1	0.1	0.1	0.1	0.1
Vitamins						
A	IU/kg	2,000	2,000	3,000	3,000	2,000
D	IU/kg	800	300	600	600	300
E	IU/kg	80	50	80	80	80

[a]Amounts or concentrations on a dry matter basis.
(From Refs. 3 and 4.)

Water

Although the NRC[6] did not address the subject of water, others[7,8] have noted that the water requirements of rabbits fed dry feed far exceed their dry matter intakes. Consumption of such diets drops precipitously if water is withheld. Water intake on dry diets is about 120 mL/kg of rabbit, or twice the amount of feed consumed. Environmental temperature also influences water consumption, increasing it by 67% between 18 and 30°C. High-quality drinking water should always be available.

Energy

For diets containing 12 to 15% digestible protein, DE and metabolizable energy (ME, DE minus urinary energy in nonruminants) are closely correlated, and ME is about 95% of DE. Diet ME and net energy (ME minus heat increment) contents are more difficult to determine than DE, so DE values are still commonly used in practical rabbit feeding.[8]

Rabbits do not utilize plant fiber as efficiently as widely assumed[6] and coprophagy (consumption of soft feces of cecal origin) does not appear to greatly influence the overall efficiency of fiber digestion.[7] Cellulose and hemicellulose digestibilities in rabbits are similar to those of rats, and less than in horses and guinea pigs. Only about 10% of neutral detergent fiber in timothy hay was digested by rabbits, compared to about 35% for horses and ponies. Rabbit growth rate is apparently optimal with diets having 13 to 25% acid detergent fiber. A minimum of 10% dietary crude fiber is needed to maximize growth rate (and to prevent enteritis and fur pulling), but over 17% depresses growth by restricting feed intake.

Starches, sugars, and lipids apparently pose no special problems for rabbits. The likelihood of a deficiency of essential fatty acids is remote, but it has been demonstrated in rabbits.

Protein

Rabbits need adequate quantities of essential amino acids in their diet for rapid growth, and nonprotein nitrogen cannot be employed usefully in grower diets.[6] Protein quality must allow essential amino acid requirements to be met. Required and optimal concentrations of some amino acids have been established for growing and lactating rabbits.[6–8] Rabbits are able to utilize 64 to 90% of the crude protein in common feedstuffs.[7] They can maintain positive nitrogen balance when fed gelatin, a protein devoid of the essential amino acid tryptophan, because of the consumption of microbial protein via coprophagy. Negative nitrogen balance occurred when coprophagy

was prevented. Increased feed intakes can compensate for low protein concentrations in diets. Therefore, it is desirable to express protein requirements per unit of energy. Growth is optimized with about 55 mg of crude protein/kcal of DE.

Minerals and Vitamins

The rabbit is unusual because serum Ca concentration reflects dietary Ca concentration, rather than being homeostatically regulated in a narrow range as in other species.[6,7] Hypocalcemia is sometimes observed in late gestation or early lactation. It is treatable with Ca-gluconate injection. However, whether an acidotic diet during late gestation would be prophylactic, as it is for a dairy cow, is not known.[8] Requirements for many minerals have not been well studied, although deficiencies and problems with excesses have often been demonstrated.

Vitamin A deficiency and toxicity have been demonstrated, but precise requirements have not been determined.[7,8] Any dietary requirement for vitamin D is likely

Table 2 Estimated nutrient requirements for rabbits (amounts are per kilogram of air-dry diet, unless otherwise specified)

Nutrient	Unit	Growth	Lactation
Water	kg	1.6	2.0
Energy	kcal	2,500	2,500
	MJ	10.5	10.5
	kJ of digestible energy/kg$^{0.75}$	950	1,200
Protein	g	170–180	170–180
Minerals			
Calcium	g	8	11.8
Phosphorus	g	5	6.6
Potassium	g	6	9
Sodium	g	2	2.2
Chlorine	g	3	3.2
Magnesium	g	3	3
Iron	mg	50	75
Zinc	mg	25	50
Copper	mg	10	10
Manganese	mg	8.5	10
Iodine	mg	0.2	0.2
Cobalt	mg	0.1	0.1
Selenium	mg	0.01	0.01
Vitamins			
A	IU	6,000	10,000
D	IU	1,000	1,000
E	mg	35	45
K	mg	1	2

(Mean or median values compiled from Refs. 6–8.)

much lower than for other species. The only practical problem encountered with vitamin D in rabbit nutrition is toxicity: 2300 to 3000 IU of vitamin D/kg are detrimental. Vitamin E deficiency has been demonstrated, but recommendations are based primarily on old data or extrapolation from other species. Vitamin K is probably not of practical concern in rabbit nutrition because it is synthesized in the cecum, and no requirement studies have been conducted.

Under practical conditions, B-complex vitamins are not dietarily essential for rabbits, but deficiencies have been demonstrated. Addition of B vitamins to commercial rabbit feeds has not shown benefits. Rabbits can synthesize vitamin C, so it is not a dietary essential either. In commercial diets, it is advisable to include a vitamin mixture that provides at least moderate concentrations of vitamins A and E to ensure that no deficiency occurs. Table 2 summarizes nutrient requirement data for rabbits.

CONCLUSION

Much remains unknown about the nutritional requirements of nonruminant herbivores. Current data, however, allow many practical dietary limitations and toxicities to be avoided in commercially important and widely distributed species, particularly horses and domestic rabbits.

REFERENCES

1. Cork, S.J.; Hume, I.D.; Faichney, G.C. Digestive Strategies of Nonruminant Herbivores: The Role of the Hindgut. In *Nutritional Ecology of Herbivores*; Jung, H.-J.G., Fahey, G.C., Jr., Eds.; Amer. Soc. Anim. Sci.; Savoy: IL, 1999; 210–260.
2. Demment, M.W.; Van Soest, P.J. A nutritional explanation for body-size patterns of ruminant and nonruminant herbivores. Am. Nat. **1985**, *125*, 641–672.
3. Lawrence, L. Feeding Horses. In *Livestock Feeds and Feeding*, 5th Ed.; Kellems, R.O., Church, D.C., Eds.; Prentice Hall: Upper Saddle River, NJ, 2002; 381–401.
4. National Research Council. *Nutrient Requirements of Horses*, 5th Rev. Ed.; Natl. Acad. Sci.: Washington, DC, 1989.
5. Ensminger, M.E.; Oldfield, J.E.; Heinemann, W.W. *Feeds and Nutrition*, 2nd Ed.; Ensminger Publ. Co.: Clovis, CA, 1990.
6. National Research Council. *Nutrient Requirements of Rabbits*, 2nd Rev. Ed.; Natl. Acad. Sci.: Washington, DC, 1977.
7. Cheeke, P.R. *Rabbit Feeding and Nutrition*; Academic Press: Orlando, FL, 1987.
8. de Blas, C.; Wiseman, J. *The Nutrition of the Rabbit*; CABI Publ.: New York, 1998.

Nutrient Requirements: Ruminants

C. L. Ferrell

United States Department of Agriculture, Agricultural Research Service, Clay Center, Nebraska, U.S.A.

INTRODUCTION

Nutrient needs of tissues of ruminants are similar to those of nonruminants. Tissues of ruminants require oxygen, water, energy, amino acids, fatty acids, minerals, and fat- and water-soluble vitamins. Dietary needs of ruminants are simpler and often cheaper than for nonruminants because of anaerobic microbial metabolism in the rumen. Microbial metabolism of dietary intake also increases the complexity of relating dietary intake to nutrients available to the animal.

WATER

Water is required by the animal for regulation of body temperature and acts as a solvent necessary for transport of nutrients, metabolites, and waste products. The requirement for water reflects needs for accretion in body tissues (e.g., growth, pregnancy) and milk production plus that lost from the animal. Water is lost from the animal by excretion as urine or feces, from the lungs as water vapor during respiration, and from skin by evaporation. Losses vary considerably and depend in part on activity, air temperature, diet, and water consumption. Because feeds contain water, and oxidation of nutrients produces water, not all water needs must be provided by drinking.

ENERGY

Energy is defined as the potential to perform work and is required to perform the ''work'' of living. Energy requirements depend on the additive needs of individual cells and vary according to physiological needs imposed upon those cells. Energy is derived from the metabolism of carbohydrates, proteins or amino acids, and fats and can be supplied from the diet, or if dietary supply is inadequate, from body tissues (fat, protein, glycogen). Carbohydrates are the primary dietary source of energy of ruminants. Dietary protein, peptides, and amino acids contribute up to about 20% to the energy supply. Fat is low (2–4%) in diets typically consumed by ruminants, and is, thus, not a major contributor to energy supplies. Fat

may be added to diets of feedlot cattle or lactating cows to increase the energy density of the diet, but dietary fat contents of greater than 8–10% may have adverse effects on rumen microbial metabolism.

Cellulose, hemicellulose, and starch are the major carbohydrates utilized by ruminants. Many species of bacteria in the rumen produce cellulase enzymes capable of hydrolyzing the β 1–4 linkages between the glucose units in cellulose and others hydrolyze the β 1–4 linkages in hemicellulose. Many species of microbes, as well as α amylases present in pancreatic secretions of all animals, hydrolyze α 1–4 linkages of starch. The symbiotic relationship between ruminants and rumen microbes allow utilization of forages and other feeds, especially those containing complex carbohydrates such as cellulose that are unusable or poorly utilized by nonruminants. Volatile fatty acids (VFA; acetate, proprionate, butyrate, etc.) are primary metabolic end-products of carbohydrate (and protein) hydrolysis by anaerobic microbes in the rumen and serve as the major energy source of ruminants. One of the major metabolic differences between ruminants and nonruminants is the reliance of ruminants on VFAs as the major substrates for oxidative metabolism and energy storage.

Little glucose is available for absorption from the digestive tract of ruminants. However, glucose is required by nervous tissue, muscle, adipose, mammary gland, and gravid uterus. Glucose requirements of ruminants are met through gluconeogenesis, primarily from proprionate, amino acids (e.g., alanine, glutamine, aspartate, glutamate), glycerol, and lactate. In spite of the lower blood glucose concentrations and extra metabolic steps required to provide glucose, requirements of ruminants appear to be similar to nonruminants.

AMINO ACIDS

It is generally assumed that tissue requirements for amino acids of ruminants are similar to those of nonruminants. However, this assumption has not been rigorously tested. Amino acids are required for synthesis of protein and other essential compounds and provide the carbon skeleton for a major proportion of glucose needed by the ruminant. Lysine, arginine, histidine, isoleucine,

Encyclopedia of Animal Science
DOI: 10.1081/E-EAS 120019736

leucine, methionine, phenylalanine, threonine, tryptophan, and valine must be supplied from the digestive tract, but specific requirements have not been well defined. Requirements have been estimated based on rate of accretion and amino acid composition of whole body protein.[1]

Ruminants have the unique ability to subsist and produce without dietary protein or amino acids due to synthesis of microbial protein from a wide variety of nitrogen (N) sources within the rumen. The sources of N that microbes utilize for protein synthesis include dietary protein and nonprotein N (NPN), as well as N recycled to the rumen via saliva or diffusion (primarily as urea). Most ruminal bacteria can use ammonia N as a source of N, but much of the N used by bacteria is derived from amino acids or peptides, if available. Ruminants can grow, reproduce, and lactate with only NPN as a source of N, but additional sources of amino acids are required to achieve maximal productivity. Rumen microbes, as well as dietary protein that escape (bypass) degradation in the rumen, supply the intestine with protein for digestion and absorption as amino acids. Microbial N composes about 40% of the nonammonia N entering the intestine on high-energy diets with high protein levels, about 60% with low protein diets, and 100% with purified, NPN-supplemented diets. Biological values of microbial protein range from about 65 to 90, with an ideal value of 100.

The quantity and quality of protein reaching the small intestine is modulated by the effects of degradation and synthesis in the rumen. Both quality and quantity of protein available to the animal may be improved by microbial metabolism if a diet containing a low level or low quality of protein is fed. Microbial action may decrease the quantity and quality of available protein when a diet containing a high level of high-quality protein is fed. The amino acid profile of microbial protein is relatively constant and well balanced relative to tissue needs, and thus is utilized very efficiently. However, dietary protein escaping ruminal degradation may be less well balanced. As with nonruminants, a poorly balanced supply of amino acids results in increased catabolism of amino acids. Unless used for synthesis of protein or other essential compounds, amino acids are catabolized with the N being converted to urea and the carbon skeleton being oxidized or used for storage. A poorly balanced amino acid supply results in inefficient use of N and is energetically costly.

MINERALS

At least 17 minerals are required by ruminants. Macrominerals (those required in large amounts) include calcium, magnesium, phosphorus, potassium, sodium, chlorine, and sulfur. Required microminerals (those required in small amounts) are chromium, cobalt, copper, iodine, iron, manganese, molybdenum, nickel, selenium, and zinc.[1–3] Other minerals—including arsenic, boron, lead, silicon, and vanadium—have been shown to be essential for one or more animal species, but there is no evidence to indicate these minerals are of practical importance in ruminant diets. Two features of ruminant nutrient requirements are noteworthy. Phytate phosphorus is not well utilized by nonruminants, but as a result of microbial fermentation, is utilized readily by ruminants. Cobalt functions as a component of vitamin B_{12}. Ruminants are not dependent on a dietary source of vitamin B_{12}, but cobalt is required for its synthesis by rumen microbes. Many of the essential minerals are usually found in typical feeds, while others must be provided by dietary supplementation for optimal animal performance. Supplementation in excess of requirements increases mineral excretion. In addition, several essential minerals (e.g., copper and selenium) are toxic at high levels, while others, although not toxic per se, interfere with absorption of other essential minerals when included in the diet in excessive amounts.

VITAMINS

Ruminants require fat-soluble vitamins (A, D, E, and K) and water-soluble vitamins (B complex), but typically only have a dietary requirement for vitamins A and E. Vitamin A is essential for normal growth and reproduction, maintenance of epithelial tissues, and bone development, and is a constituent of the visual pigment rhodopsin present in the rod cells of the retina. Vitamin A (retinol) per se does not occur in plants, but its precursors, carotenes, occur in various forms. Beta-carotene is the most widely distributed. High-quality forages provide carotenes in large amounts, but tend to be seasonal. Carotenes are rapidly destroyed by sunlight and air. Conversion of carotenes to retinol occurs in intestinal mucosal cells, but efficiency of conversion tends to be lower in ruminants than in nonruminants. Functions of vitamin E include serving as an antioxidant and in the formation of cellular membranes. Vitamin E occurs in feedstuffs as α-tocopherol. Vitamin E requirements depend on dietary concentrations of antioxidants, sulfur-containing amino acids, and selenium. Because vitamin D is synthesized by ruminants exposed to sunlight, or fed sun-cured forages, these animals rarely require vitamin D supplementation. Physiological needs of Vitamin K and the B vitamins (e.g., B_{12}, thiamin, niacin, riboflavin, pyridoxine, pantothenic acid, biotin, and choline) have been clearly demonstrated, but requirements are normally easily met by microbial synthesis in the rumen.

CONCLUSIONS

At the tissue level, nutrient requirements of ruminants are believed to be similar to those of nonruminants. However, a symbiotic relationship between the animal and microbes within the digestive tract (especially in the rumen and reticulum) results in several unique features of ruminant dietary requirements. In particular, complex carbohydrates, such as cellulose, can be effectively digested and metabolized by rumen microbes. Volatile fatty acids (VFA), by-products of microbial fermentation of carbohydrates or protein, provide a major proportion of the energy available to ruminants. Dietary protein, amino acids, or nonprotein nitrogen, such as urea, may be incorporated into microbial protein, which serves as the primary source of amino acids to ruminants. Alternatively, amino acids from the diet may escape microbial fermentation in the rumen and become available for intestinal absorption. In addition, urea produced within the animal may be recycled to the digestive tract, thus providing a source of N for microbial synthesis of amino acids. Similarly, B vitamins, vitamin K, and essential fatty acids are normally produced in sufficient quantities by microbial fermentation to meet animal requirements; however, microbial synthesis of vitamin B_{12} requires a dietary source of cobalt.

REFERENCES

1. NRC. *Nutrient Requirements of Beef Cattle*, 6th Revised Ed.; National Academy Press: Washington, DC, 2000; Update.
2. NRC. *Nutrient Requirements of Sheep*, 6th Revised Ed.; National Academy Press: Washington, DC, 1985.
3. NRC. *Nutrient Requirements of Dairy Cattle*, 6th Revised Ed.; National Academy Press: Washington, DC, 1989. Update.

Omega-3 and -6 Fatty Acids

Brian K. Speake
Peter F. Surai
Scottish Agricultural College, Ayr, U.K.

INTRODUCTION

Dietary fatty acids were originally thought to perform rather passive roles as a source of energy and cell membrane components. This view has now been transformed by the realization that omega-3 and omega-6 polyunsaturates are potent determinants of the body's physiological state, regulating fuel partitioning, inflammation, and neurological function and are, therefore, crucial determinants of health, disease, and productivity.

GENERAL ASPECTS

Structures and Nomenclature

A fatty acid molecule consists of a hydrocarbon chain with an acidic carboxyl group at one end and a terminal methyl group at the other. In the case of a saturated fatty acid, all the carbon atoms in the chain are linked by single bonds, whereas an unsaturated fatty acid is defined by the presence of one or more double bonds in the chain. Most polyunsaturated fatty acids of animal tissues belong to either the omega-6 ($\omega 6$) or omega-3 ($\omega 3$) series (also referred to as n-6 and n-3, respectively). These terms indicate the positioning of the double bonds in the chain. Thus, for an $\omega 6$ fatty acid, the double bond nearest to the methyl end is located between carbon atoms 6 and 7, counting from the methyl terminus. Similarly, the double bond nearest to the methyl end of an $\omega 3$ fatty acid forms the link between carbon atoms 3 and 4. Fatty acids are symbolized by a shorthand nomenclature. For example, linoleic acid is abbreviated to $18:2\omega 6$, indicating a chain length of 18 carbon atoms with 2 double bonds, the first double bond being located between carbons 6 and 7 from the methyl end. Other polyunsaturated fatty acids with important functions in animals are α-linolenic ($18:3\omega 3$), arachidonic ($20:4\omega 6$), eicosapentaenoic ($20:5\omega 3$), and docosahexaenoic ($22:6\omega 3$) acids. In the diets and tissues of animals, fatty acids are mainly present in the esterified form, as triacylglycerols, phospholipids, or cholesteryl esters, with only traces occurring in the free (unesterified) form.

Dietary Sources and Interconversions

Common dietary sources of the various polyunsaturated fatty acids are shown in Table 1. Vertebrate animals can synthesize saturated and monounsaturated fatty acids from dietary carbohydrate but are unable to synthesize $18:2\omega 6$ or $18:3\omega 3$. These polyunsaturates must, therefore, be provided in the diet and are referred to as essential fatty acids. Animals can, however, convert $18:2\omega 6$ to $20:4\omega 6$ via the action of desaturase and elongase enzymes.[1] The same enzymes are involved in the conversion of $18:3\omega 3$ to $20:5\omega 3$ and $22:6\omega 3$. This ability to synthesize C_{20} and C_{22} polyunsaturates from their C_{18} precursors varies greatly among animal species. Vertebrate animals are unable to perform interconversions between the $\omega 6$ and $\omega 3$ series.[1]

Functions and Health Benefits

Skin lipids (ceramides) that contain $18:2\omega 6$ perform a specific function in preventing transepidermal water loss. Dietary vegetable oils that are rich in $18:2\omega 6$ tend to reduce plasma cholesterol, probably by stimulating the hepatic uptake of low-density lipoprotein. Polyunsaturated fatty acids perform major roles as components of membrane phospholipids, where the degree of unsaturation is a key determinant of the biophysical properties of the membrane. Very high proportions of $22:6\omega 3$ are present in the phospholipids of neuronal cells of the brain and of the rod photoreceptor cells of the retina.[2] Optimal functional development of the neural tissues is dependent on adequate provision of $22:6\omega 3$ during fetal and neonatal life. Mammalian sperm phospholipids also display high proportions of $22:6\omega 3$, presumably to enhance the flexibility of the sperm tail membranes.[3]

Polyunsaturates, particularly $20:5\omega 3$ and $22:6\omega 3$, are powerful regulatory molecules. By interacting with specific transcription factors (PPARα, SREBP-1, NF-Y), they alter the pattern of gene expression in liver cells, profoundly altering the concentrations of key metabolic enzymes.[1] These changes increase the β-oxidation of fatty acids and simultaneously inhibit the synthesis of fatty acids and triacylglycerol, thereby reducing

Encyclopedia of Animal Science
DOI: 10.1081/E-EAS 120019738

Table 1 Omega-6 and -3 fatty acids: Dietary sources and metabolic functions

Name		Dietary sources	Functions
Linoleic	18:2ω6	Plant seed oils (e.g., sunflower, safflower, maize)	Energy source; skin lipids; precursor of 20:4ω6
α-linolenic	18:3ω3	Green leaves, flaxseeds, linseed oil	Energy source; precursor of 20:5ω3 and 22:6ω3
Arachidonic	20:4ω6	Meat, eggs	Membrane structure; signal transduction; gene expression; fuel partitioning; precursor of eicosanoids; proinflammatory
Eicosapentaenoic	20:5ω3	Oily fish, seafood	Gene expression; fuel partitioning; precursor of eicosanoids; anti-inflammatory; cardiovascular protection
Docosahexaenoic	22:6ω3	Oily fish, seafood	Membrane structure; brain, retina and sperm function; gene expression; fuel partitioning; anti-inflammatory; cardiovascular protection

(Based on information from Refs. 1–5.)

lipoprotein secretion. Thus, dietary fish oils can reduce plasma lipids and inhibit the accumulation of body fat.[1] Polyunsaturates also regulate cell function as a result of their conversion to eicosanoids (prostaglandins, thromboxanes, leukotrienes).[1] Eicosanoids derived from 20:4ω6 are generally more proinflammatory and prothrombotic than those derived from 20:5ω3. Dietary fish oil reduces inflammation and thrombosis by antagonising the production and action of the ω6-derived eicosanoids.[4]

The hypolipidemic, anti-inflammatory and antithrombotic effects of ω3 fatty acids, plus their antiarrhythmic and antihypertensive properties, explain the protective effects of dietary fish oil against cardiovascular disease. Beneficial effects of ω3 fatty acids in the prevention or treatment of rheumatoid arthritis, autoimmune diseases, cancers, and mental disorders have also been reported.[4]

RELEVANCE TO ANIMAL SCIENCE

Enhancing the ω3 Content of Animal Products to Benefit the Health of Consumers

During human evolution, our metabolism became adapted to a hunter-gatherer diet that provided a balanced intake of ω6 and ω3 fatty acids in a ratio of about 1:1. In the Western world, this ratio may currently be as high as 20:1.[5] Livestock raised on grain display much higher ω6:ω3 ratios in their tissues compared with meat from animals in the wild.[5] In the case of monogastric livestock, the ω3 status of their tissues is easily improved by providing a source of these fatty acids in their diets. Thus, dietary supplementation of pigs and poultry with

fish oil, fish meal, flaxseed, or certain algae readily enhances the concentration of ω3 fatty acids in the lipids of pork, chicken meat, and eggs.[5]

Modulation of the fatty acid composition of ruminant meat and milk is restricted by the extensive biohydrogenation of polyunsaturates that occurs in the rumen. This problem can be partially circumvented by encapsulation of oil supplements in a protective coating to prevent access by rumen microbes.[6] Also, there is some evidence that 20:5ω3 and 22:6ω3 are less susceptible to biohydrogenation in comparison with 18:2ω6 and 18:3ω3. Although supplementation of dairy cows with fish oil (nonencapsulated) increases the proportions of ω3 fatty acids in milk lipid, it is difficult to achieve concentrations of 22:6ω3 greater than 0.1% of milk fatty acids due to the low efficiency (3%) of transfer of this fatty acid from diet to milk.[7] Fish oil supplements result in increased concentrations of trans-fatty acids and conjugated linoleic acid in milk and also depress milk fat content.[7] Intake of linseed or fish oil by cattle produced significant increases in the concentrations of ω3 fatty acids in muscle phospholipid.[6] Cattle fed on grass have higher concentrations of ω3 fatty acids in muscle lipids compared with cattle raised on concentrates.

Improving the Health and Productivity of Livestock

Despite the massive amount of research on the role of polyunsaturates in human health, the potential for improving the health of livestock by dietary fatty acids has received limited attention. Formulated animal feeds usually have a very high ω6:ω3 ratio and often contain no 22:6ω3. Recent work has highlighted some potential benefits of ω3 supplementation for the health and productivity of the animal. For example, supplementation of sows with fish oil during pregnancy increased both the 22:6ω3 content and the weight of the piglet brain.[8] These changes were associated with a decrease in preweaning mortality, largely by a reduction in the number of piglets crushed by the sow, and possibly reflecting improved cognitive development during fetal life.[8] Supplementation of boars and cockerels with fish oil improved fertility by increasing the 22:6ω3 content, number, and fertilizing ability of spermatozoa.[3] Chickens that were fed diets rich in either ω3 or ω6 fatty acids displayed major reductions in both plasma triacylglycerol and in the weight of the abdominal fat pad compared to birds on a tallow-rich diet.[9]

CONCLUSION

With lipids occupying center stage in the relation between diet and human health, enhancing the ω3 content of meat, milk, and eggs is regarded as desirable. Furthermore, the potential to improve the health and productivity of livestock by dietary fatty acids is beginning to be evaluated.

ACKNOWLEDGMENT

We are grateful to the Scottish Executive Environment and Rural Affairs Department for financial support.

REFERENCES

1. Nakamura, M.T.; Cho, H.P.; Xu, J.; Tang, Z.; Clarke, S.D. Metabolism and functions of highly unsaturated fatty acids: An update. Lipids **2001**, *36* (9), 961–964.

2. Salem, N., Jr.; Litman, B.; Kim, H-K.; Gawrisch, K. Mechanisms of action of docosahexaenoic acid in the nervous system. Lipids **2001**, *36* (9), 945–959.

3. Speake, B.K.; Surai, P.F.; Rooke, J.A. Regulation of Avian and Mammalian Sperm Production by Dietary Fatty Acids. In *Male Fertility and Lipid Metabolism*; De Vriese, S.R., Christophe, A.B., Eds.; AOCS Press: Champaign, IL, 2003; 96–117.

4. Lands, W.E.M. Diets could prevent many diseases. Lipids **2003**, *38* (4), 317–321.

5. Simopoulos, A.P. New products from the agri-food industry: The return of n-3 fatty acids into the food supply. Lipids **1999**, *34* (Supplement), S297–S301.

6. Wood, J.D.; Enser, M.; Fisher, A.V.; Nute, G.R.; Richardson, R.I.; Sheard, P.R. Manipulating meat quality and composition. Proc. Nutr. Soc. **1999**, *58* (2), 363–370.

7. Offer, N.W.; Marsden, M.; Dixon, J.; Speake, B.K.; Thacker, F.E. Effect of dietary fat supplements on levels of n-3 polyunsaturated fatty acids, trans acids and conjugated linoleic acid in bovine milk. Anim. Sci. **1999**, *69* (3), 613–625.

8. Rooke, J.A.; Sinclair, A.G.; Edwards, S.A.; Cordoba, R.; Pkiyach, S.; Penny, P.C.; Penny, P.; Finch, A.M.; Horgan, G.W. The effect of feeding salmon oil throughout pregnancy on pre-weaning mortality of piglets. Anim. Sci. **2001**, *73* (3), 489–500.

9. Newman, R.E.; Bryden, W.L.; Fleck, E.; Ashes, J.R.; Buttemer, W.A.; Storlien, L.H.; Downing, J.A. Dietary n-3 and n-6 fatty acids alter avian metabolism: Metabolism and abdominal fat deposition. Br. J. Nutr. **2002**, *88* (1), 11–18.

Ontogeny: Adipose Tissue

Gary J. Hausman
United States Department of Agriculture, Agricultural Research Service, Athens, Georgia, U.S.A.

D. B. Hausman
University of Georgia, Athens, Georgia, U.S.A.

INTRODUCTION

Adipose tissue, now considered an endocrine organ, secretes or expresses many potential endocrine factors, including leptin and insulin-like growth factor (IGF) system proteins. Therefore, the structrual and functional aspects of adipose tissue ontogeny are important to the growing and mature animal.

FETAL AND NEONATAL DEVELOPMENT

Fat cell development commences by midgestation and is characterized by the appearance of a number of fat cell clusters, or primitive organs, which subsequently increase in number and size throughout fetal development (Table 1).[1–3] Primitive fat organs are vascular structures in presumptive adipose tissue with few or no fat cells (Fig. 1; Table 1). Fetal adipocyte development is spatially and temporally related to capillary development.[2] Although angiogenesis appears to be linked to adipogenesis, the major regulators of angiogenesis have not been examined in meat animal adipose tissue (Table 2).

Subcutaneous (SQ) depots develop before internal depots in chickens, cattle, and sheep, whereas the middle SQ layer and internal depots develop concurrently in pigs. Subcutaneous adipose tissue layers are established at the onset of adipose development and have distinct fetal and postnatal developmental patterns.[1,5]

Brown adipose tissue (BAT) is responsible, in part, for nonshivering thermogenesis in the neonate. Brown adipocytes contain more elaborate and differentiated mitochondria (Table 1)[4] than multilocular adipocytes in developing white adipose tissue (WAT; Table 1). BAT is characterized by expression of uncoupling protein (UCP-1), a mitochondrial transport protein responsible for BAT heat production. Leptin gene expression effectively marks white adipocytes since it is positively correlated with the unilocular cell morphology but inversely related to UCP-1 expression. Leptin influences many physiological processes and is primarily synthesized and secreted by WAT. BAT has not been detected in pigs and chickens but is present in neonatal ruminants and, except

for goats, is generally found only in internal fat depots. Bovine SQ originates as BAT to a degree but soon converts to WAT. At birth, sheep and cattle BAT and WAT have a mature morphology since these tissues are virtually filled with adipocytes (Table 1). BAT rapidly transforms to WAT in neonatal ruminants during the neonatal period (Table 1).

POSTNATAL DEVELOPMENT

WAT predominates in postnatal animals and adipocyte development is depot- and species-dependent (Table 3).[5–7] Adipocytes in internal depots are larger than those in the intramuscular depot, and adipocyte hypertrophy is largely responsible for fat accretion of most depots (Table 3). Generally, fat cell hypertrophy is associated with increased leptin gene expression. In the SQ depot, leptin expression responds to fasting and hormones associated with the onset of puberty.[8,9] Leptin expression traits distinguish adipose depots in sheep and cattle (Table 3).

ADIPOSE TISSUE EXPRESSION OF TRANSCRIPTION, METABOLIC, AND REGULATORY FACTORS

Adipose cell differentiation is accompanied by transcriptional activation of genes by several groups of transcription factor proteins: PPARγ, C/EBPs and ADDI/SREBP-1 (Table 2). C/EBPα, β, and PPARγ were expressed early and throughout fetal pig adipose tissue development.[3] The expression levels of several transcription factors and associated adipogenic genes increase neonatally and expression of the stearoyl coenzyme A desaturase (SCD) gene rapidly increases postnatally in several species (Table 2).

HORMONAL REGULATION OF ADIPOSE TISSUE DEVELOPMENT AND METABOLISM

Fetal hypophysectomy (hypox) increases SQ adipose tissue accretion in fetal sheep and pigs, and increases

Encyclopedia of Animal Science
DOI: 10.1081/E-EAS 120019739

Table 1 Characteristics of fetal and neonatal adipose tissue development

	WAT—cattle (C), pigs (P), and sheep (S)	BAT—cattle (C), sheep (S), and goats (G)
Fetal		
Key developmental traits	Depot-dependent development of primitive fat organs and structural differentiation of presumptive fat tissue	Depot-dependent development of primitive fat organs
Mode of accretion or expansion	C and S: hyperplasia and hypertrophy; P: hyperplasia with less hypertrophy	Hyperplasia and hypertrophy
Molecular and ultrastructural markers	Leptin; few and simple mitochondria	UCP-1; mitochondria proliferation and differentiation
Late fetal-tissue and adipocyte morphology	Moderately vascular, mature (C,S) or immature (P) tissue with either unilocular and multilocular cells (C,S) or smaller multilocular cells (P)	Very vascular, mature tissue with unilocular and multilocular cells
Neonatal		
Tissue and adipocyte morphology	Mature tissue with unilocular cells (C, P) or multilocular and unilocular cells (S)	Mature tissue with unilocular cells (C) or cells transforming from multilocular to unilocular (S)
Mode of accretion or expansion	Depot-dependent hyperplasia and hypertrophy	Hypertrophy
Accretion or expansion rate	Rapid	Relatively slow
Molecular and ultrastructural markers	Expression of leptin, transcription factors, and lipogenic enzymes	BAT-to-WAT conversion : Decreased UCP-1 expression and structural and functional mitochondrial degradation

Abbreviations: UCP-1 = uncoupling protein, WAT = white adipose tissue, BAT = brown adipose tissue.

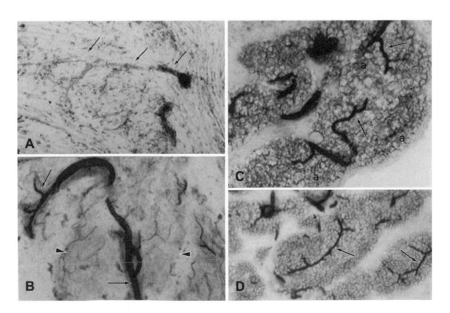

Fig. 1 Phosphatase histochemistry in cryostat sections of fetal perirenal adipose tissue from 70-day (A), 90-day (B) and 105-day (C, D) fetal pigs. Note that phosphatase reactivity is limited in arterioles (arrows) in perirenal tissue at 70 days (A), whereas more extensive phosphatase reactivity indicates that arteriolar differentiation (arrows) has clearly progressed by 90 (B) and 105 days (C, D). Areas within perirenal tissue at 90 days (B, arrowheads) can be considered primitive fat organs since there are few to no fat cells but the areas are otherwise morphologically similar to adipocyte-filled areas (a) of adipose tissue at 105 days (C). A, B, C × 300; D × 150.

Table 2 Collective reports of genes and proteins expressed during adipose tissue ontogeny

	Regulatory	Metabolism	Transcription factors
Fetal			
WAT—pigs (P) and cattle (C)	P: leptin,OBLR, IGFBP-1,-2,-3,-4,-5, IGF-I, -II, TGF-β, adipsin; C:UCP-1		P: C/EBPα, β and &, PPARγ
BAT—cattle	UCP-1, β 1-3 ARs	Cytochrome c oxidase, ADP/ATP carrier	
BAT and WAT—sheep and goats	Leptin, UCP-1, PRLR1,-2	GAPDH,VDAC, ADP/ATP carrier, cytochrome c oxidase	
Neonatal			
WAT—pigs (P) and cattle (C)	P: leptin,UCP-2,-3, GHR, IGF-I,-II ;C :PREF1, β 1-3- ARs.	P:GLUT 4,HSL, LPL,SCD, aP2; C:GLUT 1,SCD, LPL	P: C/EBPα, β and &, PPARγ, ADD1
BAT—cattle	UCP-1,[a] β 1-3- ARs	Cytochrome c oxidase, ADP/ ATP carrier	
BAT and WAT—sheep and goats	Leptin, UCP-1,[a] GR, ANG-II receptors-1,-2	11 β HSD-1,-2, cytochrome c oxidase, ADP/ATP carrier, GLUT 4	
Postnatal			
Pig WAT	Leptin, OBLR, EGF IGFBP-1,-3, bFGF, HGF, GHR, IGF-I,-II, IGF-IR, β 1-3- ARs, adipsin	SCD, ACC, ACO, FAS, LPL, ME, GLUT 1, GLUT 4	ADD1, SREBP-1, SREBP-2, PPARγ, PPARα, C/EBPα, C/EBP β
Cattle WAT	Leptin, Dlk-1-C-2, PREF1,[a] UCP-1,[a] IGF-1,NAT1, TNFα, heat shock 70 kDa protein	SCD, GLUT 4, HSL GLUT 1, LPL, ACC, ATP citrate lyase, VDAC, GDH, FAS	PPARγ 1, -2
Sheep WAT	Leptin, OBRL, UCP-2	SCD, ACC, FAS, LPL, HSL	PPARγ

Abbreviations: ADD1 = adipocyte determination and differentiation-dependent factor 1, PPAR = peroxisome proliferator activated receptor, C/EBP = CCAAT enhancing binding protein, SREBP = sterol regulatory element binding protein, FAS = fatty acid synthase, ACO = acyl-CoA oxidase, EGF = epidermal growth factor, bFGF = basic fibroblast growth factor, TGF = transforming growth factor, TNF = tumor necrosis factor, HGF = hepatocyte growth factor, GLUT = glucose transport protein, IGFBP = insulin-like growth factor binding protein, IGF- = insulin-like growth factor, IGF-1R = IGF-1 receptor, GHR = growth hormone receptor, OBR = long-form leptin receptor, HSL = hormone sensitive lipase, LPL = lipoprotein lipase, UCP = uncoupling protein, 11 β HSD-1-2 = 11 beta-hydroxysteroid dehydrogenase, SCD = stearoyl coenzyme A desaturase, ME = malic enzyme, β ARs = beta adrenergic receptors, PREF1 = preadipocyte factor 1, GDH = glutamate dehydrogenase, GAPDH = glyceraldehyde-3-phosphate dehydrogenase, aP2 = fatty acid-binding protein, ACC = acetyl CoA carboxylase, ANG-II = angiotensin, VDAC = voltage-dependent anion channel, and NAT1 = novel APOBEC-1 target-1.

[a]Undetectable. Additional genes/proteins reported: Postnatal pig adipose; low-density lipoprotein receptor, low-density lipoprotein related protein and high-density lipoprotein binding protein; postnatal cattle WAT-type III collagen and ribosomal proteins; fetal pig adipose-laminin and type IV collagen.

Table 3 Characteristics of postnatal adipose tissue development

Postnatal depots	Internal	Subcutaneous	Intramuscular/ intermuscular
Adipocyte size	Largest	Intermediate	Smallest
Mode of accretion or expansion	Early: hyperplasia and hypertrophy; later: primarily hypertrophy	Early: hyperplasia and hypertrophy; later: hypertrophy and species-dependent hyperplasia	Primarily hyperplasia with little hypertrophy
Accretion and accretion rate	Species-dependent	Dependent on location, layer and species	Slow
Lipogenesis	Intermediate	Highest	Lowest
Leptin gene expression—basal and response to fasting	Omental: moderate and increased by fasting; Perirenal: species-dependent	High to moderate and increased by fasting	Very low and not changed by fasting

fat cell size and lipogenesis in fetal pig adipose tissue. Hormone-sensitive adipogenesis begins on approximately day 70 of fetal life.[1]

Hydrocortisone and thyroxine (T4) are critical for cellular and vascular development in fetal pig adipose tissue. In contrast, T3 and cortisol are critical for establishing BAT functionality, including UCP protein expression, in fetal sheep. Growth hormone (GH) decreases lipid deposition in fetal sheep and pigs and reduces fat cell size in fetal pigs.

Adipose tissue IGF-1 and IGFBPs mediate chronic hormone effects on adipose development in fetal, neonatal, and postnatal animals, and influence the onset of fetal pig SQ adipocyte development (Table 2).[10] Expression and secretion of IGF-1 and IGFBPs by adipose tissue increase with fetal age, and many components of the IGF-GH system are expressed by postnatal pig adipose tissue (Table 2).

ONTOGENY AND REGULATION OF FETAL ADIPOSE TISSUE LEPTIN GENE EXPRESSION

Leptin gene expression in adipose tissue is developmentally regulated in fetal sheep and fetal pigs.[8] Together, hydrocortisone and T4 markedly stimulate leptin expression in fetal pigs with no influence on serum leptin levels. Insulin—but not cortisol—stimulates leptin gene expression in fetal sheep adipose as it does in growing animals.

CONCLUSION

The cellular and functional aspects of WAT and BAT ontogeny have been studied, including examination of expression of the WAT marker gene (leptin), the BAT marker gene (UCP-1), and a number of other genes associated with WAT and BAT development. The ontogeny and regulation of adipose tissue leptin gene expression have been examined.[8,9] Additional studies are necessary to determine the ontogeny of the response of leptin expression to fasting and other modulators as influenced by depot and species.

Furthermore, there is little to no information on the ontogeny of adipocyte expression of other regulatory factors expressed and secreted by rodent and human adipocytes.

REFERENCES

1. Hausman, G.J.; Hausman, D.B. Endocrine Regulation of Porcine Adipose Tissue Development: Cellular and Metabolic Aspects. In *Growth of the Pig*; Hollis, G.R., Ed.; CAB International: Wallingford, UK, 1993; 49–74.
2. Crandall, D.L.; Hausman, G.J.; Kral, J.G. A review of the microcirculation of adipose tissue: Anatomic, metabolic, and angiogenic perspectives. Microcirculation **1997**, *4*, 211–232.
3. Martin, R.J.; Hausman, G.J.; Hausman, D.B. Regulation of adipose cell development in utero. Proc. Soc. Exp. Biol. Med. **1998**, *219*, 200–210.
4. Cinti, S. Anatomy of the adipose organ. Eat. Weight Disord. **2000**, *5*, 132–142.
5. Allen, C.E.; Beitz, D.C.; Cramer, D.A.; Kaufman, R.G. *Biology of Fat in Meat Animals*; North Central Regional Research Publication, University of Wisconsin: Madison, 1976; Vol. 234.
6. Hood, R.L. Relationships among growth, adipose cell size, and lipid metabolism in ruminant adipose tissue. Fed. Proc. **1982**, *41*, 2555–2561.
7. Cartwright, A.L. Adipose cellularity in *Gallus domesticus*: Investigations to control body composition in growing chickens. J. Nutr. **1991**, *121*, 1486–1497.
8. Barb, C.R.; Hausman, G.J.; Houseknecht, K.L. Biology of leptin in the pig. Domest. Anim Endocrinol. **2001**, *21*, 297–317.
9. Chilliard, Y.; Bonnet, M.; Delavaud, C.; Faulconnier, Y.; Leroux, C.; Djiane, J.; Bocquier, F. Leptin in ruminants. Gene expression in adipose tissue and mammary gland, and regulation of plasma concentration. Domest. Anim Endocrinol. **2001**, *21*, 271–295.
10. Hausman, D.B.; DiGirolamo, M.; Bartness, T.J.; Hausman, G.J.; Martin, R.J. The biology of white adipocyte proliferation. Obes. Rev. **2001**, *2*, 239–254.

Ontogeny: Muscle

Jan E. Novakofski
Robert H. McCusker
Suzanne Broussard
University of Illinois, Urbana, Illinois, U.S.A

INTRODUCTION

Formation of skeletal muscle is called myogenesis. Precursor cells called myoblasts originate in the somitic mesoderm. Limb and abdominal muscles develop from myoblasts migrating out of somites, whereas back muscles develop from nonmigrating myoblasts. Multinucleated skeletal muscle cells are formed from fusion of mononucleated myoblasts into myotubes. Subsequent synthesis of contractile myofibrils and organization into sarcomeres within myotubes result in maturation into myofibers. Myogenesis occurs in a primary wave during embryonic development followed by a secondary wave during early fetal developments. Primary and secondary fibers are predisposed to form slow and fast contraction fibers, respectively. Innervation occurs concurrently with maturation of muscle fibers and subsequently plays an important role in survival and determination of myofiber type. Groups of myofibers separate into individual muscles surrounded by connective tissue as development continues. Myofiber number becomes fixed near birth, although additional myonuclei are added as the fibers enlarge. Nuclei are added to existing fibers by fusion of additional myoblasts called satellite cells. Myofibers grow in diameter by adding new circumferential contractile filaments and grow in length by adding new sarcomeres to the end of existing filaments. Postnatal development of contractile and metabolic properties involves sequential replacement of many fiber-type specific proteins within existing myofibers.

MYOGENESIS

Myogenesis involves three populations of precursor cells, embryonic and fetal myoblasts and postnatal satellite cells, that appear sequentially during development (Fig. 1). Embryonic myoblasts undergo extensive proliferation at the presumptive location of muscles, and then fuse into primary myofibers. Fetal myoblasts form secondary fibers and add nuclei to growing primary myofibers. Satellite cells lie beneath the basal lamina of myofibers, contribute DNA to growing myofibers, and serve as a precursor pool for muscle repair following injury.

Myoblast differentiation is accompanied by cell-cycle withdrawal followed by fusion to form myotubes with central nuclei. Contractile protein accumulation, displacement of nuclei to the periphery, and innervation result in maturation of myofibers. Embryonic myoblasts differentiate to form primary muscle fibers in early gestation, before individual muscles can be discerned. Fetal myoblasts use the surface of primary myofibers as a scaffold to align and form secondary fibers. In mammals, all primary fibers are initially slow fibers with some becoming fast fibers in fast twitch muscles. Most secondary fibers are initially fast fibers. Since there are 5 to 20 times more secondary than primary fibers, this gives rise to a common histological pattern of a small number of slow fibers surrounded by a larger number of fast fibers. The majority of myofiber formation is completed by the third trimester of development in most mammalian species. In birds, individual embryonic myoblasts are committed before fusion to forming slow, fast, or mixed primary fibers. Avian secondary fibers may also be slow, fast, or mixed. Satellite cells, which represent approximately 30% of muscle nuclei in neonates and approximately 4% in adults, do not express fiber-type characteristics until fusion with a myofiber. Postnatal muscle has a limited capacity to generate new fibers from satellite cells after injury, although a few new fibers may form one to two months after birth.

MYOFIBRILLOGENESIS

Contractile myofibrils within myofibers extend the length of the myofiber and are composed of overlapping thick and thin filaments organized into repeating units called sarcomeres. Each sarcomere is bounded by perpendicular z-lines, which organize thin filaments and attach, via titin, to the thick filaments. Z-lines extend across the muscle cell and attach by transmembrane structures to the extracellular connective tissue. Sarcomeres, which are about 2.6-μM long at rest, also serve as scaffolds for the sarcoplasmic reticulum, mitochondria, and metabolic enzymes. Myofibrillogenesis begins with aggregation of repeating units of thin filament (actin) and z-line proteins

Encyclopedia of Animal Science
DOI: 10.1081/E-EAS 120019740

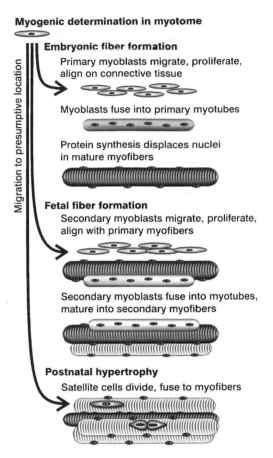

Myogenic determination in myotome

Embryonic fiber formation
Primary myoblasts migrate, proliferate, align on connective tissue

Myoblasts fuse into primary myotubes

Protein synthesis displaces nuclei in mature myofibers

Fetal fiber formation
Secondary myoblasts migrate, proliferate, align with primary myofibers

Secondary myoblasts fuse into myotubes, mature into secondary myofibers

Postnatal hypertrophy
Satellite cells divide, fuse to myofibers

Migration to presumptive location

Fig. 1 Formation of myofibers during development. Myogenic determination results in three pools of precursor cells: embryonic myoblasts, fetal myoblasts and satellite cells. Myoblasts fuse into myotubes. Synthesis of contractile proteins and organization of sarcomeres result in maturation into myofibers, which have a striated appearance under the microscope. Embryonic myoblasts form myofibers with slower contraction speeds and primarily aerobic metabolism. Fetal myoblasts organize adjacent to primary fibers and may form slow myofibers or myofibers with faster contraction and primarily anaerobic metabolism. Satellite cells proliferate; one of the daughter cells fusing with a myofiber to add myonuclei during postnatal hypertrophy or repair. (© Copyright 2003 by J. Novakofski.)

(α-actinin) beneath the sarcolemma of myotubes. Titin and then myosin are added as the nascent myofibrils migrate away from the sarcolemma and organize into sarcomeres. As muscle cells increase in length, new sarcomeres are added at the end of myofibrils.

FIBER TYPES

Myofiber type is defined by a combination of metabolic, contractile, and morphological characteristics. There are many possible combinations of characteristics but fiber type is most simply described as red (slow, oxidative, type I), intermediate (fast, oxidative and glycolytic, type IIa), or white (fast, glycolytic, type IIb). Most muscle proteins have fiber-type–specific isoforms. Fiber-type characteristics are developmentally determined but may be modulated by subsequent neural, endocrine, and mechanical influences. Myosin heavy chain (MHC), an abundant fiber-type marker, undergoes a developmental transition from embryonic to neonatal to adult isoforms. Expression of different proteins with fiber-type–specific isoforms is weakly coordinated in transitional fibers. In the embryo, slow primary fibers are larger than secondary fibers, but fast fibers become larger after birth.

MUSCLE HYPERTROPHY

The postnatal increase in myofiber size requires satellite cell fusion, DNA addition, and a protein synthesis rate greater than the rate of degradation. Newly formed myotubes are 5–10 µm in diameter, growing into 25–100 µm myofibers—a several hundredfold increase in mass. Insulin-like growth factor-I (IGF-I) is the major factor stimulating hypertrophy. IGF-I activates a number of signaling pathways including the calcineurin pathway and the phosphotidylinositiol-3 kinase pathway that increases protein synthesis. The proteasome pathway degrades most muscle proteins.

MESODERM ORIGINS

Skeletal muscles of the head, back, abdomen, and limbs have different lineages in the embryo (Fig. 2). Muscles of the head originate directly from myoblasts of the cranial mesoderm. Myoblasts that form the muscles of the limbs and trunk originate in somites. Somites result from segmentation of the paraxial mesoderm along the neural tube and notochord. The dorsal portion of the somite forms the dermomyotome, whereas the ventral portion forms the sclerotome, which is subsequently induced to form axial skeleton. The dermomyotome then segments into an inner myotome layer and outer dermatome layer. Axial muscles (i.e., longissimus, psoas) derive from the dorsomedial or epaxial portion of the myotome, whereas abdominal muscles derive from the ventrolateral or hypaxial portion of the myotome. Limb muscles derive from precursors that migrate out of the ventrolateral myotome. Anterior somites develop before posterior somites so there is a temporal gradient in myoblast migration, and forelimbs develop before hindlimbs. After

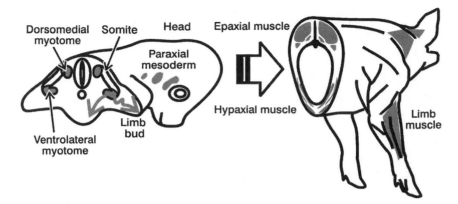

Fig. 2 Origin of muscles in the embryo. Muscles of the head, back, abdomen, and limbs arise from different developmental lineages, which are established early in embryonic development. Shaded areas in the drawing of the embryo give rise to muscles in the corresponding shaded locations of the mature animal. Muscles of the head and extraocular muscles originate from the cranial mesoderm, whereas muscles of the body and limbs derive from the myotomes on either side of the neural tube. Epaxial muscles develop from the dorsomedial portion of the myotome, whereas hypaxial muscles develop from the ventrolateral portion of the myotome. Myoblasts that form limb muscles delaminate from the ventrolateral myotome, migrate into the limbs, and undergo extensive proliferation before fusing into myofibers. Organization into individual muscles is directed by *hox* gene expression and signals from nearby mesoderm that will form connective tissue. (© Copyright 2003 by J. Novakofski.)

migration, myoblasts proliferate extensively at the location of presumptive muscles and aggregate into ventral and dorsal masses before individual muscles form. Positional clues for myoblast migration and subsequent

formation of individual muscles within limbs are provided by *hox* gene expression and cartilage derived from the limb bud mesenchyme.

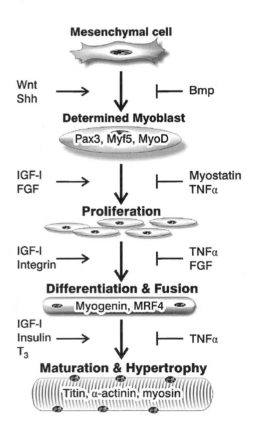

MYOGENIC DETERMINATION FACTORS

Formation of myofibers from mesenchymal precursors is controlled by growth factors that induce or inhibit

Fig. 3 Myogenesis and myogenic regulation. Each step leading to myofiber formation is controlled by growth factors that induce or inhibit myogenesis. Activators indicated by an arrow (→), inhibitors indicated by a bar (⊢). Wnt, sonic hedge hog (Shh) and bone morphogenic proteins (BMP) are secreted from the neural tube, notochord and lateral ectoderm. These secreted growth factors induce expression of myogenic regulatory transcription factors (Pax3, Myf5 and MyoD) in somatic or axial mesoderm. Subsequently, proliferation of myoblasts is regulated by insulin-like growth factor-1 (IGF-I) and fibroblast growth factor (FGF). IGF-I and integrin (a cell adhesion protein) induce expression of myogenic transcription factors, MRF4, and myogenin, essential for myoblast fusion. IGF-I is unique because it stimulates both myoblast proliferation and differentiation. Myostatin is a potent inhibitor of myoblast proliferation and myostatin inactivation results in the increased myofiber of double-muscled cattle. The proinflammatory cytokine tumor necrosis factor α (TNFα) inhibits myoblast proliferation, fusion, and synthesis of muscle specific proteins, resulting in smaller muscles. (© Copyright 2003 by J. Novakofski.)

myogenic regulatory transcription factors (MRFs) mediating the steps in myogenesis (Fig. 3). Determination of somitic mesoderm cells into myoblasts begins with induction of Myf5 and MyoD in Pax-3 positive cells of the somite by growth factors from the neural tube, notochord, and ectoderm. Although there is functional overlap, Myf5 primarily determines epaxial and MyoD determines hypaxial myoblasts. Subsequent expression of MRF4 and myogenin in determined myoblasts mediates differentiation and fusion into myofibers. MyoD and myogenin remain expressed at lower levels in mature myofibers.

Myoblast proliferation and differentiation are mutually exclusive events so myofiber formation can be increased either by stimulating myoblast proliferation or by inhibiting myoblast differentiation. Proliferation stops before fusion because elevated MRFs inhibit cell cycle proteins including cyclin-dependent kinases (CDKs), pRB, and p21. Conversely, in proliferating myoblasts, MRF activity is suppressed by Id protein or CDK phosphorylation.

Satellite cell function depends on expression of the Pax7 transcription factor, which is closely related to the Pax3 essential for myogenic determination and myoblast migration. Myf5 and MyoD are upregulated in proliferating satellite cells, whereas myogenin and MRF4 are not expressed until differentiation and fusion. Satellite cell divisions are asymmetric with fusion of one daughter cell to a myofiber while the other remains an unfused satellite cell. Asymmetry results in the segregation of Numb and differential upregulation of Pax7 and MRFs.

CONCLUSION

Major events in the ontogeny of muscle characteristics occur during embryonic and fetal development, although the bulk of muscle mass is deposited during postnatal growth. Muscles in different anatomic locations derive from different embryonic lineages. These differences are reflected in the myofiber number and mass of mature muscles and in the specific patterns of metabolic and contractile properties of the myofibers. Future insight into these complex processes will enable improvement in livestock production and achievement of biomedical goals such as replacement of diseased or damaged muscles.

REFERENCES

1. Buckingham, M.; Bajard, L.; Chang, T.; Daubas, P.; Hadchouel, J.; Meilhac, S.; Montarras, D.; Rocancourt, D.; Relaix, F. The formation of skeletal muscle: from somite to limb. J. Anat. **2003**, *202* (15), 59–68.
2. Novakofski, J.; McCusker, R. Skeletal and Muscular Systems. In *Biology of the Pig*, 2nd Ed.; Pond, W.G., Mesmann, H.J., Eds.; Cornell University Press: Ithaca, 2001; 454–502. Chap. 9.
3. *Stem Cells and Cell Signaling in Skeletal Myogenesis*; Sassoon, D.A., Ed.; Advances in Developmental Biology and Biochemistry; Elsevier: New York, 2002; Vol. 11.
4. Wigmore, P.M.; Evans, D.J. Molecular and cellular mechanisms involved in the generation of fiber diversity during myogenesis. Int. Rev. Cytol. **2002**, *216*, 175–232.

Ontogeny: Skeleton

A. M. Oberbauer
K. D. Evans
University of California, Davis, California, U.S.A.

INTRODUCTION

Bone is a "specialized form of connective tissue." The role of the skeleton is twofold: structural support and calcium homeostasis. In addition to bone, cartilage is an essential component in skeletal function. Cartilage serves as a precursor of endochondral bone formation and minimizes friction at bone joints. Bone is composed of an organic matrix of collagen and proteoglycans (osteoid) embedded with hydroxyapatite crystals containing calcium and phosphorus salts. The osteoid matrix is primarily type I collagen, whereas in cartilage tissue, the predominant component is type II collagen.

TISSUE ORIGIN

Four cell types in bone (osteoblasts, osteocytes, bone lining cells, and osteoclasts) and three in cartilage (chondroblasts, chondrocytes, and chondroclasts) are responsible for the synthesis and maintenance of bone and cartilage matrix. The osteoclasts and chondroclasts are of hemopoietic stem cell origin, whereas the remaining cell types differentiate from mesenchymal stem cells experiencing different local environmental inputs (e.g., oxygen tension or extracellular hormonal signaling).

EMBRYONIC FORMATION

Bone, the skeletal organ, is classified as being either intramembranous or endochondral in origin. Intramembranous bone is formed by the in situ differentiation of mesenchymal progenitor cells into osteoblasts that secrete osteoid; this matrix then undergoes calcification with hydroxyapatite crystal deposition.[1] In contrast, endochondral bones are embryonically formed as a cartilage anlage. Mesenchymal progenitor cells differentiate into chondroblasts and mature to chondrocytes that coalesce into a model representing a miniature version of the future bone. Chondrocytes proliferate and then mature, a process that includes hypertrophy with secretion and mineralization of matrix. Through this maturation process, the local milieu changes, inducing the death of the most centrally located chondrocytes, thereby permitting blood vessel invasion through the nutrient foramen (Fig. 1). Accompanying the vasculature are marrow stem cells, osteoblast progenitor cells, and osteoclast and chondroclast precursors. Chondroclasts locally degrade mineralized cartilage matrix, whereas osteoblasts utilize the cartilage matrix remnants as a substrate for osteoid deposition. This central invasion forms the primary center of ossification. At each of the two ends of the anlage, the vascular invasion is reiterated, generating three distinct centers of ossification: the primary and two secondary centers. The ossification centers remain distinct due to a retained cartilage disk between the primary and each secondary center. The cartilage disk, or growth plate, offers growth potential (discussed later in this article). Additional cartilage remains at the extreme ends of the anlage to become the articular cartilage essential in joint function. The bone is now defined into anatomical regions relative to the growth plates. The central region enveloping the primary center of ossification is the diaphysis. The regions encompassing the growth plate are the metaphyses, whereas the two ends of the bone are the epiphyses.[2]

GROWTH PLATE

Chondrocytes within the growth plate are organized in a precise pattern reflecting cell functionality. Randomly distributed stem cell chondrocytes lie adjacent to the epiphysis in a region termed the resting zone. Resting zone cells induced to divide produce columns of clonally expanding cells, forming the proliferative zone. The proliferative zone chondrocytes then mature in their metabolic activities, secrete additional matrix, and hypertrophy. This expansive proliferation and hypertrophy occurring in both growth plates essentially pushes the ends of the bone apart, resulting in overall elongation. The retention of cartilaginous growth plates permits elongation of bone by an internal mechanism, enabling structural support and maintenance of the physical configuration of the bone necessary for tendon and ligament insertion sites. In contrast to the endochondral growth process, intramembranous bone enlarges by appositional deposition of osteoid matrix.

Encyclopedia of Animal Science
DOI: 10.1081/E-EAS 120019742

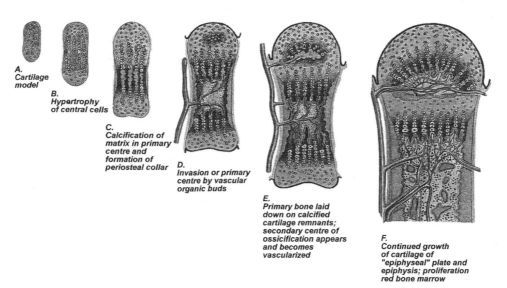

Fig. 1 Endochondral ossification stages. (Reprinted from Fig. 3.39, 37th edition of Gray's Anatomy, 1989, with permission from Elsevier.)

CELL TYPES

The osteoblast, the primary bone-forming cell, secretes type I collagen and proteoglycans to form a nonmineralized matrix that serves as scaffolding for hydroxyapatite crystal deposition by osteoblasts.[3] The osteoblast requires a surface to lay down the osteoid. As the osteoblast becomes surrounded by mineralized matrix, it changes phenotype by losing much of its protein production organelles and forming protoplasmic processes that connect via gap junctions to the adjacent protoplasmic processes of other encased osteoblasts.[4] Once surrounded by matrix, the cell is designated an osteocyte. The bulk of the osteocyte occupies a space within the bone known as the lacuna, while the protoplasmic processes occupy spaces termed canaliculi.[3] The protoplasmic process connections between osteocytes allow cellular communication, which becomes important during times of increased mechanical stress and hormonal control of serum calcium levels. In contrast to the osteoblast and osteocyte found in areas of active bone formation, bone-lining cells are present only on bone surfaces not actively forming bone. Bone-lining cells are reserve cells that differentiate into osteoblasts when needed, as during fracture repair, to actively create bone.[3] The osteoclast is the major bone resorbing cell. The osteoclast secretes acid hydrolases to dissolve the hydroxyapatite and enzymes to dissolve the protein scaffolding within bone.[5] The osteoclast maintains a polarity with only the side in contact with bone forming a ruffled membrane (Fig. 2). This ruffled edge localizes acids and enzymes permitting bone resorption within discrete sites.

BONE ELONGATION, APPOSITION, ENLARGEMENT

Bone undergoes growth in two ways. Growth in the longitudinal plane of long bones is achieved through the process of chondrocyte activity within growth plates (endochondral ossification). Widening of long bones and increased size of flat bones is achieved through a process of cell division and subsequent ossification in all directions (appositional growth).[4] Within long bones, appositional growth occurs at the periosteum accompanied by resorption at the endosteum in order for the cortical bone width at the diaphysis to maintain mechanical stability.[4] During the process of endochondral ossification, chondrocytes proliferate, hypertrophy, and mineralize. The mineralized cartilage cores produced at the metaphysis of the bone are resorbed by osteoclasts and used as scaffolding on which osteoblasts can begin building bone. As the bone lengthens, mechanical forces applied by gravity and surrounding musculature force the bone to reshape itself by resorbing the outer edges of the

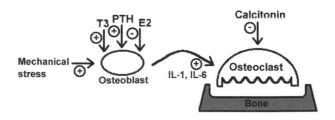

Fig. 2 Activation and communication between the osteoclast and the osteoblast: the BMU.

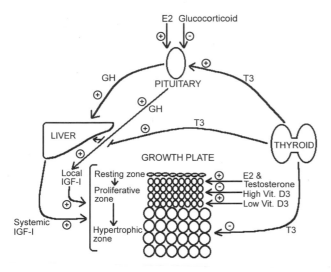

Fig. 3 Hormonal cascades involved in growth plate proliferation.

metaphysis. This process ensures that the bone retains the greatest mechanical stability in the face of normal wear and tear.[4]

The process of growth plate chondrocyte proliferation, hypertrophy, and mineralization is finely controlled through hormones that act both systemically and locally. These hormones include growth hormone (GH), insulin-like growth factor-I (IGF-I), thyroid hormone (T3), estrogen (E2), testosterone, vitamin D (Vit D3), and glucocorticoids (GCs);[6–9] the major effectors are GH and IGF-I. Growth hormone acts directly on chondrocytes to induce cell division in the resting zone and stimulates local IGF-I production by the proliferating and hypertrophic cells (Fig. 3). Growth hormone also stimulates systemic IGF-I production by the liver. Both local and systemic IGF-I promote proliferation and hypertrophy of cells within the growth plate. Estrogen (E2) directly drives chondrocyte proliferation and influences the growth plate by increasing GH release from the pituitary. Conversely, GCs inhibit GH release by the pituitary. Testosterone appears to promote growth plate closure by terminating chondrocyte proliferation after puberty.[8] Likewise, T3 acts directly on the chondrocytes to stop proliferation, although T3 stimulates the pituitary to release GH and promotes IGF-I release from the liver.

CALCIUM REGULATION

One primary function of bone is to serve as a calcium storage depot. The resorption of bone for the purpose of replenishing serum calcium levels is hormonally orchestrated. Much of the process is regulated by the osteoblast,

which signals the osteoclast (Fig. 2). The unique relationship between these two cell types is known as the BMU (basic multicellular unit).[10] The major calcium regulating hormones are parathyroid hormone (PTH) and calcitonin, with T3, E2, and cytokines contributing to calcium homeostasis.[6–9,11,12] Low serum calcium levels stimulate PTH release that, along with T3, acts to promote the release of the IL-1 and IL-6 cytokines from osteoblasts. These cytokines stimulate bone resorption by the osteoclast leading to calcium release into the fluid surrounding the osteoclast, which is transported into the circulation to replenish serum calcium levels. In contrast, E2 inhibits osteoclast resorption by impairing osteoblastic release of these cytokines. The other major calcium regulator, calcitonin, is released in response to high serum calcium levels. Calcitonin acts directly on the osteoclast to inhibit its resorbing capabilities and promote bone formation through enhancing osteoblast proliferation.[13]

MECHANICAL CONTROL

Bone constantly undergoes a process, termed remodeling. Bone is continuously resorbed by osteoclasts and replaced by osteoblasts daily. Much of the remodeling process is regulated by the osteoblast signaling the osteoclast (Fig. 2) to create the BMU.[14] The process initiates when bone experiences mechanical stress that generates microdamage. This mechanical stress ultimately determines the shape and morphology of the bone. Alterations in normal mechanical stress are sensed within the fluid of the canaliculi-connecting osteocytes. This activates the osteocytes to signal surrounding osteoblasts to recruit osteoclasts to the area. The osteoclasts bore through existing bone to the region requiring reinforcement, and together the osteoblast and osteoclast of the BMU repair and reinforce the stressed bone until it is mechanically sound. Remodeling periodically replaces old bone and microcracks, thus maintaining the overall structural integrity of the bone.

CONCLUSION

Mature skeletal size is determined by bone elongation. Bone length can be enhanced and accelerated by genetic selection for growth rate alterations or hormonal manipulation that also affect muscle deposition. Bone length must be balanced with maintaining bone strength. Disturbances in bone strength lead to undesirable consequences for human and animal health including excessive bone breakage. Overall, the skeleton is one of the most dynamic physiological systems. The constant, simultaneous, precise control over bone formation, degradation, growth, and required mineral regulation is imperative to the maintenance of healthy animals.

REFERENCES

1. Aubin, J.E.; Liu, F. The Osteoblast Lineage. In *Principles of Bone Biology*; Bilezikian, J.P., Raisz, L.G., Rodan, G.A., Eds.; Academic Press Inc.: London, 1996; 51–67.

2. Fetter, A.W; Rhinelander, F.W. Normal Bone Anatomy. In *Textbook of Small Animal Orthopaedics*; Newton, C.D., Nunamaker, D.M., Eds.; International Veterinary Information Service Ithaca: New York, 1985.

3. Marks, S.C.; Hermey, D.C. The Structure and Development of Bone. In *Principles of Bone Biology*; Bilezikian, J.P., Raisz, L.G., Rodan, G.A., Eds.; Academic Press Inc.: London, 1996; 3–14.

4. Vaughn, J. *The Physiology of Bone*, 3rd Ed.; Clarendon Press: Oxford, 1981; 17–27.

5. Tietelbaum, S.L. Bone resorption by osteoclasts. Science **2000**, *289* (5484), 1504–1508.

6. Ohlsson, C.; Bengtsson, B.-A.; Isaksson, O.G.P.; Andreassen, T.T.; Slootweg, M.C. Growth hormone and bone. Endocr. Rev. **1998**, *19* (1), 55–79.

7. Robson, H.; Siebler, T.; Shalet, S.M.; Williams, G.R. Interactions between GH, IGF-I, glucocorticoids, and thyroid hormones during skeletal growth. Pediatr. Res. **2002**, *52* (2), 137–147.

8. Siebler, T.; Robson, H.; Shalet, S.M.; Williams, G.R. Glucocorticoids, thyroid hormone and growth hormone interactions: Implications for the growth plate. Horm. Res. **2001**, *56* (Supplemental 1), 7–12.

9. Rickard, D.J.; Subramaniam, M.; Spelsberg, T.C. Molecular and cellular mechanisms of estrogen action on the skeleton. J. Cell. Biochem. **1999**, *32–33* (Supplemental), 123–132.

10. Frost, H.M. Tetracycline-based histological analysis of bone remodeling. Calcif. Tissue Res. **1969**, *3* (3), 211–237.

11. Hayden, J.M.; Mohan, S.; Baylink, D.J. The insulin–like growth factor system and the coupling of formation to resorption. Bone **1995**, *17* (Supplemental 2), 93S–98S.

12. Rodan, G.A. Introduction to bone biology. Bone **1992**, *13* (Supplemental 1), S3–S6.

13. Farley, J.; Dimai, H.P.; Stilt-Coffing, B.; Farley, P.; Pham, T.; Mohan, S. Calcitonin increases the concentration of insulin-like growth factors in serum-free cultures of human osteoblast-line cells. Calcif. Tissue Int. **2000**, *67*, 247–254.

14. Ott, S.M. Theoretical and Methodological Approach. In *Principles of Bone Biology*; Bilezikian, J.P., Raisz, L.G., Rodan, G.A., Eds.; Academic Press Inc.: London, 1996; 231–241.

Overall Contributions of Domestic Animals to Society

Duane E. Ullrey
Michigan State University, East Lansing, Michigan, U.S.A.

INTRODUCTION

The domestication of plants and animals may be the most important development in the past 13,000 years of human history. Although authorities differ in attributing dates to particular events, this domestication was a necessary prelude to the evolution of civilization as we know it. Previously, human migrations followed seasonal shifts in wild food supplies. Subsequently, settlements appeared near gardens, orchards, and pastures. Food production increased, supporting local increases in population and the spread of humans to previously unoccupied geographical regions. Increases in the efficiency of food acquisition and storage made possible the development of crafts and trades, since it was no longer necessary for every family to spend time hunting and gathering food. Ultimately, the social and political systems that evolved came to govern much of human activity.

HISTORICAL BACKGROUND

Primates of a lineage now identified as human, diverged from the great apes about 6 million years ago.[1] Not until 10,000 to 15,000 years ago was there an example of animal domestication.[2,3] This is purported to be domestication of the dog's wolflike ancestor during the hunter–gatherer period of human cultural development. The primary event initiating livestock domestication was the formation of large, relatively stable agricultural societies some 9000 to 10,000 years ago when cultivation of plants began.[2,4,5] Why it took so long is uncertain, but it has been suggested that events in the late Pleistocene may have played an important role.[1] Improved hunting skills may have depleted the supply of available prey. Discoveries in the technology of collecting, processing, and storing foods allowed societies with more effective technologies to prevail over others. Human populations were growing, and more efficient food production was required to meet increasing needs. Further, the end of the Pleistocene (11,000 B.C.) was coincident with the end of the Ice Age, and the climatic circumstances that followed were more favorable for permanent agricultural settlements and the extension of such settlements into other relatively unpopulated areas.

Beginning in about 8500 B.C., domestication of cattle, sheep, and goats began in the Near East, particularly in the Fertile Crescent, an arc of land from present-day western Syria and southern Turkey, through northeastern Iraq, to Iran.[1,2,5] Domestication of pigs took place about 9000 years ago both in Europe and in Asia.[2] Chickens were domesticated from jungle fowl in Thailand and adjacent regions about 8000 years ago, and remains of domesticated chickens have been found in neolithic sites in China dating to 6000 B.C. Llamas and alpacas were domesticated about 6000 years ago in South America.[2] Concurrently, horses were being domesticated for meat and transportation in the Ukraine.[2] Archeological evidence associating humans and silkworms dates back to about 2500 B.C. in China. Guinea pigs were domesticated about 3000 to 4000 years ago by the indigenous people of Peru for use as food and in religious ceremonies.[2] About 2500 years ago, rabbits were domesticated in southern Europe. Wild turkeys, native to North America, were transported to Europe and domesticated there about 500 years ago.[2] Additional animal species, domesticated before the time of Christ, include asses, Bactrian and dromedary camels, honey bees, bantengs, water buffalos, ducks, yaks, cats, geese, and reindeer.[5,6]

CONTRIBUTIONS OF ANIMAL DOMESTICATION

As plants and animals underwent domestication, humans acquired the power to alter their ecosystem in ways that favored their immediate needs. The balance of animal life was modified either by domestication and directed evolution or by discouraging the presence of wild animals that preyed on crops and herds. Arable areas were extended by deforestation and irrigation. Increased local production of food encouraged population growth and the formation of stable settlements. Archaeological evidence indicates that, at first, a substantial portion of animal food still came from wild animals, but hunting pressure and increasingly intensive agriculture gradually diminished local wild animal populations.

The association of humans with wild animals was long-standing and undoubtedly led to identification of

Encyclopedia of Animal Science
DOI: 10.1081/E EAS 120019743

species that were amenable to domestication. A herding instinct and a proclivity for imprinting on humans may have been important. The discovery of hoof prints of goats and sheep in the clay of a prehistoric inhabited village (Ganj-Dareh) that flourished around 7000 B.C. in the mountains of present-day western Iran provided evidence that no longer were these humans dependent on wild animals for meat.[5] Through conscious or unconscious selection, the anatomy, behavior, and productivity of these sheep and goats were modified. Not only did they provide meat and hides, as did their wild relatives, but selection for production of wool or milk added further to their societal value. Comparable changes occurred in horses and water buffalo as they were domesticated. They could not only be used for meat or milk, but could also be ridden or harnessed to ploughs and other devices that eased the physical burdens of soil preparation, planting, and harvest. Horse-mounted cavalrymen proved particularly intimidating in battle.

There are notable differences between geographical regions in the domesticated species that are present. These differences relate to the wild species that were indigenous to the region, to physiologic tolerance of the environment by their domestic counterparts, and in some regions, to religious traditions governing acceptability of particular species as food. Although there are cultural differences within and between countries in the uses of animals, their domestication enriched human society by providing companionship, recreation, materials needed for clothing, readily available food, and power to assist in labor-intensive tasks. Much of modern medical technology was derived through research with dogs, pigs, calves, and sheep. Porcine cardiac tissue has been used to replace failing valves in the human heart, and researchers now study transgenic pigs as potential organ donors for humans with terminal organ dysfunction.[7] Unfortunately, the increasing density of human populations also has been associated with the advent of epidemic diseases, some of which had their origins in, or were spread by, domestic animals.[1]

CONCLUSIONS

Domestic animals have played an integral role in the formation of modern human society. Before animal domestication, humans led a relatively nomadic existence in their search for food, absent the social and political organizations that govern current community affairs. Relief from the relentless search for food and the increased efficiency with which it was produced in stable settlements allowed for development of the trades, cultural arts, medical advances, and the various disciplines of science that now so enrich our lives.

REFERENCES

1. Diamond, J. Evolution, consequences and future of plant and animal domestication. Nature **2002**, *418*, 700–707.
2. Price, E.O. *Animal Domestication and Behavior*; CABI Publishing: New York, 2002.
3. Clutton-Brock, J. Origins of the Dog: Domestication and Early History. In *The Domestic Dog: Its Evolution, Behavior and Interactions with People*; Cambridge University Press: Cambridge, UK, 1995; 7–20.
4. Harlan, J.R. *The Living Fields: Our Agricultural Heritage*; Cambridge University Press: New York, 1995.
5. Clutton-Brock, J. *A Natural History of Domesticated Mammals*, 2nd Ed.; Cambridge University Press: Cambridge, UK, 1999.
6. Leonard, J.N. *The Emergence of Man: The First Farmers*; Time-Life Books: New York, 1973.
7. Ullrey, D.E.; Bernard, J. Other Animals, Other Uses, Other Opportunities. In *Introduction to Animal Science*; Pond, W.G., Pond, K.R, Eds.; John Wiley & Sons, Inc.: New York, 2000; 553–583.

Pathogens in Animal Products: Major Biological Hazards

John N. Sofos
Colorado State University, Fort Collins, Colorado, U.S.A.

INTRODUCTION

The most severe biological hazards in foods are pathogenic bacteria, which may cause illness as direct agents (infection) or through production of various toxins (intoxication), while additional biological hazards include parasitic and viral agents. Typical clinical symptoms of foodborne bacterial and viral diseases include acute diarrhea, abdominal cramps, vomiting, or some other manifestation in the gastrointestinal tract. In addition, syndromes associated with the central nervous system or various organs, as well as various chronic sequelae, may also be the direct or indirect result of foodborne pathogenic bacteria. Individuals with suppressed or compromised immune systems are more susceptible to severe foodborne microbial illness. Prions found in animal central nervous tissue are considered a potential newer type of hazard, leading to development of transmissible spongiform encephalopathies (TSE). According to the U.S. Centers for Disease Control and Prevention (CDC), it is estimated that for the period 1993–1997, meat and poultry were responsible for 17.3% of the total outbreaks of known vehicle of transmission and for 11.4% of the corresponding cases (www.cdc.gov).

BACTERIAL PATHOGENS

Escherichia coli O157:H7

E. coli are mostly harmless colonizers of the gastrointestinal tract of warm-blooded animals, including humans; certain strains, however, cause diarrheal illness.[1] Some strains produce Shigalike toxins (SLT) or verotoxins (VT) and are classified as enterohemorrhagic *E. coli* (EHEC) or Shigalike toxin producing (STEC), or as verocytotoxigenic (VTEC), with *E. coli* O157:H7 being the predominant EHEC serotype. *E. coli* O157:H7 are Gram-negative, facultatively anaerobic, non-spore-forming rods that are mostly motile. They can grow at temperatures of 7–46°C (optimum 35–40°C), in water activities of ≥ 0.95, and at pH values of 4.4–9.0 (optimum 6.0–7.0).[1] *E. coli*

O157:H7 usually cause illness through fecal–oral transmission or through consumption of contaminated foods, with the majority of outbreaks involving consumption of undercooked ground beef. Other foods, such as fruit juices, cantaloupe, and seed sprouts for salads, have also been associated with illness through fecal cross-contamination. Ingestion of cells (≥ 10 cells) is followed (3–9 days incubation) by mild or severe bloody diarrhea (hemorrhagic colitis) and hemolytic uremic syndrome (HUS).[1] *E. coli* O157:H7 are declared an adulterant for raw ground beef and other nonintact beef products by the U.S. Department of Agriculture Food Safety and Inspection Service (USDA/FSIS), and are estimated to cause a total of 73,000 cases of illness in the United States each year.[2]

Listeria monocytogenes

Listeria are non-spore-forming, aerobic, microaerophilic or facultatively anaerobic, Gram-positive rods that are motile by means of peritrichous flagella.[1] The organism is ubiquitous in the environment and may be harbored in many animals. Its presence in plant floors, walls, drains, condensed and standing water, and food residues on processing equipment, and its involvement in certain highly fatal (20–30%) foodborne outbreaks, make this a pathogen of major concern. As a psychrotroph, *L. monocytogenes* can grow at -1 to 45°C (optimum 30–37°C). Growth occurs at pH 4.4–9.4 and in water activities above 0.92. Foods of concern for transmission of listeriosis include non-shelf-stable, ready-to-eat meat and poultry products, deli-type foods, soft cheeses, seafood, and unpasteurized dairy products. Although there is an enteric form of listeriosis, the major concern is associated with the nonenteric infection, which affects mainly the central nervous system (meningitis, meningoencephalitis, bacteremia), and may result in stillbirth, fetal death, or spontaneous abortion in pregnant women. The infectious dose is believed to be ≥ 100 cells/g of food, and the incubation period a few days to 2–3 months.[1] The pathogen is estimated to be responsible for approximately 0.02% of the cases of foodborne illness in the United States and 28% of the deaths.[2]

Encyclopedia of Animal Science
DOI: 10.1081/E-EAS 120030467

Salmonella

This long-known pathogen is a Gram-negative, facultatively anaerobic, non-spore-forming rod; its only two species are *Salmonella enterica*, possessing six subspecies, and *Salmonella bongori*. There are approximately 2600 *Salmonella* serotypes, of which *Salmonella* Typhimurium and *Salmonella* Enteritidis are the most prevalent in the United States.[2]*Salmonella* can grow at temperatures of 5.2–46.2°C, pH values of 3.8–9.5, and in water activity ≥0.93. The primary reservoir for *Salmonella* is the gastrointestinal tract of infected animal hosts or carriers, which serve as sources of contamination for foods and the environment. Nontyphoidal *Salmonella* strains usually cause gastroenteritis after an incubation period of 5 hours to 5 days, resulting in diarrhea, nausea, mild fever, chills, vomiting, and abdominal cramping. Infectious doses of *Salmonella* (10–10,000 cells) depend on serotype, vehicle of transmission, and on the individual's susceptibility.[1] A variety of food products, including meat, poultry, and dairy products, have been implicated in the transmission of salmonellosis. *Salmonella* causes millions of illnesses and approximately 30% of the total estimated deaths from foodborne disease in the United Sates annually.[2]

Campylobacter

This organism consists of Gram-negative non-spore-forming, slender and curved rods, which, along with the single, polar flagellum located at one or both ends of the cell, cause its characteristic corkscrew-type motility.[1] As microaerophilic, *Campylobacter* grows best in environments of 2.0–5.0% oxygen and 5.0–10.0% carbon dioxide, while growth is inhibited at normal oxygen levels. It grows at 30–45°C (optimum 37–42°C), pH values of 4.9–8.0 (optimum 6.5–7.5), and in water activities above 0.91. Campylobacteriosis may result from as few as 500 cells (2–10 days incubation), and the low-fatality infection typically involves acute colitis combined with fever, malaise, abdominal pain, headache, watery or sticky diarrhea with minor traces of blood (occult), inflammation of the lamina propria, and crypt abscesses. Infection may lead to additional sequelae, including an acute paralytic disease of the peripheral nervous system known as Guillain–Barre syndrome and an autoimmune disease known as Reiter's syndrome.[1] Campylobacteriosis outbreaks have involved consumption of milk, water, and foods exposed to fecal contamination or cross-contamination.[1] Although poultry meat is considered a major source of *Campylobacter*, it is believed that a large portion of its millions of cases of foodborne illness occurs through cross-contamination.

Other Bacterial Pathogens

Several other bacterial pathogens are associated with food products of animal origin, but their contribution to foodborne disease has been overshadowed by the impact of the aforementioned four pathogens in recent years. They include additional pathogenic serotypes of *E. coli*, *Yersinia enterocolitica* (a psychrotroph of enteric origin), *Staphylococcus aureus* (a Gram-positive, heat-stable, enterotoxin-producing mesophile), *Clostridium botulinum* (a deadly, neurotoxin-producing spore-former), *Clostridium perfringens* (a common cause of gastrointestinal discomfort of short duration), and *Bacillus cereus* (a spore-forming mesophile or psychrotroph causing diarrheal or emetic illness). Detailed information on these and other pathogens of less current concern can be found in several publications[1–8] and at www.cfsan.fda.gov.

OTHER BIOLOGICAL HAZARDS

Food-producing animals may also serve as sources of parasitic and viral disease agents.[1] For example, swine may be involved in the transmission of trichinosis (*Trichinella spiralis*), sarcocystosis (*Sarcocystis* spp.), and toxoplasmosis (*Toxoplasma gondii*); and poultry of toxoplasmosis, whereas beef cattle may transmit tapeworms (*Taenia* spp.) and *Sarcocystis* spp. or serve as indirect vectors for the transmission of *Cryptosporidium parvum* (cryptosporidiosis) through water contaminated with feces.[9] Viral agents, such as Norovirus, hepatitis A, and enteroviruses, are responsible for most foodborne disease cases in the United States,[2] but their transmission is mostly associated with poor sanitation, cross-contamination during preparation and serving, or inadequate cooking.

Bovine spongiform encephalopathy (BSE) has emerged as a major animal health issue in recent years, especially because of its potential involvement in human transmissible spongiform encephalopathies (TSE) such as a new variant, Creutzfeldt–Jakob Disease (vCJD). Evidence indicates that BSE is caused by prions found in central nervous tissue, and originated in cattle fed ruminant by-products. In the 1990s, the United States established a number of measures to prevent the emergence of this problem in this country. They included a ban on importation of live ruminants and their products from countries with native BSE, immunohistochemical examinations of brains of cattle condemned for nervous system disorders, and a ban on the use of ruminant materials in meat and bone meal feeds for ruminants.[9] However, in December 2003, the first cow with BSE was detected in the United States, following another single case in Canada earlier that year. Following this event, additional measures were announced by the USDA/FSIS and the Food and

Drug Administration (FDA) in efforts to prevent spread of the problem and to better protect public health. These measures included banning use of downer (unable to stand and walk) cattle from human food, holding carcasses of cattle tested for BSE until results are confirmed, prohibiting stunning of cattle with air-injection guns, banning from the food supply specified risk materials (brain, skull, eyes, spinal cord, small intestines, etc.) of cattle over 30 months of age and the small intestine of cattle of all ages, increasing process controls for material obtained with advanced meat recovery systems, banning use of mechanically separated meat in food products, and banning from FDA-regulated foods, dietary supplements, and cosmetics use of the previous materials.

CONCLUSION

Food products of animal origin may be contaminated with biological hazards, including pathogens to human health. Such hazards include bacterial, viral, and parasitic agents, and prions associated with transmissible spongiform encephalopathies. Health problems associated with these hazards range from short-term, mild forms of gastrointestinal discomfort, to severe damage of various tissues and organs, death, chronic sequelae, or long-term medical syndromes.

ARTICLES OF FURTHER INTEREST

REFERENCES

1. Bacon, R.T.; Sofos, J.N. Characteristics of Biological Hazards. In *Food Safety Handbook*; Schmidt, R.H., Rodrick, G.E., Eds.; Wiley-Interscience: Hoboken, NJ, USA, 2003; 157–195.

2. Mead, P.S.; Slutsker, L.; Dietz, V.; McCaig, L.F.; Bresee, J.S.; Shapiro, C.; Griffin, P.M.; Tauxe, R.V. Food-related illness and death in the United States. Emerg. Infect. Dis. **1999**, *5*, 607–625.

3. Doyle, M.P. *Foodborne Bacterial Pathogens*; Marcel Dekker, Inc.: New York, NY, USA, 1989.

4. Cliver, D.O.; Riemann, H.P. *Foodborne Diseases*, 2nd Ed.; Academic Press: San Diego, CA, USA, 2002.

5. Blackburn, C.W.; McClure, P.J. *Foodborne Pathogens, Hazards, Risk Analysis and Control*; CRC Press/Woodhead Publishing Limited: Cambridge, UK, 2002.

6. Labbe, R.G.; Garcia, S. *Guide to Foodborne Pathogens*; Wiley-Interscience: New York, NY, USA, 2001.

7. Hui, Y.H; Pierson, M.D.; Gorham, J.R. *Foodborne Diseases Handbook*, 2nd Ed.; Bacterial Pathogens, Marcel Dekker, Inc.: New York, NY, USA, 2001; Vol. 1.

8. Hui, Y.H; Sattar, S.A.; Murrell, K.D.; Nip, W.-K.; Stanfield, P.S. *Foodborne Diseases Handbook*, 2nd Ed.; Viruses, Parasites, Pathogens, and HACCP, Marcel Dekker, Inc.: New York, NY, USA, 2001; Vol. 2.

9. CAST (Council for Agricultural Science and Technology). *Intervention Strategies for the Microbiological Safety of Foods of Animal Origin*; Council for Agricultural Science and Technology: Ames, IA, USA, January 2004. Issue Paper #25.

Pathogens in Animal Products: Sources and Control

John N. Sofos
Colorado State University, Fort Collins, Colorado, U.S.A.

INTRODUCTION

Food products of animal origin (i.e., fresh, processed, and ready-to-eat meat and poultry products, eggs, milk, and other dairy products) may be contaminated during harvesting, processing, and handling. Because they are rich in nutrients, they support growth of various spoilage and pathogenic microorganisms if not properly handled and preserved. Spoilage microorganisms damage product quality and lead to reduced food supplies and economic losses, whereas pathogens may cause mild, severe, brief, or chronic human illness, or death. Knowledge of sources of contamination and of the properties of foodborne pathogens allows application of proper procedures for pathogen control and enhancement of food safety. Sources and control of pathogens are addressed in this article, while major biological hazards are discussed elsewhere in this encyclopedia.

CONTAMINATION SOURCES

Animal production and product processing and handling practices result in contamination with Gram-negative and Gram-positive bacteria, yeasts, molds, parasites, and viruses, but the presence of pathogens in animal products processed under sanitary and hygienic conditions should generally be infrequent and at low levels. Contamination, however, is unpredictable. Thus, any raw, unprocessed, uncooked food should be considered as potentially contaminated with pathogens. In general, before slaughter, internal muscle tissues of healthy animals and birds can be considered sterile, whereas lymph nodes and certain organs (e.g., liver) may carry low levels of microbial contamination. In contrast, animal surfaces exposed to the environment such as hides, pelts, feathers, fleece, the mouth, and the gastrointestinal tract may be heavily contaminated.[1-5]

Contamination from soil, decaying matter, and animal waste is transmitted to water, air, pastures, and animal feeds, which may carry contamination naturally or may be cross-contaminated with manure. Additional sources of biological hazards may include rodents, mice, birds, insects, and transportation vehicles or crates for animals, which may contribute to cross-contamination, although the extent of this is unknown.[1-6] Pathogen prevalence may vary with animal type and age, geographic region, and season, and is usually higher during the warmer months. Animal manure may contaminate water used for drinking or to irrigate or wash plant crops, resulting in cross-contamination of other foods.

The extent of microbial transfer from the aforementioned sources to food products of animal origin depends on sanitation and hygienic practices; product handling and processing procedures; and conditions of storage, distribution, retailing, preparation for consumption, and serving.[1-5] Animal parts and manure serve as sources of contamination of milk, shell eggs, meat and poultry carcasses and their products, and the environment, leading to cross-contamination of other foods. Meat and poultry are contaminated during slaughtering, dressing, chilling, and cutting processes, when animals' muscles are exposed to the environment. Sources of meat contamination include air, water, feces, hides, intestines, lymph nodes, processing equipment, utensils, and humans. During milking, milk is contaminated by the animal and its environment, as well as by milking equipment and utensils. Eggs may be contaminated through shell penetration or during egg-breaking, whereas internally contaminated eggs may carry *Salmonella* serotype Enteritidis transmitted through transovarian infection of chickens.[1-3,6] The types and levels of microorganisms contaminating a product and subsequent product handling may have important consequences on product quality and safety.

CONTROL

Concern about animal food products serving as vehicles of foodborne biological hazards has led to the establishment of regulatory requirements aimed at improving their hygienic state. Recent developments have included the complete change of the U.S. meat and poultry inspection system, which has been in place since the early 1900s. The new U.S. Meat and Poultry Inspection Regulation[7] requires federally inspected meat and poultry plants to implement the hazard analysis critical control point (HACCP) system for the management of process controls.[8] The application of process controls[6,9,10] for

Encyclopedia of Animal Science
DOI: 10.1081/E-EAS 120019744

enhancement of the microbiological condition and assurance of the safety of meat and poultry products involves three approaches: 1) control of sources and processes to decrease the likelihood of contamination during product harvesting; 2) implementation of procedures to decontaminate products such as carcasses during processing; and 3) application of technologies to inactivate or control pathogens in ready-to-eat products. These approaches are applicable for pathogen control in all foods and aim at minimizing initial contamination, destroying contamination in some products, and inhibiting proliferation of contamination in others.[9–12]

Approaches to controlling bacterial pathogens in live animals include use of feed additives, diet modification, antimicrobial treatments, competitive exclusion microorganisms, treatment with bacteriophages, administration of vaccines, improved husbandry practices, etc.[12] With the exception of application of good production practices, all these approaches are still in the experimental stage. Decontamination interventions applied to meat-animal carcasses include animal cleaning; dehairing; spot-cleaning of carcasses before evisceration by knife-trimming; steaming and vacuuming; and spraying, rinsing, or deluging of carcasses before evisceration and/or before chilling with hot water, chemical solutions, or steam.[10] These processes only reduce contamination levels because it is difficult to eliminate microbial contamination and still maintain the raw state properties of foods. Processes aimed at destruction of contamination during product processing include use of heat and, to a lesser extent, ionizing radiation or high-pressure processing. Approaches aiming to inhibit microbial growth are based on low storage temperatures, drying (evaporation, concentration), binding of water levels (salting, sugaring) available for microbial growth (water activity), addition of acids (low pH), fermentation (low pH, production of antimicrobials), packaging under such modified atmospheres as vacuum, and use of chemical preservatives.[1–3,9] Parasites may be inactivated by proper cooking, freezing, irradiation, salting, or application of chemicals. Viruses can be controlled by application of proper cooking, sanitation, and hygienic procedures.

Interventions available to minimize pathogen contamination of milk include health management programs for dairy herds; employment of hygienic practices during milking, storing, and distribution of milk; and pasteurization.[6] It should be noted that pathogen-free raw milk cannot be ensured, and consumers should be advised not to drink raw milk or consume dairy products made with raw milk. Microbiological concerns associated with processed dairy products include potential survival of pathogens such as *Salmonella* in cheeses and growth of *Listeria monocytogenes* in certain soft cheeses. Whereas outbreaks of salmonellosis are rarely associated with

natural cheeses, listeriosis has been associated with consumption of fluid milk and soft cheeses when growth occurred before consumption. These concerns may be addressed through prevention of contamination after pasteurization of milk and during the manufacture of cheese products, and through control of the environment to prevent contamination.[6]

Presence of *Salmonella* Enteritidis in shell eggs is an important concern because it may be introduced through transovarian infection. The pathogen can be destroyed by proper cooking, liquid egg pasteurization, or in–shell egg pasteurization.[6] A decrease in *Salmonella* Enteritidis egg-associated illness in the United States may be the result of improved farm management practices, procedures for detecting and controlling *Salmonella* Enteritidis–contaminated flocks, timely collection of eggs, storage of eggs at low temperatures, consumer education for safe egg handling, and pasteurization of eggs from infected flocks. A significant decrease in *Salmonella* Enteritidis infections reported in the United Kingdom may be attributed to vaccination of the egg-laying flocks.[6]

CONCLUSION

Food products of animal origin are expected by nature to be contaminated with microorganisms, including some that are pathogenic to humans.[13] These pathogens may cause illness, ranging from mild gastrointestinal discomfort to severe acute or chronic illness or death. Extent, prevalence, and type of contamination are influenced by sanitary, hygienic, and processing conditions during handling of the products at all stages of the food chain. It is important to realize that control of pathogens and management of food safety risks should be based on an integrated approach that applies to all sectors—from the producer to the processor, distributor, packer, retailer, food service worker, and consumer. Interventions applied during processing include sanitation, decontamination, heating, chilling, freezing, drying, fermentation, use of chemicals as acidulants or antimicrobials, packaging, proper storage and distribution, and appropriate handling and preparation for consumption. Proper application of control processes yields products that should be safe for consumption following proper cooking and serving. Consumers should be advised to properly handle and prepare all foods, including those of animal origin, and to follow labeling instructions. Foods should be stored and handled in conditions that minimize cross-contamination (i.e., in a clean and sanitary environment), properly cooked (e.g., ground beef cooked at 160°F), and stored or held at the correct temperatures (cold: under 40°F; hot: above 140°F), and for the indicated length of time.

ARTICLES OF FURTHER INTEREST

REFERENCES

1. Sofos, J.N. Microbial Growth and Its Control in Meat Poultry and Fish. In *Quality Attributes and Their Measurements in Meat, Poultry and Fish Products*; Pearson, A.M., Dutson, T.R., Eds.; Blackie Academic and Professional: Glasgow, UK, 1994; 353–403.

2. Koutsoumanis, K.P.; Sofos, J.N. Microbial Contamination of Carcasses and Cuts. In *Encyclopedia of Meat Sciences*; Elsevier: Oxford, UK, 2004. in press.

3. Koutsoumanis, K.P.; Geornaras, I.; Sofos, J.N. Microbiology of Land Muscle Foods. In *Handbook of Food Science*; Hui, Y.H., Ed.; Marcel Dekker, Inc.: New York, NY, USA, 2004, in press.

4. ICMSF (International Commission on Microbiological Specifications for Foods). *Microorganisms in Foods 6, Microbial Ecology of Food Commodities*; Blackie Academic and Professional: London, UK, 1998.

5. Davies, A.; Board, R. *The Microbiology of Meat and Poultry*; Blackie Academic and Professional: London, UK, 1998.

6. CAST (Council for Agricultural Science and Technology). *Intervention Strategies for the Microbiological Safety of Food of Animal Origin, Issue Paper*; Council for Agricultural Science and Technology: Ames, IA, USA, January 2004. Issue Paper # 25.

7. FSIS (Food Safety and Inspection Service). Pathogen reduction; hazard analysis and critical control point (HACCP) systems: Final rule. Federal Register **1996**, *61*, 38805–38989. 9CFR Part 304.

8. NACMCF (National Advisory Committee on Microbiological Criteria for Foods). Hazard analysis and critical control point principles and application guidelines. J. Food Prot. **1998**, *61*, 762–775.

9. Juneja, V.K.; Sofos, J.N. *Control of Foodborne Microorganisms*; Marcel Dekker, Inc.: New York, NY, USA, 2002.

10. Sofos, J.N.; Smith, G.C. Nonacid meat decontamination technologies: Model studies and commercial applications. Int. J. Food Microbiol. **1998**, *44*, 171–188.

11. Samelis, J.; Sofos, J.N. Strategies to Control Stress-Adapted Pathogens. In *Microbial Stress Adaptation and Food Safety*; Yousef, A.E., Juneja, V.K., Eds.; CRC Press: Boca Raton, FL, USA, 2003.

12. Sofos, J.N. Approaches to Pre-Harvest Food Safety Assurance. In *Food Safety Assurance and Veterinary Public Health; Volume 1, Food Safety Assurance in the Pre-Harvest Phase*; Smulders, F.J.M., Collins, J.D., Eds.; Wageningen Academic Publishers: Wageningen, The Netherlands, 2002; 23–48.

13. Sofos, J.N. Pathogens in Animal Products: Major Biological Hazards. In *Encyclopedia of Animal Science*; Pond, W.G., Bell, A.W., Eds.; Marcel Dekker, Inc.: New York, 2004.

Phytases

Xin Gen Lei
Cornell University, Ithaca, New York, U.S.A.

Jesus M. Porres
Universidad de Granada, Grenada, Spain

INTRODUCTION

Phytases are meso-inositol hexaphosphate phosphohydrolases that catalyze the initiation of the stepwise phosphate splitting of phytic acid or phytate to lower inositol phosphate esters and inorganic phosphate (Fig. 1). These enzymes have emerged as effective tools to improve phosphorus nutrition and to protect the environment from phosphorus pollution in animal production. Although phosphorus is an essential nutrient to all species, 60–80% of phosphorus in feeds of plant origin is in the form of phytate (*myo*-inositol hexakisphosphate) that is poorly available to simple-stomached animals such as swine, poultry, and the preruminant calves, due to the lack of phytases in their gastrointestinal tracts. As a result, a large portion of feed phosphorus is not utilized by them and ends up in manure, causing environmental pollution. Meanwhile, expensive and nonrenewable inorganic phosphorus needs to be added to diets for these species to meet their nutrient requirements for phosphorus.

GENES, PROTEINS, AND PROPERTIES

A number of phytase genes and proteins have been identified from microorganisms and plants after the isolation of the very first phytase (PhyA) protein and DNA sequence from *Aspergillus niger*.[1] It remains unclear whether phytase is expressed in animal tissues. PhyA and most fungal phytases have molecular mass ranging from 80–120 kDa, with 10 or so *N*-glycosylation sites in the approximately 1.4-kb DNA sequences.[1] The average molecular masses of most bacterial phytases range from 40 to 55 kDa.[2] Plant phytases isolated from corn, wheat, lupine, oat, or barley have molecular sizes ranging from 47 to 76 kDa.[3] Most identified phytases, but not all, belong to a group of histidine acid phosphatases (HAPs) that feature the conserved active site hepta-peptide motif RHGXRXP and the catalytically active dipeptide HD.[1] This group of phytases catalyzes phytic acid hydrolysis in a two-step mechanism via a nucleophilic attack from the histidine in the active site of the enzyme to the scissile phosphoester bond of phytic acid. In general, fungal phytases (E.C. 3.1.3.8) initiate the splitting of the phosphate group at the C_1 or C_3 carbon of the inositol ring, and are thus called 3-phytases, whereas plant phytases (E.C. 3.1.3.26) act preferentially at the C_6 carbon, and are named 6-phytase. However, phytases isolated from *Escherichia coli*, *Lupinus albus*, or *Peniophora lycii* are exceptions to this rule. Interestingly, a soybean phytase is a purple acid phosphatase with a dinuclear iron–iron or iron–zinc center in the active site. The phytase from *Bacillus subtilis* has a six-bladed folding scaffold, and calcium ion can affect its thermostability and catalysis. As a whole, phytases show a strong ability to cleave equatorial phosphate groups, but a limited ability to hydrolyze axial phosphate groups. The optimum pH for most known phytases is in the range of 4.5–6. Exceptions are phytases from mung bean, *Enterobacter* sp., or *B. subtilis* that have their pH optimum in the neutral to alkaline range. The temperature optimum of most plant and microbial phytases ranges from 45–65°C, higher than body temperatures of animals (37–40°C). Phytase activity unit is defined by the amount of inorganic phosphate released per minute from a selected substrate under certain pH and temperature. In the case of *A. niger* PhyA, the activity is determined in 0.05–0.2 M citrate or acetate buffer, pH 5.5, at 37°C; and one unit equals the amount of enzyme that releases 1 μmol of inorganic phosphorus per minute from sodium phytate. The biochemical properties of the currently available phytases for animal feeding are summarized in Table 1.

SUBSTRATE OCCURRENCE

Phytases from *A. niger*, *Aspergillus terreus*, *E. coli* or *Bacillus* sp. seem to have a high specificity for phytic acid, whereas plant phytases and some fungal enzymes such as the one from *Aspergillus fumigatus* have a broader substrate specificity. Chemically, phytic acid refers to *myo*-inositol-1,2,3,4,5,6-hexakis dihydrogen phosphate, which contains approximately 30% phosphorus. Phytate and phytin refer to salts of phytic acid with individual or mixed

Encyclopedia of Animal Science
DOI: 10.1081/E-EAS 120019747

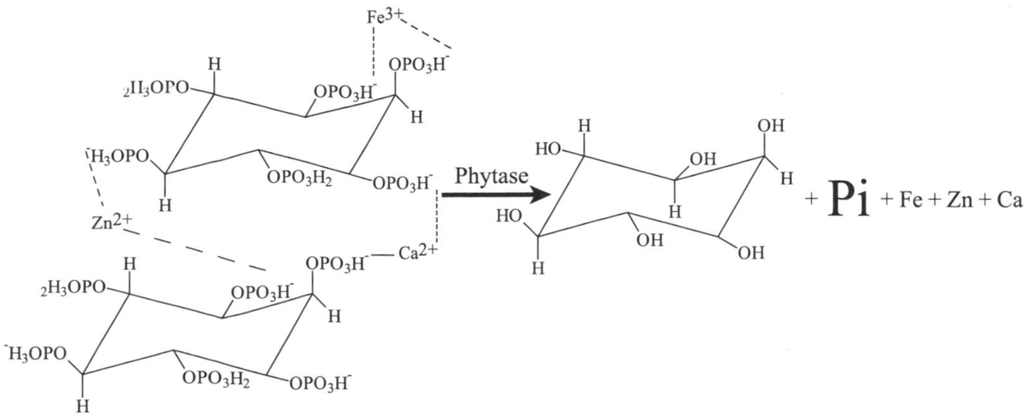

Fig. 1 Hydrolysis of phytate by phytase into inositol and phosphate. Phytate hydrolysis also releases chelated metals such as iron, zinc, and calcium.

metals such as calcium, sodium, potassium, magnesium, iron, zinc, copper, etc. In reality, all three of these compounds are indistinguishably called phytate. Total contents of phytate are 0.5–1.9% in cereals, 0.4–2.1% in legumes, 2.0–5.2% in oil seeds, and 0.4–7.5% in protein products.[4] Distribution of phytate varies with seeds. It is located in the germ of corn, in crystalloid-type globoids inside the protein bodies within the cotyledons of dicotyledoneous seeds (beans, soy, nuts, peanuts), or in the globoids of aleurone grains (protein bodies) present in the aleurone or bran layer of monocotyledoneous seeds (wheat, rice).[4] Phytate rapidly accumulates in seed ripening and serves mainly as storage of phosphorus, inositol, and minerals for the germinating seed. It may be involved in the control of inorganic phosphate levels in both developing seeds and seedlings, and it may also have antifungic and antioxidant roles.[1,4] Because of these functions of phytate and its universal abundance in all plants, caution should be given in developing low-phytate crops. However, phytate is an antinutrient factor in animal diets. With a poor availability of phosphorus, phytate also chelates divalent metals such as zinc and iron. There are twelve replaceable protons present in the phytic acid molecule: Six are dissociated in the strong acid range, one in the weak acid range, two with pK 6.8 to 7.6, and three with $pK > 10$.[5] At the neutral pH of small intestine, phytic acid is strongly negatively charged and is able to complex or bind to positively charged molecules. These complexes are rather insoluble, rendering the chelated metals unavailable for absorption.

NUTRITIONAL AND ENVIRONMENTAL BENEFITS

Numerous studies have demonstrated the effectiveness of microbial or plant phytase added to plant-based diets for swine, poultry, and fish in improving utilization of phytate-phosphorus and reducing phosphorus excretion by these animals.[6] The efficacy of different phytases varies, but the average amount of phytase needed to replace 1 g of inorganic phosphorus per kg of swine or poultry diet ranges from 500 to 1000 units.[7] With this efficacy, phytase can obviate inorganic phosphorus supplementation at least by half, saving the nonrenewable resource that may be exhausted in 80 years at the current extraction rate. More urgently, supplemental phytase reduces fecal phosphorus excretion by 30–50%, which can potentially eliminate 90,000 tons of phosphorus excreted to the environment by poultry and swine in the United States annually. In addition, phytase improves bioavailability of calcium, zinc, and iron, primarily by releasing these elements from binding to the phosphate groups of phytate. However, the effects of phytase on utilization of protein, amino acids, or energy are still controversial.

DIETARY DETERMINANTS OF EFFICACY

At least four dietary factors can modulate phytase efficacy. First, high levels of dietary calcium or calcium/phosphorus ratios reduce the effectiveness of phytase. In phytase-supplemented diets, the recommended calcium/phosphorus ratio is 1.2:1, not 2:1 as used in diets with adequate inorganic phosphorus added. Second, moderate to high levels of inorganic phosphorus may inhibit the full function of phytase. Third, supplemental organic acids such as citric acid or lactic acid enhance phytase efficacy. Those acids may reduce the pH of stomach digesta, thus providing a better environment for phytase to function, and/or to enhance the solubility of digesta phosphorus and modify the transit time of digesta in the small intestine.

Table 1 Biochemical properties of phytases currently available for use in animal diets

Origin	pH optimum	Temperature optimum (°C)	PI	M_r (kDa)[a]	Km (μM)[b]	Kcat (s^{-1})[b]	Kcat/Km (s^{-1} M^{-1})[b]
A. niger PhyA[c,d,e,f]	2.5–3; 5–5.5	55–60	4.94	66–120 (50)	27	348	1.3×10^7
A. niger PhyB[g]	2.5	63	–	269 (65)	103	628	6.1×10^6
A. fumigatus PhyA[e,h,i,j,k]	4–6.5	58–70	7.04–7.3	60–76 (49)	30	46	1.5×10^6
P. lycii[l,m]	4–4.5	50–55	3.61–4.37	71–72 (44.6)	33	2200	6.6×10^7
E. coli AppA[h,i,n,o,p,w]	2.5–4.5	55–60	6.3; 6.5	42–55 (45–48)	130 (IP6) 15 (IP5)	6209 (IP6) 6926 (IP5)	4.8×10^7 (IP6) 5×10^8 (IP5)
Bacillus sp.[q,r,s,t,u]	6–9.5	55–65	5.0–5.1; 6.5–6.8	38–47	50	26.6	5.3×10^5
Wheat[v,w]	5.2	50	–	47–65	228–300	468	1.8×10^6

[a]The values in parentheses are calculated after deglycosylation of proteins or based on the deduced peptide sequence. The value shown for A. niger phyB is the molecular mass of the tetramer. The molecular mass of the monomer is shown within parentheses.

[b]Only phytic acid (IP6) is used as the substrate for all enzymes except for E. coli AppA. Assay conditions are as follows: A. niger PhyA: 58°C, pH=5.0; A. niger PhyB: 63°C, pH=2.5; A. fumigatus PhyA: 58°C, pH=5.0; P. lycii: 58°C, pH=5.0; E. coli AppA: 35–37°C, pH=4.5; Bacillus sp: 37°C, pH=7.0; Wheat: 55°C, pH=5.15; 35°C, pH=5.0.

[c]Ullah et al. (1999) Biochem. Bioph. Res. Co. 264: 210–206.

[d]Han et al. (1999) Appl. Environ. Microbiol. 65: 1915–1918.

[e]Ullah et al. (2000) Biochem. Bioph. Res. Co. 275: 279–285.

[f]Ullah et al. (2002) Biochem. Bioph. Res. Co. 290: 1343–1348.

[g]Ullah AHJ and Sethumadhavan K (1998) Biochem. Bioph. Res. Co. 243: 458–462.

[h]Wyss et al. (1999) Appl. Environ. Microbiol. 65: 359–366.

[i]Wyss et al. (1999) Appl. Environ. Microbiol. 65: 367–373.

[j]Mullaney et al. (2000) Biochem. Bioph. Res. Co. 275: 759–763.

[k]Rodriguez et al. (2000) Biochem. Bioph. Res. Co. 268: 373–378.

[l]Lassen et al. (2001) Appl. Environ. Microbiol. 67: 4701–4707.

[m]Ullah AHJ and Sethumadhavan K (2003) Biochem. Bioph. Res. Co. 303: 46–468.

[n]Greiner et al. (1993) Arch. Biochem. Biophys. 303: 107–113.

[o]Golovan et al. (2000) Can. J. Microbiol. 46: 59–71.

[p]Rodriguez et al. (2000) Arch. Biochem. Biophys. 382: 105–112.

[q]Kerovuo et al. (1998) Appl. Environ. Microbiol. 64: 2079–2085.

[r]Kim et al. (1998) FEMS Microbiol. Lett. 162: 185–191.

[s]Kim et al. (1998) Enz. Microb. Tech. 22: 2–7.

[t]Choi et al. (2001) J. Prot. Chem. 20: 287–292.

[u]Tye et al. (2002) Appl. Microbiol. Biotechnol. 59: 190–197.

[v]Peers (1953) Biochem J. 53: 102–110.

[w]Greiner et al. (2000) J. Biotech. 84: 53–62.

In addition, organic acids may release cations chelated by phytate, reducing the amount of insoluble phytate–cation complexes that are resistant to phytase action, thereby increasing the efficacy of endogenous or supplemented phytase. Last, inclusion of hydroxylated cholecalciferol compounds has been shown to improve dietary phosphorus and zinc utilization by chicks in an additive manner with phytase. Supplementing different phytases in combination has not shown any benefit over the singular additions. However, adding phytase with other hydrolytic enzymes seems to produce a synergism. Furthermore, there are several physical forms of phytase: powder, granule, and liquid. The chemical coating of phytase to improve heat stability may somewhat compromise its release in stomach.

STORAGE AND HANDLING

Phytase should be stored under dark, cool, and dry conditions. When this is done, the enzyme may maintain good stability for 3–4 months. Refrigeration or freezing may extend its shelf life, whereas high storage temperature certainly decreases its activity. Caution should be given in storing phytase mixed with vitamin and mineral premixes, as some of their components may have deleterious effects on phytase stability. There are few reports on immune responses of workers who have inhalation exposure to phytase. The hypersensitivity symptoms can be alleviated or avoided by implementing local exhaust systems and wearing protective clothing and masks with P2 filters.[8]

DEVELOPING IDEAL PHYTASES

A phytase would be considered ideal for feed application if it were catalytically effective, proteolysis-resistant, thermostable, and cheap. The catalytic efficiency and protease susceptibility of any given phytase decide its ability to release phytate-phosphorus in the digestive tract. The thermostability of phytase determines its feasibility in feed pelleting, and the overall cost to produce the enzyme ranks its final acceptance by industry. Although there are significant differences in these features among various naturally occurring phytases, no single wild-type enzyme possesses all of the desired properties. With advances of biotechnology, there are three ways to develop effective phytases with improved properties. First, site-directed mutagenesis, based on crystal structure of phytases, has been applied to improve pH profile, thermostability, and catalytic efficiency. Second, synthetic phytases such as the experimental consensus phytase have been generated based on homologous sequences of multiple phytases. Last, new phytases can be produced by directed evolution with efficient selections. A number of heterologous expression systems have been used for phytase production. The expression hosts include plants, bacteria, fungi, and yeast.[2,9] Recently, transgenic pigs overexpressing a bacterial phytase in salivary gland have been generated.[10] If approved by regulatory agencies, this approach may serve as a sustainable and economical delivery of phytase.

CONCLUSION

There is an increasing need for phytase to improve dietary phytate-phosphorus utilization by livestock, and thus reduce their phosphorus excretion to the environment worldwide, in particular in areas of intensive animal production. Although microbial phytase supplementation has been a widespread practice in swine and poultry feeding, and to a lesser extent, in fish feeding, continuous improvements in its property and reductions in its cost are warranted. Modern biotechnology has provided great potential to develop ideal phytases and effective deliveries for specific groups of animals.

REFERENCES

1. Mullaney, E.J.; Daly, C.B.; Ullah, A.B.J. Advances in phytase research. Adv. Appl. Microbiol. **2000**, *47*, 157–199.
2. Lei, X.G.; Stahl, C.H. Biotechnological development of effective phytases for mineral nutrition and environmental protection. Appl. Microbiol. Biotechnol. **2001**, *57*, 474–481.
3. Liu, B.; Rafiq, A.; Tzeng, Y.; Rob, A. The induction and characterization of phytase and beyond. Enzyme Microb. Technol. **1998**, *22*, 415–424.
4. Reddy, N.R.; Sathe, S.K.; Salukhe, D.K. Phytates in legumes and cereals. Adv. Food Res. **1982**, *28*, 1–92. (Academic Press, New York, NY).
5. Cheryan, M. Phytic acid interactions in food systems. CRC Crit. Rev. Food Sci. Nutr. **1980**, *13*, 297–336.
6. Lei, X.G.; Stahl, C.H. Nutritional benefits of phytase and dietary determinants of its efficacy. J. Appl. Anim. Res. **2000**, *17*, 97–112.
7. Kornegay, E.T. Chapter 18: Nutritional, Environmental, and Economic Considerations for Using Phytase in Pig and Poultry Diets. In *Nutrient Management of Food Animals to Enhance and Protect the Environment*; Kornegay, E.T., Ed.; CRC, Lewis Publishing: New York, NY, 1996; 277–302.
8. Baur, X.; Melching-Kollmuss, S.; Koops, F.; Straburger, K.; Zober, A. IgE-mediated allergy to phytase—A new animal feed additive. Allergy **2002**, *57*, 943–945.
9. Pandey, A.; Szakacs, G.; Soccol, C.R.; Rodriguez-Leon, J.A.; Soccol, V.T. Production, purification and properties of microbial phytases. Bioresour. Technol. **2001**, *77*, 203–214.
10. Golovan, S.P.; Meidinger, R.; Ajakaiye, A.; Cottrill, M.; Wiederkehr, M.Z.; Barney, D.J.; Plante, C.; Pollard, J.W.; Fan, M.Z.; Hayes, M.A.; Laursen, J.; Hjorth, J.P.; Hackler, R.R.; Phillips, J.P.; Forsberg, C.W. Pigs expressing salivary phytase produce low-phosphorus manure. Nat. Biotechnol. **2001**, *19*, 741–745.

Placenta: Development

Alan W. Bell
Cornell University, Ithaca, New York, U.S.A.

INTRODUCTION

The purpose of this entry is to describe the processes of normal morphological and functional development of the placenta, the unique organ of pregnancy in higher animals. The consequences of abnormal development for fetal growth and development are also briefly considered. Examples are confined to eutherian mammals in which the placenta is most highly developed, with most emphasis on the large domestic species.

PLACENTAL FUNCTIONS

As described elsewhere in this volume,[1] the placenta acts as the conduit for exchange of nutrients and excreta between mother and fetus, as an endocrine, paracrine and autocrine regulator of many pregnancy-specific physiological functions, and as an immunological "blindfold" that serves to protect the conceptus from its maternal host. Despite considerable structural polymorphism among species,[2] the functional similarities of mammalian placentae are much greater than the differences. Emerging evidence suggests that the molecular regulation of placental development is similarly conserved among species.[3]

MORPHOLOGY

Embryonic Development

The early differentiation of trophoblast cells at the periphery of the blastocyst occurs within a week after fertilization in most domestic mammals. These cells facilitate nutrient absorption before uterine attachment and formation of the extraembryonic membranes, around the time of gastrulation.[4] Shortly before implantation in ruminants, binucleate cells appear in the predominantly uninucleate trophoblast. These cells form 15–20% of this layer throughout gestation and when mature, migrate out of the trophectoderm and fuse with uterine epithelium to produce a persistent fetomaternal syncytium. This facil-itates the delivery to maternal tissue of granules containing placental lactogen and other bioactive factors synthesized in the binucleate giant cells, thereby enabling important endocrine functions of the placenta.[5]

Shortly after the blastocyst enters the uterus, implantation is achieved by attachment of the trophoblast to the endometrium, usually before the end of the second week of gestation in domestic mammals. In large domestic mammals, the functional placenta is formed from separable trophoblastic and maternal tissues, each with distinct, albeit intimately associated, vasculature. After initial attachment, the closely apposed chorionic and endometrial epithelia progressively fold and interdigitate to form microvilli. Simultaneously, rapid development of blood vessels on both sides of the newly formed placenta allows completion of the transition from histotrophic to hemotrophic nutrition of the implanted embryo.[4]

Postembryonic Growth

After implantation, the placenta undergoes a period of explosive mitotic growth characterized by rapid synthesis and accumulation of nucleic acids and protein in trophoblastic and uterine tissues. In sheep, this period begins at around 40 days of gestation and ceases abruptly by midgestation at approximately 75 days, resulting in 50-fold and 30-fold increases in wet and dry placental mass, respectively (Fig. 1).[6] Cessation of absolute placental growth is preceded by sharp peaks in rates of DNA and protein synthesis at 50–55 days of gestation, associated with a maximal rate of dry-matter accretion (Fig. 1). In the cow, hyperplasia of the cotyledonary placenta continues into late gestation, although at a diminishing rate, whereas in the pig, macroscopic growth of the diffuse placenta is complete by about day 60 or slightly after midpregnancy.[7]

Notwithstanding some species variation in pattern and timing, in all domestic mammals the phase of major proliferative growth of the placenta occurs in early midpregnancy and precedes rapid growth of the fetus in late gestation. This is significant because the trajectory of early placental growth can determine ultimate size and functional capacity of the placenta, and fetal growth during late gestation.

Encyclopedia of Animal Science
DOI: 10.1081/E-EAS 120019748

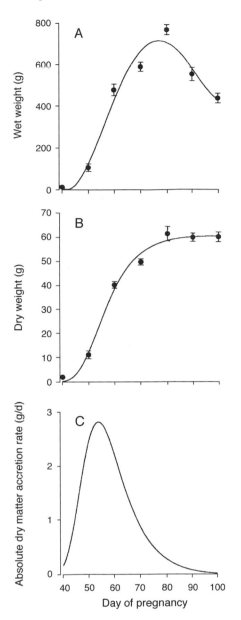

Fig. 1 Growth of the ovine placenta during midgestation, expressed in terms of (A) wet weight, (B) dry weight, and (C) rate of accretion of dry matter. (Adapted from Ref. 6.)

Tissue Remodeling and Functional Maturation in Late Gestation

The cessation or slowing of net placental growth after midgestation masks the continuing proliferative growth of the microvasculature, especially in the umbilical circulation, and the extensive remodeling that allows closer apposition of the uterine and umbilical capillaries. The wet mass of the ovine placenta actually declines during the latter half of pregnancy (Fig. 1A), mostly through loss of extracellular water associated with the loss

of hydrophilic extracellular matrix (mostly glycosoaminoglycans) from the trophoblastic villous core after about day 90 of gestation.[6] The degree of branching and total surface area of the villi and vascularization of the maternal caruncles increase during late gestation before plateauing two to three weeks before term, although vascularization of the villi continues to increase until term.[8]

Alterations in placental morphology after midpregnancy are associated with major increases in placental blood flow and functional capacity, including transfer of highly diffusible molecules and carrier-mediated transport of glucose and amino acids.[9]

REGULATION OF GROWTH AND DEVELOPMENT

Understanding of genes and their products responsible for proliferation of trophoblastic stem cells, progression from these cells to more specialized placental cell types, and differentiation of mature functions in the murine placenta has increased greatly with the recent use of transgenic and mutant mice.[10] These studies have shown that most of the genes that evolved to regulate placental development

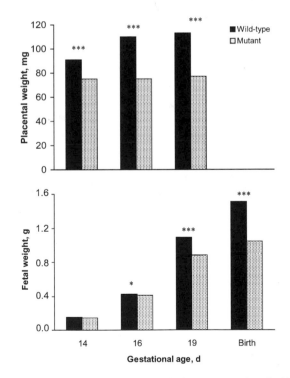

Fig. 2 Placental and fetal growth in mutant mice lacking paternal expression of the IGF-II gene in labyrinthine trophoblastic tissue of the placenta, and in their wild-type littermates. Significant differences between wild-type and mutant mice are indicated: *$P<0.05$; ***$P<0.001$. (Adapted from the data of Ref. 11.)

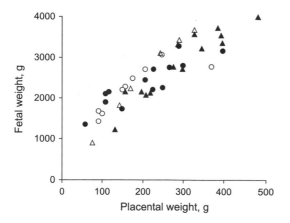

Fig. 3 Relation between fetal and placental weights in ewes representing different models of placental insufficiency during late pregnancy. Variation in placental weight was achieved by premating carunclectomy (●), chronic heat treatment (○), natural variation in litter size (▲), and overfeeding of adolescent ewes (△). (Reproduced from Ref. 15 with permission of the Society for Reproduction and Fertility.)

are either identical to ones used in other organ systems (e.g., fibroblast growth factor's control of early stem cell proliferation), were coopted to take on new functions, or arose via gene duplication to take on a specialized placental function. Preliminary evidence suggests similarity of these functions between mouse and human,[10] and probably, among other mammals.

Insulin-like growth factor II (IGF-II) may perform a special role as a regulator of placental growth and funcional capacity.[9] The IGF-II gene is paternally imprinted and abundantly expressed in multiple placental cell types. Selective deletion of a transcript specifically expressed in the trophoblast leads to dramatic stunting of placental growth, followed by fetal growth restriction in mice (Fig. 2).[11] Thus, it has been proposed that the imprinted IGF-II gene controls both the placental supply of, and the genetic demand for, maternal nutrients to the fetus.

More specific information on molecular regulation of the functional differentiation of trophoblast endocrine cells is reviewed in Soares et al.[12]

CONSEQUENCES OF ALTERED PLACENTAL DEVELOPMENT FOR FETAL GROWTH

Placental weight is a powerful determinant of fetal growth in all domestic mammals, especially during late gestation. This has been demonstrated in sheep by natural reduction of placental growth due to increased litter size, environmental heat stress, or overfeeding of adolescent ewes, and

by surgical removal of uterine caruncles before mating (Fig. 3).[9] These manipulations of placental growth have been used to identify mechanisms by which fetal growth is constrained by placental functional capacity as determined by vascular growth[13] and the development of specific nutrient transport systems.[9]

In vitro manipulation of bovine and ovine embryos has caused increased incidence of excessive fetal growth and of perinatal mortality and morbidity. Underlying mechanisms are complex and vary with the type of manipulation. However, in vitro culture of cleavage-stage embryos is a common element in most cases of large-offspring syndrome. Evidence for the involvement of abnormal placental development in this syndrome was recently reported.[14] Bovine embryos produced in vitro were more predisposed to later embryonic and early fetal mortality. During midpregnancy (days 90 and 180), increased fetal size was associated with fewer, larger placentomes with considerably greater total surface area. These observations are consistent with, but do not necessarily prove, the direct involvement of increased placental growth in large-offspring syndrome. Also, not all cases of large offspring derived from embryos manipulated in vitro have been associated with altered placental morphology.

CONCLUSIONS

Adequate placental development is critical for the growth and development of healthy, viable offspring. There is increasing awareness that placental dysfunction also may contribute to long-term "programming" of predisposition to mature-onset diseases during adulthood.[15,16] Recent progress in understanding the molecular regulation of placental development offers promise of therapies to minimize the incidence of placental insufficiency and associated intrauterine growth retardation.

ARTICLES OF FURTHER INTEREST

Placenta: Functions, p. 712
Placenta: Types, p. 716

REFERENCES

1. Ferrell, C.L. Placenta: Functions. This volume.
2. Ferrell, C.L. Placenta: Types. This volume.
3. Cross, J.C.; Baczyk, D.; Dobric, N.; Hemberger, M.; Hughes, M.; Simmons, D.G.; Yamamoto, H.; Kingdom,

J.C.P. Genes, development and evolution of the placenta. Placenta **2003**, *24*, 123–130.

4. Noden, D.M.; de Lahunta, A. *The Embryology of Domestic Animals*; Williams and Wilkins: Baltimore, USA, 1985; 1–367.

5. Wooding, F.B.P.; Flint, A.P.F. Placentation. In *Marshall's Physiology of Reproduction*, 4th Ed.; Lamming, G.E., Ed.; Chapman and Hall: London, UK, 1994; 233–460.

6. Ehrhardt, R.A.; Bell, A.W. Growth and metabolism of the ovine placenta during mid-gestation. Placenta **1995**, *16*, 727–741.

7. Knight, J.W.; Bazer, F.W.; Thatcher, W.W.; Franke, D.E.; Wallace, H.D. Conceptus development in intact and unilaterally hysterectomized gilts: Interrelations among hormonal status, placental development, fetal fluids and fetal growth. J. Anim. Sci. **1977**, *44*, 620–637.

8. Stegeman, J.H.G. Placental development in the sheep and its relation to fetal development. Bijdr. Dierkd. **1974**, *44*, 3–72.

9. Bell, A.W.; Ehrhardt, R.A. Regulation of placental nutrient transport and implications for fetal growth. Nutr. Res. Rev. **2002**, *15*, 211–230.

10. Cross, J.C.; Baczyk, D.; Dobric, N.; Hemberger, M.; Hughes, M.; Simmons, D.G.; Yamamoto, H.; Kingdom, J.C.P. Genes, development and evolution of the placenta. Placenta **2003**, *24*, 123–130.

11. Constancia, M.; Hemberger, M.; Hughes, J.; Dean, W.; Ferguson-Smith, A.; Fundele, R.; Stewart, F.; Kelsey, G.; Fowden, A.; Sibley, C.; Reik, W. Placental-specific IGF-II is a major modulator of placental and fetal growth. Nature **2002**, *417*, 945–948.

12. Soares, M.J.; Chapman, B.M.; Rasmussen, C.A.; Dai, G.; Kamei, T.; Orwig, K.E. Differentiation of trophoblast endocrine cells. Placenta **1996**, *17*, 277–289.

13. Regnault, T.R.H.; Galan, H.L.; Parker, T.A.; Anthony, R.V. Placental development in normal and compromised pregnancies—A review. Placenta **2002**, *23* (Supplement 1), S119–S129.

14. Bertolini, M.; Anderson, G.B. The placenta as a contributor to production of large calves. Theriogenology **2002**, *57*, 181–187.

15. Greenwood, P.L.; Bell, A.W. Consequences of intrauterine growth retardation for postnatal growth, metabolism and pathophysiology. Reprod., Suppl. **2003**, *61*, 195–206.

16. Godfrey, K.M. The role of the placenta in fetal programming—A review. Placenta **2002**, *23* (Supplement A), S20–S27.

Placenta: Functions

C. L. Ferrell

United States Department of Agriculture, Agricultural Research Service, Clay Center, Nebraska, U.S.A.

INTRODUCTION

The placenta has numerous functions that serve to optimize the uterine environment for conceptus growth and development. The placenta is the primary site of physiological exchange between the conceptus and parent. Exchanges include transfer of oxygen and nutrients or other substrates from the maternal blood to the conceptus, as well as transfer of carbon dioxide, and other waste products from the fetus to the parent. The placenta acts as an endocrine, autocrine, and paracrine organ. It synthesizes a large variety of hormones and other substances that are released to the maternal as well as fetal circulations. It protects the conceptus from the maternal system. The objective of this article is to summarize the major functions of the placenta and some of the mechanisms involved in performing those functions.

PROTECTION OF THE FETUS

In addition to acting as a barrier by limiting transfer of potentially damaging cells and molecules to the fetus, the trophoblast layers serve to protect the fetus from the maternal immune system. The two main mechanisms involved are production of various molecules with immunosuppressive properties (i.e., progesterone, estrogens, cytokines, and chemokines) and production of nonclassical major histocompatibility complex (MHC) molecules (e.g., HLA-G) that are thought to inhibit activities of natural killer (NK) and T cells in the decidua. Thus, the trophoblast is capable of limiting the effectiveness of the maternal immune system in both recognizing and attacking the conceptus.

PLACENTAL TRANSFER

Essentially all maternal–fetal transfer occurs via the placenta. The chorioallantoic placenta has the same transfer mechanisms found in other epithelial systems. These include passive diffusion, facilitated diffusion, active transfer, and receptor-mediated endocytosis. Most substances present in fetal or maternal blood can cross the placenta via one or more of these mechanisms.

Numerous substances traverse the placenta by simple diffusion. In general, diffusion permeability varies directly with solubility and varies inversely with molecular weight, degree of polarity, and electrical charge. Placental tissues are relatively permeable to water, some electrolytes, and lipophilic substances such as oxygen, carbon dioxide, and ethanol. These compounds equilibrate between maternal and fetal blood. Transfer of this type is limited by maternal and fetal perfusion of the placenta, and is most strongly related to the lesser flow (generally umbilical blood flow). Both fetal and maternal perfusion of the placenta, as well as placental vascularization, increase dramatically as pregnancy advances. The increased uterine and umbilical blood flows, in combination with increased placental vascularity, facilitate greater rates of transfer as fetal needs increase.[1]

For flow-limited clearance, orientation of maternal and fetal blood flow in the placenta affect the efficiency of placental transfer. Arrangements of maternal and fetal microvasculatures in placental exchange areas include countercurrent, concurrent, crosscurrent, and multivillous. The countercurrent arrangement, in which the maternal and fetal blood flows in opposite directions (horse, guinea pig), is thought to be the most efficient. Transplacental clearance of highly diffusible substances is approximately equal to umbilical blood flow. The multivillous arrangement, in which maternal blood bathes the villous branches in which fetal blood flows to, then away from the villous tips (hemochorial villous placentation; human, primates), appears to be the next most efficient. Vascular relationships in the sheep, goat, and cow are somewhat controversial, but it is generally agreed that all have relatively inefficient exchange systems. It is thought that sheep have a crosscurrent vascular arrangement. Efficiency of transfer in the cow is somewhat less than would be predicted by either concurrent or crosscurrent arrangement, suggesting significant shunting away from areas of exchange. Efficiency of transfer increases as pregnancy advances, possibly due to decreased shunting and greater vascular development, especially in the umbilical microcirculation.

Encyclopedia of Animal Science
DOI: 10.1081/E-EAS 120019749

Diffusion of hydrophilic molecules is lower than observed with lipophilic substances. Transfer of these substances, such as urea, is diffusion limited. Transfer is not greatly affected by fetal or maternal blood flows and there is incomplete equilibrium between maternal and fetal blood. There are large differences among species in placental permeability to substances having diffusion-limited clearance.

Glucose is an example of substances transferred across the placenta by carrier-mediated facilitated diffusion. Rate of transfer is considerably greater than could be accomplished by simple diffusion, but rate and direction of transfer are dependent on concentration gradient. The predominant glucose transporter protein isoforms in sheep placenta are GLUT-1 and GLUT-3.[2] Ontogenic change in GLUT-3 activity is thought to account for much of the fivefold increase in glucose transport capacity of the sheep placenta between mid and late gestation. Glucose transport is insulin and sodium independent, is stereospecific, and can be competitively inhibited by glucose analogues.

Glucose entry into gravid uterine tissues is largely determined by maternal arterial concentration, whereas transport to the fetus is determined by the transplacental concentration gradient. This concentration gradient is directly related to placental and fetal glucose metabolism, which are in turn influenced by fetal arterial glucose concentration. Thus, as fetal glucose concentration changes relative to that of the mother, placental transfer of glucose to the fetus varies inversely with placental glucose metabolism.

Placental tissues utilize oxygen and glucose at a high rate, reflecting the very high metabolic rate of those tissues. In addition to its impact on placental transfer of glucose, placental glucose metabolism has a major impact on the pattern of carbohydrates delivered to the fetus. In the sheep and cow, uteroplacental tissues utilize 65 to 80% of the glucose taken up from maternal circulation. Lactate ($\sim$35%), alanine and other nonessential amino acids ($\sim$30%), CO_2 ($\sim$20%), and fructose and various polyols ($\sim$5%) are major products of placental glucose metabolism. During midgestation, virtually all of the lactate produced by the ovine placenta is released into maternal circulation. At that time, about 70% of fetal lactate is oxidized—by both fetal (60%) and fetal placental (40%) tissues—to CO_2, with the remaining 30% of the carbon appearing primarily in nonessential amino acids, especially glutamate, glutamine, serine, and glycine. During late gestation, the fetal placenta becomes a major net source of fetal lactate, and a negligible contributor to fetal lactate disposal.

Fructose is a major form of carbohydrate in fetal blood. Fructose, as well as several polyols, is produced in fetal placental tissues from glucose in all ungulates and Cetacea,[3] and large fetal/maternal concentration ratios are maintained. The large concentration gradient is maintained, in part, by very low placental permeability.

Amino acid concentrations are higher in fetal than maternal blood, although the magnitude of the difference varies among amino acids. Observations that most amino acids taken up by the placenta are transported against a fetal/maternal concentration gradient imply the use of energy-dependent, active transport processes. Transfer of amino acids across the placenta involves mediated transport mechanisms at the microvillus and basal membrane, and perhaps diffusion. Both Na-dependent (e.g., system A, ASC, N) and Na-independent (e.g., system L, y^+, $b^{o,+}$) transporter systems have been identified.[4,5] Concentrations of amino acids in maternal and fetal blood, as well as metabolism within placental tissues, are also intimately involved in regulation of amino acid supply to the developing fetus.[6]

Iron and calcium are also transferred by active transport mechanisms. Knowledge of lipid transport and metabolism within placental tissues is limited, in part, because there are wide species differences. Lipid transport in epitheliochorial placentae appears to be much more limited than in hemochorial placentae.

Immunoglobulins and lipoproteins are transported across the placenta of some species, including primates, by endocytosis. This process serves to provide passive immunity to the fetus. In rodents, rabbits, and guinea pigs, transfer occurs via the yolk sac placenta. In ruminants, offspring receive maternal immunoglobulins only after birth via colostrum.

PLACENTAL ENDOCRINE FUNCTIONS

The placenta is a complex endocrine organ that synthesizes and metabolizes a large variety of steroid and peptide hormones as well as numerous other substances in large quantities for release into maternal and fetal circulations. Most of the substances appear to be synthesized by trophoblast elements such as the binucleate cells of sheep. The precise roles of placental and fetal hormones, the mechanisms by which they are involved with placental functions, fetal growth and development, and function and metabolism of maternal systems are discussed in more detail by Rurak.[7]

The most heavily studied protein hormones produced by the placenta are the placental lactogens and chorionic gonadotrophins. Placental lactogen is a polypeptide structurally similar to growth hormone and prolactin, and has been identified in several species, including humans, rodents, and ruminants. Placental secretion increases with increased placental size (e.g., twin vs. single pregnancy), and increases as pregnancy advances, but the pattern of secretion differs among species. Human placental lactogen (hPL) is synthesized by syncytiotrophoblast and released primarily into maternal circulation. In contrast, ovine placental lactogen (oPL) is produced by binucleate cells. Plasma levels are higher in the fetus than in the ewe until about 50 d postmating, but increases dramatically in maternal plasma as pregnancy advances. Placental lactogen cross-reacts with both growth hormone and prolactin receptors in ruminant tissues, and may act as a glucose-sparing agent that decreases peripheral sensitivity to insulin. Maternal utilization of protein is also reduced, thereby increasing amino acid availability to the conceptus.

Chorionic gonadotrophins have been heavily studied in the horse and human. Human chorionic gonadotrophin (hCG) is a double-chain glycoprotein, with the α chain identical to that in leuteinizing hormone (LH), follicle-stimulating hormone (FSH), and thyroid-stimulating hormone (TSH) and a distinct β chain. It first appears at the time of implantation and is synthesized by the blastocyst. Equine chorionic gonadotrophin (eCG or PMSG) is similar in structure to hCG and is synthesized by unique populations of binucleate trophoblast cells. Both hCG and eCG function to maintain corpora lutea function in early pregnancy until placental progesterone production is sufficient to maintain pregnancy.

Chorionic gonadotrophin is not produced by ruminants. In those species, interferon tau appears to have similar functions in pregnancy recognition and corpra lutea maintenance. Interferon tau is a 172 amino acid type I interferon that is not inducible by viruses, but is synthesized constitutively by the blastocyst trophectoderm just prior to implantation. A similar mechanism may operate in the pig.

Prolactin is produced by placental tissue of several species. Suggested roles include serving as a fetal growth hormone, stabilization of uterine prostaglandin production, and perhaps in the regulation of amnionic fluid volume. Other peptide hormones have been identified or claimed to be products of placental synthesis. Most are analogues of corresponding pituitary or hypothalamic hormones and include ACTH, FSH, TSH, and α-MSH.

Placental relaxin has been identified as a product of the placenta of humans, horses, cats, pigs, rabbits, and monkeys. It is present in low quantities in endometrial and placental tissues of the sheep, but is absent in the bovine placenta.

Steroid hormones, including estrone, estradiol, estriol, and progesterone, are produced by placental tissues in many species, although sites of production and patterns of secretion vary greatly among species. Progesterone is synthesized from maternal cholesterol, which is taken up by the trophoblast as low-density lipoprotein (LDL). Cytochrome P$_{450}$ side chain cleavage enzyme is the key enzyme in a series of reactions converting the 27-carbon cholesterol to the 21-carbon progesterone. Part of the progesterone passes to the maternal circulation, where it supplements progesterone produced by the corpus luteum. Progesterone and pregnenolone pass to the fetus, which uses these steroids to produce dehydroepiandrosterone and androstanedione, which are subsequently converted to estradiol and estriol by the placenta. In the human, ewe, cow and mare, maintenance of pregnancy is dependent on corpus luteum progesterone secretion until about 30–60, 50–60, 210–230, and 150–299 days of gestation, respectively. The goat and sow are dependent on corpus luteum production throughout pregnancy.

The key enzymes required for the conversion of the 21-carbon progestogenic steroids to the 18-carbon estrogens are 17α-hydroxylase/17,20-lyase and aromatase. There are substantial species differences in the extent to which these enzymes are present in placental tissues. In the sheep and cow, the placenta has low levels of 17α-hydroxylase/17,20-lyase during early pregnancy, thus limiting placental androstenedione production, but there is increased expression of the enzyme during late gestation. Placental androstenedione production may be supplemented by the fetal adrenal gland. Androstenedione may then be aromatized in the placenta to estrogens. In contrast, the rat placenta lacks aromatase. Thus, the placenta produces androgens during late gestation and releases them to the maternal circulation.

Placental tissues are sources of a large number of cytokines, chemokines, prostaglandins, and related factors. Regulation of arachidonic acid metabolism and prostanoid production in placental tissues is essential for the maintenance of pregnancy and initiation and progression of parturition. Cytokines (e.g., TNF-α, IL-β) and chemokines (e.g., MIP-1α) act in a coordinated fashion at multiple points of the prostanoid biosynthetic pathway to regulate prostaglandin production.[8]

CONCLUSION

The placenta combines many functional activities. It serves as a barrier to protect the fetus, but serves as the primary site of physiological exchange between the conceptus and parent. It provides the substrates for fetal metabolism and disposes of the waste products. The placenta synthesizes both peptide and steroid hormones, as well as other substances that are released to the maternal as well as the fetal circulations. The placenta grows rapidly during early gestation and adapts to increasing metabolic demands of the rapidly growing fetus. The placenta has numerous functions, and most of those functions serve to optimize the uterine environment for normal conceptus growth and development, either directly via influences on the fetus, or indirectly by modifying maternal physiological functions.

REFERENCES

1. Reynolds, L.P.; Redmer, D.A. Utero-placental vascular development and placental function. J. Anim. Sci. **1995**, *73*, 1839–1851.
2. Bell, A.W.; Ferrell, C.L.; Freetly, H.C. Pregnancy and Fetal Metabolism. In *Quantitative Aspects of Digestion and Metabolism*, 2nd Ed.; Dijkstra, J., Ed.; CAB International, 2004; *in press*.
3. Teng, C.C.; Tjoa, S.; Fennessey, P.V.; Wilkening, R.B.; Battaglia, F.C. Transplacental carbohydrate and sugar alcohol concentrations and their uptakes in ovine pregnancy. Exp. Biol. Med. **2002**, *227*, 189–195.
4. Battaglia, F.C.; Regnault, T.R.H. Placental transport and metabolism of amino acids. Placenta **2001**, *22*, 145–161.
5. Cariappa, R.; Heath-Monnig, E.; Smith, C.H. Isoforms of amino acid transporters in placental syncytiotrophoblast: Plasma membrane localization and potential role in maternal/fetal transport. Placenta **2003**, *24*, 713–726.
6. Paolini, C.L.; Meschia, G.; Fennessey, P.V.; Pike, A.W.; Teng, C.; Battaglia, F.C.; Wilkening, R.B. An in vivo study of placental transport of essential amino acids. Am. J. Physiol. **2001**, *280*, E31–E39.
7. Rurak, D.W. Development and Function of the Placenta. In *Fetal Growth and Development*; Harding, R., Bocking, A.D., Eds.; Cambridge University Press: Cambridge, UK, 2001; 17–43.
8. Keelan, J.A.; Blumenstein, M.; Helliwell, R.J.A.; Sato, T.A.; Marvin, K.W.; Mitchell, M.D. Cytokines, prostaglandins and parturition—A review. Placenta **2003**, *24* (Supplement A), S33–S46. Trophoblast Research, Vol. 17.

Placenta: Types

C. L. Ferrell

*United States Department of Agriculture, Agricultural Research Service,
Clay Center, Nebraska, U.S.A.*

INTRODUCTION

Growth and development beyond the blastocyst require a direct functional relationship between the trophoblast and the maternal blood vascular system in eutherians. Blastocysts may obtain nutrients from uterine gland secretions, but continued growth of the embryo requires an intimate interchange relationship between the embryo and uterus. The areas of close association for physiological interchange between maternal and conceptus blood constitute vascular placentation. In the majority of mammals, the definitive placenta is the chorioallantoic placenta.

The placenta, when compared to other organs of the body, differs in several respects. The placenta is formed as a result of interaction between fetal and maternal tissues within the pregnant uterus. It is of embryonic origin, but is situated outside the body of the embryo, to which it is connected by a cord of blood vessels. It is a disposable organ with a delimited lifespan, and is not innervated. It exhibits a wide variety of structural modifications such that major differences in anatomy may be found even in closely related species. Functional differences are also evident and add to an already complex situation.

Several different classification systems have been developed, based on anatomical and morphological characteristics, to differentiate types of placentae. These classifications provide only very general ideas as to differences in placental function. Two of the more commonly used systems, the first based on the number of membrane layers present and a second based on placental shape, are summarized. For more detailed and complete information, the reader is referred to the reading list at the end of this article, in particular to the classic work by Mossman.

ESTABLISHMENT OF CHORIOALLANTOIC PLACENTATION

There are several different types of chorioallantoic placentae that differ greatly in appearance. However, all chorioallantoic placentae develop from the same types of embryonic and maternal tissues and are built around a basic framework of vascular mesodermal allantoic villi.

The trophoblast, although varying greatly in structure and number of layers, is present, as are fetal mesenchyme and connective tissue, fetal blood vessels, and both fetal and maternal blood. All vascular placentae are supplied with either vitelline or allantoic vessels. Choriovitelline placental areas are usually temporary and often remain smooth (without villi). Smooth, or avillous, chorioallantoic placental areas occur temporarily in early gestation in some species, but in later gestation are supplemental to villous or labyrinthine areas. Vascular mesodermal allantoic villi are the basic framework of all definitive chorioallantoic placentae of Eutheria, whether villous, trabecular, or labyrinthine in pattern. These mesodermal villi are covered by trophoblast.

CLASSIFICATION BASED ON MEMBRANE LAYERS

Historically, Gosser's system (summarized in Table 1), based on the morphology of the interhemal membrane, is the most generally used classification system (Gosser, 1909, 1927 as cited by Mossman[1]). Gosser, using the name of the maternal tissue contiguous with the chorion as the denominator, distinguished four types of placentae: epitheliochorial, syndesmochorial, endotheliochorial, and hemochorial. This system has been challenged and modified numerous times.[2–4] Because no species having the syndesmochorial type as a major portion of a chorioallantoic placenta has been identified, this type has typically been deleted. Gosser's system became a guide for functional interpretations. Placentae having fewer numbers of layers were thought to be more efficient in interchange processes. Greater understanding of the complex nature of placental metabolism and transfer has largely dispelled that idea. The functional attributes of the placenta impact the rate at which interchange can occur; however, it is questionable whether the number of layers, or thickness, has much significance with regards to rate or efficiency of exchange. Although Gosser's system is a much battered concept, it continues to be used extensively.

Epitheliochorial placentation, observed in most hoofed mammals, moles, and lemurs, is achieved by development and growth of endometrial epithelium-lined crypts and chorioallantoic villi that fit into them. The two tissues,

Encyclopedia of Animal Science
DOI: 10.1081/E-EAS 120019750

Table 1 Classification of chorioallantoic placentae based primarily on their interhemal membranes

Epitheliochoral—3 maternal layers (epithelium, connective tissue, endothelium), 3 fetal layers (endothelium, mesenchyme, chorionic epithelium)
  Avillous (smooth chorioallantois)—extensive accessory areas in carnivores
  Villous
    Diffuse (often a very broad annulus)
      Simple villi—swine, American mole, hippopotamus, a few ruminants
      Complex villi—horses, whales, lemurs
    Cotyledonary or multiplex
      Polycotyledonary—cattle, goat, sheep, bison, antelope
      Oliocotyledonary—deer, elk, moose
Syndesmochorial—2 maternal layers (loss of epithelium), 3 fetal layers
  Unknown as the major portion of a chorioallantoic placenta
Endotheliochorial—1 maternal layer (loss of epithelium and connective tissue), 3 fetal layers
  Labyrinthine—carnivores, most bats, sloths, American anteaters
Hemochorial—maternal layers absent (except free blood), 3 fetal layers
  Labyrinthine
    Hemomonochorial—squirrels, guinea pig, chinchilla
    Hemodichorial—rabbits, beaver
    Hematrichorial—mice, rats
  Trabecular to villous
    Hemomonochorial—human, primates, and armadillos

fetal and maternal, cooperate in the process. An increase in thickness results from growth of both maternal and fetal tissues. The trophoblast and crypt epithelium usually have interdigitating cytoplasmic processes and microvilli. Both the trophoblast and epithelium become very thin locally where a maternal and fetal capillary are adjacent to one another, and trophoblastic cells (e.g., giant cells) may migrate into the uterine epithelium where they become functional cells of the endometrial cups.

Endotheliochorial placentation, such as that of carnivores and bats, typically starts with symplasmic degeneration of surface and crypt epithelium and penetration into this symplasma by chorioallantoic villi. The symplasma rapidly disappears. The trophoblast then engulfs the adjacent endometrial capillaries and becomes continuous with that of neighboring villi, thus forming a labyrinthine placenta containing maternal blood vessels lined by maternal endothelium. Further growth of both fetal and maternal tissues results in the typical thick endotheliochorial labyrinthine placenta.

Hemochorial labyrinthine placentation of superficially embedding species, such as rabbits and squirrels, starts much like that of endotheliochorial placentation. However, the endothelium of the subepithelial maternal capillaries soon ruptures, allowing the maternal blood to contact the trophoblast directly. The latter then differentiates an elaborate tubular system in which the maternal blood circulates. Invasion of the growing trophoblastic labyrinth by vascular mesodermal allantoic villi usually begins almost simultaneously with the development of the trophoblastic tubule system for maternal blood. Hemochorial villous placentation, such as that in anthropoids and primates, including humans, has a basic sequence similar to that just described, except that a greater area, two separate areas, or the entire chorion may be involved in providing the preplacental mass. A fairly well-developed circulatory system for maternal blood is formed in the preplacental trophoblast before allantoic villi appear. Placental thickening is the result of growth of the fetal trophoblast and mesodermal villi.

CLASSIFICATION BY SHAPE

Chorioallantoic placentae vary widely in shape, size, and general appearance. They have been described according to the final distribution of the chorionic villi over the endometrial surface of the fetal membranes (Fabricius, 1604, cited by Steven[3]). Fabricius recognized four main placental types, now known as Diffuse, Cotyledonary or multiplex, Zonary, and Discoid (Table 2).

In the diffuse placenta, most of the outer surface of the chorion is covered with small villi or folds, which lie in intimate contact with corresponding depressions or sulci in the uterine epithelium. This type of placenta is found in swine, peccaries, lemurs, llamas, hippopotamuses, camels, musk deer, American moles, pangolins, oriental and African Lorisidae, cetacean, and certain other mammals. The horse, a commonly cited example of this type, has also been classified as having a microcotyledonary placenta.

The cotyledonary, or multiplex placenta, is found in the majority of ruminants. The chorionic villi are restricted to a number of well-defined circular or oval areas of the chorionic sac, which are separated by less specialized areas of relatively smooth chorion. Fetal cotyledons develop normally only in those parts of the chorion overlying specialized areas of the uterus known as caruncles. Fetal cotyledons and uterine caruncles together form placental units known as placentomes. Familiar examples of this type of placentation are the cow, sheep, goat, deer, elk, moose, bison, buffalo, and giraffe.

The number of placentomes in cattle may vary from 40 to 150 (typically 80 to 100), whereas in the goat and giraffe typical ranges are 160 to 180, with a preponderance of functional placentomes occurring in the gravid horn. In sheep, the total number of placentomes varies

Table 2 Classification of chorioallantoic placentae based primarily on their shape

Diffuse (villous, epitheliochorial)	Llamas, camels, peccaries, horse (microcotyledonary; Equidae)
Multiplex or Cotyledonary (vilus epitheliochorial)	
Polycotyledonary	Cattle, bison (*Bovidae*)
Oliogocotyledonary	Deer, moose (*Cervus*)
Zonary or Annular	
Broad (villous, epitheliochorial)	
Complete (often called diffuse)	Swine (*Sus*)
Interrupted	Prairie mole (*Scalopus*)
Narrow (labyrinthine, endotheliochorial)	
Complete	Dog (*Canis*)
Interrupted	Raccoon (*Procyon*)
Discoid	
Pileate (labyrinthine, hemochorial)	Pocket gopher (*Geomys*)
Thick (labyrinthine, hemochorial)	Rat (*Rattus*)
Thick (trabecular, hemochorial)	Marmoset (*Oedipomides*)
Thick (villous, hemochorial)	Human (*Homo*)
Thick (labyrinthine, endotheliochorial)	Bear (*Ursus*)
Reniform (labyrinthine, hemochorial)	Beaver (*Castor*)
Spheroid (labyrinthine, hemochorial)	Agouti (*Dasyprocta*)
Double discoid (villous, hemochorial)	Macque (*Macaca*)
Double discoid (labyrinthine, endotheliochorial)	Mink (*Mustela*)

from about 60 to 100, with about equal distribution in both the gravid and nongravid horn. In contrast, typical numbers of placentomes in deer, moose, and reindeer are 4 to 8, usually with equal numbers in each uterine horn.

Three basic shapes of placentomes have been described—flat, convex, and concave. Flat placentomes are characteristic of pronghorn, duikers, gnu, and certain Cervidae such as the American elk, and may contain straight, slightly branched, or complexly branched villi. Convex placentomes are the most common and are characteristic of bovidae, giraffes, and many cervids. Concave placentomes are characteristic of sheep and goats. Convex and concave placentomes contain complexly branched or treelike villi. Cotyledonary placentomes generally have marginal folds of chorioallantois

covered with columnar phagocytic cytotrophoblast that apparently absorb secretions of large endometrial glands opening around the base of the caruncle. Invasive trophoblastic giant cells are common.

The zonary placenta is characteristic of the carnivores, although it is also found in quite unrelated groups. In this type, the chorionic villi, or lamellae, of the placental labyrinth are aggregated into a band of placental tissue that encircles the equatorial region of the chorionic sac. Such placental girdles may be complete, as in the dog, cat, and spotted hyena, or incomplete, as in the ferret, polar bear, brown bear, raccoon, mink, and certain Pinnipedia. Zonary placentae are also found in a limited number of noncarnivores such as the manatee and elephant.

Discoid placentae are the most localized of the placental types and are found in humans and other primates, rodents, and bats, among others.[4,5] The disk, or plate, may be single, as in humans, or double, as in the rhesus monkey.

CONCLUSIONS

The placenta is unique among mammalian organs for a number of reasons. Placentae of different species exhibit a broad diversity in structure that includes differences in cellular organization, shape, and pattern of distribution over the uterine endometrium. Placentae have been classified into three main types based on the number of layers separating maternal and fetal blood. Alternatively, placentae have been classified into four main types that relate to the degree to which the placenta is localized into a single discrete organ. Placentae differ greatly among species, yet all have the same task in maintaining and supporting embryonic and fetal growth, and appear to be equally successful in doing so.

REFERENCES

1. Mossman, H.W. *Vertebrate Fetal Membranes: Comparative Ontogeny and Morphology; Evolution; Phylogenetic Significance; Basic Functions; Research Opportunities*; Rutgers Univ. Press: New Brunswick, NJ, 1987.
2. Amaroso, E.C. Placentation. In *Marshall's Physiology of Reproduction*; Parkes, A.S., Ed.; Longmans, Green and Co.: New York, 1952; Vol. II, 127–311.
3. Steven, D.H. Anatomy of the Placental Barrier. In *Comparative Placentation*; Steven, D.H., Ed.; Academic Press: New York, 1975.
4. Rurak, D.W. Development and Function of the Placenta. In *Fetal Growth and Development*; Harding, R., Bocking, A.D., Eds.; Cambridge Univ. Press: Cambridge, 2001.
5. Ramsey, E.M. *The Placenta. Human and Animal*; Praeger Pubs.: New York, 1982.

Policy Issues: Local/State Land Use Regulation

Alyssa R. Dodd
Charles W. Abdalla
The Pennsylvania State University, University Park, Pennsylvania, U.S.A.

P

INTRODUCTION

Local land use regulation and planning is increasingly important as communities are challenged to manage population growth and residential and industrial development, and to preserve agricultural land and open spaces. Two growth trends are of increasing concern to rural communities: the accretion of urbanized areas at the fringes of rural lands and the increase in isolated, large-lot residential developments (one acre or more). Population growth is the main driver of urban sprawl. Between 1950 and 1990, U.S. population grew from 150 to 250 million. By 2050, it is expected to increase by 150 million. In the United States, local governments have primary responsibility for managing land use. This article introduces the role of government in land use regulation, describes the legal framework for the regulation of land, describes common land use controls, and highlights three land use policy issues related to agriculture: environmental impacts, nuisance impacts, and land preservation.

ROLE OF GOVERNMENT

No federal policy guides land use patterns. Although states have the legal authority to plan and regulate land use, only a few have implemented statewide planning systems.[2] State-level policies typically focus on broader land use patterns and issues. Examples include providing incentives to attract particular industries to the state and smart growth policies to curtail sprawl.[1]

In most states, primary responsibility for land use regulation and planning is delegated to local governments. They are responsible for protecting the public's health, safety, and welfare and play a major role in physical land use patterns.[2] Many utilize planning and regulatory tools to guide development and identify suitable locations for agricultural, residential, commercial, and industrial land uses.

LEGAL FRAMEWORK FOR LAND USE REGULATION

Three basic legal doctrines provide the framework for land use regulations in the United States—property rights, police power, and eminent domain. Property rights are often described as a bundle of rights that include the right to possess, use, sell, and subdivide property. Entitlements to extract minerals, cut timber, and consume water are also present. However, property rights are exclusive and limited. Some are reserved for the state, such as its right to tax the property or take it for public use.[2]

Land use controls utilize governments' police power—to legislate and regulate to protect the health, safety, and welfare of their citizens. Most states delegate these powers to local municipalities. Although some regulation is permitted, governments must balance public interest with landowners' interests and rights.[2]

Eminent domain is governments' power to take private property rights for public use. However, they cannot take these rights without just compensation. This state power is often delegated to local governments.[3] Eminent domain is important in planning, particularly in the acquisition of land to achieve land use goals. For example, it may be used to purchase easements for agricultural preservation.

LAND USE PLANNING

All states require at least some local land use planning.[1] Only some encourage or require local governments to pursue comprehensive planning, but communities usually are not required to follow these plans.[1] This may lead to undesirable patterns of land use, due to the fragmentation of local government responsibility among municipalities. For example, Michigan has approximately 1800 planning entities making these decisions with little intergovernmental coordination.[2]

Encyclopedia of Animal Science
DOI: 10.1081/E-EAS 120019754

LAND USE CONTROLS

Several planning tools and controls are available to guide development and identify suitable locations for various land uses. State-level zoning and enabling acts are often the primary tools to control land. However, other sources of power include: the state constitution, legislation that provides for home rule to distribute state power to local government, laws that authorize the exercise of police power by local government, or a doctrine of inherent powers that creates a political subdivision. Many states also have enabling acts that authorize land use controls in special situations such as floodplain zoning and historic districting.[3]

Zoning controls the location and separation of different land uses. Compatible uses such as commercial and residential may be zoned adjacent to each other. Incompatible uses such as industrial and residential may be separated to reduce potential conflicts. Zoning regulations also restrict the uses of specific parcels of land and control the intensity of development. These controls are implemented throughout the development process. Therefore, zoning plays a significant role in protecting natural and built environments, preserving property values, and managing growth.[3]

Subdivision regulation focuses primarily on residential development. These controls are implemented when one parcel of land is divided. These regulations have lasting impacts on the landscape and character of a community.[3]

Traditional land use controls, such as zoning and subdivision, do influence growth. However, local governments increasingly use management techniques, such as growth boundaries, to slow or stop growth.[3] Growth boundaries plan or mandate where urban development takes place.

Environmental land use controls aim to address development on sensitive land such as wetlands, coastal zones, floodplains, and wildlife habitat areas. Whereas various state and federal controls exist (such as the Clean Water Act), local governments are often responsible for their implementation. They are challenged to balance land development with present and future needs. For example, while a new residential development may increase the tax base, it may also strain the municipalities' drinking water supplies.[3]

State and local governments utilize aesthetic land use controls to preserve an area's beauty. For example, some have implemented billboard regulations to reduce the unsightliness of signage or require architectural design reviews. These controls regulate the appearance of structures to ensure their compatibility with surrounding areas and assess potential impact on neighboring property values.[3]

AGRICULTURE-RELATED LAND USE POLICY ISSUES

A policy issue occurs when public concern, debate, or conflict exists regarding the course of action a government, or others, should take to address a problem that affects all or a significant portion of the public. Individual land use decisions, such as building a high-density swine facility, become a policy issue when they affect others. Cumulative impacts of these decisions, such as farmers retiring and selling their land to residential developers, are common policy concerns. This section highlights three land use policy issues related to agriculture: environmental impacts, nuisance impacts, and land preservation.

Environmental Impacts

As the structure of agriculture changes, animal production facilities are increasing in scale. Larger numbers of confined animals are raised on fewer farms. More are clustering around feed mills and processing plants. These trends have led to growing public concern about the impact of agricultural land use on ground and surface water quality.[4]

Nationwide, the Clean Water Act addresses the potential water quality impacts of large-scale animal agriculture. Concentrated animal feeding operations (CAFOs) are required to obtain a National Pollutant Discharge Elimination System permit from the U.S. Environmental Protection Agency or the state government agency authorized to implement the CAFO permit program. Additionally, many states have clean streams laws, which prohibit the discharge of pollutants into surface waters. Some states have developed specific regulations to address agricultural water pollution.

Support for a statewide policy approach to address agricultural water pollution may be based on perceptions that consistent requirements across political boundaries are necessary to create a level playing field for agricultural producers. Perceptions that local government officials have limited knowledge of animal agriculture production practices may also build support for statewide requirements. Support for local control of agricultural land use may be based on perceptions that federal and state government efforts fall short of environmental performance goals for several reasons, including declining budgets; unfunded mandates; and a lack of agency monitoring, enforcement, and/or evaluation. In some cases, citizens view federal and state government intervention as onerous and unproductive, and believe individuals at the municipal level are better equipped to solve local environmental problems.[4]

Nuisance Impacts

Every state has passed some form of right-to-farm law. These laws encourage working agricultural lands, and typically aim to protect farmers from nuisance lawsuits filed by neighboring land owners.[5] A nuisance is an activity that unreasonably interferes with or disturbs a person's use and enjoyment of their own property.[6] Some right-to-farm laws restrict local governments from regulating generally accepted normal farming practices, which can be difficult to define. For example, is it normal to load animals onto trucks at midnight? This practice may cause harm to neighbors due to the truck and animal noises and spotlights.

To address growing public concern regarding the changing structure of agriculture and the impacts of odor, noise, light, and other nuisances on neighboring land owners, local governments are increasingly exercising their police powers. Zoning may separate agricultural from residential land uses. Additionally, some municipalities require specific minimum distances between residential and working farmlands to minimize potential conflicts. Problems arise when these controls are viewed as unfair or when agricultural land owners are economically burdened.

Farmland Preservation

Citizens and state and local leaders are concerned with the amount and location of land available for farming. Beyond the need for food production, the reasons for preservation include reducing the cost of infrastructure and amenities associated with providing open space.[7]

Special treatment of agricultural land is usually sought through traditional land use controls such as zoning and subdivision, with special modifications. For example, exclusive agricultural zoning, which does not allow any other uses, may be effective. However, while the goal—preserving farmland—is clear, problems may arise if farmers find the zoning too inflexible and economically unacceptable. Should farmers bare this cost so that the public may benefit from more farmland and open space?

CONCLUSION

While all states have some broad form of land use regulations, local governments are primarily responsible and have the largest impact on the landscape. Through planning and regulatory tools such as zoning, they will continue to exercise their powers to protect the public's health, safety, and welfare. In the future, local governments will continue to be challenged by increased growth, shifts in living patterns, trends in large-scale agriculture, and land use conflicts.

At this time, it is not known whether state and/or federal government will play a stronger role in land use regulation. Regardless, local governments will continue to face the four basic questions regarding land use policies:[8] What are the appropriate management goals? What is the role of government? Who should bear the cost of any management strategy? Who decides?

REFERENCES

1. Heimlich, R.E.; Anders, W.D. *Development at the Urban Fringe and Beyond: Impacts on Agriculture and Rural Land*; U.S. Department of Agriculture, Economic Research Service: Washington, DC, 2001.
2. Machemer, P.L.; Kaplowitz, M.D.; Edens, T.C. *Managing Growth and Addressing Urban Sprawl: An Overview*; Research Report; Michigan Agricultural Experiment Station, Michigan State University: East Lansing, MI, 1999; Vol. 562.
3. Juergensmeyer, J.C.; Roberts, T.E. *Land Use Planning and Control Law*; West Group: St. Paul, MN, 1998.
4. Land Use and Rural–Urban Interface Task Force of the Farm Foundation. *Land Use at the Rural–Urban Fringe*; Farm Foundation: Oak Brook, IL, 1997.
5. Prindle, A.M. State Level Farmland Protection Policy: History, Purpose, Approaches. Proceedings of the Performance of State Programs for Farmland Retention, Columbus, OH, September 10–11, 1998.
6. Andrews, G. Nuisance Law, Land Use Controls, and Environment Law Impacts on Pork Producers: A Legal Perspective. In *Industrialized Animal Agriculture, Environmental Quality, and Strategies for Collaborative Problem Solving and Conflict Resolution*; SRDC Number 208 SRIEG-10, Southern Regional Information Exchange Group-10: Knoxville, TN, 1997; Vol. 34.
7. Libby, L.W. Federal, State and Local Programs to Protect Farmland. Proceedings of What the Public Values About Farm and Ranch Land, Baltimore, MD, November 13–14, 2003.
8. Batie, S.S. Emerging Rural Environmental Issues. In *Increasing Understanding of Public Problems and Policies—1988*; Farm Foundation: Oak Brook, IL, 1998.

Policy Issues: Rural/Urban Community Effects

Jeff S. Sharp

The Ohio State University, Columbus, Ohio, U.S.A.

INTRODUCTION

Social conflict at the rural–urban interface is not new, but the increased scale of livestock production facilities and the geographic concentration of production in some regions of the United States have become headline news as communities and various levels of government seek to balance the needs of agriculture and the desires of local, nonfarm residents. As federal, state, and local governments struggle to develop policies to mitigate some of the social and environmental concerns associated with livestock production, some farmers are also attempting to develop positive social relations with nonfarm neighbors to allay some of the fears and annoyances. This article explores some of the challenges associated with livestock production at the rural–urban interface, beginning with background about some of the population and agricultural changes contributing to conflicts and then reviewing some of the impacts of large-scale livestock production facilities. The article also describes some of the policy and farmer responses aimed at mitigating the impacts and concerns associated with livestock development.

POPULATION AND AGRICULTURAL CHANGE

The population of rural and agricultural areas in the United States declined during much of the 20th century, in part due to agricultural mechanization and farm consolidation reducing the number of U.S. farms and the population residing on farms. Beginning in the 1970s, the historic trend of rural and nonmetropolitan decline reversed as many rural areas in the United States began to experience population growth, especially those regions located near urban population centers.[1] Employment opportunities in nonagricultural industries, improved transportation and communications, and a growing preference of urbanites and suburbanites for open space and rural living contributed to this population growth.[2] The loss of farmland has been one of the leading concerns associated with this pattern of population change,[1] but

perhaps a more serious concern for the livestock sector is the implication of increasing nonfarm development near or amidst livestock production.

Even as rural places have become attractive to nonfarm residents, the structure of agriculture has continued to evolve from a production system dominated by family farms to a system of increasingly large, market-oriented agribusinesses.[3] In the case of livestock production, one outcome has been the development of technologies and marketing systems that enable much larger production facilities. The development of confined animal feeding operations (CAFOs) in some communities and neighborhoods, the growing number of nonfarmers living in these open-country communities and neighborhoods, and the real or perceived negative impacts associated with CAFOs have all contributed to increasing conflict and debate concerning the permitting, regulating, and monitoring of livestock production facilities.

COMMUNITY IMPACTS AND RESPONSES

Two central community concerns associated with the existence and expansion of CAFOs are their environmental and economic impacts. In the case of the environment, the concentration of large numbers of livestock in relatively small geographic areas contributes to concerns about manure management, water quality, odor, and air quality.[4,5] Neighbor concerns about livestock odors, as they impact human health and quality of life, may be the most serious concern for the immediate neighborhood surrounding a large livestock operation, but scientific difficulties measuring and, in turn, regulating odor have limited the development of regulatory standards for managing it. As a result, much of the environmental concern about CAFOs focuses on water quality issues for which federal legislation, such as the Clean Water Act, and governmental agencies responsible for regulation and enforcement, such as the U.S. Environmental Protection Agency (EPA) and the U.S. Department of Agriculture (USDA), exist. In response to concern about the water quality and health impacts of CAFOs, the

Encyclopedia of Animal Science
DOI: 10.1081/E-EAS 120019756

Unified National Strategy was developed in 1999 to guide EPA and USDA efforts to improve existing federal CAFO rules. In December 2002, new federal rules for CAFOs aimed at improving and protecting water quality were released.

Whether the new federal rules fully address water quality and related environmental concerns of citizens and communities is yet to be known, but citizen perceptions of risk associated with odor, environmental quality, and quality of life will likely persist until the rules are perceived as effective. An additional tool available to communities to help minimize conflicts related to environmental concerns is the use of zoning in agricultural areas. Through local zoning, a community might establish rules identifying where a livestock production facility could be located or establish buffers of sufficient distance from residential areas to mitigate odor and water quality concerns.[4] Unfortunately, zoning of agricultural areas is not an option for local governments in many states because such zoning is not legally permitted in the counties, municipalities, or townships of the state. The existence of agriculture-specific zoning would enable a community to separate livestock agriculture from rural residential areas by designating the permissible areas for each activity in separate areas of the countryside. When the landscape was dominated by relatively small, diversified family farms, zoning may have seemed unneighborly and unnecessary, but as the landscape has become populated with fewer, more intensive farms next to large numbers of residences or areas that may be developed into nonfarm residences, zoning may be necessary to separate potentially incompatible land uses.

A second set of community concerns is the economic and fiscal impacts of these facilities on the community. There is some debate as to whether the economies of communities, regions, or states are better off with the replacement of small, family farm livestock operations by large livestock operations that may or may not be locally owned.[6] Specific concerns include questions about the number and quality of jobs created and the total net change in economic activity when several small livestock operations are replaced by a large one. Of course, a difficulty with these questions is that costs and benefits vary according to the level of analysis.[3] For instance, there may be a nationwide benefit to consumers that outweighs the costs to small farmers and rural communities. In response to some of these economic concerns, however, some states have implemented corporate farming laws to limit corporate involvement in farming to preserve family farming agriculture and communities. Also, increased concern about the local economic and fiscal impacts of large-scale livestock production has led some communities to more carefully weigh the potential benefits and costs before providing incentives or encouragement for this type of economic development.[5]

FARMER AND NEIGHBOR ADAPTATIONS

As should be apparent from the previous section, the various policies and policy tools available to local governments to manage some of the impacts of large-scale livestock are not well-developed in some states and localities. In addition, the effectiveness of some policies, such as the new federal environmental rules governing CAFOs, has yet to be fully understood. Further, because many conflicts related to livestock production are locality-specific with citizens requesting local action, the effectiveness of federal rules alone in quelling neighbor concerns may not be sufficient. As a result, one practical response to community concerns about livestock and other types of agricultural production in rural–urban interface settings is the use of neighboring activities to create positive rapport and facilitate communication between farmers and neighbors. Whereas neighboring activities by farmers, such as holding an open house, seeking out and meeting neighbors, or timing work to avoid conflicts with neighbor activities are unlikely to mitigate all possible concerns about odor, water quality, etc., these activities have been shown to reduce neighbor perceptions of annoyances and contribute to improved general attitudes toward local farmers.[7] Conflict resolution specialists have also observed that neighboring activities can be effective techniques for resolving conflicts instead of resorting to government or court action.[8]

CONCLUSION

To a large extent, changes in the structure of livestock production and the movement of nonfarmers into formerly rural and agricultural areas at the rural–urban interface have occurred independently. As concerns about the environmental, economic, and quality-of-life impacts of large-scale livestock have emerged at the national, state, and local level, it is apparent that future changes in the structure of livestock production will need increasingly to be sensitive to patterns of population settlement. The pattern of some livestock production locating to sparsely populated regions with reduced environmental regulation[9] may be an effective short-term strategy, but may have the long-term effect of increasing pressure at the national level for stricter environmental rules, as well as lead to greater delegation of power to local communities to manage and direct agricultural development in the communities, such as through zoning. Finding the proper balance between agricultural and residential interests may be difficult, but success or failure in finding that balance could have significant impacts on the future location of livestock production in North America and other regions of the world.[10]

REFERENCES

1. Johnson, K.M. The rural rebound. Rep. Am. **1999**, *1* (3), 1–20.
2. Audirac, I. Unsettled Views About the Fringe: Rural–Urban or Urban–Rural Frontiers? In *Contested Countryside: The Rural Urban Fringe in North America*; Furuseth, O.J., Lapping, M.B., Eds.; Ashgate Publishing Company: Brookfield, VT, 1999; 7–32.
3. Welsh, R. *The Industrial Reorganization of U.S. Agriculture: An Overview & Background Report*; Henry, A., Ed.; Wallace Institute for Alternative Agriculture: Greenbelt, MD, 1996.
4. Schwab, J. *Planning and Zoning for Concentrated Animal Feeding Operations*; American Planning Association: Washington, DC, 1998.
5. North Central Regional Center for Rural Development. *Bringing Home the Bacon*; The Kerr Center for Sustainable Agriculture: Poteau, OK, 1999.
6. Durrenberger, E.P.; Thu, K.M. The expansion of large scale hog farming in Iowa: The applicability of Goldschmidt's findings fifty years later. Human Org. **1996**, *55* (4), 409–415.
7. Sharp, J.S.; Smith, M.B. Social capital and farming at the rural–urban interface: The importance of nonfarmer and farmer relations. Agric. Syst. **2003**, *76*, 913–927.
8. Owen, L.; Howard, W.; Waldron, M. Conflicts over farming practices in Canada: The role of interactive conflict resolution approaches. J. Rural Stud. **2000**, *16*, 475–483.
9. Roe, B.; Irwin, E.G.; Sharp, J.S. Pigs in space: Modeling the spatial structure of hog production in traditional and nontraditional production regions. Am. J. Agric. Econ. **2002**, *84* (2), 259–278.
10. Blank, D.C. *The End of Agriculture in the American Portfolio*; Quorum Books: Westport, CT, 1998.

Pork: Carcass Composition and Quality

Jeffrey W. Savell
Jason M. Behrends
Texas A&M University, College Station, Texas, U.S.A.

INTRODUCTION

The pork industry continues to strive to improve the quality and palatability of pork. Composition and quality are important factors to take into account when evaluating pork carcasses. Quality can greatly affect the cost and value of pork carcasses indirectly, whether at the packing plant for export or in the local supermarket retail case. In addition, pork quality can be a determinant in consumer satisfaction. A large percentage of pork is sold in processed form (~75%), making quality and consistency extremely important to processors.

CARCASS COMPOSITION

Current market hogs continue to evolve; they are faster growing, leaner, heavier, and more muscular.[1] Stetzer and McKeith[2] reported that primary concerns about pork quality at the packing level included inconsistent weights, thin bellies, PSE (pale, soft, and exudative), too fat carcasses, and abscesses/injection sites. These concerns have been on the forefront of the industry's concerns for decades. According to Stetzer and McKeith,[2] there have been significant changes in composition of the average U.S. market hog. They reported that in the past ten years, backfat thickness has been reduced by 36% (from 27.5 to 17.6 mm), live weight has increased 4% (111.2 to 116.0 kg), and the percentage of muscle in the carcass has increased by 12% (from 49.5 to 55.5%).

The industry has struggled for years to properly segment carcasses into similar groups. The most accurate way to segment carcasses would be to rib the carcass, thus allowing a more accurate prediction of yield and quality. Regression equations have been studied to properly identify pork yield.[3,4] However, many of the factors that are used in these equations come from factors obtained only from ribbed carcasses. Despite the advantages of improved predictions, the cost and effort of ribbing pork carcasses at the current time are far greater than the industry is willing to sacrifice.

There is a trend to include compounds such as beta-agonists (phenethanolamines) to increase feed efficiency and increase muscle mass. These beta-agonists usually provide increased leanness, increased dressing percentage, improved feed utilization efficiency, and increased rate of weight gain.[5] Of the compounds, ractopamine (Paylean™) has been used based on acute metabolic responses and short-term growth responses in swine, thereby contributing to the previously mentioned beneficial factors. However, one of the major concerns with beta-agonists is meat palatability. Reducing fat in pork may lead to reduction of product quality and palatability. Compounds most extensively studied include clenbuterol, cimaterol, L-644,969, ractopamine, and salbutamol, which exhibit some degree of species specificity.[5] Ractopamine has been approved by the FDA for use in cattle and swine diets. Others have not been approved, although they are still effective in increasing carcass leanness.

Each pork packer has a specific value for carcasses. Many packers purchase hogs on an expected value of the pork carcass. Others utilize grid systems, which give premiums to those carcasses that are superior in trimness and have an average carcass weight. Systems can take many factors into account in order to assess the value of the carcass. These include systems based on cut-out value, percent lean, dressing percentage and live weight, and percent lean and carcass weight. Many packers use these systems as a tool to track the product back to the producer for carcass quality and composition improvement. With the ability of the packer to purchase the carcass on the rail, the packer is able to better assess the value of the carcass, giving those producers a premium for superior carcasses and a deduction for inferior carcasses.

MEAT QUALITY

Quality can greatly affect the cost and value of a pork carcass indirectly, whether at the packing plant for export or in your local supermarket retail case. With respect to quality, the best evaluation is one by direct observation of the characteristics in the loin eye muscle (m. longissimus thoracis) at the 10th rib. The loin eye should be slightly firm, have a slight amount of marbling (intramuscular fat), and be reddish pink in color for optimum quality.[6] In addition, subcutaneous fat should be firm. There should

Encyclopedia of Animal Science
DOI: 10.1081/E-EAS 120019758

be feathering (fat streaks) between the ribs when looking inside the thoracic cavity.[6]

Color may be the most important sensory attribute of food, and as such it, holds a preeminent position in overall pork quality. Color affects consumer judgment of sensory characteristics such as flavor, sweetness, and saltiness, as well as being an important predictor of nonsensory quality attributes such as moisture content and pigment color. Pale, soft, and exudative (PSE) meat is predominately found in pork, which has a reported incidence of 10%[7] and has recently been reported to be as high as 15.5%.[2] PSE pork is associated with an extremely rapid postmortem drop in muscle pH. PSE pork is characterized by a soft texture, a poor water-holding capacity, and pale color.[6] These conditions are caused by a rapid pH decline while the muscle temperature is still high. The looser muscle structure associated with a lower water-holding capacity results in a greater reflectance of incidental light and therefore a pale color. Water-holding capacity in pork is essential to the meat's economic benefits. The majority of the pork in the retail case today is injected with a solution, not only to enhance color, juiciness, flavor, and shelf stability, but also to increase weight of the product. If pork has low water-holding capacity, it is more difficult to get a high uptake in these processed products, thereby decreasing the value.

Moreover, PSE pork can also be related to genetics. Market hogs having high-stress conditions known as porcine stress syndrome (PSS) caused by the halothane gene produce carcasses with a high incidence of PSE pork.[6] In addition, rough handling increases PSE caused by the increase in lactic acid buildup immediately before slaughter.[8]

Solutions to solve pork quality problems continue to be a high priority in the industry. One technology that is being used is freeze chilling. Freeze chilling cools the carcass at a faster rate, slows muscle pH decline, lessens undesirable visual traits during retail display, lowers the incidence of PSE, and increases the amount of acceptable product for export. Pork carcasses are not as susceptible to thaw rigor as beef because of the increased fat on pork carcasses and their shortened time to rigor mortis. The lack of cold shortening in pork is due to the low content of red-fiber muscle.

Quality can greatly affect the end product of processed meats. As bacon production continues to increase, it is important to evaluate the trends in that sector of the industry. Bacon production is on the rise and continues to consume more of the retail case. Thicker bellies have a clear advantage when it comes to belly processing.[1] Despite these findings, it is clear that consumers visually prefer bacon produced from thinner bellies because of the appearance of less fat.[1] However, sensory evaluation found that consumers preferred bacon produced from thicker bellies versus bacon produced from thin bellies.[1] The industry must bridge the gap between production and consumption as pork bellies continue to get leaner and thinner.

Another important factor in pork quality is taint, which results from excessive concentrations of 5-alpha-androst-16-en-3-one (androstenone) and indoles, notably 3-mehylindole (skatole). Androstenone is a testicular steroid exhibiting a urine-like odor, and skatole is described as having a fecal-like odor.[9] Androstenone and skatole are often reported to be minimal in terms of the numbers of intact male pigs that have these traits. Most studies find that androstenone and skatole are major factors in boar taint. Boar taint is an unpleasant odor/flavor that can be perceived when cooking/eating the meat from some intact male pigs. Rius and Garcia-Regueiro[10] found that skatole and indole are accumulated mainly in adipose tissue, and the concentration of these compounds in the m. longissimus dorsi samples were lower than in the adipose tissue. The majority of male pigs in the United States are castrated, and therefore boar taint is not a major problem for the United States pork industry. However, the ability to identify these components of a carcass in those countries that slaughter intact males is of some concern.

CONCLUSION

There are many factors that affect pork composition and quality, but there is no single factor that can help ensure optimum pork quality. We must understand the biological basis of pork composition to help us understand how muscles work with different sources to produce the quality obtained. As consumer demand for pork increases, there is a greater push toward pork products of higher and more uniform quality. Improving the genetics of swine will continue to improve pork composition and quality, which will have a positive impact on future demand.

REFERENCES

1. Person, R.C.; Griffin, D.B.; Savell, J.W. Phase II. In *Benchmarking Value in the Pork Supply Chain—Quantitative Strategies and Opportunities to Improve Quantity*; Final Report—American Meat Science Association, 2003; 7–26.
2. Stetzer, A.J.; McKeith, F.K. Phase I. In *Benchmarking Value in the Pork Supply Chain—Quantitative Strategies and Opportunities to Improve Quantity*; Final Report—American Meat Science Association, 2003; 1–6.
3. Cross, H.R.; Smith, G.C.; Carpenter, Z.L.; Kotula, A.W. Relationship of carcass scores and measurements to five

endpoints for lean cut yields in barrow and gilt carcasses. J. Anim. Sci. **1975**, *41*, 1318–1326.

4. Edwards, R.L.; Smith, G.C.; Cross, H.R.; Carpenter, Z.L. Estimating lean in pork carcasses differing in backfat thickness. J. Anim. Sci. **1981**, *52*, 703–709.

5. Anderson, D.B.; Veenhuizen, E.L.; Jones, D.J.; Schroeder, A.L.; Hancock, D.L. The Use of Phenethanolamines to Reduce Fat and Increase Carcass Leanness in Meat Animals. In *Advances in Applied Biotechnology Series*; Library of Congress Cataloging in Publication Data, 1991; 12.

6. Savell, J.W.; Smith, G.C. *Laboratory Manual for Meat Science*, 7th Ed.; American Press: Boston, MA, 2000.

7. Meeker, D.; Sonka, S. *April 6. Pork Chain Quality Audit Progress Report*; American Meat Science Association, 1994.

8. Milligan, S.D.; Ramsey, C.B.; Miller, M.F.; Kaster, C.S.; Thomson, L.D. Resting of pigs and hot-fat trimming and accelerated chilling of carcasses to improve pork quality. J. Anim. Sci. **1998**, *76*, 74–86.

9. Bonneau, M.; Walstra, P.; Claudi-Madnussen, C.; Kempster, A.J.; Tornberg, E.; Fischer, K.; Diestre, A.; Siret, F.; Chevillon, P.; Clause, R.; Dijksterhuis, G.; Punter, P.; Matthews, K.R.; Agerhem, H.; Beague, M.P.; Olier, M.A.; Gispert, M.; Weiler, U.; von Seth, G.; Leask, H.; Font I Furnols, M.; Homer, D.B.; Cook, G.L. An international study on the importance of androstenone and skatole for boar taint: IV. Simulation studies on consumer dissatisfaction with entire male pork and the effect of sorting carcasses on the slaughter line, main conclusion and recommendation. Meat Sci. **2000**, *54*, 285–295.

10. Rius, M.A.; Garcia-Regueiro, J.A. Skatole and indole concentrations in longissimus dorsi and fat samples of pigs. Meat Sci. **2001**, *59*, 285–291.

Pork: Inspection/Processing/Marketing

Eric P. Berg
Chad A. Stahl
University of Missouri, Columbia, Missouri, U.S.A.

INTRODUCTION

The U.S. pork industry is an ever-changing entity consisting of many diverse constituents (producers, packers, wholesalers, retailers), yet it remains an enterprise driven by the single underlying principle of consumer demand. Given the hectic lifestyle of many of today's consumers, pork must be not only wholesome and safe, but also convenient, flavorful, and diverse. Therefore, animal and/or product inspection, further processing, and strategic marketing are each fundamental components of the pork industry and vital to its continued success.

INSPECTION

History

Early in history, people recognized the importance of obtaining meat from a wholesome source and the significance of proper processing techniques.[1] For example, early Mediterranean civilizations regulated and supervised slaughter and handling of meat animals.[2] It should therefore come as no surprise that the inspection process is currently regarded as an essential component in a long chain of concurrent events necessary to ensure the wholesomeness and safety of meat and meat products. United States legislation was passed in 1894 implementing a general meat inspection act for pork, yet it was not until June 1906 that the Federal Meat Inspection Act (required for all interstate and foreign commerce) was passed by the U.S. Congress. Sixty-one years and several amendments later (1967), the U.S. Congress established the Wholesome Meat Act (extending meat inspection to intrastate commerce) inevitably requiring that all meat and meat products destined for human consumption be inspected for safety and wholesomeness. More recently (1996), the Food Safety and Inspection Service of the U.S. Department of Agriculture (USDA) (the principle governmental agency designed to implement meat inspection laws) mandated that all meat-processing plants employ Pathogen Reduction and Hazard Analysis and Critical Control Point (HACCP) Systems in an attempt to diminish the incidence of physical, chemical, and biological contamination in/on meat and meat products. This mandate further fortified the safety and wholesomeness of the U.S. meat supply for both domestic and international (export) consumption.

Purpose

The purpose of inspection is to eliminate from the food supply all meat considered to be unsound, unhealthy, unwholesome, or unfit for human consumption. It is designed to: 1) protect the consumer; 2) give official assurance of wholesomeness and proper labeling; 3) detect and locate communicable diseases that may further contaminate the meat-animal population or endanger human health; and 4) minimize the presence of foodborne pathogens in meat and poultry.[3] Meat processors are required by law to utilize federal and/or state inspection systems (state inspection must be equal to or better than the federal inspection system) to ensure that the meat that passes in and out of their facility is wholesome and safe. However, facilities that choose to utilize state inspection systems are not permitted to sell and transport meat products across state lines.[4]

State and federal meat inspectors can be: 1) veterinary inspectors who have obtained a degree in Veterinary Medicine; or 2) lay inspectors (qualifications range from a high school education to food technologists with degrees from accredited universities) under the direct supervision of a veterinary inspector who has expertise in the anatomy, physiology, microbiology, and pathology of meat animals.[5] These inspectors have several responsibilities, including but not limited to: 1) facilities construction and operational sanitation; 2) antemortem (preharvest) inspection; 3) postmortem (meat and carcass) inspection; 4) product reinspection and manufacturing; 5) control of condemned product; 6) laboratory analysis; 7) marketing and labeling; 8) imported products; and 9) exotic animal inspection.[4]

Of these responsibilities, ante- and postmortem inspections are the most instrumental in preventing the sale and distribution of unwholesome or unfit product. Antemortem inspection involves the visual appraisal of livestock prior to harvest to identify animals unfit for entry into the meat supply. Animals suspected of a disease condition or

Encyclopedia of Animal Science
DOI: 10.1081/E-EAS 120019760

showing other conditions that may result in condemnation are retained and identified as "U.S. Suspect." If during the antemortem inspection an animal displays obvious symptoms of disease, the animal is identified as "U.S. Condemned."[5] Postmortem inspection involves the palpation and visual appraisal of several major lymph nodes and glands, internal organs, and other tissues. Carcasses fit for entry into the meat supply are identified as "U.S. Inspected and Passed," whereas those carcasses found to be unwholesome or unfit for human consumption are identified as "U.S. Inspected and Condemned" and eliminated from the human food chain. All condemned materials, parts, portions, organs or glands are to be: 1) rendered for inedible fats, greases, or oils; 2) made into animal feed or fertilizer (tankage); 3) destroyed by incineration; 4) chemically denatured; or 5) held at −10°F for five days and sold for animal feed.[3]

PROCESSING

Harvest

A large number of coordinated events must take place to successfully facilitate the conversion of a market hog into a safe and wholesome product. First and foremost, the animal must be humanely harvested in accordance with the Humane Slaughter Act of 1958 and the Humane Methods of Slaughter Act of 1978. Currently, the majority of market hogs sold in the United States are stunned (rendered unconscious and insensible to pain) via an electric stunning wand or by carbon dioxide anesthesia prior to exsanguination (bleeding), yet captive bolt stunners, compressed air concussion devices, and firearms are also approved stunning methods. Exsanguination is accomplished by making a small incision adjacent to the sternum, severing the carotid arteries, the jugular vein, and the anterior vena cava. This process is an essential step in the conversion of muscle to meat, altering the muscle's biochemical and physical properties and improving the keeping quality and acceptability of the product. Following exsanguination, the carcass is immersed in hot water (approximately 136–143°F), a process that converts the collagen that surrounds the hair follicle into gelatin so that the hair can be removed by either manual scraping or with a commercial dehairing machine.[3] Next, the head is removed at the atlas joint (in most instances), the bung is loosened, and the carcass is eviscerated. Evisceration consists of: 1) splitting the sternum and aitch bone; 2) loosening the gastrointestinal tract and liver; 3) cutting the diaphragm; and 4) removing the gastrointestinal tract, lungs, heart, and esophagus. The carcass is then split down the center of the vertebral column into two halves; trimmed of any blood clots,

bruises, or contaminated tissue; washed; inspected; and chilled in a cooler for approximately 24 hours.

Carcass Fabrication

The process of converting a pork carcass into closely trimmed wholesale and retail cuts (carcass fabrication) has evolved over time to respond to the ever-changing needs and wants of the consumer. It is important to note that although carcass fabrication has evolved, five basic meat-cutting principles have remained steadfast in the further processing of pork and other red meat species. These five meat-cutting principles are: 1) separate fat sections from lean sections; 2) separate tough sections from tender sections; 3) separate thick sections from thin sections; 4) separate valuable cuts from less valuable cuts; and 5) separate retail cuts by cutting across the grain, perpendicular to the predominant longitudinal orientation

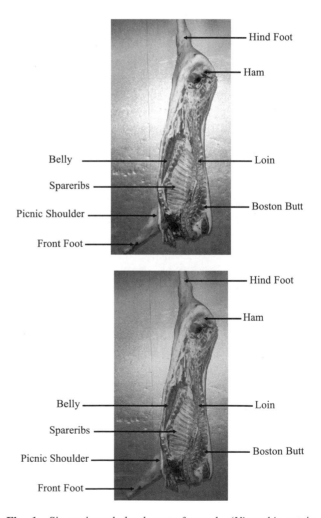

Fig. 1 Six major wholesale cuts for pork. (*View this art in color at www.dekker.com.*)

of muscle fibers within a given muscle to improve the palatability of the retail product.[3]

If processed in accordance with the appropriate industry guidelines—specifically, the Institutional Meat Purchasing Specifications (IMPS)—a pork carcass can be segmented into six major wholesale cuts (ham, loin, Boston butt, picnic shoulder, spareribs, and belly) as shown in Fig. 1. Of these wholesale cuts and their associated lean trimmings, pork can be further processed via a variety of innovative techniques to add value to an existing commodity. It is commonly accepted that 75% of the fresh pork carcass is further processed to add value to the final pork product. Such techniques consist of but are not limited to: deboning, cutting, grinding, chopping, emulsifying, pumping, curing, drying, and smoking.

MARKETING

Establishing a Market Value

The U.S. pork producer formerly marketed livestock on a live-weight basis, a concept that has all but vanished as packers shift to utilization of carcass merit pricing grids to establish an animal's monetary value. Currently, vast arrays of electronic grading equipment are at the disposal of the packer. These pieces of electronic carcass-grading equipment are capable of objectively measuring fat and muscle depth and predicting yield estimates for bone-in, closely trimmed retail cuts of the ham, loin, picnic shoulder, and Boston butt. Examples of carcass-grading equipment include but are not limited to the: 1) Fat-O-Meater (SFK; Peosta, IA); 2) UltraFOM 300 (SFK; Peosta, IA); 3) AutoFOM (SFK; Peosta, IA); 4) CVT1 with a 5049 transducer (Animal Ultrasound Services; Ithaca, NY); 5) CVT2 with a 5011 transducer (Animal Ultrasound Services; Ithaca, NY); and 6) Hennessy Optical Grading Probe (Hennessy; Auckland, NZ).

On April 2, 2001, the USDA Agriculture Marketing Service established the Livestock Mandatory Price Reporting System to ensure that market data be reported in an accurate and timely fashion to the public. The USDA Carlot report provides daily price information for various pork primal and subprimal cuts at different levels of bone-in or boneless status and various external fat-trim levels. Given that different pork-packing plants employ dissimilar cutting strategies and different electronic grading equipment, the USDA and Agriculture Marketing Service are continuously working on a statistically based method of standardizing data from specified pork carcass assessment equipment at a common end point, facilitating the consistent reporting of pork-pricing data.

Meeting Consumer Demands

Global meat consumption has and will continue to rise as the level of consumer affluence increases. Currently, pork has established itself as the international meat protein of choice, capturing more than 40% of the global market share. In an attempt to capture a greater share of the national and international consumer dollar, packers are now providing incentives to producers whose livestock meets the stringent demands of many niche and Asian markets. Additionally, a combination of sound scientific practices, further processed items, and innovative packaging systems now provide the consumer with many alternatives when selecting pork in the retail setting. Given that consumers currently demand a product that is both excellent and convenient, the pork industry has recently focused much of its research, product development, and marketing attention on precooked and microwavable items.

CONCLUSION

The U.S. pork industry can be proud of the products it produces. It is certainly one of the reasons that domestic and export demand has grown as it has. The pork industry has progressed very rapidly in response to consumer demand for lean pork that is safe, wholesome, convenient, and tasty. As a consequence, today's health-conscious consumer now perceives pork as a healthy, tasty, low-fat food staple.

REFERENCES

1. Aberle, E.D.; Forrest, J.C.; Gerrard, D.E.; Mills, E.W. Principles of Meat Science, 4th Ed.; Kendall/Hunt Publishing Co.: Dubuque, IA, 2001.
2. Hedrick, H.B.; Aberle, E.D.; Forrest, J.C.; Judge, M.D.; Merkel, R.A. Principles of Meat Science, 3rd Ed.; Kendall/ Hunt Publishing Co.: Dubuque, IA, 1994.
3. Savell, J.W.; Smith, G.C. Meat Science Laboratory Manual, 7th Ed.; American Press: Boston, MA, 2000.
4. Hale, D.S. Inspection. In Muscle Foods; Kinsman, D.M., Kotula, A.W., Breidenstein, B.C., Eds.; Chapman and Hall: New York, NY, 1994; 163–185.
5. Hale, D.S. Meat Inspection. In Facts #0413; NPPC: Des Moines, IA, 1997.

Poultry Meat: Carcass Composition and Characteristics

C. Z. Alvarado
L. D. Thompson
Texas Tech University, Lubbock, Texas, U.S.A.

INTRODUCTION

Poultry meat is defined as meat from chicken, turkey, duck, goose, guinea fowl, and pigeon. Poultry is the most consumed meat per capita in the United States, and it is one of the most consumed meats in the world. In 2002, turkey and chicken consumption has increased significantly from the early 1990s. One of the main reasons poultry meat consumption has increased in the last decade is the nutritional value of the meat. The fat in poultry meat is located in the skin and is therefore easily removable compared to other meats, enabling consumers to adopt a more low-fat type of meat in their diets. Along with this low-fat aspect, the fat in poultry meat is lower in saturated fatty acids and higher in unsaturated fatty acids. This fat deposition can vary among species and is diet-dependent. Therefore, poultry meat can easily be incorporated into a well-balanced diet to improve health.

CLASSIFICATION

Before a real understanding of the composition of poultry meat can be obtained, the classification of poultry should be discussed. In general, the market forms of poultry are based on age and weight. For ease of reference, only chickens and turkeys will be classified. Younger-type chickens include the Cornish hen (<4 weeks of age; >25% Cornish breed), broiler or fryer (6–8 weeks old; commercial chicken), roaster (8–10 weeks old; holiday bird), and the spent hen (>52 weeks of age; nonproducing layer). Turkeys are similar in the classification system, including the fryer turkey (9–16 weeks old; whole bird), roaster (16–24 weeks old; most common form), and the hen or tom turkey (>52 weeks of age; unproductive breeder birds).

PHYSICAL COMPOSITION

Yield is a method to measure profit for processors. Basically, yield is a percentage based on the amount of output divided by the amount of input. This percentage gives an estimate of efficiency to the processor. Processing efficiency, or ready-to-cook (RTC) yield, is the most popular method of determining profit for poultry processors and is based on carcass weight (output) and live weight (input). An average value for the RTC yield for processors is 70–75%, with some variation due to different processing standards from one company to another.[1] Of this 70–75% salable product, approximately 60% is meat and 40% is bone. Of this edible meat, approximately 60% is white meat and 40% is dark meat. Even though these numbers are just estimations, they are useful in determining salable product for processors.

In order for processors to obtain the highest price per carcass, the most valuable cuts should be a proportionally greater percentage of the whole carcass than the lower-priced cuts. In the United States, the most valuable meat on a poultry carcass is the breast meat. In order to maximize breast meat, processors use special genetic lines of broiler and turkeys. These genetic lines have been modified over the last several decades to increase profitability by improving feed-to-gain ratios and increasing breast meat yield. On average, breast meat accounts for 25% of the carcass, legs account for 33%, wings 14%, back and neck 17%, and giblets around 11% of the carcass weight.

COMPOSITION

Of the poultry meat species, chicken and turkey are probably the most popular species consumed in the United States. There are significant differences in meat characteristics and composition between the two. Turkey meat (skin on) is lower in fat than chicken meat (skin on), both of which are lower in fat than duck and goose meat (Table 1).

An attraction for most consumers is the leanness of chicken and turkey meat compared to red meat. Most of the fat in chicken and turkey is located in the skin, which can easily be removed. In chicken white meat, the fat is decreased from 11.1% to 1.6% with skin removal, and from 7.4% to 1.6% in turkey white meat (Table 1). However, the dark meat remains relatively higher in fat, even with the skin off. This high fat in the dark meat is due to

Encyclopedia of Animal Science
DOI: 10.1081/E-EAS 120019762

Table 1 Proximate composition and energy values of raw poultry meat from different avian species

Species	Meat type/skin	Moisture %	Protein %	Fat %	Ash %	Energy (kcal/100 g)
Chicken	Light, with skin	68.6	20.3	11.1	0.86	186
	Light, without skin	74.9	23.2	1.6	0.98	114
	Dark, with skin	65.4	16.7	18.3	0.76	237
	Dark, without skin	76.0	20.1	4.3	0.94	125
Turkey	Light, with skin	69.8	21.6	7.4	0.90	159
	Light, without skin	73.8	23.6	1.6	1.00	115
	Dark, with skin	71.1	18.9	8.8	0.86	160
	Dark, without skin	74.5	20.1	4.4	0.93	125
Duck, domesticated	All, with skin	48.5	11.5	39.3	0.68	404
	All, without skin	73.8	18.3	6.0	1.06	132
Goose, domesticated	All, with skin	49.7	15.9	33.6	0.87	371
	All, without skin	68.3	22.8	7.1	1.10	161

(From Ref. 2.)

Table 2 Composition and nutritional value of a 100-g edible portion of raw and cooked light chicken meat, with skin

Component	Raw	Roasted	Stewed	Batter-fried
Proximate				
Water, g	68.6	60.5	65.1	50.2
Protein, g	20.3	29.0	26.1	23.6
Fat, g	11.1	10.8	10.0	15.4
Carbohydrate, g	0.0	0.0	0.00	9.5
Ash, g	0.86	0.93	0.78	1.29
Energy, kcal	186	222	201	277
Minerals				
Calcium, mg	11	15	13	20
Iron, mg	0.79	1.14	0.98	1.26
Magnesium, mg	23	25	20	22
Phosphorus, mg	163	200	146	168
Potassium, mg	204	227	167	185
Sodium, mg	65	75	63	287
Zinc, mg	0.93	1.23	1.14	1.06
Copper, mg	0.04	0.053	0.044	0.061
Manganese, mg	0.018	0.018	0.018	0.055
Selenium, μg	16.4	24.1	21.2	27.2
Vitamins				
Vitamin C, mg	0.9	0.0	0.0	0.0
Thiamin, mg	0.059	0.060	0.041	0.133
Riboflavin, mg	0.086	0.118	0.112	0.147
Niacin, mg	8.908	11.134	6.935	9.156
Pantothenic acid, mg	0.794	0.926	0.535	0.794
Vitamin B6, mg	0.480	0.520	0.270	0.390
Folate, food, μg	4	3	3	6
Vitamin B12, μg	0.34	0.32	0.20	0.28
Vitamin A, IU	99	110	96	79
Vitamin E, mg	0.295	NA	0.265	NA
Lipids				
Saturated fatty acids, g	3.16	3.05	2.80	4.12
Monounsaturated, g	4.52	4.26	3.92	6.37
Polyunsaturated, g	2.34	2.31	2.12	3.60
Cholesterol, mg	67	84	74	84

NA = Data not available.
(From Ref. 2.)

Table 3 Composition and nutritional value of a 100-g edible portion of raw and roasted, light and dark turkey meat

Component	Light			Dark		
	Raw with skin	Roasted with skin	Roasted without skin	Raw with skin	Roasted with skin	Roasted without skin
Proximate						
Water, g	69.8	62.8	66.3	71.13	60.23	63.1
Protein, g	21.6	28.6	29.9	18.9	27.5	28.6
Fat, g	7.4	8.3	3.2	8.8	11.54	7.22
Carbohydrate, g	0.0	0.0	0.0	0.0	0.0	0.0
Ash, g	0.90	1.02	1.08	0.86	0.97	1.02
Energy, kcal	159	197	157	160	221	187
Minerals						
Calcium, mg	13	21	19	17	33	32
Iron, mg	1.21	1.41	1.35	1.69	2.27	2.33
Magnesium, mg	24	26	28	20	23	24
Phosphorus, mg	184	208	219	170	196	204
Potassium, mg	271	285	305	261	274	290
Sodium, mg	59	63	64	71	76	79
Zinc, mg	1.57	2.04	2.04	2.95	4.16	4.46
Copper, mg	0.075	0.048	0.042	0.137	0.023	0.023
Selenium, µg	22.4	29.1	32.1	26.4	37.8	40.9
Vitamins						
Vitamin C, mg	0.0	0.0	0.0	0.0	0.0	0.0
Thiamin, mg	0.056	.056	0.061	0.073	0.058	0.063
Riboflavin, mg	0.115	0.132	0.129	0.2002	0.235	0.248
Niacin, mg	5.137	6.289	6.838	2.855	3.53	3.649
Pantothenic acid, mg	0.615	0.626	0.667	1.033	1.160	1.286
Vitamin B6, mg	0.480	0.470	0.540	0.320	0.320	0.360
Folate, food, µg	7	6	6	10	9	9
Vitamin B12, µg	0.42	0.35	0.37	0.38	0.36	0.37
Vitamin A, IU	6	0	0	5	0	0
Vitamin E, mg	0.0141	0.134	0.09	NA	0.609	0.640
Lipids						
Saturated fatty acids, g	2.00	2.34	1.03	2.58	3.49	2.42
Monounsaturated, g	2.81	2.84	0.56	3.00	3.65	1.64
Polyunsaturated, g	1.73	2.01	0.86	2.28	3.09	2.16
Cholesterol, mg	65	76	69	72	89	85

NA = Data not available.
(From Ref. 2.)

intramuscular fat known as marbling, which is not removable. As a general rule, light meat is lower in fat and higher in protein than dark meat. This difference causes several implications for eating quality. Light meat tastes meatier because it has more meat flavor (protein) than savory flavor from fat. However, dark meat is higher in fat and has a stronger chicken flavor because most flavor compounds are located in the fat.

As the percentage of moisture increases in meat, the percentage of fat decreases. As the skin is removed from either the dark meat or the light meat, much of the fat is removed, and the moisture percentage then increases in both chicken and turkey (Table 1). Also, the higher the fat percentages in the meat, the higher the energy as measured by kcal/100 g. Therefore, as the skin

is removed, the total calories are reduced in both the light and dark chicken and turkey meat.

Poultry fat is less saturated than other animal fats. For this reason, it has a lower melting point and is less solid at room temperature compared to beef and pork fat. As an estimate, poultry meat with skin has 33% saturated fats compared to 42% in pork and 54% in beef. As for unsaturated fats (polyunsaturated and monounsaturated), poultry has 67% compared to 46% in beef and 58% in pork.[3] Tables 2 and 3 indicate the lipid content of chicken and turkey meat, respectively. Saturated fats are higher in raw chicken product when compared to raw turkey meat, both light and dark. In cooked products, however, the amount of saturated fats is really dependent upon cooking method. Since blood cholesterol levels have been associated with fats, many consumers are concerned with eating meat products. However, cholesterol in raw chicken breast is around 67 mg/100 g, whereas drumstick cholesterol is 77 mg/100 g. In turkey meat, similar results are observed in the breast, with 65 mg/100 g. However, the meat in turkey legs is higher in cholesterol (72 mg/ 100 g), which may be due to the excess intramuscular fat located in the legs. An important note is that cholesterol is found not only in fats, but also in plasma membranes surrounding the cells in lean meat. Therefore, it is not appropriate to refer to either chicken or turkey meat as lower in cholesterol than other meats.

Cooking method can affect the nutrient composition of poultry meat. Normally, water is the main component lost during cooking of poultry meat, along with some fat and collagen (heat labile). As water and some fat are lost during cooking, most of the other components of meat (protein, vitamins, and minerals) are concentrated. Tables 2 and 3 indicate the different types of cooking methods and the resulting nutrient components of chicken and turkey, respectively. Another note is that dark meat has more collagen. In younger animals, this collagen is heat labile and therefore melts during cooking. Since more collagen is lost from dark meat than from white meat, there is actually less protein in dark meat following cooking when compared to the raw product (Table 3).

A 100-g serving of roasted light chicken meat with skin is an excellent protein source, providing about 58% of the daily reference value (DRV) of protein. It also provides 17% of the RDV for fat, 15% of the RDV for saturated fat, and about one-quarter of the cholesterol allowed per day. Poultry meat is an excellent source of the minerals phosphorous and selenium and the vitamins niacin and B6, providing 20, 34, 56, and 26% of the recommended daily intake (RDI) for each nutrient, respectively.

CONCLUSION

The consumption of poultry meat, specifically chicken and turkey, has increased over the last several decades. This increase in consumption is attributable to the incorporation of poultry meat into a low-fat diet. Several factors allow poultry meat to be a leaner choice in meats, including easy removal of the skin and a higher ratio of unsaturated fats to saturated fats. With these characteristics of poultry meat, consumers are able to choose poultry meat to support a healthier lifestyle.

REFERENCES

1. Sams, A.R. Second Processing: Parts, Deboning and Portion Control. In *Poultry Meat Processing*; Sams, A.R., Ed.; CRC Press: Florida, 2001; 35–46.
2. http://www.eatchicken.com/statistics/consumption_pounds_60-02.cfm (accessed November 2003).
3. Barbut, S. Inspection, Grading, Cut Up and Composition. In *Poultry Products Processing, an Industry Guide*; Barbut, S., Ed.; CRC Press: Florida, 2002; 12–180.

Poultry Meat: Inspection/Grading

S. F. Bilgili
Auburn University, Auburn, Alabama, U.S.A.

INTRODUCTION

Consumers assume a safe food supply. The safety of meat and poultry products in the marketplace is assured by inspection activities of the Food Safety and Inspection Service (FSIS) of the U.S. Department of Agriculture (USDA). The inspection regulations and activities are designed to ensure that poultry are processed under sanitary conditions and that poultry products are wholesome, unadulterated, and properly labeled.

Grading, on the other hand, involves sorting inspected poultry and poultry products according to a set of quality characteristics. The Agricultural Marketing Service (AMS) of the USDA develops and implements the national grading standards and activities on a voluntary and fee basis. Although poultry can be graded based on individual company standards (i.e., plant grade), the use of USDA grade marks requires fee-based USDA grading services. Federal regulations and standards pertaining to the safety and quality of poultry and poultry products continue to evolve in parallel to the changing nature of poultry products and food safety concerns in the marketplace.

INSPECTION

Inspection laws and regulations pertaining to poultry were not enacted in the United States until the late 1900s because most of the poultry was produced by farmers on a small scale and sold, either live or dressed, at local markets. As poultry production and consumption increased during the last five decades, several agencies, acts, and programs were introduced by the federal government to define, regulate, and enforce inspection activities (Table 1). The Poultry Products Inspection Act of 1957 and Wholesome Poultry Products Act of 1968 basically laid out the foundation for the current poultry inspection system.[1] After the establishment of the FSIS, the inspection programs continued to evolve until 1996, when the landmark Pathogen Reduction and Hazard Analysis Critical Control Point (HACCP) System, a risk assessment-based inspection program to protect public health, was introduced.[2]

Food safety and inspection activities of the FSIS are administered through a national network of some 8000 veterinarians and inspectors. Inspection operations employees implement inspection laws in over 6000 meat and poultry plants in the United States and U.S. territories. Inspection activities of the FSIS to monitor and protect public health are:[3]

1. Ante- and postmortem inspection of poultry intended for human consumption.
2. Pathological, microbiological, and chemical analysis of poultry products for disease, infections, extraneous contaminations, drugs and other chemical residues, or any other adulteration.
3. Emergency response activities involving product retention, detention, or voluntary recall of products containing adulterants.
4. Epidemiological investigations of foodborne health hazards and disease outbreaks.
5. Public education and information programs to ensure safe handling of meat, poultry, and egg products.
6. Monitoring the effectiveness of state inspection programs to ensure equivalence to those under federal acts.
7. Implementation of cooperative food safety strategies to control hazards associated with animal production practices.
8. Monitoring foreign inspection systems and facilities that export products into the United States to ensure equivalence to national standards.
9. Inspection of imported meat and poultry products at the ports of entry into the United States.
10. Representation and coordination of inspection activities with various international health organizations, including Codex Alimentarius Commission.

In each official poultry processing facility, FSIS inspectors perform various specific tasks under the supervision of a veterinarian (inspector-in-charge). Specific in-plant inspection tasks involve: antemortem inspection of live poultry (segregation of diseased animals and separation of dead and dying animals prior to processing); postmortem inspection of poultry carcasses and internal organs (examination of internal and external

Encyclopedia of Animal Science
DOI: 10.1081/E-EAS 120019765

Table 1 History of poultry inspection and grading programs in the United States

Time	Event	Inspection program
Colonial	–	Rudimentary inspection
1924	NY Live Poultry Commission	Live poultry inspection in NY
1926	Federal Poultry Inspection Service	Inspection of NY-dressed[a] poultry
1938	USDA	Banning ''on-the-farm'' slaughter
1946	Agricultural Marketing Act	Initial grading standards
1957	Poultry Products Inspection Act	Mandatory federal inspection
1962	Talmadge-Aiken Act	State inspection programs
1968	Wholesome Poultry Products Act	Inspection of all poultry
1981	Food Safety and Inspection Service	Assumed inspection authority
1996	Pathogen reduction; HACCP ruling	HACCP and microbial testing

[a]Bled and picked poultry, without evisceration.
(Adapted from Ref. 1.)

surfaces of eviscerated carcasses and internal organs); condemnation, reinspection, and final disposition (segregation of carcass, carcass parts, or organs with signs of disease, extraneous contamination, or adulteration; and reinspection of salvaged product); sanitary slaughter and dressing (prevention of contamination of edible carcass components with digestive tract contents); chilling (prompt cooling of carcasses and their edible components, such as liver, heart, gizzard, and necks, where appropriate); plant sanitation [preoperational and operational cleaning and sanitation activities through the implementation of plant-specific Sanitation Standard Operating Procedures (SSOPs)]; residue monitoring (random screening of abdominal fat tissues for a number of potentially harmful chemicals); monitoring compliance with FSIS food safety performance standards (zero fecal contamination prior to chilling, E. coli and Salmonella testing); and verification of each plant's HACCP program.[3]

Postmortem Carcass Inspection and Disposition

By law, federal inspectors examine, bird-by-bird, the external and internal surfaces, carcasses, and organs after evisceration for signs of systemic disease conditions and/or adulterations that would make all or part of the carcass unfit for human food. Localized conditions on the carcass are removed and condemned. The criteria for causes of condemnation include:[4]

1. Tuberculosis: avian tuberculosis (TB), caused by *Mycobacterium avium,* is usually a chronic disease of birds. Avian TB has been eradicated in the United States and is rarely observed in mature birds.

2. Leukosis: this category comprises several neoplastic diseases that are caused by viruses. Marek's disease,

lymphoid leukosis, reticuloendotheliosis, and lymphoproliferative conditions cause tumors only in poultry.

3. Septicemia/toxemia: this is a general condemnation category for birds that exhibit gross signs of systemic disturbance. Carcasses condemned for this category are usually emaciated, dehydrated, and show brown discoloration of the coronary fat with pinpoint hemorrhages.

4. Airsacculitis: broad category of inflammation of the respiratory system (i.e., lungs and airsacs) of birds. Stressors during rearing and infectious agents such as *Mycoplasma*, *E. coli,* and *Chlamydia* are often isolated from affected organs.

Fig. 1 U.S. poultry inspection and grade-marks. (*View this art in color at www.dekker.com.*)

Table 2 Summary of specifications for A-quality ready-to-cook poultry

	A quality
Conformation:	Normal
Breastbone	Slight curve or dent
Back	Slight curve
Legs and wings	Normal
Fleshing:	Well fleshed, considering kind and class
Fat covering:	Well developed layer—specially between heavy feathers tracts

Defeathering:	Turkeys (feathers <3/4 in.)		Ducks and geese[a] (feathers <1/2 in.)		All other poultry (feathers <1/2 in.)	
Free of protruding feathers and hairs	Carcass	Parts	Carcass	Parts	Carcass	Parts
	4	2	8	4	4	2

Exposed flesh:[b]	Carcass		Large carcass parts[c] (halves, front and rear halves)		Other parts[c]
Weight range					
Minimum	Maximum	Breast and legs	Elsewhere	Breast and legs	Elsewhere	
None	2 lbs.	1/4 in.	1 in.	1/4 in.	1/2 in.	1/4 in.
Over 2 lbs.	6 lbs.	1/4 in.	1 1/2 in.	1/4 in.	3/4 in.	1/4 in.
Over 6 lbs.	16 lbs.	1/2 in.	2 in.	1/2 in.	1 in.	1/2 in.
Over 16 lbs.	None	1/2 in.	3 in.	1/2 in.	1 1/2 in.	1/2 in.

Discolorations: Carcass		Lightly shaded		Moderately shaded[d]	
		Breast and legs	Elsewhere	Hock of leg	Elsewhere
None	2 lbs.	3/4 in.	1 1/4 in.	1/4 in.	5/8 in.
Over 2 lbs.	6 lbs.	1 in.	2 in.	1/2 in.	1 in.
Over 6 lbs.	16 lbs.	1 1/2 in.	2 1/2 in.	3/4 in.	1 1/4 in.
Over 16 lbs.	None	2 in.	3 in.	1 in.	1 1/2 in.

Discolorations: Large carcass parts (halves, front and rear halves)		Lightly shaded		Moderately shaded[d]	
		Breast and legs	Elsewhere	Hock of leg	Elsewhere
None	2 lbs.	1/2 in.	1 in.	1/4 in.	1/2 in.
Over 2 lbs.	6 lbs.	3/4 in.	1 1/2 in.	3/8 in.	3/4 in.
Over 6 lbs.	16 lbs.	1 in.	2 in.	1/2 in.	1 in.
Over 16 lbs.	None	1 1/4 in.	2 1/2 in.	5/8 in.	1 1/4 in.

Discolorations: Other parts		Lightly shaded	Moderately shaded[d]
None	2 lbs.	1/2 in.	1/4 in.
Over 2 lbs.	6 lbs.	3/4 in.	3/8 in.
Over 6 lbs.	16 lbs.	1 in.	1/2 in.
Over 16 lbs.	None	1 1/4 in.	5/8 in.

Disjointed and broken bones:	Carcass—1 disjointed and no broken bones. Parts—thighs with back portion, legs, or leg quarters may have femur disjointed from the hip joint. Other parts—none.
Missing parts:	Wing tips and tail. In ducks and geese, the parts of the wing beyond the second joint may be removed if removed at the joint and both wings are so treated. Tail may be removed at the base.
Freezing defects:	Slight darkening on back and drumstick. Overall bright appearance. Occasional pockmarks due to drying. Occasional small areas of clear, pinkish, or reddish-colored ice.

[a]Hair or down is permitted on the carcass or part, provided the hair or down is less than 3/16 inch in length, and is scattered so that the carcass or part has a clean appearance, especially on the breast and legs.

[b]Maximum aggregate area of all exposed flesh. In addition, the carcass or part may have cuts or tears that do not expand or significantly expose flesh, provided the aggregate length of all such cuts and tears does not exceed a length tolerance equal to the permitted dimensions listed above.

[c]For all parts, trimming of skin along the edge is allowed, provided at least 75% of the normal skin cover associated with the part remains attached, and the remaining skin uniformly covers the outer surface and does not detract from the appearance of the part.

[d]Moderately shaded discolorations and discolorations due to flesh bruising are free of clots and limited to areas other than the breast and legs except for the area adjacent to the hock.

Source: From Ref. 7.

5. Synovitis: inflammation of the membranes lining joints and tendon sheets, usually caused by *Mycoplasma*. Reddened, inflamed, and swollen joints (primarily hock joint) with exudates are trimmed and condemned.

6. Cellulitis: inflammation of the subcutaneous tissues, usually due to introduction of *E.coli* through skin sores and scratches. If localized, the affected areas are trimmed. Those carcasses with diffuse lesions are condemned as a whole.

7. Tumors: carcasses with single squamous cell carcinomas, adenocarcinomas, lymphomas, or fibromas are usually trimmed. If there is evidence of metastasis, then the whole carcass is condemned.

8. Cadavers: poultry that die from causes other than slaughter are considered cadavers. Birds that die by slaughter typically have a bright, cherry-red appearance at the time they enter the scalder.

9. Overscalding: carcasses that are cooked in the scalder (usually due to a mechanical failure and line stoppage) are condemned as a whole.

10. Contamination: this category includes carcasses that are contaminated with extraneous materials (oil, paint, grease, etc.), those that cannot be inspected because of excessive contamination with digestive tract contents, and those carcasses that are mutilated by equipment.

In addition to these inspection activities, FSIS inspectors conduct prechill and postchill trim checks and carcass reinspections to make sure all carcasses meet national Finished Product Standards. Other inspection activities include monitoring plant SSOPs, HACCP implementation, and records;[5] verification activities; and corrective actions. Products fit for human consumption are allowed to carry the inspection logo, bearing the specific plant number (Fig. 1). Products found unsafe for human consumption are removed from the food chain. The FSIS uses several enforcement tools (warning letters, criminal prosecution, injunctions, withdrawal of inspection, and plant closing) when violations occur.

GRADING

Grading is defined as sorting or classifying whole poultry carcasses, parts, or further processed products according to various groups of quality characteristics.[6] These characteristics or standards provide a common language for buyers and sellers of poultry and poultry products. Through the application of uniform grading standards, the marketability of a particular product can be accomplished. Chickens, turkeys, ducks, geese, and pigeons are all eligible for grading services.

The Agricultural Marketing Service (AMS), a branch of the USDA, was authorized by legislation in 1946, driven primarily by military procurement programs for consistency in product specifications during World War II.[7] The AMS implements the federal grade standards and specifications used today on both voluntary and fee bases. Poultry products can carry an official grade mark only if grading is performed by an authorized USDA grader (Fig. 1). All poultry that is graded must first be inspected by the FSIS for wholesomeness. Quality standards are developed for a wide variety of products, including ready-to-cook (RTC) carcasses, parts, or further processed ready-to-eat entrees. RTC carcasses with processing defects (excessive feathers, skin lesions, or other trimmable defects, and those with remnants of internal organs) and with "off conditions" (slimy, putrid, or sour odors) are not graded and must be reworked. Standards of quality for RTC whole carcasses include conformation, fleshing, fat covering, exposed flesh, discolorations, disjointed or broken bones, feathers, and freezing defects (Table 2). In assessing these standards, the location, severity, and total aggregate area of each defect is taken into account. The final quality rating (A, B, or C) is based on the factor with the lowest rating.[8] Grading standards for boneless, skinless products (breast or thigh meat) include: presence of bones, tendons, cartilage, discolorations, blood clots, and other product-specific factors. Parts or components from lower-grade carcasses (i.e., B and C) may be upgraded (trimmed, deboned, portioned) to qualify as Grade A.

Because products vary in complexity and composition, customer procurement standards for further processed products may also include additional specifications. In such instances, USDA graders can include checks of class (species and age of the poultry), type (fresh or frozen), style (cut-up parts, whole muscle), metal detection, packaging integrity, labeling, net weights, portion control, temperatures, product formulations, fabrication, transportation, and storage condition. Commercial companies can also develop their own quality standards and specifications, for advertising and brand recognition. However, they will not be able to use a USDA grade mark on their products.

CONCLUSION

The poultry inspection and grading programs in the United States have evolved in parallel to the development and expansion of the modern, vertically integrated poultry industry. As new product forms (ready-to-cook and ready-to-eat) are introduced, markets (retail and grocery, fast-food, and export) are developed, and food-safety hazards (biological, physical, and chemical) are identified, the regulatory activities of the USDA will continue to change in the future.

REFERENCES

1. National Research Council. *Meat and Poultry Inspection: The Scientific Basis of the Nation's Program*; Food and Nutrition Board; National Academy Press: Washington, DC, 1985; 1–209.
2. United States Department of Agriculture. *Pathogen Reduction; Hazard Analysis and Critical Control Point (HACCP) Systems*; Final Rule; Food Safety and Inspection Service; Federal Register., 9 CFR Part 304, United States Printing Office: Washington, DC, 1996.
3. Bilgili, S.F. Poultry Meat Inspection and Grading. In *Poultry Meat Processing*, 1st Ed.; Sams, A.R., Ed.; CRC Press: Boca Raton, 2001; 47–71.
4. United States Department of Agriculture. *Poultry Postmortem Inspection*; Training Module 4, Parts 703C&904, Food Safety and Inspection Service: Washington, DC, 1999.
5. United States Department of Agriculture. *Sanitation*; 9 CFR Part 416, Food Safety and Inspection Service: Washington, DC, 1996.
6. Barbut, S. Inspection, Grading, Cut Up, and Composition. In *Poultry Products Processing: An Industry Guide*, 1st Ed.; Barbut, S., Ed.; CRC Press: Boca Raton, 2002; 129–179.
7. United States Department of Agriculture. *United States Classes, Standards, and Grades for Poultry*; Agricultural Marketing Service 2002. AMS 70.200 et seq.
8. United States Department of Agriculture. *Poultry Grading Manual*; Agriculture Handbook, Agricultural Marketing Service, 1998; Vol. 31.

Poultry Meat: Processing

Daniel L. Fletcher
University of Georgia, Athens, Georgia, U.S.A.

INTRODUCTION

On the most basic level, processing refers to the conversion of livestock to food. Although poultry were once marketed live for home slaughter and preparation, the modern industry is highly integrated, centralized, and an incredibly efficient converter of live poultry into a diverse array of consumer food products. For example, in a single day, a modern broiler processing plant can slaughter more than 250,000 birds, employ upward of 1500 people, use 2 million gallons of water, and produce over 15 tons of inedible by-products in order to produce almost a million pounds of saleable meat products. In the United States, the average consumer eats approximately 98 pounds of poultry meat (chicken and turkey) a year, compared to 119 pounds of red meat (beef and pork).

Poultry processing, or what is more commonly referred to as primary processing, is the series of steps that commences with the live bird and encompasses slaughter (killing of animals for food), evisceration, chilling, and marketing of whole, ready-to-cook carcasses. Further processing, or secondary processing, often refers to portioning of the carcass into parts and deboned meat through product formulation, further processing, and cooking.

A modern broiler processing plant is highly automated, with constantly evolving mechanization to reduce manual labor. Pronounced differences exist between plants in terms of how specific operations are accomplished. The following description is a composite of a generic plant, with the emphasis on the operations and not on how they are specifically performed.

HARVESTING

Processing begins with the removal of feed from the birds approximately 8 to 12 hours prior to slaughter. Feed withdrawal allows the bird time to void its intestinal tract and reduce the potential for gut breakage and contamination during evisceration. Feed withdrawal is closely monitored to optimize the emptying of the intestinal tract without excessive weight loss (live shrink).

After about four hours, the water is also removed, the equipment removed, the birds caught and placed in transport cages, and the cages placed on large trucks.

The birds are then transported to the processing plant to await unloading and slaughter. During holding at the farm or processing plant, fans and evaporative coolers are used to prevent overheating of the birds and to reduce heat stress mortality. In colder climates, truck covers may be used to reduce wind chill and cold stress. Table 1 summarizes the steps that are part of the harvesting and other poultry processing operations.

IMMOBILIZATION AND SLAUGHTER

The transport containers are removed from the trucks and the birds are unloaded onto a conveyor belt. From the conveyor belt, the birds are manually hung by the feet on high-speed shackle lines at the rate of approximately 140 to 180 birds per minute. Hanging is done in a low-light environment (to calm the birds) and care is exercised to reduce bird injury.

Almost immediately, the birds are electrically stunned to induce unconsciousness, reduce physical activity, and ensure humane slaughter. Gas stunning is also being used in some areas of the United States and in Europe. The neck is cut and the unconscious birds are allowed to bleed for approximately 90 seconds.

SCALDING AND PICKING

Following bleeding, the dead birds are submerged in hot water (scalding) to loosen feather attachment. Scald water is highly agitated to improve water penetration through the feathers, and scalding usually takes from one to two minutes. Immediately following scalding, the carcasses pass through a series of machines with high-speed rotating rubber fingers that remove the feathers. Care must be taken in adjusting the pickers to remove the feathers without damaging the underlying skin. Heads are usually removed immediately after picking.

TRANSFER

For hygienic reasons, the process from unloading through picking must be performed in a separate area of the plant

Encyclopedia of Animal Science
DOI: 10.1081/E-EAS 120019764

Table 1 Summary of poultry processing operations

Location	Area	Processing steps
Farm	Poultry house	Feed withdrawal
		Water withdrawal
		Catching
Transportation from farm to processing plant		
Processing plant	Live handling and immobilization	Holding sheds
		Unloading
		Shackling
	Slaughter	Stunning
		Killing (neck cut)
		Bleeding
		Scalding
		Picking
		Head removal
		Washing
		Hock removal and transfer to evisceration line
	Evisceration	Removal of preen gland (base of tail)
		Venting and opening cut
		Drawing of viscera
		INSPECTION (mandatory, USDA)
		Removal of viscera
		Giblet salvage (heart, liver, and gizzard)
		Removal of crop, trachea, and lungs
		Remove neck (to go with giblets)
		Bird washer
		Check station (look for processing errors)
		Carcasses transferred to chiller
	Chilling	Chill to below 40°F
		Removed from chiller and hung on shackles
	Packing and shipping	Sizing
		Grading (optional)
		Bulk packing
		Shipping or transfer for internal further processing
Further processing (packaging, cutting up, deboning, marinating, cooking, etc.)		
Distribution (direct distribution to outlets, warehousing, frozen storage, brokers, export)		
Marketing (grocery stores, restaurants and institutional outlets, further processing, export)		

from evisceration. Following picking, the carcasses are rinsed and then removed from the shackles by cutting the feet free at the hock joint. The carcasses are transferred to the evisceration area of the plant and rehung by the hock joint on the evisceration line.

EVISCERATION

Evisceration is essentially a disassembly of the carcass to separate the inedible portions from the edible portions of the carcass in a sanitary manner. This begins with the removal of the oil sac from the tail and venting (cutting) between the tail and around the cloaca

(commonly called the vent) to open into the abdominal cavity. The opening cut is then expanded to the posterior of the sternum (keel) and the viscera are pulled outside of the abdominal cavity, but are not detached prior to inspection.

Inspection is conducted by the USDA Food Safety and Inspection Service. The exterior, interior body cavity, and viscera of each bird are individually examined by an inspector to ensure safety and wholesomeness for human consumption. Carcasses are either passed as wholesome, trimmed or cleaned prior to passing inspection, or are condemned as unsuitable for consumption. In 1996, the inspection of poultry was enhanced by passage of what is commonly referred to as the Mega-Reg, which requires the application of Hazard Analyses, Critical Control Point (HACCP), and zero tolerance for fecal contamination to reduce the presence of human pathogens. The inspection process is currently being modernized to a more science-based system.

Following inspection, the viscera are removed. The edible viscera (giblets), including the heart, liver, and gizzard, are separated, cleaned, and chilled in a separate operation. In addition to the viscera, the lungs and trachea are also removed. The neck is removed and sent to be handled with the giblets. The carcasses are thoroughly washed inside and outside, and then checked to be sure that all inedible parts have been satisfactorily removed and there is no visible fecal contamination left on the carcass.

CHILLING

Regulations require that carcasses be rapidly chilled to below 40°F to inhibit bacterial growth. Most poultry in the United States are chilled in an ice and water bath for 45 minutes to 2 hours (immersion chilling). Since the carcasses are exposed directly to water, the USDA closely monitors water uptake. Nonimmersion, or air chilling, is commonly used in Europe and is being examined for use in the United States.

SIZING AND GRADING

As the birds exit the chiller, they are rehung on specialized shackles for weighing and sorting into lots by weight. Broilers are normally sold or further processed in designated weight categories to ensure size consistency and portion control in the final market products.

If carcasses are to be sold according to quality standards, they are generally graded at this point. Grading refers to the grouping of birds into lots with similar quality attributes. Grading can be done according to contract specifications or individual company standards, or it can be performed by the USDA Agricultural Marketing Service. Most grading standards for fresh poultry are related to processing errors resulting in broken bones, cut skin, missing parts, or discolorations that are sufficient to reduce the value of the product.

PRODUCT FORMS AND DISTRIBUTION

Traditionally, sized carcasses were marketed packed on ice in 60-pound boxes for distribution to retail outlets (grocery stores and meat markets) and food service establishments (restaurants). Carcasses were either packaged whole or cut up prior to packing for retail sales. As the market shifted from primarily a whole-bird market to a cut-up-and-further-processed market, how birds are handled following chilling has become highly variable and depends on each individual processing plant's product mix and marketing outlets.

In the early 1970s, approximately 55% of broilers were distributed as whole carcasses, 35% as cut up, and fewer than 10% further processed. Today, fewer than 10% are marketed whole, about 55% as cut up and deboned, and about 35% are further processed.

CUTTING, DEBONING, AND PACKAGING

Carcasses can be distributed whole, or the carcass can be cut up or "disassembled" into an array of possible products. Carcasses can be split (right and left halves), halved (front and back), or quartered. Often, the front half (light meat) is separated for further processing, while the rear half (dark meat) is marketed separately. Carcasses can be cut up according to specific cuts for distribution to restaurants and cooking processors. The meat can be removed from the carcasses and used as boneless, skinless raw products, or it can be further processed for food service or retail products. Raw parts can be individually prepackaged, labeled, and priced as case-ready products for immediate distribution and display in grocery stores.

FURTHER PROCESSING

Further processing generally refers to operations in which the basic commodity is cut, formulated, cooked, and/or packaged in such a way as to add value to the product. Further processing usually enhances convenience, perception of quality, and desirability to the consumer. Examples of further processing include portioning, marinating, flavoring, coating, packaging, cooking, freezing, and microwave products, to name a few.

WATER AND WASTE MANAGEMENT

Processing uses 5 to 10 gallons of water per bird, and many plants use upwards of 2 million gallons in a day. The combination of high water volume, high organic load (biochemical oxygen demand, or BOD), and waste material (blood, feathers, viscera, etc.) requires a sophisticated waste and wastewater management system. Environmental concerns relative to water and land pollution, as well as biological hazards, are consistently monitored.

CONCLUSION

Although the individual steps involved in processing poultry are not highly sophisticated, performing these operations at high speed, and in a humane and hygienic manner, is a major challenge. This is reflected in the highly technical nature of the industry's corporate structure. The current issues of food safety, animal welfare, worker conditions, environmental protection, and economics of food production are all important and must be considered when discussing the various operations involved in poultry processing.

REFERENCES

1. Barbut, S. *Poultry Products Processing*; CRC Press: Boca Raton, FL, 2002.
2. *Processing of Poultry*; Mead, G.C., Ed.; Chapman & Hall: London, 1989.
3. Mountney, G.J.; Parkhurst, C.R. *Poultry Products Technology*, 3rd Ed.; Food Products Press, Haworth Press Inc.: New York, U.S.A., 1995.
4. *Poultry-Meat Processing*; Sams, A.R., Ed.; CRC Press: Boca Raton, FL, 2001.
5. Stadelman, W.J.; Olson, V.M.; Shemwell, G.A.; Pach, S. *Egg and Poultry-Meat Processing*; Ellis Horwood Ltd: Chichester, UK, 1988.

Poultry Production: Manure and Wastewater Management

Saqib Mukhtar
Texas A&M University, College Station, Texas, U.S.A.

INTRODUCTION

Poultry production refers to raising chickens, turkeys, and ducks for meat and egg consumption. Due to the limited availability of data on duck production systems, manure and wastewater management for only chickens and turkeys is discussed in this article. Chickens raised for meat are called broilers, whereas the egg-laying hens are known as layers. Over the years, poultry production in the United States has increased steadily due to greater consumer demand for poultry products. As a result, manure production from poultry operations has also increased, despite efficient nutrition and breeding advances. Additionally, poultry operations have increased in size and are regionally concentrated. Although poultry manure constituents (nitrogen, phosphorus, and organic matter, etc.) provide natural fertilizer to plants and improve soil quality, proper manure management from poultry operations is key to reaping these benefits without adversely impacting air and water resources.

POULTRY MANURE CHARACTERISTICS

Manure with total solids (TS) of up to 4%, 4–10%, 10–20%, and more than 20% is categorized as liquid, slurry, semisolid, and solid manure, respectively.[1] Table 1 shows physicochemical properties of poultry manure.[2] As excreted, poultry manure with estimated TS content of 25% falls into the solid manure category. Other properties of excreted manure, such as total manure production and nitrogen (N), phosphorus (P), potassium (K), and volatile solids (VS), vary with type of poultry bird. For example, for the same live weight (445 kg or 1000 lb), broilers have the highest daily production of total manure, total solids (TS), VS, N, P, and K, whereas turkeys produce the lowest amount for all these properties.

Once excreted, poultry manure characteristics change further, depending on various manure management systems of collection, storage, transfer, treatment, and utilization. Depending on the type of manure management system, excreted manure may combine with feathers, spilled water and feed, process-generated wastewater (water for flushing gutters, etc.), bedding (sawdust, wood shavings, peanut hulls, etc.), and dead birds. As a result,

the properties of excreted manure differ not only within one species, but also among different types of poultry birds (Table 1). To understand these differences, a description of some poultry manure management systems is provided in the next section.

POULTRY MANURE MANAGEMENT SYSTEMS

U.S. Department of Agriculture (USDA) National Agricultural Statistics Service estimates show that from 1981 to 2001, the total number of broilers and turkeys increased by 100% and 59%, respectively.[3] Figure 1 illustrates typical poultry housing, and manure handling, storage, and disposal systems used in the United States. Solid manure is typically removed using mechanical scrapers and front-end loaders. Liquid and slurry manure is removed from the houses by pumping or by flushing with water. Poultry layer production houses containing caged birds are designed to handle manure as liquid, slurry, or solid. Liquid or slurry manure removal intervals may vary from daily to once-a-week flushing, but most layer houses may be flushed once a day for 20 minutes, using between 38 m^3 and 76 m^3 of flush water.[4] Manure from high-rise (elevated cages allowing manure removal with a tractor scraper) and belt scrape (manure removed by a belt system running under cages) houses may be handled as solid, liquid, or slurry, whereas manure from a shallow-pit layer house is handled as liquid or slurry. Liquid manure is generally flushed to a manure treatment anaerobic lagoon or a storage pond before it is land-applied as fertilizer, whereas slurry may be stored in an aboveground tank. Solid manure is generally removed once a year from the layer houses and directly applied to the land or stacked for long- or short-term storage (Fig. 1).

Broiler and turkey houses use bedding to absorb excreta and drinking water. Yearly, five to six broiler flocks and three turkey flocks are raised in poultry barns. Manure around drinkers, also known as cake, is relatively high in moisture, requiring more frequent removal (between each flock), while the remaining low-density manure pack known as clean out is generally removed once every year. The manure and bedding removed from broiler and turkey houses is known as

Encyclopedia of Animal Science
DOI: 10.1081/E-EAS 120023828

Table 1 Physicochemical properties of poultry manure

Component[a]	Layer[b]		Broiler		Turkey	
	As excreted	As removed	As excreted	As removed	As excreted	As removed
Moisture (%)	75	50	75	24	75	34
Weight (kg)	27.5	10.9	36.4	15.9	19.8	11.0
Total solids (kg)	6.9	5.5	9.1	12.0	5.0	7.3
Volatile solids (kg)	4.9	—	6.8	9.7	4.4	—
Nitrogen (kg)	0.38	0.19	0.5	0.31	0.34	0.40
Phosphorus (kg)	0.14	0.13	0.15	0.15	0.13	0.18
Potassium (kg)	0.15	0.14	0.21	0.18	0.13	0.20

—No data.

[a]Estimates based on 455 kg (1000 lb) live weight per day for all bird types.

[b]High-rise layer housing only. No bedding added to layer manure.

(Adopted from Ref. 2.)

litter. In some parts of the United States, a built-up litter-based system may be used for two to three years before a complete clean out. The litter is land-applied for fertilizing crops and pastures immediately after removal or is stored for later application.

As shown in Fig. 1, mortality from these poultry production systems may be handled using on-site incineration or composting (usually with litter as a co-composting material). The finished compost is then land-applied as fertilizer. Off-site disposal is accomplished through rendering. Burial of dead birds is prohibited in many states, but may be allowed if a large number of mortalities occur as a result of catastrophes.

POULTRY MANURE TREATMENT AND UTILIZATION

Most poultry manure is used for crop and pasture fertilization as a cost-effective alternative to inorganic mineral fertilizer. Land application also recycles nutrients, enhances soil fertility, and improves soil physical properties. However, a balance must be maintained between maximum utilization of nutrients by crops and the risk of health and environmental impacts. Proper managing of poultry manure—from its production through utilization—is the key to maintaining this balance. This includes proper design and siting of housing, manure storage, and mortality management facilities; and comprehensive nutrient management planning. Education and training of managers and operators of poultry production systems are essential for good manure management.

Manure and soils receiving manure should be tested for available nutrients before application. Application rates have typically been based on N requirements of crop. For soils testing high in P, manure application should be based

on the crop's P requirements. Manure application that exceeds a crop's ability to take up N may threaten water quality. Nitrogen as nitrate is a highly mobile compound that may cause human and animal health problems if drinking water concentrations are greater than 10 mg/l. Soil P enrichment occurs as a result of overfertilization with P. Phosphorus applied to fields as inorganic fertilizer or from manure can move into bodies of water through erosion and runoff events and can accelerate eutrophication (the natural aging process of lakes and streams), leading to excessive algae growth, oxygen deficiency, and fish mortality.

Some of the liquid or solid manure may be put to alternative uses, with or without undergoing a treatment process. Liquid manure from layer operations is sometimes stored and treated in anaerobic (oxygen-free) lagoons and further diluted with additional water, while anaerobic bacteria biodegrade volatile organic compounds. Part of the total solids in manure are settled as sludge at the lagoon bottom, while the supernatant (the liquid standing above suspended solids and sludge) can be recycled for flushing layer houses and irrigated as a source of nutrient and water for plants.

Liquid poultry manure may also be anaerobically digested in insulated, airtight containers (digesters) to produce biogas (methane and carbon dioxide). The methane gas produced with this treatment process is combustible and can be harvested to produce energy. This energy can be converted to electricity. The closed biogas digesters also control manure odors.

A small portion of the litter and straw, hay, or crop residue may be used as a carbon source for animal mortality composting, with the resulting compost used as fertilizer. In some parts of the United States, broiler litter or dried layer manure is used in the microbial mixture to supply nutrients for Agaricus mushrooms.[4]

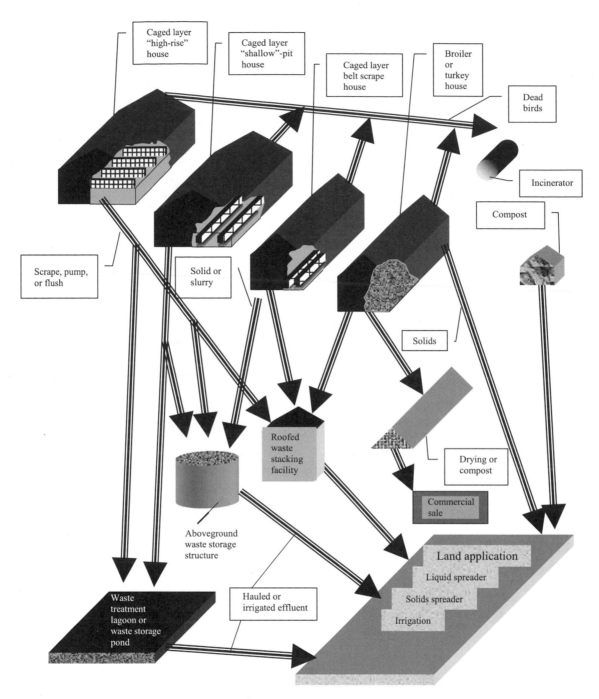

Fig. 1 Waste storage management and utilization options for poultry operations. (Adapted from USDA-NRCS Agricultural Waste Management Field Handbook, Part 651.) (*View this art in color at www.dekker.com.*)

Direct incineration of raw broiler litter with high ash content (soil and other incombustibles in the litter) in conventional furnaces has proven difficult due to incomplete combustion, slag formation, odor, gas, and particulate emissions to the environment. On a commercial scale, electric power generation plants in the United Kingdom are firing poultry litter as a furnace fuel to generate boiler steam. The ash produced from litter combustion is recovered and sold as nutrient-rich fertilizer.[5]

The feasibility of cofiring biomass (poultry litter and beef feedlot manure) with coal as a fuel for energy generation is currently being studied in the United States.[6,7] Preliminary results from small-scale boiler experiments show that blends of coal and biomass can be successfully fired, and that nitrogen oxide pollutant emissions were similar to or lower than those from firing coal only.

CONCLUSION

In the United Sates, poultry production operations have increased in size and are regionally concentrated. Poultry manure is managed as liquid or solid, depending on the manure management system and bird type. Therefore, physicochemical properties of poultry manure constituents (N, P, and K, etc.) vary from within species, and among bird types. When properly managed, poultry manure provides beneficial nutrients for plant growth, and improves soil quality without harming the natural environment. The majority of poultry manure and wastewater is land-applied as organic fertilizer. A small portion of poultry manure is treated or processed for alternative uses, such as biogas and compost for specialty crops. Incineration of litter to produce electricity is being carried out in the United Kingdom. Co-combustion of poultry litter with coal is currently being investigated.

REFERENCES

1. Lorimor, J.; Powers, W.; Sutton, A. *Manure Characteristics, MWPS-18, Section1*; Midwest Plan Service: Ames, IA, 2000; 1–23.
2. *Agricultural Waste Characteristics, Agricultural Waste Management Field Handbook, Part 651*; U.S. Department of Agriculture—Natural Resources Conservation Service: Washington, DC, 1992.
3. *Agricultural Charts and Maps*; U.S. Department of Agriculture—National Agricultural Statistics Service: Washington, DC, 2000. http://www.usda.gov/nass/aggraphs/graphics.htm (accessed October, 2003).
4. Collins, E.R., Jr.; Barker, J.C.; Carr, L.E.; Brodie, H.L.; Martin, J.H., Jr. *Poultry Waste Management Handbook*; Natural Resource, Agricultural, and Engineering Service: Ithaca, NY, 1999; 1–64.6. NRAES-132.
5. Fibrowatt Limited: London, United Kingdom. http://www.fibrowatt.com/UK-Corporate/index.html (accessed October 2003).
6. Sami, M.; Annamalai, K.; Woldridge, M. Co-firing of coal and biomass fuel blends. Prog. Energy Combust. Sci. J. **2001**, *27*, 171–214.
7. Annamalai, K.; Sweeten, J.; Mukhtar, S.; Thien, B.; Wei, G.; Piryadarsan, S.; Arumugam, S.; Heflin, K. *Co-Firing Coal: 2003. Feedlot and Litter Biomass (CFB and CLB) Fuels in Pulverized Fuel and Fixed Bed Burners*. Final Report Submitted to the U.S. Department of Energy. Grant number: DE-FG26-00NT40810.

Pregnancy: Maternal Response

Alan W. Bell
Cornell University, Ithaca, New York, U.S.A.

INTRODUCTION

Pregnancy imposes a metabolic burden on female mammals that increases with advancing gestation to a degree that is related directly to rate of conceptus growth scaled for maternal size. To accommodate the increasing nutrient demands of the fetus(es) and nonfetal conceptus tissues, the dam makes a series of coordinated metabolic adjustments in various nonuterine tissues to ensure that fetal nutrition is relatively unaffected by moderate variations in maternal nutrient intake. The homeorhetic regulation and coordination of these adaptations will be discussed. Most examples are from domestic ruminants but the general principles apply to other mammalian species.

METABOLIC ADAPTATIONS IN MATERNAL TISSUES

Glucose Metabolism

Some of the increase in hepatic gluconeogenesis in late-pregnant ruminants is due to increased voluntary feed intake.[1] However, intake is often constrained by physical factors such as diet quality and abdominal distension, as well as endocrine factors such as the surge in estrogen secretion in late pregnancy.[2] Under these or more controlled conditions of feed restriction, an increase in glucose production is sustained by increased peripheral mobilization and hepatic uptake of endogenous substrates such as amino acids from skeletal muscle and glycerol from the lipolysis of adipose triglycerides.[1,3]

Glucose utilization by muscle and adipose tissue tends to decrease during late pregnancy, especially if maternal energy intake is restricted or voluntarily declines. These tissues account for most of the approximately 20% of total glucose disposal that, in nonpregnant, nonlactating sheep, appears to be insulin-dependent. It is therefore likely that altered responses to insulin in these tissues largely account for the development of moderate insulin resistance in various parameters of whole-body glucose disposal in late-pregnant ewes.[1] This effect, which presumably mediates the so-called glucose-sparing effect of pregnancy, is exaggerated by moderate maternal undernutrition.

Mechanisms appear to involve reduced expression and, possibly, altered intracellular translocation, of the insulin-responsive glucose-transport protein, GLUT4, in muscle and adipose tissues.[4]

The increase in glucose availability created by the combination of increased hepatic production and reduced utilization in peripheral tissues is of advantage to the pregnant uterus, as well as to vital maternal tissues such as brain, because these tissues do not require insulin to facilitate the uptake and transport of glucose. Thus, a relatively normal supply of maternal glucose to the fetus can be sustained even if the dam is somewhat undernourished, especially if she has recourse to adequate lipid stores in adipose tissue.[5]

Lipid Metabolism

There is limited evidence that the lipogenic capacity of adipose tissue is enhanced during early midpregnancy in ruminants, possibly mediated by increased tissue response to insulin.[6] However, these observations are confounded in cattle by the overlapping of pregnancy and lactation, and in sheep by the possible influence of season on voluntary feed intake.[7] Even if there is not a specific enhancement of lipid synthesis and deposition during early pregnancy, there is no doubt that at this stage the well-fed animal can efficiently take advantage of adequate energy intake to deposit lipid stores in anticipation of the increased energy demands of late pregnancy and, especially, of early lactation.

During late pregnancy, adipose tissue becomes refractory to the lipogenic and antilipolytic influences of insulin and more sensitive to the lipolytic effects of adrenergic agents.[6] At least part of this increased propensity for fat mobilization is independent of energy intake and appears to be part of the regulated physiological prelude to lactation, but the general response is markedly exaggerated by maternal undernutrition.[7] In ruminants and pigs, at least, placental impermeability to nonesterified fatty acids (NEFA) prevents direct fetal access to this source of maternal stored energy. However, increased NEFA uptake and oxidation in maternal tissues allows the sparing of glucose for use in conceptus tissues as described previously.

Encyclopedia of Animal Science
DOI: 10.1081/E-EAS 120019768

Nitrogen Metabolism

Effects of pregnancy on maternal nitrogen metabolism have been less studied than those on carbohydrate and lipid supply and utilization. Increased predisposition to the mobilization of amino acids from skeletal muscle during late pregnancy can be inferred from measurements of tissue nitrogen balance in ewes.[8] This response may be permitted by the waning influences of insulin and other anabolic factors, including insulin-like growth factor 1 (IGF-1) as term approaches.[9] Coincidentally, hepatic protein synthesis is upregulated in dairy cows at a time when voluntary intake of dry matter and dietary protein is declining in the prepartum period.[10]

The dam also must dispose of the significant increase in products of nitrogen catabolism generated by conceptus tissues during late pregnancy. Fetal urea synthesis is substantial because of extensive oxidative deamination of amino acids in fetal liver and other tissues. This urea is efficiently transported by the placenta to the maternal circulation and adds directly to maternal urea destined for renal clearance and excretion. The placenta, which has little urea cycle enzyme activity, also deaminates amino acids to an extent that causes perceptible increases in maternal blood-ammonia concentrations and the need for hepatic detoxification.[3]

REGULATION AND COORDINATION OF METABOLIC ADAPTATIONS

Homeorhetic Regulation of Metabolic Adaptations to Pregnancy

The concept of homeorhesis as it applies to regulation of nutrient partitioning was elaborated by Bauman and Currie[11] and, more recently, Bauman.[12] Examples of homeorhetic regulation in pregnant animals have been reviewed previously.[1,4] Several pregnancy-related hormones, including progesterone, estradiol, and placental lactogen (PL) have been suggested as homeorhetic modulators of observed changes in tissue responses to insulin and catecholamines, and associated metabolic adaptations to the state of pregnancy in ruminants.[1] A more recently suggested candidate is leptin,[4] adipose tissue expression and plasma concentration of which increase markedly in ewes during midpregnancy, independent of nutrition and energy balance. These hormones and their proposed actions are listed in Table 1. None of these putative regulators has been shown to have the integrative, pleiotropic influences that growth hormone (GH) has in lactating ruminants.[12,13] Possibly, the combined influence of these hormones is more significant than their varying individual influences at different stages of pregnancy.

Among the sex steroids, estradiol-17β may contribute directly or indirectly to mediation of some metabolic adaptations, especially close to term when there is a pronounced surge in plasma estrogen concentrations. Treatment of ovariectomized ewes with estradiol caused a reduction in rates of adipose lipogenesis and fatty acid re-esterification. However, we were unable to discern any effect of a similar hormonal treatment on responses of glucose or NEFA metabolism in vivo to insulin or catecholamines, although basal plasma concentrations of glucose, NEFA, and glycerol were chronically elevated in treated animals.[3] Estradiol also may contribute indirectly to changes in lipid metabolism through its inhibitory effect on voluntary feed intake in late-pregnant ruminants.[2]

Definitive evidence of a homeorhetic role for PL remains elusive, but such a putative role is hard to dismiss,

Table 1 Possible homeorhetic hormones and their proposed actions on tissues during pregnancy

State	Hormone	Putative action	Tissue/response
Mid-pregnancy	Progesterone Leptin	↑ Insulin sensitivity	↑ Adipose glucose uptake ↑ Adipose lipogenesis
		↓ Catecholamine sensitivity	↓ Adipose lipolysis
Late pregnancy	Placental lactogen Estrogens	↓ Insulin sensitivity and responsiveness	↑ Liver gluconeogenesis ↓ Glucose uptake by adipose and muscle ↓ Adipose lipogenesis ↓ Muscle amino acid uptake and protein synthesis ↑ Muscle proteolysis
		↑ Catecholamine sensitivity and responsiveness	↑ Adipose lipolysis

as we have discussed elsewhere.[3] Indirect evidence for such a role includes its cross-reactivity with both GH and prolactin receptors in maternal ruminant tissues and its increased specific binding in a likely target, adipose tissue, as pregnancy advances. Cross-reactivity with the GH receptor would be consistent with the development of insulin resistance in adipose tissue since GH is a potent homeorhetic effector of this response in ruminant adipose tissue.[14] Also, moderate undernutrition enhances placental gene expression and secretion of PL in late-pregnant ewes, coincident with the decreased expression of GLUT-4 in maternal insulin-responsive tissues and exaggeration of indices of whole-body insulin resistance.[4]

The apparently pregnancy-specific increase in leptin expression and secretion by adipose tissue in sheep, together with increasing evidence that leptin modulates the metabolic actions of insulin in rodents, suggests that this peptide should be added to the list of putative homeorhetic effectors of metabolic adaptations to pregnancy. In addition, the abundant placental expression of the physiologically relevant OB-Rb form of the leptin receptor suggests that leptin may act as a direct signal of maternal energy balance to the placenta.[3]

Finally, it must be recognized that maternal adaptations to pregnancy do not occur independently from metabolic and endocrine development of the conceptus. The interplay and coordination of maternal and fetal influences is the focus of another contribution to this volume.

CONCLUSIONS

Pregnancy-induced adaptations in the metabolism of glucose, lipids, and, to a lesser extent, amino acids have been well described in ruminants and other domestic animals. These adaptations are mediated by altered responses in multiple tissues to homeostatic effectors such as insulin and catecholamines in a way that is coordinated to promote the availability of vital nutrients to the developing fetus(es). These phenomena are the hallmarks of homeorhetic regulation of nutrient partitioning in support of a chronic physiological imperative. However, the identity of the factor(s) responsible for homeorhetic modulation of metabolic adaptations to pregnancy remains to be elucidated.

ARTICLE OF FURTHER INTEREST

Female Reproduction: Maternal–Fetal Relationship, p. 408

REFERENCES

1. Bell, A.W.; Bauman, D.E. Adaptations of glucose metabolism during pregnancy and lactation. J. Mamm. Gland. Biol. Neopl. **1997**, *2* (3), 265–278.
2. Forbes, J.M. The Effects of Sex Hormones, Pregnancy, and Lactation on Digestion, Metabolism and Voluntary Intake. In *Control of Digestion and Metabolism in Ruminants*; Milligan, L.P., Grovum, W.L., Dobson, A., Eds.; Prentice-Hall: Englewood Cliffs, USA, 1986; 420–435.
3. Bell, A.W.; Ferrell, C.L.; Freetly, H.C. Pregnancy and Fetal Metabolism. In *Quantitative Aspects of Ruminant Digestion and Metabolism*, 2nd Ed.; Dijkstra, J., Forbes, J.M., France, J., Eds.; CABI Publishing: Wallingford, U.K., 2004. (in press).
4. Bell, A.W.; Ehrhardt, R.A. Regulation of Macronutrient Partitioning Between Maternal and Conceptus Tissues in the Pregnant Ruminant. In *Ruminant Physiology. Digestion, Metabolism, Growth and Reproduction*; Cronjé, P.B., Ed.; CABI Publishing: Wallingford, U.K., 2000; 275–293.
5. Bell, A.W. Pregnancy and Fetal Metabolism. In *Quantitative Aspects of Ruminant Digestion and Metabolism*; Forbes, J.M., France, J., Eds.; CAB International: Wallingford, U.K., 1993; 405–431.
6. Vernon, R.G.; Sasaki, S. Control of Responsiveness of Tissues to Hormones. In *Physiological Aspects of Digestion and Metabolism in Ruminants*; Tsuda, T., Sasaki, Y., Kawashima, R., Eds.; Academic Press: San Diego, 1991; 155–182.
7. Bell, A.W.; Bauman, D.E. Animal Models for the Study of Adipose Regulation in Pregnancy and Lactation. In *Nutrient Regulation During Pregnancy, Lactation, and Infant Growth*; Allen, L., King, J., Lönnerdal, B., Eds.; Plenum Press: New York, 1994; 71–84.
8. McNeill, D.M.; Slepetis, R.; Ehrhardt, R.A.; Smith, D.M.; Bell, A.W. Protein requirements of sheep in late pregnancy: Partitioning of nitrogen between gravid uterus and maternal tissues. J. Anim. Sci. **1997**, *75* (3), 809–816.
9. Bell, A.W.; Burhans, W.S.; Overton, T.R. Protein nutrition in late pregnancy, maternal protein reserves and lactation performance in dairy cows. Proc. Nutr. Soc. **2000**, *59* (1), 119–126.
10. Bell, A.W. Regulation of organic nutrient metabolism during transition from late pregnancy to early lactation. J. Anim. Sci. **1995**, *73* (9), 2804–2819.
11. Bauman, D.E.; Currie, W.B. Partitioning of nutrients during pregnancy and lactation: A review of mechanisms involving homeostasis and homeorhesis. J. Dairy Sci. **1980**, *63* (9), 1514–1529.
12. Bauman, D.E. Regulation of Nutrient Partitioning During Lactation: Homeostasis and Homeorhesis Revisited. In *Ruminant Physiology. Digestion, Metabolism, Growth and Reproduction*; Cronjé, P.B., Ed.; CABI Publishing: Wallingford, U.K., 2000; 311–328.
13. Bauman, D.E.; Vernon, R.G. Effects of exogenous bovine somatotropin on lactation. Annu. Rev. Nutr. **1993**, *13*, 437–461.
14. Etherton, T.D.; Bauman, D.E. Biology of somatotropin in growth and lactation of domestic animals. Physiol. Rev. **1998**, *78*, 745–761.

Pregnancy: Recognition/Signaling

M. P. Green
R. M. Roberts
University of Missouri, Columbia, Missouri, U.S.A.

INTRODUCTION

If a pregnancy is to be established successfully, a conceptus must signal its presence to the maternal system, which in turn must adjust her physiology to the needs of her developing offspring. This series of events is often termed maternal recognition of pregnancy (MRP). One crucial aspect of MRP in the domestic livestock species is that ovarian cyclicity must be interrupted and corpus luteum (CL) lifespan extended, although the embryo most likely makes its presence known to the mother well before it intervenes in events of the estrous cycle by releasing bioactive compounds "sensed" by local maternal tissues. However, embryo transfer can be completed successfully until quite late in development, suggesting that the very early signals are relatively unimportant to the long-term effects on pregnancy outcome.

CL MAINTENANCE

The timing and strength of embryonic signals probably allow the mother to evaluate the fitness of a conceptus and to terminate a pregnancy before investment is too high. Embryos that possess chromosomal abnormalities, that are developmentally stunted, or are suffering setbacks as the result of detrimental environmental and nutritional conditions in the uterus, are likely to be delayed in their development and to signal less than robustly to the mother.[1,2] Accordingly, deficient MRP signaling probably underpins much of the early embryonic loss that occurs in the first three weeks of pregnancy.

In early pregnancy, the CL is the major source of progesterone, a steroid hormone that acts on the endometrium to maintain it in a state whereby it remains receptive and provides nourishment to the embryo.[3,4] Two strategies are principally employed by conceptuses to avoid a return to cyclicity: the production of either a luteotrophic signal that promotes CL growth and activity or an antiluteolytic signal that protects the CL.[3] There are examples, e.g., dogs and marsupials, where no intervention is needed because the duration of pregnancy corresponds to the length of the luteal phase of the estrous cycle. The estrous cycles of livestock are short compared to pregnancy so that CL rescue is required.[2,5,6]

In all livestock, luteolysis is initiated by prostaglandin $F_{2\alpha}$ ($PGF_{2\alpha}$) produced in the endometrium (the lining of the uterus) toward the end of the cycle.[7] $PGF_{2\alpha}$ reaches the ovary via maternal blood, and, by mechanisms still not completely clear, causes the structural and functional demise of the progesterone-producing luteal cells. In some species, oxytocin has a role in initiating $PGF_{2\alpha}$ release from the endometrium.[7] Conceptuses ensure CL lifespan extension by either intervening in the production and/or release of $PGF_{2\alpha}$, counteracting its actions at the level of the ovary, or by a combination of strategies.[3,9]

BOVIDAE (CATTLE, SHEEP, GOAT, AND THEIR RELATIVES)

In these species, the trophectoderm (outer) cells of the conceptus begin to produce an antiluteolytic protein factor called interferon-tau (IFN-τ) at the blastocyst stage of development. Synthesis becomes maximal as the conceptus elongates in the period immediately preceding attachment of trophectoderm to the uterine wall.[5]

The progenitor IFN-τ gene duplicated from an IFN-ω gene approximately 36 million years ago (MYA). As a consequence, this gene family is unique to the Ruminantia suborder.[9] IFN-τ is expressed prior to the release of luteolytic pulses of $PGF_{2\alpha}$ from the endometrium[10] and abrogates $PGF_{2\alpha}$ release by downregulating transcription of the estrogen and oxytocin receptor genes in the uterine endometrium.[4,6,8,10] IFN-τ may simultaneously promote production of prostaglandin E_2 (PGE_2), which has a luteotrophic rather than luteolytic action on the CL and exerts a local immunosuppressive action at the maternal–conceptus interface.[5]

CAMELIDS

The camelids (camels, llamas and alpacas) diverged from the lineage leading to the true ruminant species at least

Encyclopedia of Animal Science
DOI: 10.1081/E-EAS 120019766

40 MYA.[9] The female camel is a seasonal breeder and only ovulates in response to mating. The CL develops within a few days, functionally plateaus around day 8–9 postcoitum, and then promptly regresses.[11] Thus the conceptus must initiate its signal within about a week of conception if the pregnancy is to be maintained. In nonpregnant dromedary camels, basal concentrations of $PGF_{2\alpha}$ rise and progesterone levels fall after day 8 of the cycle, thereby implicating $PGF_{2\alpha}$ as the luteolytic factor, although oxytocin appears not to be involved. The nature of the antiluteolytic signal remains unknown, but it is almost certainly not IFN-τ.

SUIDAE (PIGS AND THEIR RELATIVES)

The pig lineage diverged earlier than the camelids, about 55 MYA.[9] $PGF_{2\alpha}$ is central to the luteolytic process and can be used pharmacologically to regress pig CL to induce estrus.[3] Although pig conceptuses produce at least two forms of IFN (IFN-γ and IFN-δ), these appear not to be important in counteracting $PGF_{2\alpha}$ but probably have a local effect on the maternal immune system.[2] Instead, the unattached elongating porcine conceptuses produce large amounts of estrogen beginning about day 10 of pregnancy.[2] Estrogen increases endometrial receptors for prolactin, which cause the uterine epithelial cells to redirect their release of $PGF_{2\alpha}$ into the uterine lumen rather than basolaterally into the maternal vasculature toward the ovary and CL. Consequently, estrogen injections on days 11 to 15 of the cycle can induce a prolonged pseudopregnancy.[5] PGE_2 is also produced and may act as a luteoprotective/luteotrophic agent.[2] Doubts remain, however, as to whether the estrogen-based mechanism is the sole mechanism that prevents luteolysis in the pig.[12]

EQUIDS (HORSES AND THEIR RELATIVES)

The horse lineage diverged from the pig lineage about 80 MYA.[9] PGs synthesized by the early conceptus induce the muscular contractions that propel it from the oviduct into the uterus. The equine conceptus is unusual in that it expands spherically rather than elongating and does not assume a stationary position in the uterus until about day 18.[13] Prior to this stage, it migrates through the uterine lumen 12 to 14 times a day. Endometrial $PGF_{2\alpha}$ is the trigger for luteolysis, but there is no firm evidence for either production of an IFN or a luteoprotective role of estrogen.[13] PGE_2 production by the conceptus and uterus increases during this period and may play a role in CL maintenance. If the migration of the conceptus through the uterine lumen is physically prevented, the CL is not protected. Thus, intrauterine migration of the conceptus and possibly its direct contact with the uterine epithelium of both uterine horns is directly implicated in the suppression of luteolytic pulses of $PGF_{2\alpha}$.

APPLICATIONS AND IMPLICATIONS

The compounds responsible for MRP have the potential ability to safeguard pregnancies that are at risk. Intramuscular injections of IFN improved lambing rates and the numbers of lambs born in flocks where fertility was low, but were unhelpful in beef cattle.[14] On the other hand, IFN-τ was successful in increasing pregnancy rates after asynchronous embryo transfers in red deer.[15] Consequently, boosting the MRP signal may be useful in rescuing developmentally normal, but otherwise delayed, embryos of intra- or interspecies pregnancies for the purpose of saving endangered species or in producing hybrid or cloned animals. Finally, factors produced by the early placenta and released into the maternal bloodstream have the potential to be used as pregnancy tests.[16]

CONCLUSIONS

The production of $PGF_{2\alpha}$ by the endometrium toward the end of the estrous cycle causes the CL to regress. In pregnancy, CL lifespan is extended due to the release of conceptus factors that prevent luteolysis. In short, establishment of pregnancy depends on the ability of the conceptus to elicit a signal and of the mother to respond appropriately. This process remains poorly understood and differs across species. In a few species, biologically relevant active factors released by the conceptus have been identified, while in others they remain unknown (Table 1).

Because multiple signals undoubtedly pass between the conceptus and the mother, maternal responses are dynamic and complex. Those MRP signals that ensure

Table 1 Summary of MRP signals and the days of recognition in domestic species

Species	Days of recognition	Main signal(s)
Cattle	14–17	IFN-τ
Sheep	12–15	IFN-τ
Camels	7–8[a]	Unknown
Pigs	11–14	Estrogen and prolactin
Horses	12–14	Estrogen[a]

[a]Assumed.

extension of CL lifespan, although crucial to continuance of the pregnancy, are only the beginning of a sequence of endocrine, paracrine, and autocrine signals that direct changes in maternal physiology and ensure a successful pregnancy.

REFERENCES

1. Goff, A.K. Embryonic signals and survival. Reprod. Domest. Anim. **2002**, *37*, 133–139.

2. Bowen, J.A.; Burghardt, R.C. Cellular mechanisms of implantation in domestic farm animals. Cell Dev. Biol. **2000**, *11*, 93–104.

3. Thatcher, W.W.; Bazer, F.W.; Sharp, D.C.; Roberts, R.M. Interrelationship between uterus and conceptus to maintain corpus luteum function in early pregnancy: Sheep, cattle, pigs and horses. J. Anim. Sci. **1986**, *62* (Suppl. 2), 25–46.

4. Spencer, T.E.; Bazer, F.W. Biology of progesterone action during pregnancy recognition and maintenance of pregnancy. Front. Biosci. **2002**, *7*, D1879–D1898.

5. Roberts, R.M.; Xie, S.-C.; Mathialagan, N. Maternal recognition of pregnancy. Biol. Reprod. **1996**, *54* (2), 294–302.

6. Flint, A.P.F. Interferon, the oxytocin receptor and the maternal recognition of pregnancy in ruminants and non-ruminants: A comparative approach. Reprod. Fertil. Dev. **1995**, *7* (3), 313–318.

7. McCracken, J.A.; Custer, E.E.; Lamsa, J.C. Luteolysis: A neuroendocrine-mediated event. Physiol. Rev. **1999**, *79* (2), 264–323.

8. Mann, G.E.; Lamming, G.E.; Robinson, R.S.; Wathes, D.C. The regulation of interferon-τ production and uterine hormone receptors during early pregnancy. J. Reprod. Fertil. Suppl. **1999**, *54*, 317–328.

9. Roberts, R.M.; Ealy, A.D.; Alexenko, A.P.; Han, C.-S.; Ezashi, T. Trophoblast interferons. Placenta **1999**, *20*, 259–264.

10. Roberts, R.M.; Ezashi, T.; Rosenfeld, C.S.; Ealy, A.D.; Kubisch, H.M. The interferon-τ: Evolution of the genes and their promoters, and maternal-trophoblast interactions in control of their expression. Reprod., Suppl. **2003**, *61*, 239–251.

11. Skidmore, L.; Adams, G.P. *Recent Advances in Camelid Reproduction*; Intl. Vet. Info. Service: Ithaca, NY, 2000.

12. Zeicik, A.J. Old, new and the newest concepts of inhibition of luteolysis during early pregnancy in the pig. Domest. Anim. Endocrinol. **2002**, *23*, 265–275.

13. Allen, W.R.; Stewart, F. Equine placentation. Reprod. Fertil. Dev. **2001**, *13* (7–8), 623–634.

14. Barros, C.M.; Newton, G.R.; Thatcher, W.W.; Drost, M.; Plante, C.; Hansen, P.J. The effect of bovine interferon-1 on pregnancy rate in heifers. J. Anim. Sci. **1992**, *70* (5), 1471–1477.

15. Demmers, K.J.; Jabbour, H.N.; Deakin, D.W.; Flint, A.P.F. Production of interferon by red deer (*Cervis elaphus*) conceptuses and the effects of ρIFN-τ on the timing of luteolysis and the success of asynchronous embryo transfer. J. Reprod. Fertil. **2000**, *118* (2), 387–395.

16. Humbolt, P. Use of pregnancy specific proteins and progesterone assays to monitor pregnancy and determine the timing, frequencies and sources of embryonic mortality in ruminants. Theriogenology **2001**, *56*, 1417–1433.

Probiotics

Stanley E. Gilliland
Oklahoma State University, Stillwater, Oklahoma, U.S.A.

INTRODUCTION

The use of probiotics (also referred to as direct-fed microbials) in relation to feed supplements for animals was initiated in approximately 1974, although the suggestion for the use of such bacteria for the human diet dates much earlier. In the early 1900s, Eli Metchnikoff advocated that humans should consume milk fermented with lactobacilli in order to displace the undesirable microorganisms that may occur in the intestinal tract. Since the 1970s many feed supplements have been marketed as sources of probiotics. Unfortunately, in the late 1970s many of these products contained few, if any, viable probiotic bacteria. Thus, many reports in which probiotics were evaluated provided no conclusive evidence about their efficacy. This was in part due to low viability of the microorganism in the products and was further complicated by the fact that the probiotic bacteria, especially the lactobacilli, exhibit host-specificity, which was not considered. For example, one strain of *Lactobacillus* isolated from one animal species is not expected to function well in another animal species.

POTENTIAL BENEFITS

Interest in the use of probiotics as livestock feed supplements is largely due to a concern over use of subtherapeutic levels of antibiotics in the livestock rations. The earliest potential benefit advocated for using probiotic bacteria in the human diet was to exert control over intestinal flora. It is assumed that the same type of relationship would occur in animals. Thus the primary potential benefit of probiotics is to control intestinal infections in the livestock. Some properly selected probiotic bacteria can also increase nutrient utilization by providing enzymes in the gut capable of converting certain components of the diet into more easily used nutrients for the host animal. Some studies have suggested the possibility of feeding selected probiotic bacteria to produce certain changes in the body composition of the animals or their products such as altering the lipid composition. The specific function of probiotics may be different depending on the host animal and, more important, on the characteristics of the probiotic. Viability of the probiotic at the time of consumption is considered very important. However, the viability in feed supplements may be low.[1]

BACTERIAL SPECIES INVOLVED

Lactobacillus is the genus that contains most of the bacteria considered for use as probiotics for animals. Included in this genus as potential probiotics are *Lactobacillus acidophilus, Lactobacillus casei, Lactobacillus fermentum*, and *Lactobacillus reuteri*. Species of *Bifidobacterium*, as well as species of *Propionibacterium*, have also been tested and proposed as probiotics for certain animals. Other species of microorganisms having potential include *Streptococcus faecalis* and species of *Bacillus*. These groups of microorganisms represent the major ones that have been observed in the scientific literature related to probiotics for livestock. It is very important to remember that one particular strain of one species of a given bacterial genus should not be expected to function in all species of animal or to provide all of the potential benefits for those animals.[3] Selection of the individual strains within species to be used is thus extremely important.

PROBIOTICS FOR POULTRY

The most widely studied livestock species with respect to the use of probiotics is poultry. Much of the attention in this area has been focused on the control of salmonella in chickens. Properly selected cultures of probiotics (such as *Lactobacillus* species) can overcome those lactobacilli found in the natural flora of the birds and exert inhibitory action toward salmonella in the intestinal tract of chickens.[5] Another approach has been to culture the intestinal bacterial flora from a healthy chicken and to use this preparation to inoculate one-day-old chicks in order to establish a healthy normal flora, which helps control salmonella. The problem with this approach is possible lack of consistency in the organisms making up the preparation from one batch to another. Some refer to the use of probiotics in poultry to control pathogens as competitive exclusion. However, the mechanism by

Encyclopedia of Animal Science
DOI: 10.1081/E-EAS 120019772

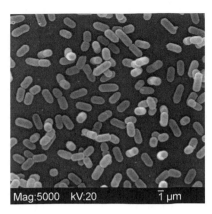

Fig. 1 *Lactobacillus acidophilus* NPC 747 is effective in reducing the frequency of occurrence of *Escherichia coli* O157:H7 in feedlot cattle.

which probiotic preparations are able to inhibit intestinal pathogens in poultry and in other animals has not been clearly defined. With regard to nutrition and growth, feeding a selected culture of *L. acidophilus* to laying hens increased egg production and feed conversion, and reduced the cholesterol level in the egg yolks.[6]

PROBIOTICS FOR SWINE

There is interest in the swine industry to find ways to control salmonella and/or other pathogens during the feeding phase.[7] Not much scientific research has been reported on this with regard to the potential for using probiotic cultures. However, feeding a mixture of *B. pseudolongum* and *L. acidophilus* to piglets decreased the frequency of mortality.[8] In the same report these probiotic organisms also increased the weight gain of the piglets. Lactobacilli are very prevalent in the duodenum, jejunum, and ileum of healthy piglets; they thus represent a part of the natural flora.[9] Feeding a culture of *L. acidophilus* selected for amylase activity to weaning-age piglets on a high-starch diet resulted in increased growth and feed efficiency.[10] Currently, efforts are underway to establish whether or not a selective culture of *L. acidophilus* would exert inhibitory action on salmonella in pigs.

PROBIOTICS FOR CATTLE

A major benefit of feeding *L. acidophilus* NPC 747 (Fig. 1) to cattle has been a significant reduction in the frequency of occurrence of *Escherichia coli* O157:H7 in feedlot cattle.[11] This is considered a very important intervention step in the feedlot cattle industry to reduce the occurrence of this pathogen on fresh meat. Probiotics, including

L. acidophilus NPC 747, have also been shown to increase daily gain and feed efficiency in feedlot cattle.[4] Feeding a mixture of selected cultures of *Propionibacterium* and *E. faecium* resulted in a trend toward reduced acidosis in feedlot cattle.[12] Feeding dairy cattle a probiotic containing *E. faecium* plus a yeast culture resulted in increased milk yield.[13] Other studies also indicate that feeding selected cultures of *L. acidophilus* resulted in increased milk yield in dairy cattle. The exact mechanism of the benefits provided by the probiotics in improving feed efficiency, growth, and milk production has not been determined.

PROBIOTICS FOR OTHER ANIMAL SPECIES

Not much appears in the scientific literature concerning the evaluation of probiotics for other animal species. Whereas there may be probiotic products available today for horses, fish, dogs, and cats, very little scientific research has been published on their efficacy. For those products that are available, host specificity may not have been considered and carefully controlled experiments to evaluate them are lacking.

CONCLUSIONS

Probiotics have the potential to provide a number of benefits for livestock as well as companion animals. One strain of one species of a bacterial culture should not, however, be expected to provide all benefits. The major group of bacteria considered for use as probiotics are in the genus *Lactobacillus*. There are many naturally occurring variations in relative functional ability among strains of each individual species within this genus. The same is true for other genera of the lactic acid bacteria. Thus, strains to be used for probiotics should be carefully selected for the ability to provide the desired benefit in the host animal. Host specificity is also very important for probiotics whose benefits require that they be able to grow and function in the intestinal tract. Probiotics should be tolerant to bile and to other material, such as stomach acids, in the digestive system. To be successfully marketed they should be easy to grow in commercial culture production facilities. Additionally, probiotics must be able to survive production, processing, storage, and delivery to the animal.

REFERENCES

1. Fuller, R. History and Development of Probiotics. In *Probiotics the Scientific Basis*, 1st Ed.; Chapman & Hall: New York, 1992; 1–8.

2. Gilliland, S.E. Enumeration and identification of lactobacilli in feed supplements marketed as sources of *Lactobacillus acidophilus*. Animal Science Research Report. Okla. Agric. Exp. Sta. MP **1981**, *108*, 192–193.

3. Gilliland, S.E. Health and nutritional benefits from lactic acid bacteria. FEMS Microbiol. Rev. **1990**, *87* (1), 175–188.

4. Krehbiel, C.R.; Rust, S.R.; Zhang, G.; Gilliland, S.E. Bacterial direct-fed microbials in ruminant diets; performance response and mode of action. J. Anim. Sci. **2003**, *81* (E. Suppl. 2), E120–E132.

5. Pascual, M.; Hugas, M.; Badiola, J.I.; Monfort, J.M.; Garriga, M. Lactobacillus salivarius CTC2197 prevents *Salmonella enteritidis* colonization in chickens. Appl. Environ. Microbiol. **1999**, *65* (11), 4981–4986.

6. Haddadin, M.S.Y.; Abdubralim, S.M.; Hashlamoun, E.A.R.; Robinson, R.K. The effect of *Lactobacillus acidophilus* on the production and chemical composition of hen's eggs. Poultry Sci. **2003**, *75* (4), 491–494.

7. Cromwell, S. Antimicrobial and Promicrobial Agents. In *Swine Nutrition*, 2nd Ed.; CRC Press: Boca Raton, FL, 2001; 401–426.

8. Abe, F.; Ishibashi, N.; Shimamura, S. Effect of administration of bifidobacteria and lactic acid bacteria to newborn calves and piglets. J. Dairy Sci. **1995**, *78* (12), 2838–2846.

9. Rojas, M.; Conway, P.L. Colonization by lactobacilli of piglet intestinal mucus. J. Appl. Bacteriol. **1996**, *81* (5), 474–480.

10. Lee, H.S.; Gilliland, S.E.; Carter, S. Amylolytic cultures of *Lactobacillus acidophilus*: Potential probiotics to improve dietary starch utilization. J. Food Sci. **2001**, *66* (2), 338–344.

11. Brashears, M.M.; Galyean, M.L.; Loneragan, G.H.; Mann, J.E.; Killinger-Mann, K. Prevalence of *Escherichia coli* O157:H7 and performance by beef feedlot cattle given *Lactobacillus* direct-fed microbials. J. Food Prot. **2003**, *66* (5), 748–754.

12. Ghorbani, G.R.; Morgavi, D.P.; Beauchemin, K.A.; Leedle, J.A.Z. Effects of bacterial direct-fed microbials on ruminal fermentation, blood variables, and the microbial populations of feedlot cattle. J. Anim. Sci. **2002**, *80* (7), 1977–1985.

13. Nocek, J.E.; Kautz, W.P.; Leedle, J.A.Z.; Block, E. Direct-fed microbial supplementation on the performance of dairy cattle during the transition period. J. Dairy Sci. **2003**, *86* (1), 331–335.

Proteins

Guoyao Wu
Jon Tate Self
Texas A&M University, College Station, Texas, U.S.A.

INTRODUCTION

Proteins are macromolecules consisting of one or more polypeptide chains synthesized from amino acids. A peptide may contain approximately 40 to more than 400 α-amino acids. The word protein originated from the Greek "proteios," meaning prime or primary. This is very appropriate, since proteins are the most fundamental component of animal tissues. Proteins play important roles in the body, including their roles in enzyme-catalyzed reactions, muscle contraction, hormone-mediated effects, cell structure, immune response, oxygen storage and transport, nutrition, metabolic regulation, and gene expression. The balance between protein synthesis and degradation determines whether a tissue grows or atrophies. Thus, knowledge of protein biochemistry and nutrition is of enormous importance for both animal agriculture and medicine.

PROTEIN STRUCTURE AND PROPERTIES

Amino acid residues in protein are linked by peptide bonds (–CO–NH–). There are four orders of protein structure:[1] primary structure (the sequence of amino acids along the polypeptide chain); secondary structure (the conformation of the polypeptide backbone); tertiary structure (the three-dimensional arrangement of protein); and quaternary structure (the spatial arrangement of polypeptide subunits). The forces stabilizing polypeptide aggregates are hydrogen and electrostatic bonds between amino acid residues.

Proteins can be classified according to their overall shape (globular or fibrous), solubility in water (hydrophobic or hydrophilic), three-dimensional structure, or biologic function (Table 1). For example, albumin and hemoglobin are globular proteins. Fibrous proteins include collagens, elastin, α-keratins (wool and hair), and β-keratins (the feathers, skin, beaks, and scales of most birds and reptiles). Collagens are rich in proline and glycine (approximately 1/3 each), and constitute approximately 30% of total proteins in animals. Keratins are rich in cysteine; wool protein contains approximately 4% sulfur.

All proteins can be denatured by heat, acids, bases, alcohols, urea, and salts of heavy metals. The suscepti-bility of proteins to heat damage is increased in the presence of carbohydrates, owing to the Maillard reaction, which involves a condensation between the carbonyl group of a reducing sugar with the free amino group of an amino acid residue (e.g., lysine).

Crude protein content in animal tissues and feeds is often obtained by multiplying the nitrogen content by a factor of 6.25, on the basis of the average nitrogen content (16%) in protein. Such calculation, however, is not very precise, because some proteins contain less or more nitrogen and because some nitrogenous compounds (e.g., ammonia, urea, amides, choline, betaine, purines, pyrimidines, nitrite, and nitrate) are neither proteins nor amino acids. The composition of amino acids in protein is often determined using liquid or gas chromatography.

PROTEIN NUTRITION AND METABOLISM

Protein Digestion and Absorption

Except for the absorption of intact immunoglobulins by the small intestine of mammalian neonates, dietary proteins have no nutritional values until they are hydrolyzed to short-chain peptides and free amino acids in the digestive tract. In nonruminants, the digestion starts in the stomach (pH=approximately 2–3), where protein is denatured by hydrochloric acid, followed by digestion with proteases (pepsins A, B, and C, and renin). The resulting large peptides enter the small intestine to be further hydrolyzed by proteases (including trypsin, chymotrypsin, elastase, carboxyl peptidases, and aminopeptidases) in an alkaline medium (owing to bile salts, pancreatic juice, and duodenal secretions). These enzymes release small peptides and considerable amounts of free amino acids. Oligopeptides composed of more than three amino acid residues are further hydrolyzed extracellularly by peptidases (located mainly on the brush border of enterocytes, and to a lesser extent, in the intestinal lumen) to form tripeptides, dipeptides, and free amino acids. Major mechanisms for the intestinal absorption of amino acids include both Na^+-dependent and Na^+-independent systems. Dipeptides and tripeptides are absorbed intact into enterocytes of the small intestine

Encyclopedia of Animal Science
DOI: 10.1081/E-EAS 120019779

Table 1 Roles of proteins in animals

Roles	Examples of proteins
Muscle contraction	Actin, myosin, tubulin
Enzyme-catalyzed reactions	Dehydrogenase, kinase, synthase
Gene expression	DNA-binding proteins, histones, repressor proteins
Hormone-mediated effects	Insulin, somatotropin, placental lactogen
Protection	Blood clotting factors, immunoglobulins, interferon
Regulation	Calmodulin, leptin, osteopontin
Storage of nutrients and O_2	Ferritin, metallothionein, myoglobin
Cell structure	Collagen, elastin, proteoglycans
Transport of nutrients and O_2	Albumin, hemoglobin, plasma lipoproteins

through H^+-gradient-driven peptide transporters. Once inside enterocytes, peptides are hydrolyzed by peptidases to form free amino acids. The small intestine transports short-chain peptides (2–3 amino acid residues) at a faster rate than free amino acids.

In ruminants, dietary protein is hydrolyzed by ruminal microbial proteases to form small peptides and free amino acids.[2] Amino acids are further degraded to form ammonia, short-chain fatty acids, and CO_2. Small peptides, amino acids, and ammonia are utilized by microorganisms in the presence of adequate energy supply (carbohydrates) to synthesize new amino acids, protein, nucleic acids, and other nitrogenous substances. The most important initial reaction for microbial ammonia assimilation is catalyzed by glutamate dehydrogenase to produce glutamate, which is then utilized to synthesize glutamine, alanine, aspartate, and asparagine by glutamine synthetase, glutamate-pyruvate transaminase, glutamate-oxaloacetate transaminase, and asparagine synthetase, respectively. These amino acids serve as substrates for the synthesis of all other amino acids by microorganisms in the presence of sulfur and adenosine 5′-triphosphate (ATP). Ruminal protozoa cannot utilize ammonia, but derive their nitrogen by engulfing bacteria and digesting them with powerful intracellular proteases. Ammonia that cannot be fixed by ruminal microorganisms is absorbed into blood for conversion into urea via the hepatic urea cycle and may be utilized by ruminal epithelial cells for biosynthetic processes. Microbial cells (bacteria and protozoa) containing proteins and amino acids, as well as undigested dietary proteins, leave the reticulorumen and omasum, and enter the abomasum and small intestine, where digestion of protein is similar to that in nonruminants.

Protein Metabolism

In both nonruminants and ruminants, there is extensive first-pass intestinal catabolism and/or utilization of the amino acids absorbed from the lumen of the small intestine, which substantially reduces their availability to extraintestinal tissues and selectively alters the patterns of amino acids in the portal vein.[3] Amino acids that enter systemic circulation may be oxidized to provide ATP and/or utilized to synthesize glucose, ketone bodies, protein, urea, uric acid, and other nitrogenous substances.

Dietary protein and energy intake regulate intracellular protein synthesis and degradation (protein turnover). At least four and two ATP molecules, respectively, are required to incorporate one amino acid into a peptide and to hydrolyze one peptide bond. Intracellular protein turnover accounts for approximately 15% and 20% of total energy expenditure in adult and growing animals, respectively. Whereas protein synthesis is well-characterized, the pathways for intracellular protein degradation are less understood.[1] Lysosomal proteases and cytosolic calpains (Ca^{2+}-dependent proteases) contribute substantially to the degradation of long-lived, endocytosed, and myofibrillar proteins. Proteasome (a multisubunit protease complex) selectively degrades intracellular proteins via the ubiquitination pathway. Protein half-lives, which range from <30 min for ornithine decarboxylase to >50–200 h for lactate dehydrogenase, are determined by N-terminal residue and physicochemical properties of a given protein.

Protein Requirements

Proportions of dietary amino acids have a profound impact on the food intake, growth, and health of animals. A limiting amino acid (one that is in the shortest supply from the diet relative to its requirement by animals) impairs the utilization of dietary protein. Likewise, an amino acid imbalance (disproportions of dietary amino acids) reduces the feed intake and growth of animals. Amino acid imbalances may occur among amino acids regardless of their structure and can be prevented by addition of one or more of the limiting amino acids to the diet. Also, an amino acid antagonism (growth depression caused by an excessive intake of an amino acid) commonly occurs among structurally related amino acids (e.g., lysine-arginine, leucine-isoleucine-valine, and threonine-tryptophan) but can be overcome by addition of a structurally similar amino acid. Thus, determining optimal amino acid patterns in the diet is very beneficial.

Nitrogen balance studies and growth trials have long been used to determine amino acid and protein requirements of animals.[4] Minimal requirements can also be

Table 2 Nutritionally essential and nonessential amino acids in monogastric animals

Monogastric mammals		Poultry	
EAA	NEAA	EAA	NEAA
Arginine[a]	Alanine	Arginine	Alanine
Histidine	Asparagine	Glycine	Asparagine
Isoleucine	Aspartate	Histidine	Aspartate
Leucine	Cysteine	Isoleucine	Cysteine
Lysine	Glutamate	Leucine	Glutamate
Methionine	Glutamine	Lysine	Glutamine
Phenylalanine	Glycine	Methionine	Serine
Threonine	Proline[b]	Phenylalanine	Tyrosine
Tryptophan	Serine	Proline	
Valine	Tyrosine	Threonine	
		Tryptophan	
		Valine	

[a]Arginine may not be required in the diet to maintain nitrogen balance in most adult mammals but its deficiency in the diet may result in metabolic, neurological, or reproductive disorders.
[b]Proline is an essential amino acid for young pigs.

estimated by factorial analysis; namely, the sum of fecal and urinary nitrogen in response to a protein-free diet (maintenance), nitrogen deposited in the body, and nitrogen excreted as animal products (e.g., milk, egg, wool, fetus growth). Most recently, direct and indirect (indicator) amino acid oxidation techniques involving radioisotopes or stable isotopes have been developed to estimate requirements of protein and essential amino acids by animals.

Amino acids are traditionally classified as nutritionally essential (indispensable) or nonessential (dispensable), on the basis of whether they need to be supplied in the diet to maintain nitrogen balance or support the maximal growth of animals (Table 2). Essential amino acids are defined as either those amino acids whose carbon skeletons cannot be synthesized by animals or those that are inadequately synthesized in animals relative to needs, and which must be provided from the diet to meet requirements for maintenance, growth, and reproduction. Conditionally essential amino acids are those that normally can be synthesized in adequate amounts by animals, but which must be provided from the diet under conditions where rates of utilization are increased relative to rates of synthesis. Nonessential amino acids are the amino acids whose carbon skeletons can be synthesized in adequate amounts by animals to meet requirements.

Collectively, an ideal protein in the diet would consist of an optimal pattern among essential amino acids that corresponds to an animal's needs. Thus, ideal proteins would likely vary with nutritional and physiological needs, including maintenance, protein accretion, egg and wool production, reproduction, and lactation. Because of extensive catabolism of amino acids by the small intestine, the pattern among amino acids in animal tissues or products is not necessarily similar to that in the diet. Thanks to Baker's seminal work,[5] the concept of ideal protein has gained acceptance for formulating swine and poultry diets in the United States and worldwide.

CONCLUSION

A major objective of animal agriculture is to produce high-quality protein products, including meats, eggs, wool, and milk. An optimal pattern among amino acids in the diet is crucial for maximizing an animal's growth and production potential while reducing the excretion of fecal and urinary nitrogenous wastes as a source of environmental pollution. Because protein is both the most expensive ingredient in diets and also a major component of cells, knowledge about protein metabolism is essential for improving the efficiency of its utilization by animals.

ACKNOWLEDGMENT

Work in our laboratory is supported in part by grants from the U.S. Department of Agriculture/National Research Initiative (USDA/NRI) and Texas A&M University.

REFERENCES

1. Voet, D.; Voet, J.G. *Biochemistry*; John Wiley & Sons, Inc.: New York, NY, 1995.
2. Stevens, C.E.; Hume, I.D. Contributions of microbes in vertebrate gastrointestinal tract to production and conservation of nutrients. Physiol. Rev. **1998**, *78*, 393–427.
3. Wu, G. Intestinal mucosal amino acid catabolism. J. Nutr. **1998**, *128*, 1249–1252.
4. Reeds, P.J.; Hutchens, T.W. Protein requirements: From nitrogen balance to functional impact. J. Nutr. **1994**, *124*, 1754S–1764S.
5. Baker, D.H. Ideal amino acid profiles for swine and poultry and their applications in feed formulation. Biokyowa Tech. Rev. **1997**, *9*, 1–24.

Quantitative Trait Loci (QTL)

Morris Soller
Ehud Lipkin
The Hebrew University of Jerusalem, Jerusalem, Israel

INTRODUCTION

Most traits of agricultural importance, such as growth rate and body composition, milk yield and composition, and egg number and quality show a continuous distribution of quantitative trait measurements in a population. Such traits are termed quantitative traits, in contrast to Mendelian traits, which typically are found in a limited number of qualitatively different forms in a population (e.g., presence or absence of horns, brown or black coat color). Genetic variation in a quantitative trait is generally attributed to allelic variation at a number of genes, in contrast to the one or two genes generally found sufficient to explain genetic variation in a Mendelian trait. Moreover, quantitative trait expression is much affected by environmental variables, again in contrast to Mendelian traits, which are generally little affected by environment. Consequently, for quantitative traits, the relationship between genotype and phenotype is complex, and the genotype of an individual cannot be inferred from its phenotype or that of its relatives. Instead, the various genes affecting a quantitative trait are individuated by mapping them to specific chromosomal locations (loci). For this reason, the term quantitative trait loci, or QTL, was proposed for the individual mapped genetic factors affecting quantitative trait value.

Mapping the QTL responsible for genetic variation in traits of agricultural importance, and using the map locations to identify the actual genes involved, is a major challenge for animal genetics. Success will provide powerful tools for understanding the physiology of trait variation, and for genetic improvement of animal stocks.

QTL MAPPING

QTL mapping means locating the specific chromosomal regions in which QTL are found. This is achieved by locating the QTL with respect to a standard set of Mendelian loci that have been previously mapped using standard genetic or physical gene-mapping procedures. These reference loci are termed genetic markers, since they identify (mark) specific chromosomal locations.

Consequently, showing that a QTL is found in the near vicinity of a specific marker (termed "linked" to the marker) is equivalent to mapping the QTL to the location of the marker. Thus, a prior requirement for QTL mapping is the availability of a comprehensive marker map. Such maps, based on DNA-level polymorphic loci, are now available for all of the major farm animals.

At present, QTL can only be mapped by using genetic (as opposed to physical) mapping procedures. Genetic mapping procedures start with an individual that is heterozygous for the marker and for the linked QTL. The genetic distance between a marker and a QTL then stands in direct proportion to the number of recombinant gene combinations (haplotypes) among the progeny of the doubly heterozygous individual, i.e., when a QTL and marker are tightly linked, recombinant haplotypes will be rare. The way in which the proportion of recombinant haplotypes among the progeny of an individual is inferred for a QTL and a linked marker is best explained by example, using the basic half-sib sire-family QTL mapping design.

Let M be a marker locus and Q a nearby linked QTL, with alleles **M** and **m** and **Q** and **q**, respectively, where allele **Q** is a positive allele that increases trait value, and allele **q** is a negative allele that decreases trait value (italics denote genes, and bold type denotes alleles). Consider a sire having haplotypes **MQ** and **mq** on a pair of homologous chromosomes carrying these genes. Let r denote the total proportion of daughters that received recombinant haplotypes **Mq** or **mQ** from their sire, and $(1-r)$ the total proportion of daughters that received the parental haplotypes, **MQ** or **mq**. Then, the following table shows the proportion of daughters carrying each of the four transmitted sire haplotypes.

Daughter type	Sire haplotype	Relative proportion among all daughters
Parental	**MQ**	$0.5(1-r)$
Recombinant	**Mq**	$0.5\,r$
Recombinant	**mQ**	$0.5\,r$
Parental	**mq**	$0.5(1-r)$

The progeny of the sire that receive the **M** marker allele from their sire will be of two types: **MQ** and **Mq**.

Encyclopedia of Animal Science
DOI: 10.1081/E-EAS 120019780

Thus, they will receive a mixture of **Q** and **q** alleles, in relative proportion $(1-r){:}r$. If *M* is close to *Q*, *r* will be small. Consequently, among these progeny, there will be a preponderance of **Q** alleles having positive effects on trait value. The opposite holds for progeny that receive the **m** marker allele from the sire; among these daughters, there will be a preponderance of **q** alleles having negative effects on trait value. The net result is that, on average, the progeny carrying the **M** marker allele are expected to show a higher trait value than the progeny carrying the **m** marker allele, the expected difference (*D*-value) being greater the closer *M* and *Q* are to one another, while *D*=0 when marker and QTL are on different chromosomes or far removed on the same chromosome.

In practice, the location of the markers in linkage to QTL is not known in advance; hence the experiment is carried out as a genome scan, in which *D*-values are calculated for a complete set of markers spanning the entire genome. A typical scan may involve 70 to 150 markers. In single-marker mapping, a QTL in a given chromosomal region is assigned the location of the marker that shows the greatest *D*-value. In interval mapping, information on all markers in a chromosomal region is used to obtain the most likely position of the QTL using advanced statistical procedures of maximum likelihood estimation and least squares regression mapping.

OTHER MAPPING DESIGNS

The granddaughter design is a variant of the half-sib design, widely used in dairy cattle QTL mapping. In this design, the half-sib family consists of the progeny-tested sons of an elite sire. The phenotype of the sons is given by the average production records of their daughters. This is a convenient design to implement because semen samples of the sire and his sons can be used as a source of DNA; semen samples of all progeny-tested sires in the United States are routinely collected in a special repository maintained by the U.S. Department of Agriculture (USDA) and made available to qualified scientists for QTL mapping. Progeny test data on the sire and his sons are also widely available through the USDA sire evaluation service. Backcross and F2 designs are implemented when mapping QTL responsible for trait differences between two populations that differ widely in trait value (such as broiler and layer chickens, disease-resistant and susceptible breeds of cattle). When the mapping population is very large and a large number of markers are followed, selective DNA pooling can reduce the genotyping load ten- to one-hundredfold.

CONFIDENCE INTERVAL OF QTL MAP LOCATION AND HIGH-RESOLUTION MAPPING OF QTL

QTL mapping gives the most likely point location for the QTL, accompanied by a confidence interval, which is an interval along the chromosome to both sides of the point location within which the QTL could actually reside. The width of this interval defines the map resolution of the experiment. In many QTL mapping experiments, the confidence interval is very large, from one-quarter to one-half of the entire chromosome.

The confidence interval can be reduced by increasing the sample size and the density of marker spacing, and by application of specialized multilocus and multitrait mapping procedures. Advanced intercross lines can also be used to improve map resolution in experimental and farm populations.

LINKAGE DISEQUILIBRIUM (LD) MAPPING AND IDENTICAL BY DESCENT (IBD) MAPPING

When marker and QTL are very close together, or when the marker is within the DNA sequence of the gene itself, a situation may arise in which there is an excess of some haplotypes and a deficiency of others across the population as a whole. This condition, termed linkage disequilibrium (LD), can be uncovered by an association test, which compares average trait value of the different genotypes at a marker across the population as a whole. Finding marker–QTL LD indicates that the marker involved is very close to the QTL. Linkage disequilibrium can be generated by the random accumulation of small changes in frequency of the various marker–QTL haplotypes over many generations. Identical by descent (IBD) mapping is based on the assumption that the mutation that produced a specific positive or negative QTL allele was a unique event that took place in a single ancestor chromosome, and will hence be in association with the specific marker alleles found in the haplotype of the ancestor chromosome within which the mutation arose. Thus, IBD mapping can lead to the very gene underlying the QTL.

RESULTS OF QTL MAPPING: NUMBER AND EFFECTS OF QTL

When all QTL mapping studies in a farm animal species are considered together and appropriate extrapolations are made, typical quantitative traits appear to be controlled by anywhere from five to a few dozen QTL. For the most part, effects of individual QTL are in the range of 1 to 3% of the trait mean. In some instances, the mapped QTL as a group are able to account for a large fraction of the observed genetic variation in the study population. Mapped QTL commonly exhibit various degrees of dominance, including overdominance; interactions (epistasis) among mapped QTL are common.

FROM QTL TO CG (CANDIDATE GENE) TO QTG (QUANTITATIVE TRAIT GENE)

When gene maps of vertebrate species, including humans, are compared, the order of the genes in large chromosomal regions (depending on the particular pair of species compared) are often found to be the same. As a result, when a QTL has been mapped to a particular chromosomal region in a particular species, it is possible to look at the comparative gene map and identify the genes that are present in the comparable region in other species. Through bioinformatic data mining, all of the functional information accumulated across all living species on the genes in a given chromosomal region can be accessed. Among these genes may be those that have functions or expression patterns that make them attractive candidates to be the actual gene underlying the QTL. This can be tested by identifying markers within these candidate genes (CG), and then testing them for association with trait value by LD mapping. Candidate genes that show strong association with trait value become putative quantitative

trait genes (QTG). Final confirmation that a putative QTG corresponds to the mapped QTL is difficult, but has been achieved successfully in a number of instances. In most cases, the identified QTG was one whose function was directly related to the physiology or development of the trait in question.

CONCLUSION

Mapping a large fraction of the QTL responsible for genetic variation in the traits of economic importance in farm animals and identifying the QTG underlying the mapped QTL are now the major challenges for farm animal genetics. The ultimate goal is to anchor 80% of the genetic variation in the traits of economic importance to specific QTL and QTG. Success in this will greatly increase our understanding of the molecular physiology of production traits, and our ability to achieve rapid and cost-effective genetic improvement.

REFERENCES

1. Falconer, D.S.; Mackay, T.S.F. *Introduction to Quantitative Genetics*, 4th Ed.; Longman Sci. and Tech.: Harlow, UK, 1996.
2. Lynch, M. *Genetics and Analysis of Quantitative Traits*; Sinauer Associates, Inc.: Sunderland, MA, 1998.
3. Weller, J.I. *Quantitative Trait Loci Analysis in Animals*; CABI Publishing: New York, NY, 2001.

Ratites: Biology, Housing, and Management

Dominique Blache
Graeme B. Martin
Irek Malecki
The University of Western Australia, Crawley, Australia

INTRODUCTION

The large flightless ostrich, emu, cassowary, and rhea, and the small flightless kiwi, compose the ratite family. The emu, ostrich, and rhea have been used in farming systems in which their biology influences management and housing. Ratite farming is in its infancy and requires further research and development to overcome inherent constraints before each species can reach its full productive potential.

BIOLOGY OF RATITES

The flat, raftlike (ratis) sternum provided the name for the family. There is no keel and the pectoral muscles are absent or vestigial. In all except rheas, the body feathers lack barbicels, so the plumage is loose and fluffy. The feathers of the emu have two shafts. The rhea and the ostrich have longer wings than the emu and they use them during elaborate displays (Fig. 1). Female emus and rheas are larger than males, but the male ostrich is the largest.[1]

All extant ratites are endemic to the Southern Hemisphere, whereas their ancestors were found in both hemispheres.[1] The ostrich, emu, and rhea are found in temperate and Mediterranean regions, but can survive in a wide range of climates.[1,2]

The ratites have very strong legs and their muscles have a specific distribution and physiology due to the mechanic constraints of bipedal locomotion. Ratites walk most of the day and can run at considerable speed (Table 1). They are nomadic and follow food availability, but are territorial during the breeding season. Ratites can also crouch, a posture between standing and sitting (Fig. 1). The females lay eggs in this position.[1,2]

Vigilant ratites stand with the neck stretched upward; their heads are very mobile and can turn almost 360 degrees. Vision is believed to be very efficient because of the elevated position of the eyes and also because of acuity. Thus, they are able to see and detect from long distances (few kilometers). Ratites are not active at night and spend most of the dark phase lying.

Rheas, emus, and ostriches can be found in groups of 30 or more, but also in smaller family groups. Ratites are very defensive when eggs or young chicks are present. Agonistic behaviors include vocalizations, body postures, and eventual charging.

The reproductive biology of ratites presents some unique features. The males have a large penile organ that erects from the cloaca and penetrates the female's cloaca during copulation. In females, sperm storage tubules in the reproductive tract allow the female to remain fertile for several days after copulation.[3] The mating system varies between species. In the wild, male ostriches and rheas form harems, but also copulate with females from other groups, whereas emus form pairs that are stable during the mating period.[1,4] Courtship is based on vocalizations and displays or postures from both sexes (Fig. 1). Ostriches reproduce during summer, but rheas and emus reproduce mainly during winter. Photoperiod is essential for the emu,[5] but is not that critical for the other ratites because, when nutrition is not limited, they breed at anytime.[1] Ratites nest on the ground in very simple nests (Fig. 1). Females lay large eggs at 2–3 day intervals. The total number of eggs laid by one female varies between species and individuals (Table 1). The number of eggs laid over a season seems to be strongly influenced by the level of fat reserves and nutrition of the female before the start of the laying period. With the exception of the ostrich, male ratites are solely responsible for incubating the clutch and raising the young (Fig. 1). Female emus leave their partner during incubation and mate with other males. Ratite chicks are precocious and the nest is usually abandoned within 48 h after hatching.[1]

The digestive system is simple and in most respects similar to that of other plant-eating birds, but ratites also consume insects and small animals.[1,2,6] The esophagus is mobile and expandable and ratites swallow their food whole. The crop is absent in all ratites, but the structure of the stomach varies among species.[6] Their appetite varies dramatically between the breeding and the nonbreeding seasons, leading to large variations in body weight, mostly due to variation in fat reserves.

Encyclopedia of Animal Science
DOI: 10.1081/E-EAS 120019782

Fig. 1 Clockwise from the top left corner. Male ostrich with his harem; one female is incubating. Male ostrich displaying courtship. Male emu displaying courtship. (*View this art in color at www.dekker.com.*)

HOUSING AND MANAGEMENT OF RATITES

The allocation of space to farmed birds varies with their age and reproductive status (Table 2). Only young chicks need access to an indoor pen. Feeding recommendations for ratites are not as precise as those for commercial poultry. Nutrient requirements are based on restricted data for ostriches and emus,[2,6] and there are no published data for rheas (Table 2). Feedstuffs of plant origin are the main constituent of the diet and, because of the requirement of

Table 1 Ratite biology

Species	Emu	Ostrich	Rhea
Number of subspecies[a]	1	4	2
Origin	Australia	Africa	Southeastern America
Farming	Yes	Yes	Yes
Sexual dimorphism	Not obvious	Yes	Not obvious
Size (m)	1.5–1.8	1.8–2.5	1.5
Weight (kg)	45–67	80–140	15–40
Number of digits per foot	3	2	3
Running speed (km/h)	45	60	45
Breeding season	Autumn–winter (SD)	Spring–summer (LD)[b]	Winter (SD)[e]
Cluch size[c] (eggs)	5–45	8–36	8–56
Egg production per female	22±5	50±20	16–30
Duration of incubation[d] (days)	56	42	30–44
Incubating sex	Male	Male and female	Male

[a]Only present subspecies.
[b]Breeding season in ostriches varies regionally in Africa and is influenced by rain and food availability.
[c]Number of eggs found in one nest.
[d]Incubation under natural conditions.
[e]SD=short-day breeder, LD=long-day breeder.
(Data from author's observations and Ref. 1.)

these large birds, a large amount of protein has to be included. Most farmed ratites are fed a pelleted diet of crushed grain and other nutrients, formulated according to age and reproductive status.[2,6,7] Usually, the diet of females is richer in energy and protein during the breeding season than during the nonbreeding season. However, this strategy might not be best considering that, naturally, the birds decrease their intake during the breeding season and replenish their reserves during the nonbreeding season. In emus, feed intake is controlled by photoperiod and increases dramatically, by at least 150% (up to 2 kg/day/bird), when the breeding season ends, allowing them to recover, within two weeks, most of the weight lost over the breeding season.[8]

Breeding management differs between countries and farms, but the relative advantages of the different strategies have not been compared scientifically. Ostriches are kept in pairs, trios (one male for two females), or colonies.[2] Emus can breed in pairs or in groups. Rheas are bred in groups because of their need for harem formation. Breeding birds are given more space because of the possibility of fighting. Reproductive failure can be due to behavioural problems, such as lack of pair formation.

Eggs are usually collected and artificially incubated to avoid the assembly of a clutch because the males become sexually inactive as they incubate. Eggs need to be cleaned and dried before being set into incubators. Damaged, under- and oversized eggs should be discarded. Storage of eggs before incubation simplifies hatchery management because it allows batch hatching. Optimal conditions for artificial incubation are known (Table 2).[2,6,7] Candling of ratite eggs is possible using commercially available devices. Recommendations for hatching conditions are not scientifically proven (Table 2), but the eggs are usually transferred to the hatcher a few days before hatch date because pipping starts 36 hours prior to hatching.

Sexual maturity is reached at 18–20 months for ostriches and emus and after 24 months for rheas (Table 2). Vent sexing can be successfully carried out within days after hatching with an accuracy of around 85%.

Table 2 Housing conditions and management of farmed emus and ostriches

Species	Emu	Ostrich
Space allocation (m²/bird)[a]		
Chicks (0–12 weeks) indoor pen	0.15–0.20	0.25–0.30
Chicks (0–12 weeks) outdoor pen	0.30	0.50
Chicks (3–6 months)	6–20	10–40
Young (6–12 months)	20–40	50–250
Yearling (12–24 months)	60–100	100–330
Breeders (>24 months)		
Free range	625–1000	500–2000
Breeding pairs	400–1200	600–2500
Maintenance requirement		
Energy (kJ/kg$^{0.75}$/day)	284	440
Nitrogen[b] (mg/kg$^{0.75}$/day)	320	320
Incubation		
Dry-bulb temperature (°C)	35.3	36.4
Relative humidity (%)	40	25–30
Air flow (m³/min/40 eggs)	0.71	1.42
Air quality (% O_2, % CO_2)	21, 0.05	21, 0.05
Rotation of the eggs		
Amplitude (degree)	180	90
Frequency (h)	4–8	1
Total egg weight lost (%)	15	15
Hatching		
Dry-bulb temperature (°C)	35	34
Relative humidity (%)	50	25–35

Space allocations vary according to feeding methods.
[a]Based on regulations and practices used by the industry.
[b]Based on nitrogen requirement of poultry.

RATITE PRODUCTION

Farming of ratites has great potential that has been exploited most often in the countries of origin of the species. Slaughter age is around 12–16 months for emus, 10–12 months for ostriches, and 18–20 months for rheas. Methods and regulations for slaughter are already in place in each country, but more development is needed to decrease the cost of slaughtering, especially plucking methods.

The products are all high quality: soft leather, meat with low-fat and high-iron content, and a fine oil that can be used as a cosmetic base for the administration of topical medicines and as an anti-inflammatory agent, a claim already supported by clinical trials for emu oil. Ostrich feathers have been successfully marketed in the past as a fashion item but this market has virtually disappeared. The meat market is still small and in need of more marketing for further expansion. There is also a need for more scientific input into management and genetic selection to improve productivity and product quality. Recent developments of sperm collection and preservation, and artificial insemination techniques specific to both ostrich and emus, provide the industry with major tools for modern methods of selection.[9]

CONCLUSION

Ratites are scientifically interesting because of their unique biological characteristics. Those same characteristics offer a unique opportunity to develop an alternative industry that might have less environmental impact than traditional, imported animal industries. These industries exist, but still need a large amount of research and development before they will be successful because ratites are not simply bigger versions of common poultry and cannot be treated as such.[10]

REFERENCES

1. Davies, S.J.J.F. *Ratites and Tinamous: Tinamidae, Rheidae, Dromaiidae, Casuariidae, Apterygidae, Struthionidae*; Oxford University Press: Oxford, 2002.
2. Deeming, D.C. *The Ostrich: Biology, Production and Health*; CAB International: Wallingford, UK, 1999.
3. Malecki, I.; Martin, G.B. Fertile period and clutch size in the Emu (*Dromaius novaehollandiae*). Emu **2002**, *102*, 165–170.
4. Blache, D.; Barrett, C.D.; Martin, G.B. Social mating system and sexual behaviour in the emu, *Dromaius novaehollandiae*. Emu **2000**, *100*, 161–168.
5. Blache, D.; Talbot, R.T.; Blackberry, M.A.; Williams, K.M.; Martin, G.B.; Sharp, P.J. Photoperiodic control of the secretion of luteinizing hormone, prolactin and testosterone in the male emu (*Dromaius novaehollandiae*), a bird that breeds on short days. J. Neuroendocrinol. **2001**, *13*, 998–1006.
6. Tully, T.N.; Shane, S.M. *Ratite: Management, Medicine and Surgery*; Krieger: Malabar, 1996.
7. Deeming, D.C. *Improving Our Understanding of Ratites in a Farming Environment*; Ratite Conference: Manchester, UK, 1996.
8. Blache, D.; Martin, G.B. Day length affects feeding behaviour and food intake in adult male emus (*Dromaius novaehollandiae*). Br. Poult. Sci. **1999**, *40*, 573–578.
9. Malecki, I.A.; Martin, G.B.; Lindsay, D.R. Semen production by the male emu (*Dromaius novohollandiae*). 1. Methods for collection of semen. Poult. Sci. **1996**, *76*, 615–621.
10. Malecki, I.; Blache, D.; Martin, G. Emu biology and farming—Developing management strategies for a valuable resource. Land Management **October 2001**, 20–21.

Ratites: Nutrition Management

James Sales
University of Maryland, College Park, Maryland, U.S.A.

INTRODUCTION

Ratites (order Struthioniformes) are flightless birds with a raftlike breastbone devoid of a keel, and can be classified into the families Struthionidae (ostriches), Dromiceiidae (emus), Rheidae (rheas), Casuariidae (cassowaries), and Apterygidae (kiwis).

DIGESTIVE PHYSIOLOGY

Despite their similarities to other birds, ratites have developed unique characteristics, such as modifications in the gastrointestinal tract, in order to survive in their natural habitat.[1] Ratites do not have teeth or a crop (the feed storage organ in other avian species). Ostriches, emus, and rheas could be considered monogastric herbivores, which means they are simple-stomached animals that have developed the ability to utilize forage. Whereas fiber fermentation appears to take place in the large intestine (colon) of the ostrich, the distal ileum serves as a fermentation organ in the emu. The most distinctive characteristic of the gastrointestinal tract of the rhea is the relatively large cecum (Table 1).

RATITE DIETS

Many different diets have been utilized in commercial ostrich production, varying from single ingredients such as alfalfa, to compound diets with several ingredients including vitamin/mineral mixtures, since the domestication of the ostrich as a farm animal around 1865 in South Africa.[2] The first book on ostrich feeds and feeding was already published in 1913 by Dowsley and Gardner.[3] Reliance on compound, commercial, manufactured diets, mostly in a pelleted form, has become the norm since the spread of ostrich farming to countries outside South Africa around 1990 and the recognition of emu farming as being technically feasible in Australia in 1987.[4] At the few pilot operations for the domestication of the rhea as a commercial farm animal in South America, a variety of compound pelleted diets, consisting mainly of alfalfa and corn meal, are fed.[5]

NUTRIENT REQUIREMENTS

The inaccuracy of earlier extrapolation of nutrient requirement specifications for poultry to ostriches and emus soon became evident from various nutrition-related problems encountered by commercial ratite farmers.[6] Studies by Cilliers[7] and O'Malley[4] revealed significant information on the energy and amino acid requirements of these two species (Tables 2 and 3).

It is evident that different diets, each with different nutrient concentrations, have to be fed at different stages of the life cycle; for example, a starter diet up to three months of age, a grower diet till slaughter age, and a breeder diet for breeder birds.

Mineral Requirements

Currently, dietary mineral, as vitamin, specifications for ratites are based on suggestions. A major problem in ostrich feeding is that calcium is very often overfed, with the result of depressed uptake of zinc and manganese. Although a total dietary calcium concentration of 2.0 to 2.5% is recommended for ostrich layers in intensive production systems, excellent laying and fertility results have been achieved with dietary calcium levels as low as 1.6% on a dry matter basis.[8] Under intensive farming conditions, leg problems seldom occur in young ostrich chicks fed a diet with calcium levels around 1.5 to 1.6%.[9]

NUTRITION OF CHICKS

Although the rearing of young ostriches is a well-established practice, high mortalities are often encountered.[9] Ostrich feed and water should be available from day one after hatch. A chopped fresh alfalfa or grass topping on feed will stimulate chicks to start eating. It was also found in rhea chicks[10] that the first few chicks required frequent stimulation, for example, by poking with a finger or pencil at the food, to induce proper feeding.

Many ostrich producers supplement the starter diet or water of the newly hatched ostrich with a booster pack containing: 1) electrolytes that will ensure that the correct

Encyclopedia of Animal Science
DOI: 10.1081/E-EAS 120019784

Table 1 Comparison of the digestive tract of ostriches, emus, and rheas

Region	Length (cm)			Relative length (% of total)		
	Ostrich	**Emu**	**Rhea**	**Ostrich**	**Emu**	**Rhea**
Small intestine	512	51	140	36	90	61
Cecum	94	7	48	6	2	21
Colon	800	28	40	57	7	17

(From Ref. 1.)

ratio of sodium to potassium will be consumed and that the absorption of moisture will be normal during these early stages of life; 2) acidification substances that will lower the pH of the digestive tract and enhance its adaptation to high-protein starter diets; 3) amylase, protease, and cellulase enzymes to ensure more efficient digestion of starch, protein, and fiber; and 4) vitamins A, D, E, and B complex to ensure immunity against infections and other diseases.[8] It is well known that ostrich chicks have poor resistance against infectious and other diseases. The

supplementation of any product, for example, yogurt, that might stimulate immunity is highly recommended.

CONCLUSION

Ratites are unique in that they resemble the characteristics of avian species with nutritional adaptations similar to that of ruminants. Despite studies on ratites that enable the modeling of energy and amino acid requirements, dietary

Table 2 Estimated dry matter intake (DMI),[a] energy (TME$_n$), and protein and amino acid requirements for maintenance and growth of African black ostriches

AGE (Days)	LW (kg)	ADG (g/b/d)	DMI (g/b/d)	TME$_n$ (MJ/kg DMI)	Prot (g/kg DMI)	Amino acids (g/kg DMI)										
						Lys	**Meth**	**Cys**	**Arg**	**Thr**	**Val**	**Isoleu**	**Leu**	**His**	**Phe**	**Tyr**
30	4.0	105	220	15.2[b]	239	10.6	3.1	2.8	9.8	6.5	7.9	8.7	14.5	3.6	8.5	4.4
60	11.0	233	440	17.5[b]	272	12.5	3.6	3.3	11.5	7.6	9.3	10.3	17.0	4.3	10.0	5.1
90	19.5	283	680	15.3[b]	224	10.8	3.2	2.8	10.1	6.6	8.2	9.0	14.7	3.8	8.7	4.5
120	28.5	300	820	14.9[b]	207	10.6	3.2	2.7	9.9	6.4	8.1	8.8	14.3	3.8	8.5	4.5
150	39.5	367	1220	12.5[b]	174	9.1	2.7	2.3	8.5	5.5	7.0	7.6	12.3	3.3	7.3	3.9
180	52.1	420	1490	12.2[b]	168	9.0	2.7	2.3	8.5	5.5	6.9	7.6	12.2	3.3	7.2	3.9
210	63.4	375	1630	11.3	148	8.5	2.6	2.1	8.0	5.1	6.6	7.2	11.4	3.1	6.8	3.7
240	73.3	330	1710	10.8	135	8.2	2.5	2.0	7.8	5.0	6.4	7.0	11.0	3.1	6.6	3.6
270	82.4	305	1760	10.7	130	8.3	2.6	2.0	7.9	5.0	6.5	7.1	11.1	3.1	6.6	3.7
300	91.0	287	1800	10.8	128	8.4	2.6	2.0	8.1	5.1	6.7	7.2	11.2	3.2	6.7	3.8
330	96.3	177	2160	8.0	85	6.3	2.0	1.5	6.1	3.8	5.1	5.4	8.4	2.4	5.0	2.9
360	99.9	120	2210	7.4	74	5.9	1.9	1.3	5.7	3.5	4.8	5.1	7.8	2.3	4.7	2.7
390	103.5	120	2250	7.4	74	5.9	1.9	1.4	5.8	3.6	4.8	5.2	7.9	2.3	4.7	2.7
420	107.0	117	2250	7.5	75	6.1	2.0	1.4	5.9	3.7	4.9	5.3	8.1	2.4	4.8	2.8
450	110.0	100	2250	7.5	73	6.1	2.0	1.4	5.9	3.7	5.0	5.3	8.0	2.4	4.8	2.8
480	112.3	77	2250	7.3	69	6.0	1.9	1.3	5.9	3.6	4.9	5.2	7.9	2.4	4.8	2.8
510	114.2	63	2250	7.3	67	6.0	1.9	1.3	5.9	3.6	4.9	5.2	7.9	2.4	4.7	2.8
540	116.0	60	2250	7.3	67	6.0	2.0	1.3	5.9	3.6	5.0	5.3	8.0	2.4	4.8	2.8
570	118.6	87	2250	7.7	74	6.4	2.1	1.4	6.2	3.8	5.2	5.6	8.4	2.5	5.1	3.0
600	120.3	57	2250	7.5	68	6.2	2.0	1.4	6.1	3.7	5.1	5.4	8.2	2.5	4.9	2.9

LW = live weight; ADG = average daily gain; DMI = dry matter intake; TME$_n$ = true metabolizable energy corrected for nitrogen retention; Prot = protein; Lys = lysine; Met = methionine; Cys = cystein; Arg = arginine; Thr = threonine; Val = valine; Isoleu = isoleucine; Leu = leucine; His = histidine; Phe = phenylalanine; Tyr = tyrosine.

[a]Based on a diet with a TME$_n$ (ostrich) content of 11.25 MJ/kg.

[b]In calculating TME$_n$ requirements from results obtained for seven-month-old birds, similar energy contents were assumed for younger birds. This assuption is incorrect, resulting in an overestimation of dietary energy requirements.

(From Ref. 7.)

Table 3 Estimated dry matter intake (DMI),[a] and protein and amino acid requirements for maintenance and growth of emus

AGE (Weeks)	LW (kg)	ADG (g/b/d)	DMI (g/b/d)	Prot (g/kg DMI)	Amino acids (g/kg DMI)					
					Lys	Met	Met+Cys	Thr	Isoleu	Leu
0–2	0.5	14	35	119	6.5	1.8	5.9	5.8	5.0	13.1
2–3	0.8	59	88	170	9.8	2.8	6.7	7.9	6.7	17.4
3–4	1.3	80	140	151	8.7	2.5	5.7	6.9	5.9	15.2
4–6	2.3	106	220	137	7.9	2.2	4.8	6.2	5.4	13.7
6–8	3.9	124	259	146	7.7	2.3	5.0	6.7	5.8	14.7
8–10	5.9	153	368	133	7.1	1.8	4.1	6.1	5.3	13.3
10–12	7.8	121	374	116	6.4	1.8	4.1	5.4	4.7	11.8
12–16	10.7	145	561	94	5.3	1.5	3.4	4.4	3.8	9.7
16–20	14.6	134	603	90	5.0	1.5	3.6	4.2	3.7	9.4
20–24	18.2	125	630	89	5.0	1.6	3.8	4.2	3.7	9.4
24–28	23.8	92	597	91	5.2	1.6	4.1	4.4	3.8	9.8
28–32	23.8	95	545	114	6.7	2.1	5.1	5.5	4.8	12.3
32–36	26.1	71	544	116	7.0	2.1	5.3	5.7	4.9	12.6
36–40	28.0	58	614	110	6.9	2.1	5.1	5.4	4.7	12.0
40–44	30.0	80	604	134	8.7	2.5	6.0	6.6	5.6	14.6
44–48	32.5	110	820	113	7.5	2.2	5.0	5.5	4.7	12.3
48–52	35.7	117	851	112	7.3	2.2	5.0	5.4	4.7	12.1
52–56	38.8	104	829	114	7.6	2.2	5.1	5.6	4.8	12.4
56–60	41.5	87	1,051	88	5.8	1.7	3.9	4.3	3.7	9.6
60–62	43.1	72	1,026	88	5.8	1.6	3.9	4.3	3.8	9.6
62–63	44.0	98	1,175	84	5.6	1.6	3.6	4.1	3.6	9.2

LW=live weight; ADG=average daily gain; DMI=dry matter intake; TME$_n$=true metabolizable energy corrected for nitrogen retention; Prot=protein; Lys=lysine; Met=methionine; Cys=cystein; Thr=threonine; Isoleu=isoleucine; Leu=leucine.
[a]Based on a diet with gross energy content of 11.5 MJ.
(From Ref. 4.)

recommendations on minerals and other nutrients are still based on data from other avian species. Different dietary nutrient concentrations are needed through the successive stages of the life cycle. Low immunity in the digestive system of the ratite chick until the age of three months is one of the reasons for high mortalities.

Of the commercial ratite species (ostriches, emus, rheas), nutritional research has mainly concentrated on the ostrich. Due to similarities in the digestive system, information obtained with ostriches could probably be extrapolated to the rhea, the least studied species.

REFERENCES

1. Angel, C.R. A review of ratite nutrition. Anim. Feed Sci. Technol. **1996**, *60*, 241–246.
2. Drenowatz, C.; Sales, J.; Sarasqueta, D.V.; Weilbrenner, A. History & Geography. In *Ratite Encyclopedia*; Drenowatz, C., Ed.; Ratite Records, Inc.: San Antonio, TX, USA, 1995; 3–29.
3. Dowsley, W.G.; Gardner, C. *Ostrich Foods and Feeding*; Crocott & Sherry: Grahamstown, South Africa, 1913.
4. O'Malley, P.J. An Estimate of the Nutritional Requirements of Emus. In *Improving Our Understanding of Ratites in a Farming Environment*; Deeming, D.C., Ed.; Ratite Conference: Oxfordshire, UK, 1996; 92–108.
5. Sales, J.; Navarro, J.L.; Bellis, L.; Manero, A.; Lizurume, M.; Martella, M.B. Carcass and component yields of rheas. Br. Poult. Sci. **1997**, *38*, 378–380.
6. Cilliers, S.C.; Angel, C.R. Basic Concepts and Recent Advances in Digestion and Nutrition. In *The Ostrich: Biology, Production and Health*; Deeming, D.C., Ed.; CAB International: Wallingford, Oxon, U.K., 1999; 105–128.
7. Cilliers, S.C. Feedstuffs Evaluation in Ostriches (*Struthio camelus*). Ph.D. Thesis; University of Stellenbosch: South Africa, 1995.
8. Smith, W.A.; Sales, J. Feeding and Feed Management. In *Practical Guide for Ostrich Management and Ostrich Products*; Smith, W.A., Ed.; An Alltech Inc. Publication, University of Stellenbosch Publishers: Stellenbosch, South Africa, 1995; 8–19.
9. Verwoerd, D.J.; Deeming, D.C.; Angel, C.R.; Perelman, B. Rearing Environments Around the World. In *The Ostrich: Biology, Production and Health*; Deeming, D.C., Ed.; CAB International: Wallingford, Oxon, U.K., 1999; 191–216.
10. Kruczek, R. Breeding Darwin's rheas at Brookfield Zoo Chicago. Int. Zoo Yearb. **1968**, *8*, 150–153.

Religious Foods: Jewish and Muslim Laws for Animal Slaughter/Welfare

Joe M. Regenstein
Cornell University, Ithaca, New York, U.S.A.

Carrie E. Regenstein
University of Wisconsin, Madison, Wisconsin, U.S.A.

Muhammad M. Chaudry
Islamic Food and Nutrition Council, Chicago, Illinois, U.S.A.

INTRODUCTION

The kosher dietary laws determine which foods are fit or proper for consumption by Jewish consumers who observe these laws. The halal dietary laws determine which foods are lawful or permitted for Muslims. The kosher and halal dietary laws both deal extensively with animal issues. More details about these laws and the additional requirements not covered in this article can be found in other sources.[1–7]

KOSHER DIETARY LAWS

Allowed Animals and the Prohibition of Blood

Ruminants with split hoofs that chew their cud, the traditional domestic birds, fish with fins and removable scales, and a few grasshoppers are generally permitted. Everything else is prohibited.

Ruminants and fowl must be slaughtered according to Jewish law by a specially trained religious slaughterer using a special knife that is very straight, very sharp, and at least twice the neck diameter in length. These animals are subsequently inspected for various defects. In the United States, a stricter inspection requirement requires smooth lungs (Glatt), i.e., less than two perforations or adhesions. The meat and poultry must be further prepared by properly removing certain veins, arteries, prohibited fats, blood, and the sciatic nerve. Therefore, only the front quarter cuts of red meat are generally used. To remove more blood, red meat and poultry are soaked and salted within a specified time period. All animal ingredients for kosher production must come from kosher-slaughtered animals. Thus, fats or oils used for kosher products are mostly obtained from plant sources.

Prohibition of Mixing Milk and Meat

"Thou shalt not seeth the kid in its mother's milk" appears three times in the Torah (the first five books of the Holy Scriptures) and is therefore considered a very serious admonition. Meat has been rabbinically extended to include poultry. Dairy includes all milk derivatives.

To keep meat and milk separate requires that the processing and handling of all food products and production equipment that are kosher fall into one of three categories: meat, dairy, or pareve (neutral).

Pareve includes all plant products plus eggs, fish, honey, and lac resin (shellac). Pareve foods can be used with either meat or dairy, except that fish cannot be mixed directly with meat. Some kosher supervision agencies do permit products without meat but made on meat equipment to be listed as "meat equipment (M.E.)."

Equipment Koshering

There are three ways to make equipment kosher and/or to change its status. Which procedure is required depends on the equipment's prior production history. Converting pareve equipment to use for meat or dairy does not require kosherization. The first and simplest equipment kosherization occurs with equipment made from materials that have only been handled cold. These require a good caustic/soap cleaning. However, materials such as ceramics, rubber, earthenware, and porcelain cannot be koshered.

Heating above 120°F is usually defined rabbinically as cooking. To kosher these items, the second form of equipment kosherization requires that the equipment be thoroughly cleaned with caustic/soap. The equipment must be left idle for 24 hours and then flooded with boiling water in the presence of a kosher supervisor. For ovens or other equipment that use fire, the third form of

Encyclopedia of Animal Science
DOI: 10.1081/E-EAS 120021146

equipment kosherization involves heating the metal until it glows with the rabbi present.

HALAL DIETARY LAWS

Prohibited and Permitted Animals; Prohibition of Blood

Meat of pigs is strictly prohibited, and so are carnivorous animals and birds of prey. Some of the animal and birds are permitted only under special circumstances, e.g., horsemeat may be allowed under certain distressing conditions. Animals fed unclean or filthy feed, e.g., sewage or tankage protein, must be fed clean feed for three to 40 days before slaughter. Eggs and milk must come from permitted animals. According to Quran, blood that pours forth is prohibited from being consumed whether from permitted or nonpermitted animals and any derivatives.

For seafood, some groups accept only fish with scales as halal, while others consider everything that lives in water, all or some of the time, as halal. Animals that live both in water and on land (e.g., amphibians) are not consumed by most Muslims.

The status of insects is unclear, except that locust is specifically mentioned as halal. The use of honey was very highly recommended by Prophet Muhammad. Other insect products are generally acceptable; however, some consider shellac and carmine makrooh offensive to their psyche.

Proper Slaughtering of Permitted Animals

There are special requirements for slaughtering the animal. It must be a halal species slaughter by a sane, adult Muslim with the name of Allah pronounced at slaughter. The throat is cut in a manner that induces rapid and complete bleeding, resulting in quick death. Generally, at least three of the four passages, i.e., carotids, jugulars, trachea, and esophagus, must be cut to give zabiha or dhabiha meat (meat acceptable for Muslim consumption).

Although kosher meat is similarly slaughtered, a prayer is not said over each animal. Thus, most Muslim scholars do not accept kosher meat as halal. In the absence of halal meats, individual Muslims may choose to purchase kosher meat products.

Islam places great emphasis on humane treatment of animals, especially before and during slaughter. Some conditions include giving the animal proper rest and water, avoiding or reducing stress, not sharpening knives in front of animals, and using a very sharp knife. The animal may only be dismembered after the blood is drained completely and the animal is lifeless. Animal-derived food ingredients must be made from Muslim-slaughtered halal animals.

Hunting of wild halal animals is permitted for the purpose of eating, but not for pleasure. Allah's name should be pronounced when ejecting the tool rather than when catching the hunt. On catching, the animal must immediately be bled by slitting the throat. If the blessing is made at the time of pulling the trigger or shooting an arrow and the hunted animal dies before the hunter reaches it, it would still be halal as long as slaughter is performed and some blood comes out. Fish and seafood may be hunted or caught by any reasonable means available as long as it is done humanely.

The requirements of proper slaughtering and bleeding are applicable to land animals and birds. Fish and other water creatures need not be ritually slaughtered. Similarly, there is no special method of killing locust.

The meat of animals that die of natural causes, diseases, from being gored by other animals, by being strangled, by falling from a height, through beating, or killed by wild beasts, is unlawful to be eaten, unless such animals are slaughtered before they become lifeless. Fish that dies of itself, if floating on water or lying on shore, is halal as long as it shows no signs of decay or deterioration.

An animal must not be slaughtered in dedication to other than Allah, or immolated to anyone other than Allah under any circumstances.

GELATIN

Gelatin is probably the most controversial kosher and halal ingredient. Gelatin can be derived from pork skin, beef bones, or beef skin along with fish skin and bones. Currently available gelatins—even if called kosher—are not acceptable to the mainstream kosher supervision organizations or to halal consumers. However, limited kosher hide gelatin is available. Similarly, at least two sources of certified halal gelatin are available.

BIOTECHNOLOGY

Rabbis and Islamic scholars currently accept products made by simple genetic engineering, e.g., chymosin (rennin) used in cheese making. The production conditions in the fermenters must still be kosher or halal, i.e., the ingredients and the fermenter, and any subsequent processing must use kosher or halal equipment and ingredients of the appropriate status. A product produced in a dairy medium would be dairy. Mainstream rabbis may approve porcine lipase made through biotechnology when it becomes available, if all the other conditions are kosher. The Muslim community is still considering the issue of products with a porcine gene; although a final ruling has not been announced, the leaning seems to be toward rejecting such materials. If the gene for a porcine-derived product were synthesized, i.e., it did not come directly from the pig, Muslim leaders are prepared to accept it. The religious leaders of both communities have not yet determined the status of more complex genetic manipulations and, therefore, such a discussion is premature.

ANIMAL WELFARE

In the United States, the Food Marketing Institute (representing the major supermarkets) and the National Council of Chain Restaurants (in conjunction with the production agriculture trade associations) has undertaken to develop a set of minimal animal welfare standards. As part of that process, a kosher/halal standard and audit requirements have been developed, based on the American Meat Institute's requirement for upright slaughter.[8] In addition, the Northeast Sheep and Goat Program at Cornell University has developed a low-cost, upright holding pen for small animals, and has identified a commercial knife appropriate for halal slaughter. The Cornell program is currently developing a poster on on-farm humane/halal slaughter that will be available in a number of different languages (e.g., English, Arabic, Persian, Spanish).

CONCLUSION

As consumers continue to refine their food requirements, more companies may well choose to provide kosher and halal food products in the marketplace.

REFERENCES

1. Chaudry, M.M. Islamic food laws: Philosophical basis and practical implications. Food Technol. **1992**, *6* (10), 92.
2. Chaudry, M.M.; Regenstein, J.M. Implications of biotechnology and genetic engineering for kosher and halal foods. Trends Food Sci. Technol. **1994**, *5*, 165–168.
3. Chaudry, M.M.; Regenstein, J.M. Muslim dietary laws: Food processing and marketing. Enc. Food Sci. **2000**, 1682–1684.
4. Regenstein, J.M. Health aspects of kosher foods. Activ. Rep. Min. Work Groups Sub-work Groups R & D Assoc. **1994**, *46* (1), 77–83.
5. Regenstein, J.M.; Regenstein, C.E. An introduction to the kosher (dietary) laws for food scientists and food processors. Food Technol. **1979**, *33* (1), 89–99.
6. Regenstein, J.M.; Regenstein, C.E. The kosher dietary laws and their implementation in the food industry. Food Technol. **1988**, *42* (6), 86, 88–94.
7. Regenstein, J.M.; Regenstein, C.E. Kosher foods and food processing. Enc. Food Sci. **2000**, 1449–1453.
8. Regenstein, J.M.; Grandin, T. Animal welfare—Kosher and halal. Inst. Food Technol. Relig. Ethnic Foods Div. Newsl. **2002**, *5* (1), 3–16.

Rumen Microbiology

Todd R. Callaway
United States Department of Agriculture, Agricultural Research Service, College Station, Texas, U.S.A.

Scott A. Martin
University of Georgia, Athens, Georgia, U.S.A.

R. C. Anderson
Tom S. Edrington
David J. Nisbet
Kenneth J. Genovese
United States Department of Agriculture, Agricultural Research Service, College Station, Texas, U.S.A.

INTRODUCTION

The ruminant animal is able to digest feeds due to a mutually beneficial relationship with microorganisms in the rumen (forestomach). These diverse microorganisms degrade and ferment feedstuffs and in turn, provide the animal with usable nutrients. The ruminal fermentation is important to the success of ruminant animals, but is inefficient. Therefore, strategies have been sought to improve the efficiency of the ruminal fermentation.

THE RUMINANT ANIMAL

The ability of the ruminant animal to utilize low-quality fibrous feedstuffs (e.g., grasses and forages) to produce a high-quality end-product (i.e., meat, milk, and wool) is the result of a mutually beneficial relationship between the mammalian host and the fermentative microbial population inhabiting the rumen (forestomach).[1] Animals equipped with a rumen include cattle, buffalo, sheep, antelope, gazelle, duiker, reindeer, deer, giraffe, and goats; other animals that consume grass (e.g., horses and donkeys) are not considered true ruminants, but rather utilize a postgastric fermentation. Mammals do not produce enzymes that degrade cellulose (a primary fibrous component of plant materials), but ruminants are able to degrade cellulose via fermentation because of the presence of the rumen and its resident microbial population.

Ruminant animals are characterized as having teeth on the bottom jaw, and a hard dental pad on the top. This arrangement of teeth results in incomplete mastication (chewing) of ingested feed. Feed is swallowed and deposited into a large pouch (the rumen) at the end of the esophagus. The rumen is a large chamber (can compose up to 30% of the mass of the animal) that is anaerobic (does not contain oxygen) and populated by a very large, diverse population of microorganisms (bacteria, protozoa, fungi, and viruses). These microorganisms degrade feeds through the process of fermentation (described subsequently). Feedstuffs in the rumen are continuously broken down into smaller and smaller pieces by microbial activity as well as regurgitation and remastication (a process known variously as ruminantion, or chewing the cud). As feed is broken down to pieces less than 1 mm in size, it passes out of the rumen and then to the abomasum (or true stomach) for further degradation and to the intestine for digestion by mammalian enzymes.

FERMENTATION: ANAEROBIC DIGESTION

Fermentation is defined as the process of substrate degradation in the absence of oxygen. The best known (to humans) fermentations involve the production of beer, wine, or vinegar (acetate), which is also an important end-product of ruminal and intestinal fermentations. Nearly all feed protein and carbohydrates can be degraded by bacteria via ruminal fermentation to produce volatile fatty acids (VFA) and microbial cells (Fig. 1). The VFA are absorbed by the host animal and provide the animal with a source of carbon and energy for maintenance and productive functions. The most important VFA to the animal are acetate (vinegar), propionate, and butyrate. Microbial cells (bodies) are washed out of the rumen along with the small feed particles and are also digested, providing the ruminant animal with an excellent source of high-quality protein (especially essential amino acids), as well as B vitamins as a by-product of fermentation. Thus, the ruminant provides the microorganisms a hospitable environment and food in exchange for the microorganisms providing nutrients derived from a low-quality feed to the animal—truly, a mutualistic relationship.

Encyclopedia of Animal Science
DOI: 10.1081/E-EAS 120019789

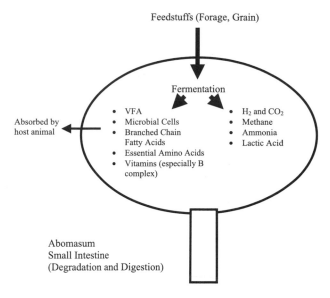

Fig. 1 Activity of the rumen.

Although the ruminal fermentation is generally beneficial to the animal, in some cases, the end-products of the ruminal fermentation can be detrimental to the animal, or even to the environment. Some bacteria ferment specific amino acids (tryptophan) and produce 3-methylindole, which can be inhaled by the animal, resulting in asphyxiation (bovine emphysema). Other problems that can be traced to production of harmful end-products of the rumen fermentation include bloat (swelling of the rumen caused by gas production) and lactic acidosis (accumulation of strong acid in the rumen, which damages the tissues of the rumen and inhibits the beneficial fermentation). Some of the ammonia produced from ruminal protein fermentation is not utilized by the animal, but is excreted in the urine and directly impacts the environment (environmental nitrogen pollution). Methane is a powerful greenhouse gas produced by ruminal microorganisms that is eructated (belched) by all ruminant animals.

MICROBIAL ECOLOGY OF THE RUMEN

The rumen is one of the most densely populated and diverse microbial ecosystems. It is composed of bacteria and protozoa (single-celled microorganisms), fungi (multicellular), and viruses. These flora and fauna break down feedstuffs by sequential colonization and synergistic effort (i.e., fungi and bacteria can colonize grass fibers, and break them down to constituent parts, which are further degraded by bacteria to produce VFA and more bacteria) (Fig. 1). The most well-understood members of the ruminal ecosystem are the bacteria and, to a lesser degree, the protozoa.

Well over 200 species of bacteria have been isolated from the rumen. However, because the rumen microbial population is very dense, many bacterial species present at very low populations probably have not been isolated. The bacterial population is extremely dense and has been estimated to be as high as 10^{10} cells/ml of ruminal fluid (that is, 10,000,000,000 bacteria/ml). Considering that the ruminal volume of a cow is 75,000 ml or greater, it is no surprise that the rumen has been characterized as the world's largest fermentation process.[2]

Ruminal bacteria can ferment nearly all dietary components, and are often grouped based on their fermentation substrate and/or the end-products of their metabolic activity (Table 1).[3] Some bacteria are generalists and can ferment many substrates fairly well (e.g., *Butyrivibrio*), while other bacteria are highly selective in what they can utilize (i.e., *Anaerovibrio*), but can ferment very rapidly. Some bacteria specialize in degrading cellulose, others primarily degrade protein in the diet, and still other species produce methane.

Protozoa are larger, multicellular microorganisms. They can ingest and ferment feedstuffs as well as bacteria and smaller protozoa and play a role in nitrogen cycling within the rumen. The exact role of protozoa in the rumen is still unclear, although they provide a home for some bacteria to attach to and can share a mutualistic relationship with these bacteria. Ruminal fungi are thought to help initiate the degradation of forage and to quickly utilize oxygen ingested with feedstuffs; however, the true significance of ruminal fungi is unclear. Whatever their role in the microbial ecosystem, each microbial species has adapted to fill a specific niche in this complex environment.

USE OF ANTIMICROBIALS TO ENHANCE FERMENTATION EFFICIENCY

The microbial fermentation allows ruminant animals to utilize low-quality feedstuffs; however, the process of fermentation is inherently inefficient. It can often require more than five pounds of feed to produce one pound of animal gain (meat) or milk. This low-feed efficiency makes ruminant production in feedlots and dairy farms quite expensive. Therefore, methods to improve the efficiency of the ruminal fermentation have been examined.

Antibiotics are antimicrobial compounds that kill or stop the growth of bacteria. Often, antibiotics are used to treat bacterial diseases in humans or in animals. In some cases, antibiotics have been used to try to increase the efficiency of the fermentation or to reduce pathogenic bacteria (both human and animal) in the gastrointestinal tract. For example, Tylosin is currently fed to cattle to reduce the incidence of *Fusobacteria necrophorum* (a bacterium responsible for liver abscesses in cattle);

Table 1 Groups of important ruminal bacteria, and the dietary components they are capable of fermenting

Dietary component	Group of bacteria	Important genera
Forage	Cellulose-fermenting species	*Ruminococcus* *Fibrobacter* *Butyrivibrio*
Forage	Hemicellulose-fermenting species	*Butyrivibrio* *Bacteroides* (*Prevotella*) *Ruminococcus*
Forage	Pectin-fermenting species	*Butyrivibrio* *Bacteroides* (*Prevotella*) *Succinovibrio* *Streptococcus*
Grain	Starch-fermenting species	*Streptococcus* *Bacteroides* (*Prevotella*) *Succinomonas* *Lactobacillus*
Any	Protein-fermenting species	*Clostridium* *Peptostreptococcus* *Bacteroides* (*Prevotella*) *Butyrivibrio* *Megasphaera*
Any	Fermentation acid-utilizing species	*Megasphaera* *Selenomonas* *Anaerovibrio*
Any	Lipid-utilizing species	*Butyrivibrio*
Any	Methane-producing species	*Methanobacterium* *Methanobrevibacter*

(Adapted from Ref. 3, among other sources.)

neomycin sulfate has been suggested to be used in feedlot cattle to reduce the human pathogenic bacterium *Escherichia coli* O157:H7.[4]

However, the use of antibiotics as animal growth promotants has come under increased scrutiny due to problems associated with antibiotic resistance (discussed elsewhere in this encyclopedia). In response to this issue, the European Union has recently (2003) enacted a ban on the use of all antimicrobial feed additives in animal rations; it remains to be seen if the United States will follow suit. Therefore, the use of antibiotics, especially those used in human medicine, to enhance the efficiency of the rumen fermentation is not widespread or encouraged.

Ionophores are the most widely used compound that can increase the efficiency of ruminant production.[5] Ionophores are antimicrobials (but not antibiotics) that inhibit Gram-positive bacteria. Because the rumen is populated by both Gram-positive and -negative bacteria, the Gram-negative bacteria gain a competitive advantage in the rumen. Due to this shift caused by ionophore treatment, ruminal methane, ammonia, and lactic acid production is reduced, and animal growth efficiency is increased. This increase in efficiency has led to the widespread use of ionophores in most feedlot cattle in the United States.

BACTERIAL PATHOGENS IN THE RUMEN

Because the rumen is ideally suited for microbial growth, it is no surprise that pathogenic bacteria can also inhabit the rumen. *E. coli* O157:H7 and *Salmonella* (many serotypes) are foodborne pathogenic bacteria that have been isolated from the rumen. Both *Salmonella* and *E. coli* O157:H7 can pose a risk to humans via direct animal contact or through consumption of contaminated meat products. Additionally, some *Salmonella* serotypes can cause severe illness in the host animal. Processing plants do an excellent job of controlling the spread of these pathogens after slaughter; however, foodborne illnesses that are associated with ruminant-derived food products still occur. Therefore, recent research has focused on strategies to reduce these pathogens in animals prior to entry into the food chain.

CONCLUSION

Our knowledge of rumen microbiology has grown immensely over the past 50 years, yet many people still regard the ruminal fermentation processes as a black box.

Like any other well-developed ecosystem, the rumen is very complex and changes imposed upon the fermentation can have unintended repercussions throughout the ecosystem, which may have a profound effect on the animal. Therefore, technologies to improve the efficiency of the ruminal fermentation proposed for the future (including introduction of designer bacteria or super-bugs that can address any perceived shortcomings of the ecosystem) need to be approached with caution. Future directions of research into the area of rumen microbiology will certainly include the use of genomics (sequencing of the DNA of ruminal microorganisms). The recent complete sequencing of the genome of predominant cellulose degrading bacteria will surely allow a greater understanding of the complex ruminal ecosystem.

ARTICLES OF FURTHER INTEREST

Digesta Processing and Fermentation, p. 282
Digestion and Absorption of Nutrients, p. 285

GI Tract: Anatomical and Functional Comparisons, p. 445
GI Tract: Animal/Microbial Symbiosis, p. 449

REFERENCES

1. Hungate, R.E. *The Rumen and Its Microbes*; Academic Press: New York, NY, 1966.
2. Weimer, P.J. Cellulose degradation by ruminal microorganisms. Crit. Rev. Biotechnol. **1992**, *12*, 189–223.
3. Yokoyama, M.G.; Johnson, K.A. Microbiology of the Rumen and Intestine. In *Microbiology of the Rumen and Intestine*; Waveland Press: Englewood Cliffs, NJ, 1988; 125–144.
4. Elder, R.O.; Keen, J.E.; Wittum, T.E.; Callaway, T.R.; Edrington, T.S.; Anderson, R.C.; Nisbet, D.J. Intervention to reduce fecal shedding of enterohemorrhagic *Escherichia coli* O157:H7 in naturally infected cattle using neomycin sulfate. J. Anim. Sci. **2002**, *80* (Suppl. 1), 15.
5. Russell, J.B.; Strobel, H.J. Effect of ionophores on ruminal fermentation. Appl. Envir. Microbiol. **1989**, *55*, 1–6.

Salmon

Barbara Grisdale-Helland
AKVAFORSK, Sunndalsøra, Norway

Ståle J. Helland
Aquaculture Protein Centre—CoE, Sunndalsøra, Norway

Kari Kolstad
AKVAFORSK, Ås, Norway

INTRODUCTION

The production of farmed salmon for food started in the 1960s, aided by experience from the production of young salmon and trout for release in rivers. Since that time, selective breeding programs and improved feeds and management have contributed to the tremendous growth in the salmon industry. During the period 1985–2001, the world production of farmed Atlantic salmon (*Salmo salar*) increased from 38,797 T to 1,025,287 T. In 2001, Norway and Chile produced 43% and 25% of the Atlantic salmon, respectively. Atlantic salmon are grown in fresh water to a size of about 70 g and are then transferred to cages in the sea where, during the next 9–12 months, they grow to a market size of 3 to 5 kg. The main ingredients in salmon feed are fish meal and fish oil, although the use of alternative sources of protein and fat is increasing. The optimal dietary protein level for salmon is higher than for terrestrial species because fish use a higher proportion of the protein for energy. Despite this, the proportion of consumed protein retained in the edible portion of salmon is about 30%, two times higher than for chickens and pigs.

PRODUCTION

The Salmonidae family includes the genera *Salmo*, *Oncorhynchus*, and *Salvelinus*, comprising the salmon, trout, and char. Atlantic salmon have been held in culture for release in rivers since the 1800s, and in a farming situation for food production since the 1960s. Atlantic salmon make up the greatest part of the world production of the various salmon species, 1,025,287 T in 2001.[1] Four countries—Norway, Chile, the United Kingdom, and Canada—produce almost 90% (Fig. 1), the rest being produced by eight other countries. Of the Pacific salmon species, the production of coho salmon (*Oncorhynchus kisutch*) (151,386 T in 2001) is greatest, 90% of it being produced by Chile (Fig. 2).[1]

The production of Atlantic salmon has increased as a result of greater numbers of fish being farmed using continuously improved genetic material, nutrition, and management. The cost of production per kg round weight (not including slaughter and packaging costs) in 1997 was US $2.495 in Norway and US $1.986 in Chile, the main differences being smolt costs and undefined miscellaneous costs.[2] Feed (including pigments, vitamins, medication, and feed transport) accounted for 51% of the production costs in Norway and 61% in Chile.[2] In 2001 in Norway, 306,328 kg salmon were produced in the sea-phase per man-year, a 58% increase from 1997.[3]

LIFE CYCLE

Most salmon are anadromous. In the wild, spawning, fertilization and hatching of roe, and an initial growth period occur in rivers. This is followed by migration to sea and the main growth period, and later, as mature fish, migration back up the river to reproduce. This cycle is duplicated in culture conditions. Mature Atlantic salmon are stripped for roe (eggs) and milt (secretion containing the sperm), these are mixed to allow fertilization, and then the eggs are hatched, all in fresh water. The alevin (young fish) lives off its yolk sac until it has developed enough to be able to consume exogenous feed. Growth continues in freshwater tanks until the fish has undergone a physiological transformation, smoltification, allowing it to survive the hyperosmotic conditions of salt water. With artificial light regimes and good husbandry, the smoltification process may be started early so that smolt are produced during the first autumn, although usually this process occurs later and the fish are not transferred to sea cages until the second spring. Atlantic salmon grow to a market size of 3 to 5 kg during a period of about 9–12 months in the sea. Fish chosen for

Encyclopedia of Animal Science
DOI: 10.1081/E-EAS 120019790

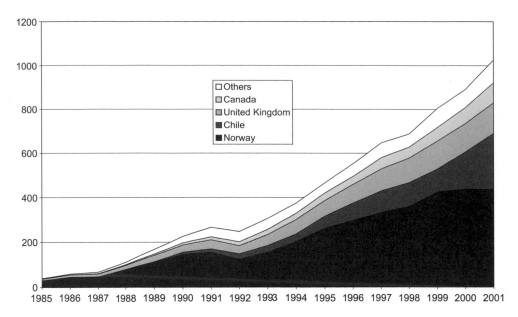

Fig. 1 World production of Atlantic salmon, in thousands of tons (round weight). (From Ref. 1.) (*View this art in color at www.dekker.com.*)

broodstock are moved back to fresh or brackish water a few months before spawning.

NUTRITION AND FEEDING

During the period 1994–1998, the feed efficiency ratio for Norwegian Atlantic salmon production was approximately 0.83 kg gain per kg dry feed.[4] The amounts of raw materials used for salmon feed production in Norway in 1999 and 2000 indicate that the average feed was made up of 40% fish meal and fish silage, 7% corn and wheat gluten, 6% various soybean products, 28% fish oil and 3% soybean oil, 12% wheat flour, and 4% vitamins, minerals, and pigment.[4] The optimal dietary protein level for salmon is higher than for terrestrial species because fish use a higher proportion of the protein for energy. Despite this, the proportion of consumed protein retained in the

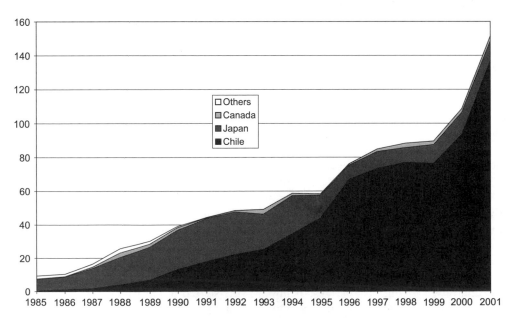

Fig. 2 World production of coho salmon, in thousands of tons (round weight). (From Ref. 1.) (*View this art in color at www.dekker.com.*)

edible portion of salmon is about 30%, two times higher than for chickens and pigs.[5] The fat level in diets for Atlantic salmon fed in sea cages has been increased from an initial level of under 10% to a current level of up to 40%, due to developments in extrusion and vacuum coating of fat. Salmon do not have a requirement for carbohydrates, but sources such as wheat and corn are added to the formulation to aid in binding of the feed and expansion during extrusion. Salmon poorly digest high levels of dietary starch.

The increase in efficiency of production of salmon has been aided by the development of computerized feeding methods and equipment. Systems are available that register the amount of feed refusal and thereby the feeding activity of the fish in the cage and subsequently, increase or decrease the ration size and/or frequency of feeding. In grow-out farms, photoperiod manipulation with underwater lights is used to delay or prevent maturation before harvest, thereby reducing or avoiding the reduction in growth and flesh quality often accompanying reproductive development.[6]

QUALITY

The main factors describing the quality of farmed salmon are color, flavor, fat content and distribution, texture, and appearance. These may be influenced by species and strain of fish, age and weight, feed composition, ration level, and genetic selection. Preference differences between markets and by the processing industry for certain characteristics influence the type of fish that are produced.

The intake of fish (and n-3 polyunsaturated fatty acids) is generally associated with a lower risk of coronary artery disease in humans, although the exact reason for this connection has not been defined.[7] Because of limited supplies of fish meal and fish oil, the use of other protein and lipid sources for fish feed, from plants for example, is expanding. The fatty acid composition of fish flesh is highly influenced by the dietary fatty acid content, though, and diets containing plant oils with higher levels of n-6 fatty acids and lower levels of n-3 fatty acids result in a reduction in the flesh n-3/n-6 fatty acid ratio. A subsequent period of feeding a diet containing only fish oil, however, may partly or completely reverse the changes in the levels of the various fatty acids caused by plant oils.[8]

BREEDING AND GENETICS

In Norway, extensive breeding experiments with Atlantic salmon and rainbow trout were started in 1971.[9] In 1975,

the first breeding program for Atlantic salmon was established. For the first two generations of selection, the breeding goal was growth rate. With an increase in growth of 14% in each generation of selection,[10] after seven generations of selection, the time needed to reach slaughter weight is now halved. The fresh water period has decreased from 16 to eight months, while the grow-out period in sea has decreased from 24 to 12 months. This has resulted in a considerable reduction in production costs, mainly through improved feed efficiency. Domestication is also an important consequence of selective breeding by selecting the highest performing individuals in each generation under famed conditions. The breeding goal is now more complex in accordance with environmental challenges and demands in the market. Characteristics such as age at sexual maturation, meat quality (fat percentage and distribution and flesh color), and disease resistance are important parts of the breeding goal. The breeding program has, from the start, been based on family selection, utilizing family information to select breeding candidates. This selection method has proven to be the most efficient in Atlantic salmon.[11] It is expected that knowledge from extensive research in the area of molecular genetics can be applied in future breeding programs.[12] Molecular information connected to important traits may be utilized to increase genetic progress. Further, the use of microsatellite DNA profiling for family identification may be possible in the future, which represents a major advance in selective breeding of aquatic species, allowing different family groups to be kept in a common tank from fertilization onward.

CONCLUSION

It is expected that the production of farmed salmon will continue to grow, despite small economic margins, as new markets are established and further improvements in production efficiency are made. An increase in the use of more readily available plant protein and fat sources and appropriate management techniques will help maintain sustainable production of this healthy, high-quality food.

ACKNOWLEDGMENT

Arne Kittelsen is gratefully acknowledged for help and discussions during the preparation of this manuscript.

ARTICLES OF FURTHER INTEREST

Aquatic Animals: Fishes—Minor, p. 55
Contributions to Society: Conversion of Feed to Food,
   p. 245

REFERENCES

1. FAO. *Aquaculture Production: Quantitites 1950–2001*;
   FAO Yearbook, Fishery Statistics, Aquaculture Production
   2001; Food and Agriculture Organisation, 2001; Vol 92/2.
   http://www.fao.org/fi/statist/fisoft/fishplus.asp (accessed
   April 2003).
2. Bjørndal, T.; Aarland, K. Salmon aquaculture in Chile.
   Aquacult. Econ. Manage. **1999**, *3*, 238–253.
3. Norwegian Directorate of Fisheries Lønnsomhetsundersø-
   kelse for matfiskproduksjon laks og ørret Økonomiske
   Analyser Fiskeoppdrett nr. 1/2002. In *Survey of Profitability in Production of Salmon and Trout*; Norwegian
   Directorate of Fisheries: Bergen, 2002; 1–71. (summary in
   English) http://www.fiskeridir.no/sider/statistikk/matfisk/
   matfisk01/index.html (accessed April 2003).
4. Waagbø, R.; Torrissen, O.J.; Austreng, E. *Fôr og
   fôrmidler—den største utfordringen for vekst i norsk
   havbruk (Feed and feed ingredients—The greatest challenge for growth in Norwegian aquaculture)*; Norges
   forskningsråd: Oslo, Norway, 2001; 1–58.
5. Austreng, E. Fôrutnytting hos laks samanlikna med
   kylling, gris og sau. (Feed utilization of salmon compared
   with chickens, pigs and sheep.) Nor. Fiskeoppdrett **1994**,
   2A, 2–3.
6. Bromage, N.; Porter, M.; Randall, C. The environmental
   regulation of maturation in farmed finfish with special
   reference to the role of photoperiod and melatonin.
   Aquaculture **2001**, *197*, 63–98.
7. Schmidt, E.B.; Christensen, J.H.; Aardestrup, I.; Madsen,
   T.; Riahi, S.; Hansen, V.E.; Skou, H.A. Marine n-3 fatty
   acids: Basic features and background. Lipids **2001**, *36S*,
   65–68.
8. Bell, J.G.; McGhee, F.; Campbell, P.J.; Sargent, J.R.
   Rapeseed oil as an alternative to marine fish oil in diets of
   post-smolt Atlantic salmon (*Salmo salar*): Changes in flesh
   fatty acid composition and effectiveness of subsequent fish
   oil "wash out." Aquaculture **2003**, *218*, 515–528.
9. Gjedrem, T. Genetic improvement of cold-water fish
   species. Aquacult. Res. **2000**, *31*, 25–33.
10. Gjerde, B.; Simianer, H.; Refstie, T. Estimates of genetic
    and phenotypic parameters for body weight, growth rate
    and sexual maturity in Atlantic salmon. Livest. Prod. Sci.
    1994, *38*, 133–143.
11. Gjerde, B.; Rye, M. Design of Breeding Programs in
    Aquaculture Species—Possibilities and Constraints. In
    *Genetics and Breeding of Mediterranean Aquaculture
    Species*; Proceedings of the Seminar of the CIHEAM
    Network on Technology of Aquaculture in the Mediterra-
    nean (TECAM), Zaragoza, Spain, 1997; Vol. 34, 181–192.
    Options Mediterr.
12. Hoyheim, B. Genetic Mapping in Salmonids, an Overview
    of the Current Research in Atlantic Salmon, Rainbow Trout
    and Brown Trout. Proceedings of the EMBO-Workshop
    on Reproduction & Early Development, Bergen, Norway,
    Oct 3–7, 1998; University of Bergen: Bergen, 1998.

Selection: Marker Assisted

R. Mark Thallman
U.S. Meat Animal Research Center, Clay Center, Nebraska, U.S.A.

INTRODUCTION

Marker-assisted selection (MAS) is the process of using the results of deoxyribonucleic acid (DNA) tests to assist in the selection of individuals to become the parents in the next generation of a genetic improvement program. The term marker refers to a location in the genome at which a specific difference in DNA sequence has been associated with an effect on the trait of interest. The word assisted implies that the selection is also influenced by other sources of information, such as phenotypes (observed or measured value) of the individuals and, in many cases, phenotypes of relatives of the individuals (which requires pedigree information). Selection methods based only on phenotypes (and optionally) pedigree will be referred to as traditional methods of selection. The additional information provided by the DNA test results should improve the accuracy of evaluating the genetic merit of the individuals in the population, and hence, should improve the rate of response to selection.

ADVANTAGES OF MARKER-ASSISTED SELECTION

Traditional methods of selection can produce very accurate evaluations of genetic merit for traits that are high in heritability (observed or measured value is a good predictor of breeding value) or for individuals that have many progeny with phenotypes recorded. However, many traits of economic importance in livestock are low or moderate (10–40%) in heritability or can only be measured postmortem, in which case, accurate genetic evaluations are only possible through progeny testing. Other important traits can only be measured late in the productive life of the individual. For these traits, accurate genetic evaluations can only be obtained after the selection decision (to produce progeny) has been made. These are the traits for which MAS is expected to accelerate the rate of genetic improvement[1,2] because the DNA testing component of MAS can be obtained and combined with marker-adjusted estimates of the parents' breeding values anytime after birth. In theory, it is possible to apply DNA testing to a few cells of an embryo and use MAS to determine whether to transfer the embryo and even to shorten the generation interval by combining MAS with germ-line manipulation.[3]

DNA tests can increase the amount of information provided by each phenotype collected, and thus, reduce the number of phenotypes required, but they do not eliminate the need for phenotypes. Marker-assisted selection has the potential to reduce the impact of antagonistic genetic correlations by concentrating selection intensity on those genes that affect one set of traits without undesirable effects on other traits.[1]

CATEGORIES OF DNA TESTS

DNA tests that could be considered for use in a MAS program can be grouped into the following general categories: functional tests, association tests, and linked marker tests.

Functional tests are those in which a polymorphism (difference in DNA sequence) being tested is the cause of an associated phenotypic difference. These tests are the easiest to apply in a breeding program, but they are also the most expensive to develop. However, a gene can have several functional polymorphisms, but the test will detect only those that it is specifically designed to detect, which implies that they are known. The process of searching a population for all of the relevant functional polymorphisms in a gene is expensive and difficult. Therefore, it should not be assumed that a functional test will account for all of the genetic variation in a particular gene.

Association tests are based on population-wide coinheritance (assumed to be due to linkage disequilibrium) of the markers being tested and the gene affecting the phenotypes. As this association may differ among breeds, the relationship within each breed in which the test will be used needs to be established, and this requires phenotypes and DNA tests on a substantial number of animals from each breed. Initially, it is likely that the associations will be established in mixed populations, representing the breeds of primary importance. In such cases, it is very important that breed differences are accounted for in the analysis; otherwise, spurious or biased associations between DNA tests and traits are likely to occur. It is

Encyclopedia of Animal Science
DOI: 10.1081/E-EAS 120019791

likely that initially, association tests will be the most widely used category of tests for production traits in livestock. Association tests are likely to eventually be converted into functional tests over time, but this is an expensive and time-consuming process. As a practical matter, it may be very difficult to determine whether a particular difference in DNA sequence is causative of phenotypic differences, or is merely associated with the differences; thus, it may not always be clear whether a particular test is a functional or an association test. However, it is not necessary to know which of these two categories a particular test belongs to because the way in which they are used is very similar.

Linked marker tests are based on the cosegregation of DNA markers and phenotypes within families. Thus, the linkage phase (the association between the markers being tested and the gene affecting the phenotypes) must be established within each family in which the markers are to be used for selection. Consequently, DNA tests must be performed on progeny with phenotypes within each family. This is the primary factor limiting the application of linked markers. Consequently, they are best suited to within-herd use by large breeding companies. Linked markers have the advantage of being the easiest and least expensive to develop. Most published QTL are currently defined by linked markers. Over time, many of these will be converted to association tests, and eventually, to functional tests.

INTEGRATION OF DNA TESTING WITH GENETIC EVALUATION SCHEMES

Quantitative traits (which include most production traits in livestock) are generally assumed to be influenced by a few genes with moderate or large effect and a greater number of genes of smaller effect. DNA tests are currently only available for a few of the genes with moderate or large effect. The aggregate effect of the remaining genes is referred to as the residual polygenic breeding value,[4] which will often account for a very substantial proportion of the genetic variance for a trait. Furthermore, with multiple genes affecting each trait and multiple traits affected by most genes, optimizing the relative selection pressure to apply to each DNA test and the residual polygenic component is not a trivial task. The most efficient way to integrate the various sources of information is a combined analysis. The marker-adjusted estimated breeding value (MAEBV) for a trait is the sum of an estimated effect of each DNA test in the analysis plus the estimated residual polygenic breeding value. Although the application of MAEBV is in its infancy, the concept is not new.[2,5]

It may be tempting to try to adjust traditional estimated breeding values (EBVs) for DNA test results. However, if a sire has a large number of progeny with phenotypes, the accuracy of his traditional EBV will be high and it will not differ substantially from his MAEBV because his total genetic merit is already well established and the DNA tests only provide information about which genes contributed to his total merit. On the other hand, a set of young sires (without progeny or phenotypes) that are candidates for progeny testing would have low-accuracy EBVs that are simply the averages of their parents' EBVs; their MAEBVs could differ substantially from their traditional EBVs. The extent to which an EBV differs from a MAEBV depends on a number of factors, so the computation of MAEBVs is best done in a genetic evaluation system that considers all relevant sources of information simultaneously.

DETERMINING WHICH DNA TESTS TO USE IN MAS

Commercial availability of a substantial number of DNA tests is a prerequisite for MAS to have a major impact on livestock breeding. However, this variety of tests implies that breeders, breed associations, and organizations that conduct genetic evaluations must decide which DNA tests are most profitable or productive for inclusion in their respective genetic improvement programs. Factors that should be considered in the decision are: amount of evidence that the effect of the test is real (not a statistical artifact), the magnitude of the effect, the frequencies of the major alleles, the percentage of genetic variation accounted for by the test, and the degree of dominance. Together, these factors determine the potential for genetic improvement and the rate at which that improvement could occur. Ideally, the above information would be estimated from animals of the breed(s) in which the test would be applied. Effects on all available traits should be reported. It is unlikely that a gene would affect only one trait, in spite of the current trend to label commercial DNA tests as being associated with only one trait.

REALISTIC EXPECTATIONS

DNA testing is not likely to make animal breeding simpler, as was initially expected, but it should make selection more effective. DNA tests are likely to change (improve) over time. As more data is acquired, estimates of the effects of test genotypes will improve. Furthermore, the association between test and functional polymorphisms is likely to be different between breeds, but these differences are likely to be discovered only after a large amount of data has been generated by using the tests widely for a number of years. To get started, the only practical approach is likely to be to use species-wide associations.

Cost will limit the adoption of DNA testing in livestock, although costs are projected to decrease substantially over the next few years.

CONCLUSION

The adoption of MAS in the livestock industries has been much slower than many would have predicted 10 to 15 years ago. However, there are several examples of application of MAS in commercial livestock populations.[6,7] Commercial DNA tests for quantitative traits are on the market for several species and MAS has the potential to substantially increase response to selection. As more tests become available over the next few years, it seems likely that MAS will become increasingly important in livestock breeding.

REFERENCES

1. Weller, J.I. *Quantitative Trait Loci Analysis in Animals*; CABI Publishing: Wallingford, UK, 2001; 217–242.
2. Smith, C. Improvement of metric traits through specific genetic loci. Anim. Prod. **1967**, *9*, 349–358.
3. Georges, M.; Massey, J.M. Velogenetics, or the synergistic use of marker assisted selection and germ-line manipulation. Theriogenology **1991**, *35*, 151–159.
4. Soller, M. The use of loci associated with quantitative effects in dairy cattle improvement. Anim. Prod. **1978**, *27*, 133–139.
5. Fernando, R.L.; Grossman, M. Marker assisted selection using best linear unbiased prediction. Genet. Sel. Evol. **1989**, *21*, 467–477.
6. Spelman, R.J. Utilization of Molecular Information in Dairy Cattle Breeding. Proceedings of the 7th World Congress on Genetics Applied to Livestock Production, Montpellier, France, Aug 19–23, 2002; 2002. CD-Rom Communication No. 22:02.
7. Boichard, D.; Fritz, S.; Rossignol, M.N.; Boscher, M.Y.; Malafosse, A.; Colleau, J.J. Implementation of Marker-Assisted Selection in French Dairy Cattle. Proceedings of the 7th World Congress on Genetics Applied to Livestock Production, Montpellier, France, Aug 19–23, 2002; 2002. CD-Rom Communication No. 22:03.

Selection: Traditional Methods

Lawrence R. Schaeffer
University of Guelph, Guelph, Ontario, Canada

INTRODUCTION

Selection is defined as any human manipulation that restricts the mating of animals such that each animal does not have an equal chance of reproducing. Only animals that reproduce influence the genetic composition of the next generation. The purpose of selection is to change the genetic composition of a livestock population to have more animals with desired characteristics.

INFINITESIMAL MODEL

Traditional selection methods have assumed that performance traits are controlled by an infinite number of gene loci, each with an equal-sized contribution to the trait of interest. Only purely additive gene action has been assumed to exist, i.e., the genetic effects that are passed to progeny. Dominance effects and other interactions between loci have been assumed to be negligible.[1]

ELEMENTS OF GENETIC CHANGE

The amount of genetic change caused by selection depends on several factors. The key equation[2] to predict response to selection, R, is

$$R = \frac{r_m i_m \sigma + r_f i_f \sigma}{L_m + L_f}$$

where r_m and r_f are the accuracies of evaluating the genetic merit of male and female animals, respectively; i_m and i_f are the intensities of selection (e.g., the top 5%) for males and females, respectively; σ is the genetic variability in the population; and L_m and L_f are the generation intervals for males and females, respectively. A generation interval is the average age of a male or female parent when a progeny of that individual can replace it in the breeding population under a particular testing scheme (Table 1).

In many livestock species, males can have larger progeny groups than females. Consequently, males can be more accurately evaluated from their more numerous progeny than females. Because fewer males are needed for matings than females, the intensity of selection on males can be much higher. Intensity of selection is a function of reproductive output compared to the number of males and females for creating the next generation. The generation intervals for males and females could be different depending on when selection decisions are made for each sex. In dairy cattle, for example, sires are not culled until their first daughters have matured, calved, and completed a full lactation of milking. Thus, sires can be six years of age or older. Cows are often culled based on their own performance, somewhere between 20 and 36 months of age.

Response to selection can be increased in several ways. Accuracy of evaluation can be increased by using more data and better methods of evaluation. Intensities of selection can be increased by selecting fewer animals from among the possible candidates. Generation intervals can be shortened by making selection decisions sooner in an animal's life. All of these factors must be balanced against the costs of achieving them.

TYPES OF SELECTION

Selection is based on different sources of information. The trait often determines the type of selection that can be applied. For example, not all traits are expressed in both sexes, such as milk production in dairy cattle, or litter size in swine and rabbits. Sex-limited traits require selection based on progeny information.

An Animal's Own Performance

Animals were originally selected on the basis of their own phenotype. That is, cows that give the most milk, sows that have the largest litters, hens that lay the most eggs, and horses that run the fastest are examples of this type of selection. Although selection on phenotypes is very easy to apply, the accuracy of phenotypes as an estimate of genetic merit is equal to the square root of heritability. Heritability is the proportion of the variability in a trait that is attributable to genetics (Table 2). For most economically important traits, heritability ranges from 0.05 to 0.50. Consequently, response to selection on an animal's own performance may not be very high. Accuracy can be improved slightly for some traits by averaging several observations taken on the same animal.

Encyclopedia of Animal Science
DOI: 10.1081/E-EAS 120019792

Table 1 Minimum possible and typical generation intervals for common livestock species[a]

Species	Sexual maturity	Gestation length	Minimum possible	Typical males	Typical females	Offspring per gestation
Cattle (*Bos taurus*)	12 mo	280 d	33 mo	6–9 yr	3–4 yr	1
Horses	15–24 mo	340 d	41–59 mo	8–12 yr	8–12 yr	1
Swine	120–250 d	112 d	19–20 mo	1.5–2 yr	1.5–2 yr	10–12
Sheep	185 d	150 d	17 mo	2–3 yr	2–4 yr	1–2
Goats	165 d	150 d	15–16 mo	2 yr	2 yr	1–2
Rabbits	125 d	31 d	11 mo	1 yr	1 yr	8–12
Chickens	140 d	In egg	11 mo	1–1.5 yr	1–1.5 yr	250
Turkey	224 d	In egg	15–16 mo	1–1.5 yr	1–1.5 yr	100
Rainbow trout	2–3 yr	In egg	3 yr	3 yr	3–4 yr	1,000

[a]Values may vary with breed within species.

Progeny Performance

For sex-limited traits, the average performance of an animal's progeny can be used. Males can generally have many dozens or hundreds of progeny and the accuracy of evaluating the genetic merit of that male can approach 100%. A disadvantage is that one has to wait until the progeny are born, grow, and make their own performance records, thereby increasing the generation interval and lowering response to selection. An optimal balance between accuracy of evaluation and generation interval has to be achieved.

Relatives' Performance

Animals' genetic merits could be evaluated using information on parents, full-sibs, or half-sibs. Accuracy of evaluation is limited by the amount of information on relatives and depends on the particular combination of relatives. Animals could be evaluated before they are old enough to be used for breeding purposes. The generation interval can be shortened using relatives' records, but accuracy of evaluation may suffer.

Combining All Sources of Information

The best method of evaluating genetic merit is through the use of an animal model.[3] An animal model is a statistical method for combining information from the animal's own performance, all other relatives, and all progeny, and at the same time, account for any nongenetic factors that might influence performance of animals, such as contemporary groups, ages, years, and seasons. Animal models make efficient use of the data and generally provide the highest probability of correctly ranking animals for genetic merit. Animal models have been used in dairy, beef, and swine since 1989 in various countries around the world. The methodology generally applied to the animal

model is called best linear unbiased prediction, or BLUP. Methodology and genetic models, however, are continually being improved.

EVALUATION OF MORE THAN ONE TRAIT

Livestock are often evaluated for many traits, such as production, reproduction, conformation, and health. Selection can be applied separately to each trait (independent culling levels), or traits may be combined into an economic index. The first step is to define the breeding goal, i.e., all of the traits that the breeder hopes to change. The next step is to identify the traits that will be in the economic index. For example, there could be five traits in the breeding goal, and 12 traits in the economic index. Traits in the breeding goal may not be measurable directly on animals, and so two or three other correlated traits are used in the economic index as indicators of the trait in the breeding goal. The genetic variability of each trait, in the breeding goal and in the index, must be known as well as the genetic correlations between all traits. A genetic correlation between two traits is an estimate of the proportion of genes that influence both traits. Relative economic weights can be computed

Table 2 Heritabilities of different kinds of traits

Low (0–0.15)	Medium (0.15–0.40)	High (0.40–0.70)
Litter size	Milk production	Carcass traits
Fertility	Growth traits	Meat tenderness
Disease susceptibility	Feed efficiency	Meat yields
Locomotion	Body lengths	Milk components
Conception rate	Racing speed	Gaits
Longevity/ survival	Egg production	Fleece weights

from figures on costs and returns using the estimated genetic correlations and genetic variabilities of traits.

Selection on an economic index leads to optimum change in economic value over all traits. Often, one trait has greater economic importance than the other traits, and so relative economic values are often debated. Economic indexes may be derived in many different ways. For example, the weights for the index may be based on the desired responses that the user seeks for each trait. Or, one or more traits, perhaps, should not change either for the better or worse, and weights can be derived to accomplish this goal. Some traits are related to each other, or to economics in a nonlinear manner. For example, legs on animals can be either too straight or too curved, but both lead to economic losses compared to an animal with desirable legs between too straight and too curved. Thus, economic indexes can be nonlinear functions.

CONSEQUENCES OF SELECTION

Selection changes the frequencies of genes that affect the traits of interest.[1] Frequency changes can raise or lower the means of traits and also increase or decrease the genetic variability of traits. Genes may affect more than one trait, directly or indirectly, so that selection will directly affect the traits of interest and will indirectly affect many other traits (i.e., correlated responses) that may not be observed in traditional record keeping. For example, many years of selection for increased milk yields in dairy cattle have caused a correlated decrease in reproductive performance. There could also have been changes in immune responses and other traits that were not observed or recorded while selection was applied to milk production.

Selection tends to choose animals that are related (because they share the same favorable genes). Breeding related animals leads to an animal that may have the same gene allele on both chromosomes. This is called homozygosity. The proportion of gene loci in an individual that are homozygous is an inbreeding coefficient. Greater homozygosity results in lower genetic variability. Inbreeding can decrease performance and increase the likelihood of undesirable genes becoming homozygous, which could result in death or greater susceptibility to diseases. Mating programs can be designed to maximize the ratio of selection response to level of inbreeding, or to minimize the increase in inbreeding per generation. Such programs dictate which males should be mated to particular females.

EFFECTIVENESS OF SELECTION

Traditional selection methods have provided rates of genetic response up to 3% of the mean per year, depending on species and trait.[4] Genetic responses are cumulative and can become appreciable over time. Expected genetic responses are often not realized because of changing economic situations that force producers to change their breeding objectives. Genetic change has been most noticeable in species with short generation intervals such as poultry and swine. Broiler chickens reach market weights significantly earlier on less feed than they did just 20 years ago, for example. Genetic responses in dairy cattle for production traits have been significant due to the ability to pick the best males on an international basis rather than within country.

CONCLUSION

Future selection programs will be improved versions of the traditional selection methods. Knowledge about individual genes, their location, the proteins they produce, and the metabolic pathways that they control will be incorporated into genetic evaluation models and will be used to shorten generation intervals such that genetic response is increased. More traits will be included in the breeding objectives so that unwanted correlated responses can be avoided. The pedigree and data files that have been created over the decades will become more valuable in discovering major quantitative trait loci (QTL). Application of DNA tests to embryos could perhaps more accurately identify superior animals and at the same time greatly shorten the generation interval. Care should be taken to completely understand the functions of individual genes because these might influence other genes in an antagonistic manner, thereby nullifying any benefits of selection using that gene. Breeders of animals will continue to select the best animals, mate the best to the best, and strive to improve livestock to near genetic perfection.

REFERENCES

1. Falconer, D.S.; Mackay, T.F.C. *Introduction to Quantitative Genetics*, 4th Ed.; Longman Group Ltd: Essex, U.K., 1996.
2. Bourdon, R.M. *Understanding Animal Breeding*; Prentice Hall, Inc.: New Jersey, 1997.
3. Henderson, C.R. *Applications of Linear Models in Animal Breeding*; University of Guelph: Canada, 1984.
4. Smith, C. Introduction: Current Animal Breeding. In *Animal Breeding Technology for the 21st Century*; Clark, A.J., Ed.; Harwood Academic Publishers: Amsterdam, 1998; 1–10.

Sheep: Breeding/Genetics—Improving Meat Production

Ronald Martin Lewis
Virginia Polytechnic Institute and State University, Blacksburg, Virginia, U.S.A.

INTRODUCTION

Since domestication, sheep have contributed to the sustenance and comfort of human society. Currently, the role of sheep enterprises in much of the world is the production of lamb meat. Besides sheep numbers, the reproductive efficiency of ewes is the key determinant to lamb output. Reproductive efficiency can be improved by crossing breeds with complementary attributes for reproductive traits. Yet benefits from crossbreeding depend on the genetic merit of the pure breeds crossed. Therefore, effective selection programs within breeds are crucial. The focus of this article is to describe those traits central to improving meat production in sheep, and genetic approaches to improve these traits.

THE CONTRIBUTION OF SHEEP

Sheep were domesticated about 12,000 years ago in Asia. Since then, sheep have been selected to fit the attributes of human husbandry systems and local environments, and to yield products deemed important. Although modern tools have improved sheep breeders' abilities to make genetic change, these basic goals have changed little over time.

Sheep contribute significantly to world needs for food, particularly meat. Grasslands account for over 30% of the global land surface and sheep provide high-quality foods from such lands that are largely unsuitable for crop production. With human populations expected to increase by one-third in the next 20 years, the contribution of sheep to food supply will need to grow.[1] Many breeds of sheep produce wool and, historically, fiber production was their primary product. However, with the important exceptions of Australia and parts of South America, wool as a commodity for trade has declined substantially. Improving the efficiency of lamb meat production is thus the aim of most sheep breeding programs.

COMPONENTS OF MEAT PRODUCTION

There are three primary factors[2] contributing to meat production: 1) the number of breeding ewes; 2) their reproductive efficiency; and 3) the slaughter weight of lambs marketed. Collectively, these factors define lamb output. Where output is ample, the quality of the carcass becomes a focus. Carcass quality is usually defined by its composition and, more marginally, its conformation.

Reproductive Efficiency

Reproductive rate is affected by the age of ewes at sexual maturity, their lambing frequency and rate, the survival of their lambs, and the length of their productive life. Of these, fertility, litter size, and lamb survival have the greatest impact on net reproductive rate.[3] Heritability estimates for such traits are in general low (less than 0.10),[4] suggesting gains from selection will be slow. Despite this, the importance of reproductive traits on lamb output compels their inclusion in breeding programs.

Fertility

Fertility is subject to ongoing natural selection since ewes that fail to conceive do not contribute to the next generation. Typically, infertility is addressed by culling barren ewes, which can be augmented by selecting rams from family lines with high fertility.

Litter Size

Among reproductive traits, litter size is the most amenable to selection. Although its heritability is low, the trait is reasonably variable, allowing relatively high selection pressure.[5] Annual gains of 1 to 2% in litter size have been achieved.[6] With improved tools for genetic evaluation available, and by basing selection decision on repeated records of litter size of ewes, larger gains are possible.

There is considerable variation between breeds in mean litter size, ranging from above one lamb to nearly four. By strategically crossing breeds, litter size can be readily increased.[7]

Regardless of the strategy followed, an optimum rather than maximum number of lambs born is the goal. The target mean litter size depends on the husbandry and feed resources available in a flock, and its season of lambing. Where litter size is too high, reduced survival and growth

Encyclopedia of Animal Science
DOI: 10.1081/E-EAS 120019796

rates in multiple births may reduce rather than increase lamb output.

Lamb Survival

Lamb mortality is often a serious problem. There are important maternal genetic factors within breeds in addition to variation between breeds that can be used to improve lamb survivability. However, optimizing mean litter size is the predominant genetic mechanism to influence lamb survival. Lambs born in larger litters have lower birth weight, which predisposes them to starvation and hypothermia during inclement weather. Losses can be reduced by supplementary feeding of litter-bearing ewes during late pregnancy and early lactation, by lambing ewes during warmer seasons in colder climates, and, where practicable, by housing ewes and applying good husbandry practices including fostering at lambing time.

Slaughter Weight

Selection to increase meat production has primarily focused on size or weight. Substantial genetic change in live weights has been achieved (Fig. 1). Increasing weight, however, does not necessarily improve efficiency of meat production. Increased weights at immature ages correspond with heavier weights at maturity and thus, increased feed costs of the breeding flock. Larger lambs also typically take longer and consume more food to achieve a target level of fatness for market. Selection for size may also adversely affect fitness and reproductive success. Although the evidence is equivocal, the genetic relation-ship between mature weight and litter size tends to be positive, while that with fertility and lamb survival negative.[4,5] In dam lines, and where fodder availability is limited, restricting increases in live weight is often desirable. By careful choice of sire breed in crossbreeding systems, weight can still be tailored to market requirements.[7]

Carcass Composition and Conformation

Strategies to alter the composition of the carcass act through direct effects on composition and indirect effects on the size at maturity. If live weight at maturity is increased, at a given immature weight, the earlier maturing tissues such as lean define a greater proportion of the body. As a corollary, at a constant level of fatness, lambs sired by breeds of larger mature size produce heavier carcasses. Composition can be altered by affecting the rate of gain of lean tissue to an immature weight, or to alter the proportion of lean in the carcass at an immature weight.[8] Crossbreeding is one useful tool to achieve that aim.

Besides carcass leanness, conformation is considered an indicator of carcass quality. Shorter blocky carcasses are perceived to have higher lean-to-bone ratio and increased muscle thickness at the same carcass weight, although the association appears weak. In some cases, better conformation carcasses are simply fatter. In contrast to carcass composition, the importance of conformation on quality is unclear. The percentage of the carcass consisting of more desirable cuts, and eating quality, appears more important than conformation.

Carcass composition cannot be measured directly and thus live weight and real-time ultrasound measurements of fat and muscle depth are often used as indicators of composition. Heritabilities are moderate to high for weight and ultrasonically measured traits,[4] and when these criteria are amalgamated into selection decisions, substantial increases in carcass lean content can be achieved. More recently, X-ray computed tomography (CT) has been introduced to sheep breeding programs, allowing a more accurate, in vivo measure of carcass composition,[8] offering further scope to accelerate genetic progress in lean meat production. However, CT is only cost-effective when used in coordination with ultrasound.

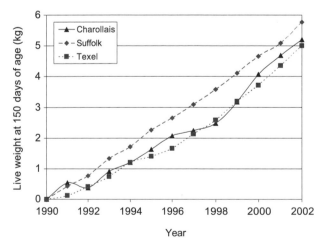

Fig. 1 Estimated genetic trends in live weight in Charollais, Suffolk, and Texel sheep in industry breeding schemes in Britain. (Data courtesy of Signet Farm Business Consultancy, Milton Keynes, UK.) (*View this art in color at www.dekker.com.*)

SIRE REFERENCING

In many countries, the size of flocks is small with little scope for intensive, within-flock selection. Furthermore,

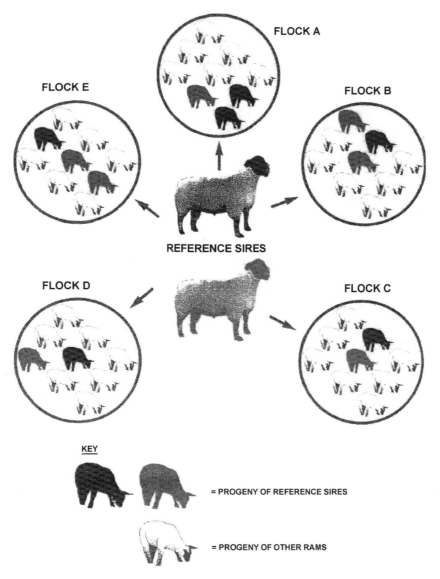

Fig. 2 Schematic diagram of sire referencing scheme in sheep where offspring of reference sires provide a benchmark for comparison across flocks. (Courtesy Scottish Agricultural College, Edinburgh, United Kingdom.)

accurate selection of animals from outside flocks is difficult due to differences in husbandry. This problem has been overcome through cooperative breeding schemes such as sire referencing schemes (SRSs). In SRSs genetic links are created among flocks by mutual use of some rams (Fig. 2). These connections allow equitable, across-flock genetic evaluations, offering a larger pool of candidates for selection for some collective breeding goal. Quicker genetic progress is thus possible.[9]

Over the last decade, SRSs have been formed in many sheep breeds, particularly in Britain. High rates of responses to selection for lean growth rate have been achieved (about 1.75% per annum in the specialized meat breeds).[10] These schemes also have the ideal structure to exploit new technologies cost-effectively, such as molecular tools and CT.

CONCLUSION

Reproductive rate is a central contributor to production efficiency in sheep enterprises. By delineating roles of breeds, reproductive efficiency and fitness can be emphasized in dam breeds, or by crossing breeds with complementary dam characteristics, while weight and composition can be improved in sire breeds. By the strategic crossing of dam and sire breeds, lambs with carcass attributes tailored to market demands can efficiently be produced.

Technologies are available to allow sheep breeders to accelerate genetic gain within their flocks. However, utilization of these tools remains limited. Cooperative breeding schemes provide an avenue to remedy that situation, which is vital to the future of sheep enterprises.

ACKNOWLEDGMENTS

The author is thankful to Geoff Simm, Maurice Shelton, and Larry Kuehn for their contributions to this manuscript.

REFERENCES

1. CAST. *Animal Agriculture and Global Food Supply*; Report No. 135, Council Agric. Sci. Tech.: Ames, IA, 1999; 1–92.
2. Shelton, M. Breeding for improvement of meat production in sheep: Preface and overview. Sheep Goat Res. J. **2002**, *17* (3), 1–5.
3. Wang, C.T.; Dickerson, G.E. Simulation of life-cycle efficiency of lamb and wool production for genetic levels of component traits. J. Anim. Sci. **1991**, *69* (11), 4324–4337.
4. Fogarty, N.M. Genetic parameters for live weight, fat and muscle measurements, wool production and reproduction. Anim. Breed. Abstr. **1995**, *63* (3), 101–143.
5. Rao, S.; Notter, D.R. Genetic analysis of litter size in targhee suffolk and polypay sheep. J. Anim. Sci. **2000**, *78* (8), 2113–2120.
6. Bradford, G.E. Selection for Litter Size. In *Genetics of Reproduction in Sheep*, 1st Ed.; Land, R.B., Robinson, D.W., Eds.; Butterworths: London, 1985; 3–18.
7. Leymaster, K.A. Breeding for improvement of meat production in sheep: Fundamental aspects of crossbreeding of sheep—Use of breed diversity to improve efficiency of meat production. Sheep Goat Res. J. **2002**, *17* (3), 50–59.
8. Simm, G. Selection for Lean Meat Production in Sheep. In *Progress in Sheep and Goat Research*, 1st Ed.; Speedy, A.W., Ed.; CAB International: Wallingford, UK, 1992; 193–215.
9. Lewis, R.M.; Simm, G. Selection strategies in sire referencing schemes in sheep. Livest. Prod. Sci. **2000**, *67* (1–2), 129–141.
10. Simm, G.; Lewis, R.M.; Collins, J.E.; Nieuwhof, G.J. Use of sire referencing schemes to select for improved carcass composition in sheep. J. Anim. Sci. **2001**, *79* (E. Suppl.), E255–E259.

Sheep: Health Management

Cleon V. Kimberling
Geri Parsons
Colorado State University, Fort Collins, Colorado, U.S.A.

S

INTRODUCTION

Sheep are one of the most common species of livestock in the world and were the first to be domesticated. Sheep inhabit many parts of the world—from the deserts of Africa to the high mountains of South America. They are adapted to a variety of management systems—from a few animals sharing a portion of the human living quarters, to groups of 1000 or more roaming the Alta Plana in the Andes, to the deserts of Outer Mongolia. Sheep vary considerably in a variety of production characteristics, temperament, longevity, herding, and mothering instincts. Not all sheep, are suited for all environments. To raise healthy sheep, it is therefore necessary to select a line or breed of sheep to match the environment and the resources that are available, or to develop a composite breed.

Climatic conditions, feed resources, management system, and desired end product (meat, milk, or fiber) dictate the type of sheep best suited for each enterprise. Each factor must be considered in order to achieve optimum production and health of the animals. Producing healthy animals starts with selection that matches the animal to the environment and available resources. First, determine the available resources and the environmental limitations; then match the type of sheep that will give optimal production with the resources available.

CLIMATIC CONDITIONS

In many parts of the world, sheep have adapted to the local environment over years of natural selection. As a result of natural and planned selection, there are many different breeds. New composite breeds have been developed to meet available resources and environmental constraints by combining strong traits from each of the parent breeds. Hair sheep do well in areas of high rainfall. Fine-wool sheep thrive in dry, temperate climates but have definite health problems in wet, damp climates. Medium- and coarse-wool sheep adapt to a wider range of climates and are utilized primarily for meat production. Fat-tail sheep are found mainly in the hot desert regions where nutritional resources are extremely limited. Milk-producing sheep are found in Europe and the Mediterranean

countries, but require specific nutritional and management resources.

FEED RESOURCES

Sheep have the ability to utilize a wide variety of feeds. The type of sheep and their production will be dictated by the available nutritional resources. In the arid parts of the world, the only feed source may be coarse bunch grasses, shrubs, and woody plants. The range of available feed sources increases dramatically in temperate zones with higher rainfall. In parts of the world, sheep production is nomadic, following the availability of feed in different seasons. Where nomadic life is not an option, feed is often harvested during the growing season and stored for availability during periods of dormancy. Crop aftermath and excess vegetable and fruit production are excellent sources of sheep feed. Studies have shown that sheep are very productive on a diet of 100% onions. This diet is lethal to cattle. Other vegetable crops work equally as well.

MANAGEMENT SYSTEMS

Management systems are dictated by climate, environmental factors, forages, and nutrition. There are basically two types of management systems—extensive and intensive—with a variety of styles within each system. Extensive systems are usually large sheep populations that utilize sparse forages in the dry, harsh, uninhabited areas of the world, where predation, limited nutritional intake, and climatic elements are the greatest factors limiting production. These sheep may have very little human contact. Health management within these systems is a total flock program; rarely is attention given to individual health needs. Many extensively managed systems will have periods of intensive management (such as at lambing time) to provide individual health care. The concentration of large populations may lead to health problems such as infections causing abortions and mastitis. Intensively managed systems usually have animals more

Encyclopedia of Animal Science
DOI: 10.1081/E-EAS 120019797

concentrated and can provide individual health care on a regular basis.

SELECTING HEALTHY BREEDING STOCK

Almost all diseases are introduced into a flock through the introduction of diseased animals. Diseased animals are inadvertently introduced through lack of professional skills to detect subclinical disease or due to a lack of affordable diagnostic tests. Prior to any introduction, make certain that the animals you are purchasing come from a healthy flock. This can be ascertained by a thorough health examination, serological testing, and health records of the flock of origin. Always require documentation of health records. Prior to introducing new animals into the flock, establish a quarantine facility adequately separated from the flock. The new animals should be observed for a minimum of 30 days. If there are conditions that need treatment or testing for disease, these can be conducted while the animals are in quarantine.

An example of introducing disease: While working with sheep in Kosovo, a diagnosis was made of ringworm, a fungal infection of the skin. The disease had never been seen in the region prior to the introduction of a group of breeding rams from Kazakhstan. Contagious Ovine Foot Rot is a prime example of a purchased disease that requires close examination. A 30–45 day quarantine, including a zinc sulfate foot soak, must be intensively managed prior to introducing these sheep into the flock. Ovine progressive pneumonia (OPP) is a more subtle disease with no apparent clinical signs early in the course of the disease. The animals should have a negative serological test prior to entry and another negative test while in quarantine. Provide strict biosecurity between the quarantine facility and the existing flock, including separate boots and equipment. Always attend to the quarantine facility last in the daily routine. The diseases will vary with the specific locality, but the measures to prevent introduction of disease are generally the same.

Genetics may predispose individual animals to certain health problems, which may spread with time if poorly managed. Scrapie is a degenerative disease of the nervous system; specific genes have been identified that play a role in this disease. Through testing and selection of QR and RR breeding stock this can be managed. Breeding stock should also be serologically tested for Spider Lamb, a genetic skeletal deformation in the lamb, requiring euthanasia. Entropion, an inversion of the eyelid, left untreated could lead to corneal ulceration of the eye. The management of this disease includes identification and treatment early in the animals' life, not breeding these animals, and culling the dams from which they come. The tendency for rectal and/or vaginal prolapse has a genetic

link as well as management causes (docking tails too short, poor nutrition and environment).

NUTRITION

Sheep are perhaps the most adaptable of all domestic livestock in terms of nutrition. They are efficient users of poor quality forages and can be very productive on a wide variety of feeds. Nutrients essential to them are water, energy, protein, vitamins, and minerals. The balance of these five ingredients is essential to good health. Any compromise in nutrition compromises health. Fortunately, the digestive process of sheep has a tremendous capacity to assimilate forages and feeds into a usable product. No living creature can survive without water. Sheep have a high requirement for water, due to the fermentation process that occurs in the rumen, and water is essential for the breakdown of fiber. If water is limited, feed consumption will decrease, resulting in poor production. In most sheep-producing areas of the world, energy is the nutrient most likely to be limited in the diet. Inadequate energy results in poor growth, reduced reproductive ability, and increased susceptibility to disease. Energy requirements depend on the size of the animal, its growth or reproductive stage, and environmental factors such as weather, shelter, and terrain. Restricting the nutritional resources of a ewe with twins or triplets leads to a health disaster. Seventy percent of fetal development occurs in the last 40–50 days of gestation. A ewe carrying twins has almost twice the nutritional requirements during this period as a ewe carrying a single fetus. Ewes have the highest requirement for energy during the last month of pregnancy and the first month of milk production. A compromise of nutrition during this period leads to pregnancy ketosis, in which both the ewe and the fetuses can be lost. In lesser cases, undernourishment leads to dystocia, weak lambs at birth, reduced colostrum production, reduced milk yield, and a decrease in mothering instincts. Proper nourishment for the ewe during the last trimester of gestation is essential for producing a healthy lamb. Because of the many factors that affect the amount of energy a sheep requires, it is important to examine animals frequently to be sure their needs are being met. Undernourishment in wooled sheep can be deceiving. Only by feeling under the wool can the condition of the animal be determined. Protein is necessary for building body tissues such as muscle, skin, hooves, and wool. Sheep derive most of the protein by digesting the microorganisms that leave their rumen. These microorganisms themselves have a requirement for either protein or nitrogen to grow and reproduce. All sheep require vitamins A, D, and E. Once the rumen becomes functional, the microorganisms synthesize almost all vitamins required for healthy production. Vitamin A deficiency causes growth retardation, retained placenta, bone malformation, reproductive failure, and night blindness. Green plants are an excellent source of beta-carotene, the precursor of vitamin A. Vitamin D, in addition to Ca and P, is required to prevent rickets in young lambs and osteomalacia in older sheep. Vitamin E is essential for the maintenance of body cell membrane integrity. The classic symptom of vitamin E deficiency in lambs is white-muscle disease. Selenium is also part of this equation. The B vitamins are normally produced by a functional rumen. Destruction of the rumen microflora can result in loss of the B vitamins, which may result in decreased appetite and polioencephalomalacia. Minerals play a major role in skeletal and nervous system functions of the body. Sixteen minerals have been classified as essential for sheep. An excellent resource for nutritional requirements can be found in the Sheep Industry Development (SID) Sheep Production Handbook.[2]

IMMUNE RESPONSE/VACCINATIONS/PARASITE CONTROL

The health of the newborn is dependent upon the health and nutritional status of the dam. Protection from the elements and the passive transfer of colostral antibody protection will ensure the new lambs a healthy start on a productive life. The dam should be vaccinated with products to protect her from the diseases prevalent in the area. The antibodies will be passed via the colostrum. For maximum protection, the lamb must receive adequate amounts of colostrum within the first 2 h of life.

Vaccinations can protect the ewe and her offspring from a variety of diseases. The selection of products and timing of administration should be determined by the veterinary health care provider who is familiar with the conditions prevalent in the area. Timing of administration should be coordinated with the desired timing of peak immune response. For maximum response, the sheep must be in good health and nutrition with minimal stress.

Successful internal and external parasite control programs depend on an understanding of the parasites involved and developing a strategic plan to control these pests. Some of the most common parasites of sheep include stomach worms, liver flukes, tapeworms, coccidia, nose bots, lice, keds, and ringworm.

CONCLUSION

Sheep are the most versatile food- and fiber-producing animals in the world. The health management of sheep is largely dependent on overall flock management. This management scheme must take into account the environment and include selection, nutrition, reproduction, sanitation, and biosecurity, which must be strictly adhered to in order to prevent the introduction and/or existence of devastating diseases.

REFERENCES

1. Kimberling, C.; Gessert, M.; Marsh, D. *Raising Healthy Sheep*, 1st. Ed.; A publication of Christian Veterinary Mission, Division of World Concern: Seattle, Washington, USA.
2. SID. *Sheep Production Handbook*; American Sheep Industries Association, Inc. American Sheep Industry, Inc.: Centennial, CO, USA, 2002 Edition; Vol. 7.
3. Kimberling. *Jenson and Swift's Diseases of Sheep*, 3rd Ed.; Lea & Febiger: Philadelphia, USA, 1988.

Sheep Milk and Milk Production: Processing and Marketing

William L. Wendorff
University of Wisconsin, Madison, Wisconsin, U.S.A.

INTRODUCTION

Currently, the total production of sheep milk in the world is approximately 8.2 million metric tons. Top sheep milk-producing countries include China, Italy, Turkey, and Greece. In the United States, the sheep milk industry is in the early stages of development. The current annual U.S. sheep milk production is estimated to be about 2000 metric tons. The majority of the sheep milk is used to produce either yogurt or various varieties of cheese.

MILK HANDLING

Sheep milk is produced under the same high hygienic standards as required for cow and goat milk. Grade A sheep milk would be required to meet the standards of <100,000/ml standard plate count (SPC) and <750,000/ml somatic cell count (SCC).[1] Normally, sheep milk would be cooled to <7°C within two hours of milking and would be transported to the processing plant every two days. Some states may allow a variance of an additional day or two at the farm before requiring transportation of the milk to the processing plant.

With seasonal production, low milk production per ewe, and a large number of producers with small herds, raw milk typically is frozen at the farm until sufficient quantities are accrued for further processing. Milk should be rapidly frozen and stored at −27°C or lower for maximum protein stability.[2] Milk frozen at −15°C exhibited protein destabilization in the milk after six months of frozen storage. Milk frozen at −27°C and stored for 12 months had quality equivalent to fresh, unfrozen milk.

Sheep milk is generally processed by one of three manufacturing processes: traditional processes at farmstead or artisinal facilities, a combination of traditional and modern processes in small plants under controlled technical conditions, or large, modern plants with advanced technologies. Regardless of the size of processing facility, good quality milk must be used to produce safe, quality products for the consumer. Raw sheep milk may be successfully pasteurized with either high-temper-ature, short-time (HTST—72°C for 15 seconds) or vat pasteurization (63°C for 30 minutes). Sensory analysis of HTST-pasteurized milk and untreated milk indicated no significant difference in flavor while vat pasteurized milk sometimes yielded a slight muttony flavor.[3] Minimal pasteurization treatments should be used for sheep milk for cheesemaking as whey proteins in sheep milk are more susceptible to heat denaturation than whey proteins from cow milk. For production of safe raw milk cheeses, processing procedures must include proper control of pH, salt content, water activity, and cheese-ripening time.[4]

YOGURT

The high solids content of sheep milk makes it a natural for production of premium yogurt products similar to the Greek-style yogurt. With solids content of 16–18% in the milk, yogurts can be produced without the need for added milk solids or stabilizers. With the higher fat in sheep yogurt, the potential harshness of the lactic acid in the yogurt may also be lessened. The nutrient content of sheep yogurt is about 50% higher than cow milk yogurt.

Sheep milk for yogurt production should be pasteurized at 91°C for 30 seconds[5] or 82°C for 30 minutes.[3] After cooling to 42–44°C, the milk is inoculated with *Streptococcus thermophilus* and *Lactobacillus delbrueckii* subsp. *bulgaricus* cultures. For set-type yogurt, the inoculated milk mixture is dispensed into cups and allowed to ferment at 44°C until the pH reaches 4.6. The yogurt is then cooled to 4°C and then stored at refrigeration temperatures until consumed. Probiotic cultures of *Lactobacillus acidophilus* or *Bifidobacterium* may also be added to the yogurt to improve the nutritional properties of the yogurt product. Very little sheep yogurt is produced by the stirred-type yogurt process.

Sheep yogurt exhibits a stronger structure to the yogurt gel and has less serum separation on storage than cow or goat yogurt.[6] Viscosity of the yogurt could be significantly increased and serum separation decreased with homogenization of the milk prior to inoculation.[7] Yogurt from sheep milk was reported to have twice the lactase activity of cow milk yogurt.[6] Yogurts produced from

Encyclopedia of Animal Science
DOI: 10.1081/E-EAS 120019794

milk pasteurized at higher temperatures tended to have a decreased rate of acid development and an increased rate of lipolysis.[5]

Since sheep milk production is seasonal, use of frozen milk may be necessary to produce yogurt throughout the year. Good quality yogurt can be produced from frozen sheep milk if the milk is frozen and stored at $-27°C$ or less for less than 12 months.[2] Seasonal variations in milk composition may impact the overall quality of the yogurt as the lactobacilli used in yogurt fermentations are sensitive to changes in milk composition.[8]

CHEESE

Traditionally, production of cheese has been the greatest market for sheep milk throughout the world. Major international varieties of cheese produced from sheep milk are Pecorino Romano, Roquefort, Manchego, and Feta. In the United States, most of the sheep milk cheeses produced are artisinal cheeses. Since the cheesemaking process involves the concentration of casein and fat in the form of curd, the high solids in sheep milk make it an outstanding source of milk for manufacturing cheese. Sheep milk is more sensitive to rennet, coagulates faster, and produces a firmer curd than cow or goat milk.[9,10] Unlike cow milk, sheep milk is not susceptible to dissociation of β-casein from the casein micelle or solubilization of calcium phosphate under cold storage.[11] Yield of cheese from sheep milk is dependent on: breed of sheep, stage of lactation, management system, milk quality, milk storage, and nutrition of the ewe.[9] Pasteurized milk cheeses will have a lower level of lipolysis and slower flavor development than raw milk cheeses. The level of free fatty acids in cheese decreases as the season progresses from winter to summer.[12] Because the supply of sheep milk is seasonal, freezing of curd at $-23°C$ for delayed ripening can be used without significant changes in cheese composition or lipolytic activity. Proteolysis does continue slowly during frozen storage with an increase in nonprotein and amino acid nitrogen.[13]

WHEY

Whey from sheep milk cheese manufacture contains more β-lactoglobulin, about the same proportion of α-lactalbumin, and lower proportions of serum albumin and immunoglobulins.[14] Whey protein concentrates from sheep whey showed significantly better foam overrun, foam stability, and gel strength than WPC from cow or goat whey.[15]

MARKETING

Sheep milk yogurt and cheese are major dairy products in many of the European and Asian countries. In many of these countries, sheep and goat milk is produced at much greater quantities than cow milk. In the United States, only about 4.3 million pounds of sheep milk is currently produced, and sheep milk yogurt and cheeses produced are considered specialty dairy products. However, over 13 million pounds of sheep milk cheeses were imported into the United States during 2001.[16] To avoid competition with imported commodity cheeses with subsidies, U.S. processors are concentrating on production of specialty and artisanal cheeses. Seasonal variations in the sheep milk production have prompted processors to use some high-quality, frozen sheep milk to adjust processing to provide for a uniform supply of products throughout the year. The greatest potential for growth in the sheep milk products market is the production of value-added specialty cheeses and premium yogurt products.

CONCLUSION

Sheep milk production is in the early stages of development within the United States. Unique properties and flavors of sheep milk are incorporated into specialty and artisanal cheeses and fermented products that cannot be produced with other sources of milk. With a continued emphasis on the special qualities of sheep milk, the market for sheep milk products should continue to grow.

REFERENCES

1. PHS/FDA. *Grade "A" Pasteurized Milk Ordinance*; Public Health Service, Food and Drug Administration, U.S. Dept. of Health and Human Services: Washington, DC, 1999.
2. Wendorff, W.L. Freezing qualities of raw ovine milk for further processing. J. Dairy Sci. **2001**, *84* (E. Suppl.), E74–E78.
3. Young, P. Pasteurization of sheep milk. Sheep Dairy News **1986**, *3* (1), 1–3.
4. Emaldi, G.C. Hygienic Quality of Dairy Products from Ewe and Goat Milk, Proc. of IDF/CIVRAL Seminar on Production and Utilization of Ewe and Goat Milk, Crete, Greece, Oct. 19–21, 1995; Inter. Dairy Federation: Brussels, Belgium, 1996; 149–158.
5. Kisza, J.; Domagaia, J.; Wszoiek, M.; Loiczak, T. Yoghurts from sheep milk. Acta Acad. Agric. Tech. Olst. **1995**, *25* (1), 78–87.

6. Kehagias, C.; Komiotis, A.; Koulouris, S.; Koroni, H.; Kazazis, J. Physio-Chemical Properties of Set Type Yogurt Made from Cow's, Ewe's and Goat's Milk. In *Production and Utilization of Ewe's and Goat's Milk*; IDF Bulletin No. 202; Inter. Dairy Federation: Brussels, Belgium, 1986; 167–169.

7. Muir, D.D.; Tamime, A.Y. Ovine milk. 3. Effect of seasonal variation of properties of set and stirred yogurts. Milchwissenschaft **1993**, *48* (10), 509–513.

8. Tamime, A.Y.; Bruce, J.; Muir, D.D. Ovine milk. 4. Seasonal changes in microbiological quality of raw milk and yogurt. Milchwissenschaft **1993**, *48* (10), 560–563.

9. Wendorff, B. *Milk Composition and Cheese Yield*; Proc. of 8th Great Lakes Dairy Sheep Symp., Nov. 7–9, 2002; Univ. of Wisconsin-Madison, 2002; 104–117.

10. Bencini, R. Factors affecting the clotting properties of sheep milk. J. Sci. Food Agric. **2002**, *82* (7), 705–719.

11. Raynal, K.; Remeuf, F. Effect of storage at 4°C on the physicochemical and renneting properties of milk: A comparison of caprine, ovine, and bovine milks. J. Dairy Res. **2000**, *67* (2), 199–207.

12. Chavarri, F.; Bustamante, M.A.; Santisteban, A.; Virto, M.; Barron, L.J.R.; de Renobales, M. Changes in free fatty acids during ripening of Idiazabal cheese manufactured at different times of the year. J. Dairy Sci. **1999**, *82* (5), 885–890.

13. Tejada, L.; Sanchez, E.; Gomez, R.; Vioque, M.; Fernandez-Salguero, J. Effect of freezing and frozen storage on chemical and microbiological characteristics in sheep milk cheese. J. Food Sci. **2002**, *67* (1), 126–129.

14. Casper, J.L.; Wendorff, W.L.; Thomas, D.L. Seasonal changes in protein composition of whey from commercial manufacture of caprine and ovine specialty cheeses. J. Dairy Sci. **1998**, *81* (12), 3117–3122.

15. Casper, J.L.; Wendorff, W.L.; Thomas, D.L. Functional properties of whey protein concentrates from caprine and ovine specialty cheese wheys. J. Dairy Sci. **1999**, *82* (2), 265–271.

16. IDFA. *Cheese Facts*, 2002 Ed.; Int. Dairy Foods Assn.: Washington, DC, 2002.

Sheep Milk and Milk Products: Composition

William L. Wendorff
University of Wisconsin, Madison, Wisconsin, U.S.A.

INTRODUCTION

Sheep milk is a high-solids milk that is well-suited for manufactured milk products, e.g., yogurt and cheese. Sheep milk generally contains twice as much fat and 40% more protein than cow or goat milk. Since sheep milk is produced on a seasonal basis, milk composition will vary throughout the lactation. Fat and protein contents increase and the lactose content decreases throughout the lactation.

SHEEP MILK

Typical milk composition for sheep in comparison to goat and cow are shown in Table 1.

Fat

The fat in sheep milk is in the form of small fat globules, 1.5–12.0 μm in diameter, present as an emulsion in the aqueous phase. The average fat globule size in sheep milk is slightly smaller than that of cow milk and varies significantly in size during lactation. Sheep milk fat is characterized by a higher content of short-chain fatty acids (C_4–C_{12}) than cow's milk fat (20–25% to 10–12%, respectively).[2] The short-chain fatty acids contribute many of the distinctive flavors observed in sheep milk and sheep milk products. Sheep milk fat also contains some volatile branched-chain fatty acids that have been associated with the flavor of lamb and some sheep milk cheeses.[3] Milk fat of sheep is white in color since it does not contain carotenoids, e.g., β-carotene, like cow milk fat. Milk produced in the early lactation (<30 days) in a mixed management system where ewes are milked once a day and the lambs are allowed to nurse the other half day results in milk with over 50% less milk fat than ewes milked twice a day since lambing.[4] In the postwean period of the lactation, fat content is comparable for all management systems.

Protein

Even though sheep milk contains approximately 40% more total protein than cow milk, the ratio of casein and whey proteins in both sheep and cow milk are similar.

Typical distribution of the various nitrogen fractions in sheep, cow, and goat milk are shown in Table 2. Sheep milk casein micelles are similar in structure to those of cow milk; however, sheep milk does contain more small micelles than cow milk. The α_{s1}, β, μ-caseins exist in sheep and cow milk in similar proportions.[2] There are slight differences in the amino acid composition of sheep and cow κ-casein, but the action with chymosin is the same for both species.[1] Of the whey proteins, sheep milk contains more β-lactoglobulin, about the same proportion of α-lactalbumin, and lower proportions of serum albumin and immunoglobulin than cow milk.[6] Relative amounts of α-lactalbumin decrease throughout the season and β-lactoglobulin rises in midseason and then gradually decreases toward the end of the lactation. Serum albumin remains fairly stable throughout the year. Sheep milk contains more urea and uric acid and less free amino acids than cow milk.[2]

Minerals

Sheep milk has a higher content of calcium, phosphorus, and potassium than cow milk. Most of the calcium in sheep milk (75–88%) is in the colloidal phase as compared to only 62–76% in cow milk.[1] Typical mineral content of various milks is shown in Table 3.

Enzymes and Vitamins

The alkaline phosphatase activity in sheep milk is about three times higher than in cow milk; however, it is more sensitive to heating at temperatures below pasteurization.[1] Other enzymes, e.g., lysozyme, peroxidase, lipase, and xanthine oxidase have lower activities in sheep milk than cow milk. Sheep milk is higher in most vitamins than cow milk.[2]

SHEEP MILK PRODUCTS

Sheep milk products possess the unique flavor and textural characteristics of some of the sheep milk components, especially from fat and protein. The short-chain (C_4–C_{12}) and branched-chain fatty acids contribute many of the distinctive flavors to manufactured sheep

Encyclopedia of Animal Science
DOI: 10.1081/E-EAS 120019793
Copyright © 2005 by Marcel Dekker, Inc. All rights reserved.

Table 1 Average gross composition of sheep, goat, and cow milk

	Sheep	Goat	Cow
Fat, %	7.1	4.1	3.8
Protein, %	5.8	3.4	3.3
Lactose, %	4.6	4.6	4.7
Ash, %	0.92	0.80	0.72
Total solids, %	18.42	12.90	12.52

(From Ref. 1.)

milk products. Flavor and functional characteristics of sheep milk products may vary widely due to the seasonal nature of the milk supply.

Yogurt

With the high solids of sheep milk, sheep yogurt possesses high gel strength and minimal syneresis compared to cow or goat yogurt. With the high fat content of sheep milk, yogurt produced from unhomogenized milk tends to form a creamy layer on the top surface of cup-set yogurt. Since sheep milk production is very seasonal, yogurt can be produced from frozen sheep milk that has been frozen and stored below $-20°C$ for less than 12 months.[8] Sheep yogurt, with high titratable acidity, may tend to have a slighty grainy body and texture due to the high level of calcium present in the sheep milk.

Cheese

Sheep milk will yield significantly more cheese due to the high solids content. Sheep milk will have a cheese yield of 16–22% in comparison to 10% for cow milk.[4] Since calcium is high in sheep milk, added calcium chloride is not required in the cheesemaking process with sheep milk. Also, less rennet or chymosin is needed to produce a satisfactory curd from sheep milk, as compared to cow or goat milk. Unlike cow milk, the β-casein in sheep milk does not reassociate at the surface of the micelle or diffuse into the interior under cold storage conditions.[9] Accordingly, sheep milk from cold storage should not have

Table 2 Average distribution of the various nitrogen fractions in milk

In % of total N	Sheep	Goat	Cow
Casein	78.5	75.6	77.8
Whey protein	16.8	15.7	17.0
Nonprotein N	4.7	8.7	5.2

(From Ref. 5.)

Table 3 Average mineral content of sheep, goat, and cow milk (100 g)

	Sheep	Goat	Cow
Calcium (mg)	193	134	119
Iron (mg)	0.10	0.05	0.05
Magnesium (mg)	18	14	13
Phosphorus (mg)	158	111	93
Potassium (mg)	136	204	152
Sodium (mg)	44	50	49
Zinc (mg)	0.57	0.30	0.38

(From Ref. 7.)

impaired rennet coagulation rates or lack of firmness of the gel. Sheep milk will produce a firmer curd than cow and goat milk and the rate of whey expulsion from the curd is slower than the other species milk. Cheese produced from sheep milk tends to be crumbly in body throughout the aging process, whereas that produced from cow milk becomes more crumbly with age.[10]

Whey

Sheep whey generally has 10–15% more solids than cow and goat whey. Typical whey protein composition is shown in Table 4.

Sheep whey protein concentrates have been reported to have significantly better foam overrun, foam stability, and gel strength than cow or goat whey protein concentrates. These characteristics may be due to the higher β-lactoglobulin content and lower ash content of sheep whey protein concentrates.[11]

Butter

Sheep milk fat has a lower iodine number than cow milk fat and is much firmer than cow milk fat,[2] thus producing a harder, more brittle butter. Sheep milk fat also does not contain as many carotenoids as cow milk fat and the white color of sheep butter is slightly unappealing for some markets.

Table 4 Whey protein distribution in sheep, goat, and cow whey (% of total protein)

Whey protein	Sheep	Goat	Cow
β-lactoglobulin	74.0%	58.6%	64.9%
α-lactalbumin	14.8	27.0	15.6
Serum albumin	4.1	4.0	6.5
Immunoglobulin	7.3	9.7	13.0

(From Ref. 6.)

CONCLUSION

With high solids, fat, and protein, sheep milk is an ideal source of milk for production of manufactured dairy products. Since sheep milk is produced seasonally, milk composition will vary throughout the year and processors will need to adjust their processing procedures to compensate for these compositional changes. With a solid understanding of sheep milk composition, processors can use the uniqueness of sheep milk to produce value-added products, e.g., specialty cheeses and traditional yogurts without added stabilizers, to expand the dairy sheep industry.

REFERENCES

1. Alichanidis, E.; Polychroniadou, A. Special Features of Dairy Products from Ewe and Goat Milk from the Physicochemical and Organoleptic Point of View, Proc. of IDF/CIVRAL Seminar on Production and Utilization of Ewe and Goat Milk, Crete, Greece, Oct. 19–21, 1995; Inter. Dairy Federation: Brussels, Belgium, 1996; 21–43.

2. Anifantakis, E.M. Physico–Chemical Characteristics of Ewe Milk Compared to Cow Milk. In *Production and Utilization of Ewe's and Goat's Milk*; IDF Bulletin No. 202, Inter. Dairy Federation: Brussels, Belgium, 1986; 42–53.

3. Ha, J.K.; Lindsay, R.C. Method for the quantitative analysis of volatile free and total branched-chain fatty acids in cheese and milk fat. J. Dairy Sci. **1990**, *73* (8), 1988–1999.

4. Wendorff, B. Milk Composition and Cheese Yield, Proc. of 8th Great Lakes Dairy Sheep Symp, Ithaca, NY, Nov. 7–9, 2002; Univ. of Wisconsin: Madison, 2002; 104–117.

5. Grappin, R. Variations of the Major Nitrogen Fractions of Goat and Ewe Milk. Proc. of IDF/CIVRAL Seminar on Production and Utilization of Ewe and Goat Milk, Crete, Greece, Oct. 19–21, 1995; Inter. Dairy Federation: Brussels, Belgium, 1996; 79–80.

6. Casper, J.L.; Wendorff, W.L.; Thomas, D.L. Seasonal changes in protein composition of whey from commercial manufacture of caprine and ovine specialty cheeses. J. Dairy Sci. **1998**, *81* (12), 3117–3122.

7. Haenlein, G.F.W. The nutritional value of sheep milk. Int. J. Anim. Sci. **2001**, *16* (2), 253–268.

8. Wendorff, W.L. Freezing qualities of raw ovine milk for further processing. J. Dairy Sci. **2001**, *84* (E Supp.), E74–E78.

9. Raynal, K.; Remeuf, F. Effect of storage at 4°C on the physicochemical and renneting properties of milk: A comparison of caprine, ovine and bovine milks. J. Dairy Res. **2000**, *67* (2), 199–207.

10. Banks, J.M.; Muir, D.D.; McNulty, D.; Dreyer, I. Sensory properties of cheddar-type cheese produced from recombined milk fat and casein fractions of bovine and ovine origin. Inter. J. Dairy Technol. **1997**, *50* (2), 73–78.

11. Casper, J.L.; Wendorff, W.L.; Thomas, D.L. Functional properties of whey protein concentrates from caprine and ovine specialty cheese wheys. J. Dairy Sci. **1999**, *82* (2), 265–271.

Sheep: Nutrition Management

Hugh Dove
CSIRO Plant Industry, Canberra, Australia

INTRODUCTION

Most sheep-production systems in the world rely on sown pasture, natural pasture, or browse as the main source of nutrients. The nutritional management of sheep therefore substantially involves the management of the amount and quality of the forage resource, as influenced by the regional climate, seasonal weather conditions, and the plant species present. In most of the world's sheep-grazing systems, the main period of pasture growth is in spring/early summer, during which pasture usually accumulates in excess of animal requirements. In winter, low temperatures will reduce or even stop pasture growth; however, the pasture that is on offer is still likely to be of moderate-to-high quality. By contrast, in climates with marked summer drought (e.g., southern Australia), there may be a large amount of forage available following spring/early summer growth, but this will be of poor quality relative to the needs of the animal.

On an individual-animal basis, the best way to optimize nutrient intake would be to match, as well as possible, the annual cycles of pasture availability and nutrient demand. However, in many grazing systems, profit derives from animal production/hectare (ha), and in order to optimize this, it is more profitable to increase stocking rates (sheep/ha) to the point that for some of the year at least, the intake of individual sheep is constrained. For example, it may be more profitable to accept the nutritional stress that results if ewes lamb well before the spring flush of pasture growth, in order to ensure that lambs are weaned onto good-quality pasture.

PASTURE FEATURES INFLUENCING NUTRIENT INTAKE

Pasture Quantity

Pasture intake by sheep increases in curvilinear fashion as the amount of pasture increases (Fig. 1), but beyond a certain amount (usually >1.2–1.5 t dry matter (DM)/ha or 4–6 cm pasture height) does not increase much because the animals are approaching their intake limit. On sparse pasture (e.g., <500 kg DM/ha), the amount eaten per bite decreases to the point that sheep can no longer compensate for smaller bite sizes by biting more often, and intakes will be markedly reduced. These general rules are strongly influenced by the physiological state of the animal; young, rapidly growing sheep, or pregnant/lactating sheep will eat more. Based on such relationships, benchmarks such as those in Table 1 have been devised as a guide for sheep producers using sown pastures.

Pasture Quality

The single most important measure of pasture nutritive value is digestibility, the proportion of the consumed pasture actually used by the animal. This usually ranges from >80% down to <40% as the season progresses and pasture plants pass from the young, vegetative stage to maturity and seed set (Fig. 2). Intake declines more rapidly at digestibilities below about 65–70%, because fiber digestion in the rumen is slower and restricts the rate at which material leaves the rumen. This means that on a pasture of low digestibility, sheep will reach their intake limit before their nutrient requirements are satisfied. Conversely, at higher pasture digestibilities, plant material passes through the rumen more rapidly, and the animal can eat more. Moreover, when herbage of higher digestibility is consumed, there is the added benefit that the metabolizable energy obtained from it by the animal is used with higher efficiency for maintenance and growth. In general, high levels of production can only be supported by pastures of 70% digestibility or above (Table 1). Pastures of 60–65% digestibility will support moderate levels of animal production, but below 55–60% digestibility, pastures will only maintain dry stock. Below 50% digestibility, weight loss is likely, regardless of the amount of pasture on offer.

In most cases, the protein content of green pasture is in the range 15–25% and probably provides soluble protein in substantial excess relative to the requirements of the rumen. By contrast, the very low protein contents (3–6% DM) in low-quality, dead pastures can fail to meet the needs of the rumen microbial population for soluble nitrogen. The rate of fiber digestion in the rumen will then be reduced and intake will fall. In this case, there is benefit in supplementing the animals with a source of soluble protein (see the following section) to increase the digestion rate and, thus, the intake of low-quality forage.

Encyclopedia of Animal Science
DOI: 10.1081/E-EAS 120019799

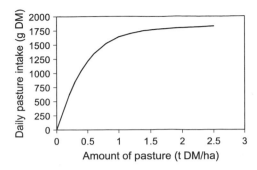

Fig. 1 Effect of amount of pasture (75% digestibility) on the intake of a 50-kg sheep. [Data derived using GrazFeed decision support tool. (From Ref. 4.)]

Legume Content

The legume (clover) content of pasture can exert a profound effect on the nutritional status of the grazing sheep. Legumes often have higher digestibilities than grasses and in addition, at a given digestibility, animals will eat about 25% more of a legume than of a grass[2] because of the faster rate of legume particle breakdown in the rumen. The products of the digestion of legumes are also used with greater efficiency for growth. This means that for growing lambs, in particular, it is important to maintain a highly digestible pasture containing high levels of legume.

GRAZING SYSTEMS

All these pasture features influence the intake and production of individual animals. However, for the sheep producer, it is ultimately production per unit area that

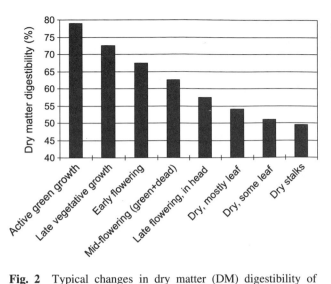

Fig. 2 Typical changes in dry matter (DM) digestibility of pasture during the growing season. (*View this art in color at www.dekker.com.*)

drives profitability. A key element in sheep nutritional management is then the identification of the stocking rate, which will strike the balance between optimum (not maximum) nutrient intake per animal, and animal production/ha.

The sheep producer must also select a system for grazing groups of animals on the available areas of pasture. Grazing management systems range from true set stocking (all the animals graze all the land all the time), through rotational grazing (animals shifted between areas at intervals of one to several weeks), to very rapid rotational grazing (large flocks or mobs of sheep graze on small areas, with frequent shifts— referred to as cell grazing or mob stocking). Which of these is the best system is the subject of continuing argument. Because most sheep-production systems

Table 1 Minimum amounts of green pasture (kg DM/ha) required for different classes of sheep[a]

	Digestibility of pasture (% DM)		
Sheep class	75	68	60
Non-pregnant, non-lactating	400	600	1,200
Ewes, mid-pregnancy	500	700	1,700
Ewes, late pregnancy	700	1,200	N[b]
Ewes, lactating, 1 lamb	1,000	1,700	N
Ewes, lactating, 2 lambs	1,500	N	N
Young stock growing at: 75 g/d	400	700	1,700
125 g/d	600	1,000	N
225 g/d	1,600	N	N

[a]Young growing stock = 4-month old, 32-kg crossbred lamb from ewe of mature live weight 55 kg.
[b]N = production target cannot be maintained under defined pasture conditions.
(Adapted from Ref. 1.)

operate below their optimum stocking rates, it is likely to be more useful to concentrate effort on defining the appropriate stocking rate for the enterprise rather than to become preoccupied with the system of grazing management.

SUPPLEMENTARY FEEDING

Supplementary feeding with pelleted feed, grain, hay, or silage is common in many sheep-grazing systems. Frequently, when sheep consume a supplement, they reduce their pasture intake.[3] The degree of this substitution may even be enough to negate the effects of the supplement. Substitution is likely to be greater when: 1) more pasture is available; 2) pasture quality is higher; 3) higher quality supplements are fed; 4) more supplement is fed; and 5) animals have a lower demand for nutrients.

Under certain circumstances, supplements can also increase forage intake if they provide a nutrient that was hitherto limiting pasture intake. For example, in sheep grazing low-quality forage (e.g., dry summer pasture) the low soluble-N content of the forage may constrain rumen fiber digestion and thus, intake. The provision of a supplement containing soluble N can overcome this constraint, so that the rate of digestion of fiber increases, the rumen empties faster, and the animal can eat more of the low-quality forage. This is referred to as complementation. It should be noted that once the supplement has met the rumen requirement for soluble N, it is likely that higher levels of supplementation will result in increasing substitution.[3]

COMPUTER-BASED AIDS TO NUTRITIONAL MANAGEMENT

The nutrition of the grazing sheep clearly involves complex interactions among the dynamics of ruminant digestion, the pasture ecosystem, and the processes of diet selection and pasture/supplement intake. One useful approach to understanding these interactions has been to build simulation models of grazing systems, and to incorporate these models into computer-based packages to help decision making. In general, this approach involves the mathematical representation of the processes of diet selection, intake, digestion, and nutrient absorption, in relation to tabulated nutrient requirements for different forms of production. A number of decision support tools are now commercially available for use by sheep producers or their advisers.[4]

CONCLUSION

In managing the nutrition of grazing sheep, the producer cannot exert the same degree of control of nutrient intake as might be practised in a beef feedlot or intensive dairy.[3,4] Intake can be increased by ensuring that sheep have access to large amounts of pasture of high digestibility and legume content. However, the focus of sheep nutritional management should not be to maximize the pasture intake of individual animals, but to optimize animal production per unit area. This will involve stocking rates that, almost certainly, will constrain the nutrient intake of individual animals. Moreover, the pasture is not only the sheep's major source of nutrients, but also the major source of the internal parasites that can dramatically reduce production and profit. It follows that sensible nutritional management of the sheep must include a program for the control of internal parasites.

REFERENCES

1. *PROGRAZE—Profitable Sustainable Grazing*; Noad, W., Ed.; New South Wales Agriculture, Meat and Livestock Australia: Dubbo, New South Wales, 1998; Segment 2, 1–6 pp.
2. Freer, M.; Jones, D.B. Feeding value of subterranean clover, lucerne, phalaris and Wimmera ryegrass for lambs. Aust. J. Exp. Agric. Anim. Husb. **1984**, *24* (125), 156–164.
3. Dove, H. Principles of Supplementary Feeding. In *Sheep Nutrition*; Freer, M., Dove, H., Eds.; CABI Publishing/CSIRO Publishing: Wallingford, UK, 2002; 119–142.
4. Freer, M. The Nutritional Management of Grazing Sheep. In *Sheep Nutrition*; Freer, M., Dove, H., Eds.; CABI Publishing/CSIRO Publishing: Wallingford, UK, 2002; 357–375.

Sheep: Reproduction Management

Lyle G. McNeal
Thomas D. Bunch
Utah State University, Logan, Utah, U.S.A.

INTRODUCTION

Reproductive management of naturally breeding sheep varies considerably throughout the world, largely due to the significant number of genetically distinct breeds and the diverse ecosystems that they inhabit. Sheep reproduction is influenced by traditional, cultural, social, and economic conditions. Once-per-year lambing is traditionally practiced in most countries, although some developed countries have resorted to accelerated lambing management strategies, i.e., three lamb crops in two years, or twice-a-year lambing.

Like all farm animals, reproductive management of sheep falls under two major constraints: genetic inheritance from its ancestors, and environmental influences, i.e., nutrition, disease, parasites, animal facilities, location and climate, human management, and perhaps most important, the season of the year. Sheep are seasonal breeders, and most breeds are short-day breeders. The photoperiod (ratio of daylight to darkness hours) is a crucial consideration in reproductive management. Animal physiologists refer to sheep as being seasonally polyestrous in their breeding patterns. The genetic evolution of the breed and the latitude of their geographic area of origin have the most influence on seasonality of breeding activity.

THE FLOCK

Reproductive management is all-encompassing with respect to the flock. In other words, in addition to the primary factors of genetics and environmental influences, the role of both the ram and the ewe must be taken into account for successful replication of their species and/or breed. When considering reproductive management of sheep, it should be reviewed within the context of gender management because of the uniqueness and functionality of both rams and ewes within the broad scope of sheep and wool production.

Reproductive management is desirable because of convenience, economics, and disease control. It involves nearly all facets of animal science. Genetics, environment, economics, and the human factor must be considered.

Each species and even breed has special characteristics that require separate management, knowledge, and skills.[1]

BREED

In a sound breeding program, based on the long-term objectives of the owner/producer, a ewe breed is selected principally for reproductive traits, and a ram is selected from a breed known for production traits. There is a wide variety of ewe breeds, each with different reproductive capabilities, that have the potential to improve flock or band performance. Examples of reproductive traits include extended breeding season (Dorset, Polypay), early onset of puberty (Finnish Landrace, Polypay), increased ovulation rate (Finnish Landrace, Romanov), and environmental suitability (Scottish Blackface, Navajo–Churro). Hormonal methods of manipulation of reproduction can be used to exploit a well-designed genetic pool, but should not be used as an alternative for poor breed selection and management.[2]

RAM REPRODUCTION

Producers often forget that the ram contributes 50% of the genetic makeup of offspring, affecting not only production traits (birth weight, average daily gain), but also the reproductive traits of potential flock replacements (semen production, ovulation rate, onset of puberty, seasonality).

The ram should be given special attention throughout the year, but especially in preparation for and during the breeding season. A veterinarian or owner who is prepared to perform a breeding soundness examination (BSE), who is knowledgeable of ram diseases, and who can make recommendations and/or decisions on ram management, can provide valuable service and input to sheep producers.[3]

A breeding soundness exam includes visual appraisal of general health and body condition, as well as a soundness check on feet, legs, eyes, jaws, and dentition. A scrotal circumference measurement is taken, along with palpation of the testicles. The testicles should palpate

Encyclopedia of Animal Science
DOI: 10.1081/E-EAS 120019800

firm, but not hard, having no signs of abscesses, injuries, orchitis, or any other condition that could affect fertility. The penis and sheath should be examined for posthitis (pizzle rot), ulcerative dermatosis, adhesions, or injury (including shearing trauma). Often, a blood sample is collected during the BSE in order to conduct a serological test for ovine sexually transmitted diseases, i.e., *Brucella ovis*. Semen samples are collected usually by electro-ejaculation and analyzed microscopically for color, percent live cells, percent motility, and percent abnormal spermatozoa. Upon palpating the scrotum, both testicles should be fully descended into the scrotal sack. At this time, a measurement is taken of the scrotum at the point of the greatest circumference, and available standard guidelines for these dimensions should be utilized. Research has shown that daughters from sires with larger testicle circumferences have higher pregnancy rates than females sired by males with smaller circumferences. Breeding soundness exam results apply only on the day the exam was conducted. Rams may be designated satisfactory, temporarily unsatisfactory, or unsatisfactory. Temporarily unsatisfactory rams may be examined again after an appropriate time, depending on the abnormality. Unsatisfactory breeders, with permanent testicular abnormalities, serological positive for *B. ovis*, scrotal hernia, sterility, etc. should be culled.[3]

Rams should be maintained separately from ewes except when breeding. The breeder rams should be sorted by age classification, i.e., virgin rams separated from mature and previously utilized breeding rams. This will reduce possible exposure to *B. ovis* from undetected, infected older rams.

Teaser rams are used to advance the breeding season, synchronize estrus in ewes, and detect the return to estrus in nonpregnant ewes. Prior to being surgically altered (vasectomy or epididymectomy), teaser rams should be carefully selected for libido and preferably chosen from breeds with an extended breeding season (Dorset, Finnish Landrace, Polypay). Teasers will breed ewes, and therefore, should be free of venereally transmitted diseases.

Artificial insemination of sheep, although not as widely practiced as in the dairy and beef cattle industries, is used in the purebred sector of the domestic sheep industry. Newer assisted reproduction technologies are being developed that will enhance the use of AI in the sheep industry.

EWE REPRODUCTION

The ratio of light to dark during a day and the absolute periods of light and dark are known to influence reproduction in many species, especially the seasonal breeders.[4] Ewes differ from cattle in that they are anestrous, which means very few come into heat (estrus) between May and July. The decrease in the light-to-dark ratio triggers hormonal change which result in ewes exhibiting estrous cycles. The two months when most ewes show estrus are October and November (temperate zone), and the fewest is between May and July. When ewes first come into estrus in August or September, they do not produce as many eggs (oocytes) and often the eggs are incompetent of normal development. Since there are very few reports of identical twins in sheep (the result of one fertilized egg dividing), two eggs must be ovulated if twins are to be conceived and born. The incidence of twinning is higher in October and November than at other times of the breeding season. There is also a higher occurrence of embryonic death in August and early September than there is later in the fall. October through early November is the ideal time interval to breed for a larger lamb crop.[5]

Ewes normally will complete an estrous cycle every 16 to 17 days until they are bred or enter the anestrous season or period. Ewes are normally receptive to a ram for 24 to 48 hours. Once conception (fertilization) occurs, the ewe will deliver a lamb between 144 to 152 days after mating.

Knowing the pregnancy status of ewes has obvious advantages. The pregnancy rate is the only true measure of flock fertility and is the basis for strategies of nutrition and feeding, utilization of labor, and facilities. Improper management of pregnant ewes often leads to pregnancy toxemia from substandard nutrition, and dystocia and fetal death due to inadequate lambing oversight, especially in bad weather or when adequate shelter is not available.

Induction and synchronization of estrus during anestrus enables some ewes to lamb three times in two years. Producing lambs out-of-season and finishing market lambs in larger and more even groups can improve profits. The induction and synchronization of estrus during seasonal anestrus is practiced by some producers in most of the major sheep-producing nations.

PREGNANCY DETECTION

Ultrasound is a highly accurate tool for pregnancy detection. The A-mode (doppler or sonar type) systems are widely used and are reliable from day 50 postconception. Real-time ultrasound (RTU) units are reliable from day 25 when used rectally and through the flank from day 35. RTU can be used to determine lamb numbers from day 40.[2]

FLOCK NUTRITION AND REPRODUCTION

Nutrition has a direct influence on incidence of estrus, ovulation rate, embryo survival, and sperm production.

Before the breeding season, reproductive management should include getting the ram into breeding condition. The sperm production cycle takes 49 days, plus an additional 11–15 days for the sperm to travel the length of the epididymis. A slowly increasing plane of nutrition, depending on the body condition score (BCS) of a ram two months before the expected breeding season, will help ensure high fertility.[3] A good BCS is when rams are neither too fat nor too thin as they enter the breeding season.

A high plane of nutrition a few days or weeks before breeding has been associated with a greater number of ovulations at breeding.[1,6] Diet influences embryonic and fetal survival during gestation and the birth weight of lambs. The nutritional level during mid- and late-pregnancy has a greater influence on fetal development than on survival.[7] A change in nutritional level after mating, whether up or down, may induce greater losses than an unchanging nutritional status held at an intermediate level.[6]

CONCLUSION

The purpose of raising sheep is for its product, i.e., meat, fiber, and milk, and they must be managed within the constraints of their seasonal breeding attributes. Photoperiod regulates the reproductive cycle of the ewe and the effects are most dramatic in the more temperate-type geographic zones. Although new technologies have been developed in an attempt to overcome the seasonal limitations, none have made a significant impact in reproductive management strategies in the commercial lamb and wool sectors. The selection and management of the ram is a very important component in reproductive management because its genetic contributions may affect half of the offspring in a given lambing season. Ram fertility and libido affect conception rates and the subsequent lamb crop. For the ewe, it is primarily the diet that affects ovulation and lambing rates and the survival of the newborn lamb.

REFERENCES

1. Dziuk, P.J.; Bellows, R.A. Management of reproduction of beef cattle, sheep and pigs. J. Anim. Sci. **1983**, *57*, 355–379.
2. Buckrell, B.C. Management of reproduction of sheep. Can. Vet. J. **1987**, *28*, 374–377.
3. Cottrell, W.O. Ram management for northeastern flocks. Cornell Vet. **1985**, *75*, 505–511.
4. Terrill, C.E. *Proceedings of Symposium on Management of Sheep and Goats*; Sheep Industry Development Program, 1977; 1–149.
5. Pope, A.L. Raising a 200% Lamb Crop—How to Get it Started. In *Proceedings 50th Annual Spooner Sheep Day, Saturday August 10, 2002*; 2002; 55–59.
6. Doney, J.M.; Gunn, R.G. Nutritional and Other Factors in Breeding Performance of Ewes. In *Environmental Factors in Mammalian Reproduction*; Gilmore, D.P., Cook, B., Eds.; MacMillan: London, 1981; 169–177.
7. Coop, I.E. *Sheep and Goat Production*; Elsevier Scientific Publishing Co.: New York, 1982; 492 pp.

Somatotropin

Dale E. Bauman
Cornell University, Ithaca, New York, U.S.A.

Frank R. Dunshea
Department of Primary Industries, Werribee, Victoria, Australia

INTRODUCTION

In the 1920s, it was discovered that a crude pituitary extract stimulated growth in rats, and this extract was referred to as somatotropin or growth hormone, after the Greek derivation meaning tissue growth.[1] Results were extended to farm animals when somatotropin (ST) was shown to enhance growth rates in pigs[2] and stimulate milk production in lactating goats[3] and cows.[4] However, the supply of ST was extremely limited until the advent of recombinant technology. In 1982, the first study with recombinant ST in domestic animals was reported, in this case bovine ST (bST) in lactating dairy cows.[5] Commercial use of bST and porcine ST (pST) began in 1994 and 1996 in the United States and Australia, respectively.

Somatotropin is a protein hormone secreted from the anterior pituitary gland under the action of growth hormone-releasing factor (stimulatory) and somatostatin (inhibitory) released from the hypothalamus. Somatotropin can vary slightly in size, generally about 191 amino acids, and the amino acid sequence also varies among species. Whereas bST and pST share a high degree of sequence similarity (ca. 90%), both have a much lower homology with human ST (ca. 65%) and hence are inactive in humans. Since ST is a protein, it is digested if consumed orally, and exogenous ST has to be administered via injection or implant.

EFFICACY OF EXOGENOUS SOMATOTROPIN

Growth

Somatotropin alters nutrient partitioning to improve growth performance and body composition, and pST has been approved commercially in 14 countries.[6,7] Exogenous pST results in dose-dependent increases in lean deposition and reductions in fat (Fig. 1). It is effective in increasing protein deposition and decreasing fat deposition in all sexes and genotypes. Although the greatest responses occur in finisher pigs (60–120 kg), exogenous pST also improves growth in younger pigs (30–60 kg). As a result of the reduction in fat deposition, there is a corresponding reduction in feed intake.[8] Since pST stimulates protein deposition in all tissues, there are increases in visceral and skin mass, and reductions in dressing percent. In general, lean tissue responses in growing ruminants have been less than in pigs, although much of these differences may relate to the difficulty of ensuring an adequate balance and quantity of amino acids to maximize response. Also, reductions in fat deposition and feed intake appear less in young ruminants compared to pigs.

There is little effect of pST on digestibility, so effects are due to an increase in the efficiency of use of dietary protein and/or an increase in the requirement of dietary protein to support the increased protein deposition. In grower pigs (30–60 kg), pST has little or no effect on dietary protein requirements, but there is an improvement in the efficiency of amino acid use. In finisher pigs (60–120 kg), pST has little effect on the efficiency of dietary protein use, but there is an increase in protein requirement commensurate with the increase in protein deposition.[6] As a consequence of the increased protein mass and protein synthesis, there is also an increase in maintenance requirement. That increase, when combined with the reduced intake, means that dietary energy may often limit the response to pST. Protein deposition in growing ruminants is virtually always limited by dietary energy consumption, and this may explain why ruminants treated with ST do not decrease feed intake, since energy spared from the reduction in lipid synthesis is partitioned toward protein deposition (or milk secretion in lactation, as discussed subsequently). Therefore, if the full benefits of exogenous ST are to be achieved, feed intake needs to be maximized regardless of species or physiological state.[9]

Lactation

Exogenous ST has been shown to enhance lactational performance in mammals ranging from laboratory animals to humans. The most extensive work is with lactating

Encyclopedia of Animal Science
DOI: 10.1081/E-EAS 120019802

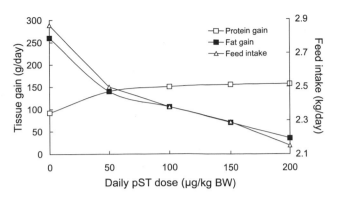

Fig. 1 Relationship between porcine somatotropin (pST) dose and parameters of growth performance. (From Ref. 9.)

cows, and bST has been approved for commercial use in 19 countries.[10,11] Commercial use over the last decade has clearly demonstrated a consistent milk response, generally about 5 kg/d, and a marked improvement in productive efficiency while maintaining normal cow health and herd life.[11] There is generally little response to bST in early lactation before peak yield, so commercial use is during the declining phase of lactation (Fig. 2).

The composition of milk is unaltered by bST treatment. Therefore, the use of bST has no impact on nutrient requirements per unit of milk or the nutritional and manufacturing properties of milk.[9,10] Responses to bST have been observed for all dairy breeds, regardless of parity and genetic potential. Cows receiving bST increase intake in an amount that matches nutrient needs for the extra milk and allows for the normal replenishment of body reserves over the lactation cycle. Thus, offering a balanced diet in adequate amounts is important; if nutrition and management are inadequate or poor, the lactational response to bST will be attenuated or even abolished.[9,10,13]

MECHANISMS

Fat and Carbohydrate

The multitude of effects that have been ascribed to ST in the regulation of growth and lactation are outlined in Table 1. Depending on physiological state, ST coordinates metabolism to partition nutrients toward lean tissue and bone during growth or toward milk synthesis during lactation. Many effects of ST are direct and mediated through changing responses to homeostatic hormones such as insulin or catecholamines. Other effects are indirect and thought to be mediated by the insulin-like growth factor (IGF) system.

Basal lipogenesis in adipose tissue from growing pigs treated with pST is decreased by up to 85%.[14] In addition, the ability of insulin to stimulate lipogenesis and glucose transport is similarly reduced in adipose tissue obtained from ST-treated animals, and this is mainly due to a decreased sensitivity to insulin. Also, ST treatment reduces rates of glucose clearance in response to an insulin or glucose challenge, and there is an augmented plasma insulin response to a glucose load. It has been suggested that the insulin resistance and resultant reduced adipose tissue lipogenesis and glucose oxidation are largely responsible for the reduction in feed intake observed in response to pST treatment.[14]

Treatment with somatotropin also causes an increase in lipolytic response to adrenergic stimulation in pigs and cattle.[10,15] In animals that are in a positive energy balance, where fat synthesis in adipose tissue is high and fat mobilization is low, effects of ST are predominantly a reduction in lipogenesis with little effect on lipolysis. On the other hand, if animals are in negative energy balance or need to draw on energy reserves, ST-treated animals have an enhanced ability to mobilize fat. Thus, the overall effect is that less nutrients are partitioned to body fat and more nutrients are available for productive functions.

Protein

Although it is well established that ST increases protein deposition and milk protein synthesis in growing and lactating animals, respectively, the precise mechanisms and extent to which effects on protein metabolism are direct or indirect via IGF-I remains an active area of investigation. Most studies suggest that in growing animals, the increase in protein deposition is due primarily

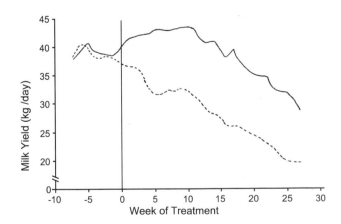

Fig. 2 Effect of bovine somatotropin (bST) on milk yield in lactating dairy cows. Commencing at week 0 (84±10 days postpartum) cows received a daily injection of excipient (dotted line) or bST (27 mg/day; solid line) for 26 weeks. (Adapted from Ref. 12.)

Table 1 Biological and production effects of somatotropin in farm animals during growth and lactation

Tissue	Physiological process affected
Skeletal muscle (growth)	↑ Protein gain
	↑ Protein synthesis
	↑ Amino acid and glucose uptake
	↑ Partial efficiency of amino acid utilization
Bone (growth)	↑ Mineral gain (paralleling tissue growth)
Mammary tissue (lactation)	↑ Milk with normal composition
	↑ Uptake of nutrients used for milk synthesis
	↑ Maintenance and activity of secretory cells
	↑ Blood flow consistent with milk yield
Adipose tissue	↓ Lipid gain
	↓ Lipid synthesis
	↑ Lipid mobilization (especially if in negative energy balance)
	↑ Catecholamine-stimulated lipolysis
	↓ Insulin-stimulated lipid synthesis and glucose metabolism
Liver	↓ Ability of glucose to inhibit gluconeogenesis
	↑ Glucose output (in lactation) to meet glucose needs
	↓ Glucose output (in growth of pigs) to meet glucose needs
Systemic effects	↓ Glucose clearance and oxidation
	↓ Insulin sensitivity
	↓ Amino acid oxidation and catabolism
	↑ Plasma glucose, insulin, IGF-I, and IGFBP-3
	↓ Plasma urea and IGFBP-2

↑=increase; ↓=decrease; IGF-I=insulin-like growth factor I; IGFBP=insulin-like growth factor binding protein. (Adapted from Refs. 10 and 15.)

to an increase in protein synthesis, with little effect on protein degradation. The increase in protein synthesis is also associated with a reduction in amino acid oxidation, so that a greater proportion of absorbed amino acids is used for protein accretion.[6,15]

Mammary Gland

Treatment of lactating cows with ST results in an increased synthesis of all milk constituents consistent with the increase in milk yield. The mechanism involves both an increase in the synthetic capacity and an improved maintenance of mammary epithelial cells. Coordinated increases in mammary blood flow and mammary uptake of nutrients also occur. The increased milk synthesis is supported by a series of orchestrated changes in other body tissues to ensure that the mammary gland is supplied with the quantity and pattern of nutrients to support milk synthesis.[10,11,13] These coordinated adaptations involve most tissues in the body, a portion of which is illustrated in Table 1.

CONCLUSIONS

Exogenous ST treatment of domestic animals markedly improves production efficiency by increasing the amount

of lean meat or milk produced per unit of feed intake. As a result, ST is used commercially in the dairy and swine industries in many countries. The mechanisms involve coordinated changes in the physiological processes, and many of these adaptations involve changes in tissue response to homeostatic signals. Overall, these orchestrated adaptations allow for a greater partitioning of nutrients for lean tissue accretion (during growth) or milk synthesis (during lactation), thereby allowing for increases in performance and productive efficiency while preserving animal well-being.

REFERENCES

1. Evans, H.M.; Simpson, M.E. Hormones of the anterior hypophysis. Am. J. Physiol. **1931**, *98*, 511–546.
2. Giles, D.D. An experiment to determine the effect of the growth hormone of the anterior lobe of the pituitary gland on swine. Am. J. Vet. Res. **1942**, *3*, 77–85.
3. Asdell, S.A. The effect of the injection of hypophyseal extract in advanced lactation. Am. J. Physiol. **1932**, *20*, 137–140.
4. Asimov, G.J.; Krouze, N.K. The lactogenic preparations from the anterior pituitary and the increase in milk yield from cows. J. Dairy Sci. **1937**, *20*, 289–306.
5. Bauman, D.E.; DeGeeter, M.J.; Peel, C.J.; Lanza, G.M.; Gorewit, R.C.; Hammond, R.W. Effect of recombinantly

derived bovine growth hormone (bGH) on lactational performance of high yielding dairy cows. J. Dairy Sci. **1982**, *65* (Suppl. 1), 121.

6. Dunshea, F.R. Nutrient requirements of pigs treated with metabolic modifiers. Proc. Nutr. Soc. Austr. **1994**, *18*, 102–114.

7. Campbell, R.G.; Johnson, R.J.; Taverner, M.R.; King, R.H. Interrelationships between exogenous porcine somatotropin (PST) administration and dietary protein and energy intake on protein deposition capacity and energy metabolism of pigs. J. Anim. Sci. **1991**, *69*, 1522–1531.

8. Boyd, R.D.; Bauman, D.E.; Fox, D.G.; Scanes, C.G. Impact of metabolism modifiers on protein accretion and protein and energy requirements of livestock. J. Anim. Sci. **1991**, *69* (Suppl. 2), 56–75.

9. National Research Council. *Metabolic Modifiers: Effects on the Nutrient Requirements of Food-Producing Animals*; Natl. Acad. Press: Washington, DC, 1994.

10. Bauman, D.E.; Vernon, R.G. Effects of exogenous bovine somatotropin on lactation. Annu. Rev. Nutr. **1993**, *13*, 437–461.

11. Bauman, D.E. Bovine somatotropin and lactation: From basic science to commercial application. Domest. Anim. Endocrinol. **1999**, *17*, 101–116.

12. Bauman, D.E.; Eppard, P.J.; DeGeeter, M.J.; Lanza, G.M. Responses of high-producing dairy cows to long-term treatment with pituitary somatotropin and recombinant somatotropin. J. Dairy Sci. **1985**, *68*, 1352–1362.

13. Burton, J.L.; McBride, B.W.; Block, E.; Glimm, D.R.; Kennelly, J.J. A review of bovine growth hormone. Can. J. Anim. Sci. **1994**, *74*, 167–201.

14. Dunshea, F.R. Effect of metabolism modifiers on lipid metabolism in the pig. J. Anim. Sci. **1993**, *71*, 1966–1977.

15. Etherton, T.D.; Bauman, D.E. Biology of somatotropin in growth and lactation of domestic animals. Physiol. Rev. **1998**, *78*, 745–761.

Spermatogenesis, Sperm Transport, and Semen

John E. Parks
Cornell University, Ithaca, New York, U.S.A.

INTRODUCTION

The principal roles of the male in reproduction are the production, maturation, and delivery of sperm for fertilization. Spermatogenesis—the proliferation and differentiation of germ cells within the testes to form haploid, free-swimming sperm—is a remarkable biological process. Once initiated at puberty, spermatogenesis proceeds throughout adult life with billions of sperm produced daily by sexually mature farm animals. Spermatogonial stem cells ensure continuity of the process when environmental factors such as high temperature disrupt testis function. Furthermore, spermatogenesis includes meiotic divisions, during which chromosome number is reduced from diploid to haploid and portions of homologous chromosomes are exchanged, producing genetically unique sperm. Following meiosis, dramatic morphological changes occur as the sperm forms, including addition of a flagellum that contributes to sperm transport and encounter with the egg. From the testis, sperm are transported through a system of excurrent ducts and, at the time of ejaculation, combined with seminal fluid to form semen. This overview will provide a glimpse of the intricate process of spermatogenesis, sperm transport, and semen characteristics that are essential aspects of male fertility.

ORGANIZATION OF THE SEMINIFEROUS TUBULE

Spermatogenesis occurs within the seminiferous tubules of the testes (Figs. 1 and 2). The intertubular area includes a vascular supply and testosterone-producing Leydig cells. A basement membrane surrounds each tubule with an outer layer of peritubular cells and a basal lamina. Within each tubule is an epithelial layer of Sertoli cells, somatic cells that provide physical and metabolic support for developing germ cells and regulate spermatogenesis. Intercellular junctions form near the base of adjacent Sertoli cells, further separating the tubule into basal and adluminal compartments and forming a blood–testis barrier. This barrier segregates diploid and haploid germ cells, thus restricting access of antibodies and preventing autoimmunity due to haploid gene expression. Germ cells are confined to spaces between adjacent Sertoli cells such that the Sertoli cell membrane conforms to the shape of the developing germ cells much like pressing one's fingertips into the side of an inflated balloon.

SPERMATOGENESIS

Spermatogenesis progresses through three phases—spermatocytogenesis, meiosis, and spermiogenesis.[1,2] Spermatocytogenesis is the mitotic divisions of spermatogonia present in the basal compartment at the onset of spermatogenesis. Spermatogonia proliferate and differentiate, becoming primary spermatocytes. Primary spermatocytes are then transported to the adluminal compartment during transient dissolution of Sertoli cell junctions. Spermatocytes proceed through first meiosis, during which four chromatids of each paired and replicated homologous chromosome form a tetrad. Chromatids of adjacent chromosome pairs often fuse at discrete points so that portions of chromatids are exchanged, contributing to the genetic variation between sperm. Secondary spermatocytes, the daughter cells of first meiosis, undergo second meiosis rapidly to form haploid round spermatids. No further DNA replication or cell division occurs in cells that have completed meiosis.

A round spermatid is genetically competent to initiate embryonic development if microinjected into a mature egg, a method of in vitro fertilization used in some cases of human infertility. However, dramatic morphological changes occur as the cytoplasm and organelles of the spermatid are extensively reorganized and modified. Key among these changes in domestic animal sperm are nuclear condensation and formation of the acrosome, mitochondrial helix, and flagellum.[2] With these changes, the spermatid gradually elongates to form a sperm.

Nuclear condensation is caused by addition of protamines to the nuclear chromatin with formation of disulfide bonds that condense the chromatin, prevent any further transcription, and impart the characteristic shape of the sperm head (typically paddle-shaped in farm animals). Formation of a flagellum, characterized by the 9+2 arrangement of microtubules typical of cilia and flagella in other cells, is directed by the distal centriole. The sperm flagellum or tail is also characterized by nine

Encyclopedia of Animal Science
DOI: 10.1081/E-EAS 120019803

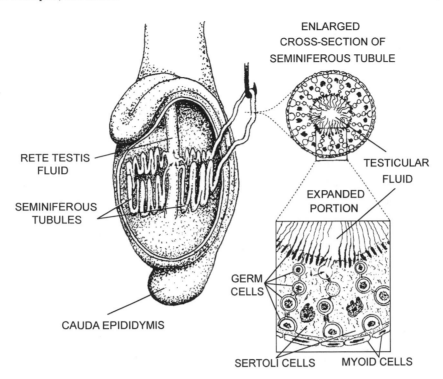

Fig. 1 Organization of the mammalian testis and excurrent ducts. (From Ref. 6, used with permission.)

coarse outer fibers that help determine the flagellar beat pattern. Vesicles elaborated by the Golgi apparatus become associated with the nucleus and ultimately form the acrosome, a lysosome-like structure that conforms to the anterior sperm head. The acrosome contains enzymes that aid in sperm penetration of the egg during fertilization. Mitochondria align end-to-end in a helical arrangement surrounding the base of the flagellum and form the sperm midpiece. Most of the spermatid cytoplasm is removed as a residual body during release of the sperm from the seminiferous tubule, referred to as spermiation.

ENDOCRINE AND PARACRINE REGULATION OF SPERMATOGENESIS

Basic aspects of neuroendocrine regulation of the hypothalamic–pituitary–gonadal axis are well established in the male. Gonadotropin releasing hormone (GnRH) from the hypothalamus stimulates release of the gonadotropins LH and FSH from the anterior pituitary gland. LH stimulates testosterone release from Leydig cells, whereas FSH stimulates Sertoli cell proliferation during development and various Sertoli cell functions.[2,3] Germ cells lack receptors for testosterone and FSH, suggesting that these hormones regulate spermatogenesis indirectly through their actions on Sertoli cells. Precise roles for

these hormones in spermatogenesis remain under investigation. FSH appears to stimulate spermatogonial proliferation, while testosterone promotes spermatid association with Sertoli cells during spermiogenesis.[4] Both hormones promote germ cell survival by inhibiting apoptosis (programmed cell death) and are necessary for quantitatively normal spermatogenesis.

KINETICS OF SPERMATOGENESIS

Quantitative and qualitative aspects of spermatogenesis have been described for many mammalian species.[1,2] Briefly, a differentiating group of spermatogonia in the basal compartment begins spermatocytogenesis within a short section of the seminiferous tubule. These cells progress along with more advanced generations of germ cells (spermatocytes and spermatids) within the same tubule section through a series of well-characterized cellular associations called stages.[1,2,5] Progression is from the basal to the adluminal compartment. Stages reappear in a cyclic pattern within a tubule section as new generations of spermatogonia enter the process. Stages also appear sequentially along the tubule length, forming a wave as the spermatogenic cycle is slightly advanced in adjacent tubule sections. The wave thus provides a mechanism for providing continuous sperm release without overfilling or occluding tubules.

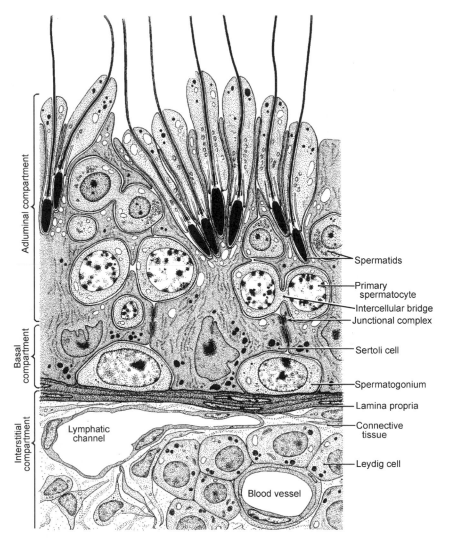

Fig. 2 Cytology of the bull testis. (From Ref. 2, used with permission.)

The exquisite timing of the cycle is intrinsically controlled and always the same within a species. Coordination of spermatogenic events is partly a function of intimate Sertoli–germ cell association and the persistence of cytoplasmic bridges between germ cells within each generation. Within a tubule section, several cycles are required for a group of spermatogonia to complete spermatogenesis and emerge as sperm, a lengthy process that takes 39 days in the boar to 61 days in the bull. The precise timing and long duration of spermatogenesis are important considerations in identifying causes for reduced semen quality and fertility.

SPERM TRANSPORT AND SEMEN

From the seminiferous tubule, sperm enter the rete testis, a network of collecting channels in the central core of farm animal testes (Fig. 1). From the rete, sperm move into a series of efferent ducts that exit the testis and converge with the initial segment of the single, highly convoluted epididymal duct. Anatomically, the epididymis is a discrete organ attached to the side of the testis and characterized by caput (head), corpus (body), and cauda (tail) regions. Changes to sperm during epididymal transit, collectively referred to as sperm maturation, are required for the acquisition of sperm motility and fertilizing ability.

Sperm transport is a function of hydrodynamic flow of male tract secretions, contraction of smooth muscle surrounding the excurrent ducts, and ciliary beat in the efferent ducts. Sperm transport from the testis through the epididymis is intrinsically regulated and requires many days.

During ejaculation, sperm are transported from the epididymis to the urethra by contractions of the vas deferens and combine with accessory sex gland secretions.

Accessory glands in farm animals include the seminal vesicles (which secrete the most fluid), the prostate, and the Cowper's glands. Seminal fluid provides a vehicle for sperm transport during ejaculation. However, numerous macromolecules are novel to or enriched in seminal fluid and have been ascribed various roles in sperm transport and fertilization.[6]

Semen, the combination of sperm and seminal fluids, can be harvested by intervention with an artificial vagina as the male mounts another animal or dummy mount, by controlled electrical stimulation of the pelvic genitalia, and other methods. Ejaculate volume averages approximately 1, 5, 100, and 200 ml in the ram, bull, stallion, and boar, respectively, with corresponding average sperm concentrations of approximately two billion, one billion, 100 million, and 200 million sperm per ml.[6] Sperm collected from farm animals is used for artificial insemination and in vitro fertilization and can be cryopreserved. In fact, the vast majority of dairy cattle in the United States are bred with frozen semen.

CONCLUSION—RECENT ADVANCES IN SPERMATOGENESIS

Basic research in the area of spermatogenesis has led to a number of exciting breakthroughs over the past decade. Among these are the discovery that spermatogonial stem cells harvested from mouse testes can be transplanted into the seminiferous tubules of a recipient male with initiation of spermatogenesis by the donor cells in the recipient testis.[7] Also, testis tissue from a variety of species can be grafted subcutaneously into immunologically tolerant mice and support complete spermatogenesis in the ectopic site.[8] Spermatogenesis in vitro remains an elusive goal, but some progress has been achieved at least through meiosis.[9] These advances will contribute to a better understanding of spermatogenesis in vivo, improvements in male fertility, and approaches to genetically modifying the male germ line.

REFERENCES

1. Johnson, L.; Walker, C.E.; Cerelli, J.S. *Spermatogenesis in the Bull. Proc. 15th Technical Conference on A.I. and Reproduction*; 1994; 9–27.
2. Senger, P.L. Endocrinology of the Male and Spermatogenesis. In *Pathways to Pregnancy and Parturition*, 1st Ed.; Current Conceptions, Inc.: Pullman, WA, 1999; 168–186.
3. Amann, R.P. Endocrine changes associated with onset of spermatogenesis in Holstein bulls. J. Dairy Sci. **1983**, *66*, 2606–2622.
4. McLachlan, R.I.; Wreford, N.G.; O'Donnell, L.; de Kretser, D.M.; Robertson, D.M. The endocrine regulation of spermatogenesis: Independent roles for testosterone and FSH. J. Endocrinol. **1996**, *148*, 1–9.
5. Bearden, H.J.; Fuquay, J.W. Spermatogenesis and Maturation of Spermatozoa. In *Applied Animal Reproduction*, 5th Ed.; Prentice Hall: Saddle River, NJ, 2000; 71–81.
6. Garner, D.L.; Hafez, E.S.E. Spermatozoa and Seminal Plasma. In *Reproduction in Farm Animals*, 6th Ed.; Hafez, E.S.E., Ed.; Lea and Febiger: Philadelphia, 1993; 165–187.
7. Brinster, R.L. Germline stem cell transplantation and transgenesis. Science **2002**, *296*, 2174–2176.
8. Honaramooz, A.; Snedaker, A.; Boiani, M.; Scholer, H.; Dobrinski, I.; Schlatt, S. Sperm from neonatal mammalian testes grafted in mice. Nature **2002**, *418*, 778.
9. Parks, J.E.; Lee, D.R.; Huang, S.; Kaproth, M.T. Prospects for spermatogenesis in vitro. Theriogenology **2003**, *59*, 73–86.

Superovulation

Ian Gordon
University College, Dublin, Republic of Ireland

INTRODUCTION

Embryo transfer (ET) technology in farm animals relies heavily on the ovarian stimulation of selected donor animals to produce the maximum number of transferable embryos after the induction of multiple ovulations (superovulation). In humans, stimulating the growth of additional follicles by gonadotropins is also an essential preliminary to in vitro fertilization (IVF). Despite extensive research efforts in the past 50 years, superovulation remains one of the weakest links in ET technology; large variability in superovulatory response to follicle-stimulating hormone (FSH) is evident in all species. One recent review has noted that the basic procedure of superovulation in cattle has undergone little improvement over the last 20 years. Factors influencing the success of superovulation include the gonadotropin preparation, its mode of administration, ovarian status, adjunct treatments (hormonal/mechanical), donor animal species, and the environment. In experimental studies, immunization against inhibin, which stimulates endogenous FSH secretion, has been shown to increase ovulation rate in the mare.

GONADOTROPINS

Serum Gonadotropin

The earliest descriptions of superovulation date back to Smith and Engle in 1927, who used crude anterior pituitary preparations to induce a fourfold increase in the ovulation rate of mice and rats A few years later, Cole and Hart demonstrated that the blood serum of pregnant mares would induce multiple ovulations in rats,[1] establishing the basis for what was to become the most widely used gonadotropin in the treatment of farm animals. This gonadotropin is commercially available in countries around the world under various trade names, e.g., Folligon (Intervet, Holland). Pregnant mare serum gonadotropin (PMSG) is a glycoprotein hormone present in the mare's circulation between days 40 and 130 of gestation and is unique as a molecule possessing both follicle-stimulating hormone (FSH) and luteinizing hormone (LH) activity. The gonadotropin is secreted by specialized trophoblastic cells that invade the mare's endometrium between days 36 and 40. For such reasons, the term equine chorionic gonadotropin (eCG) is often used now.

The preparation was used on some scale in Soviet Russia in the 1930s and 1940s to induce mild superovulation in sheep, and it is still used by farmers in many countries for that purpose.[2] Similar attempts to use serum gonadotropin in cattle to induce twin births by inducing mild superovulation proved singularly unsuccessful.[3]

FSH and LH Preparations

Effective ovarian stimulation requires knowledge of the basic concepts of follicular dynamics as well as an understanding of the respective roles of FSH and LH in regulating follicular development and ovulation. FSH stimulates follicle development by interacting with specific receptors on granulosa cells, inducing increased division of granulosa cells and aromatase activity as well as inducing expression of key genes involved in follicle maturation and the formation of LH receptors. Such receptors are essential for completion of follicle maturation and to allow ovulation to occur in response to the preovulatory surge of LH. Although recombinant bovine FSH has been used to superovulate cattle, there appears to be no technical advantage to its application in this species, where hormone cost is an important consideration. However, as noted by some observers, a recombinant product does not carry the disease risks that may be a serious consideration with pituitaries.[4] In the mare, FSH is species-specific; for that reason, equine preparations of this hormone are likely to be most effective in inducing superovulation.

Early work on superovulation in farm mammals involved comparisons between PMSG and FSH-rich pituitary extracts. Evidence favors the use of FSH, in terms of superovulatory response and embryo yield. Serum gonadotropin, due to its long biological half-life, has undesirable carry-over effects rarely found with pituitary preparations, which have a short half-life. The prolonged half-life of PMSG results in unovulated follicles secreting estradiol, leading to a disturbed

Encyclopedia of Animal Science
DOI: 10.1081/E-EAS 120019805

Table 1 Methods used to induce multiple ovulations in different species

Species	Superovulation protocols
Cattle and buffalo	FSH administered on days 8–12 of the estrous cycle. FSH treatment (4 days) initiated one day after follicle ablation or four days after estradiol/progesterone (to synchronize follicular wave emergence)
Sheep and goat	FSH administered after a period of progestagen treatment. Prostaglandin F_2-α given to regress cyclical corpus luteum
Pig	A single dose of PMSG at the start of the follicular phase of the estrous cycle (days 15–16) followed by HCG after 3–4 days.
Horse	Equine FSH administered daily for 6 days during mid-diestrus or late diestrus/early estrus.
Deer	12-day progestagen treatment with FSH administered twice daily for final four days.
Camelids	Use a combination of gonadotropin and PGF_2-α either during an induced luteal phase (GnRH/HCG) or after a simulated luteal phase (using progestagen).
Human	Downregulation of pituitary with GnRH; simultaneous administration of FSH (recombinant or urinary preparations); follicle growth monitored and HCG given to induce ovulation.

hormonal balance. In more recent times the emphasis has been with pituitary preparations having a well-defined FSH and LH content, such as Folltropin-V (Bioniche Canada, Inc.), containing a low level (20%) of LH, or Pluset (Laboratories∼Calier, S.A.), containing equal concentrations of FSH and LH.[5]

Mode of FSH Administration

Many studies in cattle have aimed at simplifying the administration of FSH, which, because of its short biological half-life, generally involves a four-day, twice-daily injection schedule. Such simplications can be important in terms of animal welfare and minimizing stress, as well as lowering labor costs on the farm. Beef cattle, for example, are less accustomed to handling than dairy cows and are often much less docile. Conventional superovulation protocols developed for domestic cattle often prove less efficient when applied to indigenous breeds of cattle or nondomestic ungulate species, due to the stress of handling.

OVARIAN STATUS

In cattle, buffaloes, horses, deer, sheep, and goats, the later stages of follicle development in the ovary occur in a wavelike pattern during the estrous cycle. In pigs, follicle growth is continuous during the cycle.[6] Each wave is characterized by the simultaneous emergence of a cohort of follicles and the establishment of one (cow) or more (sheep and goats) dominant follicles that continue to develop to ovulatory size, while apparently suppressing the growth of other antral follicles in the cohort. This is in contrast to events in the pig, where growth of ovulatory-

size follicles is limited to the follicular phase of the cycle. It is clear from many studies that the presence of large dominant follicles at the time of gonadotropin administration adversely affects superovulatory response.

One technique receiving considerable attention is the use of hormonal treatments to synchronize the follicular wave in cattle prior to initiating superovulation. Gonadotropin treatment at the time of emergence of a follicular wave has been found to be optimal. Although there is variability in the timing of emergence of the second follicular wave, most traditional superovulatory protocols begin between days 8 and 12 of the estrous cycle in order to synchronize with the second follicular wave.

ADJUNCT TREATMENTS

One hormone treatment increasingly employed in cattle superovulation to facilitate the scheduling of donor treatments is the use of estradiol in combination with progesterone to sychronize follicle wave emergence. The FSH treatment is initiated 4 days after the estrogen administration. Physical manipulation of the follicle wave is a relatively new technique, made possible by developments in ultrasound technology that permit the close monitoring of follicular characteristics in cattle. Although evidence shows that dominant follicle ablation increases superovulatory response, evidence is less encouraging in terms of the yield of transferable-quality embryos.[7]

INHIBINS

Compelling evidence emerged two decades ago that the ovary produces nonsteroidal compounds—inhibins—that are involved in regulating FSH secretion. Inhibins provide the chemical signal indicating the number of growing follicles in the ovary to the pituitary gland to reduce the secretion of FSH to the level that maintains the species-specific number of ovulations. In the mare, where application of the conventional ET technique is impeded by the lack of a suitable superovulation treatment, active immunization has been shown to increase superovulation. Active immunization against inhibin, as well as against the androgen androstenedione, is used commercially to induce mild superovulation in sheep[8] and goats.[9]

DONOR SPECIES AND ENVIRONMENT

Factors influencing superovulatory response include the donor animal itself and its environment. Response is influenced by species, nutritional status, reproductive history, age, breed, and whether it has been treated previously. In terms of species, it is well recognized that a major limitation to ET in the buffalo is the low yield of transferable-quality embryos.[10] The method of super-ovulation, although differing in detail among species, is based on administering gonadotropin when it is possible to achieve uniform follicle growth in response to FSH treatment (Table 1).

FSH preparations suitable for ruminant species, pigs, and camelids are without effect in horses.[11] In human IVF programs, pituitary down-regulation of LH and FSH by GnRH has been widely employed. Such down-regulation is usually achieved in the human patient by way of a nasal spray.[12] In farm animals, however, the requisite prolonged administration of this preparation, involving repeated injections, is currently ruled out on the basis of cost. In small ruminants, conventional protocols for superovulation generally involved an initial priming period with progesterone/progestagen-releasing devices (12 days in ewes, longer in goats) and the administration of gonadotropin prior to or around the time of progesterone/progestagen withdrawal. Responses in small ruminants and deer[13] are broadly in line with those expected in cattle, in terms of ovulation rate and yield of transferable embryos. Superovulation can be induced in the gilt and sow by administering a single dose of PMSG at the start of the follicular phase of the estrous cycle.[14] In camelids, which are induced ovulators, it is necessary to induce or simulate a luteal phase as a preliminary to the administration of gonadotropin.[15] In terms of environment, it is well established that seasonal changes in tropical and subtropical regions can markedly influence superovulatory response.

CONCLUSION

Although it is likely that a commercially available equine FSH product will soon be available for use in embryo transfer programs in mares, there seems little prospect of a significant improvement in treatment protocols in the other farm species. The extent to which pituitary down-regulation by GnRH, using suitably long-acting forms of this hormone, may favorably influence superovulatory responses in farm animal species has yet to be adequately examined. As an alternative to current methods of superovulation, the possibility exists that advancements in oocyte recovery from the live animals by transvaginal ultrasound-guided aspiration or other methods—used in conjunction with in vitro oocyte maturation, fertilization, and early embryo culture techniques—may eventually permit embryos from farm animals to be produced more easily and cheaply in the laboratory.[16]

REFERENCES

1. Cole, H.H.; Hart, G.H. The potency of blood serum of mares in progressive stages of pregnancy in effecting the sexual maturity of the immature rat. Am. J. Physiol. **1930**, 93, 57–58.
2. Gordon, I. Induction of Multiple Births in Sheep. In *Controlled Reproduction in Sheep and Goats*; CABI Publishing: Wallingford, U.K., 1996; 205–240.
3. Gordon, I. Embryo Transfer and Associated Techniques in Cattle. In *Controlled Reproduction in Cattle and Buffaloes*; CABI Publishing: Wallingford, U.K., 1996; 245–371.
4. Kanitz, W.; Becker, F.; Schneider, F.; Kanitz, E.; Leiding, C.; Nohner, H.P.; Pohland, R. Superovulation in Cattle: Practical Aspects of Gonadotropin Treatment and Insemination. In *Proceedings of the 18th Meeting European Embryo Transfer Association (Rolduc)*; 2002; 103–111.
5. Mapletoft, R.J.; Steward, B.; Adams, G.P. Superovulation in Perspective. In *Proceedings of the 18th Meeting European Embryo Transfer Association (Rolduc)*; 2002; 119–127.
6. Evans, A.C.O. Characteristics of ovarian follicle development in domestic animals. Reprod. Domest. Anim. **2003**, 38, 240–246.
7. Shaw, D.W.; Good, T.E. Recovery rates and embryo quality following dominant follicle ablation in super-ovulated cattle. Theriogenology **2000**, 53, 1521–1528.
8. Gordon, I. Embryo Transfer and Associated Techniques in Sheep. In *Controlled Reproduction in Sheep and Goats*; CABI Publishing: Wallingford, U.K., 1996; 280–329.
9. Gordon, I. Embryo Transfer and Associated Techniques in Goats. In *Controlled Reproduction in Sheep and Goats*; CABI Publishing: Wallingford, U.K., 1996; 416–439.

10. Gordon, I. Embryo Transfer and Associated Techniques in Buffaloes. In *Controlled Reproduction in Cattle and Buffaloes*; CABI Publishing: Wallingford, U.K., 1996; 467–479.

11. Gordon, I. Embryo Transfer and Associated Techniques in Horses. In *Controlled Reproduction in Horses, Deer and Camelids*; CABI Publishing: Wallingford, U.K., 1997; 139–167.

12. Wong, J.M.; Forrest, K.A.; Snabes, M.C.; Zhao, S.Z.; Gersh, G.E.; Kennedy, S.H. Efficacy of nafarelin in assisted reproductive technology: A meta-analysis. Hum. Reprod. Updat. **2001**, *7* (1), 92–101.

13. Gordon, I. Controlled Reproduction in Deer. In *Controlled Reproduction in Horses, Deer and Camelids*; CABI Publishing: Wallingford, U.K., 1997; 168–188.

14. Gordon, I. Embryo Transfer and Associated Techniques in Pigs. In *Controlled Reproduction in Pigs*; CABI Publishing: Wallingford, U.K., 1997; 183–217.

15. Gordon, I. Controlled Reproduction in Camelids. In *Controlled Reproduction in Horses, Deer and Camelids*; CABI Publishing: Wallingford, U.K., 1997; 189–208.

16. Gordon, I. *Laboratory Production of Cattle Embryos*, 2nd Ed.; No.27, Biotechnology in Agriculture Series, CABI Publishing: Wallingford, U.K., 2003; 322–381.

Swine: Behavior Management and Well-Being

Anna Kerr Johnson
National Pork Board, Des Moines, Iowa, U.S.A.

John James McGlone
Texas Tech University, Lubbock, Texas, U.S.A.

INTRODUCTION

The study of animal behavior is important in day-to-day livestock management and veterinary medicine. Ethology, or the study of animal behavior, can answer basic ethological questions or questions of interest to farmers. This article will cover beneficial and problematic behaviors displayed by swine throughout all phases of production and the importance of caretaker skills and management. A novel behavioral tool for researchers will be introduced. Finally, certification and assessment tools that can be implemented on U.S. farms to assess swine behavioral management will be described.

BENEFICIAL BEHAVIORS OF SWINE

Swine have behavioral repertoires that are rich and diverse. Some behaviors can be classified as beneficial, for example, nest building prior to farrowing and suckling of piglets by the lactating sow. Other behaviors can become problematic for individual or groups of pigs, which may even cause challenges for caretaker management. Normal and beneficial behaviors include feeding, drinking, eliminating, and resting behaviors. These behaviors, also called maintenance behaviors, are expressed by normal pigs at a certain predictable and repeatable level, depending on pig genetics and the microenvironment that is provided to the pigs.

PROBLEMATIC BEHAVIORS OF SWINE

Challenging pig behaviors can include, but are not limited to aggression, stereotypical behaviors, and tail and ear biting.

Aggression

Under confinement conditions, where swine have limited possibilities to avoid or escape from their aggressors, fighting can be injurious to pigs and therefore deleterious to both health and welfare. Aggression is a normal part of the biology of the pig and can occur at low levels throughout all phases of production. Piglets naturally begin to fight immediately after birth to establish a dominance order based on teat location. At the time of weaning piglets and regrouping of unacquainted pigs, fighting can initially occur to establish a hierarchical order. Fighting may continue if resources are perceived to be limited.[1] Certain forms of aggression can be deleterious. During farrowing, the newborn piglet can face potential savaging and cannibalism by the sow. Although the original function of such behavior is defense of the sow's own piglets, it can be a practical problem when the behavior is directed either at the caretaker or at the piglets themselves.

Stereotypies

A subset of Oral-Nasal-Facial (ONF) behaviors have sometimes been called stereotypies. Stereotypies are repetitive, relatively invariable sequences of nonfunctional behaviors, potentially indicating reduced welfare.[2] Differences among sows in the level of stereotypical behaviors, their biological significance, and causation remain unclear. Pigs within the same housing systems may vary in the average frequency of stereotypies performed, as the propensity to develop stereotypic behavior has been related to age and parity of the sow. Furthermore, stereotypies also appear to be related to individual characteristics of sows and less to housing systems.[3]

Tail and Ear Biting

Tail and ear biting is a welfare problem of growing (weaned) pigs that involves destructive chewing of penmates' tails or sometimes their ears. The injured tail or ears become attractive to other pigs in the group once the tail or ears bleed, and the syndrome grows until the bitten pig is severely injured. Tail biting, for example, occurs in two stages—a preinjury and an injury stage—and

Encyclopedia of Animal Science
DOI: 10.1081/E-EAS 120019809

it is the second stage that results in wounding and bleeding and more severe consequences such as infection, spinal abscess, paralysis, and in extreme cases, death. Potential factors predisposing tail biting are numerous: poor ventilation, breakdown in the food or water supply, poor-quality diets, absence of bedding materials, and breed type. Underlying behavioral mechanisms for tail biting are not understood.[4]

CARETAKER SKILLS AND MANAGEMENT REQUIRED FOR SWINE BEHAVIOR MANAGEMENT AND WELL-BEING

Caretakers manage the stress imposed on pigs used for farming purposes. Stress may be part of production and cannot always be avoided—for example, pigs must be transported at least once in their lifetime. Caretakers are cognizant of stress effects on performance and welfare as evidenced by disease, loss of reproduction, or low weight gain.[5] By developing management strategies designed to reduce the cost of stress, performance and, ultimately, welfare can improve. The most critical area that impacts swine welfare on farms is the careful selection, training, and skills of the caretaker. An example of the importance of caretaker skills can be seen at the time of handling. Caretakers need to know how pigs will react to human behavior to effectively move them in the desired direction and at times, to restrain them. Pigs may respond to tactile, visual, olfactory, gustatory, and auditory stimuli from their human handlers[6] and may not always understand caretaker intention. Swine that are fearful may react in a negative manner, with obvious behavioral indicators seen by the pig stopping, freezing, backing off, running away, or vocalizing.[7,8] Caretakers' behavior is strongly influenced by the attitudes they hold about the pig and these attitudes may affect job-related characteristics such as work ethic, attention to detail, and motivation to learn new skills.[7]

TOOLS TO HELP WITH SWINE BEHAVIOR MANAGEMENT AND WELL-BEING DEFINITIONS

Behavior data, acquisition, summary, and analysis are very time-consuming.[9] The researcher must decide on the classification of each behavior and this can add subjectivity or bias. Within the field of applied animal ethology and, in particular, the study of farm animal behavior, ethologists differ about what actions constitute a given behavior. This leads to a lack of consistency in comparing studies of swine behavior. Typically, at the beginning of a behavior experiment, an ethogram (a catalogue of behaviors, vocalizations, and odors issued by an animal) is developed for the species under study. Even though many dictionaries are available to assist with this process, behavior is extremely dynamic and difficult to capture using written information only and still photographs. Computer and video technology is progressing and future developments may allow totally objective measures for behavior to be collected.

An animal behavior encyclopedia has been developed to allow searching and viewing of defined (videorecorded) behaviors on the Internet. This video database is being developed to initiate a system that automatically extracts animal motion information from an input animal activity video clip using a multiobject tracking and reasoning system. Eventually, the extracted information will be analyzed and described using standard animal behavior.[9] Behavioral definitions to accompany the video clips have been reprinted or adapted from the *Dictionary of Farm Animal Behavior*.[10] The online behavioral encyclopedia is available at the Web site of the Livestock Issues Research Unit (http://www.liru.asft.ttu.edu/Refman/DB_sponsors.htm).[11] This tool can help standardize behavioral classification of swine behavior. Standardization of measurement will benefit the swine industry, which ultimately bases its swine behavior management on trained caretakers who can recognize normal and abnormal behaviors.

IMPLEMENTATION OF SWINE BEHAVIOR MANAGEMENT AND WELL-BEING ON U.S. FARMS

Two on-farm certification programs that can assess swine welfare on farm is the Certified Humane Raised and Handled certification program (http://www.certifiedhumane.

Table 1 Nine care and well-being principles of SWAP

Area		Care and Well-Being Principle (CWP)
Record keeping	1	Herd health and nutrition
	2	Caretaker training
Animal observations	3	Animal observation
	4	Body condition score
	5	Euthanasia
	6	Handling and movement
Facilities	7	Facilities
	8	Emergency support
	9	Continuing assessment and education

(From Ref. 12.)

com/) overseen by the Humane Farm Animal Care and the Animal Welfare Institute (AWI) which monitor and implement their scheme (http://www.awionline.org/farm/alternatives.htm). The National Pork Board has recognized an on-farm program called the Swine Welfare Assurance Program™ (SWAP™), which is both an educational and internal assessment program sponsored through Checkoff dollars and monitored by the National Pork Board (Table 1). It is a voluntary science-based program designed to educate pork producers and to assess and improve pig welfare (www.porkboard.org/SWAPhome).

SWAP uses swine behavioral management to help manage and improve well-being on the farm. In CWP 2, titled *Caretaker Training*, caretakers are required to work through the Pork Quality Assurance Program™. In addition, online learning courses on euthanasia, handling, and husbandry are available that explain natural pig behavior and biology and what tools a caretaker can use to reduce the stress imposed on those pigs.[12] CWP 3, titled *Animal Observations*, conducts a swine behavior test and records wounds, scratches, and abscesses. CWP 6, titled *Handling and Movement*, explains proper handling techniques required to move pigs, facility considerations, and the equipment that should be used as primary driving aids.

CONCLUSION

This article addresses the need for a standardized way of studying and recording swine behaviors at the research level and the need for sound science to be implemented back on the farm. Continued work in this area will enable caretakers to become highly skilled animal care and husbandry experts, which will continually improve swine behavior management and well-being.

REFERENCES

1. Fraser, D.; Rushen, J. Aggressive behavior. Vet. Clin. North Am., Food Anim. Pract. **1987**, *3*, 285–305.
2. Fraser, A.F.; Broom, D.M. *Farm Animal Behaviour and Welfare*, 3rd Ed.; CABI Int.: London, UK, 1990.
3. Von Borell, E.; Hurnik, J.F. Stereotypic behavior, adrenocorticol function, and open field behavior of individually confined gestating sows. Physiol. Behav. **1991**, *49*, 709–713.
4. Widowski, T.; Torrey, S. Neonatal management practices. **2002**, *1* (6). Available at http://www.porkboard.org. Accessed August 18, 2003.
5. Moberg, G.P. A review—Developing management strategies to reduce stress in pigs: A new approach utilizing the biological cost of stress. Proc. Bienn. Conf. Aust. Pig Sci. Assoc. Manipulat. Pig Prod. **1993**, *4* (IV), 116–126.
6. Hemsworth, P.H.; Gonyou, H.W. Human Contact. In *Animal Welfare*, 1st Ed.; Appleby, M.C., Hughes, B.O., Eds.; CABI Int., 1997; 205–217.
7. Hemsworth, P.H.; Coleman, G.J. *Human-Livestock Interactions. The Stockperson and the Productivity and Welfare of Intensively Farmed Animals*; CAB International: Wallingford, UK, 1993.
8. Hemsworth, P.H.; Gonyou, H.W. Human Contact. In *Animal Welfare*, 1st Ed.; Appleby, M.C., Hughes, B.O., Eds.; CABI Int., 1997; 205–217.
9. Morrow-Tesch, J.L.; Dailey, J.W.; Jiang, H. A video data base system for studying animal behavior. J. Anim. Sci. **1998**, *76*, 2605–2608.
10. Hurnik, J.F.; Webster, A.B.; Siegel, P.B. *Dictionary of Farm Animal Behavior*, 2nd Ed.; Iowa State University Press: Ames, 1995.
11. USDA-ARS. *Livestock Issues Research Unit (LBRU)*; South Plains: Lubbock, TX, 2003. Encyclopedia of Farm Animal Behavior. Available: http://www.liru.asft.ttu.edu/EFAB/default.asp. Accessed August 17, 2003.
12. National Pork Board (NPB). *Swine Welfare Assurance Program™ (SWAP™)*; 2003. Available at http://www.porkboard.org. Accessed August 17, 2003.

Swine: Breeding and Genetics

L. Ollivier
National Institute for Agricultural Research, Jouy-en-Josas, France

INTRODUCTION

The first attempts at domesticating the pig date back to the Neolithic age, i.e., circa 5000 B.C. The process of domestication includes selective breeding for specific characteristics, and may be considered a first step in genetic improvement. Pig improvement has first been the result of empirical methods employed by individual farmers. Then selection became a technique scientifically based, progressing with the knowledge of the biology involved, and particularly with the development of genetics.

An early example of breeding plans for pigs is the Danish program of 1896 for developing a new breed, the Danish Landrace, to be crossed with imported Yorkshire boars for the production of bacon. Breeding centers were then established, and official performance recording for carcass traits started in 1907. In such a scheme, one can already find the ingredients of modern pig improvement, i.e., breeding structures, breeding objectives, choice of breed combinations, and within-breed improvement by selection, as detailed later in the article.

THE ORGANIZATION OF GENETIC IMPROVEMENT

Pure-breeding, as we define it now, started in Britain in the second half of the 18th century. However, breed societies for pigs only appeared about one century later. In the course of time, breed societies became more and more constructive forces, and increasingly contributed to genetic improvement.[1]

Pig farms have specific functions in genetic improvement, according to whether they actually generate genetic changes (nucleus), or disseminate these (multiplier), or at the end, take advantage of them in a production system (producer). This three-tier breeding pyramid has been the basic structure for pig improvement in most countries for the last few decades, together with crossbreeding for exploiting heterosis effects.

Such an organization requires integrating the two upper tiers of the breeding pyramid, as achieved by independent breeding organizations (either private or cooperative) or within national schemes implemented in many countries, following the early Danish example mentioned previously.

The role played by breeding companies varies between countries. They can provide more than 50% of the replacements in some countries, compared to hardly any in others.

THE DEFINITION OF BREEDING OBJECTIVES

The breeding goals fall into two categories—reproduction and production traits—of interest to producers of weaned piglets and slaughter pigs, respectively. Reproduction traits include components of sow productivity, such as age at puberty, conception rate, number born alive per litter, number weaned, and weaning–estrus interval. Production traits include traits associated either with production costs, such as growth rate and food conversion, or with product value, such as lean content and quality of the lean and fat tissues.

The weights of the breeding goals in an overall objective define an aggregate genotype (H), made of the breeding values (A) of each element. A common practice is to use profit equations of the form:

$$P \text{ (profit)} = R \text{ (returns)} - C \text{ (costs)}$$

By taking the partial derivatives of P with respect to the n traits included as goals in R and C, economic weights are obtained and an aggregate genotype, linear in the objectives, is established,[2] i.e., $H = a_1 A_1 + a_2 A_2 + \cdots + a_n A_n$. Economic values may also be derived from life cycle efficiency models. Examples of these two approaches are given in Table 1.

In the system of specialized sire and dam lines, now extensively adopted, the choice of a breeding objective in each line is based on the profit made in the slaughter generation of the crossing system.[3] As shown in Table 2, different breeding objectives are needed in each breed for accommodating various breeding systems.

THE CHOICE OF SELECTION CRITERIA AND BREEDING VALUE ESTIMATION

A distinction is made between traits considered objectives for improvement and traits actually used in ranking the

Encyclopedia of Animal Science
DOI: 10.1081/E-EAS 120019810

Table 1 Relative importance of reproduction and production traits

	Trait	Relative importance[a]	
		a	b
Reproduction	Age at puberty	6	3
	Conception rate	14	36
	Number born alive/litter	48	34
	Piglet viability	32	27
	Total	100	100
Production	Growth rate	15	38
	Food conversion	23	20
	Carcass yield	16	12
	Lean percent	46	30
	Total	100	100

a = Profit function (France).
b = Return per slaughter pig (The Netherlands).
[a]Relative increase (%) in profitability from an increase of one phenotypic standard deviation of each trait.
(Adapted from Ref. 8.)

male and female candidates, termed criteria of selection. These two sets of traits only partly coincide, and each set includes a fairly large number of traits. Performance recording programs define the measurements to be used as selection criteria.

Reproduction performances are assessed through on-farm litter-recording systems, including litter size at birth and at weaning, and sometimes litter weights. Production traits, namely growth rate, feed efficiency, and carcass measurements, were initially recorded in central testing stations, built on the Danish model. An important step has been the advent of techniques allowing a fairly accurate evaluation of body composition by measuring fatness on the live pig.[4] This has opened the road to central performance testing stations of young boars, and to on-farm testing programs. More recently, meat quality traits

measured in slaughterhouses have been introduced into testing programs.

Pig improvement is essentially a multiple-trait selection problem, which is solved by combining performance records into an index (*I*). This index is a predictor of breeding value, chosen so as to maximize the correlation between *I* and the aggregate genotype H.[2] Eventually, selection index theory came to include methodologies accounting for unequal information among candidates and nongenetic effects and providing best linear unbiased predictions (BLUP) of breeding values.

THE DESIGN OF BREEDING PROGRAMS

Selection response depends on three parameters, i.e., selection accuracy (ρ, correlation between the aggregate genotype and the selection criterion), selection intensity (*i*, standardized selection differential), and generation interval (*t*, usually measured in years). The expected annual response, expressed in genetic standard deviation units, is

$$R_a = (i_1\rho_1 + i_2\rho_2)/(t_1 + t_2)$$

where the indices 1 and 2 refer to dams and sires, respectively. An efficient breeding program thus depends on a proper choice of evaluation methods (maximizing ρ) and replacement policies (maximizing *i* and minimizing *t*).

Production traits in pigs are measurable on both sexes either before breeding (growth rate, food conversion, and fatness), which permits individual selection, or after slaughter (lean content, lean and fat tissue characteristics), which permits only family selection. The maximum expected annual response is nearly one genetic standard deviation with individual selection for production traits. With the advent of BLUP, records from relatives such as siblings, cousins, and ancestors are used to predict breeding values with greater accuracy, and better across-farm (or -station) evaluations are also achieved. Overall,

Table 2 Relative weights of reproduction (H_1) and production (H_2) traits to accommodate four breeding systems using three different breeds

		Breed		
Breeding system (dam × sire)		A	B	C
Pure-breeding	A × A or B × B or C × C	aH_1+H_2	aH_1+H_2	aH_1+H_2
Single cross	A × C	$aH_1+0.5H_2$	–	H_2
Back cross	(A × B) × B	$aH_1+0.5H_2$	$aH_1+1.5H_2$	–
Three-way cross	(A × B) × C	$aH_1+0.5H_2$	$aH_1+0.5H_2$	H_2
Number of lines (or breeding objectives) per breed		2	3	2

a = Economic weight of H_1 relative to H_2 in a pure-breeding system.
(Adapted from Ref. 8.)

the advantage of BLUP over individual selection in genetic response has been shown to be in a range of 10–30% for most production traits.

As shown in Table 2, reproduction traits should also be included in the breeding objectives. Though most studies have so far concluded that reproduction is genetically uncorrelated with production, there are indications that this might not be a general rule, which would tend to make selection for reproduction traits increasingly worthwhile.

MARKER-ASSISTED BREEDING

Advances in molecular genetics have generated genetic maps showing highly polymorphic markers evenly spaced over the 19 chromosomes of the species.[5] Consequently, the role that individual gene or marker identifications can play in breeding schemes is enhanced, compared to classical quantitative genetics methods relying only on measurements of performances.[6]

For single-locus traits, the objective is to change gene frequency at the locus of interest by selecting the gene itself (when possible) together with nearby marker loci, a process termed marker-assisted selection (MAS). The process depends on the marker loci hitchhiking the genes of interest. This procedure has been illustrated in the elimination of the deleterious halothane gene from maternal lines, achieved in the 1980s by using biochemical markers. The pig linkage map offers several similar possibilities. Major genes for meat quality and resistance to disease are areas of particular interest.

Polygenic traits are under the control of quantitative trait loci (QTL) and the environment. Several QTL have been mapped[7] and may be exploited in selection. When all sources of gain are cumulated, considerable increases in responses may be expected from MAS.[8] This implies that the relevant QTL can be hitchhiked by the markers, as in the single-locus case examined earlier. In situations of statistical independence among loci, marker–QTL associations can be detected only within families, and lower gains in selection accuracy are obtained. The gains then result from more exact coancestry for segments of the genome including QTL.[9]

CONCLUSION

The efficiency of pig breeding programs is reflected in genetic gains reported for growth and body composition on the order of 0.5–1.5% of the mean annually.[1] No change of appreciable magnitude had been reported for litter size at birth up to a recent past in most countries, though appreciable genetic gains in piglets born per litter have recently been reported.

Further opportunities will arise from knowledge accumulated on classical, quantitative, and molecular genetics.[10] Specific challenges have to be faced for quality of lean and fat tissue or disease resistance. A better knowledge of the genome and the identification of genetic markers and functional genes are expected to complement conventional breeding plans. Pig breeding will continue to rely basically on the optimal exploitation of the pig reproductive capacity, the efficient use of breeding value evaluation tools, and an adequate management of genetic variability. A well-balanced approach will remain essential in future genetic improvement schemes.

REFERENCES

1. Sellier, P.; Rothschild, M.F. Breed Identification and Development in Pigs. In *Genetic Resources of Pig, Sheep and Goat*; Maijala, K., Ed.; World Animal Science; Elsevier: Amsterdam, 1991; Vol. 12, 125–143.
2. Hazel, L.N. The genetic basis for constructing selection indexes. Genetics **1943**, *28*, 476–490.
3. Smith, C. The use of specialised sire and dam lines in selection for meat production. Anim. Prod. **1964**, *6*, 337–344.
4. Hazel, L.N.; Kline, E.A. Mechanical measurement of fatness and carcass value on live hogs. J. Anim. Sci. **1952**, *11*, 318.
5. Archibald, A.L.; Haley, C.S. Genetic Linkage Maps. In *The Genetics of the Pig*; Rothschild, M.F., Ruvinsky, A., Eds.; CAB International: Wallingford, UK, 1998; 265–294.
6. Neimann-Sorensen, A.; Robertson, A. The association between blood groups and several production characteristics in three Danish cattle breeds. Acta Agric. Scand. **1961**, *11*, 163–196.
7. Bidanel, J.P.; Rothschild, M.F. Current status of quantitative trait locus mapping in pigs. Pig News and Information **2002**, *23* (2), 39N–54N.
8. Ollivier, L. Genetic Improvement of the Pig. In *The Genetics of the Pig*; Rothschild, M.F., Ruvinsky, A., Eds.; CAB International: Wallingford, UK, 1998; 511–540.
9. Fernando, R.L.; Grossman, M. Marker assisted selection using best linear unbiased prediction. Genet. Sel. Evol. **1989**, *21*, 467–477.
10. Rothschild, M.F.; Ruvinsky, A. *The Genetics of the Pig*; CAB International: Wallingford, UK, 1998.

Swine: Health Management

John Carr
Iowa State University, Ames, Iowa, U.S.A.

INTRODUCTION

The clinical appearance of many diseases and disorders of farmed pigs is heavily influenced by the pigs' environment. The classical concept "pathogen meets pig results in clinical disease" is nearly always incorrect. The pig industry and its servicing veterinary advisors have moved from individual animal medicine through preventive medicine into health maintenance. All of the skills learned previously still need to be employed, but veterinarians are now required to apply a degree of animal science knowledge for which they are rarely prepared.

THE PIG CLINICIAN AND HEALTH TEAM

To maintain the health of swine, the clinician needs to approach the pig unit with regard to six major areas: 1) biosecurity; 2) pig flow; 3) medicine management; 4) review of current stock health and susceptibilities; 5) competency of the stockpeople; and 6) the provision of an environment conducive to healthy pigs.

Managing the health of pigs on a farm must become the responsibility of a farm health team, which includes a veterinarian. However, the key players are the stockpeople. If their training is inadequate, disease recognition will be delayed, with potentially devastating consequences for both the pigs involved and the farm, and even nationally. This was classically demonstrated by the 2001 foot-and-mouth disease (FMD) outbreak in the United Kingdom, where failure of the producer to recognize and report clinical signs of FMD in his pigs to his local veterinarian resulted in the unnecessary deaths of 6 million animals to control the disease.[1]

BIOSECURITY

Biosecurity is a major responsibility of the farm health team, and awareness of the ease of disease spread is required for all members of the team. It is impossible (at present) to prevent the transmission of some diseases, for example, various serotypes of *Escherichia coli* or earthborne pathogens such as *Erysipelothrix rhusiopathiae*. Some diseases may spread long distances through the air, for example, parvovirus. Other pathogens are only locally spread. *Mycoplasma hyopneumoniae*, for example, will affect farms within a 3-km zone. However, for farms located in an area of low farm density, maintenance of a *M. hyopneumoniae*-free status has been possible for more than 20 years.[2] Some diseases, such as *Sarcopties scabiei* var *suis*, require direct pig contact. With modern avermectin therapies, eradication of mange on pig farms is achievable. Adequate biosecurity is the responsibility of the entire pork production chain, from the nucleus and multiplication farms, with their artificial insemination (AI) studs, to the family farm. A pathogen that is absent from the farm or area, such as pseudorabies (Aujeszky's diseases), does not require treatment or prevention. Indeed, the absence of pathogens allows for more errors in environmental management before production suffers.

PIG FLOW

The lack of animal science understanding by the veterinary profession has allowed farms to grow without regard for the biology of farmed pigs. Producers are driven by the need for an economic return and by the constraints of buildings and local legislation. Veterinarians and producers have turned to antimicrobials to balance pathogen load against health and disease. Over time, with inadequate cleaning, environments become infected with an increasing number and variety of pathogens. Eventually, the disease challenge overwhelms the natural defense mechanisms and increasing numbers of pigs present with clinical disease. The easiest way to control the pathogen load is to move clean pigs into new buildings. This is clearly impossible in a farm environment, but an approximation can be reached by adopting strict all-in/all-out procedures combined with single-source policies.

All-in/all-out is poorly understood by the farming community. The keystone must be pig flow. The provision of the pigs of the same age and health status is achieved only by minimizing the variation in pig numbers produced per batch by no more than 15% overall—5% below target output and, equally important, no more than 10% above target output. This creates stable farms and helps to reduce greed in procedures. In several parts of the world, legislation regarding stocking density, as in the European

Encyclopedia of Animal Science
DOI: 10.1081/E-EAS 120019811

Union,[3] is forcing farmers to adopt pig flow measures, because failure will result in fines and other penalties. Pig flow is a complex concept that prescribes the number of animals the farm can accommodate and then models a production method to fill these buildings.[4] The area where pig flow fails on most farms is the gilt pool; having insufficient gilts results in a reduction in output. Poor management of the gilt pool results in a glut of gilts in estrus, resulting in overproduction and overstocking of the facilities (Fig. 1).

MEDICINE MANAGEMENT

Medicine storage and usage are the cornerstone of any preventive medicine program. The diagnosis of increased coughing and mortality in finishing pigs, associated with swine influenza virus or *M. hyopneumoniane*, may result from the freezing of vaccines in the farm, veterinarian, or distributor's refrigerator. A study of farm medicine storage areas revealed that 10% of farms stored their vaccines below 0°C.[5]

The inappropriate use and overuse of needles and syringes have been demonstrated in the transmission of many pig pathogens, including porcine reproductive and respiratory syndrome virus and classical swine fever virus (Fig. 2).

STOCK HEALTH

The ability to clinically examine, recognize, and treat disease in pigs is the responsibility of the entire farm

Fig. 2 Vaccines stored in a freezing refrigerator on a farm where pigs experience finishing pneumonia, despite vaccination.

health team. Adequate training of stockpeople in the recognition of disease is a responsibility of the farm's attending veterinarian. Continual professional development is a prerequisite for the veterinarian as new diseases (postweaning multisystematic syndrome) appear and established diseases (Glasser's disease) evolve in the modern pig industry. The pig itself carries the ability to succumb to or fight disease agents. As the pig's genetic makeup becomes more understood, commercially available resistance factors will include more than just *Escherichia coli* F4 or F18 resistance.[6] A major problem in pig health management is compromised or sick pigs, who are the major sources of disease pathogens. It is essential that farms provide hospital accommodations and suitable treatment regimes to provide for these pigs.

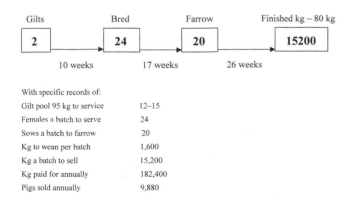

Gilts	Bred	Farrow	Finished kg – 80 kg
2	24	20	15200
10 weeks	17 weeks	26 weeks	

With specific records of:

Gilt pool 95 kg to service	12–15
Females a batch to serve	24
Sows a batch to farrow	20
Kg to wean per batch	1,600
Kg a batch to sell	15,200
Kg paid for annually	182,400
Pigs sold annually	9,880

There are some targets that have to be met: The farm weans weekly; the 90 percentile farrowing rate is 82% (the farrowing rate is over 82% ninety percent of the time); 10 piglets weaned per crate with an average weight of 8 kg at 24 days of age; a 5% postweaning mortality, therefore 95 pigs at 80-kg deadweight are paid for each week. The gilts are given 10 weeks introduction to allow for adequate compliance with biosecurity arrangements. In addition, to take finishing pigs to 80-kg deadweight requires 26 weeks.

Fig. 1 Pig flow model for a 20-sows-per-week farm.

STOCKPERSON AND STOCKMANSHIP

The fulcrum around which pig health resolves is the stockperson's abilities. Modern pig farming has a greater reliance on employed help, who may have little interest in the well-being of the pig. The National Pork Board's Swine Welfare Assurance Program initiative[7] concentrates on the pig's behavior toward the stockpeople. A caring environment promotes good health and productivity.[8]

ENVIRONMENTAL MANAGEMENT

The expression of clinical production diseases is often determined by the environmental stressors to which the pigs are subjected. Assessment of the environment can be easily achieved when the environment is broken down into its component parts: the water supply, the feeding system, the flooring, and the air (Fig. 3).

Water Supply

A supply of fresh drinking water is essential to pig health. A drinker that provides water is generally accepted as good enough by untrained stockpeople. However, the flow may be inadequate, the drinker's height inappropriate, the drinker type unsuitable, the water contaminated, or the drinker affected by stray voltage. If these factors are not recognized and corrected by the stockpeople, then performance and pig health will be negatively affected.

Feeding System

Growth rates are determined by the ability of pigs to eat. The type of feed, presentation of feed, and hygiene of feed are factors that the farm health team needs to constantly assess to ensure that health and production are maintained. In addition to swine health, feed wastage plays a key role in the profitability of swine farms, yet farms may casually waste 10% of the feed. Poorly constructed feeding systems impact the quantity and type of dust that is aerosolized during feed distribution. This can impact the health of both stock and stockpeople.

Flooring

Stocking densities for all stages of pigs are becoming a legal constraint on pig production throughout the world. Pig health improves with increased space allowance per pig, but pork output is negatively impacted. Therefore, an acceptable balance between space and production is required. As farms age, flooring and other contact surfaces (walls, doorways, and passages) become eroded, particularly around feeders and water supplies. Poor maintenance routines ultimately result in compromised pig health. Analysis of the floor would also include hygiene. The lack of all-in/all-out routines results in poor or inadequate cleaning routines and maintenance. It is only through good pig flow that sufficient time can be set aside to allow stockpeople to adequately care for the floor.

Air

Failure of the ventilation system is the classic reason for respiratory disease. Seasonal variations put tremendous pressure on the ventilation system, which fails particularly at the turn of the seasons. Managing the ventilation system requires assessment of the air variations over time with reference to the temperature, humidity, gas pollutants (NH_3, CO_2, CO, H_2S), dust and type of endotoxins.

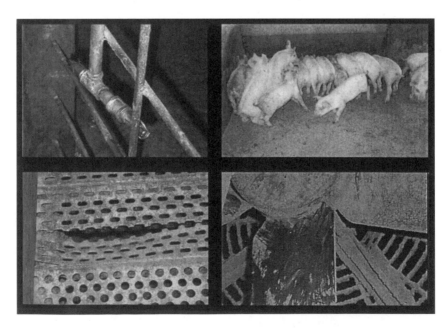

Fig. 3 Environmental management directly impacts the health of pigs. The photograph shows water that is difficult to obtain, a feeder that is too short, broken flooring, and dirty fans that reduce air flow in a building. All of these and other problems directly compromise pig health.

All buildings should be designed to provide adequate living zones for the pigs—for sleeping, eating and drinking, exercise, and dunging. The building engineers should ensure that the building works before and during pig occupancy. When failures are discovered, they should have rational improvements that can resolve the situation. Poor building orientation, particularly in cross-flow ventilation buildings, results in drafts, creating poor pig respiratory health and increased vices that necessitate tail docking to control the situation. Preweaning diarrhea is often associated with drafts and chilling of the neonatal piglet.

CONCLUSION

Swine health management maintenance requires a balance between reducing the risk of new pathogens through biosecurity; providing all-in/all-out through pig flow; requiring that medications are effective through proper use and storage; recognizing sick animals promptly; and providing excellent stockmanship and ensuring that pigs are not compromised by any failing in their environment.

REFERENCES

1. Gibbens, J.C.; Sharpe, C.E.; Wilesmith, J.W.; Mansley, L.M.; Michalopoulou, E.; Ryan, J.B.M.; Hudson, M. Descriptive epidemiology of the 2001 foot and mouth disease epidemic in Great Britain: The first five months. Vet. Rec. **2001**, *149*, 729–743.
2. Muirhead, M.R.; Alexandra, T.J.L. *Managing Pig Health and the Treatment of Disease*; 5M, 1997. ISBN 0 9530150 0 9.
3. Commission Directive 91/630/EEC laying down minimum standards for the protection of pigs Commission Directive 2001/88/EC amending Directive 91/630/EEC.
4. Carr, J. Development of pig flow models. Pig Vet. J. **1999**, *43*, 38–53.
5. Carr, J. Refrigeration management. Pig Vet. J. **1999**, *43*, 138–143.
6. EdemaGuard™; F18+*E. coli* Resistance Using PICmarq™ Technology: http://www.pic.com.
7. Pork Checkoff Swine Welfare Assurance Program™ 2003, National Pork Board.
8. Hemsworth, P.H.; Barnett, J.L. The effects of aversively handling pigs, either individually or in groups, on their behaviour, growth and corticosteroids. Appl. Anim. Behav. Sci. **1991**, *30*, 61–72.

Swine: Product Marketing

David Meisinger
Becca Hendricks
National Pork Board, Des Moines, Iowa, U.S.A.

INTRODUCTION

Market hogs and pork products are marketed and distributed over a complex pathway to customers and consumers in the United States and overseas. This article will attempt to outline some of those pathways. In addition, attention will be given to consumer attitudes about pork and some of the marketing programs that address these attitudes. Swine and pork marketing in the United States has historically been a commodity business. Pork producers have raised commodity hogs for commodity packers who provided commodity products for commodity markets. In the last few years, there has been a genuine paradigm shift in the pork industry toward production and marketing of a quality product. This shift began in 1991 with a dramatic shift to a very lean, heavily muscled hog in response to consumer demands for leaner meat. At the same time, the industry saw a shift to case-ready products with the advent of superior packaging and packaging technology. With the move toward case-ready products, there has been a lateral move toward branding, which has promoted the interest in pork quality. Retailers, packers, and further processors become very interested in quality and uniformity when their name is on the product.

LIVE HOG AND CARCASS MARKETING

There has been a significant change in the way hogs are marketed in the United States. Not many years ago, most hogs were marketed through either auction markets or terminal markets. Direct marketing—sales of pigs directly to slaughterers—was a small minority of the total marketing. Today, just the reverse is true. Essentially, all market hogs are sold direct, either delivered directly to the slaughter plant or delivered to a packer buying station. A very small percentage of hogs are sold to terminal markets, and essentially no market hogs are sold through auction markets anymore.

Of those sold direct, a growing percentage are sold under some type of contract arrangement, whether a cost-plus contract, a window contract, or just a specific market price-based contract. It is estimated that 14% of market hogs are sold on contract as opposed to 65% that are sold on the spot, which means they were sold without prior negotiations. Packers raised the remainder (19%). By the middle of the first decade of this century, spot sales will represent no more than 10% of market hogs. This is due to a desire by both producers and packers for some degree of predictability in future hog sales.[1]

Another big change that occurred is the move toward carcass marketing. Not many years ago, less than 10% of all hogs were sold on a carcass merit basis. Now the reciprocal is true. Over 90% of market hogs are sold either on a carcass merit basis or on reputation based on measurement of previous loads, or on a combination of these factors. For the latter, market hogs may be measured, but are paid for on a running average of the past three loads.

Carcass merit is established by a multitude of methods and a number of regression equations. Pork packers use a ruler to measure backfat, optical probes to measure backfat and loin depth, handheld ultrasound to measure fat and loin depth, or carcass ultrasound measurements in a sophisticated neural network of equations to estimate overall carcass lean content. The packers who use optical probe technology all use different equations based on their product use to estimate percent lean in the carcass. The interest in the Autofom for whole-carcass ultrasound estimation of percent lean in primal cuts has been based on future promises for the technology. Autofom is sophisticated software and hardware equipment and can very accurately measure the percent lean in various cuts. Packers interested in using this approach cannot currently justify the cost on the basis of paying producer suppliers more accurately, nor can they justify it on the basis of more accurate sorting and utilization of the cuts for development of different products. The primary justification has been based on the future possibility of limited manpower or the increased use of robots to do many of the manual disassembly procedures or fabrication procedures. Pigs will never be marketed as totally uniform entities. The alternative is to totally characterize the cuts so that this information can be communicated to robots that can make their movements accordingly.

DOMESTIC PORK PRODUCT MARKETING

Some of the markets available domestically are evolving as consumers' preferences change and as technology

Encyclopedia of Animal Science
DOI: 10.1081/E-EAS 120019808

allows for product development. Niche markets including natural pork, organic pork, welfare-friendly pork, antibiotic-free pork, or process-verified pork have become more commonplace. Nutraceutical uses of pork to satisfy certain nutritional needs are also receiving more attention. Fresh pork enhanced with a solution of ingredients designed to improve the tenderness, juiciness, and flavor of pork has become well accepted in the industry. Over half of all fresh pork is enhanced, and consumers have come to expect the flavor and tenderness profile associated with this technology.

Channel marketing of fresh pork can be subdivided into retail and foodservice marketing and the distributors who deliver the product to the appropriate channel. Pork is marketed about equally in the foodservice and retail markets.

Although pork is marketed at virtually every retail grocery store with a meat department and is usually the most profitable meat, pork cuts are typically underrepresented in the meat case. According to a pork industry study, pork is more of an impulsive purchase than beef or chicken. Therefore, retail pork marketing efforts should include point-of-purchase information and merchandising pieces to impact decision making at the meat case. This is also important because a growing majority of pork is case-ready, and there are typically fewer in-store meat cutters available to answer consumer questions about the product. Lead selling items in the fresh meat case at retail have been pork chops, ribs, and roasts. Because of today's consumers' busy lifestyles, many retailers are offering more and more convenience and precooked meat items. These items are typically merchandised near the fresh product. The pegboard section of the retail meat department holds the further-processed products. The lead selling processed items are cured hams, lunchmeats, bacon, and sausage. Processed products are typically sold as fixed-weight items, and fresh products are sold as random-weight items.

Foodservice marketing involves sales to commercial (limited- and full-service restaurants and travel and lodging) and noncommercial (schools, institutional foodservice, and healthcare) segments. These outlets are typically more interested in quality as defined by tenderness, juiciness, and flavor, and they are willing to pay for these quality assurances to guarantee repeat customers. Value-added product offerings are becoming more important to operators as they face labor shortages and food safety pressures. Many products being supplied to foodservice operators are now preseasoned, precooked, or preportioned by the packer or further processor who is supplying the product. Over the last several years, sausage, ham, and bacon have represented over half of the products sold in foodservice outlets. However, the fastest growing products have been ribs and bacon. Consumer trends affecting the foodservice industry include the desire for variety, taste, and experience. Almost half of the consumer food dollar is spent at foodservice outlets, and operators must provide a unique experience for their patrons. Pork fits well into most menus as it can be prepared in a variety of ways as well as in several ethnic dishes.

PORK DEMAND ENHANCEMENT STRATEGIES

A discussion of demand enhancement strategies in the pork industry must start with a historical perspective. The National Pork Producers Council (NPPC), a checkoff-funded producer group, launched its "Pork. The Other White Meat®" campaign in 1987 to reposition pork within the meat industry. Recognizing the growing popularity of poultry (consumers were appreciating its perceived nutritional benefits and versatility as highly desirable), the pork industry saw a strategic opportunity to position pork as a uniquely different entrée, competing with poultry white meat rather than with its traditional red meat competitor, beef.

It is easy to ascertain that pork is truly a white meat, because fresh pork—especially in popular cuts such as pork chops—is white in color after being cooked. Historically, pork was produced as much for the lard as for the meat. Lard was the primary fat source prior to vegetable oils and was used for cooking, as well as for munitions and other industrial purposes. The entire basis for calling attention to pork as "The Other White Meat" is to inform consumers that selected cuts of fresh pork are surprisingly lean, versatile, and convenient, and that fresh pork does fit into every diet. Given these attributes, pork does compare favorably to other white meat products.

So the concept, program, and campaign that developed not only spoke to pork's white characteristics, but also emphasized its other features that favorably position pork as a delicious break from the meal routine. The campaign educated consumers that pork offers something different. It was a significant multiple-year effort aimed at helping to expand domestic and export demand for pork and to lead the industry forward.

For more than a decade, the National Pork Board (NPB, previously the National Pork Producers Council) has remained focused and committed to the position. Today, 9 out of 10 people recognize pork as "The Other White Meat." In addition, in a recent study of the most memorable contemporary advertising campaigns undertaken by the Northwestern University Graduate School of Integrated Marketing Communications, "Pork. The Other White Meat" ranked in the top five most memorable advertising slogans in America. Not only are consumers more aware of the marketing campaign, but they rate pork 23% higher in product favorability than they did in 1994, according to an industry study. The retail value of pork has steadily grown, outpacing the rate of inflation. Production has increased 37%.

The following tables illustrate both the historical perceptions of pork (in the 1980s) and certain misconceptions that persist today.

In the mid-1980s, pork was falling off the map:
- 15 years of decline
- More than 10% erosion in market share
- Seen as being too high in cholesterol, calories, and fat
- A tired, dated image
- Not featured or promoted by key gatekeepers—retail, restaurants, and the press
- ''Second-class citizen''

Perception versus reality:

Perception:	*Reality*:
• Pork is high in calories	• Pork has 198 calories per 3 oz serving
• Pork is high in fat	• 3 oz of cooked lean pork has 9 grams of fat
• Pork is high in cholesterol	• 3 oz of pork loin contains roughly 76 milligrams of cholesterol, which is 26% of the daily allowance
• Pork is not nutritious	• 1 serving contains one-half the adult daily allowance of adult protein. Pork - has 50% more iron than chicken - is a primary source of thiamin - is high in riboflavin, zinc, and Vitamin B6

The National Pork Board continues to take the leadership in demand enhancement for fresh pork through its innovative approaches to retail, foodservice, and consumer communications. In addition to the heralded ''Pork. The Other White Meat'' promotion success story, the NPB has retail and foodservice merchandisers working to get pork a greater share of the meat case and a place on more menus.

INTERNATIONAL PORK PRODUCT MARKETING

The U.S. Meat Export Federation (USMEF) has been conducting promotions for U.S. pork since its inception in 1976. Today, USMEF has over $7 million committed specifically to promote U.S. pork worldwide. Some of these funds are used for traditional promotions (in-store retail promotions, menu promotions, seminars), while other funds are used to address market access issues and for research to determine market conditions for American pork products. Some funds are also used for administrative support for these promotions. As a result of this decades-long commitment to U.S. pork, exports have risen from 142,000 metric tons in 1980 to 728,500 metric tons in 2002. Meanwhile, the value of U.S. pork exports has jumped from $233 million in 1980 to $1.5 billion in 2002.

Up until 1991, the United States was a net importer of pork. Since then, exports have grown steadily and now represent a greater percentage of total pork production than imports. Every year, record exports are recorded and now represent over 8% of total pork production. This change has come about only because of a concerted commitment on the part of the U.S. pork industry to provide a product that fits global customers' needs for quality and safety. The United States is also viewed as a reliable supplier, with its animal disease protection and surveillance programs in place.

CONCLUSION

While the pork industry has seen various changes in the last several decades, it appears that structural change and the resulting changes in marketing have been accelerated. Producers, as well as processors, operators, and retailers, face new issues daily, including consumer demands, food safety, product quality, product traceability, and other issues. Marketing of pork and pork products in the United States and internationally is very complex and dynamic and will continue to be a major part of U.S. agriculture.

REFERENCE

1. Lawrence, J.; Grimes, G. *Production and Marketing Characteristics of US Pork Producers*; 2001; 1–19. National Pork Board website: www.porkboard.org.

Swine: Reproductive Management

William L. Flowers
North Carolina State University, Raleigh, North Carolina, U.S.A.

INTRODUCTION

Reproduction in swine is an integrated process that involves many events, including achievement of puberty and normal estrous cycles, fertilization, embryonic and fetal development during pregnancy, farrowing, and recovery of the sow's reproductive system during lactation. These events must occur in a coordinated sequence or the entire process fails. Failures of these processes cannot be measured directly, but are reflected in reductions in farrowing rates (number of sows mated that produce piglets) and/or number of pigs born alive. As a result, collection and analysis of reproductive data are key components of effective reproductive management. If done correctly, it can identify problems and reproductive events that are involved, as well as suggest solutions. Thus, reproductive management in swine involves three steps: 1) recognition of low performance; 2) determination of which processes failed; and 3) identification of management practices that must be changed to correct the problem(s).

RECOGNITION OF LOW PERFORMANCE

Identifying when reproductive performance is low requires analyses of records. This is accomplished by comparing the actual level of performance within a herd with previously established production targets and decision boundaries.[1] Production targets are goals established by swine operations that represent levels of performance that are above average. It is not uncommon for production targets to vary among farms, depending on genetics, geographic location, housing, and other factors. When reproductive performance reaches current targets, a new set is established. Therefore, the actual level of reproductive performance on a farm normally is lower than its production targets.

In contrast, decision boundaries are undesirable levels of performance that tend to be universally accepted within the swine industry. They signify that management is negatively affecting reproduction. Values above the decision boundary are interpreted as acceptable, even though they may be below the production targets. Levels below the decision boundary are interpreted as being unacceptable and indicate that immediate intervention is advisable. Suggested performance targets and decision boundaries for important measures of reproductive performance are shown in Table 1.

DETERMINATION OF REPRODUCTIVE EVENTS THAT FAILED

Determination of which physiological events in the reproductive process failed is accomplished by examining collectively the results from the decision boundary analyses for farrowing rate and litter size, as well as the length of time required for bred sows that do not become pregnant to return to estrus. The latter is referred to as the return interval. Farrowing rate and litter size are classified as either acceptable or unacceptable by comparing the actual level of performance with the decision boundaries. The return interval is designated as either regular or irregular, depending on when most of the nonpregnant sows exhibit estrus. If it is between 18 and 25 days, then the return interval is classified as regular. If it is greater than 28 days, then it is classified as irregular. Five distinct patterns or combinations emerge from examination of reproductive data collectively (Table 2).

The advantage of examining reproductive data collectively is that physiological events that failed can be identified (Table 2). The rationale for assigning specific events with a given pattern is based on the physiology associated with the establishment of pregnancy. There are two periods during which at least 5 embryos must be present in the uterus for pregnancy to be maintained.[2] The first period occurs between days 10 and 12 and the second between days 17 and 28.[3] If less than 5 embryos are present during the first 12 days, the sows will not become pregnant and return to estrus 18 to 25 days after breeding (regular returns). Sows in this situation behave as if they were never mated. In contrast, if there are adequate numbers of embryos on day 12, but not between days 17 and 28, the sows become pregnant, but the pregnancy ends prematurely. When this happens, sows don't return to estrus until 28 to 35 days after breeding (irregular returns). In essence, the return interval is the pivotal piece of information for determining which reproductive events are deficient for situations in which farrowing rate

Encyclopedia of Animal Science
DOI: 10.1081/E-EAS 120019814

Table 1 Performance targets and decision boundaries for reproductive efficiency

Reproductive measure	Targets	Decision boundary
Farrowing rate (%)	>85.0	<80.0
Number of pigs born alive per litter (litter size)	>11.0	<10.5
Number of stillborn pigs per litter (%)	<5.0	>7.5
Number of mummified fetuses per litter (%)	<1.0	>1.5

is poor. If it is regular, then physiological events prior to day 12 failed. If it is irregular, then those after day 12 were compromised.

Whenever both farrowing rate and numbers of pigs born alive are unacceptable, as is the case for patterns I and II, then most sows in the herd are affected. The deficiency probably is part of the farm's standard operating procedures. In contrast, when farrowing rate is poor, but litter size is good, only a portion of the sows are involved. Everything occurred correctly in the sows that farrowed, because litter size was normal. Therefore, the deficiency is confined to a subset of sows in the herd that did not farrow. The most common subsets evaluated are season (summer versus winter) and sow parity.

A high incidence of fetal death is a reasonable explanation for pattern III, in which farrowing rate is acceptable, but number of pigs born alive is unacceptable. As a result, the numbers of mummies and stillborn pigs per litter (Table 1) are two other reproductive measures that need to be examined. Mummies are partially decomposed piglets and stillborns are fully-formed, normal piglets that are born dead. One or both usually will be unacceptable when farrowing rate is good, but litter size is bad. If the number of mummified fetuses is high, then the problem occurred after day 50 of gestation. When fetuses die, the sow attempts to reabsorb the tissue. After day 50 of gestation, the fetal skeleton has been mostly calcified and decomposition involves

primarily soft tissues. The result is a mummified fetus. In contrast, if the number of stillborn pigs is high, then the problem occurred during the last several weeks of pregnancy or during farrowing.

EVALUATION OF MANAGEMENT PRACTICES

Finding management practices responsible for problems is the most time-consuming portion of reproductive management, because it involves a series of trial-and-error investigations. However, knowing which reproductive events might be deficient facilitates the process by reducing the number of procedures that need evaluation. Table 3 contains a summary of management practices that should be evaluated when searching for causes. The list is by no means inclusive, but it does concentrate on the most common management practices that cause failure of the physiological processes associated with reproduction.

Once a management practice is identified as a potential cause, corrective measures should be taken. Unfortunately, it normally takes about five months to see improvements in reproductive performance. This is the length of time required for sows to complete their reproductive cycle (115-day gestation, 18- to 28-day lactation, and 4- to 7-day return-to-estrus interval). As a result, subsequent analysis of reproductive performance is an important,

Table 2 Patterns of reproductive failure and their relationship to reproductive physiology

Pattern	Farrowing rate	Return interval	Number born alive	Possible reproductive events that failed
I	Unacceptable	Regular	Unacceptable	Recovery of sow reproductive tract during lactation Fertilization Embryonic development (before day 12)
II	Unacceptable	Irregular	Unacceptable	Embryonic development (between day 12 and 28)
III	Acceptable	N/A[a]	Unacceptable	Fetal development (after day 28) Farrowing
IV	Unacceptable	Regular	Acceptable	Recovery of sow reproductive tract during lactation Fertilization Embryonic development (before day 12)
V	Unacceptable	Irregular	Acceptable	Embryonic development (between day 12 and 28)

[a]Not applicable when farrowing rate is acceptable; then by default, the return interval is also.

Table 3 Common management practices associated with specific patterns of reproductive failure

Pattern	Reproductive event	Management practices
I	Recovery of sow Reproductive system during lactation Fertilization	• Lactation lengths less than 14 days • Low nutrient intake of sows during lactation • Use of low-quality semen (<70% motile and morphologically normal sperm cells) • Mating frequencies of less than once per day of estrus • Boar exposure (for detection of estrus) of less than 10 minutes per day • P.R.R.S. (Porcine Reproductive and Respiratory Syndrome)
	Embryonic development	• Full feeding after breeding • P.R.R.S. • Moving or regrouping sows after breeding (days 0 to 12)
II	Embryonic development	• Moving or regrouping sows after breeding (days 12 to 28)
III	Embryonic or fetal development	• Feed with mycotoxins (zearalenone or aflatoxin) • Leptospirosis • Parvovirus
	Farrowing	• Lack of supplemental cooling when ambient temperature >80°F • Average sow parities of four or greater (old sows) • Inducing farrowing too early with prostaglandins
IV	Recovery of sow during lactation	• Reduced feed intake during summer months • Reduced feed intake in first parity sows
	Fertilization	• Poor insemination or mating management by a few technicians • Matings late in estrus
	Embryonic mortality	• Lack of supplemental cooling when ambient temperature is >80°F
V	Embryonic mortality	• Moving or regrouping a subset of sows after breeding (days 12 to 28)

final step that confirms that changes in management have been effective. In essence, swine reproductive management begins and ends with evaluations of reproductive data.

CONCLUSION

Reproductive management in swine is deficient when reproductive measures fall below (or increase above) decision boundaries. When deficiency occurs, immediate and decisive intervention is needed, which requires analyses of reproductive records. Evaluation of farrowing rates, number of pigs born alive, and return intervals collectively result in five distinct patterns. Specific reproductive events and, thus, specific management practices are associated with each pattern, which allows for the efficient identification and correction of deficiencies

REFERENCES

1. Vinson, R.A.; Muirhead, M.R. Veterinary Services. In *Diseases of Swine*, 6th Ed.; Leman, A.D., Straw, B., Glock, R.D., Mengeling, W.L., Penny, R.H.C., Scholl, E., Eds.; Iowa State University Press: Ames, 1986; 885–912.
2. Dziuk, P.J. Effect of migration, distribution and spacing of pig embryos on pregnancy and fetal survival. J. Reprod. Fertil. **1985**, *48* (supplement), 57–63.
3. Geisert, R.D.; Zavy, M.T.; Wetteman, R.P.; Biggers, B.G. Length of pseudopregnancy and pattern of uterine protein release as influenced by time and duration of oestrogen administration in the pig. J. Reprod. Fertil. **1987**, *79*, 163–171.

Swine: Waste Management

Leonard S. Bull
North Carolina State University, Raleigh, North Carolina, U.S.A.

INTRODUCTION

The swine industry has moved rapidly toward specialized, highly concentrated production systems and a vertically integrated business organization. That trend is expected to continue not only in the United States but, as integrated companies expand offshore, the production systems developed in the United States will be replicated elsewhere. Specialized, concentrated production systems in agriculture, and especially those for poultry and swine, are responsible for the high efficiency and ability to deliver consistent products at increasingly affordable prices in all markets. Because concentrated production is often not located close to the cropland that is the site of feed production, which has historically served as the recipient of the animal waste for fertilizer, land application of waste has often exceeded the capacity of the crops growing on the land to assimilate the nutrients. This results in the possibility of surface and groundwater contamination by the nutrients and pathogens in the waste. In addition, high concentrations of animals have been associated with local concerns about emitted odors and regional concerns about emitted ammonia.

Swine production is substantially conducted in confinement facilities in which animals are housed in pens with slatted floors and without bedding. Currently, swine waste (solid and liquid), as well as spilled drinking water and feed, drops through the slats in these floors into a pit where it is held for variable lengths of time depending on the subsequent handling system. Currently used swine handling systems, new technologies, new developments, and criteria for evaluation of swine waste management systems are addressed in this article.

CURRENTLY USED SYSTEMS

Flush and Anaerobic Treatment Lagoon (Flush or Pit Recharge)

Anaerobic treatment lagoon systems, normally found in warmer climates where freezing is not a problem, are composed of a basin of volume range from 0.7–3.7 cubic feet per pound of animal contributing, depending on the type and age of the pig and the climatic zone within the

United States.[1] Lagoons are usually formed by excavation and embankment of earth to a depth of 8–10 feet (depending on the position of water table) and lined with compacted clay, rubberized fabric, or other impervious material (depending on the prevailing regulations). The lagoon receives the waste from the production facilities flushed by either release of large volumes of liquid recycled from the top portion of the lagoon (traditionally 800 gallons/flush/half of building, repeated two to six times daily) or release of 30,000–40,000 gallons of pit-recharged liquid and waste, approximately once weekly, from a recharge of lagoon liquid. In both systems, the high flow volume and the slight slope of the waste-receiving pit under the pens (1–1.5% slope) result in effective gravity waste removal from the barns. The waste streams from each of these two commonly used systems (containing less than 2% solids) may be passed through a short-retention settling basin to allow heavy solids to be retained. Once the waste materials are in the lagoon, anaerobic breakdown occurs in a complex series of reactions. While there is a loss of volatile materials from the lagoon surface (carbon dioxide, methane, ammonia, nitrogen gas, and other volatile compounds), most of the nutrients are retained in the organic phase as microbial cells (settled to bottom as sludge) or inorganic elements.[1]

Periodically, material from the lagoon is applied to cropland as a source of nutrients, with application rate governed by the requirement for nitrogen (and, more recently, phosphorus) of that specific crop. Application schedule is governed by regulations including weather and growing season. Occasionally hydraulic loading rate of the application field is a limitation.

Deep Pit Storage Systems

In areas where winter temperatures make liquid flush or pit-recharge systems impractical, waste is collected and stored under the slatted floors of the pens. In these systems, pits of depth about 6 feet are installed. Waste is allowed to accumulate for at least 6 months and up to 12 months, when it is pumped out and applied to the land (cropland on the same farm). Waste in these systems usually has a solid content of 3–6%, depending on the watering system and wastage. In these systems, there is

Encyclopedia of Animal Science
DOI: 10.1081/E-EAS 120023829

no supplemental storage or treatment site. The pit allows some anaerobic treatment to take place.

While ventilation is a major consideration in all confinement operations, those with deep pits must have careful attention. Ventilation is normally set to draw air downward through the slatted floor and to exit the building via fans located in the pit wall. This prevents escape of potentially toxic gases from the pit into the buildings.

Scraper Systems

While not used extensively, there are some production facilities that have scrapers under the slatted floors and that remove the waste materials in that manner using timed periodic scraping. Mechanical problems, maintenance, and significant odor problems in the buildings caused by the continual mixing of urine and feces have relegated those systems to minor importance.

Solid Floor with Gutter and Flush

In some older facilities, solid concrete floors are used without bedding, with the floor sloping slightly to the outside walls of the building. At the wall area is a shallow gutter of 3–5-inches depth and variable width. By locating the feeding and watering devices strategically, animal waste deposition is concentrated in the area of the gutter, and that which is not deposited there is worked toward the gutter by animal traffic and the slope of the floor. The gutter is flushed with liquid, either recycled lagoon liquid or fresh water, in a manner similar to the flush system noted earlier but with less volume released per flush.

NEW TECHNOLOGIES FOR SWINE WASTE MANAGEMENT

Concerns about concentration of swine production into "concentrated feeding operations" and possibilities of odor nuisances and extensive emissions of ammonia,[2] plus discharge of pathogens and contamination of surface and ground water with waste nutrients (especially nitrogen, phosphorus, copper, and zinc), have led to significant efforts to find economically and operationally viable alternatives to current waste management methods. While traditional swine waste management involved land application of material to meet nutrient needs of crop and/or animal feed production on the same location as where the animals were raised, the move toward separation of animal production from feed production locations has changed those practices. Waste management plans are now required for virtually any concentrated swine production facility that is economically viable in size. These plans have, until recently, been built around

the requirement for available nitrogen by the crop to be fertilized by the waste. In 2003, the Environmental Protection Agency revised the Clean Water Act[3] and included provision for regulation of waste application based on phosphorus as well as nitrogen. That process is under development at present, but it is certain that both nitrogen and phosphorus will be used in determining the amount of all animal waste that can be land-applied. The fact that many land areas that have received animal waste in the past based on nitrogen requirements have excessive levels of phosphorus poses a serious problem. Many animal operations cannot comply with the combined nitrogen and phosphorus requirements with existing land area and current animal numbers. The use of enzymes (especially phytase) in swine diets is becoming common, and this reduces phosphorus excretion by 40% or more. This practice will greatly improve, over time, the current imbalance in soil phosphorus found on many land application sites, but the remediation time will be extensive.

Increased awareness of the role of animal production in atmospheric emission of ammonia is resulting in concern not only in land application of measured waste nitrogen, but also the undesirability of loss of nitrogen as ammonia to the atmosphere with deposition elsewhere. Ammonia emission regulations are common in many countries already.[4]

Odor emission, a local issue in animal production, is the greatest concern associated with the location of swine production facilities, and one that raises significant emotional concerns and legal challenges. For that reason, swine production systems must address and significantly reduce or eliminate odor concerns beyond their property boundaries.

Modern swine production practices involve use of elevated levels of both zinc and copper in the diets for immunity enhancement in young pigs (zinc) and growth promotion (copper). The positive aspects of these additions result in significant reduction in need for antibiotic use. The negative aspect is that these metals are excreted in the waste, which, when the waste is applied to land, can result in soil accumulations that interfere with growth of some plants.

NEW DEVELOPMENTS FOR WASTE MANAGEMENT

In response to the need to address the waste management concerns noted earlier, many technologies have emerged that address some or all of the concerns using combinations of processing systems. These include but are not limited to anaerobic digestion with energy recovery (methane), gasification with synthetic or biofuel and mineral recovery, solids separation for compost development, extraction of specific fertilizer nutrients for replacement of chemical fertilizer, and water purification for recycling and reduced net usage.

CRITERIA FOR EVALUATION

Technical evaluation of swine waste management systems considered "environmentally superior" includes consideration of the following performance parameters: 1) prevention of waste discharge to surface or ground water; 2) elimination of emissions of ammonia and odors to the atmosphere; 3) elimination of discharge of pathogens and disease vectors; 4) elimination of discharge of nutrients and minerals, especially heavy metals, to soil; 5) operational and economic feasibility; and 6) acceptability for permitting by local authorities. A detailed discussion of a program that addresses all of these parameters under full-scale performance testing conditions is found in Ref. 5.

CONCLUSIONS

Swine waste management will change dramatically with the introduction of a combination of new technologies that are effective in mediating environmental concerns, pressure from the industry itself to improve its position in society, and environmental regulations at federal, state, and local levels. Rapid implementation of technologies that meet the above criteria will result in successful resolution of environmental issues associated with swine waste management while retaining the industry competitiveness on a global basis for human food production.

REFERENCES

1. Miner, R.J.; Humenik, F.J.; Overcash, M.R. *Managing Livestock Wastes to Preserve Environmental Quality*; Iowa State University Press: Ames, IA, 2000.
2. National Research Council. *Air Emissions from Animal Feeding Operations: Current Knowledge and Future Needs*; The National Academies Press: Washington, DC, 2003.
3. United States Environmental Protection Agency. *Clean Water Act*; 2002. www.epa.gov.
4. Battye, R.; Battye, W.; Overcash, C.; Fudge, S. *Development and Selection of Ammonia Emission Factors*; EC/R, Inc.: Durham, NC, 1994.
5. Williams, M.C. *Development of Environmentally Superior Technologies: Year Three Progress Report for Technology Determinations per Agreements Between the Attorney General of North Carolina and Smithfield Foods, Premium Standard Farms, and Frontline Farmers*; Raleigh, NC, 2003. www.cals,ncsu.edu/waste_mgt/.

Transgenic Animals: Improved Performance

Vernon G. Pursel
United States Department of Agriculture, Agricultural Research Service, Beltsville, Maryland, U.S.A.

INTRODUCTION

With the world's population increasing by more than 70 million people each year, modern agricultural methods that include animal biotechnology will need to be adopted if this ever-increasing population is going to avoid massive conflict over agricultural resources. The ability to isolate, clone, and transfer individual genes into farm animals provides the opportunity for scientists to produce transgenic animals with modified traits that are unattainable through genetic selection.

This article reviews progress on transfer of genes for productivity traits into farm animals, and some areas that offer promise for the future.

GROWTH-RELATED TRANSGENES

Early transgenic farm animal research was inspired by the dramatic growth of transgenic mice that expressed a growth hormone (GH) transgene.[1] A number of transgenic pigs and sheep were subsequently produced with human, bovine, rat, porcine, or ovine GH under the control of several gene promoters.[2] Although pigs expressing GH transgenes grew faster, utilized feed more efficiently, and were much leaner than their nontransgenic siblings, they were not larger and exhibited several notable health problems, which included lameness, susceptibility to stress, gastric ulcers, and reproductive problems.[2] The GH transgenic lambs did not grow faster or utilize feed more efficiently than control lambs, but they were much leaner and had serious health problems.[2]

More recently, an insulin-like growth factor-I (IGF-I) transgene has been used to produce transgenic pigs with enhanced muscle development and reduced fat in the carcass, but the transgene did not improve growth rate or feed efficiency. In contrast to the GH transgenic pigs, definitive phenotypes for the IGF-I transgenic pigs were not detected, and no gross abnormalities, pathologies, or health-related problems were encountered.[3]

MODIFICATION OF MILK COMPOSITION

Transfer of genes to alter milk composition has thus far received little research emphasis, but offers the dairy industry considerable potential for the future. A list of potential changes in milk components worthy of consideration is shown in Table 1.

About 80% of milk protein from cows is composed of caseins (S_1, S_2, and κ), and whey proteins (β-lactoglobulin, α-lactalbumin, serum albumin, and γ-globulin) make up the remaining 20%.

The caseins form the curds in cheese, whereas the whey proteins represent a less valuable by-product. Elimination of β-lactoglobulin from milk would benefit cheese production because it inhibits rennin's action on κ-casein,[4] and would benefit certain fluid milk consumers because β-lactoglobulin is responsible for some milk allergies. Removal of β-lactoglobulin from cattle is now technically feasible during transfection of fetal fibroblasts that are then used for nuclear transfer.[7]

While removal of α-lactalbumin (α-lac) from cows' milk may be beneficial for some consumers, researchers at the University of Illinois have shown that increased concentrations of lactose, which result from α-lac expression, may be beneficial for piglet growth.[8] They produced transgenic pigs that express bovine α-lactalbumin in their milk, which results in a higher milk lactose content in early lactation and a 20 to 50% greater milk yield on days 3–9 of lactation, compared to that of control sows. Weight gain of piglets suckling α-lac sows was greater at days 7 and 21 after parturition than that of control piglets. Thus, overexpression of α-lac milk protein provides a means for improving growth performance of piglets through enhanced lactation of sows.

WOOL PRODUCTION

Three transgenic approaches have been investigated for enhancing wool production or improving wool quality. The first involved transfer of bacterial genes that had the capacity to synthesize cysteine from hydrogen sulfide and serine, both of which are available in the rumen. Cysteine is the rate-limiting amino acid for wool production, so an endogenous source of this amino acid has the potential to stimulate wool growth. The second approach to improve wool production was to stimulate fiber growth by expression of an IGF-I transgene specifically in wool follicles. The third approach was to improve wool fiber quality by altering expression of wool fiber keratin and

Encyclopedia of Animal Science
DOI: 10.1081/E-EAS 120019824

837

Table 1 Some proposed modifications of milk constituents

Change	Consequence
Increase α- and β-caseins	Enhanced curd firmness for cheesemaking, improved thermal stability, and increased calcium content
Increase phosphorylation sites in caseins	Increased calcium content, improved emulsification
Introduce proteolytic sites in caseins	Increased rate of textural development to improve cheese ripening
Increase κ-casein concentration	Enhanced stability of casein aggregates, decreased micelle size, decreased gelation and coagulation
Eliminate β-lactoglobulin	Decreased high-temperature gelation, improved digestibility, decreased allergenic response, decreased primary source of cysteine in milk
Decrease α-lactalbumin	Decreased lactose, increased market potential of fluid milk, decreased ice crystal formation, compromised osmotic regulation of mammary gland
Add human lactoferrin	Enhanced iron absorption, protection against gut infections
Add human lysozyme	Increased antimicrobial activity, reduced rennet clotting time, and increased cheese yield
Add proteolytic sites to κ-casein	Increased rate of cheese ripening
Decrease expression of acetyl CoA carboxylase	Decreased fat content, improved nutritional quality, reduced milk production costs
Express immunoglobulin genes	Protection against pathogens such as salmonella and listeria
Replace bovine milk protein genes with human equivalents	Mimic human breast milk

(Source: Refs. 4–6.)

keratin-associated protein genes in the wool follicle cortex.[9] Research on the latter approach is still underway in South Australia.

ENHANCED ANIMAL HEALTH

Economic losses from diseases of farm animals have been estimated to amount to 10 to 20% of the total production costs. Use of transgenesis in farm animals holds great promise for augmenting conventional breeding techniques to confer animals with improved resistance to these diseases and thereby reduce these losses and enhance animal welfare. Unfortunately, most of the genes involved in disease resistance or susceptibility to disease are still largely unknown. In addition to naturally occurring resistance genes, transgenes could be composed of genes that enhance immune response or in vitro-designed gene products (Table 2). Several approaches that have been investigated include transfer of genes for providing

Table 2 Naturally occurring disease resistance/susceptibility genes and in vitro-designed genes conferring resistance

Resistance	Item	Genes
Type	Innate resistance	Controlling pathogen replication (e.g., interferons)
		Encoding receptors for pathogens
		Antimicrobial peptides
	Nonspecific immunity	Enhancing the level and type of the immune response (e.g., chemokines and cytokines)
		Encoding complement proteins
		Regulating phagocyte uptake and killing (e.g., NOS, Nramp)
	Specific (acquired) immunity	Encoding receptors binding directly or indirectly to antigens (T cell receptors, immunoglobulins, major histocompatibility complex, etc.)
Mechanism	Immunization (i.e., antibody production)	DNA vaccines, immunoglobulin cDNAs
	Interference with pathogen entry	Recombinant pathogen receptors, coreceptors, etc.
	Interference with pathogen replication	Antisense RNA, ribozymes, intrabodies

(Source: Ref. 10.)

resistance to influenza in pigs, preformed antibodies in pigs, viral envelope proteins in chickens and pigs, and antimicrobial peptides.[10]

As a first step toward enhancing mastitis resistance of dairy animals, researchers generated transgenic mice that secrete a potent antistaphylococcal protein, lysostaphin, into milk.[11] Lysostaphin is a peptidoglycan hydrolase normally produced by *Staphylococcus simulans* that is active against *Staphylococcus aureus* bacteria. *S. aureus* is the major contagious mastitis pathogen, accounting for more than 15% of mastitis infections, and has proved difficult to control using standard management practices. Three lines of transgenic mice were produced with an ovine β-lactoglobulin gene directing the secretion of lysostaphin into milk. Progeny of these mice exhibited substantial resistance to an intramammary challenge of *S. aureus*, with the highest expressing line being completely resistant to infection. These results clearly demonstrated the potential of a transgene to combat one of the most prevalent diseases of dairy cattle. The same lysostaphin transgene has now been used to produce transgenic dairy cattle that are currently being evaluated.

REDUCED ENVIRONMENTAL POLLUTION

In an effort to reduce phosphorus excretion in swine manure, researchers at the University of Guelph[12] constructed a transgene to provide expression of phytase in salivary glands of pigs. The saliva of these pigs contains the phytase enzyme that allows the pigs to digest the phosphorus in phytate, which is the most abundant source of phosphorus in the pig diet. Without this enzyme, phosphorus in phytate passes undigested into feces to become the single most important pollutant of swine manure. Their research showed that salivary phytase essentially provides complete digestion of dietary phytate phosphorus, relieves the requirement for inorganic phosphate supplements, and reduces fecal phosphorus output by up to 75%. These pigs offer a unique biological approach to the management of phosphorus nutrition and reduce one of the major environmental pollutants generated on swine farms.

CONCLUSION

In the past few years, transgenic research to alter carcass composition, increase milk production in sows, enhance disease resistance, and reduce excretion of phosphate in pigs has shown substantial progress. Modification of milk composition traits in dairy cattle offers considerable potential, but much of this research is dependent upon

improving the efficiency of nuclear transfer, which will distinctly reduce the cost of producing transgenic cattle.

REFERENCES

1. Palmiter, R.D.; Brinster, R.L.; Hammer, R.E.; Trumbauer, M.E.; Rosenfeld, M.G.; Birnberg, N.C.; Evans, R.M. Dramatic growth of mice that develop from eggs microinjected with metallothionein–growth hormone fusion genes. Nature **1982**, *300*, 611–615.
2. Pursel, V.G.; Rexroad, C.E., Jr. Status of research with transgenic farm animals. J. Anim. Sci. **1993**, *71* (Suppl. 3), 10–19.
3. Pursel, V.G.; Mitchell, A.D.; Wall, R.J.; Solomon, M.B.; Coleman, M.E.; Schwartz, R.J. Transgenic Research to Enhance Growth and Lean Carcass Composition in Swine. In *Molecular Farming*; Toutant, J.P., Balazs, E., Eds.; INRA: Paris, 2001; 77–86.
4. Jimenez-Flores, R.; Richardson, T. Genetic engineering of the caseins to modify the behavior of milk during processing: A review. J. Dairy Sci. **1985**, *71*, 2640–2654.
5. Yom, H-C.; Bremel, R.D. Genetic engineering of milk composition: Modification of milk components in lactating transgenic animals. Am. J. Clin. Nutr. **1993**, *58* (Suppl), 299–306.
6. Maga, E.A.; Murray, J.D. Mammary gland expression of transgenes and the potential for altering the properties of milk. Bio/Technology **1995**, *13*, 1452–1457.
7. Denning, C.; Burl, S.; Ainslie, A.; Bracken, J.; Dinnyes, A.; Fletcher, J.; King, T.; Ritchie, M.; Ritchie, W.A.; Rollo, M.; de Sousa, P.; Travers, A.; Wilmut, I.; Clark, A.J. Deletion of the alpha (1,3) galactosyl transferase (GGTA1) gene and the prion protein (PrP) gene in sheep. Nat. Biotechnol. **2001**, *19*, 559–562.
8. Noble, M.S.; Rodriguez-Zas, S.; Cook, J.B.; Bleck, G.T.; Hurley, W.L.; Wheeler, M.B. Lactational performance of first-parity transgenic gilts expressing bovine alpha-lactalbumin in their milk. J. Anim. Sci. **2002**, *80*, 1090–1096.
9. Bawden, C.S.; McLaughlan, C.J.; Walker, S.K.; Speck, P.A.; Powell, B.C.; Huson, M.J.; Jones, L.N.; Rogers, G.E. Improvement of Wool Quality by Transgenesis. In *Molecular Farming*; Toutant, J.P., Balazs, E., Eds.; INRA: Paris, 2001; 67–76.
10. Müller, M. Increasing Disease Resistance in Transgenic Domestic Animals. In *Molecular Farming*; Toutant, J.P., Balazs, E., Eds.; INRA: Paris, 2001; 87–97.
11. Kerr, D.E.; Plaut, K.; Bramley, A.J.; Williamson, C.M.; Lax, A.J.; Moore, K.; Wells, K.D.; Wall, R.J. Lysostaphin expression in mammary glands confers protection against staphylococcal infection in transgenic mice. Nat. Biotechnol. **2001**, *19*, 66–70.
12. Golovan, S.P.; Meidinger, R.G.; Ajakaiye, A.; Cottrill, M.; Wiederkehr, M.Z.; Barney, D.J.; Plante, C.; Pollard, J.W.; Fan, M.Z.; Hayes, M.A.; Laursen, J.; Hjorth, J.P.; Hacker, R.R.; Phillips, J.P.; Forsberg, C.W. Pigs expressing salivary phytase produce low-phosphorus manure. Nat. Biotechnol. **2001**, *19*, 741–745.

Transgenic Animals: Modifying the Mitochondrial Genome

Carl A. Pinkert
University of Rochester Medical Center, Rochester, New York, U.S.A.

Lawrence C. Smith
Université de Montréal, Quebec, Canada

Ian A. Trounce
University of Melbourne, Victoria, Australia

INTRODUCTION

In comparison to the techniques successfully employed for nuclear gene transgenesis in livestock over the past 20 years, the lack of comparable recombination in mitochondrial DNA (mtDNA) has, until recently, prevented its direct in vivo manipulation. The coordinated expression of single-copy nuclear gene products, together with the polyploid mtDNA gene products, is required for normal mitochondrial biogenesis and respiratory chain function. It is of great current interest to seek improved technologies for manipulating the mitochondrial genome, so that interactions of nuclear and mtDNA genotypes can be studied in experimental systems.

MITOCHONDRIAL GENETICS AND ANIMAL MODELING

Mammalian mitochondria contain between one and approximately ten copies of a closed, circular, super-coiled, double-stranded DNA that is bound to the inner mitochondrial membrane and is not associated with histones or a scaffolding protein matrix. The mtDNAs of all vertebrates are highly conserved and quite small ($\sim$16.5 kb in length) in comparison to the nuclear genome. Mammalian mitochondria have their own genetic systems, replete with a unique genetic code, genome structure, transcriptional and translational apparatus, and tRNAs. Perhaps, because of a postulated less-extensive mitochondrial DNA (mtDNA) repair system and because of the absence of protective histones, the mitochondrial genome is subject to an increased sensitivity to mutations due to metabolic (e.g., oxidative stress) and environmental (e.g., toxins, mutagens, and UV light) sources. Mitochondrial genes encode for 13 of the protein subunits that function in the mitochondrial oxidative phosphorylation

system, along with two ribosomal RNAs (rRNAs) and 22 transfer RNAs (tRNAs). Accordingly, directed modification of mitochondrial genes and/or their function would provide a powerful tool in production agriculture.[1]

Cytoplasmic-based traits in domestic animals have included growth, reproduction, and lactation. In addition, mitochondrial restriction fragment-length polymorphisms (RFLPs) were identified and associated with specific lactational characteristics in a number of dairy cattle lineages. The matrilineal inheritance of mammalian mtDNA has also been used to advantage in studies exploring the timing and geography of domestication events, as recently demonstrated for horses, where multiple domestication events appear to have occurred in the Eurasian steppe.[2] In addition, metabolic and cellular abnormalities in humans were correlated to mutations arising exclusively within the mitochondrial genome. Indeed, various diseases have been associated with mtDNA point mutations, deletions, and duplications (e.g., diabetes mellitus, myocardiopathy, and retinitis pigmentosa) as well as age-associated changes in the functional integrity of mitochondria (as seen in Parkinson's, Alzheimer's, and Huntington's diseases). As such, for both agricultural and biomedical research efforts, the ability to manipulate the mitochondrial genome and to regulate the expression of mitochondrial genes would provide one possible mode of genetic manipulation and therapy.

The creation of heteroplasmic transmitochondrial animals has developed along three lines: 1) direct mitochondrial injection into oocytes or embryos; 2) embryonic stem (ES) cell-based technologies; and 3) in relation to karyoplast or cytoplast transfer (including consequences associated with nuclear transfer or cloning experimentation; Table 1). These techniques have illustrated model systems that will provide a greater understanding of mitochondrial dynamics, leading to the development of genetically engineered production animals, and therapeutic

Encyclopedia of Animal Science
DOI: 10.1081/E-EAS 120024365

Table 1 Methods for creating mitochondrial modifications in animals

Method	Heteroplasmy/ homoplasmy detected	Germline transmission	Limitations
Mitochondrial injection into ova	Heteroplasmy	Yes	Low-level heteroplasmy
Karyoplast fusion (nuclear transfer)	Heteroplasmy	Yes	Varying efficiencies using PEG or electrofusion
Karyoplast or cytoplast transfer into ES cells and transfer	Yes	Yes	Availability of germline competent/efficient cell lines
Cytoplast/ooplasm transfer	Heteroplasmy	Yes	Varying efficiencies and low-level heteroplasmy
Sperm mediated	?	?	Rare event, aberrant recombination, or programmed destruction postfertilization

strategies for human metabolic diseases affected by aberrations in mitochondrial function.

As described in a number of recent reports,[3,4] nuclear-encoded genes and knock-out modeling have been informative in identifying novel models in mitochondrial disease pathogenesis as well as critical pathways associated with mitochondrial function. With initial characterization of these nuclear gene-encoded models, our search for a greater understanding of mitochondrial interactions and function would eventually lead us to a desire to develop methodology for mitochondria and mitochondrial gene transfer. As a first step, efficient methods to introduce foreign or altered mtDNA or genomes into somatic or germ cells would be needed.

TRANSMITOCHONDRIAL ANIMALS

To make a transmitochondrial animal, the ability to manipulate normal and mutant mitochondria in vivo has been a critical and difficult first step. In vivo mitochondrial gene transfer remains a technological hurdle in the development of mitochondria-based genetic therapies and in the generation of experimental animal models for the study of mitochondrial dynamics and mitochondria-based traits. While gene transfer has been performed in a host of cell types and organisms, transfer of nuclear DNA has been the only demonstrable form of mammalian gene transfer, short of cell fusions, to date.

Rapid segregation of mtDNA genotypes could occur in mammals and was first demonstrated in Holstein cattle where pedigree records in the industry allowed detailed analysis of maternally related individual genotypes.[5] Segregation of mtDNA was investigated in maternal lineages of heteroplasmic mice created by cytoplast fusion[6,7] and by embryonic karyoplast transplantation.[8] Although mitochondrial segregation in somatic tissues is

effective in some tissues and with increasing age, the preceding studies have shown that mtDNA heteroplasmy is maintained at stable levels throughout several generations. This would suggest that the mouse germline is not very effective in segregating mtDNA haplotypes. In cattle, however, highly heteroplasmic females will produce homoplasmic oocytes, whereas heteroplasmic bulls produce mostly heteroplasmic sperm, indicating that mtDNA segregation is very stringent in the female and practically absent in the male germline.[9] Together, these results suggest that mammalian species show variable patterns of mtDNA segregation.

In contrast to these techniques, our efforts to devise a direct mitochondria transfer technique offered certain advantages. Principally, the ability to use isolated mitochondria for the production of heteroplasmic mice would allow for investigations into the feasibility of genetic manipulation of mtDNA in vitro prior to mitochondria microinjection into zygotes.

CONCLUSIONS

Through the early 1990s, various early attempts to create transmitochondrial strains of mammalian species by introduction of foreign mitochondria into germ cells were largely unsuccessful. A number of constraints have been identified or postulated, from perturbations of biological pathways to mechanistic aspects of the specific protocols used. Since 1997, a number of laboratories have reported on methodologies used to create transmitochondrial animals. To date, methods for mitochondria isolation and interspecific transfer of mitochondria have been reported both in laboratory and domestic animal models.[3,10,11] Interestingly, early reports on development of cloned animals by nuclear transfer resulted in conflicting consequences when retrospective studies on mitochondrial transmission were reported.[12–16] Indeed, dependent upon the specific methodology employed for nuclear transfer and cytoplasm/ooplasm transfer to rescue low-quality embryos, additional models of heteroplasmy may or may not have been characterized as a consequence of mitochondrial dysfunction. As such, research independent of targeted mitochondrial genomic modifications may also help unlock mechanisms underlying the dynamics related to persistence of foreign mitochondria and maintenance of heteroplasmy in various cloning protocols.

ARTICLES OF FURTHER INTEREST

REFERENCES

1. Pinkert, C.A. Genetic Engineering of Animals. In *Handbook of Biomedical Technology and Devices*; Moore, J.E., Jr., Zouridakis, G., Eds.; CRC Press: Boca Raton, 2004; 18-1–18-12.
2. Vila, C.; Leonard, J.A.; Gotherstrom, A.; Marklund, S.; Sandberg, K.; Liden, K.; Wayne, R.K.; Ellegren, H. Widespread origins of domestic horse lineages. Science **2001**, *291* (5503), 474–477.
3. Pinkert, C.A.; Trounce, I.A. Production of transmitochondrial mice. Methods **2002**, *26* (4), 348–357.
4. Wallace, D.C. Mouse models for mitochondrial disease. Am. J. Med. Genet. **2001**, *106* (1), 71–93.
5. Olivo, P.D.; Van de Walle, M.J.; Laipis, P.J.; Hauswirth, W.W. Nucleotide sequence evidence for rapid genotypic shifts in the bovine mitochondrial DNA D-loop. Nature **1983**, *306* (5941), 400–402.
6. Jenuth, J.P.; Peterson, A.C.; Fu, K.; Shoubridge, E.A. Random genetic drift in the female germline explains the rapid segregation of mammalian mitochondrial DNA. Nat. Genet. **1996**, *14* (2), 146–151.
7. Jenuth, J.P.; Peterson, A.C.; Shoubridge, E.A. Tissue-specific selection for different mtDNA genotypes in heteroplasmic mice. Nat. Genet. **1997**, *16* (1), 93–95.
8. Meirelles, F.V.; Smith, L.C. Mitochondrial genotype segregation in a mouse heteroplasmic lineage produced by embryonic karyoplast transplantation. Genetics **1997**, *145* (2), 445–451.
9. Smith, L.C.; Bordignon, V.; Garcia, J.M.; Meirelles, F.V. Mitochondrial genotype segregation and effects during mammalian development: Applications to biotechnology. Theriogenology **2000**, *53* (1), 35–46.
10. Meirelles, F.V.; Bordignon, V.; Watanabe, Y.; Watanabe, M.; Dayan, A.; Lobo, R.B.; Garcia, J.M.; Smith, L.C. Compete replacement of the mitochondrial genotype in a *Bos indicus* calf reconstructed by nuclear transfer to a *Bos taurus* oocyte. Genetics **2001**, *158* (1), 351–356.
11. McKenzie, M.; Trounce, I.A.; Cassar, C.A.; Pinkert, C.A. Production of homoplasmic xenomitochondrial mice. Proc. Natl. Acad. Sci. USA **2004**, *101* (6), 1685–1690.
12. Hiendleder, S.; Zakhartchenko, V.; Wenigerkind, H.; Reichenbach, H.D.; Bruggerhoff, K.; Prelle, K.; Brem, G.; Stojkovic, M.; Wolf, E. Heteroplasmy in bovine fetuses produced by intra- and inter-subspecific somatic cell nuclear transfer: Neutral segregation of nuclear donor mitochondrial DNA in various tissues and evidence for recipient cow mitochondria in fetal blood. Biol. Reprod. **2003**, *68* (1), 159–166.
13. Evans, M.J.; Gurer, C.; Loike, J.D.; Wilmut, I.; Schnieke, A.E.; Schon, E.A. Mitochondrial DNA genotypes in nuclear transfer-derived cloned sheep. Nat. Genet. **1999**, *23* (1), 90–93.
14. Hiendleder, S.; Schmutz, S.M.; Erhardt, G.; Green, R.D.; Plante, Y. Transmitochondrial differences and varying levels of heteroplasmy in nuclear transfer cloned cattle. Mol. Reprod. Dev. **1999**, *54* (1), 24–31.
15. Steinborn, R.; Schinogl, P.; Zakhartchenko, V.; Achmann, R.; Schernthaner, W.; Stojkovic, M.; Wolf, E.; Muller, M.; Brem, G. Mitochondrial DNA heteroplasmy in cloned cattle produced by fetal and adult cell cloning. Nat. Genet. **2000**, *25* (3), 255–257.
16. Takeda, K.; Takahashi, S.; Onishi, A.; Goto, Y.; Miyazawa, A.; Imai, H. Dominant distribution of mitochondrial DNA from recipient oocytes in bovine embryos and offspring after nuclear transfer. J. Reprod. Fertil. **1999**, *116* (2), 253–259.

Transgenic Animals: Secreted Products

Michael J. Martin
David A. Dunn
Carl A. Pinkert
University of Rochester Medical Center, Rochester, New York, U.S.A.

INTRODUCTION

Interest in modifying traits that determine productivity of domestic animals was greatly stimulated by early experiments in which body size and growth rates were dramatically affected in transgenic mice expressing growth hormone transgenes driven by a metallothionein (MT) enhancer/promoter. From that starting point, similar attempts followed to enhance growth in farm animals by introduction of various growth factors, modulators, and their receptors. It soon became apparent that transgene regulation was an exquisite balancing act, where precise regulation of transgenes was crucial to normal development. Yet, the overexpression of various transgene products illustrated that such animals could produce biologically important molecules as efficient mammalian bioreactors, with efficiencies far greater than conventional bacterial or cell culture systems. From early studies in the mid-1980s through the 1990s, one of the main targets of genetic engineering or gene pharming efforts has involved attempts to direct expression of transgenes encoding biologically active human proteins in farm animals. To date, expression of foreign genes encoding various protein products was successfully targeted to the mammary glands of goats, sheep, cattle, and swine, yet the jump from model to achieving regulatory approval has proven most challenging.

ADVANTAGES OF RECOMBINANT PROTEIN SYNTHESIS IN TRANSGENIC ANIMALS

Several different organisms have been harnessed to produce recombinant proteins. Bacteria, yeast, fungi, plants, and cultured mammalian cells can all be reprogrammed and, if properly managed, yield relatively large amounts of recombinant proteins. Problems begin to arise, however, when one examines the ability of these organisms to posttranslationally modify and even release recombinant proteins. Bacteria, for example, are often unable to package and secrete recombinant proteins. In these instances, the recombinant protein must be physi-

cally extracted from the bacteria, a process that can be difficult and costly. Whereas yeast can secrete recombinant proteins that are glycosylated, the enzymatic pathway(s) that they utilize to accomplish protein glycosylation differs from that employed in higher plants and animals. As a result, many of the recombinant proteins produced by yeast exhibit inadequate glycosylation. Posttranslational modification of recombinant proteins produced in fungi appears to be aberrant in many instances as well. Mammalian cell lines, in contrast, typically perform posttranslational modifications of recombinant proteins that are quite similar to those observed in indigenous proteins. Primary drawbacks to the synthesis of recombinant proteins in animal cell lines include cost and the logistical challenge associated with developing and managing cell cultures for large-scale protein production.

In contrast, transgenic animals, as Louis-Marie Houdebine describes,[1] share most of the properties of animal cells in culture, exhibit appropriate posttranslational modifications of recombinant proteins, and synthesize and secrete proteins extremely efficiently. Indeed, mammary gland epithelia typically have a cell density that is 100- to 1000-fold greater than that used in mammalian cell culture bioreactors. In one recent example, 35 transgenic goats that produced a human monoclonal antibody at a concentration of 8 g/L in their milk were equivalent to an 8500-liter batch cell culture running 200 days/year with a 1 g/l final production level.[2] Thus, from a production standpoint, the amount of antibody synthesized in 170,000-liter cell culture yield was equivalent to that generated in 21,000 liters of milk from transgenic goats. Assuming a process yield of 60%, both systems would generate 100 kg of purified monoclonal antibody, yet the transgenic bioreactor was significantly more efficient.

Another obvious incentive for the production of biopharmaceuticals in transgenic livestock is their potential economic value (Table 1). The cost of human proteins obtained from donated plasma and used in replacement therapy has ranged from $4/g for serum albumin and $5000/g for antithrombin III to $150,000/g for human blood clotting factor VIII (FVIII).[4] Although the individual values of these seem dramatic, they pale in

Encyclopedia of Animal Science
DOI: 10.1081/E-EAS 120019825

Table 1 Molecular pharming projects: Potential biomedical and commercial products from transgenic farm animals

Products	Use	Commercializing firm(s)
α-1 antitrypsin	Hereditary emphysema/cystic fibrosis	(Bayer/PPL)
α-1 proteinase inhibitor	Hereditary emphysema/cystic fibrosis	(Bayer/PPL)
α-fetoprotein (rhAFP)	Myasthenia gravis, multiple sclerosis, and rheumatoid arthritis	(Merrimack/GTC)
Antithrombin III (rhATIII)	Emboli/thromboses	(GTC)
β-glucosidase	Glycogen storage disease	(Pharming)
Collagen	Rheumatoid arthritis	(Pharming)
CFTR	Ion transport/cystic fibrosis	(GTC)
Factor VIII	Hemophilia A	(ARC)
Factor IX	Blood coagulation/hemophilia	(GTC, PPL)
Fibrin, fibrinogen	Tissue sealant development	(ARC, PPL, Pharming)
Hemoglobin	Blood substitute development	(Baxter)
Lactalbumin	Food additive	(Univ. Illinois)
Lactoferrin	Immunomodulatory, antiinflammatory	(Pharming)
MSP-1 (Merozoite Surface Protein 1)	Malarial vaccine	(GTC)
Phytase (Enviropig™)	Bioremediation, pollution control	(Univ. Guelph)
Human antibodies	Biotherapeutics, biodefense	(Abgenix, Hematech, Medarex)
Human C1 inhibitor	Hereditary angioedema	(Pharming)
Human lysozyme	Antimicrobial, immune modulator	(UC-Davis)
Human protein C	Blood coagulation	(ARC, PPL)
Human serum albumin	Blood pressure, trauma/burn treatment	(Pharming; GTC)
Spider silk (Biosteel®)	Materials development	(Nexia)
tPA	Dissolve fibrin clots/heart attacks	(Genzyme)
Tissues/organs	Engineered for xenotransplantation	(Alexion, Bresagen, Novartis)
Monoclonal antibodies and immunoglobulin fusion proteins:		
5G1.1	Rheumatoid arthritis, nephritis	(Alexion/GTC)
Antegren™	Neurological disorders	(Elan/GTC)
CTLA4Ig	Rheumatoid arthritis	(Bristol Myers Squibb/GTC)
D2E7	Rheumatoid arthritis	(Abbott/GTC)
huN901	Small-cell lung cancer	(ImmunoGen/GTC)
MM-093	Myasthenia gravis, multiple sclerosis, and rheumatoid arthritis	(Merrimack/GTC)
PRO 542	HIV/AIDS	(Progenics/GTC)
Remicade®	Crohn's disease, rheumatoid arthritis	(Centocor/GTC)

(Adapted from Ref. 3.)

comparison to the projected worth of a number of recombinant structural products. Biomedical applications of Biosteel™ (Nexia Inc.), a recombinant form of dragline spider silk, produced in the milk of transgenic goats, is projected to represent $150 to $450 million in annual earnings (exclusive of military and other industrial applications).

EXPRESSION OF RECOMBINANT PROTEINS IN MILK

Since the introduction of the first exogenous genes into mice, more than 60 proteins have been produced in milk of transgenic animals. In order to target protein expression specifically to the mammary gland, a transgene typically consists of the desired protein gene fused to one of several available mammary-specific regulatory sequences.[3–7] These sequences have included: ovine BLG; murine, rat, and rabbit whey acidic protein (WAP); bovine α-s$_1$ casein; rat, rabbit, and goat β-casein; and guinea pig, ovine and caprine, and bovine α-lactalbumin. While expression of the target protein can be achieved using either a genomic DNA or cDNA coding sequence(s), the former normally yields higher levels of protein expression.

Therapeutic monoclonal antibodies produced in the mammary gland of a transgenic animal line present a potentially valuable technology. Transgenic monoclonal antibodies are produced by cloning genetic sequences for both heavy- and light-chain genes downstream of mammary gland-specific regulatory elements. Chimeric antibodies may also be produced by ligating antigen-binding region sequences from a (usually murine) monoclonal antibody to constant region sequences from a different species and/or isotype. The first transgenic mice harboring immunoglobulin genes were made in the mid-1980s.[8] Though the majority of effort and funding in this field is currently focused toward human therapeutics, veterinary use of monoclonal antibodies also shows significant promise as a developing application.

Whereas several therapeutic monoclonal antibodies have been approved for use by the U.S. Food and Drug Administration, none as yet has been approved where a transgenic animal was used as a production vehicle. Using antibody production technologies in transgenic biore-actor systems, these products target a wide range of clinical ailments and are mostly in the preclinical stage of development.

EXPRESSION OF RECOMBINANT PROTEINS IN MEDIA OTHER THAN MILK

Secretion of transgene-encoded proteins in the urine of transgenic animals was demonstrated using recombinant genes under the control of kidney-[9] or bladder-[10] specific regulatory sequences. Expression of transgenes in the kidney or bladder of transgenic animals and subsequent secretion in the urine may provide some advantages over the mammary gland as a bioreactor, as the purification of proteins from urine may be facilitated by lower lipid and protein levels in comparison to milk. Additionally, such animals can be used for production of recombinant proteins over the course of their entire life span.

RECOMBINANT PROTEIN PRODUCTION: HEALTH AND SAFETY ISSUES

In addition to being structurally and functionally analo-gous to the natural plasma-derived protein, purified recombinant proteins must be free of pathogenic organ-isms. Viral and bacterial contamination of human biopharmaceutical products produced in the blood or milk can be minimized by focusing prevention/eradication efforts on at least three levels of production: the transgenic animal donor, the medium in which the recombinant protein is produced, and the final product.[4] An initial key to minimizing the risk of contamination is to derive the transgenic donor animals from a source herd that is free from as many pathogens as possible. Maintenance of these animals in a closed facility, the implementation of strict

monitoring procedures for various pathogens, and the use of animal husbandry practices that follow generally accepted practices (GAPs) and standard operating proce-dures should greatly reduce the entry of pathogens. Though quite costly, one can develop pathogen-free herds of transgenic livestock. Such a feat was recently achieved by introducing hysterotomy-derived transgenic piglets into an elaborate SPF barrier facility.[11] Diagnostic testing of this herd over the past 3 years in this facility had revealed the absence of 35 major and minor swine pathogens including PRRS, parvovirus, leptospira, para-influenza, and *Streptococcus suis*.

CONCLUSION

While transgenic animal technology continues to open new and unexplored agricultural frontiers, molecular pharming efforts raise questions concerning regulatory and commercialization issues. Although significant advances have been made since the inception of various clinical trials, the resources required to move the projects forward and the attendant financial risks have led a number of companies to curtail product development. Various societal issues exist and will continue to influence the development of value-added animal products pro-duced through transgenesis—until transgenic products and foodstuffs are proven safe for human use and are accepted by a wide cross section of society.

ARTICLES OF FURTHER INTEREST

Biotechnology: Stem Cell and Germ Cell Technology, p. 146
Biotechnology: Transgenic Animals, p. 149
Contributions to Society: Biomedical Research Models, p. 239
Genetics: Molecular, p. 466
Molecular Biology: Animal, p. 653
Overall Contributions of Domestic Animals to Society, p. 696
Phytases, p. 704
Proteins, p. 757
Transgenic Animals: Improved Performance, p. 837

REFERENCES

1. Houdebine, L.-M. Production of pharmaceutical proteins from transgenic animals. J. Biotechnol. **1994**, *34* (3), 269–287.
2. Young, M.W.; Okita, W.B.; Brown, M.; Curling, J.M.

Production of biopharmaceutical proteins in the milk of transgenic dairy animals. BioPharm. **1997**, *10* (6), 34–38.

3. Pinkert, C.A. The history and theory of transgenic animals. Lab. Anim. **1997**, *26* (8), 29–34.

4. Clark, A.J.; Simons, P.; Wilmut, I.; Lathe, R. Pharmaceuticals from transgenic livestock. Trends Biotechnol. **1987**, *5* (1), 20–24.

5. Palmiter, R.D.; Brinster, R.L.; Hammer, R.E.; Trumbauer, M.E.; Rosenfeld, M.G.; Birnberg, N.C.; Evans, R.M. Dramatic growth of mice that develop from eggs microinjected with metallothionein-growth hormone fusion genes. Nature **1982**, *300* (5893), 611–615.

6. Martin, M.J.; Pinkert, C.A. Production of Transgenic Swine by DNA Microinjection. In *Transgenic Animal Technology: A Laboratory Handbook*, 2nd Ed.; Pinkert, C.A., Ed.; Academic Press: San Diego, 2002; 307–336.

7. Simons, J.P.; McClenaghan, M.; Clark, A.J. Alteration of the quality of milk by expression of sheep β-lactoglob-ulin in transgenic mice. Nature **1987**, *328* (6130), 530–532.

8. Storb, U.; Pinkert, C.; Arp, B.; Engler, P.; Gollahon, K.; Manz, J.; Brady, W.; Brinster, R.L. Transgenic mice with mu and kappa genes encoding antiphosphorylcholine antibodies. J. Exp. Med. **1986**, *64* (2), 627–641.

9. Zbikowska, H.M.; Soukhareva, N.; Behnam, R.; Chang, R.; Drews, R.; Lubon, H.; Hammond, D.; Soukharev, S. The use of the uromodulin promoter to target production of recombinant proteins into urine of transgenic animals. Transgenic Res. **2002**, *11* (4), 425–435.

10. Kerr, D.E.; Liang, F.; Bondioli, K.R.; Zhao, H.; Kreibich, G.; Wall, R.J.; Sun, T.T. The bladder as a bioreactor: Urothelium production and secretion of growth hormone into urine. Nat. Biotechnol. **1998**, *16* (1), 75–79.

11. Risdahl, J.; Edgerton, S.; Adams, C.; Martin, M.; Wiseman, B. Establishing a Designated Pathogen Free Swine Colony for Xenotransplantation, Proc. 17th International Pig Veterinary Society Congress (IPVS), Ames, IA, June 2–4, 2002.

Turkeys: Behavior, Management, and Well-Being

C. M. Sherwin
University of Bristol, Langford, U.K.

INTRODUCTION

Each year, many millions of turkeys are reared for eating. Methods of housing and managing these birds are diverse. Turkeys are intelligent, inquisitive, social animals, and commercial rearing often conflicts with their psychological and physiological needs. As a consequence, there are many welfare issues associated with turkey rearing, highlighted by comparing the domestic turkey with its ancestral species, the wild turkey of North America.

THE DOMESTIC TURKEY

Modern domestic turkeys have been selected primarily for large body size and rapid growth rate. Commercially, they are usually grown until they reach sexual maturity. For males, this is approximately 20 weeks of age, when they can weigh over 20 kg, compared to a 3-year-old male wild turkey that weighs a mere 9 kg. The large body weight means that domestic turkeys are unable to fly, in contrast to their wild counterparts, and natural mating is replaced by artificial insemination to prevent injury to females. Most turkeys derive from a small number of strains with homogenous white plumage, although some have retained the mottled appearance of the wild turkey.

Young domestic turkeys enthusiastically fly short distances, perch, and roost. These behaviors become less prevalent with maturation, but adults readily climb onto objects such as straw bales. Young birds perform spontaneous, frivolous running (frolicking), which has all the appearance of play. Turkeys perform a wide diversity of behaviors, including comfort behaviors such as wing-flapping, feather-ruffling, leg-stretching, and dust-bathing. They are highly social and become very distressed when isolated. Many turkey behaviors are socially facilitated, i.e., expression of a behavior by one animal increases the tendency for this behavior to be performed by others. Adults can recognize strangers[1] and placing any unfamiliar turkey into an established group will almost certainly result in that individual being attacked, sometimes fatally. Turkeys are highly vocal, and social tension within the group can be monitored by the birds' vocalizations. A high-pitched trill indicates the birds are becoming aggressive. This can develop into intense sparring, where opponents leap at each other with their large, sharp talons and try to peck or grasp the other's head. Aggression increases in frequency and severity as the birds mature. Maturing males spend a considerable proportion of their time sexually displaying. This involves fanning the tail, drooping the wings, and erecting all body feathers including the beard (a tuft of black, modified hairlike feathers on the breast). The skin of the head, neck, and caruncles becomes bright blue and red, and the snood (an erectile appendage on the forehead) elongates. The birds sneeze at regular intervals, followed by a rapid vibration of their tail. Throughout, the birds strut slowly about with the neck arched backward and the breast thrust forward, emitting their characteristic gobbling call.

COMMERCIAL REARING

Methods for rearing turkeys vary widely among producers and countries. The following is typical for the United Kingdom.

Between 1 and 7 days of age, chicks are placed into small (2.5 m), circular brooding pens to ensure they encounter food and water. To encourage feeding, they are kept under constant light for the first 48 h, and food is made widely accessible by scattering it on sheets of paper and in feeders. After several days, the pens are removed, allowing the birds access to the entire rearing shed, which may contain tens of thousands of birds. The birds remain here for several weeks, after which they are transported to another unit. To assist thermoregulation, air temperature is maintained at 35°C for the first 3 days, then lowered by approximately 3°C every 2 days to 18°C at 37 days of age, and infrared heaters are usually provided for the first few days.

The vast majority of turkeys are reared indoors in purpose-built or modified buildings, of which there are two basic types. The first type has slatted walls to allow ventilation (pole-barns). The second type has solid walls and no windows to allow lighting manipulations to optimize production (see the subsequent discussion).

Encyclopedia of Animal Science
DOI: 10.1081/E-EAS 120019827

The buildings are often very large, containing tens of thousands of birds as a single flock. The substrate is usually deep litter, e.g., wood shavings, which relies on the controlled buildup of microbial flora, requiring skillful management. Levels of CO_2 and ammonia should not exceed 5000 ppm and 5 ppm, respectively, and relative humidity should be maintained at 50–70%. Ambient temperatures for adult turkeys are usually maintained at 18–21°C. High temperatures should be avoided because the high metabolic rate of turkeys (up to 69 W/bird) makes them susceptible to heat stress, exacerbated by high stocking densities. Handling during warm conditions should be avoided. A variety of lighting schedules are used, e.g., continuous, intermittent, or long (23 h) photoperiods, to encourage feeding and accelerate growth.[2] Light intensity is usually low (e.g., <1 lux) to reduce feather-pecking (see the subsequent discussion).

WELFARE ISSUES

Intensive turkey production does not account for many of the birds' psychological and physiological needs, resulting in welfare concerns.

Turkey chicks are precocial and are sustained by yolk reserves until 3 days of age. Learning to eat and drink appropriately during this time is essential, and it is common for a proportion of chicks to die (starve-out) from failing to learn, hence the use of brooding pens. Chicks' attention can be directed by tapping on the feeders and drinkers, thus simulating the behavior of the absent mother hen.

Space allowance for turkeys is often severely limited. For example, a maximum permissible stocking density of 59.1 kg/m^2 has been suggested.[3] This approximates to three adult 20-kg birds having to share 1 m^2, despite turkeys of this weight each requiring 1700 cm^2 simply to stand without touching another bird.[4] The problems of small space allowance are exacerbated by the major influence of social facilitation—if turkeys are to feed, drink, dust-bathe, etc. simultaneously, then resources and space must be available in large quantities to avoid causing frustration.

The lighting manipulations used to optimize production can compromise welfare. Long photoperiods combined with low light intensity can result in blindness from buphthalmia (distortions of the eye morphology) or retinal detachment, and can also result in distortion of the behavioral time budget. Short photoperiods (8 h) can retard sexual development in males, and will also cause turkeys to eat in total darkness, possibly indicating an abnormally high motivation to feed resulting from selection for production characteristics. A photoperiod of 12–16 h is adequate for turkeys to consume their daily feed requirement without any obvious adverse physiological or behavioral consequences. Behavioral studies have shown that turkeys prefer light intensities higher than usually provided under commercial conditions. In addition, low intensities make it difficult for humans to adequately inspect the birds.

Feather-pecking occurs frequently among turkeys and can begin at 1 day of age. This behavior is thought to be redirected foraging behavior, caused by providing birds with an impoverished foraging environment. To reduce feather-pecking, turkeys are often beak-trimmed, which causes acute and possibly chronic pain. Feather-pecking can be considerably reduced, at least in small groups (e.g., 100 birds), by providing supplementary ultraviolet radiation (turkeys are visually sensitive to UV; humans are not), pecking substrates (e.g., straw), and visual barriers to reduce social transmission of this behavior.[5] Other pecking substrates include chains, twine, vegetable matter, or food scattered in the substrate. UV-reflective markings appear on young birds at the same time as feather-pecking becomes targeted toward these areas.[6]

Turkeys also perform head-pecking, which becomes more frequent as they sexually mature. When this occurs in small enclosures with few escape opportunities, the outcome is often rapidly fatal; healthy birds can be killed within 3 hours. Frequent monitoring is therefore essential, particularly of males approaching maturity. Head injuries receive considerable attention from other birds, and head-pecking often occurs after a relatively minor injury has been received during a fight or when lying down. Birds with fresh injuries larger than 1 cm should be closely monitored, and separation should be considered. Individuals being reintroduced after separation are often immediately reattacked—it might be impossible to reintroduce head-pecked individuals. Fatal head-pecking can occur even in small (10 birds), stable groups. Turkeys are normally reared in single-sex flocks. If a male is inadvertently placed in a female flock, he may be aggressively victimized (henpecked). Females in male groups will be repeatedly mated, during which it is highly likely she will be injured from being trampled upon.

As with broiler fowl, turkeys often become less agile and experience walking difficulties as they become older. This is due to a variety of diseases, anatomical changes from intensive selection for production traits, and poor husbandry. Sometimes, the difficulty in locomotion can become so severe that birds refuse to walk and will die of starvation or thirst unless intervention occurs. Locomotor problems cause the birds to spend long periods sitting on the substrate, which can lead to breast blisters and hock burns from high nitrogen content in the litter. These have both welfare and economic consequences. Poor litter quality can also cause foot-pad dermatitis, which can affect 98% of the flock.

Turkeys are prone to cardiovascular problems, so any physical exertion for them can be quite traumatic and may result in sudden death. Domestic turkeys should be fed commercially available diets that have been developed to meet their nutritional requirements, although they will also benefit from fresh food as dietary enrichment. Nutrient content, food quality, and feeding regimes must be carefully controlled to prevent leg abnormalities and other health and welfare problems associated with rapid growth rates.

CONCLUSION

Despite years of intensive artificial selection, which have considerably changed aspects of their morphology and behavior compared to the wild turkey, the domestic turkey is an intelligent, social animal that displays a wide range of behavior and has both psychological and physiological needs. Intensive commercial rearing conflicts with many of these needs and as a consequence, there are many compromises of welfare. Future research should include alleviation of these compromises as a priority.

ACKNOWLEDGMENT

C. M. Sherwin received the UFAW Hume Research Fellowship during preparation of this article.

REFERENCES

1. Buchwalder, T.; Huber-Eicher, B. A brief report on aggressive interactions within and between groups of domestic turkeys (*Meleagris gallopavo*). Appl. Anim. Behav. Sci. **2003**, *84*, 75–80.
2. Nixey, C. Lighting for the production and welfare of turkeys. World's Poultry Sci. J. **1994**, *50*, 292–294.
3. Farm Animal Welfare Council. *Report on the Welfare of Turkeys*; Tolworth: UK, 1995; 13–15.
4. Ellerbrock, S.; Knierim, U. Static space requirements of male meat turkeys. Vet. Rec. **2002**, *151*, 54–57.
5. Sherwin, C.M.; Lewis, P.D.; Perry, G.C. Effects of environmental enrichment, fluorescent and intermittent lighting on injurious pecking amongst male turkey poults. Br. Poultry Sci. **1999**, *40*, 592–598.
6. Sherwin, C.M.; Devereux, C.L. A preliminary investigation of ultraviolet-visible markings on domestic turkey chicks and a possible role in injurious pecking. Br. Poultry Sci. **1999**, *40*, 429–433.

Turkeys: Nutrition Management

Todd J. Applegate
Purdue University, West Lafayette, Indiana, U.S.A.

INTRODUCTION

In 1970, a male turkey averaged only 16.9 pounds and required 3.10 pounds of feed for every pound of gain at 18 weeks of age. Today, genetic and nutritional improvements have increased growth such that the average male turkey at 18 weeks of age weighs 33.4 pounds and requires only 2.52 pounds of feed for every pound of gain (Fig. 1).[1] Because average body weights for hens are only 21.75 pounds, the industry has developed separate markets and rearing practices for male and female turkeys. Turkey toms (males) are reared primarily for cut-out and further processed products, whereas hens are reared for whole-bird and parts markets. This phenomenal increase in growth has not come without its share of health, metabolic, structural, and nutritional issues. Primary issues in the area of nutrition for modern turkey production include 1) transition diets at the start of life; 2) feeding to maximize gastrointestinal (GIT) health; 3) bone integrity; 4) minimizing environmental impact; and 5) maximizing muscle mass and meat quality.

FROM THE HATCHERY TO THE FARM—MAXIMIZING EARLY GROWTH

Early access to feed and water after hatching is important to ensure that young poults have a good start and are able to realize their growth potential. Often, turkeys will hatch over a hatching window of 48 hours or more. It is not uncommon, therefore that a proportion of the poults placed (given access to food and water) on the farm have hatched nearly 48 to 72 hours prior to placement. Early hatching, hatchery services, and transportation to the farm contribute to the challenge of delivering nutrients to the poult soon after exiting the egg. During the first week after hatching, the poult's small intestine increases in weight ninefold and doubles in length.[2] Delayed access to feed greatly affects intestinal morphology and growth of the bird after feeding up to four weeks of age. Part of this delay can be attributed to damage to microvilli and crypt cell structure in the small intestine, which can be adversely affected up to nine days after hatching.

Compounds That Potentiate Early Growth

A practical approach to applying compounds to stimulate early growth has been investigated by researchers at North Carolina State University by studying the effects of in ovo administration of peptide YY. In other species, peptide YY has demonstrated effects of inhibiting gut motility and stimulating small intestinal absorption of glucose. Application of peptide YY in ovo at transfer improves body weight up to 3 days of age in the poult. Administration of nutrients into the amnion of the egg prior to when the poult imbibes the remaining amniotic fluid before hatching has positive effects on intestinal maturation and poult growth after hatch.

Starter Diet Composition

Diet composition has a profound effect on how the poult makes the transition to its new metabolic state.[3] Traditional perception by the industry is that fat supplementation should be minimized for starting hatchlings. From a digestibility standpoint, research with feeding of animal fats and animal/vegetable fat blends demonstrates that young hatchlings do not digest saturated fatty acids efficiently. However, unsaturated fatty acids are highly digestible (80 to 85%) and may actually ease the metabolic shift after hatching. Caution should be used, however, as unsaturated fats typically are easily oxidized, rendering the fat rancid. Others may contend that a high proportion of energy from carbohydrate is needed to facilitate a shift in metabolism (from deriving energy from yolk lipid to assimilation of carbohydrate from an external diet). However, when diets containing a high proportion of energy from corn (carbohydrate) are fed, researchers from Ohio State University noted that 30 to 50% of poults fed the carbohydrate-based diet have plasma glucose concentrations above 500 mg/dL 2 days after feeding, which is more than twice the normal concentration.

Because the young poult has a very high crude protein requirement (28%), nutritionists may have a tendency to include much soybean meal in starting diets. However, soybean meal contains a high proportion of nonstarch polysaccharides and is very poorly digested. Therefore,

Encyclopedia of Animal Science
DOI: 10.1081/E-EAS 120019831

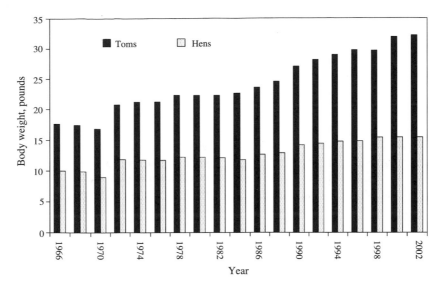

Fig. 1 Average live body weight of turkey toms (18 weeks) and hens (14 weeks). (From Ref. [1].)

prestarter or starter diets containing a high proportion of soybean meal may not provide the required amount of calculated energy and may suppress early growth. In the case of the turkey poult, the initial diet should contain less than 40% of the diet from soybean meal. Typically, formulation will include approximately 5 to 10% fish and/ or meat and bone meal. Several companies are currently marketing specialized diets to be used as the first diet at placement, or in transport boxes before arrival at the farm. These specialized diets are formulated with more easily digested nutrients, such as egg albumin as a protein source, and may also contain mixtures of bacteria (termed competitive exclusion products) to establish a normal microflora and exclude possible pathogens.

NUTRIENT IMPACT ON MUSCLE GROWTH AND QUALITY

Breast meat has become the primary retail product for commercial turkey production, so much nutritional research has focused on maximizing muscle growth and meat quality. Proteins and their component amino acids are one of the primary cost components of turkey diets, but also one of the primary drivers of muscle growth. The turkey industry typically formulates diets based on a crude protein basis, which can supply amino acids in excess of what the animal can either digest or metabolize. As research in this area progresses, however, knowledge of the amino acid digestibility of typical feed ingredients and formulating with an ideal protein ratio (theoretical exact balance of digested amino acids for metabolic needs) will allow greater precision in formulation.[4] This added

precision should considerably reduce the amount of nitrogen that is excreted by turkeys.

Additionally, recent nutritional advances have allowed the turkey industry to greatly improve the functional characteristics of turkey meat. For example, supplementation with vitamin E well above nutrient requirements for prevention of classical deficiency symptoms reduces lipid oxidation and improves the shelf life of both raw and ground turkey meat. Furthermore, vitamin E supplementation at higher concentrations in the diet reduces the incidence of pale, soft, and exudative (PSE) meat often encountered in heat-stressed birds.[5] Much of this effect can be related to alterations in glycolytic characteristics during the muscle rigor process. Other feed additives, such as betaine, show promise in aiding osmoregulation during coccidial challenges as well as providing a higher water-soluble methyl donor source, which has demonstrated effects on muscle growth in turkeys.

NUTRITION AND BONE INTEGRITY

Genetic improvements in the growth potential of commercial turkeys have not readily translated into proportional carcass growth and body conformation. For example, leg-associated disorders were a considerable issue for the industry during the late 1980s, until leg-shank width and conformation traits became selection criteria by breeding companies. Today, bone integrity is still a considerable economic issue as companies begin to market larger birds (over 40 pounds) at older ages. Nutritionally speaking, adequate dietary amino acid and protein levels have demonstrated effects on muscle growth, and they are associated with pronounced effects on the lower skeletal axis as well.[6] In fast-growing strains, spiral fractures of the femur occur in small percentages of toms between 16 and 19 weeks of age. Although it is unknown whether there is a nutritional cause, preliminary results suggest a problem in collagen fibril distribution/arrangement, along with areas of lower calcification. Other skeletal issues, such as osteomyelitis complex, are of considerable economic impact to the industry, because carcasses displaying the lesion are condemned due to a high incidence of *Staphylococcus aureus*. Supplementation with either 1,25 dihydroxy vitamin D_3 or 25-hydroxy vitamin D_3 improves skeletal integrity and reduces the incidence of osteomyelitis complex during an immune/bacterial challenge.[7]

NUTRITION AND THE ENVIRONMENT

Phosphorus (P) has emerged as an environmental issue with respect to surface-water quality. In order for animal agriculture to comply with new P-based land application regulations and the reductions in watershed scale nutrient loading imposed by total maximum daily load (TMDL) agreements in many U.S. states, it is imperative that 1) excreta P produced by the animals be minimized as much as possible through efficient animal nutrient management practices, such as dietary modification; and 2) the effects of dietary changes on the forms, availability, and transport of P in manure-amended soils be evaluated. Recent studies at Michigan State University and Purdue University demonstrate that the NRC nutrient recommendations[8] for P for turkeys are adequate for maximizing growth. Therefore, industry diets, containing at least 30% greater P, were not justified and led to substantially greater P excretion. Further reductions in litter P excretion can be achieved when microbial phytase (after reducing dietary P by 0.08%) or 25-hydroxy vitamin D_3 (after reducing dietary P by 0.03%) are fed.[9]

CONCLUSION

Nutritional issues facing the turkey industry at present include 1) transition diets at the start of life; 2) feeding to maximize GIT health; 3) maintaining bone integrity; 4) minimizing environmental impact; and 5) maximizing muscle mass and meat quality. Unfortunately, nutritional research for turkeys has not kept pace with substantial gains in performance. Fundamental research addressing bird requirements, feedstuff utilization, maintaining performance and GIT health without antibiotics, and minimizing environmental impact will be critical for the continued success of turkey production.

REFERENCES

1. Ferket, P.R. Growth of toms improves substantially. WATT Poult. USA **July 2003**, 38–48.
2. Sell, J.L. Physiological limitations and potential for improvement in gastrointestinal tract function of poultry. J. Appl. Poult. Res. **1996**, *5*, 96–101.
3. Lilburn, M.S. Ingredient quality and its impact on digestion and absorption in poultry. J. Appl. Poult. Res. **1996**, *5*, 78–81.
4. Firman, J.D.; Boling, S.D. Ideal protein in turkeys. Poult. Sci. **1998**, *77*, 105–110.
5. Olivo, R.; Soares, A.L.; Ida, E.I.; Shimokomaki, M. Dietary vitamin E inhibits poultry PSE and improves meat functional properties. J. Food Biochem. **2001**, *25*, 271–283.
6. Turner, K.A.; Lilburn, M.S. The effect of early protein restriction (zero to eight weeks) on skeletal development in turkey toms from two to eighteen weeks. Poult. Sci. **1992**, *71*, 1680–1686.
7. Huff, G.R.; Huff, W.E.; Balog, J.M.; Rath, N.C.; Xie, H.; Horst, R.L. Effect of dietary supplementation with vitamin D metabolites in and experimental model of turkey osteomyelitis complex. Poult. Sci. **2002**, *81*, 958–965.
8. National Research Council. Nutrient Requirements of Domestic Animals. In *Nutrient Requirements of Poultry*, 9th Revised Edition; National Academy Press, 1994.
9. Applegate, T.J.; Angel, R. Does dietary phytase supplementation increase phosphorus solubility in poultry manure? Proc. Carolina Poult. Nutr. Conf. **2003**, *13*, 88–104.

Ultrasound Technology: Live Animal and Carcass Evaluation

James R. Stouffer
Cornell University, Ithaca, New York, U.S.A.

INTRODUCTION

Breeders, producers, packers, retailers, and researchers are becoming more concerned about carcass traits, as the livestock industry moves closer to the concept of value-based marketing. Animal scientists have desired the ability to determine the carcass traits of composition and quality in live animals as aids in selection of breeding stock and ideal marketing time for slaughter animals, to study the mechanism of growth and development, and to understand the effect of nutrition. This has led to the development of noninvasive objective evaluation methods including ultrasound. Early ultrasound equipment was large and had limited performance capabilities. Subsequent developments have resulted in high-performance, durable, and lightweight ultrasound equipment that is associated with portable computers and sophisticated software. These systems produce rapid and accurate information for determining composition and quality characteristics of live animals and carcasses.

PROPERTIES OF ULTRASOUND

Ultrasound refers to high-frequency sound waves that are generated and received by a transducer associated with electronic equipment and, generally, a cathode ray screen. Ultrasound waves generated by the transducer are propagated through animal tissue until a slight change in density, such as tissue interfaces, will cause a portion of the ultrasound waves to be reflected back to the transducer. These signals appear on a screen in proportion to time and therefore can be measured in terms of distance and tissue depth.

EARLY EQUIPMENT

The ultrasonic reflectance technique A-mode was used for the evaluation of fat thickness of swine[1] in the late 1950s. The ultrasonic equipment used in the early studies was metal flaw detection systems. Ultrasonic waves at frequencies of 1 to 3 MHz were used to detect tissue interfaces as well as flaws in metal. This equipment was also used to evaluate beef and lambs. Clipping of hair at the examination site and the application of motor oil as a couplant was required because of the limited performance of the equipment available at that time.

Although the fat thickness was associated with a lot of the variation in composition, it soon became clear that the ability to measure lean depth and muscle area was required for increased accuracy. Subsequent studies[2] utilizing an improved technique were carried out on live market hogs and beef cattle. Depth readings of fat and muscle were made, starting at the backline and moving lateral at one-half-inch intervals and at recorded angles up to the lateral border of the rib eye muscle at specific desired rib locations on live hogs and cattle. These depth readings were then plotted on graph paper and the depths and muscle areas were plotted and measured.

The A-mode scanning, plotting, and measuring on several groups of market hogs and beef cattle[3] demonstrated that this technique offered good potential, but it required much time and effort and was not practical. This encouraged the next generation of technology. A continuous mechanical scanning procedure was developed, whereby a simulated B scan resulted from the movement of film across the signals originating from an A-mode unit in coordination with the movement of a single-element transducer on the animal. This technology was further developed and commercially marketed as the Scanogram in 1969. It was the primary ultrasonic system developed for evaluating animals that was marketed for the next decade. In order to produce a satisfactory image with the Scanogram, the animal had to remain still for approximately 10 seconds for a complete scan, and the film developed before the evaluation could be completed.

ADVANCED TECHNOLOGY

Real-time ultrasound represented a major breakthrough for noninvasive, objective animal evaluation. The medical

Encyclopedia of Animal Science
DOI: 10.1081/E-EAS 120019719

equipment industry developed ultrasonic systems that had multiple elements mounted in a linear array that could generate and receive signals from each element 15–30 times per second (i.e., real-time ultrasound). Linear array transducers of lengths up to 12.5 cm contained 64–100 elements, and a complete cross-sectional image could be produced in a fraction of a second and the frozen image viewed on the cathode ray tube of the ultrasonic unit. The real-time ultrasound equipment was used in the medical field for many diagnostic applications, and it became widely used in the livestock industry for evaluation of swine[4] and sheep although the transducer was too short to produce a complete cross-sectional image of beef cattle. A special transducer standoff guide was developed for use with the 12.5-cm transducer, which permitted the production and matching of two partial images. This technology was used for evaluating beef cattle.[5] The results were often inaccurate due to animal movement or poor operator technique. In 1990, an improved real-time ultrasonic scanner with a 17.2-cm linear transducer was developed and used for beef cattle. In 1991, this system was demonstrated for evaluating fat thickness, loin muscle area, and marbling score[6] on live cattle, sheep, and swine.

Extensive reviews of the application of ultrasound for evaluation of live beef, sheep, and swine for the previous 30 years have demonstrated the extent of the previous research and the improvements that have been realized. Topics have included the application of ultrasound for feeding and finishing animals,[7] and for the selection of breeding stock[8] and the effect on genetic improvement. Ultrasound has been used for the selection of breeding hogs for more than 20 years. Images were interpreted visually by humans and measured manually with the aid of planimeters or computers. Results have shown that automation of the process for interpreting animal ultrasonic images was feasible.

CARCASS EVALUATION

An automated evaluation system for determining fat depth and lean depth from longitudinal scans on freshly slaughtered and split pork carcasses was developed.[9] A 17.2-cm transducer mounted in a frame with a wedge-shaped standoff guide was used for longitudinally scanning pork carcasses from the tenth to last ribs two inches off and parallel to the backline. The 4°, wedge-shaped standoff guide prevented harmonic or ghost images that would have resulted in erroneous readings. The operator held the counterbalanced transducer in one hand while steadying the carcass with the other hand to ensure that the ultrasound beam from the transducer was

correctly oriented (i.e., perpendicular to the desired tissue interfaces) to produce consistent, quality images. The automated depth measurements of fat and lean provided values as accurate for predicting percent carcass lean as careful manual measurements. These automated measurements were made at line speeds of 1200 carcasses per hour. This technology has been adopted and used in multiple commercial plants for more than 5 years. A similar version of this technology is being used by most of the major swine breeding companies in the world for the selection of breeding stock.

As the performance of the ultrasonic equipment has improved in recent years, its use for determining marbling in the live animal has been developed utilizing sophisticated computers and software. Now it is common to see a complete portable system—ultrasonic scanner, transducer, laptop computer, and a few accessories—in use chuteside to evaluate live animals extensively. Marbling or intramuscular fat is the most important factor associated with beef carcass grade, and it is associated with juiciness, flavor, and tenderness of the meat when consumed by the consumer. Quality is also receiving more attention in pork and lamb. The advent of real-time ultrasound provided a method of producing speckle patterns, which was subjectively evaluated by trained ultrasound operators. More recently, software programs have been developed[10] that provide automated image grabbing and evaluation for marbling.

CONCLUSION

Ultrasound evaluation has advanced from the early equipment, which was bulky and had limited performance, to portable ultrasound units with portable computers and sophisticated software capable of making rapid and accurate evaluations of live animals and carcasses. Currently, this technology is being used in commercial feedlots to determine the optimum time to market individual beef cattle in order to realize the maximum value. Evaluation of more than 100,000 beef breeding animals is being done each year. Pork carcass evaluation is being done on rapidly moving chain lines, and robotic automation has been tested and will soon be in use. Application of this technology for beef and lambs is anticipated in the near future.

REFERENCES

1. Hazel, L.N.; Kline, E.A. Ultrasonic measurement of fatness in swine. J. Anim. Sci. **1959**, *18*, 815–819.
2. Stouffer, J.R.; Wallentine, M.V.; Wellington, G.W.;

Diekmann, A. Development and application of ultrasonic methods for measuring fat thickness and rib-eye area in cattle and hogs. J. Anim. Sci. **1961**, *20*, 758–767.

3. Stouffer, J.R.; Westervelt, R.G. A review of ultrasonic applications in animal science. J. Clin. Ultrasound **1977**, *5*, 124–128.

4. McLaren, D.G.; McKeith, F.M.; Novakoski, J. Prediction of carcass characteristics at market weight from serial real-time ultrasound measures of backfat and loin eye area in the growing pig. J. Anim. Sci. **1989**, *67*, 1657–1667.

5. Perkins, T.L.; Green, R.D.; Hamlin, K.E. Evaluation of ultrasonic estimates of carcass fat thickness and longissimus area in beef cattle. J. Anim. Sci. **1992**, *70*, 1002–1010.

6. Stouffer, J.R. Using Ultrasound to Objectively Evaluate Composition and Quality in Livestock. In *Proceedings: 21st Century Concepts Important to Meat—Animal Evaluation, University of Wisconsin, Madison, WI, Feb. 1991*; Kaufmann, R.G., Ed.; Department of Animal Science: University of Wisconsin, Madison, WI, 1991; 49–54. Publication No. 285.

7. Houghton, P.L.; Turlington, L.M. Application of ultrasound for feeding and finishing animals, a review. J. Anim. Sci. **1992**, *70*, 930–941.

8. Wilson, D.E. Application of ultrasound for genetic improvement. J. Anim. Sci. **1992**, *70*, 973–983.

9. Liu, Y.; Stouffer, J.R. Pork carcass evaluation with an automated and computerized ultrasonic system. J. Anim. Sci. **1995**, *73*, 29–38.

10. Brethour, J.R. Estimating marbling score in live cattle from ultrasound images using pattern recognition and neural network procedures. J. Anim. Sci. **1994**, *72*, 1425–1432.

11. Stouffer, J.R. History of ultrasound in animal science. J. Ultrasound Med. **2004**, *23*, 577–584.

Vitamin E—Selenium and Their Interrelationship

Donald C. Mahan
The Ohio State University, Columbus, Ohio, U.S.A.

Duane E. Ullrey
Michigan State University, Okemos, Michigan, U.S.A.

INTRODUCTION

Vitamin E is a fat-soluble nutrient found in body fat depots, plasma lipoproteins, and cell membrane phospholipids, where it serves as an important antioxidant. Selenium (Se) fulfills an antioxidant role as a component of glutathione peroxidases (GSHPx). Se is widely distributed in the body, but the most labile reservoir is in the liver. It is found in body tissue principally as selenomethionine (SeMet) or as selenocysteine (SeCys), the latter found in GSHPx. Both nutrients are discussed together because of their related functions and similar deficiency signs. However, Se and vitamin E each have unique metabolic roles, and the factors that alter the oxidative state of an animal may differentially affect their dietary needs.

VITAMIN E

Vitamin E is a collective term used for eight compounds synthesized by plants and found principally as free alcohols in lipid-containing fractions of green leaves and seeds.[1,2] Four are designated α-, β-, γ-, and δ-tocopherols (or tocols), and four are designated α-, β-, γ-, and δ-tocotrienols, differing from the tocopherols in unsaturation of the phytyl side chain. Of the various isomers, *RRR*-α-tocopherol (formerly D-α-tocopherol) has the highest biological activity in preventing fetal resorption in rats. The biological ranking of the tocopherols and tocotrienols as antioxidants is based on their ability to scavenge peroxyl radicals. Although α-tocotrienol has only about one-third of α-tocopherol's ability to prevent fetal resorption, it reportedly is equal in antioxidant activity.[3,4]

Tocopherols and tocotrienols are absorbed by mechanisms generated from fat digestion, requiring bile and pancreatic secretions. Vitamin E esters are hydrolyzed by pancreatic esterases. The dietary free alcohols and those released from the esters are subsequently incorporated into chylomicrons, assembled within the intestinal mucosa, secreted into the lymph, and transported via the thoracic duct into the blood. As circulating chylomicrons undergo catabolism, some of the newly absorbed vitamin E is transferred to lipoproteins and some remains with chylomicron remnants. Vitamin E transferred to lipoproteins during chylomicron catabolism includes all forms consumed, accounting for the presence of various tocopherols and tocotrienols in peripheral tissues. In the liver, dietary fats and tocopherols and tocotrienols in chylomicron remnants are repackaged, and *RRR*-α-tocopherol is preferentially incorporated by α-tocopherol transferase into very low density lipoproteins (VLDLs) and secreted. Following secretion of *RRR*-α-tocopherol-enriched VLDLs by the liver, peripheral tissues take up primarily *RRR*-α-tocopherol.[4]

Vitamin E is incorporated into the lipoprotein layers of cellular and subcellular membranes or deposited in adipose tissue.[1,2,4] Here they protect polyunsaturated fatty acids by interrupting peroxidative chain reactions in cell membrane phospholipids and plasma lipoproteins.[3,4] In the absence of vitamin E, polyunsaturated fatty acids are particularly susceptible to electron abstraction by free radicals. Lipid hydroperoxides (ROOH) are oxidized to peroxyl radicals (ROO), promoting further lipid hydroperoxide oxidations.[1–4] If vitamin E is present, this chain reaction is broken because the peroxyl radicals react faster with vitamin E in its reduced state (vit E–OH) than with polyunsaturated fatty acids. The result is a hydroperoxide (ROOH) and a tocopheroxyl radical (vit E–O). The tocopheroxyl radical emerges from the lipid bilayer of the cell membrane into the aqueous medium where hydrogen donors, such as glutathione or vitamin C, return it to its reduced state (vit E–OH).[4]

A deficiency of vitamin E may result in necrotizing myopathy of skeletal and cardiac muscle, placental blood vessel pathology with fetal death and resorption, degeneration of testicular epithelium, gastric ulceration, cataracts, retinal degeneration, encephalomalacia, erythrocyte hemolysis, and impaired immune function. Dairy cattle exhibit increased incidences of retained placentas and mastitis, with sows frequently exhibiting mastitis,

Encyclopedia of Animal Science
DOI: 10.1081/E-EAS 120024608

metritis, and aglactia.[5,6] Because α-tocopherol does not effectively cross the maternal–fetal barrier, the neonate has low tissue tocopherol levels and consumption of relatively tocopherol-rich colostrum is important for its postnatal welfare.[5]

Grains are generally low in *RRR*-α-tocopherol, and when stored for extensive periods, much is lost, particularly from high-moisture or acid-treated grains.[5] Although some seed oils have a relatively high tocopherol concentration, much of that in corn and soybean oils is γ-tocopherol. Young growing forages have relatively high α-tocopherol concentrations, but these decline with maturity, cutting and curing for hay, and during storage.

Cattle fed dried forage or overwintering on corn stalks and mature pasture may experience vitamin E depletion and, if sufficiently severe, will exhibit signs of deficiency.[6] Certain toxins, high dietary levels of polyunsaturated fatty acids, large excesses of dietary iron, extremes in environmental temperature, intense physical activity, and infectious diseases tend to increase oxidant stress. Collectively or individually, these factors influence the accumulation of reactive oxygen species and increase the dietary requirement for vitamin E.[3]

The principal commercial dietary vitamin E sources are the acetate or hydrogen succinate esters of all-*rac*-α-tocopherol (formerly D, L-α-tocopherol) or of *RRR*-α-tocopherol. Because of the ester linkage on the active site of the chromanol ring, these compounds are more stable in mixed feeds than free tocopherol.[5]

High dietary vitamin E levels for cows (≥ 1000 IU/day) can lower oxidized flavors in milk and reduce the incidence of intramammary infections.[6] Although high intakes of dietary vitamin E are generally considered harmless, when substantially elevated in the presence of marginal vitamin K status, they have been found to increase blood clotting time. Either vitamin E deficiencies or considerable excesses have been shown to have adverse effects on immune function in birds. Paradoxically, vitamin E in low-density lipoproteins oxidized in vitro in the absence of aqueous antioxidants may act as a prooxidant. However, prooxidant activity of high intakes of vitamin E has not yet been confirmed in vivo.[4]

SELENIUM

Selenium's (Se) nutritional history includes a period when it was considered significant only because of its toxicity and concern that it might be carcinogenic. Now it is recognized not only as an essential nutrient, but some evidence suggests that it may reduce the incidence of certain types of cancer. Selenium is not required for plant growth, but is found in plant proteins in amounts that vary with plant species, plant part, and available Se concen-

trations in soil. In grains and forages, Se is present largely as selenomethionine (SeMet), with much smaller amounts of selenocysteine (SeCyst) and other organic forms.[5,7]

Mechanisms of Se absorption are not well understood. Ruminants appear to absorb Se in either form less efficiently and more variably than nonruminants. Selenate appears to share an absorption pathway with molybdate and sulfate, and these anion antagonisms may impede Se absorption in either ruminants or nonruminants. Metabolic interactions with iron, copper, zinc, and other elements have been described, but the dietary concentrations necessary to increase requirements for Se far exceed the levels of these elements commonly found in feedstuffs. Conclusions about Se bioavailability depend on the criterion chosen. Thus, estimates of relative absorbability may be confounded by differences during digestion and in Se's postabsorptive fate.[7]

SeMet used for GSHPx synthesis is converted by transsulfuration to SeCyst and then to selenide by SeCyst β-lyase. Inorganic Se entering the cell is reduced by glutathione to selenide. Selenide may be methylated and excreted or phosphorylated by selenophosphate synthetase, followed by replacement of oxygen with Se in serine to produce SeCyst. The metabolism of selenide to SeCyst is considered to be a likely point of homeostatic Se regulation.[8]

Se is found principally as SeMet or SeCyst in the animal body. SeMet is metabolized in the general methionine pool because it appears not to be recognized as distinct from methionine. As a consequence, it does not fulfill any unique role until catabolized. SeCyst is part of the primary structure of the 11 functional selenoproteins that have been described, four of which are glutathione peroxidases. They use glutathione-reducing equivalents to catabolize hydrogen peroxide and hydroperoxides. Because oxidant molecules have functions in metabolism and in signaling pathways, the glutathione peroxidases are considered to have a regulatory role in the cell by affecting oxidant molecule concentrations. Each glutathione peroxidase appears to have a specific localization and different substrate specificities. The most abundant glutathione peroxidase, GSHPx-1, is found in the cytosol of all cells. GSHPx-2 is found predominantly in the cells of the gastrointestinal tract. GSHPx-3 is an extracellular glutathione peroxidase found in plasma and milk. GSHPx-4 is intracellular and catalyzes reduction of hydroperoxides specifically associated with phospholipids closely aligned with membrane structures. Three deiodinases involved in thyroxine metabolism have been identified as selenoproteins. Thus, a deficiency of Se may indirectly affect metabolic rate and several related physiologic processes, including parturition, tolerance to cold stress, and postnatal survival. A SeCyst-containing, NADPH-dependent selenoprotein, thioredoxin reductase, serves in animal tissues to regenerate ascorbic acid from dehydroascorbic acid.[7,8]

Selenium deficiency signs tend to overlap those seen in vitamin E deficiency. However, even with presumably adequate vitamin E intakes, very low dietary Se concentrations have been reported to result in weight loss, listlessness, alopecia, myopathy, hepatic necrosis, exudative diathesis, pancreatic fibrosis, reproductive disorders, and impaired immune function, varying with species and other aspects of diet composition.[7]

Sodium–selenite and –selenate, at levels not to exceed 0.30 ppm added Se, have been approved in the United States for incorporation into livestock diets. Recently, selenized yeast, high in SeMet, has been approved at the same added Se levels for poultry, swine, sheep, and cattle diets. As noted above, both inorganic and organic Se are effective in synthesis of selenoprotein enzymes, but SeMet released by digestion of Se-containing dietary proteins may be nonspecifically incorporated into tissue proteins, depending on the dietary ratio of methionine to SeMet. Thus, absorbed SeMet or SeMet released by catabolism of tissue proteins must undergo transulfuration to SeCyst followed by reduction to selenide to participate in synthesis of selenoprotein enzymes.[8]

ANTIOXIDANT INTERRELATIONSHIP

Any molecule with an atom that contains a single unpaired electron in its outer orbit is termed an oxidant. These atoms are unstable and have a strong attraction for the electrons of other atoms or molecules in order to regain their resting state. The process of transferring electrons to the oxidant is termed oxidation, and a new free radical is formed in the process.[3] The process can be self-perpetuating in unsaturated fatty acids found in membrane phospholipids and lipoproteins unless a more reactive electron donor, such as α-tocopherol, is introduced, whereupon the chain reaction is blocked. As described earlier, when lipid hydroperoxides are oxidized to peroxyl radicals, the peroxyl radicals react with α-tocopherol much faster than with other polyunsaturated fatty acids. The result is a corresponding organic hydroperoxide and an α-tocopheroxyl radical. The α-tocopheroxyl radical leaves the cell membrane lipid bilayer and enters the surrounding aqueous medium where glutathione peroxidase can use an electron from glutathione to restore α-tocopherol to its active or reduced state. Thus, although Se and vitamin E fulfill distinct functions, an inadequate supply of either can exacerbate the metabolic demand for the other.[8]

CONCLUSION

Because both vitamin E and selenium affect the antioxidant/prooxidant balance of cells through the mechanisms described earlier (and others), there is an interdependence in the quantitative dietary requirement for each. An inadequacy of either or both can impair animal performance, induce pathology, and increase mortality.

REFERENCES

1. Sokol, R.J. Vitamin E. In *Present Knowledge in Nutrition*, 7th Ed.; International Life Sciences Institute: Washington, DC, 1996; 130–136.
2. Chow, C.K. Vitamin E. In *Biochemical and Physiological Aspects of Human Nutrition*, 1st Ed.; W.B. Saunders Co.: Philadelphia, PA, 2000; 584–598.
3. Surai, P.F. Antioxidant Systems in the Animal Body. In *Natural Antioxidants in Avian Nutrition and Reproduction*; Nottingham Press: Nottingham, England, 2002; 1–25.
4. Traber, M.G. Vitamin E. In *Modern Nutrition in Health and Disease*, 9th Ed.; Shils, M.E., Olson, J.A., Shike, M., Ross, A.C., Eds.; Lippincott Williams & Wilkins: Baltimore, MD, 1999; 347–362.
5. Mahan, D.C. Selenium and Vitamin E in Swine Nutrition. In *Swine Nutrition*, 2nd Ed.; Lewis, A.J., Southern, L.L., Eds.; CRC Press: New York, NY, 2000; 281–314.
6. National Research Council. *Nutrient Requirements of Dairy Cattle*, 7th Ed.; National Academy Press: Washington, DC, 2001; 162–169.
7. Underwood, E.J.; Suttle, N.F. *The Mineral Nutrition of Livestock*, 3rd Ed.; CABI Publishing: New York, 1999; 421–475.
8. Burk, R.F.; Levander, O.A. Selenium. In *Modern Nutrition in Health and Disease*, 9th Ed.; Shils, M.E., Olson, J.A., Shike, M., Ross, A.C., Eds.; Lippincott Williams & Wilkins: Baltimore, MD, 1999; 265–276.

Vitamins—Fat Soluble

Donald C. Mahan
The Ohio State University, Columbus, Ohio, U.S.A.

INTRODUCTION

The fat-soluble vitamins (i.e., A, D, E, and K) are essential in the diets of domestic animals for maintenance, growth, tissue development, and reproduction, and are not involved in energy or amino acid metabolism as are the water-soluble vitamins. Meeting tissue requirements is essential, but excess supplementation could lead to toxicity situations, particularly for vitamins A and D, while none have yet been ascribed to vitamins E and K. Vitamins A, D, and K will be discussed herein, with vitamin E in a separate article.

VITAMIN A

In ancient Egypt the occurrences of an eye disorder and night blindness were resolved by the topical treatment of liver juices or consuming cooked liver. The condition existed for centuries and was reported in the Confederate Army during the American Civil War.[1] The active component in liver extract was identified as fat-soluble (1914), but was not structurally elucidated until 1930, when it was called vitamin A.

The family of compounds that exert vitamin A activity includes over 600 carotenoids ($\sim$50 are active) and various natural and synthetic vitamin A compounds.[2] The term vitamin A generically describes compounds that exhibit the biological activity of retinol (alcohol form) involved in the vision process, although the acidic form (retinoic acid) seems to perform specific functions in growth and tissue differentiation.[6] Each form shares structural similarities with retinol and its corresponding aldehyde (retinal), thus collectively referred to as retinoids. For comparative purposes, an international standard is used (1 IU=0.3 µg all-*trans* retinol). Some carotenoids have high antioxidant properties, while the retinoids do not.

Colostrum and milk provide vitamin A to the nursing animal, while synthetic vitamin A or provitamin A compounds are fed to growing and adult animals. The amount of carotenoids in forage is plentiful, but highly variable, declining with season length and plant maturity. Processing forages lowers its provitamin concentration.

Carotenoids are poorly converted to vitamin A in the intestine of domestic livestock.[3] Consequently, animals grazing pastures only have a small (<4-month) reservoir.[4]

Because the chemical structure of retinol has five double bonds and a hydroxyl group, it is readily oxidized. Commercial vitamin A is emulsified in gelatin and sugar, and is subsequently processed into a beadlet containing an antioxidant. Unprotected vitamin A is rapidly oxidized under acidic or moisture conditions when prooxidant minerals (e.g., Cu, Fe, Zn) or PUFAs or elevated nitrates are in the diet, or when feed-processing methods (friction, pressure, extrusion, steam) abuse the gelatin-coated beadlet.[5] Mycotoxins oxidize the vitamin and have produced vitamin A deficiencies in livestock.

The fat-soluble vitamin A compounds aggregate in the small intestine with other lipids from the action of pancreatic esterases and bile salts. They are transported in micellular form across the epithelial cell of the intestinal villi.[1] The absorption efficiency of synthetic vitamin A is 80 to 90%, whereas that of the carotenoids is <50%. Absorption efficiency depends largely on factors influencing lipid digestion. Retinoids are mainly retained by the liver (parenchyma and stellate) cells and, to a smaller degree, by other body cells. The major circulating form of vitamin A and carotenoids is bound to a retinol-binding protein (synthesized in liver). Lipoprotein lipase hydrolyzes the retinyl ester and facilitates its movement into cells. Only when vitamin A liver reserves are depleted does plasma retinol concentration decline.[1]

The main function ascribed to vitamin A involves the vision process, where binding proteins on the rods permit the conversion of retinol to retinal.[1–3] Its association with the membrane-bound protein opsin triggers conformational changes to rhodopsin. A series of isomerizations change the retina to light or dark sensations. Vitamin A also affects the uterine environment by promoting embryo development and enhancing their survival. The uterine endometrium secretes a retinol-binding protein that transfers up to 390 times more vitamin A between days 10 to 13 of gestation. Retinal can be irreversibly converted to retinoic acid and has been implicated in the expression of genes that determine the sequential development of the embryo.[1] The carotenoids are effective antioxidants and function by reducing free radical formation. Both

Encyclopedia of Animal Science
DOI: 10.1081/E-EAS 120019834

retinoids and carotenoids are immunomodulators by affecting both T cells and B-cell function.[2]

Signs of vitamin A deficiency include neonatal blindness (due to in utero constriction of the optic nerve), other skeletal abnormalities, poor growth, and reproductive failure (e.g., low conception, abortion, small litters in swine, stillbirths, poor semen quality). Although some of these signs are not specific for vitamin A, responses to vitamin A supplementation provide evidence for a deficiency.

The animal's ability to store vitamin A in the liver prevents a large, single ingestion from being toxic, but prolonged consumption can produce clinical symptoms of hypervitaminosis A. These include spontaneous fractures, internal hemorrhages, appetite and weight loss, thickened epithelial tissue, and increased clotting time.[2]

VITAMIN D

Technically a hormone, vitamin D was a scientific quirk that resulted in this steroid initially being classified as a vitamin. During the early 20th century, a bone abnormality (i.e., rickets) of dogs raised indoors was corrected by a dietary fat-soluble compound. It was later discovered that irradiated skin fed to rachitic rats cured the condition.[6] Although body endogenous secretions provided protection for this malady, the rapidly growing field of nutrition, the discovery of vitamin A and the B vitamins, and the use of a dietary component that prevented the deficiency resulted in this new substance being classified as a vitamin. Its discovery in 1920 and its structure in 1932 demonstrated that the steroid product was similar to the antirachetic factor (cod liver oil).

Vitamin D is a generic term for secosteroid compounds with cholecalciferol activity produced photochemically by the irradiation of 7-dehydrocholesterol present in the epidermal tissue of higher animals.[7] Plant ergocalciferol and animal cholecalciferol can be converted to vitamins D_2 and D_3, respectively. Both forms are absorbed and stored in adipose or liver tissue for several months. They can be converted by the enzyme vitamin D 25-hydroxylase to 25-hydroxyvitamin D_2 or D_3 (largely in the liver). Although both forms are biologically active in animals, more D_3 is converted to 25-dydroxyvitamin than D_2. The metabolite is further hydroxylated to 1,25-dihydroxycholecalciferol (1,25-$(OH)_2$ D_3), the active form of the vitamin in the proximal tubular cells of the kidney.[6,8] The synthesis of the active form is regulated by serum Ca, parathyroid hormone, and the circulating level of 1,25-$(OH)_2$ D_3.

Vitamin D has a biological role in regulating Ca metabolism. The parathyroid and calcitonin hormones synchronize the homeostasis of Ca and other minerals.

Vitamin D stimulates the synthesis of an intestinal Ca-binding protein, calbindin, where it directly aids in the intestinal transport of Ca and indirectly, P. Vitamin D stimulates bone osteoblasts (bone-forming cells) and mediates the activity of osteoclast cells (bone demineralization cells) through the action of 1,25-$(OH)_2$ D_3 and the parathyroid hormone.[8,10] Calcitonin inhibits Ca metabolism and subsequent bone osteoclast activity. Consequently, vitamin D has a vital role in bone mineralization and body homeostasis of Ca.

A vitamin D deficiency impairs normal Ca absorption and bone mineralization in young animals, resulting in an enlarged epiphysis.[5] As body weight increases, the bending of legs (i.e., rickets) and beaded ribs occur. In older animals, bone demineralization (i.e., osteomalacia) weakens bones, often resulting in posterior paralysis. These deficiencies are the consequences of impaired absorption of Ca, due to inadequate production of the Ca-binding protein in the intestinal mucosa and the low supply of Ca and P to the growing skeletal matrix. In the adult, the bones are demineralized because of high demands for Ca, thus mobilizing skeletal Ca reserves.[10]

High dietary vitamin D levels cause calcification of various body tissues. However, the amount necessary to achieve this toxicity is 30 to 40 times the animal's requirement. Vitamin D_3 is more toxic than D_2. Excess vitamin D stimulates bone osteoclastic activity, resulting in severe bone demineralization, bone breakage, and loss of animal performance.[4,10]

VITAMIN K

When a fat-free, low-cholesterol diet is fed to chicks, they develop a hemorrhagic condition that is cured by the addition of alfalfa meal.[9] It was demonstrated that the lipid-soluble portion of green plants and bacteria had the capacity to restore blood clotting time to normal. Although the chemical forms in green plants (K_1) and bacteria (K_2) differ, the similar quinone compounds were collectively called vitamin K. Although other commercial water-soluble forms are available, menadione bisulfite is the form most commonly added to poultry and swine diets.[5,10]

Absorption of plant and bacterial quinone compounds are dependent upon the fat digestive process, whereupon the vitamin is absorbed and transported in the lymph. Bacterial products can supply vitamin K to nonruminants practicing coprophagy, but dietary antibiotics may alter intestinal microbial synthesis of the vitamin.[10] Plants and rumen bacteria are major suppliers for ruminants on pasture, with deficiencies being rare. The consumption of moldy sweet clover hay produces a fungal metabolite (dicoumarol) that inhibits the synthesis of blood clotting factors.[4,11] All forms of vitamin K are located in the liver.[8,9]

Vitamin K modifies several liver proteins, largely involving the blood clotting factors, but its effects are posttranslational.[9] Vitamin K serves to activate the proteins, specifically at the γ-carboxyglutamate site, to increase the binding affinity of Ca ions for the clotting of blood.[9] Similar mechanisms may occur in other tissue and it probably has a role in bone mineralization.

Deficiency symptoms of vitamin K include prolonged bleeding, poor clotting, hematoma in tissue, and death from uncontrolled hemorrhages. Animal lameness, stiffness, and blood in the urine are related to the deficiency. Dicoumarol can pass the maternal–fetal barrier and the developing fetus can be affected. Because blood clotting is affected by vitamin K, the prothrombin clotting time is a rapid and useful clinical tool in detecting the deficiency.[9]

Excess vitamin K does not seem to affect any major animal species. The newer water-soluble forms may react with free tissue sulfhydryl groups and cause hemolytic anemia in liver tissue, and brain damage.

CONCLUSIONS

Each of the fat-soluble vitamins has a unique and interesting history. Their discovery was initially from deficiency observations, with chemical structures and functions later elucidated by scientific investigation. The fat-soluble vitamins are involved with tissue growth and maintenance. Grains, forages, and sunlight, in the case of vitamin D, provide animals with a supply of each vitamin, but there is great seasonal variation. Consequently, synthetic forms of each are equivalent to the active forms of the natural sources of the vitamins. The NRC publications[4,5,10,11] apply research findings to domesticated animals.

REFERENCES

1. Olson, J.A. *Vitamin A*, 7th Ed.; International Life Sciences Institute: Washington, DC, 1996; 109–119.
2. Noy, N. Vitamin A. *Biochemical and Physiological Aspects of Human Nutrition*, 1st Ed.; W.B. Sanders Co.: Philadelphia, PA, 2000; 599–623.
3. Darroch, C.S. Vitamin A in Swine Nutrition. In *Swine Nutrition*, 2nd Ed.; CRC Press: New York, NY, 2000; 263–280.
4. NRC. *Nutrient Requirements of Beef Cattle*, 7th Rev. Ed.; Natl. Acad. Press: Washington, DC, 1996; 75–78.
5. NRC. *Nutrient Requirements of Swine*, 10th Rev. Ed.; Natl. Acad. Press: Washington, DC, 1998; 71–75.
6. Norman, A.W. *Vitamin D*, 7th Ed.; International Life Sciences Institute: Washington, DC, 1996; 120–129.
7. Holick, M.F. Vitamin D. In *Biochemical and Physiological Aspects of Human Nutrition*, 1st Ed.; W.B. Sanders Co.: Philadelphia, PA, 2000; 624–639.
8. Crenshaw, T.D. Calcium, Phosphorus, Vitamin D and Vitamin K. In *Swine Nutrition*; CRC Press: New York, NY, 2000; 187–212.
9. Suttie, J.W. *Vitamin K*, 7th Ed.; International Life Sciences Institute: Washington, DC, 1996; 137–145.
10. NRC. *Nutrient Requirements of Poultry*, 9th Rev. Ed.; Natl. Acad. Press: Washington, DC, 1994; 15.
11. NRC. *Nutrient Requirements of Dairy Cattle*, 7th Rev. Ed.; Natl. Acad. Press: Washington, DC, 2001; 162–169.

Vitamins—Water Soluble: Biotin, Choline, Niacin, and Ascorbic Acid

C. Robert Dove
University of Georgia, Athens, Georgia, U.S.A.

INTRODUCTION

The water-soluble vitamins biotin, choline, niacin, and ascorbic acid are integral components of a number of metabolic systems. These vitamins serve as prosthetic groups for enzymes, a component of the liable methyl pool, and precursors to metabolically critical enzymes. These B vitamins are found in a variety of feeds at varying concentrations. Monogastric animals may require supplementation of B vitamins under some production practices. Ruminant animals do not normally need supplementation of B vitamins, as the microbes in the rumen produce a supply adequate to meet the animal's needs.

BIOTIN

Biotin was discovered as a growth factor needed for yeast, and was isolated and characterized in 1936. Biotin was also known as vitamin H and coenzyme R. Chemically, biotin is the compound hexahydro-2-oxo-1H-thieno[3,4-d]-imidazole-4-pentanoic acid.[1]

Biotin is absorbed from the small intestine by active transport at low concentrations and by simple diffusion at higher concentrations. As the animal ages, biotin absorption increases and the active transport site shifts from the ileum to the jejunum. A significant amount of biotin is synthesized by the flora of the colon; however, the bioavailability of colonic biotin is thought to be low.[1-3]

Biotin serves as the prosthetic group for enzymes involved in carboxylation reactions. Of the biotin carboxylases known to exist, only four are found in animal tissues. These include pyruvate, acetyl-CoA, propionyl-CoA, and 3-methylcrotonyl-CoA carboxylases.[2,3]

Biotin supplementation has little effect on the growth performance of growing animals. Biotin supplementation of sow diets improved reproductive performance and reduced the incidence of hoof cracks and foot pad lesions.[1] A synthetic diet, or one containing desiccated egg white or specific sulfa drugs, is required to produce a biotin deficiency. Deficiency signs that have been reported include alopecia, spasticity of the hind legs, dermatitis, skin ulcerations, a brown exudate on the skin and about the eyes, transverse cracking of the hooves, cracking and bleeding of the foot pads, diarrhea, and an inflammation of the mucous membranes of the mouth.[1,2] Studies indicate that animals can safely tolerate levels of biotin as high as 10 times the nutritional requirement.[4]

The supply of biotin to the animal is affected by the biotin content of the diet, as well as by the availability of biotin in feed ingredients and the level of synthesis by the intestinal microflora. The apparent digestibility of biotin determined at the distal ileum was 55.4, 2.7, and 3.9% in soybean meal, meat and bone meal, and canola meal, respectively; and 4.8, 4.0, and 21.6% in barley, corn, and wheat, respectively.[5]

CHOLINE

Choline is required by most animals in concentrations that far exceed what is considered the normal definition of a vitamin. However, choline will be discussed here as a vitamin, as its metabolic role is similar to many of the B vitamins. The name choline arises from the word *chole*, which is German for bile. The first demonstration of the nutritional importance of choline was reported when choline supplementation prevented the development of fatty livers in rats.[1]

Choline appears to be absorbed in the small intestine. Most animals are capable of significant biosynthesis of choline; therefore, absorption from the intestine may not be critical to the animal under normal conditions. Biosynthesis of choline is the result of the decarboxylation of the amino acid serine to ethanolamine in a pyridoxal-dependent reaction. Ethanolamine is then progressively methylated to form choline.[6] Excess dietary methionine is one of the main sources of the methyl groups used in the biosynthesis of choline.[1]

Choline is considered part of a labile methyl pool capable of contributing methyl groups for the biosynthesis of methionine and other methylated compounds, including purines and pyrimidines.[2,6] Choline is a precursor for acetylcholine and for the de novo synthesis of phosphatidylcholine and sphingomyelin. Thus, as a constituent of

Encyclopedia of Animal Science
DOI: 10.1081/E-EAS 120027690

phospholipids, choline plays a role in the structure of biological membranes.[1,2,6]

Gross observations of animals with a choline deficiency include reduction in weight gain, rough hair coats, and an unsteady and staggering gait. Examination of blood samples from deficient animals indicates a decrease in red cell, hematocrit, and hemoglobin concentrations. Upon necropsy, fat infiltration of the liver and kidney has been observed.[1,2]

Under most production conditions, choline supplementation is not needed. Choline is synthesized from excess methionine. However, choline supplementation of sow diets during gestation and lactation has proven effective in improving reproductive performance.[1]

Choline is present in all naturally occurring fats. The choline in peanut meal, canola meal, and dehulled soybean meal is 71, 24, and 83% available, respectively. The phospholipid-bound choline found in most feedstuffs and unprocessed fats is thought to be well utilized.[1,7]

NIACIN

The component of liver extracts that was successful in treating black tongue in dogs was niacinamide. It was also shown that nicotinic acid cured pellagra in humans, the parallel of black tongue in dogs. Niacin is the generic descriptor for pyridine 3-carboxylic acid and derivatives, exhibiting qualitatively the biological activity of nicotinamide.[1,8]

Nicotinic acid and nicotinamide are rapidly absorbed from the stomach and small intestine. A sodium-dependent transport occurs at low concentrations, whereas passive diffusion predominates at higher concentrations. Nicotinamide adenine dinucleotide (NAD) and NAD phosphate (NADP) are the main dietary forms of niacin and are hydrolyzed by enzymes in the intestinal mucosa to yield nicotinamide. Nicotinamide is the main form of the vitamin in the bloodstream.[1,2,8] Most mammals can synthesize niacin from excess dietary tryptophan.[9]

Nicotinamide and nicotinic acid act as precursors for the coenzymes nicotinamide adenine dinucleotide (NAD) and nicotinamide adenine dinucleotide phosphate (NADP). NAD is the coenzyme for a number of dehydrogenases participating in the metabolism of fat, carbohydrate, and amino acids. NADP also participates in dehydrogenation reactions, particularly in the hexose monophosphate shunt. The coenzymes of nicotinamide have been implicated in other biological reactions, such as the synthesis and repair of DNA and synthesis of protein.[1,2,8]

Niacin deficiency symptoms include anorexia, reduced weight gain, vomiting, diarrhea, dry skin, dermatitis, rough hair coat, hair loss, ulcerative gastritis, inflamma-

tion and necrosis of the cecum and colon, and normocytic anemia. Toxicity symptoms such as vasodilation, nausea, vomiting, and occasional skin lesions have been reported in some animals.[1,2]

Niacin is widely distributed in most plant and animal products. Cereal grains and legumes, as well as seeds, yeast, milk, and meats, are all considered to have significant concentrations of niacin. However, the niacin in many plants (including most cereal grains) may be bound and unavailable to animals.[1,2,8] Consequently, niacin is often supplemented in the diets of monogastric animals.

ASCORBIC ACID

Ascorbic acid—vitamin C—was recognized as the antiscorbutic factor in fresh fruits and vegetables as early as 1734. However, it was not until 1932 that it was isolated and identified. The term vitamin C is used as a generic descriptor for all compounds exhibiting qualitatively the biological activity of ascorbic acid.[1,10]

At low ascorbate concentrations, absorption occurs through a sodium-dependent active transport in the small intestine. At higher ascorbate concentration, absorption occurs by simple diffusion. The active transport system for dehydroascorbic acid appears to be different from the system for ascorbate.[10,11]

Ascorbic acid is a powerful, water-soluble antioxidant. An ascorbic acid deficiency may induce various liver lysosomal enzyme activities and impair the biosynthesis of collagen. Ascorbic acid enhances the formation of intracellular material, bone matrix, and tooth dentin. Ascorbic acid, due to its reducing and chelating properties, enhances the absorption of iron from the diet and may be involved in the absorption, mobilization, and distribution of other metal ions throughout the body.[1,10,11]

Ascorbic acid is not a dietary essential for most animals, as it can be synthesized from carbohydrates such as glucose and galactose. Primates and guinea pigs lack the enzyme L-gulonolactone oxidase, which is required for ascorbic acid biosynthesis. Research has suggested that under certain environmental conditions (heat or disease stress, low-energy diets), some animals may not be able to synthesize enough ascorbic acid for maximum growth. It has also been postulated that ascorbic acid supplementation may be effective in the prevention or alleviation of osteochondrosis and navel bleeding. However, no deficiency symptoms have been associated with ascorbic acid. High concentrations of ascorbic acid have been reported to result in development of toxicity signs in humans and laboratory animals. These include allergic responses, oxaluria, uricosuria, and interference with mixed-function oxidase systems.[1,12,13]

Significant concentrations of ascorbate can be found in fruits and vegetables. Data concerning the content or availability of ascorbate in cereal grains is not readily available. Estimates of the vitamin C content of foods are affected by season, storage, transport methods, and cooking practices.[10,11]

CONCLUSION

The water-soluble vitamins biotin, choline, niacin, and ascorbic acid are involved in a wide variety of metabolic processes. Each has a specific role in metabolism and synthesis of nutrients and compounds required by the animal. These vitamins are found in a wide variety of feed ingredients, but concentrations and bioavailability are influenced by processing, storage, and handling. The supplementation requirement for these vitamins depends on the species and age of the animal, and the practices and environment in which the animal is produced. Under specific production practices, supplementation of each of these vitamins to monogastric animals can be beneficial.

REFERENCES

1. Dove, C.R.; Cook, D.A. Water-Soluble Vitamins in Swine Nutrition. In *Swine Nutrition*, 2nd Ed.; Lewis, A.J., Southern, L.L., Eds.; CRC Press: New York, 2001; 315–356.
2. Standing Committee on the Scientific Evaluation of Dietary Reference Intakes and Its Panel on Folate, Other B Vitamins, and Choline and Subcommittee on Upper Reference Levels of Nutrients Food and Nutrition Board Institute of Medicine. *Dietary Reference Intakes for Thiamin, Riboflavin, Niacin, Vitamin B₆, Folate, Vitamin B₁₂, Pantothenic Acid, Biotin and Choline (1999)*; National Academy Press: Washington, DC, 2000; 374–389.
3. Mock, D.M. Biotin. In *Present Knowledge in Nutrition*, 7th Ed.; Ziegler, E.E., Filer, L.J., Jr., Eds.; ILSI Press: Washington, DC, 1996; 220–235.
4. National Research Council. Biotin. In *Vitamin Tolerance of Animals*; National Academy Press: Washington, DC, 1987; 70–73.
5. Sauer, W.C.; Mosenthin, R.; Ozimek, L. The digestibility of biotin in protein supplements and cereal grains for growing pigs. J. Anim. Sci. **1988**, *66*, 2583–2589.
6. Kuksis, A.; Mookerjea, S. Choline. In *Nutrition Reviews Present Knowledge in Nutrition*, 5th Ed.; The Nutrition Foundation, Inc.: Washington, DC, 1984; 383–399.
7. Emmert, J.L.; Baker, D.H. A chick bioassay approach for determining the bioavailable choline concentration in normal and over-heated soybean meal, canola meal, and peanut meal. J. Nutr. **1997**, *127*, 745–752.
8. Jacob, R.A.; Swendseid, M.E. Niacin. In *Present Knowledge in Nutrition*, 7th Ed.; Ziegler, E.E., Filer, L.J., Jr., Eds.; ILSI Press: Washington, DC, 1996; 184–191.
9. Van Eys, J. Nicotinic Acid. In *Handbook of Vitamins, Second Edition, Revised and Expanded*; Macklin, L.H., Ed.; Marcel Dekker: New York, 1991; 311–340.
10. Levine, M.; Rumsey, S.; Wang, Y.; Park, J.; Kwon, O.; Xu, W.; Amano, N. Vitamin C. In *Present Knowledge in Nutrition*, 7th Ed.; Ziegler, E.E., Filer, L.J., Jr., Eds.; International Life Sciences Press: Washington, DC, 1996; 146–159.
11. Panel on Dietary Antioxidants and Related Compounds, Subcommittees on Upper Reference Levels of Nutrients and Interpretation and Uses of Dietary Reference Intakes, and the Standing Committee on the Scientific Evaluation of Dietary Reference Intakes; Food and Nutrition Board, Institute of Medicine. Vitamin C. In *Dietary Reference Intakes for Vitamin C, Vitamin E, Selenium and Carotenoids*; National Academy Press: Washington, DC, 2000; 95–185.
12. National Research Council. Vitamins. In *Nutrient Requirements of Swine, Tenth Revised Edition*; National Academy Press: Washington, DC, 1998; 71–89.
13. National Research Council. Ascorbic Acid. In *Vitamin Tolerance of Animals*; National Academy Press: Washington, DC, 1987; 36–43.

Vitamins—Water Soluble: Pantothenic Acid, Folic Acid, and B$_{12}$

C. Robert Dove

University of Georgia, Athens, Georgia, U.S.A.

INTRODUCTION

The water-soluble vitamins folic acid, pantothenic acid, and B$_{12}$ are involved in a wide variety of metabolic processes. Most of these processes are involved in methyl group transfers, the formation of single carbon units, and decarboxylation and transamination pathways. Like most of the B vitamins, the initial deficiency symptoms of each include decreased growth rate and poor general health status. The B vitamins are found in plant and animal tissues in varying concentrations and availabilities. While dietary recommendations vary considerably from species to species, dietary supplementation of most of the B vitamins is recommended for monogastric species. Microorganisms in the rumen of ruminant animals produce enough B vitamins to meet the animal's needs under most production situations.

FOLIC ACID (FOLATE)

A bacterial growth factor was found in spinach leaves that prevented anemia in chicks. This factor was isolated and identified as folic acid (pteroylmonoglutamic acid). The term folate is used as a generic descriptor for folic acid and related compounds exhibiting the biological activity of folic acid.[1,2]

Intestinal absorption of folates is thought to occur at the monoglutamate level. Hydrolysis of the polyglutamates to monoglutamates occurs within the brush border membrane of the small intestine. Intestinal transport of the monoglutamyl folates is carrier-mediated and pH-dependent. Folates are absorbed by a simple diffusion mechanism when concentrations are at pharmacological levels. Absorbed folates are taken up by the liver and converted back to polyglutamate derivatives, and either retained in the liver or released into the blood or bile.[2]

The metabolic role of folic acid coenzymes in mammalian tissues is in the transfer of single carbon moieties. The coenzymatically active forms of folic acid are the tetrahydro derivatives. Specific reactions and enzymes in which these coenzymes are involved include methylation of homocysteine to methionine, the inter-

conversion of serine and glycine, the synthesis of purines and pyrimidines, and the oxidation of histidine and threonine.[1–3]

Most growing animals can obtain sufficient folic acid from feed ingredients and from bacterial synthesis in the intestine. However, reproducing animals may need more folic acid than supplied by feed ingredients. It has been demonstrated that in swine, serum folates decreased by 50% from weaning to day 60 of gestation.[4,5] The addition of 1 to 1.65 mg of folic acid/kg to a corn–soybean meal diet resulted in an improvement in the total number of pigs born and born live over three parities.[6]

Folic acid deficiency symptoms include a reduction in growth rate, fading hair color, macrocytic and normocytic anemia, leukopenial thrombopenia, reduced hematocrit, and bone marrow hyperplasia. It should be noted that a synthetic diet containing 1 to 2% of a sulfa drug or a folic acid antagonist was necessary to produce a folic acid deficiency. Folic acid is generally considered to be nontoxic, as no adverse effects have been reported following the ingestion of high levels of the vitamin in any of several species.[1]

Folates are supplied in the diet by most natural feedstuffs. However, the folate content of natural feedstuffs is highly variable and therefore should be considered an unreliable source of the vitamin. The variability of folate content in feedstuffs may be due to variety, processing, and storage differences. Bacteria in the colon appear to produce a significant amount of folates, but the contribution of bacterial folates to the animals' needs is unknown and may be very low. The apparent digestibility of folates in feedstuffs appears to be variable. The apparent availability in wheat and barley is around 80%, while most protein meals have folate apparent availabilities in the 30–60% range.[1]

PANTOTHENIC ACID

Pantothenic acid was discovered as the cure for chick pellagra. Pantothenic acid deficiencies have been reported only as a result of feeding semisynthetic diets or an antagonist to the vitamin.[2] Pantothenic acid is the

Encyclopedia of Animal Science
DOI: 10.1081/E-EAS 120027689

compound *N*-(2,4-dihydroxy-3,3-dimethyl-l-oxobutyl)-beta-alanine, also known as pantoyl-beta-alanine.[1]

Pantothenic acid is found in feedstuffs in the form of coenzyme A (CoA), acyl CoA synthetase, and acyl carrier protein. CoA is hydrolyzed in the intestinal lumen to pantothenic acid. Pantothenic acid crosses the intestinal lumen into the bloodstream by a specific sodium-dependent transport system at low concentrations. When pantothenic acid is present in the diet at higher concentrations, it is absorbed from the intestinal lumen by simple diffusion. Pantothenic acid in the bloodstream is cotransported with sodium across the cell membrane and is converted back into CoA.[1,2,7]

Pantothenic acid, in the form of pantotheine, is the functional group of the biologically active coenzyme A (CoA), acyl carrier protein, and guanosine 5'-triphosphate (GTP)-dependent acyl CoA synthetase. CoA functions as a carrier of acyl groups in enzymatic reactions involved in biological acetylations and in the synthesis of fatty acids, cholesterol, sphingosine, citrate, acetoacetate, porphyrins, and sterols, as well as in the oxidation of fatty acids, pyruvate, and alpha-ketoglutarate. Pantothenic acid, in the form of 4'-phosphopantotheine, is incorporated into acyl carrier protein, which acts as an acyl carrier in fatty acid synthesis and is also the prosthetic group of GTP-dependent acyl CoA synthetase, which converts succinyl CoA to GTP plus CoA.[2,7] The biosynthesis of the amino acids leucine, arginine, and methionine include a pantothenate-dependent step. Pantothenate donates the acetate to the N-terminal amino acid of proteins during protein synthesis.[8]

The primary symptom of a pantothenic acid deficiency in growing swine is an abnormal gait in the hind legs referred to as goose stepping.[9] Other deficiency symptoms include reduced growth, anorexia, diarrhea, dry skin, rough hair coat, alopecia, and reduced immune response.[1] Gestating and lactating gilts fed a low pantothenic acid diet developed fatty livers, enlarged adrenal glands, intramuscular hemorrhage, eccentric dilatation of the heart, rectal congestion, atrophic ovaries, and infantile uteri.[10]

Pantothenic acid is widely distributed in nature and is essential for all forms of life.[2,7] The content of pantothenic acid has been shown to be highly available in barley, wheat, and soybean meal, but it is low in corn and grain sorghum.[11] For this reason, synthetic pantothenic acid is typically added to monogastric diets in the form of calcium pantothenate. Only the d-isomer of pantothenic acid is biologically available. The d-form of calcium pantothenate has a bioavailability of 92%, whereas the racemic mixture (dl) has only 46% bioavailability.[12] Pantothenic acid is relatively stable at a neutral pH. However, cooking is reported to destroy 15–50% of the vitamin in meat, and the processing of vegetables was associated with a loss of 37–78% of the vitamin.[13]

VITAMIN B$_{12}$

Cobalt-containing compounds (corrinoids) having vitamin B$_{12}$ activity are referred to as cobalamins. Active forms of vitamin B$_{12}$ in metabolism are methylcobalamin and 5'-deoxyadenoxylcobalamin. Cyanocobalamin is the cobalamin that is normally used in supplementation and pharmaceutical preparations. Vitamin B$_{12}$ is best known for its association with Addisonian pernicious anemia.[1,2,14]

Digestion of vitamin B$_{12}$ begins in the stomach, where gastric acids and enzymes release the vitamin B$_{12}$ from its peptide bonds in food. As the protein is digested, the B$_{12}$ is freed and then bound to an intrinsic factor secreted by the gastric parietal cells. The intrinsic factor-bound vitamin B$_{12}$ is then absorbed in the ileum of the small intestine.[14]

Two coenzyme forms of vitamin B$_{12}$ are known to exist in animals. These are methylcobalamin, which functions as a methyl carrier, and 5'-deoxyadenoxylcobalamin, which serves as a hydrogen carrier. The function of methylcobalamin as a methyl carrier is the basis for the interrelationship between vitamin B$_{12}$ and folate. In one such reaction, an enzyme-bound methylcobalamin is formed as an intermediate in the transfer of the methyl moiety of N^5-methyltetrahydrofolate to homocysteine in the resynthesis of methionine. In the form of 5'-deoxyadenoxylcobalamin, vitamin B$_{12}$ is a coenzyme for methylmalonyl-CoA mutase, which catalyzes the conversion of methyl-malonyl–CoA to succinyl–CoA. This reaction is a step in the catabolism of propionyl–CoA, which is derived from the breakdown of valine and isoleucine.[1,2,14]

A vitamin B$_{12}$ deficiency in animals is evidenced by a reduction in growth rate and feed intake, rough hair coat, dermatitis, enlarged liver, extreme irritability and sensitivity to touch, and unsteadiness of gait.[1] Examination of blood samples from deficient animals has indicated normocytic anemia and high neutrophil counts, with concomitantly low lymphocyte counts. Similar to pernicious anemia in humans, a double deficiency of vitamin B$_{12}$ and folic acid has been reported to result in the development of macrocytic anemia and bone marrow hyperplasia.[2,14]

Plants and grain materials are completely devoid of naturally occurring vitamin B$_{12}$, whereas animal products and animal by-products contain varying levels of the vitamin. Vitamin B$_{12}$ found in nature is made exclusively by microorganisms. Fecal material contains high levels of vitamin B$_{12}$, but vitamin B$_{12}$ is not absorbed from the colon.[1,2,14]

CONCLUSION

Pantothenic acid, folic acid, and vitamin B_{12} have very specific roles in the metabolic processes within the body. Each of these vitamins has a unique role in the formation of compounds essential for life. The concentration and availability of these vitamins in feedstuffs is highly variable. Folic acid is normally present in amounts adequate to meet the needs of growing animals. Supplemental folic acid may be needed for reproducing animals. Pantothenic acid and vitamin B_{12} are normally supplemented in monogastric diets. Ruminant animals can produce the B vitamins they need in the rumen under most production practices. Additional research on the role of B vitamins in metabolism is ongoing.

REFERENCES

1. Dove, C.R.; Cook, D.A. Water-Soluble Vitamins in Swine Nutrition. In *Swine Nutrition*, 2nd Ed.; Lewis, A.J., Southern, L.L., Eds.; CRC Press: New York, 2001; 315–356.

2. Standing Committee on the Scientific Evaluation of Dietary Reference Intakes and Its Panel on Folate, Other B Vitamins, and Choline and Subcommittee on Upper Reference Levels of Nutrients Food and Nutrition Board Institute of Medicine. *Dietary Reference Intakes for Thiamin, Riboflavin, Niacin, Vitamin B_6, Folate, Vitamin B_{12}, Pantothenic Acid, Biotin and Choline (1999)*. National Academy Press: Washington, DC, 2000.

3. Selhub, J.; Rosenberg, I.H. Folic Acid. In *Present Knowledge in Nutrition*, 7th Ed.; Ziegler, E.E., Filer, L.J., Jr., Eds.; ILSI Press: Washington, DC, 1996; 206–219.

4. Matte, J.J.; Girard, C.L.; Brisson, G.J. Serum folates during the reproductive cycle of sows. J. Anim. Sci. **1984**, *59*, 158–163.

5. Matte, J.J.; Girard, C.L.; Brisson, G.J. Folic acid and reproductive performance of sows. J. Anim. Sci. **1984**, *59*, 1020–1025.

6. Lindemann, M.D.; Kornegay, E.T. Folic acid supplementation to diets of gestating–lactating swine over multiple parities. J. Anim. Sci. **1989**, *67*, 459–464.

7. Plesofsky-Vig, N. Pantothenic Acid. In *Present Knowledge in Nutrition*, 7th Ed; Ziegler, E.E., Filer, L.J., Jr., Eds.; ILSI Press: Washington, DC, 1996; 236–244.

8. Driessen, A.P.C.; de Jong, W.W.; Tesser, G.I.; Bloemendal, H. The mechanism of N-terminal acetylation of proteins. CRC Crit. Rev. Biochem. **1985**, *18*, 281–306.

9. Hughes, E.H.; Ittner, N.R. The minimum requirement of pantothenic acid for the growing pig. J. Anim. Sci. **1942**, *1*, 116–119.

10. Ullrey, D.E.; Becker, D.E.; Terrill, S.W.; Notzold, R.A. Dietary levels of pantothenic acid and reproductive performance of female swine. J. Nutr. **1955**, *57*, 401–414.

11. Southern, L.L.; Baker, D.H. Bioavailable pantothenic acid in cereal grains and soybean meal. J. Anim. Sci. **1981**, *53*, 403–408.

12. National Research Council. *Nutrient Requirements of Swine*, 10th Ed.; National Academy Press: Washington, DC, 1998; 75–81.

13. Tahiliani, A.G.; Beinlich, C.J. Pantothenic acid in health and disease. Vitam. Horm. **1991**, *46*, 165–228.

14. Herbert, V. Vitamin B-12. In *Present Knowledge in Nutrition*, 7th Ed.; Ziegler, E.E., Filer, L.J., Jr., Eds.; ILSI Press: Washington, DC, 1996; 191–205.

Vitamins—Water Soluble: Thiamin, Riboflavin, and B6

C. Robert Dove
University of Georgia, Athens, Georgia, U.S.A.

INTRODUCTION

The water-soluble vitamins thiamin, riboflavin, and B_6 are involved in a wide variety of metabolic processes. Most of these processes are involved in the digestion and metabolism of nutrients. Like most of the B vitamins, the initial deficiency symptoms of each include decreased growth rate and poor general health status. The B vitamins are found in plant and animal tissues in varying concentrations and availabilities. While dietary recommendations vary considerably from species to species, dietary supplementation of most of the B vitamins is recommended for monogastric species. Microorganisms in the rumen of ruminant animals produce enough B vitamins to meet the animal's needs under most production situations.

THIAMIN

Thiamin was originally known as vitamin B_1, or aneurin, and was the first B vitamin identified. Early studies of the cause of beriberi led to the discovery of thiamin. It was shown that rice bran, extracts of rice bran, or whole rice could alleviate the symptoms of beriberi. Thiamin was subsequently identified as the active factor in rice bran that prevented beriberi. The word vitamin was first coined in reference to thiamin when Casimir Funk used the term vitamine to refer to thiamin as an amine that is essential for life.[1]

Thiamin absorption takes place mostly in the jejunum of the small intestine. The thiamin phosphor–esters are completely hydrolyzed by intestinal phosphatases, and are present in the lumen of the intestine in free form. At low intestinal concentrations, active transport occurs. At higher concentrations, a passive diffusion system appears to be active.[2]

The biologically active form of thiamin is the coenzyme thiamin pyrophosphate (TPP). Thiamin, in the form of TPP, is essential for the metabolism of carbohydrates and proteins (branched-chain amino acids). Thiamin pyrophosphate also functions in the transketolase reaction of the pentose phosphate shunt, and it is believed that thiamin, in the form of thiamin triphosphate, plays a role in nerve conduction.[3]

Early symptoms of a thiamin deficiency include anorexia and an associated reduction in weight gain.[4] These nonspecific symptoms are similar to the symptoms of several other vitamin deficiencies. Other deficiency symptoms include a depression in body temperature, occasional vomiting, a flabby heart, bradycardia, hypertrophy of the heart, myocardial degeneration, and sudden death associated with heart failure. Transketolase activity has also been noted to be decreased in response to a thiamin deficiency. The most widely used and best functional test of thiamin status is the assay for erythrocyte transketolase.

Most cereal grains are rich in thiamin. However, thiamin is very heat sensitive and is easily destroyed during feed processing, especially in the presence of reducing sugars. Meat, milk, and egg products also contain significant amounts of thiamin.[1]

RIBOFLAVIN

Riboflavin was originally known as vitamin B_2, or ovoflavin. It was isolated from egg white and shown to be effective in promoting growth in rats. Dietary forms of riboflavin are mostly coenzyme derivatives that are released in the stomach and hydrolyzed by phosphatases in the small intestine. Riboflavin is absorbed by a specialized transport mechanism in the proximal small intestine. Intestinal absorption of riboflavin appears to be increased by the presence of food in the intestine.[5,6]

Riboflavin participates in metabolism as a component of flavin adenine dinucleotide (FAD) and flavin mononucleotide (FMN). As a component of FAD and FMN, riboflavin functions as a catalyst for a number of redox reactions that are critical in the metabolism of carbohydrates, proteins, and fats.[1]

Symptoms of riboflavin deficiency include a reduction in growth rate, stiffness of gait, alopecia (hair loss), seborrhea (crusty exudates), vomiting, and cataracts. Other deficiency symptoms that have been observed are increased blood neutrophil granulocytes, reduced immune response, discolored kidney and liver tissue, fatty liver, and degeneration of the myelin of the sciatic and brachial nerves. Females with severe deficiency have also been

Encyclopedia of Animal Science
DOI: 10.1081/E-EAS 120019835

shown to have collapsed follicles and degenerating ova.[5,6]

Riboflavin in feedstuffs is primarily in the form of proteins complexed with FMN and FAD. Riboflavin is found in small amounts in most plant and animal products. Organ meats and milk products contain higher levels of riboflavin. The riboflavin present in a corn–soybean meal diet was estimated to be 59% bioavailable relative to crystalline riboflavin.[7] Riboflavin photo-degrades in the presence of light, and appreciable amounts of riboflavin may be lost during the processing and storage of cereal grains and feeds.[8]

VITAMIN B$_6$

Vitamin B$_6$ is actually a group of six related compounds. These include pyridoxal, pyridoxine, and pyridoxamine and the 5′-phosphates of each of these compounds. The primary forms of vitamin B$_6$ found in animal tissue are pyridoxal phosphate (PLP) and pyridoxamine phosphate (PMP). In plant tissues, the primary forms of vitamin B$_6$ are pyridoxine and pyridoxine phosphate.[5]

Vitamin B$_6$ is absorbed from the intestinal tract by a nonsaturable, passive process. Absorption takes place mostly in the jejunum of the small intestine. The active form of vitamin B$_6$ is primarily pyridoxal phosphate (PLP), which serves as a coenzyme in many metabolic reactions. Pyridoxal phosphate is needed in amino acid metabolism, and to a lesser extent in carbohydrate and lipid metabolism. The role of PLP in lipid metabolism is as \yet unclear, but it has been shown that carcasses of deficient animals contain less lipid than those of controls.[5,9]

As with many other vitamins, a deficiency of vitamin B$_6$ results in a reduction in feed intake and growth rate. Other deficiency symptoms that have been observed include the development of brown exudates around the eyes, impaired vision, vomiting, ataxia, epileptiform seizures, coma, and death. Examination of blood samples taken from deficient animals has revealed microcytic hypochromic anemia; a reduction in albumin, hematocrit, hemoglobin, red blood cells, and lymphocytes; and an increase in gamma globulin. Other signs characteristic of vitamin B$_6$ deficiency determined at necropsy include degeneration of sensory neurons and fat infiltration of the liver.[1,5,10] A reduction in antibody production as a result of vitamin B$_6$ deficiency has also been noted. Clinical signs of a vitamin B$_6$ deficiency in young, growing animals appear within 2 to 3 weeks following the removal of the vitamin from the diet.[5] Toxicity signs, such as ataxia, muscle weakness, neuropathy, and loss of balance, have been reported.[5,10] The assay for apotyrosine decarboxyl-ase activity has been suggested as the method of choice in assessing vitamin B$_6$ status.[5]

Vitamin B$_6$ occurs in feedstuffs as pyridoxine, pyridoxal, pyridoxamine, and pyridoxal phosphate. For the chick, vitamin B$_6$ is about 40% bioavailable in corn and about 60% bioavailable in soybean meal.[11] Vitamin B$_6$ concentrations are fairly high in most cereal grains and common feed ingredients. Vitamin B$_6$ is normally present in adequate amounts and does not require supplementation. However, feed processing and storage can result in the destruction of 10% to 50% of the naturally occurring vitamin B$_6$ activity.[1]

CONCLUSION

Thiamin, riboflavin, and vitamin B$_6$ play important roles in the metabolism and efficient utilization of nutrients. These vitamins are involved in the metabolism of fats, proteins (amino acids), and carbohydrates. They are also involved in nerve conduction, vision, and heart function. Thiamin, riboflavin, and vitamin B$_6$ are present in plant and animal products, but the availability of the naturally occurring vitamins varies considerably. Pure forms of these vitamins are normally supplemented in the diets of monogastric species. Under normal production practices, ruminant animals can produce enough of these vitamins in the rumen to meet the animal's needs.

REFERENCES

1. Dove, C.R. Water-Soluble Vitamins in Swine Nutrition. In *Swine Nutrition*, 2nd Ed.; Lewis, A.J., Southern, L.L., Eds.; CRC Press: New York, 2001; 315–356.
2. Rindi, G. Thiamin. In *Present Knowledge in Nutrition*, 7th Ed.; Ziegler, E.E., Filer, L.J., Jr., Eds.; ILSI Press: Washington, DC, 1996; 160–166.
3. Bettendorff, L.; Kolb, H.A.; Schoffeniels, E. Thiamine triphosphate activated an anion channel of large unit conductance in neuroblastoma cells. J. Membr. Biol. **1993**, *136*, 281–288.
4. Hughes, E.H. The minimum requirement of thiamine for the growing pig. J. Nutr. **1940**, *2*, 239–241.
5. Standing Committee on the Scientific Evaluation of Dietary Reference Intakes and Its Panel on Folate, Other B Vitamins, and Choline and Subcommittee on Upper Reference Levels of Nutrients Food and Nutrition Board Institute of Medicine. *Dietary Reference Intakes for Thiamin, Riboflavin, Niacin, Vitamin B$_6$, Folate, Vitamin B$_{12}$, Pantothenic Acid, Biotin and Choline (1999)*; National Academy Press: Washington, DC, 2000.
6. McCormick, D.B. Riboflavin. In *Modern Nutrition in Health and Disease*, 8th Ed.; Skils, M.E., Olson, J.A.,

Shike, M., Eds.; Lea and Febiger: Philadelphia, 1994; 366–375.

7. Chung, T.K.; Baker, D.H. Riboflavin requirement of chicks fed purified amino acid and conventional corn–soybean meal diets. Poultry Sci. **1990**, *69*, 1357.

8. Rivlin, R.S. Riboflavin. In *Present Knowledge in Nutrition*, 7th Ed.; Ziegler, E.E., Filer, L.J., Jr., Eds.; ILSI Press: Washington, DC, 1996; 167–173.

9. Sauberlich, H.E. Biochemical Systems and Biochemical Detection of Deficiency. In *The Vitamins: Chemistry,* *Physiology, Pathology, Assay*, 2nd Ed.; Sebrell, W.H., Jr., Harris, R.S., Eds.; Academic Press: New York, 1968; Vol. 2, 44–80.

10. Leklem, J.E. Vitamin B_6. In *Present Knowledge in Nutrition*, 7th Ed.; Ziegler, E.E., Filer, L.J., Jr., Eds.; ILSI Press: Washington, DC, 1996; 174–183.

11. Yen, J.T.; Jensen, A.H.; Baker, D.H. Assessment of the concentration of biologically available vitamin B_6 in corn and soybean meal. J. Anim. Sci. **1976**, *42*, 866–870.

Water

Michael S. Brown
West Texas A&M University, Canyon, Texas, U.S.A.

N. Andy Cole
United States Department of Agriculture, Agricultural Research Service, Bushland, Texas, U.S.A.

L. Wayne Greene
Texas A&M University, Amarillo, Texas, U.S.A.

INTRODUCTION

The importance of water to mammalian life is highlighted by water constituting 98 to 99% of the molecules in the body. Animals may derive needed water from numerous sources such as water contained in or on feedstuffs, snow, ice, drinking water contained in surface or underground supplies, and oxidation of nutrients. Animals can lose water by excretion in urine and feces, by secretion in products such as milk and eggs, and through the insensible losses of perspiration and respiration. This article discusses the fundamental chemistry of water, water partitioning in the body, and the influences of dehydration during animal transport and water mineral composition on water balance and performance of ruminants.

CHEMISTRY OF WATER

Water functions as a critical solvent for ions and metabolites involved in osmoregulation and for digestion, metabolism, absorption, transport, and excretion of nutrients. The unequal sharing of electrons in a water molecule facilitates interaction between polar and ionic groups on molecules, and contributes to water possessing the highest dielectric constant among common solvents.[1] The dielectric constant represents the effectiveness of a solvent to reduce attraction between oppositely charged molecules by surrounding each charged species with a layer of (water) molecules, allowing the charged species to coexist in solution.[1] As a result of these characteristics, water can generally move freely between body water compartments in response to hydrostatic and osmotic pressure exerted by minerals, protein, and other ions. The high heat of vaporization (9.72 kcal/mole) and high heat capacity (1.00 cal/gram per 1°C) of water confer the ability to dissipate heat effectively and buffer core body temperature by absorbing large amounts of heat.

BODY WATER

Water content of the body is a function of body composition, and body composition varies with species, stage of production, and body condition. Body water content of animals range from approximately 40 to 80% of body weight. Neonates and lean, growing animals have the highest body water content, whereas obese animals have less body water due to displacement by adipose tissue. Adipose tissue and bone contain approximately 20% water, whereas other tissues in the body typically contain 70 to 80% water.

Total body water is partitioned into that contained within cells (intracellular) and that located outside cells (extracellular; Fig. 1). The intracellular pool comprises approximately 60% of body water and the remainder is in the extracellular pool. Extracellular water is further divided into the interstitial, plasma, and transcellular pools. Fluids contained in the digestive tract, cerebrospinal and synovial fluid, aqueous humor of the eye, bile, and renal filtrate compose transcellular fluid. The plasma pool normally represents approximately 5 to 7% of body weight, and the interstitial pool represents approximately 15% of body weight.

FATE OF INGESTED WATER

Recommendations for drinking water needs by several livestock species have been recently addressed.[2] However, majority of water in the rumen seems to be derived from saliva. Saliva secretion by cattle depends on feed intake (thus, animal weight and stage of production) and dietary forage content and form, but can range from approximately 30 to 300 L/day. However, water is also transferred rapidly from plasma and other extracellular spaces to the gastrointestinal tract in ruminants during a meal.[3] Limited data[4] suggest that only 60 to 80% of water consumed by drinking may be delivered to the

Encyclopedia of Animal Science
DOI: 10.1081/E-EAS 120019836

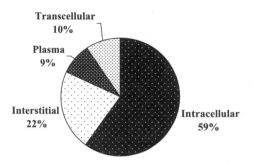

Fig. 1 Typical body water compartments (% of total body water).

rumen; the remaining proportion is presumably directed to the omasum. Within the remainder of the ruminant gut, quantitative net water absorption is greatest in the proximal small intestine, followed by the omasum and large intestine.[5] Recent data[6] indicate that the lower net water absorption in the large intestine by cattle than by sheep results from a reduced ability to retain absorbed water because more absorbed solvent/solute is drawn back into the lumen through the larger paracellular pores between colonic cells in cattle.

TRANSPORTATION-INDUCED DEHYDRATION

Transport of animals on semitrailer trucks from the site of birth to the site of growing and finishing can involve periods of up to 24 hours or more without access to water, and variable magnitudes of dehydration can occur. Feeder calves seem to lose approximately 3.3% of body weight during the loading and unloading process and can lose an additional 0.3 to 0.4% of body weight/hour of transport.[7,8] Weight losses of feeder pigs during transport can be up to 0.6% of body weight/hour.[9] Loss of gastrointestinal tract contents and carcass weight has accounted for 48 and 32%, respectively, of transport shrink by feeder steers[8] and has accounted for 62 and 27%, respectively, of transport weight loss by feeder pigs. Feces, urine, and respiration accounted for 12.6, 26, and 60% of the water loss.[10] Water accounted for 80% of weight lost by wethers during 48 hours of feed and water deprivation.[11] Of total body water loss, 57% was from the intracellular compartment and 29% was from the gastrointestinal tract. In steers deprived of water for 4 days, thiocyanate space (assumed to be extracellular space) accounted for 47% of the weight lost (total loss=16% of body weight).[12] Thiocyanate space decreased 23% and plasma volume decreased 28% during the 4-day period without water. The exchange of water within the body in response to dehydration is depicted in Fig. 2.

Water Mineral Composition

Drinking water is a source of various minerals that are generally readily available for absorption unless complexed by an interfering nutrient. Minerals ingested in water and feed are a variable mix of positively and negatively charged ions that contribute to the dietary cation–anion difference of consumed material (DCAD) and have a direct influence on fluid and acid–base balance. The DCAD is calculated as the milliequivalents (mEq) of Na^+, K^+, Ca^{++}, and Mg^{++} minus the mEq of Cl^-, $S^=$, and $P^=$.[13] As anion consumption and concentration in the body increase, cellular acidosis can occur. As the DCAD increases from negative to positive (e.g., -20 to $+100$ mEq/kg), feed intake and performance are generally increased. However, the prepartum dairy cow is one exception to the generalization. Inducing mild metabolic acidosis by feeding anionic diets before calving has been an effective means of preventing milk fever by potentiating calcium resorption from bone before the dramatic calcium needs at parturition arise.[13]

Few data are available on the contribution of water minerals to overall DCAD. Socha et al.[14] reported average mineral profiles of more than 3600 drinking water

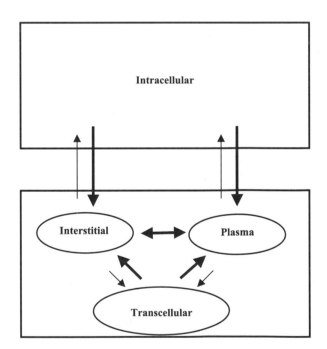

Fig. 2 Water change between body compartments during dehydration. Water is osmotically drawn from transcellular and intracellular compartments to interstitial and plasma compartments during dehydration, in response to losses by urinary and fecal excretion and insensible routes. The magnitude of reduction in compartmental volumes is dependent on the degree of dehydration.

samples collected across the United States. Assuming that a growing feedlot steer weighing approximately 300 kg and consuming 9 kg of a mixed diet (>85% dry matter) meeting mineral requirements would drink 30 L of water/day,[2] this steer would consume twice as much weight in water compared to the weight of feed consumed, and approximately 3 to 7% of calcium, sodium, and sulfur consumed would be derived from water. However, approximately 20% of chloride consumed would be derived from drinking water in this example. The DCAD calculated for the surveyed samples[14] was approximately 0.4 mEq/kg. Estimates of the contribution of drinking water minerals to overall DCAD are needed.

CONCLUSION

The polarity and ability of water to facilitate hydration of polar and ionic molecules are central to the flow of water and metabolites within the body. Saliva appears to be a greater proportion of ruminal fluid than previously thought, considering recent observations that some water consumed by drinking in nonsuckling cattle bypasses the rumen, but more intensive study is needed. The ability of sheep to form drier feces than cattle results from tighter junctions between colonic cells and a greater ability to establish an osmotic gradient to retain absorbed water. Cattle may lose approximately 3% of body weight during loading and unloading for transport, plus an additional 0.3 to 0.4% of body weight per hour of transport. Indirect data suggest that water may constitute up to 80% of this weight loss. Estimates of the contribution of drinking water minerals to overall cation–anion difference and of the influence of water cation–anion difference on animal performance are needed.

REFERENCES

1. Bohinsky, R.C. *Modern Concepts in Biochemistry*, 5th Ed.; Allyn and Bacon, Inc.: Boston, MA, 1987.

2. Parker, D.B.; Brown, M.S. Water Consumption for Livestock and Poultry Production. In *Encyclopedia of Water Science*, 1st Ed.; Stewart, B.A., Howell, T.A., Eds.; Marcel Dekker, Inc.: New York, NY, 2003.

3. Christopherson, R.J.; Webster, A.J.F. Changes during eating in oxygen consumption, cardiac function and body fluids of sheep. J. Physiol. **1972**, *221*, 441–457.

4. Zorrilla-Rios, J.J.; Garza, D.; Owens, F.N. *Fate of Drinking Water in Ruminants: Simultaneous Comparison of Two Methods to Estimate Ruminal Evasion*; Animal Science Research Report MP-129; Oklahoma Agricultural Experiment Station: Stillwater, OK, 1990; 167–169.

5. Sklan, D.; Hurwitz, S. Movement and absorption of major minerals and water in ovine gastrointestinal tract. J. Dairy Sci. **1985**, *68*, 1659–1666.

6. McKie, A.T.; Goecke, I.A.; Naftalin, R.J. Comparison of fluid absorption by bovine and ovine descending colon in vitro. Am. J. Physiol. **1991**, *261*, G433–G442.

7. Bartle, S.J.; Preston, R.L. *Feedlot Cattle Receiving Experiments, 1988–89*; Animal Science Research Report # T-5-263; Texas Tech University: Lubbock, TX, 1989; 28–30.

8. Self, H.L.; Gay, N. Shrink during shipment of feeder cattle. J. Anim. Sci. **1972**, *35*, 489–494.

9. Jesse, G.W.; Weiss, C.N.; Mayes, H.F.; Zinn, G.M. Effect of marketing treatments and transportation on feeder pig performance. J. Anim. Sci. **1990**, *68*, 611–617.

10. Mayes, H.F.; Hahn, G.L.; Becker, B.A.; Anderson, M.E.; Nienaber, J.A. A report on the effect of fasting and transportation on liveweight losses, carcass weight losses and heat production measures of slaughter hogs. Appl. Eng. Agric. **1988**, *4*, 254–258.

11. Cole, N.A. Influence of a three-day feed and water deprivation period on gut fill, tissue weights, and tissue composition in mature wethers. J. Anim. Sci. **1995**, *73*, 2548–2557.

12. Weeth, H.J.; Sawhney, D.S.; Lesperance, A.L. Changes in body fluids, excreta and kidney function of cattle deprived of water. J. Anim. Sci. **1967**, *26*, 418–423.

13. Goff, J. Factors to Concentrate on to Prevent Periparturient Disease in the Dairy Cow, Proceedings of the Mid-South Ruminant Nutrition Conference, Texas Agricultural Extension Service: College Station, TX, 1998; 63.

14. Socha, M.T.; Ensley, S.M.; Tomlinson, D.J.; Ward, T. Water composition variability may affect performance. Feedstuffs **2003**, *75* (24), 10.

Water Buffalo

Nguyen van Thu
Cantho University, Can Tho City, Vietnam

INTRODUCTION

The water buffalo is considered to be a very useful animal in many countries, supplying draft power, meat, milk, and other by-products such as hides, horn, etc. The water buffalo is closely associated with water or mud, and with smallholder farmers in the rice fields. In recent years, buffalo production has developed well, not only in Asia, but also in Europe, South America, and other continents where the buffalo has been introduced. This article aims to introduce some basic knowledge of the water buffalo, with an emphasis on its great contribution to our living standards and improved productivity that could be better exploited for a more sustainable agriculture development in the 21st century.

TAXONOMY AND TYPES

The world's buffaloes are classified into two groups, the African and the Asian, with genus names *Syncerus* and *Bubalus*, respectively. According to the zoological classification,[1] buffaloes belong to the class Mammalia, subclass Ungulata, order Artiodactila, suborder Ruminantia, family Bovidae, subfamily Bovinae, tribe Bovini. The tribe Bovini includes three groups: *Bovina* (cattle), Bubalina (the Asian buffalo), and *Syncerina* (the African buffalo). The Asian and African buffaloes are generally similar, but there are some anatomic differences. The African buffalo includes only one species, *Syncerus caffer*, while the Asian buffalo comprises three species: Anoa (*Bubalus depressicornis*) from the Island of Celebes, Tamarao (*Bubalus mindorensis*) from the Island of Mindoro, and Arni (*Bubalus Arnee*), or the Indian wild buffalo. Of these four species of African and Asian buffalo, only the India Arni buffalo has been domesticated and given the species name *bubalis*. Therefore, the domestic buffalo currently reared with the name of water buffalo is classified as *bubalus bubalis*. It is believed that the domestication of the buffalo occurred about 5000 years ago on the Indian subcontinent, and the domestication of the Swamp buffalo took place in China about 1000 years later.

The water buffalo can be classified into two breed types, the River type (2n = 50) and the Swamp type (2n = 48). River breeds consist of: 1) Asian breeds such as those in India and Pakistan (including Murrah, Nili Ravi, Surti, etc.; and 2) Mediterranean breeds found in Italy, Romania, and the Middle East. The skin of River buffaloes is black, but some specimens have a dark slate-colored skin. The horns of the River buffalo grow downward and backward, then curve upward in a spiral. The Swamp type is found mainly in China and Southeast Asia. The skin of the Swamp buffaloes is gray at birth, but becomes slate blue later. Albinoid Swamp buffaloes are quite common in some areas, for example, in the north of Thailand. Normally, the horns of Swamp buffaloes are longer than those of the River buffaloes, grow outward, and curve in a semicircle. More than 70% of the buffaloes in the world belong to the River type.[2]

MEAT, MILK, AND DRAFT ATTRIBUTES

In general, the River types are mainly used for milk in South Asian countries, while the Swamp types are used for draft power in Southeast Asian countries and China (Table 1). However, both the River and Swamp types have been used for multiple purposes such as work, milk, meat, manure, fuel, etc. by small farmers in different crop–livestock farming systems. In addition, crossbreeding programs of the River and Swamp buffaloes have shown great potential for improving meat, work, and milk outputs. Recently, the U.S. Department of Agriculture (USDA) estimated the nutritional value of water buffalo meat and compared it to beef and chicken. The findings showed that water buffalo meat has 41% less cholesterol, 92% less fat, and 56% fewer calories than traditional beef. Furthermore, there are as yet no reports on the occurrence of bovine spongiform encephalopathy (BSE), also known as mad cow disease, in buffaloes in any part of Asia.[4]

The milk yield of the buffalo is lower than that of cattle, and average milk production is 1500 kg per lactation. However, some individuals can produce 3500 kg per lactation. Buffalo milk has high nutritive value and is excellent for the preparation of dairy products. Using

Encyclopedia of Animal Science
DOI: 10.1081/E-EAS 120019837

Table 1 Plowing and harrowing performance of swamp buffaloes in the Mekong delta, Vietnam

Criteria	Sex	
	Female (n[a] = 24) Mean ± std	Male (n[a] = 24) Mean ± std
Plowing time[b] (hrs/day)	5.35 ± 0.58	5.39 ± 0.31
Plowed area (ha/pair/day)	0.29 ± 0.025	0.31 ± 0.035
Harrowing time[b] (hrs/day)	5.05 ± 0.17	5.28 ± 0.30
Harrowed area (ha/pair/day)	0.73 ± 0.167	0.77 ± 0.170

[a]In pair.
[b]With a break.
(From Ref. 3.)

buffaloes for a single purpose makes them less competitive with cattle and tractors. This is believed to be an important reason for the serious decline of the buffalo population in a number of Southeast Asian countries, including some parts of Vietnam. Alexiev reported that the Swamp-type Wenzhou buffalo in China can give an average milk yield of 1030 kg per 280-day lactation.[2] Thus, milk production of the Swamp buffalo is sufficient for family consumption. In addition, the Swamp buffalo provides draft power, and thus has potential in rural areas of China and Southeast Asian countries. In Europe and the Near East, the main purpose of raising buffaloes is for milk. Milk can be used for liquid consumption and making different cheeses or yogurt, particularly in Italy, where most of the buffalo milk is used for making a well-known cheese called Italian Mozarella, which retails at a very high price.[5,6]

The total number of buffalo in the World in 2002 was about 167,126,000 and it is increasing, particularly in India, China, Brazil, etc., where the River buffaloes are raised. However, there is a serious reduction of the Swamp buffalo population in some countries such as Thailand, Malaysia, and Cambodia due to mechanization, over-slaughtering for meat, and other reasons (Table 2).

In many cases, knowledge from studies on cattle can also be applied to buffalo research and practices. However, differences in anatomy, physiology, feeding behavior, reproductive characteristics, and productivity between the species have been reported.[8] The water buffalo is a ruminant, and the rumen–reticulum of buffaloes is similar to that of cattle. However, it is heavier than in cattle and 5–10% more capacious.[9] Studies comparing buffaloes to cattle have suggested a higher feed intake, longer retention time of feed in the digestive tract, longer rumination, less depression of cellulose digestion by soluble carbohydrates, a wider range of plant preferences, and a higher population of cellulolytic bacteria.[9] However, some authors have found no significant difference in feed digestibility between the two species. It was suggested that the better performance of buffaloes fed coarse fodder may not be related to a superior capacity for fiber digestion, but rather that they are less discriminating against plants not readily eaten by cattle. In Colombia, cattle are sometimes first used to graze pasture, whereafter buffaloes are allowed to graze the remaining and less desirable parts of the sward.[10] Recently, in a comparative study on cattle and Swamp buffaloes raised under the same village conditions, some authors reported higher bacteria, lower protozoa, and higher fungal zoospore counts in Swamp buffaloes.[11] It was also found that the Swamp buffalo can adapt better in the acid sulphate soil areas compared to the cattle and goats in the Mekong delta of Vietnam.

Based on results of a number of studies, buffalo might utilize protein more efficiently than cattle.[9] An ability of buffaloes to utilize endogenous urea more efficiently than cattle may explain in part their apparent superiority in utilizing high-fiber and low-nitrogen feed resources. It is concluded that there have been contradictory results for fiber digestion abilities of buffaloes compared to cattle. Buffaloes, however, seem to have a superior ability to consume coarse roughage, perhaps as a result of a better rumination capacity. There is evidence that urea recycling and purine excretion in buffaloes are different from those in cattle, but more comprehensive studies are lacking.

Table 2 Buffalo population (head) in the world and in selected countries (1970–2000)

	1970	1980	1990	2000
World	107,437,984	121,757,733	148,184,210	164,339,658
India	56,118,000	66,070,000	80,570,000	93,772,000
China	15,713,063	18,439,152	21,421,975	22,596,439
Brazil	118,000	495,000	1,397,097	1,102,551
Italy	48,600	88,900	112,400	201,000

(From Ref. 7.)

CONCLUSION

It may be concluded that the water buffalo has a great potential to develop in the future. A number of promising buffalo farming models have been developed in Brazil, Australia, Italy, Philippines, Colombia, etc. Valuable products of water buffaloes, such as milk, meat, draft power, and manure, are relevant for the people and our living environment, particularly with respect to the trend toward organic agriculture in many parts of the world.

REFERENCES

1. Alexiev, A. *The Water Buffalo*; St. Kliment Ohridski University Press: Sofia, 1998.
2. Chantalakhana, C. Long term breeding strategies for genetic improvement of buffaloes in developing countries. Asian-Aust. J. Anim. Sci. **1999**, *12*, 1152–1161.
3. Thu, N.V. A Study of Performance, Physiological Parameters and Economic Efficiency of Working Buffaloes in the Mekong Delta of Vietnam. In *Working Animals in Agriculture and Transport*; Pearson, R.A., Lhoste, P., Saastamoinen, M., Martin-Rosset, W., Eds.; EAAP Technical Series, Wageningen Academic Publisher, 2003; Vol. 6, 165–171.
4. Ranjhan, S.K. A Vision of buffalo production with special reference to milk and meat production. Proc. Symp. Series 1 of the 8th World Conf. Anim. Prod., Seoul, Korea, June 28–July 4, 1998; 263–270.
5. Borghese, A.; Moioli, B.; Tripadi, C. Processing and Product Development in Mediterranean Countries. In *Proceedings of the Third Asian Buffalo Congress, Kandy, Sri Lanka*, 2000; 37–46.
6. Chantalakhana, C. Long term breeding strategies for genetic improvement of buffaloes in developing countries. Asian-Aust. J. Anim. Sci. **1999**, *12* (7), 1152–1161.
7. FAO. *Live Animals. FAOstat Agriculture Data*; 2003. http://apps.fao.org/page/collections?subset=agriculture.
8. Cockrill, W.R. *The Husbandry and Health of Domestic Buffalo*; FAO: Rome, 1974.
9. Khajarern, S.; Khajarern, J.M. Feeding Swamp Buffalo for Milk Production. In *Feeding Dairy Cows in the Tropics*; FAO Animal Production and Health Paper, Wageningen Academic Publishers: The Netherlands, 1991; Vol. 86, 115–125.
10. Thu, N.V. A Study of the Use of Female Cattle and Buffalo Crusing Sugar Cane in Colombia. M.Sc. Thesis; Swedish University of Agricultural Sciences: Uppsala, Sweden, Food and Agriculture of the United Nations, 1994.
11. Wanapat, M.; Ngarmsang, A.; Korkhuntot, S.; Nontaso, N.; Wachirapakorn, C.; Keakes, G.; Rowlinson, P. A comparative study on the rumen microbial population of cattle and Swamp buffalo raised under traditional village conditions in the Northeast of Thailand. Asian-Aust. J. Anim. Sci. **2000**, *13* (7), 918–921.

Well-Being and Handling

Temple Grandin
Colorado State University, Fort Collins, Colorado, U.S.A.

INTRODUCTION

Reducing stress during handling for procedures such as vaccinations, milking, and herding will improve both animal welfare and productivity. Pigs and dairy cows that are afraid of people have reduced productivity. Pigs have lower weight gains and fewer piglets and dairy cows produce less milk. Fearfulness was assessed by measuring the animal's willingness to approach people. Cows on dairies where the employees had received training in stockmanship and animal behavior had a smaller flight zone and gave more milk.[1] The trained employees engaged in fewer negative interactions with the cows, such as hitting or yelling. Further studies have shown that wild, excitable cattle that become highly agitated in the squeeze chute had lower weight gains,[2] poor beef quality, and tougher meat.

BIOLOGICAL BASIS OF FEAR

Fear is a strong stressor and it can be detrimental to both productivity and welfare. People working with animals should take steps to reduce the animal's fear. Other stressors such as weather extremes often cannot be avoided, but livestock producers can easily reduce fear.

Fear is a basic emotion and it motivates animals to avoid predators. The amygdala is the brain's fear center.[3] If the amygdala is destroyed, the animal will no longer become fearful of things that would normally cause fear, such as sudden loud noise. It also loses learned fear responses. An example of a learned fear response is refusing to enter a squeeze chute for vaccinations because the cow was accidentally hit on the head by the headgate. In wild animals that are not accustomed to handling, destruction of the amygdala will make them act tame.

INDICATORS OF FEARFULNESS

One indicator of fearfulness in grazing animals is the size of the flight zone. Animals with larger flight zones are more fearful. Another indicator is the startle response to a sudden stimulus such as a firecracker. Some other behavioral indicators of fear are a cow struggling in a squeeze chute, sweating in horses when there is little physical exertion, flapping in caged layers, and a horse rearing when he is suddenly startled. Isolation is a strong stressor, and a single cow or lamb may run into a fence or try to jump it when it is separated from its herdmates.

Physiological measures such as cortisol in the blood can also be used as indicators of fear stress that occurs during nonpainful restraint in a squeeze chute.[4] Cortisol is a time-dependent measure and it takes 10 to 20 minutes for it to reach peak levels. It is important to differentiate between fear and pain stress. Cortisol levels can also rise in response to pain from procedures such as hot iron branding. The variable of the handling stress needs to be separated from the variable of pain caused by a procedure such as castration. Handling stress is mostly fear, and stress from castration is caused by pain and injury to tissues.

VARIATIONS IN HANDLING STRESS

Fear stress during handling can vary from almost none to extreme. Extensively raised cattle that were not accustomed to close contact with people had much higher cortisol levels when they were restrained in a squeeze chute compared to hand-reared dairy cattle.[5] Taming of an animal may reduce physiological reactivity of the nervous system. Hand-reared deer that were raised in close contact with people had significantly lower cortisol levels after restraint than free-range deer.[6]

There are three basic variables that will affect both the intensity of fear stress during handling and the size of the animal's flight zone. They are: 1) genetic factors; 2) amount of contact with people; and 3) previous experiences with handling that can be either aversive or nonaversive.

GENETIC FACTORS

The domestic phenotype has reduced responses to changes in its environment.[7] Several studies have shown that there are differences in how different breeds of cattle react to handling. Brahman cattle had higher cortisol levels after restraint than crosses of the English breeds such as

Encyclopedia of Animal Science
DOI: 10.1081/E-EAS 120019847

Hereford or Angus. Some genetic lines of cattle, pigs, or chickens are more likely to be extremely agitated during handling.

Animals that have flighty, excitable, high-fear genetics are more likely to become highly agitated when they are suddenly placed in a new situation, compared to animals with a calmer temperament. Flighty animals have to be introduced more gradually to new things to avoid agitation and panic, compared to animals with a calmer temperament.

An experiment by Ted Friend showed that measurements of epinephrine (adrenalin) showed that some pigs habituated to a novel, nonpainful swimming task where they were suddenly placed in a pool of water. The task was repeated over a series of days. In some of the pigs, the elevated epinephrine levels returned to normal and in other individuals, the epinephrine levels remained high. Some of the pigs lost their fear of swimming and others remained scared. Genetic factors may have accounted for these differences.

EFFECT OF PREVIOUS EXPERIENCES

An animal's previous experiences with handling will affect how it will react in the future. Cattle that had been accidentally bumped on the head in a squeeze chute were more reluctant to reenter the chute a month later. Sheep that had been turned upside down in a restraint device were more reluctant to reenter the facility the following year compared to sheep that were restrained in an upright position.[8]

It is important that an animal's first experience with a new person or new place be a good one. Progressive ranchers walk cows and calves through the corrals prior to doing procedures so that they will associate corrals with being fed. Sometimes painful procedures have to be done, but it is recommended that they not be associated with the animal's first experience with either a new person or a new place. A rat experiment indicated that if a rat was shocked severely the first time it entered a new arm on a maze, it would never enter that arm again. However, if the rat was fed the first time he went into the new arm and then subjected to gradually increasing shocks, he would keep entering the arm to get the food.[9]

FEAR MEMORIES

If an animal is subjected to either a frightening or a painful experience, it may form a permanent fear memory that cannot be erased.[3] This memory is formed in the lower subcortical pathway in the brain, and extinguishing the conditioned fear is difficult because it has to be suppressed by an active learning process that requires input from higher parts of the cortex. The fear memory is suppressed by the cortex, but it can sometimes reappear. Careful, quiet handling of animals will help prevent the formation of fear memories that may compromise welfare, lower productivity, or cause behavior problems, as in horses. Animals can associate certain types of clothing or a person's voice with either a frightening or a painful experience. Animals also have the ability to recognize the voice of a familiar safe person who can calm them down.

FEAR OF NOVELTY

New experiences and new things are both scary and attractive to animals. They are attractive when the animal is allowed to voluntarily approach, but frightening when suddenly introduced.[7] If a flag is placed in the middle of a large field, cattle and horses will approach it and investigate. However, if the same flag is suddenly waved next to a horse, he may become highly agitated.[7]

Animals can be trained to tolerate new things if they are gradually introduced. Cattle should become accustomed to being handled and fed by different people in different vehicles. This will help reduce stress when they are moved to a new place. Training animals to tolerate new experiences will help keep them calmer. It is important to train cattle on being moved by both people on foot and people on horses. Cattle appear to perceive a person riding a horse and a person walking on foot as two different things.

TRAIN FOR HANDLING

Training calves and pigs to handling procedures helps to produce calmer adult animals. Pigs differentiate between a person in the aisle and a person in their pens. Pigs will move more easily in and out of trucks and through chutes at a meat plant if the producer trained them by walking through their pens several times each week.

Animals will have the lowest amount of fear stress when they voluntarily cooperate with being restrained and handled. Zoos and aquariums are training animals, such as apes, lions, and dolphins, to cooperate with blood testing and veterinary procedures. Highly excitable Bongo antelope were trained to enter a box and allow blood samples to be taken when they were fed treats. Almost baseline cortisol (stress hormone) levels were obtained. The levels of glucose in the blood of trained animals was significantly lower compared to the same animal immobilized with a dart.[10]

CONCLUSIONS

Reducing fear during handling will improve animal productivity.[1] There are many different stressors that animals encounter such as stimuli that evoke fear, heat stress, cold stress, pain, or fatigue. Fear is a strong stressor and it is one stressor that is easy to reduce. Fearful animals have lower productivity. Animals remember frightening or painful events and producers should be careful to avoid creation of fear memories. An animal's first experience with a new corral or person should be low stress. Training animals to handling procedures will help reduce fear stress. Both animal welfare and productivity will be improved by reducing fear stress.

ARTICLE OF FURTHER INTEREST

Animal Handling-Behavior, p. 22

REFERENCES

1. Hemsworth, P.H.; Coleman, G.J.; Barnett, J.C.; Berg, S.; Dowling, S. The effect of cognitive behavioral interventions on the attitude and behavior of stock persons and the behavior and productivity of commercial dairy cows. J. Anim. Sci. **2002**, *80*, 68–78.

2. Voisinet, B.D.; Grandin, T.; Tatum, J.D.; O'Connor, S.F.; Struthers, J.J. Feedlot cattle with calm temperaments have higher daily weight gains than cattle with excitable temperaments. J. Anim. Sci. *75*, 892–896.

3. LeDoux, J. *The Emotional Brain*; Simon and Schuster: New York, New York, 1996.

4. Grandin, T. Assessment of stress during handling and transport. J. Anim. Sci. **1997**, *75*, 249–257.

5. Lay, D.C.; Friend, T.H.; Bowers, C.C.; Grissom, K.K.; Jenkins, O.C. A comparative physiological and behavioral study of freeze and hot iron branding using dairy cows. J. Anim. Sci. **1992**, *70*, 1121–1125.

6. Hastings, B.E.; Abott, D.E.; George, L.M.; Staler, S.G. Stress Factors influencing plasma cortisol levels and adrenal weights in Chinese water deer. Res. Vet. Sci. **1992**, *53*, 375–380.

7. Grandin, T.; Deesing, M.J. Behavioral Genetics and Animal Science. In *Genetics and the Behavior of Domestic Animals*; Grandin, T., Ed.; Academic Press: San Diego, CA, 1998; 1–30.

8. Hutson, G.D. The influence of barley food rewards on sheep movement through a handling system. Appl. Anim. Behav. Sci. **1985**, *14*, 263–273.

9. Miller, N.E. Learning resistance to pain and fear, effects of over learning exposure and rewarded exposure in context. J. Exp. Psych. **1960**, *60*, 137–142.

10. Phillips, M.; Grandin, T.; Graffam, W.; Irlbeck, N.A.; Cambre, R.C. Crate conditioning of Bongo (*Tragelaptous eurycerus*) for veterinary and husbandry procedures at Denver Zoological Garden. Zoo. Bio. **1998**, *17*, 25–32.

Well-Being Assessment: Behavioral Indicators

J. C. Swanson
M. Rassette
Kansas State University, Manhattan, Kansas, U.S.A.

INTRODUCTION

Animal well-being can be characterized as the harmony an animal is experiencing mentally and physically with its environment. Animal well-being is often used interchangeably with the term animal welfare. Domestic livestock and poultry are raised under a variety of environmental conditions that are vastly different from those of their wild ancestors. The scientific assessment of the well-being of livestock and poultry has become important to the sustainability of raising them for food. The best scientific approach and criteria to assess animal well-being have yet to achieve a scientific consensus, but it is generally accepted that behavior, physiology, health, productivity, cognition, and system ecology are indicators of animal well-being.

BEHAVIORAL INDICATORS

The repertoire of behavior expressed by a domestic animal reflects a living history of its natural and artificial selection. Generally, behavior is used to identify and assess animal needs, preferences, state of health, ability to adapt and cope with its social and physical environment, emotional state, and to gain insight into what an animal may comprehend or feel about its environment.

Several behavioral indicators are commonly cited as useful to understanding and assessing animal well-being including abnormal behavior, posture, vocalization, responsiveness, grooming and displacement behavior, preferences animals express toward features of their living environment, and the presence/absence of stereotypies.

Abnormal Behavior

The use of abnormal behavior as an indicator of well-being requires a clear knowledge of what constitutes normal behavior for a species. Species behavior is sequenced, measured, described, and recorded to construct an ethogram. The ethogram characterizes both instinctive and learned behavior displayed throughout a species' life cycle. Ethograms of wild ancestors, close relatives, or feral members of the same species are useful in studying the behavioral similarities and differences induced by domestication. An example of abnormal behavior is an outbreak of tail biting in pigs. The interpretation of behavior elicited under domestic conditions is complicated and requires that we understand the cause, developmental aspects, and function of the behavior within the construct of the evolutionary and domestic history of the species.

Posture

The posture of an animal represents a coping response to a stimulus. Posture is often coupled with other behavioral indicators such as vocalization and locomotion to assess well-being. Researchers have studied the usefulness of posture to correctly assess the amount of pain and distress an animal may experience after being subjected to common animal management procedures. For example, a behavioral method using posture was validated to assess acute pain associated with different castration procedures used on lambs.[1] Each procedure was ranked according to an established index of expected pain. Physiologic and behavioral data (including posture) were then collected for a period of 60 minutes postprocedure. The data were analyzed according to the ability to place a lamb into the correct procedure group. A combination of behavior and posture data correctly placed 79% of the lambs into their respective treatment groups.[1]

As technology advances, so too does the sophistication of using an animal's posture or movement for assessing well-being. For example, computer image analysis has been used to measure the severity of head movements of cattle undergoing various types of branding to measure their aversion to the procedure,[2] and to evaluate the thermal comfort of pigs based on their proximity to one another.[3] While assessments must be validated for other species and for different types of practices, postural measures appear to be useful behavioral indicators of well-being.

Vocalization

Animals convey a range of emotional states through various types of vocalizations. Vocalizations are context-

Encyclopedia of Animal Science
DOI: 10.1081/E-EAS 120019844

specific, and the circumstances under which vocalizations are emitted must be carefully considered. For example, a recent study compared the vocalizing of cattle in slaughter plants before and after modifications were made in animal handling procedures.[4] The data were used to evaluate the effectiveness of the plant modifications. Indeed, a reduction in observable aversive events (prod use, slippage, excessive restraint pressure) decreased the amount of vocalization behavior.[4] Other researchers have found similar uses for vocalization in different species. One study measured the occurrence and frequency of calls in piglets being castrated, and found a significantly greater rate of high-frequency calls (>1000 Hz) compared with controls who were handled similarly but not actually castrated.[5] The researchers were able to isolate the most painful part of the procedure itself, and the effect these vocalizations had on other piglets, both of which have important implications for well-being.

Responsiveness

The degree of an animal's responsiveness to stimuli also acts as an indicator of well-being. For example, the attitudes and behavior of dairy stockpersons toward cows have been researched and a correlation found between the stockperson's behaviors and the avoidance distance of cows.[6] Avoidance behavior can shed light on an animal's past relationship with humans and reflect the well-being of individuals or groups. Another example of responsiveness as an indicator of well-being comes from a study using tonic immobility.[7] Tonic immobility is a state of petrification induced by positioning a bird on its back or side—consequently, no movement is detected for a given period of time. The time until the bird recovers head movement, stands, and walks is measured. Shorter latencies to recovery indicate a better coping response by the bird. Reduced or absent responsiveness of an animal has been recognized as an indicator of poor well-being.

Grooming and Displacement Behaviors

Grooming as a social and self-maintenance behavior can reflect the relative well-being of an individual or an entire group. Disruption or abnormal manifestations of grooming are measurable events. The lack of grooming, indicated by poor hair/fur coat or feather condition, is often used as an indicator of sickness or depression for individual animals. Abnormal pulling of hair/fur or feathers or obsessive grooming activities may occur in individuals or within groups. Both are considered abnormal.

A displacement behavior is the result of frustration or behavioral disinhibition, or is performed when an animal is in conflict with how to behave in a given set of

circumstances. For example, abnormal feather pecking in laying hens may be the displaced behavior of natural foraging or dustbathing and has been used to assess different housing conditions of egg-laying hens.[8] Feather pecking in hens can lead to significant feather loss or even skin damage. Thus, the occurrence of displacement behavior and abnormal forms of grooming can be measured and used to assess well-being.

Preferences

Preference tests are valuable tools to evaluate stimuli or conditions by appealing to the desires of the animal. For example, such tests can be used to assess the effects on well-being of different enrichment devices or housing conditions. In one study, researchers tested the preferences of dairy cattle for different kinds of flooring—sand, straw, or a soft rubber mat.[9] The cows avoided sand and preferred either the mat or straw. The researchers then tested whether a preference existed between the mat and straw. They found that cattle preferred straw in winter, but in summer, cows showed no special preference for one system over the other. Preference testing of this type allows for better design of housing systems. However, extreme care must be taken when designing and drawing conclusions from such tests. For example, exposure to resource cues can affect the performance of an animal in preference tests.[10] Cues such as odors can be undetectable to humans, but obvious to animals. Carefully controlled preference tests are useful in validating the needs and choices of animals.

Stereotypies

Stereotypy is a common abnormal behavior observed in intensively farmed species and thought to be the product of impoverished environments. Stereotypies are behavior patterns repeated without variation and appear to have no obvious goal or function. Examples include bar-biting; fur, hair, or wool chewing; sham chewing; tongue lolling; and a variety of locomotion patterns such as head-weaving. Once developed, stereotypies can be difficult to extinguish, even when animals are moved into more enriched environments. This indicates an addictive quality to the behavior that requires an understanding of its neurophysiological development. Performance of stereotypic behavior is often cited as an indicator of poor well-being.

Researchers have studied stereotypies in nearly all farmed species, including those farmed for fur, such as mink raised in cages.[11] Potential remedies such as environmental enrichment are often explored to provide relief. However, the view that all stereotypies indicate poor well-being is controversial.[12–14] Performance of stereotypy could also indicate excitement or anticipation of a resource. Thus, stereotypic behaviors are complex and must be fully examined to determine the effect on well-being.

Although the motivation to stereotype in domestic species has been researched, the neurophysiological implications are only beginning to be elucidated. For example, recent studies have linked altered brain functioning and enhanced frustration to stereotypies found in caged birds.[15] Greater understanding of the disruption to brain function could eventually adjudicate the competing views on stereotypic behavior. At present, the exhibition of stereotypies in domestic animals should prompt a closer look at other well-being indicators to further assess the possibility of a poor state of well-being.

CONCLUSION

Behavior is one of several indicators used to assess animal well-being. There is still much to be learned about the behavior of our domestic livestock and poultry and what constitutes a state of good well-being or contentment. Although scientific consensus has not been reached regarding good versus poor well-being, there is general agreement that behavior provides insight into factors that promote or detract from an animal's quality of life.

REFERENCES

1. Molony, V.; Kent, J.E.; McKendrick, I.J. Validation of a method for assessment of an acute pain in lambs. Appl. Anim. Behav. Sci. **2002**, *76* (3), 215–238.
2. Schwartzkopf-Genswein, K.S.; Stookey, J.M.; Crowe, T.G.; Genswein, B.M. Comparison of image analysis, exertion force, and behavior measurements for use in the assessment of beef cattle responses to hot-iron and freeze branding. J. Anim. Sci. **1998**, *76* (4), 972–979.
3. Xin, H. Assessing swine thermal comfort by image analysis of postural behaviors. J. Anim. Sci. **1998**, *77* (supplement 2), 1–9.
4. Grandin, T. Cattle vocalizations are associated with handling and equipment problems at beef slaughter plants. Appl. Anim. Behav. Sci. **2001**, *71* (3), 191–201.
5. Weary, D.M.; Braithwaite, L.A.; Fraser, D. Vocal response to pain in piglets. Appl. Anim. Behav. Sci. **1998**, *56* (2–4), 161–172.
6. Waiblinger, S.; Menke, C.; Coleman, G. The relationship between attitudes, personal characteristics and behaviour of stockpeople and subsequent behaviour and production of dairy cows. Appl. Anim. Behav. Sci. **2002**, *79* (3), 195–219.
7. Hocking, P.M.; Maxwell, M.H.; Robertson, G.W.; Mitchell, M.A. Welfare assessment of broiler breeders that are food restricted after peak rate of lay. British Poultry Science **2002**, *43* (1), 5–15.
8. El-Lethey, H.; Aerni, V.; Jungi, T.W.; Wechsler, B. Stress and feather pecking in laying hens in relation to housing conditions. British Poultry Science **2000**, *41* (1), 22–28.
9. Manninen, E.; de Passillé, A.M.; Rushen, J.; Norring, M.; Saloniemi, H. Preferences of dairy cows kept in unheated buildings for different kinds of flooring. Appl. Anim. Behav. Sci. **2002**, *75* (4), 281–292.
10. Warburton; Mason, G.J. Is out of sight out of mind? The effects of resources cues on motivation in mink. Anim. Behav. **2003**, *65* (4), 755–762.
11. Nimon, A.J.; Broom, D.M. The welfare of farmed mink (*Mustela vison*) in relation to housing and management: A review. Animal Welfare **1999**, *8* (3), 205–228.
12. Vinke, C.M. Some comments on the review of nimon and broom on the welfare of farmed mink. Animal Welfare **2001**, *10* (3), 315–324.
13. Mason, G.J.; Mendel, M. Do Stereotypies of pigs, chickens, and mink reflect adaptive species differentiation in control of foraging? Appl. Anim. Behav. Sci. **1997**, *53* (1/2), 45–58.
14. Broom, D.M.; Nimon, A.J. Response to Vinke's short communication: Comments on mink needs and welfare indicators. Animal Welfare **2001**, *10* (3), 325–326.
15. Garner, J.P.; Mason, G.J.; Smith, R. Stereotypic route-tracing in experimentally caged songbirds correlates with general behavioural disinhibition. Anim. Behav. **2003**, *66* (4), 711–727.

Well-Being Assessment: Concepts and Definitions

John J. McGlone
Texas Tech University, Lubbock, Texas, U.S.A.

INTRODUCTION

Animal welfare and animal well-being are more or less interchangeable terms. Assessment of animal welfare seems to include some subjective assessments, while the term animal well-being is viewed as more objective in some circles. In practice, the two terms have very similar meaning to the public and most scientists.

Animal welfare/well-being assessment is often criticized by scientists as being anthropomorphic. Anthropomorphism is the ascribing of human traits to nonhumans (e.g., animals or inanimate objects). Most scientists have historically not been comfortable with assessing animal happiness or pleasure. Still, there is a need to objectively measure and assess animal well-being. From this need, the science of farm animal welfare was born. Animal cognitive experiences, including their feelings, are included in this science along with measures of physiological status (endocrine and immune status), behavior, growth, and reproduction.

HISTORICAL PERSPECTIVE

Philosophers have examined the relationship between humans and animals from moral and theological views for centuries. The modern concept of farm animal well-being began with the issuing of the Brambell report in 1965 in the United Kingdom. The group of biologists, led by Brambell, concluded that animals have "Five Freedoms." These freedoms (some would call them "rights" today) include the freedom to get up, lie down, stretch their limbs, turn around, and groom (themselves or others, depending on the species). The assignment of the original "Five Freedoms" is considered more of a moral argument than a scientific argument—there was no science to support these basic freedoms in 1965.

ANIMAL RIGHTS VS. ANIMAL WELFARE/WELL-BEING

The public and the media often confuse animal rights and animal welfare/well-being. Animals have limited legal rights and few widely agreed-upon moral rights. Animals have a legal right to not be abused or neglected. Other than that right, animals do not have the right to life or liberty. Some activist groups attribute rights to animals to the extent that they believe animals should not be eaten, exhibited, or used in research.

Animal welfare/well-being is the concern of all people who own animals. People give animals adequate environments to ensure that they have good welfare/well-being. The subject of animal welfare/well-being science is a recognized area of investigation. Those who hope to improve the lives of animals will do so through careful examination of animal welfare/well-being.

DEFINING AND ASSESSING ANIMAL WELFARE/WELL-BEING

Scientists working in the field of farm animal welfare science have struggled with defining and assessing animal welfare/well-being. The most widely-held view is that to properly assess farm animal welfare, a multidisciplinary approach is required. Measures should include behavior, physiology, growth, and reproduction. All these measures are responsive to stress to varying degrees. A sample of other views are provided here.

Duncan[1] suggested that animal welfare has to do with how animals feel—their cognitive experiences. Moberg[2] suggested that when animals experience stress, their welfare is compromised when they reach a prepathological state as measured by animal physiology and disease state (including infectious and metabolic diseases). In another view, because behavior is adaptive, simply finding a behavioral effect cannot be said to be a negative welfare situation. Only when the environment is stressful to the point that physiological changes are invoked can the animal be said to be in a state of reduced welfare, McGlone[3] argued. In another model, animal welfare has to do with behavioral needs, and when behavioral needs are met, welfare is adequate.[4] The most recent model, proposed by Curtis,[5] includes an assessment of the animals' state of being—its state relative to a continuum from a bad to a good state of being (Fig. 1). Many models of animal welfare/well-being overlap.

Encyclopedia of Animal Science
DOI: 10.1081/E-EAS 120019846

| Very good | Good | Neutral | Poor | Very poor |

Fig. 1   The continuum of states of animal welfare/well-being.

THE MULTIDISCIPLINARY APPROACH

In the multidisciplinary approach, one measures behavior, physiology, and performance and then uses all of this information to determine whether welfare/well-being is adequate. This approach is the safest approach in that several of the other models can be examined if all of these measures are collected. This approach was used recently to assess sow welfare in various housing systems using a meta-analysis of selected scientific publications.[6]

Measures of performance include, for growing animals, rates of growth and efficiency of nutrient utilization.

Table 1   Definitions in the field of animal welfare/well-being science

Name	Definition	Source[a]
Agonistic	Aggressive, submissive, and threat behaviors.	Hurnik et al.[7]
Fixed action pattern	Any action pattern typical of a given species or breed that is performed in a very similar way by its individual members. In contemporary ethology, the term "fixed action pattern" often is replaced by "modal action pattern" because of inevitable individual variations in behavior. Examples: face grooming in mice, egg retrieval in geese.	
Rights (12 definitions were given in this source)	Qualities (as adherence to duty or obedience to lawful authority) that together constitute the ideal of moral propriety or merit moral approval; something to which one has a just claim, such as the power or privilege to which one is justly entitled.	Merriam-Webster[8]
Rights (animal)	The idea that animals have a just or moral claim or privilege to certain items such as lack of abuse or neglect, life, or freedom.	
Stereotyped	Repeated behaviors shown in sequence that vary only slightly in sequence; may be caused by the environment genetics, or a combination. Examples: chewing, suckling.	
Stereotyped behavior[b]	Behavior repeated in a very constant way. The term generally is used to refer to behavior that develops as a consequence of a problem situation such as extended social isolation, low level of environmental complexity, deprivation, etc. Stereotypy also may arise from genetic predispositions, or from disease of, or damage to, the brain.	Hurnik et al.[7]
Stereotypy	Stereotyped behavior that serves no apparent function; often associated with disease or adaptation to a stressful environment. Example: navel sucking in weaned piglets.	
Welfare	The state of being of an animal. Welfare can range from very good to very bad.	
Well-being	A term used in the scientific literature to indicate animal welfare.	

[a]A source is given when the definition is widely accepted.

[b]This definition has been functionally divided into "normal" stereotyped behavior and stereotypies among farm animal welfare scientists.

Among adult animals, rates of reproduction are included in animal performance measures. Growth and reproduction are suppressed when animals are stressed.

Measures of behavior include maintenance behaviors (feeding, drinking, standing, moving, laying, and sleeping), social behaviors (agonistic and nonagonistic behaviors), goal-directed behaviors (exploration, food-searching, water-searching), preferences, emotional behaviors (fear, frustration, rage, etc.) and abnormal behaviors. Among abnormal behaviors are aberrant behaviors including tail biting, ear chewing, navel sucking, buller-steer mounting, wind sucking, and cribbing in horses, wool-picking in sheep, and a host of others. In a gray area of science, certain behaviors are considered abnormal by some authors but other authors simply conclude they have unknown cause. Included in this gray area are stereotyped behaviors that develop into stereotypies (Table 1). Examples of behaviors that clearly are stereotyped but may become stereotypies are bar biting in sows, tongue rolling in calves, and pacing among captive wild animals.

Measures of physiology include both endocrine and immune measures. Endocrine measures used in assessment of animal welfare include adrenal cortical and medullary hormones. Glucocorticoids (cortisol or corticosterone) and catecholamines are the most commonly measured endocrine measures of stress. Measures of immune status are measures of stress in that if the immune system is suppressed and a pathogenic microorganism (or even a normally nonpathogenic microorganism) is present in sufficient quantity, then the animal will become ill. Illness is clearly a state of reduced welfare/well-being. Stress suppresses the immune system and so an important measure of the animal's welfare/well-being would be its relative immune status. Examples of measures of immunity that are sensitive to stress include natural killer cell activity, neutrophil function (chemotaxis and phagocytosis), and levels of some cytokines. Other measures of immunity such as antibody response to a foreign antigen and lymphocyte proliferation in the presence of mitogen have been used in welfare/well-being assessment; however, these measures require very stressful environments to induce changes. Two examples of use of the multidisciplinary approach to assessment of animal welfare are given below.

Hicks et al.[9] examined the effects of heat stress, shipping stress, and social stress on pig behavior, immunity, and endocrine and performance measures. Pig behavior was significantly changed by all acute, mild stressors. Pig physiology was only slightly changed. Pig social stratus (dominant, intermediate, or submissive) interacted with stress treatments. Dominant pigs were heavier and less negatively influenced by stressors than were subordinate pigs. The authors concluded that behavioral changes were more consistent and reliable measures of the effects of acute stress. Stockpeople could use the behavioral responses as early indicators of reduced welfare and as a sign that interventions are required to maintain adequate animal welfare.

Mitlohner et al.[10] examined the effects of shade on cattle performance, carcass traits, physiology, and behavior while they were experiencing heat stress. The provisions of shade increased weight gain of cattle that were in a warm climate. Shade also reduced neutrophil numbers and respiratory rates and caused altered cattle behavior. Because shade increased cattle weight gain and improved some measures of physiology, one could conclude that the cattle with shade in the summertime had improved welfare/well-being.

CONCLUSIONS

Animal welfare/well-being can be examined as a science; as a legal, moral, or ethical argument; or as a subject for activism. Farm animals have the right to not be abused or neglected, but beyond that they have few agreed-upon rights. Livestock producers provide environments that are conducive to good animal welfare. Several animal welfare models are presented. Measuring animal welfare by using a multidisciplinary approach would provide information on animal behavior, physiology, and performance so that decisions about animal welfare/well-being can be made with the most possible information[11] and if possible in context with other society issues.[12]

REFERENCES

1. Duncan, I.J.H. Animal welfare defined in terms of feelings. Acta agric. Scand., A Anim. Sci. **1996**, *27*, 29–35.
2. Moberg, G.P. Suffering from stress: An approach for evaluating the welfare of an animal. Acta Agric. Scand., A Anim. Sci. **1996**, *27*, 46–49.
3. McGlone, J.J. What is animal welfare? J. Agric. Ethics **1993**, *6*, 26–36.
4. Duncan, I.J.H. Behavior and behavioral needs. Poultry Sci. **1998**, *77*, 1766–1772.
5. Curtis, S.E. Stress: State of being. Encycl. Anim. Sci. **2004**. (in press).
6. McGlone, J.J.; von Borell, E.H.; Deen, J.; Johnson, A.K.; Levis, D.G.; Meunier-Salaün, M.; Morrow, J.; Reeves, D.; Salak-Johnson, J.L.; Sundberg, P.L. Review: Compilation of the scientific literature comparing housing systems for gestating sows and gilts using measures of physiology, behavior, performance, and health. Prof. Anim. Sci. **2004**, *20*, 105–119.
7. Hurnik, J.F.; Webster, A.B.; Siegel, P.B. *Dictionary of*

Farm Animal Behavior, 2nd Ed.; Iowa State University Press: Ames, 1995.

8. Merriam-Webster. *Merriam-Webster Online Dictionary*; 2004. http://www.m-w.com/netdict.htm. Accessed March 28, 2004.

9. Hicks, T.A.; McGlone, J.J.; Whisnant, C.S.; Kattesh, H.G.; Norman, R.L. Behavioral, endocrine, immune, and performance measures for pigs exposed to acute stress. J. Anim. Sci. **1998**, *76*, 474–483.

10. Mitlöhner, F.M.; Galyean, M.L.; McGlone, J.J. Shade effects on performance, carcass traits, physiology, and behavior of heat-stressed feedlot heifers. J. Anim. Sci. **2002**, *80*, 2043–2050.

11. Brambell, F.W.R. *Report of the Technical Committee to Enquire into the Welfare of Animals Kept Under Intensive Livestock Husbandry Systems*; Command Paper, Her Majesty's Stationery Office: London, 1965; Vol. 2836.

12. McGlone, J.J. Farm animal welfare in the context of other society issues: Toward sustainable systems. Livest. Prod. Sci. **2001**, *72*, 75–81.

Well-Being Assessment: Physiological Criteria

Katherine Albro Houpt
Cornell University, Ithaca, New York, U.S.A.

INTRODUCTION

There is no single valid measure of stress (or well-being). Nevertheless, we can use physiological variables to assist in validation. The hormone most often used for measuring well-being is cortisol, the product of the mammalian adrenal cortex. One also can measure the levels of hormones and metabolites that are affected by cortisol. The sympathetic nervous system is the other major source of reactions to stress, pain, or fright.

SYMPATHETIC NERVOUS SYSTEM

There are two components to the sympathetic nervous system—neural and hormonal. The most rapid response is neural. Centers in the diencephalon (the hypothalamus, primarily) are stimulated by the frightening event, and therefore, the sympathetic pathways in the spinal cord and then the nerves of the sympathetic chain are stimulated. The neurotransmitters released by the sympathetic nerves are norepinephrine and epinephrine (adrenaline and noradrenaline are alternative names). The structures innervated by the sympathetic nerves are the blood vessels, the hair follicles, the heart and lungs, and the gastrointestinal tract. The action on the gastrointestinal tract is primarily negative: Secretion and motility are inhibited. The actions on the heart are to increase the frequency and strength of contraction and to dilate the bronchioles of the lungs. The pupils of the eyes dilate. The hair stands on end (piloerection).

Any of these reactions can be measured to assess welfare. The hormones norepinephrine and epinephrine are very quickly degraded, so blood samples need to be taken quickly and the blood kept cold and processed quickly. The hormones can also be measured in saliva, which is a less invasive method, but still involves restraint of the animal. For this reason, it is more practical and probably more valid to measure the results of sympathetic stimulation, for example, heart rate. There are heart rate monitors that can be attached to the animal with a chest band. These can be retrieved later to determine any change in heart rate or in variability of heart rate.

There can be confounding factors in any measure of stress. For example, ceiling effects can make interpretation difficult. A ceiling effect occurs when the response is already high and cannot be any higher physiologically. Branding is used for identification of beef cattle in the United States. Although the modern techniques of microchipping would also make identification possible, what the rancher needs is a symbol, unique to his ranch, that is visible from a distance. There are two methods of branding: hot-iron branding and freeze branding. Hot-iron branding destroys the hair follicles and creates a scar. Freeze branding does not destroy the hair follicles, but causes the hair to regrow white rather than pigmented. These brands are somewhat harder to read than hot-iron brands, but presumably are more humane. When the responses of beef cattle to the two types of branding were compared, the heart rate and catecholamine levels were high following both procedures. The explanation is that the restraint necessary to brand the animals was extremely stressful to all the cattle, so their response was maximal. In other words, there was a ceiling effect. When the comparison of branding methods was repeated using dairy cattle, hot-iron branding caused higher heart rate and more avoidance than freeze branding.[1] Dairy cattle are much more accustomed to the presence of humans, to restraint, and to being handled than are most beef cattle.

HYPOTHALAMIC-PITUITARY ADRENAL AXIS

Stress to the animal leads to stimulation of those hypothalamic neurons that produce corticotropin releasing factor (CRF).[2] This is carried in the hypothalamic pituitary portal system to the anterior pituitary, where it stimulates release of adrenal corticotropic hormone (ACTH). This, in turn, stimulates release of the adrenal cortical hormones, in particular cortisol (in mammals) and corticosterone (in birds). The mineral corticoids—aldosterone—may also be released to a lesser degree. This hormonal cascade will take some time (minutes to hours), in contrast to the more rapid neural activity of the sympathetic nervous system. One important question is how much does an animal's cortisol level have to rise

Encyclopedia of Animal Science
DOI: 10.1081/E-EAS 120019845

before we should consider the animal stressed. Barnett and Hemsworth[3] have suggested that a 40% increase indicates stress. One could use any increase above the normal range for the particular laboratory and species.

There are pitfalls in the use of cortisol (or any other physiological measurement), not because cortisol is not an indicator of stress, but because of confounding circumstances. For example, veal calf welfare is frequently questioned, so measuring cortisol was assumed to be a valid measure. As expected, when the calves were first placed in veal crates their cortisol was elevated, but several weeks later their cortisol was lower than age-matched calves that were housed in pens.[4] The controls had *higher* cortisol than the confined calves, probably because they had to be chased and caught before the blood samples were taken.

The method of obtaining the sample is important. If blood is taken by direct venipuncture and several attempts have to be made before the vein is punctured, the cortisol may be high for that reason. Taking blood from the anterior vena cava of a supine pig is much more likely to be stressful than taking it from the jugular vein of a horse habituated to handling and injections. Preplacement of an indwelling vascular catheter avoids some of those problems. There is a definite circadian rhythm of cortisol secretion, so that morning cannot be used as a control for afternoon. In fact, loss of the rhythmicity is another sign of stress. Twenty minutes should be allowed after the stressor for cortisol to rise.

Cortisol can be measured in other body fluids. Salivary cortisol can be collected easily by putting a cotton-tipped applicator in the animal's mouth. Urinary cortisol can be measured, but creatinine must be measured also in order to control for concentration of the urine. A low cortisol concentration in dilute urine could represent a higher plasma level than a higher level of cortisol in concentrated urine. Fecal cortisol has been measured successfully and is particularly useful when the well-being of free-ranging or wild species is to be evaluated. One advantage of measuring fecal cortisol is that cortisol production over a matter of hours is represented, rather than cortisol at a single point in time, as with a blood sample.

The actions of cortisol on the rest of the body can also be measured and used to evaluate welfare. Cortisol has effects on the liver, the fat depots, and the immune system. The hormone stimulates gluconeogenesis. Gluconeogenesis is the deamination of amino acids, freeing glucose for immediate energy. The ammonia produced forms urea, and urea can be measured as a sign of stress. In this case—cortisol stimulation—more urea is produced, but levels may be high because less is excreted. Impaired excretion would indicate a kidney problem. Therefore, when a high level of urea is detected, renal health should be evaluated before stress is diagnosed. Renal function can be measured from the specific gravity of the urine, from the presence or absence of protein in the urine, and by the ratio of urea to creatinine, a compound that rarely varies in plasma concentration.

Under the influence of cortisol, fatty acids are metabolized rather than forming more adipose tissue. These two actions, gluconeogenesis and antilipogenesis, complement the actions of the adrenal medullary hormones that stimulate glycogenolysis and lipolysis.

One of the major actions of cortisol is the reduction of inflammation, and inflammation is reduced by suppression of the immune system. The number and type of white blood cells can be measured. There are several types of white blood cells, including neutrophils and lymphocytes. The lymphocytes are the antibody-producing cells, and these are the cells suppressed by cortisol. The ratio of neutrophils to lymphocytes can therefore be used as a measure of stress. The fewer the lymphocytes, the more likely the animal is secreting more cortisol and is stressed. One can also measure the activity of white blood cells rather than simply the number of cells. Some of these measures are mitogen-induced lymphocytic proliferation and natural killer-cell cytotoxicity. These have been used to assess well-being, but the results are often inconsistent.[5]

Suppression of the immune system is the most dangerous effect of cortisol. Although the swelling and pain of inflammation will be decreased, the white blood cells that cause these signs will not be protecting the body from invasion by bacteria or viruses. Antibodies will not form complexes with foreign antigens, and bacteria will not be destroyed by phagocytosis. The result of suppression of the immune response is illness. The respiratory or gastrointestinal pathology (shipping fever) seen in newly mixed or transported animals is a result of stress-induced immunosuppression.

The adrenal glands are not the only ones stimulated by stress. Thyroid-stimulating hormone is released from the pituitary and stimulates release of thyroxine from the thyroid gland. Thyroxine increases metabolic rate and, therefore, calorigenesis. Carbohydrate stores will be utilized first, and then fat stores.

Cortisol is a useful measure of some kinds of stress, but not others. For example, cortisol increases when horses are transferred from one environment to another and when they are trailered, but chronic deprivation of water or exercise does not cause cortisol to rise or the response of cortisol to ACTH to change. Fortunately, there are other physiological values that can be used. Examples include plasma protein, which can be used to assess the effects of furosemide. Furosemide is a drug frequently administered to race horses, ostensibly to prevent exercise-induced pulmonary hemorrhage. However, it also improves the animal's performance, because the horse is 10–20 kilograms lighter in weight as a consequence of diuresis. If a horse is treated with furosemide, the loss of fluid from the circulation causes an increase in plasma protein. If horses are given limited amounts of water, as in mares used for estrogen production, they have normal plasma protein but an elevated osmotic pressure.[6]

The most recently used physiological measure of well-being is acute phase proteins. These are haptoglobins, a glycoprotein of the alpha-2-globulin fraction by haptocytes in response to stress, ACTH, and cortisol. They are elevated following castration of piglets and after transporting older pigs for more than 3 hours.

CONCLUSION

The animal whose well-being is compromised responds with a variety of physiological changes. These can be used, in combination with behavioral measures, to help us determine the optimum housing, social grouping, and transport of farm animals.

REFERENCES

1. Lay, D.C., Jr.; Friend, T.H.; Bowers, C.L.; Grissom, K.K.; Jenkins, O.C. A comparative physiological and behavioral study of freeze and hot iron branding using dairy cows. J. Anim. Sci. **1992**, *70*, 1120.
2. Dantzer, R.; Mormede, P. Stress in Domestic Animals: A Psychoneuroendocrine Approach. In *Animal Stress*; Moberg, G.P., Ed.; American Physiological Society: Bethesda, MD, 1985; 81–95.
3. Barnett, J.L.; Hemsworth, P.H. The validity of physiological and behavioral measures of animal welfare. Appl. Anim. Behav. Sci. **1990**, *20*, 177–187.
4. Stull, C.; McDonough, P. Multidisciplinary approach to evaluating welfare of veal calves in commercial facilities. J. Anim. Sci. **1994**, *72*, 2518–2524.
5. McGlone, J.J.; Salak, J.L.; Lumpkin, E.A.; Nicholson, R.I.; Gibson, M.; Normal, R.L. Shipping stress and social status effects on pig performance, plasma cortisol, natural killer cell activity, and leukocyte numbers. J. Anim. Sci. **1993**, *71* (4), 888.
6. Houpt, K.A.; Houpt, T.R.; Johnson, J.L.; Erb, H.N.; Yeon, S.C. The effect of exercise deprivation on the behaviour and physiology of straight stall confined pregnant mares. Anim. Welf. **2001**, *10*, 257–267.

Wool: Biology and Production

A. C. Schlink
N. R. Adams
CSIRO Livestock Industries, Wembley, Western Australia

INTRODUCTION

Wool is a generic description of hair from various breeds of domesticated sheep (*Ovis aries*). Wool appears to be the earliest material man used to spin and weave into clothing, with evidence of shears for harvesting wool being used around 1000 B.C. Requirement for shearing implies development of sheep with a continuously growing fleece. These developments associated with domestication have continued until this day, although wool is no longer a dominant textile fiber.

BIOLOGY

The gross morphology of a wool fiber is shown in Fig. 1.[1] The fiber is surrounded by cuticle cells that overlap in only one direction, leading to directional frictional characteristics and wool felting. The cuticle has four layers with a combined thickness of 0.5 to 0.8 µm, occupying between 6 and 16% of total fiber weight.

The cortex, composing 90% of fiber weight, consists of two cell types, ortho- (60 to 90%) and paracortex cells (10 to 40%), the latter containing higher quantities of sulphur than the former, resulting in a tougher cell with more cross-linkage. Cortex cell-type arrangement changes with increasing fiber diameter. In fine-wool Merinos, the cortical cells are arranged in a bilateral manner, and the border between cell types is arranged in helical pattern along the fiber axis. This helical pattern results in fiber crimp, with paracortex being situated in the inner part and orthocortex in the outer part of the crimp. Cortex cells have a spindlelike shape, being 45 to 95 µm long and 2 to 6 µm wide. Ortho-cortex cells rarely contain nuclear remnants and cytoplasmic residues.

At its widest point, each cortical cell contains 5 to 20 clearly separated macrofibrils embedded in intermacrofibrillar matrix material, in a hexagonal array. Macrofibrils are composed of bundles of 500 to 800 microfibrils. Microfibrils, or intermediate filaments, are composed of alpha-helical proteins of comparatively low cystine content that are linked by both disulphide and hydrogen bonds. A matrix of intermediate filament-associated proteins surrounds microfibrils and is composed of two families of nonhelical proteins, one being cystine-rich and the other, glycine- and tyrosine-rich.

Wool is almost entirely composed of a family of proteins known as alpha-keratins. Merino wool has higher cystine content than coarse wools as a result of having a larger proportion of high-sulphur alpha-keratin proteins. Amino acid composition can vary between sheep, with the growth phase of the wool follicle cycle and with the nutritional status of the sheep.

Wool fiber diameters range 10 to 80 µm and have a density of 1.304 g/cm^3, with slightly and imperfectly elliptical cross-sections. Wools with higher fiber diameter tend to be hairlike and medulated. Proteins in wool have the ability to adsorb water. At standard atmosphere of 65% relative humidity and 20°C, water regain ranges from 14 to 18%.[2]

Wool fibers are highly elastic, and if not strained by more than 30% of length for longer than one hour, they can return to their original state by soaking in water. The intrinsic strength of wool is low, varying between 50 and 300 megapascals.

Sheep wool follicles have a very long anagen phase, with 1–2% of follicles inactive at any one time. The general morphology of anagen follicles is shown in Fig. 2.[3] A connective tissue sheath surrounds the tubular down growth of epithelium, and there is a dermal papilla responsible for cell division. Blood vessels are found in the connective tissue sheath and, except in the smaller secondary follicles of Merino sheep, the dermal papilla.

Primary and secondary follicles are distinguished by their appendages and time of initiation in fetal skin. Primary follicles form first, at about 60 days postconception, and secondary follicles start 14 to 20 days later. Variable numbers of secondary follicles may form either as separate follicles or as outgrowths of other secondary follicles. Sweat glands and arrector pili muscles are appendages of primary follicles. Both follicle types have sebaceous glands. The ratio of primary to secondary follicles varies between sheep. Merino sheep with 19 µm

Encyclopedia of Animal Science
DOI: 10.1081/E-EAS 120023830

The Structure of a Merino Wool Fibre

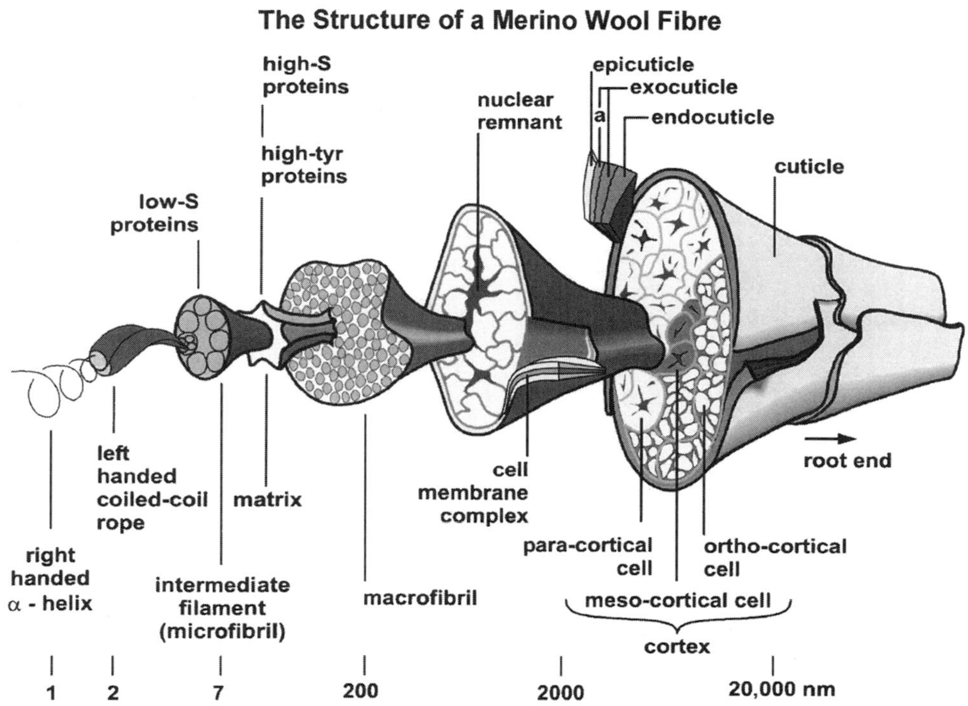

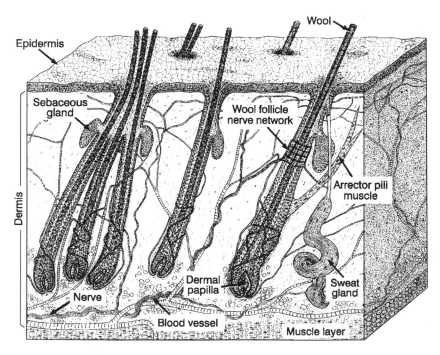

Fig. 1 Gross morphology of a Merino wool fiber. (From CSIRO Livestock Industries.) (*View this art in color at www.dekker.com.*)

Fig. 2 Diagram of skin and wool follicle groups showing primary follicles, with arrector pili muscles and sweat glands, and secondary follicles. (From CSIRO Livestock Industries.)

Table 1 Principal greasy wool-producing countries and world production from 1988 to 2002 (million kg)

Year	Australia	New Zealand	China	Eastern Europe	World
1988	916	346	209	613	2,919
1989	959	339	222	627	2,967
1990	1102	311	237	623	2,970
1991	1066	305	239	592	2,953
1992	875	296	240	526	2,989
1993	869	256	238	456	2,913
1994	829	284	240	439	2,817
1995	731	289	260	409	2,689
1996	725	275	298	263	2,541
1997	700	266	255	229	2,418
1998	684	252	277	198	2,379
1999	678	253	283	188	2,348
2000	652	237	291	187	2,303
2001	600	246	294	188	2,239
2002	565	253	293	189	2,217

(From the International Wool Textile Organization.)

wool have 80 follicles/mm^2 and a secondary to primary follicle ratio of 20:1, whereas Drysdale sheep (43 μm) have 13 follicles/mm^2 and a secondary to primary follicle ratio of 5:1.

PRODUCTION

Wool production normally occurs in areas where the pasture quality is adequate, but insufficient for meat production. Seasonal variation in clean wool growth is similar to the variation in availability of digestible dry matter per hectare, or crude protein available per hectare.[4] The amplitude in seasonal wool growth rate ranged from 20.3% in Armidale, New South Wales, to 650% in Huang Cheng, China. Peak wool growth occurred in the spring for cold, wet winter areas and in the summer in summer rainfall, tropical areas. These changes in wool growth are also seen in follicle bulb diameter, dermal papilla length, skin weight, and the incidence of active follicles in the skin.[5] Wool growth also varies between years, reflecting annual pasture production cycles, with amplitude in fleece weight between years varying from 15.8% to 118.5%.

Only 20% of the protein synthesized in skin is excreted as wool, with the remaining 80% being degraded in the skin or desquamated as epithelial cells. The value of 20% is robust for a wide range of sheep breeds and feeding levels.[6] Thus, genetic selection to increase fleece weight also increases the rate of skin protein synthesis.

Fleece weight is affected by age, pregnancy, lactation, and sex, with rams producing more wool than wethers or ewes.[7] Fiber diameter increases by 3.9 μm from 18 months to 6 years of age in rams, but for ewes the increase is 0.4 μm over the same period. Pregnancy and lactation reduce fleece weight by 30 to 600 grams and fiber diameter by 0.4 to 1.5 μm, and also affect staple strength.[8] Strong seasonal patterns in wool growth occur in many breeds, with annual rhythms synchronized by photoperiod acting through melatonin secreted by the pineal gland. Breeds such as the Merino have a reduced response to photoperiod.

Fiber diameter is the first determinant of wool price, and many wool breeding programs aim to reduce fiber diameter. Fiber diameter is changed by nutrient availability between and within years, but is mainly determined by the strain of sheep.

Seasonal variation in wool growth reduces staple strength, which is the second most important determinant of wool price. Staple strength has a strong genetic component, depending on variation in fiber diameter, fiber shedding, and the strength of individual fibers. For breeding ewes, the most critical time remains the last two weeks of pregnancy.[9]

World greasy wool production peaked in 1990, with a total production of 2970 million kilograms, and declined to 2217 million kilograms in 2002 (Table 1). On a clean wool basis, Australia and New Zealand are the world's two largest wool producers, although China produces more greasy wool than New Zealand. Australia is the dominant producer of Merino sheep in the 18- to 23-μm range for apparel production. New Zealand wool production is dominated by Romney sheep in the 30- to 38-μm range, which is suitable for carpets. China has increased wool production from 7.2% of world greasy wool in 1988 to 13.2% in 2002.

World production statistics are provided on a greasy wool basis, and greasy wool contains from 30 to 70% impurities. Wool impurities are wax, suint, dust, and vegetable matter. Sheep coats successfully reduce these contaminants. Low wool yields in countries such as China are a consequence of overnight corralling of sheep for feeding during cold winters and protection from the elements.

CONCLUSION

The average fine-wool sheep produces some 6000 kilometers of a complex protein fiber each year. This fiber is produced from wool follicles that use 20% of the protein turnover in skin. Wool is predominantly produced from grazing lands and is highly seasonal in growth. Australia is the largest producer, with 25.5% of the world production of 2217 million kilograms in 2002.

REFERENCES

1. Hocker, H. Fibre Morphology. In *Wool: Science and Technology*; Simpson, W.S., Crawshaw, G.H., Eds.; CRC Press: Cambridge, England, 2002; 60–79.

2. Heale, J.W.S. Physical Properties of Wool. In *Wool: Science and Technology*; Simpson, W.S., Crawshaw, G.H., Eds.; CRC Press: Cambridge, England, 2002; 80–129.

3. Orwin, D.F.G. Variation in Wool Follicle Morphology. In *The Biology of Wool and Hair*; Rogers, G.E., Reis, P.J., Ward, K.A., Marshall, R.C., Eds.; Chapman and Hall: New York, 1989; 227–241.

4. Schlink, A.C.; Mata, G.; Lea, J.M.; Ritchie, A.J.M. Seasonal variation in fibre diameter and length in wool of grazing Merino sheep with low or high staple strength. Aust. J. Exp. Agric. **1999**, *39*, 507–517.

5. Schlink, A.C.; Sanders, M.; Hollis, D.E. Seasonal variations in skin and wool follicle morphology of grazing Merino sheep with low or high staple strength. Asian-Australas. J. Anim. Sci. **2000**, *13* (Suppl. A), 253–256.

6. Adams, N.R.; Liu, S.; Masters, D.G. Regulation of Protein Synthesis for Wool Growth. In *Ruminant Physiology: Digestion, Metabolism, Growth and Reproduction*; Cronje, P.B., Ed.; CAB International, 2000; 255–272.

7. Corbett, J.L. Variation in Wool Growth with Physiological State. In *Physiology and Environmental Limitations to Wool Growth*; Black, J.L., Reis, P.J., Eds.; The University of New England Publishing Unit: Australia, 1979; 79–98.

8. Hynd, P.I.; Masters, D.G. Nutrition and Wool Growth. In *Sheep Nutrition*; Freer, M., Dove, H., Eds.; CAB International, 2002; 165–187.

9. Robertson, S.M.; Robards, G.E.; Wofle, E.C. The timing of nutritional restriction during reproduction influences staple strength. Aust. J. Agric. Res. **2000**, *51*, 125–132.

Xenotransplantation: Biological Barrier

Jeffrey L. Platt
Mayo Clinic, Rochester, Minnesota, U.S.A.

INTRODUCTION

Xenotransplantation, the transplantation of cells, tissues, or organs between individuals of different species, is a subject of interest because it might be used to address a shortage of human organs for transplantation and for other purposes. While the potential applications of xenotransplantation are widely appreciated, the biological hurdles have prevented all but a small number of experimental trials.

BIOLOGICAL HURDLES TO XENOTRANSPLANTATION

The biological hurdles to xenotransplantation are summarized subsequently and in recent reviews.[1,2] With certain notable exceptions, the hurdles are a direct function of the phylogenetic distance between the graft and the recipient. Because of this consideration, some have advocated using closely related species, for example, primates in the case of human recipients, as a source of xenografts. However, nonhuman primates are not sufficiently plentiful to provide organs needed to treat human disease and may harbor viruses potentially lethal to humans. Use of nonhuman primates also raises social and ethical controversy. For these reasons, many in the field of transplantation have turned to the pig as a potential source of xenografts. Swine are plentiful, and some strains, such as the mini-pig, have organs of appropriate size for use in humans. Further, the pig can be genetically engineered. This article will therefore focus on the pig, although what is mentioned for the pig would also apply to other nonprimate mammals.

IMMUNOLOGICAL HURDLES TO XENOTRANSPLANTATION

Many components of the immune system may target a xenograft (Table 1). The most important component may be xenoreactive natural antibodies. Xenoreactive natural antibodies are made by all immunocompetent humans and recognize predominantly Galα1-3Gal, a saccharide synthesized by lower mammals and New World monkeys, which have a functional α1,3galactosyltransferase. Humans and Old World monkeys lack a functional α1,3galactosyltransferase and make anti-Galα1-3Gal. Binding of anti-Galα1-3Gal antibodies activates complement. Complement activation on porcine cells is amplified because porcine complement regulatory proteins, such as decay-accelerating factor, control human complement poorly.[3] Human natural killer cells and macrophages, bearing receptors specific for porcine cell surface molecules, such as Galα1-3Gal, also react with porcine cells. Finally, xenografts provoke elicited immune responses against porcine major histocompatibility proteins.

XENOGRAFT REJECTION: SUSCEPTIBILITY AND TREATMENT

Whereas all xenografts may provoke immune responses, all xenografts are not equally susceptible to destruction by those immune responses. The critical factor determining the susceptibility of a xenograft to injury by the recipient's immune system is the nature of the blood vessels that serve the graft, and that is determined by whether the graft consists of an intact organ, free tissue, or isolated cells (Fig. 1).[1] Organ xenografts are subject to severe vascular injury (Fig. 1). This injury arises from the interaction of antibodies and complement of the recipient with the endothelial lining of blood vessels of the donor.

Hyperacute rejection is caused by the rapid activation of complement on donor blood vessels, and it typically destroys a xenograft in minutes to hours. Although hyperacute rejection is dramatic and severe, it can be prevented by depleting antidonor (Galα1-3Gal) antibodies with immunoabsorbant columns, or by inhibiting complement activation. The best way to inhibit complement is genetic engineering of swine to express human complement regulatory proteins, such as decay-accelerating factor. Some have suggested that hyperacute rejection might be prevented by knocking out α1,3GT to eradicate

Encyclopedia of Animal Science
DOI: 10.1081/E-EAS 120019851

Table 1 Immune and inflammatory components contributing to the barrier to xenotransplantation[a]

Component	Target recognized
Natural antibodies	Galα1-3Gal
Elicited antibodies	Porcine MHC, other proteins, and Galα1-3Gal
Complement	Complement fixing antibodies
Platelets	von Willebrand factor
Macrophages	Saccharides
T cells	Porcine MHC and other proteins

[a]Components organized by pig-to-human xenografts.

expression of Galα1-3Gal, but this application has yet to be tested.

When hyperacute rejection is prevented, an organ xenograft becomes subject to acute vascular rejection (AVR). AVR arises over a period of days to weeks and is caused by the interaction of host antibodies and a small amount of complement with donor blood vessels. AVR may also be caused by natural killer cells, platelets, and/or macrophages. AVR is a greater challenge than hyperacute rejection because it can be caused by very small amounts of immune reactants and may be promoted by incompat-

ibilities between complement and coagulation systems of the recipient and control proteins expressed in the donor organ.[3]

AVR has been prevented in some model systems by temporary depletion of antidonor antibodies from the recipient. Depletion of antidonor antibodies and their gradual return may bring about accommodation, a condition in which the organ acquires resistance to antibody-mediated injury.[3]

Unfortunately, accommodation has not been achieved reproducibly in pig-to-nonhuman primate organ transplants, and hence other approaches to preventing acute vascular rejection are sought. One such approach may be the induction of immunological tolerance, that is, specific immune nonresponsiveness with porcine cells. Unfortunately, tolerance to swine has yet to be achieved in primates.

Another approach to preventing acute rejection may involve eradicating donor antigen, particularly Galα1-3Gal. This end is sought by targeting the α1-3galactosyltransferase gene.[4,5] Gene knockout in swine involves targeting by homologous recombination, followed by transfer of targeted nuclei to targeting of enucleated eggs. This process, called cloning, was recently achieved and full knockout accomplished by pairing one allele of α1-3galactosyltranserase with

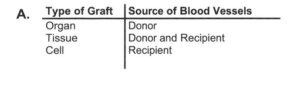

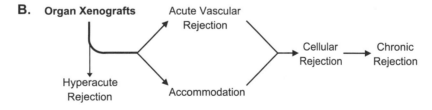

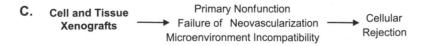

Fig. 1 Relationship between type of graft and source of blood vessels. (A) Cell and tissue transplants do not undergo humoral rejection because some or all blood vessels are of recipient origin. (B) Organ xenograft. The action of the immune system—particularly humoral immunity—on the blood vessels in organ xenografts gives rise to various types of vascular disease, including hyperacute rejection, acute vascular rejection, or accommodation and chronic rejection. Organ xenografts are also subject to cellular rejection. The figure depicts the various types of rejection in approximate temporal sequence. (C) Tissue or cell xenografts. Cell or tissue xenografts are subject to primary nonfunction and to cellular rejection, but not to the types of vascular disease shown in A and B.

spontaneous mutation in the other allele. Whether α1-3galactosyltransferase knockout pigs will truly resist AVR remains to be seen.

Xenografts are also susceptible to cellular rejection. Rejection results from immune responses to many foreign proteins, especially major histocompatibility proteins. Because all of the proteins of the pig differ to a certain extent from the proteins of humans, cell-mediated immunity might be very strong—stronger than the immune reaction against an allograft. Still, cell-mediated immunity against xenografts can apparently be controlled by immunosuppressive therapies in common use.

Organ xenografts may also be susceptible to chronic rejection. Chronic rejection arises over a period of months to years and is characterized by thickening of blood vessel walls, interstitial fibrosis, and loss of epithelial ducts. Chronic rejection is the major cause of the loss of human allografts, and some believe the occurrence would be at least as frequent and at least as severe in organ xenografts. Whether this view is correct is unknown. However, because xenografts can potentially be replaced, the implications of chronic rejection for the well-being of the recipient are not nearly so great in the case of xenotransplantation as in the case of allotransplantation.

In contrast to organ grafts, cell and tissue xenografts are mainly subject to cellular rejection.[1] Cell and tissue xenografts do not undergo hyperacute, acute vascular, or chronic rejection because they derive their blood supply mainly by ingrowth of the recipient. Because cellular rejection can be controlled by immunosuppressive therapy, cell and tissue xenografts have achieved long-term survival and have been applied clinically.

PHYSIOLOGIC BARRIERS TO XENOTRANSPLANTATION

Some xenografts may function poorly because of physiologic incompatibility with the recipient. This problem may especially plague hepatic xenografts because of the complex metabolic pathways of the liver. A related concern is that the complement, coagulation, or other proteins secreted by the xenogeneic liver might disrupt physiologic systems in the recipient. Whether or not physiology of the graft will pose a significant hurdle to xenotransplantation of the liver is unclear.

XENOTRANSPLANTATION AND ZOONOSIS

A potential hurdle to xenotransplantation that has received much attention in recent years is zoonosis, the conveying of an infectious agent, especially a virus, from the donor to the recipient.[6] Zoonosis poses a significant hurdle to use of nonhuman primates as a source of xenografts because some viruses of nonhuman primates are lethal in humans. In the case of the pig, all of the known infectious agents can potentially be eliminated, so the problem of zoonosis may not be so severe. Indeed, because infection is a regular complication of allotransplantation, the problem of infection may be less severe in the case of xenografts than it is in the case of allografts.

One exception to the relatively low risk of zoonosis is porcine endogenous retrovirus (PERV). PERV is present in the genome of all swine and may infect human cells.[7] However, while PERV can infect human cells in vitro, studies of several hundred human recipients of porcine xenografts have failed to reveal evidence that PERV can infect human cells in vivo.[8] Still, the theoretical possibility of infection has raised concerns, especially that recombination or mutation might make the virus more infectious or pathogenic. Hence, the possibility of infection and spread of PERV among humans will be intensely studied in all clinical trials.

CONCLUSION

Although xenotransplantation has been seen as a potential approach to treating organ failure for more than a century, it has not been regularly applied in human subjects. The main barrier to application is the immunological reactions of the recipient against the graft. New technologies, such as genetic engineering and cloning, offer promise for overcoming this hurdle, and thus making xenotransplantation a potential treatment for many human diseases. How xenotransplantation will weigh against other technologies, such as implantable devices and tissue engineering, for the treatment of disease remains to be determined. Regardless, genetic engineering, cloning, and other technologies developed to enable xenotransplantation to be applied may find broader use in animal science and biotechnology.

ARTICLE OF FURTHER INTEREST

Biotechnology: Xenotransplantation, p. 152

REFERENCES

1. Cascalho, M.; Platt, J.L. The immunological barrier to xenotransplantation. Immunity **2001**, *14*, 437–446.
2. Platt, J.L. Immunology of Xenotransplantation. In *Samter's*

Immunologic Diseases, 6; Lippincott Williams & Wilkins: Philadelphia, 2001; 1132–1146.

3. Platt, J.L.; Vercellotti, G.M.; Dalmasso, A.P.; Matas, A.J.; Bolman, R.M.; Najarian, J.S.; Bach, F.H. Transplantation of discordant xenografts: A review of progress. Immunol. Today **1990**, *11*, 450–456.

4. Lai, L.; Kolber-Simonds, D.; Park, K.W.; Cheong, H.T.; Greenstein, J.L.; Im, G.S.; Samuel, M.; Bonk, A.; Rieke, A.; Day, B.N.; Murphy, C.N.; Carter, D.B.; Hawley, R.J.; Prather, R.S. Production of α-1,3-galactosyltransferase knockout pigs by nuclear transfer cloning. Science **2002**, *295*, 1089–1092.

5. Phelps, C.J.; Koike, C.; Vaught, T.D.; Boone, J.; Wells, K.D.; Chen, S.H.; Ball, S.; Specht, S.M.; Polejaeva, I.A.; Monahan, J.A.; Jobst, P.M.; Sharma, S.B.; Lamborn, A.E.; Garst, A.S.; Moore, M.; Demetris, A.J.; Rudert, W.A.; Bottino, R.; Bertera, S.; Trucco, M.; Starzl, T.E.; Dai, Y.; Ayares, D.L. Production of alpha 1,3-galactosyltransferase-deficient pigs. Science **2003**, *299*, 411–414.

6. National Research Council of the National Academies. *Animal Biotechnology: Science-Based Concerns*; The National Academies Press: Washington, DC, 2002; vol.

7. Patience, C.; Takeuchi, Y.; Weiss, R.A. Infection of human cells by an endogenous retrovirus of pigs. Nat. Med. **1997**, *3*, 282–286.

8. Paradis, K.; Langford, G.; Long, Z.; Heneine, W.; Sandstrom, P.; Switzer, W.M.; Chapman, L.E.; Lockey, C.; Onions, D. Search for cross-species transmission of porcine endogenous retrovirus in patients treated with living pig tissue. Science **1999**, *285*, 1236–1241.

Yak

Gerald Wiener
Roslin Institute, Edinburgh, U.K.

Han Jianlin
International Livestock Research Institute, Nairobi, Kenya

INTRODUCTION

Yak, a species of bovidae, are the mainstay of livelihood for the nomads on the vast Qinghai-Tibetan Plateau of western China and in other countries bordering the Himalayas and to the north into Mongolia and Russia. These areas have harsh climate, short growing seasons, and high elevations. Yak withstand these extreme conditions and still remain productive.

HISTORY AND DISTRIBUTION

The yak, classified by Linnaeus in 1766 as *Bos grunniens* (on account of its grunting noises), was listed later as *Poephagus grunniens*, which recent evidence supports more strongly.[1] Both classifications remain in use.

The domestic yak is descended from wild yak, which may have been tamed by the ancient Qiang people in the Changtang area of Tibet, starting perhaps 10,000 years ago. Domestic yak herding, perhaps not too different from that practiced until recently, dates back about 4500 years.[1] From those times, the yak spread outward, but always at high altitudes, generally between 2000 m and 5000 m.

China is the main country for yak, with about 13 million animals—around 4 million each in Tibet, Qinghai, and Sichuan provinces, 900,000 in Gansu province, and relatively few in Yunnan and Xinjiang provinces. Mongolia has about 600,000 yak, and smaller populations, but of great local importance, exist in Bhutan, Nepal, northeastern India, and in some of the climatically inhospitable parts of Commonwealth of Independent States (CIS) countries.

During the late 20th century, yak were introduced into parts of the northern and western United States and Canada. There are a few very small herds in some European countries and in New Zealand. In addition, there are collections in many zoos, but few of them are viable, self-reproducing herds.

BREEDS AND BREEDING

Wild Yak

Fewer than 15,000 wild yak survive, principally in the Changtang area of Tibet and parts of the Kunlun mountains, from among former millions.[2] They have been driven to exist at elevations mostly above 4500 m by excessive hunting, albeit mostly for food. The wild yak is now a protected species, but protection is difficult and leaves them in danger of extinction.

Domestic Yak

The Chinese authorities have officially recognized 12 breeds of domestic yak, of which the Jiulong, Maiwa, Tianzhu White, Plateau, and Huanhu are best known and numerically most important. Yak in other countries are normally referred to by the name of the area in which they are found. The classification of breeds in China was based on characteristics of color, conformation, local history, distribution, and other factors, but most breeds of yak live in different parts of a vast territory (more than 2.5 million square km) and rarely intermingle or interbreed. While some of the breeds differ from each other in color and conformation, it is more difficult to say whether there is any significant genetic difference among the breeds in reproduction, survival, or performance traits. However, techniques of molecular genetics have recently started to show some degree of genetic distance between the yak populations.

Crosses and Hybrids

Crosses among yak breeds are relatively rare, but crossing with wild yak—by using the semen of captured wild yak bulls—is practiced at some breeding centers. Such crosses are larger and more vigorous than domestic yak. In times past, wild yak bulls on the perimeter of the domestic yak

Encyclopedia of Animal Science
DOI: 10.1081/E-EAS 120019852

population mated with the latter, and herders liked the crosses. Attempts are now being made, by selection, to create a new breed of yak (the Datong yak) from such crosses.

Hybridization of domestic yak with local cattle, at intermediate elevations, has been practiced for generations. The hybrids inherit some of the good characteristics from each species, but lack the adaptation of the yak to the harsh conditions at higher elevations.

Over the past 50 years or so, hybridization of yak with exotic cattle breeds, such as the Holstein or the Simmental, has been achieved on a limited scale by using artificial insemination. These hybrids are larger and more productive than the yak, but need extra feed and better management at lower altitudes than pure yak.

The male hybrids of yak and cattle are sterile and are used for draft purposes and meat. The females can be mated to either yak or cattle and are especially liked for their milk production, but their calves are not usually kept for further breeding.

MANAGEMENT

Traditionally, management follows a transhumance system dictated by the seasons, climate, topography, and sociocultural factors. During summer and early autumn, the herds are kept at higher elevations. The herders live in campsites and move as often as necessary, depending on the availability of grazing. During winter and early spring, yak are kept at lower elevations nearer the permanent homes of the herders. Some shelters are provided, especially for calves.

Formerly, the animals of several families were herded together, and milking females and their calves were kept separate from younger females and from males. Now, some of the traditional and communal systems of transhumance management are breaking down under a policy of Household Responsibility in China, in which there is individual ownership of animals and rights (though not ownership) to parcels of rangcland, some of which are fenced. It has yet to be shown whether the new system is as effective as the old in utilizing the natural resources of the rangeland.

The natural vegetation is almost the only feed available for the yak in both summer and winter. Summer is a time of plenty. The animals gain weight rapidly after severe weight loss (up to 25–30% of their liveweight) over winter and early spring, when animals can be close to starvation and deaths are common, especially in years of heavy snow. Supplementary feeds, such as hay or crop by-products, are not generally available except in very small quantities, mostly for weak animals.

ADAPTATION

The yak has adapted to high altitude (low oxygen), cold (almost no frost-free days and an annual mean temperature of 5°C), shortage of feed for up to 7 months of the year, precipitous terrain, and danger from predators. Yak conserve heat through a compact body; thick fleece of long outer hair and, in winter, an undercoat of fine down; thick skin; nonfunctioning sweat glands; and, by autumn, a layer of subcutaneous fat. Uptake of oxygen is aided by a large lung and heart, rapid breathing, and hemoglobin with a high affinity for oxygen. Pigmentation of skin and fleece (black color predominates) counteracts solar radiation. The yak's grazing habits allow use of diverse vegetation, from shrubs to the shortest grass. A special hoof shape and the yak's temperament help them in often treacherous terrain, and grouping into tight herds provides protection, especially from wolves.

PERFORMANCE

Compared to specialized dairy and beef cattle, the yak's productivity is low. There is no widespread recording of performance in yak herds, and nearly all available data stem from experimental stations and a few surveys. The values presented in this section[1] are therefore only approximate.

Reproduction

Mating takes place between June and November, with August and September being the peak months. Traditionally, the bulls run in groups and fight for possession of the females. The strongest, generally older bulls get the most mates. More controlled breeding practices, including the use of artificial insemination, have been introduced, especially for producing hybrids with exotic cattle breeds and for crossing with wild yak.

Calves are born in the spring and early summer, but their mothers are often in very poor condition at that time. Calves thus have a hard time, and those that have not put on enough weight by autumn may not survive the following winter.

In China, the majority of yak females do not show estrus until two years old and they calve first at four years old. Occurrence of estrus is greatly influenced by seasonal and environmental factors, and by the body condition of the cow. One estrus period per year is common. Cows that have not calved in the current year and others under good conditions (and in some other countries) may be polyestrous. One calf every two years is the norm, although two calves in three years is not unusual. Four to five calves, on average, are produced in a lifetime. Gestation length averages 258 days.

Body Weight

Average birth weights for calves of different breeds vary from 10 to 16 kg (with a higher range for individual animals). For one breed (Maiwa yak), weights (kg) of female yak at different ages during the warm season are reported as: birth, 11.9; 1 year, 67; 2 years, 120; 3 years, 155; 4 years, 182; 5 years, 189; and 6 years, 222. From about 3 years onward, males are significantly heavier than females, and up to twice the weight of females at maturity.

Castrated males are not usually slaughtered for meat until 4 years old in September or October, when at their fattest. Surplus females are also slaughtered then. Carcass weights vary widely as a proportion of liveweight, from around 30 to 60%.

Milk Production

Milk production is seasonal and averages among breeds from 150 to 500 kg, with fat content from 5.4 to 7.5%. Cows do not dry off completely during winter, and lactation will resume in a second year without calving again, but the cow will produce only one-half to two-thirds the quantity of milk, although it has a higher fat percentage.

Fleece

Fiber yields vary among breeds and locations, from 0.5 to 2.9 kg. The valuable down component represents 60–70% of the total fleece in calves, but can decline to as little as 20% in adults.

Other Produce

Hides, feces, blood, viscera, horn, and, to some extent, bones are all harvested.

PRODUCTS

Milk is made into butter (the main product) and various soft cheeses, mostly locally. Milk is also used skimmed or soured and made into yogurt. In Mongolia, yak milk is also fermented into an alcoholic drink. Dried milk powder is produced in factories, and in Nepal, a Swiss-style hard cheese is also produced in local factories. Milk is mostly brewed up with tea, to which butter may be added. Butter is used in cooking, as ointment, in lamps, and for sculptures in religious contexts.

Meat is eaten fresh or kept air-dried, smoked, or frozen (by nature). Meat products include a variety of sausages, often with blood added. The hair is used for ropes, blankets, and tents, and in mixtures for clothing. The hides, when tanned, are used for leather goods and to make coracles, while pelts can be used as coats. The feces are dried, and on the Qinghai-Tibetan Plateau they are the main source of fuel for heating and cooking. Yak are widely used for carrying loads and people and, in agricultural areas, for plowing.

CONCLUSIONS

Yak live on the high plateau and mountain ranges of western China and adjacent countries. The animals are adapted to withstand cold, low oxygen, often-treacherous terrain, and long periods of semistarvation. Milk yield is rarely more than needed to sustain a calf, but most of it is used for human consumption. In addition, meat and other products help to sustain the life of the nomads. Sheep and goats provide an extra source of livelihood in some areas, and horses are common for riding.

Yak are an integral part of the culture and social fabric of these regions, and they even have religious significance.

The relatively small numbers of yak kept in North America demonstrate that, contrary to received wisdom, yak can adapt to better environments and can reproduce and perform significantly better than is traditionally believed. Yak may, because of their resistance to hardship, find a role in other parts of the world.

REFERENCES

1. Cai Li; Wiener, G. *The Yak*, 2nd Ed; Regional Office for Asia and the Pacific of the Food and Agriculture Organization (FAO) of the United Nations: Bangkok, Thailand, 2003; 476. (revised and enlarge by Wiener G.; Han Jianlin; Long Ruijun) xviii.
2. Schaller, G.B. Wild Yak. In *Wildlife of the Tibetan Steppe*; University of Chicago Press: Chicago, USA, 1998; 125–142.

Zoo Animals

Harold F. Hintz
Cornell University, Ithaca, New York, U.S.A.

INTRODUCTION

Zoo has been defined as the short form for zoological garden, or a collection of living animals usually for public display, but that definition is incomplete. The mission of modern zoos includes education of the public, scientific studies, and the conservation and breeding of endangered species. Zoos remain one of the strongest links to living animals for many people. More than 26 million adults visit a zoo at least once a year. The total attendance at the member institutions of the American Zoo and Aquarium Association in 2002 was over 142 million people, which is greater than the attendance at the National Football League, Major League Baseball, National Hockey League, and National Basketball Association games combined.

HISTORY OF ZOOS

Collections of animals have been developed throughout the ages. Some consider Noah's Ark to be one of the earliest zoos. Great King Shulgi (2094–2047 B.C.) of Mesopotamia had a large zoo.[1] Ancient Egyptians were protective of many animals and built parks for lions, baboons, cattle, snakes, hippos, and crocodiles. It was suggested that every pharoh had a menagerie in his palace park, reserved for himself, his court, and foreign diplomats.[1] Queen Hatshepsut formed the first recorded animal collection expedition around 1490 B.C. Her agents returned with five ships loaded with leopards (or perhaps cheetahs), greyhounds, exotic birds, and monkeys from the present-day Somalia.[1] Ramses II (1341–1237 B.C.) is famous for the prosperity under his rule and the several temples and obelisks he had constructed. He also had a large collection of animals, which included lions, giraffes, ostriches, antelopes, monkeys, and cheetahs.[1]

Alexander the Great returned from conquests with many exotic animals, and is credited by some with founding the first public zoo. The animals were studied by Aristotle in preparation of his *Historia Animalium*. Ptolemy I, one of Alexander's generals, founded the Alexandria Zoo.

Romans, such as Caesar Augustus and Nero, collected animals for deadly games. Croke[1] can be consulted for much more zoo history information, including the zoos of Kublai Khan, Emperor Cheng Tzu, Montezuma, and the early zoos in Europe. Schonbrunn Zoo in Austria, considered to be the oldest continuously operating zoo, was founded on July 31, 1752.

The first zoo in the United States was established in Philadelphia in 1847. Efforts to build the Bronx Zoo were started before the Civil War, but it was not officially opened until 1899. The Lincoln Park Zoo in Chicago was founded in 1869, the Cincinnati Zoo in 1875, and the Cleveland Zoo in 1882. The National Zoo in Washington, D.C., was founded in 1889, in part to house gifts of animals to the President of the United States. The Denver Zoo opened in 1896. The San Diego Zoo opened in 1916, and the San Diego Wild Animal Park opened in 1972. Many of our present-day zoos were opened in the period from 1960–1990.

PRESENT STATUS OF ZOOS

Several arguments have been used for the abolishment of zoos. One argument is that "zoos by their nature are unable to give equal consideration to animals, and the animals will suffer in such husbandry systems."[2] Dr. Martha Kiley-Worthington concluded from studies on zoos that "provided the animals are kept in an ecologically, ethologically and ethically sound environment, and the costs and benefits to the individual and the environment as a whole are seriously considered there is no reason why animals should not be kept and bred in captivity."[2]

Unfortunately, not all of the animals in zoos are kept in a sound environment. Thus, another argument against zoos is that facilities in many zoos need significant renovation and more creative housing. It has been claimed that the zoo environment results in abnormal and self-destructive behavior. Many zoos, however, have made significant improvements over the old steel and concrete cages. Animals have been given more space and enriched habitats. Zoo Atlanta made many changes, but the most publicized is the change in the facility for housing the gorilla Willie B. from one of the worst in the United States to one of the best. In the new facility, Willie B. had access to green grass and trees, and was able to interact

Encyclopedia of Animal Science
DOI: 10.1081/E-EAS 120019857

with other gorillas. The San Diego Wild Animal Park has 1800 acres, which allows visitors to see herds of animals as they may have existed in the wild. There are more than 3500 animals representing 260 species in the park. The North Carolina Zoological Park has 550 acres, with exhibits such as a replicate of a short-grass prairie, with elk and bison, and an African Plains exhibit, with several species of antelope and birds. Disney's Animal Kingdom has 600 acres, and the Fossil Rim Wildlife Center has 1600 acres.

Habitat enrichment has been stressed in many zoos. Effective enrichment can increase the physical activity of animals, which results in improved physical and mental health of the animals and increased interest in the animals by zoo visitors.

Several methods have been used to enrich the environment. Exhibits have been designed to increase activity by having several levels and climbing structures. Exploration has been increased with olfactory stimulation. Fresh and dried herbs such as catnip, mint, and civet musk have been used in feline cages. The Minnesota Zoo reported that clouded leopards are stimulated by poultry seasoning; tigers love "Obsession" and "Charlie" perfumes; and tapirs, tree kangaroos, and gibbons go for banana extract. At the Honolulu Zoo, sheep, miniature horses, or llamas from the children's zoo are sometimes put in the tiger exhibit at night, when the tigers are locked in their quarters, to provide scents to which tigers react.

Encouragement of natural hunting and foraging behaviors to obtain food is a common method of enrichment. Whole dead chickens from which cats pluck the feathers is thought to decrease fur pulling. Hanging meat from the ceiling or from tall poles is used in cat exhibits, and food is often hidden in exhibits. Polar bears and cats are provided with live fish to catch. Live insects are fed to several species of animals. Meerkats at the Minnesota Zoo are provided with bug puzzles that the meerkat must roll around in just such a way as to have the bugs fall out. Elephants at the Honolulu Zoo are provided with beer barrels containing treats that require the elephant to shake the treats out. Several zoos provide chimps with artificial termite mounds. The mound can contain insects or treats such as applesauce or pie fillings that the chimps can reach with a stick through a hole in the mound.

The American Zoo and Aquarium Association (AZA), with 213 member institutions, is the largest zoo and aquarium organization in the world. The goals of AZA are to improve the care of animals in captivity, educate the public on the importance of conservation, and help preserve ecosystems around the world. Any organization that owns or cares for animals must complete an AZA accreditation or certification inspection before becoming an institutional member of AZA.[3] The inspection is a six-month-long review as well as a rigorous on-site inspection of facilities, environment, and care of animals.

Zoos are now expected to contribute to the survival of the species they display. Increased breeding of captive animals as replacements will be needed. Many species are becoming difficult or impossible to obtain from natural populations. Wild animal populations suffer from loss of habitat and poaching. Increased interaction with domestic animals results in a greater incidence of diseases such as anthrax, rinderpest, distemper, and bovine tuberculosis.

More important than maintaining the zoo population is the survival of the species in the wild. Many zoos are actively involved with reintroduction projects. The return of the Przewalski's horse, Arabian oryx, black-footed ferret, and California condor to their native habitats are often cited as successful examples of reintroduction. Unfortunately, many attempts with other species have been costly failures. Hopefully, the knowledge learned from the successes and the failures will increase the success rate of reintroduction in the future.

The number of species of animals exhibited in a zoo varies greatly among zoos. The San Diego Zoo has over 800 different species. The Denver and Houston Zoos each have over 700 species. Some zoos specialize in local animals. The Arizona–Sonora Desert Museum has animals that are native to the Sonora Desert region. Some zoos focus on certain types. Omaha's Henry Doorly Zoo has the largest facility for big cats in the United States. The Cincinnati Zoo, whose stated mission is creating adventure, conveying knowledge, and conserving nature, has a Cat House with more than 15 species of small cats and catlike animals. The San Francisco Zoo has 6220 species, of which 6000 are invertebrates.

The total number of animals of various classes in AZA member institutions in 2002 is shown in the following list:

Amphibians: 15,505
Birds: 50,412
Fish: 255,756
Invertebrates: 174,152
Mammals: 44,294
Reptiles: 28,911

ZOOS OF THE FUTURE

Predicting the future can be difficult. Croke[1] wrote, "No one knows exactly what the zoos of the future will look like. But with so much at stake, it is clear we desperately need zoos to help save the diversity of life. The question is not whether the world will have zoos in the future. The question is will the world have animals."

Kelly[4] wrote, "If zoological organizations are to continue their work to preserve biodiversity it is critical that they continue to adapt and develop, otherwise they run the risk of becoming extinct themselves.''

Conway[5] stated, ''the vision of zoos for 21st century should be to become proactive wildlife conservation caregivers and intellectual resources, to step out beyond their fences by aiding parks and reserves, to sustain animals which have lost their habitats and conduct campaigns to restore them and to provide as many key species as possible from zoo collections to be the stimulus and centerpieces of conservation efforts around the world.''

CONCLUSION

Zoo animals have provided a link to the animal world for many people. Zoos need to continue the progress on education, improved environments for zoo animals, and conservation efforts.

REFERENCES

1. Croke, V. The Modern Ark. In *The Story of Zoos: Past, Present and Future*; Scribner: New York, NY, 1997.
2. Kiley-Worthington, M. *Animals in Circuses and Zoos Chiron's World?*; Plaistow Press: London, 1990.
3. American Association of Zoological Parks and Aquariums. Silver Spring: Maryland 20910.
4. Kelly, J.D. Effective conservation in the twenty-first century: The need to be more than a zoo. One organization's approach. Int. Zoo. Yb. **1997**, *35*, 1–14.
5. Conway, W. The role of zoos in the 21st century. Int. Zoo. Yb. **2003**, *38*, 7–13.

Z

Index